ScottForesman
LITERATURE
AND INTEGRATED STUDIES

Annotated Teacher's Edition
Volume Two

American Literature

ScottForesman

Editorial Offices: Glenview, Illinois
Regional Offices: San Jose, California • Tucker, Georgia
Glenview, Illinois • Oakland, New Jersey • Dallas, Texas

Visit ScottForesman's Home Page at http://www.scottforesman.com

acknowledgments

Cover (detail): *Portrait of a Sioux* by James Bama. The Greenwich Workshop, Inc. Courtesy of The Greenwich Workshop, Inc., Shelton, CT **859c(t)** Everett Collection, Inc. **859d(t)** Bernard Boutrit/Woodfin Camp & Associates

ISBN: 0-673-29465-X
Copyright © 1997
Scott, Foresman and Company, Glenview, Illinois
All Rights Reserved. Printed in the United States of America.

1.800.554.4411
http://www.scottforesman.com

1 2 3 4 5 6 7 8 9 10 DR 03 02 01 00 99 98 97 96

ScottForesman
LITERATURE
AND INTEGRATED STUDIES

Middle School: Grade Six

Middle School: Grade Seven

Middle School: Grade Eight

Forms in Literature

World Literature

American Literature

English Literature

The cover features a detail of James Bama's *Portrait of a Sioux,* which appears in full on this page. After a distinguished career as a sports illustrator, Bama (born 1926) decided that what he most wanted to do was paint Western subjects.

ScottForesman
LITERATURE
AND INTEGRATED STUDIES

American Literature

Senior Consultants

Alan C. Purves
State University of New York at Albany

Carol Booth Olson
University of California, Irvine

Carlos E. Cortés
University of California, Riverside (Emeritus)

ScottForesman

Editorial Offices: Glenview, Illinois
Regional Offices: San Jose, California • Tucker, Georgia
Glenview, Illinois • Oakland, New Jersey • Dallas, Texas

Visit ScottForesman's Home Page at http://www.scottforesman.com

Acknowledgments

Texts

xxvi "Harrison Bergeron" from *Welcome to the Monkey House* by Kurt Vonnegut, Jr. Copyright © 1961 by Kurt Vonnegut, Jr. Reprinted by permission of Delacorte Press/Seymour Lawrence, a division of Bantam Doubleday Dell Publishing Group, Inc. **9** "This Newly Created World" by Paul Radin from *The Road of Life and Death: A Ritual Drama of the American Indians.* Copyright 1945 by Princeton University Press, renewed 1972. Reprinted by permission of Princeton University Press. **10** "I Have Killed the Deer" from *Hollering Sun* by Nancy Wood. Copyright 1972 by Nancy Wood. Reprinted by permission. **14** Excerpt from *Castaways* by Enrique Pupo-Walker. Reprinted by permission of the University of California Press and the author. **18** "Before They Got Thick" from "The White People Who Came in a Boat" by M.E. Opler from *Memoirs of the American Folklore Society.* Reproduced by permission of the American Folklore Society from the *Journal of American Folklore* 63:247, 1950. Not for further reproduction. **22** From *Great Slave Narratives* by Arna Bontemps. Copyright 1969 by Arna W. Bontemps. Reprinted by permission of Beacon Press. **31** From *Of Plymouth Plantation* by William Bradford, edited by Samuel Eliot Morison. Copyright 1952 by Samuel Eliot Morison and renewed 1980 by Emily M. Beck. Reprinted by permission of Alfred A. Knopf, Inc. **34** From *A Narrative of the Life of Mrs. Mary Jemison,* by James E. Seaver, with an introduction by June Namias. Copyright 1992 by June Namias. Published by the University of Oklahoma Press. Reprinted by permission **42** "Corn: Builder of Cities" by Mary Talbot from *Newsweek, Columbus Special Issue,* Fall/Winter 1991, page 61. Copyright © 1991 by Newsweek, Inc. All rights reserved. **43** "The Animal That Changed History" from *U.S. News & World Report,* July 8, 1991. Copyright © 1991 by U.S. News & World Report. Reprinted by permission of U.S. News & World Report.

44 From "The Buzzard and the Hawk" by Mr. Ted Williams. Reprinted by permission of The University of Georgia Press. **44** From *When Roots Die: Endangered Traditions on the Sea Islands* by Patricia Jones-Jackson. Reprinted by permission of The University of Georgia Press. **62** From *The Crucible* by Arthur Miller. Copyright 1952, 1953, 1954, renewed 1980 by Arthur Miller. Used by permission of Viking Penguin, a division of Penguin Books USA Inc. **136** "Witchcraft in Salem: A Fungus in the Rye" from *Science News.* Reprinted by permission. **205** "Lost" by David Wagoner. Reprinted by permission of the author. **205** "The Gift Outright" by Robert Frost from *The Poetry of Robert Frost,* edited by Edward Connery Lathem. Copyright © 1942 by Robert Frost. Copyright © 1970 by Lesley Frost Ballantine. Copyright © 1969 by Henry Holt and Company, Inc. Reprinted by permission of Henry Holt and Company, Inc. **207** From "This Land Is Your Land," words and music by Woody Guthrie. TRO-©-Copyright 1956 (Renewed) 1958 (Renewed) 1970 Ludlow Music, Inc., New York, New York. Reprinted by permission of The Richmond Organization. **213** "A Fable for Tomorrow" from *Silent Spring* by Rachel Carson. Copyright © 1962 by Rachel L. Carson, renewed © 1990 by Roger Christie. Reprinted by permission of Houghton Mifflin Company. All rights reserved. **214** "Return" from *Selected Poetry* by Robinson Jeffers. Copyright 1935 and renewed © 1963 by Donnan Jeffers and Garth Jeffers. Reprinted by permission of Random House, Inc. **288** From *Danse Macabre* by Stephen King. Reprinted by permission. **290** "The Thrill of Chills" by Ellen Blum Barish from *Current Health 2,* Vol. 18, No. 7, March 1992, pages 24–25. Reprinted by permission. **332** From *Behind the Blue and the Gray: The Soldier's Life in the Civil War* by Delia Ray, pages 50–56. Reprinted by permission.

continued on page 1015

iv

Senior Consultants

Alan C. Purves

Professor of Education and Humanities, State University of New York at Albany; Director of the Center for Writing and Literacy. Dr. Purves developed the concept and philosophy of the literature lessons for the series, consulted with editors, reviewed tables of contents and lesson manuscript, wrote the Assessment Handbooks, and oversaw the development and writing of the series testing strand.

Carol Booth Olson

Director, California Writing Project, Department of Education, University of California, Irvine. Dr. Olson conceptualized and developed the integrated writing strand of the program, consulted with editors, led a team of teachers in creating literature-based Writing Workshops, and reviewed final manuscript.

Carlos E. Cortés

Professor Emeritus, History, University of California, Riverside. Dr. Cortés designed and developed the multicultural strand embedded in each unit of the series and consulted with grade-level editors to implement the concepts.

Series Consultants

Visual and Media Literacy/Speaking and Listening/Critical Thinking

Harold M. Foster. Professor of English Education and Secondary Education, The University of Akron, Akron. Dr. Foster developed and wrote the Beyond Print features for all levels of the series.

ESL and LEP Strategies

James Cummins. Professor, Modern Language Centre and Curriculum Department, Ontario Institute for Studies in Education, Toronto.

Lily Wong Fillmore. Professor, Graduate School of Education, University of California at Berkeley.

Drs. Cummins and Fillmore advised on the needs of ESL and LEP students, helped develop the Building English Proficiency model for the program, and reviewed strategies and manuscript for this strand of the program.

Fine Arts/Humanities

Neil Anstead. Coordinator of the Humanitas Program, Cleveland Humanities Magnet School, Reseda, California. Mr. Anstead consulted on the fine art used in the program.

Reviewers and Contributors

Pupil and Teacher Edition

Jay Amberg, Glenbrook South High School, Glenview, Illinois **Edison Barber,** St. Anne Community High School, St. Anne, Illinois **Lois Barliant,** Albert G. Lane Technical High School, Chicago, Illinois **James Beasley,** Plant City Senior High School, Plant City, Florida **Linda Belpedio,** Oak Park/River Forest High School, Oak Park, Illinois **Richard Bruns,** Burges High School, El Paso, Texas **Kay Parks Bushman,** Ottawa High School, Ottawa, Kansas **Jesús Cardona,** John F. Kennedy High School, San Antonio, Texas **Marlene Carter,** Dorsey High School, Los Angeles, California **Patrick Cates,** Lubbock High School, Lubbock, Texas **Timothy Dohrer,** New Trier Township High School, Winnetka, Illinois **Margaret Doria,** Our Lady of Perpetual Help High School, Brooklyn, New York **Lucila Dypiangco,** Bell Senior High School, Bell, California **Judith Edminster,** Plant City Senior High School, Plant City, Florida **Mary Alice Fite,** Columbus School for Girls, Columbus, Ohio **Montserrat Fontes,** Marshall High School, Los Angeles, California **Diane Fragos,** Turkey Creek Middle School, Plant City, Florida **Joan Greenwood,** Thornton Township High School, Harvey, Illinois **William Irvin,** Pittsfield Public Schools, Pittsfield, Massachusetts **Carleton Jordan,** Montclair High School, Montclair, New Jersey **Mark Kautz,** Chapel Hill High School, Chapel Hill, North Carolina **Elaine Kay,** Bartow High School, Bartow, Florida **Roslyn Kettering,** West Lafayette Junior/Senior High School, West Lafayette, Indiana **Kristina Kostopoulos,** Lincoln Park High School, Chicago, Illinois **Julia Lloyd,** Harwood Junior High School, Bedford, Texas **John Lord,** Ocean Township High School, Oakhurst, New Jersey **Dolores Mathews,** Bloomingdale High School, Valrico, Florida **Jim McCallum,** Milford High School, Milford, Massachusetts **Monette Mehalko,** Plant City Senior High School, Plant City, Florida **Lucia Podraza,** DuSable High School, Chicago, Illinois **Frank Pool,** Anderson High School, Austin, Texas **Alice Price,** Latin School, Chicago, Illinois **Anna J. Roseboro,** The Bishop's School, La Jolla, California **Peter Sebastian,** Granite Hills High School, El Cajon, California **Rob Slater,** East Forsyth High School, Winston-Salem, North Carolina **Catherine Small,** Nicolet High School, Glendale, Wisconsin **Dennis Symkowiak,** Mundelein High School, Mundelein, Illinois **Rosetta Tetteh,** Senn High School, Chicago, Illinois **Pamela Vetters,** Harlandale High School, San Antonio, Texas **Polly Walwark,** Oak Park High School, Oak Park, Illinois **Karen Wrobleski,** San Diego High School, San Diego, California **Dru Zimmerman,** Chapel Hill High School, Chapel Hill, North Carolina

Contents

Part Two: A Tragedy at Salem

Unit 2 A New Nation

A Spirit of Independence

Also featuring John Locke, George Catlin, William Bradford, Mary
Rowlandson, Tecumseh, Thomas Cole, Erik H. Erikson, William Cullen
Bryant, Charles Kuralt, Herbert Johnson and Henry David Thoreau

Unit 3 American Classic

Part One: Romantic Truths and Terrors

Part Two: The Civil War

Unit 4 Expanding America

Part One: Letters to the World

Part Two: The Frontier

Unit 5 Breaking the Mold

Part One: Beyond the Limits

Part Two: The Harlem Renaissance

xvi

Unit 6 Modern Dilemmas

Part One: Lost in a Crowd

Part Two: The Strength of Tradition

Unit 7 Years of Change

Part One: Person to Person

Part Two: In the Midst of Struggle . . .

Unit 8 American Voices Today

Citizens of Tomorrow

Glossaries, Handbooks, and Indexes

Genre Overview

Short Stories

Poetry

Plays

Nonfiction

Folk Tales

Feature Overview

Historical Overviews

Interdisciplinary Studies

Language History

Writing Workshops

Beyond Print

Themes in American Literature

Planning Unit 5: Breaking the Mold

Literature	Integrated Language Arts			
	Literary	Writing/Grammar, Usage and Mechanics	Reading, Thinking, Listening, Speaking	Vocabulary/Spelling
The Story of an Hour *by Kate Chopin* Short Story *(average)* p. 450	Irony	Paragraph Word choice		Synonyms and antonyms
Trifles *by Susan Glaspell* Play *(average)* p. 455	Plot Foreshadowing Irony	Write an argument Essay Indefinite pronouns	Visualize Draw conclusions Recognize cause and effect Make inferences	Word pairs Understand connotation and denotation
The Revolt of "Mother" *by Mary E. Wilkins Freeman* Short Story *(easy)* p. 468	Foreshadowing Symbolism Characterization Metaphor	Compare conflict resolving methods News story Letter Commas in sentences Dialect	Compare and contrast Draw conclusions Recognize values Analyze the author's purpose Make inferences	
from Crusade for Justice *by Ida B. Wells-Barnett* Autobiography *(challenging)* p. 483	Tone	Write and support an argument Letter Epic poem Singular and plural nouns	Recognize cause and effect Draw conclusions	Using vivid verbs
The Spring and the Fall *by Edna St. Vincent Millay* Poem *(average)* p. 492 **On Thought in Harness** *by Edna St. Vincent Millay* Poem *(challenging)* p. 493	Rhythm and rhyme	Using *no, not,* and *never*	Compare and contrast	

Meeting Individual Needs

Multi-modal Activities	Mini-Lessons
Reader's theater play Exploring key concepts	Word choice
Perform the play Mock trial Identifying factual information Exploring key statements Making cultural connections Exploring character	Indefinite pronouns Plot Dramatic dialogue Understand connotation and denotation
Make blueprints List of similarities Analyzing characters Expanding vocabulary with suffixes Expanding vocabulary Creating a visual response Responding to a resolution	Commas in sentences Foreshadowing Dialect Understand sequence Plot

Create a dramatization
Sketch
Linking history and literature
Responding from different
    viewpoints
	Singular and plural
	    nouns
	Tone
	Using vivid verbs

	Using *no*, *not*, and *never*

Interdisciplinary Studies
Within Limits

Format	Content Area	Highlights	Skill
Article: **The Uprising of Women**	History and Science	Restrictions and attitudes women faced in their everyday lives.	Recognizing overgeneralizations

Article:
The Sexual Politics of Sickness
    by Barbara Ehrenreich
    and Deirdre English
	Science	Requirements of being a lady and their impact on health.	Presenting information

Article: **Teaching by the Rules**	History	Restrictions and limitations placed on women school teachers.	

Writing Workshop

Mode	Writing Format	Writing Focus	Proofreading Skills

Expository writing	An update on
	    women's roles
		Orienting your
		    audience
			Using apostrophes
			    correctly

Program Support Materials

For Every Selection	For Every Writing Workshop
Unit Resource Book Graphic Organizer Study Guide Vocabulary Worksheet Grammar Worksheet Spelling, Speaking and Listening, or Literary Language Worksheet Alternate Check Test Vocabulary Test Selection Test	**Unit Resource Book** Prewriting Worksheet Revising Strategy Worksheet Editing Strategy Worksheet Presentation Worksheet Writing Rubric **Transparency Collection** Fine Art Transparency Student Writing Model Transparencies

For Every Interdisciplinary Study	Assessment
Unit Resource Book Study Guide Mini-Lesson Skill Worksheet	**Unit Resource Book** TE Check Tests Alternate Check Test (blackline master) Vocabulary Test (blackline master) Selection Test (blackline master) **Test Generator Software** **Assessment Handbook**

Planning Unit 5: Breaking the Mold

Literature

Integrated Language Arts

	Literary	Writing/Grammar, Usage and Mechanics	Reading, Thinking, Listening, Speaking	Vocabulary/Spelling
Harlem: The Culture Capital *by James Weldon Johnson* Essay *(challenging)* p. 512	Metaphor Setting Theme	List Persuasive letter Compound-complex sentences	Make inferences Recall facts Summarize Recognize values Draw conclusions	Using synonyms with connotations
A Black Man Talks of Reaping *by Arna Bontemps* Poem *(average)* p. 524 **If We Must Die** *by Claude McKay* Poem *(average)* p. 525 **The Negro Speaks of Rivers** *by Langston Hughes* Poem *(average)* p. 526 **Harlem Wine** *by Countee Cullen* Poem *(challenging)* p. 526 **Youth** *by Langston Hughes* Poem *(easy)* p. 527 **Ma Rainey** *by Sterling A. Brown* Poem *(average)* p. 528	Meter Tone Repetition Simile	Write a poem Explain themes of Harlem Renaissance Use of dialect in writing	Fantasy and reality Visualize	Synonym Antonyms
How It Feels to Be Colored Me *by Zora Neale Hurston* Essay *(average)* p. 533	Tone Figurative language	Paragraph on author's self-esteem Paragraph on "How It Feels to Be ___ Me" Adjectives and adverbs	Make inferences Evaluate	

Meeting Individual Needs

Multi-modal Activities	Mini-Lessons
Illustrated map	Metaphor
Planning a reading strategy	Compound-complex
Visualizing the setting	sentences
Recognizing synonyms and	Using synonyms with
related words	connotations
Making personal connections	
Plan a Blues festival	Oral presentation on
Visual art	one of the selected
	poets
	Focusing on poetic
	meter
	Self-monitoring com-
	prehension
	Recognizing poetic
	language
	Analyzing dialect
Collage	Tone
Understanding figurative language	Adjectives and adverbs

Interdisciplinary Studies
Harlem Renaissance

Format	Content Area	Highlights	Skill
Art: **An Artistic Awakening**	Fine Art	These pages display a selection of African American paintings and sculptures from the Harlem Renaissance.	Using primary sources Compare and contrast print and nonprint media
Article: **Tour Director Shows Off Harlem Treasures** *by Larcelia Kabe*	Career	An elementary school principal endeavors to transform Harlem's image.	Demonstrate poise and confidence

Writing Workshop

Mode	Writing Format	Writing Focus	Proofreading Skills
Persuasive writing	A persuasive letter	Using appropriate tone	Using adjectives and adverbs correctly

Program Support Materials

For Every Selection	For Every Writing Workshop
Unit Resource Book	**Unit Resource Book**
Graphic Organizer	Prewriting Worksheet
Study Guide	Revising Strategy Worksheet
Vocabulary Worksheet	Editing Strategy Worksheet
Grammar Worksheet	Presentation Worksheet
Spelling, Speaking and Listening, or Literary Language Worksheet	Writing Rubric
Alternate Check Test	**Transparency Collection**
Vocabulary Test	Fine Art Transparency
Selection Test	Student Writing Model Transparencies

For Every Interdisciplinary Study	Assessment
Unit Resource Book	**Unit Resource Book**
Study Guide	TE Check Tests
Mini-Lesson Skill Worksheet	Alternate Check Test (blackline master)
	Vocabulary Test (blackline master)
	Selection Test (blackline master)
	Test Generator Software
	Assessment Handbook

Media and Technology

Part One Selections

The Story of an Hour

Audiotape Students may want to hear an unabridged reading of Chopin's *The Awakening*, 5 hours 30 minutes, Books in Motion, 1991.

Videotape *Kate Chopin: Five Stories of an Hour,* 26 minutes, Films for the Humanities & Sciences, 1991, consists of five versions of the short story.

Community Resources Students might be interested in hearing the experiences of someone whose daily work involves administering first aid to those who have are sick or injured. Such people might include police personnel, firefighters, paramedics, and lifeguards, doctors, nurses, emergency room personnel, and so on.

Trifles

Home Connection Students might invite a family member who quilts to visit the class, bringing examples of this traditional American folk art and describing how quilts are made, different regional and period styles, and so on.

The Revolt of "Mother"

Videotape *The Revolt of Mother,* 60 minutes, from The American Short Story Collection, Library Video Company, 1987, stars Amy Madigan.

Community Resources People in many communities today participate in re-creations of the life of various periods of the American past, such as that of the 17th-century French voyageurs, the Civil War era, or western pioneer days. Invite someone with background in 19th-century rural life to visit the class and describe what it was like to live on an American farm in the 1800s.

from Crusade for Justice

Audiotape Ida B. Wells is included on *The Negro Woman*, Scholastic/Folkways. *Vinie Burrows: Walk Together Children*, Spoken Arts, includes dramatic readings and poems spanning the black experience.

Home Connection Ida Wells-Barnett was a crusading journalist who used her newspaper as a forum to attack the evil of lynching. You might invite a broadcast or print journalist to visit the class and discuss the work of an investigative reporter.

Connections to
Custom Literature Database

For Part One "Beyond the Limits" Selections with Lessons

- "A Native of Winby" by Sarah Orne Jewett
- "Afterward" by Edith Wharton

Additional theme-based selections can be accessed on the ScottForesman database.

The Black Experience

The Negro Woman, an audiotape by Scholastic/Folkways, includes material by Ida B. Wells.

The Spring and the Fall/On Thought in Harness

Videotape Consider showing *Edna St. Vincent Millay,* 60 minutes, Films for the Humanities & Sciences, 1994.

Home Connection Edna St. Vincent Millay was a kind of unofficial "poet laureate" of the 1920s. With its cynical, defiant spirit, her verse was felt to vividly express the outlook of the decade's "new woman." For an at-home activity, students might be interested in reading and discussing some of her early poems with family members, comparing the values of a liberated woman of the 1920s with those of young women today.

Part Two Selections

Harlem: The Cultural Capital

Audiotape *God's Trombones: Seven Negro Sermons in Verse*, 90 minutes, read by five prominent African American ministers from New York, is available through Penguin-HighBridge, 1993.

Videotape Students will enjoy seeing *The Harlem Renaissance: Black Poets*, 20 minutes, Carousel Film & Video, 1980.

Community Resources The Harlem Renaissance gathered and focused the creative energy of a generation of African American artists. You might suggest that students research their own community's artistic resources and create a local cultural guide.

A Black Man Talks of Reaping/If We Must Die/The Negro Speaks of Rivers/Harlem Wine/Youth/Ma Rainey

Audiotape Arna Bontemps reads poetry of various authors in *Anthology of African American Poetry for Young People*, Smithsonian/Folkway, 1992. Ruby Dee and Ossie Davis read selected poems in *The Poetry of Langston Hughes*, Caedmon. Also consider *Langston Hughes Reads and Talks About His Poems*, Spoken Arts. *Poetry of Countee Cullen*, Caedmon/Harper Audio, features poetry performed by Ruby Dee and Ossie Davis. *Anthology of Negro Poets in the USA,* Smithsonian/Folkway, includes Countee Cullen, Sterling A. Brown, Claude McKay, and many others.

Videotape Students will enjoy *Thank You, Ma'am,* 12 minutes, BFA Films, 1976, based on the short story by Hughes. *Wild Women Don't Have the Blues*, 58 minutes, Knowledge Unlimited, 1989, traces the life and time of Ma Rainey and other legendary women.

Community Resource The poets of the Harlem Renaissance were greatly influenced by the moods and rhythms and musical forms such as blues and jazz. Interested students might use the resources of the local library to research audiotapes of early 20th century blues and jazz recordings and present a program for the class.

How It Feels to Be Colored Me

Audiotape In this 2-cassette set, students can listen to *Mules and Men* by Zora Neale Hurston, 3 hours, Caedmon/Harper Audio.

Videotape *Zora Is My Name!*, 90 minutes, PBS Video, 1989, is based on the life of Hurston.

Community Resources In addition to being a novelist, Zora Neale Hurston was also a folklorist, making several collections of traditional African American folktales. Interested students might enjoy using the resources of the local library or cultural centers to research the folklore of whatever ethnic group or groups to which they belong.

Connections to
Custom Literature Database

For Part Two "The Harlem Renaissance" Selections with Lessons
- "Life's Tragedy" and "Douglass" by Paul Laurence Dunbar
- *The Autobiography of an Ex-Colored Man,* Chapters 3–4, by James Weldon Johnson

Additional theme-based selections can be accessed on the ScottForesman database.

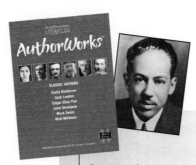

Connections to
AuthorWorks

Information about the life and times of Langston Hughes and Zora Neale Hurston is available on ScottForesman's AuthorWorks CD-ROM.

Breaking the Mold

 Art Study

The oil painting *Walking* by Charles Alston was first shown in April 1958 around the time of the Birmingham, Alabama, bus boycott.

When asked how much the civil rights movement influenced his work, Alston explained that the basically important thing to him is making a good picture.

"Whatever the theme happens to be or gets to be is inevitable, out of what your experience has been, and mine has been the experience of a black man in a fairly racist country. [However] I do try to keep the universalities that make a painting a painting uppermost."

Question What adjectives describe the figures in *Walking?* What elements of the painting bring those words to mind? *(Students might say* strong, determined, angry, hurt, courageous, *and point to the figure's postures, the bold colors, the movement from dark to light.)*

Question Make predictions about the selections in this unit based on the mood, subject, and style of this painting. What does the painting seem to say about "breaking the mold"? *(Students might predict that the selections are about social protest, experiments in style, feminism, and defying expectations or conventions.)*

UNIT 5

Breaking the Mold

Beyond the Limits
Part One, pages 446–507

The Harlem Renaissance
Part Two, pages 508–550

THEMES IN AMERICAN LITERATURE

The Search for Equality
Theme Portfolio, pages 551–561

445

THEMATIC CONNECTIONS

In the late-nineteenth and early-twentieth century, women and African Americans sometimes defied formidable legal and social conventions to win independence and realize their dreams.

Part One
Beyond the Limits

The selections in Part One present women who risked being different to do what they believed was right.

Ideas to Explore

- What were the roles of men and women?
- What drives certain people to break with tradition and define their own goals?
- What actions achieved the goals?
- Is it possible to go too far in pursuit of personal freedom?

Part Two
The Harlem Renaissance

The selections in Part Two are the creative result of a vibrant community of Harlem artists and intellectuals who lived and worked in an urban neighborhood dedicated to arts and ideas.

Ideas to Explore

- What were the social and economic conditions that fostered the existence of the Harlem Renaissance?
- What was the spirit of the Harlem artistic community?

 Art Study

The icon for Beyond the Limits is titled *Woman with a Parasol,* an oil painting by Claude Monet (1886). The icon for The Harlem Renaissance is a Harlem Renaissance head by Aaron Douglas.

EXPLORING CONCEPTS

- Women of the Progressive Era challenged confining and demeaning stereotypes about their gender and took on a wide variety of roles.
- Women made important contributions to the arts, engineered vital social reform, and became a large part of the work force during this period.
- Women in the United States received the right to vote in 1920. It took the suffragists thirty years of active, organized campaigning to convince Congress to pass the Nineteenth Amendment.

The captions describe women's contributions to art, society, and industry.

Question What stereotypes about women, as embodied in the statement "an angel in the house," do the photographs challenge? *(Possible responses: The pictures show that women are not frail or only homemakers; that they can leave the home and be political activists.)*

Art Study

This collage of images was meant to convey a sense of the energy and industry of women in the Progressive Era.

Question What is the focal point of the images and what purpose does it serve? *(The large photograph of a typist in the center of the arrangement of images is like a topic sentence in a paragraph. It sets the tone and guides the viewer's perspective on all the other women in the collage.)*

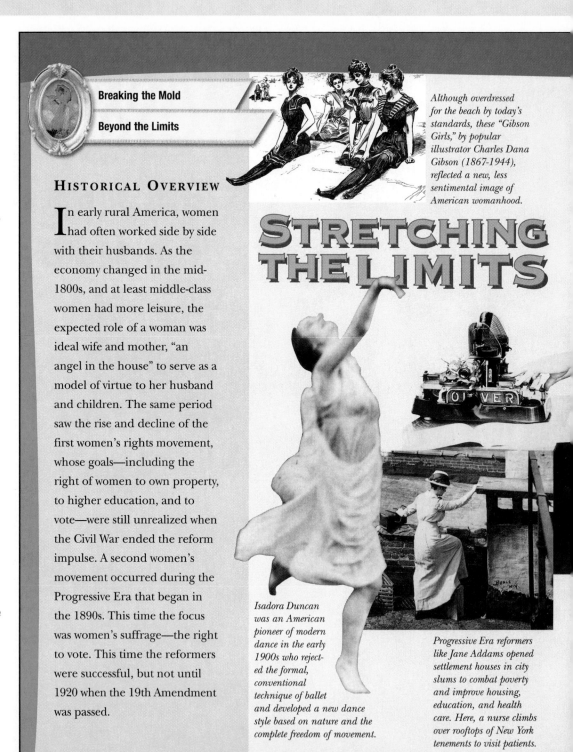

Breaking the Mold

Beyond the Limits

HISTORICAL OVERVIEW

In early rural America, women had often worked side by side with their husbands. As the economy changed in the mid-1800s, and at least middle-class women had more leisure, the expected role of a woman was ideal wife and mother, "an angel in the house" to serve as a model of virtue to her husband and children. The same period saw the rise and decline of the first women's rights movement, whose goals—including the right of women to own property, to higher education, and to vote—were still unrealized when the Civil War ended the reform impulse. A second women's movement occurred during the Progressive Era that began in the 1890s. This time the focus was women's suffrage—the right to vote. This time the reformers were successful, but not until 1920 when the 19th Amendment was passed.

Although overdressed for the beach by today's standards, these "Gibson Girls," by popular illustrator Charles Dana Gibson (1867-1944), reflected a new, less sentimental image of American womanhood.

STRETCHING THE LIMITS

Isadora Duncan was an American pioneer of modern dance in the early 1900s who rejected the formal, conventional technique of ballet and developed a new dance style based on nature and the complete freedom of movement.

Progressive Era reformers like Jane Addams opened settlement houses in city slums to combat poverty and improve housing, education, and health care. Here, a nurse climbs over rooftops of New York tenements to visit patients.

Although homemaking was still difficult on farms in the late 1800s, some women were resourceful in finding ways to make their lives easier. The woman pictured here has rigged a home-made washing machine.

In the late 1800s working women were confined to unskilled jobs in domestic service, factories, and "sweat shops." The few who could afford an education found work as teachers and nurses. The invention of the typewriter allowed women to enter the business world and by 1900 women outnumbered men in office jobs.

Suffragists often disagreed on how to get women the vote. Some supported a Constitutional amendment while others favored a state-by-state approach. Suffragists' tactics also varied from organizing petitions and parades to chaining themselves to the White House fence. When arrested they went on hunger strikes in jail and were force-fed by police.

Key Dates

1700s
Colonial law dictates that women are represented in society only by the males of the household.

1820s
Women are active outside the home as teachers and reformers.

1845
Margaret Fuller writes Woman in the Nineteenth Century, *the first American feminist book.*

1848
Seneca Falls Convention in New York discusses women's rights.

1890
National American Woman Suffrage Association is formed.

1920
The 19th Amendment passes.

Key Dates

1700s   Women are barred from owning property, attending academies of higher education, and voting.

1837   Mount Holyoke Female Seminary opens as the first school to offer women courses comparable to those taught in men's colleges.

1848   Lucretia Mott and Elizabeth Cady Stanton call the first U.S. convention for women's rights after the World Anti-Slavery Convention refuses to admit female delegates. Three hundred people, including forty men, pass a declaration proclaiming women's rights to education, property, and equality, but decide that it's too controversial to demand women's right to vote.

1920   The Nineteenth Amendment is passed: "The right of citizens of the United States to vote shall not be denied or abridged by any State on account of sex."

MATERIALS OF INTEREST
Books

American Women: Their Lives in Their Words, edited by Doreen Rappaport (HarperCollins Children's Books, 1990)

Multimedia

1995 Groliers Multimedia Encyclopedia, "Women and Voting" on CD-ROM (Groliers, 1995)

Connections to
Custom Literature Database

For further historical background, under **Background Articles,** see **Early Modern America 1870–1915.**

447

FOR ALL STUDENTS

- What limitations on your rights would you be uncomfortable with?
- What action might you take to have limitations lifted from your life?

Read together the first paragraph on page 448. Explain to students that the selections in Part One demonstrate the thoughts and actions of several women at the end of the nineteenth century.

To further explore the theme, use the transparency referenced here.

Transparency Collection
Fine Art Writing Prompt 8

For At-Risk Students

Ask students to recall stories of struggles for equal rights from history, television, movies, books, or students' personal experiences.

For Students Who Need Challenge

Have students write a position paper defining the role that they think the the U.S. government should take in improving the rights of all people.

MULTICULTURAL CONNECTION

Because of differing backgrounds and experiences, people tend to have assumptions (or "baggage") that affect how they view the world.

- Assign students "baggage" cards with labels such as *prejudice, mistrust, fear,* and *stereotype.*
- Have volunteers role-play meetings with people of different races, religions, and genders and then discuss how their "baggage" affects them and how it can be overcome.

448

Part One

Beyond the Limits

As the end of the 1800s approached, women began challenging the roles and rules that both defined and confined their gender. Feminists like Susan B. Anthony, Elizabeth Cady Stanton, and Sojourner Truth had been fighting for years to gain women's rights in education, the workplace, property ownership, and voting. Yet in every aspect of life there were still strict limits within which women were expected to live. In the following selections, you'll meet women who dared to step beyond society's limits.

Multicultural Connection While each of us is a part of one or more cultural groups, each person also finds ways to express her or his **individuality,** either within or beyond a society's expectations. How do the women in the following selections express their individuality?

448   UNIT FIVE: BREAKING THE MOLD

IDEAS THAT WORK

Motivating with Common Ground

"My students are from diverse linguistic and cultural backgrounds, so I begin by asking for their associations for the word *limits.* Then we discuss the titles of each selection in Beyond the Limits and speculate how each selection might relate to the idea of limits. I remind students to write down questions that occur to them while they are reading, and encourage them to discuss their questions with a partner after reading.

Just as we tried to find common ground with our understanding of the idea of limits, we try to find common ground with the experiences of the characters in the selections in Part One. Have students experienced a death in the family? Have them make a list of "feeling" words such as *afflicted, wept,* and *grief.* Have they ever known anyone who took action as Ida B. Wells-Barnett did in *Crusade for Justice?* Have students discuss the ways people can affect political decision-making."

Nancy Duke S. Lay
New York, New York

Before Reading

The Story of an Hour

by Kate Chopin

Kate Chopin
1851–1904

Kate Chopin did not begin to write until she was thirty-six years old. A much sought-after belle of St. Louis society, Chopin married at nineteen and had six children. In 1879, her husband Oscar died suddenly of swamp fever. Financially independent and bored with her life as a society matron, Chopin began to write. For the most part, her writing was not well-received because of the unconventional behavior of her female characters. After she died, Chopin's works were essentially forgotten, then rediscovered during the women's movement of the late 1960s.

Building Background

Breaking New Ground When Chopin embarked on a literary career, she kept her writing a secret from her circle of friends. She was afraid that she would be criticized by a society that was unprepared to see women as professionals. In 1894, certain that she had found her true vocation, and equally certain that she understood the hidden desires of women of her time, Chopin created the character of Louise and wrote her short story, "The Story of an Hour."

Literary Focus

Irony is the contrast between what appears to be and what really is. In an ironic situation, an author presents a state of affairs that is the opposite of what is expected or what seems appropriate. Using a chart similar to the one below, note examples of irony in "The Story of an Hour."

Event	What is expected	What happens

Writer's Notebook

Free at Last? Have you ever dreamed of being completely free, with absolutely no responsibilities—nothing you *have* to do and nowhere you *have* to go? What are the advantages of this type of freedom? What are the disadvantages? In your notebook, write a paragraph that explains why you would or would not want to be completely free and on your own.

The Story of an Hour   **449**

Before Reading

Building Background

Ask students to discuss women's roles in the late nineteenth century. Use a Venn diagram like the one below.

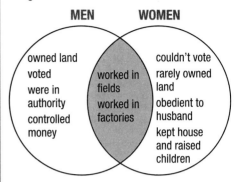

MEN   WOMEN

owned land
voted
were in
authority
controlled
money

worked in
fields
worked in
factories

couldn't vote
rarely owned
land
obedient to
husband
kept house
and raised
children

Literary Focus

Question In the story "The Gift of the Magi" a man sells his watch to buy hair combs for his wife. She sells her hair to buy him a watch chain. Is this an example of **irony?** *(yes)* Ask students to be ready to discuss the ironic ending of Chopin's story.

Writer's Notebook

Remind students to offer supporting details when writing about the advantages and disadvantages of being completely free.

More About Kate Chopin

Chopin's treatment of a woman's ambitions and motivations in *The Awakening* was very controversial. She contributed many feminist stories to literary journals.

Another work by Kate Chopin is *Bayou Folk* (1894).

SUPPORT MATERIALS OVERVIEW

Unit 5 Resource Book
- Graphic Organizer, p. 1
- Study Guide, p. 2
- Vocabulary, p. 3
- Grammar, p. 4
- Alternate Check Test, p. 5
- Vocabulary Test, p. 6
- Selection Test, pp. 7–8

Building English Proficiency
- Literature Summaries
- Activities, p. 202

Reading, Writing & Grammar SkillBook
- Reading, pp. 87–89
- Writing, pp. 121–122
- Grammar, Usage, and Mechanics, pp. 173–175

Technology
- Audiotape
- Personal Journal Software
- Custom Literature Database: An additional selection by Kate Chopin can be found on the database.
- Test Generator Software

During Reading

Selection Objectives

- To compare descriptions of thought and action
- To investigate synonyms and antonyms for vocabulary words
- To explore the theme of exceeding limits
- To identify the use of irony

Unit 5 Resource Book
Graphic Organizer, p. 1
Study Guide, p. 2

Theme Link

A nineteenth-century woman learns of her husband's death. Initially she sobs, but soon feels as though her life will now know no limits.

Vocabulary Preview

abandonment, freedom from restraint

tumultuously, violently

exalted, noble, elevated

elixir, substance supposed to have the power of lengthening life indefinitely; cure-all

unwittingly, not knowingly; unconsciously

Students can add the words and definitions to their personal word lists in the Writer's Notebook.

---

1 Reading/Thinking Skills

Compare and Contrast

Question How does Mrs. Mallard's emotional state compare to what she sees out her window? *(Possible response: She is experiencing emotional upheaval while outside birds are twittering, someone is singing, and there is "new spring life.")*

THE STORY OF AN HOUR

KATE CHOPIN

Knowing that Mrs. Mallard was afflicted with a heart trouble, great care was taken to break to her as gently as possible the news of her husband's death.

It was her sister Josephine who told her, in broken sentences; veiled hints that revealed in half concealing. Her husband's friend Richards was there, too, near her. It was he who had been in the newspaper office when intelligence of the railroad disaster was received, with Brently Mallard's name leading the list of "killed." He had only taken the time to assure himself of its truth by a second telegram, and had hastened to forestall[1] any less careful, less tender friend in bearing the sad message.

She did not hear the story as many women have heard the same, with a paralyzed inability to accept its significance. She wept at once, with sudden, wild abandonment,[2] in her sister's arms. When the storm of grief had spent itself she went away to her room alone. She would have no one follow her.

There stood, facing the open window, a comfortable, roomy armchair. Into this she sank, pressed down by a physical exhaustion that haunted her body and seemed to reach into her soul.

She could see in the open square before her house the tops of trees that were all aquiver with the new spring life. The delicious breath of rain was in the air. In the street below a peddler was crying his wares.[3] The notes of a distant song which someone was singing reached her faintly, and countless sparrows were twittering in the eaves.

There were patches of blue sky showing here and there through the clouds that had met and piled one above the other in the west facing her window.

She sat with her head thrown back upon the cushion of the chair, quite motionless, except when a sob came up into her **1** throat and shook her, as a child who has cried itself to sleep continues to sob in its dreams.

She was young, with a fair, calm face, whose lines bespoke repression and even a certain strength. But now there was a dull stare in her eyes, whose gaze was fixed away off yonder on one of those patches of blue sky. It was not a glance of reflection, but rather indicated a suspension of intelligent thought.

---

1. **forestall** (fôr stôl′), *v.* prevent by acting first.
2. abandonment (ə ban′dən mənt), *n.* freedom from restraint.
3. **crying his wares.** Street peddlers often shouted out what they were selling as they walked down the street.

SELECTION SUMMARY

The Story of an Hour

"The Story of an Hour" describes the twists and turns of thought and emotion experienced by a young woman during the hour after she learns that her husband has been suddenly killed. Because she suffers from heart disease, those around her try to shield her from the shock.

The feeling that comes over her, however, is an amazing sense of freedom that allows her to look forward, for the first time, to the rest of her life, and to hope that it is long. A further shock awaits her when a knock on the door reveals her husband.

*For summaries in other languages, see the **Building English Proficiency** book.*

Response to Caption Question   Some students may suggest that the woman in the painting appears to be experiencing the "physical exhaustion" described in the story. Others may feel the subject looks too relaxed and at ease, while the woman in the story is more emotional.

Visual Literacy   Impressionist painter John Singer Sargent used brilliantly colored oils and the contrast of light and shadow to give his impression of a woman at rest. Using broad brush strokes and a hint of detail in the woman's clothes and the furniture, he presents a warm and soothing image. Notice the bottom edge of a picture frame that runs across the entire top of the painting—holding the subject in place and forcing our eyes to rest upon her.

Question   Do the brush strokes seem to have been done quickly or slowly? *(The impression given is that most of the brush strokes were done quickly, although some students may note that the picture frame and table have more detail and that the sofa appears to have been painted in layers of color.)*

▲ How does the tone of this John Singer Sargent painting, *Repose* (1911), compare with the tone of "The Story of an Hour"?

The Story of an Hour   **451**

BUILDING ENGLISH PROFICIENCY

Exploring Key Concepts

Focusing on the idea of a character's reaction to events helps students understand the character's emotional shifts.

- Ask students to think about a time when their feelings about something or someone shifted dramatically from admiration to disdain or great liking to extreme dislike. Ask them to describe their emotions in a journal.

- Have students complete a chart like the one shown. Under "Stimulus" is the information that elicits an emotion from Mrs. Mallard. Under "Response" is the emotion she experiences. Have them add to the list when they finish reading.

MRS. MALLARD

Stimulus	Response
news of husband's death	storm of grief
something coming to her	fearful

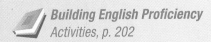

Building English Proficiency
Activities, p. 202

ESL
LEP
ELD
SAE
LD

Literary Focus

2 **Irony**

Questions

- How does Josephine think her sister is feeling? *(She thinks Mrs. Mallard is sick with grief.)*

- Why is this ironic? *(Mrs. Mallard is actually overwhelmed by a feeling of freedom.)*

Reading/Thinking Skills

3 **Summarize**

Question What kills Mrs. Mallard? *(Possible response: shock and dismay at seeing her husband alive.)*

Check Test

1. Why does the family tell Mrs. Mallard about her husband's death so gently? *(She has a weak heart and might not stand the shock.)*

2. What time of year is it and what is the weather like? *(It is spring and it's about to rain.)*

3. How do Mrs. Mallard's eyes change as she sits in the chair by the window? *(At first she looks vacant, with intelligent thought suspended. Then she becomes terrified. Finally her eyes grow keen and bright at the prospect of freedom.)*

4. How does the future now look to Mrs. Mallard as compared with the day before? *(Now she hopes her life will be long; yesterday she was afraid it would be long.)*

5. Are the doctors right in their assessment of the cause of Mrs. Mallard's death? *(No. She did not die of joy. She died because her hopes of freedom were shattered.)*

Unit 5 Resource Book
Alternate Check Test, p. 5

There was something coming to her and she was waiting for it, fearfully. What was it? She did not know; it was too subtle and elusive to name. But she felt it, creeping out of the sky, reaching toward her through the sounds, the scents, the color that filled the air.

Now her bosom rose and fell tumultuously.[4] She was beginning to recognize this thing that was approaching to possess her, and she was striving to beat it back with her will—as powerless as her two white slender hands would have been.

When she abandoned herself a little whispered word escaped her slightly parted lips. She said it over and over under her breath: "free, free, free!" The vacant stare and the look of terror that had followed it went from her eyes. They stayed keen and bright. Her pulses beat fast, and the coursing blood warmed and relaxed every inch of her body.

She did not stop to ask if it were or were not a monstrous joy that held her. A clear and exalted[5] perception enabled her to dismiss the suggestion as trivial.

She knew that she would weep again when she saw the kind, tender hands folded in death; the face that had never looked save with love upon her, fixed and gray and dead. But she saw beyond that bitter moment a long procession of years to come that would belong to her absolutely. And she opened and spread her arms out to them in welcome.

There would be no one to live for her during those coming years; she would live for herself. There would be no powerful will bending hers in that blind persistence with which men and women believe they have a right to impose a private will upon a fellow-creature. A kind intention or a cruel intention made the act seem no less a crime as she looked upon it in that brief moment of illumination.

And yet she had loved him—sometimes. Often she had not. What did it matter! What could love, the unsolved mystery, count for in face of this possession of self-assertion which she suddenly recognized as the strongest impulse of her being!

"Free! Body and soul free!" she kept whispering.

Josephine was kneeling before the closed door with her lips to the keyhole, imploring for admission. "Louise, open the door! I beg; open the door—you will make yourself ill. What are you doing, Louise? For heaven's sake open the door." **2**

"Go away. I am not making myself ill." No; she was drinking in a very elixir[6] of life through that open window.

Her fancy was running riot along those days ahead of her. Spring days, and summer days, and all sorts of days that would be her own. She breathed a quick prayer that life might be long. It was only yesterday she had thought with a shudder that life might be long.

She arose at length and opened the door to her sister's importunities. There was a feverish triumph in her eyes, and she carried herself unwittingly[7] like a goddess of Victory. She clasped her sister's waist, and together they descended the stairs. Richards stood waiting for them at the bottom.

Someone was opening the front door with a latchkey. It was Brently Mallard who entered, a little travel-stained, composedly carrying his grip-sack and umbrella. He had been far from the scene of the accident, and did not even know there had been one. He stood amazed at Josephine's piercing cry; at Richards' quick motion to screen him from the view of his wife.

But Richards was too late.

When the doctors came they said she had died of heart disease—of joy that kills. **3**

---

4. **tumultuously** (tü mul′chü əs lē), *adv.* violently.
5. **exalted** (eg zôl′təd), *adj.* noble; elevated.
6. **elixir** (i lik′sər), *n.* substance supposed to have the power of lengthening life indefinitely; cure-all.
7. **unwittingly** (un wit′ing lē), *adv.* not knowingly; unconsciously.

MINI-LESSON: GRAMMAR

To, Too, and Two

Teach Clarifying the difference between *to, too,* and *two* can help students avoid confusing them in their writing.

Activity Ideas

Ask students to work in pairs. Assign each student one page of the story. Ask students to:

- find sentences containing *to, too,* or *two*
- read sentences aloud to their partners

Partners must:

- state whether the word in question is spelled *to, too,* or *two*
- explain their response by defining the word as it is used in the story

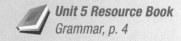
Unit 5 Resource Book
Grammar, p. 4

After Reading

Making Connections

Shaping Your Response

1. Does Louise Mallard deserve sympathy, or did she get what she deserved? Explain your opinion.

Analyzing the Story

2. How would you explain Louise's widely varied emotions in the story?

3. Find a paragraph in the story which seems to explain Louise's reaction. Analyze it carefully. Would you say it is talking about marriage, or sexism, or neither? Explain.

4. Why does Louise seem better able to express her **individuality** after she believes her husband has died?

Extending the Ideas

5. Bring "The Story of an Hour" up to the present. How might this story be different if it took place in modern times?

Literary Focus: Irony

Review the examples of **irony** you noted in your chart. Then choose one and explain why it is ironic. How does the situation—what really happens—differ from what seems appropriate or expected?

Vocabulary Study

**abandonment
tumultuously
exalted
elixir
unwittingly**

In your notebook, copy the chart shown here, providing a synonym and an antonym for each of the words.

	Synonym	Antonym
1. abandonment		
2. tumultuously		
3. exalted		
4. elixir		
5. unwittingly		

Expressing Your Ideas

Writing Choice

Writer's Notebook Update Has your attitude toward freedom changed after reading the selection? Write a paragraph that compares your thoughts about personal freedom and independence before and after reading the story.

Another Option

Reader's Theater Working in a small group, adapt "The Story of an Hour" as a **reader's theater play** and perform it for the rest of the class. Choose appropriate background music and costumes.

The Story of an Hour   **453**

After Reading

MAKING CONNECTIONS

1. Responses will vary and should be supported by the story, but most will feel she deserves sympathy.

2. Possible response: Mrs. Mallard is suddenly experiencing many new circumstances in her life. Her husband's death is sad, but the new freedom it will bring is exhilarating.

3. Possible response: In the sixth paragraph on page 452, Mrs. Mallard thinks about the constraints people put on one another in marriage. It explains why she feels freedom at being released from her marriage. Although it takes a dim view of being married, it doesn't seem to condemn only husbands.

4. Possible response: She no longer has to worry about what he will say or expect of her—nor of what society will expect of her as a married woman.

5. Some students may think it would not change much. Others may feel that both men and women now have more freedom within marriage, due to changes in the view of "a woman's place" or the acceptance of divorce. Perhaps a modern Mrs. Mallard would feel freer to investigate her feelings and her desire for freedom.

VOCABULARY STUDY

Possible Responses	Synonym	Antonym
1. abandonment	freedom	restraint
2. tumultuously	wildly	sedately
3. exalted	uplifted	depressed
4. elixir	potion	poison
5. unwittingly	innocently	knowingly

 Unit 5 Resource Book
Vocabulary p. 3
Vocabulary Test, p. 6

Selection Test

Unit 5 Resource Book
pp. 7–8

WRITING CHOICE
Writer's Notebook Update

Students may give examples from their own relationships or about others they have observed.

ANOTHER OPTION
Reader's Theater

Students might consider writing a monologue for Mrs. Mallard, through which she reveals her thoughts and emotions.

Building Background

Ask students to discuss how men and women view each other, based on gender.

Literary Focus

Plot is more than just the events that make up a play. It is also a way of revealing information about characters and theme. In this play, a man is murdered. Ask students to discuss how different people (a wife, a friend, themselves) might respond to such an event. What might their responses reveal about them?

Writer's Notebook

As students write about their response to the trial, ask them what the response reveals about themselves.

More About Susan Glaspell

- The Provincetown Players took up residence in Greenwich Village in New York City in 1916. Their theater still stands on MacDougal Street.
- Glaspell's play *Alison's House,* based on Emily Dickinson's life, won the Pulitzer Prize in 1931.

Another work by Susan Glaspell is *Suppressed Desires.*

Trifles

by Susan Glaspell

Susan Glaspell
1876?–1948

In 1915, Susan Glaspell and her husband, George Cram Cook, organized a group of Provincetown, Massachusetts artists who produced several one-act plays in a shabby wharf theater. In 1916, playwright Eugene O'Neill and poet Edna St. Vincent Millay joined the group. Over the next seven years, Glaspell wrote one play after another, many of which focused on her favorite theme of escaping imprisoning environments in order to gain individual freedom. *Trifles* was first performed by the Provincetown Players in the summer of 1916.

Building Background

Producing *Trifles* Imagine that you are the director in charge of a class production of *Trifles.* While reading Glaspell's play, keep these questions in mind: What should your sets look like? What would be an appropriate musical score? What additional stage directions will you need to give your actors? Which of your classmates would be best suited to play the five characters?

Literary Focus

Plot is the sequence of interrelated actions and events that present and resolve a conflict. As the plot unfolds, often the conflict builds to an emotional or dramatic peak—the **turning point,** or climax, which is followed by a **resolution** or denouement.

Think about plot by doing a plot structure map for a mystery story or movie you've recently read or seen. Copy the plot structure map on a sheet of paper. At each of the five points on the map, write a sentence that explains the action.

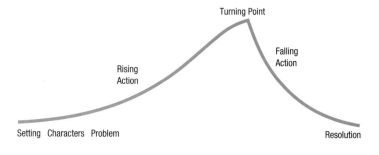

Turning Point

Rising Action

Falling Action

Setting Characters Problem

Resolution

Writer's Notebook

Guilty or Innocent? In the play you're about to read, a woman has been accused of murdering her husband. Think of a trial that you've heard about recently. If you had been a member of the jury during that trial, would you have voted guilty or innocent? Why? In your notebook, write a paragraph that explains your verdict.

SUPPORT MATERIALS OVERVIEW

Unit 5 Resource Book
- Graphic Organizer, p. 9
- Study Guide, p. 10
- Vocabulary, p. 11
- Grammar, p.12
- Alternate Check Test, p. 13
- Vocabulary Test, p. 14
- Selection Test, pp. 15–16

Building English Proficiency
- Literature Summaries
- Activities, p. 203

Reading, Writing & Grammar SkillBook
- Vocabulary, pp. 7–8
- Writing, pp. 127–129
- Grammar, Usage, and Mechanics, pp. 188–189

The World of Work
- Private Investigator, p.15
- Activity, p. 16

Technology
- Audiotape
- Personal Journal Software
- Custom Literature Database: For another selection dealing with women's issues, see Susan B. Anthony's essay "Political Economy of Women" on the database.
- Test Generator Software

TRIFLES
SUSAN GLASPELL

SCENE: The kitchen in the now abandoned farmhouse of JOHN WRIGHT, *a gloomy kitchen, and left without having been put in order—unwashed pans under the sink, a loaf of bread outside the bread-box, a dish-towel on the table—other signs of incompleted work. At the rear the outer door opens and the* SHERIFF *comes in followed by the* COUNTY ATTORNEY *and* HALE. *The* SHERIFF *and* HALE *are men in middle life, the* COUNTY ATTORNEY *is a young man; all are much bundled up and go at once to the stove. They are followed by the two women—the* SHERIFF'S *wife first; she is a slight wiry¹ woman, a thin nervous face.* MRS. HALE *is larger and would ordinarily be called more comfortable looking, but she is disturbed now and looks fearfully about as she enters. The women have come in slowly, and stand close together near the door.*

COUNTY ATTORNEY *(rubbing his hands).* This feels good. Come up to the fire, ladies.

MRS. PETERS *(after taking a step forward).* I'm not—cold.

SHERIFF *(unbuttoning his overcoat and stepping away from the stove as if to mark the beginning of official business).* Now, Mr. Hale, before we move things about, you explain to Mr. Henderson just what you saw when you came here yesterday morning.

COUNTY ATTORNEY. By the way, has anything been moved? Are things just as you left them yesterday?

SHERIFF *(looking about).* It's just the same. When it dropped below zero last night I thought I'd better send Frank out this morning to make a fire for us—no use getting pneumonia with

a big case on, but I told him not to touch anything except the stove—and you know Frank.

COUNTY ATTORNEY. Somebody should have been left here yesterday.

SHERIFF. Oh—yesterday. When I had to send Frank to Morris Center for that man who went crazy—I want you to know I had my hands full yesterday. I knew you could get back from Omaha by today and as long as I went over everything here myself—

COUNTY ATTORNEY. Well, Mr. Hale, tell just what happened when you came here yesterday morning.

HALE. Harry and I had started to town with a load of potatoes. We came along the road from my place and as I got here I said, "I'm going to see if I can't get John Wright to go in with me on a party telephone." I spoke to Wright about it once before and he put me off, saying folks talked too much anyway, and all he asked was peace and quiet—I guess you know about how much he talked himself; but I thought maybe if I went to the house and talked about it before his wife, though I said to Harry that I didn't know as what his wife wanted made much difference to John—

COUNTY ATTORNEY. Let's talk about that later, Mr. Hale. I do want to talk about that, but tell now just what happened when you got to the house.

HALE. I didn't hear or see anything; I knocked at the door, and still it was all quiet inside. I knew

---

1. wiry (wī′rē), *adj.* lean, strong, and tough.

During Reading

Selection Objectives

- To identify plot
- To analyze characters' personalities and motives
- To explore the theme of exceeding limits
- To study vocabulary through word relationships

 Unit 5 Resource Book
Graphic Organizer, p. 9
Study Guide, p. 10

Theme Link

Several characters in this play—especially the couple who figure so strongly in the plot—have gone beyond the limits of reasonable behavior. Glaspell explores their motives with a plot that asks: Who went too far?

Vocabulary Preview

wiry, lean, strong, and tough
stiffly, not easy or natural in manner
close, private, reserved
abashed, embarrassed; ashamed
scoffingly, mockingly; in a manner that makes fun to show one does not believe something

Students can add the words and definitions to their personal word lists in the Writer's Notebook.

SELECTION SUMMARY

Trifles

A man is strangled in his bed. His wife is present, but she makes no announcement or request for help, merely waiting for someone to show up. When outsiders do arrive, she is sent quickly to jail to await formal accusation. As the play opens, a contingent of officials and neighbors enters the woman's house in search of clues to a motive. The men—a neighbor, the sheriff, and a county attorney—search the bedroom after pausing to snicker over their wives' concern about the state of the suspect's preserves and half-finished quilt. The wives, left downstairs to peruse womanly "trifles," get to the heart of the matter, discovering a soured marriage and an event that may have pushed the wife beyond endurance.

 *For summaries in other languages, see the **Building English Proficiency** book.*

they must be up, it was past eight o'clock. So I knocked again, and I thought I heard somebody say, "Come in." I wasn't sure, I'm not sure yet, but I opened the door—this door *(indicating the door by which the two women are still standing)* and there in that rocker—*(pointing to it)* sat Mrs. Wright.

(They all look at the rocker.)

1 COUNTY ATTORNEY. What—was she doing?

HALE. She was rockin' back and forth. She had her apron in her hand and was kind of—pleating it.

COUNTY ATTORNEY. And how did she—look?

HALE. Well, she looked queer.

COUNTY ATTORNEY. How do you mean—queer?

HALE. Well, as if she didn't know what she was going to do next. And kind of done up.

COUNTY ATTORNEY. How did she seem to feel about your coming?

HALE. Why, I don't think she minded—one way or other. She didn't pay much attention. I said, "How do, Mrs. Wright, it's cold, ain't it?" And she said, "Is it?" and went on kind of pleating at her apron. Well, I was surprised; she didn't ask me to come up to the stove, or to set down, but just sat there, not even looking at me, so I said, "I want to see John." And then she—laughed. I guess you would call it a laugh. I thought of Harry and the team outside, so I said a little sharp: "Can't I see John?" "No," she says, kind o' dull like. "Ain't he home?" says I. "Yes," says she, "he's home." "Then why can't I see him?" I asked her, out of patience. "'Cause he's dead," says she. *"Dead?"* says I. She just nodded her head, not getting a bit excited, but rockin' back and forth. "Why—where is he?" says I, not knowing what to say. She just pointed upstairs—like that *(himself pointing to the room above)*. I got up, with the idea of going up there. I walked from there to here—then I says, "Why, what did he die of?" "He died of a rope round his neck," says she, and just went on pleatin' at her apron. Well, I went out and called Harry. I thought I might—

2 need help. We went upstairs and there he was lyin'—

COUNTY ATTORNEY. I think I'd rather have you go into that upstairs, where you can point it all out. Just go on now with the rest of the story.

HALE. Well, my first thought was to get that rope off. It looked . . . *(stops, his face twitches)* . . . but Harry, he went up to him, and he said, "No, he's dead all right, and we'd better not touch anything." So we went back downstairs. She was still sitting that same way. "Has anybody been notified?" I asked. "No," says she, unconcerned. "Who did this, Mrs. Wright?" said Harry. He said it business-like—and she stopped pleatin' of her apron. "I don't know," she says. "You don't *know?"* says Harry. "No," says she. "Weren't you sleepin' in the bed with him?" says Harry. "Yes," says she, "but I was on the inside." "Somebody slipped a rope round his neck and strangled him and you didn't wake up?" says Harry. "I didn't wake up," she said after him. We must 'a looked as if we didn't see how that could be, for after a minute she said, "I sleep sound." Harry was going to ask her more questions but I said maybe we ought to let her tell her story first to the coroner, or the sheriff, so Harry went fast as he could to Rivers' place, where there's a telephone.

COUNTY ATTORNEY. And what did Mrs. Wright do when she knew that you had gone for the coroner?

HALE. She moved from that chair to this one over here *(pointing to a small chair in the corner)* and just sat there with her hands held together and looking down. I got a feeling that I ought to make some conversation, so I said I had come in to see if John wanted to put in a telephone, and at that she started to laugh, and then she stopped and looked at me—scared. *(The* COUNTY ATTORNEY, *who has had his notebook out, makes a note.)* I dunno, maybe it wasn't scared. I wouldn't like to say it was. Soon Harry got back, and then **3** Dr. Lloyd came, and you, Mr. Peters, and so

---

MINI-LESSON: GRAMMAR

Indefinite Pronouns

Teach Point out the indefinite pronouns *somebody, anything,* and *anybody* on page 456. Ask students to name a few more indefinite pronouns *(everyone, everybody, anyone, each, other, no one, etc.).*

Question What noun could replace each indefinite pronoun named?

Activity Idea Go from general to specific with a twenty-questions game.

• Students think of a specific person or thing and describe it as *somebody* or *something.* For example: This is something that makes a sound.

• Others ask questions that help them reveal the identity of the specific person or thing. For example: Does this something make a musical sound? A "yes" answer allows the questioner to ask another question.

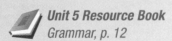
Unit 5 Resource Book
Grammar, p. 12

In Susan Glaspell's play *Trifles* Mrs. Hale says she avoided the house because it wasn't "cheerful." Does the house in Bob Timberlake's *Tulip Quilt* (1972), have that same quality that made Mrs. Hale so uncomfortable? Why or why not?

Art Study

Response to Caption Question   Some may feel it does because the room looks dark and untidy. Others may suggest that the sunshine and beautiful quilt make the room cheerful.

Visual Literacy   This painting shows the respect and admiration the artist has for the art of quilting—an art that has been the province of women all over the globe for hundreds of years. It is an art that speaks of home and family and quiet conversation—even camaraderie. The cylindrical shape of this quilt indicates it may be in a quilt hoop, which is used to keep the quilt flat and taut while quilting.

Questions

- What do the subjects of this painting tell about the person who left them in the attic room?*(Possible response: He or she is or was a quilter who probably lived a simple life.)*
- Compare the quilt with the corn. Why do you think the artist showed them together? *(Possible responses: The quilt's pattern has a similar shape. They both can be homemade or home-grown.)*
- What do you think is in the sack? *(Perhaps grain (cornmeal), the end product of the corn, or batting for the quilt.)*

BUILDING ENGLISH PROFICIENCY

Identifying Factual Information

To help students keep track of the details in this scene, have them work in groups to create a radio news report.

- Ask each group to complete a chart like the one shown.
- Have each group choose someone to play the news announcer, a reporter, and Hale or Harry being interviewed.
- Ask each group to present the earliest news of the crime. Encourage them to begin with a weather report.

Who	Hale
What	discovers that John is dead
When	
Where	
Why	
How	

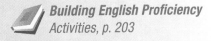 **Building English Proficiency** *Activities, p. 203*

457

Literary Element
Foreshadowing

Question Do you think the County Attorney is right in saying there is nothing important in the kitchen? *(Possible response: Probably not. He is too quick to dismiss it. The mess he finds leads him, and the audience, to wonder what else might be found.)*

5 Reader's Response
Making Personal Connections

Questions

- What is your opinion of Mr. Hale's statement about women? *(Answers will vary but will reflect students' personal views. They may also reveal an understanding of the time and place in which this play is set.)*

- How have men's opinions of women changed since this play was written? *(Answers will vary based on students' personal experience, frame of reference, and historical understanding.)*

 Art Study

Response to Caption Question
Answers will vary and may include: her life, her children, the work she has to do, and similar issues.

▲ What do you think the woman in Thomas C. Eakins' painting, *Mother* (1903), is thinking about?

I guess that's all I know that you don't.
COUNTY ATTORNEY *(looking around).* I guess we'll go upstairs first—and then out to the barn and around there. *(To the* SHERIFF.) You're convinced that there was nothing important here—nothing that would point to any motive.
SHERIFF. Nothing here but kitchen things.
(The COUNTY ATTORNEY, *after again looking around the kitchen, opens the door of a cupboard closet. He gets up on a chair and looks on a shelf. Pulls his hand away, sticky.)*

COUNTY ATTORNEY. Here's a nice mess.
(The women draw nearer.)
MRS. PETERS *(to the other woman).* Oh, her fruit; it did freeze. *(To the* LAWYER.) She worried about that when it turned so cold. She said the fire'd go out and her jars would break.
SHERIFF. Well, can you beat the woman! Held for murder and worryin' about her preserves.
COUNTY ATTORNEY. I guess before we're through she may have something more serious than preserves to worry about.
HALE. Well, women are used to worrying over trifles.
(The two women move a little closer together.)
COUNTY ATTORNEY *(with the gallantry of a young politician).* And yet, for all their worries, what would we do without the ladies? *(The women do not unbend. He goes to the sink, takes a dipperful of water from the pail and pouring it into a basin, washes his hands. Starts to wipe them on the roller-towel, turns it for a cleaner place.)* Dirty towels! *(Kicks his foot against the pans under the sink.)* Not much of a housekeeper, would you say, ladies?
MRS. HALE *(stiffly).*[2] There's a great deal of work to be done on a farm.
COUNTY ATTORNEY. To be sure. And yet *(with a little bow to her)* I know there are some Dickson County farmhouses which do not have such roller towels.
(He gives it a pull to expose its full length again.)

---

2. **stiffly** (stif´lē), *adv.* not easy or natural in manner.

MINI-LESSON: LITERARY FOCUS

Plot

Teach The interactions of characters move the plot along. This play has three distinct groupings—Mrs. Wright (and her dead husband) make up one group, and the Sheriff and County Attorney another. Each moves through the plot in different ways.

Question Which two people make up the third grouping? *(Mrs. Hale and Mrs. Peters)*

Activity Ideas

- Students can create a time line for each character or group of characters.
- Time lines should be parallel, may be of different lengths, and may have different starting points.
- Time lines may include what happened to the characters before the start of the play.
- Events that happen at the same time should line up horizontally.

MRS. HALE. These towels get dirty awful quick. Men's hands aren't always as clean as they might be.

COUNTY ATTORNEY. Ah, loyal to your sex, I see. But you and Mrs. Wright were neighbors. I suppose you were friends, too.

MRS. HALE *(shaking her head).* I've not seen much of her of late years. I've not been in this house—it's more than a year.

COUNTY ATTORNEY. And why was that? You didn't like her?

MRS. HALE. I liked her all well enough. Farmers' wives have their hands full, Mr. Henderson. And then—

COUNTY ATTORNEY. Yes—?

MRS. HALE *(looking about).* It never seemed a very cheerful place.

COUNTY ATTORNEY. No—it's not cheerful. I shouldn't say she had the homemaking instinct.

MRS. HALE. Well, I don't know as Wright had, either.

COUNTY ATTORNEY. You mean that they didn't get on very well?

MRS. HALE. No, I don't mean anything. But I don't think a place'd be any cheerfuller for John Wright's being in it.

COUNTY ATTORNEY. I'd like to talk more of that a little later. I want to get the lay of things upstairs now.

(He goes to the left, where three steps lead to a stair door.)

SHERIFF. I suppose anything Mrs. Peters does'll be all right. She was to take in some clothes for her, you know, and a few little things. We left in such a hurry yesterday.

COUNTY ATTORNEY. Yes, but I would like to see what you take, Mrs. Peters, and keep an eye out for anything that might be of use to us.

MRS. PETERS. Yes, Mr. Henderson.

(The women listen to the men's steps on the stairs, then look about the kitchen.)

MRS. HALE. I'd hate to have men coming into my kitchen, snooping around and criticising.

6 *(She arranges the pans under sink which the LAWYER had shoved out of place.)*

MRS. PETERS. Of course it's no more than their duty.

MRS. HALE. Duty's all right, but I guess that deputy sheriff that came out to make the fire might have got a little of this on. *(Gives the roller towel a pull.)* Wish I'd thought of that sooner. Seems mean to talk about her for not having things slicked up when she had to come away in such a hurry.

MRS. PETERS *(who has gone to a small table in the left rear corner of the room, and lifted one end of a towel that covers a pan).* She had bread set. *(Stands still.)*

MRS. HALE *(Eyes fixed on a loaf of bread beside the breadbox, which is on a low shelf at the other side of the room. Moves slowly toward it).* She was going to put this in there. *(Picks up loaf, then abruptly drops it. In a manner of returning to familiar things.)* It's a shame about her fruit. I wonder if it's all gone. *(Gets up on the chair and looks.)* I think there's some here that's all right, Mrs. Peters. Yes—here; *(Holding it toward the window)* this is cherries, too. *(Looking again.)* I declare I believe that's the only one. *(Gets down, bottle in her hand. Goes to the sink and wipes it off on the outside.)* She'll feel awful bad after all her hard work in the hot weather. I remember the afternoon I put up my cherries last summer.

(She puts the bottle on the big kitchen table, center of the room. With a sigh, is about to sit down in the rocking-chair. Before she is seated realizes what chair it is; with a slow look at it, steps back. The chair which she has touched rocks back and forth.)

MRS. PETERS. Well, I must get those things from the front room closet. *(She goes to the door at the right, but after looking into the other room, steps back.)* You coming with me, Mrs. Hale? You could help me carry them.

(They go in the other room; reappear, MRS. PETERS carrying a dress and skirt, MRS. HALE following with a pair of shoes.)

MRS. PETERS. My, it's cold in there.

(She puts the clothes on the big table, and hurries to the stove.)

Trifles **459**

6
Literary Focus
Plot

Questions

- What does the playwright show about Mrs. Hale and the County Attorney through the conversation between them? *(They have differing views on who bears the responsibility for making a home cheerful—the husband or the wife.)*

- What is the significance of the men going upstairs and the women staying downstairs? *(Possible response: The men have dismissed the kitchen as having no importance. They are going upstairs where the murder occurred. The women remain in their own domain—the kitchen.)*

7
Reader's Response
Making Personal Connections

Question What clues can you find about the life of a farmer's wife at this time? *(Possible responses: The house was heated only by a stove, dishes were washed by hand, bread was home-baked, and fruits were grown and preserved.)*

The World of Work

For the real-life experiences of a modern-day **private investigator**, use the pages referenced below.

The World of Work pp., 15–16

BUILDING ENGLISH PROFICIENCY

Exploring Key Statements

Draw students' attention to this key statement from page 458: "Well, women are used to worrying over trifles." Make sure that students understand the meaning of *trifles;* then use one or both of the following activities to explore Hale's words.

Activity Ideas

- Have each group draw outlines of a woman's head and a man's head. Inside each outline have them write three or four trifles that they think today's women and men worry over. Discuss the concerns they have attributed to men and women.

- Have groups of students discuss the attitude toward the opposite sex that the statement reveals. Ask them to compare it with the present-day attitudes they have outlined above.

Draw Conclusions

Question What bearing does Mrs. Wright's behavior as a young girl have on the situation being investigated now? *(She used to be lively and wear pretty clothes and now she is shabby and quiet, which may suggest that her personality has changed quite a lot—perhaps caused by her marriage to Wright.)*

MRS. HALE *(examining the skirt).* Wright was close.[3] I think maybe that's why she kept so much to herself. She didn't even belong to the Ladies' Aid. I suppose she felt she couldn't do her part, and then you don't enjoy things when you feel shabby. She used to wear pretty clothes and be lively, when she was Minnie Foster, one of the town girls singing in the choir. But that—oh, that was thirty years ago. This all you was to take in?

8

MRS. PETERS. She said she wanted an apron. Funny thing to want, for there isn't much to get you dirty in jail, goodness knows. But I suppose just to make her feel more natural. She said they was in the top drawer in this cupboard. Yes, here. And then her little shawl that always hung behind the door. *(Opens stair door and looks.)* Yes, here it is.

(Quickly shuts door leading upstairs.)

MRS. HALE *(abruptly moving toward her).* Mrs. Peters?

MRS. PETERS. Yes, Mrs. Hale?

MRS. HALE. Do you think she did it?

MRS. PETERS *(in a frightened voice).* Oh, I don't know.

MRS. HALE. Well, I don't think she did. Asking for an apron and her little shawl. Worrying about her fruit.

MRS. PETERS *(Starts to speak, glances up, where footsteps are heard in the room above. In a low voice).* Mr. Peters says it looks bad for her. Mr. Henderson is awful sarcastic in a speech and he'll make fun of her sayin' she didn't wake up.

MRS. HALE. Well, I guess John Wright didn't wake when they was slipping that rope under his neck.

MRS. PETERS. No, it's strange. It must have been done awful crafty and still. They say it was such a—funny way to kill a man, rigging it all up like that.

MRS. HALE. That's just what Mr. Hale said. There was a gun in the house. He says that's what he can't understand.

MRS. PETERS. Mr. Henderson said coming out that what was needed for the case was a motive; something to show anger, or—sudden feeling.

MRS. HALE *(who is standing by the table).* Well, I don't see any signs of anger around here. *(She puts her hand on the dish towel which lies on the table, stands looking down at the table, one half of which is clean, the other half messy.)* It's wiped to here. *(Makes a move as if to finish work, then turns and looks at loaf of bread outside the breadbox. Drops towel. In that voice of coming back to familiar things.)* Wonder how they are finding things upstairs. I hope she had it a little more red-up[4] there. You know, it seems kind of *sneaking.* Locking her up in town and then coming out here and trying to get her own house to turn against her!

MRS. PETERS. But Mrs. Hale, the law is the law.

MRS. HALE. I s'pose 'tis. *(Unbuttoning her coat.)* Better loosen up your things, Mrs. Peters. You won't feel them when you go out.

(MRS. PETERS takes off her fur tippet, goes to hang it on hook at back of room, stands looking at the under part of the small corner table.)

MRS. PETERS. She was piecing a quilt.

(She brings the large sewing basket and they look at the bright pieces.)

MRS. HALE. It's a log cabin pattern. Pretty, isn't it? I wonder if she was goin' to quilt it or just knot it?[5]

(Footsteps have been heard coming down the stairs. The SHERIFF enters followed by HALE and the COUNTY ATTORNEY.)

SHERIFF. They wonder if she was going to quilt it or just knot it!

(The men laugh, the women look abashed.)[6]

COUNTY ATTORNEY *(rubbing his hands over the stove).* Frank's fire didn't do much up there,

---

3. close (klōs), *adj.* private; reserved.
4. **red-up**, tidy, made-up.
5. **knot it**, a method of connecting the parts of a quilt.
6. abashed (ə basht′), *adj.* embarrassed; ashamed.

MINI-LESSON: SPEAKING AND LISTENING

Dramatic Dialogue

Teach Discuss with students the questions they can ask to help them understand how a character might speak a line in a play.

- What is the character reacting to?
- What are the stage directions?
- What are the words the character is using?

Activity Idea Ask students to read four or five lines spoken by Mrs. Hale and Mrs. Peters at different points in the play. Ask them to first consider

- the character's feelings and level of involvement in the situation
- the stage directions, which tell what the character is doing while she speaks and describes how she should speak
- the words the character uses and her reason for choosing each word

List the feelings evoked by Albert Pinkham Ryder's painting *The Dead Bird* (1890–1900). Are they the same as those evoked by the play? Explain.

did it? Well, let's go out to the barn and get that cleared up.

(The men go outside.)

MRS. HALE *(resentfully)*. I don't know as there's anything so strange, our takin' up our time with little things while we're waiting for them to get the evidence. *(She sits down at the big table smoothing out a block with decision.)* I don't see as it's anything to laugh about.

MRS. PETERS *(apologetically)*. Of course they've got awful important things on their minds.

(Pulls up a chair and joins MRS. HALE at the table.)

MRS. HALE *(examining another block)*. Mrs. Peters, look at this one. Here, this is the one she was working on, and look at the sewing! All the rest of it has been so nice and even. And look at this! It's all over the place! Why, it looks as if she didn't know what she was about!

(After she has said this they look at each other, then start to glance back at the door. After an instant MRS. HALE has pulled at a knot and ripped the sewing.)

MRS. PETERS. Oh, what are you doing, Mrs. Hale?

MRS. HALE *(mildly)*. Just pulling out a stitch or two that's not sewed very good. *(Threading a needle.)* Bad sewing always made me fidgety.

MRS. PETERS *(nervously)*. I don't think we ought to touch things.

MRS. HALE. I'll just finish up this end. *(Suddenly stopping and leaning forward.)* Mrs. Peters?

MRS. PETERS. Yes, Mrs. Hale?

MRS. HALE. What do you suppose she was so nervous about?

MRS. PETERS. Oh—I don't know. I don't know as she was nervous. I sometimes sew awful queer when I'm just tired. (MRS. HALE *starts to say something, looks at* MRS. PETERS, *then goes on sewing.)* Well I must get these things wrapped up. They may be through sooner than we think. *(Pulling apron and other things together.)* I wonder where I can find a piece of paper, and string.

MRS. HALE. In that cupboard, maybe.

MRS. PETERS *(looking in cupboard)*. Why, here's a bird-cage. *(Holds it up.)* Did she have a bird, Mrs. Hale?

MRS. HALE. Why, I don't know whether she did or not—I've not been here for so long. There was a man around last year selling canaries cheap, but I don't know as she took one; maybe she did. She used to sing real pretty herself.

Trifles **461**

Summarize

Question What have the women learned so far about Mrs. Wright from one other and from their "detective work"? *(Possible response: Mrs. Wright stopped in the middle of her chores, her quilting stitches became erratic just before the murder; she once sang "real pretty" and was lively and well-dressed; she probably once had a bird.)*

Evaluate

Question What are some reasons Mrs. Hale feels she should have visited Mrs. Wright? *(Mrs. Wright was childless and lonely, was married to a hard man, and lived in a cheerless home.)*

Making Personal Connections

Question Do you agree with Mrs. Peters that the bird "got sick and died"? *(Possible response: Some students may accept that explanation. Others will see the hand of Mr. Wright in the bird's death.)*

MRS. PETERS *(glancing around)*. Seems funny to think of a bird here. But she must have had one, or why would she have a cage? I wonder what happened to it.

MRS. HALE. I s'pose maybe the cat got it.

MRS. PETERS. No, she didn't have a cat. She's got that feeling some people have about cats—being afraid of them. My cat got in her room and she was real upset and asked me to take it out.

MRS. HALE. My sister Bessie was like that. Queer, ain't it?

MRS. PETERS *(examining the cage)*. Why, look at this door. It's broke. One hinge is pulled apart.

9 MRS. HALE *(looking too)*. Looks as if someone must have been rough with it.

MRS. PETERS. Why, yes.

(She brings the cage forward and puts it on the table.)

MRS. HALE. I wish if they're going to find any evidence they'd be about it. I don't like this place.

MRS. PETERS. But I'm awful glad you came with me, Mrs. Hale. It would be lonesome for me sitting here alone.

MRS. HALE. It would, wouldn't it? *(Dropping her sewing.)* But I tell you what I do wish, Mrs. Peters. I wish I had come over sometimes when *she* was here. I—*(looking around the room)*—wish I had.

MRS. PETERS. But of course you were awful busy, Mrs. Hale—your house and your children.

MRS. HALE. I could've come. I stayed away because it weren't cheerful—and that's why I ought to have come. I—I've never liked this place. Maybe because it's down in a hollow and you don't see the road. I dunno what it is, but it's a lonesome place and always was. I wish I had come over to see Minnie Foster sometimes. I can see now—

(Shakes her head.)

MRS. PETERS. Well, you mustn't reproach yourself, Mrs. Hale. Somehow we just don't see how it is with other folks until—something comes up.

MRS. HALE. Not having children makes less

work—but it makes a quiet house, and Wright out to work all day, and no company when he did come in. Did you know John Wright, Mrs. Peters? **10**

MRS. PETERS. Not to know him; I've seen him in town. They say he was a good man.

MRS. HALE. Yes—good; he didn't drink, and kept his word as well as most, I guess, and paid his debts. But he was a hard man, Mrs. Peters. Just to pass the time of day with him—*(Shivers.)* Like a raw wind that gets to the bone. *(Pauses, her eye falling on the cage.)* I should think she would 'a wanted a bird. But what do you suppose went with it?

MRS. PETERS. I don't know, unless it got sick and died. **11**

(She reaches over and swings the broken door, swings it again, both women watch it.)

MRS. HALE. You weren't raised round here, were you? (MRS. PETERS *shakes her head.*) You didn't know—her?

MRS. PETERS. Not till they brought her yesterday.

MRS. HALE. She—come to think of it, she was kind of like a bird herself—real·sweet and pretty, but kind of timid and—fluttery. How—she—did—change. *(Silence; then as if struck by a happy thought and relieved to get back to everyday things.)* Tell you what, Mrs. Peters, why don't you take the quilt in with you? It might take up her mind.

MRS. PETERS. Why, I think that's a real nice idea, Mrs. Hale. There couldn't possibly be any objection to it, could there? Now, just what would I take? I wonder if her patches are in here—and her things.

(They look in the sewing basket.)

MRS. HALE. Here's some red. I expect this has got sewing things in it. *(Brings out a fancy box.)* What a pretty box. Looks like something somebody would give you. Maybe her scissors are in here. *(Opens box. Suddenly puts her hand to her nose.)* Why—(MRS. PETERS *bends nearer, then turns her face away.)* There's something wrapped up in this piece of silk.

MRS. PETERS. Why, this isn't her scissors.

MINI-LESSON: VOCABULARY

Connotation and Denotation

Teach Discuss the difference between a word's connotation and its denotation. A dictionary definition gives the denotation of a word, while its connotation is all of the word's suggested meanings.

Activity Ideas

Explore connotation and denotation of words in the play.

- Ask students to consider the word *trifles* and to identify its denotation and connotation. Note that the word's connotation might be different depending on the character using it.

- Ask students to explore the meanings of the following words and others they may find in the play. Encourage them to consider how the word is used, by whom, and in what circumstances.

unwashed   *crazy*   *knot*

MRS. HALE (*lifting the silk*). Oh, Mrs. Peters—its—

(MRS. PETERS *bends closer.*)

MRS. PETERS. It's the bird.

MRS. HALE (*jumping up*). But, Mrs. Peters—look at it! Its neck! Look at its neck! It's all—other side *to.*

MRS. PETERS. Somebody—wrung—its—neck.

(*Their eyes meet. A look of growing comprehension, of horror. Steps are heard outside.* MRS. HALE *slips box under quilt pieces, and sinks into her chair. Enter* SHERIFF *and* COUNTY ATTORNEY. MRS. PETERS *rises.*)

12

COUNTY ATTORNEY (*as one turning from serious things to little pleasantries*). Well, ladies, have you decided whether she was going to quilt it or knot it?

MRS. PETERS. We think she was going to—knot it.

COUNTY ATTORNEY. Well, that's interesting, I'm sure. (*Seeing the birdcage.*) Has the bird flown?

MRS. HALE (*putting more quilt pieces over the box*). We think the—cat got it.

COUNTY ATTORNEY (*preoccupied*). Is there a cat?

(MRS. HALE *glances in a quick covert way at* MRS. PETERS.)

MRS. PETERS. Well, not *now.* They're superstitious, you know. They leave.

13

COUNTY ATTORNEY (*to* SHERIFF PETERS, *continuing an interrupted conversation*). No sign at all of anyone having come from the outside. Their own rope. Now let's go up again and go over it piece by piece. (*They start upstairs.*) It would have to have been someone who knew just the—

(MRS. PETERS *sits down. The two women sit there not looking at one another, but as if peering into something and at the same time holding back. When they talk now it is in the manner of feeling their way over strange ground, as if afraid of what they are saying, but as if they cannot help saying it.*)

MRS. HALE. She liked the bird. She was going to bury it in that pretty box.

MRS. PETERS (*in a whisper*). When I was a girl—my kitten—there was a boy took a hatchet, and before my eyes—and before I could get there—(*Covers her face an instant.*) If they hadn't held me back I would have—(*catches herself, looks upstairs where steps are heard, falters weakly*)—hurt him.

MRS. HALE (*with a slow look around her*). I wonder how it would seem never to have had any children around. (*Pause.*) No, Wright wouldn't like the bird—a thing that sang. She used to sing. He killed that, too.

MRS. PETERS (*moving uneasily*). We don't know who killed the bird.

MRS. HALE. I knew John Wright.

MRS. PETERS. It was an awful thing was done in this house that night, Mrs. Hale. Killing a man while he slept, slipping a rope around his neck that choked the life out of him.

MRS. HALE. His neck. Choked the life out of him. (*Her hand goes out and rests on the bird-cage.*)

MRS. PETERS (*with rising voice*). We don't know who killed him. We don't *know.*

MRS. HALE (*her own feeling not interrupted*). If there'd been years and years of nothing, then a bird to sing to you, it would be awful—still, after the bird was still.

MRS. PETERS (*something within her speaking*). I know what stillness is. When we homesteaded in Dakota, and my first baby died—after he was two years old, and me with no other then—

MRS. HALE (*moving*). How soon do you suppose they'll be through, looking for the evidence?

MRS. PETERS. I know what stillness is. (*Pulling herself back.*) The law has got to punish crime, Mrs. Hale.

MRS. HALE (*not as if answering that*). I wish you'd seen Minnie Foster when she wore a white dress with blue ribbons and stood up there in the choir and sang. (*A look around the room.*) Oh, I *wish* I'd come over here once in a while! That was a crime! That was a crime! Who's going to punish that? **14**

MRS. PETERS (*looking upstairs*). We mustn't—take on.

MRS. HALE. I might have known she needed help! I know how things can be—for women. I tell you, it's queer, Mrs. Peters. We live close together and we live far apart. We

Trifles **463**

BUILDING ENGLISH PROFICIENCY

Exploring Characters

To help students understand Minnie Wright, suggest one or more of the following activities.

- Invite students who are interested in art to draw four panels showing important events in Minnie Wright's life. The first panel should show her as young Minnie Foster.

- Discuss why Glaspell decided to keep Minnie Wright offstage. Ask a group of volunteers to plan and present a scene with Minnie on stage. Encourage them to focus on developing knowledge of her character in scenes such as Minnie bringing the canary home, or John Wright killing it.

- Encourage musical students to compose and perform a ballad or a rap song about Minnie Wright.

Questions

- Explain the irony in the playwright's choice of title. *(Possible answers: The men dismiss the women as "worrying about trifles," but the women are the ones who get to the heart of the matter. It is a supposed "trifle," a pet canary, that is the catalyst for the events.)*

- What is the irony in the last line of the play? *(The phrase "knot it"—a reference to Mrs. Wright's tying a knot in a rope and choking her husband.)*

- What is the dramatic irony in the close of the play? *(The two women, and the audience, know what really happened. The men—the formal investigators—do not.)*

Check Test

1. How were the deaths of Mr. Wright and the canary similar? *(Possible answers: Both were choked to death. Both were probably killed in a rage or out of hatred.)*

2. What clues do Mrs. Hale and Mrs. Peters put together to determine whether Mrs. Wright killed her husband? *(The unfinished chores, the poorly sewn quilt pieces, the broken cage and dead canary.)*

3. Why does each woman have sympathy for Mrs. Wright? *(Mrs. Hale knew her as a happy young woman; Mrs. Peters sympathizes with her response to silence, since she once lost a child.)*

4. Will Mrs. Wright be convicted of murder? *(Probably not, unless she confesses. The men did not find any evidence of a motive, and without it, the courts of that time and place would probably not charge her.)*

Unit 5 Resource Book
Alternate Check Test, p. 13

---

all go through the same things—it's all just a different kind of the same thing. *(Brushes her eyes, noticing the bottle of fruit, reaches out for it.)* If I was you I wouldn't tell her her fruit was gone. Tell her it *ain't.* Tell her it's all right. Take this in to prove it to her. She—she may never know whether it was broke or not.

MRS. PETERS *(Takes the bottle, looks about for something to wrap it in; takes petticoat from the clothes brought from the other room, very nervously begins winding this around the bottle. In a false voice).* My, it's a good thing the men couldn't hear us. Wouldn't they just laugh! Getting all stirred up over a little thing like a—dead canary. As if that could have anything to do with—with—wouldn't they *laugh!*

(The men are heard coming down stairs.)

MRS. HALE *(under her breath).* Maybe they would— maybe they wouldn't.

COUNTY ATTORNEY. No, Peters, it's all perfectly clear except a reason for doing it. But you know juries when it comes to women. If there was some definite thing. Something to show—something to make a story about—a thing that would connect up with this strange way of doing it—

(The women's eyes meet for an instant. Enter HALE from outer door.)

HALE. Well, I've got the team around. Pretty cold out there.

COUNTY ATTORNEY. I'm going to stay here a while by myself. *(To the SHERIFF.)* You can send Frank out for me, can't you? I want to go over everything. I'm not satisfied that we can't do better.

SHERIFF. Do you want to see what Mrs. Peters is going to take in?

(The LAWYER goes to the table, picks up the apron, laughs.)

COUNTY ATTORNEY. Oh, I guess they're not very dangerous things the ladies have picked out. *(Moves a few things about, disturbing the quilt pieces which cover the box. Steps back.)* No, Mrs. Peters doesn't need supervising. For that matter, a sheriff's wife is married to the law. Ever think of it that way, Mrs. Peters?

MRS. PETERS. Not—just that way.

SHERIFF *(chuckling).* Married to the law. *(Moves toward the other room.)* I just want you to come in here a minute, George. We ought to take a look at these windows.

COUNTY ATTORNEY. *(scoffingly)*[7] Oh, windows!

SHERIFF. We'll be right out, Mr. Hale.

(HALE goes outside. The SHERIFF follows the COUNTY ATTORNEY into the other room. Then MRS. HALE rises, hands tight together, looking intensely at MRS. PETERS, whose eyes make a slow turn, finally meeting MRS. HALE'S. A moment MRS. HALE holds her, then her own eyes point the way to where the box is concealed. Suddenly MRS. PETERS throws back quilt pieces and tries to put the box in the bag she is wearing. It is too big. She opens box, starts to take bird out, cannot touch it, goes to pieces, stands there helpless. Sound of a knob turning in the other room. MRS. HALE snatches the box and puts it in the pocket of her big coat. Enter COUNTY ATTORNEY and SHERIFF.)

COUNTY ATTORNEY *(facetiously).* Well, Henry, at least we found out that she was not going to quilt it. She was going to—what is it you call it, ladies?

MRS. HALE *(her hand against her pocket).* We call it—knot it, Mr. Henderson.

(CURTAIN)

---

7. **scoffingly** (skôf′ing lē), *adv.* mockingly; in a manner that makes fun to show one does not believe something.

After Reading

Making Connections

Shaping Your Response

1. As a class, take a vote: is Mrs. Wright guilty of murder? Discuss your theories.

Analyzing the Play

2. Why do you think this play is called *Trifles*?

3. How would you describe the sheriff's and the county attorney's attitude toward the two women?

4. Explain the significance of the canary.

5. How does Mrs. Peters's **character** change over the course of the play?

6. What cultural norms and expectations do you think helped stifle Mrs. Wright's **individuality?**

Extending the Ideas

7. Assume for the moment that Mrs. Wright is guilty of murdering her husband. Would you call it a justifiable homicide? Why or why not?

8. Were Mrs. Peters and Mrs. Hale doing the right thing when they concealed the evidence they found? Explain your answer.

Literary Focus: Plot

On a **plot** structure map like the one on page 454, map the plot of *Trifles*. At each point on the map, write a sentence that explains the action in the play.

Vocabulary Study

wiry
stiffly
close
abashed
scoffingly

Study the relationship of each of the following pairs of words; then choose another pair that has the same relationship.

1. exercise : *wiry* : :
   a. meek : mild   b. education : wise
   c. anger : sadness   d. ugly : beauty

2. comfortably : *stiffly* : :
   a. funny : humorous   b. talkative : quiet
   c. neglect : failure   d. industrious : worker

3. *close* : private : :
   a. rich : wealthy   b. lake : river
   c. cold : hot   d. notorious : obscure

4. *abashed* : proud : :
   a. instruct : train   b. joke : laughter
   c. impregnable : fortress
   d. passionate : indifferent

5. *scoffingly* : mockingly : :
   a. impediment : hindrance
   b. sunlight : glare   c. hopefully : despairingly
   d. vibrant : colors

Trifles   465

After Reading

MAKING CONNECTIONS

1. Student responses should acknowledge the clues to Mrs. Wright's motive in determining that she is guilty.

2. The play's focus is the different view of life of men and women and the things they find important, as well as the things they see as trifles.

3. Possible responses: offhand, demeaning, patronizing.

4. The canary is a beloved pet. It also symbolizes Mrs. Wright—sweet, pretty, and fluttery—and choked off by her marriage. It is killed by Mr. Wright, thus bringing about his death.

5. At first Mrs. Peters just wants to get her unpleasant task done and demurs to the men while doing so. At the end she has a sympathetic analysis of Mrs. Wright's marriage and hides the truth from the men.

6. Possible response: She was expected to live and behave as her husband wished. She had no recourse in her society but to do so.

7. Answers will vary based on students' point of view and values.

8. Answers will vary based on students' point of view and values.

VOCABULARY STUDY

1. b
2. b
3. a
4. d
5. a

More Practice   Students can use the vocabulary words to write a descriptive paragraph.

Unit 5 Resource Book
Vocabulary, p. 11
Vocabulary Test, p. 14

LITERARY FOCUS: PLOT

Students can refer to the parallel time lines they drew for the plot in the mini-lesson on page 458 and consider what is happening in each line at the climax of the play. *(Mrs. Wright is sitting in jail; the Sheriff and County Attorney are returning from their search for evidence, having found nothing; Mrs. Hale and Mrs. Peters have discovered the evidence that suggests Mrs. Wright has murdered her husband.)*

Unit 5 Resource Book
Graphic Organizer, p. 9

Selection Objectives

- To identify foreshadowing
- To analyze characters and motives
- To explore the theme of going beyond limits
- To explore the use of dialect and its effect on an audience

 Unit 5 Resource Book
Graphic Orgainzer, p. 17
Study Guide, p. 18

Theme Link

Students will encounter a husband who exceeds the limits of reasonable husbandry and a wife who confronts him by stretching the limits of propriety.

Vocabulary Preview

benevolent, kindly; charitable

infinitesimal, so small as to be almost nothing

commodious, spacious; roomy

assiduously, attentively; diligently

conclusive, decisive; convincing

sedulous, diligent; painstaking

steadfast, loyal and unwavering

pettishness, peevishness; crossness

imperturbably, calmly

furtively, done quickly and stealthily to avoid being noticed; secretly

Students can add the words and definitions to their Writer's Notebook.

1 Literary Element

Symbolism

Symbolic images and actions augment the dramatic events in this story.

Question What is symbolic about the way the man harnesses his mare? *(The mare is harnessed brusquely, with little regard for her feelings. The same can be said about the way he dismisses his wife.)*

The Revolt of "Mother"

MARY E. WILKINS FREEMAN

"Father!"

"What is it?"

"What are them men diggin' over there in the field for?"

There was a sudden dropping and enlarging of the lower part of the old man's face, as if some heavy weight had settled therein; he shut his mouth tight, and went on harnessing the great bay mare. He hustled the collar on to her neck with a jerk.

"Father!"

The old man slapped the saddle upon the mare's back.

"Look here, father, I want to know what them men are diggin' over in the field for, an' I'm goin' to know."

"I wish you'd go into the house, mother, an' 'tend to your own affairs," the old man said then. He ran his words together, and his speech was almost as inarticulate as a growl.

But the woman understood; it was her most native tongue. "I ain't goin' into the house till you tell me what them men are doin' over there in the field," said she.

Then she stood waiting. She was a small woman, short and straight-waisted like a child in her brown cotton gown. Her forehead was mild and benevolent[1] between the smooth curves of gray hair; there were meek downward lines about her nose and mouth; but her eyes, fixed upon the old man, looked as if the meekness had been the result of her own will, never of the will of another.

They were in the barn, standing before the wide open doors. The spring air, full of the smell of growing grass and unseen blossoms, came in their faces. The deep yard in front was littered with farm wagons and piles of wood; on the edges, close to the fence and the house, the grass was a vivid green, and there were some dandelions.

The old man glanced doggedly at his wife as he tightened the last buckles on the harness. She looked as immovable to him as one of the

"I wish you'd go into the house, mother, an' 'tend to your own affairs . . ."

1

---

1. benevolent (bə nev′ə lənt), *adj.* kindly; charitable.

468 UNIT FIVE: BREAKING THE MOLD

SELECTION SUMMARY

The Revolt of "Mother"

Sarah Penn, a farmer's wife, looks out from her small, cramped house one day and sees workers digging a foundation on the land where forty years ago her husband promised a new house would stand. When Sarah learns that her husband Adoniram has decided to build yet another barn, she sets out on the path toward rebellion.

The Penns' daughter Nanny is getting married soon and wants a suitable place for a wedding. The barn rises, and the small house is confining and insulting in comparison. When Adoniram is called away for a day, Sarah and her children take the "providential opportunity" to move their household into the barn.

 *For summaries in other languages, see the **Building English Proficiency** book.*

After you've read the story, decide what the woman in George Schreiber's 1939 painting *From Arkansas* has in common with Sarah in "The Revolt of 'Mother.'"

Response to Caption Question
Students may see that they are both farm women, weathered like the land. The woman in the painting looks as if she is waiting for something, just as Sarah waits for a suitable home.

Visual Literacy   In capturing the sweeping lines of the woman's blouse and apron, Schreiber sets the tone for an image of the blustery life on an Arkansas farm in the late 1930s. The barren branches of the tree mirror the tatters in the woman's apron and her loose strands of hair.

Question   This women is looking at something outside of the picture. How does she seem to be responding to what she sees? *(Answers will vary. She may be a bit expectant or eager, but seems primarily at ease and settled, as though it were someone or something she knows quite well and is not surprised to see.)*

BUILDING ENGLISH PROFICIENCY

Analyzing Characters

Use one or both of the following activities to help students understand the character of Sarah Penn.

Activity Ideas

- Have students freewrite on the topic "An Ideal Mother." Urge them to keep their responses in mind as they read so they can compare their ideal with the mother in the story.

- Have students begin a web of ideal character traits—expanding upon it after they have read the story.

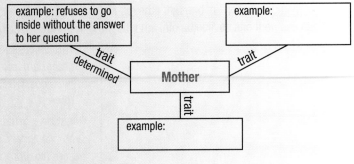

example: refuses to go inside without the answer to her question

trait
determined

Mother

trait

example:

trait

example:

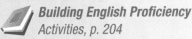

Building English Proficiency
Activities, p. 204

469

Point out the use of nonstandard language *nohow* and *afore* in the dialogue and invite students to discuss what this reveals about the characters and the characters' lives. *(Possible responses: that they are not well educated; that they are in an informal situation; that they are country folk)*

Question How do the words and description of Sarah Penn prepare you for what might come next? *(Possible response: They suggest that she is going to speak to her husband with great authority and will probably be convincing.)*

Ask students how the writer's use of run-on sentences to express Sarah Penn's thoughts reinforces the impact of those words. *(Possible response: She has so much to say after being quiet for so many years that her words pour out. The reader senses her strong feelings.)*

---

patient and steadfast[9] soul—the digging of the cellar of the new barn in the place where Adoniram forty years ago had promised her their new house should stand.

The pies were done for dinner. Adoniram and Sammy were home a few minutes after twelve o'clock. The dinner was eaten with serious haste. There was never much conversation at the table in the Penn family. Adoniram asked a blessing, and they ate promptly, then rose up and went about their work.

Sammy went back to school, taking soft sly lopes out of the yard like a rabbit. He wanted a game of marbles before school, and feared his father would give him some chores to do. Adoniram hastened to the door and called after him, but he was out of sight.

"I don't see what you let him go for, mother," said he. "I wanted him to help me unload that wood."

Adoniram went to work out in the yard unloading wood from the wagon. Sarah put away the dinner dishes, while Nanny took down her curl-papers and changed her dress. She was going down to the store to buy some more embroidery and thread.

When Nanny was gone, Mrs. Penn went to the door. "Father!" she called.
"Well, what is it!"
"I want to see you jest a minute, father."
"I can't leave this wood nohow. I've got to git it unloaded an' go for a load of gravel afore two o'clock. Sammy had ought to helped me. You hadn't ought to let him go to school so early."
"I want to see you jest a minute."
"I tell ye I can't, nohow, mother."
"Father, you come here." Sarah Penn stood in the door like a queen; she held her head as if it bore a crown; there was the patience which makes authority royal in her voice. Adoniram went.

Mrs. Penn led the way into the kitchen, and pointed to a chair. "Sit down, father," said she; "I've got somethin' I want to say to you."

He sat down heavily; his face was quite stolid, but he looked at her with restive eyes. "Well, what is it, mother?"

"I want to know what you're buildin' that new barn for, father?"

"I ain't got nothin' to say about it."

"It can't be you think you need another barn?"

"I tell ye I ain't got nothin' to say about it, mother; an' I ain't goin' to say nothing'."

"Be you goin' to buy more cows?"

Adoniram did not reply; he shut his mouth tight.

"I know you be, as well as I want to. Now, father, look here"—Sarah Penn had not sat down; she stood before her husband in the humble fashion of a Scripture woman—"I'm goin' to talk real plain to you; I never have sence I married you, but I'm goin' to now. I ain't never complained, an' I ain't goin' to complain now, but I'm goin' to talk plain. You see this room here, father; you look at it well. You see there ain't no carpet on the floor, an' you see the paper is all dirty, an' droppin' off the walls. We ain't had no new paper on it for ten year, an' then I put it on myself, an' it didn't cost but ninepence a roll. You see this room, father; it's all the one I've had to work in an' eat in an' sit in sence we was married. There ain't another woman in the whole town whose husband ain't got half the means you have but what's got better. It's all the room Nanny's got to have her company in; an' there ain't one of her mates but what's got better, an' their fathers not so able as hers is. It's all the room she'll have to be married in. What would you have thought, father, if we had had our weddin' in a room no better than this? I was married in my mother's parlor, with a carpet on the floor, an' stuffed furniture, an' a mahogany card-table. An' this is all the room my daughter will have to be married in. Look here, father!"

Sarah Penn went across the room as though it were a tragic stage. She flung open a door and disclosed a tiny bedroom, only large enough for a bed and bureau, with a path between. "There,

---

9. steadfast (sted'fast'), *adj.* loyal and unwavering.

MINI-LESSON: LITERARY FOCUS

Foreshadowing

Teach Foreshadowing—clues about coming events—is shown through the methods of dialogue, description, or narrative.

Activity Ideas

- Ask students to work in groups of four or five to create skits, each of which end with an important event.

- Encourage groups to plan their dialogue and narration to include foreshadowing clues to the later event.

- Invite groups to discuss how to use facial expressions, setting, or props to add to foreshadowing.

father," said she—"there's all the room I've had to sleep in forty year. All my children were born there—the two that died, an' the two that's livin'. I was sick with a fever there."

"I'm going to talk real plain to you; I never have sence I married you, but I'm goin' to now."

She stepped to another door and opened it. It led into the small, ill-lighted pantry. "Here," said she, "is all the buttery I've got—every place I've got for my dishes, to set away my victuals in, an' to keep my milk-pans in. Father, I've been takin' care of the milk of six cows in this place, an' now you're goin' to build a new barn, an' keep more cows, an' give me more to do in it."

She threw open another door. A narrow crooked flight of stairs wound upward from it. "There, father," said she, "I want you to look at the stairs that go up to them two unfinished chambers that are all the places our son an' daughter have had to sleep in all their lives. There ain't a prettier girl in town nor a more ladylike one than Nanny, an' that's the place she has to sleep in. It ain't so good as your horse's stall; it ain't so warm an' tight."

Sarah Penn went back and stood before her husband. "Now, father," said she, "I want to know if you think you're doin' right an' accordin' to what you profess. Here, when we was married, forty year ago, you promised me faithful that we should have a new house built in that lot over in the field before the year was out. You said you had money enough, an' you wouldn't ask me to live in no such place as this. It is forty year now, an' you've been makin' more money, an' I've been savin' of it for you ever since, an' you ain't built no house yet. You've built sheds an' cowhouses an' one new barn, an' now you're goin' to build another. Father, I want to know if you think it's right. You're lodgin' your dumb beasts

better than you are your own flesh an' blood. I want to know if you think it's right."

"I ain't got nothin' to say."

"You can't say nothin' without ownin' it ain't right, father. An' there's another thing—I ain't complained; I've got along forty year, an' I s'pose I should forty more, if it wa'n't for that—if we don't have another house. Nanny she can't live with us after she's married. She'll have to go somewheres else to live away from us, an' it don't seem as if I could have it so, noways, father. She wa'n't ever strong. She's got considerable color, but there wa'n't ever any backbone to her. I've always took the heft of everything off her, an' she ain't fit to keep house an' do everything herself. She'll be all worn out inside of a year. Think of her doin' all the washin' an' ironin' an' bakin' with them soft white hands an' arms, an' sweepin'! I can't have it so, noways, father." **11**

Mrs. Penn's face was burning; her mild eyes gleamed. She had pleaded her little cause like a Webster;[10] she had ranged from severity to pathos; but her opponent employed that obstinate silence which makes eloquence futile with mocking echoes. Adoniram arose clumsily.

"Father, ain't you got nothin' to say?" said Mrs. Penn.

"I've got to go off after that load of gravel. I can't stan' here talkin' all day."

"Father, won't you think it over, an' have a house built there instead of a barn?"

"I ain't got nothin' to say."

EVALUATE: Why do you suppose Adoniram refuses to respond to Sarah's questions? **12**

Adoniram shuffled out. Mrs. Penn went into her bedroom. When she came out, her eyes were red. She had a roll of unbleached cotton cloth. She spread it out on the kitchen table,

10. **Webster**, Daniel Webster, Congressman and famous orator of the 1800s.

11 **Reader's Response**

Making Personal Connections

Questions

- Why is it only now that Sarah Penn is demanding that her husband consider the promise he made? *(Possible responses: She wants her daughter to have a fine finished home in which to be married. She had hoped he would carry it out on his own, but building the barn shows that he never will.)*

- Why do you think Adoniram Penn hasn't kept his promise so far? *(Possible response: Students may suggest that although he meant his promise at the time, other things just keep getting in the way. Or they may feel that Adoniram does not think a promise made to his wife is as important as running a successful farm.)*

12 **Active Reading**

Evaluate

Response Perhaps because answering would be to take the questions seriously, which Adoniram refuses to do. Pehaps he thinks by not responding she will eventually give up and let him go about his business.

BUILDING ENGLISH PROFICIENCY

ESL
LEP
ELD
SAE
LD

Exploring Character

Sarah Penn goes all out in her attempt to persuade her husband to build a new house. Completing a chart like the one shown will help students understand her argument.

- Divide students into small groups. Have each group come up with three main reasons and list them on the chart.

- Call students' attention to the way in which Sarah supports each reason with specific information. Have them write one fact or example that she uses to support each reason.

Reason	Support
This house is in terrible condition.	The paper is dirty.

Art Study

13 Reading/Thinking Skills

Analyze

Question   What impact does Nanny's remark have on her mother? *(It seems to have given her mother an idea.)*

◄ Eric Sloan's *Sickle and Bucket* (1964) shows just a part of what is obviously a larger structure. The few details and objects tell a lot about what's not shown. What can you infer about the larger structure?

and began cutting out some shirts for her husband. The men over in the field had a team to help them this afternoon; she could hear their halloos. She had a scanty pattern for the shirts; she had to plan and piece the sleeves.

Nanny came home with her embroidery, and sat down with her needlework. She had taken down her curl-papers, and there was a soft roll of fair hair like an auerole[11] over her forehead; her face was as delicately fine and clear as porcelain. Suddenly she looked up, and the tender red flamed all over her face and neck. "Mother," said she.

"What say?"

"I've been thinking—I don't see how we're goin' to have any—wedding in this room. I'd be ashamed to have his folks come if we didn't have anybody else."

"Mebbe we can have some new paper before

then; I can put it on. I guess you won't have no call to be ashamed of your belongin's."

"We might have the wedding in the new barn," said Nanny, with gentle pettishness.[12] "Why, mother, what makes you look so?"

Mrs. Penn had started, and was staring at her with a curious expression. She turned again to her work, and spread out a pattern carefully on the cloth.

13

"Nothin'," said she.

Presently Adoniram clattered out of the yard in his two-wheeled dump cart, standing as proudly upright as a Roman charioteer. Mrs. Penn opened the door and stood there a minute looking out; the halloos of the men sounded louder.

It seemed to her all through the spring months that she heard nothing but the halloos and the noises of saws and hammers. The new barn grew fast. It was a fine edifice for this little village. Men came on pleasant Sundays, in their meeting suits and clean shirt bosoms, and stood around it admiringly. Mrs. Penn did not speak of it, and Adoniram did not mention it to her,

---

11. **aureole** (ôr′ē ōl), *n.* ring of light surrounding a figure or an object.
12. pettishness (pet′ish nəs), *n.* peevishness; crossness.

MINI-LESSON: WRITING STYLE

Dialect

Teach   When a writer wants the reader to hear exactly how a character speaks, he or she writes in dialect. For example, when Sarah Penn says *maybe* Freeman writes it as "mebbe."

Activity Ideas
• Ask students to read aloud a character's words, using the dialect Freeman provides.

• Discuss what dialect adds to a story and what it tells about the particular character quoted.

• Invite students to record a conversation using dialect to show how it sounds.

14 although sometimes, upon a return from inspecting it, he bore himself with injured dignity.

"It's a strange thing how your mother feels about the new barn," he said, confidentially, to Sammy one day.

Sammy only grunted after an odd fashion for a boy; he had learned it from his father.

The barn was all completed ready for use by the third week in July. Adoniram had planned to move his stock in on Wednesday; on Tuesday he received a letter which changed his plans. He came in with it early in the morning. "Sammy's been to the post-office," said he, "an' I've got a letter from Hiram." Hiram was Mrs. Penn's brother, who lived in Vermont.

"Well," said Mrs. Penn, "what does he say about the folks?"

"I guess they're all right. He says he thinks if I come up country right off there's a chance to buy jest the kind of a horse I want." He stared reflectively out of the window at the new barn.

Mrs. Penn was making pies. She went on clapping the rolling-pin into the crust, although she was very pale, and her heart beat loudly.

"I dun' know but what I'd better go," said Adoniram. "I hate to go off jest now, right in the midst of hayin', but the ten-acre lot's cut, an' I guess Rufus an' the others can git along without me three or four days. I can't get a horse round here to suit me, nohow, an' I've got to have another for all that wood-haulin' in the fall. I told Hiram to watch out, an' if he got wind of a good horse to let me know. I guess I'd better go."

"I'll get out your clean shirt an' collar," said Mrs. Penn calmly.

She laid out Adoniram's Sunday suit and his clean clothes on the bed in the little bedroom. She got his shaving-water and razor ready. At last she buttoned on his collar and fastened his black cravat.

Adoniram never wore his collar and cravat except on extra occasions. He held his head high, with a rasped dignity. When he was all ready, with his coat and hat brushed, and a lunch of pie and cheese in a paper bag, he hesitated on the threshold of the door. He looked at his wife, and his manner was defiantly apologetic. "*If* them cows come today, Sammy can drive 'em into the new barn," said he; "an' when they bring the hay up, they can pitch it in there."

"Well," replied Mrs. Penn.

Adoniram set his shaven face ahead and started. When he had cleared the doorstep, he turned and looked back with a kind of nervous solemnity. "I shall be back by Saturday if nothin' happens," said he.

"Do be careful, father," returned his wife.

She stood in the door with Nanny at her elbow and watched him out of sight. Her eyes had a strange, doubtful expression in them; her peaceful forehead was contracted. She went in, and about her baking again. Nanny sat sewing. Her wedding-day was drawing nearer, and she was getting pale and thin with her steady sewing. Her mother kept glancing at her.

"Have you got that pain in your side this mornin'?" she asked.

"A little."

Mrs. Penn's face, as she worked, changed, her perplexed forehead smoothed, her eyes were steady, her lips firmly set. She formed a maxim for herself, although incoherently with her unlettered thoughts. "Unsolicited opportunities are the guide-posts of the Lord to the new roads of life," she repeated in effect, and she **15** made up her mind to her course of action.

"S'posin' I *had* wrote to Hiram," she muttered once, when she was in the pantry—"s'posin' I had wrote, an' asked him if he knew of any horse? But I didn't, an' father's goin' wa'n't none of my doin'. It looks like a providence." Her voice rang out quite loud at the last.

"What you talkin' about, mother?" called Nanny.

"Nothin'."

Mrs. Penn hurried her baking; at eleven o'clock it was all done. The load of hay from the west field came slowly down the cart track, and drew up at the new barn. Mrs. Penn ran out. "Stop!" she screamed—"stop!"

475

---

14 Reading/Thinking Skills
Drawing Conclusions

Questions

- What does a barn of the size of the Penns mean to the village? (*Possible response: It is a symbol of good business and a strong economy.*)

- Would the response of the village be different if Penn were building a house? (*Possible response: Possibly; the villagers might see that Penn was simply providing for his family rather than taking a business risk or adding on to his existing business. They might not be as impressed.*)

15 Reading/Thinking Skills
Recognize Values

Question What reasons does Sarah Penn give herself for deciding to take action? (*Nanny is nearly ill from her hard work; the Lord has given Sarah an unsolicited opportunity; she has fulfilled all her housekeeping duties.*)

BUILDING ENGLISH PROFICIENCY

Expanding Vocabulary

To help students develop their language skills, focus on rural dialect and challenging vocabulary on these pages.

- Divide students into groups. Have them work together to "translate" the following examples of rural dialect.

   "What say?"

   "I guess you won't have no call to be ashamed . . ."

   "I dun' know but what I'd better go."

- Ask students to add the following words to their vocabulary notebooks: *edifice, perplexed, maxim,* and *unsolicited.*

WORD	MEANING
edifice	building, especially an impressive one
I work in the tallest edifice in the city.	

Question Why does Sammy go along
with his mother's wishes without doing
anything more than rolling his eyes?
*(Possible response: He can tell that she is
determined and he rolls his eyes as if to
say, "I don't know how this will end, but I
can't do anything about it.")*

Question

• The author writes, "Every builder builds
somewhat for unknown purposes, and is
in a measure a prophet." What does she
mean by this? *(Possible response:
Perhaps she means that, as a builder,
one never knows exactly how one's
building will be used.)*

• What does she mean in regard to this
story? *(Possibly that although Adoniram
didn't intend to build a house, his barn
will become one.)*

The men stopped and looked; Sammy
upreared from the top of the load, and stared at
his mother.

"Stop!" she cried out again. "Don't you put
the hay in that barn; put it in the old one."

"Why, he said to put it in here," returned
one of the hay-makers, wonderingly. He was a
young man, a neighbor's son, whom Adoniram
hired by the year to help on the farm.

"Don't you put the hay in the new barn;
there's room enough in the old one, ain't
there?" said Mrs. Penn.

"Room enough," returned the hired man, in
his thick, rustic tones. "Didn't need the new
barn, nohow, far as room's concerned. Well, I
s'pose he changed his mind." He took hold of
the horses' bridles.

Mrs. Penn went back to the house. Soon
the kitchen windows were darkened,
and a fragrance like warm honey came
into the room.

Nanny laid down her work. "I thought father
wanted them to put the hay into the new barn?"
she said, wonderingly.

"It's all right," replied her mother.

Sammy slid down from the load of hay, and
came in to see if dinner was ready.

"I ain't goin' to get a regular dinner today, as
long as father's gone," said his mother. "I've let
the fire go out. You can have some bread an' milk
an' pie. I thought we could get along." She set
out some bowls of milk, some bread and a pie on
the kitchen table. "You'd better eat your dinner
now," said she. "You might jest as well get through
with it. I want you to help me afterward."

Nanny and Sammy stared at each other. There
was something strange in their mother's manner.

Mrs. Penn did not eat anything herself. She
went into the pantry, and they heard her moving dishes while they ate. Presently she came out
with a pile of plates. She got the clothes-basket
out of the shed, and packed them in it. Nanny
and Sammy watched. She brought out cups and
saucers, and put them in with the plates.

"What you goin' to do, mother?" inquired
Nanny, in a timid voice. A sense of something
unusual made her tremble, as if it were a ghost.
Sammy rolled his eyes over his pie.

"You'll see what I'm goin' to do," replied
Mrs. Penn. "If you're through, Nanny, I want
you to go upstairs an' pack up your things; an' I
want you, Sammy, to help me take down the bed
in the bedroom."

"Oh, mother, what for?" gasped Nanny.

"You'll see."

During the next few hours a feat was performed by this simple, pious New England
mother which was equal in its way to Wolfe's
storming of the Heights of Abraham.[13] It took no
more genius and audacity[14] of bravery for Wolfe
to cheer his wondering soldiers up those steep
precipices, under the sleeping eyes of the enemy,
than for Sarah Penn, at the head of her children,
to move all their little household goods into the
new barn while her husband was away.

Nanny and Sammy followed their mother's
instructions without a murmur; indeed, they
were overawed.[15] There is a certain uncanny
and superhuman quality about all such purely
original undertakings as their mother's was to
them. Nanny went back and forth with her light
loads, and Sammy tugged with sober energy.

At five o'clock in the afternoon the little
house in which the Penns had lived for forty
years had emptied itself into the new barn.

Every builder builds somewhat for unknown
purposes, and is in a measure a prophet.

The architect of Adoniram Penn's barn, while
he designed it for the comfort of four-footed
animals, had planned better than he knew for the
comfort of humans. Sarah Penn saw at a glance its

---

13. **Wolfe's storming of the Heights of Abraham.** James
Wolfe, a British general, scored a decisive victory
against the French at Quebec in the Seven Years War
(1765–1773). He had his soldiers climb the bluffs
which were considered unscalable, taking the enemy
by surprise.
14. **audacity** (ô das′ə tē), *n.* reckless daring; boldness.
15. **overawed** (ō′vər ôd′), *adj.* overcome with awe.

MINI-LESSON: READING/THINKING SKILLS

Understand Sequence/Order of Events

Teach Sarah Penn does not really decide all at
once to move her household into the new barn.
The urge comes on her little by little through small
events laced through the plot of the story.

Activity Idea Have students list Sarah's reasons
for taking action.

• Students can place the reasons in order from
most to least important.

• Students may prefer to arrange the reasons in
chronological order.

Students may discuss other reasons for Sarah's
action that might have taken place outside the
time frame of the story.

possibilities. These great box-stalls, with quilts hung before them, would make better bedrooms than the one she had occupied for forty years, and there was a tight carriage-room. The harness-room, with its chimney and shelves, would make a kitchen of her dreams. The great middle space would make a parlor, by-and-by, fit for a palace. Upstairs there was as much room as down. With partitions and windows, what a house would there be! Sarah looked at the row of stanchions[16] before the allotted space for cows, and reflected that she would have her front entry there.

At six o'clock the stove was up in the harness-room, the kettle was boiling, and the table set for tea. It looked almost as home-like as the abandoned house across the yard had ever done. The young hired man milked, and Sarah directed him calmly to bring the milk to the new barn. He came gaping, dropping little blots of foam from the brimming pails on the grass. Before the next morning he had spread the story of Adoniram Penn's wife moving into the new barn all over the little village. Men assembled in the store and talked it over, women with shawls over their heads scuttled into each other's houses before their work was done. Any deviation from the ordinary course of life in this quiet town was enough to stop all progress in it. Everybody paused to look at the staid, independent figure on the side track. There was a difference of opinion with regard to her. Some held her to be insane; some, of a lawless and rebellious spirit.

Friday the minister went to see her. It was in the forenoon, and she was at the barn door shelling peas for dinner. She looked up and returned his salutation with dignity, then she went on with her work. She did not invite him in. The saintly expression of her face remained fixed, but there was an angry flush over it.

The minister stood awkwardly before her, and talked. She handled the peas as if they were bullets. At last she looked up, and her eyes showed the spirit that her meek front had covered for a lifetime.

"There ain't no use talkin', Mr. Hersey," said she. "I've thought it all over an' over, an' I believe I'm doin' what's right. I've made it the subject of prayer, an' it's betwixt me an' the Lord an' Adoniram. There ain't no call for nobody else to worry about it."

Every builder builds somewhat for unknown purposes, and is in a measure a prophet.

"Well, of course, if you have brought it to the Lord in prayer, and feel satisfied that you are doing right, Mrs. Penn," said the minister, helplessly. His thin gray-bearded face was pathetic. He was a sickly man; his youthful confidence had cooled; he had to scourge himself up to some of his pastoral duties as relentlessly as a Catholic ascetic, and then he was prostrated by the smart.

"I think it's right jest as much as I think it was right for our forefathers to come over from the old country 'cause they didn't have what belonged to 'em," said Mrs. Penn. She arose. The barn threshold might have been Plymouth Rock from her bearing. "I don't doubt you mean well, Mr. Hersey," said she, "but there are things people hadn't ought to interfere with. I've been a member of the church for over forty year. I've got my own mind an' my own feet, an' I'm goin' to think my own thoughts an' go my own ways, an' nobody but the Lord is goin' to dictate to me unless I've a mind to have him. Won't you come in an' set down? How is Mis' Hersey?"

"She is well, I thank you," replied the minister. He added some more perplexed apologetic remarks; then he retreated.

He could expound the intricacies of every character study in the Scriptures, he was competent to grasp the Pilgrim Fathers and all historical innovators, but Sarah Penn was beyond

---

16. **stanchion** (stăn′chən), *n.* verticle post used to secure cattle in a stall.

The Revolt of "Mother"   **477**

---

18 **Reading/Thinking Skills**
Make Inferences

Question What is the hired man's view of Adoniram Penn and his wife? *(He doesn't think Penn needed to build the farm in the first place. He spreads the news of the move to the barn throughout the village, and probably agrees with some that Sarah has a "rebellious spirit.")*

19 **Reader's Response**
Challenging the Text

Questions

• Sarah Penn compares herself to the Pilgrims landing on Plymouth Rock. From what you know of the Pilgrims, why do you think she makes this reference? *(Possible response: Because she is talking to a minister who will understand her feelings of righteousness and self-determination. Like the Pilgrims, she has left a situation where she felt oppressed to claim property she feels is hers by right.)*

• With what other historical innovators might we compare Sarah Penn? *(Responses may include any innovators who felt oppressed and who rose up to claim what they deserved—suffragists, perhaps.)*

BUILDING ENGLISH PROFICIENCY

ESL
LEP
ELD
SAE
LD

Creating a Visual Response

Making a drawing of the barn that Sarah Penn would transform into her new home will help students understand the story. They may want to use the results as the basis for the blueprints they make if they do the From Barn to Home option on page 481.

• Encourage students to match their drawing to the description of the barn as closely as possible.

• Ask them to label the objects and areas mentioned: boxstalls, bedrooms, carriage-room, harnessroom, chimney, shelves, kitchen, middle space, parlor, stanchions, and entry.

• Wherever Sarah Penn sees how a barn area might be changed to a house area, have them use two labels (for example, boxstalls/bedrooms).

• Invite comparisons of the finished drawings.

Question How do family members show their feelings about what might happen when Adoniram comes home? *(Possible responses: Sarah gets supper ready, fulfilling her duties as always; Nanny and Sammy follow Sarah around nervously but with pleasant excitement, keeping faith in their mother.)*

21 Reader's Response

Making Personal Connections

Question Does Adoniram react as you expected him to? *(Answers will vary, but will probably reflect the fact that he seems more flabbergasted than angry.)*

---

him. He could deal with primal cases, but parallel ones worsted him. But, after all, although it was aside from his province, he wondered more how Adoniram Penn would deal with his wife than how the Lord would. Everybody shared the wonder. When Adoniram's four new cows arrived, Sarah ordered three to be put in the old barn, the other in the house shed where the cooking-stove had stood. That added to the excitement. It was whispered that all four cows were domiciled in the house.

Towards sunset on Saturday, when Adoniram was expected home, there was a knot of men in the road near the new barn. The hired man had milked, but he still hung around the premises. Sarah Penn had supper all ready. There were brown-bread and baked beans and a custard pie; it was the supper Adoniram loved on a Saturday night. She had a clean calico, and she bore herself imperturbably.[17] Nanny and Sammy kept close at her heels. Their eyes were large, and Nanny was full of nervous tremors. Still there was to them more pleasant excitement than anything else. An inborn confidence in their mother over their father asserted itself.

Sammy looked out of the harness-room window. "There he is," he announced, in an awed whisper. He and Nanny peeped around the casing. Mrs. Penn kept on about her work. The children watched Adoniram leave the new horse standing in the drive while he went to the house door. It was fastened. Then he went around to the shed. That door was seldom locked, even when the family was away. The thought how her father would be confronted by the cow flashed upon Nanny. There was a hysterical sob in her throat. Adoniram emerged from the shed and stood looking about in a dazed fashion. His lips moved; he was saying something, but they could not hear what it was. The hired man was peeping around a corner of the old barn, but nobody saw him.

Adoniram took the new horse by the bridle and led him across the yard to the new barn.

Nanny and Sammy slunk close to their mother. The barn doors rolled back, and there stood Adoniram, with the long mild face of the great Canadian farm horse looking over his shoulder.

Nanny kept behind her mother, but Sammy stepped suddenly forward, and stood in front of her.

Adoniram stared at the group. "What on airth you all down here for?" said he. "What's the matter over to the house?"

"We've come here to live, father," said Sammy. His shrill voice quavered out bravely.

"What"—Adoniram sniffed—"what is it smells like cookin'?" said he. He stepped forward and looked in the open door of the harness-room. Then he turned to his wife. His old bristling face was pale and frightened. "What on airth does this mean, mother?" he gasped.

"You come in here, father," said Sarah. She led the way into the harness-room and shut the door. "Now, father," said she, "you needn't be scared. I ain't crazy. There ain't nothin' to be upset over. But we've come here to live, an' we're goin' to live here. We've got jest as good a right here as new horses an' cows. The house wa'n't fit for us to live in any longer, an' I made up my mind I wa'n't goin' to stay there. I've done my duty by you forty year, an' I'm goin' to do it now; but I'm goin' to live here. You've got to put in some windows and partitions; an' you'll have to buy some furniture."

"Why, mother!" the old man gasped.

"You'd better take your coat off an' get washed—there's the wash-basin—an' then we'll have supper."

"Why, mother!"

Sammy went past the window, leading the new horse to the old barn. The old man saw him, and shook his head speechlessly. He tried to take off his coat, but his arms seemed to lack the power. His wife helped him. She poured some water into the tin basin, and put in a piece of soap. She got the comb and brush, and smoothed his thin gray

---

17. **imperturbably** (im′pər tėr′bə bəl ē), *adv.* calmly.

MINI-LESSON: LITERARY ELEMENT

Plot

Teach The event that takes place on this page is a small one: a man returns home. It is, however, an important moment in the plot.

Activity Ideas

• Ask students to read aloud the passage in which Adoniram returns home. Encourage them to use dramatic inflection and tone to heighten the suspense and emotion.

• Invite students to share their views on what the author does to make this event the climax of the story.

• Ask students to choose a character and describe the event through his or her eyes. Students may use what the author says about the character as well as what they have learned about him or her through the plot.

A How would you describe John Steuart Curry's depiction of farm life in *Wisconsin Landscape* (1938–1939). Is it idyllic? cozy? lonesome? Explain your interpretation.

hair after he had washed. Then she put the beans, hot bread, and tea on the table. Sammy came in, and the family drew up. Adoniram sat looking dazedly at his plate, and they waited.

"Ain't you goin' to ask a blessin', father?" said Sarah.

And the old man bent his head and mumbled.

All through the meal he stopped eating at intervals, and stared furtively[18] at his wife; but he ate well. The home food tasted good to him, and his old frame was too sturdily healthy to be affected by his mind. But after supper he went out, and sat down on the step of the smaller door at the right of the barn, through which he had meant his Jerseys to pass in stately file, but which Sarah designed for her front house door, and he leaned his head on his hands.

After the supper dishes were cleared away and the milk-pans washed, Sarah went out to him. The twilight was deepening. There was a clear green glow in the sky. Before them stretched the smooth level of field; in the distance was a cluster of haystacks like the huts of a village; the air was very cool and calm and sweet. The landscape might have been an ideal one of peace.

Sarah bent over and touched her husband on one of his thin, sinewy shoulders. "Father!"

The old man's shoulders heaved; he was weeping.

"Why, don't do so, father," said Sarah.

"I'll—put up the—partitions, an'—everything you—want, mother."

Sarah put her apron up to her face; she was overcome by her own triumph.

Adoniram was like a fortress whose walls had no active resistance, and went down the instant the right besieging tools were used. "Why, mother," he said, hoarsely, "I hadn't no idee you was so set on't as all this comes to."

---

18. **furtively** (fėr′tiv lē), *adv.* done quickly and stealthily to avoid being noticed; secretly.

The Revolt of "Mother"   **479**

Response to Caption Question
Students answers will vary. Some may see the painting's broad sweep and subject as idyllic. Others may feel that the vast terrain looks lonely and isolating.

Visual Literacy   Like many American realistic painters of the 1930s, John Steuart Curry's popularity was in some ways a reaction to the abstract art of the period. His paintings depicting rural American life are among his best.

22   Reading/Thinking Skills
Analyze Character

Question   Why does Adoniram cry? *(Perhaps because he feels guilty about treating the wife he loves as he has. Perhaps because he has been put in his place. Perhaps because he is overwhelmed by feeling at his new view of Sarah.)*

Check Test

1. What factors push Sarah Penn to take action about a promise made to her forty years ago? *(the construction of the barn and Nanny's impending marriage)*

2. How does Sammy change during the course of the story? *(At first he goes along with his father; in the end he helps and supports his mother.)*

3. What does Adoniram expect Sarah will do about his decision to build a barn on the house site? *(nothing)*

4. Why does Mr. Hersey come to visit Sarah? *(As a minister, he feels he has to intervene when a member of his congregation does something that challenges the values of the time.)*

5. What impact will Sarah's decision have on Nanny? *(She will be married in a pleasant environment. She will be able to live in the house once she is married. She may now feel that she, too, can have an impact on events.)*

Unit 5 Resource Book
Alternate Check Test, p. 21

BUILDING ENGLISH PROFICIENCY

Responding to a Resolution

Wrap up discussion of this story by focusing on its resolution. Ask questions such as the following:

• What do you think of Sarah's solution to her problem? Have you ever come up with a creative solution like hers?

• How do you explain Adoniram's tears at the end of the story? Is he frustrated, sorry, or what?

• How might these events influence Nanny, who is soon to become a wife? How might they influence Sammy?

After Reading

MAKING CONNECTIONS

1. Answers will vary, but most will probably have supported Sarah.

2. She found the opportunity and the conviction to carry out her plan.

3. Possible responses: He sees that he must fulfill his promise. He finally realizes how much it means to Sarah.

4. Responses will vary. Students should support their answers with details about the characters.

5. Possible response: Sarah was a woman of her times, brought up to see men as figures of authority, and expected by society to conform to her husband's wishes.

6. Students may suggest modern ideas about women's rights or about relationships between men and women based on equality.

7. Student responses should reflect an understanding of the characters and how events have changed them. Most will suggest the couple will have a new understanding of one another.

VOCABULARY STUDY

1. benevolent
2. infinitesimal
3. commodious
4. assiduously
5. conclusive
6. sedulous
7. steadfast
8. pettishness
9. imperturbably
10. furtively

More Practice   Students can suggest words that mean the opposite or near opposite of each vocabulary word.

Unit 5 Resource Book
Vocabulary, p. 19
Vocabulary Test, p. 22

After Reading

Making Connections

Shaping Your Response

Analyzing the Story

1. As you read "The Revolt of 'Mother,'" did you find yourself applauding Sarah's actions or did you feel disapproving? Why?

2. Sarah had a lot of resentments about the new barn that she was at first willing to ignore. What do you think finally convinced her to take action?

3. Why do you suppose Adoniram agrees in the end to make the barn into a house?

4. Wilkins Freeman lamented that her characters in this story weren't realistic enough. Do you agree or disagree? Explain your answer.

5. 👁 For years Sarah never told her husband what she thought. Why do you suppose she was so reluctant to express needs and desires as an **individual?**

Extending the Ideas

6. As a modern reader, if you could speak with Sarah and Adoniram, what would you say to them? Why?

7. You are writing a continuation of this story. Will things be different now between Sarah and Adoniram? Why or why not?

Literary Focus: Foreshadowing

When Nanny joked that she might have her wedding in the new barn Sarah "started, and was staring at her [Nanny] with a curious expression." Here Wilkins Freeman **foreshadows** Sarah's revolt by allowing the reader to see that an idea is forming in her mind. Choose another example of foreshadowing to study. Write a paragraph that explains the effect of the foreshadowing on the narrative. As you write, consider these questions:

- How does the example of foreshadowing set the stage for future events?

- Foreshadowing often builds **suspense** in stories. Does it have this effect in "The Revolt of 'Mother'"?

- How does the foreshadowing affect the **mood** of the story?

Vocabulary Study

assiduously
benevolent
commodious
conclusive
furtively
imperturbably
infinitesimal
pettishness
sedulous
steadfast

Choose the word from the list that best completes each sentence.

1. A ____ person is most likely to be forgiving.

2. If a problem is ____, it could be called insignificant.

3. The ____ new barn was much larger than the old house.

4. If your boss says you are working ____, she is complimenting you.

480   UNIT FIVE: BREAKING THE MOLD

LITERARY FOCUS: FORESHADOWING

Return to the moment when Sarah decides to move her household into the barn or the moment when Adoniram returns home (see Mini-Lesson on page 478). Ask students to recall dialogue, description, or narrative that foreshadows and adds to the suspense of these moments.

Unit 5 Resource Book
Graphic Organizer, p. 17

5. "Sarah Penn washed the frying pan with a ____ air" because she had made a decision.

6. A ____ person is most likely to be hard-working.

7. A person who is ____ is definitely not unstable.

8. Though Sarah Penn was upset, she never resorted to ____.

9. If he responds to the accusation ____, his response is calm.

10. A thief works ____ because he or she is afraid of being caught.

Expressing Your Ideas

Writing Choices

Writer's Notebook Update Before reading "The Revolt of 'Mother,'" you wrote about a disagreement you once had. Are there any similarities between how you resolved your argument and how Mother and Father resolved theirs? In your notebook, compare your methods of resolving a conflict to their methods.

Front Page News Sarah Penn's move from house to barn caused quite a stir in the community. Imagine you're a reporter assigned to cover the story for the local paper. Write a front-page **news story** that describes for your readers the Penns' move. Begin by "interviewing" Sarah, Nanny, Sammy, and Adoniram. Build your story around quotes from each character. You may also want to include in your story "reactions" from members of the community: Hiram, for example, or the minister, or one of the women in the town.

Spineless or Not? Twenty-some years after she wrote "The Revolt of 'Mother,'" Wilkins Freeman said in disgust, "The backbone of the best fiction is essential truth, and 'The Revolt of "Mother"' is perfectly spineless." Would you agree? Write a **letter** to Wilkins Freeman that responds to her comment that the story is "spineless."

Other Options

From Barn to Home Review the description of the new barn in "The Revolt of 'Mother.'" Imagine you are an architect assigned to make the **blueprints** for the work that needs to be done. How will you turn this barn into a home?

Does Art Imitate Life? Think back over the three selections you've just read: "The Story of an Hour," *Trifles,* and "The Revolt of 'Mother.'" What do the three main characters—Louise, Mrs. Wright, and Sarah Penn—have in common? In small groups, brainstorm a **list** of similarities between the three women. When you've finished, look carefully at your list. Based on these three stories, what generalizations can you make about nineteenth-century American women? Do you think that women of the time felt the same quiet desperation that Louise, Mrs. Wright, and Sarah Penn all seem to feel? Why or why not? If you like, broaden your discussion to include other fictional characters of the time—Aunt Georgiana from "A Wagner Matinée," for example, or Jo from *Little Women* or Lily from Edith Wharton's *House of Mirth.* Present your group's conclusions to the rest of the class.

The Revolt of "Mother" **481**

WRITING CHOICES
Writer's Notebook Update

Students may evaluate the Penns' conflict resolution methods in light of their own efforts.

Front Page News

Remind students that a good news reporter is an objective observer. Suggest that they use quotes from townspeople to give opinions and to try to show alternative views. Remind them of the five elements of good journalism that answer the questions who?, what?, when?, where?, and why?

Spineless or Not?

As students write, encourage them to consider the time in which the story is set and also the time in which Freeman lived.

Selection Test

Unit 5 Resource Book pp. 23–24

OTHER OPTIONS
From Barn to Home

Make available chart paper so that students can create floor plans to a certain scale. Give them a point of reference by measuring the square footage of your classroom floor.

Does Art Imitate Life?

Students may also be invited to compare the authors of these stories in light of their personal histories, their goals as writers, and their place in literary history.

Building Background

Ask students

- to define *lynching*
- to talk about race relationships at the turn of the century
- to talk about the goals people seeking justice should have

Literary Focus

The **tone** of a piece of writing is often key to the author's purpose in writing it—to entertain, inform, persuade, or invite debate. In reading this selection, it is particularly helpful for students to understand the context in which Wells-Barnett wrote. It was a harrowing period of history, requiring from her such strong conviction and personal courage that she was almost stretched beyond her limits.

Writer's Notebook

As students write about heroes, ask them to consider the situations in which people behave heroically and to include characteristic actions as well as personal qualities.

More About Ida B. Wells-Barnett

- From 1889 to 1894, she was part-owner and reporter for the *Memphis Free Speech*, a newspaper famous for its anti-lynching crusades.
- In 1909, she helped found the NAACP.

Another work by Wells is *The Red Record.*

---

from Crusade for Justice

by Ida B. Wells-Barnett

Ida B. Wells-Barnett
1862–1930

A courageous and determined woman, Ida B. Wells spent her life fighting for justice. Born in Mississippi, Wells witnessed at first-hand prejudice and discrimination against African Americans. In 1878, Wells's parents and youngest brother died during a yellow fever epidemic. Although she was only fourteen, Wells took on the responsibility of raising her six siblings. In 1892, a single event dramatically changed her life. Three Memphis men, all friends of hers, were lynched. These three men were accused of a crime, kidnapped by towns-people, and shot to death. Outraged by the violence, Wells began a national campaign against the practice of lynching.

Building Background

About Lynching Lynching means the killing, most often by hanging, of a person by a mob in defiance of law and order. During the last part of the 1800s, lynchings of African Americans had become almost commonplace. In 1892 alone, 230 African Americans were lynched. Sickened by the violence, Ida B. Wells began her antilynching campaign. She traveled the world telling her audiences about the brutality of lynching and gathering support for antilynching legislation. Wells's campaign and pressure from the public resulted in many states adopting laws against lynching, though the laws were not consistently enforced. In the selection you're about to read, Wells discusses the 1909 lynching of an African American man accused of murder.

Literary Focus

Tone is the author's relationship to his or her material, to the audience, or to both. As you read *Crusade for Justice,* try to get a sense of Wells's tone. In your notebook, jot down brief answers to these questions:

1. Would you say Wells's tone in this excerpt is formal or informal?

2. Does she take her subject matter seriously? How do you know?

3. What is her attitude toward the people responsible for James's lynching?

4. How does the African American community respond to James's lynching? Is Wells satisfied with this response? How do you know?

Writer's Notebook

To Be a Hero What's your definition of a hero? What qualities would you expect to see in a heroic person? In your notebook, make a list of what you believe are the characteristics of a hero.

SUPPORT MATERIALS OVERVIEW

Unit 5 Resource Book
- Graphic Organizer, p. 25
- Study Guide, p. 26
- Vocabulary, p. 27
- Grammar, p. 28
- Alternate Check Test, p. 29
- Vocabulary Test, p. 30
- Selection Test, pp. 31-32

Building English Proficiency
- Literature Summaries
- Activities, p. 205

Reading, Writing & Grammar SkillBook
- Reading, pp. 33–36
- Writing, pp. 112–113
- Grammar, Usage, and Mechanics, pp. 180–181

Technology
- Audiotape
- Personal Journal Software
- Custom Literature Database: For other selections dealing with oppression of African Americans, see W. E. B. Du Bois on the database.
- Test Generator Software

CRUSADE FOR JUSTICE

Ida B. Wells-Barnett

During Reading

Selection Objectives

- To analyze tone
- To analyze events within a historical, social, and personal framework
- To analyze the necessity of challenging unfair limits
- To explore cause and effect within the plot of a narrative

 Unit 5 Resource Book
Study Guide, p. 26

Theme Link

The theme of going beyond prescribed limits is reflected in the actions of the author. When a lynching sets off a chain of events with racial injustice at their heart, Ida B. Wells-Barnett challenges the Illinois governor to follow the law.

Vocabulary Preview

enact, pass (a bill), giving it validity as law

prominent, well-known or conspicuous

dispossess, oust; deprive

mandatory, required by a command or order

condoning, forgiving or overlooking

Students can add the words and definitions to their personal word lists in their Writer's Notebook.

Directly after the Springfield riot,[1] at the next session of the legislature, a law was enacted[2] which provided that any sheriff who permitted a prisoner to be taken from him and lynched should be removed from office. This bill was offered by Edward D. Green, who had been sent to Springfield to represent our race. Illinois had had not only a number of lynchings, but also a three days' riot at Springfield.

In due course of time the daily press announced that a lynching had taken place in Cairo, Illinois. The body of a white woman had been found in an alley in the residential district and, following the usual custom, the police immediately looked for a Negro. Finding a shiftless, penniless colored man known as "Frog" James, who seemed unable to give a good account of himself, according to police, this man was locked up in the police station and according to the newspapers a crowd began to gather around the station and the sheriff was sent for.

Mr. Frank Davis, the sheriff, after a brief conversation with the prisoner, took him to the railroad station, got on the train, and took him up into the woods accompanied by a single deputy. They remained there overnight. Next morning, when a mob had grown to great proportions, they too went up into the country and had no trouble in locating the sheriff and his prisoner. He was placed on a train and brought back to town, accompanied by the sheriff. The newspapers announced that as the train came to a standstill, some of the mob put a rope around "Frog's" neck and dragged him out of the train and to the most prominent[3] corner of the town, where the rope was thrown over an

---

1. **Springfield riot.** The Springfield riots were three days of racial violence against African Americans in Springfield, Illinois, during August of 1908. Shortly after the riots, Wells and Mary Church Terrell organized a conference in New York City to discuss the plight of African Americans everywhere. The conference led to the formation of the NAACP.
2. enact (en akt′), *v.* pass (a bill), giving it validity as law.
3. prominent (prom′ə nənt), *adj.* well-known or conspicuous.

Crusade for Justice   **483**

SELECTION SUMMARY

Crusade for Justice

The year is 1909, the place a small Illinois town. While held by Sheriff Frank Davis, a black murder suspect is hauled away and lynched. Illinois law says that a sheriff who allows a lynching must be dispossessed of his post, but there is great support for Davis's reinstatement.

Ida B. Wells-Barnett travels to the town to muster support for Davis's dispossession and to strengthen the resolve of law officials to condemn lynching. She convinces a black Baptist minister to retract a letter he wrote in support of Davis's reinstatement. She takes her findings to court and succeeds in convincing officials to keep Davis out of office, effectively ending lynching in Illinois.

 *For summaries in other languages, see the **Building English Proficiency** book.*

1 Literary Focus
Tone

Tone is set both through the information an author chooses and the way he or she presents it. Ask students to read the description of the lynching that begins on page 483 and concludes on the top of this page.

Questions

- What word does Wells use to describe this event? *(horrible)*

- What do the word and the description of the event tell you about the author's purpose in writing this piece? *(Possible response: She wants her readers to understand what a dreadful injustice the lynching was and how she felt when she heard about it.)*

- Will this selection be an objective or subjective piece of writing? What other words would you use to describe its tone? *(The selection will be subjective. Other words might be: dramatic, emotional, involving.)*

2 Active Reading
Clarify

Response Her son convinces her that she is the only one who can affect the outcome of the situation in Cairo.

---

1 electric light arch and the body hauled up above the heads of the crowd. . . .

When the news of this horrible thing appeared in the papers, immediately a meeting was called and a telegram sent to Governor Deneen demanding that the sheriff of Alexander County be dispossessed.[4] The newspapers had already quoted the governor as saying that he did not think it mandatory[5] on him to displace the sheriff. But when our telegram reached him calling attention to the law, he immediately ousted him by telegram.

This same law provided that after the expiration of a short time, the sheriff would have the right to appear before the governor and show cause why he ought to be reinstated. We had a telegram from Governor Deneen informing us that on the following Wednesday the sheriff would appear before him demanding reinstatement. Mr. Barnett[6] spent some time urging representative men of our race to appear before the governor and fight the sheriff's reinstatement. . . .

This information was given us at the dinner table by Mr. Barnett, and he wound up his recital of his fruitless efforts that Saturday afternoon to get someone to appear by saying, "And so it would seem that you will have to go to Cairo and get the facts with which to confront the sheriff next Wednesday morning. And your train leaves at eight o'clock." I objected very strongly because I had already been accused by some of our men of jumping in ahead of them and doing work without giving them a chance.

It was not very convenient for me to be leaving home at that time, and for once I was quite willing to let them attend to the job. Mr. Barnett replied that I knew it was important that somebody gather the evidence as well as he did, but if I was not willing to go, there was nothing more to be said. He picked up the evening paper and I picked up my baby and took her upstairs to bed. As usual I not only sang her to sleep but put myself to sleep lying there beside her.

I was awakened by my oldest child, who said, "Mother, Pa says it is time to go." "Go where?" I said. He said, "To take the train to Cairo." I said, "I told your father downstairs that I was not going. I don't see why I should have to go and do the work that the others refuse." My boy was only ten years old. He and the other children had been present at the dinner table when their father told the story. He stood by the bedside a little while and then said, "Mother if you don't go nobody else will."

I looked at my child standing there by the bed reminding me of my duty, and I thought of that passage of Scripture which tells of the wisdom from the mouths of babes and sucklings. I thought if my child wanted me to go that I ought not to fall by the wayside, and I said, "Tell daddy it is too late to catch the train now, that I'll go in the morning. It is better for me to arrive in Cairo after nightfall anyway."

> **CLARIFY:** Why does Wells finally decide to go to Cairo? **2**

Next morning all four of my children accompanied my husband and me to the station and saw me start on the journey. They were intensely interested and for the first time were willing to see me leave home.

I reached Cairo after nightfall, and was driven to the home of the leading A.M.E.[7] minister, just before he went into church for his evening service. I told him why I was there and asked if he could give me any help in getting the sentiment of the colored people and investigating facts. He said that they all believed that "Frog" James had committed that murder. I asked him if he

---

4. dispossess (dis′pə zes′), *v.* oust; deprive.
5. mandatory (man′də tôr′ē), *adv.* required by a command or order.
6. **Mr. Barnett**, Ferdinand L. Barnett, Ida B. Wells's husband.
7. **A. M. E.**, African Methodist Episcopal.

MINI-LESSON: GRAMMAR

Singular and Plural Nouns

Teach Write the following nouns on the chalkboard and ask students to state whether they are singular or plural.

race	woods
police	reinstatement
crowd	information

(The words *race* and *crowd* are collective nouns and as such are singular in form. *Police* and *woods* are plural nouns. *Reinstatement* and *information* are singular nouns.)

Activity Ideas

- Ask students to write rules for identifying and forming singular and plural nouns. Suggest that their rules should be simply written and easily used by someone who is learning English.

- Invite students to list irregular singular and plural nouns.

- Have students write sentences using singular and plural nouns. The context of the sentence should help a reader identify the noun's number.

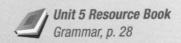
Unit 5 Resource Book
Grammar, p. 28

This photo of Ida B. Wells-Barnett and her son, Charles Aked Barnett, was taken in 1896.

3 Historical Note
Lynching

Historical Note
Lynching

- Lynching—the unlawful killing, especially hanging, of a person by a mob—goes back to the days of early white pioneers. These *vigilantes* organized themselves to combat crime in an era and setting in which there were no police.

- During and after Reconstruction (after the Civil War), the Ku Klux Klan used lynching to terrorize the African American community and keep them from participating fully in the post-slavery society. The Klan often accused those they lynched of crimes in order to justify their actions.

- Some findings indicate that more than 3,000 African Americans were lynched from the 1880s to the 1960s. Many more are believed to have remained unreported. There have been no reported lynchings since that period.

- The most intense period of lynchings occurred from 1900 to 1914, when more than a thousand people were hanged. Among the most sensational of these lynchings was the subject of this selection.

had anything upon which to base that belief. "Well," he said, "he was a worthless sort of fellow, just about the kind of a man who would do a trick like that. Anyhow, all of the colored people believe that and many of us have written letters already to the governor asking the reinstatement of the sheriff."

I sprang to my feet and asked him if he realized what he had done in condoning[8] the horrible lynching of a fellowman who was a member of his race. Did he not know that if they condoned the lynching of one man, the time might come when they would have to condone that of other men higher up, providing they were black?

I asked him if he could direct me to the home of some other colored persons; that I had been sent to see all of them, and it wouldn't be fair for me to accept reports from one man alone. He

---

8. condoning (kən dōn′ing), *n.* forgiving or overlooking.

Crusade for Justice **485**

BUILDING ENGLISH PROFICIENCY

Linking History and Literature

Help students link Ida B. Wells to other heroic women who have made a difference in the world.

Activity Ideas

- Encourage students to debate what they think a woman's role should be. Have small groups discuss the problems that women face in breaking out of traditional roles to become heroes. Encourage them to list the qualities that make certain women, like Wells, overcome these problems. As time permits, ask each group to report on a woman who is a leader in today's world.

- Invite three or four guest speakers, outstanding women of different cultural backgrounds in your community, to class. Ask them to provide background and lead a discussion on women heroes of their culture.

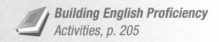
Building English Proficiency
Activities, p. 205

ESL LEP ELD SAE LD

Art Study

Response to Caption Question
Answers will vary but may include the idea that Wells was a leader of people fighting for their rights.

Questions

• Who are the people in the background? What are they doing? *(They are turn-of-the-century African Americans, perhaps protesting a lynching, campaigning for equal rights, or picketing or boycotting a discriminatory business.)*

• Look at the expression on Ida B. Wells's face in this portrait. What impression do you have of her personality? *(Possible responses: She appears to be strong, steady, wary, concerned, and determined.)*

4 Active Reading
Evaluate

Response She sees him as someone who undermines the cause by supporting lynching.

This stamp was issued by the U.S. Postal Service on February 1, 1989. What do you think is the message the artist was trying to convey about Ida B. Wells? Explain. ➤

Ida B. Wells

25
Black Heritage USA

gave me the names of one or two others, and I withdrew. I had expected to stop at his home, but after he told me that I had no desire to do so. One of the men named was Will Taylor, a druggist, whom I had known in Chicago, and I asked to be directed to his place. . . .

4 EVALUATE: What is Wells's attitude toward the minister?

Mr. Taylor and I spent the day talking with colored citizens and ended with a meeting that night. . . .

The meeting was largely attended and in my statement to them I said I had come down to be their mouthpiece; that I correctly understood how hard it would be for those who lived there to take an active part in the movement to oust the sheriff; that we were willing to take the lead

in the matter but they must give me the facts; that it would be endangering the lives of other colored people in Illinois if we did not take a stand against the all too frequent lynchings which were taking place.

I went on to say that I came because I knew that they knew of my work against lynching for fifteen years past and felt that they would talk more freely to me and trust me more fully than they would someone of whom they knew nothing. I wanted them to tell me if Mr. Frank Davis had used his great power to protect the victim of the mob; if he had at any time placed him behind bars of the county jail as the law required; and if he had sworn in any deputies to help protect his prisoner as he was obliged by law to do until such time as he could be tried by due process of law. Although the meeting lasted for two hours, and although most of those

---

MINI-LESSON: LITERARY FOCUS

Tone

Teach The things an author chooses to tell the reader can have a direct effect on the tone of the piece. For example, the author's description of falling asleep with her baby and her use of phrases from the Bible help the reader understand Wells-Barnett's attitude toward her material.

Activity Ideas

• Have students reread this quote from the selection and ask them what it adds to the overall tone.

I sprang to my feet and asked him if he realized what he had done. . . .

• Invite students to evaluate the subjective tone of this piece and to imagine how the writing might have been different if a news reporter had written it.

present and speaking were friends of Frank Davis, some of whom had been deputy sheriffs in his office, not one of them could honestly say that Frank Davis had put his prisoner in the county jail or had done anything to protect him. I therefore offered a resolution to that effect which was almost unanimously adopted. . . .

Next morning before taking the train I learned of a Baptist ministers' meeting that was being held there and decided to attend for the purpose of having them pass the same resolution. I was told that it would do no good to make the effort and that it would delay me until midnight getting into Springfield. But I went, got an opportunity to speak, offered the resolution, told of the men who had sent letters to the governor, showed how that would confuse his mind as to the attitude of the colored people on the subject, and stated clearly that all such action would mean that we would have other lynchings in Illinois whenever it suited the mob anywhere.

I asked the adoption of the resolution passed the night before. There was discussion pro and con, and finally the moderator arose and said, "Brethren, they say an honest confession is good for the soul. I, too, am one of those men who have written to the governor asking Frank Davis's reinstatement. I knew he was a friend of ours; that the man who had taken his place has turned out all Negro deputies and put in Democrats, and I was told that when the mob placed the rope around "Frog" James's neck the sheriff tried to prevent them and was knocked down for his pains. But now that the sister has shown us plainly the construction that would be placed upon that letter, I want her when she appears before the governor tomorrow to tell him that I take that letter back and hereby sign my name to this resolution." By this time the old man was shedding tears. Needless to say the resolution went through without any further objections. . . .

I entered the room at ten o'clock that morning . . . On the other side of the room there was Frank Davis, and with him one of the biggest lawyers in southern Illinois, so I was afterward told, who was also a state senator.

There was the parish priest, the state's attorney of Alexander County, the United States land commissioner, and about half a dozen other representative white men who had journeyed from Cairo to give aid and comfort to Frank Davis in his fight for reinstatement.

The governor said that they had no precedent and that he would now hear the plea to be made by the sheriff; whereupon this big lawyer proceeded to present his petition for reinstatement and backed it up with letters and telegrams from Democrats and Republicans, bankers, lawyers, doctors, editors of both daily papers, and heads of women's clubs and of men's organizations. The whole of the white population of Cairo was evidently behind Frank Davis and his demand for reinstatement.

In addition to this there were read these letters from Negro ministers and colored politicians. Special emphasis was laid upon them. Just before reading one of them the state senator said, "Your Excellency, I have known the writer of this letter since I was a boy. He has such a standing for truth and veracity in the community that if he were to tell me that black was white I would believe him, and he, too, has written to ask that Frank Davis be reinstated.". . .

When the gentlemen had finished, Governor Deneen said, "I understand Mrs. Barnett is here to represent the colored people of Illinois." Not until that moment did I realize that the burden depended upon me. It so happened that Attorney A. M. Williams, a Negro lawyer of Springfield, having heard that I was in town, came over to the Capitol to invite me to his home for dinner. Finding me by myself, he immediately camped by my side and remained with me all through the ordeal. I was indeed thankful for this help, since never before had I been confronted with a situation that called for legal knowledge.

Crusade for Justice   **487**

5 Reading/Thinking Skills

Recognize Cause and Effect

Questions

- Why was it so important to Wells that Frank Davis not be reinstated? *(If he were reinstated as sheriff, it would be a statement to all that supporting lynching was acceptable behavior on the part of an officer of the law.)*

- What were some of the things that Davis should have done to protect the victim? *(He should have placed the victim in jail, as required by law. He should also have appointed deputies to help protect the prisoner.)*

- Why does Wells insist on traveling to Springfield? *(She hopes to persuade ministers there to back her cause.)*

- Why were the letters from "colored" politicians and ministers important to the reinstatement case? *(Possible answer: If black leaders supported Davis's reinstatement, that would mean they thought he did nothing wrong.)*

BUILDING ENGLISH PROFICIENCY

Improving Comprehension

Help students track what happens on Wells's journey. Begin by dividing students into four groups.

- Ask one group to summarize what happened at the A. M. E. minister's home.

- Ask two of the groups to summarize what happens at each of the two meetings described on these pages.

Explain that the rest of the page describes the events in Springfield, where the hearing to reinstate the sheriff was held.

- Ask the fourth group to predict what will happen at the hearing.

- Have representatives from each group present the summaries orally in correct sequence, speaking from notes.

Draw Conclusions

A person combines prior understanding and new information to draw a conclusion about an issue.

Questions What are Wells's arguments to the court? *(She tells what she has discovered regarding Davis's not protecting the accused, then she presents the signature of the "colored" minister the "big" lawyer has praised—the signature which appears on her resolution.)*

7 Active Reading

Predict

Response Answers will vary. Some students may feel that Deneen will be swayed by "the whole of the white population of Cairo" to reinstate Davis. Others will assert that Wells-Barnett has argued her case so forcefully as to convince the governor.

Check Test

1. In Wells's view, what law is violated by Frank Davis? *(the law which provides that a sheriff must protect a prisoner)*

2. Why does Ida Wells have to go to Cairo? *(Representative men were asked to go and did not; she was needed to present the facts of the case and also to marshal support for the anti-lynching cause.)*

3. What is the A. M. E. minister's reason for not condemning the lynching of "Frog" James? *(He claimed the man was worthless and probably guilty.)*

4. Why does the Baptist minister retract the letter he wrote in support of Davis? *(Wells convinces him that condoning one lynching would condone them all.)*

5. What was the outcome of Wells's action? *(There were no further lynchings in Illinois.)*

Unit 5 Resource Book
Alternate Check Test, p. 29

I began by reading the brief which Mr. Barnett prepared in due legal form. I then launched out to tell of my investigation in Cairo. Before I had gotten very far the clock struck twelve, and Springfield being a country town, everything stopped so people could go home to dinner, which was served in the middle of the day. I did not go with Mr. Williams to his home but urged him to do so.

I went to his office and stayed there, getting the balance of my address in shape. At two o'clock he came for me and we went back to the Capitol. I resumed the statement of facts I had found—of the meeting held Monday night and of the resolution passed there which stated Frank Davis had not put his prisoner in the county jail or sworn in deputies to protect him although he knew there was talk of mob violence. . . .

"But that is not all, Governor; I have here the signature of that leading Baptist minister who has been so highly praised to you. I went to his meeting yesterday and when I told him what a mistake it was to seem to condone the outrage on a human being by writing a letter asking for the reinstatement of a man who permitted it to be done, he rose and admitted he had sent the letter which has been read in your hearing, but having realized his mistake he wanted me to tell you that **6** he endorsed the resolutions which I have here, and here is his name signed to them."

And then I wound up by saying, "Governor, the state of Illinois has had too many terrible lynchings within her borders within the last few years. If this man is sent back it will be an encouragement to those who resort to mob violence and will do so at any time, well knowing they will not be called to account for so doing. All the colored friends in Cairo are friends of Mr. Davis and they seem to feel that because his successor, a Democrat, has turned out all the Republican deputies, they owe their duty to the party to ask the return of a Republican sheriff. But not one of these, Mr. Davis's friends, would say that for one moment he had his prisoner in the county jail where the law demands that he should be placed or that he swore in a single deputy to help protect his life until he could be tried by law. It looked like encouragement to the mob to have the chief law officer in the county take that man up in the woods and keep him until the mob got big enough to come after him. I repeat, Governor, that if this man is reinstated, it will simply mean an increase of lynchings in the state of Illinois and an encouragement to mob violence."

When I had finished it was late in the afternoon . . . Mr. Williams said as we went down the steps, "Oh, the governor's going to send him back. I don't see how he can help it with such terrific pressure being brought to bear to have him to do so. But, by george, if I had time to dig up the law I would have furnished him so much of it that he wouldn't dare do so." I said, "We have done the best we could under the circumstances, and angels could do no more."

PREDICT: What will Governor Deneen decide to do? **7**

The following Tuesday morning Governor Deneen issued one of the finest state papers that emanated from him during his whole eight years in the Capitol. The summary of his proclamation was that Frank Davis could not be reinstated because he had not properly protected the prisoner within his keeping and that lynch law could have no place in Illinois.

That was in 1909, and from that day until the present there has been no lynching in the state. Every sheriff, whenever there seem to be any signs of the kind, immediately telegraphs the governor for troops. And to Governor Deneen belongs the credit.

MINI-LESSON: VOCABULARY

Using Vivid Verbs

Teach Wells used active, specific, vivid verbs to describe the events and emotions of her journey to Cairo.

Activity Ideas

• Ask students to find two to five sentences with very descriptive verbs and read them aloud.

• Have other students suggest synonyms that might replace these verbs and reread the sentences using the substitute verbs.

• Ask students to compare the sentences and suggest why one works better than the other.

After Reading

Making Connections

Shaping Your Response

1. Ida B. Wells battled against a very serious injustice—that of the "lynch law." If you could write a letter to any person involved in this narrative, to whom would you write, and what would you want to say?

2. What three adjectives would you use to describe Wells? Explain your choices.

Analyzing the Autobiography

3. Why do you suppose Wells's husband thought it was so important for Wells to go to Cairo to investigate?

4. Wells's child finally convinced her that she should investigate the case. Why do you think he was successful in convincing her?

5. Many prominent African Americans in Cairo at first thought that Sheriff Davis should be reinstated. Why did Wells object to this so strongly?

6. Why do you suppose Wells gives credit to Governor Deneen for ending lynching in Illinois, rather than to herself or the other crusaders?

Extending the Ideas

7. If Ida B. Wells could visit the present time, what would she like about American society? What might she want to change?

8. As a class, brainstorm a list of contemporary people who are currently leading their own crusades for justice. What are some of the characteristics these people have in common?

9. In what ways would you say Ida B. Wells went "beyond the limits" of the traditional roles for women of her time?

Literary Focus: Tone

In this excerpt from her autobiography, Wells's **tone** is formal—she obviously takes the matter of the lynching seriously and expects her readers to do the same. Look back to the notes you kept about Wells's tone while reading the selection. At certain points in her writing, Wells reveals that she is dissatisfied with the response to the lynching. Of whom is she critical? Why? How does her tone reveal her feelings?

Crusade for Justice **489**

After Reading

MAKING CONNECTIONS

1. Answers will vary but should reflect an understanding of the issues of this selection.

2. Possible responses: intelligent, brave, caring, resourceful.

3. Possible answers: He knew she could do the job right. African Americans were aware of Wells anti-lynching history and would trust her with their thoughts and support.

4. Possibly because he reminded her of her duty and she wanted to set an example for him.

5. She felt that supporting one lynching implied that lynching was acceptable under some circumstances; she wanted it outlawed under *any* circumstances.

6. Probably because she feels that his action was courageous in view of the overwhelming support for Frank Davis's reinstatement. Also, she is a humble person.

7. Answers will vary but should reflect an understanding of the gains and setbacks experienced by contemporary African Americans.

8. Answers should include intelligent, outspoken individuals fighting for justice.

9. Possible response: Women were expected to let men ask the questions and do the decision-making. Wells had been criticized by some men in her community for "jumping ahead of them." Nonetheless, she did what she felt she had to do.

LITERARY FOCUS: TONE

Remind students to analyze the information Wells includes about specific people as well as the words she uses to describe them or her response to them.

 Unit 5 Resource Book
Graphic Organizer, p. 25

489

VOCABULARY STUDY

1. condoning
2. enact
3. prominent
4. mandatory
5. dispossess

More Practice   Students can suggest words that mean the same or nearly the same as each vocabulary word.

Unit 5 Resource Book
Vocabulary, p. 27
Vocabulary Test, p. 30

WRITING CHOICES
Writer's Notebook Update

Suggest that students include at least three points in their arguments and that, as they write, they anticipate and try to dispel any objections their readers might make.

A Letter to James's Family

As students write, ask them to carefully consider information they will and will not include.

Wells the Hero

Traditional heroes are "made" by their responses to various situations as they travel through life. Students might consider other troubles Wells might have faced in her time.

Selection Test

Unit 5 Resource Book
pp. 31–32

Vocabulary Study

Choose the word from the list that best completes each sentence.

enact
prominent
dispossess
mandatory
condoning

1. Wells believed that the African American community's ____ of the sheriff's actions would lead to more violence.
2. Wells was determined that lawmakers ____ legislation that would protect the rights of African Americans.
3. Several ____ townspeople argued that Sheriff Davis should be reinstated.
4. Wells believed that it was ____ that Davis be fired for his failure to protect the prisoner.
5. Governor Deneen decided to ____ Davis of his title as sheriff.

Expressing Your Ideas

Writing Choices

Writer's Notebook Update Would you call Ida B. Wells a hero? Why or why not? Review your list of characteristics for a heroic person. Are there any changes that you'd like to make to your list? In your notebook, write a short argument about whether or not Wells could be called a hero. Support your argument with evidence from the selection.

A Letter to James's Family Imagine that Wells followed up on her work in Illinois by locating "Frog" James's family. Draft a **letter** from Wells to his family that reveals her feelings about the lynching and explains her attitude toward the crusade for justice that followed. Before you begin your letter, decide on your **tone.** How emotional would Wells have been in a letter like this? Would she have allowed her anger to show?

Wells the Hero Use this episode from Wells's autobiography as the basis for a **short story** or **epic poem** with Wells as the hero. What does she have in common with traditional epic heroes?

Other Options

Ida B. Wells and the Governor . . . Today
Arrange an imaginary meeting between Ida B. Wells and the current governor of your state. Working in pairs, brainstorm a **list** of the issues Wells might want to discuss with your governor. When you've finished your list, decide how the governor might respond to each of her points. With one person playing the role of Wells and the other playing the role of the governor, create a **dramatization** of their meeting in front of the class.

A Symbol of Wells's Crusade If you were to choose one object to symbolize Wells's crusade for justice in Illinois, what would it be? **Sketch** a picture of the object in your notebook. Include with your sketch a brief explanation of the object and how it is a symbol of Wells's crusade.

OTHER OPTIONS
Ida B. Wells and the Governor

Students may wish to consult newspapers or other resources to learn more about the governor's stand on key issues, such as hate crimes against African Americans, police brutality toward African Americans, and overpopulation of African Americans in prisons.

A Symbol of Wells's Crusade

Give students examples of symbols for ideas, such as a dove for peace, a prison door standing open, the colors of the flag from a specific African nation to symbolize African roots.

Before Reading

The Spring and the Fall
On Thought in Harness

by Edna St. Vincent Millay

Edna St. Vincent Millay
1892–1950

Born in Maine, Millay began writing verse at an early age—her mother taught her the form of a sonnet at age four. At age fourteen she published her first poem. Ten years later Millay moved to Greenwich Village in New York City and became the poetic voice of the "flaming youth" of the 1920s. Although she had some success as an actress and playwright, Millay is best remembered for her romantic poetry. She wrote about desire and death, about the self and the universe, and about the changeable emotions of rebellious youth.

Building Background

Reading Poetry When you read poetry, you do so in two ways: you read for meaning (what the poet is trying to say) and you read for structure (the poetic devices the poet uses to help illuminate meaning). Think for a moment about the poetry you've read. Which poems do you remember most vividly? List the titles on a sheet of paper. Next to each title, write a sentence that explains why the poem is memorable. Does the rhyme scheme or the structure of the poem help make it memorable? In groups, discuss what you think makes good poetry good. Make a list of the characteristics of good poetry.

Literary Focus

Rhythm and Rhyme The structure of a poem contributes to the poem's meaning. One aspect of a poem's structure, **rhythm,** is the way the poem sounds—the "beat" of the poem—when read aloud. **Rhyme** is the repetition of similar or identical sounds in the body of the poem. The pattern of rhyming words from line to line is called the **rhyme scheme** of the poem. As you read "The Spring and the Fall" and "On Thought in Harness," answer these questions:

- How should the poem sound when read aloud? Which syllables should be stressed?

- How does Millay set up her rhyme scheme? Which words rhyme? Do the rhyming words fall mostly at the ends of lines or at various places throughout the poem?

Writer's Notebook

Aspects of Love Draw a chart similar to the one shown here to list ten to fifteen words that you associate with the positive

Aspects of Love	
Positive	**Negative**

and negative aspects of love. For example, your chart may contain words like *joy, tenderness,* and *devotion,* as well as words like *betrayal, anguish,* and *sadness.* If you like, get together with some classmates and work on a group chart.

The Spring and the Fall **491**

Before Reading

Building Background

Based on their discussion of poems they find memorable, help students list characteristics of a good poem. Imagery, rhythm, rhyme, and other poetic devices should be included.

Literary Focus

Before reading Millay's poems, have students beat out the **rhythm** of one of the poems they found memorable and to find words that **rhyme**.

Writer's Notebook

It may be helpful to suggest familiar characters for students to keep in mind as they list their words, for example Romeo and Juliet.

More About Edna St. Vincent Millay

- Millay wrote verse as a child, mostly for plays she made up with her two sisters.

- Her poem "Renascence" earned her the respect of a benefactor who paid her tuition to Vassar College.

- She was an early member of the experimental theater group the Provincetown Players.

SUPPORT MATERIALS OVERVIEW

Unit 5 Resource Book
- Graphic Organizer, p.33
- Study Guide, p.34
- Vocabulary, p. 35
- Grammar, p. 36
- Alternate Check Test, p. 37
- Vocabulary Test, p. 38
- Selection Test, pp. 39–40

Building English Proficiency
- Literature Summaries
- Activities, p. 206

Reading, Writing & Grammar SkillBook
- Reading, pp. 25–28
- Writing, pp. 112–113
- Grammar, Usage, and Mechanics, pp. 240–241

Technology
- Audiotape
- Personal Journal Software
- Custom Literature Database: For other selections dealing with love and loss, see A. E Housman and William Shakespeare on the database.
- Test Generator Software

During Reading

Selection Objectives

- To compare two poems in terms of **rhythm** and **rhyme**
- To analyze the images of two love poems
- To explore the theme of going beyond limits

Unit 5 Resource Book
Study Guide, p. 34

Theme Link

One poem—written in strict rhyme and meter—describes a relationship that stays within the boundaries until one partner decides to break out. The other—written with an ear to rhyme but an irregular rhythm—is an extended metaphor that describes a relationship in which one member is tied down and the other must let go.

Vocabulary Preview

bough, one of the branches of a tree
raucous, hoarse; harsh sounding
quake, shake or tremble
degraded, lower in rank, honor, quality
forsake, give up; abandon

Students can add the words and definitions to their personal word lists in their Writer's Notebook.

The Spring and the Fall

EDNA ST. VINCENT MILLAY

In the spring of the year, in the spring
    of the year,
I walked the road beside my dear.
The trees were black where the bark
    was wet.
I see them yet, in the spring of the year.
5 He broke me a bough[1] of the blossoming
    peach
That was out of the way and hard to reach.

In the fall of the year, in the fall of
    the year,
I walked the road beside my dear.
The rooks[2] went up with a raucous[3] trill.
10 I hear them still, in the fall of the year.
He laughed at all I dared to praise,
And broke my heart, in little ways.

Year be springing or year be falling,
The bark will drip and the birds be calling.
15 There's much that's fine to see and hear
In the spring of a year, in the fall of a year.
'Tis not love's going hurts my days,
But that it went in little ways.

———————————

1. bough (bou), *n.* one of the branches of a tree.
2. **rook** (rùk), *n.* common European bird, closely resembling the crow.
3. raucous (rô′kəs), *adj.* hoarse; harsh sounding.

SELECTION SUMMARY

The Spring and the Fall and On Thoughts in Harness

The Spring and the Fall Two different poems describe two different relationships. In "The Spring and the Fall," a woman looks back on her romance with a man who brought her something wonderful "that was out of the way and hard to reach" but who also broke her heart.

On Thoughts in Harness In "On Thoughts in Harness," the release of a captive falcon parallels letting a loved one go—and not expecting to see her return.

 *For summaries in other languages, see the **Building English Proficiency** book.*

What is she doing? What is she thinking? Create a scenario for the women depicted in Theodore Robinson's *In the Garden* (1891). Use the poems for inspiration, if you wish.

On Thought in Harness

EDNA ST. VINCENT MILLAY

My falcon to my wrist
Returns
From no high air.
I sent her toward the sun that burns
5 Above the mist;
But she has not been there.

Her talons are not cold; her beak
Is closed upon no wonder;
Her head stinks of its hood, her feathers reek
10 Of me, that quake[1] at the thunder.

Degraded[2] bird, I give you back your eyes
    forever, ascend now whither you
    are tossed;
Forsake[3] this wrist, forsake this rhyme;
Soar, eat ether, see what has never been
    seen; depart, be lost,
But climb.

---

1. quake (kwāk), *v.* shake or tremble.
2. degraded (di grād′ ed), *adj.* lower in rank, honor, quality.
3. forsake (fôr sāk′), *v.* give up; abandon.

On Thought in Harness **493**

After Reading

MAKING CONNECTIONS

1. Sketches will vary but should be substantiated by the poems.

2. Responses will vary.

3. Possible responses: sadness, wistfulness, melancholy, longing

4. Possible response: Someone who has been held back by a loved one. Students can choose words associated with what the falcon symbolizes.

5. Answers will vary according to students' personal opinions, but most will agree that people must be given their freedom.

LITERARY FOCUS: RHYME AND RHYTHM

Students who are not familiar with charting rhyme and rhythm may be helped by charting a nursery rhyme, or other simple poem, with the class.

Unit 5 Resource Book
Graphic Organizer, p. 33

VOCABULARY STUDY

bough, branch, limb, arm

raucous, noisy, obstreperous, strident, uproarious

quake, tremble, shudder, cower, wince

degrade, insult, denounce, humble, humiliate

forsake, abandon, desert, spurn, denounce

More Practice Students can use vocabulary words to write a short poem of their own.

Selection Test

Unit 5 Resource Book
pp. 39–40

Transparency Collection
Fine Art Writing Prompt 8

After Reading

Making Connections

Shaping Your Response

1. In your notebook, sketch a symbol that represents the poem "The Spring and the Fall." Do the same thing for "On Thought in Harness."

2. Which poem do you most identify with? Why?

Analyzing the Poems

3. What is the **tone** of "The Spring and the Fall"?

4. What do you think the falcon **symbolizes** in "On Thought in Harness"? Defend your choice with words from the poem.

Extending the Ideas

5. What happens when a person's thoughts are kept in harness? Would you agree that we must be allowed to "soar, eat ether, see what has never been seen"? Why?

Literary Focus: Rhyme and Rhythm

When you chart the **rhyme scheme** of a poem, you label the first rhyme **a**, the second rhyme **b**, the third rhyme **c**, and so on. Here is the rhyme scheme of the first stanza of "The Spring and the Fall":

> In the spring of the year, in the spring of the year, **a**
> I walked the road beside my dear. **a**
> The trees were black where the bark was wet. **b**
> I see them yet, in the spring of the year. **a**
> He broke me a bough of the blossoming peach **c**
> That was out of the way and hard to reach. **c**

The **rhythm**—or the **meter** of a poem is measured by the metrical **foot.** Each foot contains one accented syllable and one or more unaccented syllables. You can chart the rhythm of a poem by using a ˘ to mark the unaccented syllables and a ′ to mark the accented syllables, like this:

˘ ′ ˘ ′ ˘ ′ ˘ ′ ˘ ′ ˘ ′
My fal / con to / my wrist / Re turns / From no / high air. /

In your notebook, chart the rhyme scheme of one of the two Millay poems. Then chart the rhythm of the first stanza of "On Thought in Harness."

Vocabulary Study

bough
raucous
quake
degraded
forsake

Create a word web for each of the listed words. In the middle of the web, write the word, then add synonyms for the word at the spokes. An example has been done for you.

MINI-LESSON: GRAMMAR

Using No, Not, and Never

Teach Read this sentence aloud and ask students what is wrong with it: **I never saw no bird.** *(A double negative has been used .)* The rule with negative modifiers is that you only use one per sentence.

Activity Ideas

- Have students find the negative modifiers in Millay's poems and explain how they follow the rule of correct usage.

- Invite students to collect examples of negative modifiers used incorrectly in conversations, song lyrics, and other situations.

History and Science Connections

During the late 1800s and early 1900s, women were expected to live within established limits of conduct. The following selections show the restrictions and attitudes women faced in their everyday lives.

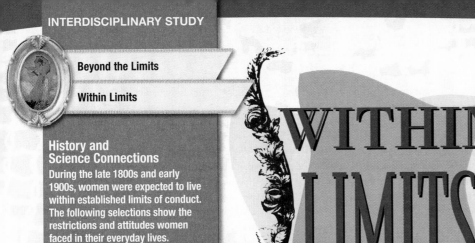

WITHIN LIMITS

The Uprising of Women

New York Times, May 5, 1912

On May 4, 1912, 10,000 women marched through New York City, demanding the right to vote. The following is the reaction of one man to the prospect of women voters.

We often hear the remark nowadays that women will get the vote, if they try hard enough andpersistently, and it is true that they will get it, and play havoc with it for themselves and society, if the men are not firm and wise enough, and, it may well be said, masculine enough to prevent them. The agitation has been on foot for many years. One does not need to be a profound student of biology to know that some women, a very small minority, have a natural inclination to usurp the social and civic function of men. But that is not true of a majority of the women in yesterday's parade, or of their thousands of sympathetic sisters who lacked the physical vigor, the courage, or the opportunity to join in the march. Their adherence to the cause is largely factitious, born of much agitation and much false theorizing. There are, however, unhappy creatures to whom the state of being a woman is naturally burdensome. Their influence would not count for so much if their less unhappy sisters, who have no real grievance against Mother Nature or society, would not give them

---

Interdisciplinary Study

Theme Link

Turn-of-the-century limits on women seem extreme today and help us see how far beyond those limits attitudes have come.

Curricular Connection: History and Science

Use the information in this interdisciplinary study to explore with students the restrictions on women and the social and scientific rationales that supported the attitudes toward women.

Terms to Know

havoc (hav′ək), very great destruction

usurp (yü zėrp′), seize and hold power or authority by force or without right

adherence (ad hir′əns), a holding to and following closely

factitious (fak tish′əs), not natural; artificial

countenance (koun′tə nəns), approve or encourage; sanction

allay (ə lā′), to put at rest; quiet

Unit 5 Resource Book
Interdisciplinary Study Guide, p. 41

BUILDING ENGLISH PROFICIENCY

Making Cultural Connections

ESL
LEP
ELD
SAE
LD

Preface the reading of "Within Limits" by encouraging students to think of parallels to the women's suffrage movement.

- Have students choose a group, such as an ethnic, cultural, or age group, that they think has been treated unfairly.

- Have students list reasons why people in that group should be kept from voting.

(Possible answers: They're not educated; they're not smart enough to vote wisely; If they get the vote, they'll want things that we don't like; we don't want to share our power with them.)

- As students read "Within Limits," have them look for similar arguments to the ones that they listed.

Art Study

Nathaniel Currier (1813–1888) and James Merritt Ives (1824–1895) designed inexpensive and extremely popular prints and wall hangings. They were successful businessmen and had a knack for selecting scenes that captured the contemporary American climate, such as Mississippi riverboat races and frontiersmen. Hundreds of copies of each scene would be hand-colored by twelve to fifteen women working in an assembly line.

Question This cartoon ridicules the idea of women doing men's work and men caring for babies. What happens to the women's femininity as they do men's work? *(Possible responses: The women are smoking, scolding, and being immodest.)*

countenance. There are numberless explanations of the conduct of otherwise nice and womanly women in this matter. There are few that can fairly be called "reasons."

We are told by some sages that education has made women discontented. It has made men discontented, too, for that matter. The equality of opportunity all men possess in this country has not allayed the discontent. There is no reason to suppose that the right to vote would allay feminine discontent. Granted the suffrage, they would demand all that the right implies. It is not possible to think of women as soldiers and sailors, police patrolmen, or firemen, although voters ought to fight if need be, but they would serve on juries and elect themselves if they could to executive offices and judgeships. Many of them are looking forward to an apportionment of high offices between the sexes. This may seem preposterous to some of the men who choose to smile complacently at the aggressiveness of the

This 1869 Currier & Ives cartoon warns that voting would create masculine, aggressive women.

women's rights adherents, but it is true. It is a state of things these men will have to cope with before they die if they do not arouse themselves and do their duty now.

We have said that the ballot will secure to woman no right that she needs and does not now possess. That is a true statement, and we hold that it is not debatable. Woman is thoroughly protected by the existing laws. Her rights as a taxpayer, a holder of property, are not in danger. Her dower rights are scrupulously upheld in the probate courts. In her pursuit of all the privileges and duties of men, however, she is deliberately endangering many rights she now enjoys without legal sanction. She receives honors and privileges which the younger man will soon learn to withhold from her when she jostles him at the polls. It will be a sad day for society when woman loses the respect she now receives from all but the basest of men. Yet yesterday's parade demonstrates that she holds male

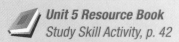

496 UNIT FIVE: BREAKING THE MOLD

MINI-LESSON: STUDY SKILLS

Recognizing Overgeneralizations

Teach Tell students that an overgeneralization occurs when the sample on which a generalization is based is too limited or unrepresentative. To help students avoid overgeneralizations in their writing or discussions, remind them

- to keep their samples large and representative
- to avoid making statements about groups unless they are certain that the statement applies to each individual in the group
- to use qualifying words such as *most, some,* or *occasionally* to limit generalizations

Activity Idea Have students identify overgeneralizations in "The Uprising of Women," such as, "They are unhappy creatures." *(Possible responses: "Education has made women discontented. It has made men discontented, too; Granted the suffrage, they would demand all that the right implies.")*

Unit 5 Resource Book
Study Skill Activity, p. 42

courtesy in slight regard, or would, if we were willing to regard the parade as a demonstration of the feelings and opinions of all our women.

Millions of men labor all their years to keep up a home, of which a woman is mistress. Poor enough the home may be, and the measure of toil its upkeep demands of the man may age him prematurely and deprive him of all the freedom which he instinctively desires. But most men throughout the civilized world have been doing their duty as husbands and fathers, as citizens, according to their lights. That the triumph of woman suffrage would tend quickly to change the point of view of these millions of plodding men is not to be doubted. If woman declares her independence, and forces the State to recognize it, the cry of the men will be "Let her uphold it and enjoy it as best she may." From the beginning "man that is born of woman" has been "of few days and full of trouble." Presumably he will continue to be born. Presumably he will continue to respect his mother, as Ishmael did. But with the opportunity afforded him by the refusal of woman to recognize his manhood as a title of supremacy in the world's affairs, he will be at pains to avoid some of the troubles which he has hitherto regarded as part of his heritage.

This we hold to be inevitable. Let the women who are not yet avowed suffragists consider it. Above all, let the complacent multitudes of men who have accepted the full responsibility of citizenship consider it. There were, at most, 10,000 women in yesterday's parade. If their cause triumphs there will be 700,000 women voters in this municipality. Have the 10,000 thought much about the measure of influence they would exert if the whole number voted under the control of their associations and environment as their intelligence impelled them to?

Teaching by the Rules

While women were struggling for career opportunities, teaching had long been an option for single women. Even so, women teachers had to live within strict limits.

Schoolteachers were expected to live up to saintly standards in private as well as public. About 1915, for example, Iva McDaniels, a schoolmarm for 15 years in one small Massachusetts community, came back after spending Thanksgiving with friends in a nearby town, to find that she had been fired for ignoring rules two and seven of those governing the conduct of female schoolteachers:

1. Do not get married.
2. Do not leave town at any time without school board permission.
3. Do not keep company with men.
4. Be home between the hours of 8 P.M. and 6 A.M.
5. Do not loiter downtown in ice cream stores.
6. Do not smoke.
7. Do not get into any carriage with any man except your father or brother.
8. Do not dress in bright colors.
9. Do not dye your hair.
10. Do not wear any dress more than two inches above the ankle.

Interdisciplinary Study **497**

Additional Background

In 1819, Emma Willard asked the New York state legislature to fund the first women's institution of higher education. When they refused, she raised the money herself and opened the Troy Female Seminary, which became a model training school for teachers.

Interdisciplinary Activity Ideas

- Students can stage a debate between *The New York Times* writer and leaders of the women's rights movement—then and now.
- Students can respond to *The New York Times* opinion of May 5, 1912, by writing letters to the editor, using current facts and perspectives.
- Teaching by the Rules can open up a discussion about whether employers have the right to know the private lives of potential employees. Students can debate the pros and cons of drug testing and lie-detector tests, investigation of arrest records, physical exams, and questions about age, marital status, and children.

BUILDING ENGLISH PROFICIENCY

Responding to Historical Details

Use one or more of the following activities to help students focus on the restrictions in Teaching by the Rules.

- Ask students to rate the rules on a scale from 1 (easiest to live by) to 10 (hardest to live by). Compare and discuss their rankings. Ask: Which rules do you think violate your personal rights the most? Why?

- Invite groups of students to present a skit that dramatizes the rules: for example, a teacher receives a marriage proposal, or explains why she has been "loitering" at the ice cream store.
- Challenge students to create and perform a rap that quotes from the regulations and perhaps uses a chorus in which the words *teaching by the rules* are included.

WITHIN LIMITS

from

The Sexual Politics of Sickness

by Barbara Ehrenreich and Deirdre English

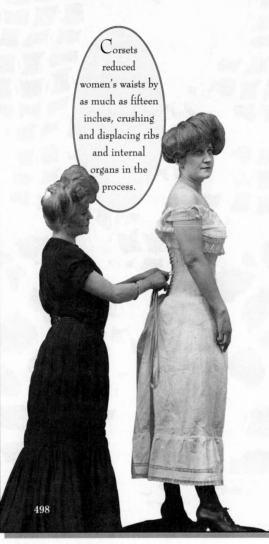

Corsets reduced women's waists by as much as fifteen inches, crushing and displacing ribs and internal organs in the process.

498

As middle- and upper-class women of the late 1800s found themselves with more leisure time and less to do, mysterious illnesses began taking over their lives. Doctors diagnosed the diseases using labels such as "neurasthenia," "dyspepsia," and "hysteria," and prescribed such cures as lying in bed several hours after every meal, staying indoors, and avoiding intellectual activity. This system kept the patients sick, the doctors wealthy, and women docile and frail.

The way [middle- and upper-class] woman was expected to live predisposed her to sickness, and sickness in turn predisposed her to continue to live as she was expected to. The delicate, affluent lady, who was completely dependent on her husband, set the sexual romanticist ideal of femininity for women of all classes.

Clear-headed feminists like Charlotte Perkins Gilman and Olive Schreiner saw a link between female invalidism and the economic situation of women in the upper classes. As they observed, poor women did not suffer from the syndrome. . . .

To Gilman's pragmatic mind, the affluent wife appeared to be a sort of tragic evolutionary anomaly, something like the dodo. She did not work; that is, there was no serious, productive work to do in the home, and the tasks which were left—keeping house, cooking and minding the children—she left as much as possible to the domestic help . . .

A successful man could have no better social ornament than an idle wife. Her delicacy, her culture, her childlike ignorance of the male world gave a man the "class" which money alone could not buy. A virtuous wife spent a hushed and peaceful life indoors, sewing, sketching, planning menus, and supervising the servants and children. The more adventurous might fill their leisure with shopping

1. Possble Response   The editor perhaps is exhibiting his own and society's fear of change, fear of shift in power, and fear that women voters would undermine the role of men in society.

2. Possible Response   Medical ignorance, social expectations, and a culture of male domination of women encouraged and promoted illness in women.

feature such stories as "The Grave of My Friend" and "Song of Dying." Society ladies cultivated a sickly countenance by drinking vinegar in quantity or, more effectively, arsenic. The loveliest heroines were those who died young, like Beth in *Little Women,* too good and too pure for life in this world.

Meanwhile, the requirements of fashion insured that the well-dressed woman would actually be as frail and ornamental as she looked. The style of wearing tight-laced corsets, which was *de riguer* throughout the last half of the century, has to be ranked somewhere close to the old Chinese practice of foot-binding for its crippling effects on the female body. A fashionable woman's corsets exerted, on the average, twenty-one pounds of pressure on her internal organs, and extremes of up to eighty-eight pounds have been measured. (Add to this the fact that a well-dressed woman wore an average of thirty-seven pounds of street clothing in the winter months, of which nineteen pounds were suspended from her tortured waist.) Some of the short-term results of tight-lacing were shortness of breath, constipation, weakness, and a tendency to violent indigestion. Among the long-term effects were bent or fractured ribs [and] displacement of the liver . . .

The theories which guided the doctor's practice from the late nineteenth century to the early twentieth century held that woman's normal state was to be sick. This was not advanced as an empirical observation, but as physiological fact. Medicine had "discovered" that female functions were inherently pathological.

John Singer Sargent's 1889-90 portrait, *Miss Elsie Palmer,* idealizes the passivity and frailty of its female subject.

excursions, luncheons, balls, and novels. A "lady" could be charming, but never brilliant; interested, but not intense. . . . By no means was such a lady to concern herself with politics, business, international affairs, or the aching injustices of the industrial work world. . . .

If you have to be idle, you might as well be sick, and sickness, in turn, legitimates idleness. From the romantic perspective, the sick woman was not that far off from the ideal woman anyway. A morbid aesthetic developed, in which sickness was seen as a source of female beauty, and, beauty—in the high-fashion sense—was in fact a source of sickness. Over and over, nineteenth-century romantic paintings feature the beautiful invalid, sensuously dropping on her cushions, eyes fixed tremulously at her husband or physician, or already gazing into the Beyond. Literature aimed at female readers lingered on the romantic pathos of illness and death; popular women's magazines

Responding

1. Why do you think the writer of the *New York Times* article was so fearful at the prospect of women voters?

2. How would you explain the extraordinary amounts of sickness in women during this time period?

BUILDING ENGLISH PROFICIENCY

Expanding Vocabulary Notebooks

Encourage students to build their own word resources in a vocabulary notebook as they read "The Sexual Politics of Sickness."

- Offer examples of words that may be completely new to them, such as *predisposed* and *pathos,* and words that may have a different meaning here, such as *domestic* and *culture.*
- Have students note these or other words, define each word, and then use it in an original sentence.

predispose	give a tendency to
My family's musical abilities predispose me to sing in the chorus.	

Language History

Teaching Objectives

- To increase awareness of gender bias in language
- To contemplate the relationship of language and society's values

Introduce

Show students a photograph of a woman. Ask students to imagine what this person did for a living, judging from her clothing, the setting, and any other clues that might give students an indication of the life that this person led.

Help students see that we make assumptions from appearance, just as we make assumptions from the words we use.

Follow Up

Have students bring in examples of gender-biased language from the media or from conversations in their lives.

Language History

The Language of Gender

 That's one small step for man, one giant leap for mankind.

Astronaut Neil Armstrong made the above statement as he took the step that made him the first person ever to walk on the moon. When he made that famous statement, did he mean one small step for human beings, in general, or one small step for males? And whom was he including with the word *mankind?*

During the 1970s womens groups began to call attention to gender biases in American English. Feminists argued that American English needed reforming to eliminate sexist language. They wanted words like *mankind* to be replaced by more universal *humankind,* and to stop the generic use of *he* to indicate all people.

Many feminists argued that we should discontinue using *man* in words that also describe the professions or abilities of women. Women fight fires, they reasoned, so the term *fireman* is incorrect. Women deliver the mail, so *mailman* should be changed to *mail carrier, spokesman* should be *spokesperson,* and so on. For years the word *authoress* was used to describe a female writer. According to feminists, the *-ess* suffix has a minimizing or trivializing effect. An *authoress* performs the same job as an *author;* a *stewardess* performs the same job as a *steward.*

Much of the language considered to reflect gender biases is disappearing. We no longer use *sculptress* and *murderess* and are beginning to drop *hostess* for the more generic *host. Flight attendant* is now used in place of *steward* and *stewardess,* and those who write poetry or act are called poets and actors, regardless of their gender. Many women now use the generic title *Ms.* before their names rather than the *Mrs.* and *Miss* titles that differentiate between married and single women, with no parallel counterparts for men.

Most linguists believe that whenever we make changes in our language, we feel motivated to make accompanying changes in society. If we use words in our language that do not favor one gender over the other, then perhaps we are one step closer to achieving gender equality in other aspects of life.

CONTENT AREA READING

Correcting Language Bias

Have students choose a fairy tale, newspaper article, or short story and rewrite it to eliminate all gender-biased language.

Just for fun, this can be taken further by eliminating all "man" syllables, such as e*man*cipation which becomes e*person*cipation. Suggest that students watch out for gender bias in names. For example, *Anderson* will become *Anderdaughter* for a female. Invite students to read their gender-free or gender-accurate rewrites aloud.

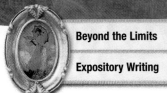

Writing Workshop

Update: Women Then and Now

Assignment You have read about what life was like for women in the past. Now write about how things have changed.

WRITER'S BLUEPRINT

Product	An update on women's roles
Purpose	To explain how life has changed for women during the last century
Audience	Men and women from the turn of the century
Specs	To write a successful paper, you should:

❑ Imagine that you have the power to send news back in time. Today you are going to update people living in the year 1900 on how women's roles have changed since their time.

❑ Begin by orienting your audience in time and space. Introduce yourself, give the date and city, and briefly describe your setting—the place where you are writing this update.

❑ Go on to review women's roles at the turn of the century and update your audience on how things have changed since then. Focus on three of these aspects: marriage, motherhood, work, education, legal rights, or other aspects of your choice.

❑ Keep in mind the limits of your audience's knowledge, and give them the background they'll need to understand what you're telling them.

❑ Conclude by giving your opinion about the direction you think women's roles are taking and how you feel about this situation.

❑ Follow the rules of grammar, usage, spelling, and mechanics. Look closely at verb forms.

1 PREWRITING

Chart women's roles. Working with a partner or small group, analyze the literature for information on women's roles at the turn of the century.

Writing Workshop **501**

Writing Workshop

WRITER'S BLUEPRINT
Specs

The Specs in the Writer's Blueprint address these writing and thinking skills:

- orienting the audience
- comparing and contrasting
- keeping to the main idea
- making judgments
- defining terms
- taking a position
- using apostrophes correctly

These Specs serve as your lesson objectives, and they form the basis for the **Assessment Criteria Specs** for a superior paper, which appear on the final TE page for this lesson. You might want to read through the *Assessment Criteria Specs* with students when you begin the lesson.

Linking Literature to Writing

Lead a discussion about what life was like for women in the past as reflected in the literature.

STEP 1 PREWRITING
Chart women's roles

After organizing the class into small groups, you might assign each of the aspects listed to a particular group. Each group could then share its information with the others.

WRITING WORKSHOP OVERVIEW

Product
Expository writing: An update on women's roles

Prewriting
Chart women's roles—Research three aspects—Try a quickwrite—Plan your essay—Consider your audience
Unit 5 Resource Book
Prewriting Worksheets pp. 43–44

Drafting
Before you draft—As you draft
Transparency Collection
Student Models for Writing Workshop 15, 16

Revising
Ask a partner—Strategy: Orienting Your Audience
Unit 5 Resource Book
Revising Worksheet p. 45

Editing
Ask a partner—Strategy: Using Apostrophes Correctly
Unit 5 Resource Book
Grammar Worksheet p. 46
Grammar Check Test p. 47

Presenting
Community Leaders
Time Line

Looking Back
Self-evaluate—Reflect—For Your Working Portfolio
Unit 5 Resource Book
Assessment Worksheet p. 48
Transparency Collection
Fine Art Writing Prompt 8

Research three aspects

If students are working with partners, have them agree on the three aspects to be covered. One of them can do the research concerning the past and the other can research concerning the present.

Try a quickwrite

Remind students that from on they'll be working on their own, working from the chart they made in the previous activity. Urge students to be sure to deal with three different aspects of women's roles.

Plan your essay

Have students summarize, in a sentence or two, their own opinions on the direction that women's roles have moved, and use these summaries in their plan.

LITERARY SOURCE
"There would be no one to live for her during those coming years; she would live for herself. There would be no powerful will bending hers in that blind persistence. . . ."
from "The Story of an Hour" by Kate Chopin

OR . . .
Have a classmate play a visitor from the turn-of-the-century. Have a conversation about the three aspects of change you selected. Then make your writing plan.

Organize your information in a chart similar to the one shown. Cover at least three of these aspects: marriage, motherhood, work, education, legal rights, or other aspects of your choice.

Turn of the Century	
Aspect	**Role**
Marriage	Submissive to husband. Life ruled by his decisions.

Research three aspects with your partner or small group. Consult history books, encyclopedias, and books on the women's movement for additional information about women's roles at the turn of the century. Also, research the state of women's roles today. Share your information and organize it in a change chart like the one shown.

Change Chart			
Aspect	**1900**	**How Things Have Changed**	**Background**
1. work	Women, as a rule, did not work outside the home.	Equal rights within the workplace and two-income families	—ERA and feminist movement —Girls encouraged to get education and seek careers

Try a quickwrite. From now on you'll be working on your own. Write for five or ten minutes. Use your change chart as a guide as you address these questions about the three aspects you chose:

- What direction do women's roles seem to be taking? Will there be more freedom in the future, or less?

- Do I approve of the direction in which things seem to be moving? Why or why not?

Plan your essay. Look back at your prewriting materials as you develop your writing plan. You might organize your notes in a plan like the one that follows.

- **Introduction** (orienting the audience)
    Who you are
    Date and city
    Description of setting

MINI-LESSON: WRITING STYLE

Orienting Your Audience

Use this mini-lesson with the "Plan your essay" activity on this page or with the Revising Strategy on page 504.

Teach   Ask students to brainstorm a list of words or concepts that are used today but were not used at the turn-of-the-century. For example: express mail, equal opportunity, fax machines, welfare, single parent, latch-key kids.

Activity Idea   Ask volunteers to role-play someone from today explaining these terms to someone at the turn of the century. Encourage students to ask each other questions.

Apply   Remind students that definitions of new terms may be a necessary part of their own papers. These explanations should be brief and easily understood.

- **Body** (updating the audience on changes)
  First aspect
  —Conditions at the turn of the century
  —Conditions today
  —Background on how changes occurred
  Second aspect
  and so on . . .

- **Conclusion** (telling the audience how you feel)
  Direction women's roles are taking
  Your opinion about this direction

Consider your audience. Look back at your plan and prewriting notes and make a list of concepts and terms you are likely to use in your paper that would not be familiar to a turn-of-the-century audience, along with a brief definition of each term. For example, as you describe the room where you're writing, you might mention a computer and a TV, two items unknown to your audience. For more ideas on considering your audience, see the Revising Strategy in Step 3 of this lesson.

DRAFTING

Before you draft, review your prewriting notes and writing plan. Then reread the Writer's Blueprint.

As you draft, don't worry about spelling or punctuation mistakes yet. Concentrate on getting the ideas from your writing plan down on paper. Here are some drafting tips.

- As you describe your setting, go beyond your immediate surroundings. Look out the window and mention things such as parking meters, street lamps, and automobiles (horseless carriages).

- Don't get bogged down in this introduction, though. Keep it brief—no more than a paragraph. Your purpose is to give your readers a taste of modern life, not an involved description and explanation.

REVISING

Ask a partner to comment on your draft before you revise it. Use the checklist on the next page as a guide.

Writing Workshop   **503**

BUILDING ENGLISH PROFICIENCY

Organizing Information

Offer these suggestions as students make their organizational decisions.

- Students already should have chosen the three aspects that they want to cover. Urge students to summarize each aspect on a note card and then experiment with arranging the cards in various ways until they are pleased with the sequence (possibly from least to most important).

- Point out that to give the best sense of closure, the conclusion should relate to the introduction. Offer guidance, as requested, as students hint at their opinion in the introduction and include a reminder of the present-day setting in the conclusion.

Consider your audience

For additional support, see the worksheets referenced below.

Unit 5 Resource Book
Prewriting Worksheet, p. 43
Prewriting Worksheet, p. 44

Connections to
Writer's Notebook

For selection-related prompts, refer to Writer's Notebook.

Connections to
Writer's Resource

For additional writing prompts, refer to Writer's Resource.

STEP 2 DRAFTING
Before you draft

Have students check off each item in the Writer's Blueprint to be sure they've included it in their plan.

As you draft

For students having difficulty getting started, you might suggest that they imagine carrying on a conversation with people from the turn-of-the-century. Have them imagine what some of their questions might be about today.

The Student Models

The **transparencies** referenced below are authentic student models. Review them with the students before they draft. These questions will help:

1. Which writer do you think does a better job of fulfilling the Specs in the Writer's Blueprint and why?

2. Look for terms the writers should have defined for their audience but didn't.

Transparency Collection
Student Models for
Writing Workshop 15, 16

STEP 3 REVISING

Ask a partner
(Peer assessment)

Encourage partners to use the checklist on page 504 and focus their comments on the three checked items.

Revising Strategy:
Orienting Your Audience

Have students explain why they agree or disagree with the changes that were made in the student model. Ask if they would have changed any other words. Urge them to look for terms that need defining in their own papers.

For additional support, see the mini-lesson at the bottom of page 502 and the worksheet referenced below.

Unit 3 Resource Book
Revising Worksheet, p. 45

Connections to
Writer's Resource

For additional writing prompts, refer to Writer's Resource.

STEP 4 EDITING

Ask a partner
(Peer assessment)

Have the class look at the proofreading marks on the back inside cover of the book. Encourage them to use these marks as they review the drafts.

✔ Did I focus on three aspects related to women's roles?

✔ Did I express my opinion on the current direction of women's roles?

✔ Am I considering my audience as I write?

Revising Strategy

Orienting Your Audience

Because your audience is not from this century, you may need to clarify some of the language you use. As you revise your work, be on the look-out for any language that may be unfamiliar to your audience. Consider these options:

• Change the term to something the audience understands.

• Explain the term—but keep these explanations brief and simple. Give your audience the information they'll need to understand your train of thought. Don't overexplain.

Notice how the writer of the student model made changes with her audience in mind.

> These changes in the household duties of women consequently
> *bringing up their children*
> affect the role that females play in ~~parenting.~~ Whereas women were
> previously expected to stay home with the children, this is not
> always the case anymore. Children now often stay in day-care
> *—places where small children are cared for while their*
> centers ~~while the mother works.~~ *parents are at work.*

STUDENT MODEL

STEP 4 EDITING

Ask a partner to review your revised draft before you edit. When you edit, look for errors in grammar, usage, spelling, and mechanics. Make sure you are using apostrophes correctly.

MINI-LESSON: GRAMMAR

Using Apostrophes Correctly

Display the following sentences and have students make any necessary corrections. Ask students to explain their answers.

1. The teams' record puts it in second place for this season. (teams' to team's)

2. The girls' problems were beginning to affect their school work. (correct)

3. Two mens' cars were hit by the bus. (mens' to men's)

4. Mr. Smith's coats were found in the back seat of the car. (correct)

5. A persons' courage can be measured in many ways. (persons' to person's)

Unit 5 Resource Book
Grammar Worksheet p. 46
Grammar Check Test p. 47

Editing Strategy

Using Apostrophes Correctly

When you edit your work, be on the lookout for problems with using apostrophes to form possessives. When you form possessive nouns, follow these rules:

1. Add **'s** to form the possessive of most singular nouns (a woman**'s** courage, one generation**'s** problems).

2. Add only an apostrophe to form the possessive of plural nouns ending in **s** (twenty senators**'** votes, their wives**'** opinions).

3. Add **'s** to form the possessive of plural nouns that do not end in **s** (many women**'s** ideas, two children**'s** mothers).

FOR REFERENCE
For more information on using apostrophes correctly, see the Language and Grammar Handbook at the back of this text.

5 PRESENTING

- Invite community leaders to your class to listen to some of your essays and present their own views.

- Include a time line with your paper, showing historical events that influenced women's roles from the turn of the century to the present.

COMPUTER TIP
Some word processing programs include a drawing program. If you have access to one, you could use it to make your time line.

6 LOOKING BACK

Self-evaluate. Look back at the Writer's Blueprint and give your paper a score on each point, from 6 (superior) to I (inadequate).

Reflect. Write answers to these questions.

✔ As you researched changes in women's roles, what did you discover about changes in men's roles?

✔ Imagine that a hundred years from now, students are asked to write the same update you did to an audience at the turn of the twentieth century about how women's roles have changed. Speculate about what such an update might say.

For Your Working Portfolio Add your update and reflection responses to your working portfolio.

ASSESSMENT CRITERIA SPECS

6 Superior   The writer of a 6 paper impressively meets these criteria:

- Provides a clear, insightful update on how women's roles have changed since the turn of the century, focusing on three specific aspects of those roles.

- Firmly orients the audience to the writer's time and place.

- Keeps in mind the limits of the audience's knowledge and provides the background they'll need to follow the writer's train of thought, including any terms that may be unfamiliar to people living at the turn of the century.

- Concludes with a carefully considered opinion as to the direction women's roles are taking in the three aspects focused on and how the writer feels about this direction.

- Makes few, if any, errors in grammar, usage, spelling, and mechanics. Uses apostrophes correctly.

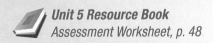

Unit 5 Resource Book
Assessment Worksheet, p. 48

Editing Strategy: Using Apostrophes Correctly

For additional support, see the mini-lesson at the bottom of page 504 and the worksheets referenced below.

Unit 5 Resource Book
Grammar Worksheet, p. 46
Grammar Check Test, p. 47

Connections to
Writer's Resource

For additional writing prompts, refer to Writer's Resource.

STEP 5 PRESENTING
Community Leaders

Have students begin with a list of community leaders that is as diverse as possible in terms of professions, races, genders, and ages.

Time Line

Suggest that students convert their time lines into posters by using different colors and pictures to highlight the historical events.

STEP 6 LOOKING BACK
Self-evaluate

The *Assessment Criteria Specs* at the bottom of this page are for a superior paper. You might want to post these in the classroom. Students can then evaluate themselves based on these criteria. For a complete scoring rubric, use the *Assessment Worksheet* referenced below.

Unit 5 Resource Book
Assessment Worksheet, p. 48

Reflect

Before students start writing individually, you may want to have them work together in small groups to predict changes.

To further explore the theme, use the Fine Art Transparency referenced below.

Transparency Collection
Fine Art Writing Prompt 8

Beyond Print

Teaching Objectives

- To analyze clues in photographs to learn about the past
- To develop skill in asking questions and listening to responses
- To make personal connections to people and events in the past

Curriculum Connections: Visual Literacy

You can use the suggestions in this article to give students practice in tapping into visual images for information about the past and to draw conclusions about values and expectations in different historical periods.

Introduce

Photographs and other visual images can provide information about the past. Explain that students can learn to look at different aspects of images, such as clothing styles, situations, and objects, to draw conclusions about specific events or periods in history. They can also use photographs in interviews to help trigger their subjects' memories.

Beyond Print

Looking at Photographs

Take a close look at the photograph of the woman on the right. What do you suppose her life was like? The photo represents an old world, far from the world you live in. Yet, you may have grandmothers or great-grandmothers who remember this world. Old photos can be a key to unlocking the past.

Exploring the Past

Use the photograph—or perhaps you have an old family photo or a photo you've found in a book that you'd rather use—to explore a world that no longer exists. Your photo should depict a time fifty or more years ago, and should have at least one person in it.

To begin, find two or more relatives, friends, or acquaintances who are old enough to remember life before World War II and are willing to be interviewed. Show them the photograph, and explain that you're trying to find out all you can about what life was like when the photo was taken. Ask questions like the following to get as much information as possible. If you are using a different photograph, you may have to adapt the questions.

Clothing Styles What time period do you think the woman's clothing belongs to? Did anyone you know—your mother or grandmother—dress like this woman? If so, describe the clothing. Was it comfortable? Was it easy to put on? What were the dresses made out of?

Situation Is this woman dressed up for a special occasion, or is she wearing everyday clothing? On what kind of an occasion might a photograph like this be taken? Do you know of any reason why she might be posed as she is, leaning on pillows with her eyes closed?

Objects Have you ever seen or owned furniture like the sofa in the picture? Does it bring back any memories? Do any of the objects in the photograph look familiar to you? What can you tell about them?

Larger Context What do you think life was like for the woman? What kinds of things might she have done for leisure? What kinds of responsibilities might she have had in the home? outside the home?

ANOTHER APPROACH

On the Internet: Cyberspace Interview

Students with access to the Internet can try a technique used by professional journalists: They can search the Internet for a bulletin board in their special field of interest and post a request for an interview.

Advise students to try to pinpoint good subjects with a clear description of their project. They should also use their skill in evaluating evidence to screen potential subjects. Once they have decided on a subject, students can conduct the interview by phone, or e-mail, sending their photograph by fax or computer.

Activity 1   You might launch this exploration of the past by inviting someone with knowledge of a particular time period into the class and letting the class interview him or her. You can introduce the person with a brief slide show of images of the time period about which he or she will speak.

Activity 2   Students might either capture their interviews on video or audio tape to preserve an oral history, or tape their monologues for a video presentation.

Follow Up

Encourage students to set their own goals for a successful interview and evaluate their own progress before and after the interview and before and after their presentation to classmates.

Personal Connection   How was the life of your mother or grandmother different from your life? What kinds of stories, if any, did your mother and grandmother tell you when you were growing up?

After your interviews,   share the information you've gathered with your classmates. The following activities are some ways you might try presenting your information.

Activity Options

Stepping Back in Time   If members of your class used the same photograph, or at least photos from the same time period, form small groups of three to five students and share the information you gathered in your interviews. Analyze the combined information and give a group oral report about what life was like when the photo was taken.

A Voice from the Past   Based on what you've learned from the photograph and from the interviews, create a personality for an individual in the photo. Create and perform a five-minute monologue in the character of the person you've invented. Include information about where you live, what you're doing in the photograph, and what your life is like.

Beyond Print   **507**

BUILDING ENGLISH PROFICIENCY

Preparing Interview Questions

The article provides some questions that students can ask interview subjects about specific photographs. But you might help students think of ways in which they can expand upon those questions to gather even more information about life in past eras.

Have students choose one question in each of the five categories. In each case, model a question that might help them gather more information, as in these examples.

- Clothing Styles: Was clothing like this bought in stores? ordered from catalogs? handed down from older relatives? homemade?
- Larger Context: How was your life different from the lives of the people shown at the time the picture was taken?
- Personal Connection: If I could travel back to the time and place of the picture, what adjustments would be hardest to make?

Ask students to share a few of the questions that turned out to be the most productive in their interviews.

EXPLORING CONCEPTS

- In the 1920s, Harlem became the artistic and intellectual capitol of African American culture.

- The spirit of the Harlem Renaissance was contagious as black writers encouraged others to join them in Harlem.

- The mood embraced both social protest and a celebration of the vibrancy of African American life.

The photographs and captions on pages 508–509 begin to tell the stories of those who contributed to the Harlem Renaissance.

Research Activity Several major Harlem Renaissance participants were from the West Indies. Marcus Garvey, Wilfrid Domingo, Claude McKay, Joel A. Rogers, and Eric Walrund all emigrated to the United States as adults. Have students research the agriculture, politics, and race relations of the early twentieth century West Indies.

Breaking the Mold

The Harlem Renaissance

Marcus Garvey

Marcus Garvey came to the U.S. in 1916 from Jamaica and organized the country's first important black nationalist movement. He formed the Universal Negro Improvement Association and his belief that blacks could only achieve equality by founding their own independent nation attracted much support in Harlem and other black communities.

A CULTURAL REVOLUTION

Duke Ellington

Edward "Duke" Ellington attracted world-wide attention as a jazz composer, pianist and band leader in the early 1900s. He went to New York in 1923 and quickly gained a reputation as an innovative band leader playing in clubs like Harlem's Cotton Club. To this day Ellington is regarded as one of the most significant figures in jazz history.

HISTORICAL OVERVIEW

In the 1920s, New York City's Harlem district, the largest African American community in the United States, also became a cultural magnet. African American actors, dancers, writers, painters, and musicians from around the country participated in an outburst of creativity that became known as the Harlem Renaissance. Many Harlem artists saw creativity as a force in their struggle against oppression, and desired to create uniquely African American traditions in the arts. Jazz rhythms, images from big-city life, and themes from African American history and folklore were important sources of inspiration. The individuals profiled here are just a few of those who made important contributions to the African American cultural revolution of the 1920s.

Aaron Douglas

Aaron Douglas was one of Harlem's most prominent visual artists in the 1920s. He came to New York in 1924 and quickly developed a unique style which reflected many different influences, including African sculpture and the works of European painters such as Gauguin, Picasso, and Matisse.

Langston Hughes

Langston Hughes was one of the first writers to accurately portray the African American experience in the U.S. through his poems, plays, and novels. He gained recognition as a major young poet of the Harlem Renaissance in the early 1920s and achieved national acclaim in 1926 with the publication of his first book, *The Weary Blues*.

Zora Neale Hurston

Novelist and folklorist Zora Neale Hurston arrived in New York in 1925 after studying at Howard University under Alaine Locke. She established herself as a figure of the Harlem Renaissance when she published short stories in the Harlem journal, Opportunity, and through her work with writers such as Langston Hughes, Claude McKay, and Jean Toomer.

Bessie Smith

Tennessee born Bessie Smith was a blues singer whose popularity in the 1920s earned her the title, "Empress of the Blues." After establishing a following in the South she went to New York in 1923 and recorded her first record, "Down Hearted Blues." It sold over a million copies and saved Columbia Records from bankruptcy. By 1927 she was the highest paid black artist in the world.

Key Dates

1916
African Americans migrate from the South to big cities in the North.

1920
Marcus Garvey organizes international convention of United Negro Improvement Association.

1921
Shuffle Along, an all-black musical, is Broadway hit.

1923
Jean Toomer's novel *Cane* is published.

1925
Alain Locke produces anthology of African American artists.

1926
Langston Hughes's The Weary Blues is published.

1927
Bessie Smith is world's highest paid black artist.

1929
Stock market crash signals start of the Great Depression and end of Harlem Renaissance.

509

Key Dates

1910   W.E.B. DuBois founds *The Crisis*, the magazine of the NAACP (National Association for the Advancement of Colored People).

1917   Three one-act plays with all African American casts are presented at the Provincetown Playhouse.

1922   *The Book of American Negro Poetry*, edited by James Weldon Johnson, is published.

1925   The first *Opportunity* awards banquet is held at which the magazine honors Zora Neale Hurston, Langston Hughes, Countee Cullen, E. Franklin Frazier, and Sterling Brown, among others.

1932   *Black and White*, a film about racial segregation in the United States, is filmed in the Soviet Union. The cast includes Langston Hughes and Taylor Gordon.

MATERIALS OF INTEREST
Books

- *When Harlem Was in Vogue* by David Levering Lewis (Oxford University Press, 1989)
- *Harlem: Negro Metropolis* by Claude McKay (Harcourt Brace Jovanovich, 1968)

Multimedia

- Compton's Encyclopedia of American History on CD-ROM, "Harlem" article

 Connections to
Custom Literature Database

For further historical background, under **Background Articles,** see **Later Modern America 1815–1945.**

Preview
The Harlem Renaissance

FOR ALL STUDENTS

- What does it mean for a community to have new life?
- What needs to be present in an intellectual and artistic community for it to have new life?

To further explore the theme, use the transparency referenced here.

Transparency Collection
Fine Art Writing Prompt 9

For At-Risk Students

Ask students something they were very excited about, for example, a movie or a book.

- Would they tell their friends about it?
- Would they want to see or read more like it?

Tell them this excitement is similar to the spirit of the Harlem Renaissance.

For Students Who Need Challenge

Invite students to research a person in their community who made a difference.

- What did this person do?
- What obstacles did this person overcome?
- What motivated this person to want to do something for the community?

MULTICULTURAL CONNECTION

Prompt students to discuss how different cultures influence our daily lives. What effects does our multicultural society have on fashion, food, the media, education, art, dance, film, music, and television?

510

Part Two

The Harlem Renaissance

In the 1920s, African American creativity sprang to the forefront of American culture in ways it never had before. An unprecedented number of African American writers were able to publish their works, African American artists flourished like never before, and blues singers and musicians gained national popularity. The capital of this creative burst of energy was New York City's Harlem, where artists, writers, musicians, and scholars gathered to share their ideas and encourage one another.

Multicultural Connection Family, social, cultural, and other **groups** help us define who we are and provide us with a sense of belonging. During the Harlem Renaissance, many African American artists, writers, and scholars were attempting to redefine what it meant to be part of the group called, at the time, "Negroes." What does each of the following works say about being part of this group?

IDEAS THAT WORK

Motivating with Rich Literature

The literature of the Harlem Renaissance brings much excitement, enlightenment, and empowerment to my students. To read and analyze great writers such as James Weldon Johnson, Langston Hughes, and Countee Cullen can truly be characterized as an illuminating experience. I use discussion and journal writing to develop concepts and expand students' understanding.

For example, Zora Neale Hurston's "How It Feels to be Colored Me" offers readers a literary piece rich in images and symbols of African American heritage and pride. Hurston's perspective is an ideal beginning for introspective discussion and journal entries of just what it is that makes us who we are. When students experience the literature on a spiritual as well as an intellectual level, then we are beginning to uncover the true essence of African American literature.

Rosetta Tetteh
Chicago, Illinois

Before Reading

Harlem: The Culture Capital

by James Weldon Johnson

James Weldon Johnson
1871–1938

James Weldon Johnson's career took many paths. He practiced law, wrote popular show tunes with his brother Rosamond—their works also include "Lift Every Voice and Sing," the song that has become the African American national anthem, and campaign songs for Theodore Roosevelt—and served as consul to Venezuela and Nicaragua. Then, in 1920, Johnson began working for the National Association for the Advancement of Colored People. While at the NAACP, he acted as mentor to many young African American writers who moved to Harlem in the 1920s, offering encouragement, advice, and often a free meal or two as the writers worked to establish themselves in a new city.

Building Background

The Great Migration Before World War I, most African Americans lived in rural areas of the South, but with the onset of the war the flood of immigrants from Europe slowed to a trickle, many workers became soldiers, and suddenly northern industries were in desperate need of workers. What came to be known as the **Great Migration** began, as hundreds of thousands of African Americans left the South and moved to northern cities, where discriminatory laws and social restrictions were less severe than in the South, and where there were unprecedented opportunities for well-paying jobs. They moved to many of the large northern industrial centers—Chicago, Detroit, New York—but, whereas in other cities African Americans could generally find housing only in the older, more worn-down neighborhoods, New York City's Harlem was a good location filled with new apartment buildings, and it quickly became one of the largest predominately black communities in the world.

Literary Focus

Metaphor In his essay, "Harlem: The Culture Capital," Johnson uses metaphor to bring freshness and vitality to his writing. A metaphor is a comparison between two basically unlike things. "A copper sky" and "a heart of stone" are examples of metaphors. As you read "Harlem: The Culture Capital," see if you can spot three examples of metaphor.

Writer's Notebook

My Kind of Town What do you like best about your hometown? What would you say are its best features? In your notebook, write a paragraph that explains what you find most appealing about your hometown.

Before Reading

Building Background

Students may have preconceived notions of Harlem from movies, the media, and books. Have students share their impressions of Harlem.

Literary Focus

Point out that **metaphors** are figurative, not literal. They can make writing vivid and graphic. On page 516, for example, Johnson calls the movement of African Americans northward a "stream of migrants." Students will use their notes after reading (p. 520).

Writer's Notebook

Suggest to students that they think of the things they would say if they were trying to convince someone to visit or move to their hometown.

More About
James Weldon Johnson

James Weldon Johnson was a prolific poet, prose writer, and editor whose works enrich the record of African American contributions to U.S. culture.

Other works
- *God's Trombones*, 1927
- *American Negro Spirituals,* 1925, 1926
- *The Autobiography of an Ex-Colored Man* (novel), 1912
- *Fifty Years and Other Poems*, 1917

SUPPORT MATERIALS OVERVIEW

Unit 5 Resource Book
- Graphic Organizer, p. 49
- Study Guide, p. 50
- Vocabulary, p. 51
- Grammar, p. 52
- Alternate Check Test, p. 53
- Vocabulary Test, p. 54
- Selection Test, pp. 55–56

Building English Proficiency
- Literature Summaries
- Activities, p. 207

Reading, Writing & Grammar Skillbook
- Reading, pp. 56–58
- Grammar, Usage, and Mechanics, pp. 168–169

Technology
- Audiotape
- Personal Journal Software
- Custom Literature Database: Part of *The Autobiography of an Ex-Colored Man* by James Weldon Johnson appears on the database.
- Test Generator Software

Van Der Zee often shot photographic portraits, recording the people of Harlem, as well as the place.

Response to Caption The photo celebrates prosperity and the luxury and style that wealth affords. The couple displays pride or satisfaction in their elegant car and coats, and the social position the belongings symbolize.

2 Literary Element

Setting

While fiction writers often create a setting, writers of nonfiction often vividly *capture* an existing setting in their descriptions. This essay focuses not only on a place, but also on a time. Ask students to identify explicit and implicit references to the historic era Johnson captures.

MULTICULTURAL NOTE

Harlem became not only a neighborhood for African Americans but also a place where cultural identity was crafted and recognized. Students may know of other places where various cultural groups established identities, such as Little Havana, an enclave of Cuban Americans in Miami, and neighborhoods with names such as Little Italy or Chinatown.

⋀ James Van Der Zee photographed his *Portrait of Couple with Raccoon Coats and Stylish Car* in 1932. What attitude toward wealth and luxury does this image convey?

2 Marshall, became famous as the headquarters of Negro talent. There gathered the actors, the musicians, the composers, the writers, the singers, dancers and vaudevillians. There one went to get a close-up of Williams and Walker, Cole and Johnson, Ernest Hogan, Will Marion Cook, Jim Europe, Aida Overton, and of others equally and less known. Paul Laurence Dunbar was frequently there whenever he was in New York. Numbers of those who love to shine by the light reflected from celebrities were always to be found. The first modern jazz band ever heard in New York, or, perhaps anywhere, was organized at The Marshall. It was a playing-singing-dancing orchestra, making the first dominant use of banjos, saxophones, clarinets and trap drums in combination, and was called The Memphis Students. Jim Europe was a member of that band, and out of it grew the famous Clef Club, of which he was the noted leader, and which for a long time monopolized the business of "entertaining" private parties and furnishing music for the new dance craze. Also in the Clef Club was "Buddy" Gilmore who originated trap drumming as it is now practised, and set hundreds of white men to juggling their sticks and doing acrobatic stunts while they

MINI-LESSON: LITERARY FOCUS

Metaphor

Teach A metaphor is a figurative comparison between two things that are not literally comparable. The similarity is implied, unlike a simile, in which something is said to be *like* something else. In a metaphor, a writer says or implies that the subject *is* the thing to which it is compared. For example, Johnson refers to people who "shine by the light reflected from celebrities" (p. 514). Celebrities are described as shining beings, luminous enough that their light reflects off their fans.

Activity Ideas

- Students can find other metaphors in the selection. (Examples: Johnson refers to other New York neighborhoods with African Americans as nests on p. 513; he calls the migration of black people to the North a stream and a wave on p. 516; he mentions a property-buying "fever" on p. 517.)

- Invite students to examine advertisements in magazines and identify any metaphors in them.

manipulated a dozen other noise-making devices aside from their drums. A good many well-known white performers frequented The Marshall and for seven or eight years the place was one of the sights of New York.

The move to Fifty-third Street was the result of the opportunity to get into newer and better houses. About 1900 the move to Harlem began, and for the same reason. Harlem had been over-built with large, new-law apartment houses, but rapid transportation to that section was very inadequate—the Lenox Avenue Subway had not yet been built—and landlords were finding difficulty in keeping houses on the east side of the section filled. Residents along and near Seventh Avenue were fairly well served by the Eighth Avenue Elevated. A colored man, in the real estate business at this time, Philip A. Payton, approached several of these landlords with the proposition[3] that he would fill their empty or partially empty houses with steady colored tenants. The suggestion was accepted, and one or two houses on One Hundred and Thirty-fourth Street east of Lenox Avenue were taken over. Gradually other houses were filled. The whites paid little attention to the movement until it began to spread west of Lenox Avenue; they then took steps to check it. They proposed through a financial organization, the Hudson Realty Company, to buy in all properties occupied by colored people and evict the tenants. The Negroes countered by similar methods. Payton formed the Afro-American Realty Company, a Negro corporation organized for the purpose of buying and leasing houses for occupancy by colored people. Under this counter stroke the opposition subsided for several years.

But the continually increasing pressure of colored people to the west over the Lenox Avenue dead line caused the opposition to break out again, but in a new and more menacing form. Several white men undertook to organize all the white people of the community for the purpose of inducing financial institutions not to lend money or renew mortgages on properties occupied by colored people. In this effort they had

considerable success, and created a situation which has not yet been completely overcome, a situation which is one of the hardest and most unjustifiable the Negro property owner in Harlem has to contend with. The Afro-American Realty Company was now defunct, but two or three colored men of means stepped into the breach. Philip A. Payton and J. C. Thomas bought two five-story apartments, dispossessed the white tenants and put in colored. J. B. Nail bought a row of five apartments and did the same thing. St. Philip's Church bought a row of thirteen apartment houses on One Hundred and Thirty-fifth Street, running from Seventh Avenue almost to Lenox.

The situation now resolved itself into an actual contest. Negroes not only continued to occupy available apartment houses, but began to purchase private dwellings between Lenox and Seventh Avenues. Then the whole movement, in the eyes of the whites, took on the aspect of an "invasion"; they became panic-stricken and began fleeing as from a plague. The presence of one colored family in a block, no matter how well bred and orderly, was sufficient to precipitate[4] a flight. House after house and block after block was actually deserted. It was a great demonstration of human beings running amuck. None of them stopped to reason why they were doing it or what would happen if they didn't. The banks and lending companies holding mortgages on these deserted houses were compelled to take them over. For some time they held these houses vacant, preferring to do that and carry the charges than to rent or sell them to colored people. But values dropped and continued to drop until at the outbreak of the war in Europe property in the northern part of Harlem had reached the nadir.[5]

---

3. proposition (prop/ə zish/ən), *n.* what is offered to be considered; proposal.
4. precipitate (pri sip/ə tāt), *v.* hasten the beginning of; bring about suddenly.
5. nadir (nā/dər), *n.* lowest point.

Harlem: The Culture Capital   **515**

3 Reader's Response
Making Personal Connections

Question   What competition or underlying conflict about real estate does Johnson describe? How do you think the situation compares to America today? *(Possible responses: Racial divisions resulted in competitions for Harlem real estate among black and white business people and residents. Many communities are integrated today; in some places, racial or cultural groups may feel they are competing for real estate. This leads to tensions in some cities and towns.)*

4 Reading/Thinking Skills
Making Inferences

Question   How does Johnson seem to judge the white flight that took place? Support your answer with details from the text. *(Possible response: He thinks it was not sensible. He describes the whites fleeing as if "from a plague," and "running amuck.")*

BUILDING ENGLISH PROFICIENCY

Visualizing the Setting

Using either of these activities may help students, especially visual learners, understand the setting.

• Discuss the photographs on pages 512 and 514. What details indicate the time setting of the selection? What images reveal social and cultural customs? *(Responses may focus on the cars, clothing, church, casino, and stores.)* Encourage students to talk about their conclusions.

• Students can convey their impressions of the Harlem of Johnson's era in art. Those not confident at depicting scenes in representational drawings, paintings, or computer art may create collages or abstract pictures. A group might assemble a bulletin board or poster display.

5 Reading/Thinking Skills
Recall Facts

Question How can readers know that Johnson is referring to World War I, not World War II, when he mentions the outbreak of war in Europe? *(He was writing before World War II, about Harlem in the years after 1900. World War I occurred between 1914 and 1918; the Second World War did not occur until after the author's death.)*

6 Literary Focus
Metaphor

Question What figurative images of water does Johnson use to describe the movement of African Americans from the South to Harlem? *(the "stream of migrants" and "the first wave . . . of Negroes")*

7 Reading/Thinking Skills
Summarize

Response With the outbreak of war, thousands of aliens rushed back to their homelands, creating a critical shortage of workers. The need was filled by bringing African American laborers from the South to northern cities.

In the meantime the Negro colony was becoming more stable; the churches were being moved from the lower part of the city; social and civic centers were being formed; and gradually a community was being evolved. **5** Following the outbreak of the war in Europe Negro Harlem received a new and tremendous impetus. Because of the war thousands of aliens in the United States rushed back to their native lands to join the colors and immigration practically ceased. The result was a critical shortage in labor. This shortage was rapidly increased as the United States went more and more largely into the business of furnishing munitions and supplies to the warring countries. To help meet this shortage of common labor Negroes were brought up from the South. The government itself took the first steps, following the practice in vogue in Germany of shifting labor according to the supply and demand in various parts of the country. The example of the government was promptly taken up by the big industrial concerns, which sent hundreds, perhaps thousands, of labor agents into the South who recruited Negroes by wholesale. I was in **6** Jacksonville, Fla., for a while at that time, and I sat one day and watched the stream of migrants passing to take the train. For hours they passed steadily, carrying flimsy suitcases, new and shiny, rusty old ones, bursting at the seams, boxes and bundles and impedimenta[6] of all sorts, including banjos, guitars, birds in cages and whatnot. Similar scenes were being enacted[7] in cities and towns all over that region. The first wave of the great exodus of Negroes from the South was on. Great numbers of these migrants headed for New York or eventually got there, and naturally the majority went up into Harlem. But the Negro population of Harlem was not swollen by migrants from the South alone; the opportunity for Negro labor exerted its pull upon the Negroes of the West Indies, and those islanders in the course of time poured into Harlem to the number of twenty-five thousand or more.

SUMMARIZE: How did World War I indirectly contribute to Harlem's population explosion? 7

These new-comers did not have to look for work; work looked for them, and at wages of which they had never even dreamed. And here is where the unlooked for, the unprecedented, the miraculous happened. According to all preconceived notions, these Negroes suddenly earning large sums of money for the first time in their lives should have had their heads turned; they should have squandered it in the most silly and absurd manners imaginable. Later, after the United States had entered the war and even Negroes in the South were making money fast, many stories in accord with the tradition came out of that section. There was the one about the colored man who went into a general store and on hearing a phonograph for the first time promptly ordered six of them, one for each child in the house. I shall not stop to discuss whether Negroes in the South did that sort of thing or not, but I do know that those who got to New York didn't. The Negroes of Harlem, for the greater part, worked and saved their money. Nobody knew how much they had saved until congestion made expansion necessary for tenants and ownership profitable for landlords, and they began to buy property. Persons who would never be suspected of having money bought property. The Rev. W. W. Brown, pastor of the Metropolitan Baptist Church, repeatedly made "Buy Property" the text of his sermons. A large part of his congregation carried out the injunction.[8] The church itself set an example by purchasing a magnificent brownstone church building on Seventh Avenue from a white

---

6. **impedimenta** (im ped′ə men′tə), *n. pl.* baggage, equipment, etc., which impedes movement or progress.
7. **enact** (en akt′), *v.* represent; act out.
8. **injunction** (in jungk′shən), *n.* an authoritative or emphatic order; command.

MINI-LESSON: GRAMMAR

Compound-Complex Sentences

Teach Review compound and complex sentences: sentences that contain two or more thoughts, expressed in clauses. Remind students that in a complex sentence, there is an independent clause and a subordinate, or dependent, clause. A **compound-complex sentence** has two or more independent clauses, like a compound sentence, and at least one subordinate clause. An example is: "These new-comers did not have to look for work; worked looked for them, and at wages of which they had never even dreamed." (p. 516)

Activity Ideas

- Have students identify the clauses in the example. Students also can find examples of compound, complex, and compound-complex sentences in the selection and identify clauses.
- Have students write compound-complex sentences that relate ideas well.

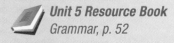

Unit 5 Resource Book
Grammar, p. 52

congregation. Buying property became a fever. At the height of this activity, that is, 1920–21, it was not an uncommon thing for a colored washerwoman or cook to go into a real estate office and lay down from one thousand to five thousand dollars on a house. "Pig Foot Mary" is a character in Harlem. Everybody who knows the corner of Lenox Avenue and One Hundred and Thirty-fifth Street knows "Mary" and her stand, and has been tempted by the smell of her pigsfeet, fried chicken and hot corn, even if he has not been a customer. "Mary," whose real name is Mrs. Mary Dean, bought the five-story apartment house at the corner of Seventh Avenue and One Hundred and Thirty-seventh Street at a price of $42,000. Later she sold it to the Y.W.C.A. for dormitory purposes. The Y.W.C.A. sold it recently to Adolph Howell, a leading colored undertaker, the price given being $72,000. Often companies of a half dozen men combined to buy a house—these combinations were and still are generally made up of West Indians—and would produce five or ten thousand dollars to put through the deal.

When the buying activity began to make itself felt, the lending companies that had been holding vacant the handsome dwellings on and abutting Seventh Avenue decided to put them on the market. The values on these houses had dropped to the lowest mark possible and they were put up at astonishingly low prices. Houses that had been bought at from $15,000 to $20,000 were sold at one-third those figures. They were quickly gobbled up. The Equitable Life Assurance Company held 106 model private houses that were designed by Stanford White. They are built with courts running straight through the block and closed off by wrought-iron gates. Every one of these houses was sold within eleven months at an aggregate[9] price of about two million dollars. Today they are probably worth about 100 percent more. And not only have private dwellings and similar apartments been bought but big elevator apartments have been taken over. Corporations have been organized for this purpose. Two of these, The Antillian Realty Company, composed of West Indian Negroes, and the Sphinx Securities Company, composed of American and West Indian Negroes, represent holdings amounting to approximately $750,000. Individual Negroes and companies in the South have invested in Harlem real estate. About two years ago a Negro institution of Savannah, Ga., bought a parcel for $115,000 which it sold a month or so ago at a profit of $110,000.

I am informed by John E. Nail, a successful colored real estate dealer of Harlem and a reliable authority, that the total value of property in Harlem owned and controlled by colored people would at a conservative estimate amount to more than sixty million dollars. These figures are amazing, especially when we take into account the short time in which they have been piled up. Twenty years ago Negroes were begging for the privilege of renting a flat in Harlem. Fifteen years ago barely a half dozen colored men owned real property in all Manhattan. And down to ten years ago the amount that had been acquired in Harlem was comparatively negligible. Today Negro Harlem is practically owned by Negroes.

The question naturally arises, "Are the Negroes going to be able to hold Harlem?" If they have been steadily driven northward for the past hundred years and out of less desirable sections, can they hold this choice bit of Manhattan Island? It is hardly probable that Negroes will hold Harlem indefinitely, but when they are forced out it will not be for the same reasons that forced them out of former quarters in New York City. The situation is entirely different and without precedent. When colored people do leave Harlem, their homes, their churches, their investments and their businesses, it will be because the land has become so valuable they can no longer afford to live on it. But the date of another move northward is very far in the future.

---

9. aggregate (ag′rə git), *adj.* total.

Harlem: The Culture Capital **517**

8

Reading/Thinking Skills
Recognizing Values

Questions What goal of African American residents and business people of Harlem during the 1920s does Johnson emphasize in the part of his essay on page 517? Does the author feel the goal was good or bad? *(Response: owning their own property; good, because it meant that Harlem's residents had a stabilizing investment in the community)*

9

Reader's Response
Making Judgments

Ask students whether they think property ownership is enough to hold a community together. Students can support their responses with ideas from Johnson's essay, as well as their own opinions. *(Possible responses: Yes; once residents own their homes and businesses, they work hard to strengthen their community. Maybe not, because selling the property could become too profitable for residents to stay; on page 517 Johnson mentions a possible future change if "the land has become so valuable they can no longer afford to live on it.")*

BUILDING ENGLISH PROFICIENCY

Recognizing Synonyms and Related Words

Help students recognize related words, including synonyms, in the selection. Here are examples from the second column on page 516.

- **unlooked for** and **unprecedented** Something unprecedented—that is, it never happened before—most likely would be "unlooked for," because people don't expect to see something that has never happened.

- **silly** and **absurd** Students can use a dictionary to compare the meanings of these words.

- **buy** and **purchase** Ask students to talk about the similarity between these synonyms.

10 Reading/Thinking Skills
Summarize

Response He says that Harlem is a self-supporting community, economically, and people are employed as individuals, not as work gangs.

11 Literary Element
Theme

This unit of the anthology, "Breaking the Mold," contains many literary selections about people who do not settle for the place or expectations imposed on them. Certainly the people of Harlem, as depicted by James Weldon Johnson, break free of limits widely accepted for African Americans of their time.

Johnson also explores themes concerning the ways in which Harlem had become distinct from other urban communities, as well as its similarities to other ethnic and cultural communities in New York and elsewhere.

Students can discuss how Johnson thinks Harlem shared attributes with places such as New York's "Italian colony," how it became a cultural community, and what was unique or special about it.

What will Harlem be and become in the meantime? Is there danger that the Negro may lose his economic status in New York and be unable to hold his property? Will Harlem become merely a famous ghetto, or will it be a center of intellectual, cultural and economic forces exerting an influence throughout the world, especially upon Negro peoples? Will it become a point of friction between the races in New York?

I think there is less danger to the Negroes of New York of losing out economically and industrially than to the Negroes of any large city in the North. In most of the big industrial centers Negroes are engaged in gang labor. They are employed by thousands in the stockyards in Chicago, by thousands in the automobile plants in Detroit; and in those cities they are likely to be the first to be let go, and in thousands, with every business depression. In New York there is hardly such a thing as gang labor among Negroes, except among the longshoremen, and it is in the longshoremen's unions, above all others, that Negroes stand on an equal footing. Employment among Negroes in New York is highly diversified;[10] in the main they are employed more as individuals than as non-integral parts of a gang. Furthermore, Harlem is gradually becoming more and more a self-supporting community. Negroes there are steadily branching out into new businesses and enterprises in which Negroes are employed. So the danger of great numbers of Negroes being thrown out of work at once, with a resulting economic crisis among them, is less in New York than in most of the large cities of the North to which Southern migrants have come.

> **10** **SUMMARIZE:** Why does Johnson believe that African Americans living in Harlem are in a better economic position than African Americans in other large cities?

These facts have an effect which goes beyond the economic and industrial situation. They have a direct bearing on the future

character of Harlem and on the question as to whether Harlem will be a point of friction between the races in New York. It is true that Harlem is a Negro community, well defined and stable; anchored to its fixed homes, churches, institutions, business and amusement places; having its own working, business and professional classes. It is experiencing a constant growth of group consciousness and community feeling. Harlem is, therefore, in many respects, typically Negro. It has many unique characteristics. It has movement, color, gayety, singing, dancing, boisterous laughter and loud talk. One of its outstanding features is brass band parades. Hardly a Sunday passes but that there are several of these parades of which many are gorgeous with regalia and insignia. Almost any excuse will do—the death of an humble member of the Elks, the laying of a cornerstone, the "turning out" of the order of this or that. In many of these characteristics it is similar to the Italian colony. But withal, Harlem grows more metropolitan and more a part of New York all the while. Why is it then that its tendency is not to become a mere "quarter"?

I shall give three reasons that seem to me to be important in their order. First, the language of Harlem is not alien; it is not Italian or Yiddish; it is English. Harlem talks American, reads American, thinks American. Second, Harlem is not physically a "quarter." It is not a section cut off. It is merely a zone through which four main arteries of the city run. Third, the fact that there is little or no gang labor gives Harlem Negroes the opportunity for individual expansion and individual contacts with the life and spirit of New York. A thousand Negroes from Mississippi put to work as a gang in a Pittsburgh steel mill will for a long time remain a thousand Negroes from Mississippi. Under the conditions that prevail in New York they would all within six months become New Yorkers. The rapidity with which Negroes

11

---

10. diversified (də vėr′sə fīd), *adj.* varied.

MINI-LESSON: VOCABULARY

Using Synonyms with Connotations

Teach Remind students that a synonym is a word having a meaning that is the same or nearly the same as that of another word. Synonyms may be interchangeable in terms of their definitions (denotations), but they may be quite different in tone or implied meaning (connotations). An example would be the synonyms *clever* and *slick*.

Activity Ideas

1. Have students consider the following vocabulary words, and list synonyms by brainstorming or using a thesaurus.

> **dilapidated** (p. 513); possible synonyms: seedy, shabby
> **precipitate** (verb, p. 515); hasten, quicken
> **cordial** (p. 519); friendly, genial, sociable

2. Students can find the sentences in which Johnson has used the words or write sentences using each word. Then they can rewrite or read each sentence, substituting each synonym for the vocabulary word. Ask: Is the meaning the same as before? Is the tone the same as before?

become good New Yorkers is one of the marvels to observers.

These three reasons form a single reason  why there is small probability that Harlem will ever be a point of race friction between the races in New York. One of the principal factors in the race riot in Chicago in 1919 was the fact that at that time there were 12,000 Negroes employed in gangs in the stockyards. There was considerable race feeling in Harlem at the time of the hegira[11] of white residents due to the "invasion," but that feeling, of course, is no more. Indeed, a number of the old white residents who didn't go or could not get away before the housing shortage struck New York are now living peacefully side by side with colored residents. In fact, in some cases white and colored tenants occupy apartments in the same house. Many white merchants still do business in thickest Harlem. On the whole, I know of no place in the country where the feeling between the races is so cordial[12] and at the same time so matter-of-fact and taken for granted. One of the surest safeguards against an outbreak in New York such as took place in so many Northern cities in the summer of 1919 is the large proportion of Negro police on duty in Harlem.

To my mind, Harlem is more than a Negro community; it is a large scale laboratory experiment in the race problem. The statement has often been made that if Negroes were transported to the North in large numbers the race problem with all of its acuteness and with new aspects would be transferred with them. Well, 175,000 Negroes live closely together in Harlem, in the heart of New York—75,000 more than live in any Southern city—and do so without any race friction. Nor is there any unusual record of crime. I once heard a captain of the 38th Police Precinct (the Harlem precinct) say that on the whole it was the most law-abiding precinct in the city. New York guarantees its Negro citizens the fundamental rights of American citizenship and protects them in the exercise of those rights. In

▲ This 1927 photograph shows a policeman at the corner of Lenox Avenue and 135th Street in Harlem.

return the Negro loves New York and is proud of it, and contributes in his way to its greatness. He still meets with discriminations, but possessing the basic rights, he knows that these discriminations will be abolished.

I believe that the Negro's advantages and opportunities are greater in Harlem than in any other place in the country, and that Harlem will become the intellectual, the cultural and the financial center for Negroes of the United States, and will exert a vital influence upon all Negro peoples.

---

11. hegira (hej′ərə), *n.* departure; flight; journey.
12. cordial (kôr′jəl), *adj.* warm and friendly in manner.

Harlem: The Culture Capital **519**

12 Reading/Thinking Skills
Drawing Conclusions

Question What does Johnson seem to think Harlem's success says about racial "friction"? *(Possible response: He thinks Harlem will not be a place of racial friction because: it is prosperous, white residents who stayed were able to live peacefully with African Americans, and many police officers were African Americans.)*

Art Study

Visual Literacy Question How does this picture convey the subject's sense of authority? *(Possible response: The officer's uniform, gesture directing traffic, and relaxed pose while standing in the street all indicate his authority.)*

Check Test

1. Did African Americans begin moving into Harlem, according to the author, in about 1850, 1875, or 1900? *(about 1900)*

2. Why did the U.S. government want people to move to New York during World War I? *(to provide workers for industry there)*

3. What did some African Americans do with part of their income during and after the war, according to the author? *(They bought property, or real estate.)*

4. What people owned most of the real estate known as "Negro Harlem," according to Johnson? *(Negroes)*

5. How did most African Americans in Harlem feel about their city, according to Johnson? *(Possible responses: They loved it. They were proud of it.)*

 *Unit 5 Resource Book*
Alternate Check Test, p. 53

BUILDING ENGLISH PROFICIENCY

Making Personal Connections

Help students understand and appreciate the essay by asking them to share ideas from their own experiences. Consider questions such as the following.

1. How does Johnson's account of Harlem compare to—or remind you of—stories of your community, background, family history, or heritage?

2. What positive cultural characteristics are present in your neighborhood or community—or in any town or place familiar to you?

Encourage students to talk or write about their ideas or stories.

Before Reading

Building Background

Discuss the term *renaissance*—a revival or period of improvement and expansion in the arts—and how it applies to the 1920s among African American writers, artists, and entertainers, especially in Harlem. Students may use information on pages 508–510 and 522.

Literary Focus

Other common poetic **meters** are *anapest* and *trochee*.

- Anapest consists of three syllables: unstressed, unstressed, stressed, as in "For the moon never beams" (Poe, "Annabel Lee").

- A trochee is two syllables: one stressed, then one unstressed, as in "Harlem."

  It may help students to write a line using each of these meters, as well as iambic.

Writer's Notebook

Encourage students to read the poems aloud, or at least to think of the sounds of the language as they read silently. Students' notes will be useful for After Reading activities.

Before Reading

A Black Man Talks of Reaping by Arna Bontemps
If We Must Die by Claude McKay
The Negro Speaks of Rivers by Langston Hughes

Harlem Wine by Countee Cullen
Youth by Langston Hughes
Ma Rainey by Sterling A. Brown

Building Background

A New Spirit In 1925, Alain Locke, an African American scholar, published a literature anthology called *The New Negro.* Many young African American writers read Locke's book and were so impressed that they followed his advice to move to Harlem. After they arrived in New York City, writers James Weldon Johnson and Claude McKay, among others, began sending letters to other black writers, encouraging *them* to move to Harlem. It was, recalls Arna Bontemps, an amazing, exhilarating period: "When acceptances from Harpers; Harcourt, Brace; Viking . . . and other front-line publishers began coming through in quick succession, the excitement among those of us who were writing was almost unbearable."

Literary Focus

Meter is the arrangement of beats, or accents, in a line of poetry. The meter of a poem is measured by **feet.** Each foot contains one accented syllable and one or more unaccented syllables. The most commonly used meter in English verse is known as **iambic.** An iamb consists of an unaccented syllable followed by an accented syllable /ˇ ′/, as in the word *delight.* Claude McKay uses **iambic** meter in "If We Must Die":

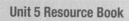

If we / must die, / O let / us no / bly die /

So that / our pre / cious blood / may not / be shed /

Begin your study of meter by reading McKay's "If We Must Die" aloud. Then, in your notebook, copy two lines from the poem, marking the unaccented and accented syllables.

Writer's Notebook

A Bit of Style Each of the poets you're about to read has a distinctive poetic style. As you read the poems, keep track of any examples of poetic devices that you find. Before you begin, you may want to review literary devices such as *rhyme, repetition, alliteration,* and *onomatopoeia* in the Glossary of Literary Terms in the back of this book.

SUPPORT MATERIALS OVERVIEW

Unit 5 Resource Book
- Graphic Organizer, p. 57
- Study Guide, p. 58
- Vocabulary, p. 59
- Grammar, p. 60
- Alternate Check Test, p. 61
- Vocabulary Test, p. 62
- Selection Test, pp. 63–64

Building English Proficiency
- Literature Summaries
- Activities, p. 208

Reading, Writing & Grammar Skillbook
- Reading, pp. 50–51
- Grammar, Usage, and Mechanics, pp. 218–219

The World of Work
- Writer, p. 17
- Activity, p. 18

Technology
- Audiotape
- Personal Journal Software
- Custom Literature Database: Works by African American writers of the times, such as W. E. B. Du Bois, appear on the database.
- Test Generator Software

Arna Bontemps
1902–1973

Arna Bontemps once described the time he spent in Harlem as his "golden years"—an exciting time of house parties, pig's knuckles, bathtub gin, and above all else, excellent conversation. After writing his novel, *God Sends Sunday,* Bontemps left New York to pursue a teaching career. He spent his later years as Head Librarian and Director of University Relations at Fisk University.

Claude McKay
1889–1948

Claude McKay was born in Jamaica, and emigrated to the United States in 1912. His novel *Home to Harlem* was perhaps the first American best-selling novel by a black writer. McKay wrote with nostalgia for Jamaica, and about city life and social protest. His poem "If We Must Die" quickly became a rallying cry for change.

Langston Hughes
1902–1967

In 1925, while working at a hotel in Washington, D.C., Langston Hughes began to publish his poems, and eventually moved to Harlem. Over the next forty years, Hughes wrote a staggering amount of verse and traveled the United States and abroad giving public readings of his poetry. Because he was considered one of the most talented poets of the 1920s and 1930s, Hughes was often called the "poet laureate" of Harlem.

Countee Cullen
1903–1946

Countee Cullen was a novelist, essayist, and much-loved poet of the Harlem Renaissance. Cullen strongly opposed the belief that African American writers should limit themselves to African American themes, yet in much of his poetry he explores what he saw as the beauty, tenderness, and joy of African American life in Harlem.

Sterling A. Brown
1901–1989

Sterling A. Brown was an influential scholar of African American writing, as well as a prolific poet. As a scholar, Brown had two main interests: African American stereotypes in literature, and the African American folk tale tradition. For his poem "Ma Rainey," Brown used his knowledge of folklore to present a unique portrait of African Americans living in the rural South.

A Black Man Talks of Reaping **523**

More About the Harlem Renaissance Poets

- **Arna Bontemps** and **Countee Cullen** collaborated on dramatic writing that evolved into the hit Broadway musical *Saint Louis Woman.*

- Some African American readers criticized **Claude McKay's** *Home to Harlem* for its portrayal of "low-life" black people in lives of debauchery, not rooted in their communities. W. E. B. Du Bois reportedly suggested that after reading it he wanted to wash up.

- **Langston Hughes** wrote "The Negro Speaks of Rivers" not long after he graduated from high school. Later his poetry became known throughout the world. He, in turn, translated works in Spanish by poets such as Gabriela Mistral and Federico García Lorca into English, for American readers.

- **Sterling Brown** wrote a classic work of literary criticism and history, *The Negro in America,* which still is studied today.

The book *The Harlem Renaissance: Hub of African-American Culture, 1920–1930* by Steven Watson (New York: Pantheon, 1995) offers more information about these and other writers of the era.

 Connections to
AuthorWorks

Langston Hughes is a featured author in the AuthorWorks CD-ROM series.

BUILDING ENGLISH PROFICIENCY

Focusing on Poetic Meter

Students who are fluent in a language besides English may be able to share information on meter in poems or songs in the other language.

- A students might write two lines of a remembered poem, rhyme, or song verse on the board and read it aloud. Other students, even if they cannot read or interpret the line, may be able to mark the stressed and unstressed syllables and determine what the meter is.

- The rhythm of metrical verse often makes it easy for readers or listeners to remember or even memorize lines. Students can illustrate this effect with lines from commercials, recited material such as the Pledge of Allegiance, or other verses.

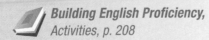 *Building English Proficiency,*
Activities, p. 208

Selection Objectives

- To consider themes of cultural history, adversity, hope, and appreciation of artistry
- To explore meter in poems
- To examine elements of poetic style
- To learn about antonyms
- To study the use of dialect

 Unit 5 Resource Book
Graphic Organizer, p. 57
Study Guide, p. 58

Theme Link

Themes explored by Harlem Renaissance poets include a yearning to honor the cultures of African and African American people.

Vocabulary Preview

accursed, hateful; troublesome
constrain, to force
dusky, somewhat dark; dark-colored
hurtle, dash or drive violently
blithe, happy; joyous

Students can add the words and definitions to their word lists in the Writer's Notebook.

1 ## Literary Element

Tone

If necessary, check to see that students know the speaker is acting as a spokesperson for black people. Students should recognize a calm and earnest tone as he relates history. The tone has a serious edge in the third stanza. Discuss with students the meaning of the closing lines. You might ask how they may relate to social issues besides farming.

"If We Must Die" has a pronounced, identifiable tone as well. Students can compare it to a rousing speech.

A BLACK MAN TALKS OF REAPING

Arna Bontemps

1

I have sown beside all waters in my day.
I planted deep, within my heart the fear
That wind or fowl would take the grain away.
I planted safe against this stark, lean year.

5 I scattered seed enough to plant the land
In rows from Canada to Mexico
But for my reaping only what the hand
Can hold at once is all that I can show.

Yet what I sowed and what the orchard yields
10 My brother's sons are gathering stalk and root,
Small wonder then my children glean[1] in fields
They have not sown, and feed on bitter fruit.

------

1. **glean** (glēn), *v.* gather (grain) left on a field by reapers.

SELECTION SUMMARY

Poems of the Harlem Renaissance

A Black Man Talks of Reaping metaphorically compares hardships of farming with the hardships and injustice experienced by African Americans.

If We Must Die suggests that a people suffering oppression and murder should die fighting back.

The Negro Speaks of Rivers presents a history of black people living in lands and civilizations along great rivers of the world and testifies to the depth of the black person's soul.

Harlem Wine presents a fantastical image of wine that flows through Harlem, driving the rhythms and tunes of music, and the movements of dance.

Youth compares the power of youth to the new light and energy of dawn.

Ma Rainey describes people flocking to hear the blues songs of Ma Rainey. It quotes a song of loneliness which moves the crowd to tears.

 *For summaries in other languages, see the **Building English Proficiency** book.*

Jacob Lawrence's *Migration of the Negro* series does include images of animosity and fighting between white and black Americans. This panel, however, concerns death caused by disease, in turn caused by privation that was part of the migration to northern cities.

Response to Caption Question
Students may note that the poem treats death as a danger to be anticipated and resisted with determination, while the painting depicts a death that has happened, with a strong impact on survivors.

IF WE MUST DIE

2

Claude McKay

If we must die, let it not be like hogs
Hunted and penned in an inglorious spot,
While round us bark the mad and hungry dogs,
Making their mock at our accursed[1] lot.
5 If we must die, O let us nobly die,
So that our precious blood may not be shed
In vain; then even the monsters we defy
Shall be constrained[2] to honor us though dead!
O kinsmen! we must meet the common foe!
10 Though far outnumbered let us show us brave,
And for their thousand blows deal one
      deathblow!
What though before us lies the open grave?
Like men we'll face the murderous, cowardly
      pack,
Pressed to the wall, dying, but fighting back!

---

1. accursed (ə kėr′sid), *adj.* hateful.
2. constrain (kən strān), *v.* force.

▲ This painting by Jacob Lawrence, panel no. 5 (1940–41) in his *Migration of the Negro* series, depicts one of the negative affects of cramped urban life. Many African Americans who moved north contracted tuberculosis. How would you compare the two treatments of death in this painting and in Claude McKay's poem?

If We Must Die **525**

2 Literary Focus
Meter

After the first line of "A Black Man Talks of Reaping," the meter is a regular iambic pentameter. Readers can strive to read it in a natural voice, and the meter will be apparent because of the accented syllables.

In "If We Must Die," lines such as 3 and 10 illustrate iambic pentameter. Other lines have some iambs, but are not metrically regular. For example, line 5 ends with the iambic "O let us nobly die." Students can read the poems, listen to syllables that are naturally stressed, and identify metrical feet.

Question Why might a poet choose to use meter that is not uniform in every line? *(Possible responses: to emphasize certain phrases and lines; to convey ideas in a style more like speech)*

BUILDING ENGLISH PROFICIENCY

Self-Monitoring Comprehension

This activity can help students evaluate their own reading and comprehension of these poems.

• Small groups of students can rewrite individual poems, either paraphrasing or summarizing them.

• The groups can share their versions by exchanging copies or reading aloud.

• Students can talk about the retellings and discuss the meanings of the poems. Encourage students to consider both literal meanings and other possible levels of meaning. For example, the Bontemps poem comments figuratively on the lives of African Americans who are not farmers.

3 Literary Element
Repetition

Question What may have been Hughes's reason for repeating the line "My soul has grown deep like the rivers"? *(Possible responses: It sounds beautiful; it states a theme; it sounds like the chorus of a song; it gains meaning by the end of the poem.)*

4 Reading/Thinking Skills
Fantasy and Reality

Questions

• What gives "Harlem Wine" elements of fantasy? *(Possible response: images of wine flowing through the Harlem streets)*

• What idea do you think is figuratively expressed by the fantasy? *(Possible response: Energy and lively enthusiasm for music gives Harlem an atmosphere of enthusiasm.)*

The Author Speaks

"Although I struggle against it, [race consciousness] colors my writing, I fear, in spite of everything I do."

Countee Cullen
in The New York Times *(1923)*

The World of Work

For the thoughts of a writer about the Harlem poets and about a writer's work, use the pages indicated here.

The World of Work
pp. 17–18

The Negro Speaks of Rivers

Langston Hughes

I've known rivers:
I've known rivers ancient as the world and older than
    the flow of human blood in human veins.

My soul has grown deep like the rivers.

5 I bathed in the Euphrates[1] when dawns were young.
I built my hut near the Congo and it lulled me to sleep.
I looked upon the Nile and raised the pyramids above it.
I heard the singing of the Mississippi when Abe Lincoln
    went down to New Orleans, and I've seen its muddy
10   bosom turn all golden in the sunset.

I've known rivers:
Ancient, dusky[2] rivers.

3 My soul has grown deep like the rivers.

---

1. **Euphrates** (yū frā′tēz), a river in southwest Asia. The Euphrates River flows through the area many believe was the birthplace or "cradle" of civilization.
2. **dusky** (dus′kē), *adj.* somewhat dark; dark-colored.

526   UNIT FIVE: BREAKING THE MOLD

Harlem Wine

Countee Cullen

This is not water running here,
These thick rebellious streams
That hurtle[1] flesh and bone past fear
Down alleyways of dreams.

5 This is a wine that must flow on
Not caring how or where,
So it has ways to flow upon
Where song is in the air.

So it can woo an artful flute
10 With loose, elastic lips,
Its measurement of joy compute
With blithe,[2] ecstatic hips.

4 _____

---

1. **hurtle** (hėr′tl), *v.* dash or drive violently.
2. **blithe** (blīṬH), *adj.* happy; joyous.

MINI-LESSON: VOCABULARY

Antonyms

Teach Remind students that a word that means the opposite of another word is its antonym. Knowing antonyms helps readers understand both words. Many words, such as *river,* have no antonyms. Other words may have more than one antonym, or at least more than one word with contrasting meanings.

Activity Idea Have groups of students write antonyms for these words from "The Negro Speaks of Rivers" and "Harlem Wine."

Groups can compare their antonyms and decide which ones are most opposite the meanings of the words as used in the poems.

Word	Possible Antonyms
ancient	new, modern
older	newer, younger
thick	thin, watery
artful	artless, clumsy
joy	sadness, sorrow
ecstatic	miserable

Youth

Langston Hughes

We have tomorrow
Bright before us
Like a flame.

Yesterday
5 A night-gone thing,
A sun-down name.

And dawn-today
Broad arch above the road
we came.

We march!

Describe the themes of this Aaron Douglas painting, *Rise Shine for Thy Light Has Come* (1932), and of Langston Hughes's poem, "Youth." Are they the same? Why or why not?

Youth   527

Aaron Douglas (1899–1979) wanted not only to become a successful artist, but also to base his art on his African and African American heritage. He did both.

Responses to Caption   Both themes concern hope, new opportunities, and action to meet those opportunities. The poem specifically focuses on youth as a time for looking ahead, and the painting may concern opportunities to do good, in a religious sense.

5 Literary Element
Simile

"We have tomorrow/Bright before us/like a flame" is a clear example of simile.

Question   How does the simile in lines 1–3 enhance the meaning of this stanza? *(Possible responses: it gives a visual image to an idea; it gives a sense of wonder, attraction, heat, or urgency.)*

6 Reader's Response
Making Personal Connections

Questions

- What is the "march" to which Hughes refers? *(Possible responses: young people moving forward, becoming active as a group; a collective effort by young African Americans to advance in life)*

- For what reasons or goals would you urge young people today to "march," or move forward together? *(Possible responses: to improve society; to fight for the environment; to gain equality for women or another group; to make sure animals are treated well; or other goals valued by students)*

BUILDING ENGLISH PROFICIENCY

Recognizing Poetic Language

In "The Negro Speaks of Rivers," the poet uses vivid phrases and connotative words that entice many readers to read slowly and savor its sounds and images. Students may benefit by talking about such words and images.

- Ask about the difference between *ancient* and *old*. Students who know other languages may know similar words

concerning great age. They can explain words like *ancient* that refer to history long ago.

- Point out images such as a soul "grown deep like the rivers" and a muddy river turning "all golden in the sunset." Invite students to convey the images in other words or in another language (that is, by translating the phrases), or in art.

527

The Blues

Like ragtime music, early blues was a musical form related to jazz. It was developed by musicians and singers such as Ma Rainey, from African roots and traditions of African Americans during and after the slavery era, with some influence of European and other American musical styles. The blues explored lives of adversity and the way people got along and persevered despite their troubles.

Visualize

Question What visual images come to mind as you read Part I of the poem? *(Possible responses: people flocking from all directions, seen in a distant or aerial view; people riding in old cars and on dusty animals, talking and enjoying themselves)*

Art Study

Romare Bearden (1912–1988) was a child in Harlem during the 1920s. His parents hosted gatherings of writers and artists of the Harlem Renaissance.

Response to Caption The joy (and music) of the poem match the mood of enjoyment (and music) in the artwork. Some students may feel that the image in the art may be more urban or stylish than the atmosphere in the poem.

Ma Rainey

Sterling Brown

I

7 When Ma Rainey[1]
Comes to town,
Folks from anyplace
Miles aroun',
5 From Cape Girardeau,
Poplar Bluff,
Flocks in to hear
Ma do her stuff;
Comes flivverin'[2] in,
10 Or ridin' mules,
Or packed in trains,
8 Picknickin' fools. . . .
That's what it's like,
Fo' miles on down,
15 To New Orleans delta
An' Mobile town,
When Ma hits
Anywheres aroun'.

---

1. **Ma Rainey.** Gertrude "Ma" Rainey (1866–1939) was a former vaudeville entertainer who sang "weird" and "strange" music, which she eventually helped propel into national prominence as the classic blues.
2. **flivverin',** driving a flivver, slang for a small, cheap automobile, especially one that is no longer new.

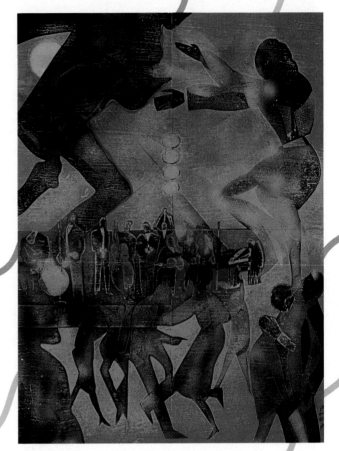

▲ Does this 1975 Romare Bearden work, *At the Savoy,* reflect the atmosphere described in Sterling Brown's poem, "Ma Rainey"? Explain your answer.

MINI-LESSON: GRAMMAR AND USAGE

Use of Dialect in Writing

Teach Some authors capture realistic and interesting speaking styles by using dialects in stories and poems. To express the spoken dialects, writers may create spellings, such as *de* for *the.* Writers may include slang or reflect informal phrasing. For example, Sterling Brown uses a style of informal African American English in passages such as "Dey comes to hear Ma Rainey. . . ." Some written dialect can be understood more easily by reading aloud. It helps to use a natural, conversational voice, not exaggerating the sounds.

Activity Idea Students can rewrite words and phrases of rural African American dialect in "Ma Rainey" in more formal English. They can discuss how well they think the poet has captured the sound of real speech.

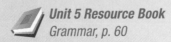
Unit 5 Resource Book
Grammar, p. 60

II

Dey comes to hear Ma Rainey from de little river settlements,
20 From blackbottom cornrows and from lumber camps;
Dey stumble in de hall, jes a-laughin' an' a-cacklin',
Cheerin' lak roarin' water, lak wind in river swamps.

An' some jokers keeps deir laughs a-goin' in de crowded aisles,
An' some folks sits dere waitin' wid deir aches an' miseries,
25 Till Ma comes out before dem, a-smilin' gold-toofed smiles
An' Long Boy ripples minors on de black an' yellow keys.

III

O Ma Rainey,
Sing yo' song;
Now you's back
30 Whah you belong,
Git way inside us,
Keep us strong. . . .
O Ma Rainey,
Li'l an' low;
35 Sing us 'bout de hard luck
Roun' our do';
Sing us 'bout de lonesome road
We mus' go. . . .

IV

I talked to a fellow, an' the fellow say,
40 "She jes' catch hold of us, somekindaway.
She sang Backwater Blues one day:

  'It rained fo' days an' de skies was dark as night,
  Trouble taken place in de lowlands at night.

  'Thundered an' lightened an' the storm begin to roll
45 *Thousan's of people ain't got no place to go.*

  'Den I went an' stood upon some high ol' lonesome hill
  An' looked down on the place where I used to live.'

An' den de folks, dey natchally bowed dey heads an' cried,
Bowed dey heavy heads, shet dey moufs up tight an' cried,
50 An' Ma lef' de stage, an' followed some de folks outside."

Dere wasn't much more de fellow say:
She jes' gits hold of us dataway.

Literary Criticism

"Sterling Brown strove . . . to erase the gap between the creative artist and the folk. Brown's portrayals of the hard life of the common man and woman [were] the most authentic, hard-boiled and fatalistic of the Renaissance."

David Levering Lewis
in The Portable Harlem Renaissance Reader *(1995)*

Check Test

1. In "A Black Man Talks of Reaping," what does the speaker say his children are eating? *(bitter fruit)*

2. In "If We Must Die," what does the speaker urge his "kinsmen" to do, if they must die? *(Possible responses: fight back, die nobly by fighting their attackers)*

3. In "The Negro Speaks of Rivers," what does the speaker compare to rivers, and how is it like the rivers? *(his/her soul, which has grown deep, like rivers)*

4. In "Harlem Wine," what image involves dancing? *(blithe, ecstatic hips)*

5. In "Ma Rainey," what do folks do when they hear of a scheduled performance by the singer? *(They travel from miles around to hear her.)*

Unit 5 Resource Book
Alternate Check Test, p. 61

BUILDING ENGLISH PROFICIENCY

Analyzing Dialect

Help students recognize the familiar English words and expressions that are written differently in the poem.

- Ask students to look for words that may appear a little different from their standard written form, such as *aroun'* and *anywheres*. Students can practice writing standard forms.

- Point out spellings the poet uses to reflect pronunciations in the poem's setting. These may include *somekindaway* (some kind of way), *natchally* (naturally), and the following examples.

Fo' (For)	lak (like)	Git (Get)	den (then)
An' (And)	deir (their)	Li'l (Little)	dey (their)
Dey (They)	yo' (your)	'bout (about)	shet (shut)
jes' (just)	Whah (Where)	do' (door)	moufs (mouths)

- Invite students to try writing a few lines in any other dialect or informal speaking style familiar to them.

After Reading

MAKING CONNECTIONS

1. Possible responses: blues, hymns, classical or other music for "A Black Man Talks of Reaping" and "If We Must Die"; any of these or jazz for "The Negro Speaks of Rivers"; jazz, rock, or rap music for "Harlem Wine"; possibly a march for "Youth"; and blues for "Ma Rainey." Responses will vary.

2. Students may base choices on who they think is inspirational, has a sense of humor, or has political wisdom.

3. Possible response: The sowing symbolizes the work African Americans have done. The reaping symbolizes the fruits of those labors, which are enjoyed by others.

4. Possible responses: to move people toward action; a recognition of the injustice suffered by African American victims of hate crimes; or courage in adversity

5. Possible responses: Hughes compares the age of the rivers with the age of the African people. He compares the scattered geography of the rivers with the many places where people of African heritage live and have lived.

6. Possible responses: hopeful, upbeat, determined

7. Possible responses: people's energy, enjoyment of life, creativity, or Harlem's soul

8. Possible responses: She sang about hardships that people related to; she shared the feelings of her audience.

9. Possible responses: adversity, suffering, marching, fighting for freedom, enjoying music, weeping together

10. Sample responses: the feelings of oppression and anger in McKay's poem; the fun in "Harlem Wine"; the love of music as in "Ma Rainey"

11. Possible responses: Johnson views Harlem from an economical viewpoint as it relates to black culture (". . . a Negro institution of Savannah, Ga., bought a parcel for $115,000 which it sold a month or two ago at a profit of $110,000"). Cullen speaks of its energy in music and dance. They both focus on the vitality of Harlem.

530

After Reading

Making Connections

Shaping Your Response

1. What musical piece would you choose to accompany an oral reading of each of these poems? Explain your choices.

2. Based on the poems you've read, which of the poets would you most want to invite to a poetry reading to be held in your school? Explain your choice.

Analyzing the Poems

3. What does the sowing and reaping **symbolize** in Bontemps's poem?

4. What emotional effect do you think McKay is trying to achieve with his poem?

5. Explain the **comparison** that Hughes makes between rivers and African heritage in "The Negro Speaks of Rivers."

6. How would you describe the **tone** of "Youth"?

7. What do you think the wine **symbolizes** in "Harlem Wine"?

8. Ma Rainey was one of the first blues singers to achieve national popularity. Based on the poem, how would you explain her popularity?

9. What kinds of shared **group** experiences do these poems both commemorate and celebrate?

Extending the Ideas

10. Which of the poems reminds you of a feeling or experience you have had? Explain your answer.

11. Compare Cullen's view of Harlem in "Harlem Wine" to Johnson's in "Harlem: The Culture Capital." Do they both see Harlem in the same way? Support your answer with examples from the literature.

Literary Focus: Meter

The **meter** of a poem can be regular or irregular. If the meter is regular, it follows a predictable pattern: / ˘ // ˘ //, for example. If the meter is irregular, its pattern is not as predictable. The meter of a poem will affect the poem's **tone**. A brisk meter can create a lighthearted, happy tone; a slow meter can create a more serious tone. Think again about the poems you've just read and then answer these questions about meter.

- Is the meter of "If We Must Die" regular or irregular?
- How does the meter of the poem contribute to its **tone?**
- How would you describe the meter of "The Negro Speaks of Rivers"? How is the meter in Hughes's poem different from the meter in McKay's poem?

LITERARY FOCUS: METER

- The meter of "If We Must Die" is irregular.
- Possible response: Meter can help express the tone or speaking style in a poem, as the fast-paced meter of "If We Must Die" expresses determination.
- Possible response: The meter of "The Negro Speaks of Rivers," with more unaccented syllables between its accented beats, has longer metrical feet. This gives the poem a slower pace and a more thoughtful, musing tone than that of "If We Must Die," which is a call to action.

Activity Idea   Students may bring in tapes of songs, with your approval. Student groups can listen to the tapes and prepare "spoken word" renditions of lines or verses, stressing the meter.

Vocabulary Study

Choose the letter of the word that is the best synonym for each numbered vocabulary word. Use your Glossary if necessary.

blithe
constrain
hurtle
dusky
accursed

1. blithe   **a.** tired   **b.** annoyed   **c.** happy   **d.** nervous
2. constrain   **a.** choose   **b.** force   **c.** restrain   **d.** separate
3. hurtle   **a.** dash   **b.** fall   **c.** dive   **d.** carry
4. dusky   **a.** foggy   **b.** dark   **c.** shady   **d.** musty
5. accursed   **a.** enchanted   **b.** pledged   **c.** spoken   **d.** hateful

Expressing Your Ideas

Writing Choices

Writer's Notebook Update Using a poem you've just read as a model, try writing a few lines of poetry. Before you begin, decide on the subject of your poem. Then, review the notes you kept about poetic devices as you were reading the selections. Use at least two poetic devices in your poem.

Hidden Meaning What were some of the major themes, or main ideas, of the Harlem Renaissance? Copy the chart below on a piece of paper. Then, working in small groups, decide on a theme for each of the poems listed and then briefly state the theme on your chart. When you've finished, look carefully at your chart. What themes do some or all of these poems have in common? In a **paragraph**, explain some of the themes of the Harlem Renaissance.

Poem	Theme
A Black Man Talks of Reaping	
If We Must Die	
The Negro Speaks of Rivers	
Youth	
Harlem Wine	
Ma Rainey	

Other Options

The Birth of the Blues During the 1920s blues music began to gain national attention. Working with a small group, plan a 1920s **Blues Fest,** playing recordings for your class and telling about the singers.

From Poem to Art Use some form of **visual art** to capture the subject matter, theme, and emotions of one of the poems you've just read. You may want to draw a picture, or create a sculpture, or even choreograph a dance.

Becoming an Expert Prepare an **oral presentation** about the life and works of one of the poets you've just read. Begin your presentation with some biographical information about the poet. Discuss some interesting details about the poet's life, as well as the poet's role in the Harlem Renaissance. Then present some of the poet's major works, offering insight about recurring themes or subject matter.

Ma Rainey   **531**

VOCABULARY STUDY

1. c. happy
2. b. force
3. a. dash
4. b. dark
5. d. hateful

More Practice It may help students understand the meaning of these vocabulary words to write a sentence using each one.

Unit 5 Resource Book
Vocabulary, p. 59
Vocabulary Test, p. 62

WRITING CHOICES
Writer's Notebook Update

To begin writing their poems, students may find it helpful to listen to music or to look at artwork that they like. They also may find a newspaper story that makes them feel a strong emotion—anger, fear, joy— and tell the story in poem form.

Hidden Meaning

Students may find that some themes of the Harlem Renaissance are moving forward, overcoming oppression, creating and enjoying music, and other celebrations of one's culture.

Selection Test

Unit 5 Resource Book
pp. 63–64

OTHER OPTIONS
The Birth of the Blues

Students also may talk about connections between the blues and contemporary forms of popular music such as rock, rap, and jazz. They may bring recordings in these genres to illustrate the connections.

From Poem to Art

When students present their art, discuss the process that took them from the written words to their interpretations, their choices of form and content.

Becoming an Expert

To research the poets' lives, students may use media center or library resources.

- Books include *The Harlem Renaissance: Hub of African-American Culture, 1920–1930* by Steven Watson (New York: Pantheon, 1995).

- Periodicals with articles about the Harlem Renaissance may be available in libraries for students willing to do serious research. They may use the *Readers' Guide to Periodical Literature* on CD-ROM or in print to begin.

Before Reading

Building Background

Hurston describes being a black student at a predominantly white college as being "a dark rock surged upon, and overswept." Have students describe what they think it would feel like to be the only student of their cultural background in a school.

Literary Focus

Point out that **tone** is created by the manner in which content is presented, not simply by the content. Hurston could have written about her topic in another tone—for example, entirely serious or sarcastic.

Writer's Notebook

Suggest to students that they picture someone they think has high self-esteem, and jot down adjectives that come to mind.

More About Zora Neale Hurston

Zora Neale Hurston's writing has been praised—and criticized—for its refusal to see African Americans as victims of social forces or stereotypes.

Other Works

- *Their Eyes Were Watching God,* 1937
- *Dust Tracks on a Road,* 1942

Connections to **AuthorWorks**

Zora Neale Hurston is a featured author in the AuthorWorks CD-ROM series.

Before Reading

How It Feels to Be Colored Me

by Zora Neale Hurston

Zora Neale Hurston
1891–1960

As a young girl growing up in southern Florida, Zora Neale Hurston loved to sit on the porch and listen in on adult "lying sessions" (daily exchanges of folk tales). Many years later, she used these stories in her own writing. Unlike other writers of the Harlem Renaissance, Hurston deliberately ignored issues of racism and discrimination in her writing. Instead, she chose to use her essays, short stories, and novels as a means of celebrating the vibrancy of African American life. Hurston spent the late 1920s and 1930s as an anthropologist, collecting and examining southern African American dialect, religious rituals, and folk tales.

Building Background

Hurston and the Harlem Renaissance At age thirty, Hurston moved to New York and became caught up in the Harlem Renaissance. She befriended other writers such as Claude McKay, Jean Toomer, and Langston Hughes and collaborated with them on various literary publications. Although her collections of folk tales were well-received by the public, she was criticized for failing to use her writing as a means of speaking out against racism and economic exploitation. Later, poet and critic Sterling Brown said that her writing about the rural South should have included, at the very least, "a few slave anecdotes that turn the tables on old marster" or "a bit of grumbling about hard work." This type of complaint about her writing made it difficult for Hurston to find publishers. By the time she died in 1960, her writing was essentially forgotten. In the 1970s, however, author Alice Walker rediscovered Hurston's works. Since Walker's rediscovery, Hurston's works have become hugely popular.

Literary Focus

Tone is the author's attitude toward his or her subject and audience. The tone of a piece of writing may be revealed by the author's word choice, the details included, or the arrangement of ideas and descriptions. As you read "How It Feels to Be Colored Me," make a few notes about Hurston's tone.

Writer's Notebook

Self-Esteem How necessary is self-esteem? Why is it important to feel good about yourself? Copy the web at the right in your log. At the end of each spoke, write an adjective that might describe a person who has high self-esteem. An example has been done for you.

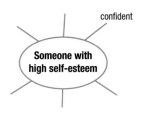

confident

Someone with high self-esteem

SUPPORT MATERIALS OVERVIEW

Unit 5 Resource Book
- Graphic Organizer, p. 65
- Study Guide, p. 66
- Vocabulary, p. 67
- Grammar, p. 68
- Alternate Check Test, p. 69
- Vocabulary Test, p. 70
- Selection Test, pp. 71–72

Building English Proficiency
- Literature Summaries
- Activities, p. 209

Reading, Writing & Grammar Skillbook
- Reading, pp. 68–69, 75–76
- Grammar, Usage, and Mechanics, pp. 229–231

Technology
- Audiotape
- Personal Journal Software
- Custom Literature Database: For a thematically related selection, see *The Colored People in America* by Ellen Watkins Harper, on the database.
- Test Generator Software

How It Feels To Be Colored Me

Zora Neale Hurston

I am colored but I offer nothing in the way of extenuating[1] circumstances except the fact that I am the only Negro in the United States whose grandfather on my mother's side was *not* an Indian chief.

I remember the very day that I became colored. Up to my thirteenth year I lived in the little Negro town of Eatonville, Florida. It is exclusively a colored town. The only white people I knew passed through going to or coming from Orlando. The native whites rode dusty horses, the Northern tourists chugged down the sandy village road in automobiles. The town knew the Southerners and never stopped chewing[2] when they passed. But the Northerners were something else again. They were peered at cautiously from behind curtains by the timid. The more venturesome[3] would come out on the porch to watch them go past and got just as much pleasure out of the tourists as the tourists got out of the village.

The front porch might seem a daring place for the rest of the town, but it was a gallery seat for me. My favorite place was atop the gate-post. Proscenium box[4] for a born first-nighter. Not only did I enjoy the show, but I didn't mind the actors knowing that I liked it. I usually spoke to them in passing. I'd wave at them and when they returned my salute, I would say something like this: "Howdy-do-well-I-thank-you-where-you-goin'?" Usually the automobile or the horse paused at this, and after a queer exchange of compliments, I would probably "go a piece of the way" with them, as we say in farthest Florida. If one of my family happened to come to the front in time to see me, of course negotiations would be rudely broken off. But even so, it is clear that I was the first

---

1. extenuating (ek sten′yū ā′ting), *adj.* making the seriousness of a fault seem less; partially excusing.
2. **chewing,** a reference to chewing sugar cane.
3. venturesome (ven′chər səm), *adj.* rash; daring.
4. **proscenium** (prō sē′nē əm) **box,** *n.* seating area in a theater directly in front of the stage.

How It Feels to Be Colored Me   533

Selection Objectives

- To explore themes of cultural or racial self-image
- To analyze an author's tone
- To examine the use of adjectives and adverbs

Unit 5 Resource Book
Graphic Organizer, p. 65
Study Guide, p. 66

Theme Link

Zora Neale Hurston writes about her own cultural consciousness as an African American, without apology. She resists conforming to any mold of expectations about how she should feel. Her voice and sentiments are part of the Harlem Renaissance.

Vocabulary Preview

extenuating, partially excusing
venturesome, rash; daring
skirmish, minor conflict or contest
rambunctious, wild and noisy
exultingly, happily; joyfully

Students can add the words and definitions to their word lists in the Writer's Notebook.

1 Literary Focus
Tone

Hurston establishes a frank, unapologetic tone about her identity in the first paragraph. She pokes fun at African Americans who seek to qualify their identity by including an American Indian among their recent ancestors.

Students may not know that many Americans do have mixed ancestry, and it was not uncommon for American Indians and African Americans to marry. Some students may not know that the word *colored* was a widely used term identifying black people.

SELECTION SUMMARY
How It Feels to Be Colored Me

The selection tells how the author's awareness of color differences among people has developed. As a child in an African American community in Florida, Hurston was hardly aware of the color of her skin. When she moved to Jacksonville at age thirteen, though, she became conscious of being "colored." She describes instances in which she is most conscious of her identity as an African American as an adult. At a predominantly white college, or listening to jazz that moves her much more deeply than it does a white friend, she is aware of the distinction. In the end, she concludes that each person is a collection of traits, however, not determined by skin color.

 For summaries in other languages, see the Building English Proficiency book.

Question What tone do Hurston's comments about her "welcome-to-our-state" greetings and the Miami Chamber of Commerce help establish? *(Possible responses: a humorous, casual, spirited, or flippant tone)*

3 **Reading/Thinking Skills**

Making Inferences

Question What point does Hurston make when she describes her interactions with the white travelers who passed through Eatonville? *(Possible response: As a young child, she acted without great regard for color differences.)*

4 **Reader's Response**

Making Personal Connections

Hurston writes that she felt most conscious of her color when she was "thrown against a sharp white background." Invite volunteers to relate experiences in which they have been in situations in which they suddenly felt different from others. Students who have moved to a new school or lived in a new country may have interesting accounts. Students should respect classmates who do not wish to share their experiences.

---

2 "welcome-to-our-state" Floridian, and I hope the Miami Chamber of Commerce will please take notice.

During this period, white people differed from colored to me only in that they rode through town and never lived there. They liked to hear me "speak pieces" and sing and wanted to see me dance the parse-me-la, and gave me generously of their small silver for doing these things, which seemed strange to me for I wanted to do them so much that I needed bribing to stop. Only they didn't know it. The colored people 3 gave me no dimes. They deplored any joyful tendencies in me, but I was their Zora nevertheless. I belonged to them, to the nearby hotels, to the county—everybody's Zora.

But changes came in the family when I was thirteen, and I was sent to school in Jacksonville. I left Eatonville, the town of the oleanders, as Zora. When I disembarked from the river-boat at Jacksonville, she was no more. It seemed that I had suffered a sea-change. I was not Zora of Orange County any more, I was now a little colored girl. I found out in certain ways. In my heart as well as in the mirror, I became a fast brown—warranted not to rub or run.

But I am not tragically colored. There is no great sorrow dammed up in my soul, nor lurking behind my eyes. I do not mind at all. I do not belong to the sobbing school of Negrohood who hold that nature has somehow given them a lowdown dirty deal and whose feelings are all hurt by it. Even in the helter-skelter skirmish[5] that is my life, I have seen that the world is to the strong regardless of a little pigmentation more or less. No, I do not weep at the world—I am too busy sharpening my oyster knife.[6]

Someone is always at my elbow reminding me that I am the granddaughter of slaves. It fails to register depression with me. Slavery is sixty years in the past. The operation was successful and the patient is doing well, thank you. The terrible struggle that made me an American out of a potential slave said "On

---

Ruby Green was a popular singer and nightclub entertainer in the late 1920s. What qualities does Green in James Chapin's 1928 painting, *Ruby Green Singing*, seem to have in common with Zora Neale Hurston in "How it Feels to Be Colored Me"? ➤

the line!" The Reconstruction said "Get set!"; and the generation before said "Go!" I am off to a flying start and I must not halt in the stretch to look behind and weep. Slavery is the price I paid for civilization, and the choice was not with me. It is a bully adventure and worth all that I have paid through my ancestors for it. No one on earth ever had a greater chance for glory. The world to be won and nothing to be lost. It is thrilling to think—to know that for any act of mine, I shall get twice as much praise and twice as much blame. It is quite exciting to hold the center of the national stage, with the spectators not knowing whether to laugh or to weep.

The position of my white neighbor is much more difficult. No brown specter pulls up a chair beside me when I sit down to eat. No dark ghost thrusts its leg against mine in bed. The game of keeping what one has is never so exciting as the game of getting.

I do not always feel colored. Even now I often achieve the unconscious Zora of Eatonville before the Hegira. I feel most colored when I am 4 thrown against a sharp white background.

For instance at Barnard.[7] "Beside the waters of the Hudson"[8] I feel my race. Among the thousand white persons, I am a dark rock surged upon, and overswept, but through it all, I remain myself. When covered by the waters, I am; and the ebb but reveals me again.

---

5. **skirmish** (skėr′mish), *n.* minor conflict or contest.
6. **sharpening my oyster knife,** an allusion to the expression "the world is my oyster."
7. **Barnard,** New York college attended by Hurston.
8. **Beside the waters of the Hudson,** an allusion to the Bible's Psalm 137: "by the waters of Babylon." In Psalm 137, the Jewish people who were forced to leave Jerusalem mourn the loss of their beloved home.

MINI-LESSON: LITERARY FOCUS

Tone

Teach Tone is the attitude an author reveals toward her or his subject. The author's tone can add emotional meaning to the ideas or information conveyed. Examples of tone are sympathy, disdain, humor, reverence, and irony.

Questions What is the difference between tone and mood? *(Possible responses: Tone is a writer's attitude toward a subject as communicated in the writing, while mood describes the atmosphere of feeling created by situations described in the work. Examples of tone are informative, serious, mocking, or praising, whereas examples of mood are suspense or peaceful calm.)*

Activity Ideas

- Students can pick three sentences from the selection that they think best convey Hurston's tone. Volunteers can discuss whether the tone varies or changes in any way in the selection.
- Students can read newspaper articles, including opinion columns and editorials, and determine what each writer's tone is.

James Chapin (1887–1975) painted many portraits depicting working people in starkly realistic settings, unlike this romanticized image of Ruby Green. Artist Grant Wood considered Chapin's portraits among the best American art.

Possible Response to Caption Question Both Hurston and Green seem to have hopeful, positive attitudes.

5 Reading/Thinking Skills
Evaluating

Questions What do you think Hurston feels about Americans who often mention the enslavement of her ancestors? *(Possible response: She seems to think they should look to the future more than the past.)*

What significance do you think the past struggles of African Americans should have today or in the near future? *(Possible responses: We should learn about how people overcame slavery and apply similar courage to problems now. I agree with Hurston that slavery is in the past.)*

Connections to
NovelWorks

NovelWorks: *Their Eyes Were Watching God* offers a rich variety of unique materials for teaching Zora Neale Hurston's acclaimed novel.

How It Feels to Be Colored Me   535

BUILDING ENGLISH PROFICIENCY

Understanding Figurative Language

Some students may need help recognizing or understanding ideas that Hurston communicates with figurative expressions and images. For example, the day she "became colored" refers to the time when she learned how she was regarded. She describes the front porch of her childhood home as a theater (p. 533). Students can talk about her images in order to comprehend them.

- Ask what Hurston means by saying that, when she went to Jacksonville, she was no longer Zora (p. 534). Allow informal peer teaching, as suitable.

- Explain that "The world is my oyster" is an expression referring to opportunities to gain advantages in life. Students can respond with an explanation of why Hurston "sharpens her oyster knife" rather than weeping at the world.

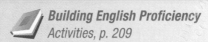
Building English Proficiency
Activities, p. 209

Sometimes it is the other way around. A white person is set down in our midst, but the contrast is just as sharp for me. For instance, when I sit in the drafty basement that is The New World Cabaret with a white person, my color comes. We enter chatting about any little nothing that we have in common and are seated by the jazz waiters. In the abrupt way that jazz orchestras have, this one plunges into a number. It loses no time in circumlocutions, but gets right down to business. It constricts the thorax and splits the heart with its tempo and narcotic harmonies. This orchestra grows rambunctious,[9] rears on its hind legs and attacks the tonal veil with primitive fury, rending it, clawing it until it breaks through to the jungle beyond. I follow those heathen—follow them exultingly.[10] I dance wildly inside myself; I yell within, I whoop; I shake my assegai[11] above my head, I hurl it true to the mark *yeeeeooww!* I am in the jungle and living in the jungle way. My face is painted red and yellow and my body is painted blue. My pulse is throbbing like a war drum. I want to slaughter something—give pain, give death to what, I do not know. But the piece ends. The men of the orchestra wipe their lips and rest their fingers. I creep back slowly to the veneer we call civilization with the last tone and find the white friend sitting motionless in his seat, smoking calmly.

"Good music they have here," he remarks, drumming the table with his fingertips.

Music. The great blobs of red and purple emotion have not touched him. He has only heard what I felt. He is far away and I see him but dimly across the ocean and the continent that have fallen between us. He is so pale in his whiteness then and I am *so* colored.

6 t certain times I have no race, I am *me.* When I set my hat at a certain angle and saunter down Seventh Avenue, Harlem City, feeling as snooty as the lions in front of the Forty-second Street Library, for instance. So far as my feelings are concerned, Peggy Hopkins Joyce[12] on the Boule Mich[13] with her gorgeous raiment, stately carriage, knees knocking together in a most aristocratic manner, has nothing on me. The cosmic Zora emerges. I belong to no race and no time. I am the eternal feminine with its string of beads.

I have no separate feeling about being an American citizen and colored. I am merely a fragment of the Great Soul that surges within the boundaries. My country, right or wrong.

Sometimes, I feel discriminated against, but it does not make me angry. It merely astonishes me. How *can* any deny themselves the pleasure of my company? It's beyond me.

But in the main, I feel like a brown bag of miscellany propped against a wall. Against a wall in company with other bags, white, red, and yellow. Pour out the contents, and there is discovered a jumble of small things priceless and worthless. A first-water diamond, an empty spool, bits of broken glass, lengths of string, a key to a door long since crumbled away, a rusty knife-blade, old shoes saved for a road that never was and never will be, a nail bent under the weight of things too heavy for any nail, a dried flower or two still a little fragrant. In your hand is the brown bag. On the ground before you is the jumble it held—so much like the jumble in the bags, could they be emptied, that all might be dumped in a single heap and the bags refilled without altering the content of any greatly. A bit of colored glass more or less would not matter. Perhaps that is how the Great Stuffer of bags filled them in the first place—who knows?

9. **rambunctious** (ram bungk′shəs), *adj.* wild and noisy.
10. **exultingly** (eg zult′ing lē), *adv.* happily; joyfully.
11. **assegai** (as′ə gī), *n.* short, broad-bladed spear of the Zulu people of southern Africa.
12. **Peggy Hopkins Joyce,** a famous American beauty of the 1920s.
13. **Boule Mich** (bül mēsh), a fashionable street in Paris.

MINI-LESSON: GRAMMAR

Adjectives and Adverbs

Teach Adjectives modify nouns (or pronouns); adverbs modify verbs, adjectives, and other adverbs. Adjectives describe qualities. Adverbs often describe the manner, frequency, or setting of an action expressed by a verb.

Activity Ideas

- Students can pick ten adjectives from the selection and write their meanings. For those that have adverb forms (with *-ly*), students can explain how the adverbs can be used.

- Students can find adverbs that Hurston uses and identify those that modify adjectives. Examples include *exclusively* in "It is exclusively a colored town" (p. 533) and *tragically* in "I am not tragically colored" (p. 534).

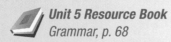
Unit 5 Resource Book
Grammar, p. 68

After Reading

Making Connections

Shaping Your Response

1. If you were going to describe Zora Neale Hurston to a friend, what five adjectives would you use? Explain your choices.

Analyzing the Essay

2. What would you say is the **theme,** or main idea, of "How It Feels to Be Colored Me"? Write one sentence that summarizes Hurston's theme.

3. Reread the last paragraph of the essay. What point is Hurston making about people of different races through her **metaphor?**

4. How would you describe the **tone** of the essay?

5. Do you think Hurston identifies herself more strongly as an individual, or as a member of a **group?** Explain your answer.

Extending the Ideas

6. Based on her essay, what advice do you think Hurston might have for people living in today's society?

Vocabulary Study

Choose the word in the column on the right that most closely resembles the meaning of the word in the left column.

extenuating
venturesome
skirmish
exultingly
rambunctious

1. extenuating   a. joyfully

2. venturesome   b. rowdy

3. skirmish   c. excusing

4. exultingly   d. daring

5. rambunctious   e. conflict

Expressing Your Ideas

Writing Choices

Writer's Notebook Update Would you say Hurston has high self-esteem? Write a paragraph that discusses her sense of self.

How It Feels . . . Write a **paragraph** about yourself expressing "How It Feels to Be _____ Me." Fill in the blank with any adjective you wish.

Another Option

My Bag Apply Hurston's "brown bag" metaphor to your own life. What would the contents of your bag be like? Make a list of the items in your bag. Then, using a combination of your own drawings and images you've cut from newspapers and magazines, create a **collage** that reveals the contents of your bag.

How It Feels to Be Colored Me   537

After Reading

MAKING CONNECTIONS

1. Possible responses: self-assured, funny, observant, philosophical, optimistic, insightful, content, thoughtful

2. Possible response: People pay more attention to skin color than a person needs to, to know herself or himself.

3. Possible response: All people regardless of skin color belong to the human race and have personal qualities.

4. Possible responses: lighthearted but serious, irreverent, unapologetic, a mixture of humor and sincerity

5. Possible response: She identifies herself more as an individual. When external factors come into play that remind her she is a person of color, she feels her group membership more strongly.

6. Possible response: She might tell people to worry less about their skin color and concentrate on what is inside them and what they can do.

VOCABULARY STUDY

1. c. excusing

2. d. daring

3. e. conflict

4. a. joyfully

5. b. rowdy

 Unit 5 Resource Book
Vocabulary, p. 67
Vocabulary Test, p. 70

Selection Test

 Unit 5 Resource Book
pp. 71–72

Transparency Collection
Fine Art Writing Prompt 9

WRITING CHOICES
Writer's Notebook Update

Students might make notes listing expressions she uses that express self-confidence.

How It Feels . . .

Students can give their paragraphs whatever tone is appropriate; it may not be the tone Hurston used.

ANOTHER OPTION
My Bag

Students can include in their lists actual objects, such as hobby or sports equipment or books, and symbolic items, such as a musical note, a sunrise, or a heart. Encourage students to create a collage that clearly conveys the ideas, experiences, or values they wish to include.

Interdisciplinary Study

Theme Link

Bold artistic vision chronicles the past, present, and future of the African American culture.

Curricular Connection: Fine Art

You can use the information in this interdisciplinary study to explore how the visual artists of the Harlem Renaissance captured the themes and spirit of this era.

 Art Study

Responses to Caption Question

Possible responses: Car headlights, streetlights, and neon signs are used as light sources in this painting.

Unit 5 Resource Book
*Interdisciplinary Study Guide,
p. 73*

 An Artistic

Fine Art Connection

The extraordinary creativity of the writers and musicians associated with the Harlem Renaissance has tended to get more attention than the achievements of the many fine African American painters and sculptors of the period. Works by a few of the most important artists appear on these pages.

Archibald J. Motley, Jr.
***Black Belt* (1934)**
The poet Countee Cullen observed that each artist had to "find his treasure where his heart lies." In his paintings, Motley chose to depict the vivid night life of big-city African American neighborhoods. What different light sources has the painter used to dramatize this scene?

538

MINI-LESSON: STUDY SKILLS

Using Primary Sources

Teach   Many of the books published during the Harlem Renaissance are still in print or can be found in libraries. Some magazines and newspapers of the day can also be found on microfilm or bound in volumes.

Activity Idea   Have each student choose his or her favorite poet from the selections, or pick one of the following other Harlem Renaissance writers.

• Zora Neale Hurston

• Jessie Redmon Fauset

• Wallace Thurman

• W.E.B. Dubois

Have each student bring in a primary source article, or excerpt of a book by this writer, that comments on African American culture and concerns. Suggest to students that they write a paragraph about what they learn from these primary sources.

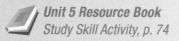 **Unit 5 Resource Book**
Study Skill Activity, p. 74

Awakening

Meta Warrick Fuller
Talking Skull (1937)
Fuller emphasized African cultural elements in her work. What might this sculpture be saying about the relationship between the individual and tradition?

BUILDING ENGLISH PROFICIENCY

ESL
LEP
ELD
SAE
LD

Making Cultural Connections

Guide students in examining and commenting on Fuller's *Talking Skull* and the relationship between the individual and tradition. Then have them use a t-chart on which to write down their own cultural traditions that relate to family, to goal setting, to choosing a career, and so on. Students can use the right-hand side of the t-chart to express how they feel about each of the traditions they wrote on the left-hand side.

Tradition	My Thoughts
All the men in my family have become farmers.	I love the farm but I want to go away to college.

Art Study

Augusta Savage
Gamin (1929)
Using as a model a child she encountered near her studio, Savage created a lively, wistful portrait of a street urchin. What do you think is the principal emotional quality the sculptor has given to this child's face?

Palmer Hayden
Fétiche et Fleurs (1932–33)
Hayden incorporated examples of traditional African sculpture and weaving in this still life. What impact do these items have in the setting in which he has placed them?

540   UNIT FIVE: BREAKING THE MOLD

MINI-LESSON: VISUAL LITERACY

Compare and Contrast Print and Nonprint Media

Teach   Written language requires that one must be able to read the language. Visual art, on the other hand, communicates more universally through images that someone from any culture can recognize.

Have students look at the art on pages 540–541. Point out images that might translate universally, for example, the boy's expression in *Gamin*, the baskets on the head of the Blackberry Woman, and Aaron Douglas's halos of light.

Activity Ideas

- Have each student bring in two pictures from magazines, newspapers, or books. The first image should be one that the student feels communicates its theme in a purely visual and universal way; the second image should be one that requires a verbal explanation, such as a caption.

- Discuss how the first picture communicates nonverbally and why the second requires verbal or written explanation.

Aaron Douglas
Aspects of Negro Life: From Slavery Through Reconstruction (1934)
Painted during the Depression, this is one of a series of four large murals depicting significant episodes in African American history. How does Douglas's composition convey a sense of optimism and faith in progress?

Richmond Barthé
Blackberry Woman (1932)
Barthé, a pioneer in choosing African American people as his subjects, here depicts a street vendor. What qualities has he given this woman?
Collection of the Whitney Museum of American Art, New York.

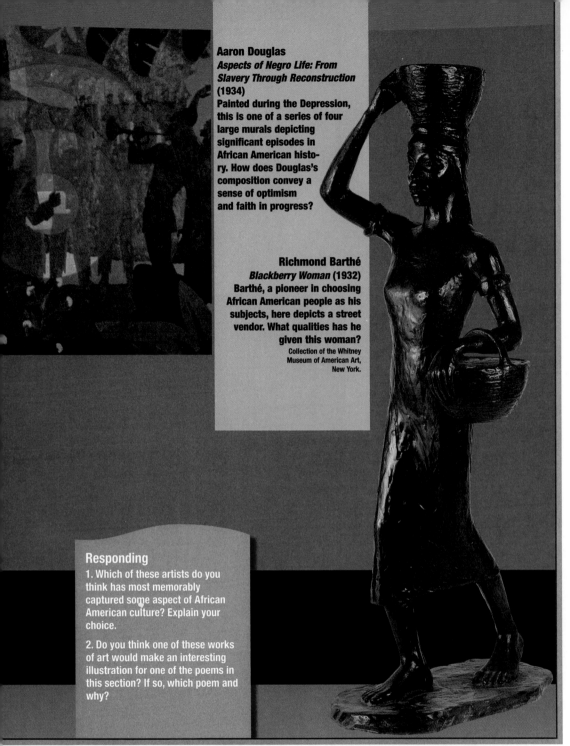

Responding

1. Which of these artists do you think has most memorably captured some aspect of African American culture? Explain your choice.

2. Do you think one of these works of art would make an interesting illustration for one of the poems in this section? If so, which poem and why?

Responses to Caption Questions
Possible responses for Aaron Douglas's *Aspects of Negro Life: From Slavery Through Reconstruction:* The mural starts with images of enslaved people picking cotton on the far left, moves through their standing up and pointing towards the capitol, fighting and becoming strong, and celebrating victory. The composition of the work adds to the sense of hope: It starts with small, huddled shapes on the far left and moves in a sweeping diagonal to the upper right corner.

Possible responses for Richmond Barthé's *Blackberry Woman:* strength, serenity, balance, beauty, a sense of movement, and hard work

Responding

1. Possible Response   Students may choose Motley for his depiction of African American social life; Fuller or Hayden for their connections to African culture; Savage or Barthé for their portraits of African American individuals; or Douglas for his sense of history and struggle.

2. Possible Response   Students' responses will vary but students should be able to support their choices with specific excerpts from the text.

BUILDING ENGLISH PROFICIENCY

Analyzing Visual Information

Use one or more of the following activities to help students focus on these artworks from the Harlem Renaissance.

- Have students explore the images and captions, left to right. Allow time for students to respond to the images and questions in their journals.

- Have students look for personal qualities that are captured in the various works. Ask: Which people in these works seem to be thoughtful? noble? enthusiastic about life?

- Ask groups of students to improvise skits in which they reveal something about the lives and values of the people depicted.

- Have volunteers suggest artwork that might represent their own cultural background. Compare their suggestions to the artwork from the Harlem Renaissance.

Interdisciplinary Study

Theme Link

Larcelia Kebe is a participator in the heritage of the Harlem Renaissance as an educator, business woman, and proud Harlem resident.

Curricular Connection: Career

You can use the information in this interdisciplinary study to discuss how students' activities might one day lead to a career.

Interdisciplinary Activity Ideas

- Suggest to students that they choose an issue about which they feel strongly and design a business that will provide profit and exposure for their issue.
- A group of students might interview a member of the school community who contributes in constructive ways and find out about his or her education, inspiration, and activities.

Responding

1. Possible Response Students might suggest that stopping at local restaurants helps to build the Harlem economy, and gives visitors a "taste" of the community.

2. Responses will vary but should be supported with specific topics that students expect to find out about on the tour they choose.

Career Connection

After the stock market crash of 1929, Harlem experienced many years of economic decline, and lost much of its reputation as a vibrant cultural center. Tour director and educator Larcelia Kebe is working to transform Harlem's image and rejuvenate the community.

Tour Director Shows Off

Harlem Treasures

In the fall of 1982 I started Harlem, Your Way! Tours Unlimited Incorporated. I was motivated to start my business because, first, I wanted to participate in the new Harlem Renaissance. Also, as an educator and administrator—I'm an elementary school principal—I looked at the very negative press Harlem had received for decades and I wanted to do something positive to dispel some of those negative images. Third, I wanted to let people know of the treasures here in Harlem.

We specialize in walking tours so that people can really see the community. A popular tour for New Yorkers is the Brownstone Tour and Workshop. I had bought and started restoring a brownstone myself in 1982. I did all the wrong things. So I take people on a tour of four or five restored brownstones in the neighborhood, and the owners talk about their homes. Afterwards we come back to my house for a workshop. Building inspectors, attorneys, architects, and designers speak. The workshops put participants closer to their dream of owning a brownstone.

Most of my clients on other kinds of tours are Europeans. Gospel tours are popular with them. They've heard of the music and want to listen to it and experience the worship service themselves. Services in European churches are not so participatory. But at a service at a Baptist church here in Harlem, the people clap, shout, talk, sing—they feel the spirit and participate.

We have a lot of history here. We have the Jumel mansion on a tour. General Washington conducted some battles of the Revolutionary War from there. The mansion is important to Harlem's history, but the furnishings are being removed and taken to museums. This is happening to several of our historical sites. The community is fighting against this.

I give a Black History Walking Tour of Harlem in February. Another special tour is A Look at the World of Malcolm X.

I feel very strongly about circulating money in the community. My guides are people of color from the community. We try to stop at local restaurants.

Many of us are hopeful about the future of Harlem. Many positive things are happening.

Larcelia Kebe

Responding

1. Why do you suppose it is so important to Larcelia Kebe to hire guides from the community and stop at local restaurants?

2. Imagine you are going to take a Harlem, Your Way! tour. What kind of tour do you want to take, and what do you want to see and do?

MINI-LESSON: SPEAKING AND LISTENING

Demonstrate Poise and Confidence

Teach Being a tour guide is like being a teacher—the guide also has to command the attention of a group and give the group information in an interesting manner. Unlike a teacher, a guide has a different class every day and needs to catch the group's attention right away. Like a teacher, a guide should speak clearly and succinctly.

Activity Idea Have each student design a tour of some aspect of his or her community. Have them present the spoken part of the tour to the class, enriching their information with interesting, little-known facts and history. Suggest that even if they don't feel completely confident, acting confident will improve their public speaking.

Writing Workshop

Calling All Artists

Assignment During the Harlem Renaissance, Harlem artists wrote to encourage other talented artists from around the country to come join them. Now put yourself in the position of one of these Harlem artists.

WRITER'S BLUEPRINT

Product	A persuasive letter
Purpose	To encourage another artist to come to Harlem
Audience	A person living during the Harlem Renaissance who is skilled in one of the fine arts
Specs	As the writer of an effective letter, you should:

❏ Choose an African-American artist (painter, sculptor, writer, dancer, musician, etc.) who actually lived in Harlem during the Harlem Renaissance. You will write your letter as if you were this artist.

❏ Choose another artist living elsewhere to write to: a well-known artist who actually lived during this era, or a fictitious African-American artist you create.

❏ Compose a letter in which you try to persuade this artist to move to Harlem. Write in a tone suitable to your reader, a fellow artist you have met once, briefly. Emphasize the advantages of Harlem's thriving arts community, economic opportunities, exciting night life, and other advantages. Use examples of real people, places, and activities to strengthen your case, including quotations from the literature.

❏ Anticipate reasons why someone might not want to move to Harlem, and counter them with logical arguments.

❏ Close by stressing what a welcome addition this artist would be to the arts community of Harlem.

❏ Follow the rules of grammar, usage, spelling, and mechanics. Avoid confusing adjectives with adverbs.

Writing Workshop   543

Writing Workshop

WRITER'S BLUEPRINT
Specs

The Specs in the Writer's Blueprint address these writing and thinking skills:

- assuming another person's point of view
- using appropriate tone
- using friendly letter format
- presenting an argument
- using persuasive reasons
- anticipating objections
- providing counter-arguments
- delivering praise
- using adjectives and adverbs correctly

These Specs serve as your lesson objectives, and they form the basis for the **Assessment Criteria Specs** for a superior paper, which appear on the final TE page for this lesson. You might want to read through the Assessment Criteria Specs with students when you begin the lesson.

Linking Literature to Writing

Lead a discussion about the many types of artists living in Harlem during this period. Have students speculate about why these artists would want to encourage other artists to join the community.

WRITING WORKSHOP OVERVIEW

Product
Persuasive writing: A persuasive letter

Prewriting
Review the literature—Anticipate possible objections—Choose a real artist—Plan your letter
Unit 5 Resource Book
Prewriting Worksheets pp. 75–76

Drafting
Before you draft—As you draft
Transparency Collection
Student Models for Writing Workshop 17, 18

Revising
Exchange drafts—Strategy: Using Appropriate Tone
Unit 5 Resource Book
Revising Worksheet p. 77

Editing
Ask a partner—Strategy: Using Adjectives and Adverbs Correctly
Unit 5 Resource Book
Grammar Worksheet p. 78
Grammar Check Test p. 79

Presenting
Read and Discuss
Poster

Looking Back
Self-evaluate—Reflect—For Your Working Portfolio
Unit 5 Resource Book
Assessment Worksheet p. 80
Transparency Collection
Fine Art Writing Prompt 9

Revising Strategy: Using Appropriate Tone

Have students work with a partner. Have one student read a letter aloud; then have the listener write down three descriptive words about the tone of the letter.

For additional support, see the mini-lesson at the bottom of page 544 and the worksheet referenced below.

Unit 5 Resource Book
Revising Worksheet, p. 77

Connections to
Writer's Resource

Refer to the Grammar, Usage, and Mechanics Handbook on Writer's Resource.

STEP 4 EDITING
Ask a partner (Peer assessment)

Review some basic proofreading marks with students that should be used in indicating changes on the drafts. Briefly discuss how students can determine whether an adjective or an adverb is needed as a modifier. Stress reading aloud and listening for whether a given word sounds right to the ear.

Revising Strategy

Using Appropriate Tone

As you reread your letter, consider how well its tone suits your audience and purpose. Aim to be enthusiastic and friendly, but not be too informal. These examples show how you can modify tone through word choice and sentence structure.

INAPPROPRIATE: bossy, disrespectful
Hey, you have <u>got</u> to head to Harlem and check out the art scene here . . .

INAPPROPRIATE: formal, pretentious
It is my pleasure to acquaint you with the advantages inherent in the environs of our fair city . . .

APPROPRIATE: warm, but respectful
I would like to invite you to join our thriving arts community here in Harlem . . .

Notice how the writer of the paragraph below revised her writing to make it more respectful.

○ *I feel that if you and your wife take the time to consider Harlem's*
~~Now that you've heard what I have to say, you've just got to~~
many advantages, you'll find yourself heading our way.
~~head north and join us. Any other decision would be ridiculous!~~

○ Speaking from personal experience, I can tell you that Harlem is an

incredible place to live. If I can provide any more information, just

○ let me know. Hope to hear from you soon!

STEP 4 EDITING

Ask a partner to review your revised draft before you edit. When you edit, watch for errors in grammar, usage, spelling, and mechanics. Make sure you haven't confused adjectives and adverbs.

MINI-LESSON: GRAMMAR

Using Adjectives and Adverbs Correctly

Write the sentence "It is a beautiful day." on the board and ask students to explain the use of *beautiful* (adjective modifying *day*). Then write the following sentences and have students make necessary corrections and explain why the corrections are necessary.

1. The sun is *real* bright today. (*really*—adverb modifying *bright*)

2. Adam wrote *badly* today. (correct—adverb modifying *wrote*)

3. Alice plays the violin *good*. (*well*—adverb modifying *plays*)

4. The mayor spoke *strongly* against the issue. (correct—adverb modifying *spoke*)

5. The wind blew *fierce* against the window. (*fiercely*—adverb modifying *blew*)

Unit 5 Resource Book
Grammar Worksheet p. 78
Grammar Check Test p. 79

Editing Strategy

Using Adjectives and Adverbs Correctly

Remember that adjectives modify nouns and that adverbs modify verbs, adjectives, and other adverbs. If you're unsure whether to use an adjective or an adverb, look at the word being modified.

FOR REFERENCE
For more information on adjectives and adverbs, see the Language and Grammar Handbook at the back of this text.

Don't write:	You could <u>live</u> quite <u>happy</u> here.
Write:	You could <u>live</u> quite <u>happily</u> here.
Don't write:	The <u>bakeries</u> down the street smell <u>deliciously</u>.
Write:	The <u>bakeries</u> down the street smell <u>delicious</u>.
Don't write:	The artists here are <u>real supportive</u>.
Write:	The artists here are <u>really supportive</u>.

STEP 5 PRESENTING

Consider these ideas for presenting your letter:

- Read your letters to each other in a small group and discuss reasons you found most persuasive and why.

- Design a poster that incorporates ideas from your letter.

STEP 6 LOOKING BACK

Self-evaluate. Look back at the Writer's Blueprint and give yourself a score on each item, from 6 (superior) to 1 (inadequate).

Reflect. Think about what you learned from writing your letter as you write answers to these questions:

✔ What are some persuasive techniques that you used in this assignment that you might use in your personal life?

✔ Do you think you would have liked living in Harlem during this period if you had been an African-American artist? Why or why not?

For Your Working Portfolio Add your persuasive letter and your reflection responses to your working portfolio.

Writing Workshop **547**

ASSESSMENT CRITERIA SPECS

Here are the criteria for a superior paper. A full six-level rubric for this paper appears on the *Assessment Worksheet* referenced below.

6 Superior   The writer of a 6 paper impressively meets these criteria:

- Is presented as a letter written from one artist who lived during the Harlem Renaissance to another.

- Is written in a tone that is at once friendly and respectful.

- Provides a variety of persuasive reasons why the reader should move to Harlem and presents them in a convincing manner.

- Backs up these reasons by citing real aspects of Harlem, including quotations from the literature.

- Effectively counters possible objections.

- Concludes with a warm, hopeful welcome.

- Uses standard letter format.

- Makes few, if any, mistakes in grammar, usage, mechanics, and spelling. Uses adjectives and adverbs correctly.

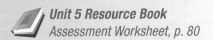

Unit 5 Resource Book
Assessment Worksheet, p. 80

Editing Strategy: Using Adjectives and Adverbs Correctly

Have students underline adjectives and adverbs to check for correct use.

For additional support, see the mini-lesson at the bottom of the previous page and the worksheets referenced below.

Unit 5 Resource Book
Grammar Worksheet, p. 78
Grammar Check Test, p. 79

Connections to
Writer's Resource

Refer to the Grammar, Usage, and Mechanics Handbook on Writer's Resource.

STEP 5 PRESENTING
Read and Discuss

Have students reflect on the artists chosen as letter writers before listening to the letters.

Poster

Have students use color, pictures, and graphics to enhance the letter details.

STEP 6 LOOKING BACK
Self-evaluate

The *Assessment Criteria Specs* at the bottom of this page are for a superior paper. You might want to post these in the classroom. Students can then evaluate themselves based on these criteria. For a complete scoring rubric, use the *Assessment Worksheet* referenced below.

Unit 5 Resource Book
Assessment Worksheet, p. 80

Reflect

You may want to let students discuss the two checked questions in a group before they write their individual responses.

To further explore the theme, use the Fine Art Transparency referenced below.

Transparency Collection
Fine Art Writing Prompt 9

547

Beyond Print

Teaching Objectives

- To improve public speaking skills
- To reflect upon and share information about the art of the Harlem Renaissance

Curricular Connection: Effective Speaking

You can use the material in this article to help students effectively speak about what they have learned of the conveyance of messages through art.

Introduce

Ask students what they think makes an effective speaker. Have they heard a speaker who captured their attention? Discuss why that person's speech interested them.

Activity Option

Students can find other poems or essays by Harlem Renaissance writers and deliver them to the class using the speaking strategies described on this page.

Students might benefit from recording their speeches beforehand on audio or videotape in order to identify which strategies they use well and which they would like to work on.

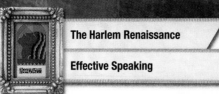
Beyond Print

Speaking Your Mind

In this Harlem Renaissance section you've seen the ideas of some of the most famous African Americans of the time expressed in the form of essays, poetry, and art. Another important way to communicate ideas is to give a speech. When giving a speech, the following strategies can help you capture and keep your audience's attention:

Rehearse Practice your speech out loud more than once. Not only does practice help you become more familiar with your material, it lets you try out different gestures and different kinds of vocal emphasis.

Get organized If you spend the first minute or so shuffling your notes, your audience may get bored and stop paying attention. Get everything in order before you walk to the front of the classroom or the stage.

Stand up straight Good posture actually helps you project your voice better. Stand on both feet so that you are balanced. If there is a desk or podium you may grasp it—lightly—but *don't* lean your weight on it.

Look at your audience Talk to your audience, not to your notes, the podium, or the floor. Pick one person and direct a sentence or two right at her or him; then pick another and another, and so on.

Speak loudly and clearly Your speech is worthless if your audience can't hear you. Try to project your voice to the back wall of the room.

Avoid meaningless vocalisms It's tempting to fill in moments of silence with *Ummm* or *Uhhh,* which may be distracting to an audience. You may not be able to avoid these altogether, but try.

Make simple, meaningful gestures While making some gestures is preferable to standing stock still, keep your gestures simple and natural.

Activity Option

Sharing Your Thoughts Choose one of the essays, poems, or artworks from this Harlem Renaissance section to react to in a five-minute speech. Explain why you like or dislike the work, what you think the artist's message is, and, if appropriate, whether you agree with the artist. Use the strategies listed above.

ANOTHER APPROACH

Professionally Speaking

Observing and then imitating a professional speaker can teach students helpful speech-making strategies. It also allows students to practice making speeches without feeling personally judged.

Encourage students to watch a video or TV broadcast of a well-known public speaker, such as a politician, news anchor, or celebrity, and evaluate the speaker using the strategies listed on page 548 as a guide. Then have students impersonate the speaker, using the speaker's words and style to demonstrate professional strategies to classmates.

Multicultural Connections

Individuality

Part One: Beyond the Limits The women in this literature convey through their actions the importance of being able to express one's individuality, whether the surrounding community or culture supports such expression or not. Mrs. Mallard in "The Story of an Hour" and Mrs. Wright in *Trifles* are victims of suppressed individuality. Sarah in "The Revolt of 'Mother'" finally takes matters into her own hands after years of suppressing her own thoughts and desires, and Ida B. Wells stands up for what she believes is right even when everyone around her seems to think she's wrong.

■ Which of these women do you think is most effective in coping with forces that suppress individuality? The least effective?

Group

Part Two: The Harlem Renaissance One of the great legacies of the Harlem Renaissance was to revitalize and reassert the strength, creativity, and pride in being African American. The artists and writers of the Harlem Renaissance helped forge a new group identity while expressing their individual talents as well. James Weldon Johnson celebrates Harlem as "the greatest Negro city in the world," Claude McKay's poem proclaims the honor and necessity of fighting back against oppressors, and Langston Hughes, Countee Cullen, and Zora Neale Hurston offer hope for the future.

■ How do you think the work of the artists and writers of this period affected and influenced African Americans across the United States?

Activities

1. Why is it sometimes hard to just "be yourself"? Considering the experiences of the women in the "Beyond the Limits" selections, along with your own experiences, work with a group to create a chart of forces in society that discourage individuality. For each "force," list a recommendation that can be used to preserve individuality.

2. What family, social, community, and cultural groups are you part of? Choose one of the groups you identify with and tell about it, including the impact the group has had on your life.

549

Unit Wrap-Up

MULTICULTURAL CONNECTION

While students are probably familiar with group movements of women and African Americans as they struggle for equal rights, it may be helpful to discuss what individuality means to different people. The following ideas and questions may facilitate discussion.

Individuality

- A woman's individuality was less important than her role as mother, wife, and homemaker.
- Expressing individuality sometimes brings improvements.

Possible Responses Ida B. Wells-Barnett effectively communicated the social injustice of lynching. The women in "Trifles" and "The Story of an Hour" destroyed themselves before gaining their individuality.

Group

- A group is a number of individuals having some unifying relationship.
- People who work together toward the same goal have more impact than a single individual.

Possible Response Their powerful example encouraged others to express their creative impulses and fostered a sense of pride in their community.

Activities

Activity 1 Suggest that students begin their charts with ideas on peer pressure and how it relates to them. Ask students how certain people in their peer groups might inhibit an individual from taking an action that might be right for him or her.

Activity 2 After students talk about the groups to which they belong, discuss times when they have asserted themselves as individuals within their groups.

Media

Suggest to students that sharing ideas for presentation of their biographies with a group will enhance their presentations.

Connections to AuthorWorks

Information for completing this project can be found on the AuthorWorks CD-ROM series.

Writing

After students have traded quizzes with their partners, have each pair choose several pertinent questions to ask the class. Conduct an open discussion and encourage all students to participate and contribute their individual thoughts on the subject.

Edutainment

Students' games might follow the format of the television show, *Jeopardy*. The answer is given first to the contestants who then supply the question, for example, Answer: The first modern jazz band ever heard in New York. Question: Who were The Memphis Students?

Art

After students have presented their collages to the class, form an exhibit in the classroom of all the work along with the writing each illustrates. Students might discuss the individual collages and express their opinions on how each one affects them.

Unit Test

Unit 5 Resource Book
New Selection, pp. 81–88
Test 1, pp. 89–90
Test 2, pp. 91–96

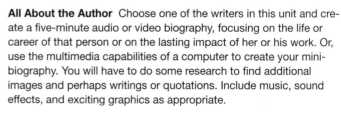

Independent and Group Projects

Media

All About the Author Choose one of the writers in this unit and create a five-minute audio or video biography, focusing on the life or career of that person or on the lasting impact of her or his work. Or, use the multimedia capabilities of a computer to create your mini-biography. You will have to do some research to find additional images and perhaps writings or quotations. Include music, sound effects, and exciting graphics as appropriate.

Writing

Quiz Exchange Working with a partner, write a thirty-question quiz that tests students' knowledge of the literature in Unit 5. Ask questions that test knowledge of important themes, events, characters, and so on, rather than minor details. When you've finished writing your questions, write an answer key with suggested responses. Trade your quiz with a partner's, and see how many of his or her questions you can answer.

Entertainment

Harlem Renaissance: The Game Create a board game, trivia game, video game or any other kind of game you wish that focuses on one or more aspects of the Harlem Renaissance. The purpose of the game, along with having fun, should be to educate the players about the personalities and events of the Harlem Renaissance.

Art

I SEE What You Mean The authors and poets in this unit use words to express their thoughts and feelings. Pick a selection that had a particular impact on you and translate the words into images. Create a collage of pictures, photographs, and objects that you feel convey the sentiments of the writer. Explain your collage to your class.

550

The SEARCH *for* EQUALITY

THEMES IN AMERICAN LITERATURE

About Thomas Jefferson

Thomas Jefferson (1743–1826) stated his commitment to democracy in these words: "I have sworn on the altar of God, eternal hostility against every form of tyranny over the mind of man."

About Elizabeth Cady Stanton

Elizabeth Cady Stanton (1815–1902) helped call the Seneca Falls Convention in 1848. The convention, held in Seneca Falls, New York, passed resolutions favoring women's rights, including the right to vote.

About the 15th Amendment

To check a backlash in the Reconstruction South aimed at destroying political gains made by African Americans after the Civil War, Congress passed the 15th Amendment to preserve voting rights for black males and electoral majorities for the Republican Party.

About the 19th Amendment

Although the Progressive-Era idealism of the early twentieth century was declining by 1920, reform triumphed in one area with the ratification of the 19th Amendment, granting women the right to vote.

About the 26th Amendment

In nine weeks in 1971—and in time for the 1972 presidential election—the required 38 states ratified the 26th Amendment, giving Americans between the ages of 18 and 21 the right to vote.

The SEARCH *for* EQUALITY

Ralph Waldo Emerson once observed that the schoolyard boast "I'm as good as you be," contained the essence of the Declaration of Independence. Human equality is the first of the "self-evident" truths recognized by the Declaration. Of course, the society that produced this document was still a very unequal one, with few civil rights for women and none for American Indians or enslaved African Americans. America's subsequent history has been a struggle to expand our notions of equality to include all Americans.

The right of citizens of the United States to vote shall not be denied or abridged by the United States or by any state on account of race, color, or previous condition of servitude.

15th Amendment (1870)

The right of citizens of the United States to vote shall not be denied or abridged by the United States or by any state on account of sex.

19th Amendment (1920)

The right of citizens of the United States, who are eighteen years or older, to vote shall not be denied or abridged by the United States or by any state on account of age.

26th Amendment (1971)

WE HOLD THESE TRUTHS TO BE SELF-EVIDENT: THAT ALL MEN ARE CREATED EQUAL; THAT THEY ARE ENDOWED BY THEIR CREATOR WITH CERTAIN UNALIENABLE RIGHTS; THAT AMONG THESE ARE LIFE, LIBERTY, AND THE PURSUIT OF HAPPINESS.

Thomas Jefferson, The Declaration of Independence (1776)

We hold these truths to be self-evident: that all men and women are created equal . . . .

Elizabeth Cady Stanton, Seneca Falls Declaration of Sentiments (1848)

552

THEME LINK TO THE LITERATURE

Some other selections in the text that deal with the theme of the search for equality are the following:

- from The Iroquois Constitution (p. 158)
- from The American Crisis (p. 170)
- from Speech in the Virginia Convention (p. 172)
- The Declaration of Independence (p. 178)
- Letter to John Adams (p. 184)
- Petition to the Massachusetts General Assembly (p. 186)

- from *Civil Disobedience* (p. 231)
- Ain't I a Woman? (p. 237)
- from What the Black Man Wants (p. 328)
- Sympathy (p. 370)
- If We Must Die (p. 525)
- How It Feels to Be Colored Me (p. 533)
- from Letter from a Birmingham Jail (p. 801)
- from *The Autobiography of Malcolm X* (p. 806)

George Caleb Bingham, Stump Speaking. *Done in the early 1850s, this is one of a series of paintings by Bingham depicting a local election in Missouri.*

About Alexis de Tocqueville

Alexis de Tocqueville (1805–1859), a Frenchman, visited the United States in the 1830s to examine model prisons that had been established in Philadelphia and Auburn, New York. He broadened his study of American society, becoming the most famous foreign observer of Jacksonian Democracy.

About Hector St. Jean de Crèvecoeur

Born in France, Crèvecoeur settled on a frontier farm in New York. Unwilling to join either party in the Revolution, he left for England in 1780, returning after the war to discover that his wife had been killed and his farm burned in an Indian raid.

No novelty in the United States struck me more vividly during my stay here than the equality of conditions. It is easy to see the immense influence of this basic fact on the whole course of society. It gives a particular turn to public opinion and a particular twist to the laws, new maxims to those who govern and particular habits to the governed.

Alexis de Tocqueville, Democracy in America *(1835)*

What, then, is the American, this new man? He is neither an European nor the descendent of an European; hence that strange mixture of blood, which you will find in no other country. I could point out to you a family whose grandfather was an Englishman, whose wife was Dutch, whose son married a French woman, and whose present four sons have four wives of different nations. . . . Here individuals of all nations are melted into a new race of men, whose labors and posterity will one day cause great changes in the world.

Hector St. Jean de Crèvecoeur,
Letters from an American Farmer *(1782)*

BUILDING ENGLISH PROFICIENCY

Debating the ERA

To help students explore the role of the U.S. Constitution in the American search for equality, you might invite them to discuss whether or not the United States needs the Equal Rights Amendment (ERA). Explain that the ERA was intended to protect women from discrimination on the basis of their sex. Although the ERA was passed by Congress in 1972, it was not ratified by the required three-quarters of the states. The class can discuss questions such as these:

1. If the ERA had been ratified, would there be less discrimination against women in American society today?

2. Do American women need constitutional safeguards like the ERA to protect their rights today?

About the Spirituals

Spirituals were religious folk songs of African Americans held in slavery. Themes of these songs include the weariness, sorrows, and pain of this world, the peace and joy of the life to come, and quests for freedom. In his essay "The Sorrow Songs" in *The Souls of Black Folk* (1903), W. E. B. Du Bois observes, "The Negro folk-song—the rhythmic cry of the slave—stands today not simply as the sole American music, but as the most beautiful expression of human experience born this side the seas."

About the Underground Railroad

The spiritual "Follow the Drinking Gourd" was used by African Americans escaping from slavery in the South to guide themselves to freedom in Canada via the "Underground Railroad," a system of escape routes run by people opposed to slavery. These people hid runaways by day and led them by night from one "station" to the next.

About the 54th Massachusetts

Almost 200,000 African Americans, most of them newly freed slaves, served in the Union armies and made a vital contribution to Northern victory. Frederick Douglass's sons Lewis and Charles served in the 54th Massachusetts Regiment and survived its costly repulse at Fort Wagner.

OH, FREEDOM!

Oh, Freedom!
Oh, Freedom!
Oh, Freedom over me!
And before I'd be a slave,
I'd be buried in my grave,
And go home to my Lord and be
free! . . .

African American Spiritual (late 1800s)

FOLLOW THE DRINKING GOURD

When the sun comes back and the first quail calls,
Follow the drinking gourd.1
The old man is a-waitin' for to carry you to freedom
If you follow the drinking gourd.

CHORUS
Follow the drinking gourd,
Follow the drinking gourd,
For the old man is a-waitin' for to carry you to freedom
If you follow the drinking gourd.

The riverbank will make a mighty good road,
The dead trees will show you the way,
And left foot, peg foot, travelling on
Just you follow the drinking gourd.

Now the river ends between two hills,
Follow the drinking gourd.
And there's another river on the other side,
Follow the drinking gourd.

Where the little river meets the great big river,
Follow the drinking gourd.
The old man is a-waitin' for to carry you to freedom,
If you follow the drinking gourd.

African American spiritual (mid–1800s)

1. **the drinking gourd,** dialect variant for the constellation also known as the Big Dipper, used by runaway slaves to guide them north.

The Price of Freedom

Lewis Douglass, son of reformer Frederick Douglass, served with the 54th Massachusetts Regiment, the first African American unit recruited by the Union. Lewis Douglass wrote to his wife after the 54th had been involved on July 18, 1863 in a bloody assault on Fort Wagner, a Confederate battery defending Charleston, South Carolina.

John Steuart Curry, Tragic Prelude. Done between 1937 and 1942, Curry's painting is dominated by the central figure of antislavery radical John Brown.

MINI-LESSON: READING/THINKING SKILLS

Recognize Values

Readers can recognize the values of writers, or people written about, by identifying statements based on deeply held beliefs or philosophies.

Teach Point out to students that the African American spirituals and Lewis Douglass's letter both reflect a belief that freedom is worth dying for. Ask them identify lines that indicate this value.

Activity Idea Have students create a banner for an antislavery society or a regimental flag for the 54th Massachusetts that conveys the importance of freedom. *(Possible response: The antislavery society banner might incorporate an image of the Big Dipper and the motto "Oh, Freedom!")*

My dear Amelia:
I have been in two fights, and am unhurt. I am about to go in another I believe tonight. Our men fought well on both occasions. The last was desperate. We charged that terrible battery on Morris island known as Fort Wagner, and were repulsed.... Jacob Carter is missing, Charles Reason wounded, Charles Whiting, Charles Creamer all wounded.

I escaped unhurt from amidst that perfect hail of shot and shell. It was terrible. I need not particularize, the papers will give a better [account] than I have time to give. My thoughts are with you often, you are as dear as ever, be good to remember it as I no doubt you will. As I said before we are on the eve of another fight and I am very busy and have just snatched a moment to write you. I must necessarily be brief. Should I fall in the next fight killed or wounded I hope I fall with my face to the foe.

This regiment has established its reputation as a fighting regiment, not a man flinched, though it was a trying time. Men fell all around me. A shell would explode and clear a space of twenty feet. Our men would close up again, but it was no use, we had to retreat, which was a very hazardous undertaking. How I got out of that fight alive I cannot tell, but I am here.

My Dear girl I hope to see you again. I must bid you farewell should I be killed. Remember if I die I die in a good cause. I wish we had a hundred thousand colored troops we would put an end to this war.

Good Bye to all. Your own loving—Write soon—

Lewis

Art Study

Visual Literacy Along with such artists as Grant Wood and Thomas Hart Benton, John Steuart Curry (1897–1946), was one of the principal American Regionalist painters of the 1930s, who turned away from European influences and sought artistic inspiration in the life of the rural Midwest and South. In his painting *Tragic Prelude*, Curry assigns a central role to John Brown in the coming of the Civil War.

Question What view of the moral character of John Brown is reflected in *Tragic Prelude*? (Possible responses: Curry's vision of Brown—with the Bible in one hand and a rifle in the other—combines good and evil; by associating Brown with forces of nature, like the tornado, Curry may be suggesting that the antislavery radical was a force beyond good or evil.)

BUILDING ENGLISH PROFICIENCY

Understanding Historical References

Some students may need help recognizing the meaning or importance of names or expressions on these pages that refer to American historical events. You might ask questions about them.

• The constellation—or group of stars that forms a shape—known as the Drinking Gourd or the Big Dipper also is called Ursa Major (Latin for the Great Bear). Why might people of the past have used the expression *drinking gourd* to refer to a dipper for water? *(Gourds, or dried fruit rinds, were used as dippers to scoop up and drink water.)*

• Who were the Union and Confederate sides in the Civil War? *(The Union was the United States, also known as the North; the Confederate army, also known as the South and the Rebels, fought for the Confederate States of America.)*

• A *battery* is a military unit that uses large mounted cannons and other guns. In Lewis Douglass's letter, he mentions explosive shells so powerful that they cleared spaces of twenty feet. What does he mean when he says that, if he dies during battle, he hopes he falls "with my face to the foe"? *(If he dies, he wants to die still fighting, rather than turning away from the enemy.)*

About Mary Elizabeth Lease and Populism

In the late 1800s, falling agricultural prices and rising costs forced many American farmers into debt. In 1892 farmers and laborers in the Midwest founded the People's, or Populist, party to advance their aims, which included federal regulation of the banks that held farm mortgages and frequently foreclosed on them. In the speech from which this passage is taken, Mary Elizabeth Lease (1853–1933)—a Populist radical once referred to as "Patrick Henry in petticoats"—demanded an end to "the accursed foreclosure system." She claimed that in Kansas "a tract thirty miles wide and ninety miles long" had been seized by loan companies in that year alone.

About Harlan Country

In 1931, with the Depression reducing the demand for coal, miners in Harlan County struck, to force mine owners to maintain wage rates. Both sides resorted to violence, and several miners were killed. It was against the background of these events that Florence Reece, the wife of a union leader, wrote her famous song, "Which Side Are You On?"

"RAISE LESS CORN AND MORE HELL!"

Mary Elizabeth Lease was a Populist famous for her fiery speeches to farmers.

This is a nation of inconsistencies. The Puritans fleeing from oppression became oppressors. We fought England for our liberty and put chains on four millions of blacks. We wiped out slavery and by our tariff laws and national banks began a system of white wage slavery worse than the first. Wall Street owns the country. It is no longer a government of the people, by the people, and for the people, but a government of Wall Street, by Wall Street, and for Wall Street. The great common people of this country are slaves, and monopoly is the master. . . . Money rules, and our . . . laws are the output of a system, which clothes rascals in robes and honesty in rags.

Mary Elizabeth Lease (1890)

WHICH SIDE ARE YOU ON?

Come all of you good workers,
Good news to you I'll tell
Of how the good old union
Has come in here to dwell.

Chorus:
Which side are you on?
Which side are you on?
Which side are you on?
Which side are you on?

My daddy was a miner
And I'm a miner's son,
And I'll stick with the union
Till every battle's won.

They say in Harlan County[1]
There are no neutrals there;
You'll either be a union man
Or a thug for J. H. Blair.[2]

Oh, workers, can you stand it?
Oh, tell me how you can.
Will you be a lousy scab[3]
Or will you be a man?

Don't scab for the bosses,
Don't listen to their lies.
Us poor folks haven't got a chance
Unless we organize.

Florence Reece (1931)

This anti-labor cartoon by Frederick Opper appeared in 1887.

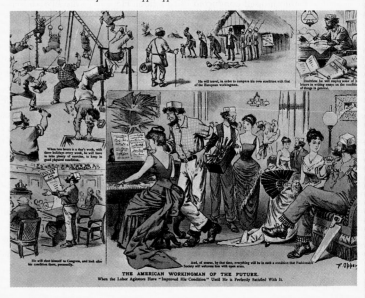

THE AMERICAN WORKINGMAN OF THE FUTURE.
When the Labor Agitators Have "Improved His Condition" Until He is Perfectly Satisfied With It.

1. **Harlan County.** Kentucky's Harlan County was the scene of bitter and frequently violent labor disputes between coal-mine operators and miners.
2. **J. H. Blair,** High Sheriff of Harlan County.
3. **scab,** non-union worker brought in to break a strike.

MINI-LESSON: READING/THINKING SKILLS

Recognize Propaganda Techniques

Recognizing propaganda techniques involves detecting systematic efforts to persuade an audience to believe or do something.

Teach Point out that political cartoons are editorials in picture form. They often employ propaganda techniques to express a point of view. Ask them to identify details in Frederick Opper's cartoon above that reflect an anti-labor outlook. *(Possible responses: the caption, which uses loaded language such as "labor agitators"; the images depicting laborers engaging in absurdly inappropriate "upper-class" pastimes)*

Activity Idea Invite students to create cartoons reflecting the point of view of either Mary Elizabeth Lease or Florence Reese. *(Sample response: an image of "Wall Street" as a huge, bloated figure in formal dress holding one end of a long chain to which many tiny figures of farmers and laborers in rags are shackled)*

Paul Davis, poster

I am 34 years old and I try to organize for the United Farm Workers.... But until two years ago, my world was still very small. I would read all these things in the papers about Cesar Chavez[1] and I would denounce him because I still had that thing about becoming a first-class patriotic citizen.... It wasn't until Chavez came to Salinas[2] where I was working in the fields, that I saw what a beautiful man he was. I went to this rally, I still intended to stay with the company. But something—I don't know—I was close to the workers. They couldn't speak English and wanted me to be their spokesman in favor of going on strike. I don't know—I just got caught up with it all, the beautiful feeling of solidarity.

Roberto Acuna (early 1970s)

1. **Cesar Chavez** (1927–1993), Chicano labor organizer who founded the United Farm Workers in 1962.

2. **Salinas,** a city in west central California.

About the United Farm Workers and Roberto Acuna

In 1965 Mexican American labor organizer Cesar Chavez (1927–1993) and his United Farm Workers began a long, bitter strike against the California grape growers. The issues of the strike had been the very low wages, the long hours, and the primitive— and often unhealthy—working conditions that were typical for farm laborers. By mid-1970, most of the growers had begun signing contracts with the union. This account by Roberto Acuna, a lettuce picker who became an organizer for the United Farm Workers, is from Studs Terkel's oral history *Working* (1974).

Art Study

Visual Literacy   This poster advertising a concert to benefit the striking grape workers was illustrated by artist Paul Davis.

Question   What adjectives might you choose to describe the image of the farm worker depicted on the poster? *(Possible responses: young, handsome, earnest, idealistic, heroic, Latino, sad, vulnerable)*

559

BUILDING ENGLISH PROFICIENCY

Interpreting a Poster

Students may interpret various details of the poster on page 559. The three most prominent lines are slogans in Spanish, meaning "Long live Chavez" (Cesar Chavez), "Long live the cause," and "Long live (or "Success to) the strike." What do the following details suggest about the intended audience?

• The poster uses Spanish and English, but the performance information is given in English.

• The performers included comedian Alan King and the singers Peter, Paul, and Mary, who performed primarily in English.

• The Spanish slogans on the poster are short and may have been familiar to many Americans of various language backgrounds, especially those who cared about labor issues in the early 1970s.

About Brown v. Board of Education

In 1954 the U.S. Supreme Court made a landmark decision in a court case called *Brown* v. *Board of Education of Topeka*, ruling that separate schools for black students and white students were unconstitutional. The *Brown* decision reversed the 1896 precedent-setting case *Plessy* v. *Ferguson,* which had stated that "separate but equal" public facilities for black and white people did not violate the 14th Amendment.

About Mary Crow Dog

Besieged by hundreds of law enforcement officers, the American Indians who occupied Wounded Knee held out for 71 days before surrendering. One Indian at Wounded Knee was Mary Crow Dog (born 1953), a Lakota Sioux. Pregnant during the siege, she delivered her child during one of the firefights. This excerpt is from her book *Lakota Women* (1973).

About Eleanor Roosevelt

A close adviser to her husband, President Franklin Roosevelt, Eleanor Roosevelt (1884–1962) helped develop guidelines for New Deal programs. A tireless humanitarian, she championed the causes of underprivileged and minority groups.

To separate [minority children] from others of similar age and qualifications solely because of their race generates a feeling of inferiority as to their status in the community that may affect their hearts and minds in a way unlikely ever to be undone. . . .

We conclude that in the field of public education, the doctrine of "separate but equal" has no place. . . .

U.S. Supreme Court, Brown *decision*

Jim Domke, The Indian and the Buffalo *(date?)*

RETURN TO WOUNDED KNEE

In early 1973, a group of American Indians seized the tiny town of Wounded Knee, South Dakota, site of an 1890 massacre of hundreds of Sioux by U.S. cavalry, to dramatize Indian grievances.

On February 27, 1973, we stood on the hill where the fate of the old Sioux Nation, Sitting Bull's and Crazy Horse's[1] nation, had been decided, and where we, ourselves, came face to face with our fate. . . . We all felt the presence of the spirits of those lying close by in the long ditch,[2] wondering whether we were about to join them, wondering when the marshals would arrive. . . . The young men tied eagle feathers to their braids, no longer unemployed kids, juvenile delinquents, or winos, but warriors.

Mary Crow Dog (1973)

No one can make you feel inferior without your consent.

Eleanor Roosevelt (1937)

1. **Sitting Bull** (1834–1890), **Crazy Horse** (1849–1877), Sioux leaders who defeated General Custer in 1876 at the Battle of Little Big Horn.

2. **ditch,** mass grave where the bodies of those killed at Wounded Knee in 1890 are buried.

MINI-LESSON: READING/THINKING SKILLS

Understand Visual Symbolism

To understand visual symbolism, viewers identify pictorial elements that signify something relatively abstract, such as a concept or idea.

Teach Explain that the image of the American Indian on Jim Domke's painting comes from the so-called "Buffalo Nickel," a U.S. coin minted from 1913 to 1938 that featured the head of an American Indian on one side and a buffalo on the other.

Activity Idea Have students hold a panel discussion exploring the following questions:

• The title of the painting is *The Indian and the Buffalo.* Why is no buffalo shown? *(Possible responses: The buffalo would be on the reverse side of the coin. The buffalo—and the Indian way of life it supported—had been nearly destroyed.)*

• Why did the artist employ an image of an Indian from a coin? *(Possible responses: The image is easily recognizable. It evokes knowledge of history. Some people don't recognize Native Americans in the population today.)*

• Given the visual symbolism of the painting, are the words "Red Power" meant to be taken ironically? Why or why not? *(Possible responses: Yes, because many Indians do not have great power in our era; no, because American Indians are striving to achieve and use power)*

AFFIRMATIVE ACTION: PRO AND CON

Perhaps the most divisive civil rights issue of the recent past has been affirmative action. Do such policies represent a correction of past injustice or are they "reverse discrimination"? The following passages argue for and against affirmative action.

The founding tenet of racism is that blacks are inferior, particularly when it comes to intellectual capability. And an underpinning of racism has been an all-out cultural onslaught on the self-esteem of blacks, to transform them from assertive and self-sufficient human beings into dependents, mere extensions of the will of the whites who choose to use them.

Affirmative action, even weakly and spottily deployed, opens doors of opportunity that would otherwise be slammed tight. As a result, the country is better and stronger. It surely is one of the most effective antidotes to the widespread habit of undervaluing the capacities of minorities and women. It also serves as a counterbalance to the tendency to overvalue, as a recruitment tool, the effectiveness and fairness of old-boy networks. . . .

Roger Wilkins (1990)

I think one of the most troubling effects of racial preferences for blacks is a kind of demoralization. Under affirmative action, the quality that earns us preferential treatment is an implied inferiority. However this inferiority is explained—and it is easily enough explained by the myriad deprivations that grew out of our oppression—it is still inferiority. There are explanations and then there is the fact. And the fact must be borne by the individual as a condition apart from the explanation. . . .

I believe another liability of affirmative action comes from the fact that it indirectly encourages blacks to exploit their own past victimization. Like implied inferiority, victimization is what justifies preference, so that to receive the benefits of preferential treatment one must, to some extent, become invested in the view of one's self as a victim. In this way, affirmative action nurtures a victim-focused identity in blacks and sends us the message that there is more power in our past suffering than in our present achievements.

Shelby Steele (1990)

RESPONDING

1. Contrast the different visions of politics expressed in the paintings Stump Speaking (page 553) and Tragic Prelude (page 555).
2. Do you agree with Booker T. Washington (page 556) that in the search for equality, economic power must come first? Why or why not?
3. Do you think that an immigrant father today would have the same confidence as Mr. Antin (page 557) that American public education would ensure his children's future success? Why or why not?
4. In your opinion, are quota systems designed to increase minority representation in higher education and the work force fair? Why or why not?
5. Is American society today moving toward greater equality among its citizens or greater inequality? Explain.

561

About Affirmative Action

Affirmative action is defined as "a program that encourages the employment of women and minorities in order to compensate for past discrimination" *(ScottForesman Advanced Dictionary).*

About Roger Wilkins

A professor of history and American culture, Roger Wilkins (born 1932) has been a long-time civil rights activist and commentator on race relations in the United States. He also served as Assistant Attorney General of the United States from 1966 to 1969.

About Shelby Steele

African American professor of English Shelby Steele (born 1946) became something of a celebrity in 1990 with the publication of his controversial book *The Content of Our Character: A New Vision of Race in America*, in which he argued against the use of white racism as a universal explanation for problems in African Americans' lives.

RESPONDING

1. Possible response: *Stump Speaking* presents an orderly view of politics based on the electoral process; *Tragic Prelude* presents a view of politics as an arena for violent visionaries.

2. Possible responses: Students who agree with Washington might argue that economic strength will lead to political power; students who disagree might feel that self-respect or legal rights must come first.

3. Possible responses: Students who agree might argue that the public schools still are the basic American institution for cultural learning and success; those who disagree might argue that American society's commitment to public education is not as universal as it once was.

4. Possible responses: Students who say they are fair might argue that minorities still are underrepresented in higher education and the workplace; students who disagree may argue that quota systems are "reverse discrimination."

5. Possible responses: Students who feel we are moving toward greater equality might point to gains made by minorities and women in recent years; students who disagree might point to developments such as a so-called "backlash" among people with power who feel that efforts to ensure equality have gone too far.

Planning Unit 6: Modern Dilemmas

Literature

Integrated Language Arts

	Literary	Writing/Grammar, Usage and Mechanics	Reading, Thinking, Listening, Speaking	Vocabulary/Spelling
The Love Song of J. Alfred Prufrock *by T. S. Eliot* Poem *(challenging)* p. 568	Allusion Figurative language	Write a poem Diagnose and prescribe a treatment Write a paragraph Ellipses Dashes	Draw conclusions	
Richard Cory *by Edwin Arlington Robinson* Poem *(easy)* p. 576 **1(a** *by E. E. Cummings* Poem *(average)* p. 577	Shapely poetry	Develop an image		
In Another Country *by Ernest Hemingway* Short Story *(average)* p. 580	Mood Metaphor Theme Irony	Write an analysis Using expressions in other languages	Compare and contrast	Word relationships
Winter Dreams *by F. Scott Fitzgerald* Short Story *(challenging)* p. 586	Character Setting, style Foreshadowing Metaphor Flashback Imagery Dialogue	Write a dialogue Write six diary entries Similarity chart Relative pronouns Descriptive adjectives	Compare and contrast Draw conclusions	Prefixes Homonyms and homophones
from Black Boy *by Richard Wright* Autobiography *(easy)* p. 605	Look who's talking (dialogue) Metaphor	Story outlines Avoiding run-on sentences	Recognize values Recognize shades of meaning	
The Jilting of Granny Weatherall *by Katherine Anne Porter* Short Story *(challenging)* p. 611	Stream of consciousness Flashback Characterization Simile Symbolism, irony	Vivid comparisons Write a eulogy Sentence fragments	Infer Cause and effect	Synonyms Connotation and denotation

Meeting Individual Needs

Multi-modal Activities	Mini-Lessons
Collage	Ellipses
Design a CD cover	Dashes
Research report	
Making personal connections	
Analyzing character	
Scrapbook	
Exploring key ideas	
Analyzing mood	Using expressions in
Analyzing key statements	other languages
Oral report	Relative pronouns
Multimedia report	Descriptive adjectives
List of quotations	Prefixes
Exploring similes and metaphors	Homonyms and homo-
Tracking story details	phones
Analyzing characters	Character
Exploring degrees of comprehension	Essential and inciden-
Making real-life connections	tal information
Expanding vocabulary notebooks	Primary and secondary
Making cultural connections	sources
Summarizing ideas	
Making personal connections	Avoiding run-on
	sentences
	Recognizing shades
	of meaning
Essay	Sentence fragments
Patchwork quilt	Synonyms
Illustrate a scene	Connotation and
Sequencing details	denotation
Exploring key concepts	
Making personal connections	

Interdisciplinary Studies
The Roaring Twenties

Format	Content Area	Highlights	Skill
Article: **The Younger Generation Runs Wild** *by Frederick Lewis Allen*	Pop Culture	This selection describes the scandalous nature of the 1920's.	Researching information
Glossary: **The Jazz Age Glossary**	Pop Culture	This is a glossary of slang that developed during the 1920's.	Presenting a speech

Writing Workshop

Mode	Writing Format	Writing Focus	Proofreading Skills
Expository writing	A cause-effect essay	Revising a thesis statement	Using commas correctly

Program Support Materials

For Every Selection	For Every Writing Workshop
Unit Resource Book	**Unit Resource Book**
Graphic Organizer	Prewriting Worksheet
Study Guide	Revising Strategy Worksheet
Vocabulary Worksheet	Editing Strategy Worksheet
Grammar Worksheet	Presentation Worksheet ·
Spelling, Speaking and Listening, or Literary Language Worksheet	Writing Rubric
Alternate Check Test	**Transparency Collection**
Vocabulary Test	Fine Art Transparency
Selection Test	Student Writing Model Transparencies

For Every Interdisciplinary Study	Assessment
Unit Resource Book	**Unit Resource Book**
Study Guide	TE Check Tests
Mini-Lesson Skill Worksheet	Alternate Check Test (blackline master)
	Vocabulary Test (blackline master)
	Selection Test (blackline master)
	Test Generator Software
	Assessment Handbook

Planning Unit 6: Modern Dilemmas

Literature	Integrated Language Arts			
	Literary	**Writing/Grammar, Usage and Mechanics**	**Reading, Thinking, Listening, Speaking**	**Vocabulary/Spelling**
Stopping by Woods on a Snowy Evening *(easy)* p. 636 **Mending Wall** *(average)* p. 637 **Birches** *(average)* p. 639 **Poems** by Robert Frost	Blank verse Rhyme Simile Narrator Symbolism	Write blank verse Describe a childhood pastime Short report Contractions	Analyze Order of events	
The Tall Men by William Faulkner Short Story *(challenging)* p. 644	Characterization Point of view Allusion Foreshadowing Theme	Create a character and write a monologue Report Slang, dialect, and informal English	Draw conclusions Analyze Make inferences Recognize values Summarize Synthesize	Using dictionaries to find meaning
Blue Winds Dancing by Thomas S. Whitecloud Autobiographical Essay *(average)* p. 658	Imagery Theme Connotation/denotation Idioms, symbolism Allusions, personification	Essay List of questions Describe a scene Commas	Recognize values Draw conclusions	Using a thesaurus
A Worn Path by Eudora Welty Short Story *(easy)* p. 667	Inferences Dialogue, simile Symbolism, mood Author's purpose Denotation/connotation Plot development	Descriptive paragraph Two page narrative Essay Dialect and formal writing	Draw conclusions Predict Compare and contrast Generalize	Context clues for word meaning
The Leader of the People by John Steinbeck Short Story *(average)* p. 676	Setting Point of view, diction Denotation/connotation Dialogue, symbolism Metaphor, hyperbole Figurative language Pun, imagery Characterization, dialect	Diagram relationships List of questions Using adverbs to intensify a narrative Distinguishing similar verbs	Predict, evaluate Make judgments Summarize Connect Draw conclusions Synthesize Compare and contrast Recognize cause and effect	Pantomime action verbs Recognize idioms
Lord Byron's Love Letter by Tennessee Williams Play *(easy)* p. 690	Diction Characterization Dialogue, allusion Recognize farce	Write a scene Write a comparison Biographical account Capitalization of names and places	Generalize Make inferences Recognize implications Compare and contrast Draw conclusions	Recognize multi-meaning words

Meeting Individual Needs

Multi-modal Activities	Mini-Lessons
Dramatic reading	Contractions
Debate	Blank verse
Play a recording	
Comprehending sounds in poetry	
Appreciating language and imagery	

Multi-modal Activities	Mini-Lessons
Research and oral report	Characterization
Reader's theater report	Using dictionaries to
Responding to characters	find meaning
Expanding vocabulary notebooks	Slang, dialect, and
Understanding character relationships	informal English
Keeping track of plot events	Summarize
Exploring key concepts	

Multi-modal Activities	Mini-Lessons
Oral presentation	Commas
Photograph	Using a thesaurus
Create a map	
Making personal connections	
Exploring key statements	
Exploring personification	

Multi-modal Activities	Mini-Lessons
Make a map	Dialect and formal
Design a board game	writing
Illustrate a scene	Inference
Analyzing characterization	Context clues for word
Making personal connections	meaning

Multi-modal Activities	Mini-Lessons
Annotated bibliography	Recognize idioms
Film review	Setting
Imagine a conversation	Using adverbs to inten-
Analyzing conflict	sify a narrative
Exploring principle parts of verbs	Distinguishing similar
Tracking plot elements	verbs
Making personal connections	The information in a
	book

Multi-modal Activities	Mini-Lessons
Oral interpretation	Recognize multi-
Oral argument	meaning words
Live performance	Diction
Improving comprehension	Capitalization of
Making personal connections	names and places
Analyzing key statements	

Interdisciplinary Studies
Life On The Home Front

Format	Content Area	Highlights	Skill
New Opportunities for African-Americans and Women *by Sybil Lewis*	History	A discussion of social and economic changes brought on by WWII.	
Children of the Home Front *by Sheril Cunning*	History	A discussion of growing up during WWII.	Note taking
Japanese Americans are "Relocated" *by Henry Murakami*	History	One man's memories of his endurances during the Japanese relocations of WWII.	Word processing

Writing Workshop

Mode	Writing Format	Writing Focus	Proofreading Skills
Expository writing	A comparison/contrast essay	Signaling comparisons and contrasts	Punctuating quotations from literature

Program Support Materials

For Every Selection	For Every Writing Workshop
Unit Resource Book	**Unit Resource Book**
Graphic Organizer	Prewriting Worksheet
Study Guide	Revising Strategy Worksheet
Vocabulary Worksheet	Editing Strategy Worksheet
Grammar Worksheet	Presentation Worksheet
Spelling, Speaking and Listening, or Literary Language Worksheet	Writing Rubric
Alternate Check Test	**Transparency Collection**
Vocabulary Test	Fine Art Transparency
Selection Test	Student Writing Model Transparencies

For Every Interdisciplinary Study	Assessment
Unit Resource Book	**Unit Resource Book**
Study Guide	TE Check Tests
Mini-Lesson Skill Worksheet	Alternate Check Test (blackline master)
	Vocabulary Test (blackline master)
	Selection Test (blackline master)
	Test Generator Software
	Assessment Handbook

Media and Technology

Part One Selections

The Love Song of J. Alfred Prufrock

Audiotape The author reads his poem in *The Love Song of J. Alfred Prufrock,* Caedmon/Harper Audio.

Home Connection How would the formal manners of someone like J. Alfred Prufrock appear in contemporary social situations? For an at-home activity, students might discuss with family members what sort of etiquette is appropriate for today's world.

Richard Cory/1(a

Audiotape Students will enjoy *Cummings Reading His Poetry,* Caedmon/Harper Audio.

Videotape *American Pioneers,* 28 minutes, Films for the Humanities & Sciences, includes the work of E. A. Robinson and others. *E.E. Cummings: The Making of a Poet,* 24 minutes, Films for the Humanities & Sciences, 1978, is an award-winning profile of the poet as told through his own words and works. *America*

in Portrait, 45 minutes, The Heritage Poetry Series, Library Video Company, 1989, features Henry Fonda and James Whitmore performing E.E. Cummings and other poets.

Home Connection What makes someone enviable? health? wealth? good looks? brains? all of the preceding? something else? For an at-home activity, students might discuss with family members what traits in people arouse envy.

In Another Country

Community Resources An ugly and futile bloodbath that decimated what became known as the "Lost Generation," World War I was a cultural watershed, shattering traditional romanticized views of war and heroism. Students might use the resources of the local library to research some aspect of this huge conflict.

Winter Dreams

Audiotape Several short stories by the author are read on *F. Scott Fitzgerald Short Stories,* 1 hour 53 minutes, Listening Library, 1990.

Videotape Students may enjoy an adaptation of Fitzgerald's novel, *The Great Gatsby,* 2 hours 26 minutes, Paramount Home Video, 1981.

from Black Boy

Audiotape An abridged reading of *Black Boy* is available on *Richard Wright,* 117 minutes, Caedmon/Harper Audio.

Videotape Consider showing *Richard Wright: Black Boy,* 30 minutes, California Newsreel, 1995.

The Jilting of Granny Weatherall

Audiotape *Collected Stories of Katherine Anne Porter,* 3 hours, Audio Partners, 1985, includes four short stories.

Videotape *The Jilting of Granny Weatherall,* 57 minutes, from The American Short Story Collection, is available from Library Video Company, 1980. *Katherine Anne Porter: The Eye of Memory,* PBS Home Video, is part of the About the Authors Collection.

Home Connection "My whole life flashed before my eyes!" is a familiar way in which a near-death experiencing, like drowning, has been described. Other people have reported seeing lights, hearing voices, feeling a wonderful serenity. For an at-home activity, students might discuss experiences of these kind with family members, examining some of the common features reported by different people who have been near death.

Connections to
Custom
Literature Database

For Part One "Lost in a Crowd" Selections with Lessons

- "Miniver Cheevy" by Edward Arlington Robinson and "Auspex" by James Russell Lowell
- "Anecdote of the Jar" by Wallace Stevens and "A narrow Fellow in the Grass" by Emily Dickinson

Additional theme-based selections can be accessed on the ScottForesman database.

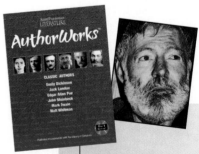

Connections to
AuthorWorks

Information about the life and times of E.E. Cummings, Ernest Hemingway, F. Scott Fitzgerald and Richard Wright is available on ScottForesman's AuthorWorks CD-ROM.

Part Two Selections

Stopping by Woods on a Snowy Evening/Mending Wall/Birches

Videotape Students will enjoy Leonard Nimoy reading Frost's *The Mending Wall*, from Aims Media, and a video portrait of the poet in *Robert Frost*, 10 minutes, Aims Media, 1972.

Community Resources Walls are one of the most characteristic products of human civilization. Students might use the resources of the local library to research some famous effort to set boundaries using walls or fences, such as the Great Wall of China, Hadrian's Wall, barbed-wire fencing on the Great Plains, or the Maginot Line.

The Tall Men

Audiotape Faulkner reads excerpts from his work and his Nobel Prize Acceptance Speech in *William Faulkner Reads*, 48 minutes, Caedmon/Harper Audio.

Videotape *A Rose for Emily*, 23 minutes, Pyramid, 1983, is a video version of a short story by Faulkner, as is *Two Soldiers*, 30 minutes, Monterey Home Video, 1992. *Bear*, 24 minutes, Aims Media, 1994, is based on the author's tale of an almost supernatural bear.

Connections to
Custom Literature Database

For Part Two "The Strength of Tradition" Selections with Lessons

- "Chicago" by Carl Sandburg
- "Discovery of a Father" by Sherwood Anderson

Additional theme-based selections can be accessed on the ScottForesman database.

Home Connection Even if the United States military continues to be an all-volunteer force, should there be some form of national service required of young people; and, if so, what kind of tasks should they undertake? For an at-home activity, students might discuss with family members the pros and cons of such a "draft."

Blue Winds Dancing

Videotape A Native American girl struggles to retain her heritage after being placed in a government school in the award-winning film, *Where the Spirit Lives,* 108 minutes, Beacon, 1991.

Community Resources Thomas Whitecloud's father was a Chippewa. The Chippewa (or Ojibway) are an American Indian people of the Great Lakes region. Students might use the resources of the local library, museum, or cultural center to learn more about the culture of the Chippewa.

A Worn Path

Audiotape The author reads "A Worn Path" and other short stories in *Eudora Welty Reads,* 98 minutes, Caedmon/Harper Audio.

Videotape *Hitch-Hikers,* 30 minutes, from The American Short Story Collection, 1989, is based on Welty's story and stars Patty Duke.

Connections to
NovelWorks

Audiotapes of *The Great Gatsby* and *Black Boy*, novels by F. Scott Fitzgerald and Richard Wright, are among the many teaching tools included in the ScottForesman NovelWorks kits.

Community Resources You might invite a community health professional—such as a clinic doctor, visiting nurse, nutritionist, or home health-care worker—to discuss the different types of services that are available.

The Leader of the People

Videotape Students will enjoy the film version of *Leader of the People*, 23 minutes, Aims Media, 1979.

Community Resources You might invite someone who has had the responsibility of managing a group of people on a trip, such as a tour guide, to visit the class.

Lord Byron's Love Letter

Audiotape The author reads excerpts and poems in *Tennessee Williams Reads*, 45 minutes, Caedmon/Harper Audio.

Videotape *Tennessee Williams: Orpheus of the American Stage*, 90 minutes, Films for the Humanities & Sciences, 1995, is a profile of the playwright. Williams' play, *The Glass Menagerie*, 2 hours 14 minutes, is available from MCA Home Video, 1988. *Whispers on the Wind,* 45 minutes, The Heritage Poetry Series, Library Video Company, 1990, features LeVar Burton and others performing the work of Tennessee Williams and other poets.

Home Connection After meeting Lord Byron, a woman described him in her diary as "mad, bad, and dangerous to know"—and then proceeded to have an affair with him! For an at-home activity, students might discuss with family members the equivalents of Lord Byron in contemporary popular culture.

Modern Dilemmas

Art Study

New York painter Edward Hopper (1882–1967) is usually associated with a painting movement called Ashcan Realism, as well as with the broader movement of American Scene painting. He applied his strong, geometric style to the depiction of the alienation and stagnancy of daily life in America. He frequently set his solitary figures in cold offices, stark hotel rooms, or empty houses. Even his rural landscapes often convey an impression of loneliness.

Edward Hopper created this famous painting, titled *Nighthawks,* in 1942. Hopper said of *Nighthawks:* "I didn't see it as particularly lonely. . . . Unconsciously, probably, I was painting the loneliness of a big city."

Ask students to relate the painting to the title of Unit 6, Modern Dilemmas.

Question How would you describe the mood of this painting? *(Possible response: It appears lonely because characters do not seem to be communicating, and the setting seems stark and cold.)*

Question What compositional elements contribute to the psychological effect of the painting? *(Possible response: the sharp angles, the contrast between the harsh light inside the coffee shop, the darkness of the night outside)*

Modern Dilemmas

Lost in a Crowd
Part One, pages 564–631

The Strength of Tradition
Part Two, pages 632–713

563

THEMATIC CONNECTIONS

As changes happened fast and furiously between the two world wars, some people found themselves alienated in an impersonal society, while others resisted change and clung to the ways of the past.

Part One
Lost in a Crowd

The selections in Part One describe the difficulty of coping with feelings of alienation in a changing society.

Ideas to Explore

- What changes were people dealing with following World War I?
- How do the authors and poets express feelings of alienation in these selections?
- What makes the characters in these selections feel alone in different stages of life?

Part Two
The Strength of Tradition

As the twentieth century rushed towards modernization, many resisted change by holding fast to traditions.

Ideas to Explore

- Does practicing the traditions of the past enrich or stifle people's lives?
- What are the authors' attitudes toward tradition in a changing society?
- Which one really wins, tradition or change?

 Art Study

The icon for Lost in a Crowd is *The Scream,* by Edvard Munch. The icon for The Strength of Tradition is *American Gothic,* by Grant Wood.

EXPLORING CONCEPTS

- Post World War I was a time of social, industrial, and political change.
- The literature of the time expresses feelings that modern people are shallow, spiritually empty, and alone.
- Those that dare to dream sometimes find themselves alone with their dreams.

The people identified in the photographs on pages 564–565 represent characteristic types of personalities during this era of extremes.

Question What characteristic social types would illustrate the end of the twentieth century? *(Responses will vary but might include Yuppies, the homeless, the sports superstar, the corporate multi-billionaire, generation X.)*

Research Activity Small groups of students might use library or online resources to find out more about the famous individuals named on pages 564–565.

Modern Dilemmas

Lost in a Crowd

Between

HISTORICAL OVERVIEW

The idealism that had prompted America's entry into World War I, "the war to end wars," was largely exhausted by 1920. The new decade saw a retreat from reform, a return to isolationism, and an outburst of unrestrained self-indulgence that earned the period the nickname "the Roaring '20s." Following the stock market crash of 1929, America suffered through the Great Depression, an economic crisis unparalleled in U.S. history. By the mid-1930s, some of the worst privation had been eased by the social welfare programs of President Franklin D. Roosevelt's New Deal, but full economic recovery did not take place until America's entry into World War II provided full employment. On the right are a few famous individuals and characteristic social types from the social scene of the 1920s and 1930s.

REVIVALIST
Cheering Prohibition, evangelist Billy Sunday declared, "Hell will be forever for rent."

ANARCHISTS
Radicals Sacco and Vanzetti (rear) were executed for murder after a questionable trial.

GANGSTER
"Machine Gun" Kelly (shown with his wife) was a notorious bank robber in the 1930s.

the Wars

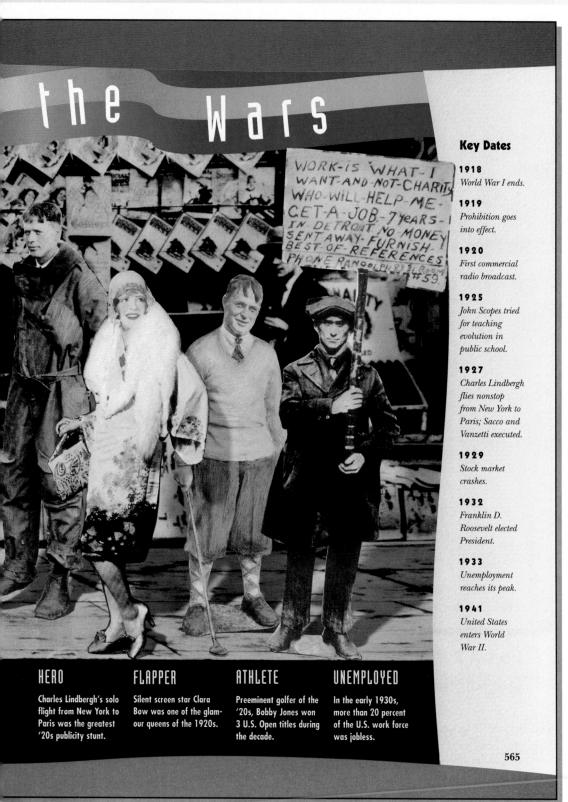

HERO
Charles Lindbergh's solo flight from New York to Paris was the greatest '20s publicity stunt.

FLAPPER
Silent screen star Clara Bow was one of the glamour queens of the 1920s.

ATHLETE
Preeminent golfer of the '20s, Bobby Jones won 3 U.S. Open titles during the decade.

UNEMPLOYED
In the early 1930s, more than 20 percent of the U.S. work force was jobless.

565

MATERIALS OF INTEREST
Books

- *The Letters of T.S. Eliot, Vol. 1: 1898–1922,* edited by Valerie Eliot (Harcourt, Brace & Co., 1988)

- *Clara Bow: Runnin' Wild* by David Stenn (Viking Penguin, 1990)

Multimedia

- *F. Scott Fitzgerald Short Stories* (2 audiocassettes) (Ingram, 1993)

- *Encarta* reference work "United States of America—The Crash of 1929" article on CD-ROM (Microsoft, 1994)

Connections to
Custom Literature Database

For further historical background, under **Background Articles,** see **Later Modern America 1815–1945.**

FOR ALL STUDENTS

- What does it mean to be urbanized?
- How would you describe an impersonal society?
- How is it possible to be in a crowd and still feel lost or alone?

Read the first paragraph on page 566 with students and explain that the selections they will be reading use different approaches to the theme of alienation.

To further explore the theme, use the transparency noted here.

Transparency Collection
Fine Art Writing Prompt 10

For At-Risk Students

Ask students how it feels to make a change: for example, a change in grade level or school or a change in activity by getting a driver's license. Discuss the positive and the negative aspects of making changes.

For Students Who Need Challenge

Encourage students to read criticism of Eliot's poem or his essay "The Social Function of Poetry" to enhance their understanding of *The Love Song of J. Alfred Prufrock.*

ॐ MULTICULTURAL CONNECTION

Among the background factors contributing to an individual's perspective are his or her culture, upbringing, education, socio-economic status, and experience. Help students increase their awareness of the influence of background by asking how the perspective of characters in Part One might change if he or she had a different background.

Part One

Lost in a Crowd

The face of the United States began changing at a faster rate than ever before between World War I and World War II. The growth of industrialization attracted people to the cities, and the jazz age ushered in new music, new language, and new values. Changes happened so rapidly that some people found themselves lost in an increasingly urbanized and impersonal society.

ॐ **Multicultural Connection** Each person has a unique **perspective** on the world and on society. As you read the following selections, notice how the main characters react to the society in which they find themselves. How do their perspectives differ from those of the people around them, and what causes them to see things differently?

IDEAS THAT WORK

Motivating with Popular Culture

"Bring the classroom theme of alienation into the realm of everyday student life by asking your high school students to think of groups in your school who differentiate themselves, such as "jocks" or the "grunge" crowd. How do they mark themselves as different? Is their differentiation destructive or constructive to themselves or those around them?

Tap into popular music and movies that share the theme of alienation by discussing the words and music of the Beatles' "Eleanor Rigby" and Simon and Garfunkel's "Richard Cory," and the movies *Rebel Without a Cause,* about teenage alienation, and *Philadelphia,* about alienation caused by the misunderstanding of AIDS."

Linda Belpedio
Oak Park, Illinois

Before Reading

The Love Song of J. Alfred Prufrock

by T. S. Eliot

T. S. Eliot
1888–1965

After graduating from Harvard, T. S. Eliot studied in France and England, and eventually became a British subject. His writing career was encouraged by Ezra Pound, poet and the acting foreign editor for *Poetry* magazine, which first published "The Love Song of J. Alfred Prufrock" in 1915. The poem reflects Eliot's feeling that modern people are shallow, their lives spiritually empty. This theme continued in Eliot's poetry until his conversion to the Anglican Church where he rediscovered faith, which he felt was the answer to the meaninglessness of modern life. In 1948 Eliot was awarded the Nobel Prize for literature.

Building Background

A Pessimistic View of the World The years during and after World War I were times of drastic social change. Industry, geared up during war time, was booming. People out to get rich quick were investing heavily in the stock market. For some citizens, eager to forget the war, it was a time to party—the "Roaring Twenties." For others, disillusioned with the war and post-war politics, it was a time to abandon the United States. Many writers and artists, including T. S. Eliot, became expatriates, living and working in Europe. It was during this time that T. S. Eliot wrote some of his most famous poems.

Literary Focus

Allusion If a news article says an investment banker has a "Midas touch," the reporter is alluding to King Midas of Greek mythology, who turned everything he touched to gold. The reporter is using a kind of shorthand to say that the banker is good at making money. A reference like this to a person, thing, event, situation, or aspect of culture, real or fictional, past or present, is an allusion. Before you read "The Love Song of J. Alfred Prufrock," find out about these topics so that you understand the allusions T. S. Eliot makes in the poem: Dante's *Inferno,* Michelangelo, John the Baptist, Lazarus, Shakespeare's characters Hamlet and Polonius, and Shakespeare's play *Twelfth Night.*

Writer's Notebook

I Should Have Said . . . J. Alfred Prufrock, the main character in the poem, is mulling over a social situation. He feels uncomfortable, and he can't say what he wants to say. Before reading the poem, think of a time when you have felt uncomfortable in a social situation. List similes or metaphors that describe how you were feeling at that time. For example, if you ran into a famous athlete and you didn't know what to say, you might describe the occasion this way: "My voice crackled like radio static and my hands shook like a washing machine in the spin cycle."

Before Reading

Building Background

Discuss with students what it means to feel shallow and empty. Record images, words, or situations that come to mind as examples of shallowness. Suggest that students take note of T. S. Eliot's portrayal of shallow people.

Literary Focus

To help students understand Eliot's literary **allusions,** they can find out more about John the Baptist in the Gospels of Mark and Matthew; Lazarus in the Gospels of Luke and John; and Prince Hamlet in Shakespeare's play *Hamlet.*

Writer's Notebook

Students might first retell their social situation experience in everyday language. Then they can revise their story by adding similes and metaphors.

More About T. S. Eliot

Although born in St. Louis, Missouri, Eliot spent most of his adult life abroad. His reputation in London was advanced when he published *Prufrock and Other Observations* in 1917. He was a poet, critic, and essayist.

Other works by T. S. Eliot include
• *Old Possum's Book of Practical Cats*
• "The Hollow Men"
• *The Wasteland*
• *The Cocktail Party*

SUPPORT MATERIALS OVERVIEW

Unit 6 Resource Book
• Graphic Organizer, p. 1
• Study Guide, p. 2
• Vocabulary, p. 3
• Grammar, p. 4
• Alternate Check Test, p. 5
• Vocabulary Test, p. 6
• Selection Test, pp. 7–8

Building English Proficiency
• Literature Summaries
• Activities, p. 210

Reading, Writing & Grammar SkillBook
• Reading, pp. 54–55
• Grammar, Usage, and Mechanics, pp. 270–271

Technology
• Audiotape
• Personal Journal Software
• Custom Literature Database
  Shakespeare's *Hamlet,* to which Prufrock refers, can be found on the database.
• Test Generator Software

Selection Objectives

- To examine a perspective of being alienated
- To identify literary allusions
- To understand the use of ellipses in writing

Unit 6 Resource Book
Graphic Organizer, p. 1
Study Guide, p. 2

Theme Link

Seemingly separated by others' inability to understand him and feeling an alienation from himself, Prufrock's love song expresses an aloneness and a personal modern dilemma.

Vocabulary Preview

etherise, make unconscious with ether fumes

tedious, long and tiring

indecision, tendency to delay or hesitate

formulated, reduced to a formula

digress, turn aside from the main subject

malinger, pretend to be sick in order to avoid work

deferential, being respectful of the judgment, opinion, or wishes of another

politic, wise in looking out for one's own interests; prudent and shrewd

meticulous, extremely and excessively careful about details

obtuse, slow in understanding; insensitive

Students can add the words and definitions to their word lists in the Writer's Notebook.

---

1 The Love Song of J. Alfred Prufrock

T. S. ELIOT

2

> *S'io credesse che mia riposta fosse*
> *A persona che mai tornasse al mondo,*
> *Questa fiamma staria senza piu scosse.*
> *Ma perciocche giammai di questo fondo*
> *Non torno vivo alcun, s' i' odo il vero,*
> *Senza tema d' infamia ti rispondo.*

Let us go then, you and I,
When the evening is spread out against the sky
Like a patient etherised upon a table;
Let us go, through certain half-deserted streets,
5 The muttering retreats
Of restless nights in one-night cheap hotels
And sawdust restaurants with oyster-shells:
Streets that follow like a tedious argument
Of insidious intent
10 To lead you to an overwhelming question . . .
Oh, do not ask, "What is it?"
Let us go and make our visit.

    In the room the women come and go
Talking of Michelangelo.

15   The yellow fog that rubs its back upon the window-panes,
The yellow smoke that rubs its muzzle on the window-panes,
Licked its tongue into the corners of the evening,
Lingered upon the pools that stand in drains,
Let fall upon its back the soot that falls from chimneys,
20 Slipped by the terrace, made a sudden leap,
And seeing that it was a soft October night,
Curled once about the house, and fell asleep.

Epigraph *S'io credesse . . . ti rispondo,* "If I believed my answer were being made to one who could ever return to the world, this flame would gleam no more; but since, if what I hear is true, never from this abyss [Hell] did living man return, I answer thee without fear of infamy." (Dante, *Inferno* XXVII, 61-66)

3 **etherised** (ē′thə rīzd′), *adj.* unconscious from ether fumes. Ether was used to anesthetize patients during operations.

8 **tedious** (tē′dē əs), *adj.* long and tiring, boring, wearisome.

13–14 **In the room . . . Michelangelo.** These lines refer to the women at the tea party which Prufrock is attending. The great Renaissance artist Michelangelo is the topic of their chatter.

568   UNIT SIX: MODERN DILEMMAS

SELECTION SUMMARY

The Love Song of J. Alfred Prufrock

An epigraph from Dante's *Inferno* opens this interior, stream-of-consciousness monologue of J. Alfred Prufrock with the comment that the speaker would not speak without the assurance that his thoughts and feelings will not be revealed. The poem reveals Prufrock's reflections on his life, how he appears to others, and his relationships with women.

Prufrock struggles between two visions of himself (half of him wants to be a romantic hero, the other half sees himself as ridiculous) until he concludes that there is no romance left for him, and he is "drowned" by life and his own self-deprecation.

 *For summaries in other languages, see the **Building English Proficiency** book.*

How would you describe the situation in Philip Evergood's 1927 painting, *Tea for Two*? What does it have in common with Prufrock's situation?

1 Historical Note
Modern Poetry

It is said that with the Prufrock poem, T. S. Eliot invented modernism in poetry. Many of Eliot's early readers were either confused or outraged by his breaking of poetic conventions to free the reader's imagination within the space of the poem.

2 Literary Focus
Allusion

In Dante's *Inferno*, quoted at the beginning of Eliot's poem, Dante is being led by the poet Virgil on a tour of hell, where he meets the punished Guido da Montefeltro. Guido speaks to Dante on the assumption that Dante will not be able to return to the world to reveal Guido's shame.

Question Why do students think Eliot opens this poem with a quote from Dante's *Inferno?* (*Possible responses: That this poem is also a confession; that the great work of Dante is a counterpoint for the shallow perspective of Prufrock*)

 Art Study

Response to Caption Questions *Tea for Two* appears to show a well-to-do couple being served by a disembodied hand; their vacant eyes are not focused on each other. There's an idleness apparent in the painting that also is reflected in Eliot's poem.

BUILDING ENGLISH PROFICIENCY

Making Personal Connections

Explain that Prufrock sees the world around him as sterile and the people as engaged in meaningless "surface" activities. He longs to perform a significant act or make a meaningful statement but fears what such exposure will mean. Help students understand Prufrock by comparing or contrasting feelings they have experienced to his feelings.

- Ask students to recall a problem or insecurity that challenged them. To get them started, they might consider characters in movies, books, or TV programs who faced such challenges.

- Suggest that students remember the self-conflict involved in a challenge, the solutions considered, and the part that their peers played in making decisions.

- Encourage students to recount the process in the form of a "dialogue with self" in their private journals. Allow for optional, voluntary sharing.

 *Building English Proficiency*
Activities, p. 210

Literary Criticism

"... For Eliot always wrote with a very strong sense of his readers. He made demands on them without which the poems are incomplete. It is no use approaching Eliot in a state of wise passiveness. You have to use your wits."

British Writers
Charles Scribners Sons, 1979–1984

3 Reading/Thinking Skills
Draw Conclusions

Question Prufrock seems to be anticipating the criticism of "they" when he thinks, "They will say: . . ." Who do you think "they" are? *(Possible response: other people whose opinions matter to Prufrock)*

4 Literary Element
Figurative Language

Question What does the image of measuring out life with coffee spoons say about the person? *(Possible responses: He is careful and meticulous about all his decisions; he only makes little, planned, safe moves in the game of life.)*

And indeed there will be time
For the yellow smoke that slides along the street,
25 Rubbing its back upon the window-panes;
There will be time, there will be time
To prepare a face to meet the faces that you meet;
There will be time to murder and create,
And time for all the works and days of hands
30 That lift and drop a question on your plate;
Time for you and time for me,
And time yet for a hundred indecisions,
And for a hundred visions and revisions,
Before the taking of a toast and tea.

35   In the room the women come and go
Talking of Michelangelo.

And indeed there will be time
To wonder, "Do I dare?" and, "Do I dare?"
Time to turn back and descend the stair,
40 With a bald spot in the middle of my hair—
[They will say: "How his hair is growing thin!"]
My morning coat, my collar mounting firmly to the chin,
My necktie rich and modest, but asserted by a simple pin—
[They will say: "But how his arms and legs are thin!"]
45 Do I dare
Disturb the universe?
In a minute there is time
For decisions and revisions which a minute will reverse.

For I have known them all already, known them all:—
50 Have known the evenings, mornings, afternoons,
I have measured out my life with coffee spoons;
I know the voices dying with a dying fall
Beneath the music from a farther room.
    So how should I presume?

55 And I have known the eyes already, known them all—
The eyes that fix you in a formulated phrase,
And when I am formulated, sprawling on a pin,
When I am pinned and wriggling on the wall,
Then how should I begin
60 To spit out all the butt-ends of my days and ways?
    And how should I presume?

32 indecision (in′di sizh′ən), *n.* tendency to delay or hesitate.

42 **morning coat,** a man's coat that tapers from the front waist downward toward tails at the back, worn for formal daytime dress.

57 formulated (fôr′myə lāt-əd), *adj.* reduced to a formula; expressed in a formula. These lines suggest that Prufrock has been scrutinized like an insect that has been classified and mounted for display.

570 UNIT SIX: MODERN DILEMMAS

MINI-LESSON: GRAMMAR

Ellipses

Teach An ellipsis is a set of marks—usually three dots or periods—in written or printed text. The plural of *ellipsis* is *ellipses*. Remind students that ellipsis points have the following uses:

- to show an omission in quoted text
- to show a lapse of time, a different location, or a change of subject matter
- to indicate a pause

Point out that some sidenotes such as the note about lines 81–83 use the three dots (an ellipsis) to show that the lines are not quoted in full. Eliot uses ellipses, however, to insert pauses and shifts in the poem.

Activity Ideas

- Point out the use of an ellipsis in line 72 and the two ellipses in line 77. Have students identify possible purposes of these ellipsis points in the poem. *(Possible response: to show pauses, and in line 77 to give the effect of the pauses in thought or interior monologue caused by tiredness)*
- Have students tell what they think are the purposes of the ellipses in lines 10 and 120.

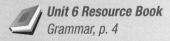
Unit 6 Resource Book
Grammar, p. 4

And I have known the arms already, known them all—
Arms that are braceleted and white and bare
[But in the lamplight, downed with light brown hair!]
65 Is it perfume from a dress
That makes me so digress?
Arms that lie along a table, or wrap about a shawl.
    And should I then presume?
    And how should I begin?

. . . . .

70 Shall I say, I have gone at dusk through narrow streets
And watched the smoke that rises from the pipes
Of lonely men in shirt-sleeves, leaning out of windows? . . .

    I should have been a pair of ragged claws
Scuttling across the floors of silent seas.

. . . . .

75 And the afternoon, the evening, sleeps so peacefully!
Smoothed by long fingers,
Asleep . . . tired . . . or it malingers,
Stretched on the floor, here beside you and me.
Should I, after tea and cakes and ices,
80 Have the strength to force the moment to its crisis?
But though I have wept and fasted, wept and prayed,
Though I have seen my head [grown slightly bald] brought in
        upon a platter,
I am no prophet—and here's no great matter;
I have seen the moment of my greatness flicker,
85 And I have seen the eternal Footman hold my coat, and snicker,
And in short, I was afraid.

    And would it have been worth it, after all,
After the cups, the marmalade, the tea,
Among the porcelain, among some talk of you and me,
90 Would it have been worth while,
To have bitten off the matter with a smile,
To have squeezed the universe into a ball   **5**
To roll it toward some overwhelming question,
To say: "I am Lazarus, come from the dead,
95 Come back to tell you all, I shall tell you all"—
If one, settling a pillow by her head,
    Should say: "That is not what I meant at all.
    That is not it, at all."   **6**

66 **digress** (dī gres′), *v.* turn aside from the main subject; to ramble.

77 **malinger** (mə ling′gər), *v.* pretend to be sick in order to avoid work.

81–83 **But though . . . no great matter.** These lines allude to John the Baptist. King Herod had him beheaded and presented the head on a platter at his stepdaughter Salome's request.

94–95 **"I am Lazarus . . . tell you all."** The biblical Lazarus lay dead in his tomb for four days until Jesus restored him to life.

The Love Song of J. Alfred Prufrock   **571**

5 Literary Focus
Allusion

Squeezing the universe into a ball is an allusion to two lines in a poem by Andrew Marvell, "To His Coy Mistress": "Let us roll all our strength and all/Our sweetness up into one ball" (lines 41–42). You may wish to have students read Marvell's entire poem.

6 Reading/Thinking Skills
Draw Conclusions

Question   What is Prufrock afraid of? *(Possible responses: being misunderstood; taking the risk of disturbing the universe and then being rejected.)*

BUILDING ENGLISH PROFICIENCY

ESL
LEP
ELD
SAE
LD

Analyzing Character

Prufrock is self-aware but indecisive. Use a graphic organizer such as the chart shown to help students "track" statements and questions that illustrate both characteristics. Help students understand that he really is giving excuses or reasons for not acting or not speaking out.

Self-Awareness Statements/Questions	Real Meaning
To prepare a face to meet other faces	Don't let your true feelings show.
"Do I dare disturb the universe?"	I can't do or say anything that would upset the order of things.

Reader's Response

Making Personal Connections

How do students feel about Prufrock, his plight, and the petty concerns he now has? *(Responses will vary. Students may identify with him, pity him, or be annoyed with him.)*

8 Literary Focus

Allusion

Remind students of mermaid and siren tales. Mermaids and sirens often are considered muses who are not necessarily all good. Does Prufrock consider the mermaids' song a potentially good or dangerous thing?

Check Test

1. Of whom do the women speak? *(Michelangelo)*

2. In what month does the poem take place? *(October)*

3. What is Prufrock afraid someone will say to him? *(That is not it at all; or, That is not what I meant, at all)*

4. What is the one decision Prufrock makes about his attire? *(to roll his trouser bottoms)*

5. To whom do the mermaids sing? *(to each other, not to Prufrock)*

Unit 6 Resource Book
Alternative Check Test, p. 5

And would it have been worth it, after all,
100 Would it have been worth while,
After the sunsets and the dooryards and the sprinkled streets,
After the novels, after the teacups, after the skirts that trail along
    the floor—
And this, and so much more?—
It is impossible to say just what I mean!
105 But as if a magic lantern threw the nerves in patterns on a
    screen:
Would it have been worth while
If one, settling a pillow or throwing off a shawl,
And turning toward the window, should say:
    "That is not it at all,
110   That is not what I meant, at all."

    . . . . .

No! I am not Prince Hamlet, nor was meant to be;
Am an attendant lord, one that will do
To swell a progress, start a scene or two,
Advise the prince; no doubt an easy tool,
115 Deferential, glad to be of use,
Politic, cautious, and meticulous;
Full of high sentence, but a bit obtuse;
At times, indeed, almost ridiculous—
Almost, at times, the Fool.

7 120   I grow old . . . I grow old . . .
I shall wear the bottoms of my trousers rolled.

    Shall I part my hair behind? Do I dare to eat a peach?
I shall wear white flannel trousers, and walk upon the beach.
8 I have heard the mermaids singing, each to each.

125   I do not think that they will sing to me.

    I have seen them riding seaward on the waves
Combing the white hair of the waves blown back
When the wind blows the water white and black.

    We have lingered in the chambers of the sea
130 By sea-girls wreathed with seaweed red and brown
Till human voices wake us, and we drown.

---

111 **Prince Hamlet,** the hero of William Shakespeare's play *Hamlet*, who set out to prove that his uncle had murdered his father. Here Prufrock envisions himself as playing a minor character rather than the lead.

115 deferential (def′ə ren′-shəl), *adj.* showing respect for the judgment, opinion, wishes of another.

116 politic (pol′ə tik), *adj.* wise in looking out for one's own interests.

116 meticulous (mə tik′yə-ləs), *adj.* extremely careful about details.

117 obtuse (əb tüs′), *adj.* slow in understanding.

MINI-LESSON: GRAMMAR

Dashes

Teach   Point out the dashes in lines 102, 103, and 118. Explain that the dash

- sets off and emphasizes supplemental information or parenthetical comments
- shows an abrupt change of thought within a sentence
- indicates a hesitation or faltering in dialogue

Activity Ideas

- Ask students what the use of dashes contributes to this poem. *(Dashes highlight the fragmentary nature and stream of consciousness of Prufrock's thoughts.)*
- Have students find the other uses of dashes in the poem and identify a reason for each use.

After Reading

Making Connections

Shaping Your Response

1. In your log, write three words that you think describe J. Alfred Prufrock. Share your words with your classmates.

2. Tea parties and morning coats are no longer in fashion. Describe where you might find a modern J. Alfred Prufrock and what he might be wearing.

Analyzing the Poem

3. Explain the extended **metaphor** that begins with line 15.

4. What do you think the fog **symbolizes** in J. Alfred Prufrock's life?

5. The words in the **epigraph** to the poem are spoken by Guido da Montefeltro, whom Dante encounters in his imaginary journey through hell. Guido is suffering eternal torment for his sins; he tells his story to Dante on the assumption that Dante, like himself, can never leave hell. In what respect is Prufrock's song likewise the confession of a soul in torment? What kinds of torment might he be suffering?

6. What kind of "overwhelming question" do you think Prufrock is trying to ask? Explain why you think so.

7. 🐾 Does Prufrock's **perspective** on society seem to differ from the people around him? Explain your answer.

Extending the Ideas

8. Select one of the following common phrases or use one of your own choosing and explain how it relates to J. Alfred Prufrock.

   • All form and no substance

   • On the outside looking in

   • Make up your mind

Literary Focus: Allusion

Writers use **allusions** to make their literature richer and more meaningful. By referring to another piece of literature or a historical character, the author makes a connection between what he or she is writing about and a familiar topic. Choose one of the allusions T. S. Eliot makes in "The Love Song of J. Alfred Prufrock," and find out its source and context. To what is the allusion referring? What connection is Eliot trying to make between Prufrock and the allusion?

MAKING CONNECTIONS

1. Possible responses: self-deprecating; wavering; inadequate; timorous; pitiful; self-conscious

2. Responses will vary: at a power lunch wearing a three-piece suit; at a cocktail party in a tuxedo.

3. The fog is presented as a cat.

4. Responses will vary: the independence of a feline who does whatever it wants regardless of time or place; the strangulation of Prufrock's unhealthy life.

5. Possible response: His life of trying to be heroic in an unheroic age torments him. The gap between his wanderings on the "half-deserted street" and the role he imagines for himself is more than he can bear.

6. Responses will vary. Maybe he questions whether or not to act. If he acted the hero and lover, would anyone accept him in that role?

7. Possible response: He is thoughtful, sensitive, and alienated. Those around him are pseudo-sophisticates, filled with ennui.

8. Possible responses: Prufrock's living in imagination while unable to bring himself to take action; a desire to make contact with the pseudo-sophisticates, who have an envied niche; Prufrock's split personality renders him frozen.

LITERARY FOCUS: ALLUSION

Suggest that students return to the margin notes of the poem, or you might share information from this teacher's annotated edition to help identify Eliot's allusions to explore further.

VOCABULARY STUDY

Vocabulary words, as used in context, should reflect correct meanings and connotations.

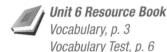

Unit 6 Resource Book
Vocabulary, p. 3
Vocabulary Test, p. 6

WRITING CHOICES
Writer's Notebook Update

To get students started, have them list words that come to mind when they think of their own experience.

Diagnosis Needed

Students might begin with a list of Prufrock's complaints, imagined or real.

What Matters?

Encourage students to make up their own lists, or add to the items listed here before ranking and writing.

Selection Test

Unit 6 Resource Book
pp. 7–8

---

deferential
politic
meticulous
obtuse
tedious
etherised
formulated
digress
malinger
indecision

Vocabulary Study

J. Alfred Prufrock uses these adjectives to describe himself: *deferential, politic, meticulous,* and *obtuse.* These words from the poem also relate to Prufrock and his life: *tedious, etherised, formulated, digress, malinger* and *indecision.* Write your own sentences using each of the listed words to describe Prufrock and his behavior. For example, Prufrock also says that he is *ridiculous.* You might write, "It is *ridiculous* that J. Alfred Prufrock worries about which way to part his hair."

Expressing Your Ideas

Writing Choices

Writer's Notebook Update Compare J. Alfred Prufrock's discomfort in a social situation with the incident you wrote about in your notebook. Then imitate T. S. Eliot's poetic style and write a poem about your experience. Try to include either a simile or a metaphor in your poem.

Diagnosis Needed What is Prufrock's problem? Write a **diagnosis** of his condition, and then write a **prescription** for his treatment that you think will help him overcome his problem.

What Matters? Everyone has different priorities in life. Look at the list below of things people value. Rank them according to the value you place on each, from most to least important. Then be J. Alfred Prufrock and rank them as you think he would. Compare the **rankings** and write a **paragraph** comparing your priorities to Prufrock's.

- job satisfaction
- social standing
- personal appearance
- wealth
- friends
- health
- education
- family

Other Options

Picture It J. Alfred Prufrock jumbles ideas and images together as he reflects on his life and his behavior. Make a **collage** using photographs and quotations from the poem to depict his inner turmoil.

Make a CD Cover T. S. Eliot himself made a recording of "The Love Song of J. Alfred Prufrock." Imagine the recording is going to be rereleased as a CD. Your job is to design the **CD cover**. It should not only catch the attention of the CD shopper, but also express the theme of the poem.

Learn About the Times Writers are influenced by the times and the places in which they live. "The Love Song of J. Alfred Prufrock" was first published in 1915, and T. S. Eliot lived in England. What was going on in the world then? Who was in power in England? What were the social standards of the day? Research what life was like in England at this time in history, and present a report to the class. Your report might be in the form of a **speech** or a **display,** or you may want to work in groups to **dramatize** some of the events and the society of the time.

574 UNIT SIX: MODERN DILEMMAS

OTHER OPTIONS
Picture It

You may wish to introduce the terms "interior monologue" and "stream of consciousness" to help students understand and describe the organization of the poem.

Make a CD Cover

The dimensions of a CD cover are 5 by 4 3/4 inches. Give students the option of designing both the front and back covers, as well as inside notes.

Learn About the Times

Suggest that students look at newspapers and magazines of the time to pick up on opinions and concerns of the people. Students might wish to extend their report to what was happening in the U.S.

Before Reading

Richard Cory by Edwin Arlington Robinson

I(a by E. E. Cummings

Edwin Arlington Robinson
1869–1935

President Theodore Roosevelt gave the young struggling poet Edward Arlington Robinson a "job" at the Custom House in New York. All Robinson had to do was show up, and then he could go home and write. By the time President Taft came into office, Robinson's poetry was famous.

E. E. Cummings
1894–1962

E. E. Cummings is famous for his innovative writing style. His name, like his poetry, sometimes appears without capitalization, but his legal name always remained capitalized, according to the E. E. Cummings Society, and it should appear that way in print.

Building Background

Variety in Poetry Both Edwin Arlington Robinson and E. E. Cummings grew up in New England and studied at Harvard. Both are highly acclaimed American poets. However, the similarities end there. Their poetic styles differ greatly. Robinson is traditional; Cummings is an innovator. Robinson's poems are matter-of-fact in their language; Cummings's poems are like puzzles to be taken apart and reassembled. Cummings, when asked to define poetry, said, "Poetry is what's different." He once wrote, "The day of the spoken lyric is past. The poem which has at last taken its place does not sing itself; it builds itself, three dimensionally, gradually, subtly, in the consciousness of the experiencer." As you read "Richard Cory" and "I(a," enjoy each poet's style and look for a common theme.

Literary Focus

Shapely Poetry Concrete poetry must be seen as well as heard because a concrete poem has a shape that is related to its subject. To hear and not see the shape of a concrete poem or the way the words are fragmented would be to miss most of the meaning. "I(a" by E. E. Cummings is an example of concrete poetry. What do you see when you look at the poem on the page? How does the shape contribute to its meaning?

Writer's Notebook

Both Edwin Arlington Robinson and E. E. Cummings explore similar themes in their poems. Before reading the poems, make a chart in which you list words that you might use to write about sadness and loneliness. Then list visual images that you might use to express that theme. Examples are provided.

Words	Images
• silent • depression • empty	• A person trapped in a doorless and windowless room

---

Before Reading

Building Background

E. E. Cummings experimented with innovations in poetry:

• He varied line length and spacing to communicate ideas.

• He created spatial pauses.

• He disregarded rules of capitalization and punctuation.

Literary Focus

Encourage students to describe how Cummings changed the words of his **concrete poem** from the way that they expect to see those words written.

Writer's Notebook

Point out that sadness and loneliness can be effectively expressed. Suggest that students write examples of this from the poems.

More About the Poets

Other poems by **Robinson** include

• "Miniver Cheevy"

• "Mr. Flood's Party"

Other poems by **Cummings** include

• "nobody loses all the time"

• "what if a much of a which of a wind"

 Connections to **AuthorWorks**

E. E. Cummings is a featured author in the AuthorWorks CD-ROM series.

SUPPORT MATERIALS OVERVIEW

Unit 6 Resource Book
• Graphic Organizer, p. 9
• Study Guide, p. 10
• Vocabulary, p. 11
• Grammar, p. 12
• Alternate Check Test, p. 13
• Vocabulary Test, p. 14
• Selection Test, pp. 15–16

Building English Proficiency
• Literature Summaries
• Activities, p. 211

Reading, Writing & Grammar SkillBook
• Reading, pp. 50–51

Technology
• Audiotape
• Personal Journal Software
• Custom Literature Database
  Additional poems by Edwin Arlington Robinson can be found on the database.
• Test Generator Software

Selection Objectives

- To analyze the expression of aloneness in poetry
- To examine concrete poetry

Unit 6 Resource Book
Graphic Organizer, p. 9
Study Guide, p. 10

Theme Link

These poems explore loneliness and the prospect of being lost in the world.

Art Study

Response to Caption Question   The statue, like Cory, is slim, clean-cut, and well-dressed. Its stiffness and unchanging facade is similar to Cory's exterior, which belies some emotional turmoil within.

---

1   **Writing Style**

Interrupters

Both Robinson and Cummings use punctuation to interrupt a sentence or a word in these poems. In "Richard Cory," dashes allow an intensifying descriptive phrase to be inserted. In "l(a" Cummings uses parentheses.

Unit 6 Resource Book
Grammar, p. 12

Richard Cory

Edwin Arlington Robinson

Whenever Richard Cory went downtown,
  We people on the pavement looked at him:
He was a gentleman from sole to crown,[1]
  Clean-favored, and imperially[2] slim.

5 And he was always quietly arrayed,[3]
  And he was always human when he talked;
But still he fluttered pulses when he said,
  "Good morning," and he glittered when
    he walked.

1 And he was rich—yes, richer than a king—
10   And admirably schooled in every grace:
In fine, we thought that he was everything
  To make us wish that we were in his place.

So on we worked, and waited for the light,
  And went without the meat, and cursed
    the bread;
15 And Richard Cory, one calm summer night,
  Went home and put a bullet through
    his head.

---

1. **crown** (kroun), *n.* the top part of a hat.
2. **imperially** (im pir′ē əl ē), *adv.* majestically, magnificently.
3. **array** (ə rā′), *v.* dress in fine clothes.

How does J. Krans's 1895 statue, *Tinsmith,* reflect the physical appearance and emotional state of Richard Cory in Edwin Arlington Robinson's poem?

576   UNIT SIX: MODERN DILEMMAS

SELECTION SUMMARY

Richard Cory, l(a

Richard Cory   The people of the town watch its most prominent citizen, Richard Cory, and note every detail about him, wishing they could trade places with him. They go through the days hating their own lives, and dreaming of living his, until one night, quite unexpectedly, Richard Cory commits suicide.

l(a   Cummings's concrete poem, "l(a," uses the oddly stacked word *loneliness,* interrupted by the observation of a leaf falling, to suggest that time passes slowly when one is lonely.

*For summaries in other languages, see the **Building English Proficiency** book.*

l(a

E. E. Cummings

2 l(a

le
af
fa

ll

s)
one
l
iness

⌃ Georgia O'Keeffe's painting, *Brown and Tan Leaves* (1928), uses the same subject matter—fallen leaves—as does Cummings's poem. Would you say the painting and poem also share a similar theme? Why or why not?

l(a   577

The poem's title might be pronounced "la" or "L.A." to clarify that it begins with the first letter of *loneliness.* Invite students to solve the poem's puzzle. What word is interrupted, and by what three-word phrase? *(loneliness; a leaf falls)*

 **Art Study**

Possible Response to Caption   The poem's main word, *loneliness,* suggests a theme about lonely people, but the painting seems to be about nature, represented by leaves.

Check Test

1. Where did people on the pavement see Richard Cory? *(downtown)*

2. What did the people on the pavement wish? *(that they could be in Richard Cory's place)*

3. What did the people on the pavement lack? *(meat to eat)*

4. How did Richard Cory die? *(He shot himself in the head.)*

5. What is the subject of "l(a"? *(Possible response: loneliness)*

 **Unit 6 Resource Book**
Alternate Check Test, p. 13

BUILDING ENGLISH PROFICIENCY

ESL
LEP
ELD
SAE
LD

Exploring Key Ideas

Making comparisons between the lives of the people and the perceived life of Richard Cory can help students understand the shocking ending of "Richard Cory."

Activity Ideas

• Have students list the material advantages that Richard Cory appears to have.

• Have students list the complaints of the people.

• Discuss why the ending is such a surprise. *(If someone seems to have everything, it is a surprise that he or she is unhappy enough to end his or her life.)*

Building English Proficiency
Activities, p. 211

After Reading

MAKING CONNECTIONS

1. Students' dialogues should deal with the irony of the people's envy.

2. Possible response: a lonely person watching a dying leaf falling from a tree

3. Students may think that much of the poem's power comes from the unexpected conclusion and the contrast between the people's view of Cory and the reality of his life.

4. Possible responses: loneliness; alienation; an unidentified personal problem

5. Possible responses: A leaf falling becomes separate from the tree and its fellow leaves. Watching a dying leaf slowly fall can mark the slow passage of time when a person is lonely.

6. Possible response: They are both about loneliness, alienation, and being separate.

7. The advice should relate to what they imagine Richard Cory would identify as his problem.

WRITING CHOICE
Writer's Notebook Update

Encourage students to examine and list elements that make up each poet's style, for example, line length, rhythm, rhyme, story, or image.

Selection Test

Unit 6 Resource Book
pp. 15–16

After Reading

Making Connections

Shaping Your
Response

1. You and a classmate are two of the "people on the pavement." What would you say to each other about Cory and his death? Perform a dialogue for the class.

2. What scene did you visualize as you read E. E. Cummings's "l(a"?

Analyzing the
Poems

3. Do you think the **ironic** ending of "Richard Cory" makes it a better poem than it would have been otherwise? Explain your answer.

4. What possible **motive** might Cory have had for killing himself?

5. What about a falling leaf makes it a suitable **symbol** for loneliness?

6. "l(a" and "Richard Cory" are very different in their poetic style. What do the two poems have in common?

Extending the
Ideas

7. If Richard Cory had confided his troubles to you before he went home that summer night, what advice might you have given to him?

Literary Focus: Concrete Poetry

Shape adds meaning to **concrete poetry.** Discuss how the shape of "l(a" contributes to its meaning. Then find other examples of concrete poetry to share with the class. How does the shape of each poem add to its meaning? "Seal" by William Jay Smith, which can be found in *A Green Place: Modern Poems* (Delacorte Press, 1982), and "Forsythia" by Mary Ellen Solt, which can be found in *A Book of Women Poets from Antiquity to Now* (Schocken Books, 1980), are both good examples of concrete poems. After the discussion, compose an original poem that uses shape to convey an idea.

Expressing Your Ideas

Writing Choice

Writer's Notebook Update Develop one of the images you listed into a poem, either using Robinson's or Cummings's style.

Another Option

Character Portraits What did Richard Cory look like? Edwin Arlington Robinson gives you clues about his character's appearance and personality. Read several other poems from Edwin Arlington Robinson's *Tilbury Town.* Draw pictures of how you visualize the characters in those poems. Copy the poems and make a **scrapbook** of the poems and the portraits.

LITERARY FOCUS: CONCRETE POETRY

Students might benefit by sketching simple shapes that they want to convey and then writing their poems to fit inside the lines of those shapes.

ANOTHER OPTION
Character Portraits

Students could choose to use other methods and media to represent Edwin Arlington Robinson's characters: for example, computer graphics, clip art, magazine pictures, paintings, and dress-up.

Before Reading

In Another Country

by Ernest Hemingway

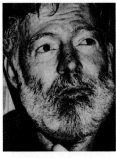

Ernest Hemingway
1899–1961

After serving in an American ambulance unit and an Italian combat unit in World War I, Ernest Hemingway became a newspaper correspondent in France. There he met F. Scott Fitzgerald, who helped Hemingway get his works published. Hemingway described his writing this way: "I always try to write on the principle of the iceberg. There is seven-eighths of it underwater for every part that shows. Anything you know, you can eliminate and it only strengthens your iceberg. It is the part that doesn't show. If a writer omits something because he does not know it, then there is a hole in the story." In addition to writing, Hemingway enjoyed fishing, boxing, hunting in Africa, and watching bullfights. A dramatic figure to the end, he died of a self-inflicted gunshot wound.

Building Background

World War I World War I began in 1914 when a Serbian nationalist assassinated the heir to the Austrian-Hungarian throne. Many European countries took sides, as you can see in the map. The United States tried to remain neutral, but two events eventually brought the U.S into the war. Tsar Nicholas of Russia was deposed from his throne, and it looked like Russia would soon be abandoning their war effort. The next day, Germany sank three American merchant ships. In April of 1917, Congress declared war. Germany finally admitted defeat and signed an armistice on November 11, 1918.

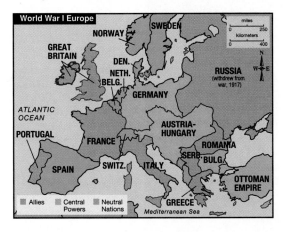

Literary Focus

Mood As you read "In Another Country," look for the details Hemingway uses to describe the setting and characters. What effect do these details have on the overall feeling—or mood—of the work?

Writer's Notebook

Rx: Hope The wounded soldiers in the story are receiving medical treatment. Write about the importance of *hope* to successful recovery.

In Another Country   **579**

Before Reading

Building Background

Help students identify the key locations of World War I on a classroom map.

Literary Focus

Alert students to look for specific images, objects, and words that Hemingway uses to shape the **mood.**

Writer's Notebook

You may wish to ask students to write separately about the role of hope in the patient and the role of hope in those giving treatment.

More About Ernest Hemingway

Hemingway couldn't join the United States army to fight in World War I because of a boxing injury. So he chose to serve in Italy as an ambulance driver, and was wounded in the knee shortly after arriving. His wound required twelve operations and a long convalescence.

Other works by Hemingway include
- *A Farewell to Arms*
- *For Whom the Bell Tolls*
- *The Old Man and the Sea*

Connections to
AuthorWorks

Ernest Hemingway is a featured author in the AuthorWorks CD-ROM series.

SUPPORT MATERIALS OVERVIEW

Unit 6 Resource Book
- Graphic Organizer, p. 17
- Study Guide, p. 18
- Vocabulary, p. 19
- Grammar, p. 20
- Alternate Check Test, p. 21
- Vocabulary Test, p. 22
- Selection Test, pp. 23–24

Building English Proficiency
- Literature Summaries
- Activities, p. 212

Reading, Writing & Grammar SkillBook
- Reading, pp. 73–74

Technology
- Audiotape
- Personal Journal Software
- Custom Literature Database
  Historical documents about the era, such as "Peace Without Victory" by Woodrow Wilson and "Interpretation of President Wilson's Fourteen Points," can be found on the database.
- Test Generator Software

Selection Objectives

- To explore the alienation of an expatriate
- To examine how mood is created
- To note the use of foreign expressions

Unit 6 Resource Book
Graphic Organizer, p. 17
Study Guide, p. 18

Theme Link

The injured soldiers in this story have a surface camaraderie but are still left feeling very much lost and separate.

Vocabulary Preview

game, wild animals, birds, or fish hunted or caught for sport or food

wither, shrivel

detached, reserved, aloof

citation, honorable mention for bravery in war

resign, submit quietly; accept and adapt without complaint

Students can add the words and definitions to their word lists in the Writer's Notebook.

1 Literary Focus
Mood

The mood is set in the first two simple, direct sentences—The war was always there; It was cold in the fall and the dark came early.

Question What mood do these first images evoke? *(Possible response: dreariness, hopelessness)*

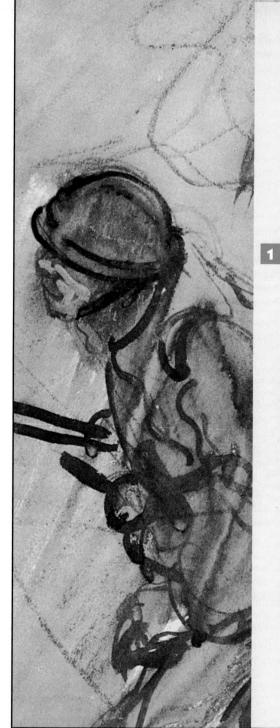

In Another Country

Ernest Hemingway

1 In the fall the war[1] was always there, but we did not go to it any more. It was cold in the fall in Milan and the dark came very early. Then the electric lights came on, and it was pleasant along the streets looking in the windows. There was much game[2] hanging outside the shops, and the snow powdered in the fur of the foxes and the wind blew their tails. The deer hung stiff and heavy and empty, and small birds blew in the wind and the wind turned their feathers. It was a cold fall and the wind came down from the mountains.

We were all at the hospital every afternoon, and there were different ways of walking across the town through the dusk to the hospital. Two of the ways were alongside canals, but they were long. Always, though, you crossed a bridge across a canal to enter the hospital. There was a choice of three bridges. On one of them a woman sold roasted chestnuts. It was warm, standing in front of her charcoal fire, and the chestnuts were warm afterward in your pocket. The hospital was very old and very beautiful, and you entered through a gate and walked across a courtyard and out a gate on the other side. There were usually funerals starting from the courtyard. Beyond the old hospital were the

---

1. **the war,** World War I (1914–1918).
2. game (gām), *n.* wild animals, birds, or fish hunted or caught for sport or food.

SELECTION SUMMARY

In Another Country

An American soldier, injured in World War I, is in Milan, Italy, a few hundred miles south of the fighting. Along with Italian officers who have been injured, he receives physical therapy on machines from an enthusiastic physician, whose expectations for recovery for his patients seem unrealistic.

The American interacts with one officer, a major with a wounded, withered hand. The major, once the finest fencer in Italy, does not believe that the machines will restore his hand. The major helps the American with his Italian grammar, and one day warns him vehemently not to marry because he should not place himself in a position of having things he can lose. The American later discovers that the major's young wife has died unexpectedly, and the major cannot reconcile himself to the loss.

 *For summaries in other languages, see the **Building English Proficiency** book.*

new brick pavilions,[3] and there we met every afternoon and were all very polite and interested in what was the matter, and sat in the machines that were to make so much difference.

The doctor came up to the machine where I was sitting and said: "What did you like best to do before the war? Did you practice a sport?"

I said: "Yes, football."

"Good," he said. "You will be able to play football again better than ever."

My knee did not bend and the leg dropped straight from the knee to the ankle without a calf, and the machine was to bend the knee and make it move as in riding a tricycle. But it did not bend yet, and instead the machine lurched when it came to the bending part. The doctor said: "That will all pass. You are a fortunate young man. You will play football again like a champion."

In the next machine was a major who had a little hand like a baby's. He winked at me when the doctor examined his hand, which was between two leather straps that bounced up and down and flapped the stiff fingers, and said: "And will I too play football, captain-doctor?" He had been a very great fencer,[4] and before the war the greatest fencer in Italy.

The doctor went to his office in the back room and brought a photograph which showed a hand that had been withered[5] almost as small as the major's, before it had taken a machine course, and after was a little larger. The major held the photograph with his good hand and looked at it very carefully. "A wound?" he asked.

"An industrial accident," the doctor said.

"Very interesting, very interesting," the major said, and handed it back to the doctor.

"You have confidence?"

"No," said the major.

There were three boys who came each day who were about the same age I was. They were all three from Milan, and one of them was to be a lawyer, and one was to be a painter, and one had intended to be a soldier, and after we were finished with the machines, sometimes we walked back together to the Café Cova, which was next door to the Scala.[6] We walked the short way through the communist quarter because we were four together. The people hated us because we were officers, and from a wineshop someone called out, *"A basso gli ufficiali!"*[7] as we passed. Another boy who walked with us sometimes and made us five wore a black silk handkerchief across his face because he had no nose then and his face was to be rebuilt. He had gone out to the front from the military academy and been wounded within an hour after he had gone into the front line for the first time. They rebuilt his face, but he came from a very old family and they could never get the nose exactly right. He went to South America and worked in a bank. But this was a long time ago, and then we did not any of us know how it was going to be afterward. We only knew then that there was always the war, but that we were not going to it anymore.

We all had the same medals, except the boy with the black silk bandage across his face, and he had not been at the front long enough to get any medals. The tall boy with a very pale face who was to be a lawyer had been a lieutenant of Arditi[8] and had three medals of the sort we each had only one of. He had lived a very long time with death and was a little detached.[9] We were all a little detached, and there was nothing that held us together except that we met every afternoon at the hospital. Although, as we walked to the Cova through the tough part of town, walking in the

---

3. **pavilion** (pə vil′yən), *n.* one of a group of buildings forming a hospital.
4. **fencer** (fens′er), *n.* sword fighter.
5. wither (wiᴛʜ′ər), *v.* shrivel.
6. **the Scala,** La Scala, Milan's world-famous opera house.
7. *"a basso gli ufficiali!"* Down with the officers! *[Italian]*
8. **Arditi,** an elite group of volunteers which served as storm troops of the Italian infantry.
9. detached (di tacht′), *adj.* reserved, aloof.

In Another Country   581

---

2 Literary Element

Characterization

The descriptions of the narrator and major emphasize the injuries for which they receive therapy. Yet the doctor speaks of recovery for the narrator.

Question Does the question of the major, who was a fencer, indicate that he shares the doctor's optimism? *(Possible response: No; he seems to be mocking the doctor.)*

3 Historical Note

Communist Quarter

Communists dominated a part of the city. The communists opposed the war. This accounts for their reaction *("A basso gli ufficiali!")* to the officers.

4 Literary Element

Theme

Often the underlying meaning of a story is not directly stated but is implied. Have students recall the theme of this part of Unit 6, Lost in a Crowd.

Question How might this passage about being detached reflect the theme? *(Possible response: The passage could mean figuratively that the soldiers are no longer fully present to their experiences and surroundings, that although they come together, they are each lost or alone.)*

BUILDING ENGLISH PROFICIENCY

Analyzing Mood

Help students understand how Hemingway creates a mood through subtle physical details and dialogue. Work with students to begin a three-column chart such as the one shown to list details and dialogue and to mark them with plus or minus signs, to indicate whether they contribute to a positive or a negative mood.

Details/Dialogue	Positive Mood +	Negative Mood –
war was always there		–
it was pleasant along the streets	+	

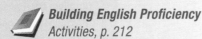
Building English Proficiency
Activities, p. 212

After Reading

MAKING CONNECTIONS

1. Possible responses: the American, because he seems so alone in a strange country; the major, for his grief and bitterness at losing his physical ability and his wife

2. The isolation of each man is shown through their individual rehabilitation on individual machines, their unshared war experiences, their personal griefs.

3. Possible responses: that the losses of the war go beyond the battlefield; that loneliness and isolation pervade modern society

4. Students may refer to the first sentence and relate the lack of connection between words and ideas to the lack of connection between people. Some students may relate the understated style to the experiences that the soldiers have but cannot share, because words do not bridge the gap between them and the other people.

5. Possible response: The soldiers' isolation is due to their role as soldiers, which they perform on behalf of society, with the result that they are alienated from society. Richard Cory's and Prufrock's alienation seems to come from internal, rather than social causes.

VOCABULARY STUDY

1. c

2. a

3. d

4. c

5. b

Unit 6 Resource Book
Vocabulary, p. 19
Vocabulary Test, p. 22

Selection Test

Unit 6 Resource Book
pp. 23–24

After Reading

Making Connections

Shaping Your Response

1. As you read "In Another Country," for which character did you have the most sympathy? Why?

Analyzing the Story

2. How does Hemingway show the loneliness of each man?

3. What do you think is the **theme** of the story?

4. Cite examples from the story that illustrate Hemingway's terse, understated **style.** Explain how this style is suited to Hemingway's theme.

Extending the Ideas

5. J. Alfred Prufrock and Richard Cory are both unhappy, lonely men. Compare their isolation to that of the soldiers in "In Another Country."

Vocabulary Study

Study the relationship of each of the following pairs of words in capital letters; then choose another pair that has the same relationship.

detached
wither
resign
citation
game

1. DEPRESSION : DETACHED : : **a.** sad : happy **b.** close : aloof **c.** virus : cold **d.** illness : cure

2. SWELL : WITHER : : **a.** bloat : shrink **b.** grape : raisin **c.** large : enormous **d.** exaggeration : silence

3. RESIGN : YIELD : : **a.** go : stop **b.** quit : apply **c.** assign : report **d.** grieve : mourn

4. CITATION : WAR : : **a.** grades : report card **b.** honorable mention : runner-up **c.** trophy : tournament **d.** medal : hero

5. DEER : GAME : : **a.** rabbit : trap **b.** hawk : predator **c.** horse : donkey **d.** tame : wild

Expressing Your Ideas

Mood Adjustment How does the mood of Childe Hassam's painting *Allies Day, May 1917* differ from the mood of "In Another Country"? Write an **analysis** describing the techniques and images the artist used to create the painting's mood.

WRITING CHOICE
Mood Adjustment

To get students started, have them write a list of words that describe the mood of the Hassam painting and a list that describes "In Another Country." Have them find and write examples or descriptions from the painting and selection for each word they wrote.

Before Reading

Winter Dreams

by F. Scott Fitzgerald

F. Scott Fitzgerald
1896–1940

F. Scott Fitzgerald wrote his novel *The Great Gatsby* while attending college at Princeton. He never finished college, but his writing brought him fame and fortune. After the success of his novel *This Side of Paradise,* Fitzgerald married Zelda Sayre, and the two took a rollercoaster ride through the Jazz Age, both at home and abroad. Both drank and partied too much, and they spent money lavishly. Their fortunes changed drastically during the Great Depression. Zelda's mental illness became unmanageable, and she was institutionalized. Fitzgerald's work was no longer popular, and he wrote screenplays in Hollywood until his early death.

Building Background

Do-Wacka-Do-Wacka-Do After the terrible years of World War I, people were ready to celebrate. Because of advances made in technology and the passage of fair labor laws, people had more leisure time. In spite of Prohibition (1919), which made making and selling alcoholic beverages illegal, "speakeasies"—private clubs where people could drink, listen to music, and dance—sprang up all over the country. Jazz blossomed as a musical style, and people danced the Charleston and the Black Bottom Rag. Henry Ford's affordable automobile made the society mobile. The thriving new movie industry created instant celebrities and fashions. Bobbed hair and flapper dresses became the rage. This was the time in which F. Scott Fitzgerald wrote, and it is the setting for "Winter Dreams."

Literary Focus

Character An author acquaints us with a **character** by describing his or her physical appearance, personality, behavior, thoughts, feelings, and speech. As you read "Winter Dreams," collect evidence to help you characterize Dexter Green and Judy Jones. Make a chart for each of them to organize your observations.

Character: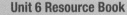

Appearance	Behavior	Speech	Thoughts

Writer's Notebook

Talk, Talk, Talk The use of dialogue makes fiction more realistic. Listen to people speaking to one another. Record bits of conversations in your notebook. Add the necessary dialogue tags to identify the speakers and to describe how they are speaking. "T. J. whispered," is an example of a dialogue tag. As you read "Winter Dreams," notice how F. Scott Fitzgerald uses dialogue to bring his characters to life.

Winter Dreams   **585**

Before Reading

Building Background

Ask students to imagine that they suddenly have lots of spending money, more free time, and an attitude that anything goes. Discuss how this might change their lives and their priorities.

Literary Focus

Note that F. Scott Fitzgerald's **characters** age from youth to maturity in this story. Students might reflect the passage of time in their charts.

Writer's Notebook

To show that we speak differently to different people, have students listen as one person speaks with a variety of people.

More About Fitzgerald

F. Scott Fitzgerald told his editor about meeting Ernest Hemingway in Paris. The editor looked up Hemingway and then published his early novels and stories.

 Connections to
AuthorWorks

F. Scott Fitzgerald is a featured author in the AuthorWorks CD-ROM series.

 Connections to
NovelWorks

NovelWorks: *The Great Gatsby* offers a rich variety of unique materials for teaching the novel.

SUPPORT MATERIALS OVERVIEW

Unit 6 Resource Book
- Graphic Organizer, p. 25
- Study Guide, p. 26
- Vocabulary, p. 27
- Grammar, p. 28
- Alternate Check Test, p. 29
- Vocabulary Test, p. 30
- Selection Test, pp. 31–32

Building English Proficiency
- Literature Summaries
- Activities, p. 213

Reading, Writing & Grammar SkillBook
- Vocabulary, pp. 11–13
- Reading, pp. 79–80
- Writing, pp. 119–120
- Grammar, Usage, and Mechanics, pp. 196–197

World of Work
- Restaurant Manager, p. 19
- Activity, p. 20

Technology
- Audiotape
- Personal Journal Software
- Custom Literature Database
  For another selection with a related theme, see "The Secret Sharer" by Joseph Conrad on the database.
- Test Generator Software

Selection Objectives

- To explore Fitzgerald's depiction of a man alone with his dreams
- To examine elements that contribute to characterization
- To be aware of realistically written dialogue
- To recognize relative pronouns

Unit 6 Resource Book
Graphic Organizer, p. 25
Study Guide, p. 26

Theme Link

The rise from country childhood to wealthy, urban lifestyle leaves Dexter Green alone with a grief for an unnamed but lost longing.

Vocabulary Preview

abruptly, unexpectedly

decisively, firmly, expressing no question or doubt

furtively, stealthily; secretly

blatantly, obviously or flagrantly

involuntarily, done in a manner that is not of one's own free will

precariously, insecurely; uncertainly

impatiently, crossly; showing a lack of patience

contemptuously, scornfully

frankly, openly; expressing one's thoughts, opinions, and feelings freely

spasmodically, in a manner characterized by sudden involuntary contractions of a muscle or muscles

Students can add the adverbs and definitions to their word lists in the Writer's Notebook.

Art Study

Illustrations by renowned illustrator J. C. Leyendecker (1874–1934) appear on this page and pages 593, 599, and 600. His commercial art helped define American styles of the early twentieth century.

Winter Dreams

F. Scott Fitzgerald

I

Some of the caddies were poor as sin and lived in one-room houses with a neurasthenic cow in the front yard, but Dexter Green's father owned the second best grocery store in Black Bear—the best one was "The Hub," patronized by the wealthy people from Sherry Island—and Dexter caddied only for pocket money.

In the fall when the days became crisp and gray, and the long Minnesota winter shut down like the white lid of a box, Dexter's skis moved over the snow that hid the fairways of the golf course. At these times the country gave him a feeling of profound melancholy— it offended him that the links should

586

SELECTION SUMMARY

Winter Dreams

In summer, Dexter Green is a golf caddy. In winter, he dreams of wealth and influence. In his fourteenth summer, he encounters the wealthy, demanding, preteen Judy Jones. When the caddy master demands that Dexter pick up Judy's clubs, Dexter quits his job. In time, he attends college in the East, becomes wealthy, and meets Judy again when he is twenty-three.

She is beautiful, and Dexter falls in love. But Judy is fickle, and he gives up hope of ever having her. He is about to be engaged to Irene Scheerer when he again encounters Judy, which ends the relationship with Irene and begins a brief, yet broken, engagement with Judy.

Years later, the now successful Dexter learns that Judy is a mistreated housewife. He realizes that there is something from long ago that is now gone forever.

 *For summaries in other languages, see the **Building English Proficiency** book.*

lie in enforced fallowness, haunted by ragged sparrows for the long season. It was dreary, too, that on the tees where the gay colors fluttered in summer there were now only the desolate sandboxes, knee-deep covered in crusted ice. When he crossed the hills the wind blew cold as misery, and if the sun was out he tramped with his eyes squinted up against the hard dimensionless glare.

In April the winter ceased abruptly.[1] The snow ran down into Black Bear Lake scarcely tarrying for the early golfers to brave the season with red and black balls. Without elation, without an interval of moist glory, the cold was gone.

Dexter knew that there was something dismal about this Northern spring, just as he knew there was something gorgeous about the fall. Fall made him clinch his hands and tremble and repeat idiotic sentences to himself, and make brisk abrupt gestures of command to imaginary audiences and armies. October filled him with hope which November raised to a sort of ecstatic triumph, and in this mood the fleeting brilliant impressions of the summer at Sherry Island were ready grist to his mill. He became a golf champion and defeated Mr. T. A. Hedrick in a marvelous match played a hundred times over the fairways of his imagination, a match each detail of which he changed about untiringly—sometimes he won with almost laughable ease, sometimes he came up magnificently from behind. Again, stepping from a Pierce-Arrow automobile, like Mr. Mortimer Jones, he strolled frigidly into the lounge of the Sherry Island Golf Club—or perhaps, surrounded by an admiring crowd, he gave an exhibition of fancy diving from the springboard of the club raft. . . . Among those who watched him in open-mouthed wonder was Mr. Mortimer Jones.

And one day it came to pass that Mr. Jones—himself and not his ghost—came up to Dexter with tears in his eyes and said that Dexter was the —— —— best caddy in the club, and wouldn't he decide not to quit if Mr. Jones made it worth his while, because every other —— —— caddy in the club lost one ball a hole for him—regularly—

"No sir," said Dexter decisively,[2] "I don't want to caddy anymore." Then, after a pause: "I'm too old."

"You're not more than fourteen. Why the devil did you decide just this morning that you wanted to quit? You promised that next week you'd go over to the state tournament with me."

"I decided I was too old."

Dexter handed in his "A Class" badge, collected what money was due him from the caddy master, and walked home to Black Bear Village.

"The best —— —— caddy I ever saw," shouted Mr. Mortimer Jones over a drink that afternoon. "Never lost a ball! Willing! Intelligent! Quiet! Honest! Grateful!"

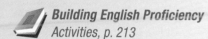

The little girl who had done this was eleven—beautifully ugly as little girls are apt to be who are destined after a few years to be inexpressibly lovely and bring no end of misery to a great number of men. The spark, however, was perceptible. There was a general ungodliness in the way her lips twisted down at the corners when she smiled, and in the—Heaven help us!—in the almost passionate quality of her eyes. Vitality is born early in such women. It was utterly in evidence now, shining through her thin frame in a sort of glow.

She had come eagerly out on to the course at nine o'clock with a white linen nurse and five small new golf clubs in a white canvas bag which the nurse was carrying. When Dexter first saw her, she was standing by the caddy house, rather ill at ease and trying to conceal the fact by engaging her nurse in an obviously unnatural conversation graced by startling and irrelevant grimaces from herself.

"Well, it's certainly a nice day, Hilda," Dexter heard her say. She drew down the corners of her mouth, smiled, and glanced furtively[3] around,

---

1. **abruptly** (ə brupt′lē), *adv.* unexpectedly.
2. **decisively** (di sī′siv lē), *adj.* firmly, expressing no question or doubt.
3. **furtively** (fėr′tiv lē), *adv.* stealthily; secretly.

Winter Dreams   **587**

---

1 Literary Focus
Character

Question How does his work at the Sherry Island Golf Club shape Dexter's character? *(Possible responses: It exposes him to rich and powerful people; it gives him perspective about those who are different from people in his own background.)*

2 Literary Element
Setting

Question What conflicts and differences does Fitzgerald's golf-club setting provide? *(Possible response: It's a setting that can bring together the well-to-do and the less well-to-do; it can illustrate dreams and aspirations of those in a lower class; it is a fantasy world set in the midst of reality.)*

The Author Speaks

"Let me tell you about the very rich. They are different from you and me. They possess and enjoy early, and it does something to them, makes them soft where we are hard, and cynical where we are trustful."

F. Scott Fitzgerald
The Rich Boy, 1926

BUILDING ENGLISH PROFICIENCY

Exploring Similes and Metaphors

Figurative language is a distinction of Fitzgerald's descriptive style. Use the following activities to encourage students to appreciate his use of language.

- Discuss the following examples from pages 586–587: poor as sin, shut down like the white lid of a box, cold as misery, grist to his mill, the fairways of his imagination. Have students try to rephrase each example in their own words.

- As students continue reading the selection, have them use their journals to record and rephrase other similes and metaphors that catch their attention. Invite sharing and whole-class discussion.

Building English Proficiency
Activities, p. 213

Making Personal Connections

Question   Do you think you would be charmed by the eleven-year-old Judy? Why or why not? *(Possible responses: yes, because she is charismatic, pretty, funny; no, because she is condescending, self-centered, spoiled)*

4 Reading/Thinking Skills
Compare and Contrast

Question   How is Judy's behavior toward her nurse different from her behavior toward Dexter? How is it the same? *(Possible responses: Judy makes small talk with her nurse, and then fights with her; with Dexter she flirts and tries to charm him. With both of them, she is haughty and acts superior.)*

---

her eyes in transit falling for an instant on Dexter.

Then to the nurse:

"Well, I guess there aren't very many people out here this morning, are there?"

The smile again—radiant, blatantly[4] artificial—convincing.

"I don't know what we're supposed to do now," said the nurse looking nowhere in particular.

"Oh, that's all right. I'll fix it up."

Dexter stood perfectly still, his mouth slightly ajar. He knew that if he moved forward a step, his stare would be in her line of vision—if he moved backward, he would lose his full view of her face. For a moment he had not realized how young she was. Now he remembered having seen her several times the year before—in bloomers.

Suddenly, involuntarily,[5] he laughed, a short abrupt laugh—then, startled by himself, he turned and began to walk quickly away.

"Boy!"

Dexter stopped.

"Boy——"

Beyond question he was addressed. Not only that, but he was treated to that absurd smile, that preposterous smile—the memory of which at least a dozen men were to carry into middle age.

"Boy, do you know where the golf teacher is?"

"He's giving a lesson."

"Well, do you know where the caddy master is?"

"He isn't here yet this morning."

"Oh." For a moment this baffled her. She stood alternately on her right and left foot.

"We'd like to get a caddy," said the nurse. "Mrs. Mortimer Jones sent us out to play golf, and we don't know how without we get a caddy."

Here she was stopped by an ominous glance from Miss Jones, followed immediately by the smile.

"There aren't any caddies here except me," said Dexter to the nurse, "and I got to stay here in charge until the caddy master gets here."

"Oh."

Miss Jones and her retinue now withdrew, and at a proper distance from Dexter became involved in a heated conversation, which was concluded by Miss Jones taking one of the clubs and hitting it on the ground with violence. For further emphasis she raised it again and was about to bring it down smartly upon the nurse's bosom, when the nurse seized the club and twisted it from her hands.

"You little mean old *thing!*" cried Miss Jones wildly.

Another argument ensued. Realizing that the elements of the comedy were implied in the scene, Dexter several times began to laugh, but each time restrained the laugh before it reached audibility. He could not resist the monstrous conviction that the little girl was justified in beating the nurse.

The situation was resolved by the fortuitous appearance of the caddy master, who was appealed to immediately by the nurse.

"Miss Jones is to have a little caddy, and this one says he can't go."

"Mr. McKenna said I was to wait here till you came," said Dexter quickly.

"Well, he's here now." Miss Jones smiled cheerfully at the caddy master. Then she dropped her bag and set off at a haughty mince toward the first tee.

"Well?" The caddy master turned to Dexter. "What you standing there like a dummy for? Go pick up the young lady's clubs."

"I don't think I'll go out today," said Dexter.

"You don't——"

"I think I'll quit."

The enormity of his decision frightened him. He was a favorite caddy, and the thirty dollars a month he earned through the summer were not to be made elsewhere around the lake. But he had received a strong emotional shock, and his perturbation required

---

4. blatantly (blāt'nt lē), *adv.* obviously or flagrantly.
5. involuntarily (in vol'ən ter'ə lē), *adv.* in a manner that is not of one's own free will.

MINI-LESSON: GRAMMAR

Relative Pronouns

Teach   A *relative pronoun* combines or relates ideas and can begin a subordinate clause. *Which, that, who, whose,* and *whom* are relative pronouns when they introduce adjective clauses.

Activity Ideas

- Have students find sentences in the story that use relative pronouns.
- Have students work in small groups to write sentences using relative pronouns. Call on each group to share their sentences with the class.

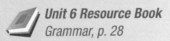
Unit 6 Resource Book
Grammar, p. 28

a violent and immediate outlet.

It is not so simple as that, either. As so frequently would be the case in the future, Dexter was unconsciously dictated to by his winter dreams.

5 CLARIFY: Why did Dexter suddenly quit his caddy job?

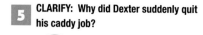

Now, of course, the quality and the seasonability of these winter dreams varied, but the stuff of them remained. They persuaded Dexter several years later to pass up a business course at the State university—his father, prospering now, would have paid his way—for the precarious advantage of attending an older and more famous university in the East, where he was bothered by his scanty funds. But do not get the impression, because his winter dreams happened to be concerned at first with musings on the rich, that there was anything merely snobbish in the boy. He wanted not association with glittering things and glittering people—he wanted the glittering things themselves. Often he reached out for the best without knowing why he wanted it—and sometimes he ran up against the mysterious denials and prohibitions in which life indulges. It is with one of those denials and not with his career as a whole that this story deals.

He made money. It was rather amazing. **6** After college he went to the city from which Black Bear Lake draws its wealthy patrons. When he was only twenty-three and had been there not quite two years, there were already people who liked to say: "Now *there's* a boy——" All about him rich men's sons were peddling bonds precariously,[6] or investing patrimonies precariously, or plodding through the two dozen volumes of the "George Washington Commercial Course," but Dexter borrowed a thousand dollars on his college degree and his confident mouth, and bought a partnership in a laundry.

It was a small laundry when he went into it, but Dexter made a specialty of learning how the English washed fine woolen golf stockings without shrinking them, and within a year he was catering to the trade that wore knickerbockers.[7] Men were insisting that their Shetland[8] hose and sweaters go to his laundry, just as they had insisted on a caddy who could find golf balls. A little later he was doing their wives' lingerie as well—and running five branches in different parts of the city. Before he was twenty-seven he owned the largest string of laundries in his section of the country. It was then that he sold out and went to New York. But the part of his story that concerns us goes back to the days when he was making his first big success.

hen he was twenty-three, Mr. Hart—one of the gray-haired men who like to say "Now there's a boy"—gave him a guest card to the Sherry Island Golf Club for a weekend. So he signed his name one day on the register, and that afternoon played golf in a foursome with Mr. Hart and Mr. Sandwood and Mr. T. A. Hedrick. He did not consider it necessary to remark that he had once carried Mr. Hart's bag over this same links, and that he knew every trap and gully with his eyes shut—but he found himself glancing at the four caddies who trailed them, trying to catch a gleam or gesture that would remind him of himself, that would lessen the gap which lay between his present and his past.

It was a curious day, slashed abruptly with fleeting, familiar impressions. One minute he had the sense of being a trespasser—in the next he was impressed by the tremendous superiority

---

6. **precariously** (pri ker′ē əs lē), *adv.* insecurely; uncertainly.
7. **knickerbockers,** full breeches gathered and banded just below the knee.
8. **Shetland,** made from the wool of Shetland sheep.

5 Active Reading
Clarify

Possible response   He cannot bear the thought of being subordinate to the demanding, coquettish little girl.

6 Geographical Note
Minnesota Connection

Minnesota is a green, fertile state bordering on Lake Superior. Fitzgerald was born in St. Paul and vacationed at White Bear Lake when he was 15 years old.

The World of Work

Dexter Green learned to manage his laundry business from the ground up. For the role of a small business **manager** today, see the pages referenced below.

The World of Work
pp. 19–20

BUILDING ENGLISH PROFICIENCY

Tracking Story Details

To assist students in following the passage of time on page 589, have them create a time line using phrases from the text that indicate time.

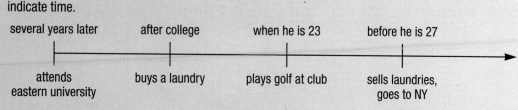

several years later — after college — when he is 23 — before he is 27

attends eastern university — buys a laundry — plays golf at club — sells laundries, goes to NY

7 Literary Element
Style

An author's style is how he or she handles language and the choices made, for example in diction, syntax, and figurative language. When Fitzgerald describes a beautiful woman, he embellishes his writing style. In this passage, he embellishes with adjectives.

Question What adjectives does Fitzgerald use to describe Judy Jones? *(passionate [eyes], down-turning [mouth], arrestingly beautiful, fluctuating and feverish [warmth], intense [life])*

8 Literary Element
Personification

Question What human quality does Fitzgerald use to personify the moon? *(He depicts the moon as a woman using a "shhh" gesture to quiet the lake.)*

---

he felt toward Mr. T. A. Hedrick, who was a bore and not even a good golfer anymore.

Then, because of a ball Mr. Hart lost near the fifteenth green, an enormous thing happened. While they were searching the stiff grasses of the rough, there was a clear call of "Fore!" from behind a hill in their rear. And as they all turned abruptly from their search a bright new ball sliced abruptly over the hill and caught Mr. T. A. Hedrick in the abdomen.

"By Gad!" cried Mr. T. A. Hedrick, "they ought to put some of these crazy women off the course. It's getting to be outrageous."

A head and a voice came up together over the hill:

"Do you mind if we go through?"

"You hit me in the stomach!" declared Mr. Hedrick wildly.

"Did I?" The girl approached the group of men. "I'm sorry. I yelled 'Fore!'"

Her glance fell casually on each of the men—then scanned the fairway for her ball.

"Did I bounce into the rough?"

It was impossible to determine whether this question was ingenuous or malicious. In a moment, however, she left no doubt, for as her partner came up over the hill she called cheerfully:

"Here I am! I'd have gone on the green except that I hit something."

As she took her stance for a short mashie[9] shot, Dexter looked at her closely. She wore a blue gingham dress, rimmed at throat and shoulders with a white edging that accentuated her tan. The quality of exaggeration, of thinness, which had made her passionate eyes and down-turning mouth absurd at eleven, was gone now. She was arrestingly beautiful. The color in her cheeks was centered like the color in a picture—it was not a "high" color, but a sort of fluctuating and feverish warmth, so shaded that it seemed at any moment it would recede and disappear. This color and the mobility of her mouth gave a continual impression of flux, of intense life, of passionate vitality—balanced only partially by the sad luxury of her eyes.

She swung her mashie impatiently[10] and without interest, pitching the ball into a sand pit on the other side of the green. With a quick, insincere smile and a careless "Thank you!" she went on after it.

"That Judy Jones!" remarked Mr. Hedrick on the next tee, as they waited—some moments—for her to play on ahead. "All she needs is to be turned up and spanked for six months and then to be married off to an old-fashioned cavalry captain."

"My, she's good-looking!" said Mr. Sandwood, who was just over thirty.

"Good-looking!" cried Mr. Hedrick contemptuously,[11] "she always looks as if she wanted to be kissed! Turning those big cow eyes on every calf in town!"

It was doubtful if Mr. Hedrick intended a reference to the maternal instinct.

"She'd play pretty good golf if she'd try," said Mr. Sandwood.

"She has no form," said Mr. Hedrick solemnly.

"She has a nice figure," said Mr. Sandwood.

"Better thank the Lord she doesn't drive a swifter ball," said Mr. Hart, winking at Dexter.

Later in the afternoon the sun went down with a riotous swirl of gold and varying blues and scarlets, and left the dry, rustling night of western summer. Dexter watched from the veranda of the Golf Club, watched the even overlap of the waters in the little wind, silver molasses under the harvest moon. Then the moon held a finger to her lips and the lake became a clear pool, pale and quiet. Dexter put on his bathing suit and swam out to the farthest raft, where he stretched dripping on the wet canvas of the springboard.

There was a fish jumping and a star shining and the lights around the lake were gleaming.

---

9. **mashie,** a kind of golf club.
10. impatiently (im pā′shənt lē), *adv.* crossly; in a manner showing a lack of patience.
11. contemptuously (kən temp′chŭ əs lē), *adv.* scornfully.

MINI-LESSON: WRITING STYLE

Descriptive Adjectives

Teach One of the ways an author's writing style is defined is through visual descriptions. Using color in interesting ways makes an author's writing unique and vivid. Finding new words to describe colors adds specificity to a writer's style. For instance, Fitzgerald uses the words *butternut* and *dull platinum*, adding sensory details that the words *tan* or *white* would have left out.

Activity Idea Have each student list an object in the room, such as a pencil, plant, radiator, chair, or computer. Then have students think of unusual ways to suggest the colors of these objects. For instance, rather than "green" plant, they may come up with "jade" plant.

Over on a dark peninsula a piano was playing the songs of last summer and of summers before that—songs from *Chin-Chin* and *The Count of Luxemburg* and *The Chocolate Soldier*[12]—and because the sound of a piano over a stretch of water had always seemed beautiful to Dexter, he lay perfectly quiet and listened.

The tune the piano was playing at that moment had been gay and new five years before when Dexter was a sophomore at college. They had played it at a prom once when he could not afford the luxury of proms, and he had stood outside the gymnasium and listened. The sound of the tune precipitated in him a sort of ecstasy, and it was with that ecstasy he viewed what happened to him now. It was a mood of intense appreciation, a sense that, for once, he was magnificently attuned to life and that everything about him was radiating a brightness and a glamor he might never know again.

A low, pale oblong detached itself suddenly from the darkness of the Island, spitting forth the reverberate sound of a racing motorboat. Two white streamers of cleft water rolled themselves out behind it and almost immediately the boat was beside him, drowning out the hot tinkle of the piano in the drone of its spray. Dexter raising himself on his arms was aware of a figure standing at the wheel, of two dark eyes regarding him over the lengthening space of water—then the boat had gone by and was sweeping in an immense and purposeless circle of spray round and round in the middle of the lake. With equal eccentricity one of the circles flattened out and headed back toward the raft.

"Who's that?" she called, shutting off her motor. She was so near now that Dexter could see her bathing suit, which consisted apparently of pink rompers.

The nose of the boat bumped the raft, and as the latter tilted rakishly, he was precipitated toward her. With different degrees of interest they recognized each other.

"Aren't you one of those men we played through this afternoon?" she demanded.

He was.

"Well, do you know how to drive a motorboat? Because if you do, I wish you'd drive this one so I can ride on the surfboard behind. My name is Judy Jones"—she favored him with an absurd smirk—rather, what tried to be a smirk, for, twist her mouth as she might, it was not grotesque, it was merely beautiful—"and I live in a house over there on the Island, and in that house there is a man waiting for me. When he drove up at the door, I drove out of the dock because he says I'm his ideal."

There was a fish jumping and a star shining and the lights around the lake were gleaming. Dexter sat beside Judy Jones and she explained how her boat was driven. Then she was in the water, swimming to the floating surfboard with a sinuous crawl. Watching her was without effort to the eye, watching a branch waving or a sea gull flying. Her arms, burned to butternut, moved sinuously among the dull platinum ripples, elbow appearing first, casting the forearm back with a cadence of falling water, then reaching out and down, stabbing a path ahead.

They moved out into the lake; turning, Dexter saw that she was kneeling on the low rear of the now uptilted surfboard.

"Go faster," she called, "fast as it'll go."

Obediently he jammed the lever forward and the white spray mounted at the bow. When he looked around again, the girl was standing up on the rushing board, her arms spread wide, her eyes lifted toward the moon.

"It's awful cold," she shouted. "What's your name?"

He told her.

"Well, why don't you come to dinner tomorrow night?"

His heart turned over like the flywheel of the boat, and, for the second time, her casual whim gave a new direction to his life.

---

12. *Chin-Chin . . . Soldier,* popular musicals and light operas of the day.

Winter Dreams **591**

9

10

9 Reader's Response
Making Personal Connections

Music is a powerful catalyst for bringing memories to life. Even though the piano tune playing in this scene is not named, readers can relate to Dexter's experience. Discuss with students different kinds of music and the feelings and memories they connect with it.

10 Literary Focus
Character

Question How does Judy's insistence of "Go faster, fast as it'll go" reflect her character? *(Possible response: It tells us she is reckless and enjoys danger and speed.)*

BUILDING ENGLISH PROFICIENCY

Analyzing Characters

To help students grasp the complexities of Judy Jones's character, suggest that they keep track of her qualities, appearance, and people's reactions on the chart shown here. Encourage students to continue adding information as they read the selection.

Judy Jones		
Qualities	**Appearance**	**People's Reactions to Her**
ingenious	wearing a pink bathing suit	irritation
cheerful		
thoughtless		

Next evening while he waited for her to come downstairs, Dexter peopled the soft deep summer room and the sun porch that opened from it with the men who had already loved Judy Jones. He knew the sort of men they were—the men who when he first went to college had entered from the great prep schools with graceful clothes and the deep tan of healthy summers. He had seen that, in one sense, he was better than these men. He was newer and stronger. Yet in acknowledging to himself that he wished his children to be like them, he was admitting that he was but the rough, strong stuff from which they eternally sprang.

When the time had come for him to wear good clothes, he had known who were the best tailors in America, and the best tailors in America had made him the suit he wore this evening. He had acquired that particular reserve peculiar to his university, that set it off from other universities. He recognized the value to him of such a mannerism and he had adopted it; he knew that to be careless in dress and manner required more confidence than to be careful. But carelessness was for his children. His mother's name had been Krimslich. She was a Bohemian of the peasant class and she had talked broken English to the end of her days. Her son must keep to the set patterns.

At a little after seven Judy Jones came downstairs. She wore a blue silk afternoon dress, and he was disappointed at first that she had not put on something more elaborate. This feeling was accentuated when, after a brief greeting, she went to the door of a butler's pantry and pushing it open called: "You can serve dinner, Martha." He had rather expected that a butler would announce dinner, that there would be a cocktail. Then he put these thoughts behind him as they sat down side by side on a lounge and looked at each other.

"Father and Mother won't be here," she said thoughtfully.

J.C. Leyendecker was an illustrator whose Arrow Collar and shirt ads made him famous in the early 1900s. The illustrations for F. Scott Fitzgerald's "Winter Dreams" are examples of Leyendecker's work. ➤

He remembered the last time he had seen her father, and he was glad the parents were not to be here tonight—they might wonder who he was. He had been born in Keeble, a Minnesota village fifty miles farther north, and he always gave Keeble as his home instead of Black Bear Village. Country towns were well enough to come from if they weren't inconveniently in sight and used as footstools by fashionable lakes.

They talked of his university, which she had visited frequently during the past two years, and of the nearby city which supplied Sherry Island with its patrons, and whither Dexter would return next day to his prospering laundries.

EVALUATE: How does the grown-up Judy compare to Dexter's recollection of her as a child?

During dinner she slipped into a moody depression which gave Dexter a feeling of uneasiness. Whatever petulance she uttered in her throaty voice worried him. Whatever she smiled at—at him, at a chicken liver, at nothing—it disturbed him that her smile could have no root in mirth, or even in amusement. When the scarlet corners of her lips curved down, it was less a smile than an invitation to a kiss.

Then, after dinner, she led him out on the dark sun porch and deliberately changed the atmosphere.

"Do you mind if I weep a little?" she said.

"I'm afraid I'm boring you," he responded quickly.

"You're not. I like you. But I've just had a terrible afternoon. There was a man I cared about,

MINI-LESSON: VOCABULARY

Prefixes

Teach   Learning about prefixes may help students understand the uses and meanings of words. A prefix is an element affixed to the beginning of a base word which alters the meaning of that word. Write these prefixes on the board with their definitions:

- *sub*—"under" or "less than"
- *anti*—"against" or "the reverse of"
- *un*—"not" or "the opposite of"
- *pre*—"before"

Activity Ideas

- Write the following words on the board and have students figure out definitions, using their knowledge of prefixes.

submarine	anticonvulsant
antisegregation	uncoiled
unostentatious	prewar

- Have students find words containing prefixes on pages 292–293. Remind them to use their knowledge about prefixes to figure out the meanings of the words from the text.

Question What information in Judy's comments about marriage might foreshadow later events in the story? *(Possible response: The fact that Judy has intended to marry a lot of men, but didn't, might foreshadow similar intentions toward Dexter.)*

 **Art Study**

J.C. (Joseph Christian) Leyendecker was a German-born American artist. Although his pictures reflect the style and fashions associated with the 1910s and 1920s, they appeal to many advertising designers as "classics" today.

and this afternoon he told me out of a clear sky that he was poor as a church mouse. He'd never even hinted it before. Does this sound horribly mundane?"

"Perhaps he was afraid to tell you."

14 "Suppose he was," she answered. "He didn't start right. You see, if I'd thought of him as poor—well, I've been mad about loads of poor men, and fully intended to marry them all. But in this case, I hadn't thought of him that way, and my interest in him wasn't strong enough to survive the shock. As if a girl calmly informed her fiancé that she was a widow. He might not object to widows, but——"

"Let's start right," she interrupted herself suddenly. "Who are you, anyhow?"

For a moment Dexter hesitated. Then:

"I'm nobody," he announced. "My career is largely a matter of futures."

"Are you poor?"

"No," he said frankly,[13] "I'm probably making more money than any man my age in the Northwest. I know that's an obnoxious remark, but you advised me to start right."

There was a pause. Then she smiled and the corners of her mouth drooped and an almost imperceptible sway brought her closer to him, looking up into his eyes. A lump rose in Dexter's throat, and he waited breathless for the

---

13. frankly (frangk lē), *adv.* openly; expressing one's thoughts, opinions, and feelings freely.

Winter Dreams **593**

BUILDING ENGLISH PROFICIENCY

Exploring Degrees of Comparison

Adjectives and adverbs that compare two things usually have an *-er* ending. Those that show the highest degree of quality when three or more things are compared usually end in *-est*.

Ask students to place the following words from pages 592–593 into the chart and then complete the chart. Answers appear in parentheses.

Word	Compares two	Shows best of three or more
great	(greater)	(greatest)
clear	(clearer)	(clearest)
poor	(poorer	(poorest)
close	(closer)	(closest)
strong	(stronger)	(strongest)

Questions

- What is Fitzgerald telling us about Judy in this sentence? *(Possible responses: Judy doesn't need anyone but herself; she is basically alone, and feeds off the youthful love presented to her.)*

- Do you now find Judy a sympathetic or an unsympathetic character? Why? *(Responses will vary. This explanation provides more depth to her character and an idea that she is merely trying to survive.)*

16 Literary Element
Metaphor

The metaphor of love as a drug is an old one. Here Fitzgerald is saying that Judy induces a dreamy trance in Dexter, rather than invigorating him.

---

experiment, facing the unpredictable compound that would form mysteriously from the elements of their lips. Then he saw—she communicated her excitement to him, lavishly, deeply, with kisses that were not a promise but a fulfillment. They aroused in him not hunger demanding renewal but surfeit[14] that would demand more surfeit . . . kisses that were like charity, creating want by holding back nothing at all.

It did not take him many hours to decide that he had wanted Judy Jones ever since he was a proud, desirous little boy.

IV

It began like that—and continued, with varying shades of intensity, on such a note right up to the denouement.[15] Dexter surrendered a part of himself to the most direct and unprincipled personality with which he had ever come in contact. Whatever Judy wanted, she went after with the full pressure of her charm. There was no divergence of method, no jockeying for position or premeditation of effects—there was a very little mental side to any of her affairs. She simply made men conscious to the highest degree of her physical loveliness. Dexter had no desire to change her. Her deficiencies were knit up with a passionate energy that transcended and justified them.

When, as Judy's head lay against his shoulder that first night, she whispered, "I don't know what's the matter with me. Last night I thought I was in love with a man and tonight I think I'm in love with you——"—it seemed to him a beautiful and romantic thing to say. It was the exquisite excitability that for the moment he controlled and owned. But a week later he was compelled to view this same quality in a different light. She took him in her roadster to a picnic supper, and after supper she disappeared, likewise in her roadster, with another man. Dexter became enormously upset and was scarcely able to be decently civil to the other people present. When she assured him that she had not kissed the other man, he knew she was lying—yet he was glad that she had taken the trouble to lie to him.

He was, as he found before the summer ended, one of a varying dozen who circulated about her. Each of them had at one time been favored above all others—about half of them still basked in the solace of occasional sentimental revivals. Whenever one showed signs of dropping out through long neglect, she granted him a brief honeyed hour, which encouraged him to tag along for a year or so longer. Judy made these forays upon the helpless and defeated without malice, indeed half unconscious that there was anything mischievous in what she did.

When a new man came to town, everyone dropped out—dates were automatically cancelled.

The helpless part of trying to do anything about it was that she did it all herself. She was not a girl who could be "won" in the kinetic sense—she was proof against cleverness, she was proof against charm; if any of these assailed her too strongly, she would immediately resolve the affair to a physical basis, and under the magic of her physical splendor the strong as well as the brilliant played her game and not their own. She was entertained only by the gratification of her desires and by the direct exercise of her own charm. Perhaps from so much youthful love, so many youthful lovers, she had come, in self-defense, to nourish herself wholly from within. **15**

Succeeding Dexter's first exhilaration came restlessness and dissatisfaction. The helpless ecstasy of losing himself in her was opiate rather than tonic. It was fortunate for his work during the winter that those moments of ecstasy came infrequently. Early in their acquaintance it had seemed for a while that there was a deep and spontaneous mutual attraction—that first August, for example—three days of long evenings on her dusky veranda, of strange wan kisses through the late afternoon, in shadowy alcoves or behind the **16**

---

14. **surfeit** (sûr′fit), *n.* overindulgence.
15. **denouement** (dā′nŭ mänt′), *n.* solution of a plot in a story, play, situation, etc.

MINI-LESSON: VOCABULARY

Homonyms and Homophones

Teach   Homonyms are words that are spelled the same and sound the same but have different definitions, such as *bear* meaning "to carry," and *bear* meaning "the animal." Homophones are words that are pronounced the same way whether or not they are spelled identically. *Pear*, meaning "a fruit," and *pare*, meaning "to cut off," are homophones.

Activity Idea   Divide the class into small groups, and assign one or more of the following words from "Winter Dreams" to each group. Have them find the word's homophone, and determine whether it is also a homonym. Some words may have more than one homophone. Suggested answers are in italics.

guest, *guessed*	fore, *four, for*
made, *maid*	club, *club*
stare, *stair*	bore, *boar*
pale, *pail*	mind, *mined*
rough, *ruff*	hours, *ours*

protecting trellises of the garden arbors, of mornings when she was fresh as a dream and almost shy at meeting him in the clarity of the rising day. There was all the ecstasy of an engagement about it, sharpened by his realization that there was no engagement. It was during those three days that, for the first time, he had asked her to marry him. She said "maybe some day," she said "kiss me," she said "I'd like to marry you," she said "I love you"— she said—nothing.

The three days were interrupted by the arrival of a New York man who visited at her house for half September. To Dexter's agony, rumor engaged them. The man was the son of the president of a great trust company. But at the end of a month it was reported that Judy was yawning. At a dance one night she sat all evening in a motorboat with a local beau, while the New Yorker searched the club for her frantically. She told the local beau that she was bored with her visitor, and two days later he left. She was seen with him at the station, and it was reported that he looked very mournful indeed.

On this note the summer ended. Dexter was twenty-four, and he found himself increasingly in a position to do as he wished. He joined two clubs in the city and lived at one of them. Though he was by no means an integral part of the stag lines at these clubs, he managed to be on hand at dances where Judy Jones was likely to appear. He could have gone out socially as much as he liked—he was an eligible young man, now, and popular with downtown fathers. His confessed devotion to Judy Jones had rather solidified his position. But he had no social aspirations and rather despised the dancing men who were always on tap for the Thursday or Saturday parties and who filled in at dinners with the younger married set. Already he was playing with the idea of going East to New York. He wanted to take Judy Jones with him. No disillusion as to the world in which she had grown up could cure his illusion as to her desirability.

Remember that—for only in the light of it can what he did for her be understood.

Eighteen months after he first met Judy Jones, he became engaged to another girl. Her name was Irene Scheerer, and her father was one of the men who had always believed in Dexter. Irene was light-haired and sweet and honorable, and a little stout, and she had two suitors whom she pleasantly relinquished when Dexter formally asked her to marry him.

Summer, fall, winter, spring, another summer, another fall—so much he had given of his active life to the incorrigible lips of Judy Jones. She had treated him with interest, with encouragement, with malice, with indifference, with contempt. She had inflicted on him the innumerable little slights and indignities possible in such a case—as if in revenge for having ever cared for him at all. She had beckoned him and yawned at him and beckoned him again and he had responded often with bitterness and narrowed eyes. She had brought him ecstatic happiness and intolerable agony of spirit. She had caused him untold inconvenience and not a little trouble. She had insulted him, and she had ridden over him, and she had played his interest in her against his interest in his work—for fun. She had done everything to him except to criticize him—this she had not done—it seemed to him only because it might have sullied the utter indifference she manifested and sincerely felt toward him.

When autumn had come and gone again, it occurred to him that he could not have Judy Jones. He had to beat this into his mind but he convinced himself at last. He lay awake at night for a while and argued it over. He told himself the trouble and pain she had caused him, he enumerated her glaring deficiencies as a wife. Then he said to himself that he loved her, and after a while he fell asleep. For a week, lest he imagine her husky voice over the telephone or her eyes opposite him at lunch, he worked hard and late, and at night he went to his office and plotted out his years.

At the end of a week he went to a dance and cut in on her once. For almost the first time

17 Literary Element
Flashback

This paragraph is part of a flashback which brings us through a year and a half of Dexter's life with Judy Jones.

Question   Why do you think Fitzgerald chooses to tell these events in flashback? *(Possible responses: Readers can better know why Dexter is engaged to Irene after seeing what eighteen months with Judy was like; also, readers can see the contrast between Judy, who torments Dexter, and Irene, who is a calm, honorable person.)*

18 Reader's Response
Making Personal Connections

Everyone has had the experience of wanting something they know is impossible. This could be a particular person, or a skill, or an object. Discuss with students the experience and feelings of not being able to have something they want.

BUILDING ENGLISH PROFICIENCY

Making Real-Life Connections

Help students understand why Dexter continues to love Judy, despite her obvious mistreatment of him.

- Have students recall movies, TV programs, or books that portray a relationship in which one character is mesmerized by another character. Ask: What qualities in both characters make such a relationship possible?

- Encourage students to name and discuss famous people who seem "perfect" in their public lives, but who appear less than perfect in their private lives.

19

Literary Focus
Character

Question How does Dexter change once he decides not to pursue Judy? *(Possible response: He is more confident, self-important, occupied by business, and pragmatic.)*

20

Active Reading
Clarify

Response Dexter likes Irene's popularity and feels comfortable and secure with her.

21

Literary Element
Imagery

Point out to students the imagery of gold surrounding Judy.

Question What images does the idea of gold evoke? *(Possible responses: wealth, warmth, a trophy, something precious)*

---

since they had met he did not ask her to sit out with him or tell her that she was lovely. It hurt him that she did not miss these things—that was all. He was not jealous when he saw that there was a new man tonight. He had been hardened against jealousy long before.

He stayed late at the dance. He sat for an hour with Irene Scheerer and talked about books and about music. He knew very little about either. But he was beginning to be master of his own time now, and he had a rather priggish notion that he—the young and already fabulously successful Dexter Green—should know more about such things.

That was in October, when he was twenty-five. In January, Dexter and Irene became engaged. It was to be announced in June, and they were to be married three months later.

The Minnesota winter prolonged itself interminably, and it was almost May when the winds came soft and the snow ran down into Black Bear Lake at last. For the first time in over a year Dexter was enjoying a certain tranquility of spirit. Judy Jones had been in Florida, and afterward in Hot Springs, and somewhere she had been engaged, and somewhere she had broken it off. At first, when Dexter had definitely given her up, it had made him sad that people still linked them together and asked for news of her, but when he began to be placed at dinner next to Irene Scheerer, people didn't ask him about her anymore—they told him about her. He ceased to be an authority on her.

May at last. Dexter walked the streets at night when the darkness was damp as rain, wondering that so soon, with so little done, so much of ecstasy had gone from him. May one year back had been marked by Judy's poignant, unforgivable yet forgiven turbulence—it had been one of those rare times when he fancied she had grown to care for him. That old penny's worth of happiness he had spent for this bushel of content. He knew that Irene would be no more than a curtain spread behind him, a hand moving among gleaming teacups, a voice

calling to children . . . fire and loveliness were gone, the magic of nights and the wonder of the varying hours and seasons . . . slender lips, down-turning, dropping to his lips and bearing him up into a heaven of eyes. . . . The thing was deep in him. He was too strong and alive for it to die lightly.

In the middle of May when the weather balanced for a few days on the thin bridge that led to deep summer, he turned in one night at Irene's house. Their engagement was to be announced in a week now—no one would be surprised at it. And tonight they would sit together on the lounge at the University Club and look on for an hour at the dancers. It gave him a sense of solidity to go with her—she was so sturdily popular, so intensely "great."

CLARIFY: What does Dexter like about Irene Scheerer? **20**

He mounted the steps of the brownstone house and stepped inside.

"Irene," he called.

Mrs. Scheerer came out of the living room to meet him.

"Dexter," she said. "Irene's gone upstairs with a splitting headache. She wanted to go with you but I made her go to bed."

"Nothing serious, I——"

"Oh, no. She's going to play golf with you in the morning. You can spare her for just one night, can't you, Dexter?"

Her smile was kind. She and Dexter liked each other. In the living room he talked for a moment before he said good night.

Returning to the University Club, where he had rooms, he stood in the doorway for a moment and watched the dancers. He leaned against the doorpost, nodded at a man or two—yawned.

"Hello, darling."

The familiar voice at his elbow startled him. Judy Jones had left a man and crossed the room to him—Judy Jones, a slender enameled doll in **21**

MINI-LESSON: LITERARY FOCUS

Character

Teach Much of what makes characters unique and three-dimensional is how they change. In "Winter Dreams," Dexter goes through several major changes, and some more subtle ones. Showing us how Dexter is changed by events is one of Fitzgerald's ways of giving us insight into the character.

Activity Ideas

• Have students make a list of all the major events that change Dexter in "Winter Dreams," such as encountering the eleven-year-old Judy, and going to school in the East.

• Divide the class into small groups and have students brainstorm alternative ways Dexter could have responded to the events that changed him.

• Have students discuss how Dexter's character would be different with each alternative change. For example, if Dexter had continued caddying, he might have gone on to get a job at the club and may never have moved away from Black Bear Lake.

cloth of gold: gold in a band at her head, gold in two slipper points at her dress's hem. The fragile glow of her face seemed to blossom as she smiled at him. A breeze of warmth and light blew through the room. His hands in the pockets of his dinner jacket tightened spasmodically.[16] He was filled with a sudden excitement.

"When did you get back?" he asked casually.

"Come here and I'll tell you about it."

She turned and he followed her. She had been away—he could have wept at the wonder of her return. She had passed through enchanted streets, doing things that were like provocative music. All mysterious happenings, all fresh and quickening hopes, had gone away with her, come back with her now.

She turned in the doorway.

"Have you a car here? If you haven't, I have."

"I have a coupé."

In then, with a rustle of golden cloth. He slammed the door. Into so many cars she had stepped—like this—like that—her back against the leather, so—her elbow resting on the door—waiting. She would have been soiled long since had there been anything to soil her—except herself—but this was her own self outpouring.

With an effort he forced himself to start the car and back into the street. This was nothing, he must remember. She had done this before, and he had put her behind him, as he would have crossed a bad account from his books.

*H*e drove slowly downtown, and, affecting abstraction, traversed the deserted streets of the business section, peopled here and there where a movie was giving out its crowd or where consumptive or pugilistic youth lounged in front of pool halls. The clink of glasses and the slap of hands on the bars issued from saloons, cloisters of glazed glass and dirty yellow light.

She was watching him closely and the silence was embarrassing, yet in this crisis he could find no casual word with which to profane the hour.

At a convenient turning he began to zigzag back toward the University Club.

"Have you missed me?" she asked suddenly. [22]

"Everybody missed you."

He wondered if she knew of Irene Scheerer. She had been back only a day—her absence had been almost contemporaneous with his engagement.

"What a remark!" Judy laughed sadly—without sadness. She looked at him searchingly. He became absorbed in the dashboard.

"You're handsomer than you used to be," she said thoughtfully. "Dexter, you have the most rememberable eyes."

He could have laughed at this, but he did not laugh. It was the sort of thing that was said to sophomores. Yet it stabbed at him.

"I'm awfully tired of everything, darling." She called everyone darling, endowing the endearment with careless, individual camaraderie. "I wish you'd marry me."

The directness of this confused him. He should have told her now that he was going to marry another girl, but he could not tell her. He could as easily have sworn that he had never loved her. [23]

"I think we'd get along," she continued, on the same note, "unless probably you've forgotten me and fallen in love with another girl."

Her confidence was obviously enormous. She had said, in effect, that she found such a thing impossible to believe, that if it were true he had merely committed a childish indiscretion—and probably to show off. She would forgive him, because it was not a matter of any moment but rather something to be brushed aside lightly.

"Of course, you could never love anybody but me," she continued, "I like the way you love me. Oh, Dexter, have you forgotten last year?"

"No, I haven't forgotten."

"Neither have I!"

---

16. **spasmodically** (spaz modʹik lē), *adv.* in a manner characterized by sudden, involuntary contractions of a muscle or muscles.

22 Literary Element
Dialogue

Discuss with students how a conversation can have much more depth than the surface meaning suggests. In this dialogue, Judy is in a subtle tug-of-war with Dexter, trying to determine if he is still emotionally attached to her. With his reply, Dexter attempts to hold her at arm's length.

23 Reader's Response
Making Personal Connections

Question   At this point, do you think Judy will succeed in pulling Dexter away from Irene? What do you hope he does? *(Possible responses: I hope he stays with Irene because she's good for him; I hope he leaves Irene and pursues Judy, because he doesn't really love Irene.)*

BUILDING ENGLISH PROFICIENCY

ESL LEP ELD SAE LD

Expanding Vocabulary Notebooks

Encourage students to expand their vocabulary notebooks by adding words from "Winter Dreams" that they find unusual or difficult.

- Offer these examples from pages 596–597:

priggish	poignant
provocative	prolonged
fancied	abstraction
interminably	sturdily
pugilistic	

- Suggest that students record the words, the meanings, and a sample sentence for each. Encourage the use of a dictionary.

fancied	imagined

Peter was clumsy, yet he <u>fancied</u> himself a great acrobat.

Style

Rather than saying that the Joneses' home is merely *big* or *fancy*, Fitzgerald describes it with grand words, such as *somnolent, gorgeous*, and *drenched with the splendor of the damp moonlight*. Remind students of the similar grand descriptions of Judy's beauty.

25 Literary Focus
Character

"Winter Dreams" is a coming-of-age story in which we see Dexter go through many changes. Here he changes again.

Questions

- How would you describe Dexter at this point in his life? *(He becomes hardened and invulnerable, but accepting of his situation.)*
- How is this different or the same as the teenage Dexter at the beginning of the story? *(Possible response: As a teen, he was looking for adoration and dreaming of wealth and influence; he no longer pursues elusive fantasies.)*

Was she sincerely moved—or was she carried along by the wave of her own acting?

"I wish we could be like that again," she said, and he forced himself to answer:

"I don't think we can."

"I suppose not. . . . I hear you're giving Irene Scheerer a violent rush."

There was not the faintest emphasis on the name, yet Dexter was suddenly ashamed.

"Oh, take me home," cried Judy suddenly; "I don't want to go back to that idiotic dance—with those children."

Then, as he turned up the street that led to the residence district, Judy began to cry quietly to herself. He had never seen her cry before.

24 The dark street lightened, the dwellings of the rich loomed up around them, he stopped his coupé in front of the great white bulk of the Mortimer Joneses' house, somnolent, gorgeous, drenched with the splendor of the damp moonlight. Its solidity startled him. The strong walls, the steel of the girders, the breadth and beam and pomp of it were there only to bring out the contrast with the young beauty beside him. It was sturdy to accentuate her slightness—as if to show what a breeze could be generated by a butterfly's wing.

He sat perfectly quiet, his nerves in wild clamor, afraid that if he moved, he would find her irresistibly in his arms. Two tears had rolled down her wet face and trembled on her upper lip.

"I'm more beautiful than anybody else," she said brokenly, "why can't I be happy?" Her moist eyes tore at his stability—her mouth turned slowly downward with an exquisite sadness: "I'd like to marry you if you'll have me, Dexter. I suppose you think I'm not worth having, but I'll be so beautiful for you, Dexter."

A million phrases of anger, pride, passion, hatred, tenderness fought on his lips. Then a perfect wave of emotion washed over him, carrying off with it a sediment of wisdom, of convention, of doubt, of honor. This was his girl who was speaking, his own, his beautiful, his pride.

598 Unit Six: Modern Dilemmas

Would this 1913 ad by J.C. Leyendecker best portray Dexter with Judy or with Irene? Explain your choice. ➤

"Won't you come in?" He heard her draw in her breath sharply.

Waiting.

"All right," his voice was trembling, "I'll come in."

V

It was strange that neither when it was over nor a long time afterward did he regret that night. Looking at it from the perspective of ten years, the fact that Judy's flare for him endured just one month seemed of little importance. Nor did it matter that by his yielding he subjected himself to a deeper agony in the end and gave serious hurt to Irene Scheerer and to Irene's parents, who had befriended him. There was nothing sufficiently pictorial about Irene's grief to stamp itself on his mind.

25 Dexter was at bottom hard minded. The attitude of the city on his action was of no importance to him, not because he was going to leave the city, but because any outside attitude on the situation seemed superficial. He was completely indifferent to popular opinion. Nor, when he had seen that it was no use, that he did not possess in himself the power to move fundamentally or to hold Judy Jones, did he bear any malice toward her. He loved her, and he would love her until the day he was too old for loving—but he could not have her. So he tasted the deep pain that is reserved only for the strong, just as he had tasted for a little while the deep happiness.

Even the ultimate falsity of the grounds upon which Judy terminated the engagement that she did not want to "take him away" from Irene—Judy who had wanted nothing else—did not revolt him. He was beyond any revulsion or any amusement.

MINI-LESSON: READING/THINKING SKILLS

Essential and Incidental Information

Teach Essential information gives us the facts of who, why, where, when, and how in a story. Incidental information includes vivid descriptions and details that make a story more interesting and entertaining.

Activity Idea Have students read the following excerpt from page 598 of the selection. Have them focus on essential and incidental information.

"Looking at it from the perspective of ten years, the fact that Judy's flare for him endured just one month seemed of little importance. Nor did it matter that by his yielding he subjected himself to a deeper agony in the end and gave serious hurt to Irene Scheerer and to Irene's parents, who had befriended him."

Ask: What is the essential and incidental information in this excerpt? *(Students' answers might include Dexter's being reunited with Judy for only a month and his breaking off his relationship with Irene as essential information. They might include the one-month duration and Irene's parents' grief as incidental.)*

Response to Caption Question
Students might say this portrays Dexter with Judy because of the woman's coquettishness and very stylish posture. Others might say this portrays Dexter with Irene because the man appears disinterested or distracted.

BUILDING ENGLISH PROFICIENCY

Making Cultural Connections

Judy's rhetorical question—"I'm more beautiful than anybody else . . ., why can't I be happy?"—is one that seems to be universal. Lead students to consider this issue with the following questions:

- What is the most important quality you would want in a "significant other"?

- Where does beauty rate as a desirable quality in a partner?

- Do you think that Judy is right in thinking that because she is physically attractive she should be happy? Why or why not?

- What qualities does any culture familiar to you consider necessary for a desirable partner? How are those qualities alike or different from those in Fitzgerald's story?

He went East in February with the intention of selling out his laundries and settling in New York—but the war came to America in March and changed his plans. He returned to the West, handed over the management of the business to his partner, and went into the first officers' training camp in late April. He was one of those young thousands who greeted the war with a certain amount of relief, welcoming the liberation from webs of tangled emotion.

VI

This story is not his biography, remember, although things creep into it which have nothing to do with those dreams he had when he was young. We are almost done with them and with him now. There is only one more incident to be related here, and it happens seven years farther on.

It took place in New York, where he had done well—so well that there were no barriers too high for him. He was thirty-two years old, and, except for one flying trip immediately after the war, he had not been West in seven years. A man named Devlin from Detroit came into his office to see him in a business way, and then and there this incident occurred, and closed out, so to speak, this particular side of his life.

"So you're from the Middle West," said the man Devlin with careless curiosity. "That's funny—I thought men like you were probably born and raised on Wall Street. You know—wife of one of my best friends in Detroit came from your city. I was an usher at the wedding."

Dexter waited with no apprehension of what was coming.

"Judy Simms," said Devlin with no particular interest; "Judy Jones she was once."

"Yes, I knew her." A dull impatience spread over him. He had heard, of course, that she was married—perhaps deliberately he had heard no more.

"Awfully nice girl," brooded Devlin meaninglessly, "I'm sort of sorry for her."

In what ways does this man from an Arrow Collar advertisement by J.C. Leyendecker (1919) resemble Dexter Green at the end of the story?

"Why?" Something in Dexter was alert, receptive, at once.

"Oh, Lud Simms has gone to pieces in a way. I don't mean he ill-uses her, but he drinks and runs around——"

"Doesn't she run around?"

"No. Stays at home with her kids."

"Oh."

"She's a little too old for him," said Devlin.

"Too old!" cried Dexter. "Why, man, she's only twenty-seven."

He was possessed with a wild notion of rushing out into the streets and taking a train to Detroit. He rose to his feet spasmodically.

"I guess you're busy," Devlin apologized quickly. "I didn't realize——"

"No, I'm not busy," said Dexter, steadying his voice. "I'm not busy at all. Not busy at all. Did

MINI-LESSON: STUDY SKILLS

Primary and Secondary Sources

Teach   Remind students that when doing research, facts that are generally unknown need to be supported with their sources, that is, where the information was found. There are primary sources, such as documents, journals, letters, and autobiographies, that state the words of the person actually involved in the event being researched, and secondary sources, which are the words of someone who has examined a primary source and then commented on it or depictions of primary sources.

Activity Ideas

- Have students bring in examples of primary-source material about the 1920s.
- Ask students to discuss how they found their source, and what, if any, problems they encountered in finding their material.

you say she was—twenty-seven? No, I said she was twenty-seven."

"Yes, you did," agreed Devlin dryly.

"Go on, then. Go on."

"What do you mean?"

"About Judy Jones."

Devlin looked at him helplessly.

"Well, that's—I told you all there is to it. He treats her like the devil. Oh, they're not going to get divorced or anything. When he's particularly outrageous she forgives him. In fact, I'm inclined to think she loves him. She was a pretty girl when she first came to Detroit."

A pretty girl! The phrase struck Dexter as ludicrous.

"Isn't she—a pretty girl anymore?"

"Oh, she's all right."

"Look here," said Dexter, sitting down suddenly. "I don't understand. You say she was a 'pretty girl' and now you say she's 'all right.' I don't understand what you mean—Judy Jones wasn't a pretty girl, at all. She was a great beauty. Why, I knew her. She was——"

Devlin laughed pleasantly.

"I'm not trying to start a row," he said. "I think Judy's a nice girl and I like her. I can't understand how a man like Lud Simms could fall madly in love with her, but he did." Then he added: "Most of the women like her."

Dexter looked closely at Devlin, thinking wildly that there must be a reason for this, some insensitivity in the man or some private malice.

"Lots of women fade just like *that*," Devlin snapped his fingers. "You must have seen it happen. Perhaps I've forgotten how pretty she was at her wedding. I've seen her so much since then, you see. She has nice eyes."

A sort of dullness settled down upon Dexter. For the first time in his life he felt like getting very drunk. He knew that he was laughing loudly at something Devlin had said, but he did not know what it was or why it was funny. When, in a few minutes, Devlin went he lay down on his lounge and looked out the window at the New York skyline into which the sun was sinking in dull lovely shades of pink and gold.

He had thought that having nothing else to lose he was invulnerable at last—but he knew that he had just lost something more, as surely as if he had married Judy Jones and seen her fade away before his eyes.

The dream was gone. Something had been taken from him. In a sort of panic he pushed the palms of his hands into his eyes and tried to bring up a picture of the waters lapping on Sherry Island and the moonlit veranda, and gingham on the golf links and the dry sun and the gold color of her neck's soft down. And her mouth damp to his kisses and her eyes plaintive with melancholy and her freshness like new fine linen in the morning. Why, these things were no longer in the world! They had existed and they existed no longer.

For the first time in years the tears were streaming down his face. But they were for himself now. He did not care about mouth and eyes and moving hands. He wanted to care, and he could not care. For he had gone away and he could never go back anymore. The gates were closed, the sun was gone down, and there was no beauty but the gray beauty of steel that withstands all time. Even the grief he could have borne was left behind in the country of illusion, of youth, of the richness of life, where his winter dreams had flourished.

"Long ago," he said, "long ago, there was something in me, but now that thing is gone. Now that thing is gone, that thing is gone. I cannot cry. I cannot care. That thing will come back no more."

26 Reading/Thinking Skills
Draw Conclusions

Question What do you think the "thing" inside of Dexter is? *(Possible responses: passion, the part of him that dreamed and cared; the elusive fantasy of idealized love)*

Check Test

1. What is the content of Dexter's winter dreams? *(He dreams of being wealthy and powerful like the people at the golf club.)*

2. How old is Dexter when he first meets Judy? *(fourteen)*

3. How does Dexter earn his fortune? *(In a laundry business that caters to wealthy golfers.)*

4. Where does Dexter first see Judy as an adult? *(at the Sherry Island Golf Club)*

5. What does the business associate tell Dexter about Judy? *(He says Judy is a married housewife who is treated badly by her husband, and is no longer beautiful.)*

Unit 6 Resource Book
Alternate Check Test, p. 29

BUILDING ENGLISH PROFICIENCY

Summarizing Ideas

Wrap up this story by discussing the idea of unattainable, unrequited love. Ask questions such as

- How do you think Dexter views himself and his unrequited love for Judy? Why?
- Do you consider his unrequited love admirable or ridiculous? Why?
- Do you think Judy is deserving of the life she is reported to have? Why or why not?
- What do you think the rest of life will be like for Dexter? for Judy?

After Reading

MAKING CONNECTIONS

1. Responses will vary. Some students may wish to be friends with Judy because she is pretty, active, and rich. Others might not because she is disloyal and self-centered.

2. He is attracted to her beauty, her family's wealth and social status, and maybe also because she is unattainable.

3. Possible responses: Winter dreams are his fantasy of being wealthy and important. His dreams fall apart when, as in winter when things seem to die, his romantic ideal dies.

4. He has a need to impress her perhaps because he feels insecure about his position in society.

5. Responses will vary. Students might say he is marrying someone unthreatening, proper, and stable.

6. He has lost his last illusion about the desirability of the fantasy world Judy represented to him.

7. Possible responses: He would have been happier because he would not be alone and would have a family; he would be unhappy because he would always wish for something else.

8. Responses will vary. Students who aspire to make fortunes and move away from their families may share Dexter's perspective. Others may feel he is materialistic, placing too much emphasis on wealth, status, and physical beauty.

After Reading

Making Connections

Shaping Your Response

1. Would you want Judy Jones for a friend? Why or why not?

2. What do you think makes Judy Jones so appealing to Dexter Green?

Analyzing the Story

3. When Dexter gave up caddying, he was "unconsciously dictated to by his *winter dreams*." Why do you think these words are the title of the story, and what do you think the title means?

4. Why do you think Dexter tells Judy that "I'm probably making more money than any man my age in the Northwest"?

5. Why do you think Dexter becomes engaged to Irene Scheerer?

6. After Dexter hears about Judy Jones Simms from a business associate, he is bereft. "The dream was gone. Something had been taken from him." What do you think Dexter has lost?

Extending the Ideas

7. Would Dexter have been happier if he had married Irene? Explain your answer.

8. ☞ Compare Dexter Green's **perspective** on life to your own. What kinds of things are most important to Dexter, and are his values the same as or different than yours?

Literary Focus: Character

Use the charts you made to write a gossip-column article describing Dexter Green and Judy Jones.

Vocabulary Study

Complete each sentence with the adverb from the list that matches the context of the sentence.

decisively
spasmodically
blatantly
precariously
contemptuously
furtively
involuntarily
impatiently
abruptly
frankly

1. Dexter couldn't wait to have Judy as his wife. "I absolutely have to marry Judy," Dexter said to himself ____.

2. Mr. Scheerer—Irene's father—scorned Dexter's attentions to Judy, and eyed Dexter ____ as he escorted Judy out of the club.

3. Judy obviously did not love Dexter, and lied ____ when she told him that she wanted to marry him.

4. Mr. Mortimer Jones seemed to have little control over his movements, and gripped his golf club ____.

5. Dexter's uncertain feelings for Irene were ____ balanced against his infatuation with Judy Jones.

6. Dexter didn't want anyone to see him looking, so he glanced ____ around the room to see if anyone noticed him leaving with Judy.

602 UNIT SIX: MODERN DILEMMAS

LITERARY FOCUS: CHARACTER

Students should incorporate what they know about Dexter and Judy to place them in character-appropriate situations, surrounded by plausible people and doing plausible activities. Encourage students to include "direct quotations" from the characters in their column.

Suggest that they use research about styles and trends of the 1920s to add realistic details to their gossip column. They might illustrate the column with a drawing of Dexter and Judy dancing, dining, or strolling together.

7. Without warning, Judy stopped the speedboat ____, almost hitting the raft.

8. Dexter couldn't help himself, and he laughed ____ when young Judy called him "Boy!"

9. Judy Jones was quite certain she wanted to leave when she said ____, "Let's escape from this boring party right now."

10. "To answer your question, Judy, I'm making a lot of money," said Dexter ____, expressing himself freely.

Expressing Your Ideas

Writing Choices

Writer's Notebook Update Reread the dialogue you recorded in your notebook. Then try your hand at writing your own realistic dialogue. Imagine that Dexter runs into Irene Scheerer the summer after their break-up. Write a conversation that they might have.

Take a Peek Although Judy Jones doesn't seem introspective, perhaps she kept a diary. Be Judy and write six **diary entries**—one to follow each of the six sections of the story.

Art Imitates Life Much of F. Scott Fitzgerald's writing is autobiographical. Find out more about his life and make a **chart** listing the similarities between the characters and events in "Winter Dreams" and F. Scott Fitzgerald's life.

Similarities	
Events in "Winter Dreams"	Events in Fitzgerald's life

Other Options

The Jazz Age Work with a small group to research the roots of jazz as a musical style and define it. Then find recordings of famous jazz musicians of the 1920s. Give an **oral report** and play some of the recordings for the class.

The Roaring Twenties What were the highlights of the 1920s? Create a **multimedia report** showing the fashions of the day, the major political events, entertainment trends, famous people, and so on.

Women of the Jazz Age At the time this story took place, men did not generally consider women their equals. Make a **list of quotations** from the story that represent attitudes toward women. For example, Mr. Hedrick says of Judy, "All she needs is to be turned up and spanked for six months and then to be married off to an old-fashioned cavalry captain."

Winter Dreams **603**

Before Reading

Building Background

Discuss with students the historical and cultural influences of the period of Richard Wright's life (1908–1960).

- The Great Migration from the South to the Northern urban centers
- The legacy of the Harlem Renaissance

Literary Focus

Through Wright's **dialogue** we get to know his classmates, editor, and family. Have students give examples of vivid dialogue from the story.

Writer's Notebook

Students might find it easier to write plot titles first and then their plot ideas.

More About Richard Wright

A New York stage production of Wright's 1940 novel, *Native Son,* was produced by John Houseman and directed by Orson Welles in 1941.

Connections to
AuthorWorks

Richard Wright is a featured author in the AuthorWorks CD-ROM series.

Connections to
NovelWorks

NovelWorks: *Black Boy* offers a rich variety of materials for teaching the novel.

Before Reading

from Black Boy

by Richard Wright

Richard Wright
1908–1960

All four of Richard Wright's grandparents were born into slavery. His father was a sharecropper who deserted the family when Wright was five, and his mother fell ill and was eventually paralyzed. Wright and his brother were passed from relative to orphanage to relative until, at age fifteen, he went out on his own. After moving about the country, he eventually went to New York to pursue his writing career. Wright's most famous book, *Native Son,* was published in 1940, followed by *Black Boy* in 1944. Wright continued writing and traveled extensively, later moving his family to France to escape the racial discrimination they encountered in the United States.

Building Background

Set the Scene *Black Boy* is the autobiographical account of Richard Wright's life. The incident in this excerpt occurred when Wright was in the eighth grade at Smith Robertson Junior High School in Jackson, Mississippi. Wright and his mother lived with his grandmother, a strict Seventh-Day Adventist. For Wright's family poverty was a way of life. Keeping food on the table and the rent paid were the primary goals. There was no time for "foolish dreams" like writing. Racial discrimination was enforced by law. Ambition was not rewarded. In spite of this hostile environment, the seeds of Wright's future career as a writer began to grow.

Literary Focus

Look Who's Talking Dialogue, the conversation between two or more people in a literary work, can serve many purposes. It can help to characterize both the speaker and those spoken about, it can create a mood or atmosphere, it can move the plot forward, and it can develop a theme. As you read this excerpt from *Black Boy,* think about the purposes of the dialogue. What does it contribute to the story of Wright's life?

Writer's Notebook

What's In a Name? Richard Wright was bored, so he decided to write a story. He wrote it in three days and gave it a title that really caught the reader's eye. In your notebook jot down several plot ideas that you might like to develop into a story. Then write an eye-catching title that you think would be appropriate for each idea.

SUPPORT MATERIALS OVERVIEW

Unit 6 Resource Book
- Graphic Organizer, p. 33
- Study Guide, p. 34
- Vocabulary, p. 35
- Grammar, p. 36
- Alternate Check Test, p. 37
- Vocabulary Test, p. 38
- Selection Test, pp. 39–40

Building English Proficiency
- Literature Summaries
- Activities, p. 214

Reading, Writing & Grammar SkillBook
- Reading, pp. 59–61
- Grammar, Usage, and Mechanics, pp. 152–153

Technology
- Audiotape
- Personal Journal Software
- Custom Literature Database
  For a selection with a related theme, see "My Struggle for an Education," by Booker T. Washington, on the database.
- Test Generator Software

FROM

Black Boy

RICHARD WRIGHT

The eighth grade days flowed in their hungry path and I grew more conscious of myself; I sat in classes, bored, wondering, dreaming. One long dry afternoon I took out my composition book and told myself that I would write a story; it was sheer idleness that led me to it. What would the story be about? It resolved itself into a plot about a villain who wanted a widow's home and I called it *The Voodoo of Hell's Half-Acre*. It was crudely atmospheric, emotional, intuitively psychological, and stemmed from pure feeling. I finished it in three days and then wondered what to do with it.

The local Negro newspaper! That's it . . . I sailed into the office and shoved my ragged composition book under the nose of the man who called himself the editor.

"What is that?" he asked.

"A story," I said.

"A news story?"

"No, fiction."

"All right. I'll read it," he said.

He pushed my composition book back on his desk and looked at me curiously, sucking at his pipe.

"But I want you to read it *now*," I said.

He blinked. I had no idea how newspapers were run. I thought that one took a story to an editor and he sat down then and there and read it and said yes or no.

"I'll read this and let you know about it tomorrow," he said.

I was disappointed; I had taken time to write it and he seemed distant and uninterested.

"Give me the story," I said, reaching for it.

He turned from me, took up the book and read ten pages or more.

"Won't you come in tomorrow?" he asked. "I'll have it finished then."

I honestly relented.[1]

"All right," I said. "I'll stop in tomorrow."

I left with the conviction[2] that he would not read it. Now, where else could I take it after he had turned it down? The next afternoon, en route to my job, I stepped into the newspaper office.

"Where's my story?" I asked.

"It's in galleys," he said.

"What's that?" I asked; I did not know what galleys were.

"It's set up in type," he said. "We're publishing it."

"How much money will I get?" I asked, excited.

"We can't pay for manuscript," he said.

"But you sell your papers for money," I said with logic.

"Yes, but we're young in business," he explained.

"But you're asking me to *give* you my story, but you don't *give* your papers away," I said.

He laughed.

"Look, you're just starting. This story will put your name before our readers. Now, that's something," he said.

---

1. relent (ri lent′), *v.* give in.
2. conviction (kən vik′shən), *n.* firm belief, certainty.

Black Boy **605**

During Reading

Selection Objectives

- To discuss how determination and aspiration can contribute to being alone in a crowd
- To explore the purposes of dialogue
- To learn to avoid writing run-on sentences

 Unit 6 Resource Book
Graphic Organizer, p. 33
Study Guide, p. 34

Theme Link

Young Richard Wright finds himself alone without support when he uses his imagination.

Vocabulary Preview

relent, give in

conviction, firm belief, certainty

alien, strange; foreign

hedge, avoid giving a direct answer

contemptuous, showing the feeling that a person, act, or thing is mean, low, or worthless

naive, not sophisticated

aspiration, longing; ambition

taboo, prohibited; banned

articulate, able to put one's thoughts into words easily and clearly

yearning, strong desire; longing

Students can add the words and meanings to their word lists in the Writer's Notebook.

SELECTION SUMMARY

Black Boy

In this excerpt from *Black Boy*, Richard Wright describes writing his first story. Out of the boredom of his eighth-grade classroom, he writes a story entitled "The Voodoo of Hell's Half-Acre." He takes his story to the editor of the local Negro newspaper, who agrees to print it in three parts. Richard wants to be paid, but all the editor offers him is exposure.

When the story is published, Richard's classmates don't believe the story is Richard's idea and don't understand why he wants to write. His Granny believes writing made-up stories is the devil's work. His mother is worried that writing will make him seem foolish. Even though he receives not one encouraging word, he still aspires to move North and become a writer. He begins to reject the limited ambitions allowed for black people and feels he is on the verge of major change.

 *For summaries in other languages, see the **Building English Proficiency** book.*

Literary Focus

Dialogue

Dialogue can help to create a mood or atmosphere. The dialogue of the class-mates helps to set a mood of disbelief, suspicion, and nonsupport.

Question What contributes to making Wright's dialogue with his classmates humorous? *(Possible responses: the repetition, the fact that they continue to challenge what they don't understand, the short sentences)*

Reading/Thinking Skills

Recognize Values

Questions

- In Granny's opinion, what is wrong with made-up stories? *(Granny believes any made-up story is a lie.)*
- What evidence of her values is in Granny's statements? *(She is concerned with how her grandson speaks; she believes that writing is the devil's work.)*

"But if the story is good enough to sell to your readers, then you ought to give me some of the money you get from it," I insisted.

He laughed again and I sensed that I was amusing him.

"I'm going to offer you something more valuable than money," he said. "I'll give you a chance to learn to write."

I was pleased, but I still thought he was taking advantage of me.

"When will you publish my story?"

"I'm dividing it into three installments," he said. "The first installment appears this week. But the main thing is this: Will you get news for me on a space rate basis?"

"I work mornings and evenings for three dollars a week," I said.

"Oh," he said. "Then you better keep that. But what are you doing this summer?"

"Nothing."

"Then come to see me before you take another job," he said. "And write some more stories."

A few days later my classmates came to me with baffled eyes, holding copies of the *Southern Register* in their hands.

"Did you really write that story?" they asked
1 me.

"Yes."

"Why?"

"Because I wanted to."

"Where did you get it from?"

"I made it up."

"You didn't. You copied it out of a book."

"If I had, no one would publish it."

"But what are they publishing it for?"

"So people can read it."

"Who told you to do that?"

"Nobody."

"Then why did you do it?"

"Because I wanted to," I said again.

They were convinced that I had not told them the truth. We had never had any instruction in literary matters at school; the literature

---

of the nation or the Negro had never been mentioned. My schoolmates could not understand why anyone would want to write a story; and, above all, they could not understand why I had called it *The Voodoo of Hell's Half-Acre.* The mood out of which a story was written was the most alien[3] thing conceivable to them. They looked at me with new eyes, and a distance, a suspiciousness came between us. If I had thought anything in writing the story, I had thought that perhaps it would make me more acceptable to them, and now it was cutting me off from them more completely than ever.

At home the effects were no less disturbing. Granny came into my room early one morning and sat on the edge of my bed.

"Richard, what is this you're putting in the papers?" she asked.

"A story," I said.

"About what?"

"It's just a story, granny."

"But they tell me it's been in three times."

"It's the same story. It's in three parts."

"But what is it about?" she insisted.

I hedged,[4] fearful of getting into a religious argument.

"It's just a story I made up," I said.

"Then it's a lie," she said.

"Oh, Christ," I said.

"You must get out of this house if you take the name of the Lord in vain," she said.

"Granny, please . . . I'm sorry," I pleaded. "But it's hard to tell you about the story. You see, granny, everybody knows that the story isn't true, but . . ."

"Then why write it?" she asked.

"Because people might want to read it."

"That's the Devil's work," she said and left. **2**

My mother also was worried.

"Son, you ought to be more serious," she said. "You're growing up now and you won't be able to get jobs if you let people think that

---

3. **alien** (ā′lyən), *adj.* strange; foreign.
4. **hedge** (hej), *v.* avoid giving a direct answer.

MINI-LESSON: GRAMMAR

Avoiding Run-On Sentences

Teach Richard Wright tells his story with some long sentences. He combines clauses, using conjunctions such as *and,* as well as semicolons or other punctuation. He avoids run-on sentences. Remind students to avoid run-on sentences by creating compound sentences using semicolons or conjunctions with commas. Run-ons confuse readers by omitting punctuation or conjunctions needed to clearly join clauses.

Activity Ideas

- Have students find compound sentences in this selection, for example: "We had never had any instruction in literary matters at school; the literature of the nation or the Negro had never been mentioned." (p. 606)

- Have students add a semicolon and a comma where needed in the following sentence. *(semicolon after "schooling"; comma after "nation")* I was in my fifteenth year in terms of schooling I was far behind the average youth of the nation but I did not know that.

- Encourage students to examine their own writing for run-on sentences and to correct the punctuation.

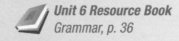

Unit 6 Resource Book
Grammar, p. 36

What thoughts, moods, or emotions do you think are portrayed in Hughie Lee Smith's, *Portrait of a Boy* (1938)? Explain your answer.

you're weak-minded. Suppose the superintendent of schools would ask you to teach here in Jackson, and he found out that you had been writing stories?"

I could not answer her.

"I'll be all right, mama," I said.

Uncle Tom, though surprised, was highly critical and contemptuous.[5] The story had no point, he said. And whoever heard of a story by the title of *The Voodoo of Hell's Half-Acre?* Aunt

---

5. **contemptuous** (kən temp′chŭ əs), *adj.* showing the feeling that a person, act, or thing is mean, low, or worthless.

3 Reader's Response
Making Personal Connections

Questions

- What kind of support is Richard getting for his writing? *(Other than from the publisher, so far it is negative.)*

- What position would you take about Wright's writing? Would you be a supporter or a detractor? Why? *(Responses will vary.)*

Art Study

Response to Caption Question
Responses will vary. Students should support their interpretations with evidence of something visual in the portrait, for example, his crossed arms make him appear determined; the set of his down-turned mouth may express sadness or disappointment.

The Author speaks

". . . I don 't know if the book I'm working on now will be a good book or a bad book. And I really don't care. The mere writing of it will be more fun and a deeper satisfaction than any praise or blame from anybody."

Richard Wright
from "How 'Bigger' was Born"
New York, March 7, 1940

BUILDING ENGLISH PROFICIENCY

Making Personal Connections

The following activity ideas will help students understand the reactions of Richard's friends and family and how those reactions dampen Richard's own pleasure at being published.

- Ask students to recall a time when they have had a positive experience, for example, being chosen for membership in a sports team or school club or receiving an award.

- Suggest that students write two lists in their journals—one for adjectives describing their feelings about the experience, and the other for adjectives describing the reactions of friends or relatives.

- Encourage students to write about or discuss how any negative reactions to their positive experience might have affected their own feelings.

Building English Proficiency Activities, p. 214

The Harlem Connection

Although the Harlem Renaissance is usually marked as the period following World War I through the economic collapse of 1929, it actually had a lasting influence. Wright moved from Chicago to Harlem in 1937, where he became the Harlem editor of the *Daily Worker,* a Communist newspaper, and befriended the young writer, Ralph Ellison.

5 Literary Element

Metaphor

Questions

- What does the metaphor of the train describe? *(Possible response: Wright's own unstoppable life, headed into dangerous territory, ignoring all warnings that might slow him or stop him.)*

- Do you think it is an effective metaphor? Why? *(Possible response: It gives a sense of things happening fast, and momentum without control.)*

Check Test

1. What is "The Voodoo of Hell's Half-Acre"? *(a story written by Richard Wright)*

2. How is Richard "paid" by the newspaper? *(He receives exposure and the prospect of a summer job.)*

3. What effect does Richard's story have on his relationship with his classmates? *(Their disbelief and noncomprehension of why he wants to write cuts him off from them.)*

4. How do Richard's grandmother and mother respond to his story? *(His grandmother says writing is the devil's work. His mother worries that he will seem foolish.)*

5. What does Richard want most to do with his life? *(Possible responses: to move to the North and write books; to be recognized by others)*

 Unit 6 Resource Book
Alternate Check Test, p. 37

608

Addie said that it was a sin for anyone to use the word "hell" and what was wrong with me was that I had nobody to guide me. She blamed the whole thing upon my upbringing.

In the end I was so angry that I refused to talk about the story. From no quarter, with the exception of the Negro newspaper editor, had there come a single encouraging word. It was rumored that the principal wanted to know why I had used the word "hell." I felt that I had committed a crime. Had I been conscious of the full extent to which I was pushing against the current of my environment, I would have been frightened altogether out of my attempts at writing. But my reactions were limited to the attitude of the people about me, and I did not speculate or generalize.

4 I dreamed of going north and writing books, novels. The North symbolized to me all that I had not felt and seen; it had no relation whatever to what actually existed. Yet, by imagining a place where everything was possible, I kept hope alive in me. But where had I got this notion of doing something in the future, of going away from home and accomplishing something that would be recognized by others? I had, of course, read my Horatio Alger[6] stories, my pulp stories, and I knew my Get-Rich-Quick Wallingford series from cover to cover, though I had sense enough not to hope to get rich; even to my naive[7] imagination that possibility was too remote. I knew that I lived in a country in which the aspirations[8] of black people were limited, marked-off. Yet I felt that I had to go somewhere and do something to redeem my being alive.

I was building up in me a dream which the entire educational system of the South had been rigged to stifle. I was feeling the very thing that the state of Mississippi had spent millions of dollars to make sure that I would never feel; I was becoming aware of the thing that the Jim Crow laws[9] had been drafted and passed to keep out of my consciousness; I was acting on impulses that southern senators in the nation's capital had striven to keep out of Negro life; I was beginning to dream the dreams that the state had said were wrong, that the schools had said were taboo.[10]

Had I been articulate[11] about my ultimate aspirations, no doubt someone would have told me what I was bargaining for; but nobody seemed to know, and least of all did I. My classmates felt that I was doing something that was vaguely wrong, but they did not know how to express it. As the outside world grew more meaningful, I became more concerned, tense; and my classmates and my teachers would say: "Why do you ask so many questions?" Or: "Keep quiet."

I was in my fifteenth year; in terms of schooling I was far behind the average youth of the nation, but I did not know that. In me was shaping a yearning[12] for a kind of consciousness, a mode of being that the way of life about me had said could not be, must not be, and upon which the penalty of death had been placed. Somewhere in the dead of the southern night my life had switched onto the wrong track and, without **5** my knowing it, the locomotive of my heart was rushing down a dangerously steep slope, heading for a collision, heedless of the warning red lights that blinked all about me, the sirens and the bells and the screams that filled the air.

---

6. **Horatio Alger** (1834–1899), American author of a series of inspirational books for boys.
7. naive (nä ēv′), *adj.* not sophisticated.
8. aspiration (as′ pə rā′shən), *n.* a longing; ambition.
9. **Jim Crow laws.** "Jim Crow" was a term used by many whites to refer to African Americans. In the late 1800s and early 1900s many Southern states passed laws, called Jim Crow laws, mandating segregation by race in schools, public places, and so on.
10. taboo (tə bü′), *adj.* prohibited; banned.
11. articulate (är tik′yə lit), *adj.* able to put one's thoughts into words easily and clearly.
12. yearning (yėr′ning), *n.* strong desire; longing.

MINI-LESSON: VOCABULARY

Recognize Shades of Meaning

Teach Discuss with students how an author's choice of words contributes to his or her writing style and form of expression. Remind students that there often are many different ways to say something.

Activity Ideas

- Have students choose ten words that particularly strike them in this excerpt from *Black Boy* and then write a paragraph using these words. Share the paragraphs with the class and discuss any trends or patterns of the words that students picked.

- Ask students to choose a synonym for each word they selected and have them use the synonym to replace the word in the selection sentence. Do students think the substitution has changed the sentence?

After Reading

Making Connections

Shaping Your Response

1. What would you say to young Richard Wright if he were in your class and got a story published in the local newspaper?

Analyzing the Autobiography

2. How does Wright **characterize** the editor of the *Southern Register*?

3. Richard Wright, disappointed by people's response to his first story, attempts to justify their reactions. Why does he think they don't appreciate his writing?

4. Why do you think young Wright's **perspective** on life is so different from that of his family and peers?

Extending the Ideas

5. If Richard Wright were a fifteen-year-old now writing his first story, how do you think his life might be different?

Vocabulary Study

Answer these questions about Richard Wright. Refer to the Glossary if necessary to find the meanings of the italicized vocabulary words.

naive
taboo
relent
aspiration
articulate
contemptuous
alien
hedge
conviction
yearning

1. How is Richard Wright *naive* in thinking that publishing his story will benefit him?

2. What kind of language is *taboo* in Granny's house?

3. Should the editor *relent* and pay Richard Wright for his story?

4. What was Richard Wright's main *aspiration*?

5. Why was being *articulate* not valued in Wright's community?

6. What was it about Wright's story that provoked such a *contemptuous* response by his family?

7. Why was becoming a writer an *alien* ambition in Wright's school?

8. Wright had to *hedge* when his grandmother asked what his story was about. Why?

9. Explain Wright's *conviction* about the educational system he experienced.

10. Describe the *yearning* Wright began to feel when he was fifteen.

Expressing Your Ideas

Writer's Notebook Update Choose one of the ideas you selected and develop it into a **story outline**. Think of two titles for the story, one that is outrageous, like "The Voodoo of Hell's Half Acre," and another that is more subtle.

Black Boy **609**

WRITING CHOICE
Writer's Notebook Update

A screenwriter's "pitch" is an exciting summary of a story plot in one or two sentences. Have students pitch their titles and stories to the class.

After Reading

MAKING CONNECTIONS

1. Possible responses: congratulate him; ask him to read the story aloud

2. He is a businessman, but wants to give Wright a chance; he's not overly warm and kind, but encouraging.

3. Possible responses: People don't understand him, haven't been taught anything about Negro literature, and think writing is blasphemous.

4. Possible response: He has read much literature and knows the world is larger than his environment.

5. Possible responses: He might receive family support and teacher encouragement, and have outlets for his writing.

VOCABULARY STUDY

1. He believes that he will be respected and paid.

2. Using the Lord's name in vain

3. Students may answer yes or no.

4. To move North and be a writer

5. It was not a skill that was taught to or expected of them.

6. It was fiction and had the word *hell* in the title.

7. It was not part of the world they lived in; it was not "useful."

8. He knew she would disapprove.

9. He believed it was stifling, and designed to reinforce the status quo.

10. He wanted to be different, move away, and be a great writer.

Unit 6 Resource Book
Vocabulary, p. 35
Vocabulary Test, p. 38

Selection Test

Unit 6 Resource Book
pp. 39–40

Stream of Consciousness

These vivid images begin Granny Weatherall's stream of consciousness. Invite students to watch for the uneven and illogical flow of her thoughts, sensations, memories, and emotional associations.

2 Active Reading

Evaluate

She doesn't want her family to see that side of her personality.

3 Literary Element

Flashback

In the middle of the wash of memories comes this very clear flashback.

Question Why do you think this flash-back is included? *(Students may say it shows that Granny is not afraid of death; she has made her peace with it and said good-bye to her children. It also shows tenacity in that she's been at death's doorstep before and survived.)*

"What'd you say, Mother?" Granny felt her face tying up in hard knots. "Can't a body think, I'd like to know?"

"I thought you might want something."

"I do. I want a lot of things. First off, go away and don't whisper."

1 She lay and drowsed, hoping in her sleep that the children would keep out and let her rest a minute. It had been a long day. Not that she was tired. It was always pleasant to snatch a minute now and then. There was always so much to be done, let me see: tomorrow.

Tomorrow was far away and there was nothing to trouble about. Things were finished somehow when the time came; thank God there was always a little margin over for peace: then a person could spread out the plan of life and tuck in the edges orderly. It was good to have everything clean and folded away, with the hair brushes and tonic bottles sitting straight on the white embroidered linen: the day started without fuss and the pantry shelves laid out with rows of jelly glasses and brown jugs and white stone-china jars with blue whirligigs and words painted on them: coffee, tea, sugar, ginger, cinnamon, allspice: and the bronze clock with the lion on top nicely dusted off. The dust that lion could collect in twenty-four hours! The box in the attic with all those letters tied up, well, she'd have to go through that tomorrow. All those letters—George's letters and John's letters and her letters to them both—lying around for the children to find afterward made her uneasy. Yes, that would be tomorrow's business. No use to let them know how silly she had been once.

> **2** EVALUATE: Why doesn't Granny Weatherall want her children to find her old love letters?

While she was rummaging² around, she found death in her mind and it felt clammy and unfamiliar. She had spent so much time preparing for death there was no need for bringing it up again.

---

3 Let it take care of itself now. When she was sixty, she had felt very old, finished, and went around making farewell trips to see her children and grandchildren, with a secret in her mind: This is the very last of your mother, children! Then she made her will and came down with a long fever. That was all just a notion like a lot of other things, but it was lucky too, for she had once and for all got over the idea of dying for a long time. Now she couldn't be worried. She hoped she had better sense now. Her father had lived to be one hundred and two years old and had drunk a noggin of strong hot toddy³ on his last birthday. He told the reporters it was his daily habit, and he owed his long life to that. He had made quite a scandal and was very pleased about it. She believed she'd just plague⁴ Cornelia a little.

"Cornelia! Cornelia!" No footsteps, but a sudden hand on her cheek. "Bless you, where have you been?"

"Here, Mother."

"Well, Cornelia, I want a noggin of hot toddy."

"Are you cold, darling?"

"I'm chilly, Cornelia. Lying in bed stops the circulation. I must have told you that a thousand times."

Well, she could just hear Cornelia telling her husband that Mother was getting a little childish and they'd have to humor⁵ her. The thing that most annoyed her was that Cornelia thought she was deaf, dumb, and blind. Little hasty glances and tiny gestures tossed around her and over her head saying, "Don't cross her, let her have her way, she's eighty years old," and she sitting there as if she lived in a thin glass cage. Sometimes Granny almost made up her mind to pack up and move back to her own house where nobody

---

2. **rummage** (rum′ij), *v.* search thoroughly by moving things about.
3. **noggin of hot toddy,** a small cup of a drink made from an alcoholic beverage, hot water, sugar, and spices.
4. **plague** (plāg), *v.* annoy or bother.
5. **humor** (hyū′mər), *v.* give in to the whims of a person; indulge.

MINI-LESSON: GRAMMAR

Sentence Fragments

Teach A sentence fragment is a phrase or clause that appears as a sentence, but lacks either a subject or a verb, or is a dependent clause.

Although sentence fragments are grammatically incorrect, an author may use them as part of a writing style. Katherine Anne Porter uses sentence fragments in her stream-of-consciousness prose, for example, "Not that she was tired," and "No footsteps, but a sudden hand on her cheek."

Activity Ideas

- Have students identify five sentence fragments in "The Jilting of Granny Weatherall" and write them on the chalkboard. Then have students add words to the sentence fragments to make them into complete sentences.

- Discuss with students the extent that Porter's sentence fragments lose effectiveness for their purpose in this story when they are made into complete sentences, and how it alters her style.

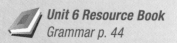

Unit 6 Resource Book
Grammar p. 44

List five adjectives that describe this woman in Grant Wood's painting, *Victorian Survivor* (1931). Which of those words, if any, could also describe Granny Weatherall? ➤

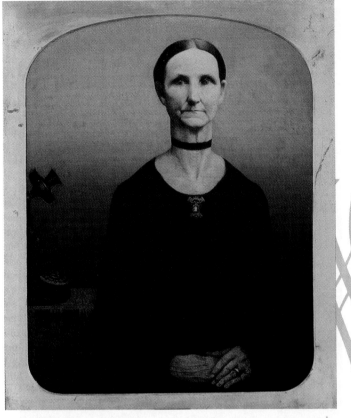

could remind her every minute that she was old. Wait, wait, Cornelia, till your own children whisper behind your back!

In her day she had kept a better house and had got more work done. She wasn't too old yet for Lydia to be driving eighty miles for advice when one of the children jumped the track, and Jimmy still dropped in and talked things over: "Now, Mammy, you've a good business head, I want to know what you think of this? . . ." Old. Cornelia couldn't change the furniture around without asking. Little things, little things! They had been so sweet when they were little. Granny wished the old days were back again with the children young and everything to be done over. It had been a hard pull, but not too much for her. When she thought of all the food she had cooked, and all the clothes she had cut and sewed, and all the gardens she had made—well, the children showed it. There they were, made out of her, and they couldn't get away from that. Sometimes she wanted to see John again and point to them and say, Well, I didn't do so badly, did I? But that would have to wait. That was for tomorrow. She used to think of him as a man, but now all the children were older than their father, and he would be a child beside her if she saw him now. It seemed strange and there was something wrong in the idea. Why, he couldn't possibly recognize her. She had fenced in a hundred acres once, digging the postholes herself and clamping the wires with just a Negro boy to help. That changed a woman. John would be looking for a young woman with the peaked Spanish comb in her hair and the painted fan. Digging postholes changed a woman. Riding country roads in the winter when women had their babies was another thing: sitting up nights with sick horses and sick Negroes and sick children and hardly ever losing one. John, I hardly ever lost one of them! John would see that in a minute, that would be something he could understand, she wouldn't have to explain anything! **4**

CLARIFY: How could the children be older than their father? **5**

The Jilting of Granny Weatherall   **613**

Responses to Caption Question
Possible responses: Adjectives for the painting: stern, unrelenting, severe, proper, no-nonsense, determined. Adjectives that also describe Granny Weatherall: stern, no-nonsense, determined

Grant Wood (1892–1942) is best known for his painting *American Gothic*, which has become one of the best-known pieces of American art.

4 Reading/Thinking Skills
Infer

Question   What is implied by the statement "she wouldn't have to explain anything"? *(Students may suggest that John will see the years of work and struggle in her and understand why she looks as she does.)*

5 Active Reading
Clarify

He died at an age that was younger than they are now.

BUILDING ENGLISH PROFICIENCY

Sequencing Details

Students might have difficulty sorting out time sequence in Porter's stream-of-consciousness technique. Suggest that they use a chart to organize the events. Encourage them to mark each mention of the jilting episode with an asterisk.

In the Past	Happening Now	Might Happen in the Future
had once been silly	nearly asleep in bed	go through box of letters

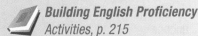

📖 *Building English Proficiency*
Activities, p. 215

9 Literary Focus
Stream of Consciousness

Porter connects events in unlikely ways, and Granny's wandering in and out of reality with little sense of elapsed time adds to the reader's sense of continuous flow of thought.

Question Granny Weatherall regresses to the time of the birth of one of her children. What other life event could "My time has come" refer to? *(Possible response: imminent death)*

10 Active Reading
Evaluate

She wants him to know she did well without him.

11 Literary Element
Simile

Similes compare two unlike things in order to tell us more about what they have in common. Granny compares the room to a picture she had seen.

Question What are Granny's perceptions as suggested by this simile of a picture? *(distance, an unreal feeling, distortion of reality)*

---

kiss, when Cornelia began whispering from a long way off, "Oh, is there anything you want to tell me? Is there anything I can do for you?"

Yes, she had changed her mind after sixty years and she would like to see George. I want you to find George. Find him and be sure to tell him I forgot him. I want him to know I had my husband just the same and my children and my house like any other woman. A good house too and a good husband that I loved and fine children out of him. Better than I hoped for even. Tell him I was given back everything he took away and more. Oh, no, oh, God, no, there was something else besides the house and the man and the children. Oh, surely they were not all? What was it? Something not given back. . . . Her breath crowded down under her ribs and grew into a monstrous frightening shape with cutting edges; it bored up into her head, and the agony was unbelievable: Yes, John, get the doctor now, no more talk, my time has come.

9

10 EVALUATE: Why does Granny Weatherall make this contradictory statement: "Find him and be sure to tell him I forgot him"? What does she want?

When this one was born, it should be the last. The last. It should have been born first, for it was the one she had truly wanted. Everything came in good time. Nothing left out, left over. She was strong, in three days she would be as well as ever. Better. A woman needed milk in her to have her full health.

"Mother, do you hear me?"

"I've been telling you——"

"Mother, Father Connolly's here."

"I went to Holy Communion only last week. Tell him I'm not so sinful as all that."

"Father just wants to speak to you."

He could speak as much as he pleased. It was like him to drop in and inquire about her soul as if it were a teething baby, and then stay on for a cup of tea and a round of cards and gossip. He always had a funny story of some sort, usually about an Irishman who made his little mistakes and confessed them, and the point lay in some absurd thing he would blurt out in the confessional showing his struggles between native piety and original sin. Granny felt easy about her soul. Cornelia, where are your manners? Give Father Connolly a chair. She had her secret comfortable understanding with a few favorite saints who cleared a straight road to God for her. All as surely signed and sealed as the papers for the new Forty Acres. Forever . . . heirs and assigns forever. Since the day the wedding cake was not cut, but thrown out and wasted. The whole bottom dropped out of the world, and there she was blind and sweating with nothing under her feet and the walls falling away. His hand had caught her under the breast, she had not fallen, there was the freshly polished floor with the green rug on it, just as before. He had cursed like a sailor's parrot and said, "I'll kill him for you." Don't lay a hand on him, for my sake leave something to God. "Now, Ellen, you must believe what I tell you. . . ."

So there was nothing, nothing to worry about any more, except sometimes in the night one of the children screamed in a nightmare, and they both hustled out shaking and hunting for the matches and calling, "There, wait a minute, here we are!" John, get the doctor now, Hapsy's time has come. But there was Hapsy standing by the bed in a white cap. "Cornelia, tell Hapsy to take off her cap. I can't see her plain."

Her eyes opened very wide and the room stood out like a picture she had seen somewhere. Dark colors with the shadows rising toward the ceiling in long angles. The tall black dresser gleamed with nothing on it but John's picture, enlarged from a little one, with John's eyes very black when they should have been blue. You never saw him, so how do you know how he looked? But the man insisted the copy was perfect, it was very rich and handsome. For a picture, yes, but it's not my husband. The table by the bed had a linen cover and a candle and a crucifix. The light was blue from Cornelia's silk lampshades.

11

MINI-LESSON: VOCABULARY

Connotation and Denotation

Teach The denotation of a word is its literal definition. A word's connotation is the unspoken or unwritten added feeling or meaning that is associated with the word. Often, the connotation has a less tangible and more emotional meaning.

Activity Idea Write the following words on the blackboard. Ask students to write a denotation and connotation for each one in their notebooks, and then share the results with the class. (The connotation is underlined.)

childish *(like a child; immature, silly)*

home *(dwelling place; place where one feels comfortable, safe)*

rummage *(to search through things by moving them about; to make a mess)*

golden *(made from gold; excellent, perfect, wonderful)*

No sort of light at all, just frippery. You had to live forty years with kerosene lamps to appreciate honest electricity. She felt very strong and she saw Doctor Harry with a rosy nimbus around him.

"You look like a saint, Doctor Harry, and I vow that's as near as you'll ever come to it."

"She's saying something."

"I heard you, Cornelia. What's all this carrying on?"

"Father Connolly's saying——"

Cornelia's voice staggered and bumped like a cart in a bad road. It rounded corners and turned back again and arrived nowhere. Granny stepped up in the cart very lightly and reached for the reins, but a man sat beside her and she knew him by his hands, driving the cart. She did not look in his face, for she knew without seeing, but looked instead down the road where the trees leaned over and bowed to each other and a thousand birds were singing a Mass. She felt like singing too, but she put her hand in the bosom of her dress and pulled out a rosary, and Father Connolly murmured Latin in a very solemn[11] voice and tickled her feet.[12] My God, will you stop that nonsense? I'm a married woman. What if he did run away and leave me to face the priest by myself? I found another a whole world better. I wouldn't have exchanged my husband for anybody except St. Michael himself, and you may tell him that for me with a thank you in the bargain.

Light flashed on her closed eyelids, and a deep roaring shook her. Cornelia, is that lightning? I hear thunder. There's going to be a storm. Close all the windows. Call the children in. . . . "Mother, here we are, all of us." "Is that you, Hapsy?" "Oh, no, I'm Lydia. We drove as fast as we could." Their faces drifted above her, drifted away. The rosary fell out of her hands and Lydia put it back. Jimmy tried to help, their hands fumbled together, and Granny closed two fingers around Jimmy's thumb. Beads wouldn't do, it must be something alive. She was so amazed her thoughts ran round and round. So, my dear Lord, this is my death and I wasn't even thinking about it. My children have come to see me die. But I can't, it's

not time. Oh, I always hated surprises. I wanted to give Cornelia the amethyst set—Cornelia, you're to have the amethyst set, but Hapsy's to wear it when she wants, and, Doctor Harry, do shut up. Nobody sent for you. Oh, my dear Lord, do wait a minute. I meant to do something about the Forty Acres, Jimmy doesn't need it and Lydia will later on, with that worthless husband of hers. I meant to finish the altar cloth and send six bottles of wine to Sister Borgia for her dyspepsia. I want to send six bottles of wine to Sister Borgia, Father Connolly, now don't let me forget.

Cornelia's voice made short turns and tilted over and crashed. "Oh, Mother, oh, Mother, oh, Mother. . . ."

"I'm not going, Cornelia. I'm taken by surprise. I can't go."

You'll see Hapsy again. What about her? "I thought you'd never come." Granny made a long journey outward, looking for Hapsy. What if I don't find her? What then? Her heart sank down and down, there was no bottom to death, she couldn't come to the end of it. The blue light from Cornelia's lampshade drew into a tiny point in the center of her brain, it flickered and winked like an eye, quietly it fluttered and dwindled.[13] Granny lay curled down within herself, amazed and watchful, staring at the point of light that was herself; her body was now only a deeper mass of shadow in an endless darkness and this darkness would curl around the light and swallow it up. God, give a sign!

For the second time there was no sign. Again no bridegroom and the priest in the house. She could not remember any other sorrow because this grief wiped them all away. Oh, no, there's nothing more cruel than this—I'll never forgive it. She stretched herself with a deep breath and blew out the light.

---

11. **solemn** (sol′əm), *adj.* done with form and ceremony.
12. **Father Connolly . . . feet,** The priest is administering the sacrament for the dying, which includes anointing the hands and feet.
13. **dwindle** (dwin′dl), *v.* shrink; diminish.

The Jilting of Granny Weatherall   **617**

12 Literary Element
Symbolism

This reference to a cart and driver might remind students of the carriage and driver in Emily Dickinson's poem, "Because I could not stop for Death."

Question   Who is the man in the cart? *(Students may recognize him as Death.)*

13 Literary Element
Irony

In this ironic moment, Granny experiences the priest's touch as a flirtation, when he is really administering the sacrament for the dying.

Check Test

1. What is Cornelia's relationship to Granny Weatherall? *(She is Granny's daughter.)*

2. What did George and John send to Granny? *(love letters)*

3. What did George do to Granny on their wedding day? *(He jilted her.)*

4. Who is Hapsy? *(She is Granny's deceased daughter.)*

5. What is Granny's dying thought? *(She thinks only of the jilting and her grief from it.)*

Unit 6 Resource Book
Alternate Check Test, p. 45

BUILDING ENGLISH PROFICIENCY

Making Personal Connections

Use one or both of the following activities to help students expand their personal understanding of the story.

Activity Ideas

- Suggest that students interview senior citizens that they know about their "first love." Questions might include: How did you meet? Did that relationship end—and, if so, how? Was "jilting" considered a serious offense when you were my age?

- Students might want to work in pairs to create the old love letters mentioned on page 612. Challenge students to include George's explanation for missing the wedding, Ellen's reply, and Ellen's letter accepting John.

Interdisciplinary Study

Theme Link

Children who grew to adulthood in the 1920s found themselves in a crowd that was finding new ways to live and deal with the challenges of their generation.

Curricular Connection: Pop Culture

You can use this interdisciplinary study to explore with students the shocking new popular culture introduced by young people of the Roaring Twenties.

Terms to Know

insidious (in sid′ē əs), working secretly or subtly

consternation (kon′stər nā′shən), great dismay

furtive (fėr′tiv), secret

brazen (brā′zn), having no shame

depraved (di prāvd′), morally bad; corrupt

Unit 6 Resource Book
Interdisciplinary Study Guide, p. 49

Pop Culture Connection

The excitement and terror of World War I left a lasting impression on the minds of a whole generation of young Americans. Traditional values and codes of behavior seemed outdated to 1920s youth, and their new ways shocked their elders. In the following passage from his book, *Only Yesterday*, Frederick Lewis Allen describes the new enemy that had invaded American society.

THE YOUNGER GENERATION Runs Wild

by Frederick Lewis Allen

The war [World War I] had not long been over when cries of alarm from parents, teachers, and moral preceptors began to rend the air. For the boys and girls just growing out of adolescence were making mincemeat of [the moral] code.

MINI-LESSON: STUDY SKILLS

Researching Information

Teach   While doing research on popular culture of the 1920s, students may find it difficult to locate information or they may reach a dead end. Suggest they use the following strategies to develop new leads:

- Brainstorm for new categories that their topic may fit into, which will provide avenues for further investigation.
- Check bibliographies at the end of encyclopedia articles, journal articles, or nonfiction books.
- Check a thesaurus for additional terms or words that can be used to expand a card catalog or computer search.

- Review encyclopedia and journal articles for cross-references.
- Ask a librarian.

Activity Ideas

- Have students create a checklist of the above strategies to use while doing research.
- When students reach dead ends with their individual research, have them collaborate with partners in developing additional avenues of research.

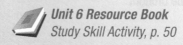
Unit 6 Resource Book
Study Skill Activity, p. 50

The dresses that the girls—and for that matter most of the older women—were wearing seemed alarming enough. In July, 1920, a fashion writer reported in the *New York Times* that "the American woman . . . has lifted her skirts far beyond any modest limitation," which was another way of saying that the hem was now all of nine inches above the ground. It was freely predicted that skirts would come down again in the winter of 1920–1921, but instead they climbed a few scandalous inches farther. The flappers wore thin dresses, short-sleeved and occasionally (in the evening) sleeveless; some of the wilder young things rolled their stockings below their knees, revealing to the shocked eyes of virtue a fleeting glance of shin-bones and knee-cap; and many of them were visibly using cosmetics. "The intoxication of rouge," earnestly explained Dorothy Speare in *Dancers in the Dark,* "is an insidious vintage known to more girls than mere man can ever believe." Useless for frantic parents to insist that no lady did such things; the answer was that the daughters of ladies were doing it, and even retouching their masterpieces in public. Some of them, further-more, were abandoning their corsets. "The men won't dance with you if you wear a corset," they were quoted as saying.

The current mode in dancing created still more consternation. Not the romantic violin but the barbaric saxophone now dom-inated the orchestra, and to its passionate crooning and wailing the fox-trotters moved in what the editor of the Hobart College

Herald disgustedly called a "syncopated embrace." No longer did even an inch of space separate them; they danced as if glued together, body to body, cheek to cheek. Cried the *Catholic Telegraph* of Cincinnati in righteous indignation, "The music is sensuous, the embracing of partners—the female only half dressed—is absolutely indecent; and the motions—they are such as may not be described, with any respect for propriety, in a family newspaper. Suffice it to say that there are certain houses appropriate for such dances; but those houses have been closed by law." . . .

It was not until F. Scott Fitzgerald, who had hardly grad-uated from Princeton and ought to know what his generation were doing, brought out *This Side of Paradise* in April, 1920, that fathers and mothers realized fully what was afoot and how long it had been going on . . . . "None of the Victorian mothers—and most of the mothers were Victorian—had any idea how casually their daughters were accustomed to be kissed," wrote Fitzgerald. ". . . Amory saw girls doing things that even in his memory would have been impossible: eating three-o'clock, after-dance suppers in impossible cafés, talking of every side of life with an air half of earnestness, half of mockery, yet with a furtive excitement that Amory considered stood for a real moral let-down. But he never realized how widespread it was until he saw the cities between New York and Chicago as one vast juvenile intrigue." The book caused a shudder to run

down the national spine; did not Mr. Fitzgerald represent one of his well-nurtured heroines as brazenly confessing, "I've kissed dozens of men. I suppose I'll kiss dozens more" . . .

It was incredible. It was abominable. What did it all mean? Was every decent standard being thrown over? Mothers read the scarlet words and wondered if they themselves "had any idea how often their daughters were accustomed to be kissed." . . . But no, this must be an exaggerated account of the misconduct of some especially depraved group. Nice girls couldn't behave like that and talk openly about passion. But in due course other books appeared to substantiate the findings of Mr. Fitzgerald; *Dancers in the Dark, The Plastic Age, Flaming Youth.* Magazine articles and newspapers reiterat-ed the scandal. To be sure, there were plenty of communities where nice girls did not, in actual fact, "behave like that"; and even in the more sophisticated urban centers there were plenty of girls who did not. Nevertheless, there was enough fire beneath the smoke of these sensational revelations to make the Problem of the Younger Generation a topic of anxious discussion from coast to coast.

Responding

1. Do you think the older generation was overreacting to the youth of the 1920s? Why or why not?

2. How do the concerns of today's parents compare with those of the older generation in the 1920s?

Additional Background

Flappers first appeared at least forty years before the 1920s. The word *flapper,* which was originally used to describe a young duck just learning to fly by flapping its wings wildly, was used in the 1880s to describe a young girl who broke with the pinned-up hair fashion of the time to let her hair hang loose and blow wildly in the wind.

In France around 1900, a flapper was a very loose woman with bobbed hair and a short skirt. Soon, however, the term was being applied to any independent, modern woman who, in unladylike rebellion, smoked, drank, wanted to vote, and believed in women's rights.

The flappers of the Roaring Twenties, also known as jazz babies, provided the most well-known interpretation of the term.

Research Topics

- Fads of the 1920s
- Gangsters and racketeers of the 1920s
- Dance crazes of the 1920s
- Events and causes of the stock market crash of October 29, 1929

Responding

1. Possible Response Students may agree or disagree but should recognize that the morality of the younger generation broke sharply from that of previous generations.

2. Possible Response The concerns are different, and those of the 1920s might seem tame to the concerns of today's parents.

BUILDING ENGLISH PROFICIENCY

Checking Comprehension

This article contains factual details about an era that perhaps seems old-fashioned. You might help students evaluate their under-standing by having them complete these sentences, either in writing or through discussion.

- "Flappers" became the symbol of the postwar era in the United States because _____.

- _____ made the music and dance styles that became popular during that time rather shocking.

- F. Scott Fitzgerald brought these trends to the attention of the general public when he _____.

- Traditional parents began to wonder _____.

- The "Problem of the Younger Generation" was that _____.

Interdisciplinary Study

Theme Link

Alienated from the previous generation, the rebellious young people of the Roaring Twenties felt free to innovate on the English language.

Curricular Connection: Pop Culture

This interdisciplinary study offers an opportunity to explore the evolving language of popular culture.

Additional Background

Flappers avoided saying yes or no. Instead, they would respond with a long, drawn-out "pos-i-tive-ly" or "ab-so-lute-ly." And sometimes, they combined the response by saying "poss-a-loot-ly."

Here are some additional terms to share with students.

- jazz babies: flappers
- cakeater, jazzbo, jellybean: various terms for a flapper's boyfriend
- sheba: an especially attractive woman
- sheik: an especially attractive man

Pop Culture Connection

The new ways of the 1920s called for a new vocabulary. The younger generation considered the established ways of their elders to be nonsense, and invented creative new ways to say "nonsense." Their exuberance and easy attitude toward life were reflected in their words as well. The following list includes some of the terms coined during this era.

Roaring Twenties

DRUGSTORE COWBOY

ALARM CLOCK — a persistent worrier; a chaperone.

ALL WET — wrong; arguing a mistaken notion.

AND HOW! — yes, indeed!

APPLESAUCE — a term of derogation; nonsense.

BADGE — police officer.

BALLOON SOUP — empty talk, nonsense; same as applesauce.

BALONEY — nonsense, same as applesauce and balloon soup.

BEE'S KNEES — a marvelous person or thing.

BIG CHEESE — an important, influential person.

BLIND DATE — a date with an unknown person of the opposite sex.

BOOK WORM — a person who spends much time reading or studying.

BRAWL — a wild party or celebration.

BREEZER — an open-topped car.

BUM RAP — a false accusation or conviction.

BUNK — nonsense (a shortened form of *bunkum,* which is also spelled *buncombe,* from the name of a North Carolina county whose representative in Congress from 1819–1821 kept making long-winded and pointless speeches "for Buncombe").

CAKE — a male flirt.

CARRY A TORCH — to love someone who does not return one's affections.

CAT'S MEOW — anything first-rate; similar to bee's knees.

CHEATERS — eyeglasses.

COPACETIC — very good, excellent.

CRACKERS — crazy or eccentric.

622   UNIT SIX: MODERN DILEMMAS

MINI-LESSON: SPEAKING AND LISTENING

Presenting a Speech

Teach When preparing to deliver an informational report, urge students to use an audio or video recorder during practice to help them evaluate their delivery of the following elements.

- Emphasis: Are important words and ideas stressed?
- Pauses: Do I use pauses effectively to emphasize ideas?
- Tone: Is my tone appropriate to my subject and purpose?

- Loudness: Am I talking loudly enough to be heard?
- Articulation: Am I enunciating clearly?
- Pace: Is the speed of my delivery too fast or too slow?

Activity Idea As students prepare oral reports on 1920s culture, have them work in pairs or small groups to analyze each other's delivery and to offer constructive suggestions for improvement.

Glossary

HOOCH

ALL WET

CRUSH – a sudden romantic feeling for another person.

DAD – fellow; friend.

DRUGSTORE COWBOY – a fashionably dressed young man who hangs around public places trying to pick up young women.

FAN THE AIR – to chatter; gossip.

FLAPPER – a young woman of the 1920s who dressed unconventionally – with short skirts and rolled stockings – and behaved with considerable freedom.

FLAT TIRE – a boring person.

FRAME – to make someone seem guilty through false evidence.

GATECRASHER – a person who attends parties and other events without an invitation.

GUSSIE UP – to dress up.

HEEBIE-JEEBIES – a nervous feeling; the jitters.

HEP – informed; wise.

HOOCH – bootleg liquor (from Hoochinoo, an Alaskan Indian tribe who made liquor).

JAKE – fine, okay (commonly used in the phrase "everything's jake").

JALOPY – an old automobile.

KEEN – excellent; wonderful.

LOUNGE LIZARD – a ladies' man.

MAIN DRAG – the busiest or chief street of a city or town.

PINCH – to arrest.

REAL McCOY, THE – the real thing; the genuine article (comes either from a Scottish clan leader named MacKay; a boxer named Kid McCoy, who had a rival with the same name; or a bootlegger named McCoy who did not dilute his liquor).

RITZY – smart; stylish (from *Ritz*, the name of the palatial hotels founded by César Ritz, 1850–1918, Swiss-born hotel manager).

RUN-AROUND – evasion or indefinite postponement of an action, especially in response to a request.

SCRAM – to leave at once (from scramble).

SPEAKEASY – a saloon or bar illegally selling alcohol.

SPIFFY – having a smart, elegantly fashionable appearance.

SWELL – excellent; first-rate.

WHOOPEE – boisterous, jovial fun.

FLAPPER

Responding

1. Which of these terms have endured the test of time and are still used today?

2. What are some modern-day equivalents to these terms and expressions? What new words and phrases would be included in a "modern age" glossary?

Responding

1. **Possible Responses** *all wet, and how, baloney, blind date, book worm, bum rap, crush, frame, runaround.* Students should be able to use the words in contemporary sentences.

2. Students should list slang and jargon that are common among people of their age group.

Interdisciplinary Activity Ideas

- Invite students to work in a group to learn about and report on the music of the 1920s. Encourage them to investigate the variety of trends in music and to collect representative recordings of jazz, blues, big band, and other music to play for the class. Musically skilled students might perform some songs. Others might demonstrate and teach the dances of the day.

- Ask students to work in a group to learn about clothing fashions of the 1920s. Students might create a fashion display, using sketches, paintings, or models of male and female clothing. Have students display the fashions to the class and give historical commentary, explaining the origin and changes in these fashions throughout the decade.

BUILDING ENGLISH PROFICIENCY

ESL
LEP
ELD
SAE
LD

Exploring Slang

Use one or more of the following activities to help students focus on the slang of the Roaring Twenties.

- Ask students to comment orally or in their journals on any terms that they find unfamiliar, unusual, or funny.

- Have volunteers create drawings that illustrate terms of their choice.

- Work with students to classify the terms; for example, words for types of problematic people (such as *alarm clock, flat tire,* and *gatecrasher*) and words that compliment (such as *bee's knees, copacetic, jake,* and *ritzy).*

- Invite pairs or small groups of students to create sentences that use terms from the glossary; for example, "You've got to be *crackers* to have a *crush* on a *flat tire* like that!"

STEP 3 REVISING

Ask a partner
(Peer assessment)

After reading the entire paper, have students comment on the thesis statement: Does it get the reader's interest? Does the writer express his or her views of the causes of the character's alienation? Is the statement specific?

Revising Strategy:
Revising a Thesis Statement

Have students listen as you read the student model aloud, both with and without the corrections. Discuss how the corrections make the statement more specific and limiting.

For additional support, see the mini-lesson at the bottom of this page and the worksheet referenced below.

Unit 6 Resource Book
Revising Worksheet, p. 53

Connections to
Writer's Resource

Refer to the Grammar, Usage, and Mechanics Handbook on Writer's Resource.

Ask a partner for comments on your draft before you revise it. Pay special attention to the thesis statement.

Revising Strategy

Revising a Thesis Statement

Your thesis statement must be sufficiently limited and specific. Here is an example of the development of a thesis statement (based on Hemingway's "In Another Country"):

Thesis Statement	Sufficiently Limited and Specific?
The soldier's alienation is caused by a variety of factors.	Unworkable. Way too broad and general. The writer needs to define what "a variety of factors" means.
The alien world that surrounds the soldier makes him feel lost and detached from society.	Better. "The alien world that surrounds the soldier" is a bit more specific and limited, but still too vague.
The unfriendly and wounded people who populate the world are the chief causes of the soldier's alienation.	Workable. The writer now has something definite to fasten on—the "unfriendly and wounded people." The rest of the essay can focus on these people, the chief contributors to his alienation.

Notice how the writer of this student model has revised his thesis statement to make it more limited and specific.

> When people do not think like their peers, they sometimes become alienated because they are misunderstood and viewed as being dangerous. In the story "Black Boy" by Richard Wright, ~~Richard~~ ^Richard's desire to be and do more than people told him that he was capable of doing alienates him from his^ ~~is alienated from his family and friends because they believe he is~~ family and friends. ~~different from them.~~

STUDENT MODEL

MINI-LESSON: WRITING STYLE

Revising a Thesis Statement

Teach Write thesis statements on the board for one or two of the selections and apply the criteria in the lesson to the thesis statement. Let students discuss the appropriateness of the thesis statement and make suggestions to revise and improve it.

Activity Idea Place students in small groups. Let students in each group choose a story or an article from a magazine or newspaper. Have the group write a thesis statement for the article and revise it to make it more accurate and interesting.

Apply Remind students to carefully analyze their own thesis sentences, just as they did in the group.

4 EDITING

Ask a partner to review your revised draft before you edit. When you edit, watch for errors in grammar, usage, spelling, and mechanics. Pay special attention to errors with commas.

Editing Strategy

Using Commas Correctly

Use commas to avoid, not cause, confusion. Take care to use a comma when it's needed for sense—and not to add needless commas that end up confusing the reader. For example:

No commas needed: Some people want to live their lives, in a way that they consider, to be dangerous.

Edited: Some people want to live their lives in a way that they consider to be dangerous.

Commas needed: In the first instance I've mentioned because Richard yearns to see the world outside of his home town Jackson he loses the support of his family and friends.

Edited: In the first instance I've mentioned, because Richard yearns to see the world outside of his home town, Jackson, he loses the support of his family and friends.

Notice how the writer of the student model made corrections with commas to avoid confusion. Look for these same kinds of comma-confusion errors when you edit your writing.

> **FOR REFERENCE**
> More rules for using commas can be found in the Language and Grammar Handbook at the back of this text.

○   Richard's family and friends cannot understand him. His

○   dreams‸of becoming a writer‸reach past Jackson into new places

   where he believes he can encounter new things‸things that will

○   broaden and deepen his experience. Richard dreams of going to the

   North‸a place where he feels that anything is possible.

STUDENT MODEL

Writing Workshop   **629**

STEP 4 EDITING

Ask a partner (Peer assessment)

Have students read their partner's paper specifically to look for correct comma usage.

Editing Strategy: Using Commas Correctly

After reading the entire paper, have partners discuss any comma usage that they feel could be confusing to the reader and how to correct it.

For additional support, see the mini-lesson at the bottom of this page and the worksheets referenced below.

📖 ***Unit 6 Resource Book***
Grammar Worksheet, p. 54
Grammar Check Test, p. 55

💿 Connections to
Writer's Resource

Refer to the Grammar, Usage, and Mechanics Handbook on Writer's Resource.

MINI-LESSON: GRAMMAR

Using Commas Correctly

Have students correct the comma usage in the following sentences. Some sentences may already be correct.

- Our English teacher said, that Ernest Hemingway was often difficult to understand. (a paraphrase, so no comma after *said*)

- I read <u>The Old Man and the Sea</u> because I had heard a lot about it but I didn't really understand it. (comma needed between *it* and *but* because of coordinating compound)

- It is interesting that great writers like Hemingway, and Tennessee Williams led such troubled lives. (not a series of three or more, so no comma after *Hemingway*)

- What the author does does matter to the publisher. (comma needed between *does* and *does* to avoid confusion)

📖 ***Unit 6 Resource Book***
Grammar Worksheet p. 54
Grammar Check Test p. 55

629

STEP 5 PRESENTING
Read and Discuss

In each group, have students make a chart showing the similarities and the differences in the conclusions that they reached.

Poster

On the poster, students might use pictures or stories from contemporary life to illustrate the same causes that were revealed in the selections.

STEP 6 LOOKING BACK
Self-evaluate

The *Assessment Criteria Specs* at the bottom of this page are for a superior paper. You might want to post these in the classroom. Students can then evaluate themselves based on these criteria. For a complete scoring rubric, use the *Assessment Worksheet* referenced below.

Unit 6 Resource Book
Assessment Worksheet, p. 56

Reflect

You may want to have the students work in small groups first, especially in discussing the second checked question, before they begin writing their own responses.

To further explore the theme, use the Fine Art Transparency referenced below.

Transparency Collection
Fine Art Writing Prompt 10

Consider these ideas for presenting your paper.

- Meet with students in your class who chose the same character you did. Read your essays to each other and compare your conclusions.

- Find at least two other students who each wrote about different characters, and form a small group. Make a list of the causes of each character's alienation. Then draw some conclusions about what causes alienation. Make a poster to illustrate these causes, and share it with the class.

STEP **6** LOOKING BACK

Self-evaluate. What grade would *you* give your paper? Look back at the Writer's Blueprint and give yourself a score on each item, from 6 (superior) to 1 (inadequate).

Reflect. Think about what you learned from writing your essay as you write answers to these questions:

✔ What did you learn about alienation by writing this paper? Will you do or react to anything differently as a result of exploring this topic? Why or why not?

✔ In what ways are your feelings or the feelings of today's youth similar to or different from the feelings expressed in the literature you read?

For Your Working Portfolio Add your essay and your reflection responses to your working portfolio.

ASSESSMENT CRITERIA SPECS

6 Superior   The writer of a 6 paper impressively meets these criteria:

- Focuses on one particular character's alienation throughout, never losing focus.
- Has an intriguing opening that highlights something specific about the character's alienation.
- Includes a clear, concise thesis statement of the causes of the character's alienation, which serves as the guiding force for the rest of the essay.
- Describes in insightful detail both the inner and outer causes of the character's alienation.

- Provides a convincing description of what the character does and says that signals his or her alienation.
- Firmly supports conclusions and opinions with specific details from the selection, including quotations where appropriate.
- Ends by restating the thesis with fresh new insights.
- Makes few, if any, errors in grammar, usage, spelling, and mechanics. Uses commas correctly.

Beyond Print

The Wonders of Word Processing

When Ernest Hemingway was a young writer struggling to make a living in Paris, a suitcase full of his manuscripts was lost on a train. Since Hemingway had no other copies, he lost several years' worth of work. Today, thanks to word processing programs, writers can save their work on a hard drive or file server, back it up on floppy disks, and print it out as hard copy.

The true power of word processors, however, lies not in their ability to preserve documents, but in their ability to make writing easier and more efficient. The following tips can help you make the most of the word processor you use:

- When you're working on a rough draft, don't worry about mistakes. Correcting, moving, and editing text can be done later, so let yourself go and *just write!*

- Use the spelling checker on your word processor, but proofread your work as well. Why? Be cause they spill checker wood knot find any miss steaks in this sentience, that's way. Are you convinced?

- Save your documents frequently as you work, since power outages and system errors can wipe out unsaved work. Back up important documents by putting a copy on a server or on an extra floppy disk.

- Limit your use of fonts. Use different font styles like outline, shadow, bold, and italic only when needed. Too many fonts can make a document confusing to read.

- Learn how to use word-processing tools such as automatic page numbers, footnotes, centered headings, and even charts and graphs.

Activity Options

Word-Processed Homework If you've never done this before, try to compose your next writing assignment entirely on the computer.

How-To Handbook Spend some time exploring all of the capabilities of your word processing program, then write a user-friendly "User's Guide." Create the handbook, of course, using your word processor, then share it with your classmates.

Beyond Print **631**

Beyond Print

Teaching Objectives

- To understand the capabilities and advantages of word processing
- To develop word processing skills

Curricular Connection: Technology

You can use the information in this article to help students understand the advantages of using word processing and to develop useful computer skills.

Introduce

Discuss students' methods for the physical process of writing a report, short story, essay, or other class assignment. Ask what problems and drawbacks they encounter and list them on the board. Then ask students to read the article. When they've finished you may wish to review their list and discuss how word processing might eliminate or minimize the problems they encounter.

Activity Options

Activity 1 As students compose their assignments, advise them to focus on getting their ideas down and to ignore mechanical mistakes. They might also avoid trying to make every word choice exact. These corrections and improvements can be made during revision.

Activity 2 Suggest that students write their User Guides with friendly terminology and accessible formats, such as bulleted lists and bold headings. Students might wish to share ideas and software discoveries with each other so that their guides will be as complete and useful as possible.

ANOTHER APPROACH

Without Word Processors: Exploring Potential

If students do not have access to word processors, they can investigate the types and capabilities of computers and software available on the market. Small groups of students might work together to visit computer stores, read consumer reports and surveys, interview computer users, and do library research to learn about available technology. Suggest that students use the following criteria for comparison.

- capability
- ease of use
- advantages
- disadvantages

When research is completed, have students share their findings in a class discussion or a sales presentation.

EXPLORING CONCEPTS

- Regional writers give us unforgettable characters and snapshots of a time and place.
- Regional culture and traditions occasionally clash with the modern world.
- Sometimes, people caught up in the modern world find themselves searching for lost traditions.

Point out that the images and descriptions of art forms on pages 632–633 illustrate regional characteristics.

Question Does each region of the United States have a distinctive culture? *(Responses may vary, but students should give reasons and examples to support their answers.)*

Research Activity Encourage groups of students to select one of the regions identified on pages 632–633 and do further research to identify writers, musicians, painters, and other artists from that region.

Modern Dilemmas

The Strength of Tradition

The STRENGTH of TRADITION

HISTORICAL OVERVIEW

In the early 1900s, the impact of movies, radio, magazines, and advertising was to homogenize American culture. Despite this tendency, regional cultural traditions that emphasized the unique characteristics of different parts of the country thrived in the period between World War I and World War II. The regionalist ideal was expressed by Southern poet Allen Tate: "Only a return to the provinces, to the small, self-contained centers of life, will put the all-destroying abstraction America to rest." During the Great Depression of the 1930s, a number of New Deal programs, notably the Works Progress Administration (WPA), funded a wide variety of regional cultural projects. Among the WPA programs were the Federal Writers Project, the Federal Arts Projects, and the Federal Theatre Project, which supported a wide variety of regional cultural efforts.

The Far West

The Grapes of Wrath by John Steinbeck, which describes the migration of Dust Bowl farmers to California, is a classic of 20th century American regionalism. Migrant life was also recorded by photographer Dorothea Lange.

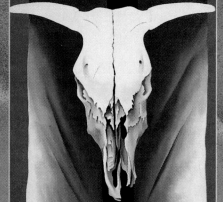

The Southwest

In the late 1920s Georgia O'Keeffe began painting the mountains, flowers, cloud forms, and bleached bones of desert animals in a monumental style that combines realism and abstraction.

The Midwest

In works such as *North of Boston*, poet Robert Frost evoked the landscapes and folkways of rural New England. This area was also the subject of many of the paintings of Edward Hopper such as *Corn Hill* (1930).

The industrial Midwest is celebrated in Diego Rivera's *Detroit Industry* (1932-33).

New England

In a series of recordings beginning in the later 1920s, the Carter Family preserved the musical culture of the Appalachian region.

Appalachia

In novels and stories set in his fictional Yoknapatawpha County, William Faulkner vividly recreated rural Mississippi. Writers such as Tennessee Williams, Flannery O'Connor, and Eudora Welty demonstrated the continuing strength of regionalism in Southern literature.

The South

Key Dates

1927
The Carter Family begins recording Appalachian music.

late 1920s
Georgia O'Keeffe begins painting in the Southwest.

1933
Diego Rivera completes mural Detroit Industry.

mid 1930s
Dust Bowl develops in Great Plains.

1935
Works Progress Administration established.

mid 1930s
Dorothea Lange begins photographing migrant farmers.

late 1930s
Federal Writers Project supports regional culture.

1939
The Grapes of Wrath is published.

633

Key Dates

1924   Artist Edward Hopper gives his first one-man show. A major subject for Hopper then and afterwards was the loneliness and isolation of New England's small towns.

1929   William Faulkner writes *Sartoris*, the first of his novels set in the fictional Mississippi county of Yoknapatawpha.

1935   The Federal Writers Project begins. More than 6,000 writers participate during its four year span.

1935–1939   The Federal Theatre Project spends forty-six million dollars producing more than 800 works.

1940   John Steinbeck receives Pulitzer Prize for Literature for *The Grapes of Wrath*.

1943   WPA terminated by President Roosevelt.

MATERIALS OF INTEREST
Books

- *Imagined Places: Journeys into Literary America* by Michael Pearson (University Press of Mississippi, 1991)
- *Writers on World War Two: An Anthology*, edited by Mordechai Richler (Random House, 1993)

Multimedia

Appalachian Journey, written, directed, and produced by Alan Lomax (PBS Home Video, 1990)

Connections to
Custom Literature Database

For further historical background, under **Background Articles**, see **Later Modern America 1815–1945**.

FOR ALL STUDENTS

Remind students that traditions are the handing down of beliefs, opinions, customs, and stories from parents to children.

- Ask students to reflect on traditions in their own lives.
- What family traditions have outlasted changes in family life or in society?

To further explore the theme, use the transparency referenced here.

Transparency Collection
Fine Art Writing Prompt 11

For At-Risk Students

Ask students to discuss school traditions.

- Does the school honor or practice any traditions concerning academics, sports, or social activities?
- Have any traditions changed in the time they have been attending the school? What prompted the changes?

For Students Who Need Challenge

Have students interview a person born before World War II to discuss changes that person has seen in American government or politics.

MULTICULTURAL CONNECTION

As students read the selections, ask them to think about communication styles and traditions in relation to lifestyle. Can communication and traditions be classified as urban or rural? Do differences break down if people are seen as individuals rather than as members of a group?

Part Two

The Strength of Tradition

While American society was rapidly changing between the wars, many individuals found strength in maintaining the traditions and customs of their cultures and regions. Particularly in rural America, people resisted the changes caused by rapid industrialization, and chose to hold on to the wisdom and ways of older generations.

Multicultural Connection The way we communicate with each other depends a lot on our individual experiences and our cultural backgrounds. In the following selections, notice how **communication** styles differ between the individuals and groups depicted. What in these selections leads to successful communication, and what causes communication to break down?

IDEAS THAT WORK

Motivating with Discovery

"To provide students with a sense of discovery, put them to work uncovering common threads in a variety of selections. Finding recurring themes, images, or character types amounts to an exercise in critical thinking and primary research.

With students organized into working groups of two or three, I provide hints or suggestions so that it becomes almost a "dependent study" assignment, and I set a time limit. When time is up, I have students write or orally report their findings.

In the selections of The Strength of Tradition, students might discover decision-making, the inner strengths of characters, or each author's use of imagery. Praise what students discover, and don't be surprised when they find something that you haven't ever considered before this."

John R. Lord
Ocean, New Jersey

Before Reading

Stopping by Woods on a Snowy Evening
Mending Wall
Birches

by Robert Frost

Robert Frost
1874–1963

Born in San Francisco, ten-year-old Robert Frost moved with his mother and sister to his grandfather's farm in Massachusetts following his father's death. For twenty years, while farming, teaching, and working in a bobbin factory, Frost was a mostly unknown and unsuccessful poet. Then in 1912 he made a big decision. Frost sold the farm and moved with his wife and four children to England. There he could "write and be poor without further scandal in the family." Two books of Frost's poetry were published in England, *A Boy's Will* in 1913 and *North of Boston* in 1914. When Frost returned to the United States, he was famous. This Yankee farmer/poet won the Pulitzer Prize four times.

Building Background

Think Yankee What do you visualize when you think of New England? Rocky farmland? cold, snowy winters? rutted roads? deep woods? wild Atlantic waters? Robert Frost was a Yankee; his home was New England. His poems are populated with tough, hard-working people whose words are spare. Although Frost is sometimes considered a regional writer because he wrote about the New England landscape as well as the customs, dress, and speech of its people, his poems are rich in universal meanings. As you read these three poems by Robert Frost, reflect on how his insights relate to you today.

Literary Focus

Blank Verse At times Robert Frost's poems sound almost as if the poet were chatting with you. To achieve this natural sound, Frost often uses **blank verse,** which is unrhymed iambic pentameter. Each unrhymed line has five feet or ten syllables, the first syllable in each pair unaccented and the second accented. A line of blank verse sounds like this: ta Dum ta Dum ta Dum ta Dum ta Dum. Notice the rhythm in the first two lines of "Birches."

> When I see birches bend to left and right
>
> Across the lines of straighter darker trees

Now look ahead at the first few lines of "Mending Wall" and "Stopping by Woods on a Snowy Evening." Which one is written in blank verse? How do you know?

Writer's Notebook

Your Backdrop Good writers write about what they know, and Robert Frost is no exception. A New England farmer at heart, Frost uses the New England landscape and Yankee farmers as a backdrop for his reflections on life. What things in your surroundings inspire you? Look around and then jot down some possible topics.

Before Reading

Building Background

Poet Randall Jarrell wrote of Frost, "When you know Frost's poems you know surprisingly well how the world seemed to one man." Frost's use of common language and everyday imagery allows his poetry to be read on many levels.

Literary Focus

Because **blank verse** doesn't rhyme, it may seem easy to write. However, it requires a skillful use of pauses, accents, and meaningful word groupings in order to keep the rhythm from becoming monotonous. *("Mending Wall" is written in blank verse for the most part, with five feet, ten syllables, per line.)*

Writer's Notebook

Point out to students that their "backdrop" can be geographic (a region of the country; rural, suburban, urban) or more personal (school or home life, music, movies, sports).

More About Robert Frost

- Frost was christened Robert Lee Frost after General Robert E. Lee.
- He had no formal schooling until the age of ten.

Connections to
AuthorWorks

Robert Frost is a featured author in the AuthorWorks CD-ROM.

SUPPORT MATERIALS OVERVIEW

Unit 6 Resource Book
- Graphic Organizer, p. 57
- Study Guide, p. 58
- Vocabulary, p. 59
- Grammar, p. 60
- Alternate Check Test, p. 61
- Vocabulary Test, p. 62
- Selection Test, pp. 63–63

Building English Proficiency
- Literature Summaries
- Activities, p. 216

Reading, Writing & Grammar SkillBook
- Vocabulary, pp. 9–10
- Reading, pp. 48–49
- Writing, pp. 119–120
- Grammar, Usage, and Mechanics, pp. 184–185

Technology
- Audiotape
- Personal Journal Software
- Custom Literature Database: Additional poems by Robert Frost can be found on the database.
- Test Generator Software

During Reading

Selection Objectives

- To explore the theme of holding on to traditions
- To identify examples of blank verse
- To analyze the use of symbolism
- To discuss our relationship to one another and to nature

 Unit 6 Resource Book
Graphic Organizer, p. 57
Study Guide, p. 58

Theme Link

Although Frost seems to write about a simpler time in America, his poems, which draw on traditional subjects and images, make the reader wonder if those times really were so uncomplicated. He raises questions about issues that are relevant today.

1 Literary Element

Rhyme

In the first three stanzas of this poem, three of the four lines rhyme, and the end sound in the third line of each is picked up in the following stanza.

Questions

- What is the rhyme scheme in the first stanza of the poem? *(aaba)*
- What is the rhyme scheme in the rest of the poem? *(bbcb, ccdc, dddd)*

Literary Criticism

"The speaker is caught between his desire to remain still, peacefully held by the serene beauty of the woods, and his contrasting need to leave, to return to his responsibilities. In a similar way, the poem's rhyme is caught between a surge forward toward a new sound and a return to a sound repeated earlier. The pull and counterpull of the rhyme reflect the speaker's ambivalence."

Robert DiYanni
Modern American Poets:
Their Voices and Visions

636

STOPPING BY WOODS ON A SNOWY EVENING

ROBERT FROST

Whose woods these are I think I know.
His house is in the village, though;
He will not see me stopping here
To watch his woods fill up with snow.

5 My little horse must think it queer
To stop without a farmhouse near
Between the woods and frozen lake
The darkest evening of the year.

He gives his harness bells a shake
10 To ask if there is some mistake.
The only other sound's the sweep
Of easy wind and downy flake.

The woods are lovely, dark, and deep,
But I have promises to keep,
1 15 And miles to go before I sleep,
And miles to go before I sleep.

SELECTION SUMMARY

Poems by Robert Frost

Frost writes about his rugged and simple New England surroundings. There is an undercurrent of melancholy in these poems, and an understanding that this traditional landscape is bursting with irony and ambiguity. People may yearn for the simple life, but human nature moves us toward the more complex.

Stopping by Woods on a Snowy Evening   The narrator stops to admire the woods filling with snow, wishing he could linger, but the responsibilities of his life beckon.

Mending Wall   An everyday discussion between two neighbors becomes the metaphor for the nature of communication and barriers.

Birches   This poem is both a nostalgic look at the carefree days of boyhood and a lament about the ravages of nature on humans and trees.

 *For summaries in other languages, see the **Building English Proficiency** book.*

This barn which stood isolated from other farm buildings was the inspiration for Eric Sloane's painting, *Hill Farm Barn*. Could the stone wall in his painting resemble one that may have inspired Robert Frost's poem, "Mending Wall"? Why or why not?

MENDING WALL

ROBERT FROST

2 Something there is that doesn't love a wall,
That sends the frozen-ground-swell under it
And spills the upper boulders in the sun,
And makes gaps even two can pass abreast.
5 The work of hunters is another thing:
I have come after them and made repair
Where they have left not one stone on a stone,
But they would have the rabbit out of hiding,
To please the yelping dogs. The gaps I mean,

 **Art Study**

Response to Caption Question   Most students will say that although the wall in the picture is also made of stone, it seems in much greater disrepair than the one in Frost's poem and would not be as high. It really doesn't look much like a wall at all.

Visual Literacy   During the 1930s, Eric Sloane became interested in weather. This led to his paintings of cloud formations, which he called "cloudscapes." He even studied meteorology at the Massachusetts Institute of Technology and published several illustrated books on weather. He often used oil on canvas, employing a pencil or a razor blade to work the wet paint.

Question   Where is the sun in this painting and which way is the wind blowing? *(Possible answer: The sun is at the left of the painting and judging by the grass, the wind is moving from left to right.)*

2 **Writing Style**
Interpretation

By inverting the word order, Frost draws attention to this opening line, making a more dramatic statement. Note also that he says *something* rather than *someone*.

Question   What is that something that doesn't love a wall? *(Possible responses: a personality trait, nature, the elements, the seasons, hunters, the ground.)*

BUILDING ENGLISH PROFICIENCY

Comparing Sounds in Poetry

ESL
LEP
ELD
SAE
LD

Help students explore how Frost uses sound to enhance his poems.

- Ask volunteers to read aloud "Stopping by Woods on a Snowy Evening" and "Mending Wall" (or use the Audiotape). Have students discuss music that they think would complement the mood of each poem.

- Have students work together to complete the chart shown. Ask each group to study one sound effect in both poems and to share what they find out.

Sound Effects	"Stopping by Woods on a Snowy Evening"	"Mending Wall"
Rhyming Lines	lines 1, 2, and 4 in stanzas 1-3	no end rhyme
Rhythm Pattern		
Alliteration		

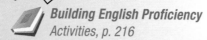 *Building English Proficiency Activities*, p. 216

3 Reading/Thinking Skills
Analyze

Questions

- Who initiates the yearly chore of repairing the wall? *(the narrator)*

- What might you conclude from that? *(Possibly that is important to the narrator to keep the wall up or that he enjoys this ritual contact with his neighbor.)*

- Describe the two neighbors as they work on the wall *(Each one stays on his side of the wall. They are separated by the wall, but they are working together. It is almost like a game, with rules regarding who stands where. They are divided also by a difference of opinion as to what it means to be a neighbor.)*

4 Literary Element
Simile

Questions

- To what does the narrator compare the neighbor and what does this simile mean? *(to "an old-stone savage armed"; perhaps it means that he is living in the past, in a time when walls were useful and men had to be brutal to protect themselves)*

- What does this suggest about the need for a wall? *(Perhaps that the neighbor [and his ideas] are primitive and threatening; therefore suggesting that walls are needed for defense against enemies.)*

5 Reader's Response
Challenging the Text

Question   What do you think the wall represents? *(Students might answer the wall stands for communication [or lack of same], boundaries, barriers, sense of self, or defenses.)*

---

10   No one has seen them made or heard them made,
  But at spring mending-time we find them there.
  I let my neighbor know beyond the hill;
  And on a day we meet to walk the line
  And set the wall between us once again.

3 15   We keep the wall between us as we go.
  To each the boulders that have fallen to each.
  And some are loaves and some so nearly balls
  We have to use a spell to make them balance:
  "Stay where you are until our backs are turned!"
20   We wear our fingers rough with handling them.
  Oh, just another kind of outdoor game,
  One on a side. It comes to little more:
  There where it is we do not need the wall:
  He is all pine and I am apple orchard.
25   My apple trees will never get across
  And eat the cones under his pines, I tell him.
  He only says, "Good fences make good neighbors."
  Spring is the mischief in me, and I wonder
  If I could put a notion in his head:
30   "*Why* do they make good neighbors? Isn't it
  Where there are cows? But here there are no cows.
  Before I built a wall I'd ask to know
  What I was walling in or walling out,
  And to whom I was like to give offense.
35   Something there is that doesn't love a wall,
  That wants it down." I could say "Elves" to him,
  But it's not elves exactly, and I'd rather
  He said it for himself. I see him there,
  Bringing a stone grasped firmly by the top

4 40   In each hand, like an old-stone savage armed.
  He moves in darkness as it seems to me,
  Not of woods only and the shade of trees.
  He will not go behind his father's saying,
  And he likes having thought of it so well

5 45   He says again, "Good fences make good neighbors."

MINI-LESSON: GRAMMAR
Contractions

Teach   The apostrophe in a contraction shows where letters have been left out in order to form a single word from two words. In some instances in these poems, students must use context to distinguish between a contraction and a possessive.

Questions

- What is the only contraction in "Stopping by Woods"? What two words does it stand for? *(sound's; sound is)*

- Find three contractions in "Mending Wall." *(doesn't, Isn't, I'd, doesn't, it's, I'd)*

- What does the word *boy's* mean in line 3 of "Birches"? *(boy has)*

Activity Idea   Have students rewrite these phrases using contractions:

- She has finished. *(She's finished.)*
- He will not. *(He won't.)*
- Coffee is brewing. *(Coffee's brewing.)*
- Where does it hurt? *(Where's it hurt?)*

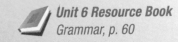
Unit 6 Resource Book
Grammar, p. 60

What would you say is the appeal of birch trees that would inspire a painting like Neil Welliver's *The Birches* (1977) or a poem like Robert Frost's "Birches"? ➤

BIRCHES

ROBERT FROST

When I see birches bend to left and right
Across the lines of straighter darker trees,
I like to think some boy's been swinging them.
But swinging doesn't bend them down to stay
5 As ice storms do. Often you must have seen them
Loaded with ice a sunny winter morning
After a rain. They click upon themselves
As the breeze rises, and turn many-colored
As the stir cracks and crazes their enamel.
10 Soon the sun's warmth makes them shed crystal shells
Shattering and avalanching on the snow crust—
Such heaps of broken glass to sweep away
You'd think the inner dome of heaven had fallen.
They are dragged to the withered bracken[1] by the load,

---

1. **bracken** (brak′ən), *n.* a large, coarse fern common on hillsides, in woods, etc.

Birches   639

BUILDING ENGLISH PROFICIENCY

ESL
LEP
ELD
SAE
LD

Appreciating Language and Imagery

One way to allow students to share poetic elements that appeal to them is to stage a "Quaker reading."

• Ask students to write down passages that contain images that strike them as very vivid, moving, impressive, or unusual.

• Have students share a passage or passages that they have chosen by standing and reading them aloud.

• To extend the activity, ask students to choose an image from one of the passages they have heard and draw it. The class can then guess the phrase illustrated by each image. You might want to display these images in sequence.

8 Literary Element
Narrator

Question How would you describe the narrator of this poem? *(Possible responses: He is an older man who is nostalgic and worn out. He no longer climbs trees. He misses being a boy. He'd like a chance to do it all again.)*

9 Literary Element
Symbolism

Question What does the birch tree symbolize in this poem? *(Possible responses: the passage of time, life, adversity, memories.)*

10 Reader's Response
Making Personal Connections

Question What do you think being a swinger of birches means in the last line? *(Possibly that birch swingers are adaptable, "go with the flow," enjoy life, do not make a permanent mark, as nature does, but temporarily influence the environment.)*

Check Test

1. Why must the narrator move on in the first poem? *(He has lots of responsibilities he must fulfill.)*

2. What two points of view about walls are given in "Mending Wall"? *(Something doesn't love them and good fences make good neighbors.)*

3. Why does the narrator think a wall is unnecessary? *(Neither neighbor has livestock to keep in or out, they only have trees.)*

4. What is the difference between trees bent by boys swinging or by an ice storm? *(Trees bent by the storm stay bent.)*

5. How would the narrator like to die, or "go," in "Birches"? *(He'd like to climb a birch tree towards heaven and be set down.)*

 Unit 6 Resource Book
Alternate Check Test, p. 61

640

---

15 And they seem not to break; though once they are bowed
So low for long, they never right themselves:
You may see their trunks arching in the woods
Years afterwards, trailing their leaves on the ground
Like girls on hands and knees that throw their hair
20 Before them over their heads to dry in the sun.
But I was going to say when Truth broke in
With all her matter of fact about the ice storm,
I should prefer to have some boy bend them
As he went out and in to fetch the cows—
25 Some boy too far from town to learn baseball,
Whose only play was what he found himself,
Summer or winter, and could play alone.
One by one he subdued his father's trees
By riding them down over and over again
30 Until he took the stiffness out of them,
And not one but hung limp, not one was left
For him to conquer. He learned all there was
To learn about not launching out too soon
And so not carrying the tree away
35 Clear to the ground. He always kept his poise
To the top branches, climbing carefully
With the same pains you use to fill a cup
Up to the brim, and even above the brim.
Then he flung outward, feet first, with a swish,
40 Kicking his way down through the air to the ground.
So was I once myself a swinger of birches.
And so I dream of going back to be.
It's when I'm weary of considerations,
And life is too much like a pathless wood
45 Where your face burns and tickles with the cobwebs
Broken across it, and one eye is weeping
From a twig's having lashed across it open. **7**
I'd like to get away from earth awhile
And then come back to it and begin over.
50 May no fate willfully misunderstand me
And half grant what I wish and snatch me away
Not to return. Earth's the right place for love:
I don't know where it's likely to go better.
I'd like to go by climbing a birch tree, **8**
55 And climb black branches up a snow-white trunk
Toward heaven, till the tree could bear no more,
But dipped its top and set me down again.
That would be good both going and coming back.
One could do worse than be a swinger of birches. **9**

MINI-LESSON: LITERARY FOCUS

Blank Verse

Teach Have students reread the description of blank verse on page 635. When determining the meter of a poem, mark each unaccented syllable with the symbol ⌣ and each accented syllable with the symbol ´. The feet are divided by a slash mark /. Show students how to mark the first few lines of "Birches."

⌣ ´ ⌣ ´ ⌣ ´ ⌣ ´ ⌣ ´
When I see birch/ es bend/ to left/ and right

⌣ ´ ⌣ ´ ⌣ ´ ⌣ ´ ⌣ ´
A cross/ the lines/ of straight/ er dark/ er trees

Activity Idea Have students mark five to ten more lines of the poem with these symbols. In some lines, words that are typically two syllables may be read as one to preserve the meter. However, note that Frost clearly does deviate from iambic pentameter in some places.

After Reading

Making Connections

Shaping Your Response

1. Which of the three Frost poems do you like the best? Why?

2. Two opposing opinions are expressed in "Mending Wall": "Good fences make good neighbors" and "Something there is that doesn't love a wall." Which opinion do you hold? Why? Survey the class to see whether your classmates agree.

Analyzing the Poems

3. What examples of **alliteration,** the repetition of initial sounds *(lovely, ladies),* can you find in "Stopping by Woods on a Snowy Evening"?

4. What effect does the **repetition** in the last two lines of "Stopping by Woods on a Snowy Evening" have?

5. How does the speaker in "Mending Wall" **characterize** his neighbor?

6. What **images, metaphors,** and **similes** describe the effect of ice storms on birches in the poem "Birches"?

7. How would you describe the **mood** of "Birches" in lines 43–47?

Extending the Ideas

8. Compare the three Frost poems. Do they have a common **theme?** Explain your answer.

9. Robert Frost writes about a stone fence, a traveler in a snowy woods, and a stand of birches. What three things characteristic of your geographic region could you substitute for Frost's topics?

10. In "Mending Wall," two neighbors repair a wall between their property. What kinds of metaphorical walls sometimes impede **communication** between people? How can such "walls" be torn down?

Literary Focus: Blank Verse

Robert Frost uses **blank verse,** but he occasionally alternates iambic pentameter with other rhythms to convey a conversational quality. Read "Birches" aloud. In which line does Frost begin to deviate from iambic pentameter? In which line does he return to it? What would you say is the effect of the variations in rhythm in this poem?

Birches   641

LITERARY FOCUS
Blank Verse

Frost varies the rhythm in the fifth line, but returns to it in the seventh line. He deviates again in line fourteen and returns to it in line sixteen. The break in the rhythm slows the poem down in those places where heaviness or slower motion is suggested by the images.

Unit 6 Resource Book
Graphic Organizer, p. 57

After Reading

MAKING CONNECTIONS

1. Students' responses will vary.

2. Answers will depend on the student's sense of personal space, safety, and viewpoint about how people treat one another.

3. Examples of alliteration include: his/house; He/here; watch/woods; my/must; his/harness; dark/deep. You may want to point out that alliteration does not have to be initial sounds, for example, so<u>me/mi</u>stake and wind/and/downy flake.

4. Students may respond that the repetition emphasizes the thought, conveys a sense of sadness or regret, or completes the rhyme scheme.

5. Possible response: He is a man who keeps to himself and follows the ways of his father. He methodically and resolutely returns the stones to the wall without questioning—unable or unwilling to learn new ways.

6. Images: lines of straight, dark trees, sunny winter morning after a rain, trunks arching, kicking; black branches, snow-white trunk. Metaphors: shed crystal shells, heaps of broken glass. Similes: like girls on hands and knees, like a pathless wood.

7. Possible responses: despair, weariness, regret, pain

8. Possible responses: They seem to be concerned with trying to make one's way in a difficult world, full of loss, pain, and distance between people (or people and their dreams).

9. City-dwellers may list modes of mass transport, building styles, traffic sound, neighborhood smells.

10. Students might answer that the poem is also about communication and the emotional walls or defenses we build around ourselves to keep people at a distance.

Selection Test

Unit 6 Resource Book
pp. 63–64

WRITING CHOICES
Writer's Notebook Update

Remind students that blank verse does not rhyme, but must have a cadence, even if they deviate from it occasionally.

Childhood Pastimes

Remind student writers to use sensory images as they describe a childhood activity. What did they most love to do and what did doing it feel like? What did they see, hear, touch, and smell as they were engaged in that activity? How do they feel as they look back at the experience?

Local Poetry

Local colleges, independent bookstores, or libraries may provide information about the work of local poets.

Expressing Your Ideas

Writing Choices

Writer's Notebook Update Choose one of the topics you listed in your Writer's Notebook. Then write ten lines of blank verse about it. For example, if you have chosen *school* as one of your topics, you might begin with this line: "Today I got to school at eight o'clock." You may vary the rhythm occasionally to keep the verse from becoming monotonous.

Childhood Pastimes The speaker in "Birches" was a swinger of birches as a boy. What was your favorite pastime as a child? Were you a skipper of stones, a comic book kid, or something else? Write a **description** of your childhood pastime.

Local Poetry Who is your local poet laureate? Find out more about a poet from your community, state, or region at a library or bookstore. Then write a short **report** on the poet's life and work.

Other Options

Step into the Poem Choose one of the three Frost poems to present to the class. Prepare a **dramatic reading** of the poem, or you might try memorizing it.

Don't Fence Me In Your neighbors are circulating a petition to take down all the fences in your community. However, an opposition group is forming to keep the fences up and add more! Which side will you take? Prepare your arguments and then **debate** a classmate with an opposing viewpoint.

New England Scenes Find and play for the class parts of a **recording** of either of the following works for orchestra by American composers: *Three Places in New England* by Charles Ives or *New England Triptych* by William Schuman. Have your classmates draw what they visualize as they listen.

OTHER OPTIONS
Step into the Poem

For "Birches" or "Mending Wall," you may want to suggest they select part of the poem, so that they do not choose "Stopping by Woods" simply because of its brevity. Encourage students who do not want to memorize an entire poem to memorize their favorite stanzas.

Don't Fence Me In

Remind students that in a debate, no one is right or wrong. But each side must have solid arguments to support its stand. Students can use oral arguments or any visuals they can think of, such as photos and drawings to show the effect of building or removing walls.

New England Scenes

While music is playing, ask students to write down images that come to mind.

Before Reading

The Tall Men

by William Faulkner

William Faulkner
1897–1962

Like Robert Frost, William Faulkner is often considered a regionalist. Born near Oxford, Mississippi, he spent most of his life there. He began by writing poetry and then a novel about World War I. Writer Sherwood Anderson, who was a roommate of Faulkner's in New Orleans, convinced him to write about "that little patch up there in Mississippi where you started from." Following Anderson's advice, Faulkner created Yoknapatawpha County, Mississippi, and peopled it with unforgettable characters. Some of the Yoknapatawpha novels are *Sartoris, The Sound and the Fury, As I Lay Dying,* and *Sanctuary.* Faulkner won the Nobel Prize for literature in 1950.

Building Background

A "New Deal" for Farmers When President Franklin Roosevelt took office in 1933, the United States was on the verge of economic collapse. Neither business nor agriculture had recovered from the stock market crash of 1929. To help farmers, Roosevelt's administration implemented the Agricultural Adjustment Act (AAA). Based on the economic principle of supply and demand—when an item is scarce, the price will rise, and when plentiful, the price will fall—the AAA sought to control the supply of crops in the country by paying farmers cash subsidies to *not* plant certain crops, thereby driving up prices. The McCallum family, the farmers in "The Tall Men," chose not to participate in the farm subsidy program.

Literary Focus

Characterization The method an author uses to develop his or her characters is called **characterization.** A writer may describe a character's appearance, personality, behavior, thoughts, feelings, or speech. *Flat characters* are one-dimensional and lacking in complexity. *Round characters* are multi-faceted, with realistic emotions and behavior. Choose one of the main characters in "The Tall Men," and find story passages that show examples of Faulkner's methods of characterization.

Writer's Notebook

Skillet or Fry Pan? To establish the setting of the rural South in the 1940s and to develop his characters, William Faulkner uses **dialect.** Dialect is a form of speech characteristic of a particular region or group. For example, one of the characters in Faulkner's story refers to a *demijohn,* a kind of bottle. Another character says, "This here ain't hurt none to speak of since I got a-holt of this *johnny-jug.*" Do you or the people in your area have names for things that are different from names used in other areas? In your notebook, write words, phrases, or expressions that you think might be dialect.

The Tall Men **643**

Before Reading

Building Background

Ask students if they have followed debates among political candidates about the level of government involvement in people's lives.

- Discuss the role of welfare, how it can help or hurt people.
- Discuss farm subsidies and the role they play in the U.S. economy.

Literary Focus

Encourage students to describe ways that authors show who their characters are. Elicit ideas about physical description, past histories, speech, and actions as methods of **characterization.**

Writer's Notebook

Explain that after reading the story, students will be using the examples of dialect they write down to create a monologue for a character.

More About William Faulkner

Faulkner never completed high school, but he was an avid reader. He could barely support his family on the sales of his books, and in the 1930s and 1940s he wrote Hollywood screenplays. By 1944 only one of his seventeen books was still in print. Interest was revived in 1948, with the publication of *The Portable Faulkner.*

SUPPORT MATERIALS OVERVIEW

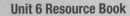

Unit 6 Resource Book
- Graphic Organizer, p. 65
- Study Guide, p. 66
- Vocabulary, p. 67
- Grammar, p. 68
- Alternate Check Test, p. 69
- Vocabulary Test, p. 70
- Selection Test, pp. 71–72

Building English Proficiency
- Literature Summaries
- Activities, p. 217

Reading, Writing & Grammar SkillBook
- Vocabulary, pp. 9–10
- Reading, pp. 90–91
- Writing, pp. 137–138
- Grammar, Usage, and Mechanics, pp. 173–175

Technology
- Audiotape
- Personal Journal Software
- Custom Literature Database: For another selection dealing with American tradition, see the First Inaugural Address of Franklin Delano Roosevelt on the database.
- Test Generator Software

During Reading

Selection Objectives

- To read an American regional story
- To analyze characterization
- To understand point of view
- To interpret informal English, slang, and dialect in the context of a story

 Unit 6 Resource Book
Graphic Organizer, p. 65
Study Guide, p. 66

Theme Link

In this Depression-era story, a family strives to keep up the tradition of high standards set by their independent, principled ancestors, while facing changes in their nation's expectations.

Vocabulary Preview

jeopardize, put in danger; risk

relinquish, give up; let go

discern, perceive the difference between two or more things

seethe, be excited; be disturbed

expedite, do or perform quickly

cease, come to an end or stop

evade, avoid by cleverness; elude

cite, summon officially to appear in court

speculative, reflective

stabilize, prevent changes in, hold steady

   Students can add the words and definitions to their personal word lists in their Writer's Notebooks.

Dorothea Lange was an influential documentary photographer who is renowned for her photographs of destitute victims of the Great Depression of the 1930s. This 1938 photograph is from Lange's collection.

644   UNIT SIX: MODERN DILEMMAS

SELECTION SUMMARY

The Tall Men

"The Tall Men" is the story of the all-male McCallum family. A draft investigator has come to their farm with the local marshal to arrest Anse and Lucius McCallum for draft evasion. The stranger views the McCallums as people who cheat the government. Arriving on the farm, the investigator finds that Buddy, the boys' father, must have his leg amputated due to an accident. Buddy takes care of business first—he sends the boys to enlist. They leave obediently. With only whiskey to dull the pain, Buddy's leg is amputated. As the marshal and the investigator bury the leg, the marshal recounts the McCallum family history. Old Anse was a confederate Civil War veteran and Buddy was wounded in World War I. The McCallums always "stand tall," refusing government aid and subsidies not to grow cotton. The two men then return to town.

 *For summaries in other languages, see the **Building English Proficiency** book.*

THE TALL MEN

William Faulkner

They passed the dark bulk of the cotton gin. Then they saw the lamplit house and the other car, the doctor's coupé, just stopping at the gate, and they could hear the hound baying.

"Here we are," the old deputy marshal said.

"What's that other car?" the younger man said, the stranger, the state draft[1] investigator.

"Doctor Schofield's," the marshal said. "Lee McCallum asked me to send him out when I telephoned we were coming."

"You mean you warned them?" the investigator said. "You telephoned ahead that I was coming out with a warrant for these two evaders? Is this how you carry out the orders of the United States Government?"

The marshal was a lean, clean old man who chewed tobacco, who had been born and lived in the county all his life.

"I understood all you wanted was to arrest these two McCallum boys and bring them back to town," he said.

1 CLARIFY: Why does the state investigator intend to arrest the McCallum boys?

"It was!" the investigator said. "And now you have warned them, given them a chance to run. Possibly put the Government to the expense of hunting them down with troops. Have you forgotten that you are under a bond yourself?"

"I ain't forgot it," the marshal said. "And ever since we left Jefferson I been trying to tell you something for you not to forget. But I reckon it will take these McCallums to impress that on you. . . . Pull in behind the other car. We'll try to find out first just how sick whoever it is that is sick is."

The investigator drew up behind the other car and switched off and blacked out his lights. "These people," he said. Then he thought, *But this doddering, tobacco-chewing old man is one of them, too, despite the honor and pride of his office, which should have made him different.* So he didn't speak it aloud, removing the keys and getting out of the car, and then locking the car itself, rolling the windows up first, thinking, *These people who lie about and conceal the ownership of land and property in order to hold relief jobs which they have no intention of performing, standing on their constitutional rights against having to work, who jeopardize[2] the very job itself through petty and transparent subterfuge to acquire a free mattress which they intend to attempt to sell; who would relinquish[3]*

---

1. **draft**, *n.* selection of persons for some special purpose. Soldiers are supplied to the army by draft during periods of war.
2. jeopardize (jep′ər dīz), *v.* put in danger; risk.
3. relinquish (ri ling′kwish), *v.* give up; let go.

Dialect

Questions

• Find two examples of dialect in this paragraph. *(we was running, something went whang, I never knowed nothing else, a heap of us racked up, this here ain't hurt none to speak of since I got ahold of this johnny-jug)*

• What does the use of dialect show you about Buddy? *(He is a simple man, at home with himself and comfortable among his family and friends.)*

11 **Literary Focus**

Characterization

Questions

• How would you characterize the McCallums? *(They are quiet, powerful, serious, responsible, close-knit, and intense.)*

• What words does Faulkner use to describe them? *(tremendous men, not big, not tall, looking quietly, faces bearing an almost identical stamp of kinship)*

• Has your assessment of Buddy's character changed any? *(Most will say he seems even more heroic at this point, what with his war wounds and his acceptance of the imminent amputation of his leg.)*

"No," the doctor said. "He's had too much already."

"Pour me some whisky, Jackson," the man on the bed said. He puffed steadily at the pipe, looking at the investigator. "You come from the Government?" he said.

"Yes," the investigator said. "They should have registered. That's all required of them yet. They did not——" His voice ceased,[8] while the seven pairs of eyes contemplated him, and the man on the bed puffed steadily.

…the seven pairs of eyes contemplated him …

"We would have still been here," the man on the bed said. "We wasn't going to run." He turned his head. The two youths were standing side by side at the foot of the bed. "Anse, Lucius," he said.

To the investigator it sounded as if they answered as one, "Yes, father."

"This gentleman has come all the way from Jackson to say the Government is ready for you. I reckon the quickest place to enlist will be Memphis. Go upstairs and pack."

The investigator started, moved forward, "Wait!" he cried.

But Jackson, the eldest, had forestalled him. He said, "Wait," also, and now they were not looking at the investigator. They were looking at the doctor.

"What about his leg?" Jackson said.

"Look at it," the doctor said. "He almost amputated it himself. It won't wait. And he can't be moved now. I'll need my nurse to help me, and some ether, provided he hasn't had too much whisky to stand the anesthetic too. One of you can drive to town in my car. I'll telephone——"

"Ether?" the man on the bed said. "What for? You just said yourself it's pretty near off now. I could whet up one of Jackson's butcher knives and finish it myself, with another drink or two. Go on. Finish it."

"You couldn't stand any more shock," the doctor said. "This is whisky talking now."

"Shucks," the other said. "One day in France we was running through a wheat field and I saw the machine gun, coming across the wheat, and I tried to jump it like you would jump a fence rail somebody was swinging at your middle, only I never made it. And I was on the ground then, and along toward dark that begun to hurt, only about that time something went whang on the back of my helmet, like when you hit an anvil, so I never knowed nothing else until I woke up. There was a heap of us racked up along a bank outside a field dressing station, only it took a long time for the doctor to get around to all of us, and by that time it was hurting bad. This here ain't hurt none to speak of since I got a-holt of this johnny-jug. You go on and finish it. If it's help you need, Stuart and Rafe will help you. . . . Pour me a drink, Jackson."

This time the doctor raised the demijohn and examined the level of the liquor. "There's a good quart gone," he said. "If you've drunk a quart of whisky since four o'clock, I doubt if you could stand the anesthetic. Do you think you could stand it if I finished it now?"

"Yes, finish it. I've ruined it; I want to get shut of it."[9]

The doctor looked about at the others, at the still, identical faces watching him. "If I had him in town, in the hospital, with a nurse to watch him, I'd probably wait until he got over this first shock and got the whisky out of his system. But he can't be moved now, and I can't stop the bleeding like this, and even if I had ether or a local anesthetic——"

"Shucks," the man on the bed said. "God never made no better local nor general comfort or anesthetic neither than what's in this johnny-jug. And this ain't Jackson's leg nor Stuart's nor

10

11

---

8. cease (sēs), *v.* come to an end or stop.
9. **get shut of it,** colloquial expression meaning "get rid of it," or "get it over with."

MINI-LESSON: VOCABULARY

Using the Dictionary to Find Meaning

Teach Most words in the English language have various meanings. You can find these meanings in a dictionary, with the most common or accepted definition listed first.

Activity Idea Divide the class into small groups and assign one of more of these words from the selection to each group:

cease	cite	discern	evade	expedite
jeopardize	relinquish	seethe	stabilize	

Ask each group to

• check the dictionary for the main definition

• check for secondary definitions

• choose which definition most closely fits the word as used in the selection

▲ Do these tenant farmers in Dorothea Lange's 1937 photograph fill the picture the way the "tremendous men" encountered by the investigator filled Buddy's room in William Faulkner's story, "The Tall Men"? Why or why not?

12 Reading/Thinking Skills
Make Inferences

Why do you think the doctor asks permission from the oldest brother, Jackson, even though Buddy insists that his leg be cut off? *(Possible answers: He thought Buddy was too drunk or in too much pain or shock to make a sound decision. That was the way things were done there.)*

13 Reader's Response
Making Personal Connections

Question Throughout the story, there have been many references to the McCallums looking at the investigator. How do you think the investigator feels about having their eyes on him so much? *(He probably feels uncomfortable, like an outsider or intruder, threatened, vulnerable, angry, and nervous.)*

Rafe's nor Lee's. It's mine. I done started it; I reckon I can finish cutting it off any way I want to."

12 But the doctor was still looking at Jackson. "Well, Mr. McCallum?" he said. "You're the oldest."

But it was Stuart who answered. "Yes," he said. "Finish it. What do you want? Hot water, I reckon."

"Yes," the doctor said. "Some clean sheets. Have you got a big table you can move in here?"

"The kitchen table," the man who had met them at the door said. "Me and the boys——"

"Wait," the man on the bed said. "The boys won't have time to help you." He looked at them again. "Anse, Lucius," he said.

Again it seemed to the investigator that they answered as one, "Yes, father."

"This gentleman yonder is beginning to look **13** impatient. You better start. Come to think of it, you won't need to pack. You will have uniforms in a day or two. Take the truck. There won't be nobody to drive you to Memphis and bring the truck back, so you can leave it at the Gayoso Feed Company until we can send for it. I'd like for you to enlist into the old Sixth Infantry, where I used to be. But I reckon that's too much to hope, and you'll just have to chance where

The Tall Men **649**

BUILDING ENGLISH PROFICIENCY

Understanding Characters' Relationships

ESL LEP ELD SAE LD

To help students identify the seven McCallum men, have them work in groups to copy and complete the graphic organizer shown. Here, in no particular order, is a list of their names.

Lucius   Stuart   Rafe   Buddy
Jackson   Anse   Lee

• Ask students to write the name of each McCallum on the chart in a place that shows his relationship to the others. *(Students should note that Jackson, Stuart, Lee, Rafe, and Buddy are brothers and that*

Anse and Lucius are Buddy's sons.)

• Have them write a brief description of each McCallum.

The McCallum Family

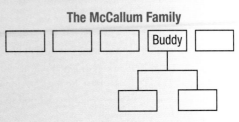

14 Literary Focus
Characterization

Question Why does Buddy think the government will "do right" by his sons? *(Possible answers: They took care of him when he was hurt in the war in France. He believes in the government because it stands for his country. People didn't question the government then as they do today.)*

15 Reading/Thinking Skills
Analyze

Question What does Buddy mean when he tells the boys to remember their names and not take "nothing from no man"? *(Don't forget who you are and where you came from; be proud. Obey your officers, but don't let anyone push you around.)*

16 Reading/Thinking Skills
Recognize Values

Question Do you think the investigator would like to drop the charges? Why or why not? *(Answers may vary. Most will say no, he believes in the letter of the law and in following proper procedure. Some may say yes, because he sees that they now intend to do the right thing.)*

17 Active Reading
Clarify

Response They are going to Memphis to enlist in the Army. Pearson says it is too late for that. Because they failed to register with the selective service, he has an arrest warrant for them.

650

---

14 they send you. But it likely won't matter, once you are in. The Government done right by me in my day, and it will do right by you. You just enlist wherever they want to send you, need you, and obey your sergeants and officers until you find out how to be soldiers. Obey them, but **15** remember your name and don't take nothing from no man. You can go now."

"Wait!" the investigator cried again; again he started, moved forward into the center of the room. "I protest this! I'm sorry about Mr. McCallum's accident. I'm sorry about the whole business. But it's out of my hands and out of his hands now. This charge, failure to register according to law, has been made and the warrant issued. It cannot be evaded[10] this way. The course of the action must be completed before any other step can be taken. They should have thought of this when these boys failed to register. If Mr. Gombault refuses to serve this warrant, I will serve it myself and take these men back to Jefferson with me to answer this charge as made. And I must warn Mr. Gombault that he will be cited[11] for contempt."

The old marshal turned, his shaggy eyebrows beetling again, speaking down to the investigator as if he were a child, "Ain't you found out yet that me or you neither ain't going nowhere for a while?"

"What?" the investigator cried. He looked about at the grave faces once more contemplating him with that remote and speculative[12] regard. "Am I being threatened?" he cried.

"Ain't anybody paying any attention to you **16** at all," the marshal said. "Now you just be quiet for a while, and you will be all right, and after a while we can go back to town."

So he stopped again and stood while the grave, contemplative faces freed him once more of that impersonal and unbearable regard, and saw the two youths approach the bed and bend down in turn and kiss their father on the mouth, and then turn as one and leave the room, passing him without even looking at

650   Unit Six: Modern Dilemmas

---

him. And sitting in the lamplit hall beside the old marshal, the bedroom door closed now, he heard the truck start up and back and turn and go down the road, the sound of it dying away, ceasing, leaving the still, hot night—the Mississippi Indian summer, which had already outlasted half of November—filled with the loud last shrilling of the summer's cicadas, as though they, too, were aware of the imminent season of cold weather and of death.

CLARIFY: What do Anse and Lucius intend to do, and why is this upsetting to Mr. Pearson? **17**

"I remember old Anse," the marshal said pleasantly, chattily, in that tone in which an adult addresses a strange child. "He's been dead fifteen-sixteen years now. He was about sixteen when the old war broke out, and he walked all the way to Virginia to get into it. He could have enlisted and fought right here at home, but his ma was a Carter, so wouldn't nothing do him but to go all the way back to Virginia to do his fighting, even though he hadn't never seen Virginia before himself; walked all the way back to a land he hadn't never ever seen before and enlisted in Stonewall Jackson's army and stayed in it all through the Valley, and right up to Chancellorsville, where them Carolina boys shot Jackson by mistake, and right on up to that morning in 'Sixty-five when Sheridan's cavalry blocked the road from Appomattox to the Valley, where they might have got away again. And he walked back to Mississippi with just about what he had carried away with him when he left, and he got married and built the first story of this house—this here log story we're in right now—and started getting them boys—

---

10. **evade** (i vād′), *v.* avoid by cleverness; elude.
11. **cite** (sīt), *v.* summon officially to appear in court.
12. **speculative** (spek′yə lā′tiv), *adj.* reflective.

MINI-LESSON: GRAMMAR
Slang, Dialect, and Informal English

Teach   Guide students to identify the investigator's speech as standard English and to compare his way of speaking with the informal dialogue of the other characters.

Activity Ideas

- Ask students to write a paragraph of Pearson's thoughts (the words in italics) or his spoken words, as if he were a local rather than a stranger to the McCallums and the marshal.

- Have students write a section of the marshal's or Buddy McCallum's speech in standard English, correcting any grammar mistakes.

- Ask students to write or speak a character's words using the informal English spoken around school.

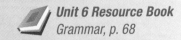

Unit 6 Resource Book
Grammar, p. 68

650

18 Jackson and Stuart and Raphael and Lee and Buddy.

"Buddy come along late, late enough to be in the other war, in France in it. You heard him in there. He brought back two medals, an American medal and a French one, and no man knows till yet how he got them, just what he done. I don't believe he even told Jackson and Stuart and them. He hadn't hardly got back home, with them numbers on his uniform and the wound stripes and them two medals, before he had found him a girl, found her right off, and a year later them twin boys was born, the livin', spittin' image of old Anse McCallum. If old Anse had just been about seventy-five years younger, the three of them might have been triblets. I remember them—two little critters exactly alike, and wild as spikehorn bucks, running around here day and night both with a pack of coon dogs until they got big enough to help Buddy and Stuart and Lee with the farm and the gin, and Rafe with the horses and mules, when he would breed and raise and train them and take them to Memphis to sell, right on up to three, four years back, when they went to the agricultural college for a year to learn more about whiteface cattle.

"That was after Buddy and them had quit raising cotton. I remember that too. It was when the Government first begun to interfere with how a man farmed his own land, raised his cotton. Stabilizing[13] the price, using up the surplus, they called it, giving a man advice and help, whether he wanted it or not. You may have noticed them boys in yonder tonight; curious folks almost, you might call them. That first year, when county agents come out here and tried to explain it to Buddy and Lee and Stuart, explaining how they would cut down the crop, **19** but that the Government would pay farmers the difference, and so they would actually be better off than trying to farm by themselves.

"'Why, we're much obliged,' Buddy says.

'But we don't need no help. We'll just make the cotton like we always done; if we can't make a crop of it, that will just be our lookout and our loss, and we'll try again.'

"So they wouldn't sign no papers nor no cards nor nothing. They just went on and made the cotton like old Anse had taught them to; it was like they just couldn't believe that the Government aimed to help a man whether he wanted help or not, aimed to interfere with how much of anything he could make by hard work on his own land, making the crop and ginning it right here in their own gin, like they had always done, and hauling it to town to sell, hauling it all the way into Jefferson before they found out they couldn't sell it because, in the first place, they had made too much of it and, in the second place, they never had no card to sell what they would have been allowed. So they hauled it back. The gin wouldn't hold all of it, so they put some of it under Rafe's mule shed and they put the rest of it right here in the hall where we are setting now, where they would have to walk around it all winter and keep themselves reminded to be sho and fill out that card next time. **20**

... they just couldn't believe that the Government aimed to help a man whether he wanted help or not ...

"Only next year they didn't fill out no papers neither. It was like they still couldn't believe it, still believed in the freedom and liberty to make or break according to a man's fitness and will to work, guaranteed by the Government that old Anse had tried to tear in two once and failed, and

---

13. **stabilize** (stā′bə līz), v. prevent changes in, hold steady.

The Tall Men   **651**

18 Literary Focus
Characterization

Questions
• What does the story of "old Anse" joining Stonewall Jackson's army say about Anse? *(Possible response: He was a stubborn, honorable man. As a teenager, when the Civil War broke out, he put duty above all else and walked to Virginia to serve, because his family came from there.)*

• Why is the marshal telling the story of "old Anse"? *(He wants Pearson to know what kind of people Buddy and his sons come from and that family and honor are important to them.)*

19 Reading/Thinking Skills
Analyze

Question What is the marshal's opinion of the government's attempts to stabilize prices? What words tell you this? *(The marshal doesn't like the government policy. He calls it interference and says the government gave advice whether or not a farmer wanted it.)*

20 Reading/Thinking Skills
Recognize Cause and Effect

Question As a result of refusing government help, what happened to the McCallums' cotton farming? *(They couldn't sell their cotton because they had too much and they didn't have a card. They had to store the cotton all around their farm.)*

BUILDING ENGLISH PROFICIENCY

Keeping Track of Plot Events

The following activities may help students keep track of the shifts between present and past events in the story.

Activity Ideas
• Have students add old Anse, his mother, his wife, and Buddy's wife to the McCallum family chart they began earlier (see page T649).

• Ask students, working in groups, to summarize two events in the paragraph beginning *"I remember old Anse"* on page 651 and ending with . . . *trying to farm by themselves.* . . . (You may want to assign one group to summarize each event.) Have the groups write each event on a large sheet of paper and number them in order.

Summarize

Questions

- According to the marshal, why does Buddy visit Lawyer Gavin Stevens? *(to try to find out why the Government won't let them sell their cotton)*

- Why did the McCallum brothers abide by Jackson's decision? *(They thought he was speaking for what their father would want, since he was the oldest.)*

22 **Reader's Response**

Making Personal Connections

Question Do you agree that Old Anse would want the boys to put the cotton land into pasture? *(Most students will agree that Anse, like his sons, was the type of man who would want to decide how to run his farm.)*

LITERARY CRITICISM

In "The Tall Men" the investigator is an important agent in the development of the action. He has come with the old deputy to the McCallum farm to arrest Buddy's boys, Anse and Lucius, for failing to register for the draft. But "The Tall Men" is not really his story; the core of the work is the family itself and the values it epitomizes. The investigator remains on the periphery . . . He is a necessary but somewhat obvious narrative <u>device</u> for the development of the platitudinous thematic material of the story.

James Ferguson
Faulkner's Short Fiction
The University of Tennessee Press, 1991

⋀ This photograph shows cotton waiting to be processed at a cotton gin near Orangeburg, South Carolina.

admitted in good faith he had failed and taken the consequences, and that had give Buddy a medal and taken care of him when he was far away from home in a strange land and hurt.

"So they made that second crop. And they couldn't sell it to nobody neither because they never had no cards. This time they built a special shed to put it under, and I remember how in that second winter Buddy come to town one day to see Lawyer Gavin Stevens. Not for legal advice how to sue the Government or somebody into buying the cotton, even if they never had no card for it, but just to find out why. 'I was for going ahead and signing up for it,' Buddy says.

'If that's going to be the new rule. But we talked it over, and Jackson ain't no farmer, but he knowed father longer than the rest of us, and he said father would have said no, and I reckon now he would have been right.' 21

"So they didn't raise any more cotton; they had a plenty of it to last a while—twenty-two bales, I think it was. That was when they went into whiteface cattle, putting old Anse's cotton land into pasture, because that's what he would have wanted them to do if the only way they could raise cotton was by the Government telling them how much they could raise and how much they could sell it for, and where, and 22

MINI-LESSON: LITERARY FOCUS

Characterization

Teach The central character of a story is sometimes called the hero or protagonist and usually faces some type of conflict.

Questions

- Who is the hero of this story? *(Buddy McCallum or the entire McCallum family)*

- Which phrase best sums up the conflict for the hero (or heroes) in "The Tall Men?"

  a. person against self

  b. person against person

  c. person against society

  d. person against nature *(Response: c)*

Activity Idea Ask students to describe the conflict another main character faces in a story, film, or television show.

when, and then pay them for not doing the work they didn't do. Only even when they didn't raise cotton, every year the county agent's young fellow would come out to measure the pasture crops they planted so he could pay them for that, even if they never had no not-cotton to be paid for. Except that he never measured no crop on this place. 'You're welcome to look at what we are doing,' Buddy says. 'But don't draw it down on your map.'

"'But you can get money for this,' the young fellow says. 'The Government wants to pay you for planting all this.'

"'We are aiming to get money for it,' Buddy says. 'When we can't, we will try something else. But not from the Government. Give that to them that want to take it. We can make out.'

"And that's about all. Them twenty-two bales of orphan cotton are down yonder in the gin right now, because there's room for it in the gin now because they ain't using the gin no more. And them boys grew up and went off a year to the agricultural college to learn right about whiteface cattle, and then come back to the rest of them—these here curious folks living off here to themselves, with the rest of the world all full of pretty neon lights burning night and day both, and easy, quick money scattering itself around everywhere for any man to grab a little, and every man with a shiny new automobile already wore out and throwed away and the new one delivered before the first one was even paid for, and everywhere a fine loud grabble and snatch of AAA and WPA[14] and a dozen other three-letter reasons for a man not to work. Then this here draft comes along, and these curious folks ain't got around to signing that neither, and you come all the way up from Jackson with your paper all signed and regular, and we come out here, and after a while we can go back to town. A man gets around, don't he?"

"Yes," the investigator said. "Do you suppose we can go back to town now?"

"No," the marshal told him in that same kindly tone, "not just yet. But we can leave after a while. Of course you will miss your train. But there will be another one tomorrow."

He rose, though the investigator had heard nothing. The investigator watched him go down the hall and open the bedroom door and enter and close it behind him. The investigator sat quietly, listening to the night sounds and looking at the closed door until it opened presently and the marshal came back, carrying something in a bloody sheet, carrying it gingerly.

"Here," he said. "Hold it a minute."

"It's bloody," the investigator said.

"That's all right," the marshal said. "We can wash when we get through." So the investigator took the bundle and stood holding it while he watched the old marshal go back down the hall and on through it and vanish and return presently with a lighted lantern and a shovel. "Come along," he said. "We're pretty near through now."

The investigator followed him out of the house and across the yard, carrying gingerly the bloody, shattered, heavy bundle in which it still seemed to him he could feel some warmth of life, the marshal striding on ahead, the lantern swinging against his leg, the shadow of his striding scissoring and enormous along the earth, his voice still coming back over his shoulder, chatty and cheerful, "Yes, sir. A man gets around and he sees a heap; a heap of folks in a heap of situations. The trouble is, we done got into the habit of confusing the situations with the folks. Take yourself, now," he said in that same kindly tone, chatty and easy; "you mean all right. You just went and got yourself all fogged up with rules and regulations. That's our trouble. We done invented ourselves so many

---

14. **AAA** and **WPA,** Agricultural Adjustment Act, which paid farmers to reduce their crops, and the Works Progress Administration, which created public service projects in order to employ people and restore their self-respect. Both programs were instituted under President Franklin D. Roosevelt to help bring the country out of the Great Depression.

The Tall Men   **653**

VOCABULARY STUDY

1. stabilize
2. cease
3. relinquish
4. jeopardize
5. evade
6. expedite
7. speculative
8. discern
9. cite
10. seethe

More Practice   Have students change vocabulary words (all verbs) into nouns. (*cessation, citation, discernment, evasion, jeopardy, relinquishment, seething, stabilization or stability*)

 Unit 6 Resource Book
Vocabulary, p. 67
Vocabulary Test, p. 70

WRITING CHOICES
Writer's Notebook Update

Help students to imagine their characters before beginning their monologue. What is the character's background, age, attitudes, opinions? What does the character look and sound like? Encourage students to read dialogue aloud, or to use a tape recorder, for practice.

Respectfully Submitted

Students' reports could take one of two approaches: the investigator gives a factual account of what happened, or the investigator "fudges" in order to cover himself. Have some students read their reports aloud. Discuss which versions seem the most consistent with the character.

Vocabulary Study

On a piece of paper, write the verb that best completes each sentence. Use the Glossary if you need help.

cease
cite
discern
evade
expedite
jeopardize
relinquish
seethe
stabilize
speculative

1. The doctor attempted to ____ the patient's blood pressure.
2. Mr. Pearson wondered when the hounds' barking would ____.
3. The McCallum family refused to ____ control of their cotton crop to the government.
4. When there is a military draft, draft evaders ____ their future because they are breaking the law.
5. The McCallums did not intend to ____ military service; they didn't see the point in registering for the draft when there wasn't a war.
6. It will ____ the registration process if you bring current identification.
7. As time passed, the state draft investigator became less rigid and more ____ about why the men didn't register for the draft.
8. Could Mr. Pearson ____ the difference between the letter of the law and the spirit of the law?
9. Mr. Pearson intended to ask a judge to ____ the marshal for contempt.
10. Mr. Pearson began to ____ when he realized the marshal's intent to save the McCallum boys from arrest.

Expressing Your Ideas

Writing Choices

Writer's Notebook Update Review the examples of dialect that you wrote in your notebook. Then create a character who might use that dialect and write a monologue for him or her.

Respectfully Submitted As a government employee, Mr. Pearson would probably have to write a report about the McCallum boys to submit to his superior. What do you suppose he would write in order to explain why he did not arrest them? What version of the story will he tell? Assume that you are Pearson and write a **report** for the McCallum file.

Other Options

Farm Subsidies Research the history of farm subsidies. Why did the government institute them? How do they work? How have they changed over the years? How do they affect the nation's economy? Prepare an **oral report** summarizing your research on the topic.

Reader's Theater Select a scene from "The Tall Men" that would make a good **reader's theater production.** Assign the parts of the narrator and characters, rehearse the scene, and present it to the class.

OTHER OPTIONS
Farm Subsidies

Encourage students to use a periodicals index or Internet search, as well as an encyclopedia, to look up the history of farm subsidies. You might want to suggest that they discuss contemporary issues also.

Reader's Theater

For practice in script writing, encourage students to write a draft of the scene, complete with stage directions for each actor.

Before Reading

Blue Winds Dancing

by Thomas S. Whitecloud

Thomas S. Whitecloud
1914–1972

Thomas S. Whitecloud was born in New York. His father was a Chippewa Indian and his mother was white. His parents divorced when Whitecloud's father, who had a law degree from Yale, decided to return to the Lac du Flambeau Reservation and live with the Chippewa people. Whitecloud began working when he was ten, and he held a variety of jobs: farm worker, truck driver, and boxer, to name a few. He flunked out of the University of New Mexico, but eventually graduated from the University of Redlands in California. It was during this time that he wrote "Blue Winds Dancing," which won first prize in a Phi Beta Kappa essay contest. He went on to earn his medical degree and practiced medicine in the military as an Indian Service physician and in private practice.

Building Background

Who Am I? As a child of two different cultures, Thomas Whitecloud grew up in two different worlds. The customs and values of his relatives on the Lac du Flambeau Reservation were quite different from those he encountered at school and on the job. While he was attending school, Whitecloud missed his family, his community, and his people's ways and values. Discouraged and homesick, Whitecloud followed an impulse to hop a freight train and go home for Christmas. This essay recounts his trip back home and his reflections on the differences between white and American Indian society.

Literary Focus

Imagery "And there is a fall wind blowing in my heart." This line from Thomas Whitecloud's essay makes the reader feel a chill, brisk wind. Whitecloud uses **imagery,** descriptions that appeal to the senses, throughout "Blue Winds Dancing." In this case, the image is figurative. A wind isn't really blowing in his heart; his heart feels restless because he is homesick. As you read the essay, look for other sensory images. Which are literal and which are figurative? To which sense does each appeal: sight, hearing, touch (or motion), taste, or smell? Use a chart like this to record the images from the essay.

Image	Sense to Which It Appeals

Writer's Notebook

Culture Shock Imagine this scene: You are far away from home, living with people in a culture different from your own, and today is an important family day. Maybe it is your birthday or a holiday. Take three minutes to write about how you feel, and what you miss most about home.

Blue Winds Dancing **657**

Before Reading

Building Background

For students of mixed racial, ethnic, or religious background, the weighing of one side of the one's culture against another may be familiar. Encourage students to discuss similarities and differences in outlook, attitude, and ways of life from one culture to the other.

Literary Focus

Guide students to define the difference between literal and figurative images, and to suggest examples of each. A literal image presents a factual sensory picture of a scene or situation. A figurative image creates an imaginary picture, often by comparing a situation or feeling to a familiar but seemingly dissimilar situation.

Discuss the title of the piece as **imagery.** What senses does it appeal to? *(Students may answer that it appeals to the senses of sight and touch.)*

Writer's Notebook

Encourage students to use their imaginations to picture what they love about their homes.

More About Thomas S. Whitecloud

Whitecloud had a difficult childhood and adolescence, attending and being expelled from numerous schools. He eventually earned a medical degree from Tulane University in New Orleans.

SUPPORT MATERIALS OVERVIEW

Unit 6 Resource Book
- Graphic Organizer, p. 73
- Study Guide, p. 74
- Vocabulary, p. 75
- Grammar, p. 76
- Alternate Check Test, p. 77
- Vocabulary Test, p. 78
- Selection Test, pp. 79–80

Building English Proficiency
- Literature Summaries
- Activities, p. 218

Reading, Writing & Grammar SkillBook
- Vocabulary, pp. 5–6
- Reading, pp. 50–51
- Writing, pp. 123–124
- Grammar, Usage, and Mechanics, pp. 262–265

Technology
- Audiotape
- Personal Journal Software
- Custom Literature Database: For another selection dealing with American Indian traditions, see "A Short Narration of My Last Journey to the Western Country" by Hendrick Aupaumut on the database.
- Test Generator Software

Selection Objectives

- To explore the importance of imagery in descriptive writing
- To identify literal and figurative images
- To compare the author's experience of two different cultures
- To analyze mood in the narration

Unit 6 Resource Book
Graphic Organizer, p. 73
Study Guide, p. 74

Theme Link

Strength of tradition is reflected in the narrator's struggle to find acceptance in two worlds and two heritages.

Vocabulary Preview

maelstrom, a turbulent whirlpool

radical, person favoring extreme changes or reforms

pulsate, beat; throb

serene, calm, peaceful

rapt, so busy thinking of or enjoying one thing that one does not know what else is happening

Students can add the words and definitions in their personal word lists to the Writer's Notebook.

---

1 Literary Element
Theme

Question What is Whitecloud saying about living in the "outside" world as opposed to being in his home? *(In the outside world, he is separated from nature; life is rigid and ordered. At home, there is freedom and the beauty of living with the elements.)*

Blue Winds Dancing

Thomas S. Whitecloud

There is a moon out tonight. Moon and stars and clouds tipped with moonlight. And there is a fall wind blowing in my heart. Ever since this evening, when against a fading sky I saw geese wedge southward. They were going home. . . . Now I try to study, but against the pages I see them again, driving southward. Going home.

Across the valley there are heavy mountains holding up the night sky, and beyond the mountains there is home. Home, and peace, and the beat of drums, and blue winds dancing over snow fields. The Indian lodge will fill with my people, and our gods will come and sit among them. I should be there then. I should be at home.

But home is beyond the mountains, and I am here. Here where fall hides in the valleys, and winter never comes down from the mountains. Here where all the trees grow in rows; the palms stand stiffly by the roadsides, and in the groves the orange trees line in military rows, and endlessly bear fruit. Beautiful, yes; there is always beauty in order, in rows of growing things! But it is the beauty of captivity. A pine fighting for existence on a windy knoll is much more beautiful.

In my Wisconsin, the leaves change before the snows come. In the air there is the smell of wild rice and venison cooking; and when the winds come whispering through the forests, they carry the smell of rotting leaves. In the evenings, the loon calls, lonely; and birds sing their last songs before leaving. Bears dig roots and eat late fall berries, fattening for their long winter sleep. Later, when the first snows fall, one awakens in the morning to find the world white and beautiful and clean. Then one can look back over his trail and see the tracks following. In the woods there are tracks of deer and snowshoe rabbits, and long streaks where partridges slide to alight. Chipmunks make tiny footprints on the limbs; and one can hear squirrels busy in hollow trees, sorting acorns. Soft lake waves wash the shores, and sunsets burst each evening over the lakes, and make them look as if they were afire.

That land which is my home! Beautiful, calm—where there is no hurry

---

SELECTION SUMMARY

Blue Winds Dancing

While away at college, the narrator becomes unhappy—homesick for the calmer, more meaningful way of life of the Chippewa of Wisconsin. Images of nature figure strongly in this piece because the narrator is strongly connected to the land he left. He refers to the winds and snows of his reservation. Although he decides to make his way home by hopping trains, he is anxious about his homecoming because he doesn't know if he fits there either. By the end, he is united with his people, at least temporarily. He has heard the old woman under the ice, which signifies that he is truly home.

*For summaries in other languages, see the **Building English Proficiency** book.*

After you've finished the story, come back to this image, Richard Red Owl's acrylic, *Lost in Dance* (1994). Does it match the mood of the end of "Blue Winds Dancing"? Why or why not?

Blue Winds Dancing   659

Response to Caption Question   Most students will agree that the painting does match the mood at story's end in that the narrator finally joins the rhythmic dance of his people, whirling under the lights.

Visual Literacy   Turn Richard Red Owl's painting upsidedown and you will see that there really is no top, no bottom, no obvious left or right side. The dancer twirls in a stream of blue and red, and the viewer hovers over her like a passing cloud.

Question   Does the dancer seem lost in the dance, or has she found something? *(The question is open to interpretation. She has lost herself in the dance, but probably found a larger connectedness or deeper understanding of things.)*

BUILDING ENGLISH PROFICIENCY

Making Personal Connections

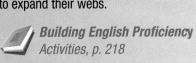

Home is an important idea in this essay. Suggest that students first make a personal connection by thinking about the place, situations, traditions, and people that mean *home* to them and recording those thoughts in a semantic web. As they read the essay, they can jot down Whitecloud's words and phrases to expand their webs.

Building English Proficiency
Activities, p. 218

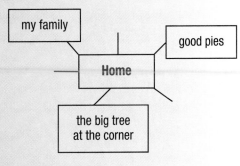

to get anywhere, no driving to keep up in a race that knows no ending and no goal. No classes where men talk and talk, and then stop now and then to hear their own words come back to them from the students. No constant peering into the maelstrom[1] of one's mind; no worries about grades and honors; no hysterical preparing for life until that life is half over; no anxiety about one's place in the thing they call Society.

I hear again the ring of axes in deep woods, the crunch of snow beneath my feet. I feel again the smooth velvet of ghost-birch bark. I hear the rhythm of the drums. . . . I am tired. I am weary of trying to keep up this bluff of being civilized. Being civilized means trying to do everything you don't want to, never doing anything you want to. It means dancing to the strings of custom and tradition; it means living in houses and never knowing or caring who is next door. These civilized white men want us to be like them—always dissatisfied, getting a hill and wanting a mountain.

Then again, maybe I am not tired. Maybe I'm licked. Maybe I am just not smart enough to grasp these things that go to make up civilization. Maybe I am just too lazy to think hard enough to keep up.

Still, I know my people have many things that civilization has taken from the whites. They know how to give; how to tear one's piece of meat in two and share it with one's brother. They know how to sing—how to make each man his own songs and sing them; for their music they do not have to listen to other men singing over a radio. They know how to make things with their hands, how to shape beads into design and make a thing of beauty from a piece of birch bark.

But we are inferior. It is terrible to have to feel inferior; to have to read reports of intelligence tests, and learn that one's race is behind. It is terrible to sit in classes and hear men tell you that your people worship sticks of wood—that your gods are all false, that the Manitou[2] forgot your people and did not write them a book.

I am tired. I want to walk again among the ghost-birches. I want to see the leaves turn in autumn, the smoke rise from the lodgehouses, and to feel the blue winds. I want to hear the drums; I want to hear the drums and feel the blue whispering winds.

There is a train wailing into the night. The trains go across the mountains. It would be easy to catch a freight. They will say he has gone back to the blanket; I don't care. The dance at Christmas. . . .

> *There is a train wailing into the night. . . . It would be easy to catch a freight.*

A bunch of bums warming at a tiny fire talk politics and women and joke about the Relief and the WPA[3] and smoke cigarettes. These men in caps and overcoats and dirty overalls living on the outskirts of civilization are free, but they pay the price of being free in civilization. They are outcasts. I remember a sociology professor lecturing on adjustment to society; hobos and prostitutes and criminals are individuals who never adjusted, he said. He could learn a lot if he came and listened to a bunch of bums talk. He would learn that work and a woman and a place to hang his hat are all the ordinary man wants. These are all he wants, but other men are not content to let him want only these. He must be taught to want radios and automobiles and a new suit every spring. Progress would stop if he did not want these things. I listen to hear if there is any talk of communism or socialism in the hobo jungles. There is none. At best there is a sort of disgusted philosophy about life. They

---

1. **maelstrom** (māl′strəm), *n.* a turbulent whirlpool.
2. **Manitou** (man′ə tü), Great Spirit; deity.
3. **Relief** and **the WPA,** "Relief" refers to the Civil Works Administration (CWA), a forerunner of the Works Progress Administration (WPA). Both were federal jobs projects to help the unemployed during the Depression.

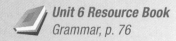

seem to think there should be a better distribution of wealth, or more work, or something. But they are not rabid about it. The radicals[4] live in the cities.

I find a fellow headed for Albuquerque, and talk road-talk with him. "It is hard to ride fruit cars. Bums break in. Better to wait for a cattle car going back to the Middle West, and ride that." We catch the next east-bound and walk the tops until we find a cattle car. Inside, we crouch near the forward wall, huddle, and try to sleep. I feel peaceful and content at last. I am going home. The cattle car rocks. I sleep.

5Morning and the desert. Noon and the Salton Sea, lying more lifeless than a mirage under a somber sun in a pale sky. Skeleton mountains rearing on the skyline, thrusting out of the desert floor, all rock and shadow and edges. Desert. Good country for an 6Indian reservation. . . .

Yuma and the muddy Colorado. Night again, and I wait shivering for the dawn.

Phoenix. Pima country. Mountains that look like cardboard sets on a forgotten stage. Tucson. Papago country. Giant cacti that look like petrified hitchhikers along the highways. Apache country. At El Paso my road-buddy decides to go on to Houston. I leave him, and head north to the mesa country. Las Cruces and the terrible Organ Mountains, jagged peaks that instill fear and wondering. Albuquerque. Pueblos along the Rio Grande. On the boardwalk there are some Indian women in colored sashes selling bits of pottery. The stone age offering its art to the twentieth century. They hold up a piece and fix the tourists with black eyes until, embarrassed, he buys or turns away. I feel suddenly angry that my people should have to do such things for a living. . . .

Santa Fe trains are fast, and they keep them pretty clean of bums. I decide to hurry and ride passenger coaltenders. Hide in the dark, judge the speed of the train as it leaves, and then dash out, and catch it. I hug the cold steel wall of the

tender and think of the roaring fire in the engine ahead, and of the passengers back in the dining car reading their papers over hot coffee. Beneath me there is blur of rails. Death would come quick if my hands should freeze and I fall. Up over the Sangre De Cristo range, around cliffs and through canyons to Denver. Bitter cold here, and I must watch out for Denver Bob. He is railroad bull who has thrown bums from fast freights. I miss him. It is too cold, I suppose. On north to the Sioux country.

Small towns lit for the coming Christmas. On the streets of one I see a beam-shouldered young farmer gazing into a window filled with shining silver toasters. He is tall and wears a blue shirt 7buttoned, with no tie. His young wife by his side looks at him hopefully. He wants decorations for his place to hang his hat to please his woman. . . .

Northward again. Minnesota, and great white fields of snow; frozen lakes, and dawn running into dusk without noon. Long forests wearing white. Bitter cold, and one night the northern lights.[5] I am nearing home.

I reach Woodruff at midnight. Suddenly I am afraid, now that I am but twenty miles from home. Afraid of what my father will say, afraid of being looked on as a stranger by my own people. I sit by a fire and think about myself and all the other young Indians. We just don't seem to fit in anywhere—certainly not among the whites, and not among the older people. I think again about the learned sociology professor and his professing. So many things seem to be clear now that I am away from school and do not have to worry about some man's opinion of my ideas. It is easy to think while looking at dancing flames.

Morning. I spend the day cleaning up, and buying some presents for my family with what is

---

4. **radical** (rad′ə kəl), *n.* person favoring extreme changes or reforms.
5. **northern lights,** aurora borealis; streamers or bands of light appearing in the sky at night, especially in polar regions.

5
Geographical Note
The Salton Sea

The Salton Sea is a shallow lake in the Imperial Valley of the southern California desert. It was formed by the diversion of the Colorado River onto a salt-covered depression. It is 265 feet below sea level.

6
Literary Focus
Imagery

Question   Contrast the image of the desert with the images Whitecloud gave earlier of his own reservation in Wisconsin. *(Possible responses: The desert is bare mountains, hard edges, dry and hot. His own land is clean, cold, snowy, and teeming with life.)*

7
Literary Element
Symbolism

Question   What do you think the "beam-shouldered young farmer" and his wife symbolize? *(Possible answer: They seem to represent the attitudes and desires of white America—people who want "decorations" in order to please (and possibly impress) others; they symbolize the acquisitiveness of our age.)*

BUILDING ENGLISH PROFICIENCY

Exploring Key Statements

Draw students' attention to this key statement on page 660: "He would learn that work and a woman and a place to hang his hat are all the ordinary man wants."

- Have students discuss in small groups what they think men want most in life and what women want most. Encourage them to record their responses on a T-chart.

- Ask them to review their T-charts after finishing the essay. Encourage them to explain any revisions that they want to make.

Men want . . .	Women want . . .

Question Whitecloud writes, "A gift is a gift, if a man buys it with his last quarter." What do you think he means by that? *(Possible answers: He is contrasting the meaning of a gift with the commercialism of Christmas in the modern world. He is saying that a gift is something you want to give. It doesn't matter how much you spend.)*

9 **Literary Element**

Allusions

Solitude is one of the central allusions of this essay.

Question The author says you can never be lonely if you love the snow and the pines. What does he mean? *(Possible responses: You are filled with joy or awe in their presence; you are surrounded by the spirits of nature.)*

 Reading/Thinking Skills

Draw Conclusions

Questions

- How does Whitecloud's mood change in this paragraph? *(Possible responses: He brightens up as soon as he turns his back on the city and walks into the woods. He has chosen between the village and the city.)*

- Why does Whitecloud laugh as he goes into the woods? *(Possible responses: He is relieved; he feels free; he is laughing at the foolishness of city people.)*

8 left of my money. Nothing much, but a gift is a gift, if a man buys it with his last quarter. I wait until evening, then start up the track toward home.

Christmas Eve comes in on a north wind. Snow clouds hang over the pines, and the night comes early. Walking along the railroad bed, I feel the calm peace of snowbound forests on either side of me. I take my time; I am back in a world where time does not mean so much now. I am alone; alone but not nearly so lonely as I was back on the campus at school. Those are never lonely who love the snow and the pines; never lonely when the pines are wearing white shawls and snow crunches coldly underfoot. In the woods I know there are the tracks of deer and rabbit; I know that if I leave the rails and go into the woods I shall find them. I walk along feeling glad because my legs are light and my feet seem to know that they are home. A deer comes out of the woods just ahead of me, and stands silhouetted on the rails. The North, I feel, has welcomed me home. I watch him and am glad that I do not wish for a gun. He goes into the woods quietly, leaving only the design of his tracks in the snow. I walk on. Now and then I pass a field, white under the night sky, with houses at the far end. Snow comes from the chimneys of the houses, and I try to tell what sort of wood each is burning by the smoke; some burn pine, others aspen, others tamarack. There is one from which comes black coal smoke that rises lazily and drifts out over the tops of the trees. I like to watch houses and try to imagine what might be happening in them.

Just as a light snow begins to fall, I cross the reservation boundary; somehow it seems as though I have stepped into another world. Deep woods in a white-and-black winter night. A faint trail leading to the village.

The railroad on which I stand comes from a city sprawled by a lake—a city with a million people who walk around without seeing one another; a city sucking the life from all the country around; a city with stores and police and intellectuals and criminals and movies and apartment houses; a city with its politics and libraries and zoos.

I cross the reservation boundary; somehow it seems as though I have stepped into another world.

Laughing, I go into the woods. As I cross a **10** frozen lake I begin to hear the drums. Soft in the night the drums beat. It is like the pulse beat of the world. The white line of the lake ends at a black forest, and above the trees the blue winds are dancing.

I come to the outlying houses of the village. Simple box houses, etched black in the night. From one or two windows soft lamp light falls on the snow. Christmas here, too, but it does not mean much; not much in the way of parties and presents. Joe Sky will get drunk. Alex Bodidash will buy his children red mittens and a new sled. Alex is a Carlisle man, and tries to keep his home up to white standards. White standards. Funny that my people should be ever falling farther behind. The more they try to imitate whites the more tragic the result. Yet they want us to be imitation white men. About all we imitate well are their vices.

The village is not a sight to instill pride, yet I am not ashamed; one can never be ashamed of his own people when he knows they have dreams as beautiful as white snow on a tall pine.

Father and my brother and sister are seated around the table as I walk in. Father stares at me for a moment, then I am in his arms, crying on his shoulder. I give them the presents I have brought, and my throat tightens as I watch my sister save carefully bits of red string from the packages. I hide my feelings by wrestling with my brother when he strikes my shoulder in token of affection. Father looks at me, and I

MINI-LESSON: VOCABULARY

Using a Thesaurus

Teach Demonstrate the use of a thesaurus as a valuable tool for finding words that are similar in meaning and for discussing the nuances of words.

Activity Ideas

- Have students look up synonyms for each of these words: *maelstrom, radical, pulsate, serene,* and *rapt.*

- Ask students to compare the organization and definitions of one thesaurus with another or with a crossword puzzle dictionary.

know he has many questions, but he seems to know why I have come. He tells me to go on alone to the lodge, and he will follow.

I walk along the trail to the lodge, watching the northern lights forming in the heavens. White waving ribbons that seem to pulsate[6] with the rhythm of the drums. Clean snow creaks beneath my feet, and a soft wind sighs through the trees, singing to me. Everything seems to say "Be happy! You are home now—you are free. You are among friends—we are your friends; we, the trees, and the snow, and the lights." I follow the trail to the lodge. My feet are light, my heart seems to sing to the music, and I hold my head high. Across white snow fields blue winds are dancing.

Before the lodge door I stop, afraid. I wonder if my people will remember me. I wonder—"Am I Indian, or am I white?" I stand before the door a long time. I hear the ice groan on the lake, and remember the story of the old woman who is under the ice, trying to get out, so she can punish some runaway lovers. I think to myself, "If I am white I will not believe that story; if I am Indian, I will know that there is an old woman under the ice." I listen for a while, and I know that there is an old woman under the ice. I look again at the lights, and go in.

Inside the lodge there are many Indians. Some sit on benches around the walls, others dance in the center of the floor around a drum. Nobody seems to notice me. It seems as though I were among a people I have never seen before. Heavy women with long black hair. Women with children on their knees—small children that watch with intent black eyes the movements of the dancers, whose small faces are solemn and serene.[7] The faces of the old people are serene, too, and their eyes are merry and bright. I look at the old men. Straight, dressed in dark trousers and beaded velvet vests, wearing soft moccasins.

Dark, lined faces intent on the music. I wonder if I am at all like them. They dance on, lifting their feet to the rhythm of the drums, swaying lightly, looking upward. I look at their eyes, and am startled at the rapt[8] attention to the rhythm of the music.

The dance stops. The men walk back to the walls, and talk in low tones or with their hands. There is little conversation, yet everyone seems to be sharing some secret. A woman looks at a small boy wandering away, and he comes back to her.

Strange, I think, and then remember. These people are not sharing words—they are sharing a mood. Everyone is happy. I am so used to white people that it seems strange so many people could be together without someone talking. These Indians are happy because they are together, and because the night is beautiful outside, and the music is beautiful. I try hard to forget school and white people, and be one of these—my people. I try to forget everything but the night, and it is a part of me; that I am one with my people and we are all a part of something universal. I watch eyes, and see now that the old people are speaking to me. They nod slightly, imperceptibly, and their eyes laugh into mine. I look around the room. All the eyes are friendly; they all laugh. No one questions my being here. The drums begin to beat again, and I catch the invitation in the eyes of the old men. My feet begin to lift to the rhythm, and I look out beyond the walls into the night and see the lights. I am happy. It is beautiful. I am home.

---

6. **pulsate** (pul′sāt), *v.* beat; throb.
7. **serene** (sə rēn′), *adj.* peaceful, calm.
8. **rapt** (rapt), *adj.* so busy thinking of or enjoying one thing that one does not know what else is happening.

Blue Winds Dancing   **663**

In Native American cultures, elements of nature are often endowed with qualities of human beings. Point out to students that authors often personify nature, machines, and so on. For example, *the leaves whispered.*

Questions   What verb does Whitecloud use to endow the lake with a human quality? *(Response: groan)*

Check Test

1. What does Whitecloud miss in the beginning of the essay? *(his home)*

2. Why is he tired of living in the "civilized" world? *(Everyone is in a rush to go nowhere; there are too many people and too much of doing what you should instead of what you want to.)*

3. Why does Whitecloud become afraid as he gets closer to home? *(He is afraid that the people there will not accept him and that he will not feel at home.)*

4. How does Whitecloud determine whether he belongs with white people or Indians? *(by checking his interpretation of Indian lore)*

5. Why does the silence of the lodge seem so strange to Whitecloud at first? *(He is used to the talk of white people and has forgotten that people can be together without speaking.)*

Unit 6 Resource Book
Alternate Check Test, p. 77

BUILDING ENGLISH PROFICIENCY

ESL
LEP
ELD
SAE
LD

Exploring Personification

Recognizing personification—a figure of speech that talks about something nonhuman as if it were a person—is important to understanding the closeness that Whitecloud feels to nature.

- Call on a volunteer to read aloud the first full paragraph on page 663. Define personification; ask students to find examples in the paragraph.

- Invite students to try substituting a different "human" action for the ones underlined below.

  Smoke <u>climbs</u> slowly.

  A soft wind <u>sighs</u>.

  My heart seems to <u>sing</u>.

  I hear the ice <u>groan</u>.

OTI
Edu

Stude
topic,
towa

Imp

Stude
medi

Before Reading

Building Background

Ask students about their personal travels from a trip to the store to a long hike in the woods. You might discuss other journeys, both long and short, that students have encountered in literature and in movies.

Literary Focus

Suggest that students organize a chart to help them make **inferences** about what they read.

Facts	Assumptions	Inference
what we know	prior assumptions	logical conclusions

Writer's Notebook

Suggest that students take careful notes the next time they travel the path between school and home, recording sensory impressions.

More About Eudora Welty

Welty once said, "I am a writer who came of a sheltered life. A sheltered life can be a daring life as well. For all daring starts from within." Her father's interest in meteorology and folk omens influenced her to use the imagery of weather. Other works by Welty include:

- *The Optimist's Daughter,* 1972
- *One Writer's Beginnings,* 1984

Before Reading

A Worn Path

by Eudora Welty

Eudora Welty
born 1909

"One day I saw a solitary old woman. . . . She was walking. I saw her at middle distance, in a winter country landscape, and watched her slowly make her way across my line of vision. That sight of her made me write the story," wrote Eudora Welty about her inspiration for "A Worn Path." Welty, like Faulkner, was from Mississippi, and many of her stories are set in the South. Born in Jackson, she attended the University of Wisconsin and then went to New York to study journalism. When she returned to Jackson, she worked as a photographer for the Works Progress Administration (WPA). Her first collection of stories, *A Curtain of Green,* was published in 1941.

Building Background

A Country Mile, and Then Some How far do you have to travel to shop or go to a restaurant? How do you get there—by walking, driving, or taking public transportation? And how long does it take? Phoenix Jackson, the main character in "A Worn Path," is an old, frail woman who lives in the backwoods of Mississippi. She has no car, there is no public transportation, and she lives miles from town. Wooded hills surround her house; beyond that are fields of cotton and corn. The path that leads from her house to town is one she has traveled many times.

Literary Focus

Inferences Writers don't spell out everything. Readers must make inferences, or draw reasonable conclusions based on clues provided by a writer. Such inferences may or may not be accurate, but good readers make them, and adjust their conclusions if necessary. As you read "A Worn Path," make some inferences about Phoenix and her trip from the information provided.

Writer's Notebook

A Sensory Experience Eudora Welty writes descriptions that appeal to all of the senses. For example, a cane's tapping is "like the chirping of a solitary bird" (sound), and ". . . cones dropped as light as feathers" (touch or motion). Before you read "A Worn Path," write in your notebook a list of sensory words, phrases, or sentences that describe the route you take to school.

SUPPORT MATERIALS OVERVIEW

Unit 6 Resource Book
- Graphic Organizer, p. 81
- Study Guide, p. 82
- Vocabulary, p. 83
- Grammar, p. 84
- Alternate Check Test, p. 85
- Vocabulary Test, p. 86
- Selection Test, pp. 87–88

Building English Proficiency
- Literature Summaries
- Activities, p. 219

Reading, Writing & Grammar SkillBook
- Vocabulary, pp. 3–4
- Reading, pp. 79–80
- Writing, pp. 134–136
- Grammar, Usage, and Mechanics, pp. 202–203

Technology
- Audiotape
- Personal Journal Software
- Custom Literature Database: For selections dealing with race relations in the past, see Paul Lawrence Dunbar and Solomon Northup on the database.
- Test Generator Software

EUDORA WELTY

A Worn Path

It was December—a bright frozen day in the early morning. Far out in the country there was an old Negro woman with her head tied in a red rag, coming along a path through the pinewoods. Her name was Phoenix Jackson. She was very old and small and she walked slowly in the dark pine shadows, moving a little from side to side in her steps, with the balanced heaviness and lightness of a pendulum in a grandfather clock. She carried a thin, small cane made from an umbrella, and with this she kept tapping the frozen earth in front of her. This made a grave and persistent noise in the still air, that seemed meditative like the chirping of a solitary little bird.

She wore a dark striped dress reaching down to her shoe tops, and an equally long apron of bleached sugar sacks, with a full pocket: all neat and tidy, but every time she took a step she might have fallen over her shoelaces, which dragged from her unlaced shoes. She looked straight ahead. Her eyes were blue with age. Her skin had a pattern all its own of numberless branching wrinkles and as though a whole little tree stood in the middle of her forehead, but a golden color ran underneath, and the two knobs of her cheeks were illumined by a yellow burning under the dark. Under the red rag her hair came down on her neck in the frailest of ringlets, still black, and with an odor like copper.

Now and then there was a quivering in the thicket. Old Phoenix said, "Out of my way, all you foxes, owls, beetles, jack rabbits, coons and wild animals! . . . Keep out from under these feet, little bobwhites. . . . Keep the big wild hogs out of my path. Don't let none of those

come running my direction. I got a long way." Under her small black-freckled hand her cane, limber as a buggy whip, would switch at the bush as if to rouse up any hiding things.

On she went. The woods were deep and still. The sun made the pine needles almost too bright to look at, up where the wind rocked. The cones dropped as light as feathers. Down in the hollow[1] was the mourning dove—it was not too late for him.

The path ran up a hill. "Seem like there is chains about my feet, time I get this far," she said, in the voice of argument old people keep to use with themselves. "Something always take a hold of me on this hill—pleads I should stay."

After she got to the top, she turned and gave a full, severe look behind her where she had come. "Up through pines," she said at length. "Now down through oaks."

Her eyes opened their widest, and she started down gently. But before she got to the bottom of the hill a bush caught her dress.

Her fingers were busy and intent, but her skirts were full and long, so that before she could pull them free in one place they were caught in another. It was not possible to allow the dress to tear. "I in the thorny bush," she said. "Thorns, you doing your appointed work. Never want to let folks pass, no sir. Old eyes thought you was a pretty little *green* bush."

Finally, trembling all over, she stood free, and after a moment dared to stoop for her cane.

---

1. **hollow** (hol′ō), *n.* a low place between hills.

A Worn Path   **667**

Selection Objectives

- To explore tradition and love as inspirations for heroism
- To recognize inferences
- To investigate verb forms
- To explore imagery

Unit 6 Resource Book
Graphic Organizer, p. 81
Study Guide, p. 82

Theme Link

An old woman's journey to retrieve medicine for her grandson proves that tradition, duty, and love can triumph over mighty obstacles.

1 Literary Element

Dialogue

Much of Phoenix's conversation is directed toward plants, animals, and other voiceless objects.

Question   Why does Phoenix react so calmly to the thorn bush? *(Possible answers: She accepts that the thorn bush is acting according to nature's design. She's been among these thorns before and knows how to handle them.)*

SELECTION SUMMARY

A Worn Path

A frail old woman named Phoenix Jackson, armed with a makeshift walking stick, journeys slowly and painstakingly from her home in the hilly back country of Mississippi into the town of Natchez. Along the way, she crosses a creek on a log, crawls under a barbed wire fence, navigates uncharted fields, survives the charge of an angry dog, and outwits a rude young hunter. By chance she sees a nickel fall from the hunter's pocket and she manages to pick it up when he isn't looking. Arriving at her destination, a doctor's office, she becomes momentarily confused, forgetting

her purpose. She finally retrieves the medicine for her sick grandson— the sole purpose of her trip. The attendant gives Phoenix a nickel, which, together with the hunter's nickel, is enough to buy a simple gift for her grandson. She turns around to begin the grueling return journey home.

For summaries in other languages, see the **Building English Proficiency** *book.*

WRITING CHOICES

Writer's Notebook Update

Suggest that students use the notes that they compiled to help them with their descriptions. Remind students of the intense mood that Welty creates by using strong natural images.

Return of the Hunter

You might suggest that students organize a character trait web to clarify the personality of the hunter before they attempt to write a narrative from his point of view.

Your Point of View

Ask students to decide what they consider to be the main idea of the story. The thesis of their essay will depend on their response. Suggest that they draw a main idea map to organize supporting details.

Selection Test

 *Unit 6 Resource Book*
pp. 87–88

Expressing Your Ideas

Writing Choices

Writer's Notebook Update Compare the sensory words, phrases, and sentences you wrote in your log with those of your classmates. Reflect on a trip that you make every day. What are the sights, sounds, and smells that you experience on that route? Write a **descriptive paragraph** that makes your routine trip sound unusual.

Return of the Hunter Imagine that you are the hunter who meets Phoenix and helps her to her feet. You have returned home and are telling your family about the encounter with the old woman. In a **narrative** of a page or two, try to capture the relaxed, conversational tone that the man would probably use. Before you begin writing, reread that section of the story to review what happened and what was said.

Your Point of View Some readers feel that "A Worn Path" would be somehow "better" if Phoenix's grandson were dead. Others are sure the boy must be alive. Still others think it makes no difference to the story. Write an **essay** of at least four paragraphs for a literary magazine in which you support one of these three positions. Consider the purpose of Phoenix's trip, her devotion and single-mindedness, the outcome of the story, and the irony that the boy's death would provide.

Other Options

Turn Right, Then Left What if Phoenix cannot make the next trip for the medicine? She gives you the directions so that you can go in her place. Make a **map** of the path from Phoenix's place to the doctor's office so that you can find your way.

Obstacle Game Review the story and **list** all of the hazards Phoenix Jackson encountered on this trip or on other trips she has taken along this path. Then design a **board game** with the object of the game to get Phoenix from her home on the Natchez Trace to the doctor's office. Make the board and any cards or game pieces you might need.

A Path of Pictures Work with a group and select the most memorable scenes along the path. Each of you choose one scene, illustrate it, and provide a quote from the story as a caption. Display the **illustrations** for your class.

OTHER OPTIONS

Turn Right, Then Left

Suggest that students be creative, modeling their maps after old treasure maps that depict the potential hazards of each new passage with illustrations and clever labels.

Obstacle Game

You might suggest that students create an alternative to each of Phoenix's triumphs. For example, the game could include the possibilities of falling from the log into the creek, never being helped from the ditch, or being chased back by a real ghost.

A Path of Pictures

Have students research the rural areas of Mississippi. They can use photographs and descriptions of the area around Natchez to inspire their imaginations.

Before Reading

The Leader of the People

by John Steinbeck

John Steinbeck
1902–1968

"If there is a magic in story writing, and I am convinced that there is, no one has ever been able to reduce it to a recipe that can be passed from one person to another," wrote John Steinbeck in a letter to one of his professors at Stanford University. Born in Salinas, California, Steinbeck struggled through the early days of the Depression working as a hod-carrier, surveyor, and fruit picker. As a writer, he populated his stories and novels with poor and working-class people. However, his characters, such as those in *Of Mice and Men* and *The Grapes of Wrath,* which won a Pulitzer Prize, show a love for life and a dignity that goes beyond their humble circumstances.

Building Background

The End of the Trail The discovery of gold in 1848 and the Homestead Act in 1862, with the promise of free land, enticed thousands of people to Oregon and California. Artists and writers glorified these pioneers. But once these pioneers began to move across the land, the West changed. Buffalo hunters killed off most of the herds, altering forever the lives of the Plains Indians. Broken treaties and government mandates forced Indians off their lands and onto reservations. The "Wild West" didn't last long—soon the frontier was officially declared closed and the pioneers were stopped in their tracks by the Pacific Ocean.

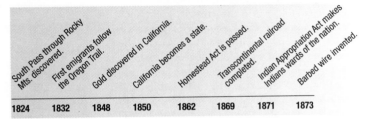

South Pass through Rocky Mts. discovered.	First emigrants follow the Oregon Trail.	Gold discovered in California.	California becomes a state.	Homestead Act is passed.	Transcontinental railroad completed.	Indian Appropriation Act makes Indians wards of the nation.	Barbed wire invented.
1824	1832	1848	1850	1862	1869	1871	1873

Literary Focus

Setting The time and place in which the action of a narrative takes place is the setting. "The Leader of the People" takes place on a ranch in Salinas, California, sometime in the 1920s or 1930s. Before you begin reading the story, find Salinas on a map. What is the countryside around it like? How close is it to the ocean? As you read, notice how Steinbeck describes the setting. Ask yourself: What effect does the setting have on the mood of the story? How does it help to reveal character? Does it affect the plot in any way?

Writer's Notebook

All in the Family In your notebook, jot down the first words you think of when you hear each of these phrases describing family relationships: father–son, father–daughter, father-in-law–son-in-law, husband–wife, and grandfather–grandson.

The Leader of the People **675**

Before Reading

Building Background

Discuss the frontier crossing from different points of view, for example: a pioneer who struck gold and resettled in California; a Plains Indian displaced from his home; a mother whose daughter died along the way.

Literary Focus

The **setting** of a story impacts on the plot and characters. Only fifteen miles from the ocean, Salinas is surrounded by mountains.

Writer's Notebook

Point out that family relationships are affected by setting. Have students imagine a setting for each of the listed relationships, for example, a father and son playing basketball in a gym.

More About John Steinbeck

Morte d'Arthur by Malory was the first book that Steinbeck owned, and he cited it as a great influence on his work.

Connections to AuthorWorks

John Steinbeck is a featured author in the AuthorWorks CD-ROM.

Connections to NovelWorks

Material for teaching *The Pearl* and *The Grapes of Wrath* is in NovelWorks.

SUPPORT MATERIALS OVERVIEW

Unit 6 Resource Book
- Graphic Organizer, p. 89
- Study Guide, p. 90
- Vocabulary, p. 91
- Grammar, p. 92
- Alternate Check Test, p. 93
- Vocabulary Test, p. 94
- Selection Test, pp. 95–96

Building English Proficiency
- Literature Summaries
- Activities, p. 220

Reading, Writing & Grammar SkillBook
- Vocabulary, pp. 7–8
- Reading, pp. 70–72
- Writing, pp. 119–120
- Grammar, Usage, and Mechanics, pp. 202–203

The World of Work
- Truck Driver, p. 21
- Activity, p. 22

Technology
- Audiotape
- Personal Journal Software
- Custom Literature Database: For another selection dealing with the tradition of going off to seek one's fortune, see the Jack London story "Where the Trail Forks" on the database.
- Test Generator Software

Selection Objectives

- To understand how setting affects mood, character, and plot
- To investigate verb usage
- To examine the conflict between tradition and change

Unit 6 Resource Book
Study Guide, p. 90

Theme Link

When a boy's father criticizes his grandfather for dwelling in the past, three generations come into conflict over the importance of tradition.

Vocabulary Preview

emerge, come into view, come out
peer, look closely to see clearly
convene, meet for some purpose
sidle, move sideways
mimic, make fun of by imitating

Students can add the words and definitions to their Writer's Notebooks.

1 Literary Element
Point of View

The author tells this story through a third-person limited omniscient point of view.

Question What does this passage say about the author's attitude toward Jody? *(It seems to convey an understanding and acceptance of the boy.)*

JOHN STEINBECK
The Leader

O n Saturday afternoon Billy Buck, the ranch hand, raked together the last of the old year's haystack and pitched small forkfuls over the wire fence to a few mildly interested cattle. High in the air small clouds like puffs of cannon smoke were driven eastward by the March wind. The wind could be heard whishing in the brush on the ridge crests, but no breath of it penetrated down into the ranch cup.

The little boy, Jody, emerged[1] from the house eating a thick piece of buttered bread. He saw Billy working on the last of the haystack. Jody tramped down scuffling his shoes in a way he had been told was destructive to good shoe leather. A flock of white pigeons flew out of the black cypress tree as Jody passed, and circled the tree and landed again. A half-grown tortoiseshell cat leaped from the bunkhouse porch, galloped on stiff legs across the road, whirled and galloped back again. Jody picked up a stone to help the game along, but he was too late, for the cat was under the porch before the stone could be discharged. He threw the stone into the cypress tree and started the white pigeons on another whirling flight.

Arriving at the used-up haystack, the boy leaned against the barbed-wire fence. "Will that be all of it, do you think?" he asked.

The middle-aged ranch hand stopped his careful raking and stuck his fork into the ground. He took off his black hat and smoothed down his

---

1. emerge (i mėrj´), *v.* come into view; come out.

Does David DeMatteo's painting of the Santa Ynez Valley in California depict a place where you'd like to live? Why or why not? ➤

SELECTION SUMMARY

The Leader of the People

One Saturday afternoon in March, an energetic young boy named Jody Tiflin welcomes his maternal grandfather to his family's ranch in the Salinas Valley. Jody's father, Carl, is less hospitable, complaining to his wife that Grandfather talks too much about his pioneering days of the past. That night, Jody's grandfather once again reminisces about leading a wagon train to California years ago. Jody welcomes the adventurous stories even though he has already heard them many times. The ranch hand, Billy Buck, and Jody's mother listen politely but without real enthusiasm. Carl is irritated by the old man's repetitive narrative. He interrupts and tries to redirect the conversation. The next morning Grandfather overhears Carl criticizing his tales, and he takes it very hard. Jody sympathizes and identifies with his grandfather and is thus awakened to new feelings of compassion and generosity.

*For summaries in other languages, see the **Building English Proficiency** book.*

of the People

hair. "Nothing left of it that isn't soggy from ground moisture," he said. He replaced his hat and rubbed his dry leathery hands together.

"Ought to be plenty mice," Jody suggested.

"Lousy with them," said Billy. "Just crawling with mice."

"Well, maybe, when you get all through, I could call the dogs and hunt the mice."

"Sure, I guess you could," said Billy Buck. He lifted a forkful of the damp ground hay and threw it into the air. Instantly three mice leaped out and burrowed frantically under the hay again.

Jody sighed with satisfaction. Those plump, sleek, arrogant mice were doomed. For eight months they had lived and multiplied in the haystack. They had been immune from cats, from traps, from poison, and from Jody. They had grown smug in their security, overbearing and fat. Now the time of disaster had come; they would not survive another day.

Billy looked up at the top of the hills that surrounded the ranch. "Maybe you better ask your father before you do it," he suggested.

"Well, where is he? I'll ask him now."

"He rode up to the ridge ranch after dinner. He'll be back pretty soon."

Jody slumped against the fence post. "I don't think he'd care."

As Billy went back to his work he said ominously, "You'd better ask him anyway. You know how he is." **2**

Jody did know. His father, Carl Tiflin, insisted upon giving permission for anything that was done on the ranch, whether it was important or not. Jody sagged farther against the post until he was sitting on the ground. He looked up at the little puffs of wind-driven cloud. "Is it like to rain, Billy?" **3**

Art Study

The Santa Ynez Mountains extend along the coast of Southern California, west of the Sierra Madre Mountains, about 250 miles south of Salinas

Response to Caption Question
Answers should reflect the student's ability to make inferences about the kind of life one would live in the environment of the painting.

Visual Literary DeMatteo's painting presents a strong contrast between light and shadow. He believes that light, "intensified and diminished to a delicate balance," makes a painting come to life.

2 Reading/Thinking Skills
Predict

Question When Billy Buck says, "You know how he is," he creates an air of suspense around Jody's father. What do you think the father will be like? *(Possible response: Students might guess that Jody's father is strict and likes things done his way.)*

3 Literary Element
Diction

Question What does the author's use of the verbs "slumped" and "sagged" suggest about the boy's relationship with his father? *(Possible responses: He doesn't often get what he wants from his father. He sees his father as somewhat of an adversary.)*

BUILDING ENGLISH PROFICIENCY

Analyzing Conflict

Help students keep track of the conflicts in this story.

- Explain that conflict—a clash between opposing forces—is at the heart of most good stories. In **external conflicts,** a character struggles against a person, an animal, a natural force, or a whole society. An **internal conflict** goes on inside a character's mind.

- Divide students into groups; ask each group to come up with examples of the kinds of conflicts listed above in real life.

- Ask students to find two conflicts introduced on page 677. *(Jody against the mice; Jody against his father)* As they read, have them keep track of how these conflicts develop and to find other conflicts that are important to Steinbeck's plot.

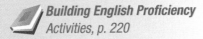
Building English Proficiency Activities, p. 220

Evaluate

Question Why do you think Billy Buck fails to respond to Jody's bold profanity? *(Possible responses: He probably disapproves, but realizes that it is normal for a boy to try to act like a grown-up by swearing. He doesn't want to call attention to it.)*

Connotation/Denotation

Discuss the connotations of the phrase "I'll keep him busy if he isn't careful."

Question What effect does Carl intend to create with this statement? *(Possible response: He is trying to intimidate his son so that Jody will learn to mind his own business.)*

Make Judgments

Question Why do you think Mr. Tiflin reacts so fiercely to Jody's interruption? *(Possible responses: He is ashamed of his inability to defend himself against his wife's anger, so he turns his own anger towards his son; or he is very annoyed about his father-in-law's arrival and it angers him that his son is excited about the stories the old man will tell.)*

"It might. The wind's good for it, but not strong enough."

"Well, I hope it don't rain until after I kill those damn mice." He looked over his shoulder to see whether Billy had noticed the mature profanity. Billy worked on without comment.

Jody turned back and looked at the side-hill where the road from the outside world came down. The hill was washed with lean March sunshine. Silver thistles, blue lupins and a few poppies bloomed among the sage bushes. Halfway up the hill Jody could see Doubletree Mutt, the black dog, digging in a squirrel hole. He paddled for a while and then paused to kick bursts of dirt out between his hind legs, and he dug with an earnestness which belied the knowledge he must have had that no dog had ever caught a squirrel by digging in a hole.

*S*uddenly, while Jody watched, the black dog stiffened, and backed out of the hole and looked up the hill toward the cleft in the ridge where the road came through. Jody looked up too. For a moment Carl Tiflin on horseback stood out against the pale sky and then he moved down the road toward the house. He carried something white in his hand.

The boy started to his feet. "He's got a letter," Jody cried. He trotted away toward the ranch house, for the letter would probably be read aloud and he wanted to be there. He reached the house before his father did, and ran in. He heard Carl dismount from his creaking saddle and slap the horse on the side to send it to the barn where Billy would unsaddle it and turn it out.

Jody ran into the kitchen. "We got a letter!" he cried.

His mother looked up from a pan of beans. "Who has?"

"Father has. I saw it in his hand."

Carl strode into the kitchen then, and Jody's mother asked, "Who's the letter from, Carl?"

He frowned quickly. "How did you know there was a letter?"

She nodded her head in the boy's direction. "Big-Britches Jody told me."

Jody was embarrassed.

His father looked down at him contemptuously. "He *is* getting to be a Big-Britches," Carl said. "He's minding everybody's business but his own. Got his big nose into everything."

Mrs. Tiflin relented a little, "Well, he hasn't enough to keep him busy. Who's the letter from?"

Carl still frowned on Jody. "I'll keep him busy if he isn't careful." He held out a sealed letter. "I guess it's from your father."

Mrs. Tiflin took a hairpin from her head and slit open the flap. Her lips pursed judiciously. Jody saw her eyes snap back and forth over the lines. "He says," she translated, "he says he's going to drive out Saturday to stay for a little while. Why, this is Saturday. The letter must have been delayed." She looked at the postmark. "This was mailed day before yesterday. It should have been here yesterday." She looked up questioningly at her husband, and then her face darkened angrily. "Now what have you got that look on you for? He doesn't come often."

Carl turned his eyes away from her anger. He could be stern with her most of the time, but when occasionally her temper arose, he could not combat it.

"What's the matter with you?" she demanded again.

In his explanation there was a tone of apology Jody himself might have used. "It's just that he talks," Carl said lamely. "Just talks."

"Well, what of it? You talk yourself."

"Sure I do. But your father only talks about one thing."

"Indians!" Jody broke in excitedly. "Indians and crossing the plains!"

Carl turned fiercely on him. "You get out, Mr. Big-Britches! Go on, now! Get out!"

Jody went miserably out the back door and closed the screen with elaborate quietness. Under the kitchen window his shamed, downcast eyes fell upon a curiously shaped stone, a stone of such

---

MINI-LESSON: VOCABULARY

Recognize Idioms

Teach Have students analyze the following sentences on page 678: He *is* getting to be a Big-Britches," Carl said. "He's minding everybody's business but his own."

Explain that an idiom is an expression peculiar to a language that takes on a meaning beyond the literal meaning of its parts. This idiom is related to another idiom, to be "too big for one's britches."

Questions
- What is the literal meaning of big-britches? *(big trousers)*
- What does this idiom connote? *(someone who is overconfident or trying to appear older and wiser than he is)*

Activity Ideas
- Have students brainstorm similar idioms or words that could be used in this context. *(Possible responses: know-it-all, smarty-pants, busybody)*
- Have students find other idioms in this and other stories they have read. They can then read them to the class and ask for definitions.

fascination that he squatted down and picked it up and turned it over in his hands.

The voices came clearly to him through the open kitchen window. "Jody's damn well right," he heard his father say. "Just Indians and crossing the plains. I've heard that story about how the horses got driven off about a thousand times. He just goes on and on, and he never changes a word in the things he tells."

When Mrs. Tiflin answered, her tone was so changed that Jody, outside the window, looked up from his study of the stone. Her voice had become soft and explanatory. Jody knew how her face would have changed to match the tone. She said quietly, "Look at it this way, Carl. That was the big thing in my father's life. He led a wagon train clear across the plains to the coast, and when it was finished, his life was done. It was a big thing to do, but it didn't last long enough. Look!" she continued, "it's as though he was born to do that, and after he finished it, there wasn't anything more for him to do but think about it and talk about it. If there'd been any farther west to go, he'd have gone. He's told me so himself. But at last there was the ocean. He lives right by the ocean where he had to stop."

> *He led a wagon train clear across the plains to the coast, and when it was finished, his life was done.*

She had caught Carl, caught him and entangled him in her soft tone.

"I've seen him," he agreed quietly. "He goes down and stares off west over the ocean." His voice sharpened a little. "And then he goes up to the Horseshoe Club in Pacific Grove, and he tells people how the Indians drove off the horses."

She tried to catch him again. "Well, it's everything to him. You might be patient with him and pretend to listen."

Carl turned impatiently away. "Well, if it gets too bad, I can always go down to the bunkhouse and sit with Billy," he said irritably. He walked through the house and slammed the front door after him.

Jody ran to his chores. He dumped the grain to the chickens without chasing any of them. He gathered the eggs from the nests. He trotted into the house with the wood and interlaced it so carefully in the wood-box that two armloads seemed to fill it to overflowing.

His mother had finished the beans by now. She stirred up the fire and brushed off the stove top with a turkey wing. Jody peered² cautiously at her to see whether any rancor toward him remained. "Is he coming today?" Jody asked.

"That's what his letter said."

"Maybe I better walk up the road to meet him."

Mrs. Tiflin clanged the stove lid shut. "That would be nice," she said. "He'd probably like to be met."

"I guess I'll just do it then."

Outside, Jody whistled shrilly to the dogs. "Come on up the hill," he commanded. The two dogs waved their tails and ran ahead. Along the roadside the sage had tender new tips. Jody tore off some pieces and rubbed them on his hands until the air was filled with the sharp wild smell. With a rush the dogs leaped from the road and yapped into the brush after a rabbit. That was the last Jody saw of them, for when they failed to catch the rabbit, they went back home.

Jody plodded on up the hill toward the ridge top. When he reached the little cleft where the road came through, the afternoon wind struck him and blew up his hair and ruffled his shirt. He looked down on the little hills and ridges below and then out at the huge green Salinas Valley.³ He could see the white town of Salinas

---

2. peer (pēr), v. look closely to see clearly.
3. **Salinas Valley,** an agriculturally rich valley in California.

The Leader of the People **679**

7 Literary Element
Dialogue

Point to the places where tone of voice indicates a shift in the power struggle between Mr. and Mrs. Tiflin. For example, "she had . . . entangled him in her soft tone" and "his voice sharpened a little."

8 Reading/Thinking Skills
Summarize

Question What reasons does Mrs. Tiflin give for her father's repetitive stories? *(Possible response: He has nothing left but to think and talk about his experience. There are no other adventures for him.)*

9 Reading/Thinking Skills
Connect

Question Does Jody's manner toward the dogs reflect the way he has been treated today? *(Most students will agree that Jody's shrill command to the dogs is a reflection of his father's treatment of him.)*

10 Literary Element
Symbolism

Discuss the sage plant's "tender new tips" as a symbol of youth and innocence.

Question How does the author use this symbol to illustrate an aspect of Jody's character? *(Possible response: His tearing of the sage shows a desire to destroy.)*

BUILDING ENGLISH PROFICIENCY

Exploring Principal Parts of Verbs

ESL LEP ELD SAE LD

Use "The Leader of the People" to help students review verb forms.

- Explain the difference between present, past, and past participle verb forms.
- Draw the chart shown at the right, which lists verb forms from page 679, on the board. Leave blanks where answers in parentheses are shown.)
- Work with students to complete the chart.

Present	Past	Past Participle
(carry)	carried	*(carried)*
(catch)	*(caught)*	caught
(go)	went	*(gone)*
has	*(had)*	*(had)*
(notice)	*(noticed)*	noticed
(run)	ran	*(run)*
(see)	saw	*(seen)*
(take)	took	*(taken)*

Art Study

Taken in 1939 in Bozeman, Montana, this photograph captures some of the weather-beaten grit and confidence of the American cowpoke.

Response to Caption Question
Students will probably say that this fellow and grandfather would have a lot in common, including traveling long distances over rough terrain, the spirit of adventure, and determination.

11 Literary Focus
Setting

Point out that the appearance and disappearance of the approaching wagon climbing the nearby hill creates an element of suspense.

12 Reading/Thinking Skills
Draw Conclusions

Question Why does the man climb down and release the horse? *(Possible response: Climbing hills has exhausted the horse so the man lightens the load by walking.)*

13 Reading/Thinking Skills
Synthesize

Note this passage as a significant indication of Grandfather's character and disposition. Discuss how old age might affect a person's ability to change course, both literally and figuratively. Suggest that students keep this character trait in mind as they continue reading.

Question Based on this description of Grandfather, does he now seem more or less like the man in photograph? *(Most students will say less like him. Grandfather seems more dapper in his suit, gaiters, and tie. His eyes are "merry," but both men have "granite dignity.")*

far out in the flat and the flash of its windows under the waning sun. Directly below him, in an oak tree, a crow congress had convened.[4] The tree was black with crows all cawing at once. Then Jody's eyes followed the wagon road down from the ridge where he stood, and lost it behind a hill, and picked it up again on the other side. On that distant stretch he saw a cart slowly pulled by a bay horse. It disappeared behind the hill. Jody sat down on the ground and watched the place where the cart would reappear again. The wind sang on the hilltops and the puffball clouds hurried eastward.

Then the cart came into sight and stopped. A man dressed in black dismounted from the seat and walked to the horse's head. Although it was so faraway, Jody knew he had unhooked the checkrein, for the horse's head dropped forward. The horse moved on, and the man walked slowly up the hill beside it. Jody gave a glad cry and ran down the road toward them. The squirrels bumped along off the road, and a roadrunner flirted its tail and raced over the edge of the hill and sailed out like a glider.

Jody tried to leap into the middle of his shadow at every step. A stone rolled under his foot and he went down. Around a little bend he raced, and there, a short distance ahead, were his grandfather and the cart. The boy dropped from his unseemly running and approached at a dignified walk.

The horse plodded stumble-footedly up the hill and the old man walked beside it. In the lowering sun their giant shadows flickered darkly behind them. The grandfather was dressed in a black broadcloth suit and he wore kid congress gaiters and a black tie on a short, hard collar. He carried his black slouch hat in his hand. His white beard was cropped close and his white eyebrows overhung his eyes like

▲ Arthur Rothstein's 1939 photograph is of Frank Lotta, an old-time cowpuncher. What might this man and Grandfather in Steinbeck's story have in common?

mustaches. The blue eyes were sternly merry. About the whole face and figure there was a granite dignity, so that every motion seemed an impossible thing. Once at rest, it seemed the old man would be stone, would never move again. His steps were slow and certain. Once made, no step could ever be retraced; once headed in a direction, the path would never bend nor the pace increase nor slow.

When Jody appeared around the bend, Grandfather waved his hat slowly in welcome, and he called, "Why, Jody! Come down to meet me, have you?"

Jody sidled[5] near and turned and matched

---

4. **convene** (kən vēn′), *v.* meet for some purpose.
5. **sidle** (sī′dl), *v.* move sideways.

MINI-LESSON: LITERARY FOCUS

Setting

Teach Have students examine this passage from page 680:

Jody sat on the ground and watched the place where the cart would reappear again. The wind sang on the hilltops and the puffball clouds hurried eastward.

Explain that the "puffball clouds" appear repeatedly as natural elements that connect the story's setting to its plot. The image of the wind driving the clouds eastward foreshadows Grandfather's lament that "Westering has died

out of the people"; equating the drive westward with a strength of spirit. The wind drives the clouds east throughout the story, reinforcing Grandfather's fears.

Activity Idea Ask students to find the first mention of these clouds in the story *(page 676 . . . small clouds like puffs of cannon smoke were driven eastward. . .).* Ask them to be aware of this important aspect of the setting as they continue reading.

his step to the old man's step and stiffened his body and dragged his heels a little. "Yes, sir," he said. "We got your letter only today."

"Should have been here yesterday," said Grandfather. "It certainly should. How are all the folks?"

"They're fine, sir." He hesitated and then suggested shyly, "Would you like to come on a mouse hunt tomorrow, sir?"

"Mouse hunt, Jody?" Grandfather chuckled. "Have the people of this generation come down to hunting mice? They aren't very strong, the new people, but I hardly thought mice would be  game for them."

"No, sir. It's just play. The haystack's gone. I'm going to drive out the mice to the dogs. And you can watch, or even beat the hay a little."

The stern, merry eyes turned down on him. "I see. You don't eat them, then. You haven't come to that yet."

Jody explained, "The dogs eat them, sir. It wouldn't be much like hunting Indians, I guess."

"No, not much—but then later, when the troops were hunting Indians and shooting children and burning teepees, it wasn't much different from your mouse hunt."

They topped the rise and started down into the ranch cup, and they lost the sun from their shoulders. "You've grown," Grandfather said. "Nearly an inch, I should say."

"More," Jody boasted. "Where they mark me on the door, I'm up more than an inch since Thanksgiving even."

Grandfather's rich throaty voice said, "Maybe you're getting too much water and turning to pith and stalk. Wait until you head out, and then we'll see."

Jody looked quickly into the old man's face to see whether his feelings should be hurt, but there was no will to injure, no punishing nor putting-in-your-place light in the keen blue eyes. "We might kill a pig," Jody suggested.

"Oh, no! I couldn't let you do that. You're just humoring me. It isn't the time and you know it."

"You know Riley, the big boar, sir?"

"Yes. I remember Riley well."

"Well, Riley ate a hole into that same haystack, and it fell down on him and smothered him."

"Pigs do that when they can," said Grandfather.

"Riley was a nice pig, for a boar, sir. I rode him sometimes, and he didn't mind."

A door slammed at the house below them, and they saw Jody's mother standing on the porch waving her apron in welcome. And they saw Carl Tiflin walking up from the barn to be at the house for the arrival.

The sun had disappeared from the hills by now. The blue smoke from the house chimney hung in flat layers in the purpling ranch cup. The puffball clouds, dropped by the falling wind, hung listlessly in the sky.

*B*illy Buck came out of the bunkhouse and flung a washbasin of soapy water on the ground. He had been shaving in midweek, for Billy held Grandfather in reverence, and Grandfather said that Billy was one of the few men of the new generation who had not gone soft. Although Billy was in middle age, Grandfather considered him a boy. Now Billy was hurrying toward the house too.

When Jody and Grandfather arrived, the three were waiting for them in front of the yard gate.

Carl said, "Hello, sir. We've been looking for you."

Mrs. Tiflin kissed Grandfather on the side of his beard, and stood still while his big hand patted her shoulder. Billy shook hands solemnly, grinning under his straw mustache. "I'll put up your horse," said Billy, and he led the rig away.

Grandfather watched him go, and then, turning back to the group, he said as he had said a hundred times before, "There's a good boy. I knew his father, old Mule-tail Buck. I never knew why they called him Mule-tail except he packed mules."

Mrs. Tiflin turned and led the way into the house. "How long are you going to stay, Father? Your letter didn't say."

The Leader of the People **681**

14 Reader's Response
Making Personal Connections

Ask students if they have grandparents or older relatives who comment on the faults of the younger generation. Discuss the differences between how people live today compared to the life their elderly relatives remember from their youth.

15 Reading/Thinking Skills
Connect

Question   What moral lesson is Grandfather suggesting about Jody's idea of "play"? *(Perhaps that it is a cruel and unnecessary.)*

16 Reader's Response
Challenging the Text

Question   Discuss Jody's fear of ridicule. Do you feel sorry for him? Does he deserve ridicule? *(Answers will vary, but should reflect an ability to connect the boy's behavior to the way he has been treated.)*

BUILDING ENGLISH PROFICIENCY

Tracking Plot Elements

Making a story map like the one shown will help students keep track of the story's elements as they read. At this point, students have enough information to write notes about setting, characters, and two events. The problem, which is also the major conflict, may not be clear until page 682.

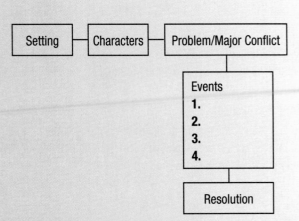

Setting — Characters — Problem/Major Conflict

Events
1.
2.
3.
4.

Resolution

Metaphor

Discuss the way that Carl reacts to the moth—decisively and with little feeling.

Question How does Carl's killing of the moth serve as a metaphor for his treat-ment of Grandfather? *(Possible response: He is impatient, and he regards Grandfather's stories as a nuisance; he therefore "breaks" Grandfather's sentence in order to shut him up, just as he has broken the moth.)*

Hyperbole

Explain that although the narrator exagger-ates Jody's "heroism" to create irony, it is still a bold move for the boy.

Question What inspires Jody to assert himself? *(Possible response: He empathizes with Grandfather because Carl had humiliated him too earlier that day.)*

Draw Conclusions

Question Why does everyone else remain silent? *(Possible response: Because they've heard the story before and don't want to encourage Grandfather to tell it again.)*

"Well, I don't know. I thought I'd stay about two weeks. But I never stay as long as I think I'm going to."

In a short while they were sitting at the white oilcloth table eating their supper. The lamp with the tin reflector hung over the table. Outside the dining-room windows the big moths battered softly against the glass.

Grandfather cut his steak into tiny pieces and chewed slowly. "I'm hungry," he said. "Driving out here got my appetite up. It's like when we were crossing. We all got so hungry every night we could hardly wait to let the meat get done. I could eat about five pounds of buffalo meat every night."

"It's moving around does it," said Billy. "My father was a government packer. I helped him when I was a kid. Just the two of us could about clean up a deer's ham."

"I knew your father, Billy," said Grandfather. "A fine man he was. They called him Mule-tail Buck. I don't know why, except he packed mules."

"That was it," Billy agreed. "He packed mules."

Grandfather put down his knife and fork, and looked around the table. "I remember one time we ran out of meat——" His voice dropped to a curious low singsong, dropped into a tonal groove the story had worn for itself. "There was no buffalo, no antelope, not even rabbits. The hunters couldn't even shoot a coyote. That was the time for the leader to be on the watch. I was the leader, and I kept my eyes open. Know why? Well, just the minute the people began to get hungry they'd start slaughtering the team oxen. Do you believe that? I've heard of parties that just ate up their draft cattle. Started from the middle and worked toward the ends. Finally they'd eat the lead pair, and then the wheelers. The leader of a party had to keep them from doing that."

In some manner a big moth got into the room and circled the hanging kerosene lamp. Billy got up and tried to clap it between his hands. Carl **[17]** struck with a cupped palm and caught the moth and broke it. He walked to the window and dropped it out.

"As I was saying," Grandfather began again, but Carl interrupted him. "You'd better eat some more meat. All the rest of us are ready for our pudding."

Jody saw a flash of anger in his mother's eyes. Grandfather picked up his knife and fork. "I'm pretty hungry, all right," he said. "I'll tell you about that later."

When supper was over, when the family and Billy Buck sat in front of the fireplace in the other room, Jody anxiously watched Grandfather. He saw the signs he knew. The bearded head leaned forward; the eyes lost their sternness and looked wonderingly into the fire; the big lean fingers laced themselves on the black knees.

"I wonder," he began, "I just wonder whether I ever told you how those thieving Piutes drove off thirty-five of our horses."

"I think you did," Carl interrupted. "Wasn't it just before you went up into the Tahoe country?"

Grandfather turned quickly toward his son-in-law. "That's right. I guess I must have told you that story."

"Lots of times," Carl said cruelly, and he avoided his wife's eyes. But he felt the angry eyes on him, and he said, "'Course I'd like to hear it again."

Grandfather looked back at the fire. His fin-gers unlaced and laced again. Jody knew how he felt, how his insides were collapsed and empty. Hadn't Jody been called a Big-Britches that very afternoon? He arose to heroism and **[18]** opened himself to the term Big-Britches again. "Tell about Indians," he said softly.

Grandfather's eyes grew stern again. "Boys always want to hear about Indians. It was a job for men, but boys want to hear about it. Well, let's see. Did I ever tell you how I wanted each wagon to carry a long iron plate?"

Everyone but Jody remained silent. Jody said, "No. You didn't." **[19]**

"Well, when the Indians attacked, we always put the wagons in a circle and fought from between the wheels. I thought that if every wagon carried a long plate with rifle holes, the

---

MINI-LESSON: WRITING STYLE

Using Adverbs to Intensify a Narrative

Teach Have students examine the author's use of adverbs in the following sentences on page 678.

"His father looked down at him <u>contemptuously</u>."

"Her lips pursed <u>judiciously</u>."

"Jody broke in <u>excitedly</u>."

Explain that these adverbs (underlined) offer the perceptive reader insight into a character's personality. Explain that Steinbeck's lucid writing style relies heavily on the careful choice of adverbs.

Question What do the adverbs tell about the subject of the sentence? *(Possible responses: Jody's father is scornful; his mother is levelheaded; Jody is enthusiastic and energetic.)*

Activity Ideas

- Have students find examples of other adverbs that deepen the story's meaning.
- Have students choose another adverb for each sentence and discuss how it changes the meaning.

What interpretation of "westering" does Samuel Colman present in his 1872 painting, *Ships of the Plains*? Does he focus on the difficulties or on the grandeur of "westering"?

men could stand the plates on the outside of the wheels when the wagons were in the circle and they would be protected. It would save lives and that would make up for the extra weight of the iron. But of course the party wouldn't do it. No party had done it before and they couldn't see why they should go to the expense. They lived to regret it, too."

20 Jody looked at his mother, and knew from her expression that she was not listening at all. Carl picked at a callus on his thumb and Billy Buck watched a spider crawling up the wall.

Grandfather's tone dropped into its narrative groove again. Jody knew in advance exactly what words would fall. The story droned on, speeded up for the attack, grew sad over the wounds, struck a dirge at the burials on the great plains. Jody sat quietly watching Grandfather. The stern blue eyes were detached. He looked as though he were not very interested in the story himself. **21**

When it was finished, when the pause had been politely respected as the frontier of the story, Billy Buck stood up and stretched and hitched his trousers. "I guess I'll turn in," he said. Then he faced Grandfather. "I've got an old powder horn and a cap and ball pistol down **22**

The Leader of the People **683**

Art Study

Samuel Colman studied painting under Asher Durand, a Hudson River School painter. Beginning in about 1870 he began his travels to the American West, where *Ships of the Plains* was painted.

Response to Caption Question A possible response might be that both elements are captured here. Colman depicts the life as cumbersome, grueling, and grand. The spirit of forging ahead despite recalcitrant cattle and dusty roads is captured.

20 Literary Focus
Setting

Question Describe your mental picture of the room in which the family is sitting. Recall details that enrich your image of life inside the house. *(Details might include: the spider crawling up the wall; the hanging kerosene lamp; the fireplace.)*

21 Literary Element
Figurative Language

Point out that the author's playful style exaggerates Grandfather's long-windedness. You might ask students to demonstrate their impression of how the story droned on, speeded up, grew sad, and struck a dirge.

22 Literary Element
Pun

Question Can you find the pun in this paragraph? *(Response: the pause is called the "frontier of the story," meaning that Grandfather had reached his destination— the end of the story.)*

BUILDING ENGLISH PROFICIENCY

Linking Past and Present

When Grandfather says, "It's like when we were crossing," he attempts to make a connection between his past and his present. Invite students to do something of the same.

- If students know how their ancestors or families came to the United States, have them tell or write about that "crossing." Ask: Does the "crossing" influence your thinking as much as Grandfather's did his? Why or why not?

- Students who prefer more imaginative storytelling may wish to collaborate on writing or telling a science-fiction story about an interstellar "crossing." Urge them to let their stories reveal how the "crossing" affected the pioneers of the future.

Compare and Contrast

Question Compare and contrast Billy Buck's treatment of Grandfather to Carl's. *(Possible response: Billy Buck politely listens to Grandfather's stories. He tries to be friendly. Carl interrupts and tries to steer Grandfather away from his stories. Carl only extends himself under his wife's influence.)*

24 **Literary Element**

Imagery

Point out that Steinbeck uses sensory images of nature to reinforce the plot of the story. For example, the wind rises and the tree groans as Jody's consciousness drifts from reality, represented by the dog scratching his fleas, back into the world of dreams.

The World of Work

Young boys in Jody's time didn't have comic books to read, but they are very popular with the kids of today. For the real-life experiences of a **comic book store owner,** use the pages referenced below.

The World of Work
pp. 21–22

---

to the bunkhouse. Did I ever show them to you?"

Grandfather nodded slowly. "Yes, I think you did, Billy. Reminds me of a pistol I had when I was leading the people across." Billy stood politely until the little story was done, and then he said, "Good night," and went out of the house.

A race of giants had lived then, fearless men, men of a staunchness unknown in this day.

Carl Tiflin tried to turn the conversation then. "How's the country between here and Monterey? I've heard it's pretty dry."

"It is dry," said Grandfather. "There's not a drop of water in the Laguna Seca. But it's a long pull from '87. The whole country was powder then, and in '61 I believe all the coyotes starved to death. We had fifteen inches of rain this year."

23 "Yes, but it all came too early. We could do with some now." Carl's eye fell on Jody. "Hadn't you better be getting to bed?"

Jody stood up obediently. "Can I kill the mice in the old haystack, sir?"

"Mice? Oh! Sure, kill them all off. Billy said there isn't any good hay left."

Jody exchanged a secret and satisfying look with Grandfather. "I'll kill every one tomorrow," he promised.

Jody lay in his bed and thought of the impossible world of Indians and buffaloes, a world that had ceased to be forever. He wished he could have been living in the heroic time, but he knew he was not of heroic timber. No one living now, save possibly Billy Buck, was worthy to do the things that had been done. A race of giants had lived then, fearless men, men of a staunchness unknown in this day. Jody thought of the wide plains and of the wagons moving across like centipedes. He thought of Grandfather on a huge

684 UNIT SIX: MODERN DILEMMAS

white horse, marshaling the people. Across his mind marched the great phantoms, and they marched off the earth and they were gone.

He came back to the ranch for a moment, then. He heard the dull rushing sound that space and silence make. He heard one of the dogs, out in the doghouse, scratching a flea and bumping his elbow against the floor with every stroke. Then the wind arose again and the black cypress groaned and Jody went to sleep.

24

He was up half an hour before the triangle sounded for breakfast. His mother was rattling the stove to make the flames roar when Jody went through the kitchen. "You're up early," she said. "Where are you going?"

"Out to get a good stick. We're going to kill the mice today."

"Who is 'we'?"

"Why, Grandfather and I."

"So you've got him in it. You always like to have someone in with you in case there's blame to share."

"I'll be right back," said Jody. "I just want to have a good stick ready for after breakfast."

He closed the screen door after him and went out into the cool blue morning. The birds were noisy in the dawn and the ranch cats came down from the hill like blunt snakes. They had been hunting gophers in the dark, and although the four cats were full of gopher meat, they sat in a semicircle at the back door and mewed piteously for milk. Doubletree Mutt and Smasher moved sniffing along the edge of the brush, performing the duty with rigid ceremony, but when Jody whistled, their heads jerked up and their tails waved. They plunged down to him, wriggling their skins and yawning. Jody patted their heads seriously, and moved on to the weathered scrap pile. He selected an old broom handle and a short piece

---

MINI-LESSON: GRAMMAR

Distinguishing Similar Verbs: lie/lay; sit/set; let/leave

Teach Have students examine the following sentences:

Jody lay in his bed and thought of . . . Indians and buffaloes.

Carl laid his mush spoon on the table and touched his. . . .

Explain that *lay* is the past tense of the verb to *lie* (to recline in a lying position) and *laid* is the past tense of the verb *lay* (to put or to place something). Point out two other difficult verb pairs: *sit* (to rest in an upright position) and *set* (to put or place something); *let* (to allow) and *leave* (to go away).

Activity Idea Have students write a descriptive paragraph about something in nature using these verbs pairs.

Infinitive	Present Participle	Past Participle
to lie	lying	(have) lain
to lay	laying	(have) laid
to sit	sitting	(have) sat
to set	setting	(have) set
to let	letting	(have) let
to leave	leaving	(have) left

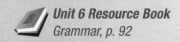

Unit 6 Resource Book
Grammar, p. 92

of inch-square scrap wood. From his pocket he took a shoelace and tied the ends of the sticks loosely together to make a flail. He whistled his new weapon through the air and struck the ground experimentally, while the dogs leaped aside and whined with apprehension.

Jody turned and started down past the house toward the old haystack ground to look over the field of slaughter, but Billy Buck, sitting patiently on the back steps, called to him, "You better come back. It's only a couple of minutes till breakfast."

Jody changed his course and moved toward the house. He leaned his flail against the steps. "That's to drive the mice out," he said. "I'll bet they're fat. I'll bet they don't know what's going to happen to them today."

"No, nor you either," Billy remarked philosophically, "nor me, nor anyone."

Jody was staggered by this thought. He knew it was true. His imagination twitched away from the mouse hunt. Then his mother came out on the back porch and struck the triangle, and all thoughts fell in a heap.

Grandfather hadn't appeared at the table when they sat down. Billy nodded at his empty chair. "He's all right? He isn't sick?"

"He takes a long time to dress," said Mrs. Tiflin. "He combs his whiskers and rubs up his shoes and brushes his clothes."

Carl scattered sugar on his mush. "A man that's led a wagon train across the plains has got to be pretty careful how he dresses."

Mrs. Tiflin turned on him. "Don't do that, Carl! Please don't!" There was more of threat than of request in her tone. And the threat irritated Carl.

"Well, how many times do I have to listen to the story of the iron plates, and the thirty-five horses? That time's done. Why can't he forget it, now it's done?" He grew angrier while he talked, and his voice rose. "Why does he have to tell them over and over? He came across the plains. All right! Now it's finished. Nobody wants to hear about it over and over."

The door into the kitchen closed softly. The four at the table sat frozen. Carl laid his mush spoon on the table and touched his chin with his fingers.

Then the kitchen door opened and Grandfather walked in. His mouth smiled tightly and his eyes were squinted. "Good morning," he said, and he sat down and looked at his mush dish.

Carl could not leave it there. "Did—did you hear what I said?"

Grandfather jerked a little nod.

"I don't know what got into me, sir. I didn't mean it. I was just being funny."

Jody glanced in shame at his mother, and he saw that she was looking at Carl, and that she wasn't breathing. It was an awful thing that he was doing. He was tearing himself to pieces to talk like that. It was a terrible thing to him to retract a word, but to retract it in shame was infinitely worse.

Grandfather looked sidewise. "I'm trying to get right side up," he said gently. "I'm not being mad. I don't mind what you said, but it might be true, and I would mind that."

"It isn't true," said Carl. "I'm not feeling well this morning. I'm sorry I said it."

"Don't be sorry, Carl. An old man doesn't see things sometimes. Maybe you're right. The crossing is finished. Maybe it should be forgotten, now it's done."

Carl got up from the table. "I've had enough to eat. I'm going to work. Take your time, Billy!" He walked quickly out of the dining room. Billy gulped the rest of his food and followed soon after. But Jody could not leave his chair.

"Won't you tell any more stories?" Jody asked.

"Why, sure I'll tell them, but only when—I'm sure people want to hear them."

"I like to hear them, sir."

"Oh! Of course you do, but you're a little boy. It was a job for men, but only the little boys like to hear about it."

Jody got up from his place. "I'll wait outside for you, sir. I've got a good stick for those mice."

The Leader of the People   **685**

25

---

30 Literary Element
Characterization

Explain that a *dynamic* character changes during the course of the story's action.

Question Is Jody a dynamic character? Why or why not? *(Possible response: Yes. He can now see beyond himself and empathize with his grandfather's sadness.)*

Check Test

1. Who is Billy Buck? *(the ranch hand on the Tiflin farm)*

2. What is Jody planning to hunt and kill? *(the mice in the haystack)*

3. Why doesn't Carl want Grandfather to visit? (*He finds the old man's repetitive stories irritating.*)

4. Who is "The Leader of the People?" *(Jody's grandfather)*

5. How does Grandfather find out that Carl doesn't like his stories? *(He overhears Carl at the breakfast table.)*

Unit 6 Resource Book
Alternative Check Test, p. 93

He waited by the gate until the old man came out on the porch. "Let's go down and kill the mice now," Jody called.

"I think I'll just sit in the sun, Jody. You go kill the mice."

"You can use my stick if you like."

"No, I'll just sit here a while."

Jody turned disconsolately away, and walked down toward the old haystack. He tried to whip up his enthusiasm with thoughts of the fat juicy mice. He beat the ground with his flail. The dogs coaxed and whined about him, but he could not go. Back at the house he could see Grandfather sitting on the porch, looking small and thin and black.

Jody gave up and went to sit on the steps at the old man's feet.

"Back already? Did you kill the mice?"

"No, sir. I'll kill them some other day."

*T*he morning flies buzzed close to the ground, and the ants dashed about in front of the steps. The heavy smell of sage slipped down the hill. The porch boards grew warm in the sunshine.

Jody hardly knew when Grandfather started to talk. "I shouldn't stay here, feeling the way I do." He examined his strong old hands. "I feel as though the crossing wasn't worth doing." His eyes moved up the side-hill and stopped on a motionless hawk perched on a dead limb. "I tell those old stories, but they're not what I want to tell. I only know how I want people to feel when I tell them.

"It wasn't the Indians that were important, nor adventures, nor even getting out here. It was a whole bunch of people made into one big crawling beast. And I was the head. It was westering and westering. Every man wanted something for himself, but the big beast that was all of them wanted only westering. I was the leader, but if I hadn't been there, someone else would have been the head. The thing had to have a head.

"Under the little bushes the shadows were

black at white noonday. When we saw the mountains at last, we cried—all of us. But it wasn't getting here that mattered, it was movement and westering.

"We carried life out here and set it down the way those ants carry eggs. And I was the leader. The westering was as big as God, and the slow steps that made the movement piled up and piled up until the continent was crossed.

"Then we came down to the sea, and it was done." He stopped and wiped his eyes until the rims were red. "That's what I should be telling instead of stories."

When Jody spoke, Grandfather stared and looked down at him. "Maybe I could lead the people some day," Jody said.

The old man smiled. "There's no place to go. There's the ocean to stop you. There's a line of old men along the shore hating the ocean because it stopped them."

"In boats I might, sir."

"No place to go, Jody. Every place is taken. But that's not the worst—no, not the worst. Westering has died out of the people. Westering isn't a hunger any more. It's all done. Your father is right. It is finished." He laced his fingers on his knee and looked at them.

Jody felt very sad. "If you'd like a glass of lemonade, I could make it for you."

Grandfather was about to refuse, and then he saw Jody's face. "That would be nice," he said. "Yes, it would be nice to drink a lemonade."

Jody ran into the kitchen where his mother was wiping the last of the breakfast dishes. "Can I have a lemon to make a lemonade for Grandfather?"

His mother mimicked—[6] "And another lemon to make a lemonade for you."

"No, ma'am. I don't want one."

"Jody! You're sick!" Then she stopped suddenly. "Take a lemon out of the cooler," she said softly. "Here, I'll reach the squeezer down to you." **30**

---

6. mimic (mim′ik), *v.* make fun of by imitating.

MINI-LESSON: STUDY SKILLS

The Information in a Book

Teach Students who want to learn more about Western trailblazers will have an easier time finding information if they are familiar with the various parts of a book. Have a few reference books on hand as you discuss the chart at the right.

Using these features will help students determine if a reference work contains the information they need.

Activity Idea Have students pair up with a reference book. One partner calls out the various parts for the other partner to find.

Book Part	Information It Gives
Copyright page	tells when book was published (and how current the information is)
Table of contents	lists the chapters, parts, or selections included in the book
Preface (or Forward)	tells what the book is about
Glossary	defines words used in the book
Index	lists the topics discussed in the book and where you can find them

After Reading

Making Connections

Shaping Your Response

1. Write five adjectives that you think describe Jody. Then do the same thing for Carl Tiflin, Mrs. Tiflin, and Grandfather.

2. Being a parent isn't easy, and some people are better at it than others. Where would you place Carl Tiflin on this "parent performance scale"? Where would you place Mrs. Tiflin? Explain.

poor ⟷ excellent

Analyzing the Story

3. Why do you think Jody doesn't believe himself to be "of heroic timber"?

4. What **character** traits show through in Jody's interactions with the adults in his life?

5. What can you **infer** is the reason for the change in Jody's attitude about killing mice?

6. At the beginning of the story Jody sees his grandfather as a "giant shadow." Near the end of the story, Jody sees his grandfather looking "small and thin." How would you explain this change in Jody's perception?

Extending the Ideas

7. The westward movement was over long before your grandparents were born. What were the major events that took place during their young adulthood that made a lasting impression on them?

Literary Focus: Setting

The time (year, season, and time of day) and place in which the action of a narrative occurs is called **setting.**

- What effect does the setting have on the mood of the story?
- How does setting help to reveal character?
- Does the setting affect the plot in any way?

Vocabulary Study

convene
emerge
mimic
peer
sidle

Work with a small group to pantomime each of the action verbs at the left, and have the class identify the verb. As a follow-up, write original sentences using the verbs.

The Leader of the People   **687**

LITERARY FOCUS: SETTING

- Possible response: The forces of nature found in the rural valley, such as the hills, the sunlight and shadows, the animals and wind, all serve to enhance the mood as it shifts from excitement into tension and finally into sadness.

- Possible response: The way that the characters interact with their surroundings reveals different aspects of their character. Carl appears silhouetted on the hill, establishing his austerity. Grandfather sits silently on the shaded porch, illustrating his

sadness. Jody hurries through his chores, demonstrating his excitement.

- Possible response: Yes, because the isolated, rural setting makes it more likely that the family would gather after dinner and entertain themselves with idle conversation. It is during this family time that Grandfather grates on Carl's nerves.

Unit 6 Resource Book
Graphic Organizer, p. 81

After Reading

MAKING CONNECTIONS

1. Possible responses: Jody: curious, mischievous, energetic, sincere, innocent. Carl Tiflin: strict, rigid, angry, impatient, cowardly. Mrs. Tiflin: understanding, protective, strict, forthright. Grandfather: gentle, kind, repetitive, sad, verbose.

2. Students will probably give Carl Tiflin poor ratings based on his interactions with both Grandfather and Jody. Mrs. Tiflin's rating will vary according to students' interpretation of her comments to Jody and her conflict with Carl, but will be higher.

3. Possible responses: He believes Grandfather, who dismisses the "new people" of the younger generation as having gone "soft." He hasn't yet been tested.

4. Answers will vary, but should include respect for authority, perceptiveness, curiosity, and a desire for approval.

5. Possible response: He hasn't the stomach for it after seeing how his father's cruelty hurt his grandfather.

6. Possible response: He sees his father reduce his grandfather's spirit, originally that of a "giant" leading a wagon train westward, to that of a confused and hurt old man. His grandfather is no longer bigger than life. He has become an ordinary man.

7. Answers might include the Depression, World War II, and the drought in the Dust Bowl, among others.

VOCABULARY STUDY

Answers will vary. Gestures should convey the following actions:

convene: coming together
emerge: coming out
mimic: imitating
peer: looking closely
sidle: moving sideways

Unit 6 Resource Book
Vocabulary, p. 91
Vocabulary Test, p. 94

WRITING CHOICES
Writer's Notebook Update

Have students write a second sentence that describes how the relationship might be affected by setting. (For example: Jody's father is strict because he has to keep the boy from getting hurt on the ranch.)

What I Want to Know

You might have students research the history of the frontier and attempt to provide answers to each other's questions.

Selection Test

Unit 6 Resource Book
pp. 95–96

Expressing Your Ideas ─────────

Writing Choices

Writer's Notebook Update Did the words you associated with different family relationships fit the Tiflin family? Enlarge and copy the following diagram into your notebook. On the arrows write **sentences** that explain how the characters relate to each other. A sample sentence is provided here.

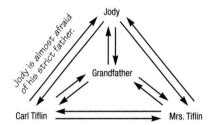

Jody

Jody is almost afraid of his strict father.

Grandfather

Carl Tiflin ←————————→ Mrs. Tiflin

What I Want to Know
If you could talk to Jody's grandfather about his experience, what would you ask him? Make a **list of questions** that you would ask about traveling across the country in a covered wagon.

Other Options

Read On With a partner, write an **annotated bibliography** of selected Steinbeck works. If possible, display a collection of his books in the classroom along with the bibliography.

At the Movies *The Red Pony,* from which "The Leader of the People" is taken, was made into a film. With a partner, view the film and **review** it orally for the class.

Campfire Conversation Study the William Ranney painting *The Old Scout's Tale.* What do you suppose they are discussing? Make up names for the characters in the painting and imagine a **conversation** that they might be having about the trip west. With a group of classmates perform the conversation for the rest of the class.

OTHER OPTIONS
Read On

You might suggest that students research the life of John Steinbeck, so that they can accompany their annotations with accompanying biographical references to the writer's life.

At the Movies

Suggest that students consider the following factors when they rate the film: screenplay adaptation, sets, casting, acting, photography, and musical score.

Campfire Conversation

Some students may prefer to do a visual comparison of this painting and the painting by Samuel Colman on page 683.

Before Reading

Lord Byron's Love Letter

by Tennessee Williams

Tennessee Williams
1911–1983

Because his traveling salesman father was away much of the time, Thomas Lanier Williams lived in Columbus, Mississippi, in the home of his maternal grandparents. Later, however, the family moved to St. Louis. The children had trouble adjusting to city life, and to their father who often drank and gambled. Thomas found an escape in writing. After graduating from college, he moved to New York to write professionally, publishing his works as "Tennessee" Williams, a name he chose because his paternal ancestors were some of the original settlers of Tennessee. Williams is best known for his plays, which are filled with Southern romantics who cannot adjust to the modern South.

Building Background

How Scandalous! Strikingly handsome, with a reputation for wickedness and free thought, the English Romantic poet Lord Byron embodied in his life and in his writings the figure subsequently known as the "Byronic hero": a moody, turbulent individual, self-exiled from society after exhausting all possibilities of human excitement, and tormented by remorse over secret sins committed in the past.

Enjoying his role as the favorite of London society, Byron gained the reputation of being one who was "mad, bad, and dangerous to know." He dressed as he felt a poet should and cultivated a deliberately mysterious air. After several love affairs, he married the nobly born, very proper Annabella Milbanke. After one year of marriage, his wife returned to her parents with their newborn daughter. The circumstances of the separation scandalized English society and led to Byron's decision, in 1816, to leave England for good. Byron went to Greece, where he committed his money and energies to the Greek's war of liberation from Turkish rule until his death from illness on April 19, 1824, at the age of thirty-six.

Literary Focus

Diction In *Lord Byron's Love Letter,* Tennessee Williams includes characters from different walks of life. One way that Williams contrasted these characters was through diction, his choice of words and phrases. As you read the play, notice the language used by each character.

Writer's Notebook

Fraud! A *con artist* is someone who gains a person's confidence and then swindles him or her out of money. For example, there are con artists who pose as tradesmen and prey on elderly homeowners by collecting money for making unnecessary home repairs. Preview the characters and the setting of *Lord Byron's Love Letter.* In your notebook predict which of the characters might be a con artist and what you think the "con" might involve.

Lord Byron's Love Letter   **689**

Before Reading

Building Background

Located in Louisiana on the east bank of the Mississippi, the city of New Orleans has expanded around its original site, the historic French Quarter. New Orleans attracts many tourists during Mardi Gras, the annual period of carnival which precedes Ash Wednesday and the subsequent fasting period of Lent. This play takes place during Mardi Gras.

Literary Focus

Remind students that characters' **diction** will vary according to:

- the audience they are addressing
- the topic of their discussion
- the effect the author wishes to create with their words

Writer's Notebook

Encourage students to keep a list of the sets and the props that the spinster and the old woman use to enact their "play-within-a-play."

More About Tennessee Williams

Williams won two Pulitzer Prizes in his career, for *A Streetcar Named Desire* in 1947 and for *Cat on a Hot Tin Roof* in 1955.

Other works
- *Orpheus Descending* (1957)
- *Night of the Iguana* (1961)

SUPPORT MATERIALS OVERVIEW

Unit 6 Resource Book
- Graphic Organizer, p. 97
- Study Guide, p. 98
- Vocabulary, p. 99
- Grammar, p. 100
- Alternate Check Test, p. 101
- Vocabulary Test, p. 102
- Selection Test, pp.103–104

Building English Proficiency
- Literature Summaries
- Activities, p. 221

Reading, Writing & Grammar SkillBook
- Vocabulary, pp. 7–8
- Reading, pp. 75–76
- Writing, pp. 121–122
- Grammar, Usage, and Mechanics, pp. 259–259

Technology
- Audiotape
- Personal Journal Software
- Custom Literature Database: For a collection of poems by Lord Byron, see the database.
- Test Generator Software

Selection Objectives

- To explore capitalization
- To identify and understand the literary function of diction
- To investigate plot and characterization
- To explore the commercial application of tradition

Unit 6 Resource Book
Study Guide, p. 98

Theme Link

Drawing on the romantic shock value of Lord Byron's bohemian tradition, a spinster and an old woman attempt to exploit a tourist by showing one of his love letters.

Vocabulary Preview

turbulent, stormy; tempestuous

exile, banish; force to leave one's country or home

ambiguous, having several possible interpretations; lacking definiteness

averted, turned away or turned aside

compel, drive or urge with force

suffuse, overspread

azure, the clear blue color of the unclouded sky

tranquil, calm; peaceful

stupor, a dazed condition

oblivious, not mindful; unaware

Students can add the words and definitions to their personal word lists in the Writer's Notebook.

LORD BYRON'S
Love Letter

TENNESSEE WILLIAMS

CHARACTERS

THE SPINSTER
THE OLD WOMAN
THE MATRON
THE HUSBAND

(SCENE: The parlor of a faded old residence in the French Quarter of New Orleans in the late nineteenth century. The shuttered doors of the room open directly upon the sidewalk and the noise of the Mardi Gras[1] festivities can be faintly distinguished. The interior is very dusky. Beside a rose-shaded lamp, the SPINSTER,[2] *a woman of forty, is sewing. In the opposite corner, completely motionless, the* OLD WOMAN *sits in a black silk dress. The doorbell tinkles.)*

SPINSTER *(rising).* It's probably someone coming to look at the letter.
OLD WOMAN *(rising on her cane).* Give me time to get out.
(She withdraws gradually behind the curtains. One of her claw-like hands remains visible, holding a curtain slightly open so that she can watch the visitors. The SPINSTER *opens the door and the* MATRON, *a middle-aged woman, walks into the room.)*
SPINSTER. Won't you come in?
MATRON. Thank you.

SPINSTER. You're from out of town?
MATRON. Oh, yes, we're all the way from Milwaukee. We've come for Mardi Gras, my husband and I. *(She suddenly notices a stuffed canary in its tiny pink cage.)* Oh, this poor little bird in such a tiny cage! It's much too small to keep a canary in!
SPINSTER. It isn't a live canary.
OLD WOMAN *(from behind the curtain).* No. It's stuffed.
MATRON. Oh. *(She self-consciously touches a stuffed bird on her hat.)* Winston is out there dilly-dallying on the street, afraid he'll miss the parade. The parade comes by here, don't it?
SPINSTER. Yes, unfortunately it does.
MATRON. I noticed your sign at the door. Is it true that you have one of Lord Byron's love letters?
SPINSTER. Yes.
MATRON. How very interesting! How did you get it?
SPINSTER. It was written to my grandmother, Irénée Marguerite de Poitevent.

---

1. **Mardi Gras** (mär′dē grä′), the last day before Lent; Shrove Tuesday. It is celebrated with parades and festivities.
2. **spinster** (spin′stər), *n.* an older, unmarried woman.

690   UNIT SIX: MODERN DILEMMAS

SELECTION SUMMARY

Lord Byron's Love Letter

A matronly tourist enters a dusky New Orleans apartment to see Lord Byron's love letter, which is advertised on the door. She is greeted by a spinster and an old woman who keeps herself hidden behind a curtain. The quirky hostesses acquaint the tourist with some of Byron's romantic adventures. The tourist calls her husband in from the street, where he has been waiting for the Mardi Gras parade. The spinster reads from the diary of her grandmother, which describes her love affair with Byron in Greece. After building the tourist's interest with poems and tales, the two women show her the envelope of the purported love letter. Before they can convince her to pay them for their show-and-tell act, the tourist rushes into the street after her husband, who is lured outside by the parade.

*For summaries in other languages, see the **Building English Proficiency** book.*

 Art Study

Audrey Flack's painting, *Truman's Teachers* (1964), was inspired by a magazine photograph. How might this painting portray the women differently than a photograph would?

Visual Literacy A pioneer in the Photo-Realistic painting movement of the 1960s, Audrey Flack often uses photographs as the source for her paintings. Here, the sun shines on her subjects, and they appear to be looking straight into a camera. Unlike some other Realists, Flack handles pigment in a painterly way. Her subjects "speak to [us] about the human condition."

Response to Caption Question The painter has emphasized the lines in their faces and the shadows on their torsos. The color has a softer, less realistic quality than do most photographs. A photograph could not show the foreground and background in such sharp focus.

Historical Note
1
Byron, Shelley, and Keats

Like Lord Byron, Percy Shelley was a great English Romantic poet whose radical philosophies forced him into exile. He drowned in the Italian Gulf of Spezia. Byron and another close friend cremated Shelley's body and buried it in the same Roman cemetery where John Keats, another well-known British Romantic poet, had been buried two years earlier.

MATRON. How very interesting! Where did she meet Lord Byron?

SPINSTER. On the steps of the Acropolis[3] in Athens.

MATRON. How very, very interesting! I didn't know that Lord Byron was ever in Greece.

SPINSTER. Lord Byron spent the final years of his turbulent[4] life in Greece.

OLD WOMAN *(still behind the curtains).* He was exiled[5] from England!

1 SPINSTER. Yes, he went into voluntary exile from England.

OLD WOMAN. Because of scandalous gossip in the Regent's court.

SPINSTER. Yes, involving his half-sister!

OLD WOMAN. It was false—completely.

SPINSTER. It was never confirmed.

OLD WOMAN. He was a passionate man but not an evil man.

---

3. **Acropolis** (ə krop′ə lis), the high, fortified part of Athens on which the Parthenon was built.
4. **turbulent** (tėr′byə lənt), stormy; tempestuous.
5. **exile** (eg′zīl), *v.* banish; force to leave one's country or home.

Lord Byron's Love Letter   **691**

BUILDING ENGLISH PROFICIENCY

Improving Comprehension

The following activity will help students read details for information at the outset of the play.

- Ask students to divide into two groups and read pages 690–691 together. Next, have them list three questions they have about the characters, setting, or situation.

- Have the groups exchange questions. Ask them to use their skills at predicting—and their imaginations—to come up with answers to the questions that they receive.

Group 1's Questions	Group 2's Answers
Why is Lord Byron so important to the spinster?	
Why does the old woman speak from behind the curtain?	

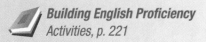 *Building English Proficiency* Activities, p. 221

Characterization

Question How does the author use the device of repetition to characterize the matron? (*Possible response: She keeps saying, "How very interesting," perhaps for want of anything better to say, perhaps because she is easily impressed or gullible, perhaps because she is looking for a "literary" souvenir of her trip to New Orleans.*)

Dialogue

Point out that a playwright must rely on dialogue to convey conflict between the characters.

Questions

- How would you describe the old woman's tone of voice? (*Possible responses: impatient, frustrated, anxious*)

- What does her warning to the spinster suggest about their motives? (*Possible responses: that they do not want to give too much away; that they are trying to trick the matron into something*)

SPINSTER. Morals are such ambiguous[6] matters, I think.

MATRON. Won't the lady behind the curtains come in?

SPINSTER. You'll have to excuse her. She prefers to stay out.

MATRON (*stiffly*). Oh, I see. What was Lord Byron doing in Greece, may I ask?

OLD WOMAN (*proudly*). Fighting for Freedom!

SPINSTER. Yes, Lord Byron went to Greece to join the force that fought against the infidels.[7]

OLD WOMAN. He gave his life in defense of the universal cause of freedom!

MATRON. What was that, did she say?

SPINSTER (*repeating automatically*). He gave his life in defense of the universal cause of freedom.

MATRON. Oh, how very interesting!

OLD WOMAN. Also he swam the Hellespont.[8]

SPINSTER. Yes.

OLD WOMAN. And burned the body of the poet Shelley, who was drowned in a storm on the Mediterranean with a volume of Keats in his pocket!

MATRON (*incredulously*). Pardon?

SPINSTER (*repeating*). And burned the body of the poet Shelley who was drowned in a storm on the Mediterranean with a volume of Keats in his pocket.

MATRON. Oh. How very, very interesting! Indeed, I'd like so much to have my husband hear it. Do you mind if I just step out for a moment to call him in?

SPINSTER. Please do.

2 (*The* MATRON *steps out quickly, calling, "Winston! Winston!"*)

OLD WOMAN (*poking her head out for a moment*). Watch them carefully! Keep a sharp eye on them!

SPINSTER. Yes. Be still.

(*The* MATRON *returns with her* HUSBAND *who has been drinking and wears a paper cap sprinkled with confetti.*)

MATRON. Winston, remove that cap. Sit down on the sofa. These ladies are going to show us Lord Byron's love letter.

SPINSTER. Shall I proceed?

MATRON. Oh, yes. This—uh—is my husband— Mr. Tutwiler.

SPINSTER (*coldly*). How do you do.

MATRON. I am *Mrs.* Tutwiler.

SPINSTER. Of course. Please keep your seat.

MATRON (*nervously*). He's been—celebrating a little.

OLD WOMAN (*shaking the curtain that conceals her*). Ask him please to be careful with his cigar.

SPINSTER. Oh, that's all right, you may use this bowl for your ashes.

OLD WOMAN. Smoking is such an unnecessary habit!

HUSBAND. Uh!

MATRON. This lady was telling us how her grandmother happened to meet Lord Byron. In Italy, wasn't it?

SPINSTER. No.

OLD WOMAN (*firmly*). In Greece, in Athens, on the steps of the Acropolis! We've mentioned that *twice*, I believe. Ariadne, you may read them a passage from the journal first.

SPINSTER. Yes.

OLD WOMAN. But please be careful what you choose to read! **3**

(*The* SPINSTER *has removed from the secretary a volume wrapped in tissue and tied with ribbon.*)

SPINSTER. Like many other young American girls of that day and this, my grandmother went to Europe.

OLD WOMAN. The year before she was going to be presented to society!

MATRON. How old was she?

OLD WOMAN. Sixteen! Barely sixteen! She was very beautiful too! Please show her the picture, show these people the picture! It's in the front of the journal.

(*The* SPINSTER *removes the picture from the book and*

---

6. **ambiguous** (am bigʹyŭ əs), having several possible interpretations; lacking definiteness.
7. **infidel** (inʹfə dəl), *n.* person who does not accept a particular faith.
8. **Hellespont** (helʹi spont), ancient name for the Dardanelles, the strait in Northwest Turkey which connects the Sea of Marmara with the Aegean Sea.

MINI-LESSON: VOCABULARY

Recognize Multi-meaning Words

Teach Direct students' attention to the following sentence on page 692: *The Spinster has removed a volume wrapped in tissue from the secretary.*

Explain that since some words have more than one meaning, it is necessary to judge a word's meaning by its context.

Questions

- What is the meaning of the word *secretary* in this context? (*Response: a desk with a small bookcase on top*)

- What is another possible meaning of this word? (*Response: a person employed to execute the administrative affairs of a business or organization*)

Activity Idea Have students find other multi-meaning words that appear in the selection. (Examples: *passage*, p. 692; *journal*, p. 692) _hands it to the_ MATRON.)

MATRON (_taking a look_). What a lovely young girl. (_Passing it to her_ HUSBAND.) Don't you think it resembles Agnes a little?

HUSBAND. Uh!

4 OLD WOMAN. Watch out! Ariadne, you'll have to _watch_ the man. I believe he's been drinking. I _do_ believe that he's been——

HUSBAND (_truculently_). Yeah? What is she saying back there?

MATRON (_touching his arm warningly_). Winston! Be quiet.

SPINSTER (_quickly_). Near the end of her tour, my grandmother and her aunt went to Greece, to study the classic remains of the oldest civilization.

OLD WOMAN (_correcting_). The oldest _European_ civilization.

SPINSTER. It was an early morning in April of the year eighteen hundred and——

OLD WOMAN. Twenty-seven!

SPINSTER. Yes. In my grandmother's journal she mentions——

OLD WOMAN. Read it, read it, _read_ it.

MATRON. Yes, _please_ read it to us.

SPINSTER. I'm trying to find the place, if you'll just be patient.

5 MATRON. Certainly, excuse me. (_She punches her_ HUSBAND _who is nodding._) Winston!

SPINSTER. Ah, here it is.

OLD WOMAN. Be _careful!_ Remember where to _stop_ at, Ariadne!

SPINSTER. Shhh! (_She adjusts her glasses and seats herself by the lamp._) "We set out early that morning to inspect the ruins of the Acropolis. I know I shall never forget how extraordinarily pure the atmosphere was that morning. It seemed as though the world were not very old, but very, very young, almost as though the world had been newly created. There was a taste of earliness in the air, a feeling of freshness, exhilarating my senses, exalting my spirit. How shall I tell you, dear Diary, the way the sky looked? It was almost as though I had moistened the tip of

my pen in a shallow bowl full of milk, so delicate was the blue in the dome of the heavens. The sun was barely up yet, a tentative breeze disturbed the ends of my scarf, the plumes of the marvelous hat which I had bought in Paris and thrilled me with pride whenever I saw them reflected! The papers that morning, we read them over our coffee before we left the hotel, had spoken of possible war, but it seemed unlikely, unreal: nothing was real, indeed, but the spell of golden antiquity and rose-colored romance that breathed from this fabulous city." **6**

OLD WOMAN. Skip that part! Get on to where she meets him!

SPINSTER. Yes . . . (_She turns several pages and continues._) "Out of the tongues of ancients, the lyrical voices of many long-ago poets who dreamed of the world of ideals, who had in their hearts the pure and absolute image—"

OLD WOMAN. _Skip_ that part! Slip down to where——

SPINSTER. Yes! _Here! Do_ let us manage without any more _interruptions!_ "The carriage came to a halt at the foot of the hill and my aunt, not being too well——"

OLD WOMAN. She had a sore throat that morning.

SPINSTER. "—preferred to remain with the driver while I undertook the rather steep climb on foot. As I ascended the long and crumbling flight of old stone steps——"

OLD WOMAN. Yes, yes, that's the place! (_The_ SPINSTER _looks up in annoyance. The_ OLD WOMAN's _cane taps impatiently behind the curtains._) Go on, Ariadne!

SPINSTER. "I could not help observing continually above me a man who walked with a barely perceptible limp—"

OLD WOMAN (_in hushed wonder_). Yes—Lord Byron!

SPINSTER. "—and as he turned now and then to observe beneath him the lovely Panorama——"

OLD WOMAN. Actually he was watching the girl behind him.

SPINSTER. (_sharply_). Will you please let me finish!

Lord Byron's Love Letter **693**

---

4 Literary Element
Allusion

Explain that the spinster's name alludes to a figure from Greek mythology. Ariadne, the daughter of King Minos, helped the hero Theseus find his way through the labyrinth and kill the Minotaur. Theseus married her but soon deserted her.

Question What is this an appropriate name for the spinster? (_Possible responses: She is capitalizing on her supposed connection to Lord Byron, who supposedly wooed her grandmother on the steps of the Acropolis in Greece. Being a spinster, perhaps she has also been deserted. These two women are leading the matron through a kind of whimsical labyrinth._)

5 Literary Element
Recognizing Farce

Explain that farce is a comedic form in which ridiculous, often stereotyped characters get into farfetched situations and create humor through slapstick and clowning.

Question What aspects of the husband's character lend a farcical element to the play? (_Possible responses: the cap and the confetti, his drunkenness, the fact that he is nodding off, his grunted responses_)

6 Literary Focus
Diction

Question How would you describe the diction of the grandmother's diary? (_Possible response: It is flowery, verbose, poetic, and childishly romantic._)

BUILDING ENGLISH PROFICIENCY

Making Personal Connections

ESL
LEP
ELD
SAE
LD

Help students relate a young girl's excitement in meeting Lord Byron to meeting a present-day celebrity.

• Ask students to meet in groups and share stories of meetings with celebrities. If they never have met anyone famous, ask them to name a celebrity they would like to meet and then fantasize a meeting. (Invite group members to ask questions that might fill in details.)

• Have students begin to fill out a chart like the one shown. (Make sure they include the surprise ending on page 696.)

	Meeting Byron	Meeting (Celebrity)
Time/Place		
Things Said		
Actions		
Results		

Question How would you describe the relationship between the spinster and the old woman? *(Possible response: The old woman is in control, and her aggressive behavior agitates and confuses the spinster.)*

8 Literary Element
Stage Directions

Explain that stage directions not only help the performers to interpret their roles, but also provide the reader with clues to understanding the plot.

Questions

- How does the direction for the old woman to speak *hoarsely* change the mood? *(Possible response: Her passion adds an element of rising suspense to the spinster's reading.)*
- How does the image of her "bony fingers" and hand "widening the aperture" of the curtain affect the plot? *(Possible response: It suggests that in her excitement she is forgetting to maintain the barrier between herself and the Tutwilers.)*

9 Reading/Thinking Skills
Infer

Question Why do the spinster and the old woman refuse to read the rest of the journal? *(Possible responses: It describes intimate romantic relations between the diarist and Lord Byron. It does not contain any reference to Lord Byron. They want to move on to the point where they can collect some money.)*

(There is no answer from behind the curtains, and she continues to read.) "I was irresistibly impressed by the unusual nobility and refinement of his features!"

(She turns a page.)

OLD WOMAN. The handsomest man that ever walked the earth!

(She emphasizes the speech with three slow but loud taps of her cane.)

SPINSTER *(flurriedly)*. "The strength and grace of his throat, like that of a statue, the classic outlines of his profile, the sensitive lips and the slightly dilated nostrils, the dark lock of hair that fell down over his forehead in such a way that——"

OLD WOMAN *(tapping her cane rapidly)*. Skip that, it goes on for pages!

SPINSTER. ". . . When he had reached the very summit[9] of the Acropolis he spread out his arms in a great, magnificent gesture like a young god. Now, thought I to myself, Apollo[10] has come to earth in modern dress."

OLD WOMAN. Go on, skip that, get on to where she *meets* him!

SPINSTER. "Fearing to interrupt his poetic trance, I slackened[11] my pace and pretended to watch the view. I kept my look thus carefully averted[12] until the narrowness of the steps compelled[13] me to move close by him."

OLD WOMAN. Of course he pretended not to see she was coming!

SPINSTER. "Then finally I faced him."

OLD WOMAN. Yes!

SPINSTER. "Our eyes came together!"

OLD WOMAN. Yes! Yes! That's the part!

SPINSTER. "A thing which I don't understand had occurred between us, a flush as of recognition swept through my whole being! Suffused[14] my——"

OLD WOMAN. Yes . . . Yes, that's the part!

SPINSTER. "'Pardon me,' he exclaimed, 'you have dropped your glove!' And indeed to my surprise I found that I had, and as he returned it to me, his fingers ever so lightly pressed the cups of my palm."

694 UNIT SIX: MODERN DILEMMAS

OLD WOMAN *(hoarsely)*. Yes!

(Her bony fingers clutch higher up on the curtain, the other hand also appears, slightly widening the aperture.)

SPINSTER. "Believe me, dear Diary, I became quite faint and breathless, I almost wondered if I could continue my lonely walk through the ruins. Perhaps I stumbled, perhaps I swayed a little. I leaned for a moment against the side of a column. The sun seemed terribly brilliant, it hurt my eyes. Close behind me I heard that voice again, almost it seemed I could feel his breath on my——"

OLD WOMAN. Stop *there!* That will be quite enough!

(The SPINSTER closes the journal.)

MATRON. Oh, is that all?

OLD WOMAN. There's a great deal more that's not to be read to people.

MATRON. Oh.

SPINSTER. I'm sorry. I'll show you the letter.

MATRON. How nice! I'm dying to see it! Winston? *Do sit up!*

(He has nearly fallen asleep. The SPINSTER produces from the cabinet another small packet which she unfolds. It contains the letter. She hands it to the MATRON, who starts to open it.)

OLD WOMAN. Watch out, watch *out*, that woman can't *open* the letter!

SPINSTER. No, no, please, you mustn't. The contents of the letter are strictly private. I'll hold it over here at a little distance so you can see the writing.

OLD WOMAN. Not too close, she's holding up her glasses!

(The MATRON quickly lowers her lorgnette.)

SPINSTER. Only a short while later Byron was killed.

MATRON. How did he die?

---

9. **summit** (sum′it), *n.* the highest point; top.
10. **Apollo** (ə pol′ō), the Greek god of the sun. Apollo was considered the highest type of youthful, manly beauty.
11. **slacken** (slak′ən), *v.* become slower.
12. **averted** (ə vėrt′əd), *adj.* turned away or turned aside.
13. **compel** (kəm pel′), *v.* drive or urge with force.
14. **suffuse** (sə fyüz′), *v.* overspread.

MINI-LESSON: LITERARY FOCUS

Diction

Teach Have students analyze the following passage from page 694:

"Fearing to interrupt his poetic trance, I slackened my pace and pretended to watch the view. I kept my look thus carefully averted until the narrowness of the steps compelled me to move close by him."

Explain that the author could have expressed this idea in any number of different ways but none would not have created the same effect.

Question How does the diary's elaborate diction affect the matron? *(Response: She gets even more caught up in the romance.)*

Activity Idea Have students rewrite this passage using less formal language. *(Possible example: I didn't want to snap him out of his daydream, so I backed off and looked away. I tried to keep my distance, but the steps were so narrow that I had to squeeze by him.)*

◄ Does the style of Sandra Burshell's 1994 pastel, *Tranquil Corner,* match the atmosphere of the parlor in the play? Why or why not?

MATRON. Tch-tch-tch! How dreadful! I think that was foolish of her.
(The cane taps furiously behind the curtains.) **10**
SPINSTER. You don't understand. When a life is completed, it ought to be put away. It's like a sonnet. When you've written the final couplet, why go on any further? You only destroy the part that's already written!
OLD WOMAN. Read them a poem, the sonnet your grandmother wrote to the memory of Lord Byron.
SPINSTER. Would you be interested?
MATRON. We'd adore it—truly!
SPINSTER. It's called "Enchantment."
MATRON *(she assumes a rapt[15] expression).* Aahhh!
SPINSTER *(reciting).*

Un saison enchanté! I mused, Beguiled
Seemed Time herself, her erstwhile errant ways
Briefly forgotten, she stayed here and smiled,
Caught in a net of blue and golden days.

OLD WOMAN. Not blue and golden—gold and *azure*[16] days!
SPINSTER.

Caught in a net—of gold and azure days! **11**

But I lacked wit to see how lightly shoon
Were Time and you, to vagrancy so used——

---

15. **rapt** (rapt), *adj.* so busy thinking of or enjoying one thing that one does not know what else is happening.
16. azure (azh′ər), *adj.* the clear blue color of the unclouded sky.

OLD WOMAN. He was killed in action, defending the cause of freedom!
(This is uttered so strongly the HUSBAND *starts.)*
SPINSTER. When my grandmother received the news of Lord Byron's death in battle, she retired from the world and remained in complete seclusion for the rest of her life.

Lord Byron's Love Letter   **695**

Art Study

Visual Literacy   Sandra Burshell, who lives in Louisiana, is known for her moody, dimly lit "roomscapes." She has said that when looking for a subject, she searches for the opportunity to work with "chiaroscoro," the interplay between light and shadow.

Response to Caption Question   Most students will agree that the dark gentility of the painting does match the atmosphere of the play.

10 Reading/Thinking Skills
Recognize Implications

Question   Why does the old woman become furious at this remark? *(Possible responses: She is so emotionally attached to the story that she cannot bear criticism of any aspect of it. She identifies completely with anyone who wants to remain in seclusion. Perhaps she is annoyed by the tourists' resistance to her scheme.)*

11 Literary Focus
Diction

Explain that the old woman's correction is based on diction. Discuss how the word *azure* creates a different effect than the word *blue.*

BUILDING ENGLISH PROFICIENCY

Analyzing Key Statements

On page 695 the spinster says to the matron,
"You don't understand. When a life is completed, it ought to be put away."
Help students focus on this key statement.

• Point out the irony in the statement. Explain that an ironic statement says one thing but means another. Ask: What might the spinster really mean? *(Possibly that she is tired of telling the story or that she wishes that she could be free of the past.)*

• Invite students to compare the matron and the spinster. As part of the discussion, invite students to share their knowledge about the roles that married and unmarried women played in the past and play today.

12 Reading/Thinking Skills
Compare and Contrast

Compare the mood created by the sonnet to that of the passing parade.

Question How does the author use simile to emphasize this contrast? *(Possible response: He suggests that the parade breaks the spell of the sonnet, which is emotionally transporting the old woman to the distant past.)*

13 Reading/Thinking Skills
Draw Conclusions

Explain that there are two ways to interpret this last sentence:

- the letter is really from Lord Byron, who is Ariadne's grandfather, and the old woman, Ariadne's grandmother, is his aged paramour.
- the letter is a fake, from Ariadne's actual grandfather, and the old woman and the spinster created this elaborate hoax to extort money from gullible romantics like the matron.

Question How do you interpret the ending? *(Answers will vary.)*

Check Test

1. Why are the tourists visiting New Orleans? *(to experience Mardi Gras)*

2. Who is sitting behind the curtain? *(the old woman)*

3. Why does the husband keep falling asleep? *(He's had too much to drink.)*

4. According to the spinster, where did her grandmother meet Lord Byron? *(on the steps of the Acropolis)*

5. Does the matron pay the spinster and the old woman their fee for displaying the letter? *(no)*

Unit 6 Resource Book
Alternate Check Test, p. 101

696

(The OLD WOMAN *begins to accompany in a hoarse undertone. Faint band music can be heard.)*

That by the touch of one October moon
From summer's tranquil[17] spell you might be
   loosed!

OLD WOMAN *(rising stridently with intense feeling above the* SPINSTER'S *voice).*

Think you love is writ on my soul with chalk,
To be washed off by a few parting tears?

Then you know not with what slow step I walk.
The barren way of those hibernal years—

My life a vanished interlude, a shell
Whose walls are your first kiss—and last
   farewell!

(The band, leading the parade, has started down the street, growing rapidly louder. It passes by like the heedless, turbulent years. The HUSBAND, *roused from his stupor,[18] lunges to the door.)*

12 MATRON. What's that, what's that? The *parade?*
(The HUSBAND *slaps the paper cap on his head and rushes for the door.)*
HUSBAND *(at the door).* Come on, Mama, you'll miss it!
SPINSTER *(quickly).* We usually accept—you understand?—a small sum of money, just anything that you happen to think you can spare.
OLD WOMAN. Stop him! He's gone outside!
(The HUSBAND *has escaped to the street. The band blares through the door.)*
SPINSTER *(extending her hand).* Please—a dollar . . .

OLD WOMAN. *Fifty cents!*
SPINSTER. Or a *quarter!*
MATRON *(paying no attention to them).* Oh, my goodness—Winston! He's *disappeared* in the crowd! Winston—*Winston! Excuse* me! *(She rushes out onto the door sill.)* Winston! Oh, my goodness gracious, he's off again!
SPINSTER *(quickly).* We usually accept a little money for the display of the letter. Whatever you feel that you are able to give. As a matter of fact it's all that we have to *live* on!
OLD WOMAN *(loudly).* One dollar!
SPINSTER. Fifty cents—or a quarter!
MATRON *(oblivious,[19] at the door).* Winston! *Winston!* Heavenly days. *Good-bye!*
(She rushes out on the street. The SPINSTER *follows to the door and shields her eyes from the light as she looks after the* MATRON. *A stream of confetti is tossed through the doorway into her face. Trumpets blare. She slams the door shut and bolts it.)*
SPINSTER. Canaille! . . . Canaille!
OLD WOMAN. Gone? Without paying? *Cheated* us? *(She parts the curtains.)*
SPINSTER. *Yes*—the *canaille!*[20]
(She fastidiously plucks the thread of confetti from her shoulder. The OLD WOMAN *steps from behind the curtain, rigid with anger.)*
OLD WOMAN. Ariadne, my letter! You've dropped **13** my letter! Your grandfather's letter is lying on the floor!

---

17. tranquil (trang′kwəl), *adj.* calm; peaceful.
18. stupor (stü′pər), *n.* a dazed condition.
19. oblivious (ə bliv′ē əs), *adj.* not mindful; unaware.
20. canaille (kə nēl′), riffraff, scoundrel.

MINI-LESSON: GRAMMAR
Capitalization of Names and Places

Teach Remind students that proper nouns and proper adjectives must be capitalized. Look over the chart at the right.

Question Can you suggest a proper adjective for Acropolis? *(Response: There really isn't one, although Acropolis-like could suffice.)*

Activity Idea Have students look through this and other selections and find other examples of common and proper nouns and proper adjectives that would complete the chart.

Common Noun	Proper Noun	Proper Adjective
country	Greece	Grecian
city	Athens	Athenian
man	Lord Byron	Byronic
sea	Mediterranean	Mediterranean
temple	Acropolis	

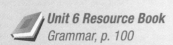
Unit 6 Resource Book
Grammar, p. 100

After Reading

Making Connections

Shaping Your Response

1. Poll the class to see who believes the letter was from Lord Byron and who believes it was a fake. Ask your classmates to explain their opinions.

2. If you could have a part in this play, which would you choose? Why?

Analyzing the Play

3. What do you think the curtain that the old woman hides behind **symbolizes?**

4. Notice the **diction** in the play. Whose words are the most poetic? Whose are the least poetic?

5. How would you describe the **characters** of the spinster and the old woman?

6. How would you **characterize** the Tutwilers?

7. Ariadne calls Mrs. Tutwiler a *canaille,* or scoundrel. Who do *you* think is a *canaille* in this play, and why?

Extending the Ideas

8. Lord Byron was a romantic hero in his day. He was handsome, athletic, artistic, and notorious. Describe someone you would consider to be a contemporary romantic hero.

Vocabulary Study

Choose the response that best answers the question or completes the sentence.

azure
stupor
exile
suffuse
averted
turbulent
ambiguous
compel
tranquil
oblivious

1. What might the old woman describe as *azure?*

   a. Lord Byron's hair   **b.** the Grecian sky   **c.** clumps of grass

2. Mr. Tutwiler was in a *stupor.* Which word best describes his state?

   a. tranquil   **b.** turbulent   **c.** oblivious

3. A *tranquil* home would be:

   a. peaceful and calm   **b.** buzzing with excitement   **c.** untidy

4. Lord Byron chose to *exile* himself from England and would never ____.

   a. leave   **b.** complain   **c.** return

5. You can tell that Mr. Tutwiler is *oblivious* to the conversation, because he:

   a. likes parades   **b.** pays no attention   **c.** despises Lord Byron

6. Which of the following would definitely <u>not</u> be described as *turbulent?*

   a. the parade   **b.** the old woman's mood
   c. Mr. Tutwiler's interest in the letter

Lord Byron's Love Letter   **697**

After Reading

MAKING CONNECTIONS

1. Answers will vary. Students should back up their opinions with supporting details based on characterization, dialogue, and plot.

2. Answers will vary. More students might choose the old woman because, although she sits behind the curtain, she has the most intriguing character.

3. Possible response: The curtain symbolizes the barrier between her fantasy world of Romantic poets and love affairs and the reality of her present circumstances.

4. Possible response: The young diarist's words are the most poetic. The wife's speech is very pedestrian and her husband is almost completely inarticulate.

5. Possible response: The spinster is rigid and politely cold; the old woman is outspoken, aggressive, and passionate.

6. Possible response: The Tutwilers are not very bright, are flighty, and self-interested.

7. Answers will vary. Some students may find the old woman a scoundrel for trying to pull off this scheme. Others might find the husband a scoundrel for being so rude and disinterested. Some might say Mrs. Tutwiler is the *canaille* for not giving the ladies something for their elaborate show.

8. Students may choose actors or musical performers to represent their idea of a modern hero.

VOCABULARY STUDY

1. b

2. c

3. a

4. c

5. b

6. c

7. a

8. b

9. a

10. c

Unit 6 Resource Book
Vocabulary, p. 99
Vocabulary Test, p. 102

7. The ladies may have noticed Mrs. Tutwiler ____ with embarrassment at her husband's behavior.

   a. *suffuse* **b.** *averted* **c.** *compel*

8. The young woman glimpsed Lord Byron through ____ eyes.

   a. *suffuse* **b.** *averted* **c.** *compel*

9. An *ambiguous* message is:

   a. unclear **b.** clear **c.** silent

10. The best synonym for "force" is:

    a. *suffuse* **b.** *averted* **c.** *compel*

Expressing Your Ideas

Writing Choices

Writer's Notebook Update Imagine that the police received a complaint about the two women, and a police officer had to visit them to check out the situation. Write a scene for the three characters expressing what you think might be said in such a confrontation.

Williams at His Best Either read a copy of *The Glass Menagerie* by Tennessee Williams, or watch a videotape of the movie adaptation. Write a **comparison** of it and *Lord Byron's Love Letter.*

More About Lord Byron The Building Background article preceding the play provides a brief biography of Lord Byron. To round out your knowledge of this romantic poet, research his life and write your own **biographical account.**

Other Options

In His Own Words Although the play is titled *Lord Byron's Love Letter,* the audience doesn't hear one word written by Lord Byron. Work with a small group of students and read some of Lord Byron's poetry or letters. Practice reading them aloud, and then present an **oral interpretation** of them to the class.

Tourist Trap Imagine that the New Orleans Chamber of Commerce has gotten complaints about the old woman and the spinster for running a "scam." Would you as a chamber member vote to allow them to continue their business or put a stop to it? Choose your position, prepare an **oral argument,** and present your argument to the class.

The Play's the Thing Plays are meant to be performed, not read silently. Work with a small group of students and perform *Lord Byron's Love Letter.* Depending on the available recording equipment and class time, produce either a live **performance,** a videotaped production, or an audiotaped "radio play."

OTHER OPTIONS

In His Own Words

A number of Byron's poems can be found on the database that accompanies this book. Students might also find good examples in the following books:

- Bloom, Harold, ed., *George Gordon, Lord Byron* (1986)
- Marchand, Leslie, ed. *Lord Byron: Selected Letters and Journals* (1984)

Tourist Trap

Ask students to recall their own experiences with hoaxes, pretenses, and practical jokes. Do they feel that they should have been protected from these situations by the law? Or do they feel in retrospect that the experiences are worthwhile either as lessons or as adventures?

The Play's the Thing

Encourage students to provide themselves with sets and props that approximate those that are outlined in the stage directions, for example, a makeshift curtain, a cane, an envelope, a volume that resembles a diary, confetti, and a party hat.

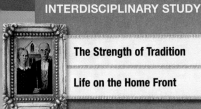

The Strength of Tradition

Life on the Home Front

History Connection

World War II began for the United States on December 7, 1941, when Japan attacked Pearl Harbor. The war's effects on Americans at home were as diverse as the people themselves. The following pages relate some of these home front experiences.

New Opportunities for African Americans and Women

Sybil Lewis

The need for more industrial workers provided new and better paying jobs for many African Americans and women. Sybil Lewis details some of the economic and social changes of the time.

H ad it not been for the war I don't think blacks would be in the position they are now. The war and defense work gave black people opportunities to work on jobs they never had before. It gave them opportunity to do things they never experienced before.

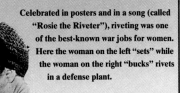

We Can Do It!

WAR PRODUCTION CO-ORDINATING COMMITTEE

Recruitment posters urged women to "roll up their sleeves" and join the work force to aid the war effort. By 1944 more than a third of the nation's workers were women.

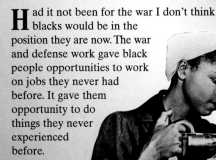

Celebrated in posters and in a song (called "Rosie the Riveter"), riveting was one of the best-known war jobs for women. Here the woman on the left "sets" while the woman on the right "bucks" rivets in a defense plant.

Interdisciplinary Study

Theme Link

The strength of tradition can be a powerful obstacle to social change. Sometimes, however, great historical events, such as war, force changes on society.

Curricular Connection: History

You can use this interdisciplinary study to explore the effects of World War II on people on the home front.

Terms to know

Victrola (vik trō′lə), trademark for an early phonograph

storm troopers, members of the private army formed by Adolf Hitler about 1923 and disbanded in 1934

troopship, (trüp′ship′), ship used to carry soldiers

Unit 6 Resource Book
Interdisciplinary Study Guide, p. 105

BUILDING ENGLISH PROFICIENCY

Making Real-Life Connections

The accounts on pages 699–703 shed light on some human aspects of World War II. You can introduce or expand upon these accounts by having students' relatives or people from the community share memories of their experiences with the class. You might wish to assemble a panel of people to field students' questions. Students might prepare questions such as these.

- How did you hear about the United States' entry into the war?
- How aware were you of the war's progress?
- Did you have relatives or friends who served overseas? What happened to them?
- What did you do for fun at home, especially given the wartime shortages?
- How did the war change your family's life? your own life?

Additional Background

Women in the Workplace Before World War II began, women made up about one-fourth of the American work force. Almost all the jobs were low-paying. When men went into the army, the jobs had to be filled and millions of women entered the work force.

Government policy provided equal pay for equal work, and women made tremendous strides toward achieving equality. When the war ended, many of the women returned to being housewives, and others were forced into lower-paying jobs. However, the advances made during the war were never lost entirely.

Rosie the Riveter Working women during World War II were hailed as Rosie the Riveter, or Rosie for short. The name came from a popular patriotic song, "Rosie the Riveter."

According to legend, the real Rosie was a riveter named Rosie Bonavita who hammered 3,345 rivets into a fighter plane's wing in six hours.

New Opportunites . . . Continued

They made more money and began to experience a different lifestyle. Their expectations changed. Money will do that. You could sense that they would no longer be satisfied with the way they had lived before.

When I got my first paycheck, I'd never seen that much money before, not even in the bank, because I'd never been in a bank too much. I don't recall exactly what it was in the aircraft plant, but it was more than three hundred dollars a month, and later, in the shipyard, it was even more.

To be able to buy what you wanted, your clothing and shoes, all this was just a different way of life.

When I first got my paycheck I bought everything that I thought I had ever wanted, but in particular I bought shoes. I wore a large size as a child and I could never be fitted properly for shoes. The woman I worked for in Oklahoma wore beautiful shoes, and I remember thinking then that when I got a chance to make some money I was going to buy shoes first. So my first paycheck I bought

mostly shoes. And it felt very good. To be honest, today I still buy more shoes than anything else.

Other experiences I had during the war were important, too, like having to rivet with a white farm girl from Arkansas and both of us having to relate to each other in ways that we had never experienced before. Although we had our differences we both learned to work together and talk together. We learned that despite our hostilities and resentments we could open up to each other and get along. As I look back

★ ★

CHILDREN OF THE HOME FRONT

SHERIL JANKOVSKY CUNNING

The world turned upside down for the children of the home front. Many of their families were broken up as fathers and older brothers went off to war. In the following excerpt Sheril Jankovsky Cunning talks about growing up during the war.

As a child growing up during the war in Long Beach, California, I lived constantly with the fear we might be invaded or bombed. We lived only three blocks from the beach,

and before the war started we would walk down there with our mother and play in the waves and sand. But during the war the whole coast was blocked off from civilian use. All along the bluffs, they set up giant antiaircraft artillery and camouflage netting which to a small child appeared to be several stories high. You couldn't see the ocean anymore. All you could see was the guns and camouflage.

We also had air raid alerts which made the possibility of invasion seem very real. Because Pearl Harbor had been bombed and California was the Pacific and close to the Japanese, we felt we could have a surprise air attack at any minute.

My father was the block air raid warden. I'll never forget the fear I felt as he went out during air raid alert and left the family huddled in the hallway. The sirens would go off, the searchlights would sweep the sky, and Daddy would don his gas mask and his big hard hat and goggles and go out to protect the neighborhood.

Although we had blackout curtains, my parents didn't really trust them not to leak light. So we sat in a hall closet with all the doors closed in order to be able to have the lights on. We had a wind-up Victrola which we'd take in there with us. My mother would sing to us to keep up our spirits. But we couldn't help being afraid for our father. And afraid for ourselves.

MINI-LESSON: STUDY SKILLS

Note Taking

Teach As students prepare for research assignments, review note-taking skills, reminding them that writing notes on index cards is a useful method that allows for the convenient ordering of ideas. Suggest that students keep in mind the following suggestions when they take notes.

- Record the source on each card.
- Write concisely, using abbreviations and symbols and leaving out unnecessary words.
- Paraphrase information, but be careful that ideas are accurate.
- Write direct quotes exactly and compare the notes with the original to ensure that the quotation is accurate.

Activity Idea Encourage students to choose one of the research topics suggested for this interdisciplinary study and concentrate on effective note-taking as they do the research. Have students use index cards and follow the guidelines suggested in this mini-lesson.

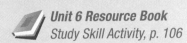

Unit 6 Resource Book
Study Skill Activity, p. 106

now I feel that experience was meaningful to me and meaningful to her. She learned that Negroes were people, too, and I saw her as a person also, and we both gained from it.

I also saw in California that black women were working in jobs that I had never seen in the South, not only defense work but working in nice hotels as waitresses, working in the post office, doing clerical work. So I realized there were a lot of things women could do besides housework. I saw black people accepted in the school system and accepted in other kinds of jobs that they had not been accepted in before. It's too bad it took a war to motivate people to move here to want to make more of their lives, but if it had not been for the war offering better jobs and opportunities, some people would have never left the South. They would have had nothing to move for.

After I graduated from college I returned to California and started applying for civil-service jobs. Had it not been for the war I probably would have ended up a schoolteacher in rural Oklahoma, but the impact of the war changed my life, gave me an opportunity to leave my small town and discover there was another way of life. It financed my college education and opened my eyes to opportunities I could take advantage of when the war was over.

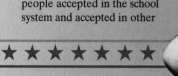

Our prime protector was out protecting someone else. It gave us the feeling of being abandoned. The searchlights and sirens struck great fear in our hearts and yet it was exciting.

Many of our games involved war themes. We made hideouts and plans (and alternate plans) in the event Long Beach would be invaded or bombed. My sister and I planned for situations in which we might be like the poor, starving children of Europe we saw in the news-reels, living without parents, in rags, in bombed-out buildings. We were convinced

Children participated wholeheartedly in supporting the nation's war effort by collecting recyclables such as scrap metal which eventually found its way into war machinery.

BUILDING ENGLISH PROFICIENCY

Linking Past and Present

As the photograph on page 701 shows, young people of the wartime era got involved in supporting the Allied cause. Challenge students to find out about a cause that they could be involved in today.

• As a class, brainstorm a list of challenges that the United States faces at home today such as children's rights or the fight against drug abuse.

• Have students choose two challenges, and then divide the class into two teams, one for each challenge. Ask each team to discuss how they, as high-school students, might support their cause.

• Have representatives from each team present a plan of action. Then work with students to follow through on one or two suggestions and to share the results.

Additional Background

Although Japanese Americans were forced to remain in internment camps during the war, President Roosevelt allowed Japanese Americans to serve in the U.S. armed forces. Thousands volunteered, and the 442nd Japanese American Regimental Combat Team was formed. The regiment served in Europe and was one of the most highly decorated combat units of the war.

In 1948, the Japanese American Evacuation Claims Act allowed $2,500 to individuals as compensation for their losses while they were in the camps.

In 1988, the Civil Liberties Act provided compensatory payments of $20,000 and an apology to surviving Japanese Americans who had been in the internment camps.

Research Topics

- The Japanese internment and relocation camps of World War II
- World War II posters encouraging support of the war effort
- The United Service Organization (USO)
- The War Production Board, scarcity at home, rationing, and restrictions on the manufacture of consumer goods
- Civil Liberties Act of 1988

Children . . . Continued

that if attacked only children would survive and all adults would be killed.

We had a back closet that we figured was the safest place in the house to hide in case of invasion. My mother stored all her old clothes in there in big rubber garment bags. We figured that nobody would find us behind those bags. But just in case they did, we kept a bottle of ketchup in the closet. We were going to douse ourselves with it and lie there as if we had already been bloodied and killed, so that they would walk away and not stick their bayonets into us.

What was funny is we always thought it would be the Germans who would invade. Although Japan was on the other side of that ocean out there in our front yard, we had very strong visions of storm troopers in big boots invading our shores. The Japanese were going to bomb us, but it was the Nazis who were going to open that closet door and see two little dead girls. I'm sure that came from the newsreels and *Life* magazine. *Life* came every week to deliver the war to our doorstep and replenish our fear.

The war also brought my first experience of death. I remember the day that we got the news that my cousin was killed when his troopship was torpedoed. Yet there were so many stories and movies around about someone coming back after being declared dead that I thought, Well, maybe they'll discover Jimmy alive someday. My mother tried to make me realize. "No, Jimmy is really dead. He was in the middle of the ocean. There isn't going to be any finding Jimmy." And I remember her crying, saying things like "He was so young, he never hurt anybody, and he never had a chance to grow up and be a man." It was a long time after the war before I gave up my hope that he would return.

JAPANESE AMERICANS ARE "RELOCATED"

HENRY MURAKAMI

In 1942, 110,000 people of Japanese ancestry were sent to internment camps across the western United States. In the following excerpt, Henry Murakami remembers the events endured by his family.

After Pearl Harbor we were ordered not to go out fishing. We put away all the nets, tied the boats, and all you had to do was stay home and watch what was going on. It was worse than terrible. You could do nothing. Day after day you just had to stay around the house, and that's all.

On February 11, I was outside the house, holding my year-and-a-half daughter in my arms. And a big flock of tall American men came around. One of them had a piece of paper in his hand, and he started asking me who lives where, where is this man, and so on. So I said, "What is this?" and he said, "We're just asking a few questions." I asked, "Is my name on the list?" And he asked, "What's your name?" So I told him. He was checking the names, and he found it. So right there he said, "You come with us for just a little while and you'll come right back." I called my wife and she came on the porch and I asked the FBI man if I could go in and put my shoes on. I had no socks, just Japanese slippers. And the FBI man said, "No, you don't need to change. You'll come right back." I believed what they said. I couldn't argue. So I handed the baby to my wife and I went with them.

They took us to the immigration office in San Pedro. We were there two days and two nights, then they put us all in old trains. Two days and two nights more we traveled. No window, all closed; you couldn't look outside. And suddenly the trains stopped and the guards said, "Get out." We came out, and all you could see was white, noth-

---

MINI-LESSON: TECHNOLOGY

Word Processing

Teach Discuss with students how they can use the full capabilities of their classroom computers in creating graphically interesting documents. Most programs include predesigned templates to aid in development of newsletters, reports, and other documents. These can all be customized, or entirely new templates can be developed.

Additionally, many programs allow for the creation of tables, charts, and diagrams. Drawing programs add the ability to create original artwork. These programs vary widely in sophistication and difficulty. Most programs also permit the importation of existing images from sources such as the World Wide Web and CD-ROM.

If your computers are equipped with a scanner, images existing in print media can be added to documents. Guide students in experimenting to learn the capabilities of their computers and software.

Activity Idea Challenge students to create customized documents and to incorporate charts, tables, photographs, and other graphic images into the reports and presentations they prepare for this interdisciplinary study.

This painting, *Boys With Kite* (1944), was created by the non-Japanese wife of a detainee who chose to accompany her husband into the relocation camps.

ing but white. You couldn't even see houses or buildings. Just snow. They said eight feet high. And we found out it was Bismarck, North Dakota, and it was twenty-nine degrees below zero, and I was walking on the snow in my bare feet and slippers.

They took us to Fort Lincoln, and we had to go to the mess hall where hundreds of people were standing in line. You know how hard it is to stand only fifteen or twenty minutes in cold like that? Within a week I had frostbite. I couldn't walk anymore.

Why? We hadn't done anything wrong. We obeyed the laws. None of us were spies. We didn't know anything about those things. But we were all arrested because we carried fishermen's licenses.

After I was at Fort Lincoln a few weeks I received a letter from my wife that she had

forty-eight hours' notice to evacuate from the island. She was eight months pregnant and there was nothing she could do. So she abandoned everything. Pregnant and with four children, how much could she carry? So she took the children and one suitcase and they all went to the camp the government had built at the Santa Anita Racetrack.

They were there about sixty days, then they were sent to Manzanar. In July I was sent to Manzanar and joined my family, and my new son who was born in May. And we were really joyous . . .

After the war I came back to California, but I couldn't fish anymore. I had no gear to start with. I had no money. How could I go back to fishing? None of the old Japanese fishermen ever went back.

My own loss I can say, was $55,000 or more. Minimum. In 1940 I bought three new sets of nets. One was for tuna, one for mackerel, and one for sardines. The mackerel and sardine nets each cost $15,000; the tuna net cost about $25,000, because it had all heavyweight webbings. I worked so hard to pay for them. I bought everything by cash. I didn't like that credit business.

Each of the nets we kept in a big flatbed truck on the street where we lived. The day I was arrested I saw with my own eyes my three sets of nets sitting on the flatbeds. I saw them. When we were sent to Fort Lincoln I asked the FBI men about my nets. They said, "Don't worry. Everything is going to be taken care of." But I never saw the nets again, nor my brand-new 1941 Plymouth, nor our furniture. It all just disappeared. I lost everything. But I don't blame anyone. It was a war. We had nothing to do with the war, but we were its victims.

Responding
1. How were the experiences of the individuals similar? Different?

2. How do you think wartime experiences affected the lives of women, African Americans, and Japanese Americans after the war?

Responding

1. Possible response For all, the war brought great changes. For some the changes were positive, providing great opportunities. For others, the effects of the war were a realization of the meaning of war and death. For many Japanese Americans, the effects were devastating, as they lost their possessions and most of their civil liberties.

2. Possible response Students' responses may reflect the idea that once changes begin to occur, the effects can never be completely reversed.

Interdisciplinary Activity Ideas

- Have students work in groups to examine the effect of World War II on minorities at home and in the armed forces. Students might look at the impact of the war on Japanese Americans, African Americans, and Native Americans. Urge students to investigate both the positive and negative effects.

- Challenge students to investigate daily life on the home front in their communities during World War II. Students might interview grandparents and other relatives or neighbors, read about daily events reported in newspapers from the time, or gather information from local museums and historical societies. Have students work together to prepare a multimedia presentation of their findings.

BUILDING ENGLISH PROFICIENCY

Drawing Conclusions

The World War II era sometimes is remembered with nostalgia. Help students understand that it also was a time when the difficulties and horrors of war were evident.

- Begin a semantic web for the word *war*.
- Have students reread the personal accounts on pages 699–703 to look for underlying fears, difficulties, and personal pain, and have them enter these ideas on their webs.
- Have groups of students draw conclusions

about war from the four personal accounts, giving special attention to conclusions that two or more accounts share.

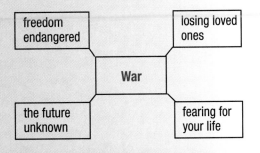

freedom endangered — War — losing loved ones

the future unknown — War — fearing for your life

Writing Workshop

WRITER'S BLUEPRINT
Specs

The Specs in the Writer's Blueprint address these writing and thinking skills:

- Identifying opposing points of view
- comparing and contrasting
- using quotations from literature
- connecting literature to life experience
- summarizing
- making judgments
- punctuating quotations correctly

These Specs serve as your lesson objectives, and they form the basis for the **Assessment Criteria Specs** for a superior paper, which appear on the final TE page for this lesson. You might want to read through the Assessment Criteria Specs with students when you begin the lesson.

Linking Literature to Writing

Lead a discussion about differing points of view as reflected in the literature. Have students summarize or read aloud examples from the selections.

The Strength of Tradition

Expository Writing

Writing Workshop

Point-Counterpoint

Assignment Write an essay in which you compare and contrast differing points of view about the same issue, based on one of the selections in this part of the unit.

WRITER'S BLUEPRINT

Product	A comparison/contrast essay
Purpose	To analyze and evaluate differing points of view
Audience	People who've read the literature
Specs	To write a successful essay, you should:

❑ Choose one of these topics:

— differing points of view about fences and neighbors in "Mending Wall"

— differing points of view about the law in "The Tall Men" (for example, the investigator's and the deputy's)

— another topic of your choice involving differing points of view, drawn from one of the selections

❑ Begin your paper by identifying the issue and describing the two differing points of view in the selection that you've chosen to deal with. Use quotations to illustrate each point of view. Take care to signal comparisons and contrasts.

❑ Go on to discuss your own reactions to each point of view. Illustrate your reactions with specific examples from experiences in your own life.

❑ Conclude with a summary of the merits of each point of view. Then tell which point of view you favor and why.

❑ Follow the rules of grammar, usage, spelling, and mechanics. Punctuate quotations from literature correctly.

WRITING WORKSHOP OVERVIEW

Product
Expository writing: A comparison/contrast essay

Prewriting
Review the literature—Compare and contrast—Walk in someone else's shoes—List the merits of each position—Formulate your own opinion—Plan your essay—Ask a partner
Unit 6 Resource Book
Prewriting Worksheets pp. 107–108

Drafting
Before you draft—As you draft
Transparency Collection
Student Models for Writing Workshop 21, 22

Revising
Ask a partner—Strategy: Signalling Comparisons and Contrasts
Unit 6 Resource Book
Revising Worksheet p. 109

Editing
Ask a partner—Strategy: Punctuating Quotations from Literature
Unit 6 Resource Book
Grammar Worksheet p. 110
Grammar Check Test p. 111

Presenting
Read and Discuss
Bumper Sticker

Looking Back
Self-evaluate—Reflect—For Your Working Portfolio
Unit 6 Resource Book
Assessment Worksheet p. 112
Transparency Collection
Fine Art Writing Prompt 11

STEP 1 PREWRITING

Review the literature selections to identify differing points of view about the same issue. Note that *differing* doesn't necessarily mean *opposite.* Characters may disagree on some aspects of an issue and agree on others. Just be sure that the two points of view show significant differences. When you finish, look over your notes and choose your topic: the issue and the differing points about it held by two characters.

Compare and contrast the two points of view you chose. Reread the selection closely to find examples of similarities and differences. Include at least two quotations for each character. These quotations should show why your characters firmly believe in the views they hold. Record your examples in a Venn diagram. In the overlapping area in the middle, list aspects of the issue that both characters agree on, as in the example that follows.

Issue: Whether good fences make good neighbors

LITERARY SOURCE
"My apple trees will never get across/And eat the cones under his pines, I tell him./He only says, 'Good fences make good neighbors'"
from "Mending Wall" by Robert Frost

Narrator's View — Do we really need a wall? *and so on . . .*

Both — need to mend wall in spring *and so on . . .*

Neighbor's View — We need walls to get along. *and so on . . .*

Walk in someone else's shoes. Refer to your Venn diagram and try to see each character's point of view. Write for five minutes as if you were one of the characters expressing your point of view. Then switch roles and do the same for the other character.

Notice how the writer of the student model on the next page captured one character's point of view from "The Tall Men."

OR . . .
With a partner listening, take on one character's point of view and improvise what the character would say if asked to explain his or her position. Then try it again as the other character you've chosen.

STEP 1 PREWRITING
Review the literature

Before students begin working individually, have volunteers write on the board the title of each selection and the major issue presented in each selection. For additional support, see the worksheet referenced below.

Unit 6 Resource Book
Prewriting Worksheet, p. 107

Compare and contrast

Point out how some of the information in the Venn diagram has been drawn from the Literary Source. Model this process of extracting information from the literature.

Walk in someone else's shoes

Between quickwrites, give students a few minutes to talk in groups about the point of view of the other character. They will probably need to gather their thoughts before they can write about a different point of view.

BUILDING ENGLISH PROFICIENCY

ESL LEP ELD SAE LD

Using Prewriting Helps

Draw attention to some of the prewriting helps provided on page 705.

- In the Literary Source note, point out that the excerpt presents two different (not necessarily opposing) points of view. Discuss with students how each speaker's point of view is supported in "Mending Wall" (especially how the neighbor's ideas are based upon tradition more than upon insightful thinking).

- Encourage pairs of students who wish to try the Or . . . activity to record their improvisations. Urge them to review the tape a few times, taking notes that might be useful to their essays.

List the merits of each position

You might tell the students to think about the list as though they were preparing for a debate. They need to present a positive case for both sides of the issue.

Formulate your own opinion

If students find it difficult to relate the points of view to a personal experience, perhaps they could first relate them to experiences of family members, friends, or from another piece of literature. For additional support, see the worksheet referenced below.

Unit 6 Resource Book
Prewriting Worksheet, p. 108

Plan your essay

Remind students that their plans are a beginning point for their drafts. The plans may be modified as the students continue to work.

> The investigator is dead serious about the law. He doesn't want to give an inch. He plays it by the book, as the TV cops say, always on the lookout for violators. He thinks people ought to live up to their legal obligations no matter what, and if they don't, they ought to suffer the consequences.

STUDENT MODEL

List the merits of each position. Use your quickwrite as a guide. Consider each point of view in a positive light and make a list of reasons why someone might take that position.

Formulate your own opinion. Look over your list of reasons in favor of each point of view and jot down notes on your reactions. Think of experiences you've had in your own life and complete these sentences:

A time in my life when I was confronted with this issue was when _____.

My point of view about the issue at that time was _____.

The way I feel about it now is _____.

Then ask yourself: *Which point of view comes closer to my own position?* Explain your decision to a partner, discuss it, and take notes on your discussion.

Plan your essay, using a three-part outline like the one shown.

- **Introduction**
  The issue
  The first point of view
    —Quotations from the text
  The second point of view
    —Quotations from the text

- **Body**
  Reactions to first point of view
    —examples from your own experience
  Reactions to second point of view
    —examples from your own experience

- **Conclusion**
  Merits of first point of view
  Merits of second point of view
  Which one you favor
  Why

MINI-LESSON: WRITING STYLE

Signalling Comparisons and Contrasts

Use this mini-lesson in conjunction with the Revising Strategy on page 708.

Teach Ask students to brainstorm a list of words that signal comparisons and contrasts and write the list on the board.

Activity Idea Have students look through other stories or articles to find examples of sentences using these compare and contrast words. Students can write their examples on the board or on a posterboard and explain to the class the relationship between the parts of the sentence signalled by the compare and contrast words.

Apply Remind students to use a variety of signal words in their own writing. Have students look over their papers to make sure they have used transitions to show the comparison and contrast relationships.

Ask **a partner** to review your plan.

✔ Have I described two differing points of view presented in a selection?

✔ Do my quotations illustrate and support my claims?

✔ Do I demonstrate which point of view I prefer?

Use your partner's comments to help you revise your plan.

STEP 2 DRAFTING

Before you draft, review the Writer's Blueprint and your prewriting materials. Be sure your plan takes into account each point in the blueprint.

As you draft, consider these ideas:

- Write your introduction as if it were being spoken by two characters from the selection who hold differing points of view, with each character making a brief statement that summarizes his or her position on the issue. Then write the rest of the essay in your own voice.

- Write your introduction by relating an incident from your own experience when you dealt with the issue at hand.

- Remember that your audience is familiar with the selection, so don't spend a lot of time summarizing the plot. Get right to the heart of the issue and stay there.

- Be sure you state comparisons and contrasts clearly. See the Revising Strategy in Step 3 of this lesson.

STEP 3 REVISING

Ask a partner for comments on your draft before you revise it.

✔ Have I used specific examples to illustrate each point of view?

✔ Have I concluded with a summary of the merits of each point of view and an explanation of which one I favor and why?

✔ Do I state comparisons and contrasts clearly?

After reviewing them, partners might work together in refining their plans by talking about the weak areas and looking back at the original selections.

Connections to
Writer's Notebook

For selection-related prompts, refer to Writer's Notebook.

Connections to
Writer's Resource

For additional writing prompts, refer to Writer's Resource.

STEP 2 DRAFTING
The Student Models

The **transparencies** referenced below are authentic student models. Review them with the students before they draft. These questions will help:

1. How does the writer of model 21 illustrate her reactions with examples from experiences in her own life?

2. Look over model 22 for how effectively the writer signals comparisons and contrasts.

3. Look over both models to see whether quotations from the literature are punctuated correctly.

Transparency Collection
Student Models for Writing Workshop 21, 22

STEP 3 REVISING

Ask a partner
(Peer assessment)

Have partners focus on consistency: that the specific examples and the stated comparisons and contrasts present consistent points of view for the two characters from the selection.

BUILDING ENGLISH PROFICIENCY

Supporting Main Ideas

Use this feature with the "Plan your essay" step on page 706. As students plan their responses to the two points of view, remind them of the importance of supporting their ideas.

1. Explain that although their reactions are based on their opinions, those opinions should be based on fact—and that their own experiences are valid. Thus, reactions that can be summarized only as "I think so because I think so" are inappropriate.

2. Encourage students to avoid vague generalizations, such as "Everyone knows that . . ." Urge them to be specific (although they may want to avoid naming names of people who would be embarrassed about being named in the essay).

Revising Strategy: Signalling Comparisons and Contrasts

Signalling comparisons and contrasts for the reader might be compared to road signs along the way that keep the driver moving in the right direction. The signals should give clear and concise directions to the readers. For additional support, see the mini-lesson at the bottom of page 706 and the worksheet referenced below.

Unit 6 Resource Book
Revising Worksheet, p. 109

Connections to
Writer's Resource

Refer to the Grammar, Usage, and Mechanics Handbook on Writer's Resource.

STEP 4 EDITING
Ask a partner (Peer assessment)

You might have students edit in small groups, with each group member looking at each paper for one specific editing aspect, such as subject-verb agreement or punctuation.

Revising Strategy

Signalling Comparisons and Contrasts

When you look over your draft, look for words and phrases like the ones listed below. You can use them to signal similarities (comparisons) and differences (contrasts) between the two points of view. Use them to make it easier for your readers to follow your train of thought.

Comparison Words	Contrast Words
like, likewise, just as, as, also, both, similarly, in the same way, as well, compared with	unlike, however, otherwise, although, but, yet, still, on the other hand, in contrast, even though

Notice how the writer of the student model has added a comparison-contrast signal during revision.

> In this story the investigator represents what a police officer should be like in today's society. He is a strict, hard core, "don't mess with me" type of guy. He will obey the law and make sure that
> *On the other hand,*
> the law is obeyed. The deputy marshal represents a humanitarian
> *also*
> officer. He is an officer who cares about the law but cares about the well being of the criminals more.

STUDENT MODEL

STEP 4 EDITING

Ask a partner to review your revised draft before you edit. When you edit, look for errors in grammar, usage, spelling, and mechanics. Look closely for errors in punctuating quotations from literature.

MINI-LESSON: GRAMMAR

Punctuating Quotations from Literature

Have students generate a short list of reminders on correctly punctuating quotations in a paragraph. Then write on the board two short quotations taken from selections in this unit: one of prose and one of poetry. Give titles and page references so students can consult the texts if they choose to. Repeat the same procedure, using two long quotations.

In groups, assign one of the quotes to each group and have students write a short paragraph that includes the quote assigned to them. When students have finished the paragraphs, have them exchange papers with other groups to check the punctuation of the quotation. Students should correctly punctuate all quotations.

Unit 6 Resource Book
Grammar Worksheet p. 110
Grammar Check Test p. 111

Editing Strategy

Punctuating Quotations from Literature

The way you punctuate a quotation depends on the length of the quoted material. For short quotations (less than 4 lines of prose or 3 lines of poetry), enclose the quoted material in quotation marks and run it in. For longer quotations, instead of using quotation marks, set the quoted material off by indenting it from the left margin:

FOR REFERENCE
More information about punctuating literary quotations can be found in the Language and Grammar Handbook in the back of this text.

○ The narrator drives home his view of the wall as a

barrier in the following passage:

STUDENT MODEL

○ And on a day we meet to walk the line

And set the wall between us once again.

○ We keep the wall between us as we go.

To each the boulders that have fallen to each.

COMPUTER TIP
Many word processors allow you to indent text by changing the margins for individual paragraphs without using tabs. Consult your manual to find out how.

STEP 5 PRESENTING

- Find other classmates who wrote about the same selection as you. Read your essays aloud and discuss your points of view.

- Design a bumper sticker that promotes the point of view you favor.

STEP 6 LOOKING BACK

Self-evaluate. Look back at the Writer's Blueprint and give yourself a score for each item, from 6 (superior) to 1 (inadequate).

Reflect. Write about how your own point of view did or did not change during the writing of this essay.

For Your Working Portfolio Add your comparison/contrast essay and your reflection responses to your working portfolio.

ASSESSMENT CRITERIA SPECS

Here are the criteria for a superior paper. A full six-level rubric for this paper appears on the *Assessment Worksheet* referenced below.

6 Superior   The writer of a 6 paper impressively meets these criteria:

- Focuses on two clearly differing points of view from the literature. Maintains this focus throughout the essay.

- Insightfully compares and contrasts these differing views, using quotations where appropriate.

- Effectively signals comparisons and contrasts.

- Discusses the writer's own feelings about both views by using specific examples from the writer's life.

- Shows a real understanding of the merits of each point of view.

- Clearly states the view the writer favors.

- Makes few, if any, mistakes in grammar, usage, spelling, and mechanics. Punctuates quotations from literature correctly.

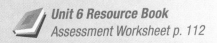
Unit 6 Resource Book
Assessment Worksheet p. 112

Editing Strategy: Punctuating Quotations from Literature

For additional support, see the mini-lesson at the bottom of page 708 and the worksheets referenced below.

Unit 6 Resource Book
Grammar Worksheet, p. 110
Grammar Check Test, p. 111

Connections to
Writer's Resource

Refer to the Grammar, Usage, and Mechanics Handbook on Writer's Resource.

STEP 5 PRESENTING
Read and Discuss

Remind students of the difference between a discussion and an argument: that in a discussion, such as the one they'll be having, the aim is to clarify points of view, not refute them.

STEP 6 LOOKING BACK
Self-evaluate

The *Assessment Criteria Specs* at the bottom of this page are for a superior paper. You might want to post these in the classroom. Students can then evaluate themselves based on these criteria. For a complete scoring rubric, use the *Assessment Worksheet* referenced below.

Unit 6 Resource Book
Assessment Worksheet, p. 112

Reflect

Before having students write their responses, you might poll the class to see how many students did change their points of view while writing the essay.

To further explore the theme, use the Fine Art Transparency referenced below.

Transparency Collection
Fine Art Writing Prompt 11

Beyond Print

Teaching Objectives

- To understand the purposes of propaganda
- To be aware of how a message is influenced by propaganda
- To analyze a piece of propaganda

Curricular Connection: Critical Thinking

You can use the material in this article to guide students in recognizing and understanding propaganda. Encourage students to spend time examining the poster on page 711 and giving thoughtful answers to the text questions that ask them to analyze it. Remind them to also examine their own emotional responses and discuss whether they think the poster has the same emotional impact today that it did during World War II.

Introduce

Invite students to describe favorite television commercials. Ask students to tell what the product or service is and how the commercial makes them feel about the product. Emphasize that television commercials are carefully written and filmed to create a precise response among viewers.

Discuss whether using propaganda to persuade viewers to buy a product is useful or not useful, or right or wrong.

Encourage students to be critical consumers of today's advertising by applying these elements of analysis to commercials and print advertising that they see every day.

Beyond Print

Propaganda

What do you think of when you hear the term *propaganda?* Propaganda is a systematic effort to spread opinions or beliefs. Often people have negative associations with the word *propaganda,* but it is really just a tool with which to convince or motivate people, and can be used for both good causes and bad.

The trouble with propaganda is that it often distorts reality. It may take very complex issues and oversimplify them, dividing them into categories of good and evil. It also tends to exploit people's emotions and insecurities, for instance, making people feel threatened when they may not be in real danger, or making them feel they are lacking something and need to buy a certain product to make up for it.

Propaganda surrounds you every day. It is your job to be able to analyze the message the propaganda is attempting to deliver, then choose whether or not you agree. Start by analyzing the World War II poster on the facing page.

Analyzing the Poster

Initial Response What is your first reaction to the poster? What feelings do you associate with the images? Are they positive, negative, or both?

Analyzing the Figures The two hands represent the United States' two major enemies during World War II. The hand in the upper right has Nazi Germany's swastika symbol on it, and the one on the bottom left has a sun, a symbol Japan uses on its flag. What do the portrayal of the two hands say about the two countries and their intentions?

Whom would you say the mother and baby are supposed to be? What qualities do they portray? What do their facial expressions suggest? Looking at the figures symbolically, what do you think the hands symbolize? What might the woman and baby symbolize?

Analyzing the Message What is this poster telling its viewers? Victory bonds were bonds individuals could buy to help fund the war effort. What does the poster suggest will happen if the viewers do *not* buy victory bonds?

ANOTHER APPROACH

Audio Propaganda

As an alternative to the analysis of visual propaganda, you might emphasize nonvisual propaganda from the radio. Record a radio commercial, public-service announcement, or news editorial. Through class discussion, have students analyze the audio propaganda, using the criteria on pages 710–711.

As an alternative, record just the audio of a television commercial to emphasize the role of language, sound effects, and music in persuasion.

KEEP
THESE
HANDS
OFF!

BUY *the New* VICTORY BONDS

Evaluating the Propaganda In what ways does the poster reflect reality? distort reality? Do you agree with the poster's message? Is it furthering a worthy cause? Explain.

Activity Option

Today's Propaganda Today's world is filled with propaganda—on television, radio, billboards, pamphlets, books, even on the Internet. It comes in the form of advertisements, political materials, public service announcements, and so on. Choose a piece of propaganda to analyze for your classmates. Tell your initial response, what is going on in the piece, what the message is, and your opinion of the effectiveness and worth of the message.

Activity Option

The following chart can help students organize their analyses of the propaganda they have chosen. Students may need to adjust the chart to fit their particular piece of propaganda; for example, graphic information can be replaced with audio information for radio propaganda.

Initial Response
positive or negative feelings?
image associations?
Analyze Graphic Information
What graphics are used?
What do they represent?
What qualities are associated with the graphics?
Analyze the Message
sponsor or source of information?
clear or subtle?
fact or opinion?
positive or negative?
Evaluate the Propaganda
Is reality reflected or distorted?
Do you agree with the message?

BUILDING ENGLISH PROFICIENCY

ESL
LEP
ELD
SAE
LD

Exploring Visual Propaganda

Use one or both of the following activities to help students grasp the analytical process on pages 710–711.

- As students look closely at the poster, ask them to jot down notes in their journals about anything they want to express about the poster. Then have students circle comments that seem to relate to the various elements described, for example, the use of symbols, the emotional content of the poster, its realism, and its message.

- Invite students to imagine themselves as a poster artist. Ask: If the government asked you to submit a poster for a World War II propaganda campaign, what would your poster's message be? What images or graphics would your poster include?

Unit Wrap-Up

☀ MULTICULTURAL CONNECTION

Students may know intuitively but may need help verbalizing the concept that people have different perspectives and that these perspectives influence communication, as explored in Parts One and Two of Unit 6. The following ideas and questions may facilitate discussion.

Perspective

- One man's ceiling is another man's floor. What is trash to one is treasure to another.
- Differences of perspective exist between individuals within the same cultural group as well as between those of different cultural groups.

Possible Response Students should support their choices with a rationale and specific examples from the selections.

Communication

- Communication occurs both verbally and nonverbally.
- When people are not familiar with another's communication habits, communication may fail.

Possible responses Obstacles to communication may include not being open to others' ideas; having expectations that aren't met; having different standards of behavior or moral values. Overcoming may include effort on each side and finding common ground.

Activities

Activity 1 Suggest that students choose dramatic situations that are likely to evoke strong reactions. You may wish to vary the activity by having students present more than two impressions, or by having the group present the same drama a second time with members switching perspectives.

Activity 2 Send students into the field to take notes on people engaged in communication. Encourage students to find as many different situations as they can, and, using a prearranged criteria list, have them make observations about what people say, how they say it, and what their body language says.

☀ Multicultural Connections

Perspective

Part One: Lost in a Crowd J. Alfred Prufrock attends a tea-party, but from his perspective it almost seems more like an ordeal than an enjoyable social event. From the perspective of those around him Richard Cory has all that life has to offer, yet in the end it's clear that he has miseries others cannot see. Granny Weatherall's perspective drifts in and out of reality as her death approaches.

■ Which of the selections in this section provide the most interesting perspective, or way of looking at things? Explain your choice.

Communication

Part Two: The Strength of Tradition The way individuals communicate depends a great deal on their cultural background. The narrator and the neighbor in Frost's "Mending Wall" communicate over a wall. The McCallums in "The Tall Men" communicate as much through glances and gestures as through words. When Thomas Whitecloud returns to his home in Wisconsin, he notices his community's habit of communicating welcome and acceptance without words. The differences in communication styles between the two women and their guests provide humor in *Lord Byron's Love Letter.*

■ What are the greatest obstacles to communication in this section, and how are these obstacles overcome?

Activities

Work in small groups on the following activities.

1. Often two people can have very different impressions of the same thing. For instance, to someone who likes thrills, riding a roller-coaster could be a great time, whereas to someone who is afraid of heights, it could be a nightmare. In your group, think of times when a difference in perspectives led to a misunderstanding. Choose one of the situations to dramatize.

2. Society has rules and customs about how to communicate when on the phone, in a library, online, writing a letter, in a movie theater, talking to an authority figure, to a baby, and so on. Make a list of as many situations as you can think of that call for a particular style of communication. Compare lists with the rest of your class.

Independent and Group Projects

Writing

Disillusionment When someone or something has not lived up to our expectations, this can cause disillusionment. Look back over the selections by T. S. Eliot, Edwin Arlington Robinson, Ernest Hemingway, and F. Scott Fitzgerald. Why are the characters they have created disillusioned? In an essay, compare and contrast how each author has treated this theme.

Entertainment

Literary Pursuits In this unit you have been introduced to some of the most famous American writers of the twentieth century. Use your knowledge of the writers and the literature presented in this unit to create a "Literary Pursuits" game. Create categories that you would like to develop like "Expatriate Writers," "Regional Writers," "Memorable Characters," "Famous Lines," and so on. Then write ten questions for each category, each question on a separate index card. Make up rules of play for the game, and play it in class.

Geography

Mapping the Literary Scene Make a literary map showing the areas of the United States that the writers in this unit described. Begin by tracing a U.S. map, then highlight the states, cities, and locales that the authors wrote about. Make feature boxes on the margin of the map that describe each author and the memorable regional characters that he or she wrote about. Alternatively, you can use software to create the literary map and author/region cards.

Drama

Be the Writer Hal Holbrook, a well-known actor, has toured the country performing as writer Mark Twain. Choose one of the writers in this unit that you would like to become and create a monologue to present to the class. As part of the production, create a costume, set a scene, and provide appropriate background music. Your monologue should include autobiographical information as well as a discussion of the stories or poetry you have written. As a finale, read a favorite passage from one of your writer's stories or poems.

713

Writing

Encourage students to consider the following questions.

- What ideals did the characters hold?
- Were the ideals betrayed?
- How did the betrayal take place?

Entertainment

Students may want to base their games on another format, or they might create a computer or multimedia game. Suggest that groups begin with a brainstorming session for a variety of ways to format the game.

Geography

Students may want to embellish their maps by adding the following information.

- Geographic, political, or socio-economic features of the region
- Placing the literature title next to each story's setting
- Other regional authors and literature they have read

Drama

Suggest that students take the following steps to prepare for their performance.

- Research the author's life and find good quotations to use in your monologue.
- Read several works by the author.
- Practice delivering the monologue until you are comfortable with your presentation.

 Connections to
AuthorWorks

Information for completing these projects can be found in the AuthorWorks CD-ROM series.

 Unit Test

Unit 6 Resource Book
New Selection, pp. 113–120
Test 1, pp. 121–122
Test 2, pp. 123–128

Planning Unit 7: Years of Change

Literature	Integrated Language Arts			
	Literary	**Writing/Grammar, Usage and Mechanics**	**Reading, Thinking, Listening, Speaking**	**Vocabulary/Spelling**
The Life You Save May Be Your Own *by Flannery O'Connor* Short Story *(challenging)* p. 720	Diction, characterization Simile, irony Tone, dialogue Satirical humor, conflict	Paragraph on conflict Write a continuation Using commas in addresses and names	Make connections Identify author's purpose Visualize	Antonym
I Stand Here Ironing *by Tillie Olsen* Short Story *(average)* p. 732	Interior monologue Diction Irony Rhythm and repetition	Short essay Essay on character development Description Pronouns and antecedents	Draw conclusions Recall details Make inferences Compare and contrast Identify author's point of view	Word analogies Understand connotations and denotations
Separating *by John Updike* Short Story *(average)* p. 742	Point of view Extended metaphor Symbolism, plot Characterization Irony, setting, tone	Venn diagram Write an essay Using irregular plurals	Make inferences Make judgments Recall details Make connections Analyze	Expand reading vocabulary
from The Woman Warrior *by Maxine Hong Kingston* Autobiographical Essay *(average)* p. 754	Symbolism	List of rules Distinguishing and spelling homophones	Clarify Compare and contrast	
Everyday Use *by Alice Walker* Short Story *(average)* p. 760	Figurative language Imagery and characters Diction, irony Conflict, dialogue	Significance of names Write a summary End punctuation	Reader's response Make connections Make inferences Recognize values	Word relationships Recognize shades of meaning
Mirror *by Sylvia Plath* Poem *(challenging)* p. 771 **One Art** *by Elizabeth Bishop* Poem *(average)* p. 772 **Legacies** *by Nikki Giovanni* Poem *(average)* p. 773 **Leaves** *by Sam Hamod* Poem *(easy)* p. 774 **To Jesus Villanueva, with Love** *by Alma Luz Villanueva* Poem *(average)* p. 775	Personification Repetition Symbolism Tone	Analyze a poem Poem or personal narrative Write letters	Understand sequence Make inferences Connect Generalize	Answer questions Understand colloquialisms

Meeting Individual Needs

Multi-modal Activities	Mini-Lessons
Draw a wedding portrait Dialogue Making predictions Understanding dialect and double negatives Recognizing irony Understanding a turning point in the story	Using commas in addresses and names Diction Readers theater Considering complex themes
Deliver a speech Oral reading Stand-up comic routine Understanding time shifts Understanding causes and effects Exploring key concepts	Pronouns and antecedents Interior monologue
Bar or line graph Monologue Exploring key concepts Exploring a character Related words and parts of speech Exploring conflict	Expanding reading vocabulary Using irregular plurals Point of view
Make a graph and map Making cultural connections Compare and contrast schools	Distinguishing and spelling homophones
Create a dialogue Quilt design Exploring characterization Exploring relationships among characters Making cultural connections	Figurative language End punctuation Recognize shades of meaning
Poetry reading Create an illustration Oral or hyperstudio report Exploring key concepts Orally interpreting a poem Celebrating family or friends	Understanding colloquialisms Writing letters Personification

Interdisciplinary Studies
Television Takes Over

Format	Content Area	Highlights	Skill
Article: **Life After Television** by John Brooks	Pop Culture	This article discusses the growth in popularity of television.	Using videos as reference sources
Collage: **What's on TV?**	Pop Culture	These pages show television programs that became popular.	Use appropriate speaking and listening behavior

Writing Workshop

Mode	Writing Format	Writing Focus	Proofreading Skills
Persuasive writing	A literary critique	Writing in the active voice	Comparative forms of adjectives and adverbs

Program Support Materials

For Every Selection	For Every Writing Workshop
Unit Resource Book Graphic Organizer Study Guide Vocabulary Worksheet Grammar Worksheet Spelling, Speaking and Listening, or Literary Language Worksheet Alternate Check Test Vocabulary Test Selection Test	**Unit Resource Book** Prewriting Worksheet Revising Strategy Worksheet Editing Strategy Worksheet Presentation Worksheet Writing Rubric **Transparency Collection** Fine Art Transparency Student Writing Model Transparencies

For Every Interdisciplinary Study	Assessment
Unit Resource Book Study Guide Mini-Lesson Skill Worksheet	**Unit Resource Book** TE Check Tests Alternate Check Test (blackline master) Vocabulary Test (blackline master) Selection Test (blackline master) **Test Generator Software** **Assessment Handbook**

Planning Unit 7: Years of Change

Literature

Integrated Language Arts

	Literary	Writing/Grammar, Usage and Mechanics	Reading, Thinking, Listening, Speaking	Vocabulary/Spelling
from To Be Young, Gifted and Black *by Lorraine Hansberry* Autobiographical Essay *(average)* p. 794	Point of view Imagery Tone Archetype	Self-portrait Active and passive verbs	Draw conclusions Classify Evaluate author's point of view	
from Letter from a Birmingham Jail *by Martin Luther King, Jr.* Letter *(challenging)* p. 800 **from The Autobiography of Malcolm X** *by Malcolm X* Autobiography *(challenging)* p. 806	Allusion Style Repetition Metaphor Imagery Tone	Essay Create a dialogue Writing a formal letter	Identify author's purpose Recognize use of persuasion Make judgments Recognize values Cause and effect Identify alternatives	Latin root words
On the Rainy River *by Tim O'Brien* Short Story *(average)* p. 812	Dialogue, narrator Plot, tone Symbolism, imagery Style, simile Characterization Diction, point of view Irony	Compare decisions Write a letter Three diary entries Make a list Action verbs Write a fictional memoir	Recognize assumptions and implications Predict outcome Infer	Write a letter Expand reading vocabulary Recognize idioms
from Where the Ashes Are *by Nguyễn Qúi Dú'c* Autobiography *(challenging)* p. 828	Imagery, dialogue Characterization Style, narrator Symbolism	Three stanza poem Write a review Character study Analyze grammatical structure	Infer Make judgments	Expand vocabulary using structural analysis
Village *by Estela Portillo Trambley* Short Story *(easy)* p. 838	Theme, setting Imagery, dialogue Symbolism, plot	Affixes	Infer	Word relationships Etymology

Meeting Individual Needs

Multi-modal Activities	Mini-Lessons
Exploring key concepts Exploring an author's thoughts	Active and passive verbs
Television special Musical accompaniment Planning a reading strategy Improving comprehension Analyzing parallelism Comparing author	Writing a formal letter Interpretive reading Latin root words Outlining an essay
Oral report Create a poster In-depth interviews Exploring key concepts Analyzing sensory detail Exploring sentence variety Expanding vocabulary notebooks Exploring punctuation for dialogue Making personal connections	Action verbs Expanding reading vocabulary Making lists Examining dialogue Recognize idioms Writing a fictional memoir
Stage production Bulletin board display Debate the issue Making personal connections Exploring suspense Understanding characters	Analyzing grammatical structure Expanding vocabulary using structural analysis Relate literature to personal experience
Exploring sentence fragments Mapping a plot Contrasting viewpoints	Affixes Etymology

Interdisciplinary Studies
Time of Turmoil 1955-1975

Format	Content Area	Highlights	Skill
Time line: **The Pace of Change**	History	A time line charting some memorable events that occurred during the 60s and 70s.	Listening to a speech Primary and secondary sources Comparing and contrasting

Writing Workshop

Mode	Writing Format	Writing Focus	Proofreading Skills
Narrative writing	An interview	When to quote directly and when to paraphrase	Punctuating direct quotations

Program Support Materials

For Every Selection	For Every Writing Workshop
Unit Resource Book Graphic Organizer Study Guide Vocabulary Worksheet Grammar Worksheet Spelling, Speaking and Listening, or Literary Language Worksheet Alternate Check Test Vocabulary Test Selection Test	**Unit Resource Book** Prewriting Worksheet Revising Strategy Worksheet Editing Strategy Worksheet Presentation Worksheet Writing Rubric **Transparency Collection** Fine Art Transparency Student Writing Model Transparencies

For Every Interdisciplinary Study	Assessment
Unit Resource Book Study Guide Mini-Lesson Skill Worksheet	**Unit Resource Book** TE Check Tests Alternate Check Test (blackline master) Vocabulary Test (blackline master) Selection Test (blackline master) **Test Generator Software** **Assessment Handbook**

Part One Selections

The Life You Save May Be Your Own

Audiotape *O'Connor* is included in Selected Shorts, Volume III, 150 minutes, American Audio Prose Library, 1993.

Videotape *The Displaced Person,* 58 minutes, from The American Short Story Collection, Library Video Company, 1976, is based on O'Connor's story and stars John Houseman.

Community Resources Working on Mrs. Crater's old Ford, Mr. Shiftlet compares it favorably to the current products of automobile assembly lines. Actually, it was Henry Ford who first employed assembly-line methods in making cars. Students might use the resources of the local library to research the early history of the American automobile industry, focusing on the revolutionary impact of the assembly line and the Model-T Ford.

I Stand Here Ironing

Audiotape *I Stand Here Ironing,* 1 hour 17 minutes, American Audio Prose Library, includes an interview and the author reading.

Home Connection The experience of childhood illness affects people in different ways. The limitations imposed by sickness or injury may frustrate most people, but for some they contribute to the development of creativity. For an at-home activity, students might discuss with family members the different ways in which their own childhood experiences with illness have affected them.

Separating

Audiotape Hear the author reading his work, including "Separating," in *John Updike Reads Selected Stories*, 169 minutes, Random House, 1986. Also consider an interview with the author in *John Updike*, 25 minutes, Tapes for Readers.

Videotape *Too Far to Go,* 100 minutes, is an adaptation of stories by Updike, Library Video Company, 1978.

Community Resources Is breaking up hard to do? Students might be interested in hearing someone discuss this question who is professionally involved in advising couples who are involved in separating, such as lawyers, members of the clergy, counselors, advice columnists, and so on.

from The Woman Warrior

Audiotape The author talks about her books, including *The Woman Warrior*, and about growing up Chinese in America in *Maxine Hong Kingston*, 53 minutes, Pacifica Tape Library.

Videotape *The Stories of Maxine Hong Kingston: The Power of the Word,* 60 minutes, PBS Video, is an extended interview with the author by Bill Moyers.

Community Resources Students might use the resources of the local library, cultural center, or art center to learn a few Chinese ideographs and the materials and methods used by calligraphers to create them.

Everyday Use

Audiotape Students will want to listen to *Alice Walker Reads*, 36 minutes, American Audio Prose Library, in which the author reads her poetry and short stories.

Videotape An interview and in-depth portrait of the author is presented in *Alice Walker,* 30 minutes, California Newsreel, 1992.

Home Connection Students might invite a family member who is interested in American antiques to visit the class and discuss what an antique is (as opposed to collectibles in general), what different types of American antiques are collected, what makes them valuable, and so on.

Mirror/One Art/Legacies/Leaves/To Jesus Villanueva, with Love

Videotape *With a Feminine Touch*, 45 minutes, The Heritage Poetry Series, Library Video Company, 1989, features Valerie Harper and Claire Bloom performing Sylvia Plath and other poets. *Sylvia*

Connections to
Custom Literature Database

For Part One "Person to Person" Selections with Lessons

• The Truman Doctrine by Harry S. Truman

• "The Death of the Hired Man" by Robert Frost

Additional theme-based selections can be accessed on the ScottForesman database.

Connections to
AuthorWorks

Information about the life and times of Flannery O'Connor and Lorraine Hansberry is available on ScottForesman's AuthorWorks CD-ROM.

Plath: Letters Home, 90 minutes, Films for the Humanities & Sciences, focuses on letters written by the poet to her mother.

Audiotape Nikki Giovanni reads her poetry in *Cotton Candy on a Rainy Day* and *The Reason I Like Chocolate*, both from Folkways/Smithsonian.

Home Connection What things from your childhood are you most grateful for having kept? What things do you most regret losing? For an at-home activity, students might explore these questions with family members.

Part Two Selections

from To Be Young, Gifted and Black

Audiotape James Earl Jones reads the words of the author in *To Be Young, Gifted, and Black*, 2 hours 30 minutes, Harper, 1990.

Videotape Students might want to see *A Raisin in the Sun*, 2 hours 8 minutes, Columbia/Tri-Star, 1961, based on the play by Hansberry, starring Sidney Poitier. *Lorraine Hansberry: The Black Experience in Creation of Drama*, 35 minutes, Films for the Humanities & Sciences, documents her life and work.

from Letter from a Birmingham Jail/ from The Autobiography of Malcolm X

Audiotape Students will enjoy hearing Coretta Scott King read from her book, *My Life with Martin Luther King*, in a cassette offered by Caedmon/Harper Audio.

Videotape Students will enjoy viewing *Martin Luther King: An Amazing Grace*, 60 minutes, Facets Multimedia Inc., 1991. Also consider *Speeches of Martin Luther King, Jr.*, 60 minutes, from the In Their Own Worlds Series, Library Video Company and *Martin Luther King, Jr.: Letter from Birmingham Jail*, 25 minutes, Coronet/MTI, 1988. Students would enjoy the video biography, *Malcolm X (Black Americans of Achievement series)*, 30 minutes, Schlessinger Video Productions, which includes archival footage and period music. The daughters of Martin Luther King, Jr., Medgar Evers, and Malcolm X talk about their fathers in *Daughters of the Black Revolution*, 28 minutes, Films for the Humanities & Sciences, 1990.

Computer Software Consider using the CD-ROM, *Malcolm X: By Any Means Necessary*, available for Macintosh from Scholastic, and *Autobiography of Malcolm X*, CD-ROM from Voyager for IBM and Macintosh.

On the Rainy River

Audiotape *Going After Cacciato*, Harper Audio, is a reading of O'Brien's book about peace and freedom during the Vietnam War era.

Videotape *Not on the Frontline*, 30 minutes, Great Plains Network, 1991, gives accounts from five women who served in Vietnam.

from Where the Ashes Are

Audiotape Huynh Quang Nhuong reads his collection of short stories about his childhood in Vietnam in *The Land I Lost*, 52 minutes, American Audio Prose Library.

Community Resources Although the United States was able to counterattack successfully and overcome the Viet Cong Tet Offensive, it was nevertheless a major political defeat for the Johnson Administration and all those who wanted to sustain the American commitment to continue the war in Vietnam. Students might use the resources of the local library to research the impact of Tet on the American home front.

Village

Videotape *The Bicycle Doctors*, 28 minutes, Carousel, 1991, documents the daily life of a Vietnamese medical family.

Computer Software *Vietnam*, CD-ROM for MPC, Medio, 1994, investigates the forces, personalities, and events in the war in a riveting multimedia presentation.

Connections to
Custom
Literature Database
For Part Two "In the Midst of Struggle…" Selections with Lessons
- Civil Rights Act of 1964
- The Meaning of July Fourth for the Negro by Frederick Douglass

Additional theme-based selections can be accessed on the ScottForesman database.

Connections to
NovelWorks
An audiotape of *A Raisin in the Sun*, a play by Lorraine Hansberry, is one of the many teaching tools included in the ScottForesman NovelWorks kit.

Years of Change

 ## Art Study

This painting, *Hot Fudge Sundae,* (1972) is part of the movement known as Photorealism, also known as "new realism," and "super-realism." The artist, Ralph Goings, approaches a modern ice cream parlor with incredible attention to detail, sharpness, and precision, without making social or moral comment on his subject.

Realism is characterized by this dispassionate approach, and often depicts the mundane scenes of people's everyday lives.

Question How does Goings's faithfulness to reality give the painting a surreal feeling? *(Possible response: The car in the parking lot takes on a menacing character. The elevation of everyday things to great importance makes them seem larger than life.)*

Question What elements of this painting reveal its time period? *(Possible response: the models of the cars, the arched facade of the Safeway grocery store, the woman's clothing)*

Question If you were to read a social message into this realistic "snapshot," what would it be? *(Possible response: The suburban American landscape has an isolated feel and is cold and unfriendly; there is an emphasis on glass, metal, and consumerism.)*

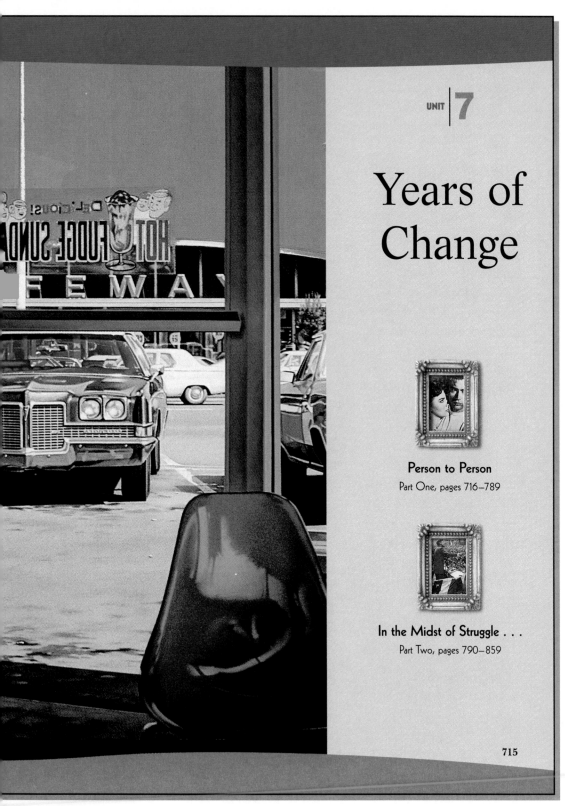

UNIT 7

Years of Change

Person to Person
Part One, pages 716–789

In the Midst of Struggle . . .
Part Two, pages 790–859

715

THEMATIC CONNECTIONS

Political and social unrest both at home and abroad led Americans to re-evaluate their relationships to each other and to demand a restructuring of American society.

Part One
Person to Person

The selections in Part One show how circumstances and turmoil of the outer world cause people to question their relationships with their families, with each other, and with their inner selves.

Ideas to Explore

- Which characters try to force their will on the changing world around them?
- Which characters are victims of change?

Part Two
In the Midst of Struggle

The selections in Part Two reveal the complexity and challenge that individuals faced during the turbulent years of the Civil Rights movement and the Vietnam war.

Ideas to Explore

- How did each writer view the events of the 1960s in America?
- How did each writer overcome obstacles to change?
- What relevance do the social ideas in these selections have in America today?

 *Art Study*

The icon for Person to Person is a photo of actors James Dean and Natalie Wood from the movie *Rebel Without a Cause.* The icon for In the Midst of Struggle… shows former President John F. Kennedy making a speech.

EXPLORING CONCEPTS

- The end of World War II sparked a period of growth in America that included population expansion, technological innovation, and economic prosperity.

- The literature of the 1950s and 1960s reflects changes in social attitudes among American readers.

- Character's inner lives are out of kilter with the affluence of society around them.

- Cultures clash as heritage conflicts with an American upbringing.

Art Study

"Iconography" refers to the identification and interpretation of symbols, themes, and subject matter in the visual arts. In the late 50s and 60s the artists of the *Pop Art* movement began to capture and portray contemporary culture by taking their iconography from television, comic books, magazines, and advertising.

Questions Which of the images on pages 716–717 would you identify as pop icons? What do they stand for? *(Possible response: All are icons and students should interpret what they stand for, for example, Marilyn Monroe of the 1950s is an icon for glamour, fame, and a feminine ideal.)*

Years of Change

Person to Person

POSTWAR CULTURE

HISTORICAL OVERVIEW

In the 15 years following World War II, America experienced huge changes. A postwar baby boom created the future audience for the youth culture of the 1950s and '60s. The landscape was altered by interstate highways, suburban subdivisions, drive-in theaters, and shopping malls. Television changed the way Americans entertained themselves, and eventually how they saw themselves and the world. The increasing dominance of the American economy by large corporations created affluence but also left many workers feeling anonymous and powerless. There was a pervasive feeling of complacency, symbolized by the comfortable families seen on television, but also an under-current of revolt that appeared in Beatnik literature, movies about teenage rebels, and rock 'n' roll.

SPUTNIK I

When the Soviets beat the United States into space by launching a satellite in 1957, Americans criticized the direction of the U.S. economy and the quality of American education.

JACKIE ROBINSON

Baseball finally lived up to its nickname of "the national pastime" in 1947 when Jackie Robinson became the first African American to play in the major leagues.

JACK KEROUAC

Beatnik writer Jack Kerouac celebrated nonconformity and criticized the consumer culture of the 1950s in novels like *On the Road*.

OZZIE AND HARRIET

Serious family problems were remote from the comfortable, suburban version of domestic life presented in the 1950s by TV situation comedies like *Ozzie and Harriet*.

ELVIS PRESLEY

In the mid–1950s, rock 'n' roll music became a craze as teenagers went wild for such stars as Elvis Presley, whose recording of "Heartbreak Hotel" became the best-selling record in America in 1956.

MARILYN MONROE

With the feminist movement of the 1960s still in the future, the most visible image of women in the postwar period remained glamorous Hollywood stars like Marilyn Monroe.

Key Dates

1947
Major league baseball is racially integrated.

1952
Eisenhower is elected President.

1953
Two out of three American homes have television.

1955
"Rock Around the Clock" is the first rock 'n' roll hit.

1956
Congress approves interstate highway system.

1957
Kerouac's On the Road *is published; Soviet Union launches* Sputnik I.

1960
Presidential campaign debates between candidates John F. Kennedy and Richard M. Nixon are televised.

717

Key Dates

1950–1953   The Korean War

1953   Arthur Miller's play, *The Crucible*, was published.

1955   The Montgomery Bus Boycott and the emergence of a young minister named Martin Luther King, Jr.

1956   Beat poetry chants rebellion against the self-satisfied culture of the 1950s.

1958   National Defense Education Act was passed.

1959   Lorraine Hansberry's *A Raisin in the Sun,* was the first Broadway performance of a play by a contemporary black playwright.

MATERIALS OF INTEREST
Books

- *Rockin' in Time: A Social History of Rock and Roll*, David P. Szatmary (Prentice Hall, 1991)
- *John Updike: A Study of the Short Fiction,* Robert M. Luscher (Twayne, 1993)
- *Flannery O'Connor Short Stories* (Macmillan Publishing Co. Inc., 1995)

Multimedia

American Graffiti, video recording (MCA Home Video, 1985)

 Connections to
Custom Literature Database

For further historical background, under **Background Articles,** see **Postwar America 1945– .**

Person to Person

FOR ALL STUDENTS

- Why might family relationships contain a complex mixture of emotional experiences?
- How does a family's circumstances in the outside world affect its relationships at home?

To further explore the theme, use the transparency referenced here.

Transparency Collection
Fine Art Writing Prompt 12

For At-Risk Students

Have students choose a family member with whom they have frequent interaction. Have them write a "positive" (feels good) and "negative" (feels bad) chart, listing examples of experiences and interactions for each category.

For Students Who Need Challenge

Encourage students to research demographic and social changes in the American family from the years 1945 to 1980.

MULTICULTURAL CONNECTION

Cultural traditions often pass through families, sometimes through artifacts like the quilt in "Everyday Use," or sometimes through attitudes, like the cold rationality that Dickie inherits from his mother in "Separating."

Encourage students to look for cultural links between the characters in the selections of Part One.

Part One

Person to Person

The way Americans relate with one another—among family members, friends, acquaintances, and even the way we relate to ourselves—has long been a source of inspiration for American writers. The following selections each provide insights into different kinds of person-to-person relationships.

Multicultural Connection Our cultural heritage—including our family, community, and customs—can affect our **interactions** with others. In which of the following selections do cultural factors enhance the person-to-person interactions, and in which do they seem to inhibit or complicate interactions?

IDEAS THAT WORK

Motivating with Viewpoint

Person to Person highlights the complexities of parenting in post–World War II society. I like to use this literature as an opportunity for students to explore the generation gap, especially from a parents' point of view.

We begin with a generation study starting with the students' generation. We gather together in small groups, and I ask each group to create lists of their generation's heroes, inventions, fads, and events. Then each group investigates similar elements of a decade from the twentieth century and presents its findings to the class.

With this as background, students can begin to analyze their own parents. I ask them to write brief descriptions of their parents and to see the world from their parent's point of view. As we read the selections, I ask, "What is causing the separation of generations?" The leap from the literature to the students' own experience is made, and they begin to see parenting in a new light.

Timothy A. Dohrer
Mundelein, Illinois

Before Reading

The Life You Save May Be Your Own

by Flannery O'Connor

Flannery O'Connor
1925–1964

Flannery O'Connor once said, "Whenever I'm asked why Southern writers particularly have a penchant for writing about freaks, I say it is because we are still able to recognize one." O'Connor was born in Savannah, Georgia. Educated in convent schools, her religious upbringing had a profound impact on her writing, and the theme of salvation is explored throughout her works. O'Connor attended Georgia State College for Women and the State University of Iowa. Her first novel and most famous single work, *Wise Blood,* was published in 1952. She won a National Book Award in 1972 for *The Complete Stories.* In 1950, O'Connor was diagnosed with lupus. She died at the age of thirty-nine.

Building Background

Who Is Being Saved? ". . . she could tell, even from a distance, that he was a tramp and no one to be afraid of." That is Mrs. Lucynell Crater's first impression of Mr. Shiftlet as he approaches her home. But things are not what they seem in O'Connor's stories, which often contain deep psychological complexities. Critic C. Hugh Holman wrote that "Flannery O'Connor's world is the world of people rendered grotesque by their inability to satisfy their spiritual hungers." As you read "The Life You Save May Be Your Own," make some inferences about the characters and their motives. Is Mr. Shiftlet a complex character, or is he entirely predictable? Is Mrs. Crater shrewd or naive?

Literary Focus

Diction Flannery O'Connor's fiction is distinguished by her careful choice of words. Consider Mr. Shiftlet's name, for example. The name sounds almost like the word *shiftless.* What clue might this give you about his character? This thoughtful choice of words and phrases, which considers both the connotative and denotative meanings of words as well as levels of usage, is called **diction.**

Writer's Notebook

Good and Evil Much of literature through the ages deals with the conflict between good and evil. The Biblical accounts of Adam and Eve and the serpent and of Cain's murder of Abel are just the beginning. In your writer's notebook, write examples of stories, novels, movies, television shows, and even video games that you have read, seen, or played that deal with good versus evil. Explain how good and evil are portrayed in these examples.

The Life You Save May Be Your Own   **719**

Before Reading

Building Background

Students may be familiar with grotesques—strange characters often with odd or unattractive traits—in horror stories and psychological dramas. In this story the author uses a realistic style to present grotesque characters.

Literary Focus

O'Connor's **diction** supports her subtle but powerful imagery, as in the woman's looking toward a "piercing sunset." In the story O'Connor also carefully captures the speaking style of her characters. For example, the man introduces himself by saying, "Name Tom T. Shiftlet." The author crafts her story to depict characters vividly.

Writer's Notebook

Have students review the villains in each of their examples and list any common characteristics. What traits comprise traditional or popular images of evil?

More About Flannery O'Connor

Other works by O'Connor include the novel *The Violent Bear It Away* (1960) and short stories collected in *A Good Man Is Hard to Find* (1955).

Connections to
AuthorWorks

Flannery O'Connor is a featured author in the AuthorWorks CD-ROM series.

SUPPORT MATERIALS OVERVIEW

Unit 7 Resource Book
- Graphic Organizer, p. 1
- Study Guide, p. 1
- Vocabulary, p. 1
- Grammar, p. 4
- Alternate Check Test, p. 5
- Vocabulary Test, p. 6
- Selection Test, pp. 7–8

Building English Proficiency
- Literature Summaries
- Activities, p. 222

Reading, Writing & Grammar SkillBook
- Vocabulary, pp. 5–6
- Reading, pp. 79–80
- Writing, pp. 117–118
- Grammar, Usage, and Mechanics, pp. 262–265

Technology
- Audiotape
- Personal Journal Software
- Custom Literature Database: Biblical selections about themes in the story appear on the database.
- Test Generator Software

THE LIFE YOU SAVE MAY BE YOUR OWN

Flannery O'Connor

The old woman and her daughter were sitting on their porch when Mr. Shiftlet came up their road for the first time. The old woman slid to the edge of her chair and leaned forward, shading her eyes from the piercing sunset with her hand. The daughter could not see far in front of her and continued to play with her fingers. Although the old woman lived in this desolate[1] spot with only her daughter and she had never seen Mr. Shiftlet before, she could tell, even from a distance, that he was a tramp and no one to be afraid of. His left coat sleeve was folded up to show that there was only half an arm in it and his gaunt[2] figure listed slightly to the side as if the breeze were pushing him. He had on a black town suit and a brown felt hat that was turned up in the front and down in the back and he carried a tin tool box by a handle. He came on, at an amble, up her road, his face turned toward the sun which appeared to be balancing itself on the peak of a small mountain.

The old woman didn't change her position until he was almost into her yard; then she rose with one hand fisted on her hip. The daughter, a large girl in a short blue organdy dress, saw him all at once and jumped up and began to stamp and point and make excited speechless sounds.

Mr. Shiftlet stopped just inside the yard and set his box on the ground and tipped his hat at her as if she were not in the least afflicted; then he turned toward the old woman and swung the hat all the way off. He had long black slick hair that hung flat from a part in the middle to beyond the tips of his ears on either side. His face descended in forehead for more than half its length and ended suddenly with his features just balanced over a jutting steel-trap jaw. He seemed to be a young man but he had a look of

---

1. desolate (des′ə lit), *adj.* deserted.
2. gaunt (gônt), *adj.* very thin and bony.

1

SELECTION SUMMARY

The Life You Save May Be Your Own

A wily one-armed tramp comes upon an old southern country house and works as a handyman in exchange for a place to stay. The old woman who owns the house sees him as a prospective husband for her daughter, who is mentally handicapped. The man, Mr. Shiftlet, is kind to the daughter and performs repairs. He even manages to fix an old car, in which he has been sleeping. The old woman, Mrs. Crater, uses the automobile to bribe Shiftlet into marrying her daughter. She gives him money to take her daughter on a honey- moon. He marries the daughter but deserts her when she falls asleep in a roadside diner on the way to Mobile. He then picks up a hitchhiker and starts to lecture him about the virtues of a good mother. The hitchhiker tells him to go to the devil and jumps out of the moving car. Depressed, Shiftlet prays for the Lord to remove sinners from the earth as he drives into a thunderstorm.

 *For summaries in other languages, see the **Building English Proficiency** book.*

After reading "The Life You Save May Be Your Own," decide whether you think Mrs. Crater's first impression of Mr. Shiftlet describes the man in Billy Morrow Jackson's 1958 painting, *The Interloper.*

Responses to Caption   Some students may judge the pictured man as resembling "a tramp and no one to be afraid of," as Mrs. Crater thinks of Shiftlet. Others are unlikely to see the figure as a harmless tramp.

Visual Literacy   Ask students to consider the weight that a title can carry, when it is the only verbal element of an artwork.

Questions   Do you think *The Interloper* is an appropriate title for this painting? What other titles might fit this painting? *(Encourage students to give reasons for their responses.)*

2 Literary Element
Simile

O'Connor compares the young woman's eye color to that of a peacock, a vivid image. Some readers may feel this descriptive detail points out an attractiveness in an otherwise pitiable character.

composed dissatisfaction as if he understood life thoroughly.

"Good evening," the old woman said. She was about the size of a cedar fence post and she had a man's gray hat pulled down low over her head.

The tramp stood looking at her and didn't answer. He turned his back and faced the sunset. He swung both his whole and his short arm up slowly so that they indicated an expanse of sky and his figure formed a crooked cross. The old woman watched him with her arms folded across her chest as if she were the owner of the sun, and the daughter watched, her head thrust forward and her fat helpless hands hanging at the wrists. She had long pink-gold hair and eyes **2** as blue as a peacock's neck.

He held the pose for almost fifty seconds and then he picked up his box and came on to

The Life You Save May Be Your Own   **721**

BUILDING ENGLISH PROFICIENCY

Making Predictions

Readers who think about what may happen next in a story are attentive and can understand it better, even if their predictions turn out to be inaccurate. Help students make predictions based on the character descriptions and action of the opening paragraphs. Encourage students to anticipate likely events but not to worry if the story surprises them. The "grotesque" or unusual characters in this story may not act in ways typical of conventional fiction. The following considerations may help.

- Shiftlet carries a tool box. What might he want? *(Possible response: odd jobs; work)*
- The woman is described as old. Is her daughter more likely to be a child or an adult? *(an adult)*
- The narrator says that the woman "lived in this desolate spot with only her daughter." Is it likely that they are rich, financially comfortable, or poor? *(poor)*

Allow students to discuss their plot expectations.

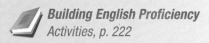 *Building English Proficiency*
Activities, p. 222

Make Connections

O'Connor reportedly considered the title "The World Is Almost Rotten" for this story. Students may want to keep this comment by Shiftlet in mind as they continue reading. Ask students to compare his actions to his self-righteous statements.

4 Literary Focus

Diction

Diction is the manner of expressing ideas in words. Three kinds of diction mark this story. The narrator relates the story with a very expressive and somewhat formal choice of words and phrasing. One character sometimes speaks formally, seeking impressive phrasing. At other times the characters speak naturally, in an informal English dialect, omitting words as is common in conversation.

Questions

- How does the narrator reveal Shiftlet's interest in the car as he introduces himself? *(In one sentence, the narrator tells that he murmurs his name and looks at the tires.)*

- What philosophical statements does he make in this conversation? *(Possible responses: He refers to the sunset, the changes and rottenness of the world, the idea that doctors studying the heart don't know more about it than others, and the tendency of some people to lie.)*

---

the porch and dropped down on the bottom step. "Lady," he said in a firm nasal voice, "I'd give a fortune to live where I could see me a sun do that every evening."

"Does it every evening," the old woman said and sat back down. The daughter sat down too and watched him with a cautious sly look as if he were a bird that had come up very close. He leaned to one side, rooting in his pants pocket, and in a second he brought out a package of chewing gum and offered her a piece. She took it and unpeeled it and began to chew without taking her eyes off him. He offered the old woman a piece but she only raised her upper lip to indicate she had no teeth.

Mr. Shiftlet's pale sharp glance had already passed over everything in the yard—the pump near the corner of the house and the big fig tree that three or four chickens were preparing to roost in—and had moved to a shed where he saw the square rusted back of an automobile. "You ladies drive?" he asked.

"That car ain't run in fifteen years," the old woman said. "The day my husband died, it quit running."

3 "Nothing is like it used to be, lady," he said. "The world is almost rotten."

"That's right," the old woman said. "You from around here?"

4 "Name Tom T. Shiftlet," he murmured, looking at the tires.

"I'm pleased to meet you," the old woman said. "Name Lucynell Crater and daughter Lucynell Crater. What you doing around here, Mr. Shiftlet?"

He judged the car to be about a 1928 or '29 Ford. "Lady," he said, and turned and gave her his full attention, "lemme tell you something. There's one of these doctors in Atlanta that's taken a knife and cut the human heart—the human heart," he repeated, leaning forward, "out of a man's chest and held it in his hand," and he held his hand out, palm up, as if it were slightly weighted with the human heart, "and

studied it like it was a day-old chicken, and, lady," he said, allowing a long significant pause in which his head slid forward and his clay-colored eyes brightened, "he don't know no more about it than you or me."

"That's right," the old woman said.

"Why, if he was to take that knife and cut into every corner of it, he still wouldn't know no more than you or me. What you want to bet?"

"Nothing," the old woman said wisely. "Where you come from, Mr. Shiftlet?"

He didn't answer. He reached into his pocket and brought out a sack of tobacco and a package of cigarette papers and rolled himself a cigarette, expertly with one hand, and attached it in a hanging position to his upper lip. Then he took a box of wooden matches from his pocket and struck one on his shoe. He held the burning match as if he were studying the mystery of flame while it traveled dangerously toward his skin. The daughter began to make loud noises and to point to his hand and shake her finger at him, but when the flame was just before touching him, he leaned down with his hand cupped over it as if he were going to set fire to his nose and lit the cigarette.

He flipped away the dead match and blew a stream of gray into the evening. A sly look came over his face. "Lady," he said, "nowadays, people'll do anything anyways. I can tell you my name is Tom T. Shiftlet and I come from Tarwater, Tennessee, but you never have seen me before: how you know I ain't lying? How you know my name ain't Aaron Sparks, lady, and I come from Singleberry, Georgia, or how you know it's not George Speeds and I come from Lucy, Alabama, or how you know I ain't Thompson Bright from Toolafalls, Mississippi?"

"I don't know nothing about you," the old woman muttered, irked.[3]

"Lady," he said, "people don't care how they lie. Maybe the best I can tell you is, I'm a man; but listen, lady," he said and paused and made

---

3. **irked** (ėrkd), *adj.* disgusted, annoyed.

MINI-LESSON: GRAMMAR

Using Commas in Addresses and Names

Teach　Use Shiftlet's speech (page 722): "How you know my name ain't Aaron Sparks, lady, and I come from Singleberry, Georgia, . . . or how you know I ain't Thompson Bright from Toolafalls, Mississippi?" In the middle of a sentence, the city name and state name are followed by commas.

- Remind students of commas in place names and addresses. A comma separates a city or town name from its state, province, or country name. (A ZIP code is not preceded by a comma.)

- Point out that a title such as *Jr.* following a name is separated from the rest of the sentence by a pair of commas. For example, "My name is Lee Jones, Jr., from Omaha, Nebraska, sir."

Activity Idea　Have students work in groups to make up lists of personal names, place names, and addresses. Include titles such as *M.D., R.N.* (Registered Nurse), *Jr.,* and *Sr.* Have each group incorporate its names into a brief story, using commas as appropriate.

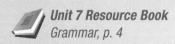

Unit 7 Resource Book
Grammar, p. 4

his tone more ominous still, "what is a man?"

The old woman began to gum a seed. "What you carry in that tin box, Mr. Shiftlet?" she asked.

"Tools," he said, put back. "I'm a carpenter."

"Well, if you come out here to work, I'll be able to feed you and give you a place to sleep but I can't pay. I'll tell you that before you begin," she said.

There was no answer at once and no particular expression on his face. He leaned back against the two-by-four that helped support the porch roof. "Lady," he said slowly, "there's some men that some things mean more to them than money." The old woman rocked without comment, and the daughter watched the trigger that moved up and down in his neck. He told the old woman then that all most people were interested in was money, but he asked what a man was made for. He asked her if a man was made for money, or what. He asked her what she thought she was made for but she didn't answer, she only [5] sat rocking and wondered if a one-armed man could put a new roof on her garden house. He asked a lot of questions that she didn't answer. He told her that he was twenty-eight years old and had lived a varied life. He had been a gospel singer, a foreman on the railroad, an assistant in an undertaking parlor, and he had come over the radio for three months with Uncle Roy and his Red Creek Wranglers. He said he had fought and bled in the Arm Service of his country and visited every foreign land and that everywhere he had seen people that didn't care if they did a thing one way or another. He said he hadn't [6] been raised thataway.

A fat yellow moon appeared on the branches of the fig tree as if it were going to roost there with the chickens. He said that a man had to escape to the country to see the world whole and that he wished he lived in a desolate place like this where he could see the sun go

...there's some men that some things mean more to them than money.

down every evening like God made it to do.

"Are you married or are you single?" the old woman asked.

There was a long silence. "Lady," he asked finally, "where would you find you an innocent woman today? I wouldn't have any of this trash I could just pick up."

The daughter was leaning very far down, hanging her head almost between her knees, watching him through a triangular door she had made in her overturned hair; and she suddenly fell in a heap on the floor and began to whimper. Mr. Shiftlet straightened her out and [7] helped her get back in the chair.

"Is she your baby girl?" he asked.

"My only," the old woman said, "and she's the sweetest girl in the world. I wouldn't give her up for nothing on earth. She's smart too. She can sweep the floor, cook, wash, feed the chickens, and hoe. I wouldn't give her up for a casket of jewels."

"No," he said kindly, "don't ever let any man take her away from you."

"Any man come after her," the old woman said, "'ll have to stay around the place."

Mr. Shiftlet's eye in the darkness was focused on a part of the automobile bumper that glittered in the distance. "Lady," he said, jerking his short arm up as if he could point with it to her house and yard and pump, "there ain't a broken thing on this plantation that I couldn't fix for you, one-arm jackleg or not. I'm a man," he said with a sullen[4] dignity, "even if I ain't a whole one. I got," he said, tapping his knuckles on the floor to emphasize the immensity of what he was going to say, "a moral intelligence!" and his face pierced out of the darkness into a shaft of doorlight and he stared at her as if he were astonished himself at this impossible truth.

The old woman was not impressed with the phrase. "I told you you could hang around and

---

4. sullen (sul'ən), *adj.* showing resentment; somber.

The Life You Save May Be Your Own **723**

[5] **Literary Element**
Characterization

Question What do Mrs. Crater's thoughts as Shiftlet speaks reveal about her? *(Possible response: She doesn't care what he says; she is trying to figure out what she can get from him.)*

[6] **Literary Element**
Irony

Question What contrasts does the author create between the way Shiftlet depicts himself and the image of him that the narrator provides? *(Possible response: He poses as a moral man in a rotten world, who wasn't "raised thataway," and who can't find an innocent woman. His words and actions suggest that he is a wanderer, more interested in the car than the people, and familiar with falsehood.)*

[7] **Reading/Thinking Skills**
Identify Author's Purpose

O'Connor injects irreverent humor into the story. One example is the town names—Tarwater, Singleberry, Lucy, and Toolafalls. Another is the juxtaposition of images and comments about serious topics such as religion, ethics, and marriage with details such as Mrs. Crater bluntly telling Shiftlet she can't pay for work.

Question Who represents an "innocent woman," the kind Shiftlet claims he cannot find? *(Lucynell Crater, the daughter)*

BUILDING ENGLISH PROFICIENCY

Understanding Dialect and Double Negatives

Advise students, if necessary, that the characters' English has regional and informal characteristics, such as the following. Clarify differences between these conversational attributes and formal English.

- Colloquialisms such as *ain't* and *lemme* (let me)
- Omitted words in statements such as "Name Lucynell Crater and daughter Lucynell Crater" (for "My name is Lucynell Crater, and this is my daughter, Lucynell Crater") and "What you want to bet?" (for "What do you" or "What would you want to bet?")
- Double negatives, in statements such as "I don't know nothing about you" and "he don't know no more about it than you or me"

Activity Students can work with partners to find sentences with informal or nonstandard English—such as omitted words and double negatives—and rewrite them in formal English. Here are sample sentences from the story.

- Does it every evening. (page 722)
- You ladies drive? (page 722)
- That car ain't run in fifteen years. (page 722)
- I wouldn't give her up for nothing on earth. (page 723)
- Any man come after her'll have to stay around the place. (page 723)

723

Possible Responses   She wants him to fix things around her house and maybe marry her daughter. He wants food, shelter, and a chance to fix—or maybe get—her car.

9 Literary Element
Tone

Questions

• The narrator describes the evening sky from a perspective reflecting Mrs. Crater's view of "her" mountains and the moon leaving her chickens. What do these details reveal about Mrs. Crater? *(Possible responses: that she thinks of the world only in terms of herself; that she is arrogant)*

• How would you describe the author's tone? *(Possible responses: ironic, amused)*

10 Historical Note
The Assembly Line

In 1913 Henry Ford revolutionized the production of automobiles by refining the moving assembly line method, which required standardization and interchange-ability of parts. The synchronized assembly line required a division of labor which assigned each worker to a specific and repetitive task, such as tightening a bolt or welding a joint. Contrary to Shiftlet's contention, mass assembly decreased the average price of cars.

11 Active Reading
Clarify

Possible Response   She wants to stir up a romance or get her daughter married.

---

work for food," she said, "if you don't mind sleeping in that car yonder."

"Why listen, Lady," he said with a grin of delight, "the monks of old slept in their coffins!"

"They wasn't as advanced as we are," the old woman said.

> **8** EVALUATE: Based on their conversations, what do you think Mrs. Crater wants from Mr. Shiftlet? What do you think Mr. Shiftlet wants from Mrs. Crater?

The next morning he began on the roof of the garden house while Lucynell, the daughter, sat on a rock and watched him work. He had not been around a week before the change he had made in the place was apparent. He had patched the front and back steps, built a new hog pen, restored a fence, and taught Lucynell, who was completely deaf and had never said a word in her life, to say the word *bird*. The big rosy-faced girl followed him everywhere, saying "Burrttddt ddbirrrttdt," and clapping her hands. The old woman watched from a distance, secretly pleased. She was ravenous[5] for a son-in-law.

Mr. Shiftlet slept on the hard narrow back seat of the car with his feet out the side window. He had his razor and a can of water on a crate that served him as a bedside table and he put up a piece of mirror against the back glass and kept his coat neatly on a hanger that he hung over one of the windows.

9 In the evenings he sat on the steps and talked while the old woman and Lucynell rocked violently in their chairs on either side of him. The old woman's three mountains were black against the dark blue sky and were visited off and on by various planets and by the moon after it had left the chickens. Mr. Shiftlet pointed out that the reason he had improved this plantation was because he had taken a personal interest in it. He said he was even going to make the automobile run.

He had raised the hood and studied the mechanism and he said he could tell that the car

had been built in the days when cars were really built. You take now, he said, one man puts in one bolt and another man puts in another bolt and another man puts in another bolt so that it's a man for a bolt. That's why you have to pay so much for a car: you're paying all those men. Now if you didn't have to pay for but one man, you could get you a cheaper car and one that had had a personal interest taken in it, and it would be a better car. The old woman agreed with him that this was so. **10**

Mr. Shiftlet said that the trouble with the world was that nobody cared, or stopped and took any trouble. He said he never would have been able to teach Lucynell to say a word if he hadn't cared and stopped long enough.

"Teach her to say something else," the old woman said.

"What you want her to say next?" Mr. Shiftlet asked.

The old woman's smile was broad and toothless and suggestive. "Teach her to say 'sugarpie,' " she said.

Mr. Shiftlet already knew what was on her mind.

> CLARIFY: What is on Mrs. Crater's mind? **11**

The next day he began to tinker with the automobile and that evening he told her that if she would buy a fan belt, he would be able to make the car run.

The old woman said she would give him the money. "You see that girl yonder?" she asked, pointing to Lucynell who was sitting on the floor a foot away, watching him, her eyes blue even in the dark. "If it was ever a man wanted to take her away, I would say, 'No man on earth is going to take that sweet girl of mine away from me!' but if he was to say, 'Lady, I don't want to take her away, I want her right here,' I would say, 'Mister, I don't blame you none. I wouldn't pass

---

5. **ravenous** (rav′ə nəs), *adj.* very hungry; greedy.

MINI-LESSON: LITERARY FOCUS

Diction

Teach   Point out that O'Connor carefully chooses words to describe characters and develop thematic unity. For example, the narrator states that Mrs. Crater is "ravenous for a son-in-law."

Question   What does the adjective *ravenous* suggest about the woman? *(Possible response: Her desire to get her daughter married is like the hunger of a starving predator who will do anything to catch the prey.)*

Activity Idea   Students can select a description such as one of the following and explain how any

of the author's word choices make the description more vivid or meaningful.

• Shiftlet sleeping on the car's "hard narrow back seat"

• The two women rocking "violently" in their chairs beside Shiftlet

• Shiftlet's explanation that he had taken "a personal interest" in "this plantation"

• The old woman's "broad and toothless and suggestive" smile

Aaron Bohrod (1908–1992) was a realist painter who grew up in Chicago and later lived in Wisconsin. He painted urban scenes, war scenes of D-Day combat, and other paintings, including *trompe l'oeil* ("tricks the eye") works.

Responses to Caption   Similarities include the desolate appearance, need for repairs, and old car.

▲ Does the setting in Aaron Bohrod's painting, *Landscape Near Chicago* (1934), remind you of Mrs. Crater's place? Why or why not?

12 Literary Element
Dialogue

Discuss the manner in which Shiftlet often answers a question with a question, or responds to a statement with an opinion on an unrelated topic.

Question   What does Shiftlet's use of language suggest about his character? *(Possible responses: He steers conversation indirectly toward his hidden goals; he likes to hear himself talk; he listens only for his own purposes.)*

13 Literary Element
Characterization

Ask students to discuss what Mrs. Crater's answer about her daughter's age indicates, and how Mr. Shiftlet's expression as he drives the car from the shed reveals more about his character.

up a chance to live in a permanent place and get the sweetest girl in the world myself. You ain't no fool,' I would say."

"How old is she?" Mr. Shiftlet asked casually.

"Fifteen, sixteen," the old woman said. The girl was nearly thirty but because of her innocence it was impossible to guess.

"It would be a good idea to paint it too," Mr. Shiftlet remarked. "You don't want it to rust out."

"We'll see about that later," the old woman said.

The next day he walked into town and returned with the parts he needed and a can of gasoline. Late in the afternoon, terrible noises issued from the shed and the old woman rushed out of the house, thinking Lucynell was somewhere having a fit. Lucynell was sitting on a chicken crate, stamping her feet and screaming, "Burrrddttt! bddurrddtttt!" but her fuss was drowned out by the car. With a volley of blasts it emerged from the shed, moving in a fierce and stately[6] way. Mr. Shiftlet was in the driver's seat, sitting very erect. He had an expression of serious modesty on his face as if he had just raised the dead.

That night, rocking on the porch, the old

_____

6. stately (stāt′lē), *adj.* having dignity; imposing; majestic.

The Life You Save May Be Your Own   **725**

BUILDING ENGLISH PROFICIENCY

Recognizing Irony

Students may need help understanding that they should not accept at face value the things the characters say in this story. Shiftlet continually speaks and acts in ways intended to impress Mrs. Crater. She speaks and acts in a campaign to arrange a marriage between her daughter and the man who arrives at their home.

Activity Ideas

• Students can work in small groups to find statements with which Shiftlet is trying to impress the old woman with his intelligence, his skills as a carpenter or repairman, or his moral values.

• Likewise students can find statements that are part of the old woman's effort to make a match between young Lucynell and Shiftlet.

• Interested students can compare statements and actions in the story to the moves in a chess game or another tactical interaction between the man and the old woman.

14

Literary Element

Satirical Humor

While this story is not a conventional satire aimed at promoting social reform, it does contain humor that some critics consider satirical.

Mrs. Crater's praise of her mute daughter as a potentially ideal wife—who couldn't sass her husband or use foul language—has been called a satirical jab at traditional gender roles, including the ideal of a quiet, passive wife.

The stereotype of a man resisting marriage is used but distorted here. The discussion of marriage doesn't include the prospective bride, and Shiftlet voices his reluctance in noble terms that are not borne out by his actions in the rest of the story.

Literary Element

Simile

Questions To what does the narrator compare the descriptive words "poor disabled friendless drifting man" entering Shiftlet's head? *(a group of buzzards settling in the top of a tree)*

To what does Shiftlet compare a man's body and spirit, in his reply? *(He compares the body to a house and the spirit to a car "always on the move.")*

A vivid simile about Shiftlet's smile also appears on this page.

---

woman began her business at once. "You want you an innocent woman, don't you?" she asked sympathetically. "You don't want none of this trash."

"No'm, I don't," Mr. Shiftlet said.

"One that can't talk," she continued, "can't sass you back or use foul language. That's the kind for you to have. Right there," and she pointed to Lucynell sitting cross-legged in her chair, holding both feet in her hands.

"That's right," he admitted. "She wouldn't give me any trouble."

"Saturday," the old woman said, "you and her and me can drive into town and get married."

Mr. Shiftlet eased his position on the steps.

"I can't get married right now," he said. "Everything you want to do takes money and I ain't got any."

"What you need with money?" she asked.

"It takes money," he said. "Some people'll do anything anyhow these days, but the way I think, I wouldn't marry no woman that I couldn't take on a trip like she was somebody. I mean take her to a hotel and treat her. I wouldn't marry the Duchesser Windsor,[7] he said firmly, "unless I could take her to a hotel and give her something good to eat.

"I was raised thataway and there ain't a thing I can do about it. My old mother taught me how to do."

"Lucynell don't even know what a hotel is," the old woman muttered. "Listen here, Mr. Shiftlet," she said, sliding forward in her chair, "you'd be getting a permanent house and a deep well and the most innocent girl in the world. You don't need no money. Lemme tell you something: there ain't any place in the world for a poor disabled friendless drifting man."

The ugly words settled in Mr. Shiftlet's head like a group of buzzards in the top of a tree. He didn't answer at once. He rolled himself a cigarette and lit it and then he said in an even voice, "Lady, a man is divided into two parts, body and spirit."

> . . . the spirit, lady, is like a automobile: always on the move, always. . . .

The old woman clamped her gums together.

"A body and a spirit," he repeated. "The body, lady, is like a house: it don't go anywhere; but the spirit, lady, is like a automobile: always on the move, always. . . ."

"Listen, Mr. Shiftlet," she said, "my well never goes dry and my house is always warm in the winter and there's no mortgage on a thing about this place. You can go to the courthouse and see for yourself. And yonder under that shed is a fine automobile." She laid the bait carefully. "You can have it painted by Saturday. I'll pay for the paint."

In the darkness, Mr. Shiftlet's smile stretched like a weary snake waking up by a fire. After a second he recalled himself and said, "I'm only saying a man's spirit means more to him than anything else. I would have to take my wife off for the weekend without no regards at all for cost. I got to follow where my spirit says to go."

"I'll give you fifteen dollars for a weekend trip," the old woman said in a crabbed voice. "That's the best I can do."

"That wouldn't hardly pay for more than the gas and the hotel," he said. "It wouldn't feed her."

"Seventeen-fifty," the old woman said. "That's all I got so it isn't any use you trying to milk me. You can take a lunch."

Mr. Shiftlet was deeply hurt by the word *milk.* He didn't doubt that she had more money sewed up in her mattress, but he had already told her he was not interested in her money. "I'll make that do," he said and rose and walked off without treating with her further.

On Saturday the three of them drove into town in the car that the paint had barely dried on and Mr. Shiftlet and Lucynell were married

---

7. **Duchesser Windsor.** The Duchess of Windsor was a member of the British royal family.

MINI-LESSON: SPEAKING AND LISTENING

Readers Theater

Teach Students can relate to and better understand O'Connor's characters by reading their dialogue dramatically. Explain or remind students that Readers Theater calls for readers to take the roles of characters and narrator(s) to read a selection or passage. The narrator or narrators read the narrative portions, and each character-reader reads his or her character's lines. There is no need to memorize parts, act out the movements, or speak in regional accents.

Apply Volunteers may read a short scene containing dialogue from the story. Then small groups can select other important scenes to prepare.

Activity Idea Groups can dramatically read their passages. Students then can compare their impressions of the characters.

in the Ordinary's office while the old woman witnessed. As they came out of the courthouse, Mr. Shiftlet began twisting his neck in his collar. He looked morose[8] and bitter as if he had been insulted while someone held him. "That didn't satisfy me none," he said. "That was just something a woman in an office did, nothing but paper and blood tests. What do they know about my blood? If they was to take my heart and cut it out," he said, "they wouldn't know a thing about me. It didn't satisfy me at all."

"It satisfied the law," the old woman said sharply.

"The law," Mr. Shiftlet said and spit. "It's the law that don't satisfy me."

He had painted the car dark green with a yellow band around it just under the windows. The three of them climbed in the front seat and the old woman said, "Don't Lucynell look pretty? Looks like a baby doll." Lucynell was dressed up in a white dress that her mother had uprooted from a trunk and there was a Panama hat on her head with a bunch of red wooden cherries on the brim. Every now and then her placid[9] expression was changed by a sly isolated little thought like a shoot of green in the desert. "You got a prize!" the old woman said.

Mr. Shiftlet didn't even look at her.

They drove back to the house to let the old woman off and pick up the lunch. When they were ready to leave, she stood staring at the window of the car, with her fingers clenched around the glass. Tears began to seep sideways out of her eyes and run along the dirty creases in her face. "I ain't ever been parted with her for two days before," she said.

Mr. Shiftlet started the motor.

"And I wouldn't let no man have her but you because I seen you would do right. Goodby, Sugarbaby," she said, clutching at the sleeve of the white dress. Lucynell looked straight at her and didn't seem to see her there at all. Mr. Shiftlet eased the car forward so that she had to move her hands.

SUMMARIZE: How would you describe the change that has come over Mr. Shiftlet?

The early afternoon was clear and open and surrounded by pale blue sky. Although the car would go only thirty miles an hour, Mr. Shiftlet imagined a terrific climb and dip and swerve that went entirely to his head so that he forgot his morning bitterness. He had always wanted an automobile but he had never been able to afford one before. He drove very fast because he wanted to make Mobile by nightfall.

Occasionally he stopped his thought long enough to look at Lucynell in the seat beside him. She had eaten the lunch as soon as they were out of the yard and now she was pulling the cherries off the hat one by one and throwing them out the window. He became depressed in spite of the car. He had driven about a hundred miles when he decided that she must be hungry again and at the next small town they came to, he stopped in front of an aluminum-painted eating place called The Hot Spot and took her in and ordered her a plate of ham and grits. The ride had made her sleepy and as soon as she got up on the stool, she rested her head on the counter and shut her eyes. There was no one in The Hot Spot but Mr. Shiftlet and the boy behind the counter, a pale youth with a greasy rag hung over his shoulder. Before he could dish up the food, she was snoring gently.

"Give it to her when she wakes up," Mr. Shiftlet said. "I'll pay for it now."

The boy bent over her and stared at the long pink-gold hair and the half-shut sleeping eyes. Then he looked up and stared at Mr. Shiftlet. "She looks like an angel of Gawd," he murmured. "Hitchhiker," Mr. Shiftlet explained. "I can't wait. I got to make Tuscaloosa."

The boy bent over again and very carefully

---

8. morose (mə rōs′), *adj.* gloomy; sullen; ill-humored.
9. placid (plas′id), *adj.* pleasantly calm or peaceful.

The Life You Save May Be Your Own **727**

16 Reading/Thinking Skills
Visualize

- Ask students to visualize Shiftlet's movements and expression after the marriage.
- Students can portray their impressions of Shiftlet's expression with their own faces or in drawings.

17 Literary Element
Conflict

The plot involves the conflict between Mrs. Crater's and Mr. Shiftlet's desires. Tension is high at this point, because Mrs. Crater is still trying to secure her victory, and Mr. Shiftlet is feeling trapped and pressured.

Question Why does the old woman compliment Lucynell's appearance? *(Possible response: She hopes to cajole Shiftlet into thinking he made a good decision.)*

18 Active Reading
Summarize

Possible Response Mr. Shiftlet has abandoned his polite facade and has stopped trying to impress Mrs. Crater. Impatient to be on his way, he cruelly ignores her emotional outburst.

19 Reader's Response
Evaluate

Questions How does Shiftlet leaving Lucynell in the diner make you feel about him? *(Possible response: I lose all respect for him, because he is abandoning a defenseless person far from her home, and he lies to the boy about it.)*

BUILDING ENGLISH PROFICIENCY

Understanding a Turning Point in the Story

It is important that students understand the significance of Shiftlet's actions as he stops at the Hot Spot diner and then leaves. If necessary, help students comprehend that what he explains to the boy is very different from his real intent.

Activity Idea Groups of students can read the story scene aloud, with one or more narrators, a reader for the lines spoken by Shiftlet, and a reader of the lines of the counter boy.

Each of these readers can stop at any time and explain what the character thinks or knows is happening. A student reading the narrator's part might clarify any points that are not clear.

VOCABULARY STUDY

1. f. frantic
2. i. cheerful
3. g. stout
4. e. populous
5. d. chilly
6. a. pleased
7. c. appreciate
8. b. satiated
9. i. cheerful
10. h. undignified

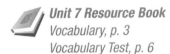

Unit 7 Resource Book
Vocabulary, p. 3
Vocabulary Test, p. 6

WRITING CHOICES

Writer's Notebook Update

Suggest that students use examples of symbolism, simile, and imagery from the story to support their argument. Remind students that O'Connor's writing is influenced by her religion. For example, how do images such as the smile as a "snake waking by a fire," "the angel of Gawd," and the "crooked cross" fit into students' responses?

Missing Persons

You might suggest that gifted students research literary criticism of O'Connor's work to discover her original ending to this story, which is more sinister than the revised version.

Selection Test

Unit 7 Resource Book
pp. 7–8

Vocabulary Study

Match each vocabulary word from the first column with an antonym from the second column. Use the Glossary or a dictionary for help. You will use one answer twice.

desolate
gaunt
irked
morose
placid
ravenous
rue
stately
sullen
sultry

1. placid   a. pleased
2. sullen   b. satiated
3. gaunt   c. appreciate
4. desolate   d. chilly
5. sultry   e. populous
6. irked   f. frantic
7. rue   g. stout
8. ravenous   h. undignified
9. morose   i. cheerful
10. stately

Expressing Your Ideas

Writing Choices

Writer's Notebook Update Is Mr. Shiftlet evil? Mrs. Crater? You listed literature, movies, television shows, and video games that deal with the conflict of good versus evil. Do you want to add this story to the list? Write a paragraph explaining whether and how you think this story develops the conflict between good and evil.

Part Two Imagine Mrs. Crater's dismay when the new Mr. and Mrs. Shiftlet fail to return home from their honeymoon. Write a **continuation of the story** explaining what Mrs. Crater does next and what ultimately happens to Lucynell and Mr. Shiftlet.

Other Options

Wedding Portrait Mr. Shiftlet and Lucynell did not have wedding photographs taken. Imagine that you are a portrait artist. Make a **color drawing** of the bride and bridegroom on their wedding day. Under the pictures, write the quotes that guided you.

Sheriff's Report When Shiftlet and Lucynell did not return, Mrs. Crater probably reported the incident to the local sheriff. Work with a classmate to create a **dialogue** between Mrs. Crater and the sheriff, including an explanation about Lucynell, Mr. Shiftlet, and the wedding. Perform your dialogue for the class.

730   Unit Seven: Years of Change

OTHER OPTIONS

Wedding Portrait

Instruct students to pay close attention to the details that O'Connor carefully includes in her physical descriptions.

You also might suggest that students draw a cartoon that captures an event from the story, such as the wedding or the resurrection of the old car.

Sheriff's Reports

Remind students to be faithful to the characterization of Mrs. Crater as it is developed in the story. Do students think she would tell the truth? How might her anger towards Mr. Shiftlet affect the veracity of her report? Do students think she would show remorse?

Before Reading

I Stand Here Ironing

by Tillie Olsen

Tillie Olsen
born 1913

Tillie Olsen began writing her first novel when she was nineteen, but put it aside after her marriage to Jack Olsen and the birth of their four daughters. For twenty years there was no time for writing. In addition to caring for her family, Olsen worked as a typist in San Francisco. She never lost her desire to write, however, and was able to begin writing again when she earned a creative writing fellowship to Stanford University in 1956. A Ford grant enabled her to quit her office job in 1959 and write full time. *Tell Me a Riddle,* which includes "I Stand Here Ironing," was published in 1961 when Olsen was forty-eight. Olsen has taught at Amherst, Stanford, MIT, and the University of Massachusetts.

Building Background

Doing the Best I Can Parenthood is often idealized in magazine ads and television shows: a beautiful, well-dressed, young woman cuddles a cherubic, smiling child in a beautifully furnished home. In the background, painting the baby's room, is the handsome, loving, attentive father. Reality is often very different. Interview your own or other parents about the difficulties and rewards of parenting. Work with a partner to develop questions to ask them. After the interviews are completed, discuss the parents' responses in class, and make a chart recording the most difficult and most rewarding parts of being a parent.

Parenthood	
Most Difficult	Most Rewarding

Literary Focus

Interior Monologue "I Stand Here Ironing" is told entirely through the narrator's thoughts, or stream of consciousness, as she reviews crucial events in her daughter Emily's life. One technique for presenting stream of consciousness is **interior monologue,** the recording of the emotional experiences of a character. The reader is made aware of the character's private thoughts, which are never spoken aloud. As you read "I Stand Here Ironing," decide whether this is an effective technique for the story.

Writer's Notebook

Childhood Memories Emily, the narrator's daughter, is a high school student. Before you begin reading her mother's reflections on Emily's childhood, talk to family members about your childhood. What do they remember about you at various ages? Write about some of these events in your notebook.

I Stand Here Ironing **731**

Before Reading

Building Background

Some parents may not want to be interviewed; advise students to respect their wishes.

Explain that the story was written in 1952, when many people were less accepting of single, working mothers. Discuss the effects of social change on the challenges of parenthood.

Literary Focus

Ask students if they have ever composed a speech in their heads before meeting with an adult. Note that the narrator addresses her **interior monologue** to someone referred to as "you," possibly a counselor at her daughter Emily's school. The mother's tone suggests that this listener is sitting in judgment as the mother explains details of her parenting.

Writer's Notebook

Students also can write about events they remember from their childhood. Do they recall the same events as their parents? What makes these moments memorable?

More About Tillie Olsen

Jobs that Tillie Olsen has had in her life include packinghouse worker, punch-press operator, trimmer in a slaughterhouse, shaker in a laundry, secretary, and waitress. Another work by Olsen is "Tell Me a Riddle," an O. Henry Award story, 1961.

SUPPORT MATERIALS OVERVIEW

Unit 7 Resource Book
- Graphic Organizer, p. 9
- Study Guide, p. 10
- Vocabulary, p. 11
- Grammar, p. 12
- Alternate Check Test, p. 13
- Vocabulary Test, p. 14
- Selection Test, pp. 15–16

Building English Proficiency
- Literature Summaries
- Activities, p. 223

Reading, Writing & Grammar SkillBook
- Reading, pp. 41–45
- Grammar, Usage and Mechanics, pp. 198–199

Technology
- Audiotape
- Personal Journal Software
- Custom Literature Database: Several Edgar Lee Masters poems with interior monologues appear on the database.
- Test Generator Software

Selection Objectives

- To explore a mother's perspective on the challenges of motherhood
- To examine the perseverance of family members in the face of hardship
- To appreciate interior monologue as a literary form
- To recognize clear reference between pronouns and antecedents

Unit 7 Resource Book
Graphic Organizer, p. 9
Study Guide, p. 10

Theme Link

Olsen depicts a personal mother-daughter relationship as the mother reviews interactions, milestones, and mishaps of her daughter's life.

Vocabulary Preview

homely, not good-looking; plain

ecstasy, condition of very great joy; overwhelming delight

implore, beg or pray earnestly for

somber, melancholy; dismal

anonymity, condition or quality of being unknown, nameless

Students can add the words and definitions to their word lists in the Writer's Notebook.

1 Active Reading
Clarify

Possible Responses a guidance counselor, a teacher, a school administrator, or an employer

---

I STAND HERE IRONING

TILLIE OLSEN

I stand here ironing, and what you asked me moves tormented back and forth with the iron.

"I wish you could manage the time to come in and talk with me about your daughter. I'm sure you can help me understand her. She's a youngster who needs help and whom I'm deeply interested in helping."

"Who needs help." Even if I came, what good would it do? You think because I am her mother I have a key, or that in some way you could use me as a key? She has lived for nineteen years. There is all that life that has happened outside of me, beyond me.

1 **CLARIFY:** To whom do you think the narrator is responding?

And when is there time to remember, to sift, to weigh, to estimate, to total? I will start and there will be an interruption and I will have to gather it all together again. Or I will become engulfed with all I did or did not do, with what should have been and what cannot be helped.

She was a beautiful baby. The first and only one of our five that was beautiful at birth. You do not guess how new and uneasy her tenancy in her now-loveliness. You did not know her all those years she was thought homely,[1] or see her poring over her baby pictures, making me tell her over and over how beautiful she had been—and would be, I would tell her—and was now, to the seeing eye. But the seeing eyes were few or nonexistent. Including mine.

I nursed her. They feel that's important nowadays. I nursed all the children, but with her, with all the fierce rigidity of first motherhood, I did like the books then said. Though her cries battered me to trembling and my breasts ached with swollenness, I waited till the clock decreed.

Why do I put that first? I do not even know if it matters, or if it explains anything.

She was a beautiful baby. She blew shining bubbles of sound. She loved motion, loved light, loved color and music and textures. She would lie on the floor in her blue overalls, patting the surface so hard in ecstasy[2] her hands and feet would

---

1. **homely** (hōm′lē), *adj.* not good-looking; plain.
2. **ecstasy** (ek′stə sē), *n.* condition of very great joy; overwhelming delight.

SELECTION SUMMARY

I Stand Here Ironing

The narrator's nineteen-year-old daughter, Emily, is having trouble in school. A school staff member has requested a conference with Emily's mother. As if rehearsing her response, the mother stands at the ironing board, reviewing the sad facts of Emily's childhood. Themes of separation, alienation, and disease shape the mother's memories. She is apologetic about past separations over which she was powerless. Emily has survived her difficulties by developing a sharp sense of humor. She has transformed her pain into a talent for entertainment. The mother is uncertain how to help her daughter's comedic career but seems certain that Emily will find her way. When Emily briefly wanders into the room where her mother is pensively ironing, she seems buoyant but fatalistic. The narrator wishes that her daughter will come to know that she has the power to shape her own destiny.

*For summaries in other languages, see the **Building English Proficiency** book.*

Art Study

Edgar Degas (1834–1917) was a French Impressionist. Due to his classical training in artistic rendering, he strove for technical discipline. His studies of ballerinas reveal a preoccupation with impressions of space and form presented from unexpected angles.

Possible Response to Caption   Yes, the woman is alone, able to think, and in a world of her own, like the woman in the story.

Visual Literacy   A defining feature of the French Impressionist movement was its radical insistence that any scene that offered an opportunity to explore color, form, and light was a valid subject for a painting. This all-embracing eye differed from another tradition in art that called for art to depict "dignified" subject matter.

Question   What qualities make this scene, *Woman Ironing,* an interesting subject for a painting? *(Possible responses: the woman's concentration and diligence, the relationship between the human figure and the light from the background, the interest in details of life)*

Does the mood of Edgar Degas's painting, *Woman Ironing* (1892), resemble that of the story? Explain.

I Stand Here Ironing   **733**

BUILDING ENGLISH PROFICIENCY

Understanding Time Shifts

Throughout this story, the mother's thoughts travel back and forth between past and present. To help students recognize time shifts, ask students in small groups to begin T-charts. Students can read to find three details of events long ago and three details about what is happening in the story's present time. Students can write brief summaries of the incidents or details in columns of the chart.

Past	Present
My first baby was beautiful. I was a 19-year-old mother.	I am worried about my daughter.

 Building English Proficiencies Activities, p. 223

2 Historical Note
The Depression

- During 1933, one American worker in every four was unemployed.
- Between 1929 and 1932 about 11,000 U.S. banks failed.

3 Literary Element
Diction

Discuss how the mother must have felt separated from her baby all day. She describes the child's "weeping that could not be comforted," illustrating misery.

Question How does the word *lacerations* affect her description of her daughter's day care, "the lacerations of group life in the nurseries"? (*Possible response: It makes her daughter's experiences sound as painful as wounds, cuts, or tearing.*)

4 Literary Elements
Rhythm and Repetition

A volunteer might read the paragraph containing the repeated word *Momma* while imitating the action of ironing. How might the narrator move the iron and think the lines at the same time?

5 Literary Element
Clarify

Response She got married and started a new family.

---

blur. She was a miracle to me, but when she was eight months old, I had to leave her daytimes with the woman downstairs, to whom she was no miracle at all, for I worked or looked for work and for Emily's father, who "could no longer endure" (he wrote in his goodbye note) "sharing want with us."

2 I was nineteen. It was the pre-relief, pre-WPA[3] world of the depression. I would start running as soon as I got off the streetcar, running up the stairs, the place smelling sour, and awake or asleep to startle awake, when she saw me, she would break into a clogged weeping that could not be comforted, a weeping I can yet hear.

After a while I found a job hashing[4] at night so I could be with her days, and it was better. But it came to where I had to bring her to his family and leave her.

It took a long time to raise the money for her fare back. Then she got chicken pox, and I had to wait longer. When she finally came, I hardly knew her, walking quick and nervous like her father, looking like her father, thin, and dressed in a shoddy red that yellowed her skin and glared at the pockmarks. All the baby loveliness gone.

She was two. Old enough for nursery school they said, and I did not know then what I know now—the fatigue of the long day, and the lacer-3 ations of group life in the nurseries that are only parking places for children.

Except that it would have made no difference if I had known. It was the only place there was. It was the only way we could be together, the only way I could hold a job.

And even without knowing, I knew. I knew the teacher was evil because all these years it has curdled into my memory, the little boy hunched in the corner, her rasp, "Why aren't you outside, because Alvin hits you? That's no reason, go out, scaredy." I knew Emily hated it even if she did not clutch and implore[5] "Don't go, Mommy" like the other children, mornings.

She always had a reason why we should stay home. Momma, you look sick. Momma, I feel sick. Momma, the teachers aren't there today,

they're sick. Momma, there was a fire there last 4 night. Momma, it's a holiday today, no school, they told me.

But never a direct protest, never rebellion. I think of our others in their three-, four-year-oldness—the explosions, the tempers, the denunciations, the demands—and I feel suddenly ill. I put the iron down. What in me demanded that goodness in her? And what was the cost, the cost to her of such goodness?

The old man living in the back once said in his gentle way: "You should smile at Emily more when you look at her." What *was* in my face when I looked at her? I loved her. There were all the acts of love.

It was only with the others I remembered what he said, and it was the face of joy, and not of care or tightness or worry I turned to them—too late for Emily. She does not smile easily, let alone almost always as her brothers and sisters do. Her face is closed and somber,[6] but when she wants, how fluid. You must have seen it in her pantomimes; you spoke of her rare gift for comedy on the stage that rouses a laughter out of the audience so dear they applaud and applaud and do not want to let her go.

Where does it come from, that comedy? There was none of it in her when she came back to me that second time, after I had had to send her away again. She had a new daddy now to learn to love, and I think perhaps it was a better time.

CLARIFY: How did the narrator's life change at this point in time? 5

Except when we left her alone nights, telling ourselves she was old enough.

"Can't you go some other time, Mommy, like

---

3. **relief, WPA,** relief programs established to help the poor and unemployed during the Great Depression.
4. **hashing,** a slang term for waitressing.
5. implore (im plôr′), *v.* beg or pray earnestly for.
6. somber (som′bər), *adj.* melancholy; dismal.

MINI-LESSON: GRAMMAR

Pronouns and Antecedents

Teach Have students study the pronouns in the following sentences on page 734.

"The old man living in the back once said in his gentle way: 'You should smile at Emily more when you look at her.'"

"It was only with the others I remembered what he said, and it was the face of joy, and not of care or tightness or worry I turned to them—too late for Emily. She does not smile easily, let alone almost always as her brothers and sisters do."

Explain that readers know who is represented by each person pronoun: *his, you, her, I, he, them, she.* A pronoun must clearly refer to its proper antecedent. The old man is referred to as *he.*

Questions

- Who does the pronoun *I* refer to? (*the mother who is telling the story*)
- Who do the pronouns *them* and the *others* refer to? How do you know? (*Possible response: Emily's brothers and sisters; brothers and sisters are mentioned in this part of the story.*)
- Who does the pronoun *she* refer to? How do you know? (*Emily; the mother's commentary is about Emily; she is a singular feminine pronoun.*)

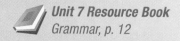
Unit 7 Resource Book
Grammar, p. 12

tomorrow?" she would ask. "Will it be just a little while you'll be gone? Do you promise?"

The time we came back, the front door open, the clock on the floor in the hall. She rigid awake. "It wasn't just a little while. I didn't cry. Three times I called you, just three times, and then I ran downstairs to open the door so you could come faster. The clock talked loud. I threw it away; it scared me when it talked."

6

She said the clock talked loud again that night when I went to the hospital to have Susan. She was delirious with the fever that comes before red measles, but she was fully conscious all the week I was gone and the week after we were home, when she could not come near the new baby or me.

She did not get well. She stayed skeleton thin, not wanting to eat, and night after night she had nightmares. She would call for me, and I would rouse from exhaustion to sleepily call back, "You're all right, darling—go to sleep—it's just a dream" and if she still called, in a sterner voice, "now go to sleep Emily, there's nothing to hurt you." Twice, only twice, when I had to get up for Susan anyhow, I went in to sit with her.

Now, when it is too late (as if she would let me hold and comfort her like I do the others), I get up and go to her at once at her moan or restless stirring. "Are you awake, Emily? Can I get you something?" And the answer is always the same: "No, I'm all right, go back to sleep, Mother."

They persuaded me at the clinic to send her away to a convalescent home in the country where "she can have the kind of food and care you can't manage for her, and you'll be free to concentrate on the new baby." They still send children to that place. I see pictures on the society page of sleek young women planning affairs to raise money for it, or dancing at the affairs, or decorating Easter eggs or filling Christmas stockings for the children.

They never have a picture of the children, so I do not know if the girls still wear those gigantic red bows and the ravaged looks on the every other Sunday when parents can come to visit "unless otherwise notified"—as we were notified the first six weeks.

Oh, it is a handsome place, green lawns and tall trees and fluted flower beds. High up on the balconies of each cottage the children stand, the girls in their red bows and white dresses, the boys in white suits and giant red ties. The parents stand below shrieking up to be heard and the children shriek down to be heard, and between them the invisible wall "Not to Be Contaminated by Parental Germs or Physical Affection." **7**

There was a tiny girl who always stood hand in hand with Emily. Her parents never came. One visit she was gone. "They moved her to Rose Cottage," Emily shouted in explanation. "They don't like you to love anybody here."

She wrote once a week, the labored writing of a seven-year-old. "I am fine. How is the baby. If I write my leter nicly I will have a star. Love." There never was a star. We wrote every other day, letters she could never hold or keep but only hear read—once. "We simply do not have room for children to keep any personal possessions," they patiently explained when we pieced one Sunday's shrieking together to plead how much it would mean to Emily, who loved so to keep things, to be allowed to keep her letters and cards.

They don't like you to love anybody here.

Each visit she looked frailer. "She isn't eating," they told us. (They had runny eggs for breakfast or mush with lumps, Emily said later; I'd hold it in my mouth and not swallow. Nothing ever tasted good, just when they had chicken.) **8**

It took us eight months to get her released home, and only the fact that she gained back so little of her seven lost pounds convinced the social worker.

I Stand Here Ironing **735**

---

6 **Reader's Response**
Making Personal Connections

Discuss the fantasy of the clock. Ask if students recall ever being afraid of imaginary dangers when they were children.

Question What "talking" was the child hearing? *(the ticking of the clock)*

---

7 **Historical Note**
Quarantine

Explain that Emily was quarantined because she had contracted a contagious disease. Before the advent of routine vaccination and today's antibiotics, childhood infections such as measles, mumps, and polio could be epidemic. To control their spread, medical authorities did not allow contact between the people who were ill and others, even their family members.

---

8 **Literary Element**
Irony

Question The mother had been told that at the convalescent home Emily could "have the kind of food and care you can't manage for her." What details does the narrator offer that cast an ironic light on that promise? *(Possible responses: "the ravaged looks" of the shrieking children; the signs ordering no contact or affection between parents and patients; the runny eggs and mush with lumps; the insensitivity of the staff; and Emily's frail look)*

BUILDING ENGLISH PROFICIENCY

ESL
LEP
ELD
SAE
LD

Understanding Causes and Effects

Help students keep track of events in Emily's early childhood and the effects these events have on her. Pairs or groups of students can become "experts" on particular parts of Emily's early life.

- Four periods are shown on the chart. Model the ways readers can recognize parts of the daughter's life in the history being recounted by her mother. For example, page 734 begins with what happened when she was eight months old.

- Each pair or group of students can make a quick chart for one period. They can record what happened and the effect her mother describes.

Time	What Happened	Effects on Emily
8 months to 2 years		
In nursery school		
When her mother remarries		
At the convalescent home		

Identify Author's Point of View

Explain that this story was written in the early 1950s, when many people were concerned about nuclear bombs and the Cold War.

Question How does Emily's casual statement reveal the political context of the story? *(Possible response: She is flippant and jaded about the atrocity and despair of war.)*

Check Test

1. What inspired the narrator to review the details of her daughter's life? *(Someone asked to speak to her about her daughter.)*

2. Why did the narrator send her baby to live with relatives? *(Because she could not work and take care of an infant at the same time)*

3. Why did the narrator and her new husband send Emily to a convalescent home? *(They were persuaded to by a clinic staff because they had a new baby, and Emily had the red measles.)*

4. Who is Susan? *(the narrator's second daughter)*

5. What hidden talent does Emily discover? *(She is a gifted comedian.)*

Unit 7 Resource Book
Alternate Check Test, p. 13

---

to make me laugh, or out of her despair, she would imitate happenings or types at school.

I think I said once: "Why don't you do something like this in the school amateur shows?" One morning she phoned me at work, hardly understandable through the weeping: "Mother, I did it. I won, I won; they gave me first prize; they clapped and clapped and wouldn't let me go."

Now suddenly she was Somebody, and as imprisoned in her difference as she had been in her anonymity.[9]

She began to be asked to perform at other high schools, even in colleges, then at city and statewide affairs. The first one we went to, I only recognized her that first moment when thin, shy, she almost drowned herself into the curtains. Then: Was this Emily? the control, the command, the convulsing and deadly clowning, the spell, then the roaring, stamping audience, unwilling to let this rare and precious laughter out of their lives.

Afterward: You ought to do something about her with a gift like that—but without money or knowing how, what does one do? We have left it all to her, and the gift has as often eddied inside, clogged and clotted, as been used and growing.

She is coming. She runs up the stairs two at a time with her light, graceful step, and I know she is happy tonight. Whatever it was that occasioned your call did not happen today.

"Aren't you ever going to finish the ironing, Mother? Whistler[10] painted his mother in a rocker. I'd have to paint mine standing over an ironing board." This is one of her communicative nights, and she tells me everything and nothing as she fixes herself a plate of food out of the icebox.

She is so lovely. Why did you want me to come in at all? Why were you concerned? She will find her way.

She starts up the stairs to bed. "Don't get *me* up with the rest in the morning." "But I thought you were having midterms." "Oh, those," she

comes back in, kisses me, and says quite lightly, "in a couple of years when we'll all be atom-dead, they won't matter a bit."

She has said it before. She *believes* it. But because I have been dredging the past, and all that compounds a human being is so heavy and meaningful to me, I cannot endure it tonight.

I will never total it all. I will never come in to say: She was a child seldom smiled at. Her father left me before she was a year old. I had to work away from her her first six years when there was work, or I sent her home and to his relatives. There were years she had care she hated. She was dark and thin and foreign-looking in a world where the prestige went to blondness and curly hair and dimples; she was slow where glibness was prized. She was a child of anxious, not proud, love. We were poor and could not afford for her the soil of easy growth. I was a young mother, I was a distracted mother. There were other children pushing up, demanding. Her younger sister seemed all that she was not. There were years she did not let me touch her. She kept too much in herself; her life has been such she had to keep too much in herself. My wisdom came too late. She has much to her and probably little will come of it. She is a child of her age, of depression, of war, of fear.

Let her be. So all that is in her will not bloom—but in how many does it? There is still enough left to live by. Only help her to know—help make it so there is cause for her to know—that she is more than this dress on the ironing board, helpless before the iron.

---

9. anonymity (an′ə nim′ə tē), *n.* condition or quality of being unknown, nameless.
10. **Whistler,** James McNeill Whistler (1834–1903), an American painter and etcher who is best known for his painting which shows his mother sitting in a rocking chair.

MINI-LESSON: VOCABULARY

Understand Connotations and Denotations

Teach Explain that Tillie Olsen often takes advantage of the connotative powers of words. A connotation is an added or implied meaning or impression that a word carries, beyond its denotation—its literal definition. For example, *home* means a place where someone lives, but the word *home* has rich emotional meanings for most people.

Apply Ask students to analyze the connotations of each italicized word in these phrases from the story. For example, how might *huge* sound worse than *large* as a descriptive word for a school? Do the words *chubby* and *fat* have the same impact?

• Running out to that *huge* school

• (every little girl was supposed to look . . .) a *chubby* blonde replica of Shirley Temple

• her *light,* graceful step

Activity Idea Have students work in pairs to brainstorm groups of words that have commonly recognized connotations. Then each pair can write a character sketch, using connotative words to enrich the description of a made-up person. Encourage students to pay attention to connotative differences between synonyms such as *thin, slim, slender, lean, lanky, skinny,* and *gaunt.*

After Reading

Making Connections

Shaping Your Response

1. If you could change one part of Emily's childhood to make it easier for her, what part would you change? Why?

Analyzing the Story

2. Describe the **setting** of "I Stand Here Ironing."

3. Which of the events could the narrator have changed to make Emily's childhood better, and which were beyond her control? Explain.

4. Explain the narrator's wish for her daughter: "Only help her to know—help make it so there is cause for her to know—that she is more than this dress on the ironing board, helpless before the iron."

Extending the Ideas

5. In your opinion, are single mothers in today's society better off than the narrator was? Explain your response.

6. What do you think Emily will be doing in ten years? Explain why you think so.

Literary Focus: Interior Monologue

Interior monologue is a technique for presenting a character's stream of consciousness or private thoughts. Keeping in mind the story, answer these questions:

- What is the advantage of reading a character's uncensored thoughts?
- Do you find this technique for relating a story appealing? Why or why not?

Vocabulary Study

Analogies express relationships. Notice the relationships between these pairs of words.

     MOVEMENT : PANTOMIME : : WORDS : DIALOGUE

Movement is the means of expression for *pantomime,* just as *words* are the means of expression for *dialogue.*

Use the vocabulary words in the list to complete the following analogies on your paper. Refer to your Glossary for help.

**anonymity
ecstasy
homely
implore
somber**

1. FAME : MOVIE STAR : : ____ : moviegoer
2. GIVE : DONATE : : beg : ____
3. ROSE BUSH : BEAUTIFUL : : crabgrass : ____
4. ORANGE : VIVID : : gray : ____
5. FEAR : TERROR : : happiness : ____

I Stand Here Ironing   **739**

After Reading

MAKING CONNECTIONS

1. Responses may include keeping her from being separated from her mother.

2. at an ironing board in a multi-leveled home, apparently on a hill in a large city

3. Possible responses: She might have listened more, smiled at Emily more, not left her alone some nights, or maybe even had fewer children. She was powerless over the fact that Emily's father abandoned them, her resulting poverty, Emily's illness, her husband going to war, and her family demanding so much work and attention.

4. Possible response: She wants her daughter to feel empowered, to know that she can survive and prosper despite the actions of others or the blows of circumstance.

5. Possible responses: Yes, because changing social and economic patterns have made single motherhood more acceptable. Institutional changes, such as day care and maternity leave, have eased some pressure on mothers. No; because factors such as poverty and lack of child support still are problems.

6. Possible responses: She will have a family of her own; she will be a famous stand-up comedian; she will be friends with her mother.

VOCABULARY STUDY

1. anonymity
2. implore
3. homely
4. somber
5. ecstasy

Unit 7 Resource Book
Vocabulary, p. 11
Vocabulary Test, p. 14

LITERARY FOCUS: INTERIOR MONOLOGUE

- Possible responses: Readers get deep views into the character's ideas, feelings, and memories. It helps you to understand the perspective from which the narrator is viewing the events of the story.

- Responses will vary. Some students may appreciate the informality or intimacy of this narrative style, while others may find the restricted point of view incomplete.

WRITING CHOICES

Writer's Notebook Update

You might give students the option of writing their stories in the form of an interior monologue.

Developing Character

Suggest that students draw a Main Idea map, with their thesis at the top. For example: "Character formation is the direct result of parental guidance." Supporting details can be placed under separate headings, such as My Experience, Psychology, Statistics, and Plans for My Children.

Some students may not know that Anne Frank (1929–1945) was a girl who hid with her Jewish family from Nazi persecution in the Netherlands from 1942 until 1944. She kept a famous diary during that time. She died in a Nazi concentration camp.

Susan's Point of View

Remind students that a mother's view of her child is subjective and informed by emotion. Encourage them to try to form their impression of Susan's character based on the facts in the story and try to imagine Susan's perspective.

Selection Test

Unit 7 Resource Book
pp. 15–16

Expressing Your Ideas

Writing Choices

Writer's Notebook Update Review the childhood stories that you recorded in your notebook. Choose a particularly vivid one, and describe it in a short essay.

Developing Character Anne Frank wrote the following words in her diary. "[Daddy] said: 'All children must look after their own upbringing.' Parents can only give good advice or put them on the right paths, but the final forming of a person's character lies in [his or her] own hands." Analyze this viewpoint in an **essay,** thinking not only about your own experiences but the way you might bring up children of your own.

Susan's Point of View "I Stand Here Ironing" is told from Emily's mother's point of view. Other characters might describe Emily differently. Write a **description** of her from her younger sister Susan's point of view.

Other Options

The Ideal Childhood Prepare and deliver a **speech** on what childhood ought to be. Imagine that your audience is a segment of national television viewers, even though you will be delivering your speech for your class. Consider finding some quotes about childhood and including them in your essay.

Growing Up With several partners, prepare an **oral reading** of parts of "I Stand Here Ironing," with each reader choosing a section that recounts Emily's different ages. The first reader might begin with paragraph five and read through paragraph eleven. The next reader would then begin with paragraph twelve, and so on.

The Stand-up Comic Emily's mother mentions the child actress Shirley Temple, who was popular when Emily was growing up. Examine this picture of her, then rent or borrow a Shirley Temple movie on videotape and watch it. Invent a **routine** that Emily might use in her stand-up comedy act relating to Shirley Temple, and perform it for the class.

OTHER OPTIONS

The Ideal Childhood

- Students might research childhood through the ages. How have the activities, rights, and health of children changed throughout history?
- Students might take a multicultural approach by researching the roles and responsibilities of children in various cultures.

Growing Up

Students can practice their oral interpretations together and individually. They may want to videotape or audiotape the readings.

The Stand-Up Comic

Popular Shirley Temple movies include *Little Miss Marker* (1934), *Curly Top* (1935), *The Little Colonel* (1935), *Dimples* (1936), and *Rebecca of Sunnybrook Farm* (1938). Interested students may want to read Shirley Temple Black's autobiography, *Child Star* (Warner, 1989).

Before Reading

Separating

by John Updike

John Updike
born 1932

John Updike says the goal of his writing is "to transcribe middleness with all its grits, bumps, and anonymities, in all its fullness of satisfaction and mystery." He grew up in Pennsylvania, and went to Harvard, where he was the editor of the Harvard *Lampoon*. His work includes poetry, short stories, essays, and novels, and the topic of much of his work is life in the suburbs. His most famous books are the novels in the series about car salesman Harry "Rabbit" Angstrom. The third book in the series, *Rabbit Is Rich,* won a Pulitzer Prize, an American Book Award, and a commendation from the National Book Critics circle.

Building Background

Till Death Us Do Part The institutions of marriage and family have changed dramatically in the last twenty-five years. This graph, taken from information in *Fatherless America* by David Blankenhorn, illustrates the change in family structure for children in the United States. Updike records the human side of these statistics in "Separating."

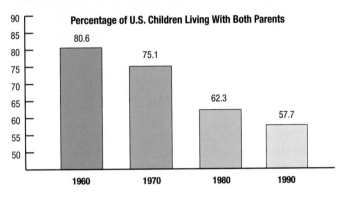

Percentage of U.S. Children Living With Both Parents

Year	Percentage
1960	80.6
1970	75.1
1980	62.3
1990	57.7

Literary Focus

Point of View The vantage point from which an author tells a story is called **point of view.** This vantage point is established through an author's choice of narrator. A story may be related by a character (*first-person point of view*) or by a narrator who does not participate in the action (*third-person point of view*). The third-person narrator may be *omniscient*—that is, able to see into the thoughts of all of the characters; *limited*—confined to a single character's perceptions; or *objective,* describing only what can be seen. As you read "Separating," identify the point of view used by John Updike.

Writer's Notebook

Prime Time Families Do television shows portray realistic family situations? Should they? In your notebook jot down the names of some television shows in which the characters are family members. Then note which ones you think portray a realistic family situation.

Separating   **741**

Before Reading

Building Background

You might discuss factors that have contributed to family changes, such as these.

- Laws that allow "no-fault" divorces
- Records on fathers not living with their children
- Women in the work force, less dependent on a husband as "breadwinner"

Literary Focus

Students who don't readily appreciate how **point of view** affects stories may consider the various accounts of a two-car traffic accident that would be given by the two drivers (both first-person points of view), as well as an unbiased witness (third-person objective) and an imagined all-knowing witness (third-person omniscient). *("Separating" is narrated from a third-person limited point of view.)*

Writer's Notebook

Students may include shows from the 1960s and 1970s, seen in syndication and cable TV. They might organize the shows according to the decades of their production.

More About John Updike

After twenty-one years of marriage and raising four children, Updike and his wife Mary were divorced.

Other works by Updike include:

- *The Witches of Eastwick,* 1985
- *Rabbit Redux,* 1971

SUPPORT MATERIALS OVERVIEW

Unit 7 Resource Book
- Graphic Organizer, p. 17
- Study Guide, p. 18
- Vocabulary, p. 19
- Grammar, p. 20
- Alternate Check Test, p. 21
- Vocabulary Test, p. 22
- Selection Test, pp. 23–24

Building English Proficiency
- Literature Summaries
- Activities, p. 224

Reading, Writing & Grammar SkillBook
- Vocabulary, pp. 7–8
- Reading, pp. 70–72
- Grammar, Usage, and Mechanics, pp. 184–185

Technology
- Audiotape
- Personal Journal Software
- Custom Literature Database: For another literary treatment of themes in the story, see the poem "Life's Tragedy" by Paul Laurence Dunbar on the database.
- Test Generator Software

Selection Objectives

- To consider the impact of marital problems on a family with children
- To understand the use of point of view as a powerful narrative tool
- To examine the use of literary elements
- To review irregular plural nouns

 Unit 7 Resource Book
Graphic Organizer, p. 17
Study Guide, p. 18

Theme Link

This story depicts the person-to-person interactions and emotions of parents and their four children in the face of the disclosure that the father and mother are separating.

Vocabulary Preview

rivulet, a very small stream

rebuke, express disapproval of

atrociously, shockingly badly

diaphanous, transparent

crucial, very important; critical

Students can add the words and definitions to their word lists in the Writer's Notebook.

1 Literary Focus
Point of View

Students should recognize third-person point of view early in the story. Whether it is omniscient or limited may take a few pages of reading. Students will see Richard's thoughts revealed. Joan's thoughts are related mainly as Richard knows them.

JOHN UPDIKE   1

The day was fair. Brilliant. All that June the weather had mocked the Maples' internal misery with solid sunlight—golden shafts and cascades of green in which their conversations had wormed unseeing, their sad murmuring selves the only stain in Nature. Usually by this time of the year they had acquired tans; but when they met their elder daughter's plane on her return from a year in England they were almost as pale as she, though Judith was too dazzled by the sunny opulent jumble of her native land to notice. They did not spoil her homecoming by telling her immediately. Wait a few days, let her recover from jet lag, had been one of their formulations, in that string of gray dialogues—over coffee, over cocktails, over Cointreau[1]—that had shaped the strategy of their dissolution, while the earth performed its annual stunt of renewal unnoticed beyond their closed windows. Richard had thought to leave at Easter; Joan had insisted they wait until the four children were at last assembled, with all exams passed and ceremonies attended, and the bauble of summer to console them. So he had drudged away, in love, in dread, repairing screens, getting the mowers sharpened, rolling and patching their new tennis court.

The court, clay, had come through its first winter pitted and wind-swept bare of redcoat. Years ago the Maples had observed how often, among their friends, divorce followed a dramatic home improvement, as if the marriage were making one last effort to live; their own worst crisis had come amid the plaster dust and exposed plumbing of a kitchen renovation. Yet,

a summer ago, as canary-yellow bulldozers gaily churned a grassy, daisy-dotted knoll into a muddy plateau, and a crew of pigtailed young men raked and tamped clay into a plane, this transformation did not strike them as ominous, but festive in its impudence; their marriage

SEPARATING

could rend the earth for fun. The next spring, waking each day at dawn to a sliding sensation as if the bed were being tipped, Richard found the barren tennis court—its nets and tapes still rolled in the barn—an environment congruous with his mood of purposeful desolation, and the crumbling of handfuls of clay into cracks and holes (dogs had frolicked on the court in a thaw; rivulets[2] had eroded trenches) an activity suitably elemental and interminable.[3] In his sealed heart he hoped the day would never come.

Now it was here. A Friday. Judith was reacclimated; all four children were assembled before jobs and camps and visits again scattered them. Joan thought they should be told one by one. Richard was for making an announcement at the table. She said, "I think just making an announcement is a cop-out. They'll start quarreling and playing to each other instead of focusing. They're

---

1. **Cointreau** (kwôn´trō´), brand name of an expensive orange-flavored liquor.
2. rivulet (riv´yə lit), *n.* a very small stream.
3. **interminable** (in tėr´mə nə bəl), *adj.* unceasing; endless.

SELECTION SUMMARY
Separating

After a tortuous period of waiting and worrying, Richard and Joan Maple have decided the time has come to inform their four young-adult or teenaged children that they are separating. They have waited for their daughter Judith to return from a year abroad. They have planned to personally disclose the news to each child. After performing chores around the house, Richard bungles the plan by crying during his daughter's "welcome home" dinner. Three of the children learn the terrible news. Daughters Judith and Margaret accept it calmly, but son John reacts with hurt and anger. Then he comes to terms with it. Later that night Richard picks up his older son, Dickie, at the train station. Father and son discuss the sad news in the car and again in the son's bedroom, where a kiss and hot tears bring the tragedy of the separation home.

 For summaries in other languages, see the Building English Proficiency book.

Fairfield Porter (1907–1975), the son of a well-known architect and second cousin to the poet T.S. Eliot, was the brother of photographer Eliot Porter (see page 227). Despite his associations with avant-garde artists in New York, Fairfield Porter's style remained conservative and representational. He painted with flat, broad brush strokes and an attention to spotted sunlight.

Possible Response to Caption The people facing different directions do seem separated by attitude, despite their nearness.

Visual Literacy The poet John Ashberry stated that Porter's work proves "there are no rules for anything, no ideas in art, just objects and materials that combine, like people, in somewhat mysterious ways."

Question What kind of mystery might the images of these people depicted in paint create for viewers? *(Possible responses: a mystery about why the people are feeling and acting as they are; questions about who these people are, what has happened, and what will happen next)*

⋀ Does Fairfield Porter's 1962 painting, *A Day Indoors,* portray a feeling of separation or separateness? Explain your answer.

Separating **743**

BUILDING ENGLISH PROFICIENCY

Exploring Key Concepts

ESL LEP ELD SAE LD

As students read, they can make semantic webs to record and understand information about the Maple family and family relationships. The beginnings of two webs are shown. Students also might include in discussion or in their notes their own thoughts about societal issues such as parents separating. Encourage students to respect those who do not want to reveal personal views.

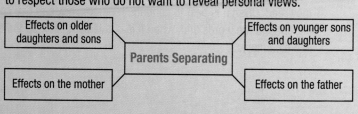

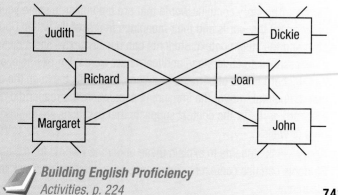

Building English Proficiency
Activities, p. 224

743

Questions

- How do Joan's and Richard's responses in this situation compare or contrast? *(Possible responses: Joan is factual, matter-of-fact, and in control. Richard is emotional, crying, and not able to make sense of what's being said.)*

- How do Joan and Richard compare to common stereotypes of men and women? *(Possible response: They provide a contrast to stereotypes of women as emotional and men as stoic and unwilling to cry.)*

9 Reading/Thinking Skills
Make Judgments

Questions

- Why does John act like a clown? *(Possible response: He has drunk champagne, is overcome with emotion, and does not know how to express it.)*

- Why does he light the matches in his mother's face? *(Possible response: He is angry and hurt; he may feel like retaliating against her, as she acts calm and collected in this crisis.)*

---

distances at the table had grown immense—"You knew, you always knew," but the clenching at the back of his throat prevented him from making sense of it. From afar he heard Joan talking, levelly, sensibly, reciting what they had prepared: it was a separation for the summer, an experiment. She and Daddy both agreed it would be good for them; they needed space and time to think; they liked each other but did not make each other happy enough, somehow.

Judith, imitating her mother's factual tone, but in her youth off-key, too cool, said, "I think it's silly. You should either live together or get divorced."

. . . THEY LIKED EACH OTHER BUT DID NOT MAKE EACH OTHER HAPPY ENOUGH, SOMEHOW.

Richard's crying, like a wave that has crested and crashed, had become tumultuous; but it was overtopped by another tumult, for John, who had been so reserved, now grew larger and larger at the table. Perhaps his younger sister's being credited with knowing set him off. "Why didn't you *tell* us?" he asked, in a large round voice quite unlike his own. "You should have *told* us you weren't getting along."

Richard was startled into attempting to force words through his tears. "We *do* get along, that's the trouble, so it doesn't show even to us—" *That we do not love each other* was the rest of the sentence; he couldn't finish it.

8 Joan finished for him, in her style. "And we've always, *especially*, loved our children."

John was not mollified. "What do you care about *us?*" he boomed. "We're just little things you *had*." His sisters' laughing forced a laugh from him, which he turned hard and parodistic. "Ha ha *ha*." Richard and Joan realized simultaneously that the child was drunk, on Judith's homecoming champagne. Feeling bound to

keep the center of the stage, John took a cigarette from Judith's pack, poked it into his mouth, let it hang from his lower lip, and squinted like a gangster.

"You're not little things we had," Richard called to him. "You're the whole point. But you're grown. Or almost."

The boy was lighting matches. Instead of holding them to his cigarette (for they had never seen him smoke; being "good" had been his way of setting himself apart), he held them to his mother's face, closer and closer, for her to blow out. Then he lit the whole folder—a hiss and then a torch, held against his mother's face. **9**

Prismed by tears, the flame filled Richard's vision; he didn't know how it was extinguished. He heard Margaret say, "Oh stop showing off," and saw John, in response, break the cigarette in two and put the halves entirely into his mouth and chew, sticking out his tongue to display the shreds to his sister.

Joan talked to him, reasoning—a fountain of reason, unintelligible. "Talked about it for years . . . our children must help us . . . Daddy and I both want . . ." As the boy listened, he carefully wadded a paper napkin into the leaves of his salad, fashioned a ball of paper and lettuce, and popped it into his mouth, looking around the table for the expected laughter. None came. Judith said, "Be mature," and dismissed a plume of smoke.

Richard got up from this stifling table and led the boy outside. Though the house was in twilight, the outdoors still brimmed with light, the lovely waste light of high summer. Both laughing, he supervised John's spitting out the lettuce and paper and tobacco into the pachysandra. He took him by the hand—a square gritty hand, but for its softness a man's. Yet, it held on. They ran together up into the field, past the tennis court. The raw banking left by the bulldozers was dotted with daisies. Past the court and a flat stretch where they used to play family baseball stood a

---

MINI-LESSON: GRAMMAR

Using Irregular Plurals

Teach Use examples from the selection to review the plural forms of some nouns.

- The nouns *species* and *pachysandra* each have one form that can be used as singular and plural: "each . . . species of grass distinct as illumination on parchment" (p. 747); "spitting out the lettuce . . . into the pachysandra" (p. 746)

- Collective nouns such as *family,* referring to individuals together, are singular in American English: The Maple family goes to church in town.

- Many people do not know that last names have regular plural forms. The plural of the name *Maple* is *Maples* (no apostrophe). The plural possessive form of *Maple* is *Maples',* as in "the Maples' house." The singular possessive form of *Maple* is *Maple's,* as in "John Maple's salad."

Activity Idea Students can suggest nouns with irregular plural forms for a class list.

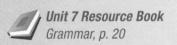
Unit 7 Resource Book
Grammar, p. 20

Could the child in Fairfield Porter's painting, *Under the Elms* (1971-1972) portray any of the children in the story? Why or why not? ➤

soft green rise glorious in the sun, each weed and species of grass distinct as illumination on parchment. "I'm sorry, so sorry," Richard cried. "You were the only one who ever tried to help me with all the damn jobs around this place."

Sobbing, safe within his tears and the champagne, John explained. "It's not just the separation, it's the whole crummy year. I *hate* that school, you can't make any friends, the history teacher's a scud."[9]

They sat on the crest of the rise, shaking and warm from their tears but easier in their voices, and Richard tried to focus on the child's sad year— the weekdays long with homework, the weekends spent in his room with model airplanes, while his parents murmured down below, nursing their separation. How selfish, how blind, Richard thought; his eyes felt scoured. He told his son, "We'll think about getting you transferred. Life's too short to be miserable."

They had said what they could, but did not want the moment to heal, and talked on, about the school, about the tennis court, whether it would ever again be as good as it had been that first summer. They walked to inspect it and pressed a few more tapes more firmly down. A little stiltedly, perhaps trying now to make too much of the moment, Richard led the boy to the spot in the field where the view was best, of the metallic blue river, the emerald marsh, the scattered islands velvety with shadow in the low light, the white bits of beach far away. "See," he said. "It goes on being beautiful. It'll be here tomorrow."

"I know," John answered, impatiently. The moment had closed.

Back in the house, the others had opened some white wine, the champagne being drunk,

---

9. **scud,** a slang term for an undesirable teacher.

Separating   **747**

BUILDING ENGLISH PROFICIENCY

Related Words and Parts of Speech

"Separating" offers a chance for a quick review of word structure and parts of speech. For example, the words *tumultuous* and *tumult* both appear in one sentence (page 746). Students may be able to identify *tumult* as a noun and *tumultuous* as an adjective built from the noun and the suffix *-ous* (in this case *-uous*).

Students can use other words in this part of the story to talk about and write related words. As they learn new forms, they can add words and notes about their meanings to their word lists in the Writer's Notebook. Examples of words in the story are shown here, with related words.

- separation, separate
- factual, fact
- especially, special
- gangster, gang
- folder, fold
- glorious, glory
- parodistic, parody
- metallic, metal
- velvety, velvet
- impatiently, impatient, patient

---

10 Literary Element
Irony

You might discuss the irony that surfaces as John and Richard talk. At the moment they may be communicating more than they normally do. The impending separation probably will make such comfortable communication difficult.

🎨 *Art Study*

Possible Responses to Caption
Students may imagine the child representing either John outside with his father, or Margaret, who is described as "gazing at her father as if from the other side of a pane of glass." Either could have this expression, which might be interpreted as sad or pensive.

Artist Fairfield Porter depicted a girl with short hair. It is not a picture of any character in the story.

Visual Literacy   The painting is entitled *Under the Elms,* but the girl is pictured in sunlight, while the space under the trees is in shadow.

Question   Where are your eyes drawn in the painting? *(Possible responses: Some viewers' eyes are drawn to the face, while other viewers first look toward the shade beyond the girl. There is no single "approved" way to view the painting. Its title suggests that the artist paid attention to both parts of the scene.)*

11 Literary Element
Setting

Students can discuss the images of beauty in the description of land around the Maples' house. The setting reinforces readers' knowledge about the characters' economic circumstances.

Questions

- What fact does Richard fail to mention as he expresses relief that even Judith did not mention a third person as a possible reason for the separation? *(Richard and another woman apparently are romantically involved.)*

- What tone do you think Joan might have used in her response, "That *was* touching"? *(Possible response: sarcastic)*

13 Literary Element
Metaphor

Point out the mountain that Richard faces—and that moves inside him—and discuss what it represents. Students may consider it his emotions, his discomfort in anticipation of telling another son about the separation, or his grief.

14 Literary Focus
Point of View

Question Is it clear who expresses this thought about Joan giving Richard courage–the narrator or Richard? *(Possible response: It is not clear; the narrator is so intimately describing the protagonist's thoughts that the point of view seems to merge with Richard's.)*

---

and still sat at the table, the three females, gossiping. Where Joan sat had become the head. She turned, showing him a tearless face, and asked, "All right?"

"We're fine," he said, resenting it, though relieved, that the party went on without him.

In bed she explained, "I couldn't cry I guess because I cried so much all spring. It really wasn't fair. It's your idea, and you made it look as though I was kicking you out."

"I'm sorry," he said. "I couldn't stop. I wanted to but couldn't."

"You *didn't* want to. You loved it. You were having your way, making a general announcement."

"I love having it over," he admitted. "God, those kids were great. So brave and funny." John, returned to the house, had settled to a model airplane in his room, and kept shouting down to them, "I'm OK. No sweat." "And the way," Richard went on, cozy in his relief, "they never questioned the reasons we gave. No thought of a third person. Not even Judith."

12 "That *was* touching," Joan said.

He gave her a hug. "You were great too. Very reassuring to everybody. Thank you." Guiltily, he realized he did not feel separated.

"You still have Dickie to do," she told him. These words set before him a black mountain in the darkness; its cold breath, its near weight affected his chest. Of the four children, his elder son was most nearly his conscience. Joan did not need to add, "That's one piece of your dirty work I won't do for you."

"I know. I'll do it. You go to sleep."

Within minutes, her breathing slowed, became oblivious and deep. It was quarter to midnight. Dickie's train from the concert would come in at one-fourteen. Richard set the alarm for one. He had slept atrociously[10] for weeks. But whenever he closed his lids some glimpse of the last hours scorched them—Judith exhaling toward the ceiling in a kind of aversion. Bean's mute staring, the sunstruck growth in the field where he and John had rested. The mountain **13** before him moved closer, moved within him; he

was huge, momentous. The ache at the back of his throat felt stale. His wife slept as if slain beside him. When, exasperated by his hot lids, his crowded heart, he rose from bed and dressed, she awoke enough to turn over. He told her then, "Joan, if I could undo it all, I would."

"Where would you begin?" she asked. There **14** was no place. Giving him courage, she was always giving him courage. He put on shoes without socks in the dark. The children were breathing in their rooms, the downstairs was hollow. In their confusion they had left lights burning. He turned off all but one, the kitchen overhead. The car started. He had hoped it wouldn't. He met only moonlight on the road; it seemed a diaphanous[11] companion, flickering in the leaves along the roadside, haunting his rearview mirror like a pursuer, melting under his headlights. The center of town, not quite deserted, was eerie at this hour. A young cop in uniform kept company with a gang of T-shirted kids on the steps of the bank. Across from the railroad station, several bars kept open. Customers, mostly young, passed in and out of the warm night, savoring summer's novelty. Voices shouted from cars as they passed; an immense conversation seemed in progress. Richard parked and in his weariness put his head on the passenger seat, out of the commotion and wheeling lights. It was as when, in the movies, an assassin grimly carries his mission through the jostle of a carnival—except the movies cannot show the precipitous, palpable slope you cling to within. You cannot climb back down; you can only fall. The synthetic fabric of the car seat, warmed by his cheek, confided to him an ancient, distant scent of vanilla.

A train whistle caused him to lift his head. It was on time; he had hoped it would be late. The slender draw-gates descended. The bell of approach tingled happily. The great metal body, horizontally fluted, rocked to a stop, and sleepy

---

10. **atrociously** (ə trō′shes lē), *adv.* shockingly badly.
11. **diaphanous** (dī af′ə nəs), *adj.* transparent.

MINI-LESSON: LITERARY FOCUS

Point of View

Teach Explain that the limited third-person point of view in this story restricts the narrator to Richard's perspective. Wherever Richard goes, the narrative follows. The narrator has access to the thoughts of Richard *only*. Richard is somewhat aware of other characters' thoughts, which we learn through his impressions of them.

Apply Discuss this passage on page 748:

"It was as when, in the movies, an assassin grimly carries his mission through the jostle of a carnival—except the movies cannot show the precipitous, palpable slope you cling to within."

Question What does this figurative image reveal about Richard's mood as he awaits his son's train? *(Possible response: He is caught up in anticipation of telling his son troubling news and is aware that it may hurt his son, despite the pleasant setting and people he sees in the town.)*

Activity Idea Students can describe what Dickie—or Joan or the other children, if they are awake—may be thinking at this moment in the story. The contrast can demonstrate the story's point of view.

teenagers disembarked, his son among them. Dickie did not show surprise that his father was meeting him at this terrible hour. He sauntered to the car with two friends, both taller than he. He said "Hi" to his father and took the passenger's seat with an exhausted promptness that expressed gratitude. The friends got in the back, and Richard was grateful; a few more minutes' postponement would be won by driving them home.

RICHARD HAD FEARED THAT HIS TEARS WOULD RETURN AND CHOKE HIM . . .

He asked, "How was the concert?"

"Groovy," one boy said from the back seat.

15 "It was OK," Dickie said, moderate by nature, so reasonable that in his childhood the unreason of the world had given him headaches, stomachaches, nausea. When the second friend had been dropped off at his dark house, the boy blurted, "Dad, my eyes are killing me with hay fever! I'm out there cutting that grass all day!"

"Do we still have those drops?"

"They didn't do any good last summer."

"They might this." Richard swung a U-turn on the empty street. The drive home took a few minutes. The mountain was here, in his throat. "Richard," he said, and felt the boy, slumped and rubbing his eyes, go tense at his tone, "I didn't come to meet you just to make your life easier. I came because your mother and I have some news for you, and you're a hard man to get ahold of these days. It's sad news."

"That's OK." The reassurance came out soft, but quick, as if released from the tip of a spring.

Richard had feared that his tears would return and choke him, but the boy's manliness **16** set an example, and his voice issued forth steady and dry. "It's sad news, but it needn't be tragic

news, at least for you. It should have no practical effect on your life, though it's bound to have an emotional effect. You'll work at your job, and go back to school in September. Your mother and I are really proud of what you're making of your life; we don't want that to change at all."

"Yeah," the boy said lightly, on the intake of his breath, holding himself up. They turned the corner; the church they went to loomed like a gutted fort. The home of the woman Richard hoped to marry stood across the green. Her bedroom light burned.

"Your mother and I," he said, "have decided to separate. For the summer. Nothing legal, no divorce yet. We want to see how it feels. For some years now, we haven't been doing enough for each other, making each other as happy as we should be. Have you sensed that?"

"No," the boy said. It was an honest, unemotional answer: true or false in a quiz.

Glad for the factual basis, Richard pursued, even garrulously, the details. His apartment across town, his utter accessibility, the split vacation arrangements, the advantages to the children, the added mobility and variety of the summer. Dickie listened, absorbing. "Do the others know?"

"Yes."

"How did they take it?"

"The girls pretty calmly. John flipped out; he shouted and ate a cigarette and made a salad out of his napkin and told us how much he hated school."

His brother chuckled. "He did?"

"Yeah. The school issue was more upsetting for him than Mom and me. He seemed to feel better for having exploded."

"He did?" The repetition was the first sign that he was stunned.

"Yes. Dickie, I want to tell you something. This last hour, waiting for your train to get in, has been about the worst of my life. I hate this. *Hate* it. My father would have died before doing it to me." He felt immensely lighter, saying this. **17** He had dumped the mountain on the boy. They

Separating   **749**

15 Reading/Thinking Skills
Make Connections

Questions Which of his parents may have given Dickie this trait, reasonableness? *(Possible response: His mother, who is described as rational and levelheaded)*

16 Reader's Response
Making Personal Connections

You might point out that this is the second time Richard has been inspired by the behavior of one of his sons. John "rebuked" him with his honesty, and now Dickie's "manliness" gives him the courage to speak.

Question It is common to acknowledge that children learn from their parents. Do you think parents also learn from—or can be inspired by—their sons and daughters? *(Students probably will respond that parents do learn from their children.)*

17 Literary Element
Tone

The narrator has shared with readers many of Richard's thoughts. Occasionally the narrator reveals Richard's motivations, even those that are not ideal or honorable. Direct students' attention to the line about dumping the "mountain" on his son.

Question Does the narrator's tone suggest complete sympathy with Richard's perspective? *(Possible response: No; the narrator reveals how Richard sometimes thinks and acts selfishly. However, this may indicate Richard's awareness of his somewhat selfish acts.)*

BUILDING ENGLISH PROFICIENCY

ESL
LEP
ELD
SAE
LD

Exploring Conflict

Help students recognize the story's important conflicts as they talk about these questions.

- In what parts of the story has the subdued conflict between Joan and Richard been most clearly seen? *(their conversations about how to tell the children and how Richard caused the separation to be revealed at dinner)*

- What detail on page 749 tells why Richard is leaving Joan? *(On the way home from the train station, he passes "the home of*

the woman Richard hoped to marry.")

- What conflicts within the children has the announced separation caused? *(Each faces the inner conflict of surviving the hurt caused by the breakup of their family.)*

- Most of the story involves Richard's thoughts. What conflict is going on within him? *(Discussion may involve his love of his family versus his love of another woman, his guilt over hurting his family, and his unsure feelings about the future.)*

Question   Why do you think Richard finds the sound of the door closing "sickening"? *(Possible response: He would rather see a sign of Dickie's emotion; Dickie's calm response makes his father uncomfortable.)*

Check Test

1. What news are Joan and Richard going to break to their children? *(that they are separating; that their life together in marriage will end)*

2. Where has their older daughter, Judith, been for the past year? *(England)*

3. How does Richard spoil the plan to tell the children individually? *(by crying at the dinner table)*

4. Which son or daughter acts most upset about the news? *(John)*

5. Where does Richard break the news to Dickie? *(in the car on the way back from the train station)*

Unit 7 Resource Book
Alternate Check Test, p. 21

were home. Moving swiftly as a shadow, Dickie was out of the car, through the bright kitchen. Richard called after him, "Want a glass of milk or anything?"

"No thanks."

"Want to call the course tomorrow and say you're too sick to work?"

In his father's ear he moaned one word, the crucial, intelligent word: Why?

"No, that's all right." The answer was faint, delivered at the door to his room; Richard listened for the slam that went with a tantrum. The door closed normally, gently. The sound was sickening.

Joan had sunk into that first deep trough of sleep and was slow to awake. Richard had to repeat, "I told him."

"What did he say?"

"Nothing much. Could you go say goodnight to him? Please."

She left their room, without putting on a bathrobe. He sluggishly changed back into his pajamas and walked down the hall. Dickie was already in bed, Joan was sitting beside him, and the boy's bedside clock radio was murmuring music. When she stood, an inexplicable light—the moon?—outlined her body through the nightie. Richard sat on the warm place she had indented on the child's narrow mattress. He asked him, "Do you want the radio on like that?"

"It always is."

"Doesn't it keep you awake? It would me."

"No."

"Are you sleepy?"

"Yeah."

"Good. Sure you want to get up and go to work? You've had a big night."

"I want to."

Away at school this winter he had learned for the first time that you can go short of sleep and live. As an infant he had slept with an immobile, sweating intensity that had alarmed his baby sitters. In adolescence he had often been the first of the four children to go to bed. Even now, he would go slack in the middle of a television show, his sprawled legs hairy and brown. "OK. Good boy. Dickie, listen. I love you so much, I never knew how much until now. No matter how this works out, I'll always be with you. Really."

Richard bent to kiss an averted face but his son, sinewy, turned and with wet cheeks embraced him and gave him a kiss, on the lips, passionate as a woman's. In his father's ear he moaned one word, the crucial,[12] intelligent word: *"Why?"*

Why. It was a whistle of wind in a crack, a knife thrust, a window thrown open on emptiness. The white face was gone, the darkness was featureless. Richard had forgotten why.

---

12. **crucial** (krü′shəl), *adj.* very important; critical.

After Reading

Making Connections

Shaping Your Response

1. Does the story "Separating" strike you as realistic or unrealistic? Explain your opinion.

Analyzing the Story

2. Choose a passage that you think is a good example of Updike's ability to describe emotion, and explain how he achieves this.

3. How would you **characterize** Richard? Joan? Use details from the story to support your descriptions.

4. What do you think is the basic **conflict** in the story?

5. 👆 Describe the **interactions** between the characters in this story. Would you say they communicate well with each other or not? Explain your answer.

Extending the Ideas

6. Do you think the Maples will go through with a divorce, or do you think they will reconcile? Be prepared to support your opinion with information from the story.

7. How do you think the children will be affected by the absence of their father?

Literary Focus: Point of View

Point of View is the vantage point from which a story is told. A story may be told from first- or third-person point of view, and a third-person narrator may be omniscient, limited, or objective. Answer the following questions about the story:

- Is the narrator in this story able to see into the minds of all the characters?
- Is the point of view limited to a single character's perceptions?
- Does the narrator describe only what can be seen, without any attempt to describe emotions or reactions?
- Who is the narrator and from what point of view is the story told?

LITERARY FOCUS: POINT OF VIEW

You might point out that in a skillful narrative the reader gets caught up in the writing, and the narrator seems to disappear.

Responses to Questions

- No
- Yes; Richard's
- No
- The narrator is not identified; the story is told from a third-person limited point of view.

MAKING CONNECTIONS

1. Possible response: Realistic, because it presents each character's human traits and actions in convincing ways

2. Possible responses: Each child's reaction to hearing of the separation shows a way that a person that age might feel about their parents splitting up. The images in the last paragraph describe the downhearted confusion that Richard feels at that moment.

3. Possible responses: Richard is emotional and introspective; he thinks about guilt and pain—and analyzes what he sees—throughout the story. Yet he has trouble taking responsibility. Joan is organized and in control of herself (p. 744 description); levelheaded (p. 746, talking to children); somewhat bitter now (p. 748 dialogue with Richard); and tender and loving (p. 750).

4. Possible response: Richard's internal conflict over leaving his family is central to every scene.

5. Possible responses: They speak easily and communicate but often find it painful to share their feelings. They communicate indirectly, not dwelling long on painful topics. They manage to show love for each other in nonverbal ways.

6. Possible responses: The fact that the marriage has been faltering for a while, and that Richard has a mistress, seem to indicate that they will divorce. Richard's and Joan's concern for the children and even for one another leave open a possibility of reconciling.

7. Possible response: John and Margaret probably will be more seriously affected than the older children, who are nearly on their own. Their adjustment will depend on Richard's accessibility.

During Reading

Selection Objectives

- To consider the challenges cultural customs pose to people of another culture
- To explore complex symbolism
- To distinguish and spell homophones

Unit 7 Resource Book
Graphic Organizer, p. 25
Study Guide, p. 26

Theme Link

The narrator struggles to find a voice as she assimilates into the American school system, which has little tolerance for the manners and beliefs of a young Chinese American girl. The Person to Person theme is explored as she finds her voice.

Vocabulary Preview

frenum, fold of membrane beneath the tongue

tauten, tighten

tamper, meddle improperly

intricacy, intricate nature or condition; complexity

assuredly, confidently, boldly

resolve, break into parts or components

ideograph, a graphic symbol that represents a thing or an idea directly, without representing the sounds of the word for the thing or idea

nonexistent, having no being or existence

mute, not making any sound, silent

teak, (adj.) made of hard, durable, yellowish-brown wood from a large tree that grows in the East Indies

Students can add the words to their word lists in the Writer's Notebook.

Literary Focus

1 ### Symbolism

The narrator recounts how her mother cut her frenum. Such a cut would have been made for a practical purpose, not a symbolic one. The act became symbolic in the girl's mind, and she shares the symbolism by focusing on it so extensively.

754

THE WOMAN WARRIOR

MAXINE HONG KINGSTON

Long ago in China, knot-makers tied string into buttons and frogs, and rope into bell pulls. There was one knot so complicated that it blinded the knot-maker. Finally an emperor outlawed this cruel knot, and the nobles could not order it anymore. If I had lived in China, I would have been an outlaw knot-maker.

Maybe that's why my mother cut my tongue. She pushed my tongue up and sliced the frenum.[1] Or maybe she snipped it with a pair of nail scissors. I don't remember her doing it, only her telling me about it, but all during childhood I felt sorry for the baby whose mother waited with scissors or knife in hand for it to cry—and then, when its mouth was wide open like a baby bird's, cut. The Chinese say "a ready tongue is an evil."

I used to curl up my tongue in front of the mirror and tauten[2] my frenum into a white line, itself as thin as a razor blade. I saw no scars in my mouth. I thought perhaps I had had two frena, and she had cut one. I made other children open their mouths so I could compare theirs to mine. I saw perfect pink membranes stretching into precise edges that looked easy enough to cut. Sometimes I felt very proud that my mother committed such a powerful act upon me. At other times I was terrified—the first thing my mother did when she saw me was to cut my tongue.

"Why did you do that to me, Mother?"

"I told you."

"Tell me again."

"I cut it so you would not be tongue-tied. Your tongue would be able to move in any language. You'll be able to speak languages that are completely different from one another. You'll be able to pronounce anything. Your frenum looked too tight to do those things, so I cut it." **1**

"But isn't 'a ready tongue an evil'?"

"Things are different in this ghost country."[3]

"Did it hurt me? Did I cry and bleed?"

"I don't remember. Probably."

She didn't cut the other children's. When I asked cousins and other Chinese children whether their mothers had cut their tongues loose, they said, "What?"

"Why didn't you cut my brothers' and sisters' tongues?"

"They didn't need it."

"Why not? Were theirs longer than mine?"

"Why don't you quit blabbering and get to work?"

If my mother was not lying she should have cut more, scraped away the rest of the frenum skin, because I have a terrible time talking. Or she should not have cut at all, tampering[4] with my speech. When I went to kindergarten and had to speak English for the first time, I became silent. A dumbness—a shame—still cracks my voice in two, even when I want to say "hello" casually, or ask an easy question in front of the check-out counter, or ask directions of a bus driver. I stand frozen, or I hold up the line with the complete, grammatical sentence that comes squeaking out at impossible length. "What did you say?" says the cab driver, or "Speak up," so I have to perform again, only weaker the second time. A telephone call makes my throat bleed

---

1. frenum (frē′nəm), *n.* fold of membrane beneath the tongue.
2. tauten (tôt′n), *v.* tighten.
3. **ghost country.** Chinese immigrants commonly referred to white Americans as *ghosts.*
4. tamper (tam′pər), *v.* meddle improperly.

SELECTION SUMMARY

The Woman Warrior

A Chinese American woman describes her childhood struggle with speaking. Her mother told her that, to help her daughter speak various languages, she had cut the membrane under her tongue when she was an infant. She describes her experiences at an American grade school, where the teachers could not understand her perpetual silence. Other behavior, such as painting her artwork black and challenging a patriotic song lyric, further confuses her intolerant teachers. In Chinese school, however, the narrator discovers a freedom and comfort among her fellow Chinese American students. She finally manages to stand up and recite a lesson before her class, shakily, proving her resolve to find, use, and project her own voice.

*For summaries in other languages, see the **Building English Proficiency** book.*

Artist Tomie Arai once explained that a central character in Asian American art is "the sojourner, forever foreign, uprooted and marginal . . ." Does her 1988 silkscreen, *Laundryman's Daughter,* reflect that idea? If so, how?

and takes up that day's courage. It spoils my day with self-disgust when I hear my broken voice come skittering out into the open. It makes people wince to hear it. I'm getting better, though. Recently I asked the postman for special-issue stamps; I've waited since childhood for postmen to give me some of their own accord. I am making progress, a little every day.

My silence was thickest—total—during the three years that I covered my school paintings with black paint. I painted layers of black over houses and flowers and suns, and when I drew on the blackboard, I put a layer of chalk on top. I was making a stage curtain, and it was the moment before the curtain parted or rose. The teachers called my parents to school, and I saw they had

The Woman Warrior   **755**

🎨 *Art Study*

Tomie Arai created this silkscreened image of a photograph taken in New York City. The images of buildings reflect urban America, juxtaposed with Chinese images. The artwork is part of "Memory-in-Progress: A Mother/Daughter Project," which was displayed at the Chinatown History Project in New York in 1989.

Response to Caption   The art does reflect a "foreign" image of people in America, wearing traditional Chinese clothes and surrounded by images that suggest carrying China and America with them, rather than being rooted firmly in one or the other.

2 **Historical Note**
Asian Americans

Asian Americans are people whose origins are traced to countries of Asia and Asian Pacific Islands, such as China, Japan, Vietnam, Korea, Cambodia, Laos, Thailand, and the Philippines. Although Asian Americans have been settling in the United States at least since the mid-nineteenth century, larger populations have immigrated since discriminatory government quotas were lifted in 1965.

3 **Reading/Thinking Skills**
Clarify

Questions

• How does the narrator explain her covering of art with black paint? *(Possible response: She sees it as a stage curtain covering her art, as if it were the moment before the curtain would be opened.)*

• During the time when she used black paint, was she communicating with language at school? *(No; she says her "silence was thickest—total" at the time.)*

BUILDING ENGLISH PROFICIENCY

Making Cultural Connections

Help students talk about the experiences of people who immigrate or otherwise enter a cultural setting that is at first unfamiliar to them.

• Some students may be willing and able to share their own experiences of adjusting to new cultural surroundings. It is important not to single students out on the basis of their culture or immigrant background, because many students do not welcome such attention imposed on them.

• Many students who have not personally experienced migration from one cultural setting to another still may know of experiences of relatives or ancestors.

• Students may find on a map or globe various places important to their cultural heritage.

📖 *Building English Proficiency*
Activities, p. 225

After Reading

MAKING CONNECTIONS

1. Possible responses: Ask her about her favorite animals, colors, or other interests; give her personal attention and show patience; involve her in word games or songs; ask what the black paint showed.

2. Possible responses: her discomfort in a school she didn't understand; the expectations of teachers and other students who didn't understand her culture; her feeling that silence was part of being a Chinese girl; and other cultural barriers

3. Possible response: Despite her mother's drastic action, she has great trouble speaking.

4. Possible response: She is rebellious and would find a way to communicate, even if it were not approved.

5. Possible responses: Schools now have programs such as "English as a Second Language" or bilingual education to help students learn and achieve skills in English and other subjects.

VOCABULARY STUDY

1. c. forehead

2. c. brass

3. a. ignore

4. b. deaf

5. a. cut

6. b. carefully

7. b. real

8. a. photograph

9. a. simplification

10. c. disappear

Unit 7 Resource Book
Vocabulary, p. 27
Vocabulary Test, p. 30

Selection Test

Unit 7 Resource Book
pp. 31–32

After Reading

Making Connections

Shaping Your Response

1. If you were the young Kingston's teacher, what would you have done to try to encourage her to speak?

Analyzing the Autobiography

2. What factors inhibit young Kingston's **interactions** with others?

3. What is the **irony** in the notion that Kingston's mother cut her frenum to free her tongue?

4. What do you think Kingston means when she says she would be an "outlaw knot maker"?

Extending the Ideas

5. How have schools changed since Kingston's schooling in the 1940s to accommodate students whose home language is not English?

Vocabulary Study

Choose the word least related in meaning to the vocabulary word.

frenum
teak
tamper
mute
tauten
assuredly
nonexistent
ideograph
intricacy
resolve

	a.	b.	c.
1. *frenum*	tongue	palate	forehead
2. *teak*	oak	mahogany	brass
3. *tamper*	ignore	meddle	interfere
4. *mute*	dumb	deaf	silent
5. *tauten*	cut	stretch	tighten
6. *assuredly*	confidently	carefully	certainly
7. *nonexistent*	imaginary	real	unreal
8. *ideograph*	photograph	pictograph	symbol
9. *intricacy*	simplification	entanglement	complication
10. *resolve*	divide	separate	disappear

Expressing Your Ideas

Writing Choice

Writer's Notebook Update As a child, were you ever in a situation where being too quiet or talking too much got you into trouble? Write a list of rules telling when it's best to talk and when it's best to be silent.

Another Option

California, Here I Come Research the immigration of Chinese people to California in the first half of the 1900s. Make a **graph** showing the immigration trends, and prepare a **map** of California that shows the major destinations of the immigrants.

WRITING CHOICE
Writer's Notebook Update

To enrich the writing, students might write a few sentences explaining why each rule may or may not make sense to a young child.

ANOTHER OPTION
California, Here I Come

Students also might research the Chinatown communities in major metropolitan areas such as San Francisco or New York City and Chicago. Suggest that students research the cross-cultural blend of Chinese and American influences within these communities.

Before Reading

Everyday Use

by Alice Walker

Alice Walker
born 1944

Alice Walker was born in Eatonton, Georgia, the eighth child of sharecroppers. When she was eight, Walker was blinded in her right eye as a result of a BB gun accident. This incident left her physically and emotionally scarred, and it was at this time that she turned to journal writing. From the late 1960s to the mid-1970s she taught writing and African American studies at a number of universities. In her poetry, short stories, novels, and essays she often focuses on the themes of racism and sexism, and her main characters are usually African American women, as in her novel *The Color Purple,* which won a Pulitzer Prize and was made into a movie.

Building Background

Forty Acres and a Mule Although the Emancipation Proclamation freed all enslaved African Americans, daily life was not much changed for them in the South after the Civil War. Land-reform plans which promised to give former slaves "40 acres and a mule" did not materialize. Many former slaves stayed on the plantations as laborers. Others worked as sharecroppers, farming a plot of land for the owner in exchange for part of the crops. Still others worked in factories springing up in the South, getting paid very low wages. Opportunities were better in the North and in the West. The industrial boom, along with slowed immigration, that accompanied World War I offered African Americans unprecedented opportunities for employment. The price of this economic gain, however, often included leaving behind relatives and friendships, as well as rural traditions and ways of living.

Literary Focus

Figurative Language Figurative language is the use of words apart from their ordinary, literal meanings to add freshness or vitality to a piece of writing. Some common figures of speech are **hyperbole, simile,** and **metaphor.** Hyperbole is obvious exaggeration: "The noise of the jack hammer was so loud it could have awakened the dead." A simile is a comparison using *like* or *as:* "The trees lined the driveway like soldiers standing at attention." A metaphor is an implied comparison: "She wept a storm of tears." As you read "Everyday Use," look for examples of figurative language.

Writer's Notebook

That Certain Something If you could choose one item from your childhood home to take with you when you move out, what would it be? In your log write a description of the object you would choose, and explain its significance to you.

Everyday Use **759**

SUPPORT MATERIALS OVERVIEW

Unit 7 Resource Book
- Graphic Organizer, p. 33
- Study Guide, p. 34
- Vocabulary, p. 35
- Grammar, p. 36
- Alternate Check Test, p. 37
- Vocabulary Test, p. 38
- Selection Test, pp. 39–40

Building English Proficiency
- Literature Summaries
- Activities, p. 226

Reading, Writing & Grammar SkillBook
- Reading, pp. 66–67
- Grammar, Usage, and Mechanics, pp. 173–175

Technology
- Audiotape
- Personal Journal Software
- Test Generator Software

Selection Objectives

- To examine themes of cultural heritage and of parent-child relationships
- To appreciate the power of figurative language
- To recognize clear uses of end punctuation in sentences and exclamations

 Unit 7 Resource Book
Graphic Organizer, p. 33
Study Guide, p. 34

Theme Link

The story examines a rural woman's insights about cultural heritage and family issues as she deals with personal conflicts involving her adult daughters.

Vocabulary Preview

organdy, a fine, thin, stiff, transparent material, used for dresses, curtains, and so on

furtive, sly, stealthy

oppress, keep down unjustly or by cruelty

doctrine, a principle taught by a church, nation, or group of persons; belief

alcove, a small room opening out of a larger room

Students can add the words and meanings to their word lists in the Writer's Notebook.

1 Literary Elements
Imagery and Characters

Students who can use help appreciating characterization might note details and images in a chart under each character's name. Examples are shown.

Mama	Maggie	Dee
Big-boned woman with rough, man-working hands	Burn scars Eyeing her sister with envy	Would look anyone in the eye

---

EVERYDAY USE

Alice Walker

 will wait for her in the yard that Maggie and I made so clean and wavy yesterday afternoon. A yard like this is more comfortable than most people know. It is not just a yard. It is like an extended living room. When the clay is swept clean as a floor and the fine sand around the edges lined with tiny, irregular grooves, anyone can come and sit and look up into the elm tree and wait for the breezes that never come inside the house.

Maggie will be nervous until after her sister goes: she will stand hopelessly in corners, homely and ashamed of the burn scars down her arms and legs, eyeing her sister with a mixture of envy and awe. She thinks her sister has held life always in the palm of one hand, that "no" is a word the world never learned to say to her.

You've no doubt seen those TV shows where the child who has "made it" is confronted,[1] as a surprise, by her own mother and father, tottering in weakly from backstage. (A pleasant surprise, of course: What would they do if parent and child came on the show only to curse out and insult each other?) On TV mother and child embrace and smile into each other's faces. Sometimes the mother and father weep, the child wraps them in her arms and leans across the table to tell how she would not have made it without their help. I have seen these programs.

Sometimes I dream a dream in which Dee and I are suddenly brought together on a TV program of this sort. Out of a dark and softseated limousine I am ushered into a bright room filled with many people. There I meet a smiling, gray, sporty man like Johnny Carson who shakes my hand and tells me what a fine girl I have. Then we are on the stage and Dee is embracing me with tears in her eyes. She pins on my dress a large orchid, even though she has told me once that she thinks orchids are tacky flowers.

In real life I am a large, big-boned woman with rough, man-working hands. In the winter I wear flannel nightgowns to bed and overalls during the day. I can kill and clean a hog as mercilessly as a man. My fat keeps me hot in zero weather. I can work outside all day, breaking ice to get water for washing; I can eat pork liver cooked over the open fire minutes after it comes steaming from the hog. One winter I knocked a bull calf straight in the brain between the eyes with a sledgehammer and had the meat hung up to chill before nightfall. But of course all this does not show on television. I am the way my daughter would want me to be: a hundred pounds lighter, my skin like an uncooked barley pancake. My hair glistens in the hot, bright lights. Johnny Carson has much to do to keep up with my quick and witty tongue.

But that is a mistake. I know even before I wake up. Who ever knew a Johnson with a quick tongue? Who can even imagine me looking a strange white man in the eye? It seems to me I have talked to them always with one foot raised in flight, with my head turned in whichever way is farthest from them. Dee, though. She would always look anyone in the eye. Hesitation was no part of her nature. **1**

"How do I look, Mama?" Maggie says, showing

---

1. **confront** (kən frunt′), *v.* bring face to face; place before.

SELECTION SUMMARY

Everyday Use

A rural African American woman describes the conflict that arises when Dee, her stylish, educated daughter, returns for a visit. Her other daughter, Maggie, a shy and self-effacing burn victim, is overwhelmed by her aggressive sister. Dee arrives with her boyfriend, who boldly greets Maggie and later refuses to eat their food for religious reasons. Dee, intrusive from the moment she arrives, takes snapshots of the house, her family, and the cow as she greets her mother. She announces her new name, Wangero, that symbolizes her liberation from the oppression of her Southern heritage. She appropriates a butter churn as an addition to her home decorations, ignoring the fact that her mother and sister still use it. When she tries to take two handmade quilts, the narrator stops her. She has promised these to Maggie. The narrator realizes that Maggie has a deeper appreciation of her heritage.

 For summaries in other languages, see the Building English Proficiency book.

What details in Hubert Shuptrine's 1985 portrait, *Mama Agnes*, match the story?

Possible Responses to Caption Any of the following details are similar to Mama in the story. The woman is African American, old enough to have grown children, and large. She sits outside her house as if her yard is "like an extended living room." She appears to be thoughtful, and she is called Mama.

Visual Literacy The portrait resembles some literature, in that a person is portrayed and the viewer can imagine her character and more of the setting. Students may imagine what is just out of the frame and describe or draw the surroundings. Are there other people present? Is there a road or street? Artist Hubert Shuptrine has created a warm, realistic portrait that places Mama Agnes at a house. It is up to viewers to picture the rest of the setting, if they wish.

BUILDING ENGLISH PROFICIENCY

Exploring Characterization

Mama is the narrator of the story and a fascinating character in her own right. Have students focus on the way Walker characterizes her. Students can begin a character traits web about Mama (or about Maggie or Dee).

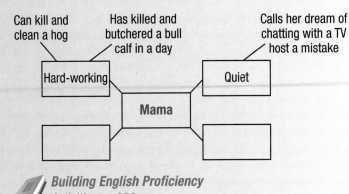

Building English Proficiency
Activities, p. 226

761

2 Literary Element
Diction

The narrator uses expressive language to recount events, describe her daughters and their experiences, and reveal her own attitudes.

Question What does the phrase "some careless person rich enough to own a car" suggest about Mama's opinion of the importance of wealth? *(Possible response: She is poor enough to consider a car a luxury item, but she does not regard rich people as better than others.)*

Discuss the words that Mama chooses to describe Dee's efforts to teach her family: *burned, pressed, shove, forced.*

Question How would you describe Mama's feelings about Dee? *(Possible response: She resents Dee's way of forcing ideas on Maggie and herself.)*

3 Literary Element
Irony

Question Why is Dee's use of the word *choose* ironic? *(Possible response: The narrator is poor; she doesn't feel she and Maggie have a lot of choice about where to live.)*

---

just enough of her thin body enveloped in pink skirt and red blouse for me to know she's there, almost hidden by the door.

"Come out into the yard," I say.

Have you ever seen a lame animal, perhaps a dog run over by some careless person rich enough to own a car, sidle up to someone who is ignorant enough to be kind to him? That is the way Maggie walks. She has been like this, chin on chest, eyes on ground, feet in shuffle, ever since the fire that burned the other house to the ground.

Dee is lighter than Maggie, with nicer hair and a fuller figure. She's a woman now, though sometimes I forget. How long ago was it that the other house burned? Ten, twelve years? Sometimes I can still hear the flames and feel Maggie's arms sticking to me, her hair smoking and her dress falling off her in little black paper flakes. Her eyes seemed stretched open, blazed open by the flames reflected in them. And Dee. I see her standing off under the sweet gum tree she used to dig gum out of; a look of concentration on her face as she watched the last dingy gray board of the house fall in toward the red-hot brick chimney. Why don't you do a dance around the ashes? I'd wanted to ask her. She had hated the house that much.

I used to think she hated Maggie, too. But that was before we raised the money, the church and me, to send her to Augusta to school. She used to read to us without pity; forcing words, lies, other folks' habits, whole lives upon us two, sitting trapped and ignorant underneath her voice. She washed us in the river of make-believe, burned us with a lot of knowledge we didn't necessarily need to know. Pressed us to her with the serious way she read, to shove us away at just the moment, like dimwits, we **2** seemed about to understand.

Dee wanted nice things. A yellow organdy² dress to wear to her graduation from high school; black pumps to match a green suit she'd

> At sixteen she had a style of her own—and knew what style was.

made from an old suit somebody gave me. She was determined to stare down any disaster in her efforts. Her eyelids would not flicker for minutes at a time. Often I fought off the temptation to shake her. At sixteen she had a style of her own—and knew what style was.

I never had an education myself. After second grade the school was closed down. Don't ask me why: in 1927 colored asked fewer questions than they do now. Sometimes Maggie reads to me. She stumbles along good-naturedly but can't see well. She knows she is not bright. Like good looks and money, quickness passed her by. She will marry John Thomas (who has mossy teeth in an earnest face), and then I'll be free to sit here and I guess just sing church songs to myself. Although I never was a good singer. Never could carry a tune. I was always better at a man's job. I used to love to milk till I was hooked in the side in '49. Cows are soothing and slow and don't bother you, unless you try to milk them the wrong way.

I have deliberately turned my back on the house. It is three rooms, just like the one that burned, except the roof is tin; they don't make shingle roofs any more. There are no real windows, just some holes cut in the sides, like the portholes in a ship, but not round and not square, with rawhide holding the shutters up on the outside. This house is in a pasture, too, like the other one. No doubt when Dee sees it she will want to tear it down. She wrote me once that no matter where we "choose" to live, she **3** will manage to come see us. But she will never bring her friends. Maggie and I thought about this and Maggie asked me, "Mama, when did Dee ever *have* any friends?"

She had a few. Furtive³ boys in pink shirts hanging about on washday after school. Nervous

---

2. **organdy** (ôr′gən dē′), *n.* a fine, thin, stiff, transparent material, used for dresses, curtains, etc.
3. **furtive** (fėr′tiv), *adj.* sly, stealthy.

MINI-LESSON: LITERARY FOCUS

Figurative Language

Teach Have students examine the images in the following sentences from the story. Help students identify the metaphorical images, the example of hyperbole (or figurative exaggeration), and the simile.

- She washed us in the river of make-believe, burned us with a lot of knowledge we didn't necessarily need to know. *(a pair of metaphors)*
- This house is in a pasture, too, like the other one. No doubt when Dee sees it she will want to tear it down. *(hyperbole)*
- [Her sister's hair] is black as night and around the edges are two long pigtails that rope about like small lizards disappearing behind her ears. *(The image of the pigtails contains a simile.)*

Explain that if these sentences were rewritten without figurative language, they might have a similar meaning, but they would lose much of their descriptive power.

Activity Idea Have students try to rewrite the above sentences without using figurative language. *(For example: No doubt Dee won't like it.)* Compare the results to the originals.

girls who never laughed. Impressed with her they worshipped the well-turned phrase, the cute shape, the scalding humor that erupted like bubbles in lye. She read to them.

When she was courting Jimmy T, she didn't have much time to pay to us, but turned all her fault-finding power on him. He *flew* to marry a cheap city girl from a family of ignorant flashy people. She hardly had time to recompose herself.

When she comes I will meet—but there they are!

Maggie attempts to make a dash for the house, in her shuffling way, but I stay her with my hand. "Come back here," I say. And she stops and tries to dig a well in the sand with her toe.

 PREDICT: What do you think the reunion between the narrator and her daughter Dee will be like?

It is hard to see them clearly through the strong sun. But even the first glimpse of leg out of the car tells me it is Dee. Her feet were always neat-looking, as if God himself had shaped them with a certain style. From the other side of the car comes a short, stocky man. Hair is all over his head a foot long and hanging from his chin like a kinky mule tail. I hear Maggie suck in her breath. "Uhnnnh," is what it sounds like. Like when you see the wriggling end of a snake just in front of your foot on the road. "Uhnnnh."

Dee next. A dress down to the ground, in this hot weather. A dress so loud it hurts my **5** eyes. There are yellows and oranges enough to throw back the light of the sun. I feel my whole face warming from the heat waves it throws out. Earrings gold, too, and hanging down to her shoulders. Bracelets dangling and making noises when she moves her arm up to shake the folds of the dress out of her armpits. The dress is loose and flows, and as she walks closer, I like it. I hear Maggie go "Uhnnnh" again. It is her sister's hair. It stands straight up like the wool

on a sheep. It is black as night and around the edges are two long pigtails that rope about like small lizards disappearing behind her ears.

"Wa-su-zo-Tean-o!" she says, coming on in that gliding way the dress makes her move. The short, stocky fellow with the hair to his navel is all grinning and he follows up with "Asalamalakim,[4] my mother and sister!" He moves to hug Maggie but she falls back, right up against the back of my chair. I feel her trembling there and when I look up I see the perspiration falling off her chin.

"Don't get up," says Dee. Since I am stout it takes something of a push. You can see me trying to move a second or two before I make it. She turns, showing white heels through her sandals, and goes back to the car. Out she peeks next with a Polaroid. She stoops down quickly and lines up picture after picture of me sitting there in front of the house with Maggie cowering behind me. She never takes a shot without making sure the house is included. When a cow comes nibbling around the edge of the yard she snaps it and me and Maggie *and* the house. Then she puts the Polaroid in the back seat of the car, and comes up and kisses me on the **6** forehead.

Meanwhile Asalamalakim is going through motions with Maggie's hand. Maggie's hand is as limp as a fish, and probably as cold, dispite the sweat, and she keeps trying to pull it back. It looks like Asalamalakim wants to shake hands but wants to do it fancy. Or maybe he don't know how people shake hands. Anyhow, he soon gives up on Maggie.

"Well," I say. "Dee."

"No, Mama," She says. "Not 'Dee,' Wangero Leewanika Kemanjo!"

"What happened to 'Dee'?" I wanted to know.

"She's dead," Wangero said. "I couldn't bear

---

4. **Wa-su-zo-Tean-o! . . . Asalamalakim!** Black Muslim greetings.

4 Active Reading
Predict

Possible response: It probably will be tense and awkward. Dee may be critical.

5 Literary Focus
Figurative Language

Question What hyperbole, or figurative exaggeration, does Mama use as she describes Dee's dress? *(Possible response: She says the colors are so loud and bright that they hurt her eyes, throw back the sun's light, and throw out heat waves.)*

6 Reading/Thinking Skills
Reader's Response

Clarify the sequence of events with students: the daughter takes a series of pictures before she has even hugged or kissed her mother. Ask students to consider the time, place, and feelings that usually surround a family snapshot.

Question Do you think Dee greets her mother and sister appropriately? Why or why not? *(Possible response: Students may think it rude for Dee to objectify her mother and sister, as if she is recording information rather than personally greeting them.)*

BUILDING ENGLISH PROFICIENCY

Exploring Relationships Among Characters

Students can clarify how members of the family relate to one another by using a character diagram. Pairs of students might draw the diagram and write along each arrow a word or phrase that describes how each person seems to feel about the person to whom the arrow points.

As students talk about the characters, they may change their minds or gain new insights. If students disagree, two diagrams may reflect their views, or they can ask the class to reach consensus.

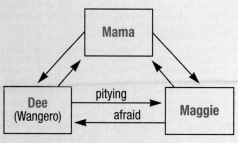

7 Active Reading
Clarify

Possible response: She wanted to create a new identity for herself that is not connected to slavery and the white South. The name she has chosen apparently is of African origin.

8 Literary Element
Conflict

Discuss the tension between the narrator and her guests. Mama seems conscious of Dee's and the young man's disdain.

- Why does Mama stand up to him at this point? (Possible response: He is patronizing and interfering with her point.)
- What sort of eye signals do you think he and Wangero are exchanging over the narrator's head? (Possible response: a rolling of the eyes, as if to say, "Isn't she something?")

9 Reading/Thinking Skills
Make Connections

Question Why does Dee suddenly remember what she wanted from her mother's house? (Possible response: She places her hand on the butter dish, which reminds her of the churn.)

Students should recognize the irony when Dee (Wangero) reveals that she "needs" the churn top as a decoration (p. 765). Her mother and sister actually use it to make butter, its designed purpose.

---

it any longer, being named after the people who oppress[5] me."

7 CLARIFY: Why did Dee change her name?

"You know as well as me you was named after your aunt Dicie," I said. Dicie is my sister. She named Dee. We called her "Big Dee" after Dee was born.

"But who was *she* named after?" asked Wangero.

"I guess after Grandma Dee," I said.

"And who was she named after?" asked Wangero.

"Her mother," I said, and saw Wangero was getting tired. "That's about as far back as I can trace it," I said. Though, in fact, I probably could have carried it back beyond the Civil War through the branches.

"Well," said Asalamalakim, "there you are."

"Uhnnnh," I heard Maggie say.

"There I was not," I said, "before 'Dicie' cropped up in our family, so why should I try to trace it that far back?"

He just stood there grinning, looking down on me like somebody inspecting a Model A car. **8** Every once in a while he and Wangero sent eye signals over my head.

"How do you pronounce this name?" I asked.

"You don't have to call me by it if you don't want to," said Wangero.

"Why shouldn't I?" I asked. "If it's what you want us to call you, we'll call you."

"I know it might sound awkward at first," said Wangero.

"I'll get used to it," I said. "Ream it out again."

Well, soon we got the name out of the way. Asalamalakim had a name twice as long and three times as hard. After I tripped over it two or three times he told me to just call him Hakim-a-barber. I wanted to ask him was he a barber, but I didn't really think he was, so I didn't ask.

"You must belong to those beef-cattle peoples

---

down the road," I said. They said "Asalamalakim" when they met you, too, but they didn't shake hands. Always too busy: feeding the cattle, fixing the fences, putting up salt-lick shelters, throwing down hay. When the white folks poisoned some of the herd the men stayed up all night with rifles in their hands. I walked a mile and a half just to see the sight.

Hakim-a-barber said, "I accept some of their doctrines,[6] but farming and raising cattle is not my style." (They didn't tell me, and I didn't ask, whether Wangero [Dee] had really gone and married him.)

We sat down to eat and right away he said he didn't eat collards[7] and pork was unclean. Wangero, though, went on through the chitlins[8] and corn bread, the greens and everything else. She talked a blue streak over the sweet potatoes. Everything delighted her. Even the fact that we still used the benches her daddy made for the table when we couldn't afford to buy chairs.

"Oh, Mama!" she cried. Then turned to Hakim-a-barber. "I never knew how lovely these benches are. You can feel the rump prints," she said, running her hands underneath her and along the bench. Then she gave a sigh and her hand closed over Grandma Dee's butter dish. "That's it!" she said. "I knew there was something I wanted to ask you if I could have." She jumped up from the table and went over in the corner where the churn stood, the milk in it clabber[9] by now. She looked at the churn and **9** looked at it.

"This churn top is what I need," she said. "Didn't Uncle Buddy whittle it out of a tree you all used to have?"

"Yes," I said.

---

5. **oppress** (ə pres′), *v.* keep down unjustly or by cruelty.
6. **doctrine** (dok′trən), *n.* a principle taught by a church, nation, or group of persons; belief.
7. **collards** (kol′ərds), *n.* the fleshy leaves of the kale plant, cooked as greens.
8. **chitlins, chitterlings** (chit′linz), *n.* parts of the small intestines of pigs, calves, etc., cooked as food.
9. **clabber** (klab′ər), *n.* thick, sour milk.

MINI-LESSON: GRAMMAR

End Punctuation

Teach   Point out that writers use clear application of end punctuation in story dialogue to establish characters' tone of voice.

- As Wangero (Dee) presses her mother for information to prove a point about the name Dee, she asks insistent questions ending in question marks: "But who was *she* named after?" and "And who was she named after?"

- The comma in Mama's statement to Dee's friend, "You must belong to those beef-cattle peoples down the road," stands for a period. That is, she is making a statement, not asking a question. The connection between this man and the people down the road probably makes sense to her, and she avoids directly asking him a question about it.

Questions   What does the exclamation point in Dee's comment "That's it!" reveal about her feeling concerning the butter churn top? (Possible response: She is excited at the chance to get it.)

Activity Idea   Students can create comic strips with dialogue that uses periods, question marks, and exclamation points in clear and expressive ways.

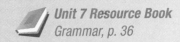 *Unit 7 Resource Book*
Grammar, p. 36

"Uh huh," she said happily. "And I want the dasher,[10] too."

"Uncle Buddy whittle that, too?" asked the barber.

Dee (Wangero) looked up at me.

"Aunt Dee's first husband whittled the dash," said Maggie so low you almost couldn't hear her. "His name was Henry, but they called him Stash."

"Maggie's brain is like an elephant's," Wangero said, laughing. "I can use the churn top as a centerpiece for the alcove[11] table," she said, sliding a plate over the churn, "and I'll think of something artistic to do with the dasher."

When she finished wrapping the dasher the handle stuck out. I took it for a moment in my hands. You didn't even have to look close to see where hands pushing the dasher up and down to make butter had left a kind of sink in the wood. In fact, there were a lot of small sinks; you could see where thumbs and fingers had sunk into the wood. It was beautiful light yellow wood, from a tree that grew in the yard where Big Dee and Stash had lived.

After dinner Dee (Wangero) went to the trunk at the foot of my bed and started rifling through it. Maggie hung back in the kitchen over the dishpan. Out came Wangero with two quilts. They had been pieced by Grandma Dee and then Big Dee and me had hung them on the quilt frames on the front porch and quilted them. One was in the Lone Star pattern. The other was Walk Around the Mountain. In both of them were scraps of dresses Grandma Dee had worn fifty and more years ago. Bits and pieces of Grandpa Jarrell's paisley shirts. And one teeny faded blue piece, about the size of a penny matchbox, that was from Great Grandpa Ezra's uniform that he wore in the Civil War.

"Mama," Wangero said sweet as a bird. "Can I have these old quilts?"

List five words that describe the physical features of the scene in this painting, *Gilley's House* (about 1976), by Bob Timberlake. Then list another five that describe the feeling you get from this painting. Are your lists similar or different from each other?

I heard something fall in the kitchen, and a minute later the kitchen door slammed.

"Why don't you take one or two of the others?" I asked. "These old things was just done by me and Big Dee from some tops your grandma pieced before she died."

"No," said Wangero. "I don't want those. They are stitched around the borders by machine."

---

10. **dasher** (dash′ər), *n.* device for stirring the cream in a churn.
11. alcove (al′kōv), *n.* a small room opening out of a larger room.

10 Literary Element

10 Literary Element
Dialogue

Discuss the author's use of dialogue to contrast the characters of the two daughters.

- This is the first time Maggie has the courage to say anything other than, "Uhnnnnh."
- Wangero's (or Dee's) response is casual, almost thoughtless, and dismissive.

Art Study

North Carolina painter Bob Timberlake didn't even visit an art gallery until he was 30, but he established himself as a respected "rural realist" soon after his professional debut in 1971. Since then, he has designed postage stamps, written books, and worked on the "Keep America Beautiful" campaign.

Possible Responses to Caption   For physical features: *old-fashioned, rural* (or *country*), *rustic, shabby, peaceful, colorful;* for feelings: *calm, curious, isolated, peaceful, nostalgic,* and so on

11 Reading/Thinking Skills
Make Inferences

Question   Who is making these noises? Why? *(Possible response: Maggie; Dee's selfish appropriation of the quilts is making Maggie angry.)*

BUILDING ENGLISH PROFICIENCY

Making Cultural Connections

Help students recognize the value of the quilts to the characters, if necessary. Discuss how people appreciate hand-crafted items and sometimes pass them as heirlooms from one generation to another.

Activity Ideas

- Students can vote on which sister they think should receive the quilts. Students can talk about why the quilts may be important in different ways to both sisters.

- Invite interested students to explain or demonstrate phases of quilt making. Pictures or samples of handmade quilts can be shown.
- Invite students to bring pictures (or objects, if suitable) to display any kind of folk art they or their family members value.

Recognize Values

Discuss the irony of Dee's accusation about the "everyday use" of the quilts. Mama responds that Maggie is better able to appreciate her grandmother's quilts because she knows how to make and use quilts herself.

Question What point is the author making about the heritage of the rural South? *(Possible response: People shouldn't simply appropriate and objectify their cultural inheritance; they must learn and appreciate it and pass their knowledge along to the next generation.)*

Check Test

1. How did Maggie get her scars? *(in a fire)*

2. Why did Dee have a hard time forming friendships? *(Possible responses: because she was aggressive and critical; because of her fault-finding)*

3. Who is Wangero? *(Dee)*

4. Why does Dee want the butter churn top? *(She thinks it will make a quaint table decoration.)*

5. To whom does the narrator give her precious quilts? *(Maggie)*

Unit 7 Resource Book
Alternate Check Test, p. 37

"That'll make them last better," I said.

"That's not the point," said Wangero. "These are all pieces of dresses Grandma used to wear. She did all this stitching by hand. Imagine!" She held the quilts securely in her arms, stroking them.

"Some of the pieces, like those lavender ones, come from old clothes her mother handed down to her," I said, moving up to touch the quilts. Dee (Wangero) moved back just enough so that I couldn't reach the quilts. They already belonged to her.

"Imagine!" she breathed again, clutching them closely to her bosom.

"The truth is," I said, "I promised to give them quilts to Maggie, for when she marries John Thomas."

She gasped like a bee had stung her.

"Maggie can't appreciate these quilts!" she said. "She'd probably be backward enough to put them to everyday use."

"I reckon she would," I said. "God knows I been saving 'em for long enough with nobody using 'em. I hope she will!" I didn't want to bring up how I had offered Dee (Wangero) a quilt when she went away to college. Then she had told me they were old-fashioned, out of style.

"But they're *priceless!*" she was saying now, furiously; for she had a temper. "Maggie would put them on the bed and in five years they'd be in rags. Less than that!"

"She can always make some more," I said. "Maggie knows how to quilt."

Dee (Wangero) looked at me with hatred. "You just will not understand. The point is these quilts, *these* quilts!"

"Well," I said, stumped. "What would *you* do with them?"

"Hang them," she said. As if that was the only thing you *could* do with quilts.

Maggie by now was standing in the door. I could almost hear the sound her feet made as they scraped over each other.

"She can have them, Mama," she said, like somebody used to never winning anything, or having anything reserved for her. "I can 'member Grandma Dee without the quilts."

I looked at her hard. She had filled her bottom lip with checkerberry snuff and it gave her face a kind of dopey, hangdog look. It was Grandma Dee and Big Dee who taught her how to quilt herself. She stood there with her scarred hands hidden in the folds of her skirt. She looked at her sister with something like fear but wasn't mad at her. This was Maggie's portion. This was the way she knew God to work.

When I looked at her like that something hit me in the top of my head and ran down to the soles of my feet. Just like when I'm in church and the spirit of God touches me and I get happy and shout. I did something I never had done before: hugged Maggie to me, then dragged her on into the room, snatched the quilts out of Miss Wangero's hands and dumped them into Maggie's lap. Maggie just sat there on the bed with her mouth open.

"Take one or two of the others," I said to Dee.

But she turned without a word and went out to Hakim-a-barber.

"You just don't understand," she said, as Maggie and I came out to the car.

"What don't I understand?" I wanted to know.

"Your heritage," she said. And then she turned to Maggie, kissed her, and said, "You ought to try to make something of yourself, too, Maggie. It's really a new day for us. But from the way you and Mama still live you'd never know it."

She put on some sunglasses that hid everything above the tip of her nose and her chin.

Maggie smiled; maybe at the sunglasses. But a real smile, not scared. After we watched the car dust settle I asked Maggie to bring me a dip of snuff. And then the two of us sat there just enjoying, until it was time to go in the house and go to bed.

MINI-LESSON: VOCABULARY

Recognize Shades of Meaning

Teach Explain that this story's author often conveys a negative impression of Dee without directly criticizing her. One way that she achieves this is by taking advantage of words' shades of meaning, revealing Dee's craftiness through irony.

For example, at first, Dee sweetly asks, "Mama, can I have these old quilts?" A few paragraphs later, she shouts, "They're priceless, priceless!" She was trying to manipulate her mother by using the word *old*. It is their antique quality that makes them so valuable.

Apply Have students examine this sentence: "I can use the churn top as a centerpiece for the alcove table," she said, sliding a plate over the churn, "and I'll think of something *artistic* to do with the dasher."

Question How does the word *artistic* cast an negative light on Dee? *(Possible response: Dee won't use the dasher for its intended purpose; instead she'll do something artistic, which Mama probably considers less useful and perhaps phony.)*

Activity Idea Have students find other examples of words in the story that have ironic shades of meaning.

After Reading

Making Connections

Shaping Your Response

1. Write five adjectives that you would use to describe Dee. Then write five adjectives to describe the narrator and five to describe Maggie.

Analyzing the Story

2. What is the significance of the title "Everyday Use"?

3. What do you think is the purpose of Dee's visit with her mother and sister? Explain.

4. What do you think the narrator realizes about herself during her argument with Dee over the quilts?

5. 🔥 How does cultural heritage play a part in the **interactions** between Dee and her family?

Extending the Ideas

6. Dee is an ambitious person. Explain when, in your opinion, ambition is a good quality and when it is a bad quality.

Literary Focus: Figurative Language

Skim the story to find examples of similes, metaphors, and hyperbole. Make a chart like the one below in your notebook and add to it as you find examples of each kind of figure of speech.

Similes	Metaphors	Hyperbole
yard like an extended living room (p. 760)		

Vocabulary Study

Study the relationship between the first word pair for each item, then choose the word that completes the second pair so that it expresses a similar relationship.

furtive
organdy
alcove
doctrine
oppress

1. photogenic : model : : *furtive* : ____
   - **a.** photographer
   - **b.** farmer
   - **c.** spy
   - **d.** writer

2. burlap : homely : : *organdy* : ____
   - **a.** corduroy
   - **b.** beautiful
   - **c.** ugly
   - **d.** cozy

3. cove : lake : : *alcove* : ____
   - **a.** river
   - **b.** room
   - **c.** neighborhood
   - **d.** porch

4. rule : school : : *doctrine* : ____
   - **a.** belief
   - **b.** education
   - **c.** medicine
   - **d.** religion

5. lower : raise : : *oppress* : ____
   - **a.** elevate
   - **b.** repress
   - **c.** compress
   - **d.** enslave

Everyday Use **767**

After Reading

MAKING CONNECTIONS

1. Possible response: Dee—aggressive, selfish, stylish, rude, inconsiderate; Mama (narrator)—patient, wise, introspective, generous, honest; Maggie—insecure, self-deprecating, wounded, afraid, quiet

2. It refers to the quilts, which Maggie would use for their functional value, and Dee would hang up as works of "folk art" but not use.

3. Possible response: She wants to "rediscover" her roots and collect souvenirs because these are fashionable things to do.

4. Possible response: She realizes that she has not resisted Dee's aggressiveness or made clear her love or attention for Maggie.

5. Possible response: Dee considers her cultural heritage to be a fashionable African American style. Maggie and Mama represent the old-fashioned tradition that Dee has tried to escape, although she considers it a kind of gallery of art pieces.

6. Responses may reflect the positive aspects of education, travel, and a desire to rise above poverty. Negative aspects of ambition may include selfishness, aggressive behavior, and lack of consideration of others' needs.

VOCABULARY STUDY

1. c. spy
2. b. beautiful
3. b. room
4. d. religion
5. a. elevate

Unit 7 Resource Book
Vocabulary, p. 35
Vocabulary Test, p. 38

LITERARY FOCUS:
FIGURATIVE LANGUAGE

Many teachers emphasize students' abilities to appreciate the differences between figurative language and language used in literal ways, rather than focusing primarily on differences among similes, metaphors, hyperbole, and other figures of speech. Students who recognize the imaginative qualities of figurative language become more skilled readers.

WRITING CHOICES

Writer's Notebook Update

Suggest that students discuss their names with their parents or guardians. Is there a history of the name within the family? Does the name reflect a particular cultural heritage? Students can consider how their families or friends might react if they decided to change their names.

Don't Stop Now

Some students may prefer to read an essay of Walker's, from a collection such as *In Search of Our Mothers' Gardens*. Students who read both fiction and nonfiction may consider how Walker's fiction develops any political views expressed in her essays.

Selection Test

 **Unit 7 Resource Book**
pp. 39–40

Expressing Your Ideas

Writing Choices

Writer's Notebook Update Families have significant material things, like the item you described in your notebook, but one intangible thing that families have is their name. Write a paragraph explaining the significance of your name—both your given name and your family name. If you, like Dee, don't like your name, write about the name you would like to have, and why you would like it.

Don't Stop Now Alice Walker has written several volumes of short stories, including *In Love and Trouble: Stories of Black Women* and *You Can't Keep a Good Woman Down*. Choose another story written by Walker, read it, and write a **summary** of it.

Other Options

Maggie Speaks Maggie doesn't say much during the course of the story. Work with a partner to create a **dialogue** that Maggie might have with her fiancé, John Thomas, discussing the events of the day. Take on the roles of the two characters and perform your dialogue for the class.

Stitching Up History One of the quilts Dee wanted was in the Lone Star pattern like the one pictured here. Research the history of quilt patterns in the United States. Some are simple blocks of cloth, and others are made with complicated designs and intricate stitchwork. Create a **quilt square,** either on graph paper or with cloth, and explain to your class the significance of the pattern. Or, use your imagination to create an **original quilt design** on paper or with cloth. Be sure to title your design.

OTHER OPTIONS

Maggie Speaks

- Students may enrich their dialogue with figurative language—for example, similes, metaphors, and hyperbole.
- Remind students to make their characters convincing by keeping the story's setting and characterization in mind as they write.

Stitching Up History

Books that offer information about quilts include the following titles and many others.

- Anderson, Suzy M. *A Collector's Guide to Quilts* (Chilton, 1991)
- *Quilter's Complete Guide* (Oxmoor House, 1993)
- Shogren, Linda. *Quilt Pattern Index* (Pieceful Pleasures, 1981)

Before Reading

Mirror by Sylvia Plath

One Art by Elizabeth Bishop

Legacies by Nikki Giovanni

Leaves by Sam Hamod

To Jesus Villanueva, with Love by Alma Luz Villanueva

Building Background

Deep Thoughts Introspection is the art of looking within one's heart and soul and reflecting on what is there. *Who is important to me? What is important to me? What should I do? How should I behave?* All of these are questions we ask ourselves in introspective moments. The five poems you are about to read are different in tone, form, and style, but each is the result of the poet's introspection about a relationship in his or her life.

Literary Focus

Personification Just as the mirror in "Snow White" comes alive and speaks, the mirror in Sylvia Plath's poem "Mirror" tells about the woman who looks into it. This technique of attributing human qualities to nonhuman or nonliving things is called **personification.** As you read "Mirror," note details that make this technique effective for conveying the meaning of the poem. What relationship is explored in this poem?

Writer's Notebook

Poetic License Poets take some liberties with language. They may disregard the rules of punctuation, grammar, or capitalization to achieve the effect they desire. They may or may not impose a rhythm and/or rhyme on their words. Before reading the following poems, copy a favorite short poem into your notebook. Does the poet take any liberties with the conventions of language? As you read the five poems that follow, try to answer these questions:

- Which of the poems disregard the conventions of capitalization and punctuation?
- Which of the poems are more structured?
- Which poems use conversational language or colloquial speech in them?
- What difference do these things make?

Mirror **769**

Before Reading

Building Background

Students may discuss connections between poetry and song. Songs often are poems put to music, and there is a musical quality to poetry. Ask students if any songs or poems remind them of special relationships.

Literary Focus

To review **personification,** ask students to imagine other objects that might have interesting things to say if they were given a human voice—for example: a steering wheel, a telephone, a kitchen sink, or a chair in a principal's office.

Response to Question on Pupil Page
the relationship between a woman and a mirror she uses, or between the woman and herself

Writer's Notebook

Responses to Questions on Pupil Page

- "Legacies," "Leaves," and "To Jesus Villanueva, with Love" disregard conventions of capitalization or punctuation.
- "Mirror" and "One Art" are more structured.
- "Legacies," "Leaves," and "To Jesus Villanueva, with Love" use informal language.
- The less formal poems may be easier to read or understand quickly. The more structured poems gain depth from their subtle imagery and adherence to meter.

SUPPORT MATERIALS OVERVIEW

Unit 7 Resource Book
- Graphic Organizer, p. 41
- Study Guide, p. 42
- Vocabulary, p. 43
- Grammar, p. 44
- Alternate Check Test, p. 45
- Vocabulary Test, p. 46
- Selection Test, pp. 47–48

Building English Proficiency
- Literature Summaries
- Activities, p. 227

Reading, Writing & Grammar SkillBook
- Reading, pp. 41–45, 75–76

Technology
- Audiotape
- Personal Journal Software
- Custom Literature Database: Other poems about personal relationships, by poets such as Robert Frost and Edwin Arlington Robinson, appear on the database.
- Test Generator Software

More About the Poets

- When **Sylvia Plath** was eighteen, she published a story in *Seventeen* magazine and a poem in *The Christian Science Monitor*. Other works by Plath are *The Bell Jar,* 1963, and *Ariel,* 1965.

- Although **Elizabeth Bishop** started writing poetry when she was eight, her literary career really got started when she was twelve—she won a five-dollar gold piece from the American Legion for an essay on "Americanism." Other poems by Bishop are found in *North and South—A Cold Spring,* 1955, and *Collected Poems,* 1969.

- **Nikki Giovanni** self-published her first book of poems, *Black Feeling, Black Talk,* in 1968 with the financial assistance of friends and family members. Other works by Giovanni are *Cotton Candy on a Rainy Day,* 1978, and *Those Who Ride the Night Winds,* 1983.

- **Hamod** has written television scripts, as well as several books of poetry, including *Dying with the Wrong Name,* 1980. His father was an imam, or priest, of the Muslim faith.

- **Alma Luz Villanueva,** a strong believer in the creative powers of the unconscious, keeps dream journals that she writes in poetry form. Her other works include *Weeping Woman, La Lorrona and Other Stories,* 1993, and *Bloodroot,* 1977.

Sylvia Plath
1932–1963

When her father died suddenly when she was eight, Sylvia Plath began writing poetry as "a new way of being happy." She won a Fulbright scholarship to Cambridge University, where she met and married English poet Ted Hughes. She battled chronic depression her whole life, and killed herself at the age of thirty-one.

Elizabeth Bishop
1911–1979

Elizabeth Bishop's father died when she was eight months old, and her mother was committed to a mental institution in 1916. She was raised by relatives. After college, Bishop made a trip to Europe that whetted her appetite for adventure. A later two-week trip to Brazil stretched into a fifteen-year stay. Bishop's poetry won many awards, among them the Pulitzer Prize and the National Book Award.

Nikki Giovanni
born 1943

Nikki Giovanni enrolled in Fisk University when she was sixteen. When she was suspended for leaving the campus without permission to visit her sick grandmother, she quit college, disgusted with the rigid rules. She later returned to Fisk and began to write poetry. She presently teaches at Virginia Polytechnic and State University.

Sam Hamod
born 1936

Born in his parents' boardinghouse in Gary, Indiana, Lebanese American poet Sam Hamod has said, "My earliest recollections are of my father, mother, and maternal grandfather, plus a lot of guys who roomed at the hotel and ate with us—gandy dancers, railroad firemen and engineers, open-hearth workers—everything—and from every nationality in the world." Hamod is currently a professor of English at Howard University.

Alma Luz Villanueva
born 1944

In her poetry, novels, and short stories, Villanueva relates her experiences as a woman in a male-dominated society, as part of an extended family, as a mother of four, and as a Chicana in a white society. Her novel, *The Ultraviolet Sky,* won an American Book Award in 1989. She teaches at the University of California at Santa Cruz.

SELECTION SUMMARY

Mirror; One Art; Legacies; Leaves; To Jesus Villanueva, With Love

Mirror   The speaker, a personified mirror, describes the anguish of the woman who approaches it daily to observe her aging reflection in its uncompromising surface.

One Art   Although the speaker boasts of her easy recovery from losses of intensifying degree, she then confesses her inability to face the loss of a dear friend with such stoicism.

Legacies   An old woman tries to teach her granddaughter how to make rolls. The little girl refuses, because she wants to depend on her grandmother forever. The old woman, unaware of her granddaughter's feelings, is irked by her apparent obstinacy.

Leaves   The speaker describes the discovery process that follows the death of his father. He has found grape leaves his father picked, stored in a freezer. Sifting through mementos, records, and memories, he rediscovers his unknown links to his father and to his Arabic heritage.

To Jesus Villanueva, with Love   This poem memorializes the poet's Mexican grandmother with a tribute to her humor, beauty, courage, and power in the face of death.

*For summaries in other languages, see the **Building English Proficiency** book.*

What do you think is happening in George Tooker's painting, *Mirror II* (1963)? Write an explanation that tells your view of the relationship between the young woman, the old woman, and the mirror. ➤

Mirror

Sylvia Plath

1 I am silver and exact. I have no preconceptions.[1]
Whatever I see I swallow immediately
Just as it is, unmisted by love or dislike.
I am not cruel, only truthful—
5 The eye of a little god, four-cornered.
Most of the time I meditate[2] on the opposite wall.
It is pink, with speckles. I have looked at it so long
I think it is a part of my heart. But it flickers.
Faces and darkness separate us over and over.

10 Now I am a lake. A woman bends over me,
Searching my reaches for what she really is.
Then she turns to those liars, the candles or the moon.
I see her back, and reflect it faithfully.
She rewards me with tears and an agitation of hands.
15 I am important to her. She comes and goes.
Each morning it is her face that replaces the darkness.
In me she has drowned a young girl, and in me an old woman
Rises toward her day after day, like a terrible fish.

---

1. **preconception** (prē′kən sep′shən), *n.* idea or opinion formed beforehand.
2. **meditate** (med′ə tāt), *v.* engage in deep and serious thought.

Mirror **771**

Selection Objectives

- To examine poems that deal with themes of love and loss between people
- To consider the use of personification
- To review a standard format for writing personal or informal letters

📖 **Unit 7 Resource Book**
Graphic Organizer, p. 41
Study Guide, p. 42

Theme Link

The theme "Person to Person" is explored in poems that convey mixtures of emotions that accompany changes during youth, lost opportunities, the end of a relationship, and the death of a loved one.

Vocabulary Preview

preconception, idea or opinion formed beforehand

meditate, engage in deep and serious thought

evident, easy to see or understand

repentant, feeling regret; sorry for wrongdoing

persistently, continually

Students can add the words and meanings to their lists in the Writer's Notebook.

Art Study

Possible Responses to Caption The woman may see a similarity in her face to an older relative's appearance, or maybe she foresees her own aging face.

BUILDING ENGLISH PROFICIENCY

Exploring Key Concepts

A central idea in "Mirror" concerns youth and age. The topic of aging can allow students to practice writing or conversing about a subject that virtually everyone thinks about. Students may consider differing ideas about aging in various cultures.

Activity Ideas

- Students can draw one person at three stages of life, either gazing into a mirror or involved in activities they consider typical

for each age. Then students can talk about the pictures, examining them for stereotypes or other aspects of interest.

- Students can portray people of various ages talking about the benefits of each part of life or the attitudes toward aging in different cultures familar to students.

📖 **Building English Proficiency**
Activities, p. 227

1 Literary Focus
Personification

Students can imagine a person studying his or her own face in a mirror, feeling hope for improving or maintaining one's appearance. To consider such an experience from another perspective, the poet imagines what a mirror (and reflecting lake) might see and think.

2 Literary Element
Repetition

Point out that each repetition of "The art of losing isn't hard to master" carries more weight as the poem progresses. Have students examine how the context affects tone and meaning.

3 Reading/Thinking Skills
Understand Sequence

Question   How does the poet escalate the amount or power of loss from the beginning to the end of the poem? *(Possible response: Each new stanza describes the loss of something larger or more valuable than the preceding loss.)*

4 Reading/Thinking Skills
Make Inferences

What does the parenthetical command "*Write* it!" suggest about the speaker? *(Possible response: She has to force herself to express her distress about this loss, even though she has been saying she has mastered the art of losing.)*

One Art

Elizabeth Bishop

The art of losing isn't hard to master;
so many things seem filled with the intent
to be lost that their loss is no disaster.

Lose something every day. Accept the fluster
5 of lost door keys, the hour badly spent.
The art of losing isn't hard to master.

Then practice losing farther, losing faster:
places, and names, and where it was you meant
to travel. None of these will bring disaster.

10 I lost my mother's watch. And look! my last, or
next-to-last, of three loved houses went.
The art of losing isn't hard to master.

I lost two cities, lovely ones. And, vaster,
some realms I owned, two rivers, a continent.
15 I miss them, but it wasn't a disaster.

—Even losing you (the joking voice, a gesture
I love) I shan't have lied. It's evident[1]
the art of losing's not too hard to master
though it may look like (*Write* it!) like disaster.

---

1. **evident** (ev′ə dənt), *adj.* easy to see or understand.

MINI-LESSON: VOCABULARY

Understanding Colloquialisms

Teach   Discuss the conversational style of the poems by Giovanni, Hamod, and Villanueva. Explain that each poet presents the English language through a cultural perspective. The informal style allows the poets to include colloquialisms or phrases that reflect the way informal English is casually spoken by people in a certain region or cultural group. Examples are shown here.

- Giovanni spells *you* as *chu* to suggest a pronunciation (p. 773).
- Hamod uses *up till,* an equivalent of *until* (p. 774).
- Villanueva quotes her grandmother's use of the term *gringos,* referring to North American people, or non-Hispanic people (p. 775).

Activity Idea   Students can list phrases and words they use in everyday speech that might not turn up in the dictionary. You may want to advise students, in advance, of restrictions that you deem appropriate.

⑤ *Legacies*

Nikki Giovanni

her grandmother called her from the
    playground
    "yes, ma'am"
    "i want chu to learn how to make rolls,"
      said the old
woman proudly
5 but the little girl didn't want
to learn how because she knew
even if she couldn't say it that
that would mean when the old one died
    she would be less
dependent on her spirit so
10 she said
    "i don't want to know how to make
      no rolls"
with her lips poked out
and the old woman wiped her hands on
her apron saying "lord
15   these children"
and neither of them ever
said what they meant
and i guess nobody ever does

⋀ What feeling would you say the artist, Lois Mailou Jones, has
captured in her 1943 oil painting, *Jennie?* How does the work
convey the feeling?

Questions How does the title relate to
the events described in the poem? Is the
title ironic? *(Possible response: The grandmother is trying to bequeath a legacy, her
recipe for baking rolls, to her granddaughter. Because the poem recounts an episode
is which the legacy is not passed successfully, there may be irony in this title.)*

Art Study

**Possible Response to Caption
Questions** The artist has captured
a warm feeling of appreciation for family, home, or mother's care. She has
portrayed the careful preparation of food
and has used warm colors and a homey
setting.

Legacies **773**

ESL
LEP
ELD
SAE
LD

BUILDING ENGLISH PROFICIENCY

Orally Interpreting a Poem

To help students carefully consider the sound and meaning of each
poem, you might invite students to read the poems aloud.

- Various readers each can select one of the poems and rehearse it
  before a small audience of one or two classmates. Allow students
  to talk about the meaning and sound of each poem. Students may
  prepare by informally paraphrasing parts of the poems before
  clearly reading the poems themselves.

- Then students can read the poems before a larger group such
  as the whole class. You may suggest that students audiotape the
  readings. Students who can play music may provide suitable
  background instrumentals for the readings, if possible.

Symbolism

Discuss the poet's use of objects to represent his father. The grape leaves of the title, the quoted letter, and an Arabic grammar book all reflect interests of the speaker's father. As they represent his father to him, so too they can symbolize his relationship with his father—and the idea that parent-child bonds do not end upon the parent's death—to readers.

Questions

- What might the grape leaves represent to the speaker in the poem? *(Possible response: The leaves are gifts from the father that keep turning up, symbolizing his presence and care that was apparent during his life.)*
- What might the Arabic grammar book represent? *(Possible response: It may symbolize the speaker's Arabic heritage, his father's cultural legacy to the speaker and his family.)*

Leaves
Hamod

FOR DAVID, LAURA, AND SALLY

Tonight, Sally and I are making stuffed
grapeleaves, we get out a package, it's
drying out, I've been saving it in the freezer, it's
one of the last things my father ever picked in this
5   life—they're over five years old
and up till now
we just kept finding packages of them in the
freezer, as if he were still picking them
somewhere   packing them
10   carefully to send us
making sure they didn't break into pieces.

      * * *

"To my Dar Garnchildn
Davd and Lura
from Thr Jido"
15   twisted on tablet paper
between the lines
in this English lettering
hard for him even to print,
I keep this small torn record,
20   this piece of paper stays in the upstairs storage,
one of the few pieces of American
my father ever wrote. We find his Arabic letters
all over the place, even in the files we find
letters to him in English, one I found from Charles Atlas[1]
25   telling him, in 1932,
"Of course, Mr. Hamod, you too can build
your muscles like mine . . ."

      * * *

Last week my mother told me, when I was
asking why I became a poet, "But don't you remember,
30   your father made up poems, don't you remember him
singing in the car as we drove—those were poems."

6 Even now, at night, I sometimes
get out the Arabic grammar book
though it seems so late.

_____

1. **Charles Atlas,** a famous bodybuilder.

MINI-LESSON: GRAMMAR

Writing Letters

Teach   Have students consider the note from the speaker's father to his grandchildren in "Leaves." While this grandfather's spelling and punctuation may reflect his unfamiliarity with English, he does incorporate standard aspects of personal letter format into his note. Review the standard format for personal letters. Informal letters customarily include these parts.

- The date and a salutation, or greeting, above the body of the letter: The greeting appears at the left and often begins with the word *Dear,* followed by the addressee's name and a comma.
- The body of the letter, in one or more paragraphs

- A closing word or phrase (such as *Sincerely*) at the right, followed by a comma, and the writer's signed name on the next line

A well-written letter is clear, handwritten legibly or typed, and free of spelling and other errors. Similar qualities in electronic mail can make it easy to read.

Activity Idea   Have partners write brief letters to one another, each describing one of the poems and what it expresses about personal relationships.

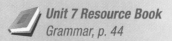
Unit 7 Resource Book
Grammar, p. 44

What effect do the colors in Fatima Del Real's 1988 painting, *Tacos Sabrosos*, have on the mood of the painting? ➤

To Jesus Villanueva, with Love

Alma Luz Villanueva

my first vivid memory of you
mamacita,
we made tortillas together
yours, perfect and round
5 mine, irregular and fat
we laughed
and named them: *ose, pajarito, gatito.*[1]
my last vivid memory of you
   (except for the very last
10   sacred memory
    i won't share)
mamacita
beautiful, thick, long, gray hair
the eyes gone sad
15 with flashes of fury
when they wouldn't let you
have your chilis, your onions, your peppers
   —what do these damned gringos[2]
      know of *my* stomach?—
so when I came to comb
20 your beautiful, thick, long, gray hair

as we sat for hours
(it soothed you
my hand
on your hair)
25 I brought you your chilis, your onions,
       your peppers.
and they'd always catch you
because you'd forget
and leave it lying open.
they'd scold you like a child
30 and you'd be embarrassed like a child
silent, repentant,[3] angry
and secretly waiting for my visit, the new
      supplies
we laughed at our secret

---

1. *ose, pajarito, gatito,* the Spanish words for bear (oso), little bird, little cat.
2. *gringos,* Spanish word for English-speaking people.
3. **repentant** (ri pen′tənt), *adj.* feeling regret; sorry for wrongdoing.

To Jesus Villanueva, with Love   775

The title *Tacos Sabrosos* means "delicious tacos."

Possible Response to Caption Question   The vibrant colors give the painting a warm and pleasant mood.

7 Reading/Thinking Skills
Generalize

You might discuss the emphasis on the preparation of food as a bonding ritual between family members.

Question   Why does learning to prepare savory foods leave such a strong impression on many children? *(Possible response: When elders start to teach children how to prepare their own food, it is an activity that helps children take steps toward adulthood, often in comfortable, affectionate family surroundings. It may also build bonds between generations.)*

8 Reading/Thinking Skills
Make Inferences

Villanueva, who was raised primarily by her grandmother whose name was Jesus, called her grandmother *mamacita,* an affectionate name for "mother."

Questions
• Where did the speaker visit her grandmother? *(Possible response: a hospital)*
• Who scolded her for eating spicy foods? *(Possible response: the doctors and nurses)*

BUILDING ENGLISH PROFICIENCY

Celebrating Family or Friends

Just as the poets recall legacies or fond moments with loved ones in these poems, students may have memories they can capture in a poem or journal entry.

Invite students to write a short account of something they have received as a legacy from someone they have cared about. The topic may be a bit of courage gained during an adventure with a relative or friend, a physical trait such as hair color, a symbolic object, or a pleasing memory.

Students can record it in a poem, in prose, or in words with art. Students who are comfortable sharing this writing may contribute the work to a class display or booklet.

Question   What tone is suggested by the repetition of the word *and? (Possible responses: frustration, anger, impatience, assertiveness)*

Check Test

1. In the poem "Mirror," who is speaking? *(A mirror, and the lake it becomes)*

2. What is the "One Art" that the speaker has tried to master, in the poem of that title? *(The art of losing)*

3. In "Legacies," what does the grandmother want to teach the little girl? *(How to make rolls)*

4. What are the "Leaves" in Hamod's poem? *(Grape leaves picked by his father before the father died)*

5. What kind of relative or friend is the speaker addressing in "To Jesus Villanueva, with Love"? *(Her grandmother)*

Unit 7 Resource Book
Alternate Check Test, p. 45

---

        we always laughed
35   you and I
        you never could understand
        the rules
        at clinics, welfare offices, schools
        any of it.
40 I did.
        you lie. you push. you get.
        I learned to do all this by
        the third clinic day of being persistently[4]
        sent to the back of the line by 5 in the
            afternoon
45 and being so close to done by 8 in the
            morning.
        so my lungs grew larger
        and my voice got louder
        and a doctor consented
        to see an old lady,
50 and the welfare would give you the money
        and the landlady would remember to
            spray for cockroaches
9 and the store would charge the food till
            the check came
        and the bank might cash the check if I got
            the nice man this time
        and I'd order hot dogs and Cokes for us
55 at the old "Crystal Palace" on Market
            Street
        and we'd sit on the steps
        by the rear exit, laughing
                you and I

        mamacita,
60 I remember you proudly at Christmas
        time, church at midnight services:
        you wear a plain black dress
        your hair down, straight and silver
        (you always wore it up
65 tied in a kerchief,
        knotted to the side)
        your face shining, your eyes clear,
        your vision intact.

        ----

        4. persistently (pər sis′tənt lē), *adv.* continually.

        you play Death.
70 you are Death.
        you quote long stanzas from a poem
                I've long
        forgotten;
        even fitful babies hush
        such is the power of your voice,
75 your presence
        fills us all.
        the special, pregnant
        silence.
        eyes and hands lifted up
80 imploringly and passionately
        the vision and power
        offered to us,
        eyes and hands cast down
        it flows through you
85 to us,
        a gift.

        your daughter, my mother
        told me a story I'd never
        heard before;
90   you were leaving Mexico
        with your husband and two
        older children, pregnant
        with my mother.
        the U.S. customs officer
95   undid everything you so
        preciously packed, you
        took a sack, blew it up
        and when he asked about
        the contents of the sack,
100   well, you popped it with
        your hand and shouted
        MEXICAN AIR!

        aiiiiiiiiii mamacita, Jesus,
        I won't forget my visions and reality.
105 to lie, to push, to get
        just isn't
        enough.

MINI-LESSON: LITERARY FOCUS

Personification

Teach   Point out that personification in literary works often is not as obvious as it is in Plath's "Mirror." Often a poet briefly personifies an object, a natural force, or an idea. For example, in "To Jesus Villanueva, with Love," the speaker recalls her grandmother's recital at a Christmas service, in which she played Death. The speaker refers to a personified version of death, common in folk traditions.

Apply   Ask students to describe popular personifications of Death. *(Possible description: a skeletal or faceless figure in a long, black, hooded robe, with a staff or a walking stick, that stands silently beside a person's death bed)*

Activity Idea   Have students brainstorm and perhaps illustrate common cultural personifications of other abstract concepts, such as Wisdom, Love, War, Justice, and Crime.

After Reading

Making Connections

Shaping Your Response

1. Which one of these five poems had the greatest impact on you? Why?

2. If you were to associate emotions with these poems, what would they be? Make a chart like the one shown here in your notebook and fill it in. Be prepared to explain your choices.

Poem	Emotion
"Mirror"	
"One Art"	

Analyzing the Poems

3. What relationship does the poem "The Mirror" explore?

4. Describe the **tone** of the first five stanzas of "One Art." How does it change in the last stanza?

5. What do you learn about Hamod's father from each stanza of "Leaves"?

6. What is the **point of view** of each poem?

7. ☝ Describe the person-to-person **interactions** discussed in each poem.

Extending the Ideas

8. The poems by Hamod, Villanueva, and Giovanni all portray memorable relationships. If you were to write a poem describing a relationship that you have, who would it be about? What is special about that relationship?

Literary Focus: Personification

The mirror in the poem "Mirror" is **personified,** or given human attributes. Reread the first stanza and list all the phrases that describe what human things the mirror does.

LITERARY FOCUS: PERSONIFICATION

Possible Responses:

- have no preconceptions
- see . . . swallow
- [I am] truthful
- meditate on the opposite wall
- look at it
- I think
- my heart

MAKING CONNECTIONS

1. Responses will vary; they may reflect emotional identification or appreciation of a poet's use of language.

2. Possible responses:

"Mirror"—anguish

"One Art"—determination

"Legacies"—frustration

"Leaves"—regret

"To Jesus Villanueva"—affection

3. Possible responses: the relationship between a person and that person's reflected image; a person's relationship with herself

4. Possible response: The tone is one of carefree (or careless) confidence, as if losses don't matter; it changes to uncertainty.

5. Possible response: In the first stanza, that he is dead and that he cared for his son's family; in the second, that he was Arabic, he wrote letters, and he was more comfortable with his native language than English; in the third, that he wrote poetry in Arabic

6. First-person point of view in "Mirror," "One Art," "Leaves," and "To Jesus Villanueva, with Love"; third-person limited point of view in "Legacies"

7. Possible responses: "Mirror" describes an interaction between a woman and herself.

In "One Art," the speaker has lost a dear friend.

"Legacies" describes an interaction between a girl and her grandmother, who wants to teach her to bake rolls.

The speaker in "Leaves" is learning about his father, who has died.

Villanueva's poem shows the gifts that the speaker receives as she helps her grandmother deal with old age and illness.

8. Responses will vary but may reflect interesting people or the emotional impacts students have experienced.

VOCABULARY STUDY

Possible Responses:

1. the art of losing

2. She is not comfortable with her appearance.

3. Sample preconceptions: Aging makes people upset; people lose physical stamina as they age; people lose mental quickness, and so on.

4. Sample words and phrases: "I am sorry," "I didn't mean it," and "Forgive me."

5. Constantly

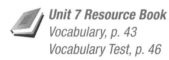

Unit 7 Resource Book
Vocabulary, p. 43
Vocabulary Test, p. 46

WRITING CHOICES
Writer's Notebook Update

Suggest that students analyze the poem that they understand best or that has the strongest effect on them. You might have students write comments that describe how deeper analysis affected their initial understanding of the poem's meaning.

A Tribute

Interested students may try to employ any of the literary techniques that they could analyze in their Writer's Notebook; such as figurative language, rhythm, and rhyme.

Selection Test

Unit 7 Resource Book
pp. 47–48

Transparency Collection
Fine Art Writing Prompt 12

778

Vocabulary Study

Answer the following questions. Use the Glossary for help with the italicized vocabulary words.

meditate
evident
preconception
repentant
persistently

1. What does the narrator of "One Art" *meditate* about?

2. What fact is *evident* near the end of the poem about the woman described in "Mirror"?

3. Describe a common *preconception* about aging.

4. What words might a *repentant* person say to someone he or she has harmed?

5. If a patient calls the doctor *persistently,* does he or she call occasionally, reluctantly, or constantly?

Expressing Your Ideas

Writing Choices

Writer's Notebook Update Choose one of the five poems in this section and write an analysis of it. Discuss the form of the poem and any special techniques used by the poet. Consider the point of view, the use of dialect or colloquial speech, figurative language, rhythm, and rhyme, and tell how these things might relate to the poem's meaning.

A Tribute Hamod, Giovanni, and Villanueva each wrote a poem as a tribute to a close relative. Choose a family member or friend that you would like to honor. Either write an original **poem** or a **personal narrative** telling an anecdote about your relationship.

Other Options

Voices of the Twentieth Century Go to the library and find another poem by one of these five poets, or choose a poem by a different twentieth-century poet. Work with a small group to present a **poetry reading** of several poems.

Picture the Poem What do you visualize when you read each of these poems? Choose one of the poems and create an **illustration** that captures the emotions represented in the poem and presents the setting.

Cultural Legacies Hamod's father came from Lebanon and Villanueva's grandmother came from Mexico. Choose one of these countries and research its history, geography, and culture, and look into the lives of Americans whose ancestors came from that country. Either present an **oral report** to the class or create a **hyperstudio report** presenting your findings.

OTHER OPTIONS
Voices of the Twentieth Century

Other twentieth-century poets you might suggest: Gwendolyn Brooks, Anne Sexton, Robert Lowell, Theodore Roethke, John Ashberry, and Adrienne Rich.

Picture the Poem

If a number of students choose to illustrate the poem, they may want to wait until after they create their art before comparing their impressions.

Cultural Legacies

You might suggest that students research some of the recipes that are described in the poems: tortillas with chilis, onions, and peppers; stuffed grape leaves; and baked rolls.

Multimedia reports are electronic documents that can contain text, pictures, audio elements such as speech and music, and video material. Among the software tools to assemble multimedia documents are HyperStudio (Roger Wagner Publishing) and The Multimedia Workshop (Davidson & Associates). Students should be aware of copyright restrictions on the use of many media materials.

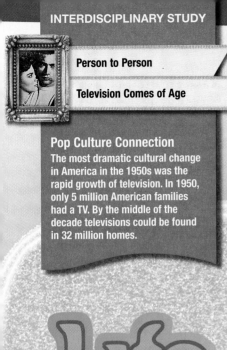

Person to Person

Television Comes of Age

Pop Culture Connection
The most dramatic cultural change in America in the 1950s was the rapid growth of television. In 1950, only 5 million American families had a TV. By the middle of the decade televisions could be found in 32 million homes.

The most striking thing about the arrival of television on the American scene was certainly the almost apocalyptic suddenness with which it became a fully established part of our national life, complete with a huge audience and an established minority opposition, affecting not only all our other communications media and the whole world of our popular arts but also our manners, morals, habits, ways of thinking.

Life After Television

John Brooks

Children have been one of the most enthusiastic portions of television's mass audience since its arrival in the early 1950s.

Interdisciplinary Study   **779**

Interdisciplinary Study

Theme Link

Americans turn to television for person-to-person communication.

Curricular Connection: Pop Culture

You can use the information in this inter-disciplinary study to explore with students the beginning years of television in America.

Additional Background

- Television is first known as "sight radio," "radio moving pictures," or "radiovision."
- In 1939, NBC makes its first regular broadcast featuring President Franklin D. Roosevelt.
- In 1945, at the end of World War II, there are 5,000 televisions in U.S. homes.
- 1947 marks the debut of commercial television with 16 stations.

Unit 7 Resource Book
Interdisciplinary Study Guide, p. 49

BUILDING ENGLISH PROFICIENCY

Making Personal Connections

Capitalize on students' interest and knowledge of television.

- Have students create a semantic web arising from the word *televi-sion.* Encourage them to jot down words, images, or comments that they associate with watching TV.

- As volunteers share responses, encourage students to see how important TV is to most of them and to try to imagine what the world was like before its invention.

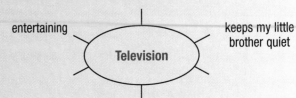

entertaining — **Television** — keeps my little brother quiet

Additional Background

Uncle Miltie By fall, 1948, Milton Berle captured over 90 percent of the viewing audience for his show *Texaco Star Theater.* It had an estimated viewing audience of nearly 4.5 million people.

TV Dinners Before World War II, refrigerators had very small freezer compartments, so people did not buy even the few frozen foods that were available. But when canned goods became rationed because of the metal shortage during World War II, frozen foods became more appealing.

Frozen dinners were easy to prepare and serve in front of the television, and they became known as "TV dinners."

By comparison, the much chronicled automobile revolution earlier in the century had been [very gradual]....As late as 1948 there were still fewer than 20 TV stations on the air, and only 172,000 families had receiving sets. Then the explosion began. During 1949 and 1950 sets were installed at a rate sometimes as high as a quarter of a million a month. In June, 1950, there were more than 100 stations operating in 38 states; coaxial cable, the device by which reception is extended beyond a station's normal range and network broadcasting is made possible, reached along the East Coast from Boston to Richmond, and westward as far as Milwaukee and St. Louis; and the census of that year found 5 million families with TV sets in the house.

What happened next is already history. Set ownership rose at a rate of roughly 5 million a year during the 1950s. Here, surely, was something totally unprecedented in world history. Neither in this nation nor in any other had anything like 5 million families per year ever acquired for the first time any wholly new thing of any sort....

There were moments in the late Fifties, when television had become all-pervasive and yet still retained the sheen of a new toy, when it seemed almost to bring our national life to a halt. The year 1954 saw the "TV dinner" make its appearance; it also saw the city of Toledo make the astonishing discovery that water consumption rose startlingly during certain three-minute periods that turned out to be the time of commercials during popular programs. In a small town that I know of, at certain hours no one was to be seen in the streets; the stores and restaurants were almost deserted, and a strange hush fell; and even a telephone call was generally answered curtly and with ill grace. No one could be very much surprised at the results of a national survey made by Westinghouse Electric shortly after the beginning of the 1960s. More man-hours per year in the United States, Westinghouse found, were being spent watching TV than were spent working for pay....

Almost as sudden as the arrival of TV was the emergence of the critical counterattack.... In particular, the attacks had been, and continued to be, focused on the effects on children, an audience so numerous and so devoted that some TV men say they constitute, collectively, a virtual tyranny dictating the timing and nature of programming. Does the child ... who sits mesmerized in front of the screen 20 or 30 hours a week, suffer any lasting effects from the experience? Are the eyes damaged? Does the violence of the programs predispose to a life of crime? Does the passivity of the act of watching damage initiative? While none of these charges has been definitely proved, none has been definitely proved false. A report to the American Academy of Pediatrics in the fall of 1964 declared that excessive television watching can lead to a specific physical sickness—the "tired-child syndrome," characterized by fatigue, headache, loss of appetite, and vomiting, and curable only by abstinence from television. Nor is excessive exposure to such hazards an exclusively American phenomenon; a United Nations study published in 1965 showed that childhood TV-watching habits in Japan and England are about the same as here.

MINI-LESSON: STUDY SKILLS

Using Videos as Reference Sources

Teach Students may find that they need specialized types of references for research about early television. They may want to access videotapes of early shows so they can see them for themselves. They may find early shows on stations that broadcast reruns, as well as in video stores, libraries, or broadcast museums.

Activity Idea Have students pick one early, popular television show for which they can get a video. Have them report on what they learn about attitudes, fashion, concerns, and family structures of the 1950s or 1960s from the show that they view.

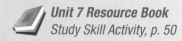

Unit 7 Resource Book
Study Skill Activity, p. 50

What's on TV?

What were so many Americans watching with such devotion during the 1950s? Many of the new programs were adapted from radio shows and vaudeville comedy, while others struck out in new directions, taking advantage of the abilities of the new TV medium. The following are a few of the shows that left their mark on the '50s.

SITUATION COMEDIES

In 1951 film and radio comedienne Lucille Ball tried out the new medium with a television sit-com featuring her as the wacky wife of a Cuban bandleader played by her real-life husband Desi Arnaz. *I Love Lucy* was among the most successful programs in television history, remaining the number one show on TV throughout the early '50s and appearing in syndicated reruns ever since.

Television has never paid much attention to working-class America. A notable exception was *The Honeymooners*, a sit-com set in the run-down apartment of bus driver Ralph Cramden and his wife Alice. This program, starring Jackie Gleason as Ralph, began as a popular comedy sketch on Gleason's variety program and later became a series in its own right. While not as successful as an independent program, it remains one of the best remembered sit-coms of the 1950s.

Additional Background

- Of the first four successful situation comedies, three portray ethnic minorities: Jewish, Swedish, and Black families.
- Television is first broadcast in color in 1951 when CBS showed a zoo, a football game, and a Picasso painting.
- Canned laughter is introduced in 1950 on a show called "Hank McCune Show."
- The Nielsen Ratings are introduced in 1952.

BUILDING ENGLISH PROFICIENCY

Analyzing Cause and Effect

Students may find it easier to keep track of the details in "Life After Television" or to check their comprehension of the article if they think about the causes and effects that author John Brooks discusses. Encourage students to record the information on a t-chart. Point out that a cause may have more than one effect and vice-versa.

Cause	Effect
Americans become fascinated with TV	5 million sets per year are bought
	TV dinners gain acceptance

New programs in the 1950s included the following. How many of these have students seen in syndication?

- *Garroway at Large*
- *The Jack Benny Show*
- *You Bet Your Life*
- *The Roy Rogers Show*
- *The Adventures of Superman*
- *Mr. Wizard*
- *The George Burns and Gracie Allen Show*
- *The Adventures of Ozzie and Harriet*
- *Make Room for Daddy*
- *Lassie*
- *The Mickey Mouse Club*
- *Captain Kangaroo*
- *Father Knows Best*
- *Leave It to Beaver*
- *The Donna Reed Show*
- *The Many Loves of Dobie Gillis*
- *The Twilight Zone*

Interdisciplinary Activity Ideas

- Have students chart their own television watching behavior for a week. What did they watch? How long did they watch? Did they do anything else while the television was on?
- Suggest that students investigate the facilities and programming of your local cable television community access channel.

QUIZ AND GAME SHOWS

Quiz programs and game shows had long been featured on radio. But radio's *$64 Question* underwent a huge inflation in moving to television in the summer of 1955. TV's *$64,000 Question* was an overnight hit. As a recent history of television observes, "The appeal of seeing ordinary people sweating through complex questions to reach huge sums of money was enormous." In the late 1950s a scandal erupted concerning rigging of the big-money quiz shows and their popularity abruptly waned.

One of the best known TV game shows was *What's My Line?*, where a celebrity panel attempted to guess the occupations of the contestants. The wit of regular panelists such as actress Arlene Francis proved engaging and *What's My Line?* ran for 18 seasons.

MINI-LESSON: SPEAKING AND LISTENING

Use Appropriate Speaking and Listening Behavior

Teach Have students look at the two photographs of quiz and game shows on page 782. Point out that shows such as these require contestants to follow detailed rules for speaking and listening that are much more structured than the rules for ordinary conversation.

Activity Ideas

- Have students brainstorm rules of conduct that they think might have been in effect for each of the shows pictured.
- Have students write the producers of a current game show for a copy of rules for contestants. Have them compare what they find out to the rules they brainstormed in class.

AND NOW FOR THE NEWS . . .

Journalist Edward R. Murrow became famous for his dramatic radio news broadcasts from wartime London. On November 18, 1951, he premiered his television news program, *See It Now*, with a striking demonstration of the potential of the new medium, showing simultaneous live shots of both the Atlantic and Pacific Ocean and commenting that "no journalistic age was ever given a weapon for truth with quite the scope of this fledgling television." Murrow's style of television journalism proved its worth in 1954, when he used it to expose the smear tactics of anticommunist crusader Senator Joseph McCarthy.

Responding

1. Does TV have the same impact on society today that it had back in the 50s? Why or why not?

2. Early criticism of TV warned that it could become "the opiate of the people" and "would corrupt the morals of the young." Looking back, were the concerns of TV critics valid? What new criticisms have been sounded about TV?

783

BUILDING ENGLISH PROFICIENCY

Responding to Visual Cues

Use one or more of the following activities to help students discuss the photos and captions on pages 781–783.

- Invite comments about each of the television shows and/or personalities shown. Encourage students not to focus merely on the styles of the era but to suggest why they think each program or person was popular.

- Ask students to name one or more situation comedies, quiz and game shows, and news programs that are popular today. Ask students to notice what the text says about each show. Ask: Can the same things be said about the modern shows?

- Have students name other TV genres that attract viewers today. Examples might include soap operas, talk shows, children's shows, medical dramas, and crime dramas. Students might enjoy finding out how those genres were represented in the 1950s.

Writing Workshop

WRITER'S BLUEPRINT
Specs

The Specs in the Writer's Blueprint address these writing and thinking skills:

- establishing criteria for judgment
- taking a position
- supporting a position
- anticipating objections
- summarizing
- using an authoritative tone
- using the active voice
- using comparative forms of adjectives and adverbs

These Specs serve as your lesson objectives, and they form the basis for the **Assessment Criteria Specs** for a superior paper, which appear on the final TE page for this lesson. You might want to read through the Assessment Criteria Specs with students when you begin the lesson.

Linking Literature to Writing

Lead a discussion about characteristics of true-to-life relationships as reflected in the literature. Have students find examples in the selections to summarize or read aloud for the class. Have students discuss the elements of the relationships in the literature that seem the most realistic.

Person to Person

Persuasive Writing

Writing Workshop

You Be the Judge

Assignment In their stories in this part of the unit, Tillie Olson, John Updike, Alice Walker, and Maxine Hong Kingston write about person-to-person relationships. Which author created the most true-to-life relationship? You be the judge.

WRITER'S BLUEPRINT

Product	A literary critique
Purpose	To present convincingly your views on how a fiction writer makes a person-to-person relationship seem true-to-life
Audience	People who have read the literature
Specs	As the writer of an effective critique, you should:

❏ Establish your own criteria for what makes a relationship in a story seem true-to-life and then, based on these criteria, decide which person-to-person relationship in the four stories is most realistic.

❏ Begin your written critique by declaring your choice and describing the criteria you used in making it.

❏ Go on to describe this relationship and explain why you consider it the most realistic. Support your position with quotations from the stories.

❏ Anticipate reasons why others might disagree, and provide counter-arguments.

❏ Conclude with a summary of your main points and a strong statement of support for your choice, using an authoritative tone that demands serious consideration. Write in the active voice.

❏ Follow the rules of grammar for correct usage, spelling, and mechanics. Pay special attention to the comparative forms of adjectives and adverbs.

WRITING WORKSHOP OVERVIEW

Product
Persuasive writing: A literary critique

Prewriting
Establish criteria—Discuss your criteria—Make your judgment—Revisit the story you chose—Listen to opposing viewpoints—Plan your essay
Unit 7 Resource Book
Prewriting Worksheets pp. 51–52

Drafting
Start writing
Transparency Collection
Student Models for Writing Workshop 23, 24

Revising
Ask a partner—Strategy: Writing in the Active Voice
Unit 7 Resource Book
Revising Worksheet p. 53

Editing
Ask a partner—Strategy: Comparative Forms of Adjectives and Adverbs
Unit 7 Resource Book
Grammar Worksheet p. 54
Grammar Check Test p. 55

Presenting
Poster
Discussion

Looking Back
Self-evaluate—Reflect—For Your Working Portfolio
Unit 7 Resource Book
Assessment Worksheet p. 56
Transparency Collection
Fine Art Writing Prompt 12

Establish criteria for a realistic relationship. Ask yourself: *What makes the writing about this relationship realistic?* Review the Olson, Updike, Walker, and Kingston stories and make notes on details that seem true-to-life. Organize your notes into a chart like the one shown.

Realistic Details

Story/Characters	Characterization	Dialogue	Actions
"I Stand Here Ironing" —Emily's mother and Emily	". . . and she tells me everything and nothing . . ." (Superficial conversation is like this.)	" ' . . . I did it. I won, I won . . .' " (repeating things when you get excited)	mother does everyday chore of ironing

Now look over your chart and draw conclusions. These conclusions will become your criteria for judgment. Here is part of one student's list:

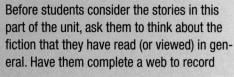

Characterization: All four stories involve characters who have problems communicating. In real life, that happens a lot. One person says one thing and the other person hears something else. The result is they never quite connect.

Dialogue: The characters in these stories speak like real people do. For example,

> **LITERARY SOURCE**
> "This is one of her communicative nights, and she tells me everything and nothing as she fixes herself a plate of food out of the icebox."
> from "I Stand Here Ironing" by Tillie Olsen

Discuss your criteria. With a small group, discuss each other's criteria for realistic writing about relationships. Use group members' comments and observations to help you revise and sharpen your criteria.

Make your judgment. Using the criteria you've developed, rank each relationship somewhere on the following scale. Your highest-ranked relationship is the one you'll present.

1   2   3   4   5   6   7   8   9   10

Totally Unreal   Totally Real

STEP 1 PREWRITING
Establish criteria

Have students select two TV series they watch regularly that portray human relationships. Have them list details that are realistic and details that are unrealistic about the relationships in the programs.

Discuss your criteria

Before breaking into groups, have students brainstorm criteria for realistic writing about relationships, building on the previous activity. The group can use the list to help expand their discussion about relationships in the selections.

Make your judgment

You might have students confer with a partner at this point and explain their rankings based on the criteria they've chosen—to be sure they're on solid ground. For additional support, see the worksheet referenced below.

📖 *Unit 7 Resource Book*
Prewriting Worksheet, p. 51

BUILDING ENGLISH PROFICIENCY

Exploring Key Concepts

Before students consider the stories in this part of the unit, ask them to think about the fiction that they have read (or viewed) in general. Have them complete a web to record their thoughts about what makes a story true to life; then urge them to apply those standards to the four stories named.

Revisit the story you chose

Have students organize details from the selections into four columns, headed: Characterization, Setting, Dialogue, Plot. After each detail, students should indicate "R" for realistic and "U" for unrealistic.

Listen to opposing viewpoints

After groups have listened to classmates' reasons, allow a few minutes for them to organize their counter-arguments. Each counter-argument should be supported by an example from the literature. For additional support, see the worksheet referenced below.

Unit 7 Resource Book
Prewriting Worksheet, p. 52

Plan your essay

Have students review their prewriting notes before beginning their plans for their essays.

Connections to
Writer's Notebook

For selection-related prompts, refer to Writer's Notebook.

Connections to
Writer's Resource

For additional writing prompts, refer to Writer's Resource.

STEP 2 DRAFTING
Start writing

Have students review the body section of their plans. Suggest that they present reasons supporting the idea that theirs is the most realistic relationship in order from the least convincing to the most convincing.

786

Revisit the story you chose and make more detailed notes on characterization, setting, dialogue, and plot.

Listen to opposing viewpoints and prepare counter-arguments. Meet with a group of classmates who've chosen a different relationship and discuss your differing viewpoints. Listen carefully to your classmates' reasons for choosing a different relationship, and make notes on counter-arguments you'll be providing in your critique.

Plan your essay. Organize your thoughts in a three-part outline like the one shown:

- **Introduction**
  Your choice
  Your criteria

- **Body**
  Description of the relationship
  Why it's the most realistic
  —characterization (with supporting details and quotations)
  —dialogue (with supporting details and quotations)
  —actions (with supporting details and quotations)
  Reasons others might disagree
  Counter-arguments

- **Conclusion**
  Summary of main points from body
  Closing statement of support for your choice

> **OR . . .**
> In addition to taking notes on each opposing viewpoint, complete this written statement: I disagree with your choice because ___.

 **STEP 2 DRAFTING**

Start writing. As you draft, concentrate on developing a persuasive argument. The following tips may help you get started:

- Begin your critique with a quote from the story that you feel exemplifies realistic writing about a relationship. Then state your choice.

- When you finish the introduction and body, pause and review. Check your main points against the points listed in the Conclusion part of your plan. You may find that your main points have changed. If so, revise the last part of your plan before writing the conclusion.

- Approach your critique as you would a formal argument or debate. Write in a strong, persuasive tone in the active voice. See the Revising Strategy in Step 3 of this lesson.

MINI-LESSON: WRITING STYLE

Writing in the Active Voice

Teach   Demonstrate the difference between active and passive voice by having volunteers create sentence-pairs similar to the example pair in the Revising Strategy feature on page 787.

Activity Idea   Display this paragraph and have students revise it to make it more forceful and direct.

> Begun by us one rainy day in May was our fateful journey. Had by us was a lofty goal. Wanted to be seen by us were whales off the California coast. Closely gathered around by the ten of us was the captain's table. Out on this table by the captain was spread the map. Pointed to by the captain's gnarled hand was a spot several miles out to sea. Made by him was a tiny drawing of a whale there. Dreamed of by me that night was nothing but whales.

Apply   Have students look carefully at their drafts with the idea of making them more forceful and direct.

Ask a partner for comments on your draft before you revise it. Pay special attention to writing in the active voice.

Revising Strategy

Writing in the Active Voice

Verbs in the active voice express action done *by* the subject of the sentence, while verbs in the passive voice show action done *to* the subject. In general, the active voice makes writing clearer, more concise, and more forceful. For example:

Passive: A descriptive language was created by Emily.

Active: Emily created her own descriptive language.

As you revise, check to see that you're writing in the active voice. Notice how this writer made his critique more forceful and direct by changing passive-voice sentences to the active voice.

~~Nothing was suspected by~~ the eldest daughter, Judith, and so *suspected nothing* ~~she continued to be protected by~~ her family. They recalled pushing *continued to protect her* her in a carriage nineteen years earlier.

 STUDENT MODEL

STEP 4 EDITING

Ask a partner to review your revised draft before you edit. As you edit, pay special attention to the comparative forms of adjectives and adverbs.

The Student Models

The **transparencies** referenced below are authentic student models. Review them with the students before they draft. These questions will help:

1. Which writer do you think came closer to fulfilling the Specs in the Writer's Blueprint and why?

2. Which writer do you think wrote more forcefully and directly and why?

3. Look closely at the final paragraph of model 23 for technical mistakes and for awkward or unclear phrasing.

 Transparency Collection
Student Models for Writing
Workshop 23, 24

STEP 3 REVISING

Ask a partner
(Peer assessment)

Suggest that partners meet after reading one another's drafts for a short discussion focusing specifically on the persuasiveness of the arguments.

Revising Strategy:
Writing in the Active Voice

For additional support, see the mini-lesson at the bottom of page 786 and the worksheet referenced below.

 Unit 7 Resource Book
Revising Worksheet, p. 53

Connections to
Writer's Resource

Refer to the Grammar, Usage, and Mechanics Handbook on Writer's Resource.

STEP 4 EDITING

Ask a partner
(Peer assessment)

Write five frequently used proofreading marks on the board. Have student volunteers explain when each mark is used and write a sentence on the board to demonstrate.

ESL
LEP
ELD
SAE
LD

MINI-LESSON: GRAMMAR

Comparative Forms of Adjectives and Adverbs

Use this mini-lesson in conjunction with the Editing Strategy feature on the next page.

Display the following sentences and have students make necessary corrections.

1. The puppy scratches at the door less often during the day. (correct)

2. My new truck is more heavier than my old truck. (*more heavier* to *heavier*)

3. The school bus arrives more earlier than the city bus. (*more earlier* to *earlier*)

4. The sun is brighter in the living room at this time of day. (correct)

5. Our team is playing better this season than it has in years. (correct)

 Unit 7 Resource Book
Grammar Worksheet p. 54
Grammar Check Test p. 55

787

Editing Strategy: Comparative Forms of Adjectives and Adverbs

For additional support, see the mini-lesson at the bottom of page 787 and the worksheets referenced below.

Unit 7 Resource Book
Grammar Worksheet, p. 54
Grammar Check Test, p. 55

Connections to
Writer's Resource

Refer to the Grammar, Usage, and Mechanics Handbook on Writer's Resource.

STEP 5 PRESENTING
Poster

After students complete the list of criteria, suggest that they include two examples from the selections that demonstrate the criteria.

STEP 6 LOOKING BACK
Self-evaluate

The *Assessment Criteria Specs* at the bottom of this page are for a superior paper. You might want to post these in the classroom. Students can then evaluate themselves based on these criteria. For a complete scoring rubric, use the *Assessment Worksheet* referenced below.

Unit 7 Resource Book
Assessment Worksheet, p. 56

Reflect

Remind students that what they believe to be important in a fictional portrayal of a relationship may help them discover what is important to them in their own relationships.

To further explore the theme, use the Fine Art Transparency referenced below.

Transparency Collection
Fine Art Writing Prompt 12

788

Editing Strategy

FOR REFERENCE
You'll find more rules for using comparative forms of adjectives and adverbs in the Language and Grammar Handbook at the back of this text.

Comparative Forms of Adjectives and Adverbs

Avoid the common mistake of using "more" or "less" with adjectives or adverbs that are already in the comparative form. For example:

Incorrect: Her burdens were <u>more bigger</u> when Emily was small.
Correct: Her burdens were <u>bigger</u> when Emily was small.

Incorrect: Ronnie's crying during the night occurs <u>less oftener</u> now.
Correct: Ronnie's crying during the night occurs <u>less often</u> now.

STEP 5 PRESENTING

- Read your critique aloud to a small group of classmates who chose different relationships, and discuss the similarities among the criteria you each chose. Come up with a list of criteria for fiction which portrays a realistic relationship that you all agree on and turn it into a poster to be displayed in the classroom.

- Work up a short TV-style thumbs-up thumbs-down discussion in which you and a classmate, as literary critics, describe your disagreements over one of the selections, and present your discussion to the class.

STEP 6 LOOKING BACK

Self-evaluate. Look back at the Writer's Blueprint and give yourself a score on each point, from 6 (superior) to 1 (inadequate).

Reflect. Think about what you learned from writing your critique as you write answers to these questions.

✔ Looking back at the stories, which relationship was least true-to-life? Explain why.

✔ Think about the relationships you have in your own life. Which one do you feel is the most important and why?

For Your Working Portfolio Add your critique and your reflection responses to your working portfolio.

ASSESSMENT CRITERIA SPECS

Here are the criteria for a superior paper. A full six-level rubric for this paper appears on the *Assessment Worksheet* referenced below.

6 Superior   The writer of a 6 paper impressively meets these criteria:

- Establishes clear, well-reasoned criteria for judgment.

- Takes a solid position on which relationship is most realistic, based on these criteria.

- Backs up this position with examples and quotations from the literature that help clarify as well as support this position.

- Acknowledges and effectively refutes possible counter-arguments in ways that further serve to support and clarify the writer's position.

- Concludes with a forceful, convincing restatement of position.

- Writes with authority, using the active voice.

- Makes few, if any, mistakes in grammar, usage, mechanics, and spelling. Uses the comparative forms of adjectives and adverbs correctly.

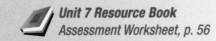

Unit 7 Resource Book
Assessment Worksheet, p. 56

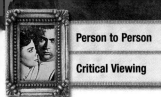

Beyond Print

Looking at Television

Why do some TV shows bomb, while others return to entertain us year after year? The best shows maintain a life of their own in reruns and videos even after they're canceled. What makes them last?

Some of the shows you read about from the fifties—shows like *I Love Lucy* and *The Honeymooners*—are still popular in reruns today. *M*A*S*H*, a series about a medical unit in the Korean War, lasted longer than the actual Korean War did. In the eighties shows like *The Cosby Show* and *Cheers* were memorable, while more recent hits like *Roseanne, The Simpsons, Seinfeld, Friends,* and *E.R.* came back season after season. Why do some last while others fail? To unravel this TV mystery, analyze your favorite television program using the following criteria:

Characters What makes the characters so interesting? Why are viewers willing to spend time with them week after week? Consider personality, lifestyle, sense of humor, commitment, zaniness, and appearance.

Themes Why are the weekly stories so interesting to viewers? What universal human conditions does the show manage to describe? What interesting and unusual twists does the show depict? How do the stories develop? How do the beginnings, middles, and endings make viewers feel satisfied?

Composition and Editing What does the show look like? What do viewers see that is both comfortable and interesting? How does the show keep moving? How are transitions handled? Describe the overall visual appeal of the show.

Other Criteria Apply any other criteria you feel is important to a successful, long term television show.

Activity Option

Your Analysis Share your analysis of your favorite television program with classmates. If it's a relatively new program, use your analysis to convince classmates of the potential of the show to become a classic. Unfortunately, only time can prove you right, but in a few years you may find yourself to be a great predictor of quality television.

Beyond Print   **789**

Teaching Objectives

- To practice critical viewing
- To use and create criteria for evaluation
- To make a prediction based on a critical evaluation

Curricular Connection: Critical Viewing

You can use the material in this article to give students practice in critically viewing and responding to television.

Introduce

Invite students to discuss television programs that have enjoyed a long life. Begin by brainstorming a list of programs that have been or were on the air for years. Ask students why they think each of the programs they named remained on television. Then have students read the article. Encourage them to apply the criteria to shows on their lists.

Activity Option

Encourage students to read and use the criteria in terms of the type of television show they will anaylze. If they pick a game, sports, or news show, they may need to tailor the criteria to fit the show.

ANOTHER APPROACH

Without Television: Critical Viewing of Other Entertainment

Students can learn more about critical viewing by analyzing another form of visual entertainment. Students could choose to analyze a movie in terms of its box office popularity, or live entertainment such as a comedian or a band in terms of long-term success.

Students should adapt the evaluation criteria to fit the kind of entertainment they have chosen to evaluate.

Historical Overview

EXPLORING CONCEPTS

- The two decades from the mid-50s to the mid-70s were marked by political, social, and cultural change in the U.S.
- Social and political protest took both nonviolent and violent forms.
- The war in Vietnam and violence at home divided the country and disturbed our individual consciences.

Art Study

Question Why do you think this particular photograph has remained a lasting symbol of anti-war protest? *(Possible responses: because the contrast between the flowers and the guns is so striking; because the symbolism of the flowers and guns is universally understood)*

Question What does the statement on the bumper sticker mean? *(Possible response: Either acquiesce to American foreign policy, i.e., the war in Vietnam, or find another place to live.)*

Years of Change

In the Midst of Struggle . . .

A Stormy Era

HISTORICAL OVERVIEW

The period from the mid-1950s to the mid-1970s was a political, social, and cultural watershed for the United States, as Americans found themselves challenged by a variety of issues. At home, inspired by the African American civil rights movement, a variety of groups, including women, American Indians, and Latinos sought greater freedom and equality. Internationally, U. S. involvement in the Southeast Asian country of Vietnam resulted in America's longest and most divisive war, producing stalemate on the battlefield and protest at home. Beginning with the assassination of President Kennedy, violence haunted American politics during this period. But it was also a hopeful time, in which many Americans felt that by coming together with optimism and good will they could change their society.

An anti-war protest and a popular pro-war bumper sticker reflect two views of the Vietnam War. ➤

Key Dates

1954
Supreme Court outlaws racially segregated schools.

1955
Montgomery bus boycott begins.

1962
Cesar Chavez organizes United Farm Workers.

1963
Civil rights march on Washington, D.C. takes place. President Kennedy assassinated.

1966
National Organization for Women founded.

1968
Martin Luther King, Jr., assassinated. Anti-war protests mark Democratic Convention.

1970
First Earth Day observed.

1973
American Indians occupy Wounded Knee.

1975
United States withdraws from Vietnam.

791

AMERICA:
LOVE IT OR LEAVE IT

Key Dates

1955   The United States agrees to help train the South Vietnamese army.

1960   Black students sit-in at a "whites-only" lunch counter.

1962   Rachel Carson publishes the ecological warning, *Silent Spring.*

1963   Assassination of civil rights leader Medgar Evers.

1964   Freedom workers Chaney, Schwerner, and Goodman killed in Mississippi.

1965   President Johnson orders continuous bombing of North Vietnam; Malcolm X assassinated.

1968   Presidential candidate Robert F. Kennedy assassinated; Shirley Chisholm becomes the first black woman elected to Congress.

1974   President Nixon resigns.

MATERIALS OF INTEREST
Books

- *The Fire Next Time* by James Baldwin (Dell, 1962 and 1963)
- *The Fifties: A Women's Oral History* by Brett Harvey (HarperCollins, 1993)
- *The Sixties Reader* by James Haskins and Kathleen Benson (Viking, 1988)

Multimedia

- *Vietnam: A Television History* 13 video recordings (WGBH, 1983)

 Connections to
Custom Literature Database

For further historical background, under **Background Articles,** see **Postwar America 1945–.**

FOR ALL STUDENTS

- What does the word *struggle* mean to you?
- What political and social struggles are you aware of?

Read together the first paragraph. Explain to students that the selections they will be reading explore six individual struggles brought about by the political and social struggles of the 1960s and 1970s.

To further explore the theme, use the transparency referenced here.

Transparency Collection
Fine Art Writing Prompt 13

For At-Risk Students

Ask students to turn to pages 846–850 and discuss what the photographs reveal about the 1950s, 60s, and 70s.

For Students Who Need Challenge

Invite students to find recordings of the songs of the 1960s and 1970s to compile a musical retrospective of the issues of the day. You might suggest these artists: Bob Dylan, Joan Baez, Pete Seeger, Phil Ochs, and Helen Reddy.

ᘒ MULTICULTURAL CONNECTION

Encourage students to compare the issues of various groups who were involved in the struggles of the 1960s and 70s, for example, younger and older generations; whites, blacks, Hispanics, and Native Americans; pro-war and antiwar supporters; women and men.

Part Two

In the Midst of Struggle . . .

The 1960s and '70s proved to be very turbulent decades for the United States as African Americans began to demand the rights they fought for in the Civil War but were never fully granted; as young Americans began protesting a war they didn't understand or support and yet were forced, if drafted, to fight; as women began demanding equal opportunities in the workplace and in society. The following selections describe individuals in the midst of these struggles.

ᘒ **Multicultural Connection** In times of great social upheaval, individuals often find themselves in the position of having to make difficult **choices.** As they are caught between society's expectations and personal convictions, note the kinds of choices the individuals in the following selections face.

IDEAS THAT WORK

Motivating with Eyewitness Accounts

Get back to the '50s and '60s through eyewitness accounts. Have students search out people who will give firsthand accounts of their experiences during this time. The eyewitnesses might have memorabilia to share or photographs that will spark a discussion on fashion, activities, and lifestyle. Students might ask several people to tell where they were when they learned that John F. Kennedy or Martin Luther King, Jr., had been shot.

Eyewitness accounts can help you achieve the responses that you want from students, and create an impact that will stay with students for a long time.

Marion P. Fleming
Hempstead, New York

Before Reading

To Be Young, Gifted and Black

by Lorraine Hansberry

Lorraine Hansberry
1930–1965

Lorraine Hansberry's mother and father were both political activists determined to fight racism. When she was eight years old, her family moved to an all-white neighborhood on Chicago's South Side to fight racial segregation. Angry neighbors threw bricks and stones at the family's new home. When the lower courts ordered the family to move, Hansberry's father took their case to the U.S. Supreme Court. In the famous *Hansberry* v. *Lee* decision, the Court declared that neighborhood segregation was unconstitutional. In *To Be Young, Gifted and Black,* Hansberry discusses her family's political activism and the effect it had on her life.

Building Background

Hansberry's Legacy When Lorraine Hansberry died of cancer at age 34, she left behind three file cabinets of manuscripts. One of her last notes read: "If anything should happen—before 'tis done—may I trust that all commas and periods will be placed and someone will complete my thoughts. . . . This last should be the least difficult—since there are so many who think as I do . . . " After she died, Hansberry's husband, Robert Nemiroff, gathered together many of these manuscripts and published them under the title *To Be Young, Gifted and Black.*

Literary Focus

Point of View In literature, a story is told by a narrator from a particular point of view, or vantage point. The story may be related by a character in his or her own words *(first-person point of view)* or by a narrator who is not a character and stands anonymously outside the action *(third-person point of view).* The third-person point of view may be either *omniscient* (able to see into the minds of all characters), *limited* (confined to a single character's perspective), or *objective* (a factual, eyewitness account).

Copy the chart below. Fill it in with examples from your reading of each type of point of view. Then, after you've read "To Be Young, Gifted and Black," identify the point of view that is used.

Point of View	Selection Name	What You Know About the Narrator
first-person		
third-person *omniscient*		
third-person *limited*		
third-person *objective*		

Writer's Notebook

Family Ideals In her essay Hansberry mentions the ideals and attitudes her parents instilled in their children. In your notebook, make a list of the ideals you would like to instill in your children someday.

To Be Young, Gifted and Black **793**

Before Reading

Building Background

Encourage students to consider what they would leave behind if they were to leave the world today.

Literary Focus

Discuss with students how most literature written in the first person contains both *subjective* and *objective* statements. Ask them to consider the differences between limited and objective **points of view** and to find examples in the selection.

Writer's Notebook

Encourage students to consider the ideals their parents tried to instill in them and to what extent they were successful.

More About Lorraine Hansberry

Hansberry was the first black woman to have a play produced on Broadway. The play was *A Raisin in the Sun*, written in 1959.

Connections to
AuthorWorks

Lorraine Hansberry is a featured author in the AuthorWorks CD-ROM.

Connections to
NovelWorks

Material for teaching *A Raisin in the Sun* is in NovelWorks.

SUPPORT MATERIALS OVERVIEW

Unit 7 Resource Book
- Graphic Organizer, p. 57
- Study Guide, p. 58
- Vocabulary, p. 59
- Grammar, p. 60
- Alternate Check Test, p. 61
- Vocabulary Test, p. 62
- Selection Test, pp. 63–64

Building English Proficiency
- Literature Summaries
- Activities, p. 228

Reading, Writing & Grammar SkillBook
- Reading, pp. 70–72
- Writing, pp.112–113
- Grammar, Usage, and Mechanics, pp.204–205

Technology
- Audiotape
- Personal Journal Software
- Custom Literature Database: For another selection dealing with the struggle for equality, see *Brown v. Board of Education of Topeka* (1954) on the database.
- Test Generator Software

During Reading

Unit 7 Resource Book
Study Guide, p. 58

Selection Objectives

- To understand point of view
- To explore the theme of struggle as experienced by a black girl growing up in Chicago in the 1930s and 1940s.
- To identify and use active and passive verbs

Theme Link

Lorraine Hansberry and her family found themselves in the midst of a struggle when they integrated a white Chicago neighborhood.

Vocabulary Preview

restrictive, confining; limiting

covenant, solemn agreement; compact

pummel, strike or beat; beat with the fists

presume, dare; take liberties

deride, scorn; ridicule

Students can add the words and definitions to their personal word lists in the Writer's Notebook.

Art Study

Answer to Caption Question Answers will vary, but pattern, color, texture, African, American, signs, geometric, washing, and collage are possibilities. Statements will vary also, but something along the lines of: The artist presents American street scenes and interiors and African images to give an impression of *Black Manhattan*.

Visual Literacy Born in 1914, Romare Bearden studied in New York and at the Sorbonne in Paris, where he met Brancusi and Braque. Bearden was deeply effected by the Civil Rights Movement of the 1960s. During this period he produced collages that draw on African masks and icons as well as cityscapes, capturing the daily lives of African Americans.

794

To Be YOUNG, GIFTED AND BLACK
Lorraine Hansberry

What do the individual details and faces in Romare Bearden's 1969 collage, *Black Manhattan* remind you of? Jot down any words or thoughts the images call to mind, then write a statement about why you think Romare Bearden brought these images together in his collage.

SELECTION SUMMARY

To Be Young, Gifted and Black

In this excerpt, Hansberry describes the Southside of Chicago where she grew up. She describes her parents as proud and responsible, but rarely loving—concerned primarily with their children's awareness of family and race. As the youngest of four children, separated by seven years from her closest sibling, Hansberry learned to play alone or with the other children in her neighborhood. She tells of hot summer evenings when her family would sleep in the park, her parents telling stories of growing up in the South. She describes her father, so brilliant and commanding that she finds it difficult to imagine him afraid. Finally, in a letter to *The New York Times* written in 1964, she reveals the period in her childhood spent in daily persecution by neighbors as her father fought to win a Supreme Court case that would allow his family to live in a white neighborhood.

 *For summaries in other languages, see the **Building English Proficiency** book.*

Chicago: Southside Summers

1 For some time now—I think since I was a child—I have been possessed of the desire to put down the stuff of my life. That is a commonplace impulse, apparently, among persons of massive self-interest; sooner or later we all do it. And, I am quite certain, there is only one internal quarrel: how much of the truth to tell? How much, how much, how much! It *is* brutal, in sober uncompromising moments, to reflect on the comedy of concern we all enact when it comes to our precious images!

Even so, when such vanity as propels the writing of such memoirs is examined, certainly one would wish at least to have some boast of social serviceability on one's side. I shall set down in these pages what shall seem to me to be the truth of my life and essences . . . which are to be found, first of all, on the Southside of Chicago, where I was born. . . .

2 All travelers to my city should ride the elevated trains that race along the back ways of Chicago. The lives you can look into!

I think you could find the tempo of my people on their back porches. The honesty of their living is there in the shabbiness. Scrubbed porches that sag and look their danger. Dirty gray wood steps. And always a line of white and pink clothes scrubbed so well, waving in the dirty wind of the city.

My people are poor. And they are tired. And they are determined to live.

Our Southside is a place apart: each piece of our living is a protest.

3 I was born on May 19, 1930, the last of four children.

Of love and my parents there is little to be written: their relationship to the children was utilitarian.[1] We were fed and housed and dressed and outfitted with more cash than our associates and that was all. We were also vaguely taught certain vague absolutes: that we were better than no one but infinitely superior to everyone; that we were the products of the proudest and most mistreated of the races of man; that there was nothing enormously difficult about life; that one *succeeded* as a matter of course.

Life was not a struggle—it was something that one *did*. One won an argument because, if facts gave out, one invented them—with color! The only sinful people in the world were dull people. And, above all, there were two things which were never to be betrayed: the family and the race. But of love, there was nothing ever said.

If we were sick, we were sternly, impersonally and carefully nursed and doctored back to health. Fevers, toothaches were attended to with urgency and importance; one always felt *important* in my family. Mother came with a tray to your room with the soup and Vick's salve or gave the enemas in a steaming bathroom. But we were not fondled, any of us—head held to breast, fingers about that head—until we were grown, all of us, and my father died.

At his funeral I at last, in my memory, saw my mother hold her sons that way, and for the first time in her life my sister held me in her arms I think. We were not a loving people: we were passionate in our hostilities and affinities,[2] but the caress embarrassed us.

We have changed little. . . .

4 Seven years separated the nearest of my brothers and sisters and myself; I wear, I am sure, the earmarks of that familial station to this day. Little has been written or thought to my knowledge about children who

---

1. **utilitarian** (yū til′ə ter′ē ən), *adj.* designed for usefulness rather than beauty.
2. **affinity** (ə fin′ə tē), *n.* attraction to people or things.

To Be Young, Gifted and Black **795**

---

1 Reading/Thinking Skills
Draw Conclusions

Discuss with students Hansberry's view of memoirs as presented in Section 1 of the essay.

Questions

• What do you think Hansberry means when she says that writing about oneself "is a commonplace impulse, apparently, among persons of massive self-interest; sooner or later we all do it"? *(Possible response: that all people are massively self-interested and, at some point, feel compelled to write about their lives)*

• How would you define Hansberry's view of a memoir-writer's goal? *(Possible response: to transcend vanity and self-interest in order to reveal things which are true and have social worth)*

2 Literary Element
Imagery

Discuss imagery—the vivid sensory details that arouse feelings—with students.

Question In Section 2, what kinds of images does Hansberry use to describe her neighbors and their struggle? *(Possible response: She uses contrasting images—scrubbed porches that sag and scrubbed clothes hanging in the dirty wind—to evoke the struggle of a determined people against an oppressive environment.)*

3 Literary Element
Tone

Remind students that tone is the author's attitude, either stated or implied, toward his or her subject matter and audience.

Question What is the tone in Section 3, and what does it tell the reader about how the author feels about her upbringing? *(Students might respond that Hansberry's tone is one of regret over the absence of affection or demonstrative love in her family.)*

BUILDING ENGLISH PROFICIENCY

Exploring Key Concepts

ESL LEP ELD SAE LD

Exploring different ways that families interact will help students better understand the diversity of all families.

• Draw a T-chart on the chalkboard. Label it as shown at right.

• Have students contribute ways in which fictional families (on TV, in movies, in books, and so on) relate to one another.

• Ask students to list ways in which the Hansberrys interact.

• Make comparisons.

TV, Movies	Hansberry Family
talk about love	material needs met
hugging	cared for when sick
presents	taught pride in race and family

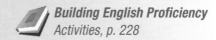
Building English Proficiency
Activities, p. 228

795

Classify

Point out to students that since Hansberry's time much has been written about the impact of a child's numerical place in the family, including profiles of only children and children born first, last, and in the middle.

Question Based on what Hansberry writes about being the youngest child by seven years, come up with a profile of such a child. *(Profiles will vary, but might include feelings of being left out, unwanted, pampered, patronized, having to try harder, and so on.)*

5 Literary Element

Archetype

An archetype is an image, story pattern, or character type that recurs frequently in literature and evokes strong associations in the reader.

Ask students to consider Hansberry's description of her father talking about the stars, and her use of the phrase "as fathers must."

Question Can you describe the archetypal image evoked and name a similar father in another story you have read? *(Possible response: He is a serious father of great depth who, relaxes occasionally to share his knowledge with his children. Another such father is Atticus Finch in To Kill a Mockingbird.)*

6 Literary Focus

Point of View

Help students see that Hansberry's point of view is *subjective,* influenced by her own feelings. Point out such phrases as *I think now, looking back; my father's . . . image in my mind; seemed; I was quite certain.*

Question How does Hansberry's subjectivity affect what she writes? *(Possible answer: Her writing is as much about her father's effect on her as it is about her father.)*

occupy that place: the last born separated by an uncommon length of time from the next youngest. I suspect we are probably a race apart.

The last born is an object toy which comes in years when brothers and sisters who are seven, ten, twelve years older are old enough to appreciate it rather than poke out its eyes. They do not mind diapering you the first two years, but by the time you are five you are a pest that has to be attended to in the washroom, taken to the movies, and "sat with" at night. You are not a person—you are a nuisance who is not particular fun anymore. Consequently, you swiftly learn to play alone. . . .

5 My childhood Southside summers were the ordinary city kind, full of the street games which other rememberers have turned into fine ballets these days, and rhymes that anticipated what some people insist on calling modern poetry:

> Oh, Mary Mack, Mack, Mack
> With the silver buttons, buttons, buttons
> All down her back, back, back.
> She asked her mother, mother, mother
> For fifteen cents, cents, cents
> To see the elephant, elephant, elephant
> Jump the fence, fence, fence.
> Well, he jumped so high, high, high
> 'Til he touched the sky, sky, sky
> And he didn't come back, back, back
> 'Til the Fourth of Ju—ly, ly, ly!

I remember skinny little Southside bodies by the fives and tens of us panting the delicious hours away:

"May I?"

And the voice of authority: "Yes, you may—you may take one giant step."

One drew in all one's breath and tightened one's fist and pulled the small body against the heavens, stretching, straining all the muscles in the legs to make—one giant step.

It is a long time. One forgets the reason for the game. (For children's games are always

explicit in their reasons for being. To play is to win something. Or not to be "it." Or to be high pointer, or outdoer or, sometimes—just *the winner.* But after a time one forgets.)

Why was it important to take a small step, a teeny step, or the most desired of all—one GIANT step?

A giant step to *where?*

6 Evenings were spent mainly on the back porches where screen doors slammed in the darkness with those really very special summertime sounds. And, sometimes, when Chicago nights got too steamy, the whole family got into the car and went to the park and slept out in the open on blankets. Those were, of course, the best times of all because the grownups were invariably reminded of having been children in the South and told the best stories then. And it was also cool and sweet to be on the grass and there was usually the scent of freshly cut lemons or melons in the air. Daddy would lie on his back, as fathers must, and explain about how men thought the stars above us came to be and how far away they were.

I never did learn to believe that anything could be as far away as *that.* Especially the stars. . . .

7 The man that I remember was an educated soul, though I think now, looking back, that it was as much a matter of the physical bearing of my father as his command of information and of thought that left that impression upon me. I know nothing of the "assurance of kings" and will not use that metaphor on account of it. Suffice it to say that my father's enduring image in my mind is that of a man whom kings might have imitated and properly created their own flattering descriptions of. A man who always seemed to be doing something brilliant and/or unusual to such an extent that to be doing something brilliant and/or unusual was the way I assumed fathers behaved.

He digested the laws of the State of Illinois and put them into little booklets. He invented

MINI-LESSON: GRAMMAR

Active and Passive Verbs

Teach An active verb phrase is used when the subject *performs* the action described by the verb. A passive verb phrase is used when the subject *receives* the action being performed. Passive verb phrases are formed with the helping verb *to be* and the past participle of the verb. Help students find passive verbs phrases on pages 795–796. *(We were fed and housed. . . .; things that were never to be betrayed. . . .; reminded of having been children. . . .)*

Question How does Hansberry's use of the passive voice affect the selection? *(Possible answer: It helps the reader realize she is not recounting hard facts but memories full of emotion.)*

Activity Idea Have students find other sentences using passive verbs and rewrite them using active verbs. Talk about how this might change the meaning.

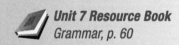

Unit 7 Resource Book
Grammar, p. 60

complicated pumps and railroad devices. He could talk at length on American history and private enterprise (to which he utterly subscribed). And he carried his head in such a way that I was quite certain that there was nothing he was afraid of. Even writing this, how profoundly it shocks my inner sense to realize suddenly that *my father,* like all men, must have known *fear.* . . .

8   April 23, 1964

To the Editor,
The *New York Times:*

[7] *With reference to civil disobedience and the Congress of Racial Equality stall-in:*

. . . My father was typical of a generation of Negroes who believed that the "American way" could successfully be made to work to democratize the United States. Thus, twenty-five years ago, he spent a small personal fortune, his considerable talents, and many years of his life fighting, in association with NAACP[3] attorneys, Chicago's "restrictive[4] covenants"[5] in one of this nation's ugliest ghettos.

That fight also required that our family occupy the disputed property in a hellishly hostile "white neighborhood" in which, literally, howling mobs surrounded our house. One of their missiles almost took the life of the then eight-year-old signer of this letter. My memories of this "correct" way of fighting white supremacy in America include being spat at, cursed, and pummeled[6] in the daily trek to and from school. And I also remember my desperate and courageous mother, patrolling our house all night with a loaded German luger, doggedly guarding her four children, while my father fought the respectable part of the battle in the Washington court.

The fact that my father and the NAACP "won" a Supreme Court decision, in a now famous case which bears his name in the lawbooks, is—ironically—the sort of "progress" our satisfied friends allude to when they presume[7] to deride[8] the more radical means of struggle. The cost, in emotional turmoil, time and money, which led to my father's early death as a permanently embittered exile in a foreign country when he saw that after such sacrificial efforts the Negroes of Chicago were as ghetto-locked as ever, does not seem to figure in their calculations.

That is the reality that I am faced with when I now read that some Negroes my own age and younger say that we must now lie down in the streets, tie up traffic, do whatever we can—take to the hills with guns if necessary—and fight back. Fatuous[9] people remark these days on our "bitterness." Why, of course we are bitter. The entire situation suggests that the nation be reminded of the too little noted final lines of Langston Hughes's[10] mighty poem.

What happens to a dream deferred?
Does it dry up
Like a raisin in the sun?
Or fester like a sore—
And then run?
Does it stink like rotten meat?
Or crust and sugar over—
Like a syrupy sweet?
Maybe it just sags
Like a heavy load.

Or does it explode?

Sincerely,

3. **NAACP,** National Association for the Advancement of Colored People.
4. restrictive (ri strik′tiv), *adj.* confining; limiting.
5. covenant (kuv′ə nənt), *n.* solemn agreement; compact.
6. pummel (pum′əl), *v.* strike or beat; beat with the fists.
7. presume (pri züm′), *v.* dare; take liberties.
8. deride (di rīd′), *v.* scorn; ridicule.
9. fatuous (fach′ü əs), *adj.* stupid but self-satisfied.
10. **Langston Hughes's mighty poem,** refers to "Harlem," later published under the title "Dream Deferred."

To Be Young, Gifted and Black   **797**

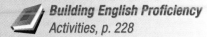

After Reading

MAKING CONNECTIONS

1. Most students will relate to such events as moving to a new neighborhood, playing children's games in the street, or listening to a parent's stories. Some may sympathize with being ostracized by neighbors or schoolmates.

2. Most students will say that she is very proud of her parents for the strength and integrity they demonstrated and the awareness of racial issues they instilled in her. They may also note that she is not so proud of their emotional coolness and the "vague absolutes" they preached.

3. The connection between Hughes' lines and the black experience that Hansberry relates is that for some (perhaps her father) the American "dream" festered and sagged, while for others in the 1960s it "exploded" into militarism.

4. Some students may feel that progress has been made in race relations, with increasing awareness of the evils of racism—laws prohibiting discrimination, and more social interaction between people of all races. Others may respond that racial tensions have continued to escalate, separatist movements abound, and racial violence still occurs.

VOCABULARY STUDY

1. covenant

2. restrictive

3. pummel

4. deride

5. presume

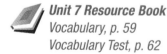

Unit 7 Resource Book
Vocabulary, p. 59
Vocabulary Test, p. 62

After Reading

Making Connections

Shaping Your Response	**1.** Which events in Hansberry's life can you relate to the most? Explain your answer.
Analyzing the Essay	**2.** Would you say Hansberry is proud of her upbringing? Explain.
	3. What connection do you think Hansberry makes between Langston Hughes's poem, "A Dream Deferred," and her experiences?
Extending the Ideas	**4.** From your experience or observation, write a brief summary indicating how you think race relations have changed since Hansberry's time.

Vocabulary Study

Use the vocabulary words in the list to complete the paragraph.

presume
restrictive
covenant
pummel
deride

Lorraine Hansberry's father spent much of his life fighting a discriminatory __(1)__ of Chicago's housing laws. To protest the __(2)__ policy, the Hansberrys moved to an all-white neighborhood. Neighbors would routinely taunt, curse, and __(3)__ the Hansberry children. Thinking back on her experiences, Hansberry wonders how critics have the nerve to __(4)__ the more radical means of protest. How can they __(5)__ to criticize if they've never been the victim of racial injustice?

Expressing Your Ideas

Picture Yourself Look carefully at Hansberry's self-portrait. Why do you suppose she chose to use the classified section of a newspaper as a background for her sketch? What would you choose as a backdrop for your own self-portrait? A shopping bag? The cover of a sports magazine? An art museum brochure? Sketch a **self-portrait,** using paper of your choice. Include an explanation of your composition.

798   UNIT SEVEN: YEARS OF CHANGE

Picture Yourself

Answers to this question will vary. She may have liked the textural quality of newsprint paper. Since she sketched herself reading the paper she may have thought this background would add dimension.

It may be symbolic of searching for something. Perhaps she didn't have sketch paper and began drawing on what was handy. Help students find the right creative medium for their self-portraits.

Before Reading

from **Letter from a Birmingham Jail** by Martin Luther King, Jr.

from **The Autobiography of Malcolm X**

Martin Luther King, Jr.
1928–1968

When he was 26 years old, Martin Luther King, Jr. led a successful boycott of the Montgomery, Alabama city bus line to protest discrimination against African American riders. King spent the next 11 years leading nonviolent protest against racism. Four years after he won the 1964 Nobel Peace Prize, King was assassinated. On his tombstone is a line from his famous "I Have a Dream" speech: "Free at last, free at last, thank God Almighty, I'm free at last."

Malcolm X
1925–1965

When he was 21 years old, Malcolm Little, later known as Malcolm X, was imprisoned for burglary. While in prison he adopted the beliefs of the Nation of Islam, which preached the separation of the races. After his release, Malcolm acted as a spokesperson for the Nation of Islam until he began to question their separatist beliefs. In 1965 he was assassinated. Three men, including two members of the Nation of Islam, were sentenced to life in prison for Malcolm's murder.

Building Background

The Civil Rights Movement How much do you know about the Civil Rights Movement of the 1950s and 1960s? As a class, work together to complete the chart below. Elect a secretary to copy the chart on the board and keep notes about your class discussion. Use the "What We Want to Find Out" column to keep track of events that you need to research. After you finish reading the selections, return to your class chart to make corrections or additions as necessary.

Event	What We Know	What We Want to Find Out
1. *Brown* v. *Board of Education*		
2. Rosa Parks arrested		
3. Sit-ins at lunch counters		
4. The March on Washington		
5. "I Have a Dream" Speech		
6. The Nation of Islam		
7. "Black Power" movement		

Literary Focus

Allusion An allusion is a reference to a person, thing, event, situation, or aspect of culture. Allusions may be drawn from art, myth, literature, history, religion, or any aspect of culture. For example, in "Letter from a Birmingham Jail," King makes an allusion to the Apostle Paul and the journey he embarks upon in order to preach the gospel of Jesus Christ. As you read "Letter from a Birmingham Jail," watch for more examples of allusion. List each example in your notebook.

Writer's Notebook

Two Crusaders for Justice How was King's crusade different from Malcolm X's? Make some notes about King's and Malcolm X's struggles for freedom in your notebook.

Letter from a Birmingham Jail   **799**

Before Reading

Building Background

If students have access to a computer, suggest that they consult a multimedia encyclopedia on CD-ROM for information about the Civil Rights Movement. Such encyclopedias will have relevant articles as well as video clips.

Literary Focus

Lead a class discussion on the purpose of **allusion,** asking students to consider the kinds of allusions that are most effective. Confirm that writers use allusion to involve their audiences, not to confuse them. King knew that his readers had a deep understanding of the Bible.

Writer's Notebook

To organize their notes, students may want to create headings such as: *Background, Ideology, Goals, Methods, Successes,* and *Failures.*

More About the Authors

Martin Luther King, Jr., considered by many the founder of the Civil Rights Movement, was greatly influenced by Gandhi's teachings. He and his father were co-pastors of the Ebenezer Baptist Church in Atlanta, Georgia.

When **Malcolm X** was six years old his father was killed—some believe because of his support of Black Nationalism. A pilgrimage to Mecca inspired Malcolm X to reject racial separatism in 1964.

SUPPORT MATERIALS OVERVIEW

Unit 7 Resource Book
- Graphic Organizer, p. 65
- Study Guide, p. 66
- Vocabulary, p. 67
- Grammar, p. 68
- Alternate Check Test, p. 69
- Vocabulary Test, p. 70
- Selection Test, pp. 71–72

Building English Proficiency
- Literature Summaries
- Activities, p. 229

Reading, Writing & Grammar SkillBook
- Vocabulary, pp. 19–20
- Reading, pp. 75–76
- Writing, pp. 139–141
- Grammar, Usage, and Mechanics, pp. 260–261

Technology
- Audiotape
- Personal Journal Software
- Custom Literature Database: For other selections dealing with the struggle for equality, see the historical documents concerning the Civil Rights Act of 1964 and the *NAACP v. Alabama* on the database.
- Test Generator Software

Selection Objectives

- To recognize and understand the use of allusion
- To learn about the Civil Rights Movement
- To explore the struggles of Martin Luther King, Jr., and Malcolm X
- To write a formal letter
- To expand vocabulary by using structural analysis

Unit 7 Resource Book
Study Guide, p. 66

Theme Link

Black leaders Martin Luther King, Jr., and Malcolm X describe their struggles—private and public.

Vocabulary Preview

gainsay, deny; contradict

impunity, freedom from punishment

pathos, quality that arouses a feeling of pity or sadness

degenerating, worsening

corroding, eating away gradually

complacency, self-satisfaction; a sense of security

repudiate, refuse to accept; reject

ominous, unfavorable; threatening

fomenter, one who stirs up trouble

smugness, overly pleased with one's own goodness, cleverness, respectability, etc.

Students can add the words and definitions to their Writer's Notebooks.

Letter from a Birmingham Jail

DR. MARTIN LUTHER KING, JR.

By 1963, Dr. Martin Luther King, Jr. and other civil rights leaders had grown tired of waiting for President John F. Kennedy to take action on issues concerning civil rights for African Americans. King and his associates organized massive demonstrations to protest racial discrimination in Birmingham, Alabama. Police used dogs and fire hoses to drive back the peaceful protesters, many of whom were children. King, among others, was jailed for his participation in the protest. While in prison, King wrote a letter to the citizens of Birmingham. In his letter, King responds to the opinion of several Alabama clergymen that the battle for integration should take place in the courts, rather than on the streets.

My Dear Fellow Clergymen,

While confined here in the Birmingham city jail, I came across your recent statement calling our present activities "unwise and untimely." Seldom, if ever, do I pause to answer criticism of my work and ideas. If I sought to answer all of the criticisms that cross my desk, my secretaries would be engaged in little else in the course of the day, and I would have no time for constructive work. But since I feel that you are men of genuine good will and your criticisms are sincerely set forth, I would like to answer your statement in what I hope will be patient and reasonable terms.

1

I think I should give the reason for my being in Birmingham, since you have been influenced by the argument of "outsiders coming in." I have the honor of serving as president of the Southern Christian Leadership Conference, an organization operating in every southern state, with headquarters in Atlanta, Georgia. We have some eighty-five affiliate organizations all across the South—one being the Alabama Christian Movement for Human Rights. Whenever necessary and possible we share staff, educational and financial resources with our affiliates. Several months ago our local affiliate here in Birmingham invited us to be on call to engage in a nonviolent

2

This is a section of Don Miller's *King Mural* which was unveiled on the first national celebration of Dr. Martin Luther King, Jr.'s birthday on January 20, 1986. The mural depicts some of the significant people and events in King's life and is exhibited at the King Memorial Library in Washington, D.C. ➤

SELECTION SUMMARY

Letter from a Birmingham Jail, The Autobiography of Malcolm X

Letter from a Birmingham Jail Martin Luther King, Jr., addresses his 1963 letter to Alabama clergymen who criticized his Birmingham civil rights demonstrations—for which he was jailed. He justifies his presence as an "outsider" in Alabama, explaining that he is a member of a network of civil rights groups and he is an American responding to the needs of fellow Americans. He then presents the "four basic steps" in a nonviolent campaign—collecting facts, negotiation, self-purification, and direct action—and tells how each applied to the situation in Birmingham. After describing how nonviolent action is a reasonable middle ground between complacency and militarism, he argues that change cannot be delayed—his people want freedom.

The Autobiography of Malcolm X In this excerpt from his autobiography, Malcolm X describes how a pilgrimage to Mecca changed his goal from black militancy to interracial harmony. He criticizes the white press for overlooking his new ideas in favor of sensational headlines and catch phrases. Anger, he says, has a time and purpose. Violence can be justified when necessary. Finally, he prophesies his own violent death.

*For summaries in other languages, see the **Building English Proficiency** book.*

Direct students' attention to the introduction and opening paragraph of King's letter.

Question How does King present his purpose for writing his "Letter from a Birmingham Jail"? *(He says that he wants to respond to what he feels is sincere and well-intentioned criticism by these clergymen of the demonstrations for which he was jailed.)*

🎨 Art Study

Just in front of the large image of Dr. King can be seen his wife, Coretta, and their four children. Depicted on the right are demonstrators being hosed and protesters of all ages being held in jail.

2 Historical Note
The Southern Christian Leadership Conference

Formed by Dr. King in 1957 in Atlanta, Georgia, the Southern Christian Leadership Conference (SCLC) was created to encourage nonviolent action in support of civil rights, including marches, voter-registration drives, and boycotts of unfair businesses.

BUILDING ENGLISH PROFICIENCY

Planning a Reading Strategy

To help students understand the selection, have them make a K-W-L chart. Allow time for class discussion about prior knowledge. To guide discussion, ask questions like these:

• What kind of family did Dr. King come from?

• How were Dr. King's protests different from others?

• Why did Dr. King become a hero?

After reading, students can share responses and complete the chart in small groups.

What We **K**now	What We **W**ant to Know	What We **L**earned
Dr. King's birthday is a federal holiday.	Why do we celebrate his birthday?	because he was a great American leader

direct-action program if such were deemed necessary. We readily consented and when the hour came we lived up to our promises. So I am here, along with several members of my staff, because we were invited here. I am here because I have basic organizational ties here.

Beyond this, I am in Birmingham because injustice is here. Just as the eighth-century prophets left their little villages and carried their "thus saith the Lord" far beyond the boundaries of their hometowns; and just as the Apostle Paul left his little village of Tarsus and carried the gospel of Jesus Christ to practically every hamlet and city of the Graeco-Roman world, I too am compelled to carry the gospel of freedom beyond my particular hometown. Like Paul, I must constantly respond to the Macedonian call for aid.

Moreover, I am cognizant of the interrelatedness of all communities and states. I cannot sit idly by in Atlanta and not be concerned about what happens in Birmingham. Injustice anywhere is a threat to justice everywhere. We are caught in an inescapable network of mutuality, tied in a single garment of destiny. Whatever affects one directly affects all indirectly. Never again can we afford to live with the narrow, provincial "outside agitator" idea. Anyone who lives in the United States can never be considered an outsider anywhere in this country.

You deplore the demonstrations that are presently taking place in Birmingham. But I am sorry that your statement did not express a similar concern for the conditions that brought the demonstrations into being. I am sure that each of you would want to go beyond the superficial social analyst who looks merely at effects, and does not grapple with underlying causes. I would not hesitate to say that it is unfortunate that so-called demonstrations are taking place in Birmingham at this time, but I would say in

> **Injustice anywhere is a threat to justice everywhere.**

more emphatic terms that it is even more unfortunate that the white power structure of this city left the Negro community with no other alternative.

In any nonviolent campaign there are four basic steps: (1) collection of the facts to determine whether injustices are alive, (2) negotiation, (3) self-purification, and (4) direct action. We have gone through all of these steps in Birmingham. There can be no gainsaying[1] of the fact that racial injustice engulfs this community.

Birmingham is probably the most thoroughly segregated city in the United States. Its ugly record of police brutality is known in every section of this country. Its unjust treatment of Negroes in the courts is a notorious reality. There have been more unsolved bombings of Negro homes and churches in Birmingham than any city in this nation. These are the hard, brutal and unbelievable facts. On the basis of these conditions Negro leaders sought to negotiate with the city fathers. But the political leaders consistently refused to engage in good faith negotiation.

Then came the opportunity last September to talk with some of the leaders of the economic community. In these negotiating sessions certain promises were made by the merchants—such as the promise to remove the humiliating racial signs from the stores. On the basis of these promises Rev. Shuttlesworth and the leaders of the Alabama Christian Movement for Human Rights agreed to call a moratorium[2] on any type of demonstrations. As the weeks and months unfolded we realized that we were the victims of a broken promise. The signs remained. Like so many experiences of the past we were

---

1. **gainsay** (gān′sā′), *v.* deny; contradict.
2. **moratorium** (môr′ə tôr′ē əm), *n.* temporary cessation of action on any issue.

MINI-LESSON: GRAMMAR

Writing a Formal Letter

Teach Review with students the elements of a formal letter. If needed, go over the rules for capitalization within a letter.

Activity Idea Have students write similar letters to organizations, requesting catalogs, brochures, and so forth. College-bound students might write application requests. Encourage students to be sure they've included all elements. Verify names, addresses, and titles. Have classmates proofread one another's letters.

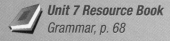

Unit 7 Resource Book
Grammar, p. 68

Heading ──────────────→ *123 West Canal St.*
Boise, Idaho 83705
*October 3, 199_*

Inside address → *Central Librarian*
King Memorial Library
901 George St. NW
Washington, D.C. 20001

Salutation → *Dear Central Librarian,*
Please send a color copy of the King Mural by Don Miller to the above address.

Body → *I am studying Dr. King in class and would like to hang this picture on the classroom wall. Thank you.*

Closing ──────────────→ *Sincerely,*
Signature ──────────────→ *Gail John*

confronted with blasted hopes, and the dark shadow of a deep disappointment settled upon us. So we had no alternative except that of preparing for direct action, whereby we would present our very bodies as a means of laying our case before the conscience of the local and national community. We were not unmindful of the difficulties involved. So we decided to go through a process of self-purification. We started having workshops on nonviolence and repeatedly asked ourselves the questions, "Are you able to accept blows without retaliating?" "Are you able to endure the ordeals of jail?" We decided to set our direct-action program around the Easter season, realizing that with the exception of Christmas, this was the largest shopping period of the year. Knowing that a strong economic withdrawal program would be the by-product of direct action, we felt that this was the best time to bring pressure on the merchants for the needed changes. Then it occurred to us that the March election was ahead and so we speedily decided to postpone action until after election day. When we discovered that Mr. Connor was in the run-off, we decided again to postpone action so that the demonstrations could not be used to cloud the issues. At this time we agreed to begin our nonviolent witness the day after the run-off.

This reveals that we did not move irresponsibly into direct action. We too wanted to see Mr. Connor defeated; so we went through postponement after postponement to aid in this community need. After this we felt that direct action could be delayed no longer.

 You may well ask, "Why direct action? Why sit-ins, marches, etc.? Isn't negotiation a better path?" You are exactly right in your call for negotiation. Indeed, this is the purpose of direct action. Nonviolent direct action seeks to create such a crisis and establish such creative tension that a community that has constantly refused to negotiate is forced to confront the issue. It seeks so to dramatize the issue that it can no longer be ignored. I just referred to the creation of tension as a part of the work of the nonviolent resister. This may sound rather shocking. But I must confess that I am not afraid of the word *tension.* I have earnestly worked and preached against violent tension, but there is a type of constructive nonviolent tension that is necessary for growth. Just as Socrates felt that it was necessary to create a tension in the mind so that individuals could rise from the bondage of myths and half-truths to the unfettered realm of creative analysis and objective appraisal, we must see the need of having nonviolent gadflies[3] to create the kind of tension in society that will help men to rise from the dark depths of prejudice and racism to the majestic heights of understanding and brotherhood. So the purpose of the direct action is to create a situation so crisis-packed that it will inevitably open the door to negotiation. We, therefore, concur with you in your call for negotiation. Too long has our beloved Southland been bogged down in the tragic attempt to live in monologue rather than dialogue.

One of the basic points in your statement is that our acts are untimely. Some have asked, "Why didn't you give the new administration time to act?" The only answer that I can give to this inquiry is that the new administration must be prodded about as much as the outgoing one before it acts. We will be sadly mistaken if we feel that the election of Mr. Boutwell will bring the millennium to Birmingham. While Mr. Boutwell is much more articulate and gentle than Mr. Connor, they are both segregationists, dedicated to the task of maintaining the status quo. The hope I see in Mr. Boutwell is that he will be reasonable enough to see the futility of massive resistance to desegregation. But he will not see this without pressure from the devotees of civil rights. My friends, I must say to you that we have not made a single gain in civil rights without determined legal and nonviolent pressure. History is

---

3. **gadfly** (gad′flī), *n.* person who goads others to action with irritating or annoying remarks.

Question How does King present his rationale for taking direct action in Birmingham? *(After presenting a breakdown of the four basic steps in a nonviolent campaign, he shows how each step naturally led to the next—resulting in no alternative but to take action.)*

7 Literary Focus
Allusion

Discuss with students how King's allusion to Socrates—whose philosophies are part of the foundation of accepted Western thought—helps him to advance his argument that nonviolent tension is necessary for growth. Socrates lends legitimacy to King's statements.

8 Reading/Thinking Skills
Identify Author's Purpose

Question How does King use the concept of negotiation to serve his argument? *(He uses it to suggest that he and his opponents really agree, arguing that the purpose of the direct action he sanctions is to bring about the negotiation encouraged by his opponents.)*

9 Reader's Response
Making Personal Connections

Question Having read the letter to this point, do you find King convincing? *(Most students will say yes, because he presents his case so well and it is such a worthwhile cause. Others may feel that they have to read on to decide.)*

BUILDING ENGLISH PROFICIENCY

Improving Comprehension

To help students share their understanding, divide them into seven groups, and assign each group one paragraph. (Combine the two short paragraphs on page 802, and the short paragraph on page 803 with the one following it.)

- Ask each group to become an expert on its assigned paragraph, looking up unfamiliar words, researching any allusions, and summarizing King's ideas in two sentences.

- Have each group decide on one thing to teach the class about the paragraph—for example, allusions, vocabulary, or organization (facts, examples, reasons, events). Ask each group to also generate one question to guide the class's reading of the paragraph.

- Let each group decide on a way to present its assigned paragraph, limiting teaching time to two or three minutes each.

Alex Haley and Roots

Alex Haley, Malcolm X's partner in the writing of *The Autobiography of Malcolm X,* later wrote the world-famous book *Roots: The Saga of an American Family* (1976). Containing twelve years of research, it combined fact and fiction to tell the history of Haley's family beginning in Africa in the 1700s. The final episode of the eight-part television drama based on *Roots* that appeared in 1977 was one of the most-watched programs in TV history.

 **Art Study**

Writer, photographer, and film maker, Gordon Parks has covered much of the American scene from the 1950s through the 1990s. America's first black photo-journalist, his camera became "the voice of the black ghetto."

Response to Caption Question
Students' answers will vary, but may include: public speaker, assured, friendly, positive, and thoughtful.

The Autobiography of Malcolm X

Malcolm X

In 1963 Alex Haley approached Malcolm X with the idea of collaborating on writing an autobiography of Malcolm's life. Malcolm agreed to the project, though he was reluctant at first. In The Autobiography of Malcolm X, first published in 1964, Malcolm details the story of his life and reveals why he chose to become a spokesperson for African Americans. The selection that follows is an excerpt from the last section of his autobiography.

MINI-LESSON: VOCABULARY

Latin Root Words

Teach   Encourage students to use a dictionary to investigate the roots of vocabulary words. Latin may be a dead language, but Latin roots are alive and well in many English words.

Activity Idea   Divide the class into groups. Assign the following words from the selections to each group: *moratorium, impunity, degenerate, foment,* and *repudiate.* Ask students to create a chart like the one at the right. Then have them consult a dictionary to look up the words, identify their meanings, the Latin root word, and its meaning.

Word	Meaning	Latin Root	Meaning
moratorium	temporary delay	*morari*	to delay

On the streets, after my speeches, in the faces and the voices of the people I met—even those who would pump my hands and want my autograph—I would feel the wait-and-see attitude. I would feel—and I understood—their uncertainty about where I stood. Since the Civil War's "freedom" the black man has gone down so many fruitless paths. His leaders, very largely, had failed him. The religion of Christianity had failed him. The black man was scarred, he was cautious, he was apprehensive.

I understood it better now than I had before. In the Holy World, away from America's race problem, was the first time I ever had been able to think clearly about the basic divisions of white people in America, and how their attitudes and their motives related to, and affected Negroes. In my thirty-nine years on this earth,  the Holy City of Mecca had been the first time I had ever stood before the Creator of All and felt like a complete human being.

In that peace of the Holy World—in fact, the very night I have mentioned when I lay awake surrounded by snoring brother pilgrims—my mind took me back to personal memories I would have thought were gone forever . . . as far back, even, as when I was just a little boy, eight or nine years old. Out behind our house, out in the country from Lansing, Michigan, there was an old, grassy "Hector's Hill," we called it—which may still be there. I remembered there in the Holy World how I used to lie on the top of Hector's Hill, and look up at the sky, at the clouds moving over me, and daydream, all kinds of things. And then, in a funny contrast of recollections, I remembered how years later, when I was in prison, I used to lie on my cell bunk—this would be especially when I was in solitary: what we convicts called "The Hole"—and I would picture myself talking to large crowds. I don't have any idea why such previsions came to me. But they did. To tell that to anyone then would have sounded crazy. Even I

◄ What qualities does Gordon Parks's 1963 photograph of Malcolm X portray?

didn't have, myself, the slightest inkling. . . .

In Mecca, too, I had played back for myself the twelve years I had spent with Elijah Muhammad as if it were a motion picture. I guess it would be impossible for anyone ever to realize fully how complete was my belief in Elijah Muhammad. I believed in him not only as a leader in the ordinary *human* sense, but also I believed in him as a *divine* leader. I believed he had no human weaknesses or faults, and that, therefore, he could make no mistakes and that he could do no wrong. There on a Holy World hilltop, I realized how very dangerous it is for people to hold any human being in such esteem, especially to consider anyone some sort of "divinely guided" and "protected" person.

My thinking had been opened up wide in Mecca. In the long letters I wrote to friends, I tried to convey to them my new insights into the American black man's struggle and his problems, as well as the depths of my search for truth and justice.

"I've had enough of someone else's propaganda," I had written to these friends. "I'm for truth, no matter who tells it. I'm for justice, no matter who it is for or against. I'm a human being first and foremost, and as such I'm for whoever and whatever benefits humanity *as a whole*."

Largely, the American white man's press refused to convey that I was now attempting to teach Negroes a new direction. With the 1964 "long, hot summer" steadily producing new incidents, I was constantly accused of "stirring up Negroes." Every time I had another radio or television microphone at my mouth, when I was asked about "stirring up Negroes" or "inciting violence," I'd get hot.

"It takes no one to stir up the sociological dynamite that stems from the unemployment, bad housing, and inferior education already in the ghettoes. This explosively criminal condition has existed for so long, it needs no fuse; it fuses itself; it spontaneously combusts from within itself. . . ."

They called me "the angriest Negro in

The Autobiography of Malcolm X   **807**

🔊 **MULTICULTURAL NOTE**

Located in Saudi Arabia, Mecca, the birthplace of the Muslim prophet Muhammad, is the holy city of the Islam faith. Each year, over a million Muslims participate in the *hajj* (pilgrimage) to Mecca, where they visit the *al-Haram* (Great Mosque), the site of a holy shrine and well. Only Muslims are permitted to enter Mecca.

16 Literary Element
Style

Style, or the distinctive handling of language by an author, involves diction, figurative language, syntax, and so on. Encourage students to consider how Malcolm X's writing style differs from that of Martin Luther King, Jr. Much of *The Autobiography of Malcolm X* was dictated by Malcolm X to Alex Haley.

17 Reading/Thinking Skills
Cause and Effect

Question How does Malcolm account for his change in thinking—that is, from valuing only black people to valuing "humanity as a whole"? *(He says that being in Mecca opened up his mind and caused him to realize that he had been overly influenced by Elijah Muhammad. He is interested in truth and justice.)*

BUILDING ENGLISH PROFICIENCY

ESL
LEP
ELD
SAE
LD

Comparing Authors

To help students compare and contrast Martin Luther King, Jr., and Malcolm X, have them work together in groups to create Venn diagrams. Ask students to use only details given in these passages; alternatively, before you assign the Venn diagrams, have a group of students research and present a panel discussion on the lives and deeds of both men.

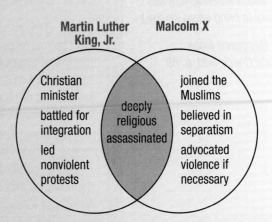

Martin Luther King, Jr.: Christian minister; battled for integration; led nonviolent protests

deeply religious; assassinated

Malcolm X: joined the Muslims; believed in separatism; advocated violence if necessary

VOCABULARY STUDY

1. b
2. c
3. a
4. c
5. a
6. a
7. a
8. b
9. b
10. a

More Practice Students can use the vocabulary words to write a short speech.

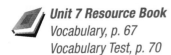
Unit 7 Resource Book
Vocabulary, p. 67
Vocabulary Test, p. 70

WRITING CHOICES
Writer's Notebook Update

Encourage students to examine their own backgrounds, ideologies, and goals and compare them with those of each leader.

Leader to Leader

Remind students that style involves *diction,* formal or casual, *syntax,* or grammatical patterns, *figurative language,* such as metaphors, similes, and hyperbole. Encourage students to take these elements into account when writing their dialogues.

Selection Test

Unit 7 Resource Book
pp. 71–72

Vocabulary Study

Using your Glossary if necessary, choose the word that is most nearly the same as the numbered vocabulary word.

gainsay
impunity
pathos
degenerating
repudiate
corroding
ominous
fomenter
smugness
complacency

1. gainsay	**a.** agree	**b.** contradict	**c.** acknowledge
2. impunity	**a.** punishment	**b.** confine	**c.** exemption
3. pathos	**a.** sadness	**b.** fury	**c.** progressive
4. degenerating	**a.** improving	**b.** creating	**c.** worsening
5. repudiate	**a.** reject	**b.** repeat	**c.** redo
6. corroding	**a.** gnawing	**b.** concealing	**c.** influencing
7. ominous	**a.** threatening	**b.** noisy	**c.** ugly
8. fomenter	**a.** foe	**b.** instigator	**c.** detractor
9. smugness	**a.** happiness	**b.** conceit	**c.** resentment
10. complacency	**a.** contentment	**b.** joy	**c.** worry

Expressing Your Ideas

Writing Choices

Writer's Notebook Update Now that you've read the excerpts from "Letter from a Birmingham Jail" and *The Autobiography of Malcolm X,* you may want to make some changes to what you've written in your notebook. Review the notes you made about King and Malcolm X, and decide which leader you agree with most.

Leader to Leader Martin Luther King and Malcolm X both had distinctive ways of expressing themselves. Create a one-page **dialogue** between the two leaders, using "Letter from a Birmingham Jail" and *The Autobiography of Malcolm X* as models for each man's style. Before you begin, choose the topic for their dialogue. For example, you may decide to have the two leaders speak to each other about the use of violence in the fight for racial justice. Team with a partner to perform your dialogue for the class.

Other Options

Telling Their Stories You are the producer of a **television special,** focusing on the lives and times of Dr. Martin Luther King, Jr. and Malcolm X. Working in small groups, prepare for your show. You'll need biographical information about both men, as well as an understanding of their work and philosophies. Plan some visuals for the show, either art of your own creation or art that you find in a library. Write a script for your show including quotes from their writings, then videotape your show. Play the video for your class.

Musical Accompaniment What music would you choose to accompany an oral reading of King's letter? of Malcolm X's autobiography? Choose two different **musical accompaniments** for the selections. Play the music for the class, offering a brief explanation for your choices.

OTHER OPTIONS
Telling Their Stories

Suggest to students that they delegate different responsibilities to the various members of their groups. For example, two students might work as researchers, one might serve as art director, obtaining visuals for the show; one could be the writer and script the show based on the researchers' notes; and a final student could act as executive director, coordinating the various elements and videotaping the show.

Musical Accompaniment

Students who choose this option might want to combine with those who have chosen the option above and supply the music for their video.

Before Reading

On the Rainy River

by Tim O'Brien

Tim O'Brien
born 1946

Born in Austin, Minnesota, Tim O'Brien was drafted to serve in Vietnam immediately following his graduation from college. He served for two years as a soldier with the United States infantry. When he returned home from the war, O'Brien began to write about his experiences. In his writing about the war, O'Brien explores the human element of the conflict in Vietnam—the fear, the confusion, and the isolation that many of the soldiers who served in Vietnam experienced. "On the Rainy River" (a chapter from his 1990 book, *The Things They Carried*) is narrated by a character named Tim O'Brien, who the author says is not himself. According to O'Brien, "On the Rainy River" is a **fictional memoir** of a tumultuous time in American history.

Building Background

The Vietnam War In the Vietnam War, which lasted from the mid-1950s until 1975, Communist-ruled North Vietnam fought to take control of non-Communist South Vietnam. The United States government feared that if one Southeast Asian nation fell to the Communists, other nations would fall as well. As a result, the U. S. government sent financial assistance to the government of South Vietnam. Later, when it seemed that South Vietnam might collapse, President Lyndon Johnson ordered combat troops to Vietnam. The Vietnam War caused tremendous controversy in the United States. Many Americans, especially young people, staged protests against the war. Many of those who were drafted to serve in Vietnam refused to go and sought refuge in countries such as Canada. In the story you're about to read, a young man struggles with the question of what to do after he is drafted to fight in Vietnam.

Literary Focus

Dialogue Conversation between two or more people in a literary work is called **dialogue**. Dialogue can serve many purposes, among them:

- characterization, both of those speaking and of those spoken about;
- the creation of mood or atmosphere;
- the advancement of plot;
- the development of theme.

As you read "On the Rainy River," watch for the dialogue between the two main characters. What does their dialogue reveal about their characters? What can you learn about the theme from the dialogue?

Writer's Notebook

Making Decisions Before reading "On the Rainy River," think about a time in your life when you've had to make a tough decision. In your notebook, write how you felt about the decision. Then make a list of the people in your life who influenced your decision. Did you do what *you* wanted to do, or did you do what others thought you should do? Why?

On the Rainy River **811**

Before Reading

Building Background

Ask students if they have seen movies or television shows about the Vietnam War and to discuss their impressions.

Literary Focus

Discuss with students some of the choices writers make in creating **dialogue,** and some of the elements readers can look for in evaluating it. For example: Is the dialogue stilted or natural? Is it formal or casual? Does the writer handle dialect successfully?

Writer's Notebook

Ask students to consider what is involved in making a decision: Defining the decision to be made, listing pros and cons, considering possible outcomes, etc.

More About Tim O'Brien

To some degree, the Vietnam War plays a part in all of O'Brien's books. He believes that good writing "requires a sense of passion, and my passion as a human being and as a writer intersect in Vietnam. . . ." He won the National Book Award in 1978 for his novel *Going After Cacciato.*

Other Works

- *If I Die in a Combat Zone, Box Me Up and Send Me Home* (1973)
- *Northern Lights* (1974)

SUPPORT MATERIALS OVERVIEW

Unit 7 Resource Book
- Graphic Organizer, p. 73
- Study Guide, p. 74
- Vocabulary, p. 75
- Grammar, p. 76
- Alternate Check Test, p. 77
- Vocabulary Test, p. 78
- Selection Test, pp. 79–80

Building English Proficiency
- Literature Summaries
- Activities, p. 230

Reading, Writing & Grammar SkillBook
- Vocabulary, pp. 9–10
- Reading, pp. 37–40
- Writing, pp. 132–133
- Grammar, Usage, and Mechanics, pp. 216–217

The World of Work
- Resort Operator and Owner, p. 25
- Activity, p. 26

Technology
- Audiotape
- Personal Journal Software
- Custom Literature Database: For another selection dealing with the war in Vietnam, see the Speech at Johns Hopkins University, April 7, 1965, by Lyndon Johnson on the database.
- Test Generator Software

During Reading

Selection Objectives

- To discuss the functions of dialogue
- To learn about the Vietnam War
- To explore a character's internal struggle
- To learn about the use of action verbs

Unit 7 Resource Book
Graphic Organizer, 73
Study Guide, p. 74

Theme Link

A young man struggles to decide whether to respond to the draft or desert to Canada.

Vocabulary Preview

conviction, firmly-held belief

removal, emotional distance

censure, expression of disapproval

acquiescence, consent given without making objections; assent

platitude, dull or commonplace remark, especially one given out solemnly as if it were fresh and important

treasonous, traitorous; involving betrayal of one's country

adrenaline, hormone which speeds up the heartbeat and thereby increases bodily energy

preoccupied, absorbed; engrossed

reticence, tendency to be silent or say little; reserved in speech

comport, conduct (oneself) in a certain manner; behave

Students can add the words and definitions to their Writer's Notebooks.

ON THE RAINY RIVER

Tim O'Brien

This is one story I've never told before. Not to anyone. Not to my parents, not to my brother or sister, not even to my wife. To go into it, I've always thought, would only cause embarrassment for all of us, a sudden need to be elsewhere, which is the natural response to a confession. Even now, I'll admit, the story makes me squirm. For more than twenty years I've had to live with it, feeling the shame, trying to push it away, and so by this act of remembrance, by putting the facts down on paper, I'm hoping to relieve at least some of the pressure on my dreams. Still, it's a hard story to tell. All of us, I suppose, like to believe that in a moral emergency we will behave like the heroes of our youth, bravely and forthrightly, without thought of personal loss or discredit. Certainly that was my conviction back in the summer of 1968. Tim O'Brien: a secret hero. The Lone Ranger. If the stakes ever became high enough—if the evil were evil enough, if the good were good enough—I would simply tap a secret reservoir of courage that had been accumulating inside me over the years. Courage, I seemed to think, comes to us in finite quantities, like an inheritance, and by being frugal and stashing it away and letting it earn interest, we steadily increase our moral capital in preparation for that day when the account must be drawn down. It was a comforting theory. It dispensed with all those bothersome little acts of daily courage; it offered hope and grace to the repetitive coward; it justified the past while amortizing[1] the future.

In June of 1968, a month after graduating from Macalester College, I was drafted to fight a war I hated. I was twenty-one years old. Young, yes, and politically naive, but even so the

---

1. **amortize** (am′ər tīz), *v.* set aside quantities of money at regular intervals, to accumulate a larger sum.

SELECTION SUMMARY

On the Rainy River

As a 21-year-old college graduate living in a small Minnesota town in 1968, Tim O'Brien hated the Vietnam War—and somehow believed he would never have to fight in it. The story begins when he is drafted. Soon afterward, he is overcome with panic at the slaughterhouse where he works, and he flees his hometown, driving north. Stopping at an old fishing resort in Northern Minnesota, he encounters Elroy Berdahl, an elderly man of few words and great insight. During the six days he spends with Berdahl—who never questions why he is there, but provides him with an "Emergency Fund" by paying him for odd jobs he has done around the resort—a decision becomes more and more imminent. On the sixth day, Berdahl takes the young man on the Rainy River, which divides the United States from Canada, ostensibly for a fishing trip. O'Brien soon realizes that they have crossed the Canadian border. In a momentous second, he sees that he will not be able to dive into the river and leave his old life behind, but is destined to do what others consider to be right. He leaves Minnesota and goes to war, with deep regrets over his lack of courage.

For summaries in other languages, see the Building English Proficiency book.

 What kind of mood, thoughts, or feelings do you think the young man in this painting, *Bellamy 9* (1988), is experiencing? How does artist Glenn Priestly convey his state of mind?

American war in Vietnam seemed to me wrong. Certain blood was being shed for uncertain reasons. I saw no unity of purpose, no consensus on matters of philosophy or history or law. The very facts were shrouded in uncertainty: Was it a civil war? A war of national liberation or simple aggression? Who started it, and when, and why? What really happened to the USS *Maddox* on that dark night in the Gulf of Tonkin? Was Ho Chi Minh[2] a Communist stooge, or a nationalist savior, or both, or neither? What about the Geneva Accords?[3] What about SEATO[4] and the Cold

2. **Ho Chi Minh** (hō′chē′min′), Communist president of North Vietnam from 1954 to 1969.
3. **Geneva Accords.** In 1954, France and the Democratic Republic of Vietnam agreed to divide Vietnam into two parts: the north was given to the communists, and the south was given to the Saigon government. Under the terms of the agreement, the country was to be reunified in 1956.
4. **SEATO,** the Southeast Asia Treaty Organization, formed in 1954. SEATO brought Thailand, Pakistan, and the Philippines into alliance with the United States, Britain, France, Australia, and New Zealand. SEATO was formed for defense against aggression in southeastern Asia and the southwestern Pacific.

On the Rainy River   **813**

 Art Study

Response to Caption Question
Answers will vary, but may include: He appears dazed and unhappy, perhaps worried, or depressed. The artist conveys this by having him look off into space, away from the viewer. Also his body language suggests that he has withdrawn within himself or is sagging under the weight of his troubles.

1 **Literary Element**
Narrator

Discuss with students what the narrator reveals about himself in the first two pages of the story. Ask students why they think O'Brien may have chosen to create a fictional character with his own name rather than writing an autobiographical memoir or inventing a fictional name. *(Students may respond that the narrator shows himself to be a man of conscience who for many years has been hiding a secret which plagues him. We know that he is married, because he mentions a wife; we know that he has a college education and takes ideas seriously. Students may suggest that O'Brien created a fictional version of himself to tell a story that is based upon fact, but not always factual; in this way, he is able to take certain liberties—use poetic license—for the sake of the story. The fictional Tim O'Brien may also be the author's way of distancing himself sufficiently from his own story to have the necessary perspective to tell it.)*

BUILDING ENGLISH PROFICIENCY

Exploring Key Concepts

Considering the impact of war will help students better understand the main character and theme in this story.

Activity Ideas
- Have students in small groups share ideas and feelings about wars (causes, effects, winners, losers) that they or family members have read about or witnessed.
- Ask students to draw a picture of what war means to them.
- Have students create a semantic web with WAR at the center.

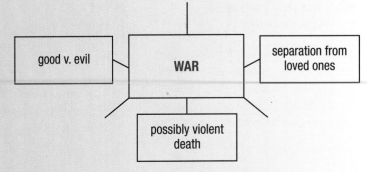

Recognize Assumptions and Implications

Question Who are the "smart men in pinstripes" and why does O'Brien use this phrase to describe them? *(Students may respond that they are the so-called leaders of the country—the politicians, businessmen, etc. O'Brien uses this statement to reduce them to a somewhat comic image.)*

3 Literary Element

Plot

Discuss with students the three basic elements of plot: conflict, climax, and resolution (or dénouement).

Question What conflict does Tim O'Brien present? *(Possible response: The main character is drafted to fight a war he cannot morally support.)*

EDITORIAL NOTE A sentence in the second paragraph has been edited. The sentence originally read, "I was a liberal, for Christ sake."

4 Literary Element

Tone

Questions

• What is the narrator's attitude toward being drafted? *(Possible responses: astonished, outraged, devastated)*

• What is his attitude toward his audience? *(Possibly one of kinship, perhaps apologetic or needing to explain things. He is trying to foster understanding.)*

5 Reader's Response

Making Personal Connections

Question Why do you think Tim replies "Nothing" when his father asks his plans? *(Possibilities: He cannot put his feelings into words. He doesn't want to upset his father. He feels he must face this alone.)*

814

---

2 War? What about dominoes?[5] America was divided on these and a thousand other issues, and the debate had spilled out across the floor of the United States Senate and into the streets, and smart men in pinstripes could not agree on even the most fundamental matters of public policy. The only certainty that summer was moral confusion. It was my view then, and still is, that you don't make war without knowing why. Knowledge, of course, is always imperfect, but it seemed to me that when a nation goes to war it must have reasonable confidence in the justice and imperative of its cause. You can't fix your mistakes. Once people are dead, you can't make them undead.

In any case those were my convictions,[6] and back in college I had taken a modest stand against the war. Nothing radical, no hothead stuff, just ringing a few doorbells for Gene McCarthy,[7] composing a few tedious, uninspired editorials for the campus newspaper. Oddly, though, it was almost entirely an intellectual activity. I brought some energy to it, of course, but it was the energy that accompanies almost any abstract endeavor; I felt no personal danger; I felt no sense of an impending crisis in my life. Stupidly, with a kind of smug removal[8] that I can't begin to fathom, I assumed that the problems of killing and dying did not fall within my special province.

3 The draft notice arrived on June 17, 1968. It was a humid afternoon, I remember, cloudy and very quiet, and I'd just come in from a round of golf. My mother and father were having lunch out in the kitchen. I remember opening up the letter, scanning the first few lines, feeling the blood go thick behind my eyes. I remember a sound in my head. It wasn't thinking, just a silent howl. A million things all at once—I was too *good* for this war. Too smart, too compassionate, too everything. It couldn't happen. I was above it. I had the world licked—Phi Beta Kappa and summa cum laude[9] and president of the student body and a full-ride scholarship for grad studies at Harvard. A mistake, maybe—a

814 UNIT SEVEN: YEARS OF CHANGE

foul-up in the paperwork. I was no soldier. I hated Boy Scouts. I hated camping out. I hated dirt and tents and mosquitoes. The sight of blood made me queasy, and I couldn't tolerate authority, and I didn't know a rifle from a slingshot. I was a *liberal:* If they needed fresh bodies, why not draft some back-to-the-stone-age hawk? Or some dumb jingo in his hard hat and Bomb Hanoi button, or one of LBJ's[10] pretty daughters, or Westmoreland's[11] whole handsome family—nephews and nieces and baby grandson. There should be a law, I thought. If you support a war, if you think it's worth the price, that's fine, but you have to put your own precious fluids on the line. You have to head for the front and hook up with an infantry unit and help spill the blood. And you have to bring along your wife, or your kids, or your lover. A *law,* I thought. **4**

I remember the rage in my stomach. Later it burned down to a smoldering self-pity, then to numbness. At dinner that night my father asked what my plans were. **5**

"Nothing," I said. "Wait."

I spent the summer of 1968 working in an Armour meat-packing plant in my hometown of Worthington, Minnesota. The plant specialized in pork products, and for eight hours a day I stood on a quarter-mile assembly line—more properly, a disassembly line—removing blood clots from the necks of dead pigs. My job title, I believe, was Declotter. After slaughter, the

---

5. **dominoes,** supporters of the war believed that if South Vietnam fell under Communist control, other countries would also fall "like a row of dominoes."
6. **conviction** (kən vik′shən), *n.* firmly held belief.
7. **Gene McCarthy.** Senator Eugene McCarthy was an early candidate in the 1968 presidential elections. He spoke out strongly against the war in Vietnam.
8. **removal** (ri mü′vəl), *n.* emotional distance.
9. **Phi Beta Kappa and summa cum laude,** honors for outstanding students.
10. **LBJ,** Lyndon Baines Johnson, President of the United States from 1963 to 1969.
11. **Westmoreland,** General William Westmoreland, commander of the U. S. ground troops in South Vietnam.

MINI-LESSON: GRAMMAR

Action Verbs

Teach Action verbs describe something that occurs in a limited time and has a beginning and an end. They serve three grammatical functions. First, they act as the main action word in a sentence. Secondly, they serve a secondary but independent function in a clause. Finally, they appear in verb phrases, where they are sometimes combined with auxiliary verbs such as *be, do,* and *have.* Here are some examples:

  . . . my father asked what my plans were.

  . . . I headed straight west along the Rainy River,

which separates Minnesota from Canada. . . .

At night, when I couldn't sleep, I'd sometimes carry on fierce arguments with those people. . . .

Ask students to find the main action verbs in the sentences. *(asked, headed, carry on)* Which is an action verb in an independent clause? *(sleep)*

Activity Idea Have students find each kind of action verb in the selection.

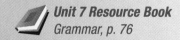

Unit 7 Resource Book
Grammar, p. 76

hogs were decapitated, split down the length of the belly, pried open, eviscerated,[12] and strung up by the hind hocks on a high conveyer belt. Then gravity took over. By the time a carcass reached my spot on the line, the fluids had mostly drained out, everything except for thick clots of blood in the neck and upper chest cavity. To remove the stuff, I used a kind of water gun. The machine was heavy, maybe eighty pounds, and was suspended from the ceiling by a heavy rubber cord. There was some bounce to it, an elastic up-and-down give, and the trick was to maneuver the gun with your whole body, not lifting with the arms, just letting the rubber cord do the work for you. At one end was a trigger; at the muzzle end was a small nozzle and a steel roller brush. As a carcass passed by, you'd lean forward and swing the gun up against the clots and squeeze the trigger, all in one motion, and the brush would whirl and water would come shooting out and you'd hear a quick splattering sound as the clots dissolved into a fine red mist. It was not pleasant work. Goggles were a necessity, and a rubber apron, but even so it was like standing for eight hours a day under a lukewarm blood-shower. At night I'd go home smelling of pig. It wouldn't go away. Even after a hot bath, scrubbing hard, the stink was always there—like old bacon, or sausage, a dense greasy pig-stink that soaked deep into my skin and hair. Among other things, I remember, it was tough getting dates that summer. I felt isolated; I spent a lot of time alone. And there was also that draft notice tucked away in my wallet.

In the evenings I'd sometimes borrow my father's car and drive aimlessly around town, feeling sorry for myself, thinking about the war and the pig factory and how my life seemed to be collapsing toward slaughter. I felt paralyzed. All around me the options seemed to be narrowing, as if I were hurtling down a huge black funnel, the whole world squeezing in tight. There was no happy way out. The government had ended most graduate school deferments; the waiting lists for the National Guard and

Reserves were impossibly long; my health was solid; I didn't qualify for CO[13] status—no religious grounds, no history as a pacifist. Moreover, I could not claim to be opposed to war as a matter of general principle. There were occasions, I believed, when a nation was justified in using military force to achieve its ends, to stop a Hitler or some comparable evil, and I told myself that in such circumstances I would've willingly marched off to the battle. The problem, though, was that a draft board did not let you choose your war.

Beyond all this, or at the very center, was the raw fact of terror. I did not want to die. Not ever. But certainly not then, not there, not in a wrong war. Driving up Main Street, past the courthouse and the Ben Franklin store, I sometimes felt the fear spreading inside me like weeds. I imagined myself dead. I imagined myself doing things I could not do—charging an enemy position, taking aim at another human being.

Beyond all this . . . was the raw fact of terror. I did not want to die.

At some point in mid-July I began thinking seriously about Canada. The border lay a few hundred miles north, an eight-hour drive. Both my conscience and my instincts were telling me to make a break for it, just take off and run like hell and never stop. In the beginning the idea seemed purely abstract, the word Canada printing itself out in my head; but after a time I could see particular shapes and images, the sorry details of my own future—a hotel room in Winnipeg, a battered old suitcase, my father's eyes as I tried to explain myself over the telephone. I could almost hear his voice, and my mother's. Run, I'd think. Then I'd think, Impossible. Then a second later I'd think, *Run.*

---

12. **eviscerate** (i vis′ə rāt′) *v.* remove the internal organs.
13. **CO,** conscientious objector: person with moral or religious objections to serving in the armed forces.

On the Rainy River   **815**

6 Literary Element
Symbolism

Symbolism involves the use of a concrete object, action, or character to stand for an abstract concept or idea. Ask students to consider O'Brien's job at the meat-packing plant and the imagery the author uses to describe it.

Question   What does this job symbolize? *(Possible response:The systematic slaughter of pigs symbolizes the horrors of war, involving many similar sights, sounds, and even smells.)*

7 Historical Note
The Draft for the Vietnam War

The draft for the Vietnam War was determined by a lottery system established in 1969. During that time, young men could sometimes obtain official status as conscientious objectors based on their ethics; however, if their objections were specific to the war in Vietnam, status could not be granted. As a result, many men of draftable age left the United States, often sneaking across the Canadian border.

BUILDING ENGLISH PROFICIENCY

Analyzing Sensory Detail

Help students understand that a writer uses sensory details to make an experience come alive for the reader.

- Let students share reactions to Tim's job. Be sure they see how the job relates to his draft problem. (His "life seemed to be collapsing toward slaughter.")

- Explain that O'Brien uses details of sight, sound, and smell to give us the feeling that we are experiencing Tim's job. Have students work together in groups to complete the graphic organizer shown.

Sights	Sounds	Smells
split down the length of the belly	a quick spattering sound	dense greasy pig-stink

13 Literary Element
Characterization

Characterization refers to the methods—involving speech, thoughts, and behavior—that an author uses to develop the personality of a character.

Question What does O'Brien reveal about Berdahl—and how does he do it—in these two paragraphs? (*Possible response: He evokes Berdahl's essence, as well as the mood that surrounds him. He describes his silences and his compact way of speaking. He also uses descriptive details to convey Berdahl's intelligence.*)

14 Reader's Response
Challenging the Text

Questions

- What do you think Berdahl means when he says, "There's Jesus"? (*Possible responses: Perhaps he sees the owl as a symbol of Christ [or the Holy Ghost] rising from the dead and hovering in the air; perhaps he means that nature can offer redemptive possibilities; perhaps that in the world around us miraculous things happen in the fluttering of a wing.*)

- What part of O'Brien's description of Berdahl does this bit of dialogue support? (*That when he speaks at all, he has "a way of compressing large thoughts into small, cryptic packets of language."*)

We spent six days together at the Tip Top Lodge. Just the two of us. Tourist season was over, and there were no boats on the river, and the wilderness seemed to withdraw into a great permanent stillness. Over those six days Elroy Berdahl and I took most of our meals together. In the mornings we sometimes went out on long hikes into the woods, and at night we played Scrabble or listened to records or sat reading in front of his big stone fireplace. At times I felt the awkwardness of an intruder, but Elroy accepted me into his quiet routine without fuss or ceremony. He took my presence for granted, the same way he might've sheltered a stray cat—no wasted sighs or pity—and there was never any talk about it. Just the opposite. What I remember more than anything is the man's willful, almost ferocious silence. In all that time together, all those hours, he never asked the obvious questions: Why was I there? Why alone? Why so preoccupied?[20] If Elroy was curious about any of this, he was careful never to put it into words.

My hunch, though, is that he already knew. At least the basics. After all, it was 1968, and guys were burning draft cards, and Canada was just a boat ride away. Elroy Berdahl was no hick. His bedroom, I remember, was cluttered with books and newspapers. He killed me at the Scrabble board, barely concentrating, and on those occasions when speech was necessary he had a way of compressing large thoughts into small, cryptic packets of language. One evening, just at sunset, he pointed up at an owl circling over the violet-lighted forest to the west.

"Hey, O'Brien," he said. "There's Jesus."

The man was sharp—he didn't miss much. Those razor eyes. Now and then he'd catch me staring out at the river, at the far shore, and I could almost hear the tumblers clicking in his head. Maybe I'm wrong, but I doubt it.

One thing for certain, he knew I was in desperate trouble. And he knew I couldn't talk about it. The wrong word—or even the right word—and I would've disappeared. I was wired and jittery. My skin felt too tight. After supper one evening I vomited and went back to my cabin and lay down for a few moments and then vomited again; another time, in the middle of the afternoon, I began sweating and couldn't shut it off. I went through whole days feeling dizzy with sorrow. I couldn't sleep; I couldn't lie still. At night I'd toss around in bed, half awake, half dreaming, imagining how I'd sneak down to the beach and quietly push one of the old man's boats out into the river and start paddling my way toward Canada. There were times when I thought I'd gone off the psychic edge. I couldn't tell up from down, I was just falling, and late in the night I'd lie there watching weird pictures spin through my head. Getting chased by the Border Patrol—helicopters and searchlights and barking dogs—I'd be crashing through the woods, I'd be down on my hands and knees—people shouting out my name—the law closing in on all sides—my hometown draft board and the FBI and the Royal Canadian Mounted Police. It all seemed crazy and impossible. Twenty-one years old, an ordinary kid with all the ordinary dreams and ambitions, and all I wanted was to live the life I was born to—a mainstream life—I loved baseball and hamburgers and cherry Cokes—and now I was off on the margins of exile, leaving my country forever, and it seemed so impossible and terrible and sad.

I'm not sure how I made it through those six days. Most of it I can't remember. On two or three afternoons, to pass some time, I helped Elroy get the place ready for winter, sweeping down the cabins and hauling in the boats, little chores that kept my body moving. The days were cool and bright. The nights were very dark. One morning the old man showed me how to split and stack firewood, and for several hours we just worked in silence out behind his house. At one point, I remember, Elroy put down his maul and looked at me for a long time, his lips

---

20. **preoccupied** (prē ok′yə pīd), *adj.* absorbed; engrossed.

MINI-LESSON: READING/THINKING SKILLS

Making Lists

Teach Direct students' attention to the sentence in the second column on this page that begins "Twenty-one years old. . . ." Discuss how the author uses a list to illustrate who he is, what he loves, and what he sees as his destiny.

Activity Idea Instruct students to make lists representing their own lives. Ask them to

- describe the kinds of people they are, illustrating their descriptions with lists of the things they love
- add illustrations to their lists
- trade lists anonymously and try to guess who wrote the list they have

Review some of the descriptions of Elroy Berdahl. Do you envision a man like the one in Doug Brega's portrait, *Emerson* (1986)? Why or why not?

On the Rainy River **819**

Art Study

Answer to Caption Question Many students will agree that Brega's portrait brings Berdahl to mind. This man has Berdahl's sympathetic look and wears similar clothes. He doesn't look as old or shrunken, however, and does not appear to be bald.

Visual Literacy In this realistic portrait, the subject, Emerson, is captured in a thoughtful pose. Like Berdahl, he appears to be a solitary man—conveyed by the shadow that slightly obscures his eyes and face. Despite the shadow, his eyes reveal much about him, including compassion and sadness.

Question What might this man be looking at? *(Answers will vary, but it seems to be something that does not please him.)*

The World of Work

For the real-life experiences of a **resort owner and operator** use the pages referenced below.

 The World of Work *pp. 25–26*

BUILDING ENGLISH PROFICIENCY

Expanding Vocabulary Notebooks

Students can continue to add unusual words and expressions to their vocabulary notebooks.

- Have students divide into small groups. Ask them to find five words or expressions on page 818 that they think some classmates may not know (for example, *hick, compressing, cryptic, tumblers clicking, psychic, mainstream life*). Have them check a dictionary and write definitions for the words they listed.

- See how many words were chosen by more than one group. List only these words on the chalkboard, and have students add them, with definitions, to their vocabulary notebooks.

- For an added challenge, have students attempt to write sample sentences using two of the words in each sentence.

Point of View

Lead a class discussion on the shifts of perspective or point of view in the first six paragraphs on this page.

Questions

- What is the narrator's point of view in the first paragraph? *(Possible response: He describes things as seen from very close up; he presents an almost magnified view.)*

- What is the effect of this perspective? *(Students may respond that it enables the reader to experience the narrator's moment of decision almost in slow motion, as we sometimes experience the most important moments of our lives.)*

- What is the effect when for the first time O'Brien includes the second person—or you—in his story? *(Possible response: It is surprising; it stops the story's action mid-moment. It makes the reader feel as though he is listening to a friend.)*

- Why do you think the author chose to use this device? *(Students may suggest that the author wanted his readers to be truly involved in—to feel—the most climactic moment in the story. It is also a way of ensuring the reader's attention, of drawing one in.)*

I remember staring at the old man, then at my hands, then at Canada. The shoreline was dense with brush and timber. I could see tiny red berries on the bushes. I could see a squirrel up in one of the birch trees, a big crow looking at me from a boulder along the river. That close—twenty yards—and I could see the delicate latticework of the leaves, the texture of the soil, the browned needles beneath the pines, the configurations of geology and human history. Twenty yards. I could've done it. I could've jumped and started swimming for my life. Inside me, in my chest, I felt a terrible squeezing pressure. Even now, as I write this, I can still feel that tightness. And I want you to feel it—the wind coming off the river, the waves, the silence, the wooded frontier. You're at the bow of a boat on the Rainy River. You're twenty-one years old, you're scared, and there's a hard squeezing pressure in our chest.

What would you do?

Would you jump? Would you feel pity for yourself? Would you think about your family and your childhood and your dreams and all you're leaving behind? Would it hurt? Would it feel like dying? Would you cry, as I did?

I tried to swallow it back. I tried to smile, except I was crying.

Now, perhaps, you can understand why I've never told this story before. It's not just the embarrassment of tears. That's part of it, no doubt, but what embarrasses me much more, and always will, is the paralysis that took my heart. A moral freeze: I couldn't decide, I couldn't act, I couldn't comport[22] myself with even a pretense of modest human dignity.

20 All I could do was cry. Quietly, not bawling, just the chest-chokes.

At the rear of the boat Elroy Berdahl pretended not to notice. He held a fishing rod in his hands, his head bowed to hide his eyes. He kept humming a soft, monotonous little tune. Everywhere, it seemed, in the trees and water and sky, a great worldwide sadness came pressing down on me, a crushing sorrow, sorrow like I had never known it before. And what was so sad, I realized, was that Canada had become a pitiful fantasy. Silly and hopeless. It was no longer a possibility. Right then, with the shore so close, I understood that I would not do what I should do. I would not swim away from my hometown and my country and my life. I would not be brave. That old image of myself as a hero, as a man of conscience and courage, all that was just a threadbare pipe dream. Bobbing there on the Rainy River, looking back at the Minnesota shore, I felt a sudden swell of helplessness come over me, a drowning sensation, as if I had toppled overboard and was being swept away by the silver waves. Chunks of my own history flashed by. I saw a seven-year-old boy in a white cowboy hat and a Lone Ranger mask and a pair of holstered six-shooters; I saw a twelve-year-old Little League shortstop pivoting to turn a double play; I saw a sixteen-year-old kid decked out for his first prom, looking spiffy in a white tux and a black bow tie, his hair cut short and flat, his shoes freshly polished. My whole life seemed to spill out into the river, swirling away from me, everything I had ever been or ever wanted to be. I couldn't get my breath; I couldn't stay afloat; I couldn't tell which way to swim. A hallucination, I suppose, but it was as real as anything I would ever feel. I saw my parents calling to me from the far shoreline. I saw my brother and sister, all the townsfolk, the mayor and the entire Chamber of Commerce and all my old teachers and girlfriends and high school buddies. Like some weird sporting event: everybody screaming from the sidelines, rooting me on—a loud stadium roar. Hotdogs and popcorn—stadium smells, stadium heat. A squad of cheerleaders did cartwheels along the banks of the Rainy River; they had megaphones and pompoms and smooth brown thighs. The crowd swayed left and right. A marching band played fight songs. All my aunts and uncles were there, and

---

22. **comport** (kəm pôrt′), *v.* conduct (oneself) in a certain manner; behave.

MINI-LESSON: VOCABULARY

Recognize Idioms

Teach Remind students that idioms are figures of speech that cannot be understood from the ordinary meanings of the words in them. Idioms are often derived from culturally-shared ideas and activities. Direct students' attention to this phrase:

. . . all that was just a threadbare pipe dream . . .

Discuss the fact that *threadbare*, *pipe*, and *dream* all have very distinct meanings when used separately, but together they create an entirely new and very explicit image of lost hope.

Activity Ideas

- Invite students to find other idioms in this and other selections.
- Have them share their findings with the class and analyze the meanings of each idiom discussed.

Response to Caption Question
Students will probably say that the mood is tranquil, still, or perhaps a bit moody or ominous.

21 Literary Element
Style

Questions

- What is the effect of O'Brien's long list of people that begins on page 822 and ends on 824? *(Possible response: By listing these many and disparate people—real people, fictional people, people from his own and our country's past, as well as from his future—O'Brien creates a visual time line for the reader. It is a parade of supporters who have contributed to making him who he is and will be.)*

- Why do you think the author uses only one sentence to describe much of his vision? *(Possible response: His vision comes over him in a rush, with little continuity. His sentence flows and swirls, like the river, unbroken by pauses. Words and vision stretch from the distant past to the imminent future with no particular order or symmetry.)*

How would you describe the mood of Ken Moylan's 1995 painting, *Boundary Lake?* Is it the same as, or does it contrast with, the mood of the story?

Abraham Lincoln, and Saint George, and a nine-year-old girl named Linda who had died of a brain tumor back in fifth grade, and several members of the United States Senate, and a blind poet scribbling notes, and LBJ, and Huck Finn, and Abbie Hoffman, and all the dead soldiers back from the grave, and the many thousands who were later to die—villagers with terrible burns, little kids without arms or legs— yes, and the Joint Chiefs of Staff were there, and a couple of popes, and a first lieutenant named Jimmy Cross, and the last surviving veteran of the American Civil War, and Jane Fonda dressed up as Barbarella, and an old man sprawled beside a pigpen, and my grandfather, and Gary Cooper, and a kind-faced woman carrying an umbrella and a copy of Plato's *Republic*, and a million ferocious citizens waving flags of all **21**

On the Rainy River **823**

BUILDING ENGLISH PROFICIENCY

Making Personal Connections

On page 822, Tim asks, "What would you do?" Invite students to imagine that they all have been drafted to fight a war that they hate. Ask: What might be your reasons for fighting or refusing to fight? On the graphic organizer shown, have them list either Tim's reasons or their own reasons for serving or not serving in such a war. Have them write either *TIM* or *ME* between the two blocks of reasons.

FIGHT
- Everyone expects it.
- Be patriotic.
- Others are dying for you.

→ **TIM** ←

DON'T FIGHT
- You may get killed.
- Your whole life is ahead of you.
- This war is wrong.

WRITING CHOICES

Writer's Notebook Update

Encourage students to compare the steps involved in each decision-making process. How were they similar and how were they different?

A Letter from Vietnam

You might encourage students to do library research to find letters written home by real soldiers fighting real wars. Assign each student to present one such letter to the class for discussion.

Berdahl's Perspective

Tell students to consider how Berdahl's style of speaking might relate to his style of writing. As an intelligent man, would he write in an intellectual or literary style? Or would he write as he speaks—sparely and colloquially?

The Things He Carried

You might suggest that students brainstorm an intangible associated with or symbolized by each physical item. For example, a family photograph might represent memories, weapons could symbolize bravado, and a religious medal could stand for faith.

Selection Test

Unit 7 Resource Book
pp. 79–80

Expressing Your Ideas

Writing Choices

Writer's Notebook Update Before you read "On the Rainy River," you wrote about an important decision you once made. In one or two paragraphs, write a comparison between the decision the character O'Brien made and the decision you made. How did each of you arrive at your decisions?

A Letter from Vietnam Imagine you are O'Brien. You've been shipped out to the steamy jungles of Vietnam. Write a **letter** home, telling your parents about the war, about your experiences. What will you talk about in your letter? What will your tone be like? Will you be bitter? Will you be upbeat? Will you reveal your fear, or will you put up a brave front?

Berdahl's Perspective O'Brien isn't able to say much about Berdahl, and is only able to make a few guesses about what he is thinking. What do *you* think Berdahl's opinion of O'Brien is? If Berdahl had been keeping a journal, what might he have written about O'Brien? Write three **diary entries** for Berdahl, one for the first night of O'Brien's stay, one for the night after O'Brien refuses to take Berdahl's money, and one for the night after O'Brien leaves.

The Things He Carried "On the Rainy River" is a chapter from the author Tim O'Brien's book, *The Things They Carried.* The title of the book refers to the things a soldier takes into combat—not necessarily all physical items like weapons, but also intangibles such as fear, confusion, and memories. Working in small groups, make a **list** of the tangible and intangible things your group thinks the character O'Brien might have carried with him to Vietnam. Present your list to the rest of the class, explaining each item.

Other Options

O'Brien's Approval Rating When he's on the boat, O'Brien has a vision of a crowd of people watching him. Choose one of the historical figures or events mentioned and research information about it. Give an **oral report** of your findings, including visual prompts such as maps, charts, or photos.

Designer for a Day You are a graphic designer assigned to create a **poster** that promotes the Hollywood film *On the Rainy River.* What will you draw that will capture the interest of the movie-going public? Using a piece of tag board, create your poster. When you've finished your art, add a few lines of text— whatever you think will best promote the film.

Looking Back Do some in-depth **interviews** about the Vietnam War. Ask family members, neighbors, and teachers about their opinions of the war. Did they support the war in Vietnam? Why or why not? In retrospect, do they think the Vietnam War needed to be fought? As a class, write a list of at least ten interview questions, and then each student can interview up to five people. Capture your interviews on video camera, and then play the tape for your class. Your class may also want to compile the survey results on a **chart.**

OTHER OPTIONS

O'Brien's Approval Rating

In preparing their reports, encourage students to consult books, magazine articles, and, if available, computer sources such as CD-ROM multimedia encyclopedias and the Internet.

Designer for a Day

Encourage students to examine past and present movie posters for ideas on how to write promotional text. Old movie posters can often be observed at specialized stores, film museums, and movie theaters.

Looking Back

Remind students of some of the techniques for successful interviewing—for example, looking directly at the interviewee; making sure that he or she has completed the answer to one question before asking the next; and avoiding distracting personal habits such as fidgeting or doodling during the interview.

Before Reading

from Where the Ashes Are

by Nguyên Qúi Dú'c

Nguyên Qúi Dú'c
born 1959

Nguyên Qúi Dú'c was born to an upper-class Vietnamese family. His mother was a school principal; his father was a high-ranking civil servant in the South Vietnamese government. During the Tet offensive, Dú'c's father was seized by the Vietcong and imprisoned for sixteen years. Dú'c's mother, no longer allowed to teach school, began selling noodles in the street. At age eighteen, Dú'c moved to the United States where he eventually became a reporter for National Public Radio. In his first book, *Where the Ashes Are,* Dú'c describes the profound effect the Vietnam War had on his family.

Building Background

The Tet Offensive In late January of 1968, during the Vietnamese holiday of Tet, the Vietcong attacked all the major cities in South Vietnam simultaneously. Most of the people of South Vietnam were caught off-guard by the Tet offensive because they believed the holiday of Tet would be held sacred and a cease-fire agreement would be honored by the government of North Vietnam. The destruction of lives and property during Tet was overwhelming; thousands of civilians were killed or made homeless, and entire cities were leveled. In his autobiography, Nguyên Qúi Dú'c—who was nine years old in 1968—describes the terrifying days of the Tet offensive.

Literary Focus

Imagery Nguyên Qúi Dú'c uses imagery—word pictures that appeal to any of the senses—to bring vividness to the frightening scenes he describes. Imagery may appeal to the reader's sense of sight, hearing, taste, smell, or motor activity (motion or feeling). Using a web similar to the one below, make some notes about Dú'c's use of imagery as you read his story.

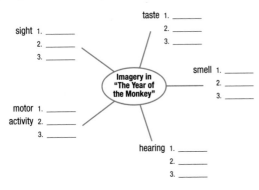

Writer's Notebook

In your notebook, make a list of the words and images that you associate with war and its affects on people and property.

Where the Ashes Are   **827**

Before Reading

Building Background

You might mention to students that Egypt and Syria used a similar military strategy five years later to start the October War in 1973. They caught Israelis off-guard by attacking on Yom Kippur (the Day of Atonement), the holiest day of the Jewish year.

Literary Focus

Discuss with students how **imagery** is one way for writers to *show* rather than simply *tell* about people, places, and things, creating a fuller and more complete experience for their readers.

Writer's Notebook

You might encourage students to *freewrite* for five minutes before making their lists, reacting quickly and without critical concern to the word *war*. Students can use the results as the basis for their lists.

More About Nguyên Qúi Dú'c

When Nguyên Qúi Dú'c arrived in the United States, he possessed only a smattering of English; old, torn bell-bottoms; and an overwhelming sense of loss. He lived with his older brother and his family, who had also taken in his sister Dieu-Hà. For a time, his closest companion was his brother's three-year-old son, Donnie.

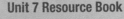

SUPPORT MATERIALS OVERVIEW

Unit 7 Resource Book
- Graphic Organizer, p. 81
- Study Guide, p. 82
- Vocabulary, p. 83
- Grammar, p. 84
- Alternate Check Test, p. 85
- Vocabulary Test, p. 86
- Selection Test, pp. 87–88

Building English Proficiency
- Literature Summaries
- Activities, p. 231

Reading, Writing & Grammar SkillBook
- Vocabulary, pp. 14–16
- Reading, pp. 41–45
- Writing, pp. 137–138
- Grammar, Usage, and Mechanics, pp. 144–145

Technology
- Audiotape
- Personal Journal Software
- Custom Literature Database: For another selection dealing with an Asian nation at war, see "Recruiting Officer of Shih-hao" by Tu Fu on the database. Also see the war poems of Siegfried Sassoon and Wilfred Owen on the database.
- Test Generator Software

During Reading

Selection Objectives

- To identify the use of imagery
- To explore the struggle experienced by a family during war
- To analyze grammatical structures by diagramming sentences

 Unit 7 Resource Book
Graphic Organizer, p. 81
Study Guide, p. 82

Theme Link

When the Tet Offensive surprises the Nguyên family on a holiday visit, nine-year-old Dú'c finds himself In a struggle that will change his family forever.

Vocabulary Preview

defunct, no longer in use

escalation, act of increasing or expanding rapidly in stages

intricately, elaborately

affiliation, association or connection with a group or organization

opulence, wealth; riches

Students can add the words and definitions to their Writer's Notebooks.

1 Literary Element
Dialogue

Question What is the effect of Dú'c's opening his story with dialogue? *(It creates a quick and dramatic beginning, pulling the reader immediately into the action.)*

Where the Ashes Are

Nguyên Qúi Dú'c

1

"Wake up, wake up!" my mother shouted. "We've got to get out of here! How can you sleep through all this?" She pulled the covers off me, handed me my clothes, and rushed out of the room.

"Wait!" I cried out, throwing off my pajamas. One leg in and one out of my dark blue school trousers, I stumbled over to my sister Dieu-Hà's room. My mother was yelling, "Are you deaf? Get out! We're going downstairs!"

It was five in the morning. Explosions and gunfire echoed through the high-ceilinged rooms of the government guest house. Arched corridors surrounded the twenty bedrooms on the second floor of the massive French-style mansion. My parents had taken the master suite at the end of the hall while my two sisters and I had large rooms next to one another. We had arrived at the end of January 1968, two days before the lunar New Year. Our family were the only guests in the building. Rather than having us stay at my grandfather's small house, my father felt we would be safer at the guest house, where extra platoons of local soldiers had been assigned to protect him. He also preferred the guest house because it was built along the bank of the river in Hue, the old imperial city, and away

828   UNIT SEVEN: YEARS OF CHANGE

SELECTION SUMMARY

Where the Ashes Are

Nguyên Qúi Dú'c recalls how his family was torn apart by the 1968 Tet Offensive. The author was nine-years-old at the time; his father worked as a civilian deputy to a South Vietnamese governor. Dú'c describes how his father chose, despite threats of increasing military activity, to take his wife and children to visit his parents in the city of Hué. He assumed that there would be no problem during the New Year's holiday, but, wanting to be cautious, brought his family to stay at a local government guest house where they would be guarded by soldiers. Dú'c describes how the holiday fireworks turned to gunfire as the Vietcong invaded the area. The family was among those captured, and Dú'c, his mother, and his sisters were

held in a nearby basement, while his father was imprisoned in the government house. Dú'c tells of his mother's strength and courage, protecting her children—including Dú'c's older sister, who was mentally ill—and allaying their fears. Eventually the family was allowed to see Dú'c's father before he was taken away for "re-education." At the close of the section, Dú'c describes his father, hands bound to his body as he is led away by Communist soldiers. Assured that they would only be parted for a short time, the family would not be reunited for sixteen years.

 *For Summaries in other Languages, see the **Building English Proficiency** book.*

Response to Caption Question Most
students will see that they appear to be
very troubled and anxious, huddling
close to one another for support. They
are eager and alert, and appear to be
looking toward someone or something
that they hope will help them.

Visual Literacy Notice how tightly
the photographer has framed this image,
giving the viewer a feeling of confine-
ment. The colorful shirt and staunch
pose of the woman in the foreground
gives one the sense that she is the
leader (perhaps the mother) of the
group.

Question What do you think these
people might be thinking or getting
ready to say? *(Possible response:
The girl may be about to ask the older
woman what is going to happen to them.
The boys appear to be wondering what
is going on. The older woman looks as
though she is about to ask for [or
demand] information.)*

This photograph by William Albert Allard shows South Vietnamese refugees arriving in Hong Kong in 1979. What do their expressions and body language relate about what they're experiencing?

Where the Ashes Are **829**

BUILDING ENGLISH PROFICIENCY

Making Personal Connections

The writer describes what happened to his family in 1968 when Vietcong soldiers attacked Hue. Help students think about what happened to their own families in the 1960s and in the decades since then.

- Ask students to draw a time line like the one shown.
- Have them record one important family event in the space marking each decade.

My family immigrated to the U.S.	My family got its first TV.	I was born!	
My parents married.	My grandfather died.	My sister was born!	
1960s	1970s	1980s	1990s

Response The visit is risky because Dú'c's father has been warned that there may be increasing military action. However, he assumes that he and his family will be safe because it is the New Year's holiday and both sides have agreed to stop fighting.

3 Geographical Note
The Rice Fields of Southern Vietnam

Located in Southeast Asia, southern Vietnam contains the large delta of the Mekong River. Temperatures are tropical—ranging from 79 degrees Fahrenheit (26 degrees Celsius) to 85 degrees Fahrenheit (30 degrees Celsius) throughout the year. As a result, the land is well suited to the cultivation of rice, the export of which is the country's main source of income.

4 Literary Focus
Imagery

Discuss with students the senses Dú'c appeals to when he describes his family's flight downstairs in response to gunfire. *(Responses may include the following— Sight: the marble steps and carved banister, the elephant tusks in the vestibule, the view of the Sông Hu'o'ng River, the dark foliage visible from the window, the orange and red fire of the rockets; Sound: the explosions of the firecrackers and gunfire, Dieu-Hà's scream; Motor activity: the race downstairs, the chilly wind in the reception hall)*

---

from the town's noisy center. The nearby train station was defunct,[1] since the war had disrupted all but a few railway lines.

For many years my father had been working for the government of South Viet Nam. Assigned to central Viet Nam as a civilian deputy to the military governor, he was based in Dà Nang, a coastal town just over an hour's drive from Hue. He sent us to visit his parents there regularly, especially at holidays. He came along on this holiday visit—for the lunar New Year, Tet, in 1968.

Although my father had been warned about a possible escalation[2] in the fighting, he said to my mother: "There's a ceasefire. It's New Year's. We'll be safe." But he abandoned his plan to drive and instead arranged for a flight to Hue. We'd landed at the Phú Bài airport in midafternoon.

2 SUMMARIZE: What possible dangers does the visit present? Why does the family decide to proceed with the visit?

The road into town had been taken over by an endless convoy of tanks and army trucks transporting U.S. soldiers, most likely toward Khe Sanh, an American base that had been under siege for several months. Along with a few other civilian cars, small trucks, and innumerable[3] motorcycles, we inched our way toward Hue. I kept looking out the car window, glimpsing rice fields here and there. Mostly, though, the view was blocked by the olive green steel of tanks and trucks.

My mother sought to distract us. "You kids are going to be spoiled this year. I bet your grandparents will have lots of treats for you. But I want you to behave."

Settled in at the guest house, on the second night of our stay my mother and sisters and I fell asleep just after twelve, insulated by its thick walls and heavy curtains. Endless rounds of firecrackers went off as the people of Hue

celebrated the arrival of Tet. No one knew that along with the Year of the Monkey, the dreaded Viet Cong soldiers had also arrived. No one could tell when the firecrackers stopped and the gunfire began.

Dieu-Hà and I followed my mother into my other sister's room. Dieu-Qùynh had buried herself under a pile of blankets. Ma shook her. "Come on, we're going downstairs!" As she started to rifle through Dieu-Qùynh's drawers, grabbing clothes for her to change into, she said to Dieu-Hà and me, "Go see if your father's downstairs, and stay with him!"

We rushed down the corridors toward the double staircase. Its marble steps formed a half-circle framed by an intricately[4] carved banister. A bullet shattered a porthole as we skipped down the steps. Dieu-Hà screamed. Pieces of glass and marble flew by. We raced past the elephant tusks in the huge vestibule and toward the reception hall. A chilly wind blew through the huge room. Someone had opened the drapes and shutters of the dozens of windows rising from knee level to ten feet above my head, each framing a view of the River of Perfume, Sông Hu'o'ng.

In the somber light I could make out dark foliage swaying by the riverbank as a coat of morning mist rose above the water. Nature paints winter scenes in Hue in shades of gray, but this morning I could see rapid bursts of orange and red fire coming from behind the bushes. A flare shot out from the far distance. Exploding with a thud, it hung from a small parachute and cast a brilliant midday light over a large area of the river as it floated down. Rockets exploded across the burning sky and fell to the ground in rapid succession. Deafened, Dieu-Hà and I dove **4**

---

1. **defunct** (di fungkt'), *adj.* no longer in use.
2. **escalation** (es'kə lā'shən), *n.* act of increasing or expanding rapidly in stages.
3. **innumerable** (i nü'mər ə bəl), *adj.* too many to count.
4. **intricately** (in'trə kit lē), *adv.* elaborately.

MINI-LESSON: GRAMMAR
Analyzing Grammatical Structure

Teach Diagramming sentences can help students understand the parts of a sentence and different parts of speech. Draw the diagrams to the right on the board.

The most basic diagram divides a simple sentence into subject and predicate. More complicated diagrams divide complex sentences into branches.

Activity Invite students to diagram other sentences from the selection.

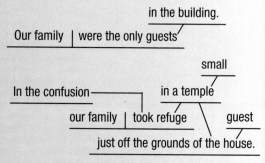

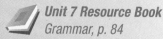

Unit 7 Resource Book
Grammar, p. 84

behind an antique cabinet at the end of the room. My father had been nowhere in sight.

That night he had stayed up late to read a French book that contrasted two warriors: North Viet Nam's famed general Võ Nguyên Giáp and William Westmoreland, commander of the U.S. ground troops in South Viet Nam. Just before four o'clock Cha[5] had left his bed and gone up to the rooftop terrace, where he marveled at the red and green tracers flying across the sky like shooting stars. Despite his interest in the generals, he had little understanding of the role of flares and tracers as tools of warfare. They were simply a beautiful sight as they burst over the night sky.

"Your father's still up there. Been on that roof an hour! He'll get killed!" Ma wailed as she came down the staircase. Seeing the open windows, she took us into a chamber behind the reception room. "Where's Dieu-Quỳnh?" she exclaimed. "She was just on the stairs with me!"

In the midst of the gunfire and explosions, my sister had gone back to bed—a mad thing to do, since bullets were now flying indoors. By 1968, however, most of what Dieu-Quỳnh did was irrational. For four years she had been showing signs of mental illness. Ordering Dieu-Hà and me to sit still, my mother dashed back upstairs. A bullet came through Dieu-Quỳnh's room, hitting the lamp on her bedstand. Sparks flew in all directions. Ma grabbed my older sister by the wrist and led her downstairs, calling out to my father all the while.

"We shouldn't worry too much," he said in his usual unruffled tone when he entered the room a few minutes later. When he had finally left the roof, he went downstairs to look for the butler, then into an office off the living room. "I called the provincial office; they say the fighting is far away."

"Look out the windows!" my mother shot back.

"I did," Cha replied, still calm and composed. "Our soldiers are still at their posts." From the rooftop he had been able to see men in green surrounding the guest house.

We gathered together, crouching on the floor. No one spoke. My father glanced at the spacious desk and heavy armchairs, hoping to hide behind the furniture until the gunfire died down.

Between explosions came the sound of someone knocking at the front door. My parents put out their arms. We sat still. The pounding grew louder. After a moment of hesitation, Ma stood up. "It's our soldiers," she declared. "Come on!" My sisters followed her through the reception area to the vestibule. As my father and I reached the door to the reception room, we heard her scream.

My father led me back to the office in the back, locking the door behind him as quietly as possible. We went to the desk, and I held his hand as we lowered ourselves behind it. My father didn't know what else to do. Spotting a steel safe in the corner of the room, he went over to open it, then without a word closed it again. Not even a nine-year-old boy could fit inside.

"I have a young son in the house," my mother was explaining to the intruders in the vestibule, Viet Cong soldiers in olive green uniforms. They wore no insignia or badges that showed affiliation[6] or rank. Whether because of the darkness or distance, his poor eyesight, or his unfamiliarity with military matters, my father had mistaken them for our own Southern Republican Army troops.

One of the soldiers now threatened to shoot anyone still hiding in the house. "Tell us where everyone is and you'll be safe, Sister," he assured my mother.

"Please, please don't hurt us, please!" she begged. "Just let me go find my son."

Cha groped behind the heavy dark green drapes along the office wall, where a set of double doors opened onto a hallway. We tiptoed through the hall to the doors that led outside. My father **6**

---

5. **Cha**, Father. *[Vietnamese]*
6. **affiliation** (ə fil′ē ā′shən) *n.* association or connection with a group or organization.

5 Literary Element
Characterization

Ask students to consider how Dú'c characterizes the members of his family in the first column of page 831.

Question How does each member's response to the gunfire serve to represent his or her personality? *(Possible responses: The father is calm, studious, inexperienced in military matters, and perhaps a bit of a dreamer, reacting to the beauty of the flares and tracers and neglecting to come down from the roof when the gunfire starts. The mother is practical and emotional, a woman of action who mobilizes her family for safety. Sister Dieu-Quỳnh's mental instability is illustrated by her ignoring the crisis and trying to go back to bed. Dú'c and Dieu-Hà are hiding behind a cabinet, as frightened children will.)*

6 Literary Element
Style

Style refers to the distinctive handling of language by an author, involving choices made regarding diction, syntax, and so on.

Question What is your impression of Dú'c 's writing style, based on the episode where the soldiers arrive at the mansion. *(Students may use words such as* straightforward, clear, emotional, *and* involved *to describe Dú'c's style, noting how he uses everyday language; short, simple sentences with strong action verbs; and dramatic dialogue.)*

BUILDING ENGLISH PROFICIENCY

Exploring Suspense

Help students recognize that a well-written narrative keeps you in suspense about what will happen next.

- Ask students to divide into groups of four.
- Have them create a chart like the one at the right, using the left-hand column to list five events on pages 830–831 in chronological order.

- Have each group review the events it listed. Beside each event, ask students to note in the right-hand column a question that makes them want to keep reading until they find the answer.

Events	Questions
The family arrives in Hue.	Will the enemy attack?

832

7 Historical Note

Ho Chí Minh and Charles de Gaulle

Ho Chí Minh [*Hoh Chee Min*] was the president of North Vietnam from 1945 to 1969. Charles de Gaulle was the president of France from 1958 to 1969. From 1946–1954, Ho led the North Vietnamese government in an ultimately successful battle against France for its independence from French Indochina. When the French soldier says to the Vietcong soldiers that de Gaulle and Ho are friends, he may be suggesting that France no longer bears North Vietnam any malice.

8 Active Reading

Clarify

Response   Because if the soldiers were to discover his high rank in the South Vietnamese government, they might take revenge against him and his family.

9 Reading/Thinking Skills

Infer

Question   What do you think the Vietcong woman means when she says, "We'll take care of you"? *(Possible response: She is using irony to threaten Dú'c's father that now that he has been captured, he will be brought down to size—losing his elevated position and the material possessions that she, as a Communist, views as decadent or criminal. She may be threatening to kill him.)*

---

motioned me out first, then carefully closed the doors behind him. I ran down the steps and turned toward the hedges that separated the guest house grounds from the riverbank. "Hey, boy!" someone cried. I turned. A Viet Cong soldier sitting cross-legged pointed his rifle at me. I ran back to my father.

Back in the hallway inside the house, Cha quietly approached each door to the offices surrounding the reception area. A gun muzzle protruded from one, and we backed off. The doorway to yet another office also had a gun muzzle poking out from it. There was no escape.

Out in the courtyard it was still dark. Dozens of people in nightclothes shivered in the early morning dampness. Slowly the soldiers separated families from one another. The guest house was to be used as a temporary holding center. More people were brought into the courtyard. A disheveled[7] Frenchman of about thirty entered the area barefooted, a trench coat thrown on over his pajamas. Hands clasped together, he tried to explain his situation to two Viet Cong soldiers. "De Gaulle, Ho Chí Minh,[8] *amis*," he kept saying. "Friends."

The two Viet Cong waved him away. One of them shouted, *"Không biet tieng dâu!"*[9] They did not speak any foreign languages.

"They're regular soldiers," my father whispered to a man next to him, whose crisp white shirt was tucked into pajama trousers. "Such a strong northern accent."

"You're right," the man whispered back. "The way they call everybody 'Sister' and 'Brother' is strange." The men and women before us were not part of the so-called National Liberation Front[10] within South Viet Nam. Ho Chí Minh was now sending in troops from the North for an outright offensive, a full invasion.

In the confusion our family took refuge in a small temple just off the grounds of the guest house. Searching through his wallet, my father took out all his business cards and hid them under a mat. "Just say you're a teacher," whispered my mother.

CLARIFY: Why does Dú'c's father want to hide his identity from the soldiers? 8

He never had the chance. When a Viet Cong woman found us in the temple a little more than an hour later, she jabbed her index finger into his chest. "You, Brother, I know who you are," she said. "The Party and the Revolution will be generous to all those willing to confess their crimes against the People."

"The Party" could only be the Communist party headquartered in Hà Noi. The enemy's arm had now reached into the heart of Hue. "Don't lie!" the woman continued. Putting her finger up to my father's nose, she said, "Brother, we know—you're the general staying in this house. Such opulence.[11] We'll take care of you." 9

We lost track of the time as the soldiers sorted out all the people gathered in front of the guest house. At last, however, they accepted my father's protestations that he was not a general but a government functionary. He and the other men were taken inside the mansion. Women and children were sent to a neighboring building, down into a long rectangular basement with extremely thick walls and a single narrow door at one end. The rocket explosions had ceased, but the sound of gunfire continued. We had become accustomed to it and no longer jumped at the bursts from automatic weapons. Ten families followed each other below ground. I ended up leading the way into the darkness.

---

7. **disheveled** (də shev′əld), *adj.* rumpled; disordered.
8. **De Gaulle, Ho Chi Minh.** Charles de Gaulle was president of France from 1959 to 1969. Ho Chi Minh was president of North Vietnam from 1954 to 1969.
9. *Không biet tieng dâu,* I do not speak any foreign languages. *[Vietnamese]*
10. **National Liberation Front,** a political organization formed by the Vietcong in South Vietnam.
11 opulence (op′yə ləns), *n.* wealth; riches.

MINI-LESSON: VOCABULARY

Expand Vocabulary Using Structural Analysis

Teach   Discuss with students how suffixes can be added to create various grammatical forms from the same basic root.

Write the following nouns from the selection on the board: *escalation, affiliation, opulence.*

Activity Idea   Challenge students to

• Use a dictionary to find the words' roots, meanings, and origins.

• Brainstorm other grammatical forms of the words, such as adjectives and verbs.

• Analyze the words to figure out which suffixes are commonly used to form which parts of speech.

Word	Root	Meaning	Origin	Other forms
escalation				
affiliation				
opulence				

"Go to the far end. Go!" my mother urged me, and made sure that Dieu-Qùynh stayed with us. She knew that, on capturing a town, the Communists would use residents as workers to support military operations. Women would be sent to look for food, or nurse the wounded. If not required to take up arms themselves, men would have to gather the wounded and the dead. Dieu-Qùynh, a tall girl of eighteen, was at risk of being drafted for such service. Turning to the family behind her, my mother explained. "My daughter is ill. A big girl, but not all that wise." It was an explanation she would feel compelled to repeat often in the next days. I finally settled for a spot below a minuscule[12] window with iron bars. In the damp, cavernous basement, the tiny hole let in a faint ray of the light that signaled the first day of the Year of the Monkey.

Throughout that day and most of the next night the adults carried on a whispered debate, trying to make sense out of what had happened. "They can't win," the guest house chauffeur pronounced. "I bet they'll retreat soon. The Americans will bomb, and our troops will rescue us in a few days." My mother listened dispassionately. She sighed often, and refused to eat any of the food the family next to us offered. Busy with their prisoners in the mansion, the soldiers left us alone.

On our second day of captivity, a female voice shouted into the basement. "Mrs. Dai! Is there a Mrs. Dai down there?" My mother picked her way toward the door. "Your husband's up in the house. He wants to see you," the voice announced. My mother went up alone, warning me to keep my sister Dieu-Qùynh from wandering out. During the night, Dieu-Qùynh had been difficult, continually demanding hot water. For the last year or so she had been obsessed with matters of hygiene, compulsively washing her hands as well as any household utensils before she would use them. Finally realizing that this was a luxury, she now sat silent and withdrawn. I asked Dieu-Hà to stay with her, then went to sit at the door to wait for my mother.

The guns had gone quiet at some point without anyone noticing. More soldiers had arrived in the compound and were now setting up a crude hospital. A stretched-out army poncho served as an awning, sheltering three bamboo cots that had been shoved together. The soldiers put a mat of woven branches and leaves on top of the cots, enlarging the surface to accommodate five wounded men. Looking like pallbearers carrying a white porcelain coffin, three young men and a woman in civilian clothes brought in an ancient French bathtub. They filled the tub half full of water, warning us not to use it. No one seemed to be in charge, yet a lot of orders were being issued. Sitting by the door of the basement, I watched the men and women from the North. From the way they handled the everyday artifacts of city life, they must have spent years in the jungle. One came with a beer can with a pull tab on its top. He shook it, hearing the sound of sloshing liquid inside. When he pulled the tab and the beer exploded, he threw the can on the ground and ran away. "It's a grenade! A grenade!" he yelled. I dared not laugh.

Later, I watched two men struggle to start a motorized tricycle. They tried to push it, but the gears were engaged. They gave up after a while and walked away. Half an hour later they came back on two bicycles whose frames had been lashed together with branches, with which they were hauling a few bags of New Year's food: cakes of sticky rice stuffed with pork and green beans and wrapped in banana leaves. I was wondering who the food was for when my mother came back. "What are you doing here?" she asked, roughing up my hair. "We're going up to see your father in a while." She did not sound excited. After checking on my sisters, she set about looking for food for my father.

"Ma, what are they going to do with him?" I asked. I repeated the question again and again, [11]

---

12. **minuscule** (mi nus'kyŭl), *adj.* extremely small.

---

10 Literary Focus
Imagery

Question To which of his readers' senses does Dú'c appeal when he describes the spot where he and his siblings hid from the attention of the Vietcong? What images does he use? *(Possible responses: Sight—the tiny window with iron bars, the cavernous basement, the faint ray of light from outside; Motor activity: the dampness of the basement; Touch—the damp, cavernous basement)*

11 Literary Element
Narrator

Invite students to discuss what the narrator reveals when he describes himself as a nine-year-old child in a terrifying situation on page 833.

Questions

- What is the young Dú'c feeling? *(Possible responses: He is afraid and confused. He is concerned about his father and wants to know more about a situation which he doesn't understand.)*

- How would you describe the narrator's attitude toward himself as a child? *(Students may respond that he seems sympathetic with the child he once was, evoking for the reader a little boy afraid to laugh at the enemies' jokes and tugging at his mother's arm for information about his father.)*

BUILDING ENGLISH PROFICIENCY

Understanding Characters

Help students understand how the members of Dú'c's family relate to one another.

- Have students draw a family chart showing the five members of Dú'c's family (Dú'c himself, his father, his mother, and his two sisters). See the example at the right.

- Ask students to imagine that they are inside the mind of each family member during any of the events on these pages. Have them write down one or two thoughts for each person.

PERSON	THOUGHT
Dú'c	
Dú'c's father	"How can I make them believe I'm not a general?"
Dú'c's mother	
Dieu-Qùynh	
Dieu-Hà	"I wish Dú'c would stay with me. I'm so scared."

Questions

- What do you think the Vietcong mean by "re-education?" *(Students may respond that it is a euphemism for brainwashing.)*

- Why does Dú'c's mother tell him re-education is like school? *(Possible response: She wants to protect him.)*

13 Literary Element
Symbolism

Questions

- What do you think Dú'c's mother's jewelry and toilet case symbolize to the Vietcong? *(Possible response: Opulence and the domination of the wealthy over society.)*

- What might these items symbolize in the story of Dú'c's family? *(Perhaps the family's future—one of meaningless destruction and loss.)*

Check Test

1. Where are Dú'c and his family when the Tet Offensive begins? *(at a government guest house in the city of Hué)*

2. What is Dú'c's father's job? *(He is a civil servant for the government of South Vietnam.)*

3. Why isn't Dú'c's father concerned when the soldiers knock at the door of the guest house? *(He had seen them from the roof when the fighting began and had mistaken them for allies.)*

4. Where do the Vietcong force the members of Dú'c's family to stay? *(Dú'c's father is kept inside the mansion where the family has been living. The rest of the family is held in the basement of a local building.)*

5. What is wrong with the water the Vietcong allow Dú'c's mother to bring his father? *(It contains the disinfectant that was used to wash soldiers' wounds.)*

Unit 7 Resource Book
Alternate Check Test, p. 85

but my mother would only shake her head; finally she responded, "Oh, he'll be all right. They said all he needed was a few days of re-education. They're taking him somewhere, but he'll be back."

Taken where? Would we be rescued first? Would they let him go? I didn't think she knew the answers to my questions. I tugged at her sleeve. "Ma, what's 're-education'?"

12 She glanced at the wounded Viet Cong lying beneath the poncho. "It's like school, that's all. Now help me with this pot."

Spoiled since her youth by household servants, my mother had rarely gone near a kitchen. Now she was cooking a big pot of rice she had secured from a woman in the basement. The Viet Cong had set up a few clay burners and gave us some coal. Other than the rice, there was nothing to cook. We ate it with pickled leeks and cucumber, which normally accompanied fancier foods during Tet. The rice tasted of the river water my mother had used to cook it in. The Viet Cong had allowed her only a small amount of water from the bathtub to take to my father. She was happy to have cleaner water for him to drink—until she tasted it. It smelled of Mercurochrome, the red disinfectant common in Viet Nam. The soldiers had used the water to wash the wounds of injured men, then poured back unused portions, now laced with Mercurochrome. She found a tiny bit of tea to steep in the water and packed some rice into a big bowl for my father.

I sensed that my father was happy to see us, but his face showed no such emotion. He took the woven basket Ma handed him, which contained a towel, two T-shirts, and a pair of pants

she had found on her previous trip to the guest house to see him. "There's no need—you will be well provided for," a Viet Cong cadre[12] said. "You'll be in re-education for just a short time. Now that the region is liberated, you'll be allowed to come back soon."

In the big hall across from the master suite, my father kept caressing my head. I couldn't think of much to say. Some prisoners crouched along the wall, watching us. Others were curled up on the floor like shrimps. My mother gave my father the bowl of rice and the tea. I waited to see if he could taste the Mercurochrome, but I couldn't tell from his expression.

I glanced around my parents' bedroom. It had been turned upside down. The book my father had been reading about Giáp and Westmoreland still lay by his bed. My mother's jewelry and toilet case had had a hole gashed through it with a crude knife. **13**

"Your mother will take you over to your grandparents' in a few days," Cha said. "I'll be back after a time."

L ater, sometime past midnight, Communist soldiers took my father and a dozen other men away. Standing on a stool with my mother at my side, I watched through the tiny basement window. A rope was hooked through my father's elbows and tied behind his back, while his wrists were bound together in front of his chest. He was also tied to the man in front of him. It would be sixteen years before I saw him again.

---

12. **cadre** (kad′rē), *n.* persons trained for organizing or expanding an organization such as a political party.

MINI-LESSON: READING/THINKING

Relate Literature to Personal Experience

Teach Discuss with students how Nguyên Qúi Dú'c uses imagery and dialogue to re-create a situation in which he and his family were in danger. Review the specific stylistic devices he uses to involve his readers: e.g. simple sentences, strong, active verbs; and ordinary language.

Activity Idea Ask students to imitate Dú'c's style, writing a few paragraphs to describe a situation in which they and one or more others found themselves in the midst of a crisis. Explain that the crisis need not be as serious or life-threatening as that faced by Dú'c and his family. Subjects could include being stuck on a subway or elevator during a power failure or accidentally disturbing a hive of bees while playing baseball.

After Reading

Making Connections

Shaping Your Response

1. What three questions would you like to ask Dú'c about the events he describes?

Analyzing the Autobiography

2. What adjectives would you use to describe Dú'c's mother?

3. Why do you think Dú'c hesitates to reveal to his father how frightened he feels?

4. Describe Dú'c's narrative **style.** Would you call him an *emotional* or a *dispassionate* narrator? Why?

Extending the Ideas

5. Compare Dú'c's writing to Tim O'Brien's "On the Rainy River." In what ways are the two selections similar? In what ways are they different?

6. After arriving in the United States, what do you think Dú'c might have wanted to tell the American people about the Vietnam War? Explain.

Literary Focus: Imagery

Look over the notes you took about Dú'c's use of **imagery.** What effect does the imagery have on his story? Now try using imagery in your own writing. Write a **paragraph** that describes an incident in your own life. In your paragraph, use a series of images that appeal to the different senses. Then give your paragraph to a classmate to read. Can your classmate spot the imagery in your writing?

Vocabulary Study

From the lettered word list below, choose a word that is most nearly the opposite of each numbered vocabulary word. Use your Glossary if necessary.

escalation
defunct
affiliation
intricately
opulence

1. escalation
2. defunct
3. affiliation
4. intricately
5. opulence

a. separateness
b. poverty
c. decrease
d. viable
e. simply

After Reading

MAKING CONNECTIONS

1. Students may propose such questions as: *How were you and your sisters treated by the Vietcong?* or *What happened to your family after your father was taken away?*

2. Students may use words such as: *protective, innovative, emotional,* and *brave.*

3. Possible response: He is trying to be brave.

4. Students may respond that Dú'c is an emotional narrator, who tells his story in a direct and involved style.

5. Possible response: The selections are similar in that both center around the Vietnam War, both involve a difficult struggle, and both are told from the first-person limited point of view. They are different in that O'Brien's struggle involves a decision, whereas Dú'c is given no choice over his destiny. O'Brien's struggle is a spiritual or internal one, while Dú'c's is physical or external.

6. Students may suggest that Dú'c would have wanted Americans to know how the war in which their country participated affected the civilians who were caught in its action. He also may have wanted to express that the Vietcong were guilty of atrocities and America's help was, indeed, warranted.

VOCABULARY STUDY

1. c
2. d
3. a
4. e
5. b

More Practice   Students can suggest synonyms for each vocabulary word.

Unit 7 Resource Book
Vocabulary, p. 83
Vocabulary Test, p. 86

LITERARY FOCUS: IMAGERY

Once again, students might prepare by using *freewriting,* jotting down as many concrete words and phrases as come to mind to describe their experiences. They can then select the most interesting or evocative images from their writing to include in their descriptive paragraphs.

Building English Proficiency
Graphic Organizer, p. 81

Writer's Notebook Update

Encourage students to find other poems about war at the library. The poems of Siegfried Sassoon and Wilfred Owen are a good place to start, some of which are available on the Custom Literature Database. Each student might copy a poem to present to the class, describing its imagery and how it affected him or her.

Write a Review

Remind students of the parts of a review: the name of the author and selection, a summary of the work, critical analysis, and, if possible, biographical information about the author.

The Young Author

Tell students that their essays will be fictional memoirs (like Tim O'Brien's "On the Rainy River"), using facts as the basis for speculation and a real person as the model for a fictional character.

Expressing Your Ideas

Writing Choices

Writer's Notebook Update Review the list of words and images that you associate with war. Then use these words and images in a two- or three-stanza poem about war.

Write a Review Write a **review** of the excerpt for a literary magazine. In your review, explain how you think Dú'c's memoir is relevant today, more than thirty years after the Vietnam War's end.

The Young Author Do a **character study** of Dú'c, the nine-year-old boy. Begin by listing everything you know about him. Describe his personality, his place in the family, and his attitude toward the war. What do you think his life was like before the war? Is he strong enough to help care for the family after his father is taken away? When you've finished your notes, write a short personality sketch of Dú'c.

Other Options

On Stage As a class, do a **stage production** of the excerpt from *Where the Ashes Are.* Divide yourselves into several small groups, with each group responsible for one part of the production: actors, set designers, script, playbill, costumes, music, and so on. You may also want to choose a narrator who will give background information to your audience.

Bulletin Board Art Using sketches of your own, pictures you've cut from magazines, and captions that you generate on a computer, create a **bulletin board display** that reflects the action—and emotions—of Dú'c's story.

Why Did We Leave Vietnam? General William Westmoreland, whom Dú'c mentions in his memoir, was furious when the United States began its withdrawal of troops from Vietnam. In 1976 Westmoreland said, "Press and television . . . created an aura not of victory but of defeat and timid officials in Washington listened more to the media than to their own representatives on the scene." [Westmoreland: *A Soldier Reports,* 1976.] Was Westmoreland correct? Why *did* the United States abandon its efforts in Vietnam? Was it because it was an "unwinnable" war, or was it because the American public, through protest, forced the United States government to back out? In small groups, research the question. Then divide your group into two teams and prepare to **debate** the issue in front of the class.

OTHER OPTIONS

On Stage

In adapting the selection, remind students to account for both *dialogue* and *imagery.* Imagery might be represented through backdrops, props, pre-recorded sound effects, and so forth.

Bulletin Board Art

If students brought war poems to class during the Writer's Notebook Update activity, they might incorporate appropriate excerpts into the display.

Why Did We Leave Vietnam?

Help students prepare for the debate with a list of suggestions. These might include:

- Summarize your position.
- Research primary sources of information—such as speeches, interviews, and memoirs—as well as hard facts, such as statistics.
- Try to understand both sides of the argument, so that you can anticipate and prepare responses for what your opponents might say.
- Arrange the information you plan to present on index cards.

Before Reading

Village

by Estela Portillo Trambley

Estela Portillo Trambley
born 1936

Estela Portillo Trambley was born in El Paso, Texas. Raised primarily by her grandparents, Portillo Trambley returned to her parents at age twelve, then was married just out of high school. She earned a Bachelor's degree in English in 1956 and a Master's degree in English in 1978, both from the University of Texas at El Paso. Her book *Rain of Scorpions and Other Writings*, first published in 1975, is generally recognized as the first work of fiction published by a Chicana, or Mexican American woman. Portillo Trambley recently revised this collection, rewriting some of the stories and adding several new ones under the title *Rain of Scorpions and Other Stories.* "Village" is one of the new stories that appears in this collection.

Building Background

American Troops in Vietnam In 1965, the United States government began sending combat troops to Vietnam. Three years later, there were close to 540,000 U.S. troops stationed in Vietnam. Most of the Vietnam War was fought in the jungle. Soldiers lived in makeshift huts or army tents and usually tried to set up camp in jungle clearings. The jungles of Vietnam are hot and humid places, full of biting and stinging insects. Excursions into the jungle were extremely difficult and often unbearably uncomfortable. Although American troops stationed in Vietnam lived with the constant fear of an attack by the Vietcong, they were also bored and homesick a great deal of the time. "Some GI's," wrote Cathleen Cordova, who worked as a club director in Vietnam in 1968 and 1969, "say this war could have, and should have, been won by now if it weren't for the politicians meddling in military matters. Others are opposed to the war and don't think we should be here. . . . Actually, the majority of the guys aren't concerned with issues, moral judgments or politics. Most of them are young guys who didn't want to come here, and they just want to get out in one piece." By the time the United States pulled out of Vietnam in 1973, 58,000 American men and women had been killed.

Literary Focus

Theme The theme of a literary work is its underlying main idea. A theme may be directly stated but is more often implied. Plot, characters, tone, and setting all contribute to theme. As you read "The Village," try to get a sense of the theme. What point is the author making? In your notebook, jot down examples of dialogue, description, and action that contribute to the story's theme.

Writer's Notebook

The Controversy at Home The Vietnam War caused a tremendous amount of controversy in the United States. In your notebook, list some of the reasons why you think the Vietnam War was so controversial. Why did people protest the war? Why were many soldiers reluctant to fight this war?

Village **837**

Before Reading

Building Background

Students may be interested to learn that:

- College students, members of religious organizations, and peace activists were among the main groups of Americans who opposed the war in Vietnam.
- Only a small percentage of those opposed to the war were revolutionaries who supported Ho Chí Minh.

Literary Focus

Tell students that in many cases, the **theme** of a literary work can be stated as a conflict. Examples might be change versus stasis or isolation versus reaching out to others. Suggest that students try using this form to express the theme of "Village."

Writer's Notebook

If they have not done so previously, students should research the Vietnam War. Provide reference books.

More About Estela Portillo Trambley

Some critics accuse Portillo Trambley of painting an overly optimistic view of Chicano life. Her response to this is that she is looking at larger issues than the antagonism between Anglos and Chicanos. She writes of the human yearning for inner peace, understanding, and balance. Other works include the drama *The Day of the Swallows* (1971) and the novel *Trini* (1986).

SUPPORT MATERIALS OVERVIEW

Unit 7 Resource Book
- Graphic Organizer, p. 89
- Study Guide, p. 90
- Vocabulary, p. 91
- Grammar, p. 92
- Alternate Check Test, p. 93
- Vocabulary Test, p. 94
- Selection Test, pp. 95–96

Building English Proficiency
- Literature Summaries
- Activities, p. 232

Reading, Writing & Grammar SkillBook
- Vocabulary, pp. 9–10
- Reading, pp. 41–45
- Writing, pp. 112–113
- Grammar, Usage, and Mechanics, pp. 11–13, 14–16

Technology
- Audiotape
- Personal Journal Software
- Custom Literature Database: For another selection dealing with the struggles with one's conscience, see *Everyman* written in around 1500, on the database.
- Test Generator Software

Selection Objectives

- To identify the theme of a literary work
- To explore the struggle between loyalty to one's country and concern for others
- To explore words of Spanish origin

Unit 7 Resource Book
Graphic Organizer, p. 89
Study Guide, p. 90

Theme Link

A soldier in Vietnam is ordered to attack a civilian village. He struggles between his duty and his beliefs.

Vocabulary Preview

pyre, large pile of burnable material

discord, lack of harmony; contradiction

tumult, emotional disturbance

indiscernible, not distinguishable; imperceptible

disdain, a feeling of scorn

Students can add the words and definitions to their Writer's Notebook.

1 Literary Element

Setting

Question How does the author introduce the setting of the story? *(Possible response: She presents it as a foreign, enemy city, which nevertheless feels tranquil and familiar to the soldier Rico.)*

VILLAGE

ESTELA PORTILLO TRAMBLEY

The title of the 1984 painting on the facing page by Rachael Romero is *He Who Feels It Knows It.* Explain what you think this means. Could the same title apply to Rico in the story? Why or why not?

838 UNIT SEVEN: YEARS OF CHANGE

Rico stood on top of a bluff overlooking Mai Cao.[1] The whole of the wide horizon was immersed in a rosy haze. His platoon was returning from an all night patrol. They had scoured the area in a radius of thirty-two miles, following the length of the canal system along the delta, furtively on the lookout for an enemy attack. On their way back, they had stopped to rest, smoke, drink warm beer after parking the carryalls[2] along the edge of the climb leading to the top of the bluff. The hill was good cover, seemingly safe.

Harry was behind him on the rocky slope. Then the sound of thunder overhead. It wasn't thunder, but a squadron of their own helicopters on the usual run. Rico and Harry sat down to watch the planes go by. After that, a stillness, a special kind of silence. Rico knew it well, the same kind of stillness that was part of him back home, the kind of stillness that makes a man part of his world—river, clearing, sun, wind. The stillness of a village early in the morning—barrio[3] stillness, the first stirrings of life that come with dawn. Harry was looking down at the village of Mai Cao.

"Makes me homesick . . ." Harry lighted a cigarette.

Rico was surprised. He thought Harry was a city dude. Chicago, no less. "I don't see no freeway or neon lights."

"I'm just sick of doing nothing in this damned war."

No action yet. But who wanted action? Rico had been transformed into a soldier, but he knew he was no soldier. He had been trained to kill the enemy in Vietnam. He watched the first curl of smoke coming out of one of the chimneys. They were the enemy down there. Rico didn't believe it. He would never believe it. Perhaps because there had been no confrontation with Viet Cong soldiers or village people. Harry flicked away his cigarette and started down the slope. He turned, waiting for Rico to follow him. "Coming?"

"I'll be down after a while."

"Suit yourself." Harry walked swiftly down the bluff, his feet carrying with them the dirt yieldings in a flurry of small pebbles and loose earth. Rico was relieved. He needed some time by himself, to think things out. But Harry was right. To come

---

1. **Mai Cao** (mī kou′).
2. **carryall** (kar′ē ôl), *n.* enclosed truck-like vehicle.
3. **barrio** (bär′ē ō), *n.* in the United States, a section of a city inhabited chiefly by Spanish-speaking people.

SELECTION SUMMARY

Village

In "Village" Estela Portillo Trambley describes the moral struggle experienced by an American soldier in the Vietnam War. As his platoon prepares to attack the village of Mai Cao, Rico cannot overcome his sense that it is wrong to destroy these people. Standing on a hill overlooking the village, he observes a woman walking in the sun with her child. He recalls his mother, who struggled to cross the Mexican border before his own birth so that he could grow up American. He thinks of what he has been told about the villagers. They are the enemy, ready to murder him. He thinks about his duty, but his instincts tell him that it is wrong to attack

this village. When he approaches his sergeant to question the attack, Rico is brusquely told to follow orders. When the moment of attack arrives, the sergeant raises his arm as a signal. In a split second, Rico turns and shoots the lifted arm. Rico is shackled to a cot when his comrade comes to visit. He tells Rico that he was crazy to act as he did. He now faces prison. Rico responds that he is free inside.

 *For summaries in other languages, see the **Building English Proficiency** book.*

EDITORIAL NOTE   In the sixth paragraph on page 838, the word *damned* in paragraph five was substituted for *goddamned*.

Art Study

Response to Caption Question

Responses will vary, but could include the idea that to truly understand something one must have a spiritual as well as an intellectual understanding of it. If one understands something within one's heart then one understands it fully. Because Rico sees this village not as "other" or enemy territory but as a familiar place that feels a part of him, he seems to be a person who understands things deeply, a man who feels and knows.

Visual Literacy   This brown-skinned man wearing blood-stained barbed-wire looks out at the viewer with piercing blue eyes. Is it a crown of thorns wrapped around his hat? Is he about to be crucified? Or has he been resurrected? Clearly, he is serene and compassionate, although the riotous background would indicate that trouble follows him. Discuss who this man might be and what he might be doing with the students.

BUILDING ENGLISH PROFICIENCY

Exploring Sentence Fragments

Help students identify and avoid using sentence fragments in their writing. Review the rules of a complete sentence.

- Read aloud the second paragraph on page 838. Ask volunteers to identify groups of words that look like sentences but really are fragments.
- Have students revise the fragments, changing them into complete sentences.
- Discuss the reasons writers use fragments —to create realistic dialogue or to give the impression of fragments of thought. Emphasize that students should only use fragments when appropriate.

ESL
LEP
ELD
SAE
LD

IT'S A SENTENCE IF . . .

It has a SUBJECT.
It has a VERB.
It expresses a COMPLETE THOUGHT.

 Building English Proficiency
Activities, p. 232

2 Literary Element
Imagery

Imagery refers to the sensory details that provide vividness and arouse the reader's emotions. Discuss with students the imagery that invokes the potential violence of Rico's situation.

Questions

- To which of the reader's senses does Portillo appeal? *(Students may respond that the author appeals to the sense of feeling and sight by providing vivid images of violent actions.)*

- What parts of speech does she use to evoke the experience of killing, and what do many of the words have in common? *(Possible response: verbs:* strangle, slit, grind, mash, *and* stomp; *nouns:* lick, garrote, throat, heel, face, brains, rib cage, *and* bone splinters. *They have harsh, hard vowel sounds.)*

3 Literary Focus
Theme

Question   What conflict does Rico experience when he contemplates attacking Mai Cao? *(Possible response: He is torn between the warnings that the villagers are waiting to kill him, and his own innate sense that Mai Cao is a peaceful village full of people like himself.)*

---

across an ocean just to do routine checks, to patrol ground where there was no real danger . . . it could get pretty bad. The enemy was hundreds of miles away. The enemy! He remembered the combat bible—kill or be killed. Down a man—the lethal lick: a garotte[4] strangling is neater and more quiet than the slitting of a throat; grind your heel against a face to mash the brains. Stomp the rib cage to carve the heart with bone splinters. Kill . . .

Hey, who was kidding who? They almost made him believe it back at boot camp in the States. In fact, only a short while ago, only that morning he had crouched down along the growth following a mangrove[5] swamp, fearing an unseen enemy, ready to kill. Only that morning. But now, looking down at the peaceful village with its small rice field, its scattered huts, something had struck deep, something beyond the logic of war and enemy, something deep in his guts.

He had been cautioned. The rows of thatched huts were not really peoples' homes, but "hootches," makeshift temporary stays built by the makeshift enemy. But then they were real enemies. There were too many dead Americans to prove it. The hootches didn't matter. The people didn't matter. These people knew how to pick up their sticks and go. Go where? Then how many of these villages had been bulldozed? Flattened by gunfire? Good pyre[6] for napalm,[7] these Vietnamese villages. A new kind of battleground.

Rico looked down and saw huts that were homes, clustered in an intimacy that he knew well. The village of Mai Cao was no different than Valverde, the barrio where he had grown up. A woman came out of a hut, walking straight and with a certain grace, a child on her shoulder. She was walking toward a stream east of the slope. She stopped along the path and looked up to say something to the child. It struck him again, the feeling a bond—people all the same everywhere.

The same scent from the earth, the same warmth from the sun, a woman walking with a child—his mother, Trini. His little mother who had left Tarahumara country and crossed the Barranca del Cobre, taking with her the seeds from the hills of Batopilas,[8] withstanding suffering, danger—for what? A dream—a piece of ground in the land of plenty, the United States of America. She had waded across the Rio Grande from Juarez, Mexico, to El Paso, Texas, when she felt the birth pangs of his coming. He had been born a citizen because his mother had had a dream. She had made the dream come true—an acre of river land in Valverde, on the edge of the border. His mother, like the earth and the sun, mattered. The woman with the child on her shoulder mattered. Every human life in the village mattered. He knew this not only with the mind but with the heart.

Rico remembered a warning from combat training, from the weary, wounded soldiers who had fought and killed and survived, soldiers sent to Saigon, waiting to go home. His company had been flown to Saigon before being sent to the front. And this was the front, villages like Mai Cao. He felt relieved knowing that the fighting was hundreds of miles away from the people in Mai Cao—but the warning was still there:

Watch out for pregnant women with machine guns. Toothless old women are experts with the knife between the shoulders. Begging children with hidden grenades, the unseen VC hiding in the hootches—village people were not people; they were the enemy. The woman who knew the child on her shoulder, who knew the path to the

---

4. **garotte** (gə rōt′), *n.* a cord or wire used for strangling.
5. **mangrove** (mang′grōv), *n.* tropical trees or shrubs that have branches that send down many roots which look like additional trunks.
6. **pyre** (pīr), *n.* large pile of burnable material.
7. **napalm** (nā′päm), *n.* jellied gasoline used for making incendiary bombs and in flamethrowers.
8. **Tarahumara** (tär′ä hä mär′ä) . . . **Barranca del Cobre** (bä rän′ka del kō′brä) . . . **Batopilas** (bä′tō pē′läs); places in Mexico.

MINI-LESSON: GRAMMAR

Affixes

Teach   Explain to students that affixes include *prefixes*—additions to the beginnings of word bases, and *suffixes*—additions to their endings. While suffixes tend to change only the grammatical form of a word—for example, the verb *love* to the adjective *lovable* or the adverb *lovely*—prefixes usually alter the meaning of the word.

There are two kinds of suffixes: *inflectional suffixes*—such as *-s*, *-ed*, and *-er* (when added to verbs), and *derivational suffixes*—such as *-ence*, *-ness*, *-ive*, *-able*, *-ize*, *-ly*, and so forth.

Activity Ideas

- Have students find examples in the selection of words containing each of the three affixes described at the left.
- Have students find two words with suffixes.
- Discuss how each prefix and suffix affects the meaning of the word.

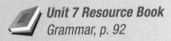

Unit 7 Resource Book
Grammar, p. 92

door, who knew the coming of the sun—she was the enemy.

It was a discord[9] not to be believed by instinct or intuition. And Rico was an Indian, the son of a Tarahumara chieftain. Theirs was a world of instinct and intuitive decisions. Suddenly he heard the sounds of motors. He looked to the other side of the slope, down to the road where the carryalls had started queuing[10] their way back to the post. Rico ran down the hill to join his company.

In his dream, Sergeant Keever was shouting, "Heller, heller . . ." Rico woke with a start. It wasn't a dream. The men around him were scrambling out of the pup tent. Outside, most of the men were lining up in uneven formation. Rico saw a communiqué[11] in the sergeant's hand. Next to Keever was a lieutenant from communications headquarters. Keever was reading the communiqué:

"Special mission 72 . . . for Company C, platoon 2, assigned at 22 hours. Move into the village of Mai Cao, field manual description—hill 72. Destroy the village."

No! It was crazy. Why? Just words on a piece of paper. Keever had to tell him why. There had to be a reason. Had the enemy come this far? It was impossible. Only that morning he had stood on the slope. He caught up with Keever, blurting out, "Why? I mean—why must we destroy it?"

Sergeant Keever stopped in his tracks and turned steel blue eyes at Rico. "What you say?"

"Why?"

"You just follow orders, savvy?"[11]

"Are the Viet Cong . . ."

"Did you hear me? You want trouble, Private?"

"There's people . . ."

"I don't believe you, soldier. But OK. Tell you as much as I know. We gotta erase the village in case the Viet Cong come this way. That way they won't use it as a stronghold. Now move . . ."

Keever walked away from him, his lips tight in some kind of disgust. Rico did not follow this time. He went to get his gear and join the men in one of the carryalls. Three carryalls for the assault—three carryalls moving up the same road. Rico felt the weight and hardness of his carbine. Now it had a strange, hideous meaning. The machine guns were some kind of nightmare. The mission was to kill and burn and erase all memories. Rico swallowed a guilt that rose from the marrow—with it, all kinds of fear. He had to do something, something to stop it, but he didn't know what. And with all these feelings, a certain reluctance to do anything but follow orders. In the darkness, his lips formed words from the anthem, "My country, 'tis of thee . . ."

They came to the point where the tree lines straggled between two hills that rose darkly against the moon. Rico wondered if all the men were of one mind—one mind to kill. . . . Was he a coward? No! It was not killing the enemy that his whole being was rejecting, but firing machine guns into a village of sleeping people . . . people. Rico remembered only the week before, returning from their usual patrol, the men from the company had stopped at the stream, mingling with the children, old men, and women of the village. There had been an innocence about the whole thing. His voice broke the silence in the carryall, a voice harsh and feverish. "We can get the people out of there. Help them evacuate . . ."

"Shut up." Harry's voice was tight, impatient.

The carryalls traveled through tall, undulant grass following the dirt road that led to the edge of the bluff. It was not all tall grass. Once in a while trees appeared again, clumped around scrub bushes. Ten miles out the carryalls stopped. It was still a mile's walk to the bluff in the darkness, but they had to avoid detection. Sergeant Keever was leading the party. Rico,

---

9. **discord** (dis′kôrd), *n.* lack of harmony; contradiction.
10. **queue** (kyü), *v.* follow in a line.
10. **communiqué** (kə myü′nə kā′), *n.* official communication.
11. **savvy** (sav′ē), *v.* slang for understand.

Village **841**

4 Literary Focus
Theme

Ask students to consider how the information about Rico in this paragraph clarifies the theme. *(Students may say Portillo presents Rico's essential qualities—his tradition and history—against what he has been told in the army.)*

EDITORIAL NOTE "Now move . . . ," at the bottom of the first paragraph, originally read "Now move your ass. . . ."

5 Literary Element
Dialogue

Questions

- What does this dialogue reveal about Sergeant Keever and about Rico? *(Possible response: It shows Keever to be a tough, aggressive man of duty, disgusted with Rico's questions. Rico is unable to put aside his instincts and follow blindly.)*
- How does the dialogue advance the story's theme? *(Students may respond that it adds fuel to the conflict between duty and conviction.)*

6 Literary Element
Symbolism

Question Which side of Rico's conflict is symbolized by his singing the national anthem? *(his allegiance to his country)*

BUILDING ENGLISH PROFICIENCY

Mapping a Plot

Creating a plot map will help students understand the structure of this short story. Have them work in pairs to complete elements of the plot map below.

- Ask students to fill in the setting, major character, problem, and rising action (two events).
- Have each pair predict what they think will happen at the climax and in the falling action of the story.

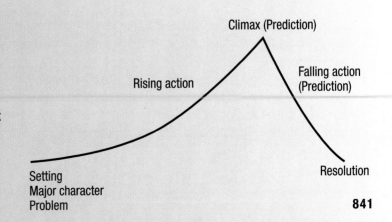

Climax (Prediction)

Rising action

Falling action (Prediction)

Resolution

Setting
Major character
Problem

Infer

Question What does Rico mean when he recalls his friend's war medals and thinks, "They weren't worth a nickel"? *(He may mean not only that old medals have no monetary value, but that victory in battle is a worthless achievement.)*

8 Literary Element

Imagery

Discuss with students the images Portillo uses to evoke Rico's sensations as he waits for the order to attack.

Questions

- How do these images affect Rico? *(They seem to heighten his senses— he hears the splashing water, smells the burning wood, sees the huts awash in moonlight.)*

- What simile does the author use to describe the advancing soldiers? *(She uses the simile of dancing grasshoppers.)*

EDITORIAL NOTE "That . . .—get him," in the second paragraph, originally read "That fucking bastard—get him."

9 Literary Element

Plot

Question What is the climax in "Village"? *(Rico shooting his sergeant's arm)*

---

almost at the rear, knew he had to catch up to him. He had to stop him. Harry was ahead of him, a silent black bundle walking stealthily through rutted ground to discharge his duty. For a second, Rico hesitated. That was the easy thing to do—to carry out his duty—to die a hero, to do his duty blindly and survive. Hell, why not? He knew what happened to men who backed down in battle. But he wasn't backing down. Hell, what else was it? How often had he heard it among the gringos[12] in his company?

"You Mexican? Hey, you Mexicans are real fighters. I mean, everybody knows Mexicans have guts . . ."

A myth perhaps. But no. He thought of the old guys who had fought in World War II. Many of them were on welfare back in the barrio. But, man! Did they have medals! He had never seen so many purple hearts. He remembered old Toque, the wino, who had tried to pawn his medals to buy a bottle. No way, man. They weren't worth a nickel.

He quickly edged past Harry, pushing the men ahead of him to reach the sergeant. He was running, tall grass brushing his shoulder, tall grass that swayed peacefully like wheat. The figure of Sergeant Keever was in front of him now. There was a sudden impulse to reach out and hold him back. But the sergeant had stopped. Rico did not touch him but whispered hoarsely, desperately in the dark. "Let's get the people out—evacuate . . ."

"What the hell . . ." Keever's voice was ice. He recognized Rico and hissed, "Get back to your position, soldier, or I'll shoot you myself."

Rico did as he was told, almost unaware of the men around him. But at a distance he heard something splashing in the water of the canal, in his nostrils the smell of sweet burnt wood. He looked toward the clearing and saw the cluster of huts bathed in moonlight. In the same moonlight, he saw Keever giving signals. In the gloom, he saw the figures of the men carrying machine guns. They looked like dancing grasshoppers as

they ran ahead to position themselves on the bluff. He felt like yelling, "For Christ's sake! Where is the enemy?"

The taste of blood in his mouth—he suddenly realized he had bitten his quivering lower lip. As soon as Sergeant Keever gave the signal, all sixteen men would open fire on the huts— machine guns, carbines—everything would be erased. No more Mai Cao. The execution of duty without question, without alternative. They were positioned on the south slope, Sergeant Keever up ahead, squatting on his heels, looking at his watch. He raised himself, after a quick glance at the men. As Sergeant Keever raised his hand to give the signal for attack, Rico felt the cold metallic deadness of his rifle. His hands began to tremble as he released the safety catch. Sergeant Keever was on the rise just above him. Rico stared at the sergeant's arm, raised, ready to fall—the signal to fire. The cross-fire was inside Rico, a heavy dosed tumult[13]—destroy the village, erase all memory. There was ash in his mouth. Once the arm came down, there was no turning back.

In a split second, Rico turned his rifle at a forty-degree angle and fired at the sergeant's arm. Keever half turned with the impact of the bullet, then fell to his knees. In a whooping whisper the old-timer soldier blew out the words, "That . . .—get him." He got up and signaled the platoon back to the carryalls as two men grabbed Rico, one hitting him on the side of his head with the butt of his rifle. Rico felt the sting of the blow as they pinned his arm back and forced him to walk the path back to the carryall. He did not resist. There was a lump in his throat, and he blinked back tears, tears of relief. The memory of the village would not be erased. Someone shouted in the dark, "They're on to us. There's an old man with a lantern and others coming out of the hootches . . ."

---

12. **gringo** (gring′gō), *n.* a term in Spanish, often considered offensive, for a foreigner, especially an American or Englishman.

13. **tumult** (tŭ′mult), *n.* emotional disturbance.

MINI-LESSON: VOCABULARY

Etymology

Teach The story "Village" can be used as the basis for a lesson about Spanish-language words that have become an accepted part of the English language.

Apply Direct students attention to the words *barrio* and *gringo* in the selection. Discuss the difference between most foreign words, which are italicized in writing, and words such as the aforementioned, which have become common in English usage.

Activity Ideas

- Invite students to brainstorm common Spanish words and terms.
- Divide the words among students.
- Have each student check a dictionary to see if his or her words have accepted English-language meanings, either the same as or similar to their original Spanish meanings.

"People—just people . . ." Rico whispered, wanting to shout it, wanting to tell them that he had done the right thing. But the heaviness that filled his senses was the weight of the truth. He was a traitor—a maniac. He had shot his superior in a battle crisis. He was being carried almost bodily back to the truck. He glanced at the thick brush along the road, thinking that somewhere beyond it was a rice field, and beyond that a mangrove swamp. There was a madman inside his soul that made him think of rice fields and mangrove swamps instead of what he had done. Not once did he look up. Everyone around him was strangely quiet and remote. Only the sound of trudging feet.

In the carryall, the faces of the men sitting around Rico were indiscernible[14] in the dark, but he imagined their eyes, wide, confused, peering through the dark at him with a wakefulness that questioned what he had done. Did they know his reason? Did they care? The truck suddenly lurched. Deep in the gut, Rico felt a growing fear. He choked back a hysteria rising from the diaphragm. The incessant bumping of the carryalls as they moved unevenly on the dirt road accused him, too. He looked up into a night sky and watched the moon eerily weave in and out of tree branches. The darkness was like his fear. It had no solutions.

 ack on the post, Sergeant Keever and a medic passed by Rico, already handcuffed, without any sign of recognition. Sergeant Keever had already erased him from existence. The wheels of justice would take their course. Rico had been placed under arrest, temporarily shackled to a cot in one of the tents. Three days later he was moved to a makeshift bamboo hut, with a guard in front of the hut at all times. His buddies brought in food like strangers, awkward in their silence, anxious to leave him alone. He felt like some kind of

poisonous bug. Only Harry came by to see him after a week.

"You dumb jerk, were you on locoweed?" Harry asked in disgust.

"I didn't want people killed, that's all."

"Hell that's no reason, those chinks aren't even—even . . ."

"Even what?" Rico demanded. He almost screamed it a second time. "Even what?"

"Take it easy, will you? You better go for a section 8." Harry was putting him aside like everyone else. "They're sending you back to the States next week. You'll have to face Keever sometime this afternoon. I thought I'd better let you know."

"Thanks." Rico knew the hopelessness of it all. There was still the nagging question he had to ask. "Listen, nobody tells me anything. Did you all go back to Mai Cao? I mean, is it still there?"

"Still there. Orders from headquarters to forget it. The enemy were spotted taking an opposite direction. But nobody's going to call you a hero, you understand? What you did was crud. You're no soldier. You'll never be a soldier."

Rico said nothing to defend himself. He began to scratch the area around the steel rings on his ankles. Harry was scowling at him. He said it again, almost shouting, "I said, you'll never be a soldier."

"So?" There was soft disdain[15] in Rico's voice.

"You blew it, man. You'll be locked up for a long, long time."

"Maybe . . ." Rico's voice was without concern. "Don't you care?"

"I'm free inside, Harry." Rico laughed in relief. "Free . . ."

Harry shrugged, peering at Rico unbelievingly, then turned and walked out of the hut.

---

14. **indiscernible** (in′də zėr′nə bəl), *adj.* not distinguishable; imperceptible.

15. **disdain** (dis dān′), *n.* a feeling of scorn.

Village **843**

10 Literary Element
Symbolism

Questions

- Why does Rico think of rice fields and mangrove swamps instead of the repercussions of his traitorous actions? *(Possible responses: He associates these things with the humanity of the Vietnamese people; they are symbols of the lives he saved by refusing to kill.)*

- What might the village symbolize? *(Possible responses: humanity, human beings, human harmony, or balance)*

EDITORIAL NOTE "You dumb jerk," at the top of the second column, originally read "You dumb ass. . . ."

11 Literary Element
Dialogue

Question How does the dialogue characterize Harry? *(Possible responses: It shows him to be unsympathetic, unable to view the "other" as worthwhile or human.)*

Check Test

1. Where is Rico at the opening of the story? *(He's on a hill looking at the village of Mai Cao.)*

2. What does Portillo tell us about Rico's past? *(He is from the barrio of Valverde, on the American side of the Mexican border. His mother struggled to cross the border before his birth so that he would have a better life in America. His father was a Tarahumara chief.)*

3. What is Sergeant Keever's response when Rico asks why the platoon must destroy the village? *(He is annoyed that Rico is questioning his orders.)*

4. What does Rico do just before Keever completes the signal to attack? *(He turns and shoots him in the arm.)*

5. Where is Rico at the story's end? *(He is a prisoner in one of the tents.)*

 *Unit 7 Resource Book*
Alternate Check Test, p. 93

BUILDING ENGLISH PROFICIENCY

Contrasting Viewpoints

Help students understand conflicting viewpoints by having them generate both questions and answers from two points of view.

- Divide the class into groups. Have each group generate questions Keever might have for Rico. Encourage them to consider how Rico might answer these questions.

- Have each group choose one of their members to play the role of Keever and another to be Rico. Let the others in the group coach these characters with notes.

- Match a student playing Keever with one playing Rico. Have Keever question Rico and Rico answer. After all groups have had a turn, have them switch viewpoints.

After Reading

MAKING CONNECTIONS

1. Students may say that they would have made Keever receptive to Rico's objections or that they might have forestalled the events until the orders to halt the attack came from headquarters.

2. Possible responses: Yes: because he shot his commanding officer. No: because he saved his fellow soldiers from being forced to commit an immoral act.

3. Students should be aware that Rico is disturbed because they are attacking ordinary people, whom he cannot see as different from himself or his own family.

4. Students may feel that Rico's background as the son of an immigrant and an Indian chieftain sway his decision, or that he is simply more thoughtful than his comrades, who unquestioningly accept an "us against them" attitude.

5. Possible response: Because Rico has committed an act that Keever finds unthinkable, he dismisses him much as he dismisses the villagers to whom he cannot relate.

6. Students should be aware that although Rico knows that he may spend the rest of his life physically imprisoned, he is content because he has freed his spirit or soul by being true to himself.

7. Possible response: Both Rico and Tim reject the definitions of heroism or courage of those around them. Both are unable to rationalize killing others. However, when the crucial moment arrives, Rico is able to face the condemnation of his society and follow his heart, whereas Tim cannot.

8. Students may respond that the next chapter would deal with Rico's trial, or court martial, in which he would explain his actions. The fact that the village did not need to be destroyed after all might extenuate his prison sentence.

844

After Reading

Making Connections

Shaping Your Response

1. If you could be the hand of fate, how would you change the events of this story?

2. As a class, take a vote: Is Rico a traitor to his platoon? Be prepared to explain your opinion.

Analyzing the Story

3. What bothers Rico about the orders to level the village?

4. 👣 Why does Rico make a **choice** that is different from that of his comrades?

5. Why do you suppose Keever ignores Rico after he has been placed under arrest?

6. Explain what you think Rico means when he says, "I'm free inside."

Extending the Ideas

7. Compare Rico's feelings about the Vietnam War to the character Tim O'Brien's feelings. How are they similar and different?

8. Now Rico is back in the United States. If there were another chapter to this story, what would happen to Rico?

Literary Focus: Theme

What is the **theme,** or main idea, of "Village"? Write a sentence that explains the theme, and list the clues you found in the text that helped reveal the theme. Keep in mind that elements such as plot, character, dialogue, and setting can all contribute to the theme.

Vocabulary Study

pyre
discord
tumult
indiscernable
disdain

Study the relationship of each of the following pairs of words, then choose another pair that has the same relationship.

1. BRANCH : PYRE :: **a.** dream : snore **b.** water : fire **c.** transient : permanent **d.** raindrop : flood

2. DISCORD : CONFLICT :: **a.** unremitting : boredom **b.** ostentatious : opulent **c.** prodigious : tiny **d.** talented : cellist

3. DISTURBANCE : TUMULT :: **a.** politician : power **b.** wise : foolish **c.** anger : shout **d.** horror : terror

4. INDISCERNIBLE : FEATURES :: **a.** superfluous : needed **b.** corpulent : physique **c.** transgression : infraction **d.** accurate : correct

5. SCORN : DISDAIN :: **a.** disorganized : orderly **b.** vengeful : bully **c.** ethereal : music **d.** exhort : urge

---

LITERARY FOCUS: THEME

If students use the form suggested in Before Reading, their statements might include duty versus integrity to self, logic versus intuition, the head versus the heart, or the individual versus society to arrive at the conclusion that the theme of "Village" is that of doing what you believe to be honorable not what others tell you is right.

Expressing Your Ideas

Writing Choices

Writer's Notebook Update Based on the list you made of some of the reasons why the Vietnam War caused so much controversy in the United States and on your reading of Portillo Trambley's short story, write a summary of the controversy that could be included in an encyclopedia entry about the Vietnam War under the heading "Vietnam War: Dissent and Protest." Your summary should be no longer than one paragraph.

Recent Revelations In 1995, Robert McNamara, former United States Secretary of Defense under President Johnson, revealed that as early as 1967 he had concluded that the Vietnam War was unwinnable and that the combat strategies he had helped design were "wrong, terribly wrong." McNamara says in his 1995 autobiography, *In Retrospect,* that he deeply regrets United States involvement in Vietnam. Imagine that you are Rico. Write a **letter** to McNamara explaining why you agree or disagree with him.

Other Options

Vietnam Today Working with a partner, prepare a **presentation** of today's Vietnam, using maps and other visual aids as necessary. In your presentation, include an explanation of current diplomatic relations between the United States and Vietnam.

Divergent Viewpoints In "Village," Rico sees Mai Cao in two different ways. At times he views the village as a quiet, innocent place. At other times he attempts to see the village as his fellow soldiers do—a place of "begging children with hidden grenades, the unseen VC hiding in the hootches . . ." Divide a large piece of paper into two sections. On the left hand side of the paper, make a **sketch** of the village that represents the way Rico sees it. On the right-hand side, make a sketch of the village that represents the way Rico has been *ordered* to see it.

A Memorial The Vietnam Veterans Memorial in Washington, D.C. includes two black granite walls inscribed with the names of all Americans who died in the Vietnam War, or who remained classified as missing in action when the walls were built. If you were asked to create a Vietnam Veterans Memorial for your town, what would it be? Sketch your memorial. Include with your design an explanation of the materials you would use. Then write an inscription for a plaque that might accompany the memorial.

Village **845**

WRITING CHOICES
Writer's Notebook Update

Summaries should include answers to the basic questions *who, what, where, when, why,* and *how,* listing such facts as the kinds of people who objected to the war, the forms their protests took, the reasons for their dissent, and the years when dissent was strongest and most visible.

Recent Revelations

Most letters will indicate agreement with McNamara, stressing that it is morally wrong to attack civilians and their homes. Encourage students to use the proper form for a formal letter, as discussed in the Grammar Mini-lesson on page 802 of this unit.

OTHER OPTIONS
Vietnam Today

If students have access to a computer, suggest that they research their topic using a CD-ROM multimedia encyclopedia or the Internet.

Divergent Viewpoints

Students might use some of the following techniques to create artistic contrast: Content—a peaceful, sleeping village versus one with menacing people hiding behind every hut and tree; Color—soft tones or pastels versus harsh reds and black; Technique—fluid lines versus disconnected slashes, and degree of realism or abstraction.

A Memorial

Students may be interested to learn that the Vietnam Veterans Memorial was designed by Maya Yang Lin, who later created the Civil Rights Memorial in Montgomery, Alabama. Lin's plan for the monument was selected while she was still an architecture student at Yale. Expenses for its construction were paid by the Vietnam Veterans Memorial Fund.

Interdisciplinary Study

Theme Link

The civil rights, American Indian, and women's movements and the anti-Vietnam War and National Farm Workers protests emerged or exploded during the 1960s and 1970s.

Curricular Connection: History

You can use this interdisciplinary study to explore how people and government responded during two decades of struggle.

Terms to Know

boycott (boi′kot), combine against (a person, business, nation, etc.) in agreement not to buy from, sell to, or associate with and try to keep others from doing so for purposes of coercion and punishment

sit-in, a sitting down and refusing to move, especially in a public place, as a form of protest against racial discrimination or government policies

counterculture, the culture made up primarily of young people who reject many of the established values and customs of modern society

martial law, rule by the army or militia with special military courts instead of the usual civil authorities

Unit 7 Resource Book
Interdisciplinary Study Skills,
p. 97

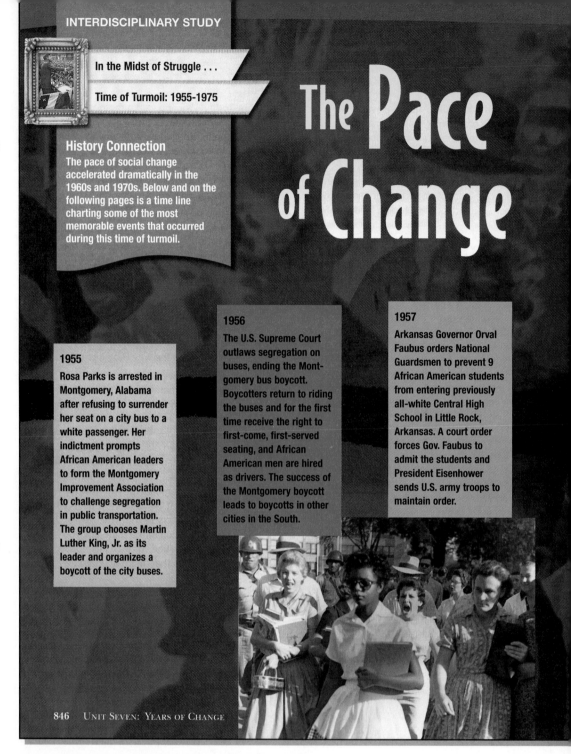

In the Midst of Struggle . . .

Time of Turmoil: 1955-1975

History Connection

The pace of social change accelerated dramatically in the 1960s and 1970s. Below and on the following pages is a time line charting some of the most memorable events that occurred during this time of turmoil.

The Pace of Change

1955

Rosa Parks is arrested in Montgomery, Alabama after refusing to surrender her seat on a city bus to a white passenger. Her indictment prompts African American leaders to form the Montgomery Improvement Association to challenge segregation in public transportation. The group chooses Martin Luther King, Jr. as its leader and organizes a boycott of the city buses.

1956

The U.S. Supreme Court outlaws segregation on buses, ending the Montgomery bus boycott. Boycotters return to riding the buses and for the first time receive the right to first-come, first-served seating, and African American men are hired as drivers. The success of the Montgomery boycott leads to boycotts in other cities in the South.

1957

Arkansas Governor Orval Faubus orders National Guardsmen to prevent 9 African American students from entering previously all-white Central High School in Little Rock, Arkansas. A court order forces Gov. Faubus to admit the students and President Eisenhower sends U.S. army troops to maintain order.

MINI-LESSON: SPEAKING AND LISTENING

Listening to a Speech

Teach   Explain to students that the persuasiveness of a speech comes from a number of different aspects. The content, the style, the rhetorical devices used, and the voice and personal charisma of the speaker are some of the factors that make a speech powerful.

Explain that listening critically requires an analysis of the role of these factors in the effectiveness of the speech. If you are persuaded, it is important to know why.

Activity Idea   Play a recording of Martin Luther King, Jr.'s speech "I Have a Dream." If possible, view a video recording so students can see as well as hear King and the audience. Have students listen to the speech once through just to experience it. Then have them listen several more times and use the categories suggested above to analyze the sources of the effectiveness of the speech.

1960

College and high school students begin staging peaceful demonstrations known as sit-ins, in which they sit at segregated lunch counters and refuse to leave until served. Trained not to fight back when harassed or attacked, these protesters endure beatings and arrests but are successful at desegregating some lunch counters and other public facilities. The success of early sit-ins leads to a movement that spreads to cities across the South during the early part of the decade. Other forms of nonviolent protest emerge such as Freedom Rides on interstate buses and mass freedom marches.

1962

During the fall, federal troops are sent to Oxford, Mississippi when a large mob of whites riots in violent protest against the admission of African American student James Meredith to the University of Mississippi.

1962

Folk singer Bob Dylan writes the song "Blowin' in the Wind," which becomes an unofficial anthem of the civil rights movement.

1963

In June NAACP leader Medger Evers is shot to death in Jackson, Mississippi.

1963

During the summer civil rights leader A. Philip Randolph organizes the March on Washington for Jobs and Freedom. On August 28 more than 250,000 people gather at the Lincoln Memorial where Dr. Martin Luther King, Jr., delivers his "I Have a Dream" speech.

THE FREEWHEELIN' BOB DYLAN

I have a dream...

BUILDING ENGLISH PROFICIENCY

ESL
LEP
ELD
SAE
LD

Responding to Historical Detail

A great deal of historical information is presented on pages 846–850. Encourage students to use their dialogue journals to respond to details that catch their attention. For example, in the left-hand column of a t-chart, they could note dates, places, and events; in the right-hand column, they could express an opinion, jot down a question, and so on. Invite volunteers to share their comments.

Fact/Detail	My Response
1960: Students "sit in" at segregated lunch counters.	This is civil disobedience, right?

Additional Background

Cesar Chavez (1927–1993) was the son of a migrant farm worker and attended over 30 elementary schools. He began organizing farm workers in 1962, and he founded the United Farm Workers.

NOW (National Organization for Women) was founded in 1966 with Betty Friedan as its first president. NOW aims at achieving "full equality for women in truly equal partnership with men." NOW tried to gain passage of the Equal Rights Amendment, but it was defeated in the House of Representatives on November 15, 1983.

1965

U.S. involvement in Vietnam increases as President Johnson orders sustained bombing of North Vietnam and the deployment of the first American combat troops. Claiming that it would be dishonorable not to come to the aid of South Vietnam, President Johnson begins an escalation of American forces that commits nearly 200,000 troops by year's end, and continues for the next three years.

1965

Labor leader Cesar Chavez and the National Farm Workers Association join with Filipino grape pickers to strike against growers' unfair wage practices. The strike, which quickly gains national attention and becomes known as "La Causa" or the Cause, lasts 3 years when Chavez, in an effort to heighten public awareness of the workers' cause, initiates a nation-wide boycott of table grapes. The boycott helps end the strike in 1970.

1966

The National Organization for Women (NOW) forms to pressure the Equal Employment Opportunity Commission to enforce a law prohibiting sex discrimination. With its president, Betty Friedan—author of *The Feminine Mystique,* a book that three years earlier charged society's institutions with conditioning women to believe they could become nothing other than housewives and mothers—the group pledges to "bring women into full participation in the mainstream of American society . . . now."

1967

The protest movement against the Vietnam War grows with more marches, sit-ins, and demonstrations against U.S. presence in Vietnam. American men—eligible to be drafted into the army at the age of 18—publicly tear up or burn their draft cards. Renowned pediatrician Dr. Benjamin Spock and poet Allen Ginsburg are among more than 500 arrested at an antiwar protest in New York. A poll at year's end reveals for the first time that most Americans believe that getting involved in Vietnam was a mistake.

HELL no we won't go!

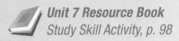

Sisterhood

MINI-LESSON: STUDY SKILLS

Primary and Secondary Sources

Teach Point out to students that the capsules of history in this interdisciplinary study provide only a very broad, simplistic understanding of events that were complex and had far-reaching consequences. In order to better understand historical events that are described briefly in secondary sources, it is important to consult primary sources as well as longer, more detailed secondary sources.

Activity Idea Have students work together in small groups to find and suggest three primary and secondary sources that would help them gain a greater understanding of each event on pages 646–650.

Unit 7 Resource Book
Study Skill Activity, p. 98

1968

The police, FBI, and CIA infiltrate meetings of antiwar protest organizers and use information to disrupt planned demonstrations. In Chicago, some 10,000 antiwar protesters converge in August to demonstrate at the Democratic National Convention. Chicago's Mayor Richard J. Daley orders 12,000 police and 5000 National Guardsmen to prevent protesters from disturbing the convention. Violence erupts as demonstrators break through police barriers and police attack protesters.

1968

African American athletes consider boycotting the summer Olympic Games in Mexico City to protest racism in the United States. Although the boycott is canceled, U.S. Olympic champions Tommie Smith and John Carlos make their own protest at the medals ceremony when they bow their heads and raise black-gloved fists during the playing of their national anthem. Their Black Power salute prompts the international Olympic committee to force the U.S. committee to suspend the two runners from the team.

1969

Nearly 500,000 members of America's counterculture —a social revolt that developed earlier in the decade among young people mostly opposed to the Vietnam War, individualism, and capitalism, and in favor of communal living—unite for the Woodstock Music and Art Fair in New York. The three day festival becomes a symbol of solidarity for a generation in revolt against "the establishment." Several months later, in contrast to the peaceful atmosphere of Woodstock, violence disrupts a free concert at the Altamont Speedway in California and a man is murdered by a member of the Hell's Angels—a motorcycle gang hired to keep order at the concert.

1970

President Nixon announces that U.S. forces have launched a surprise attack on Vietnamese communists' military headquarters in Cambodia. The announcement reignites the antiwar movement. National student strikes are organized and students close down college campuses across the nation. Four students are killed at Kent State University, Ohio, by National Guardsmen called in to enforce martial law.

4 dead in Ohio

Interdisciplinary Activity Ideas

- Suggest that students find out more about U.S. involvement in Vietnam, take a pro war or anti war position, and present a series of campaign speeches that speak to the issue.
- In the midst of the struggle was the exciting race to the moon. Have students draw a time line showing the progression of the U.S. space program.

Additional Background

America first became involved in Vietnam when Americans helped the French retake control of French Indochina (Vietnam, Cambodia, and Laos). At first the United States helped primarily with financial support. Then as Vietnamese Communists, known as Viet Cong, began incursions and guerrilla warfare, President Kennedy added military advisers.

The war escalated, and in 1965, the United States had 184,000 troops in Southeast Asia.

BUILDING ENGLISH PROFICIENCY

Analyzing Visual Information

Use one or more of the following activities to help students understand the information behind the historic photographs.

- Ask students how they think each picture represents a social or political change.
- Ask groups of students to choose a photograph and create a news report for the event as it might appear on a nightly news program.

Additional Background

The American Indian Movement was created in 1968 by several Objiwa Indians in Minnesota to fight racial discrimination against American Indians in urban areas.

Watergate In June 1972, five burglars broke into the Democratic National Committee headquarters in the Washington, D.C. Watergate office building. When ties between the burglars and the Committee to Re-elect the President became known, suspicions about President Nixon were aroused.

Responding

1. Possible Response The wide variety of social struggles indicates that turmoil was inevitable.

2. Responses will vary and can prompt discussion as to why some pictures define an event.

1973
Members of the American Indian Movement (AIM) take over the town of Wounded Knee, South Dakota, site of an 1890 massacre of 300 Sioux by the United States army cavalry, and occupy the town for seventy-one days. The group is part of a new spirit of political militancy among American Indians that rises during the late 1960s and early 1970s to protest problems faced by American Indians, namely high unemployment, poor conditions on reservations, and violations of federal land and hunting treaties by states.

1974
President Richard M. Nixon becomes the first American president to resign from office. Nixon had become linked to a major scandal named for the Watergate office complex in Washington, D.C.

1975
The communist North Vietnamese launch their final great offensive and the South Vietnamese army collapses. Panic spreads through Saigon as the communists march into the South Vietnamese capital. The United States evacuates its remaining diplomatic and military personnel as thousands of South Vietnamese desperately attempt to board U.S. helicopters to escape.

Responding
1. Was the turmoil during this period of United States history avoidable or inevitable? Explain.

2. The photograph on page 849 of a shocked and grief-stricken girl kneeling beside the body of one of the students killed at Kent State has come to define that event in the American memory. What recent events have been shaped in the public consciousness by vivid images?

850

MINI-LESSON: VISUAL LITERACY

Comparing and Contrasting

Teach Point out that comparing and contrasting two images that have some similarities and some differences can help students better understand both photographs.

Activity Idea Have students compare and contrast the photo at the top right of page 850 with the photograph at the bottom left of page 850. What similarities and differences do they find? Students might begin by comparing and contrasting the moods of the two photographs. (*Possible response: There is pomp and circumstance surrounding the President's flight, and desperation, pushing and shoving as people try to save lives during the evacuation.*)

Language History

Euphemisms: Polite and Deadly Language

 As for your criticism of our pacification, you are right that war is devastating. But we are doing everything we can to limit that.

At first glance, one hardly notices that this quote by President Lyndon Johnson is talking about the violent death of American soldiers and others in Vietnam. During wars, government and military leaders use many euphemisms—mild or indirect expressions used in place of harsh, direct ones—to direct their own attention, as well as the public's, away from the brutal reality of war.

In the early years of the Vietnam War the U.S. government referred to the fighting in Vietnam as a *police action* to avoid calling it war. The Pentagon coined many euphemisms designed to obscure what was really happening in Vietnam. Mercenaries—soldiers serving for pay in a foreign army—were known as *civilian irregular defense soldiers*, refugees were *ambient noncombatant personnel*, and dead civilians were called *collateral damage*. Spraying an area with machine-gun fire was known as *reconnaissance by fire;* a *traumatic amputation* occurred when a soldier's arm or leg was blown off. Perhaps most chilling of all: *aluminum transfer containers* was the term for coffins used to transport dead soldiers home.

Soldiers stationed in Vietnam used euphemisms as a way of protecting themselves from the difficulty of their mission. A *birdfarm* was an aircraft carrier loaded with weapons, A Vietcong (enemy) soldier was a *hard-hat* and a Vietnamese home was called a *hooch.*

Euphemisms don't only occur during times of war, of course. Whenever there's an unpleasant task to do, you can be sure euphemisms will be created to describe it. Whereas in the past companies might *fire* or *lay off* employees, today they are more likely to *down-size*. A politician may not admit to wanting to raise taxes, but may see a need for *revenue enhancement*. The danger in euphemisms, of course, is that they shield us from realities that we are sometimes better off confronting head-on, and may lull us into doing nothing when we should be taking action.

Language History   **851**

Language History

Teaching Objectives
- To recognize euphemisms
- To understand the use of euphemisms

Introduce

Present a simple example of a direct and euphemistic communication, for example
- die
- laid to rest
- pass on
- kick the bucket
- go on to their eternal glory

Ask students to talk about the kinds of circumstances where they would find euphemisms in use. Then have students read the article and consider the relationship between the words that were used and the concept to which the words referred.

Follow Up

Ask students to translate the common into the euphemistic. Students might take a school announcement, school rules, or even a portion of a folk or fairy tale and rewrite it into a palatable piece of mild and indirect prose.

CONTENT AREA READING

Domestic Employment (Homework)

Encourage students to follow the news in newspapers, news magazines, and on radio and television to find examples of euphemisms. Ask students to bring in the examples that they find and post them in the classroom along with the euphemism's more direct meaning.

Writing Workshop

WRITER'S BLUEPRINT
Specs

The Specs in the Writer's Blueprint address these writing and thinking skills:

- researching
- questioning
- interviewing
- orienting the reader
- paraphrasing
- evaluating evidence
- making judgments
- punctuating quotations correctly

These Specs serve as your lesson objectives, and they form the basis for the **Assessment Criteria Specs** for a superior paper, which appear on the final TE page for this lesson. You might want to read through the Assessment Criteria Specs with students when you begin the lesson.

Linking Literature to Writing

Lead a discussion about the personalities, events, and issues of the 1960s as reflected in the literature. Have students find examples in the selections to summarize or read aloud for the class.

STEP 1 PREWRITING
Choose your subject

Encourage students to include people of different professions, races, and genders in brainstorming a list of possible subjects born before 1945.

In the Midst of Struggle . . .

Narrative Writing

Writing Workshop

Reflecting on the Sixties

Assignment Work in a small group to explore the 1960s.

> ## WRITER'S BLUEPRINT
>
> | | |
> |---|---|
> | Product | An interview |
> | Purpose | To present personal reflections on the 1960s by someone who lived during that era |
> | Audience | Anyone with an interest in the 1960s |
> | Specs | As the creators of a successful interview, your group should: |
>
> ❑ Choose someone born before 1945 who is willing to be interviewed about the 1960s.
>
> ❑ Research and prepare interview questions about personalities, events, and issues of the 1960s. Then interview your subject, focusing on his or her personal reflections about the personalities, events, and issues from your research.
>
> ❑ Begin your paper by introducing your subject. Give background on who the person is now, and who the person was then. Then write your interview, using a mix of descriptive details, paraphrases, and direct quotations.
>
> ❑ Conclude by telling whether you would have liked to have lived during the 1960s and why.
>
> ❑ Follow the rules of grammar, usage, spelling, and mechanics. Take care to punctuate quotations correctly.

STEP 1 PREWRITING

Choose your subject. Brainstorm a list of people born before 1945 who are well-known to members of your group. When you make your choice, be sure to contact him or her right away and arrange for a live interview. (See the Or . . . option at the bottom of the next page.)

WRITING WORKSHOP OVERVIEW

Product
Narrative writing: An interview

Prewriting
Choose your subject—Review the literature—Research the 1960s—Develop interview questions—Interview your subject
Unit 7 Resource Book
Prewriting Worksheets
pp. 99–100

Drafting
Draft the introduction—Draft the interview—Draft the conclusion
Transparency Collection
Student Models for Writing Workshop 25, 26

Revising
Ask another group—Strategy: When to Quote Directly and When to Paraphrase
Unit 7 Resource Book
Revising Worksheet p. 101

Editing
Ask another group—Strategy: Punctuating Direct Quotations
Unit 7 Resource Book
Grammar Worksheet p. 102
Grammar Check Test p. 103

Presenting
Magazine Article
Copy to Subject

Looking Back
Self-evaluate—Reflect—For Your Working Portfolio
Unit 7 Resource Book
Assessment Worksheet p. 104
Transparency Collection
Fine Art Writing Prompt 13

Review the literature in this part of the unit, as well as the Interdisciplinary Study, to start developing interview questions. What events, issues, and personalities from the 1960s do the authors focus on? In a group, brainstorm ideas and organize them in a chart like this one:

1960s		
Events	**Issues**	**Personalities**
Vietnam War	—U.S. and French involvement in Vietnam —U.S. citizens' reactions to involvement in Vietnam	Diem

LITERARY SOURCE

"They didn't know the first thing about Diem's tyranny, or the nature of Vietnamese nationalism, or the long colonialism of the French— . . . it was a war to stop the Communists, plain and simple, which was how they liked things. . . ."
from "On the Rainy River" by Tim O'Brien

Research the 1960s. Consult other sources to add to your chart. Consider books; magazine and newspaper articles; 1960s TV shows, movies, and music; online sources; and other people you know who lived during the era. Along the way, gather together photographs and other illustrations from magazines and newspapers of the time to use when you present your interview.

Develop interview questions. Working as a group, develop a list of interview questions that focus on those issues, events, and personalities that your research indicates are the most interesting and prominent. Here are some tips:

- Write each question on a separate piece of paper to give plenty of room to take notes on the answers.

- If you know your subject has detailed knowledge about a particular issue, plan to ask a number of questions about it. (See the first Or . . . option.)

- Include questions that focus on your subject's background: who he or is now (occupation, interests, accomplishments), and who he or she was then, in the 1960s. You'll need this information when you draft your introduction.

Interview your subject. Be on time and be prepared. If your subject agrees, take his or her picture to use when you present the interview. If you plan to tape-record the interview, be sure you have your subject's permission beforehand. Here are more interview tips:

- Tape-record the interview, if you can, to ensure the accuracy of the information and of the direct quotes you will use.

- Whether you tape the interview or not, take careful notes.

OR . . .
Give your subject an idea of the topics you plan to focus on and ask him or her for some initial reactions. Use these reactions to help you formulate your questions.

OR . . .
If your subject can't be interviewed in person, arrange to conduct the interview by phone. A third option is to submit a list of questions by mail first and then follow up with a phone interview.

Review the literature

Allow students to brainstorm, writing their thoughts on the board. Then have them place the items listed on the board into the appropriate columns in their own charts. Have them look back at the selections to complete any blanks in the chart.

Research the 1960s

Help students assemble a list of possible sources: people and places where they might find information on the 1960s. For additional support, see the worksheet referenced below.

Unit 7 Resource Book
Prewriting Worksheet, p. 99

Develop interview questions

Have students jot down what they already know about their subjects. Based on these notes, have students predict what issues or events may have been significant in the subjects' lives during the 1960s. For additional support, see the worksheet referenced below.

Unit 7 Resource Book
Prewriting Worksheet, p. 100

Interview your subject

Students might practice interviewing by doing some role-playing with a partner. The interviewee and interviewer could pick a current issue of interest to use for asking questions and taking notes during an interview.

Connections to
Writer's Notebook
For selection-related prompts, refer to Writer's Notebook.

Connections to
Writer's Resource
For additional writing prompts, refer to Writer's Resource.

BUILDING ENGLISH PROFICIENCY

ESL
LEP
ELD
SAE
LD

Planning a Research Strategy

Encourage students to prepare questions that will help guide their research. Offer these examples, based on the Writer's Blueprint; have students suggest others.

Personalities: Whose records, movies, and TV shows were the most popular? Which politicians and sports figures did many people greatly admire—or dislike?

Events: Which topics turn up repeatedly in news magazines of the time? Which events could complete this statement: *The world was never the same after _____ ?*

Issues: What causes brought people together for rallies? What sorts of messages appeared on T-shirts and bumper stickers?

STEP 2 DRAFTING
Draft the introduction

Suggest that students begin with the subject now and finish with the subject in the 1960s, thus leading the reader from the present back into the period that will be covered during the interview that will follow.

Draft the interview

Remind students that direct quotes from their subjects will add more life to their drafts if they are proceeded by colorful and descriptive details about the subject's appearance, mannerisms, and movements.

Draft the conclusion

Have students make a chart, heading one column "Reasons why I would like to have lived in the 1960s" and the other "Reasons why I would not like to have lived in the 1960s." These lists can then be used to support students' conclusions.

The Student Models

The **transparencies** referenced below are authentic student models. Review them with students before they draft. These questions will help:

1. What prominent feature of the Writer's Blueprint did both writers fail to include? (direct quotations)

2. Which writer does a better job of giving background information about the subject? Point out examples.

3. Which writer gives you a better feel for the personality of the subject? Why is this so?

Transparency Collection
Student Models for Writing
Workshop 25, 26

STEP 3 REVISING
Ask another group
(Peer assessment)

After reading the drafts, suggest that groups meet together and discuss whether additional information needs to be included to present a more complete picture of the subject.

- Although it's important to prepare your questions in advance, listen carefully to the answers. Don't focus so intently on asking the next question on your list that you fail to ask the follow-up questions that will add the necessary detail and depth to enrich the interview.

- Make notes on your subject's appearance and mannerisms.

OR . . .
If you've taped the interview, edit the actual tape before you draft. Eliminate extraneous information and rearrange the order to create a smooth narrative flow. Then write your draft from this edited tape.

STEP 2 DRAFTING

Draft the introduction. Be sure to include background information about who your subject is now (occupation, interests, accomplishments), and who your subject was then, in the 1960s.

Draft the interview. Use a format that mixes descriptive details about the subject's appearance and mannerisms, paraphrases of what was said, and direct quotations. For example:

> paraphrase
>
> We asked if he'd ever seen the Beatles in person. He ran a hand through his salt and pepper hair and furrowed his brow, then raised a hand in the air. "Once, yes," he said. "It was in my college days—in Chicago." He smiled at the thought, lowering his arm and settling back in his chair. "Let's see now . . ."
>
> descriptive detail   direct quotation

STUDENT MODEL

Look ahead to the Revising Strategy in Step 3 of this lesson for tips on when to paraphrase material and when to quote directly.

Draft the conclusion. Separately, complete this sentence:

From our research and interview I get the impression that I would/would not like to have lived then because _____.

Then share your impressions and draft your conclusion.

STEP 3 REVISING

Ask another group to comment on your draft before you revise it. Use the checklist on the next page as a guide.

MINI-LESSON: WRITING STYLE
Quoting Versus Paraphrasing

Teach   Go over the Revising Strategy feature on page 855 to point out the differences between quoting directly and paraphrasing.

Activity Idea   Get together published interviews in books, newspapers, and magazines and have students find examples of direct quotations and paraphrases. Choose several to model and discuss. Have students concentrate on how the direct quotations reveal the personalities of the people being interviewed and how the paraphrases help set up the sections of direct quotation.

Apply   Urge students to look over their drafts and mark places where they might want to change quoted material to paraphrased material, and vice-versa.

✔ Did we start by introducing our subject, then and now?

✔ Does our interview focus on issues, events, and personalities of the 1960s?

✔ Have we presented our interview as a mix of descriptive details, paraphrases, and direct quotations?

Revising Strategy

When to Quote Directly and When to Paraphrase

A paraphrase is a summary of what was said (I asked him what happened next), while a direct quotation gives the speaker's exact words ("We got into the car"). Paraphrases are used to move the interview along smoothly and to lead into—set up—direct quotations. For example:

○   We asked Eddie for more details about the rally. At first he couldn't

    recall anything and we talked about how hard it is to remember things you

○   haven't thought about in a long while. Then a thought came to him. "Yes,

    now I remember," he said. "Things started to get scary when the protesters

○   began chanting. . . ."

STUDENT MODEL

Look back at your draft and see if you can move things along more smoothly by mixing paraphrases and direct quotations.

STEP 4 EDITING

Ask another group to review your revised draft before you edit. When you edit, look for errors in grammar, usage, spelling, and mechanics. Look at each sentence to make sure you are punctuating direct quotations correctly.

Revising Strategy: When to Quote Directly and When to Paraphrase

As students listen (but do not read along), read the student model aloud and have a student volunteer identify which part of the paragraph is paraphrased and which part is a direct quote. Discuss how the quote adds to the paragraph.

For additional support, see the mini-lesson at the bottom of page 854 and the worksheet referenced below.

 *Unit 7 Resource Book*
Revising Worksheet, p. 101

 Connections to
Writer's Resource

Refer to the Grammar, Usage, and Mechanics Handbook on Writer's Resource.

STEP 4 EDITING
**Ask another group
(Peer assessment)**

Make sure all group members read each other's drafts.

MINI-LESSON: GRAMMAR

Punctuating Direct Quotations

Displays the following sentences and have students make necessary corrections.

1. "I will be here for three days, she said. I don't want to be disturbed by anyone." ("I will be here for three days," she said. "I don't want to be disturbed by anyone.")

2. The fireman shouted, There are still two people in the house! (The fireman shouted, "There are still two people in the house!")

3. "I am from England," Portia said. (correct)

4. "It has been raining for three days. Mike told us on the phone. The temperature has not been above forty. And everybody is in a bad mood." ("It has been raining for three days," Mike told us on the phone. "The temperature has not been above forty. And everybody is in a bad mood.")

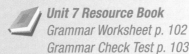 *Unit 7 Resource Book*
Grammar Worksheet p. 102
Grammar Check Test p. 103

Editing Strategy: Punctuating Direct Quotations

For additional support, see the mini-lesson at the bottom of page 855 and the worksheets referenced below.

Unit 7 Resource Book
Grammar Worksheet, p. 102
Grammar Check Test, p. 103

Connections to
Writer's Resource

Refer to the Grammar, Usage, and Mechanics Handbook on Writer's Resource.

STEP 5 PRESENTING
Magazine Article

Have students arrange their layouts for the articles with a balance between words and pictures, so the articles will look appealing to readers before they begin reading them.

Copy to Subject

Allow students time to write thank-you notes to subjects.

STEP 6 LOOKING BACK
Self-evaluate

The *Assessment Criteria Specs* at the bottom of this page are for a superior paper. You might want to post these in the classroom. Students can then evaluate themselves based on these criteria. For a complete scoring rubric, use the *Assessment Worksheet* referenced below.

Unit 7 Resource Book
Assessment Worksheet, p. 104

Reflect

You may want to have the groups discuss the second checked question before starting to write their answers individually.

To further explore the theme, use the Fine Art Transparency referenced below.

Transparency Collection
Fine Art Writing Prompt 13

856

Editing Strategy

FOR REFERENCE
For more information on punctuating direct quotations, see the Language and Grammar Handbook at the back of this text.

Punctuating Direct Quotations

Follow these rules for punctuating direct quotations:

- If a quotation is uninterrupted, put quotation marks only at the beginning and end of the entire quotation, no matter how many sentences are in it: "No, I don't think so. I'd like to, though."

- If a quotation is interrupted by a speaker tag or some other words that are not part of the actual quotation, use a separate set of quotation marks for each part: "No, I don't think so," he said. "I'd like to, though."

COMPUTER TIP
If you do a magazine article presentation, plan your layout in advance and format your text so that it wraps around and along the sides of your illustrations.

STEP 5 PRESENTING

- Turn your materials into a magazine article, with captioned visuals, including a photograph of your subject. (See the Computer Tip.)

- Present a copy of your written material to your subject.

STEP 6 LOOKING BACK

Self-evaluate. What grade would *you* give your paper? Look back at the Writer's Blueprint and give yourself a score on each point, from 6 (superior) to 1 (inadequate).

Reflect. Think about what you've learned from writing this interview as you write answers to these questions.

✔ How does what you know of life in the 1960s compare with life today? What are some similarities? some differences?

✔ What are some lessons you learned about the art of interviewing? Next time you conduct an interview, what will you do differently?

For Your Working Portfolio Add your interview and reflection responses to your working portfolio.

ASSESSMENT CRITERIA SPECS

Here are the criteria for a superior paper. A full six-level rubric for this paper appears on the *Assessment Worksheet* referenced below.
6 Superior The writer of a 6 paper impressively meets these criteria:

- Orients the reader by drawing concise portraits of the subject now and during the 1960s.
- Presents an interview that gives insights into the subject's personality as well as past experiences, incorporating a smooth flow of descriptive details, paraphrasing, and direct quotations.

- Shows real knowledge of the 1960s acquired through extensive research.
- Concludes with personal reactions to the 1960s that show that the writer has gained genuine insights from the research, interviewing, and writing.
- Makes few, if any, mistakes in grammar, usage, spelling, and mechanics. Punctuates quotations correctly.

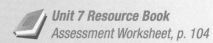

Unit 7 Resource Book
Assessment Worksheet, p. 104

Beyond Print

Multimedia Presentations

You are living in an age in which modern technology—computers, VCRs, CD ROMs, and programs with multimedia capabilities—can transform traditional reports and speeches into exciting media events. Whenever you use a combination of media to communicate to an audience, you are making a multimedia presentation. This includes speeches, posters, slides, video, projected images, graphs, recordings, or even skits.

The computer is a powerful tool in producing any multimedia presentation. You can hook up the computer to a projection unit in order to use the program during an oral presentation and provide animation, special effects, sound, and video. You might engage your audience with an interactive program in which viewers manipulate the type and order of information they receive by clicking a button.

Since each piece of media you add makes the presentation more complex, be thoughtful and organized in preparing your materials. Save only the most important information for posters or computer screens. Avoid materials that are cluttered or confusing.

Here are some hints for using multimedia in oral presentations.

- Use pictures and music that will supplement the information, not distract the audience.

- Use large type (for readability) and important heads (for emphasis) in projections. Present additional details orally or in handouts.

- Use concise, clear, and correctly spelled text.

- Plan, organize, and practice presenting your material.

- Project your voice so that everyone can hear.

Activity Option

- Prepare a multimedia presentation on one of the topics or famous personalities you've encountered in this section. Prepare a speech; then add one or more other media. You might use, for example, a slide, picture, or video footage from the Vietnam War, a recording of a speech by Malcolm X or King, or music from the 1960s.

Beyond Print   857

Beyond Print

Teaching Objectives

- To recognize ways to use technology to create multimedia presentations
- To follow guidelines for improving multimedia presentations

Curricular Connection: Technology Skills

You can use the material in this article to give students practice in preparing multimedia presentations using modern technology.

Introduce

Computers, VCRs, and CD-ROMs are technologies offering alternative ways to enhance presentations. Have students brainstorm different forms that a class presentation could take. Then have them read the article and add more ideas to their lists. They can keep their lists as a reference for the next time they prepare a presentation.

Activity Option

Encourage students to check the following resources for ideas and information for their presentation.

- *The 1950s: Picture History of the 20th Century* by Richard Tames (Watts, 1990)
- *Eyes on the Prize Civil Rights Reader,* ed. Clayborne Carson. (Viking Penguin, 1991)
- *Making Sense of the Sixties: Breaking Boundaries, Testing Limits* Video—60 minutes (PBS)
- *Panati's Parade of Fads, Follies, and Manias: The Origins of Our Most Cherished Obsessions* by Charles Panati (HarperCollins, 1991)

ANOTHER APPROACH

Without Technology: Do It Yourself

Students who do not have access to computers, slide projectors, tape recorders, VCRs, and other technology can still enhance their presentations by thoughtful use of multimedia. They can introduce music and sound effects that they themselves provide, invite guests with special knowledge of their topic for a panel discussion, provide demonstrations, and share thoughtfully prepared posters and charts.

Unit Wrap-Up

☞ MULTICULTURAL CONNECTION

Students may have made choices and had interactions without full awareness of the cultural factors that shaped them. The following ideas and questions may facilitate discussion of the interactions and choices dealt with in Parts One and Two of Unit 7.

Interactions

- Social change may make interactions difficult.
- Different generations may have different understandings of their cultural heritage.

Possible Response   Students may mention "To Jesus Villanueva with Love" or "Everyday Use" as examples of heritage and personal choice leading to positive interactions.

Choices

- Moral training, emotional and psychological state, age, and beliefs also influence choices.
- Choices can be hard for different reasons: some are hard to make; others are hard to live with.
- Sometimes we find out too late that we have made poor choices.

Possible Response   Students may think that Tim O'Brien's decision was the most difficult because he wasn't sure within himself what was the right decision.

Activities

Activity 1   Ask students to consider and perhaps include in their dramatization both the interactions between people that happen when both people are present, and the introspective interaction that occurs when one person thinks about or plans to interact with the other.

Activity 2   Students may find it easiest to deal with an issue that they have personally faced.

☞ Multicultural Connections

Interactions

Part One: Person to Person Cultural factors influence the way people interact. In "I Stand Here Ironing," society's attempts to help the mother seem only to further alienate her from her daughter. Tension over different cultural values cause trouble for Dee and her mother in "Everyday Use." Young Maxine Hong Kingston's cultural heritage makes her interactions with teachers and other students difficult.

■ In which selections does cultural heritage—in the forms of family, community, and customs—seem to support and enhance positive interactions between people?

Choices

Part Two: In the Midst of Struggle . . . How we make choices is influenced both by our cultures of origin and the society around us. Lorraine Hansberry's father chose to fight for racial integration, even when it put his own family in danger. In "On the Rainy River," Tim O'Brien's personal convictions told him that the war in Vietnam was wrong, but community pressure was so strong that he chose to go to war anyway. Rico in "Village" was caught between the army, personal convictions, and his cultural heritage as he made his choices.

■ Which individual in this section do you think faced the most difficult choices? Explain.

Activities

Work in small groups on the following activities.

1. Choose the selection from Part One that you think presents the *worst* example of interactions between people. Do a dramatization of the selection, but, during the dramatization, stop the action in places where your group thinks the interactions could be improved, and explain what the people should have done instead.

2. Making the right choice can be tough sometimes. Choose an issue of interest to your group that involves a personal choice. Some examples of issues might be drug use, joining a gang, standing up against injustice, and so on. Make a list of the cultural and social pressures that help individuals make the right choice, and those that lead individuals in the wrong direction.

Independent and Group Projects

Art

The Essence of the Work Of all the works in Unit 7, which one had the greatest impact on you? Choose the piece that you thought was the most powerful and create a visual work of art that expresses your thoughts or impressions of the literature. Choose any medium you wish—sculpture, collage, painting, drawing, and so on. Exhibit your work in the classroom. Can your classmates tell which piece of literature your artwork relates to?

Music

Music of the Era Many of the musicians who were popular in the 1960s and early 1970s tried to capture the social upheaval of the times in their music. Artists such as the Beatles, the Rolling Stones, Bob Dylan, and Joan Baez sang about the Vietnam War, race relations, and the anger that many young people felt toward the "establishment." Working with a partner, put together an audio montage that you feel best reflects the Vietnam War era. Play them for your class and analyze the lyrics, telling how they relate to the issues of the times.

Drama

Sneak Preview Working with a group of students, create a video "sneak preview" of Unit 7, as if to capture the interest of students who have not yet read the literature. Choose some of the highlights of the literature—your favorite scenes from stories, poems, and so on, and present them in the form of a video. You may want to read the passages dramatically, or actually dramatize some scenes. Include some of your own thoughts and impressions about the works in Unit 7 as well. You may wish to include music and art in your video.

Multimedia

The Author's Life Choose one of the authors from this unit to research. Gather information about the author's life and times, most well-known works, motivation for writing, and so on. Present your information in a hypertext report, using pictures, sound, and text, if possible.

859

Art

Students should choose a medium based on factors such as

- choosing a medium that they can work in comfortably or skillfully
- choosing a medium which will help to convey their thoughts and feelings

Music

Encourage students to interview adults who remember the music of the era for suggestions of specific songs that might cast a light on the social upheaval.

Drama

To help students focus on what they might include in their previews, encourage them to ask themselves these questions.

- What kinds of things do they want a preview to tell them?
- What kinds of things do they prefer to discover for themselves?

Multimedia

Encourage students to check reference sources for

- quotations from the authors
- critical commentary on their works
- biographical information
- lists of publications

Connections to
AuthorWorks

Information for completing this project can be found on AuthorWorks CD-ROM series.

Unit Test

Unit 7 Resource Book
New Selection, pp. 105–112
Test 1, pp. 113–114
Test 2, pp. 115–120

Planning Unit 8: American Voices Today

Literature

Integrated Language Arts

Literature	Literary	Writing/Grammar, Usage and Mechanics	Reading, Thinking, Listening, Speaking	Vocabulary/Spelling
Teenage Wasteland *by Anne Tyler* Short Story *(average)* p. 866	Mood Point of view Characterization Allusion, theme Foreshadowing	Advice Write a sequel Policy handbook Possessive nouns	Draw conclusions Make inferences	Connotation and denotation
Gary Keillor *by Garrison Keillor* Short Story *(easy)* p. 876	Hyperbole, style Characterization Idiom, repetition Figurative language Point of view, irony	Revise humorous narrative Summary Yearbook signing Punctuation: Colons	Recognize cause and effect Infer Visualize	Use new vocabulary in writing
Salvador Late or Early *by Sandra Cisneros* Short Story *(average)* p. 888	Figurative language Style	Essay Dialogue Recognize run-on sentences		
Poems *by Martín Espada* *(easy)* p. 893 *by Cathy Song* *(challenging)* p. 894 *by Barbara Kingsolver* *(average)* p. 896 *by Ana Castillo* *(easy)* p. 898	Theme Metaphor Imagery	Poem about self Informative subtitles Subordinate and coordinate clauses	Compare and contrast	Connotation and denotation
Mother Tongue *by Amy Tan* Autobiographical Essay *(average)* p. 902	Denotation and connotation Diction Theme	Paragraph Movie review Subject/verb agreement	Anticipate objections Recognize values Compare and contrast Draw conclusions Analyze	Analogies
This Is What It Means to Say Phoenix, Arizona *by Sherman Alexie* Short Story *(average)* p. 911	Flashback, plot Characterization Symbolism, imagery Flash-forward, theme Figurative language	Explanatory paragraph Sermon/speech Research report Consistent verb tense	Infer Levels of meaning	Expanding vocabulary
Top of the Food Chain *by T. Coraghessan Boyle* Short Story *(challenging)* p. 923	Hyperbole Tone Characterization	Environmental concerns Report Recognizing/avoiding jargon	Infer Recognize values Make judgments	Crossword puzzle Recognize idioms
A Blizzard Under Blue Sky *by Pam Houston* Short Story *(easy)* p. 930	Setting Characterization Imagery	Prose description Postcard messages Indefinite pronoun-verb agreement	Recognize values	
The Janitor *by August Wilson* Play *(challenging)* p. 936	Allusion Character	Speech Journal entry Parallel construction		

Meeting Individual Needs

Multi-modal Activities	Mini-Lessons
Create dialogue Oral critique Understanding specialized vocabulary Analyzing characters Making cultural connections	Connotation and denotation Mood Possessive nouns
Recognizing irony and humor Tracking shifts in time Exploring mood Presenting humorous readings	Hyperbole Punctuation: Colons Use new vocabulary in writing
Short speech Create a likeness of Salvador Understanding figurative language	Recognize run-on sentences
Panel discussion Electronic mail messages Exploring imagery Appreciating language and imagery	Make analogies Subordinate and coor- dinate clauses Connotation and denotation
Create a travel brochure Exploring an author's opinions Improving comprehension Exploring verbal phrases	Subject/verb agreement Draw conclusions
Retell story Prepare a dialogue Understanding cause and effect Analyzing dialogue Making cultural connections	Expanding vocab- ulary Consistent verb tense Flashback Order of events
Illustrated diagram Understanding story sequence Analyzing tone	Recognizing and avoiding jargon Recognize idioms
Weather report Oral report Understand key terms Exploring key concepts	Indefinite pronoun- verb agreement
Making cultural connections	Parallel construction

Interdisciplinary Studies
A Glimpse into the Future

Format	Content Area	Highlights	Skill
Article: **The Way We Will Be**	Future	An exploration of pos- sibilities for America's future.	
Article: **Future Technology: Dream or Nightmare?**	Future	The advantages and disadvantages of life in a technological age.	Reading aloud for the class
Article: **Future Fashions**	Future	Discussion of what fashions of the future may look like.	Information through illustration
Article: **The Changing Face of America** by Raul José Lopez	Career	The effects of increas- ing cultural diversity on the American society.	Graphing statistics

Writing Workshop

Mode	Writing Format	Writing Focus	Proofreading Skills
Narrative writing	A poem	Using imagery and figures of speech	Avoiding careless spelling mistakes

Program Support Materials

For Every Selection	For Every Writing Workshop
Unit Resource Book Graphic Organizer Study Guide Vocabulary Worksheet Grammar Worksheet Spelling, Speaking and Listening, or Literary Language Worksheet Alternate Check Test Vocabulary Test Selection Test	**Unit Resource Book** Prewriting Worksheet Revising Strategy Worksheet Editing Strategy Worksheet Presentation Worksheet Writing Rubric **Transparency Collection** Fine Art Transparency Student Writing Model Transparencies

For Every Interdisciplinary Study	Assessment
Unit Resource Book Study Guide Mini-Lesson Skill Worksheet	**Unit Resource Book** TE Check Tests Alternate Check Test (blackline master) Vocabulary Test (blackline master) Selection Test (blackline master) **Test Generator Software** **Assessment Handbook**

Teenage Wasteland

Audiotape Anne Tyler's *The Clock Winder*, 3 hours, is available from Random House.

Videotape *Breathing Lessons*, 98 minutes, Library Video Company, 1994, stars James Garner and Joanne Woodward and is based on Tyler's novel of the same name.

Community Resources You might invite someone from the community who works with troubled teenagers, such as a counselor or therapist, to visit the class and discuss some of the problems young people face and what can be done to address them.

Gary Keillor

Audiotape Garrison Keillor reads excerpts from his humorous work in *Lake Wobegon USA*, 5 hours, Minnesota Public Radio, 1993.

Community Resources Students might like to use the local library to explore the work of other American humorists who have written about high school and other aspects of teen-age life. One is Jean Shepherd, whose books *In God We Trust, All Others Pay Cash* and *Wanda Hickey's Night of Golden Memories and Other Disasters* deal collect often hilarious accounts of his experiences growing up in Northern Indiana.

Salvador Late or Early

Audiotape Students will enjoy hearing the author read her work in *Sandra Cisneros Reads*, 3 hours, Random House. Also consider the short stories read by the author on *The House on Mango Street*, 3 hours, Random House, 1992.

Coca-Cola and Coco Frío/Lost Sister/Naming Myself/Red Wagons

Audiotape The author reads from her novel and talks about her culture in *Ana Castillo Reads*, 30 minutes, A Moveable Feast, 1993.

Mother Tongue

Audiotape The author reads an unabridged version of her novel, *The Kitchen God's Wife*, 18 hours, Dove Audio, 1991.

Videotape *The Joy Luck Club*, 139 minutes, Hollywood Pictures Home Video, 1994, is based on Amy Tan's novel.

This Is What It Means to Say Phoenix, Arizona

Home Connection For an at-home activity, students might discuss with family members the people in their pasts with whom they have had differences. Have these differences ever been reconciled? If so, how were they resolved?

Top of the Food Chain

Audiotape Students may enjoy an abridged reading by Boyle of his novel, *The Road to Wellville*, 3 hours, Penguin-HighBridge, 1993.

Connections to
Custom Literature Database

For "Citizens of Tomorrow" Selections with Lessons

- from *Looking Back* by Edward Bellamy
- John F. Kennedy's Inaugural Address by John F. Kennedy

Additional theme-based selections can be accessed on the ScottForesman database.

Connections to
NovelWorks

An audiotape of *The Joy Luck Club*, one of Amy Tan's novels, is one of the may teaching tools included in the ScottForesman Novelworks kit.

Videotape *T. Corraghessan Boyle*, 30 minutes, Facets Multimedia, 1991, profiles this American writer.

Community Resources The environmental chain of events in "Top of the Food Chain" begins when American officials use DDT to deal with insect infestation on a tropical island. Students might use the resources of the local library to research the history of the rise and fall of the reputation of DDT as a pesticide cure-all.

A Blizzard Under Blue Sky

Audiotape Hear the author reading her work in *Pam Houston*, 30 minutes, New Letters.

Home Connection "It was so cold that . . ." Everyone has had to endure extreme weather conditions—heat, cold, wind, rain, snow—at one time or another. For an at-home activity, students might discuss with other family members different experiences of bad weather and the methods they used to cope with them.

The Janitor

Videotape Experience an interview and in-depth portrait of the playright in *August Wilson*, 22 minutes, *California Newsreel,* 1992, and in *August Wilson: A World of Ideas*, 30 minutes, PBS Video.

Welcome to Lake Wobegon

Garrison Keillor's radio broadcasts are excerpted on *Lake Wobegon USA,* available from Minnesota Public Radio.

Two Views of August Wilson

The videos *August Wilson* and *August Wilson: A World of Ideas* present in-depth looks at the famous playright.

American Voices Today

 ## Art Study

Oak Street Beach (1976) is a carefully cut and stitched felt, velvet, and corduroy appliqué wall hanging by Laura Lynch (1949–). Lynch is best known for her appliqué pictures of urban life, which take her six to twelve months to complete.

This panoramic view of Oak Street Beach in Chicago, Illinois, is 84" x 100" and shows crowds milling about on the sand along Lake Michigan and a variety of vehicles on busy Lake Shore Drive. The bathers and boaters appear framed by endless sky and water.

Visual Literacy Lynch's scenes are rather unrealistic, perhaps portraying the city the way city dwellers would like it to be rather than how it actually is.

Question How does this artwork portray an idealistic view? *(Possible responses: The traffic appears to be orderly; everyone is enjoying themselves; the colors are bright and clean; there is no evidence of personal conflicts or urban problems.)*

American Voices Today

Citizens of Tomorrow
Pages 862–954

THEMES IN AMERICAN LITERATURE

The Media
Theme Portfolio, pages 955–965

861

THEMATIC CONNECTIONS

Citizens of tomorrow come from many backgrounds that color their insights and influence their visions for a changing America.

Citizens of Tomorrow

The literature of today's authors asks us to take an introspective look at our backgrounds, our childhood experiences, and our ancestry to help us make sense of the past and prepare for the future.

Ideas to Explore

- Why might teen years be called a wasteland?
- Is there pain as well as pleasure in the memories of our youth?
- What are the identifying moments that make up a heritage?
- Where do we go from here?

Art Study

The icon for Citizens of Tomorrow is titled *Family Unit* by Diana Ong.

EXPLORING CONCEPTS

- Unity is an ideal that has not yet been realized.
- Unity and diversity need to be brought into balance.
- Diversity provides society with a rich array of traditions and understandings.
- We are products of both our childhood and our heritage.
- We can better understand ourselves when we better understand our cultural backgrounds.
- What is our responsibility to the future?

Question How would you describe your heritage? *(Responses will vary but students should be able to articulate a cultural identity.)*

Research Activity Have students find out more about the authors in Unit 8, read more of their work, and give book talks or write book reviews that include biographical information. Reviews could be compiled into a single volume for class distribution.

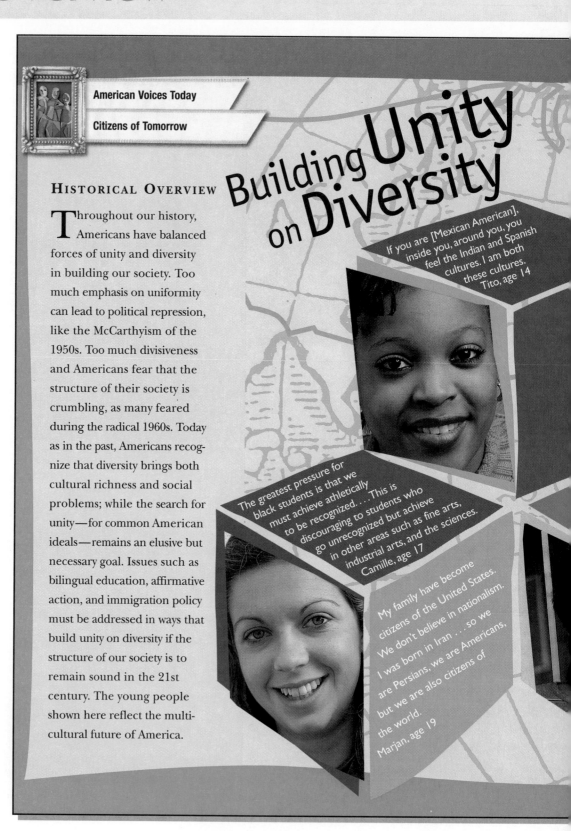

American Voices Today

Citizens of Tomorrow

Building Unity on Diversity

HISTORICAL OVERVIEW

Throughout our history, Americans have balanced forces of unity and diversity in building our society. Too much emphasis on uniformity can lead to political repression, like the McCarthyism of the 1950s. Too much divisiveness and Americans fear that the structure of their society is crumbling, as many feared during the radical 1960s. Today as in the past, Americans recognize that diversity brings both cultural richness and social problems; while the search for unity—for common American ideals—remains an elusive but necessary goal. Issues such as bilingual education, affirmative action, and immigration policy must be addressed in ways that build unity on diversity if the structure of our society is to remain sound in the 21st century. The young people shown here reflect the multicultural future of America.

If you are [Mexican American], inside you, around you, you feel the Indian and Spanish cultures. I am both these cultures.
Tito, age 14

The greatest pressure for black students is that we must achieve athletically to be recognized.... This is discouraging to students who go unrecognized but achieve in other areas such as fine arts, industrial arts, and the sciences.
Camille, age 17

My family have become citizens of the United States. We don't believe in nationalism. I was born in Iran ... so we are Persians, we are Americans, but we are also citizens of the world.
Marjan, age 19

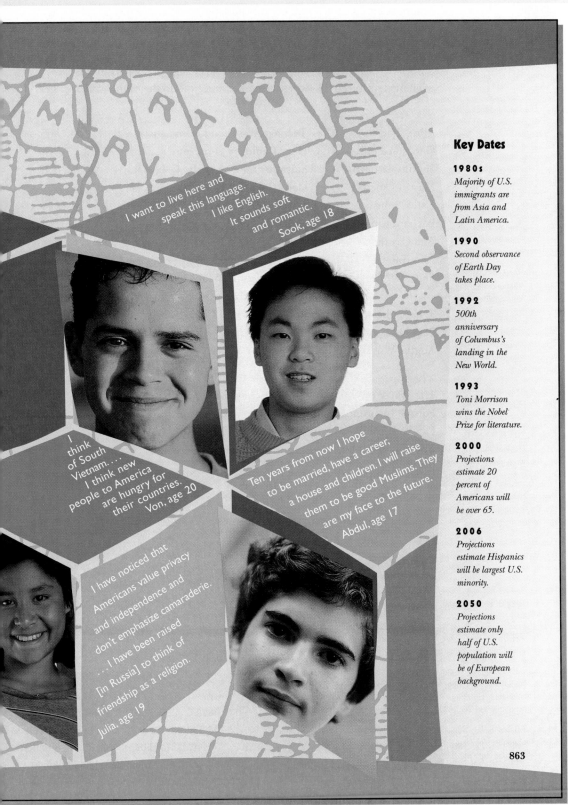

I want to live here and speak this language. I like English. It sounds soft and romantic.
Sook, age 18

I think of South Vietnam.... I think new people to America are hungry for their countries.
Von, age 20

Ten years from now I hope to be married, have a career, a house and children. I will raise them to be good Muslims. They are my face to the future.
Abdul, age 17

I have noticed that Americans value privacy and independence and don't emphasize camaraderie. ... I have been raised [in Russia] to think of friendship as a religion.
Julia, age 19

Key Dates

1980s
Majority of U.S. immigrants are from Asia and Latin America.

1990
Second observance of Earth Day takes place.

1992
500th anniversary of Columbus's landing in the New World.

1993
Toni Morrison wins the Nobel Prize for literature.

2000
Projections estimate 20 percent of Americans will be over 65.

2006
Projections estimate Hispanics will be largest U.S. minority.

2050
Projections estimate only half of U.S. population will be of European background.

863

Key Dates

1981–1990   7,338,000 people immigrated to the United States. Of those, 1,655,700 came from Mexico. Then, in the early 1990s, immigration from Mexico increased sharply, with nearly 1 million people arriving in 1991 alone.

1981–1990   European immigrants made up 10.4% of the total number of immigrants.

MATERIALS OF INTEREST

Books

Into a Strange Land: Unaccompanied Refugee Youth in America by Brent Ashabranner and Melissa Ashabranner (Dodd, Mead & Company, 1987)

Multimedia

Smithsonian's America: An Interactive Exhibition of American History and Culture (Smithsonian Institution, 1994)

Connections to
Custom Literature Database

For further historical background, under **Background Articles,** see **Postwar America 1945–.**

FOR ALL STUDENTS

Invite students to read the first paragraph on page 864 and then share their predictions for the future.

- What will the world be like 20 years from now? *(Responses will vary, but might include the role of computers, hi-tech communication; possible wars, political changes.)*
- What do you think you'll be doing in 20 years? *(Responses will vary. Ask students what events they think will lead to their predictions.)*

To further explore the theme, use the transparency referenced here.

Transparency Collection
Fine Art Writing Prompt 14

For At-Risk Students

Ask students to plan a time capsule that will describe their lives today to a future generation.

For Students Who Need Challenge

Students might investigate an aspect of American culture that has changed from 1776 to the present.

- How has education changed?
- How have the roles of women and minority groups changed?

⚙ MULTICULTURAL CONNECTION

The characters in the poems on pages 893–898 cope with cultural change.

Question What events might cause someone to have to cope with a cultural change? *(Possible responses: changes due to emigration to a new country or area; new political thought such as the vote for women; war; and society's expectations)*

864

Citizens of Tomorrow

Americans are facing a new century and a new millennium. The following selections present a cross-section of the lives and experiences of a changing America, and offer important insights for the citizens of tomorrow.

⚙ Multicultural Connection How does **cultural change** play a part in the lives of characters in the following selections, and how do they cope with change?

IDEAS THAT WORK

Motivating with Drama

Using drama in the classroom can help students know the characters of the literature perhaps better than they know themselves. The following assignment helps students to get inside of these characters.

The first part of the assignment is to create a setting for two or more of the characters from the stories. The environment they choose should allow the characters to express their views, for example, a Nobel Prize winner's dinner or a sinking ship.

Then have students create a situation that moves the characters to action. I have students use a play format for their ideas, and in addition to dialogue, I expect students to include stage directions for movement and mannerisms, as well as notes on costumes and props.

The backbone of this assignment should reflect an understanding of what the characters are about and the ideas they embody.

Montserrat Fontes
Glendale, California

Before Reading

Teenage Wasteland

by Anne Tyler

Anne Tyler
born 1941

Anne Tyler grew up in North Carolina, attended Duke University in Raleigh and Columbia University in New York, and in 1963 married Taghi Mohammed Modarressi, a psychiatrist and writer. They and their two daughters settled in Baltimore, Maryland in 1967. Baltimore has been the setting for most of Tyler's novels. The family is at the center of Tyler's fiction, and her quirky characters endure the crises in their lives. Tyler's novels are both popular and critically acclaimed. *Dinner at the Homesick Restaurant* (1982) was nominated for the Pulitzer Prize, and *Breathing Lessons* (1988) won it. *The Accidental Tourist* (1985), which was made into a movie starring William Hurt, won the National Book Critics Circle Award.

Building Background

You're the Parent Imagine you are a parent, and your teenage son or daughter is having problems in school. Your child's grades have been steadily slipping, he or she has been caught skipping classes, and you suspect your child is smoking or drinking. What should you, as a parent, do when you see these signs of trouble? As a class, brainstorm ways to cope with these problems. Use a web like the one shown to record your ideas.

Best ways to cope with your teenage son or daughter's problems.

Literary Focus

Mood "When I opened the door after school, I was greeted with the tempting aroma of chocolate chip cookies cooling on the counter and the pleasant chatter of my mother playing with my twin brothers at the kitchen table." The preceding sentence establishes a cozy, cheerful mood. The kitchen setting is warm and inviting. The image of a mother playing with her children is heartwarming. The sensory description of the aroma of baking cookies is appealing, and the connotation associated with baking cookies—that of dispensing love—adds to the overall mood. In addition, the choice of words—*greeted, tempting aroma,* and *pleasant chatter*—contributes to the cheerful mood. As you read "Teenage Wasteland," identify the mood of the story and notice how Anne Tyler establishes that mood.

Writer's Notebook

Heart to Heart Once again, you're the parent, and your teenager is having problems in school—getting bad grades, cutting classes, smoking, drinking, and so on. You just can't seem to talk to each other, so you try a different route—you write a letter. What will you say to your teenager to try to make a difference in his or her life? Write your letter in your notebook.

Teenage Wasteland **865**

SUPPORT MATERIALS OVERVIEW

Unit 8 Resource Book
- Graphic Organizer, p. 1
- Study Guide, p. 2
- Vocabulary, p. 3
- Grammar, p. 4
- Alternate Check Test, p. 5
- Vocabulary Test, p. 6
- Selection Test, pp. 7–8

Building English Proficiency
- Literature Summaries
- Activities, p. 233

Reading, Writing & Grammar Skillbook
- Reading, pp. 73–74
- Grammar, Usage, and Mechanics, pp. 182–185

Technology
- Audiotape
- Personal Journal Software
- Custom Literature Database
  For a contrasting treatment of students, a parent, and school, see "An Immigrant Goes to School" by Mary Antin on the database.
- Test Generator Software

Before Reading

Building Background

Students may consider rewards for good behavior, responses to unacceptable behavior, processes such as counseling, and so forth.

Literary Focus

Remind students that the **mood,** or atmosphere, of a literary work can be created by
- descriptions of a setting or settings
- characters' words and actions

A story's mood can change or intensify as the story unfolds.

Writer's Notebook

Invite discussion of expressing feelings through a letter. Is it easier to say what you really feel on paper or in a computer message than it is in person? Why or why not?

More About Anne Tyler

Anne Tyler has said that the heroes in her books "are first the ones who manage to endure and second the ones who somehow are able to grant other people the privacy of the space around them and yet produce some warmth."

Another work by Anne Tyler with a teenage protagonist is *Saint Maybe* (novel, 1991).

During Reading

Selection Objectives

- To explore themes of adolescent alienation and parental concern
- To appreciate mood in a literary work
- To consider denotations and connotations of words
- To recognize forms of possessive nouns

Unit 8 Resource Book
Graphic Organizer, p. 1
Study Guide, p. 2

Theme Link

Parents can recognize their children as citizens of the future, but preparations for that future may be tough for alienated adolescents. In the story, a mother seeks to stem her son's downward slide, in and out of school. Her best intentions don't come to pass.

Vocabulary Preview

morass, a difficult situation; a puzzling mess

amiably, in a pleasant and agreeable way

forlorn, wretched in feeling or looks; unhappy

talisman, anything that acts as a charm

vindictive, feeling a strong tendency toward revenge

Students can add the words and definitions to their word lists in the Writer's Notebook.

---

1 ## Literary Element

Point of View

Questions

- Is the story told from the first-person or third-person point of view? *(third-person)*
- Which character's perspective does the narrator emphasize? *(Donny's mother, Daisy's)*
- How does the point of view affect how Donny's actions are portrayed? *(His actions are considered serious problems.)*

TEENAGE WASTELAND

Anne Tyler

He used to have very blond hair—almost white—cut shorter than other children's so that on his crown a little cowlick always stood up to catch the light. But this was when he was small. As he grew older, his hair grew darker, and he wore it longer—past his collar even. It hung in lank, taffy-colored ropes around his face, which was still an endearing face, fine-featured, the eyes an unusual aqua blue. But his cheeks, of course, were no longer round, and a sharp new Adam's apple jogged in his throat when he talked.

In October, they called from the private school he attended to request a conference with his parents. Daisy went alone; her husband was at work. Clutching her purse, she sat on the principal's couch and learned that Donny was noisy, lazy, and disruptive, always fooling around with his friends, and he wouldn't respond in class.

In the past, before her children were born, Daisy had been a fourth-grade teacher. It shamed her now to sit before this principal as a parent, a delinquent parent, a parent who struck Mr. Lanham, no doubt, as unseeing or uncaring. "It isn't that we're not concerned," she said. "Both of us are. And we've done what we could, whatever we could think of. We don't let him watch TV on school nights. We don't let him talk on the phone till he's finished his homework. But he tells us he doesn't *have* any homework or he did it all in **1** study hall. How are we to know what to believe?"

From early October through November, at Mr. Lanham's suggestion, Daisy checked Donny's assignments every day. She sat next to him as he worked, trying to be encouraging, sagging inwardly as she saw the poor quality of everything he did—the sloppy mistakes in math, the illogical leaps in his English themes, the history questions left blank if they required any research.

Daisy was often late starting supper, and she couldn't give as much attention to Donny's younger sister. "You'll never guess what happened at . . ." Amanda would begin, and Daisy would have to tell her, "Not now, honey."

By the time her husband Matt came home, she'd be snappish. She would recite the day's hardships—the fuzzy instructions in English, the botched history map, the <u>morass</u>[1] of unsolvable algebra equations. Matt would look surprised and confused, and Daisy would gradually wind down. There was no way, really, to convey how exhausting all this was.

In December, the school called again. This time, they wanted Matt to come as well. She and Matt had to sit on Mr. Lanham's couch like two bad children and listen to the news: Donny had improved only slightly, raising a D in history to a C, and a C in algebra to a B-minus. What was worse, he had developed new problems. He had cut classes on a least three occasions. Smoked in the furnace room. Helped Sonny Barnett break

---

1. morass (mə ras′), *n.* a difficult situation; puzzling mess.

SELECTION SUMMARY

Teenage Wasteland

Daisy Coble tells how her fifteen-year-old son Donny is having trouble in a private high school. He is noisy, lazy, and disruptive. He cuts classes, smokes in the furnace room, and is suspected of drinking on occasion. At the school's suggestion, his parents take him to a psychologist and then hire an adult tutor. Cal, the tutor, hits it off with Donny, but Daisy fails to see positive results. In fact, Donny's grades slip further. In April, the teenager is expelled from school. The Cobles place him in another school and fire the tutor. By June, Donny has vanished, and the police assume he's run away. Three months later he is still missing and Daisy is wondering "what went wrong, where they made their first mistake."

For summaries in other languages, see the Building English Proficiency book.

◄ What is the boy feeling in Alex Katz's 1972 painting, *Ada and Vincent in the Car?* What is the woman feeling? What clues from the painting support your ideas?

Art Study

Alex Katz was born in New York in 1927. His personal style combines realism with a deliberate naïveté.

Possible Responses to Caption

The boy may be feeling bored, mildly curious about something happening nearby, or wanting to be somewhere else. The woman may be waiting for someone or feeling thoughtful. Their facial expressions and hands are clues, although neither is showing a strong emotion.

Visual Literacy   This work can illustrate that in art realism may include the depiction of people, places, and things with a simplicity similar to cartoon art but a tone that does not parody or exaggerate features as cartoon art does. Note the background seen through the car windows. It is stylized, limiting the focus to the people and the car interior.

---

2 **Literary Focus**

Mood

Discuss with students the description of Daisy and Matt. Point out that it sketches a picture of the couple in the reader's mind, but it also contributes to the mood of sadness that permeates the story. Although the two seem to be decent people, Daisy thinks they are "failures."

---

into a freshman's locker. And last week, during athletics, he and three friends had been seen off the school grounds; when they returned, the coach had smelled beer on their breath.

Daisy and Matt sat silent, shocked. Matt rubbed his forehead with his fingertips. Imagine, Daisy thought, how they must look to Mr. Lanham: an overweight housewife in a cotton dress and a too-tall, too-thin insurance agent in a baggy, frayed suit. Failures, both of them—the kind of people who are always hurrying to catch up, missing the point of things that everyone else grasps at once. She wished she'd worn nylons instead of knee socks.

It was arranged that Donny would visit a psychologist for testing. Mr. Lanham knew just the person. He would set this boy straight, he said.

When they stood to leave, Daisy held her stomach in and gave Mr. Lanham a firm, responsible handshake.

Donny said the psychologist was a jackass and the tests were really dumb; but he kept all three of his appointments, and when it was time for the follow-up conference with the psychologist and both parents, Donny combed his hair and seemed unusually sober and subdued. The psychologist said Donny had no serious emotional problems. He was merely going through a difficult period in his life. He required some academic help and a better sense of self-worth. For this reason, he was suggesting a man named Calvin Beadle, a tutor with considerable psychological training.

In the car going home, Donny said he'd be damned if he'd let them drag him to some stupid fairy tutor. His father told him to watch his language in front of his mother.

That night, Daisy lay awake pondering the term "self-worth." She had always been free with her praise. She had always told Donny he had talent, was smart, was good with his hands. She had made a big to-do over every little gift he gave her. In fact, maybe she had gone too far, although, Lord knows, she had meant every word. Was that his trouble?

She remembered when Amanda was born.

BUILDING ENGLISH PROFICIENCY

Understanding Specialized Vocabulary

To present the topic of teenage alienation, author Anne Tyler uses mental health and behavioral terms that may be unfamiliar to some students. For example, Donny sees a *psychologist,* who mentions the boy's *sense of self-worth* to the parents. In an unusual usage, the mother refers to herself as if she is seen as a *delinquent* parent. Students can investigate the meanings of these terms.

- Invite students to list unfamiliar words and phrases that concern counseling, behavior, and emotional health in a chart.
- Ask students to invite a school counselor or an expert from the community to advise them about possible meanings. This counselor or other expert might be invited to speak to the class.

- Students also can use dictionaries to find definitions and then write the meanings in their own words.

Term	Meaning
delinquent	not living up to a duty
psychologist	scientist who studies people's minds

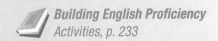

Building English Proficiency
Activities, p. 233

Draw Conclusions

Question   What does Daisy find difficult about being a parent? *(Possible responses: You only have one chance to raise your kids; you can't go back and do it over. You don't know whether to praise your children too much or too little; there's no "cookbook" that tells you the right way to do things.)*

Making Personal Connections

• Discuss Cal and his house with students: Does he seem like someone who relates well to teenagers? Why? *(Possible responses: Yes; he dresses like them; he talks to Donny as if he were a peer; his house seems set up to welcome teenagers and encourage them to spend time there.)*

• Ask: Would you like to have a tutor like Cal? *(Responses will vary.)*

The Author Speaks

"I want to live other lives. I've never quite believed that one chance is all I get. Writing is my way of taking chances."

Anne Tyler
quoted in Current Biography, *1981*

Donny had acted lost and bewildered. Daisy had been alert to that, of course, but still, a new baby keeps you so busy. Had she really done all she could have? She longed—she ached—for a time machine. Given one more chance, she'd do it perfectly—hug him more, praise him more, or perhaps praise him less. Oh, who can say . . .

The tutor told Donny to call him Cal. All his kids did he said. Daisy thought for a second that he meant his own children, then realized her mistake. He seemed too young, anyhow, to be a family man. He wore a heavy brown handlebar mustache. His hair was as long and stringy as Donny's, and his jeans as faded. Wire-rimmed spectacles slid down his nose. He lounged in a canvas director's chair with his fingers laced across his chest, and he casually, amiably² questioned Donny, who sat upright and glaring in an armchair.

"So they're getting on your back at school," said Cal. "Making a big deal about anything you do wrong."

"Right," said Donny.

"Any idea why that would be?"

"Oh, well, you know, stuff like homework and all," Donny said.

"You don't do your homework?"

"Oh well, I might do it sometimes but not just exactly like they want it." Donny sat forward and said, "It's like a prison there, you know? You've got to go to every class, you can never step off the school grounds."

"You cut classes sometimes?"

"Sometimes," Donny said, with a glance at his parents.

Cal didn't seemed perturbed.³ "Well," he said, "I'll tell you what. Let's you and me try working together three nights a week. Think you could handle that? We'll see if we can show that school of yours a thing or two. Give it a month; then if you don't like it, we'll stop. If *I* don't like it, we'll stop. I mean, sometimes people just don't get along, right? What do you say to that?"

"Okay," Donny said. He seemed pleased.

"Make it seven o'clock till eight, Monday, Wednesday, and Friday," Cal told Matt and Daisy. They nodded. Cal shambled to his feet, gave them a little salute, and showed them to the door.

This was where he lived as well as worked, evidently. The interview had taken place in the dining room, which had been transformed into a kind of office. Passing the living room, Daisy winced at the rock music she had been hearing, without registering it, ever since she had entered the house. She looked in and saw a boy about Donny's age lying on a sofa with a book. Another boy and a girl were playing Ping-Pong in front of the fireplace. "You have several here together?" Daisy asked Cal.

"Oh, sometimes they stay on after their sessions, just to rap. They're a pretty sociable group, all in all. Plenty of goof-offs like young Donny here."

He cuffed Donny's shoulder playfully. Donny flushed and grinned.

Climbing into the car, Daisy asked Donny, "Well? What did you think?"

But Donny had returned to his old evasive⁴ self. He jerked his chin toward the garage. "Look," he said. "He's got a basketball net."

Now on Mondays, Wednesdays, and Fridays, they had supper early—the instant Matt came home. Sometimes, they had to leave before they were really finished. Amanda would still be eating her dessert. "Bye, honey. Sorry," Daisy would tell her.

Cal's first bill sent a flutter of panic through Daisy's chest, but it was worth it, of course. Just look at Donny's face when they picked him up: alight and full of interest. The principal telephoned Daisy to tell her how Donny had improved. "Of course, it hasn't shown up in his

---

2. **amiably** (āʹmē ə blē), *adv.* in a pleasant and agreeable way.
3. **perturbed** (pər tėrbdʹ), *adj.* uneasy or troubled.
4. **evasive** (i vāʹsiv), *adj.* tending or trying to avoid by cleverness; misleading.

MINI-LESSON: VOCABULARY

Connotation and Denotation

Teach   Review with students that some words have both denotative and connotative meanings. A denotation is a literal or dictionary definition. Connotations include the inferences, implications, or feelings associated with a word. Part of a writer's craft is choosing words that evoke images and associations in the minds of readers.

Question   What is the denotative meaning of "stringy" on page 868: "His hair was as long and stringy as Donny's . . ."? *(string-like; resembling a string)* What is its connotative meaning? *(When applied to hair, the word "stringy" implies the hair is unkempt, perhaps dirty.)*

Activity Ideas

• Work as a class to think of other words that people apply to hair. Decide if the words have a negative, positive, or neutral connotation. *(Possible words: shiny, long, curly, straight, tresses, auburn, bouncy, body, blonde, raven, luster, dishwater)*

• Have student pairs find other instances of words in the story that Tyler may have chosen for their connotative meaning. The pairs can report their results to the class, explaining each word's denotative and connotative meanings.

grades yet, but several of the teachers have noticed how his attitude's changed. Yes sir, I think we're onto something here."

At home, Donny didn't act much different. He still seemed to have a low opinion of his parents. But Daisy supposed that was unavoidable— part of being fifteen. He said his parents were too "controlling"—a word that made Daisy give him a sudden look. He said they acted like wardens. On weekends, they enforced a curfew. And any time he went to a party, they always telephoned first to see if adults would be supervising. "For God's sake!" he said. "Don't you trust me?"

"It isn't a matter of trust, honey . . ." But there was no explaining to him.

His tutor called one afternoon. "I get the sense," he said, "that this kid's feeling . . . underestimated, you know? Like you folks expect the worst of him. I'm thinking we ought to give him more rope."

"But see, he's still so suggestible," Daisy said. "When his friends suggest some mischief—smoking or drinking or such—why, he just finds it very hard not to go along with them."

"Mrs. Coble," the tutor said, "I think this kid is hurting. You know? Here's a serious, sensitive kid, telling you he'd like to take on some grown-up challenges, and you're giving him the message that he can't be trusted. Don't you understand how that hurts?"

"Oh," said Daisy.

"It undermines his self-esteem—don't you realize that?"

"Well, I guess you're right," said Daisy. She saw Donny suddenly from a whole new angle: his pathetically poor posture, that slouch so **⑤** forlorn[5] that his shoulders seemed about to meet his chin . . . oh, wasn't it awful being young? She'd had a miserable adolescence herself and had always sworn no child of hers would ever be that unhappy.

They let Donny stay out later, they didn't call ahead to see if the parties were supervised, and they were careful not to grill him about his evening. The tutor had set down so many rules! They were not allowed any questions at all about any aspect of school, nor were they to speak with his teachers. If a teacher had some complaint, she should phone Cal. Only one teacher disobeyed—the history teacher, Miss Evans. She called one morning in February. "I'm a little concerned about Donny, Mrs. Coble."

"Oh, I'm sorry, Miss Evans, but Donny's tutor handles these things now . . ."

"I always deal directly with the parents. You are the parent," Miss Evans said, speaking very slowly and distinctly. "Now, here is the problem. Back when you were helping Donny with his homework, his grades rose from a D to a C, but now they've slipped back, and they're closer to an F."

"They are?"

"I think you should start overseeing his homework again."

She saw Donny suddenly from a whole new angle . . .

"But Donny's tutor says . . ."

"It's nice that Donny has a tutor, but you should still be in charge of his homework. With you, he learned it. Then he passed his tests. With the tutor, well, it seems the tutor is more of a crutch. 'Donny,' I say, 'a quiz is coming up on Friday. Hadn't you better be listening instead of talking?' 'That's okay, Miss Evans,' he says. 'I have a tutor now.' Like a talisman![6] I really think **⑥** you ought to take over, Mrs. Coble."

"I see," said Daisy. "Well, I'll think about that. Thank you for calling."

Hanging up, she felt a rush of anger at Donny. A talisman! For a talisman, she'd given up all luxuries, all that time with her daughter, her evenings at home!

She dialed Cal's number. He sounded muzzy.

---

5. **forlorn** (fôr lôrn′), *adj.* wretched in feeling or looks; unhappy.
6. **talisman** (tal′is mən), *n.* anything that acts as a charm.

Teenage Wasteland **869**

Allusion

The Who, a British rock and roll group, have influenced popular music with songs such as "My Generation" in the 1960s and "Teenage Wasteland" in the 1970s, as well as a rock opera, *Tommy* (1969). In the story, the song title "Teenage Wasteland" takes on personal meanings for the characters.

Question How does the image of a "teenage wasteland" contribute to the story's mood? (*Possible response: It introduces images of alienation and perhaps wasted opportunities for young people.*)

The allusion to music is a clue to the story's time setting, which may be the early 1980s. It was first published in 1983.

Foreshadowing

Donny's expulsion may not surprise readers; Tyler has given hints that something like it might happen.

Question What incidents or dialogue have foreshadowed Donny's expulsion? (*Possible responses: Daisy stops supervising Donny, on Cal's advice; Miss Evans says that Donny's grades have slipped; Cal's students look like "hoodlums" to Daisy; other students at Cal's have gotten into trouble.*)

870

"I'm sorry I woke you," she told him, "but Donny's history teacher just called. She says he isn't doing well."

"She should have dealt with me."

"She wants me to start supervising his homework again. His grades are slipping."

"Yes," said the tutor, "but you and I both know there's more to it than mere grades, don't we? I care about the *whole* child—his happiness, his self-esteem. The grades will come. Just give them time."

When she hung up, it was Miss Evans she was angry at. What a narrow woman!

It was Cal this, Cal that, Cal says this, Cal and I did that. Cal lent Donny an album by the Who. He took Donny and two other pupils to a rock concert. In March, when Donny began to talk endlessly on the phone with a girl named Miriam, Cal even let Miriam come to one of the tutoring sessions. Daisy was touched that Cal would grow so involved in Donny's life, but she was also a little hurt, because she had offered to have Miriam to dinner and Donny had refused. Now he asked them to drive her to Cal's house without a qualm.

This Miriam was an unappealing girl with blurry lipstick and masses of rough red hair. She wore a short, bulky jacket that would not have been out of place on a motorcycle. During the trip to Cal's she was silent, but coming back, she was more talkative. "What a neat guy, and what a house! All those kids hanging out, like a club. And the stereo playing rock . . . gosh, he's not like a grown-up at all! Married and divorced and everything, but you'd think he was our own age."

"Mr. Beadle was married?" Daisy asked.

"Yeah, to this really controlling lady. She didn't understand him a bit."

"No, I guess not," Daisy said.

Spring came, and the students who hung around at Cal's drifted out to the basketball net above the garage. Sometimes, when Daisy and Matt arrived to pick up Donny, they'd find him there with the others—spiky and excited,

jittering on his toes beneath the backboard. It was staying light much longer now, and the neighboring fence cast narrow bars across the bright grass. Loud music would be spilling from Cal's windows. Once it was the Who, which Daisy recognized from the time that Donny had borrowed the album. "*Teenage Wasteland,*" she said aloud, identifying the song, and Matt gave a short, dry laugh. "It certainly is," he said. He'd misunderstood; he thought she was commenting on the scene spread before them. In fact, she might have been. The players looked like hoodlums, even her son. Why, one of Cal's students had recently been knifed in a tavern. One had been shipped off to boarding school in midterm; two had been withdrawn by their parents. On the other hand, Donny had mentioned someone who'd been studying with Cal for five years. "Five years!" said Daisy. "Doesn't anyone ever stop needing him?"

Donny looked at her. Lately, whatever she said about Cal was read as criticism. "You're just feeling competitive," he said. "And controlling."

She bit her lip and said no more.

In April, the principal called to tell her that Donny had been expelled. There had been a locker check, and in Donny's locker they found five cans of beer and half a pack of cigarettes. With Donny's previous record, this offense meant expulsion.

Daisy gripped the receiver tightly and said, "Well, where is he now?"

"We've sent him home," said Mr. Lanham. "He's packed up all his belongings, and he's coming home on foot."

Daisy wondered what she would say to him. She felt him looming closer and closer, bringing this brand-new situation that no one had prepared her to handle. What other place would take him? Could they enter him in a public school? What were the rules? She stood at the living room window, waiting for him to show up. Gradually, she realized that he was taking too long. She checked the clock. She stared up the street again.

MINI-LESSON: LITERARY FOCUS

Mood

Teach The mood, or atmosphere, of a story is created by the description of settings, the actions and words of characters, and the author's tone.

Questions

• What is the dominant mood in "Teenage Wasteland"? (*Possible responses: sadness, futility, subdued family conflict*)

• How does the author create this mood? (*Possible response: Daisy's thoughts, the actions of characters, and the family's inability to solve the problem all help to create the*

mood. *Daisy sadly describes her frustrations; and Donny walks with a slouch and takes little interest in school, resulting in little success. Even the attempts to help seem misdirected.*)

Activity Idea Have students imagine a cheerful, successful teenage son or daughter and compare that image to the description of Donny at the bottom of page 869. Then they can compare and contrast the different moods that stories about the two teenage characters might evoke.

When an hour had passed, she phoned the school. Mr. Lanham's secretary answered and told her in a grave, sympathetic voice that yes, Donny Coble had most definitely gone home. Daisy called her husband. He was out of the office. She went back to the window and thought a while, and then she called Donny's tutor.

"Donny's been expelled from school," she said, "and now I don't know where he's gone. I wonder if you've heard from him?"

There was a long silence. "Donny's with me, Mrs. Coble," he finally said.

"With you? How'd he get there?"

"He hailed a cab, and I paid the driver."

"Could I speak to him, please?"

There was another silence. "Maybe it'd be better if we had a conference," Cal said.

"I don't *want* a conference. I've been standing at the window picturing him dead or kidnapped or something, and now you tell me you want a—"

"Donny is very, very upset. Understandably so," said Cal. "Believe me, Mrs. Coble, this is not what it seems. Have you asked Donny's side of the story?"

"Well, of course not, how could I? He went running off to you instead."

"Because he didn't feel he'd be listened to."

"But I haven't even—"

"Why don't you come out and talk? The three of us," said Cal, "will try to get this thing in perspective."

"Well, all right," Daisy said. But she wasn't as reluctant as she sounded. Already, she felt soothed by the calm way Cal was taking this.

Cal answered the doorbell at once. He said, "Hi, there," and led her into the dining room. Donny sat slumped in a chair, chewing the knuckle of one thumb. "Hello, Donny," Daisy said. He flicked his eyes in her direction.

"Sit here, Mrs. Coble," said Cal, placing her opposite Donny. He himself remained standing, restlessly pacing. "So," he said.

Daisy stole a look at Donny. His lips were swollen, as if he'd been crying.

After you've finished reading the entire story, decide where in the story this painting, *Ada Behind the Screen Door* (1985) by Alex Katz, best fits. Explain your answer.

"You know," Cal told Daisy, "I kind of expected something like this. That's a very punitive school you've got him in—you realize that. And any half-decent lawyer will tell you they've violated his civil rights. Locker checks! Where's their search warrant?"

"But if the rule is—" Daisy said.

"Well, anyhow, let him tell you his side."

She looked at Donny. He said, "It wasn't my fault. I promise."

"They said your locker was full of beer."

"It was a put-up job! See, there's this guy that doesn't like me. He put all these beers in my

Teenage Wasteland **871**

9 Reader's Response

Making Personal Connections

Invite a discussion of Donny's actions after being expelled. Students can think about what they would have done under similar circumstances. If they could give Donny advice, what would they say?

Art Study

Possible Response to Caption The painting could illustrate the scene in which Daisy looks for Donny to arrive home from school after being expelled.

10 Reading/Thinking Skills

Draw Conclusions

Ask students to debate or discuss Donny's guilt, based on knowledge of his character and previous actions.

Questions Is Donny guilty? Is Cal right about the school? Should Daisy believe Donny when he says it wasn't his fault? (*Students may be skeptical about Donny's denial.*)

BUILDING ENGLISH PROFICIENCY

Making Cultural Connections

Encourage students to consider the story's theme of teenage alienation in America.

Activity Ideas

• Invite students to share attitudes about adolescence—the teenage years—in cultural settings familiar to them, such as their extended families, neighborhoods, and ethnic, religious, or cultural groups. What are teenagers expected to do, own, and contribute to their households in various lands, economic groups, and families?

• Invite students who have lived in other countries to create webs on the board to explore the images of "typical" American teenagers that are held by people abroad. Students also might

comment about how Donny would act or express his feelings about teenage life if he were living in another country or culture.

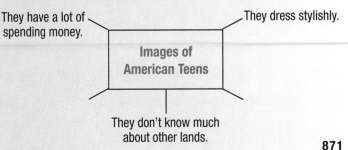
They have a lot of spending money.
They dress stylishly.
Images of American Teens
They don't know much about other lands.

Question What do you think is the theme of "Teenage Wasteland"? *(Possible responses: Some young people have difficulty conforming to society's expectations despite their parents' efforts; at a certain age, some children no longer accept the influence of their parents; a young person may have trouble choosing a healthy path; parents may find it hard to help their children.)*

Check Test

1. What is Donny's problem early in the story? *(He is having difficulty in school.)*

2. What do school officials suggest, to resolve Donny's troubles? *(a visit to a psychologist and the help of a tutor)*

3. Who is Cal? *(the tutor Donny visits regularly)*

4. Does Cal's help solve Donny's problems at school? Explain. *(No; Donny's grades and attitude become worse, and he gets expelled.)*

5. What does Donny do at the end of the story? *(He vanishes, and the police assume he has run away.)*

Unit 8 Resource Book
Alternate Check Test, p. 5

---

locker and started a rumor going, so Mr. Lanham ordered a locker check."

"What was the boy's name?" Daisy asked.

"Huh?"

"Mrs. Coble, take my word, the situation is not so unusual," Cal said. "You can't imagine how vindictive[7] kids can be sometimes."

"What was the boy's *name,*" said Daisy, "so that I can ask Mr. Lanham if that's who suggested he run a locker check."

"You don't believe me," Donny said.

"And how'd this boy get your combination in the first place?"

"Frankly," said Cal, "I wouldn't be surprised to learn the school was in on it. Any kid that marches to a different drummer, why, they'd just love an excuse to get rid of him. The school is where I lay the blame."

"Doesn't *Donny* ever get blamed?"

"Now, Mrs. Coble, you heard what he—"

"Forget it," Donny told Cal. "You can see she doesn't trust me."

Daisy drew in a breath to say that of course she trusted him—a reflex. But she knew that bold-faced, wide-eyed look of Donny's. He had worn that look when he was small, denying some petty misdeed with the evidence plain as day all around him. Still, it was hard for her to accuse him outright. She temporized and said, "The only thing I'm sure of is that they've kicked you out of school, and now I don't know what we're going to do."

"We'll fight it," said Cal.

"We can't. Even you must see we can't."

"I could apply to Brantly," Donny said.

Cal stopped his pacing to beam down at him. "Brantly! Yes. They're really onto where a kid is coming from, at Brantly. Why, *I* could get you into Brantly. I work with a lot of their students."

Daisy had never heard of Brantly, but already she didn't like it. And she didn't like Cal's smile, which struck her now as feverish and avid[8]—a smile of hunger.

On the fifteenth of April, they entered Donny in a public school, and they stopped his tutoring sessions. Donny fought both decisions bitterly. Cal,

surprisingly enough, did not object. He admitted he'd made no headway with Donny and said it was because Donny was emotionally disturbed.

Donny went to his new school every morning, plodding off alone with his head down. He did his assignments, and he earned average grades, but he gathered no friends, joined no clubs. There was something exhausted and defeated about him.

The first week in June, during final exams, Donny vanished. He simply didn't come home one afternoon, and no one at school remembered seeing him. The police were reassuring, and for the first few days, they worked hard. They combed Donny's sad, messy room for clues; they visited Miriam and Cal. But then they started talking about the number of kids who ran away every year. Hundreds, just in this city. "He'll show up, if he wants to," they said. "If he doesn't, he won't."

Evidently, Donny didn't want to.

It's been three months now and still no word. Matt and Daisy still look for him in every crowd of awkward, heartbreaking teenage boys. Every time the phone rings, they imagine it might be Donny. Both parents have aged. Donny's sister seems to be staying away from home as much as possible.

At night, Daisy lies awake and goes over Donny's life. She is trying to figure out what went wrong, where they made their first mistake. Often, she finds herself blaming Cal, although she knows he didn't begin it. Then at other times she excuses him, for without him, Donny might have left earlier. Who really knows? In the end, she can only sigh and search for a cooler spot on the pillow. As she falls asleep, she occasionally glimpses something in the corner of her vision. It's something fleet and round, a ball—a basketball. It flies up, it sinks through the hoop, descends, lands in a yard littered with last year's leaves and striped with bars of sunlight as white as bones, bleached and parched and cleanly picked. **11**

---

7. vindictive (vin dik′tiv), *adj.* feeling a strong tendency toward revenge.

8. **avid** (av′id), *adj.* extremely eager; greatly desirous.

MINI-LESSON: GRAMMAR

Possessive Nouns

Teach Review the rules for forming possessive nouns.

To form the possessive of **singular nouns,** add an apostrophe and *s* (*'s*):
a junior's locker, Donny Coble's tutor, Cass's car

To form the possessive for **a pair of nouns:**
- In the case of joint possession, add *'s* to the second noun of the pair.
Cal and his wife's marriage, Daisy and Matt's house
- In the case of individual possession, make each noun possessive.
a boy's and a girl's books, Matt's and Daisy's wallets

To form the possessive of **plural nouns:**
- Add an apostrophe to a noun that forms its plural by adding *s.*
the girls' team, the Cobles' house
- If a noun's plural is formed in a way other than by adding *s,* add *'s* to the plural of the noun: *men's lockers, mice's tails, the Joneses' car*

Activity Idea Have students in small groups write exercises or quizzes on possessive nouns. The groups can exchange papers and take each other's tests.

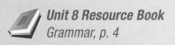
Unit 8 Resource Book
Grammar, p. 4

After Reading

After Reading

Making Connections

Shaping Your Response

1. Cal seems to think Donny is a sensitive, misunderstood youngster who needs more trust and freedom. Daisy seems to think Donny needs more guidance and discipline. With which character do you agree? Explain your answer.

2. Why do you think Donny ran away?

Analyzing the Story

3. What do you think is the significance of the title "Teenage Wasteland"?

4. Notice how Tyler **characterizes** the two Coble parents during the second meeting with the principal. What are these two characters like, and how might their personalities be affecting Donny?

5. Why do you think Daisy and Matt Coble listen to Cal's advice even though it contradicts what they think is the right way to raise Donny?

6. Identify the **point of view** used in the story and explain why you think Tyler chose to use that point of view.

7. This story leaves a lot of questions unanswered. Why do you think Tyler chose to leave Donny's story unresolved?

Extending the Ideas

8. Who do you think is responsible for the behavior of a teenager, the teenager, the teachers, or the parents? Explain your reasoning.

9. Times changed between Daisy Coble's teenage years and Donny's. How would you describe the changes that happened in the culture at large during this period?

Literary Focus: Mood

Anne Tyler uses details about the characters and the settings in "Teenage Wasteland" to establish the **mood** of the story. Describe what you think is the mood of the story, and then make a list of details that help to create that mood.

MAKING CONNECTIONS

1. Students should consider Donny's actions, his attitude before and after meeting Cal, and the fact that ultimately Donny runs away.

2. Possible response: He obviously was unhappy with school and may have seen running away as a solution to his problems. He may want to feel free to do what he wants.

3. Possible response: Donny seems caught in a sort of wasteland; he can't relate to his parents or schools; his actions aren't leading to success, but responsible adults haven't reached him.

4. The parents seem to be well-intentioned, but ineffectual. Their inability to make firm decisions or act authoritatively may have been emulated by Donny.

5. Possible responses: They don't have confidence in their ability to raise Donny, and they repeatedly accept the guidance of others. Cal is said to be an expert, recommended by a psychologist.

6. The story is told from the third-person, limited point of view, revealing Daisy's perspective. This point of view shows a parent's pain at her inability to help her son as he heads down a troubled path.

7. Possible responses: The story is about problems, not solutions. Maybe she does not have answers for problems like Daisy's and Donny's. She may want each reader to make up his or her mind about Donny's and his parent's decisions.

8. Responses will vary; students may say that each person is responsible for his or her own behavior.

9. Note: If the story is set in the early 1980s, Daisy may have been a teenager in the 1950s. Possible responses: Popular music and media such as TV shows became more daring. More young people rebelled openly or questioned authority. More ideas about families, raising children, and behavior were publicized.

LITERARY FOCUS: MOOD

Invite students to share their impressions of the story. They may note that the overall mood is one of sadness or regret for wasted opportunities. Tyler creates the mood through details such as these:

- The title and image of a "teenage wasteland"
- The parents described as "failures" (overweight or too thin)
- Daisy wondering if Donny might have missed love and support at a crucial time in his development, after his sister was born
- Donny's "forlorn" slouch—seeming to need something nobody is able to give him
- The attitude and effect of Cal, who repeatedly criticizes Donny's parents, teachers, and school
- Donny disappearing
- Donny's sister "staying away from home as much as possible" at the end, implying that she may be having troubles
- Images that bother Daisy, such as the loud music and the dream described in the last paragraph

VOCABULARY STUDY

1. c. mouse : rodent

2. b. placid : calm

3. d. brown : eyes

4. a. quickly : move

5. d. catastrophe : destruction

More Practice Students can write an antonym for each vocabulary word.

Unit 8 Resource Book
Vocabulary, p. 3
Vocabulary Test, p. 6

WRITING CHOICES
Writer's Notebook Update

Students might use ideas from the semantic web they created in Building Background on page 865.

Tying Up Loose Ends

Students may want to write their sequels from Donny's point of view. Discuss how changing the point of view changes the perspective from which the reader views Donny's problems.

School Policy

Students might refer to an existing school handbook for ideas. If their suggestions vary greatly from current policy, suggest that they present their ideas with supporting reasons to school administrators.

Selection Test

Unit 8 Resource Book
pp. 7–8

Vocabulary Study

Choose the pair of words that best expresses a relationship similar to that of the numbered pair.

forlorn
morass
amiably
talisman
vindictive

1. RABBIT'S FOOT : TALISMAN : : **a.** lucky : unlucky **b.** black cat : misfortune **c.** mouse : rodent **d.** toe : foot

2. FORLORN : UNHAPPY : : **a.** miserable : happy **b.** placid : calm **c.** lonely : contented **d.** misery : company

3. VINDICTIVE : PERSONALITY : : **a.** glove : mitten **b.** revenge : anger **c.** strong : handsome **d.** brown : eyes

4. AMIABLY : CHAT : : **a.** quickly : move **b.** yell : shout **c.** whisper : talk **d.** dutifully : faithfully

5. MORASS : CONFUSION : : **a.** messy : bedroom **b.** reconstruction : devastation **c.** simple : complex **d.** catastrophe : destruction

Expressing Your Ideas

Writing Choices

Writer's Notebook Update If you were Donny's parents, what would you have done differently to help him get on the right track? Based on what you'd do and say as a parent, write a note of advice to the Coble parents.

Tying Up Loose Ends Write a **sequel** to this story that resolves some of the questions left at the end of the story. Why was Donny so unhappy, and why was he behaving so badly? Who was helping him most, his parents or Cal? Why did he run away? Where did he go, and what became of him? Share your story sequel with the class.

School Policy How should a school handle a student who is having problems like Donny's? In a group, write a **policy handbook** you think schools should use as a guide for dealing with students like Donny.

Other Options

A Telling Conversation With a partner, create a **dialogue** between Cal and Donny in one of their tutoring sessions that reveals the personalities of both characters. Perform your dialogue for the class.

Background Music Anne Tyler alludes to music that was popular with teenagers in the past. What contemporary music do you think represents teenage life today? Prepare a **musical program** of contemporary songs about teenage life, play the songs for the class, and explain why you chose them.

Literature About Teens Stories and novels about teenagers and their problems abound. Choose a novel or short story about teenage life, read it, and present an **oral critique** to the class telling whether or not the selection is an accurate representation of teen life.

874 UNIT EIGHT: AMERICAN VOICES TODAY

OTHER OPTIONS
A Telling Conversation

Suggest that students begin by rereading the story and taking notes whenever their character is described. They can use the notes as a starting point in creating their versions of the characters.

Background Music

Students may be asked to limit the portion of their program to be played in class to a few short selections, especially if a number of students choose this activity. Some teachers like to preview the recordings and judge their appropriateness in advance.

Literature About Teens

Students might consider a larger question: Is there one "typical" representation of teen life? Discuss how, within the United States, the lives of teenagers in cities, suburbs, and rural areas may differ. Teenagers from various families, regions, and cultural groups also may live comparable or contrasting lives. When critiquing the novel or story, students may explain whether a character's life is similar to theirs or not, and how this affects their perceptions.

Before Reading

Gary Keillor

by Garrison Keillor

Garrison Keillor
born 1942

"That's the news from Lake
Wobegon, where all the women
are strong, the men are good-
looking, and all the children are
above average." That line is
how Garrison Keillor closes his
national radio show, "A Prairie
Home Companion," during
which he tells the weekly news
about Lake Wobegon's imaginary residents. Although he is
now known as *Garrison*, he
was actually christened *Gary*.
He changed his name when he
submitted poetry to his junior
high school newspaper. "It was
in a school and at a time when
boys didn't write poetry . . . I
was trying to hide behind a
name that meant strength and
'don't give me a hard time
about this.' " Keillor's story,
"Gary Keillor," is a fictionalized
account of the author's youth.

Building Background

A Slice of Life in the Fifties The 1950s were prosperous years in
the United States. Dwight D. Eisenhower, better known as Ike, was
President. Men and women who had served in World War II came
home, attended college on the G.I. Bill, got good jobs, married and
started families, and moved into the new subdivisions which were
springing up all over the country. The baby boom had begun. On the
entertainment scene, movies were still popular, and television, a relatively new invention, was finding its way into homes throughout the
country. By the mid-1950s rock-and-roll music had become popular,
and Elvis Presley was the king of rock-and-roll. Fashion in the fifties
was formal compared to fashion today; no one except a farmer or
rancher would dream of wearing blue jeans. It was during this decade
that the young Garrison Keillor grew up.

Literary Focus

Hyperbole When you say, "Traffic was so slow it took forever to get
home," you are using hyperbole, or exaggeration, to cause a humorous, satiric, dramatic, or sentimental effect. It didn't really take
forever; you are just being dramatic. Garrison Keillor uses hyperbole
for humorous effect in his story. As you read "Gary Keillor," note as
many examples as you can of hyperbole.

Writer's Notebook

What's So Funny? Think of the funniest thing that you have ever
seen or that has happened to you. What made the incident funny?
Now think of a way to describe the incident so that someone else
will think it is funny too. Write your humorous description in your
notebook.

Gary Keillor   **875**

Before Reading

Building Background

Invite students to share fads, images,
fashions, songs, and events of the fifties.
You might ask questions such as: Where
do you get your impressions of the fifties?
*(Possible responses: TV, movies, parents,
other relatives, adult friends, family photos)*

Literary Focus

Stress that **hyperbole** involves exaggeration so great that it is figurative language.

Question Can you think of a kind of story
that is built on hyperbole? *(the tall tale)*

Writer's Notebook

Discuss what makes comical things funny.
Students might suggest the following:

- odd or unexpected happenings
- poking fun at excessive pride, fear,
  or other traits
- hyperbole
- slapstick physical gags

More About
Garrison Keillor

Keillor put himself through the University
of Minnesota by working for the college
radio station. Later it was his radio shows
that made his name as a writer and comic.
Other works by the author include:

- "News from Lake Wobegon"
  (cassette, 1983)
- *A Prairie Home Companion: The Last
  Show* (videocassette, 1987)

SUPPORT MATERIALS OVERVIEW

Unit 8 Resource Book
- Graphic Organizer, p. 9
- Study Guide, p. 10
- Vocabulary, p. 11
- Grammar, p. 12
- Alternate Check Test, p. 13
- Vocabulary Test, p. 14
- Selection Test, pp. 15–16

Building English Proficiency
- Literature Summaries
- Activities, p. 234

Reading, Writing & Grammar Skillbook
- Reading, pp. 77–78
- Grammar, Usage, and Mechanics,
  pp. 266–267

Technology
- Audiotape
- Personal Journal Software
- Custom Literature Database
  For a different treatment of themes of pride
  and talent, see "Fable" by Ralph Waldo
  Emerson on the database.
- Test Generator Software

Selection Objectives

- To appreciate an informal, humorous story about a young person's pranks, attitudes, and interest in performing
- To recognize examples of hyperbole
- To learn about uses of colons

Unit 8 Resource Book
Graphic Organizer, p. 9
Study Guide, p. 10

Theme Link

The theme of Citizens of Tomorrow is explored by Garrison Keillor as he describes his entry into show business—a less-than-serious recital in a high-school talent show.

Vocabulary Preview

subtle, so fine or delicate as to elude observation or analysis

prevail, win out; triumph

enterprising, showing initiative and readiness to undertake a project or venture

surly, bad-tempered

gravity, serious or critical character; importance

rendition, a performance of a musical score or dramatic piece

erupt, burst forth

demented, insane; crazy

improvise, make up on the spur of the moment; perform without preparation

pandemonium, wild disorder or lawless confusion

Students can add the words to their lists in the Writer's Notebook.

1 Literary Element
Style

Question What does the opening paragraph reveal about Keillor's style? *(Students may note his informal style of storytelling, his wry tone, and his use of exaggeration—"the metabolism of a wolverine" and "muskmelon, which smelled rotten and loathsome.")*

876

Gary Keillor

GARRISON KEILLOR

When I was sixteen years old, I stood six feet two inches tall and weighed a hundred and forty pounds. I was intense and had the metabolism of a wolverine. I ate two or three lunches a day and three full dinners at night, as my family sat around the kitchen table and observed, and I cleaned off their plates too when they had poor appetites or were finicky. There was no food I disliked except muskmelon, which smelled rotten and loathsome. Everything else I ate. (It was Minnesota so we didn't have seafood, except fish sticks, of course.) I was a remarkable person. I was a junior in high school, Class of 1960. I was smart, so smart that poor grades didn't bother me in the slightest; I considered them no reflection on my intelligence. I read four books a week, and I sometimes walked home from school, all twelve miles, so I could relive favorite chapters out loud, stride along the shoulder of the highway past the potato farms, and say brilliant and outrageous things, and

sing in a big throbbing voice great songs like "Til There Was You" and "Love Me Tender."

I had no wish to sing in front of an audience, songs were a private thing with me. I was an intense person, filled with powerful feelings, and I assumed that I would live alone for the rest of my life, perhaps in a monastery, silent, swishing around in a cassock, my heart broken by a tragic love affair with someone like Natalie Wood, my life dedicated to God.

I was a lucky boy. I had learned this two years before on a car trip to Colorado. My Uncle Earl and Aunt Myrna drove there that summer—he had been stationed in Colorado Springs during the war—along with my cousins Gordon and Mel, and I got to go too. I won that trip by dropping over to their house and being extremely nice. I'd say, "Here, let me wash those dishes." I'd say, "Boy, I'm sure in a mood to mow a lawn." And then she'd offer me a glass of nectar and a piece of angel food cake and I'd eat it and say, "Boy, I was looking at *National Geographic* the

SELECTION SUMMARY

Gary Keillor

In a rambling, humorous style, Garrison Keillor recounts events that occurred when he was sixteen, participating in a high-school talent show. Gary is interested in performing in the show because he secretly loves the chairperson, a girl named Dede Petersen. Unfortunately for him, Dede has a boyfriend, so Keillor never professes his love. He is asked to recite a poem in the show, right after Dede's boyfriend's performance of the song "All Shook Up." The boyfriend, Bill, brings the

house down with his rendition of the Elvis Presley hit, but then Bill makes the mistake of singing another song, which Gary fouls up by slowing down the music. The audience roars with laughter to Bill's anger. Keillor follows with a humorous rendition of the Walt Whitman poem and is a great success.

 *For summaries in other languages, see the **Building English Proficiency** Book.*

other night and they had a big article on Colorado. It was so interesting. Just the different rock formations and things. I don't see how people can look at those mountains and not know there's a God." And she'd smile at me, a good boy who mowed lawns and whose faith was pure, and I got to go. Of course my brothers and sisters were fit to be tied. "How come he gets to go? We never get to go. Oh no, we have to stay here all summer and work in the garden while he goes riding out to Colorado." They just didn't get it. Trips to Colorado don't fall in your lap. You've got to go out and earn Colorado.

We took off on the trip, and I was a very good passenger. I sat in the favored front seat between my aunt and uncle, looking at the scenery for hours, no stains on my clothes, my face clean, a good strong bladder, never got carsick, and had a subtle[1] sideways technique for picking my nose—you'd never see it even if you looked straight at me. Far off, the mountains appeared, shining on the horizon for almost a whole day, and then we rose up into them—

---

1. **subtle** (sut'l), *adj.* so fine or delicate as to elude observation or analysis.

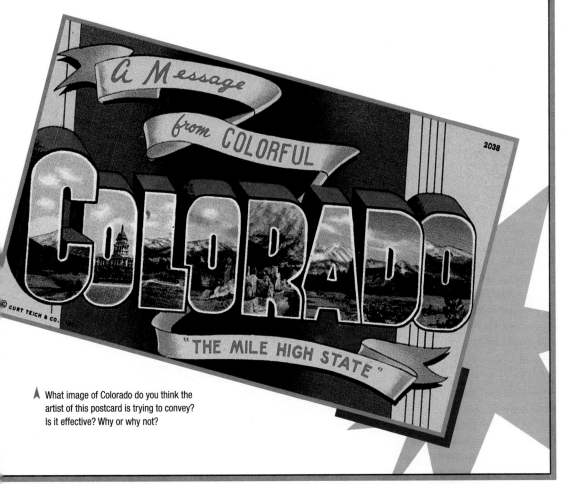

▲ What image of Colorado do you think the artist of this postcard is trying to convey? Is it effective? Why or why not?

2 Literary Element
Characterization

Question What does the narrator reveal about himself in describing how he "earned" the trip to Colorado? *(Possible responses: He is clever and sneaky, hard-working when the reward is disproportionately large, and persistent. He uses a combination of flattery and helpfulness to entice his aunt and uncle into asking him to go on the trip.)*

Art Study

Possible Response to Caption the image of a colorful place worth visiting for its mountains, natural beauty, and other attractions

This card, published by Curt Teich & Company, is one of many thousands of postcards in an archive donated by the company to the Lake County Museum in Illinois. Scholars of popular culture use the collection for research, and museum visitors see samples in a gallery.

BUILDING ENGLISH PROFICIENCY

Recognizing Irony and Humor

You might help students understand Keillor's story by recognizing his humorous use of language.

Activity Ideas

- Model the process of reading for ironic humor by reading a passage or two aloud and sharing your thoughts. Examples include Keillor's comments about the number of meals he ate as his family "sat around the kitchen table and observed" (p. 876) and how he played up to his aunt and uncle and then concludes, "You've got to go out and earn Colorado" (p. 877).

- Invite students to explain idioms such as *cleaned off their plates, dropping over to their house, fit to be tied, (they) just didn't get it,* and *fall in your lap.* Help students understand how they help characterize the young Keillor as a scamp who endears himself to others for his own benefit.

- As students become more familiar with his style, volunteers may want to read aloud for partners or small groups, illustrating the humor with tone of voice.

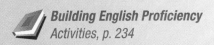

Building English Proficiency Activities, p. 234

Hyperbole

Draw attention to fanciful statements in Keillor's fourteen-page love letter to Dede.

Questions

- How do you think Keillor as an adult regards the pledge in the letter of "a spiritual friendship that would last forever"? *(Responses may include that the adult Keillor knows he was making an exaggerated promise.)*

- What effect does the line about "our souls communing over vast distances" have in the story? *(Possible response: It pokes gentle humor at the letter from the lovestruck sixteen-year-old.)*

Characterization

Garrison Keillor, an adult who works in the entertainment industry, undoubtedly knows a lot about how people become successful in that business. In this discussion of Barbara Lee, however, he reflects his perspective as a youth.

Question   From what the narrator tells about Barbara Lee, is it true that there's "no doubt about" whether she was "Broadway bound"? *(Possible response: No; she can sing, dance, do the splits, and play the marimba, but these skills and the impression made on her classmates are not enough to guarantee being "Broadway bound.")*

---

snowcapped peaks, like the last scene in a western in which justice and romance prevail,[2] and when we reached Denver (*EL. 5280,* the sign said, exactly a mile), we ate dinner at a Chinese restaurant and my fortune cookie said: "You are enterprising[3]—take advantage of it." Well, there it was in a nutshell.

The mountains were startling in their whiteness and steepness, the valleys dark in the late afternoon, the peaks glittering in pure sunlight, beautiful stands of light gray-green aspen floating like fog, and my aunt took a picture of me with trees and mountains behind me. Just me, tall and intense. You would never guess I was from Minnesota. I thought, "This is my lucky picture. I'll keep it the rest of my life."

I had been in love with Dede for two years, in an intense and secret way.

My family lived in the country, along the Mississippi River between Minneapolis and Tryon, and I attended New Tryon High School, which was bulging under a tidal wave of children from new subdivisions on the other side of the river, places with names like Riverview Estates and Woodlawn and Forest Hills. Our side, South Tryon Township, along the West River Road, was still rural, truck farms, and scattered houses on big rolling tracts, and we West River Roaders were the cream of the school. The editor of the school paper, *The Beacon,* Elaine Eggert, was one of us; so were the stars of the debate team and the speech team, three of the class officers, and the chairperson of the spring talent show, Dede Petersen, who rode on my bus.

I had been in love with Dede for two years, in an intense and secret way. She had bouncy blonde hair and wore soft sweaters, plaid skirts, penny loafers and knee socks. One winter day I wrote her a fourteen-page letter (single-spaced) saying that she was my ideal of womanhood, a

person of pure taste, excellent judgment, stunning beauty, and natural intelligence, a woman to whom I could pledge myself in a spiritual friendship that would last forever no matter what. If the friendship should turn into physical love, good, and if not, fine. We would be friends for the rest of our lives, our souls communing over vast distances. **3**

I did not, after long thought, give her the letter. I guessed that she might laugh at it and also that her boyfriend Bill Swenson might pound me into the ground. He was an intense person too.

One afternoon riding home on the bus, sitting behind her, I heard her complain to her pal Marcy about the miseries of planning the April talent show. Bill Swenson would be in it, lip-synching "All Shook Up,"[4] and he was terrific, but there wasn't much other talent around, nothing compared to last year, when all those guys sang "Bali Hai" with the coconuts on their chests, and the skit about school lunch when the kids pretended to vomit and out came green confetti, and of course last year there had been Barbara Lee. Barbara Lee was the most talented person ever to graduate from our school. She danced, she sang, she did the splits, she played the marimba. She was Broadway bound, no doubt about it. **4**

I leaned forward and said, "Well, I think we have lots of talent." Oh? like who, for example? she said. I said, "Well, I could do something." *You?* she said. "Or I could get together with some other kids and we could do a skit." *Like what?* she said. I said, "Oh, I don't know. Something about the school burning down. It all depends."

---

2. **prevail** (pri vāl′), *v.* win out; triumph.
3. **enterprising** (en′tər prī′zing), *adj.* showing initiative and readiness to undertake a project or venture.
4. **"All Shook Up,"** a rock-and-roll song made famous by singer Elvis Presley, who was popular in the 1950s and 1960s.

MINI-LESSON: LITERARY FOCUS

Hyperbole

Teach   Have students reread the definition of hyperbole on page 875: exaggeration used to create a humorous, satiric, dramatic, or sentimental effect. A hyperbolic statement is not meant literally; it is figurative overstatement.

Apply   Ask students to generate examples of hyperbole. For example:

- He saw a big snake and jumped higher than a housetop.

- She ran so fast, she was crossing the finish line before the starter finished saying "go."

Activity Idea   Have students write brief stories or poems that employ hyperbole. Discuss whether the results are humorous, dramatic, or sentimental, and why.

"That doesn't sound funny to me," she said. Marcy didn't think it was funny either.

What burned my toast was her saying *"You?"* when I volunteered to be in her talent show. I was only being helpful, I was not claiming to be another Barbara Lee. I had no interest in the stage at all until I heard her incredulity and amusement— *"You?"*—and then I was interested in being interested. A spiritual friendship with Dede was out of the question, if she thought I was the sort of guy you could say *"You?"* to.

No one in our family sang or performed for entertainment, only for the glory of God and only in groups, never solo. We were Christian people; we did not go in for show. But I was an intense young man. Intensity was my guiding principle. And when I thought about joining that monastery after Natalie Wood rejected me and spending my life in the woodshop making sturdy chairs and tables, I thought that perhaps I ought to get in the talent show at New Tryon High first, get a whiff of show business before I gave my life to God.

It was one of those ugly and treacherous springs in the Midwest, when winter refuses to quit, like a big surly[5] drunk who heads for home and then staggers back for another round and a few more songs that everyone has heard before. It was cold and wet, and we sat day after day in dim airless classrooms, the fluorescent lights turned on at midday, the murky sky and bare trees filling the big classroom windows, pools of oil-slicked rain in the parking lot, the grass in front dead, the Stars and Stripes hanging limp and wet like laundry. In plane geometry, I was lost in the wilderness, had been lost since Christmas, and in history, we were slogging through World War I, and in English class, we were memorizing poems. "These are treasures you will carry with you forever," said Miss Rasmussen, a big woman in a blue knit suit. In her wanderings around the classroom as she talked about poetry and metaphor, she often stopped in the aisle and stood looming above me, her voice overhead, her hand resting on my desk, her puffy white hand and red knuckles and short ringless fingers. Her stopping there indicated, I knew, her fondness for me. I was the only student of hers who wrote poems. She had even suggested that I memorize and recite one of my own poems. I declined. Part of the memorization assignment was reciting the poem in front of the class. My poems were far too intense and personal to be said out loud in front of people. I was memorizing Whitman's elegy on the death of Abraham Lincoln, "O Captain! My Captain!" I walked home through the rain one cold day crying out, "O Captain! my Captain! our fearful trip is done, / The ship has weather'd every rack, the prize we sought is won."

One day a fuel oil truck backed into our driveway and got stuck in the mud and the driver put it into forward gear and got dug in deeper. He gunned it in reverse and gunned it forward and rocked the truck loose and pulled forward and unwound his hose and started filling our fuel oil tank, but meanwhile he had left deep ruts in my mother's garden and the front yard. She was home alone, washing clothes. She heard the grinding and roaring from down in the laundry room and came outdoors to find her garden dug up and the tulips and irises destroyed, and the driver looked at her and said, "You ought to do something about your driveway." Not a word of apology, acted like it was the driveway's fault. My mother was the quietest, politest person ever, she felt that raising your voice indicated a flawed character, but she put her hands on her hips and said, "Mister, if you can't figure out how to drive a truck, then they oughta find you a job you'd be able to handle." And she told him to get out and she would be sending the company a bill for the flower garden. And he did. And she did. And the company sent us a check and an apology from the general manager, a Harold L. Bergstrom.

---

5. **surly** (sėr′lē), *adj.* bad-tempered.

Gary Keillor **879**

5 Literary Element
Idiom

An idiom is an expression in a given lan-guage that is grammatically peculiar or that cannot be understood from the meanings of its elements. Point out to students that Keillor uses idioms as part of his informal style.

- "What burned my toast. . . ." (p. 879)
- "Well, there it was in a nutshell." (p. 878)

6 Literary Element
Repetition

Students may note that Keillor keeps using the word *intense* as a comic motif. He has described himself, his love for Dede, and Dede's boyfriend Bill as intense. Perhaps he remembers sixteen as an age of intense feelings.

7 Literary Element
Figurative Language

Questions

- To what does Keillor compare the wintry spring weather? *(to a big surly drunk who refuses to quit)*
- What effect does the figurative image have? *(Possible response: It is humorous and descriptive; the reader has a clear image of how unpleasant the spring was, but the comparison also is comical.)*

BUILDING ENGLISH PROFICIENCY

ESL
LEP
ELD
SAE
LD

Tracking Shifts in Time

Some students may have difficulty with the time shifts in the story. Most of the story deals with the talent show when Gary Keillor is sixteen. Yet there are scenes of his trip to Colorado two years earlier, as well as a driveway confrontation between Keillor's mother and a fuel-oil truck driver. This latter event apparently took place when Keillor was sixteen. Students can keep track of the sequence by making a simple time line or chart. They can briefly identify events in order. A possible format is shown.

Two years earlier	When Gary is sixteen		
Gary goes to Colorado with his aunt and uncle.	He learns about the talent show.	He memorizes "O Captain! My Captain!"	His mother reacts to the truck driver.

Recognize Cause and Effect

A wacky cause-and-effect sequence leads Keillor to conclude that he should try show business. Encourage students to diagram the sequence in order to more fully appreciate the anecdote's wry humor. The diagram might look like this:

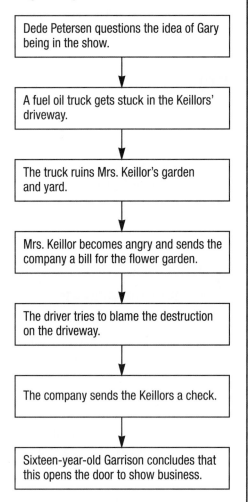

> Dede Petersen questions the idea of Gary being in the show.

> A fuel oil truck gets stuck in the Keillors' driveway.

> The truck ruins Mrs. Keillor's garden and yard.

> Mrs. Keillor becomes angry and sends the company a bill for the flower garden.

> The driver tries to blame the destruction on the driveway.

> The company sends the Keillors a check.

> Sixteen-year-old Garrison concludes that this opens the door to show business.

It was the first time in my memory that my mother had fought back and raised her voice to a stranger, a watershed[6] moment for me. I heard the story from our neighbor, Mr. Couture, and I admired her so much for standing up to the jerk and defending our family's honor. Her principles had always told her to be quiet and polite and turn the other cheek and never make trouble, but there comes a time to let go of principle and do the right thing. To me, this seemed **8** to open the door to show business.

And then, about a week before the talent show, suddenly I was in. The real power behind the show wasn't Dede, it was Miss Rasmussen, my teacher, the adviser to the talent show, and the day I stood before the class and recited "O Captain! My Captain!" she told Dede to put me in the show. The next day, Miss Rasmussen had me stand up in class and recite it again. It was one of the finest pieces of oral interpretation she had ever seen, she said. She sat in a back corner of the room, her head bowed, her eyes closed, as I stood in front and with dry mouth launched the Captain's ship again, and she did not see the kids smirking and gagging and retching and pulling long invisible skeins of snot from their nostrils and when my Captain died and I got to "O the bleeding drops of red, / Where on the deck my Captain lies, / Fallen cold and dead," they rolled their eyes and clutched at their hearts and died. Then, when she stood up, her eyes moist, and clapped, they all clapped too. "Wasn't that good!" she cried. "You really liked it, didn't you! Oh, I'm glad you did! He's going to recite it in the talent show, too! Won't that be nice!" A couple of boys in front clapped their hands over their mouths and pretended to lose their lunch. They seemed to speak for most of the class.

So I was in the talent show, which I wanted to be, but with an inferior piece of material. I suggested to Miss Rasmussen that "O Captain! My Captain!" might not be right for the talent show audience, that maybe I could find a humorous

poem, and she said, "Oh, it'll be just fine," not realizing the gravity[7] of the situation. "Never give up on beauty," she said. "Never compromise your standards out of fear that someone may not understand." Teachers were full of useless advice like that.

I tried not to think about "O Captain." I experimented with combing my hair a new way, with the part on the right. I was handsome at certain angles, I thought, and a right-hand part would emphasize a good angle. I stood at the bathroom mirror, a small mirror in my hand, and experimented holding my head cocked back and aimed up and to the right, a pose favored by seniors in their graduation pictures, which looked good from either side, and reciting "O Captain" with my head at that angle. I had good skin except when it flared up, which it did two days before the show, and it took a long time to repair the damage. There were six children in our family and only one bathroom, but I spent fifteen minutes behind a locked door doing surgery and applying alcohol and cold packs and skin-toned cream. The little kids stood banging on the door, pleading to use the toilet. I said, "Well, how bad do you have to go?" I was the one in show business, after all.

So I was in the talent show, which I wanted to be, but with an inferior piece of material.

I worked on "O Captain" so that every line was set in my head. I recited it to myself in the mirror ("O Captain! O Captain! the fateful day is done, / Your blemishes have disappeared, the skin you sought is won") and for my mother, who said I was holding my head at an unnatural angle, and then, the Friday night before the show, I recited it at a

---

6. **watershed** (wô′tər shed′), *n.* point at which a notable change takes place.
7. **gravity** (grav′ə tē), *n.* serious or critical character; importance.

MINI-LESSON: GRAMMAR

Punctuation: Colons

Teach   Explain that a colon is a mark of introduction. Whatever follows the colon—a list, clause, phrase, or the lines of a poem, for example—is linked with some element that precedes it. Some uses of colons are explained here:

- A colon may introduce a clause or phrase that explains or illustrates what has gone before it.

  Time was of the essence: a decision had to be made.

- A colon may direct attention to an appositive.

  I have only one request: a pizza.

- A colon can introduce a series.

The following states are participating: California, Florida, Indiana, Maryland, Texas, and Wyoming.

Be prepared to do the following: swim 100 yards, bike 10 miles, and run 1 mile.

- A colon can be used to introduce a long quotation, as on page 881.

Activity Idea   Have students work in small groups. Each group can generate an example illustrating each use for colons given above. Groups then can trade papers to check that the colons have been used properly.

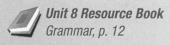
Unit 8 Resource Book
Grammar, p. 12

party at Elaine Eggert's house, and there my interpretation of "O Captain! My Captain!" took a sharp turn toward the English stage.

Miss Rasmussen loved a recording of Sir John Gielgud reading "Favourites of English Poetry" and she played it once for our class, a whole hour of it, and from that day, all the boys in the class loved to do English accents. A little lisp, endless dramatic pauses, fruity inflections including shrill birdlike tones of wonderment, and instead of the vowel *o* that delicious English *aaooovw*, a bleating sound not found anywhere in American speech. In the cafeteria, when my friend Ralph Moody came to the table where all of us West River Road rats sat, he stood holding his tray, peering down at us and the welter of milk cartons and comic books and ice cream wrappers and uneaten macaroni-cheese lunches, and after a long pause he cried "Aaaaoooooww," with a shudder, a great man forced to sit among savages. So at the party, surrounded by kids from the debate team and the newspaper, the cream of West River Road society, when Elaine had said for the sixth time, "Do the poem you're going to do on Monday," I reached back for Ralph's *Aaooovw* and did "O Captain" as Sir John might have done it:

Aoowww Cap-tin, myyyyy Cap-tin,

aower————feeah-fool twip eez done!

Th' sheep has wethah'd————eviddy rack!

th' priiiiiiize we sot————eez won!

But————aaaooooooooowwwww

th' bleeeeeeeding drrrops————of rrred————

wheahhhh————

on th' deck————

myyyy Captin liiiiiiies————

fallin————

caaaooooowwwld————

and————————ded!

It was a good party poem. I recited it in the basement, and then everyone upstairs had to come down and hear it, and then Elaine had to call up a friend of hers in the city and I did it on the phone. It got better. "Miss Rasmussen is going to burst a blood vessel," said Elaine. She was a true rebel, despite the editorials she wrote extolling the value of team play and school spirit. I was starting to see some of the virtues in her that I had previously imagined in Dede Petersen.

Bill Swenson had worked for weeks on "All Shook Up," and he looked cool and capable backstage before the curtain went up. His hair was slicked down, he wore heavy eye makeup, and he was dressed in a white suit with gold trim, without a single wrinkle in it. He stood, holding his arms out to the sides, avoiding wrinkling, and practiced moving his lips to "A-wella bless my soul, what'sa wrong with me? I'm itching like a man on a fuzzy tree." Dede knelt, shining his black shoes.

He pretended to be surprised to see me. "What are you doing here? You running the p.a. or what?"

I told him I would be in the show, reciting a poem by Walt Whitman.

"Who? Twitman?" No. Whitman, I said.

"Well, I'm glad I don't have to follow that," he said, with heavy sarcasm. He glanced at my outfit, brown corduroy pants, a green plaid cotton shirt, a charcoal gray sweater vest, and said, "You better change into your stage clothes though."

"These are my stage clothes," I said.

"Oh," he said, his eyebrows raised. "Oh." He smiled. "Well, good luck." He did not know how much luck I had. I had my lucky picture in my pocket, the one of me in the mountains.

Dede brushed his forehead with face powder and poofed up his hair. She gave him a light kiss on the lips. "You're going to be great," she said. He smiled. He had no doubt about that. She had put him high on the program, right after "America the Beautiful," a dramatic choral

Gary Keillor **881**

9 **Literary Focus**
Hyperbole

Questions

- What does Elaine mean when she predicts that Miss Rasmussen will burst a blood vessel? (*that Miss Rasmussen will be extremely upset*)

- Is the use of hyperbole effective in this instance? Why or why not? (*Possible response: Yes; the phrase vividly conveys how angry or upset the teacher will be.*)

10 **Reading/Thinking Skills**
Infer

Discuss Bill's attitude toward Keillor. Later, students can remember this dialogue; it may explain Keillor's sabotage of Bill's encore.

Question What can you infer from Bill's conversation with Keillor? (*Bill obviously doesn't like or respect Gary very much; he is patronizing and insulting to Keillor.*)

BUILDING ENGLISH PROFICIENCY

Exploring Mood

Help students recognize that Keillor creates a mood of anticipation by setting up opposing expectations. Students should know that the Whitman poem is a serious work. Students who can answer the following questions, as the story goes on, will understand the action and the mood.

- How does the reaction of Miss Rasmussen to Keillor's reading of the poem differ from the reactions of other students?

- Would Miss Rasmussen likely enjoy the kind of reading of the poem Gary does at the party?

- How might Gary Keillor be feeling about Bill Swenson after Bill criticizes Gary's clothes and planned talent show act?

Elvis Presley (1935–1977) was the most famous figure in rock and roll before the 1960s. He began recording for Sun Records in 1954. By 1956, hits such as "Hound Dog," "Heartbreak Hotel," and "Love Me Tender" made him a star. His vocal style was influenced by Southern blues, gospel music, country music, and rhythm and blues. Presley was as well-known for his physical movements while performing as for his singing, a fact illustrated by this photograph.

11 **Literary Element**
Style

One of the hallmarks of Keillor's style is the number of details—frequently amusing—that he includes. Draw students' attention to the program of the talent show. They may appreciate the wild disparity of performances: "America the Beautiful," a patriotic song; *Antigone,* a Greek tragic play, "Nobody Knows the Trouble I've Seen," an African American spiritual; Rodgers and Hammerstein music; an Elvis Presley imitator; and Keillor's fake British reading of a poem.

reading from *Antigone,* a solo trumpet rendition[8] of "Nobody Knows the Trouble I've Seen," and a medley of Rodgers and Hammerstein songs performed on the piano by Cheryl Ann Hansen. **11** Then Bill would electrify the crowd with "All Shook Up," and then I would do "O Captain."

He was Mr. Cool. After Cheryl Ann Hansen's interminable medley, which kids clapped and cheered for only because they knew that her mother had recently died of cancer, Bill grinned at Dede and bounced out on stage and yelled, "Helllll-ooo baby!" in a Big Bopper voice, and the audience clapped and yelled "Hellllloo baby!" and he yelled, "You knowwwwwwwww what I like!" and he was a big hit in the first five seconds. He

---

8. **rendition** (ren dish′ən), *n.* a performance of a musical score or dramatic piece.

◄ This photograph of Elvis Presley was taken by Bob Verlin in 1956, the same year Presley achieved national recognition with his best-selling record, "Heartbreak Hotel."

MINI-LESSON: VOCABULARY

Use New Vocabulary in Writing

Teach Using vocabulary from the selection in another context can help students become comfortable with words they may not have used much before. These words from the selection may have been unfamiliar to many students.

subtle	rendition
prevail	erupt
enterprising	demented
surly	improvise
gravity	pandemonium

Activity Ideas

Have students use four or five words from the vocabulary list to do either of the following.

• Write a summary of Keillor's talent show or any other performance they have seen or heard.

• Give a humorous oral report of their participation in a talent show, musical, concert, play, or other performance.

said it again, "Helllllllllooo baby!" and the audience yelled back, "Helllllllllooo baby!" And then Dede carefully set the phonograph needle on the record of "All Shook Up" and Elvis's hoody voice blasted out in the auditorium and Bill started shimmying across the stage and tossing his head like a dustmop. "My friends say I'm acting queer as a bug, I'm in love—huh! I'm all shook up," and on the *huh* he stuck both arms in the air and threw his hip to the left, *huh,* and the audience sang along on the "hmm hmm hmm—oh—yeah yeah"—he was the star of the show right there. Dede ran to look out through a hole in the curtain, leaving me standing by the record player. She was so thrilled, she hopped up and down and squealed.

I could see part of him out there, his white suit hanging loose, the red socks flashing, him pulling out the red satin hanky and tossing it into the audience, *hmmm hmmm hmmm oh yeah yeah,* and at the end the whole auditorium stood up and screamed. He came off stage bright with sweat, grinning, and went back out and made three deep bows, and threw his hip, *huh,* and came off and Dede wiped his face with a towel and kissed him, and the audience was still screaming and whistling and yelling, "More! More!" and right then Bill made his fateful decision. He went out and did his other number.

It was "Vaya con Dios" by the Conquistadores. Dede put the needle down and the guitars throbbed, and the audience clapped, but Bill hadn't worked as hard on "Vaya con Dios" as on "All Shook Up" and his lips didn't synch very well, but the main problem was that "Vaya con Dios" was "Vaya con Dios," and after "All Shook Up" it seemed like a joke, especially since the Conquistadores were a trio and Bill wasn't. Kids started to laugh, and Bill got mad—perhaps "Vaya con Dios" meant a lot to him personally—and his grim face and his clenched fists made "Vaya con Dios" seem even zanier. Dede ran to the hole in the curtain to see where the hooting and light booing were coming from, and there, standing by the record player,

I thought I would help poor Bill out by lightly touching the record with my finger and making the music go flat and sour for a moment.

It was miraculous, the effect this had, like pressing a laugh button. I touched the black vinyl rim and the music warbled, and fifty feet away, people erupted[9] in fits of happiness. I did it again. How wonderful to hear people laugh! and to be able to give them this precious gift of laughter so easily. Then I discovered a speed control that let me slow it down and speed it up. The singers sounded demented,[10] in love one moment, carsick the next. The audience thought this was a stitch. But Bill sort of went to pieces. One prime qualification for a show business career, I would think, is the ability to improvise[11] and go with the audience, but Bill Swenson did not have that ability. Here he was, rescued from his drippy encore, magically transformed into comedy, and he was too rigid to recognize what a hit he was. His lips stopped moving. He shook his fist at someone in the wings, perhaps me, and yelled a common vulgar expression at someone in the crowd, and wheeled around and walked off.

I didn't care to meet him, so I walked fast right past him onto the stage, and coming out of the bright light into the dark, he didn't see me until I was out of reach. There was still some heavy booing when I arrived at the microphone, and I made a deep English-actor type of bow, with princely flourishes and flutters, and they laughed, and then they were mine all the way. I held on to them for dear life for the next two minutes. I sailed into "O Captain," in my ripest and fruitiest accent, with roundhouse gestures, outflung arms, hand clapped to the forehead ————I cried:

AOOWWW CAP-TIN, MYYYYY CAP-TIN,

---

9. **erupt** (i rupt′), *v.* burst forth.
10. **demented** (di men′tid), *adj.* insane; crazy.
11. **improvise** (im′prə vīz), *v.* make up on the spur of the moment; perform without preparation.

Gary Keillor   **883**

12 **Reading/Thinking Skills**

Visualize

Some students may not appreciate that this is an on-target imitation of Presley's style. If possible, show photos or video clips of a Presley performance. You might invite a volunteer to draw a picture of Bill Swenson's Presley act.

13 **Reading/Thinking Skills**

Infer

Question   Although Keillor plays an unkind trick, he also seems to learn something about himself in the process. What is it? *(that he likes to make people laugh)*

14 **Literary Element**

Point of View

Keillor's sabotage of Bill Swenson's act is presented from the author's point of view. Students should note that Bill undoubtedly would tell the anecdote differently.

Question   What does Keillor think Bill should have done to respond to the audience and the changing music? *(He says Bill should have improvised, turning the song into a comedy act.)*

BUILDING ENGLISH PROFICIENCY

ESL
LEP
ELD
SAE
LD

Presenting Humorous Readings

Students may want to try reading a serious work for humorous effect, either privately or for an audience of classmates. You may want to judge in advance whether any particular work or style of reading is appropriate for your class.

1. Discuss Keillor's description of his presentation. He mentions his vocal qualities and his gestures.

2. Invite students to choose a serious poem and practice reading it for humorous effect.

3. Students may want to present their readings in small groups or before the class.

Irony

Keillor ends with an ironic description of his "modest" self waiting in the back of the auditorium "patiently" enduring other students' attention and congratulations. Then the teacher who loves the poem talks to him. Readers might expect that she would be angry about his reading.

Question How does Miss Rasmussen feel about Gary's reading of the poem? *(Possible responses: She wonders why he changed it, guesses that he forgot a line, and is curious about his voice, but she is pleased the audience liked it. She doesn't get the joke.)*

Check Test

1. Why did Keillor help his aunt and uncle—and act virtuously around them? *(to be invited on a trip to Colorado)*

2. Where does the main action in "Gary Keillor" take place? *(at a high school talent show)*

3. What does Keillor plan to perform? *(a reading of a poem, "O Captain! My Captain!")*

4. Who is Bill Swenson? *(Dede's boyfriend, who imitates Elvis in the show)*

5. What does Keillor do to Bill? *(During Bill's encore, Keillor changes the tempo of the music to make Bill's performance funny.)*

Unit 8 Resource Book
Alternate Check Test, p. 13

884

AOWER————FEEAH-FOOL TWIP EEZ DONE!

TH' SHEEP HAS WETHAH'D————EVIDDY

  RACK!

TH' PRIIIIIIIZE WE SOT————EEZ WON!

BUT——— ———AAAAOOOOOOOWWWWW

TH' BLLEEEEEEEDING DRRROPS————

OF RRRED————

WHEAHH————

ON TH' DECK————

BEEEL SWEN-SON LIIIIIIIIES————

FALLIN————

CAAAOOOOWWWLD

————————AND————

————DED!

It wasn't a kind or generous thing to do, but it was successful, especially the "AAAAAOOOO-OOOWWWWW" and also the part about Bill Swenson, and at the end there was shouting and whistling and pandemonium,[12] and I left the stage with the audience wanting more, but I had witnessed the perils of success, and did not consider an encore. "Go out and take a bow," said Miss Rasmussen, and out I went, and came back off. Dede and Bill were gone. Dede was not feeling well, said Miss Rasmussen.

I watched the rest of the show standing at the back of the auditorium. The act after me was a girl from the wrong side of the river who did a humorous oral interpretation entitled "Granny on the Phone with Her Minister." The girl had painted big surprise eyebrows and a big red mouth on her so we would know it was comedy, and as the sketch went on, she shrieked to remind us that it was humorous. The joke was that Granny was hard-of-hearing and got the words wrong. Then came an accordionist, a plump young man named David Lee, Barbara's cousin, who was a little overambitious with "Lady of Spain" and should have left out two or three of the variations, and a tap dancer who tapped to a recording of "Nola" and who made the mistake of starting the number all over again after she had made a mistake. I enjoyed watching these dogs, strictly from a professional point of view. And then the choir returned to sing "Climb Every Mountain," and then Miss Rasmussen stood and spoke about the importance of encouraging those with talent and how lucky we should feel to have them in our midst to bring beauty and meaning to our lives. And then the lights came up, and my classmates piled into the aisles and headed for the door and saw me standing in back, modest me, looking off toward the stage. Almost every one of them said how good I was as they trooped past—clapped my shoulder, said, hey, you were great, you should've done more, that was funny—and I stood and patiently endured their attention until the auditorium was empty and then I went home.

"You changed the poem a little," Miss Rasmussen said the next day. "Did you forget the line?" "Yes," I said. "Your voice sounded funny," she said. I told her I was nervous. "Oh well," she said, "they seemed to like it anyway."

"Thank you," I said, "thank you very much."

15

---

12. **pandemonium** (pan′də mō′nē əm), *n.* wild disorder or lawless confusion.

After Reading

Making Connections

Shaping Your Response

1. How would you describe the young Gary Keillor? Write five adjectives that you would use to tell about him. Then write five adjectives each to describe Bill Swenson, Dede Peterson, and Miss Rasmussen.

2. Choose what you think is the most humorous part of the story and prepare to read it to the class.

Analyzing the Story

3. Gary Keillor describes himself as *intense*. What do you think he means by that?

4. One way that Garrison Keillor introduces humor into his writing is by relating humorous incidents. Find several examples.

5. What is the **point of view** in "Gary Keillor"? How would the selection be different if it were told from another point of view?

6. What does the picture of Gary in Colorado seem to **symbolize** to him?

Extending the Ideas

7. Compare the **tone** of "Teenage Wasteland" to that of "Gary Keillor." How would you explain the differences?

8. If you were to write about a humorous incident that took place at your high school, what would it be?

Literary Focus: Hyperbole

Garrison Keillor's use of hyperbole, or obvious exaggeration, is one of the reasons his story is so funny. Make a list of examples of his use of hyperbole. Then, find examples of hyperbole in other sources, either from magazine or newspaper cartoons, or from jokes or tall tales. Share one of your examples with the class.

Vocabulary Study

demented
enterprising
erupt
gravity
improvise
prevail
pandemonium
rendition
subtle
surly

Use the vocabulary words in the list to complete these statements that Bill Swenson and Miss Rasmussen might have made about Gary Keillor.

"That Gary Keillor is __(1)__," said Bill Swenson, the Elvis impersonator, in a __(2)__ voice. "I could strangle him for ruining my __(3)__ of 'Vaya con Dios.' Did you hear the laughter __(4)__ when the music slowed down and then speeded up? That idiot had better steer clear of me!"

"Well," said Miss Rasmussen, "Gary Keillor's sense of humor is not exactly __(5)__. First of all the __(6)__ young man decided to improve the talent show. He turned a serious song into a comedy by varying the speed on the record player. Needless to say, the audience loved it,

---

LITERARY FOCUS: HYPERBOLE

Examples of hyperbole from "Gary Keillor":

- *"I ate two or three lunches a day and three full dinners at night. . . ."* (p. 876)
- *"I assumed that I would live alone for the rest of my life, perhaps in a monastery, silent, swishing around in a cassock, my heart broken by a tragic love affair with someone like Natalie Wood. . . ."* (p. 876)
- *"We would be friends for the rest of our lives, our souls communing over vast distances."* (p. 878)
- *"She danced, she sang, she did the splits, she played the marimba. She was Broadway bound, no doubt about it."* (p. 878)

After Reading

MAKING CONNECTIONS

1. Responses may include: Keillor—intense, dramatic, funny, persistent, comic, tall; Swenson—conceited, intense, patronizing, "too cool," dramatic; Petersen—pretty, blonde, stuck-up, thoughtless, silly; Miss Rasmussen—old-fashioned, big, naive, powerful

2. Choices may vary; invite students to explain why they think their choice is humorous.

3. Possible response: He feels things deeply.

4. Possible responses: his Colorado trip; the fake British reading of the poem; the sabotage of Bill Swenson's act

5. First-person point of view, from Keillor's perspective; Dede or Bill probably would present Keillor in a harsh light, perhaps as a nerd who ruined Bill's act; Miss Rasmussen probably wouldn't have known why Bill's music and Keillor's voice sounded funny.

6. Possible responses: good luck because he was fortunate to take the trip; himself as an interesting or exotic person—"You would never guess I was from Minnesota."

7. Possible response: "Teenage Wasteland" is poignant and serious, because it concerns tragic events; "Gary Keillor" is ironic and amused, because it concerns silly and trivial incidents.

8. Responses will vary; students can consider what makes an incident humorous.

VOCABULARY STUDY

1. demented
2. surly
3. rendition
4. erupt
5. subtle
6. enterprising
7. pandemonium
8. prevail
9. gravity
10. improvise

More Practice   Students can suggest a synonym for each vocabulary word.

Unit 8 Resource Book
Vocabulary, p. 11
Vocabulary Test, p. 14

Writer's Notebook Update

Have students recap the discussions on what makes a humorous incident funny (see page 875 and, on this page, question 8). Students can use this information and any tips they picked up in reading the selection to increase the humor of their own narratives.

Tune In

Keillor's recordings include:

- "News from Lake Wobegon" (cassette), Minnesota Public Radio, 1983
- "Gospel Birds and Other News of Lake Wobegon" (cassette), Minnesota Public Radio, 1985
- "Prairie Home Companion: The Final Performance" (cassette), Minnesota Public Radio, 1987
- "A Prairie Home Companion: The Last Show" (videocassette), Disney Home Video, 1987

Yearbook Signing

Students should consider Keillor's traits, such as his humor, and the story's events, as well as the likely attitude of the other characters.

Selection Test

Unit 8 Resource Book,
pp. 15–16

---

and __(7)__ broke out in the auditorium. Although the poor lip synch performer was ready to attack Gary, cooler heads were able to __(8)__. The lip synch performer left in a huff. I don't think Gary realized the __(9)__ of the situation. Anyway, Gary then proceeded to his talent show number, a reading of a famous poem. He began to __(10)__ on his delivery, and he had the audience in stitches. What a comedian!"

Expressing Your Ideas

Writing Choices

Writer's Notebook Update Reread the humorous incident you recorded in your log before reading "Gary Keillor." How could you improve your narrative? Does it need more colorful descriptions? Could you use exaggeration for humorous effect? Revise your humorous narrative to make it even funnier. Write the final draft in your notebook.

Tune In Check out one of Garrison Keillor's recordings of his radio show, "A Prairie Home Companion," from your library. Listen to several episodes and then write a **summary** of your favorite show.

Yearbook Signing Gary Keillor was quite a character. What do you think that Elaine Eggert, one of Gary's West River Road buddies, might have written in his yearbook at the end of this year? What would Bill Swanson write? Dede Peterson? Miss Rasmussen? Be these characters and write **notes** to Gary in his yearbook.

Other Options

It's All in the Delivery Find a copy of Walt Whitman's poem "O Captain! My Captain!", about the death of Abraham Lincoln. Prepare an **oral interpretation** of the poem to present to the class. Choose whether you would like to present it as Miss Rasmussen would like it, as Gary Keillor performed it for the talent show, or an original interpretation.

High School Happenings Telling a funny story requires different skills than writing one. Imagine that your high school has a radio show and you are the host. Prepare a three- to five- minute **"humor spot"** about things you have observed around your school. Tape your show and then play the tape for the class.

Lively Allusions Throughout his narrative Garrison refers to songs and singers that were popular in the 1950s. If you are familiar with the songs, his story is even funnier. Do some research and find recordings of as many of the songs as you can. Work with a partner to make an **oral presentation** explaining the origins of the songs and playing parts of each of them.

OTHER OPTIONS

It's All in the Delivery

Students can discuss the effect of each interpretation. Is it funny? sad? dramatic? poignant? Encourage the class to analyze why the interpretation had the particular effect it did.

High School Happenings

You may want to advise students not to mock people at the school without the subjects' agreement.

Students can prepare by watching comics on television. They might ask themselves:

- How do comics "time" their jokes?
- What sorts of jokes or anecdotes seem to draw the most laughter?

Lively Allusions

Students may find recordings at a library, a college music department, or in the collection of a relative who is a music fan.

Before Reading

Salvador Late or Early

by Sandra Cisneros

Sandra Cisneros
born 1954

The daughter of a Mexican father and a Chicana mother, Sandra Cisneros studied writing at Loyola University in Chicago, and then went to the University of Iowa for graduate school. As she listened to her classmates in the Iowa Writer's Workshop describe their childhood homes as part of an assignment, Cisneros realized that their middle and upper class childhoods were nothing like her experiences as an urban Chicana. As she once said, "I'm trying to write the stories that haven't been written. I feel like a cartographer. I'm determined to fill a literary void." Some of her books are *The House on Mango Street*, *My Wicked, Wicked Ways*, and *Woman Hollering Creek and Other Stories*.

Building Background

The Author's Heritage More than eighteen million Mexican Americans currently live in the United States. The long, rich history which intertwines the countries and peoples of Mexico and the United States began in 1540 when the Spanish explorer Coronado marched into what is now New Mexico. Mexicans, descendants of both European explorers and Indians, settled in many areas of the Southwest as well as parts of the Midwest. Often lumped together with other Spanish-speaking peoples, the children of Mexican Americans created the word *Chicano* (*Chicana* for the feminine form) to define themselves. Sandra Cisneros, the author of "Salvador Late or Early," shares the experiences of Chicano life in her prose and her poetry.

Literary Focus

Figurative Language Sandra Cisneros writes both poetry and prose, and her poetic talents spill over into her fiction. She uses figurative language, the use of words apart from their ordinary, literal meanings, to add freshness, conciseness, and vitality to her writing. For example, she describes homes as being "the color of bad weather," which not only brings to mind a dark, dreary color, but also creates a feeling of uneasiness. As you read "Salvador Late or Early," notice how Cisneros uses figurative language to create a vivid picture of Salvador's life.

Writer's Notebook

On the Economic Edge What images come to mind when you think of the word *poverty*? What is life like for families who are struggling to get by? Before reading "Salvador Late or Early," write down your impressions of what it means to live in poverty.

Before Reading

Building Background

Invite students to share knowledge of achievements by Mexican Americans. Among the many who have contributed to American culture, students may be interested in former U.S. Surgeon General Antonia Novello, athletes Nancy Lopez and Fernando Valenzuela, labor leader Cesar Chavez, entertainers Edward James Olmos and Selena, and writers Pat Mora and Gary Soto.

Literary Focus

You might tell students that Cisneros feels her stories are almost like poems. Examples of her use of figurative language include:

- [A body's] "geography of scars"
- "the hundred balloons of happiness, the single guitar of grief"

Writer's Notebook

Encourage students to discuss stereotypes of poverty and what each person can do to accept people of all socioeconomic classes with an open mind.

More About Sandra Cisneros

Cisneros won the 1985 American Book Award for *The House on Mango Street*.

SUPPORT MATERIALS OVERVIEW

Unit 8 Resource Book
- Graphic Organizer, p. 17
- Study Guide, p. 18
- Vocabulary, p. 19
- Grammar, p. 20
- Alternate Check Test, p. 21
- Vocabulary Test, p. 22
- Selection Test, pp. 23–24

Building English Proficiency
- Literature Summaries
- Activities, p. 235

Reading, Writing & Grammar Skillbook
- Reading, pp. 59–61
- Grammar, Usage, and Mechanics, pp. 170–172

Technology
- Audiotape
- Personal Journal Software
- Test Generator Software

Selection Objectives

- To appreciate a word portrait of a young character with many responsibilities
- To understand the use of figurative language
- To recognize run-on sentences

Unit 8 Resource Book
Graphic Organizer, p. 17
Study Guide, p. 18

Theme Link

Cisneros presents a citizen of tomorrow— a boy—who is burdened with responsibilities. He handles his burdens with care that is not recognized by many people around him.

1 Literary Focus

Figurative Language

Have students note examples of the author's figurative language. Encourage them to describe how Cisneros builds an image of Salvador in the reader's mind's eye.

Question   How do you think Salvador's "string of brothers" appear, when he brings them from their beds? *(Possible responses: They may be moving in a line; Salvador may be pulling them together.)*

2 Literary Element

Style

Draw attention to the author's style, which is like a stream of consciousness. The effect resembles someone thinking about Salvador. There also is a sense of rushing, which may capture the pace of Salvador's life.

Question   What qualities of Salvador are emphasized? *(Possible responses: He's responsible and busy. He lacks friends. He has happiness and grief within him. Inside he's like other boys, but outside he must act older than his years.)*

888

Salvador
Late or Early

Sandra Cisneros

1 **Salvador** with eyes the color of caterpillar, Salvador of the crooked hair and crooked teeth, Salvador whose name the teacher cannot remember, is a boy who is no one's friend, runs along somewhere in that vague direction where homes are the color of bad weather, lives behind a raw wood doorway, shakes the sleepy brothers awake, ties their shoes, combs their hair with water, feeds them milk and corn flakes from a tin cup in the dim dark of the morning.

Salvador, late or early, sooner or later arrives with the string of younger brothers ready. Helps his mama, who is busy with the business of the baby. Tugs the arms of Cecilio, Arturito, makes them hurry, because today, like yesterday, Arturito has dropped the cigar box of crayons, has let go the hundred little fingers of red, green, yellow, blue, and nub of black sticks that tumble and spill over and beyond the asphalt puddles until the crossing-guard lady holds back the blur of traffic for Salvador to collect them again.

2 **Salvador** inside that wrinkled shirt, inside the throat that must clear itself and apologize each time it speaks, inside that forty-pound body of boy with its geography of scars, its history of hurt, limbs stuffed with feathers and rags, in what part of the eyes, in what part of the heart, in that cage of the chest where something throbs with both fists and knows only what Salvador knows, inside that body too small to contain the hundred balloons of happiness, the single guitar of grief, is a boy like any other disappearing out the door, beside the schoolyard gate, where he has told his brothers they must wait. Collects the hands of Cecilio and Arturito, scuttles off dodging the many schoolyard colors, the elbows and wrists crisscrossing, the several shoes running. Grows small and smaller to the eye, dissolves into the bright horizon, flutters in the air before disappearing like a memory of kites.

In the image at the right, why do you think Antonio Bernis combined real objects with painted images in his 1974 mixed-media work, *Juanito en la Laguna?* How would you describe the effect of the combined materials?

888   UNIT EIGHT: AMERICAN VOICES TODAY

MINI-LESSON: GRAMMAR

Recognizing Run-On Sentences

Teach   This selection creates a sense of someone thinking. It includes many predicates and phrases separated by commas. It is not written in formal English, but the style works well.

In formal written English, run-on sentences are avoided. Run-ons often join clauses without proper punctuation or conjunctions. They are difficult to read and understand. For example:

Salvador arrived at school he was late because of his brothers.

This sentence may be corrected in several ways:

- *Salvador arrived at school late, because he was helping his brothers.*
- *Salvador arrived at school. He was late, because he helped his brothers.*

Activity Idea   Students can write a sentence in formal English describing Salvador. Then they can read each other's sentences, noticing structure.

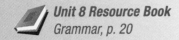

Unit 8 Resource Book
Grammar, p. 20

BERNI '74

 **Art Study**

Antonio Berni has given the artwork (oil painting and collage on wood) a third dimension, affixing materials along the shoreline. The title translated into English is *Juanito in the Lagoon.*

Possible Responses to Caption Questions   The artist may have wanted to show litter despoiling the scene. The effect is one of dimension or depth to the clutter, a rich texture to the image, and a suggestion of hazard to the boy.

Check Test

1. Is Salvador described as a boy who probably is popular among his schoolmates? *(No; he is described as "no one's friend.")*

2. Why is Salvador often "late or early"? *(He has to get his brothers ready for school, as well as himself.)*

3. Why does Salvador take care of his brothers? *(They are younger, and his mother is busy with a new baby.)*

4. What does one of the boys drop? *(a box full of crayons)*

5. Who are Cecilio and Arturito? *(Salvador's brothers)*

 Unit 8 Resource Book
Alternate Check Test, p. 21

BUILDING ENGLISH PROFICIENCY

Understanding Figurative Language

Encourage students to recognize figurative language that achieves a descriptive effect by not using words literally. Students can examine descriptive, literal details and contrast them to images created with figurative language.

- Literal details include Salvador's crooked teeth and how he feeds his brothers cereal and milk from "a tin cup in the dim dark."

- An example of figurative language is the image of crayons as "the hundred little fingers of red, green, yellow, blue. . . ." Ask: How are crayons like fingers? *(Possible responses: They are shaped like fingers, they are together like fingers, and Arturito may hold them in his hand the way he clutches his brother's fingers.)*

 Building English Proficiency
Book Activities, p. 235

 For summaries of the selection in English and other languages, see the **Building English Proficiency** *book.*

ESL
LEP
ELD
SAE
LD

After Reading

MAKING CONNECTIONS

1. Students might choose some of the metaphors and similes that Cisneros uses to describe Salvador, such as "limbs stuffed with feathers and rags."

2. Possible responses: Appearance—dark eyes, poorly cut hair, crooked teeth, 40 pounds, scarred, ragged; personality—responsible, caring, helpful, friendless, a mix of anger and happiness

3. Possible responses: Salvador is himself inside, no matter how the outside world sees him. He is a boy who cannot control his environment; his lateness or earliness depends on his younger brothers.

4. Possible responses: Story—action, strong characterization, and paragraph format; poem—figurative language, an emphasis on images rather than plot, and a length as short as many poems

5. Responses will vary. Point out that children's workloads may vary with cultural setting and socioeconomic status.

WRITING CHOICES
Writer's Notebook Update

Responses will vary. Students may note that Salvador lives where "homes are the color of bad weather" and that his limbs are "stuffed with feathers and rags." He may seem underweight, which may be a sign of poverty.

Best Friends

Although students may focus on the negative (Salvador's responsibilities or poverty), they also should note positive aspects of his life (for example, his reliability and strong family connections).

Selection Test

Unit 8 Resource Book
pp. 23–24

After Reading

Making Connections

Shaping Your Response

1. If you were going to illustrate this story, what images and materials would you use? Describe your illustration.

Analyzing the Story

2. Sandra Cisneros paints a vivid picture of her **character** Salvador in only three paragraphs. Describe his appearance and personality.

3. What do you think is the significance of the title, "Salvador Late or Early"?

4. In some ways "Salvador Late or Early" seems like a story, and in other ways it seems like a poem. What elements does it have in common with each of these **genres?**

Extending the Ideas

5. Salvador has a lot of responsibility for a young boy. What tasks or chores do you think 10- or 12-year-old children should have?

Expressing Your Ideas

Writing Choices

Writer's Notebook Update Review your thoughts about poverty that you described in your notebook. Would you say Salvador's family is impoverished or not? Write a paragraph explaining your thoughts about Salvador's family.

Best Friends With a partner, create a best friend for Salvador. Then create and perform a **dialogue** between the two, allowing Salvador to share his thoughts about his family, his school, and his life.

Other Options

Show-and-Tell Imagine you are Arturito. You must tell about a family member for "show and tell." Give a short **speech** to the class about Salvador as you think Arturito might.

A Portrait of Salvador Create a likeness of Salvador in the form of a **painting,** a **papier-mâché or clay sculpture,** or a **drawing.** In your creation, try to capture the personality and mood Cisneros has caught in her story.

OTHER OPTIONS
Show and Tell

Students can prepare by brainstorming how Salvador would appear to Arturito. They might come up with a list including notes like these: big brother, makes us do things, nice, takes care of us. Students also may consider objects Arturito could use in his "show and tell" speech, such as photos, his cigar box, or other items.

A Portrait of Salvador

Before students begin, ask them to describe the mood of "Salvador Late or Early." *(poignant, moving, heartfelt)* After the likenesses are completed, students might display them in a class art gallery.

Before Reading

Coca-Cola and Coco Frío by Martín Espada

Lost Sister by Cathy Song

Naming Myself by Barbara Kingsolver

Red Wagons by Ana Castillo

Building Background

The Shadows of the Past What convergence of experiences has made you the person you are today? We are each a product of our past, both of our childhood and of our family heritage. The narrators of the poems in this section each examine something in his or her past that has made a difference in some way. Think about the influences in your life—people, places, and events. Use a pie chart to apportion the impact of each influence on your life. For example, the young girl in the Unit 7 poem "Legacies" (page 773), looking back as an adult, might apportion her pie chart this way. Be prepared to discuss your chart in class.

Literary Focus

Theme The deeper, underlying meaning of a poem is its theme. A theme is usually not stated explicitly, but is implied. Also, a theme of a poem is not its subject but rather an observation about that subject. For example, the subject of the poem "Legacies" on page 773 is a grandmother's desire to teach her granddaughter how to make biscuits. One statement of its theme might be, "Family members express their love in different ways." As you read the four poems that follow, think about what you think is the theme of each one.

Writer's Notebook

Who Are You? If you were the topic of a poem, what words might a poet use to accurately express your individuality? In your notebook make a list of five nouns, five verbs, five adjectives, and five adverbs that could be used in the poem about you.

Coca-Cola and Coco Frío   **891**

Before Reading

Building Background

Students should consider the following for inclusion in their pie charts:

- family
- friends
- heritage
- events
- teachers and influential adults
- neighborhood
- hobbies and sports
- culture, including books, movies, and so on

Literary Focus

To analyze the theme, students might consider these questions:

- Does the title of the work reveal the theme?
- Is the theme presented directly or indirectly?
- Do images or metaphors point to a theme?

Writer's Notebook

Students will use their lists to write poetry about themselves on page 900. Suggest they revise their lists as they read the following poems if new ideas occur to them.

SUPPORT MATERIALS OVERVIEW

Unit 8 Resource Book
- Graphic Organizer, p. 25
- Study Guide, p. 26
- Vocabulary, p. 27
- Grammar, p. 28
- Alternate Check Test, p. 29
- Vocabulary Test, p. 30
- Selection Test, pp. 31–32

Building English Proficiency
- Literature Summaries
- Activities, p. 236

Reading, Writing & Grammar SkillBook
- Vocabulary, pp. 7–8
- Reading, pp. 48–49
- Writing, pp. 121–122
- Grammar, Usage, and Mechanics, pp. 160–161

Technology
- Audiotape
- Personal Journal Software
- Custom Literature Database: For another selection dealing with retaining one's identity, see "Blues Ain't No Mockin Bird" by Toni Cade Bambara on the database.
- Test Generator Software

More About the Poets

- **Martín Espada**   Espada graduated from the University of Wisconsin with an undergraduate degree and from Northeastern University with a law degree. He gives readings of his poetry at colleges and universities in the Boston area.

- **Cathy Song**   The importance of family and the rootlessness of life for an immigrant in an alien culture are themes that recur in many of Cathy Song's poems. A graduate of Wellesley College and Boston University, Song has taught creative writing at a number of universities.

- **Barbara Kingsolver**   wrote her first novel, *The Bean Trees*, while suffering insomnia. To occupy herself during periods of sleeplessness, she wrote in a closet with her typewriter on her knees so as not to disturb her sleeping husband. Another work by Barbara Kingsolver is *Holding the Line: Women in the Great Arizona Mine Strike of 1983* (nonfiction, 1989).

- **Ana Castillo**   is also the editor (with Cherrie Moraga) of a well-received anthology of Hispanic writing called *This Bridge Called My Back (Este Puente, Mi Espalda: Voces de Mujeres Tercermundistas en Los Estados Unidos)*, published in 1988. Other poetry by Ana Castillo includes "Zero Makes Me Hungry" (1975) and "We Would Like You to Know" (1994).

Martín Espada
born 1957

Martín Espada is a tenant lawyer in Boston, and he also teaches classes in Latino poetry at local colleges and universities. Born in Brooklyn, New York, of Puerto Rican and Jewish parentage, Espada writes mostly about working class people, many of them immigrants. His poetry collections include *The Immigrant Iceboy's Bolero* (1982), *Trumpets from the Islands of Their Eviction* (1987), *Rebellion Is a Circle of a Lover's Hands* (1990), and *City of Coughing and Dead Radiators* (1993).

Cathy Song
born 1955

"Lost Sister" is taken from Cathy Song's poetry collection *Picture Bride,* which won the Yale Series of Younger Poets Award in 1982. In the title poem Song reveals some of her family history. Her grandmother was a mail-order bride—a "picture bride"—from Korea who was sent for by Song's grandfather in Hawaii. Song herself was born and raised in Honolulu, Hawaii. Her poetry reflects the tug-of-war between the cultural ties to Asia and life in modern Hawaii.

Barbara Kingsolver
born 1955

Although Barbara Kingsolver studied to be a biologist, she always loved writing. She began writing short stories and essays as a child and has kept a personal journal since she was eight. Her books include the novels *The Bean Trees* (1988), *Animal Dreams* (1990), and *Pigs in Heaven* (1993); a short story collection, *Homeland and Other Stories* (1989); nonfiction works; and a poetry collection called *Another America* (1994). Most of Kingsolver's writing features characters who are struggling to survive economically, psychologically, or politically.

Ana Castillo
born 1953

Born in Chicago of Mexican American parents, Ana Castillo's professional training is in art education and social science. In addition to writing, Castillo also dances, and she sometimes performs her poetry set to music. Her poetry collections include *Otro Canto* (1977), *The Invitation* (1979), *Pajaros Enganosos* (1983), and *Women Are Not Roses* (1984). She has also published a collection called *My Father Was a Toltec* (1995), in which the poem "Red Wagons" appears.

Coca-Cola and Coco Frío

MARTÍN ESPADA

 Which Puerto Rico do you think this painting, *Merengue in Boca Chica* (1983) by Rafael Ferrer, most resembles—the one where aunts serve Coca-Cola, or the one that enjoys Coco Frío? Explain your answer.

On his first visit to Puerto Rico,
island of family folklore,
the fat boy wandered
from table to table
5   with his mouth open.
At every table, some great-aunt
would steer him with cool spotted hands
to a glass of Coca-Cola.
One even sang to him, in all the English
10 she could remember, a Coca-Cola jingle
from the forties. He drank obediently,
    though
he was bored with this potion, familiar
from soda fountains in Brooklyn.

Then, at a roadside stand off the beach,
    the fat boy

15 opened his mouth to coco frío, a coconut
chilled, then scalped by a machete
so that a straw could inhale the clear milk.
The boy tilted the green shell overhead
and drooled coconut milk down his chin;
20 suddenly, Puerto Rico was not Coca-Cola
or Brooklyn, and neither was he.

For years afterward, the boy marveled at
    an island
where the people drank Coca-Cola
and sang jingles from World War II
25 in a language they did not speak,
while so many coconuts in the trees
sagged heavy with milk, swollen
and unsuckled.

Coca-Cola and Coco Frío   **893**

SELECTION SUMMARY

Coca-Cola and Coco Frío, Lost Sister, Naming Myself, Red Wagons

Coca-Cola and Coco Frío   Espada writes of a boy's first visit to Puerto Rico and the American soft drink everyone there seems to favor. After drinking chilled coconut milk, he wonders why Puerto Ricans have forsaken this luscious fruit of their culture.

Lost Sister   Song reflects on a woman who left China to find freedom and equality in America. Here she also found loneliness, alienation, and the realization that she needed China too.

Naming Myself   Barbara Kingsolver ponders her last name and its rich family history.

Red Wagons   Ana Castillo considers the contrast between the playful red wagon used by children in her schoolbooks and the red wagon pulled by her father hauling kerosene to heat their home.

 *For summaries in other languages, see the **Building English Proficiency** book.*

During Reading

Selection Objectives

- To analyze four poems about how yesterday influences tomorrow
- To identify a poem's theme
- To understand analogies

 *Unit 8 Resource Book*
Graphic Organizer, p. 25
Study Guide, p. 26

Theme Link

The poets reflect on the past and its influence on the present and the future.

Vocabulary Preview

dormant, in a state of rest or inactivity
redundant, needlessly repetitive
inundate, overspread, as if with a flood
meager, poor or scanty; sparse
unremitting, never stopping

   Students can add the words and definitions to their personal word lists in the Writer's Notebook.

Art Study

Response to Caption Question   It could represent both. The merengue band is a rich symbol of Puerto Rican culture, and the environment is that of "Coco Frío." The sunbathing woman seems to be enjoying the fruits of this culture as the band serenades her, but she is not a part of it. She seems to be the "Coca-Cola" in the painting.

Visual Literacy   Ferrer was born in Santurce, Puerto Rico. Since the 1980s his work has reflected the dynamics between the life of the people of the Caribbean and the tourist trade.

1   Literary Focus
Theme

Question   What is the poem's theme? (*Possible response: People should not forsake their own cultures.*)

893

2 Literary Element
Metaphor

Invite comments on the metaphor of the woman who diluted "jade green with the blue of the Pacific."

Questions

- What does jade stand for in the poem? *(China)*
- What does the Pacific stand for? *(the United States, since the woman had to cross the Pacific to reach this country)*
- What does the metaphor mean? *(Possible response: Although the woman retained her Chinese heritage, it is now mixed or "diluted" with American culture and customs.)*

3 Reader's Response
Making Personal Connections

Question   Why do you think the poet calls this poem "Lost Sister"? *(Possible response: The woman in the poem is lost to the China that she once knew. She has lost that part of her life. The poet may think of the lonely woman as a sister—either as a relative or as a sister in the broader sense.)*

Lost Sister 3
CATHY SONG

1.

In China,
even the peasants
named their first daughters,
Jade—
5 the stone that in the far fields
could moisten the dry season,
could make men move mountains
for the healing green of the inner hills,
glistening like slices of winter melon.

10 And the daughters were grateful:
they never left home.
To move freely was a luxury
stolen from them at birth.
Instead, they gathered patience,
15 learning to walk in shoes
the size of teacups,
without breaking—
the arc of their movements
as dormant¹ as the rooted willow,
20 as redundant² as the farmyard hens.
But they travelled far
in surviving,
learning to stretch the family rice,
to quiet the demons,
25 the noisy stomachs.

2.

There is a sister
across the ocean,
who relinquished her name,
diluting jade green
30 with the blue of the Pacific.
Rising with a tide of locusts,
she swarmed with others
to inundate³ another shore.

In America,
35 there are many roads
and women can stride along with men.

But in another wilderness,
the possibilities,
the loneliness,
40 can strangulate like jungle vines.
The meager⁴ provisions and sentiments
of once belonging:
fermented⁵ roots, mahjong⁶ tiles and fire crackers;
cannot shake away the ghosts,
45 sets but a flimsy household
in a forest of nightless cities.
A giant snake rattles above,
spewing black clouds into your kitchen.
Dough faced landlords
50 slip in and out of your keyholes,
making claims you don't understand,
tapping into your communication systems
of laundry lines and restaurant chains.
You find you need China:
55 your one fragile identification,
a jade link
handcuffed to your wrist.

You remember your mother
who walked for centuries,
60 footless—
and like her,
you have left no footprints,
but only because
there is an ocean inbetween,
65 the unremitting⁷ space of your rebellion. 4

---

1. **dormant** (dôr′mənt), *adj.* in a state of rest or inactivity.
2. **redundant** (ri dun′dənt), *adj.* needlessly repetitive.
3. **inundate** (in′un dāt), *v.* overspread as if with a flood.

---

4. **meager** (mē′gər), *adj.* poor or scanty; sparse.
5. **fermented** (fər ment′əd), *adj.* chemically changed by yeast, enzymes, or bacteria changing sugars to alcohol.
6. **mahjong** (mä′zhong′), *n.* game played with tiles.
7. **unremitting** (un′ri mit′ing), *adj.* never stopping.

MINI-LESSON: CRITICAL THINKING

Make Analogies

Teach   Review that an analogy is a resemblance between two or more things that are otherwise not alike. Discuss analogies that may be made between the two poems that students have read thus far. For example, the jade in "Lost Sister" represents the author's heritage just as the coconut milk represents the culture of Puerto Rico in "Coca-Cola and Coco Frío."

Activity Idea   Have students make other analogies between these two poems and the two that follow. To get started, suggest they consider images, theme, and style. Encourage them to see that looking for analogies can provide a deeper insight into the poems.

Theme

Discuss the theme of Song's poem with students.

Questions

- What do you think is the poem's theme? *(Possible responses: America offers new opportunities, but also means a loss of Chinese culture.)*
- What is the significance of jade? *(Possible response: Jade stands both for China and for the woman's Chinese heritage.)*

Art Study

Response to Caption Question
Students probably will relate the painting to the poem. It appears to contrast a woman's new life (in America) to a woman's life in China. The boat and the woman in costume represent China. The numbers appear to be street numbers in California, where many Chinese Americans immigrated.

Visual Literacy   Artist Hung Liu (born 1948 in Manchuria) based her images on a young Chinese American woman in a turn-of-the-century photograph taken in Chinatown, San Francisco, and a Chinese woman, an imperial concubine, from a painting of the Tang dynasty era (A.D. 618–906). The street sign numbers match the years of the Tang dynasty.

▲ In this painting, *Tang Ren Jie* (1988) by Hung Lui, what story might the artist be trying to tell? Who is the woman in the center, where and when is she living, and what is her relationship to the boat, the traditionally dressed woman, and the numbers?

BUILDING ENGLISH PROFICIENCY

Exploring Imagery

Song begins her poem by referring to jade—traditionally, a green stone. There are many other "green" images. Work with students to construct a web of images that Song links to that color. Then have them discuss that color's symbolic value—both in "Lost Sister" and in their own thinking.

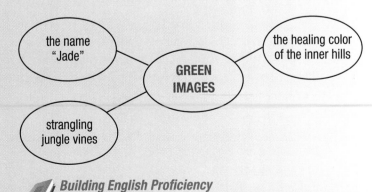

the name "Jade" — GREEN IMAGES — the healing color of the inner hills

strangling jungle vines

📖 *Building English Proficiency*
Activities, p. 236

Discuss Kingsolver's use of imagery with students, noting how the details create a picture of the narrator's grandparents and explain the importance to her of her family name.

Questions

- What images does Kingsolver use to describe her grandfather and grandmother? *(Grandfather = restless, Virginian, thief, inventor. Grandmother= nameless, ink-braided, button-clothed)*

- How does Kingsolver think of her name? *(Possible response: She compares it to her soul and considers how it evokes her family history.)*

6 Literary Focus
Theme

Encourage students to connect Kingsolver's images with the theme.

Question   What do you think is the poem's theme? *(Possible responses: One's family name is part of one's heritage and as such should not be shed lightly.)*

Naming Myself

Barbara Kingsolver

I have guarded my name as people
in other times kept their own clipped hair,
believing the soul could be scattered
if they were careless.

5   I knew my first ancestor.
His legend. I have touched
his boots and moustache, the grandfather
whose people owned slaves and cotton.
He was restless in Virginia
10 among the gentleman brothers, until
one peppered, flaming autumn he stole a horse,
rode over the mountains to marry
a leaf-eyed Cherokee.
The theft was forgiven but never
15 the Indian blood. He lost his family's name
and invented mine, gave it fruit and seeds.
I never knew the grandmother.
Her photograph has ink-thin braids
and buttoned clothes, and nothing that she
      was called.

20 I could shed my name in the middle of life,
the ordinary thing, and it would flee
along with childhood and dead grandmothers
to that Limbo[1] for discontinued maiden names.[2]

But it would grow restless there.
25 I know this. It would ride over leaf smoke
      mountains
and steal horses.

_____

1. **Limbo** (lim′bō), *n.* the dwelling place of souls kept from Heaven; place for persons and things forgotten, cast aside, or out of date.
2. **maiden name,** a woman's surname before her marriage.

MINI-LESSON: GRAMMAR

Subordinate and Coordinate Clauses

Teach   Review with students that a clause is a group of words that has a subject and a predicate. A subordinate clause is incomplete and is used with a main clause to express a related idea. Coordinate clauses have equal rank in a sentence.

This sentence from "Red Wagons" has two subordinate clauses; the sentence would make sense without them, although each adds to the meaning of the main clause:

Father pulled it to the gas station <u>when he was home</u> and <u>if there was money</u>.

This sentence from "Naming Myself" contains coordinate clauses, each of which is of equal importance to the meaning of the sentence:

I could shed my name in the middle of life, . . . and it would flee along with childhood and dead grandmothers. . . .

Some phrases has been omitted here, to clearly show the basic clauses.

Activity Idea   Have students write descriptions of their parents or two friends, using at least one subordinate clause and one pair of coordinate clauses. They can underline any subordinate clauses once and any coordinate clauses twice.

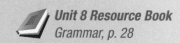

Unit 8 Resource Book
Grammar, p. 28

Poniendome un Nombre

Barbara Kingsolver

▲ What story might Jaune Quick-To-See Smith be telling in her 1992 composition *Red Horse*?

He protegido mi nombre como la gente
de otras épocas guardaba mechones de su
    cabello,
creyendo que el alma podía fugarse
si no tenían cuidado.

5 Conocí a mi primer antepasado.
Su leyenda. He tocado
sus botas y el mostacho, el abuelo
cuya familia era dueña de esclavos y algodón.
Se sentía inquieto en Virginia
10 entre sus hermanos aristócratas, hasta que
un otoño llameante robó un caballo,
y galopó sobre las montañas para desposar
a una cheroki de ojos en forma de hojas.
El robo fue perdonado, pero nunca
15 la sangre indígena. Perdió el nombre de
    familia
e inventó el mío, le dió frutos y semillas.
Nunca conocí a la abuela.
Su fotografía tiene delgadas trenzas color tinta
y ropas abotonadas, y ningún nombre por
    el cual se le conociera.

20 Podría deshacerme de mi nombre en la mitad
    de la vida,
la cosa más común, y desaparecería
junto con la niñez y las abuelas muertas
hacia ese limbo creado para los nombres
    de soltera fuera de circulación.

Pero se inquietaría allí.
25 Lo sé. Cabalgaría sobre montañas con humo
    de hojas
para robar caballos.

7

Poniendome un Nombre   897

Question If you were writing a poem, what might a red wagon (or another toy) stand for? *(Responses will vary.)*

9 Literary Focus

Theme

Discuss the theme of Castillo's poem. Have students consider the red wagon and its contrasting uses in the school primer and the narrator's home. (*The textbook wagon is part of an idealized version of childhood, the narrator's real childhood is different .*)

Check Test

1. What is coco frío? *(fresh, chilled coconut milk)*

2. What was a common first name for a Chinese girl? *(Jade)*

3. What objects stand for one's heritage in "Coca-Cola and Coco Frío" and "Lost Sister"? *(coco frío; jade)*

4. What is the origin of the narrator's last name in "Naming Myself"? *(An ancestor married a Cherokee woman and was disowned by his family. He invented a last name for his new family.)*

5. What was the red wagon used for in the narrator's home? *(to pull kerosene cans)*

Unit 8 Resource Book
Alternate Check Test, p. 29

---

8 # RED WAGONS

Ana Castillo

c. 1958

In grammar school primers[1]
the red wagon
was for children
pulled along
5 past lawns on a sunny day.
Father drove into
the driveway. "Look,
Father, look!"
Silly Sally pulled Tim
10 on the red wagon.

Out of school,
the red wagon carried
kerosene cans
to heat the flat.[2]
15 Father pulled it to the gas
station
when he was home
and if there was money.

If not, children went to bed
20 in silly coats
silly socks; in the morning
were already dressed
for school.

---

1. **primer** (prim′ər), *n.* a first book in reading.
2. **flat** (flat), *n.* apartment.

MINI-LESSON: VOCABULARY

Connotation and Denotation

Teach Ask students to define *denotation* and *connotation*. (*Denotation is a word's exact definition. Connotation refers to the inferences, implications, or feelings associated with the word.*) Point out that poetry is particularly dependent on the connotations of words. Discuss that considering the connotations of key words (such as "red wagon") can help students decipher the poem's meaning.

Questions

• What is the denotative meaning of "red wagon" on page 898? *(a low four-wheel vehicle with an open rectangular body and a long handle made for play)*

• What is its connotative meaning in Castillo's poem? *(Possible responses: in textbooks—fun, a carefree life, a life of plenty; at home—work, heat, necessities of life)*

• How is this related to the poem's theme? *(The wagon's connotative meaning in each situation—in schoolbooks and at home—points up the contrast between the idealized world of books and the narrator's world at home.)*

Activity Idea Have students choose a word that has important connotations to them and explain why in a poem or in a prose paragraph.

After Reading

After Reading

Making Connections

Shaping Your Response

1. Choose one of the poems and write three questions you would like to ask the narrator.

2. What sensory image do you recall most vividly from these poems? Cite the lines that created the **imagery.**

Analyzing the Poems

3. **Summarize** what astonished the boy in "Coca-Cola and Coco Frío."

4. Explain the **comparison** that Ana Castillo develops in "Red Wagons."

5. In "Lost Sister" the narrator says that even Chinese peasants named their first daughters "Jade." What is **ironic** about this?

6. **Compare** the two places described in "Lost Sister."

7. What example of **personification** can you find in "Naming Myself"?

8. **Summarize** the narrator's reasons for keeping her maiden name.

9. Choose two of the four poems and explain the **changes** the characters experience. Tell how cultural heritage plays a part in or is effected by the changes.

Extending the Ideas

10. The United States has in the past been called a "melting pot" because it has received many peoples from different lands who then become "Americans." Think about the notion of "assimilation," or becoming part of a larger group. What do you think are the advantages and disadvantages of assimilation? Cite examples from the poems to support your opinions.

Literary Focus: Theme

Think about the underlying meaning of each of the poems. Then complete the following chart by stating the subject and writing a statement of theme for each poem. Do any of the poems share common themes?

Poem	Subject	Statement of Theme
"Coca-Cola and Coco Frío"		
"Lost Sister"		
"Red Wagons"		
"Naming Myself"		

MAKING CONNECTIONS

1. Responses will vary. Students might choose the poem that holds the most personal meaning for them.

2. Possible images: the cold coconut milk in "Coca-Cola and Coco Frío"; the jade in "Lost Sister"; the name riding over mountains and stealing horses in "Naming Myself"; the red wagon in "Red Wagons"

3. That the people would drink Coca-Cola while leaving delicious coconuts to rot on trees.

4. The red wagon of the textbook was part of an idealized version of childhood; at home, the red wagon was used for work, not play. It represents the contrast between fantasy and reality.

5. Jade is an expensive mineral that the peasants would have never been able to afford.

6. China is seen as constricting for women, but it also holds family and friends; the United States offers a woman more freedom but the people are strangers who practice unfamiliar customs and make "claims you don't understand."

7. The poet personifies a name, writing that if discarded, it would "ride over leaf smoke mountains and steal horses."

8. The name represents her family heritage.

9. Possible advantages: greater freedom, a chance to become better off than one was in the old country; Possible disadvantages: loss of one's own culture and heritage, loss of family ties and support.

LITERARY FOCUS: THEME

Unit 8 Resource Book
Graphic Organizer, p. 25

Remind students to consider a poem's title, images, and conclusions in considering its theme.

Possible chart:

Poem	Subject	Statement of Theme
"Coca-Cola and Coco Frío"	the effect the USA has on Puerto Rico	People should treasure their own culture
"Lost Sister"	freedom and equality versus loss and alienation for the immigrant	In embracing American culture, it is important to also honor one's heritage.
"Red Wagons"	the difference between idealized American culture and the real experience	Not everyone has the idealized childhood pictured in books.
"Naming Myself"	how the narrator got her name and why it is important	One's family name is an important part of one's heritage.

VOCABULARY STUDY

1. redundant
2. dormant
3. inundate
4. meager
5. unremitting

More Practice   Students can write an antonym for each vocabulary word, then use the antonym in a sentence.

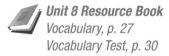
Unit 8 Resource Book
Vocabulary, p. 27
Vocabulary Test, p. 30

WRITING CHOICES
Writer's Notebook Update

Encourage students to use the four poems as models. Their poems can focus on their own heritage, neighborhoods, or families. You might collect the poems into a class literary magazine.

You Can't Judge a Book by Its Cover

Responses will vary, but the subtitle probably will elucidate the poem's theme.

Selection Test

Unit 8 Resource Book
Selection Test, pp. 31–32

Vocabulary Study

Write the word from the list that could replace the italicized word or words in each sentence.

dormant
meager
inundate
redundant
unremitting

1. My comment about Puerto Rico was *repetitious* because Ana already answered the teacher's question.
2. The flower seed was *inactive* throughout the winter, but began to grow in the spring.
3. Radio and television broadcasts *bombard* their audiences with commercials.
4. Dinner was usually a *small* portion of potatoes and corn.
5. The anxiety caused by the loss of family support and cultural familiarity is *constant* for many people who emigrate to the United States.

Expressing Your Ideas

Writing Choices

Writer's Notebook Update   Use the words that you wrote in your writer's notebook to write a poem about yourself. It can be rhymed or unrhymed, long or short. If you are not the poetic type, write a descriptive paragraph about yourself.

You Can't Judge a Book by Its Cover
Sometimes a book will have a subtitle that further explains the book's topic. For example, an autobiography by a basketball referee entitled *The Last Word* might have the subtitle *I Make the Calls.* Write informative **subtitles** for the four poems you have just read.

Other Options

Meeting of Minds   In groups of four, find out all you can about the four authors in this cluster, including becoming familiar with their other works. Then, based on what you learn, dramatize a **panel discussion** between the four, discussing what they think it means to be American in today's multicultural society.

Conversing on the Net   Imagine that two of the narrators or characters from these poems have found each other on a bulletin board or newsgroup of the Internet and begin writing to each other. What will they say to each other? With a partner, choose two of the poem's personalities and write a series of **electronic mail messages** to and from each other. Be sure to use the information in the poems as a basis for your discussion.

OTHER OPTIONS
Meeting of Minds

Students can find information about authors in reference works such as *Something About the Author, Contemporary Authors, Contemporary Literary Criticism,* and *Current Biography Yearbook.* They also might consider writing the author's publisher or agent for information.

Conversing on the Net

Encourage students to visualize the poet they choose before beginning. They should reread the poet's biography and poem, looking for answers to questions such as:

• How old is the poet?
• Where is the poet from?
• What is the poet like?

Before Reading

Mother Tongue

by Amy Tan

Amy Tan
Born 1952

Amy Tan was born in Oakland, California, to parents who had recently emigrated from China. Tan won her first literary contest when she was eight. She has since worked as a consultant, writer, editor, and publisher. Tan comments on her writing: "The kind of writing I do is very dream-like. . . . I focus on a specific image, and that image takes me into a scene. Then I begin to see the scene and I ask myself, "What's to your right? What's to your left? and I open up into this fictional world . . . and let it go where it wants to go, wherever the characters want to go." Tan's latest work of fiction is *The Hundred Secret Senses* (1995).

Building Background

What Languages Do You Speak? In "Mother Tongue," the essay you are about to read, Amy Tan talks about "all the Englishes" she grew up with. Analyze the Englishes that you use. Think about how you speak to your parents, your teachers, your friends, and younger children. Do the vocabularies differ? How about the sentence structure and grammar you use? Does your family have ethnic words or expressions infused into its English? For example, does your grandmother call a scarf a *babushka,* or is your uncle referred to as *tío?* Does your English have a regional flavor—a Texas twang, a Chicago accent, or a Southern drawl? Tape-record or make a written transcript of three short conversations between you and an adult non-family member, between you and a friend, and between you and a family member. How do the Englishes that you use compare to each other?

Literary Focus

Denotation and Connotation Words not only have denotations, or literal meanings, but also connotations, or emotional associations. For example, in the phrase *mother tongue,* the denotative meaning of the word *mother* is: "derived from one's mother; native." However, the word may also connote feelings of warmth and goodness. As you read the essay, notice the connotations of the words *broken* and *limited* as Tan uses them to describe her mother's English.

Writer's Notebook

Know Your Audience Imagine that you are supposed to present a report to the class about contemporary music and provide taped examples. During the middle of your report, the audiotape breaks, ruining your presentation. How would you write about the situation in a letter to your brother who is away at college? How would you write about it if you were writing to the manufacturer of the audiotape? Choose one of these situations and write a sample letter in your notebook.

Mother Tongue **901**

During Reading

Selection Objectives

- To analyze a word's denotations and connotations
- To draw conclusions based on evidence
- To understand issues faced by the citizens of today and tomorrow.

 **Unit 8 Resource Book**
Study Guide, p. 34

Theme Link

Amy Tan reflects on the many forms of the English language in considering the challenges faced by Citizens of Tomorrow.

Vocabulary Preview

transcribe, set down in writing

belie, give a false idea of; misrepresent

portfolio, holdings in the form of stocks, bonds, etc.

impeccable, free from fault; irreproachable

insular, standing alone like an island; isolated

semantic, having to do with the meaning of words

hone, to perfect or make more effective

quandary, state of perplexity or uncertainty; dilemma

nascent, in the process of coming into existence; emerging

Students can add the words and definitions to their Writer's Notebooks.

---

1 Reading/Thinking
Anticipate Objections

Point out the way in which the author antcipates objections. She provides credentials and admits what she is not.

Questions

- What are the author's credentials? *(She is a writer, someone who thinks about and uses language a great deal.)*
- What objections might people raise to her writing this essay? *(She is not an English scholar; she's not a linguist.)*

902

MOTHER Tongue

Amy Tan

I AM NOT a scholar of English or literature. I cannot give you much more than personal opinions on the English language and its variations in this country or others.

I am a writer. And by that definition, I am someone who has always loved language. I am fascinated by language in daily life. I spend a great deal of my time thinking about the power of language—the way it can evoke an emotion, a visual image, a complex idea, or a simple truth. Language is the tool of my trade. And I use them all—all the Englishes I grew up with.

1

Recently, I was made keenly aware of the different Englishes I do use. I was giving a talk to a large group of people, the same talk I had already given to half a dozen other groups. The nature of the talk was about my writing, my life, and my book, *The Joy Luck Club.* The talk was going along well enough, until I remembered one major difference that made the whole talk sound wrong. My mother was in the room.

This 1991 work by Pacita Abad is titled *How Mali Lost Her Accent.* Based on the details in the work, what else do you think Mali may have lost, and what does she seem to have gained?

902   UNIT EIGHT: AMERICAN VOICES TODAY

SELECTION SUMMARY

Mother Tongue

Amy Tan considers both her mother tongue and her mother's tongue, and their effects on her development. She describes her mother's "limited English," and shares incidents in which her mother had difficulty being understood. She also considers why Asian Americans are so prominent in mathematics and science, and under-represented in writing programs. She concludes with a description of the English in her novel *The Joy Luck Club*, explaining that she strove to include "all the Englishes I grew up with." She knew she had succeeded when her mother read the book and declared it "So easy to read."

 *For summaries in other languages, see The **Building English Proficiency** book.*

 **Art Study**

Response to Caption Question
Students may suggest that Mali may have lost her own cultural identity—at least in the setting she finds herself in here. Judging by the way she is dressed, her facial expression, and her surroundings, she appears to be a typical American college student. She seems to be gaining a top-notch education—perhaps at the expense of her past.

Visual Literacy Pacita Abad used acrylic, oil, and collage on stitched and padded canvas to create *How Mali Lost Her Accent.* The resulting image—of a young woman in a kaleidoscope of color surrounded by the collegiate symbols of hard work and success (Harvard, Yale, UCLA, and so on)—gives the viewer a sense of excitement, movement, and perhaps frenzy. Mali may be facing a dilemma that many foreign-born young people face, making sense of the changes and challenges of a new culture. Must one forsake the old for this new life? The young woman looking out at us from this painting appears proud, determined, and optimistic about it all.

BUILDING ENGLISH PROFICIENCY

Exploring an Author's Opinions

Tan fills her selection with statements about language in general, the English language in particular, and her feelings about both. Encourage students to keep track of these statements and to agree or disagree with them, using their own experiences to support their opinions. Students may simply list Tan's statements and comment on them orally. Encourage students who are capable of doing so to construct a chart such as the following.

Statement	Agree/Disagree	Reason
I [have] always loved language.	Not sure	I haven't thought much about it.
I use different kinds of English.	Agree	I use the language of my family at home and English at school.

Response Students should note that Tan is using formal, standard English, a type of English she and her mother do not use at home. She may worry that she sounds pretentious or that her mother won't understand her, although later in the essay she explains that her mother understands standard English very well.

3 Literary Element
Diction

Elicit that Tan's use of "mother tongue" is a play on words that also makes a point: A *mother tongue* is a person's first language; but the particular form of English her mother speaks is Tan's "mother tongue."

4 Reading/Thinking
Recognize Values

Questions

• According to Tan, what is wrong about describing the nonstandard English of an immigrant as "broken"? *(Possible response: It implies that their English is damaged and needs to be fixed.)*

• Do you agree or disagree with her opinion? Why? *(Responses will vary. Some may agree with Tan that nonstandard English is simply another form of English. Others may feel that nonstandard English is "broken" or limited, because it does limit the ability of the listener to understand the speaker.)*

And it was perhaps the first time she had heard me give a lengthy speech, using the kind of English I have never used with her. I was saying things like, "The intersection of memory upon imagination" and "There is an aspect of my fiction that relates to thus-and-thus"—a speech filled with carefully wrought grammatical phrases, burdened, it suddenly seemed to me, with nominalized forms, past perfect tenses, conditional phrases, all the forms of standard English that I had learned in school and through books, the forms of English I did not use at home with my mother.

2 CLARIFY: What difference does having her mother in the audience make to Amy Tan?

Just last week, I was walking down the street with my mother, and again I found myself conscious of the English I was using, the English I do use with her. We were talking about the price of new and used furniture and I heard myself saying this: "Not waste money that way." My husband was with us as well, and he didn't notice any switch in my English. And then I realized why. It's because over the twenty years we've been together I've often used that same kind of English with him, and sometimes he even uses it with me. It has become our language of intimacy, a different sort of English that relates to family talk, the language I grew up with.

So you'll have some idea of what this family talk I heard sounds like, I'll quote what my mother said during a recent conversation which I videotaped and then transcribed.[1] During this conversation, my mother was talking about a political gangster in Shanghai who had the same last name as her family's, Du, and how the gangster in his early years wanted to be adopted by her family, which was rich by comparison. Later, the gangster became more powerful, far richer than my mother's family, and one day showed up at my mother's wedding to pay his respects. Here's what she said in part:

"Du Yusong having business like fruit stand. Like off the street kind. He is Du like Du Zong—but not Tsung-ming Island people. The local people call putong, the river east side, he belong to that side local people. That man want to ask Du Zong father take him in like become own family. Du Zong father wasn't look down on him, but didn't take seriously, until that man big like become a mafia. Now important person, very hard to inviting him. Chinese way, came only to show respect, don't stay for dinner. Respect for making big celebration, he shows up. Mean gives lots of respect. Chinese custom. Chinese social life that way. If too important won't have to stay too long. He come to my wedding. I didn't see, I heard it. I gone to boy's side, they have YMCA dinner. Chinese age I was nineteen."

You should know that my mother's expressive command of English belies[2] how much she actually understands. She reads the *Forbes* report, listens to *Wall Street Week*, converses daily with her stockbroker, reads all of Shirley MacLaine's books with ease—all kinds of things I can't begin to understand. Yet some of my friends tell me they understand 50 percent of what my mother says. Some say they understand 80 to 90 percent. Some say they understand none of it, as if she were speaking pure Chinese. But to me, my mother's English is perfectly clear, perfectly natural. It's my mother tongue. Her language, as I hear it, is vivid, direct, full of observation and imagery. That was the language that helped shape the way I saw things, expressed things, made sense of the world. **3**

LATELY, I'VE BEEN GIVING more thought to the kind of English my mother speaks. Like others, I have described it to people as "broken" or "fractured" English. But I wince when I say that. It has always bothered me that I can think of no way to describe it other than "broken," as if it were damaged and needed to be fixed, as if **4**

---

1. transcribe (tran skrīb′), *v.* set down in writing.
2. belie (bi lī′), *v.* give a false idea of; misrepresent.

MINI-LESSON: GRAMMAR

Subject/Verb Agreement

Teach Review that in standard written English, verbs agree in number and person with their grammatical subjects. For example:

Helen *goes* to the store.   I *went* to the store.

The boys *go* to the store.   You *will go* to the store.

This can be tricky when the verb is not immediately after the subject. Write the sentence below on the board, stressing that the verb must refer back to the subject, *not* to the nearest noun:

Helen, one of the group's leaders, *goes* to the store.

Collective nouns, such as *team* or *family*, usually take singular verbs, unless the emphasis is on the individuals rather than on the unit itself:

The family *has agreed* to go to the store together.

The family *have been arguing* among themselves about going to the store.

Activity Idea Have students work in pairs to find examples of subject-verb agreement and disagreement in "Mother Tongue." Have them rewrite any sentences that do not follow standard English conventions. (Stress that the English used by Tan's mother is not substandard but unconventional.)

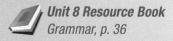
Unit 8 Resource Book
Grammar, p. 36

it lacked a certain wholeness and soundness. I've heard other terms used, "limited English," for example. But they seem just as bad, as if everything is limited, including people's perceptions of the limited English speaker.

> . . . to me, my mother's English is perfectly clear, perfectly natural. It's my mother tongue.

I know this for a fact, because when I was growing up, my mother's "limited" English limited *my* perception of her. I was ashamed of her English. I believed that her English reflected the quality of what she had to say. That is, because she expressed them imperfectly, her thoughts were imperfect. And I had plenty of empirical evidence to support me: the fact that people in department stores, at banks, and at restaurants did not take her seriously, did not give her good service, pretended not to understand her, or even acted as if they did not hear her.

My mother has long realized the limitations of her English as well. When I was fifteen, she used to have me call people on the phone to pretend I was she. In this guise, I was forced to ask for information or even to complain and yell at people who had been rude to her. One time it was a call to her stockbroker in New York. She had cashed out her small portfolio[3] and it just so happened we were going to go to New York the next week, our very first trip outside California. I had to get on the phone and say in an adolescent voice that was not very convincing, "This is Mrs. Tan."

And my mother was standing in the back whispering loudly, "Why he don't send me check, already two weeks late. So mad he lie to me, losing me money."

And then I said in perfect English, "Yes, I'm getting rather concerned. You had agreed to send the check two weeks ago, but it hasn't arrived."

Then she began to talk more loudly. "What he want. I come to New York tell him front of his boss, you cheating me?" And I was trying to calm her down, make her be quiet, while telling the stockbroker, "I can't tolerate any more excuses. If I don't receive the check immediately, I am going to have to speak to your manager when I'm in New York next week." And sure enough, the following week there we were in front of this astonished stockbroker, and I was sitting there red-faced and quiet, and my mother, the real Mrs. Tan, was shouting at his boss in her impeccable[4] broken English.

EVALUATE: How can Amy Tan's mother's English be both "broken" and "impeccable"? 7

We used a similar routine just five days ago, for a situation that was far less humorous. My mother had gone to the hospital for an appointment, to find out about a benign brain tumor a CAT scan had revealed a month ago. She said she had spoken very good English, her best English, no mistakes. Still, she said, the hospital did not apologize when they said they had lost the CAT scan and she had come for nothing. She said they did not seem to have any sympathy when she told them she was anxious to know the exact diagnosis, since her husband and son had both died of brain tumors. She said they would not give her any more information until the next time and she would have to make another appointment for that. So she said she would not leave until the doctor called her daughter. She wouldn't budge. And when the doctor finally called her daughter, me, who spoke in perfect English—lo and behold—we had assurances the CAT scan would be found, promises that a

---

3. **portfolio** (pôrt fōʹlē ō), *n.* holdings in the form of stocks, bonds, etc.
4. **impeccable** (im pekʹə bəl), *adj.* free from fault; irreproachable.

Mother Tongue **905**

8 Reading/Thinking

Draw Conclusions

At the end of this page, Tan writes about being asked these questions: "Why [aren't there] more Asian Americans represented in American literature? Why do so many Chinese students go into engineering?" Discuss these questions with students before they read her thoughts on this issue.

Questions

- What is the easy conclusion that might be drawn from the fact that many Chinese students study engineering but not literature? *(Possible response: that they are genetically or environmentally predisposed to do well in math and poorly in language arts)*

- What explanation do you think Tan might offer? *(Perhaps that Asian American students are steered away from language arts by parents or teachers. Perhaps they are more comfortable with math than with language arts and literature.)*

9 Reading/Thinking

Analyze

Have students note the author's purpose for writing this essay: to explain why there are not more Asian Americans writing American literature.

Question What device does Tan use to convey her opinion to the reader? *(Possible response: She uses personal anecdotes, relating the external forces acting upon her as she grew up—nonstandard English spoken at home, teachers who steered her toward math and science, aptitude tests that indicated greater ability in science than in language—to explain why Asian Americans in general are not literary.)*

906

---

8 conference call on Monday would be held, and apologies for any suffering my mother had gone through for a most regrettable mistake.

I think my mother's English almost had an effect on limiting my possibilities in life as well. Sociologists and linguists probably will tell you that a person's developing language skills are more influenced by peers. But I do think that the language spoken in the family, especially in immigrant families which are more insular,[5] plays a large role in shaping the language of the child. And I believe that it affected my results on achievement tests, IQ tests, and the SAT. While my English skills were never judged as poor, compared to math, English could not be considered my strong suit. In grade school I did moderately well, getting perhaps B's, sometimes B-pluses, in English and scoring perhaps in the sixtieth or seventieth percentile on achievement tests. But those scores were not good enough to override the opinion that my true abilities lay in math and science, because in those areas I achieved A's and scored in the ninetieth percentile or higher.

This was understandable. Math is precise: there is only one correct answer. Whereas, for me at least, the answers on English tests were always a judgment call, a matter of opinion and personal experience. Those tests were constructed around items like fill-in-the-blank sentence completion, such as, "Even though Tom was _____, Mary thought he was _____." And the correct answer always seemed to be the most bland combinations of thoughts, for example, "Even though Tom was shy, Mary thought he was charming," with the grammatical structure "even though" limiting the correct answer to some sort of semantic opposites, so you wouldn't get answers like, "Even though Tom was foolish, Mary thought he was ridiculous." Well, according to my mother, there were very few limitations as to what Tom could have been and what Mary might have thought of him. So I never did well on tests like that.

The same was true with word analogies, pairs of words in which you were supposed to find some sort of logical, semantic[6] relationship—for example, "*Sunset* is to *nightfall* as _____ is to _____." And here you would be presented with a list of four possible pairs, one of which showed the same kind of relationship: *red* is to *stoplight, bus* is to *arrival, chills* is to *fever, yawn* is to *boring*. Well, I could never think that way. I knew what the tests were asking, but I could not block out of my mind the images already created by the first pair, "*sunset* is to *nightfall*"—and I would see a burst of colors against a darkening sky, the moon rising, the lowering of a curtain of stars. And all the other pairs of words—red, bus, stoplight, boring—just threw up a mass of confusing images, making it impossible for me to sort out something as logical as saying: "A sunset precedes nightfall" is the same as "a chill precedes a fever." The only way I would have gotten that answer right would have been to imagine an associative situation, for example, my being disobedient and staying out past sunset, catching a chill at night, which turns into feverish pneumonia as punishment, which indeed did happen to me.

9

. . . the correct answer always seemed to be the most bland . . .

I HAVE BEEN THINKING about all this lately, about my mother's English, about achievement tests. Because lately I've been asked, as a writer, why there are not more Asian Americans represented in American literature. Why are there so few Asian Americans enrolled in creative writing programs? Why do so many Chinese students go into engineering? Well, these are broad sociological questions I can't begin to

---

5. insular (in′sə lər), *adj.* standing alone like an island; isolated.
6. semantic (sə man′tik), *adj.* having to do with the meaning of words.

906 UNIT EIGHT: AMERICAN VOICES TODAY

MINI-LESSON: CRITICAL THINKING

Draw Conclusions

Teach Review that a conclusion is a deduction based on available facts and evidence. A persuasive essay such as "Mother Tongue" uses facts, anecdotes, and examples to reach one or more conclusions. Analyzing the evidence presented can help the reader draw her or his own conclusions. Discuss what evidence Tan presents for her conclusion that her mother understands a great deal more English than her spoken English indicates (see page 904). *(Students might note that Mrs. Tan reads the* Forbes Report, *listens to*

Wall Street Week, *converses with her stockbroker, and reads books written for adults in English.)*

Question How did this evidence affect your acceptance of Amy Tan's conclusion? *(Possible response: The evidence is convincing, making the reader likely to accept the author's conclusion.)*

Activity Idea Have pairs find other conclusions drawn by Tan and present the evidence that supports her conclusions. Have them explain whether the evidence is convincing or not.

answer. But I have noticed in surveys—in fact, just last week—that Asian students, as a whole, always do significantly better on math achievement tests than in English. And this makes me think that there are other Asian American students whose English spoken in the home might also be described as "broken" or "limited." And perhaps they also have teachers who are steering them away from writing and into math and science, which is what happened to me.

 SUMMARIZE: How does Amy Tan think her "mother tongue" affected her academically?

Fortunately, I happen to be rebellious in nature and enjoy the challenge of disproving assumptions made about me. I became an English major my first year in college, after being enrolled as pre-med. I started writing nonfiction as a freelancer the week after I was told by my former boss that writing was my worst skill and I should hone[7] my talents toward account management.

But it wasn't until 1985 that I finally began to write fiction. And at first I wrote using what I thought to be wittily crafted sentences, sentences that would finally prove I had mastery over the English language. Here's an example from the first draft of a story that later made its way into *The Joy Luck Club,* but without this line: "That was my mental quandary[8] in its nascent[9] state." A terrible line, which I can barely pronounce.

Fortunately, for reasons I won't get into today, I later decided I should envision a reader for the stories I would write. And the reader I decided upon was my mother, because these were stories about mothers. So with this reader in mind—and in fact she did read my early drafts—I began to write stories using all the Englishes I grew up with: the English I spoke to my mother, which for lack of a better term might be described as "simple"; the English she used with me, which for lack of a better term might be described as "broken"; my translation of her Chinese, which could certainly be described as "watered down"; and what I imagined to be her translation of her Chinese if she could speak in perfect English, her internal language, and for that I sought to preserve the essence, but neither an English nor a Chinese structure. I wanted to capture what language ability tests can never reveal: her intent, her passion, her imagery, the rhythms of her speech and the nature of her thoughts.

Fortunately, I happen to be rebellious in nature . . .

Apart from what any critic had to say about my writing, I knew I had succeeded where it counted when my mother finished reading my book and gave me her verdict: "So easy to read." **12**

---

7. **hone** (hōn), *v.* to perfect or make more effective.
8. **quandary** (kwon′dər ē), *n.* state of perplexity or uncertainty; dilemma.
9. **nascent** (nas′nt), *adj.* in the process of coming into existence; emerging.

Mother Tongue   **907**

After Reading

MAKING CONNECTIONS

1. Possible responses: determined, pugnacious, proud (of Amy), vivid, direct, practical, smart

2. Du Yusong owned a fruit stand. He wanted to be adopted by Mrs. Tan's father, who didn't take him seriously until Du Yusong became a powerful gangster. Then they invited him to Mrs. Tan's first wedding. She didn't see him, since she was with her husband's family at their dinner.

3. Possible response: Language is a personal expression. Nonstandard English is as rich and vivid as standard English.

4. She was ashamed of her mother's English as a child, especially since Americans often did not take her seriously or ignored her. As an adult she realizes that her mother is a passionate, intelligent person.

5. Stockbroker: He underestimates Mrs. Tan and perhaps tries to cheat her, or at least does not explain things sufficiently. Hospital personnel: They are rude and do not listen to her. They are disrespectful.

6. Tan's mother uses colorful, nonstandard English. Amy uses polite, formal, standard English. Amy makes the call because her mother is aware that non-Chinese respond with more respect and attention to people who use standard English.

7. Responses will vary. Students might think about the power of words to hurt, to comfort, and to express feelings, needs, and desires.

8. Possible response: be patient, respectful, and understanding; the person is probably just as intelligent as you, but is unable to communicate as well in English.

After Reading

Making Connections

Shaping Your Response

1. What five adjectives would you use to describe Amy Tan's mother?

2. Can you understand Tan's mother? Retell her story about Du Yusong in your own words.

Analyzing the Essay

3. **Summarize** the point that Tan is trying to make about language.

4. How does Tan's childhood perception of her mother differ from her adult perception?

5. Describe either the New York stockbroker or the hospital personnel and their treatment of Tan's mother.

6. Compare the words that Tan's mother uses to tell Amy what to tell the stockbroker over the phone to the words Amy uses in the conversation. How would you describe the difference?

Extending the Ideas

7. Amy Tan refers to the "power of language." Do you see language as powerful? Explain.

8. What advice would you give to people about communicating with people whose first language is not English?

Literary Focus: Denotation and Connotation

Review the paragraph in which Amy Tan describes her mother's English. Why does she have a problem with referring to it as "broken" or "limited" or "fractured"?

LITERARY FOCUS: DENOTATION AND CONNOTATION

Students can locate the paragraph on the bottom of page 904. *(Possible response: These words all have the negative connotation of something damaged that needs to be fixed. Tan dislikes this connotation, since she believes her mother's English is vivid, direct, and full of imagery.)*

 Unit 8 Resource Book
Graphic Organizer, p. 33

Vocabulary Study

Amy Tan would hate this exercise; however, you are probably an expert on analogies by now. Use the list of vocabulary words to complete each analogy. One word will be used twice.

portfolio
transcribe
impeccable
insular
quandary
semantic
belie
hone
nascent

1. recipe : cookbook : : stock : _____
2. imperfect : flawed : : perfect : _____
3. behavior : psychological : : words : _____
4. peninsula : connected : : island : _____
5. scene : photograph : : speech : _____
6. answer : question : : certainty : _____
7. knife : sharpen : : talent : _____
8. deception : misperception : : hide : _____
9. tree : mature : : seedling : _____
10. outgoing : social : : shy : _____

Expressing Your Ideas

Writing Choices

Writer's Notebook Update When you write a letter, you have a very specific audience in mind. Review the letter you wrote before reading the essay by Amy Tan. How did you tailor your language to fit the recipient of your letter, either a college-aged sibling or a manufacturer? Write a paragraph explaining how the letter you didn't write would be different from the letter you did write.

Thumbs Up, Thumbs Down Borrow or rent a copy of the movie version of Amy Tan's book *The Joy Luck Club.* Watch it and then write a **movie review** to post in your classroom.

Another Option

A Trip to China Amy Tan didn't visit China until she was an adult. She said of her visit, "As soon as my feet touched China, I became Chinese." If you were to visit China, what would you like to see? Using a travel guide and a map, and any other resources you can find about China, create a **travel brochure**—including a daily itinerary of cities and sights as well as photographs—that advertises the China trip you would like to take.

Mother Tongue 909

VOCABULARY STUDY

1. portfolio
2. impeccable
3. semantic
4. insular
5. transcribe
6. quandary
7. hone
8. belie
9. nascent
10. insular

More Practice Students can divide into groups and create a word web for one of the vocabulary words. Then each group can share its results with the class.

Unit 8 Resource Book
Vocabulary, p. 35
Vocabulary Test, p. 38

WRITING CHOICES
Writer's Notebook Update

Students should realize that their choice of words and sentence structure depends on whom they are writing to. The sibling would probably receive an informal, conversational letter, while the manufacturer should receive a formal letter clearly detailing the writer's complaint.

Thumbs Up, Thumbs Down

Students' reviews should include a summary of the movie and their opinion of it.

Unit 8 Resource Book
Selection Test, pp. 39–40

ANOTHER OPTION
A Trip to China

Suggest that students visit or call a travel agent for information on China. Also suggest using an encyclopedia and other reference works. Students will probably include Beijing, China's capital, in their brochures. Other cities might include Shanghai and Guangzhou (Canton) along the eastern coast. They might also wish to visit the Tibetan plateau, the Inner Mongolian tableland, or the central plain of Manchuria. To see how the Chinese live, they might sail up major rivers, including the Huang He (Yellow River) in north China, the Yangzi River in central China, and the Si and Pearl Rivers in south China.

Before Reading

Building Background

Native American culture was dealt a harmful blow when Indian children were forced to attend government-run boarding schools. Forbidden to speak their own language, many could not speak to their families when they returned home.

Literary Focus

Suggest students jot down a few notes each time a **flashback** occurs in the story. They can use these notes to make the story map in the activity on page 919.

Writer's Notebook

Invite a discussion of why childhood friends may grow apart. It may be because people mature at different rates, so that an old friend may seem "babyish." Teenagers may begin to explore new interests, which may lead to new friends and a rift with old ones.

More About Sherman Alexie

The Lone Ranger and Tonto Fistfight in Heaven, the collection from which this story is taken, won a PEN/Hemingway Award for Best First Book of Fiction and a 1994 Lila Wallace-Reader's Digest Writers' Award. Alexie has also been a poetry fellow in Washington State and the recipient of a grant from the National Endowment for the Arts.

Before Reading
This Is What It Means to Say Phoenix, Arizona

by Sherman Alexie

Sherman Alexie
born 1966

Writer Sherman Alexie explains, "I am a Spokane/Coeur d'Alene Indian from Wellpinit, Washington, where I live on the Spokane Indian Reservation. Everything I do now, writing and otherwise, has its origin in that." Alexie attended Gonzaga University and received a B.A. from Washington State University in 1991. He has written a number of books of poetry: *The Business of Fancy Dancing* (1992), *I Would Steal Horses* (1992), *Old Shirts and New Skins* (1993), and *First Indian on the Moon* (1993). The story "This Is What It Means to Say Phoenix, Arizona" is taken from his collection of short stories, *The Lone Ranger and Tonto Fistfight in Heaven* (1993).

Building Background

Reservation Life The Spokane and Coeur d'Alene Indians originally lived along the river valleys on the Columbia Plateau, which is bordered on the east by the Rocky Mountains and on the west by the Cascade Mountains. After the Coeur d'Alene War in 1858 they were forced to live on reservations. With the best lands reserved for white settlers, railroads, and mining interests, the Indians on the reservations were left with few means of economic self-sufficiency. Poverty, despair, and alcoholism are some of the problems that the reservation system has created. This is the reality of reservation life about which Sherman Alexie writes.

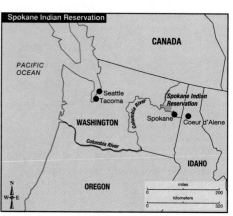

Literary Focus

Flashback Flashbacks are interruptions in a narrative that show events that happened previously. As you read "This Is What It Means to Say Phoenix, Arizona," notice each flashback and reflect on why the author chooses to include it.

Writer's Notebook

Growing Up The two main characters in the story you are about to read are childhood friends who grew apart. In your notebook write about a childhood friend of yours. What did he or she look like? What did you enjoy doing together? Are you still friends? Write a paragraph about it.

SUPPORT MATERIALS OVERVIEW

Unit 8 Resource Book
- Graphic Organizer, p. 41
- Study Guide, p. 42
- Vocabulary, p. 43
- Grammar, p. 44
- Alternate Check Test, p. 45
- Vocabulary Test, p. 46
- Selection Test, pp. 47–48

Building English Proficiency
- Literature Summaries
- Activities, p. 238

Reading, Writing & Grammar SkillBook
- Vocabulary, pp. 9–10
- Reading, pp. 81–81
- Writing, pp. 137–138
- Grammar, Usage, and Mechanics, pp. 202–203

Technology
- Audiotape
- Personal Journal Software
- Custom Literature Database: For other selections dealing with Native American myths and legends, see "Raven's Adventures" by Franz Boas and "Glooscap" by Silas Rand on the database.
- Test Generator Software

THIS IS WHAT IT MEANS TO SAY PHOENIX, ARIZONA

SHERMAN ALEXIE

Just after Victor lost his job at the BIA,[1] he also found out that his father had died of a heart attack in Phoenix, Arizona. Victor hadn't seen his father in a few years, only talked to him on the telephone once or twice, but there still was a genetic[2] pain, which was soon to be pain as real and immediate as a broken bone.

Victor didn't have any money. Who does have money on a reservation, except the cigarette and fireworks salespeople? His father had a savings account waiting to be claimed, but Victor needed to find a way to get to Phoenix. Victor's mother was just as poor as he was, and the rest of his family didn't have any use at all for him. So Victor called the Tribal Council.

"Listen," Victor said. "My father just died. I need some money to get to Phoenix to make arrangements."

"Now, Victor," the council said. "You know we're having a difficult time financially."

"But I thought the council had special funds set aside for stuff like this."

"Now, Victor, we do have some money available for the proper return of tribal members' bodies. But I don't think we have enough to bring your father all the way back from Phoenix."

"Well," Victor said. "It ain't going to cost all that much. He had to be cremated.[3] Things were kind of ugly. He died of a heart attack in his trailer and nobody found him for a week. It was really hot, too. You get the picture."

"Now, Victor, we're sorry for your loss and the circumstances. But we can really only afford to give you one hundred dollars."

"That's not even enough for a plane ticket."

"Well, you might consider driving down to Phoenix."

"I don't have a car. Besides, I was going to drive my father's pickup back up here."

"Now, Victor," the council said. "We're sure there is somebody who could drive you to Phoenix. Or is there somebody who could lend you the rest of the money?"

"You know there ain't nobody around with that kind of money."

"Well, we're sorry, Victor, but that's the best we can do."

Victor accepted the Tribal Council's offer. What else could he do? So he signed the proper papers, picked up his check, and walked over to the Trading Post to cash it.

While Victor stood in line, he watched Thomas Builds-the-Fire standing near the magazine rack, talking to himself. Like he always did. Thomas was a storyteller that nobody wanted to listen to. That's like being a dentist in a town where everybody has false teeth.

Victor and Thomas Builds-the-Fire were the same age, had grown up and played in the dirt

---

1. **BIA,** Bureau of Indian Affairs.
2. genetic (jə net′ik), *adj.* having to do with origin and natural growth.
3. cremate (krē′māt), *v.* to burn a dead body to ashes.

This Is What It Means to Say Phoenix, Arizona **911**

During Reading

Selection Objectives

- To see the connection between yesterday, today, and tomorrow
- To analyze the role of flashbacks in a plot
- To use consistent verb tenses
- To use graphic organizers to keep track of events in a story

 Unit 8 Resource Book *Study Guide, p. 42*

Theme Link

The theme of Citizens of Tomorrow is explored when a young American Indian man travels to Phoenix, Arizona, with a childhood friend to retrieve his father's remains. They consider their past and their future.

Vocabulary Preview

genetic, having to do with origin and natural growth

cremate, to burn a dead body to ashes

boycott, to abstain from using, buying, participating in, or dealing with to express protest

hover, hang fluttering or suspended in air

altitude, height above earth's surface

1 | Literary Element
Plot

Review that the plot's exposition provides necessary background material for the reader. Exposition establishes setting, mood, and provides information about the characters and their problems.

Questions

- Where does the story begin? *(on a reservation)*
- What is Victor's problem? *(His father has died and Victor would like to claim his body, savings account, and truck, but he lacks the money to travel to Phoenix.)*

912

2 Literary Element
Characterization

Thomas seems to be an unusual person. Encourage students to note Alexie's characterization of the man.

Questions

- What special powers does Thomas seem to have? *(the ability to foretell the future and to read other people's minds)*
- Why don't some of the other Indians talk to Thomas? *(They don't want to hear the stories he tells over and over again.)*

3 Literary Focus
Flashback

Discuss with students the time shift here. The rest of this page and the top of the page to follow contain a flashback to Victor's youth.

Question Where are we now in time and what words suggest this? *(The story has shifted to the past; Victor is thinking about Thomas Builds-the-Fire as a ten-year-old boy.)*

4 Historical Note
Native Americans and the American Revolution

The Treaty of Paris that formally ended the American Revolution in 1783 paid no attention to Indian rights or interests. The British, who had promised to protect tribal land rights, sold out their Indian allies, ceding their lands to the United States and Spain. The new American nation believed it had beaten both the British and the Indians, although it had defeated no tribe. The Americans treated the Indian lands as spoils of war, giving the land away to veterans as bounties instead of cash. Within five years, the new nation was already forcing some Native Americans to live on small reservations.

---

together. Ever since Victor could remember, it was Thomas who always had something to say.

Once, when they were seven years old, when Victor's father still lived with the family, Thomas closed his eyes and told Victor this story: "Your father's heart is weak. He is afraid of his own family. He is afraid of you. Late at night he sits in the dark. Watches the television until there's nothing but that white noise. Sometimes he feels like he wants to buy a motorcycle and ride away. He wants to run and hide. He doesn't want to be found."

Thomas Builds-the-Fire had known that Victor's father was going to leave, knew it before anyone. Now Victor stood in the Trading Post with a one-hundred-dollar check in his hand, wondering if Thomas knew that Victor's father was dead, if he knew what was going to happen next.

Just then Thomas looked at Victor, smiled, and walked over to him.

"Victor, I'm sorry about your father," Thomas said.

"How did you know about it?" Victor asked.

"I heard it on the wind. I heard it from the birds. I felt it in the sunlight. Also, your mother was just in here crying."

"Oh," Victor said and looked around the Trading Post. All the other Indians stared, surprised that Victor was even talking to Thomas. Nobody talked to Thomas anymore because he told the same damn stories over and over again. Victor was embarrassed, but he thought that Thomas might be able to help him. Victor felt a **2** sudden need for tradition.

"I can lend you the money you need," Thomas said suddenly. "But you have to take me with you."

"I can't take your money," Victor said. "I mean, I haven't hardly talked to you in years. We're not really friends anymore."

"I didn't say we were friends. I said you had to take me with you."

"Let me think about it."

Victor went home with his one hundred dollars and sat at the kitchen table. He held his head in his hands and thought about Thomas Builds-the-Fire, remembered little details, tears

---

and scars, the bicycle they shared for a summer, so many stories.

Thomas Builds-the-Fire sat on the bicycle, **3** waited in Victor's yard. He was ten years old and skinny. His hair was dirty because it was the Fourth of July.

"Victor," Thomas yelled. "Hurry up. We're going to miss the fireworks."

After a few minutes, Victor ran out of his house, jumped the porch railing, and landed gracefully on the sidewalk.

"And the judges award him a 9.95, the highest score of the summer," Thomas said, clapped, laughed.

"That was perfect, cousin," Victor said. "And it's my turn to ride the bike."

Thomas gave up the bike and they headed for the fairgrounds. It was nearly dark and the fireworks were about to start.

"You know," Thomas said. "It's strange how us Indians celebrate the Fourth of July. It ain't **4** like it was *our* independence everybody was fighting for."

"You think about things too much," Victor said. "It's just supposed to be fun. Maybe Junior will be there."

"Which Junior? Everybody on this reservation is named Junior."

And they both laughed.

The fireworks were small, hardly more than a few bottle rockets and a fountain. But it was enough for two Indian boys. Years later, they would need much more.

Afterwards, sitting in the dark, fighting off mosquitoes, Victor turned to Thomas Builds-the-Fire.

"Hey," Victor said. "Tell me a story."

Thomas closed his eyes and told this story: "There were these two Indian boys who wanted **5** to be warriors. But it was too late to be warriors in the old way. All the horses were gone. So the two Indian boys stole a car and drove to the city. They parked the stolen car in front of the police station and then hitchhiked back home to the

---

MINI-LESSON: VOCABULARY

Expand Vocabulary

Teach Point out to students that words often share roots. Once you learn the root word, it is easy to remember related words. Ask a volunteer to find *cremate* in a dictionary. Have the student find and read related words such as *crematory* (a furnace for cremating).

Activity Idea Divide the class into groups. Assign one of these words to each group: *altitude, genetic, boycott, hover.* Ask each group to look up its word in a dictionary and locate any related words. For example, for *altitude* the group might list *altimeter* (an instrument for measuring altitude) and *altiplano* (a high plateau or plain).

Response to Caption Question Most students will respond that the young man in the painting looks as though he may be thinking of those "exploits." He wears his hair in a traditional American Indian way, but he also wears the current "uniform" of the young, a T-shirt and jacket. The cracked and peeling wall may symbolize the dreary environment he finds himself in and the lack of options for doing "brave and courageous things."

Visual Literacy Instead of the traditional background one might expect in a portrait of a Native American—plains, mountains, or forest—Bama has painted a bleak and barren wall. It is a startling contrast to the imposing figure in the foreground. It is a concrete representation of the enormous challenges the young man faces in finding his true path.

5 Multicultural Note
Trickster Tales

Discuss with students the Native American tradition of telling tribal myths and legends. The adventurous trickster is a common character in many of these legends. Discuss Glooscap, a Micmac trickster, or the many animal characters that served this same role, such as Rabbit, Coyote, or Raven.

▲ Artist James Bama refers to his painting, *A Sioux Indian,* as showing "a guy who would like to have exploits like Crazy Horse and do brave and courageous things but has no vehicle for doing it anymore." How do the painting's images convey that sentiment?

This Is What It Means to Say Phoenix, Arizona **913**

BUILDING ENGLISH PROFICIENCY

Understanding Cause and Effect

The death of Victor's father begins a series of cause-and-effect events that drive the story's plot. Encourage students to create a cause-effect chart like the one here.

Ask students to continue charting the story's main events in this way.

> Cause: His father has died.
> ↓
> Effect: Victor must go to Phoenix.
> ↓
> Cause: The Tribal Council only gives Victor part of the money he needs to get to Phoenix.
> ↓
> Effect: Victor must take Thomas's money and Thomas.
> ↓
> Cause:
> ↓
> Effect:

Discuss with students how the story Thomas tells fits into the legend of the trickster and how it relates to them.

Questions

- The boys' friends and parents tell them how brave they are. Does this seem realistic to you? *(Most students will say it's not realistic. The boys take a risk, just like the trickster, and suffer no adverse consequences. Students may note a ten-year-old tells the story.)*

- Do you find the story sad? Explain. *(Some may find it sad that the boys can't be warriors in the old way and are reduced to stealing cars to prove their bravery.)*

7 Literary Element
Symbolism

Question What does Victor mean when he says, "All I need is stars"? *(Possible response: Literally, he means that he could find his way by the light of the stars. He may also mean that he would prefer the reservation were less modern, more in tune with the old ways.)*

8 Literary Focus
Flashback

In this flashback the boys are five years older than in the first flashback.

9 Reader's Response
Making Personal Connections

Questions

- Why do you think Victor beat Thomas up? *(Most will say that he had no real reason, except that he was drunk and probably unhappy.)*

- What do you learn about Thomas through this incident? *(Possible responses; He's a kid that others pick on; he's no good at defending himself; he's stoical about it all.)*

914

---

reservation. When they got back, all their friends cheered and their parents' eyes shone with pride. *You were very brave,* everybody said to the two Indian boys. *Very brave.*"

"Ya-hey," Victor said. "That's a good one. I wish I could be a warrior."

"Me, too," Thomas said.

They went home together in the dark, Thomas on the bike now, Victor on foot. They walked through shadows and light from streetlamps.

"We've come a long ways," Thomas said. "We have outdoor lighting."

"All I need is the stars," Victor said. "And besides, you still think about things too much."

They separated then, each headed for home, both laughing all the way.

V ictor sat at his kitchen table. He counted his one hundred dollars again and again. He knew he needed more to make it to Phoenix and back. He knew he needed Thomas Builds-the-Fire. So he put his money in his wallet and opened the front door to find Thomas on the porch.

"Ya-hey, Victor," Thomas said. "I knew you'd call me."

Thomas walked into the living room and sat down on Victor's favorite chair.

"I've got some money saved up," Thomas said. "It's enough to get us down there, but you have to get us back."

"I've got this hundred dollars," Victor said. "And my dad had a savings account I'm going to claim."

"How much in your dad's account?"

"Enough. A few hundred."

"Sounds good. When we leaving?"

When they were fifteen and had long since stopped being friends, Victor and Thomas got into a fistfight. That is, Victor was really drunk and beat Thomas up for no reason at all. All the other Indian boys stood around and watched it happen. Junior was there and so were Lester, Seymour, and a lot of others. The beating might

914 UNIT EIGHT: AMERICAN VOICES TODAY

---

have gone on until Thomas was dead if Norma Many Horses hadn't come along and stopped it.

"Hey, you boys," Norma yelled and jumped out of her car. "Leave him alone."

If it had been someone else, even another man, the Indian boys would've just ignored the warnings. But Norma was a warrior. She was powerful. She could have picked up any two of the boys and smashed their skulls together. But worse than that, she would have dragged them all over to some tipi, and made them listen to some elder tell a dusty old story.

The Indian boys scattered, and Norma walked over to Thomas and picked him up.

"Hey, little man, are you okay?" she asked.

Thomas gave her a thumbs up.

"Why they always picking on you?"

Thomas shook his head, closed his eyes, but no stories came to him, no words or music. He just wanted to go home, to lie in his bed and let his dreams tell his stories for him.

Thomas Builds-the-Fire and Victor sat next to each other in the airplane, coach section. A tiny white woman had the window seat. She was busy twisting her body into pretzels. She was flexible.

"I have to ask," Thomas said, and Victor closed his eyes in embarrassment.

"Don't," Victor said.

"Excuse me, miss," Thomas asked. "Are you a gymnast or something?"

"There's no something about it," she said. "I was first alternate on the 1980 Olympic team."

"Really?" Thomas asked.

"Really."

"I mean, you used to be a world-class athlete?" Thomas asked.

"My husband still thinks I am."

Thomas Builds-the-Fire smiled. She was a mental gymnast, too. She pulled her leg straight up against her body so that she could've kissed her kneecap.

"I wish I could do that," Thomas said.

Victor was ready to jump out of the plane. Thomas, that crazy Indian storyteller with ratty

---

MINI-LESSON: GRAMMAR

Consistent Verb Tense

Teach The tense of a verb expresses a specific time distinction. Once a writer chooses to write in a particular tense, he or she should stay in that tense unless there is a change in time. Have students read the paragraph on page 914 that begins: "Victor sat at his kitchen table." Have them note each verb and its tense. *(sat, counted, knew, needed, put, opened—all past tense)*

Next, draw students' attention to a passage with dialogue. Have them note that the dialogue is in the present tense, although the rest of the passage remains in the past.

Activity Idea Have students write a paragraph telling what they did last night or last week. Then ask them to underline the verbs and tell in which tense they are writing.

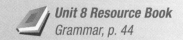
Unit 8 Resource Book
Grammar, p. 44

old braids and broken teeth, was flirting with a beautiful Olympic gymnast. Nobody back home on the reservation would ever believe it.

"Well," the gymnast said. "It's easy. Try it."

Thomas grabbed at his leg and tried to pull it up into the same position as the gymnast. He couldn't even come close, which made Victor and the gymnast laugh.

"Hey," she asked. "You two are Indian, right?"

"Full-blood," Victor said.

"Not me," Thomas said. "I'm half magician on my mother's side and half clown on my father's."

They all laughed.

"What are your names?" she asked.

"Victor and Thomas."

"Mine is Cathy. Pleased to meet you all."

The three of them talked for the duration of the flight. Cathy the gymnast complained about the government, how they screwed the 1980 Olympic team by boycotting.[4]

"Sounds like you all got a lot in common with Indians," Thomas said.

Nobody laughed.

After the plane landed in Phoenix and they had all found their way to the terminal, Cathy the gymnast smiled and waved good-bye.

"She was really nice," Thomas said.

10 "Yeah, but everybody talks to everybody on airplanes," Victor said. "It's too bad we can't always be that way."

"You always used to tell me I think too much," Thomas said. "Now it sounds like you do."

"Maybe I caught it from you."

"Yeah."

Thomas and Victor rode in a taxi to the trailer where Victor's father died.

"Listen," Victor said as they stopped in front of the trailer. "I never told you I was sorry for beating you up that time."

"Oh, it was nothing. We were just kids and you were drunk."

"Yeah, but I'm still sorry."

"That's all right."

Victor paid for the taxi and the two of them stood in the hot Phoenix summer. They could smell the trailer.

"This ain't going to be nice," Victor said. "You don't have to go in."

"You're going to need help."

Victor walked to the front door and opened it. The stink rolled out and made them both gag. Victor's father had lain in that trailer for a week in hundred-degree temperatures before anyone found him. And the only reason anyone found him was because of the smell. They needed dental records to identify him. That's exactly what the coroner said. They needed dental records. 11

"Oh, man," Victor said. "I don't know if I can do this."

"Well, then don't."

"But there might be something valuable in there."

"I thought his money was in the bank."

"It is. I was talking about pictures and letters and stuff like that."

"Oh," Thomas said as he held his breath and followed Victor into the trailer.

When Victor was twelve, he stepped into an underground wasp nest. His foot was caught in the hole, and no matter how hard he struggled, Victor couldn't pull free. He might have died there, stung a thousand times, if Thomas Builds-the-Fire had not come by. 12

"Run," Thomas yelled and pulled Victor's foot from the hole. They ran then, hard as they ever had, faster than Billy Mills, faster than Jim Thorpe,[5] faster than the wasps could fly.

Victor and Thomas ran until they couldn't breathe, ran until it was cold and dark outside, ran until they were lost and it took hours to find

---

4. **boycott** (boi′kot), *v.* to abstain from using, buying, participating, or dealing with to express protest.
5. **Billy Mills . . . Jim Thorpe,** both U.S. Olympians, both American Indians, Thorpe won gold medals in 1912 and Mills in 1964.

This Is What It Means to Say Phoenix, Arizona **915**

10
Reader's Response
Making Personal Connections

Questions

- What point is Victor making here? *(Possible response: that most of the time people are too distant, too unfriendly)*

- Do you agree with Victor ? Explain. *(Some students might prefer a friendlier world, while others may feel brief conversation with strangers doesn't matter much one way or the other.)*

11
Literary Element
Imagery

Draw students' attention to the senses Alexie engages with this description—the sense of smell *(the stink)* and the sense of touch *(hot day).*

Question Why do you think the author included this unpleasant imagery? *(Perhaps because it adds to the realism of the story, increasing its believability. It also juxtaposes the vital, complex man that Thomas will later remember and talk about vividly.)*

12
Literary Focus
Flashback

Point out another shift in time here. The boys are three years younger than in the previous flashback.

BUILDING ENGLISH PROFICIENCY

The First Americans

Encourage students to learn about and share their knowledge of Native Americans.

Activity Ideas

- Discuss the place of Native Americans in United States history. Decide how to find answers to questions that the discussion raises; then assign any questions to student pairs. Do the answers support or deny what is in the selection?

- Suggest that students pair up to visit the library and find books and magazine articles about contemporary Native American life.

- Obtain the address of the Spokane Indian Reservation from a Washington directory. Work with students as a class to draft a letter asking for information about the Spokane/Coeur d'Alene Indians. (Students can use this information should they choose to write the research report described on page 921.)

Invite students to consider how the reader's understanding of Thomas has increased throughout the story.

Question What did you think of Thomas at the beginning of the story? How do you feel about him now? *(Students probably began the story accepting Victor's evaluation of Thomas as a strange, irritating person. Now they may be beginning to understand, and even like, Thomas.)*

14 Literary Element

Flash-Forward

Victor and Thomas are now in the trailer. Once here, the memories of Victor's father bring to life a strong and vital force.

15 Literary Element

Theme

Present and past are rapidly interchanging at this point, as Thomas tells a pivotal story about Victor's dad. It makes explicit one of the story's major themes—that people should take care of one another.

16 Reading/Thinking

Infer

Review the principle that an inference is made based on given information and the reader's own experiences.

Question Why does Victor smile? *(Possibly because he has decided that he had a good father, on the whole.)*

17 Reader's Response

Make Personal Connections

Question Why do the boys hate Thomas for his courage? *(Students might note that the boys are jealous and a bit afraid of Thomas's gifts, and don't know how to deal with their feelings.)*

916

---

13 their way home. All the way back, Victor counted his stings.

"Seven," Victor said. "My lucky number."

14 Victor didn't find much to keep in the trailer. Only a photo album and a stereo. Everything else had that smell stuck in it or was useless anyway.

"I guess this is all," Victor said. "It ain't much."

"Better than nothing," Thomas said.

"Yea, and I do have the pickup."

"Yeah," Thomas said. "It's in good shape."

"Dad was good about that stuff."

"Yeah, I remember your dad."

"Really?" Victor asked. "What do you remember?"

15 Thomas Builds-the-Fire closed his eyes and told this story: "I remember when I had this dream that told me to go to Spokane, to stand by the Falls in the middle of the city and wait for a sign. I knew I had to go there but I didn't have a car. Didn't have a license. I was only thirteen. So I walked all the way, took me all day, and I finally made it to the Falls. I stood there for an hour waiting. Then your dad came walking up. *What the hell are you doing here?* he asked me. I said, *Waiting for a vision.* Then your father said, *All you're going to get here is mugged.* So he drove me over to Denny's, bought me dinner, and then drove me home to the reservation. For a long time I was mad because I thought my dreams had lied to me. But they didn't. Your dad was my vision. *Take care of each other* is what my dreams were saying. *Take care of each other.*"

Victor was quiet for a long time. He searched his mind for memories of his father, found the good ones, found a few bad ones, added it all up, and smiled. **16**

"My father never told me about finding you in Spokane," Victor said.

"He said he wouldn't tell anybody. Didn't want me to get in trouble. But he said I had to watch out for you as part of the deal."

"Really?"

"Really. Your father said you would need the help. He was right."

916 Unit Eight: American Voices Today

"That's why you came down here with me, isn't it?" Victor asked.

"I came because of your father."

Victor and Thomas climbed into the pickup, drove over to the bank, and claimed the three hundred dollars in the savings account.

Thomas Builds-the-Fire could fly.

Once, he jumped off the roof of the tribal school and flapped his arms like a crazy eagle. And he flew. For a second, he hovered,[6] suspended above all the other Indian boys who were too smart or too scared to jump.

"He's flying," Junior yelled, and Seymour was busy looking for the trick wires or mirrors. But it was real. As real as the dirt when Thomas lost altitude[7] and crashed to the ground.

He broke his arm in two places.

"He broke his wing," Victor chanted, and the other Indian boys joined in, made it a tribal song.

"He broke his wing, he broke his wing, he broke his wing," all the Indian boys chanted as they ran off, flapping their wings, wishing they could fly, too. They hated Thomas for his courage, his brief moment as a bird. Everybody has dreams about flying. Thomas flew. **17**

One of his dreams came true for just a second, just enough to make it real.

Victor's father, his ashes, fit in one wooden box with enough left over to fill a cardboard box.

"He always was a big man," Thomas said.

Victor carried part of his father and Thomas carried the rest out to the pickup. They set him down carefully behind the seats, put a cowboy hat on the wooden box and a Dodgers cap on the cardboard box. That's the way it was supposed to be.

"Ready to head back home," Victor asked.

"It's going to be a long drive."

"Yeah, take a couple days, maybe."

"We can take turns," Thomas said.

---

6. **hover** (huv′ər), v. hang fluttering or suspended in air.
7. **altitude** (al′tə tüd), n. height above the earth's surface.

MINI-LESSON: LITERARY FOCUS

Flashback

Teach Review that a flashback serves to shed light on characters and events of the present by providing background information. A flashback may provide details of exposition, offer insight into characters' motives, and comment on actions in the present. Have students find and discuss the flashbacks in the story and the dramatic weight flashbacks lend it.

Activity Idea Have students write a passage about their week so far, inserting at least one flashback.

"Okay," Victor said, but they didn't take turns. Victor drove for sixteen hours straight north, made it halfway up Nevada toward home before he finally pulled over.

"Hey, Thomas," Victor said. "You got to drive for a while."

"Okay."

Thomas Builds-the-Fire slid behind the wheel and started off down the road. All through Nevada, Thomas and Victor had been amazed at the lack of animal life, at the absence of water, of movement.

"Where is everything?" Victor had asked more than once.

Now when Thomas was finally driving they saw the first animal, maybe the only animal in Nevada. It was a long-eared jackrabbit.

"Look," Victor yelled. "It's alive."

Thomas and Victor were busy congratulating themselves on their discovery when the jackrabbit darted out into the road and under the wheels of the pickup.

"Stop the damn car," Victor yelled, and Thomas did stop, backed the pickup to the dead jackrabbit.

"Oh man, he's dead," Victor said as he looked at the squashed animal.

"Really dead."

"The only thing alive in this whole state and we just killed it."

"I don't know," Thomas said. "I think it was suicide."

Victor looked around the desert, sniffed the air, felt the emptiness and loneliness, and nodded his head.

"Yeah," Victor said. "It had to be suicide."

"I can't believe this," Thomas said. "You drive for a thousand miles and there ain't even any bugs smashed on the windshield. I drive for ten seconds and kill the only living thing in Nevada."

"Yeah," Victor said. "Maybe I should drive."

"Maybe you should."

Thomas Builds-the-Fire walked through the corridors of the tribal school by himself. Nobody wanted to be anywhere near him because of all those stories. Story after story.

Thomas closed his eyes and this story came to him: "We are all given one thing by which our lives are measured, one determination. Mine are the stories which can change or not change the world. It doesn't matter which as long as I continue to tell the stories. My father, he died on Okinawa in World War II, died fighting for this country, which had tried to kill him for years. My mother, she died giving birth to me, died while I was still inside her. She pushed me out into the world with her last breath. I have no brothers or sisters. I have only my stories which came to me before I even had the words to speak. I learned a thousand stories before I took my first thousand steps. They are all I have. It's all I can do."

Thomas Builds-the-Fire told his stories to all those who would stop and listen. He kept telling them long after people had stopped listening. **18**

Victor and Thomas made it back to the reservation just as the sun was rising. It was the beginning of a new day on earth. **19**

"Good morning," Thomas said.

"Good morning."

The tribe was waking up, ready for work, eating breakfast, reading the newspaper, just like everybody else does. Willene LeBret was out in her garden wearing a bathrobe. She waved when Thomas and Victor drove by.

"Crazy Indians made it," she said to herself and went back to her roses.

Victor stopped the pickup in front of Thomas Builds-the-Fire's HUD[8] house. They both yawned, stretched a little, shook dust from their bodies.

"I'm tired," Victor said.

"Of everything," Thomas added.

They both searched for words to end the journey. Victor needed to thank Thomas for his

---

8. **HUD,** Housing and Urban Development, a department of the U.S. government.

Literary Element
18 **Characterization**

The transformation of Thomas from an unsympathetic to a sympathetic character is completed with this last flashback.

Question What do you think of Thomas now? *(Possible response: He seems to be more of a noble dreamer than a crazy person. The reader may even feel sorry for him; he is driven to tell stories to which no one listens.)*

Reading/Thinking Skills
19 **Infer**

Question What might you infer about the future from the author's description of Thomas and Victor's arrival home? *(The sun is rising, things are buzzing, and it's "the beginning of a new day on earth." This portends, if not a complete reconciliation of the two men, at least a better understanding between them and perhaps a deeper appreciation of life in general.)*

EDITORIAL NOTE: Two sentences on this page have been edited. "Stop the damn car" originally was written as "Stop the goddamn car." The sentence "It was the beginning of a new day on earth" originally also said, "but the same old shit on the reservation."

BUILDING ENGLISH PROFICIENCY

Analyzing Dialogue

Alexie reveals a great deal about his characters through their dialogue. Help students use the dialogue to tell them more about the characters and their relationships.

- Read aloud, or have a volunteer read aloud, the first exchange between Thomas and Victor on the plane (page 915).
- Point out that Thomas's use of the phrase *have to* indicates a curiosity so strong it's a command.

- Ask students what characteristic of Victor's is revealed by his embarrassed response of "Don't." *(He could be shy or prefer not to draw attention to himself.)*
- Have student pairs find and read other examples of such dialogue on other pages.

Art Study

Response to Caption Question   Some students may say that the mood of the piece is one of adventure, expansion, or exploration. Others may assert that it seems boring, repetitive, or barren.

Question   If you were traveling on this road, what would you like to see over the next hill? *(Answers will vary, but will probably be along the lines of "something different than what appears in these ten prints.")*

20 | Literary Element
Figurative Language

This paragraph is rich in figurative language.

Question   Can you find examples of simile, metaphor, personification, and hyperbole in this paragraph? *(Simile: rise like a salmon, shine like silver, like a rainbow; Metaphor: he will rise; Personification: a salmon as Victor's father; Hyperbole: leap over the bridge, over me)*

EDITORIAL NOTE: The sentence in the left column, "I know your friends would give you too much trouble" has been edited. It originally said, "I know your friends would give you too much shit about it."

help, for the money, and make the promise to pay it all back.

"Don't worry about the money," Thomas said. "It don't make any difference anyhow."

"Probably not, enit?"

"Nope."

Victor knew that Thomas would remain the crazy storyteller who talked to dogs and cats, who listened to the wind and pine trees. Victor knew that he couldn't really be friends with Thomas, even after all that had happened. It was cruel but it was real. As real as the ashes, as Victor's father, sitting behind the seats.

"I know how it is," Thomas said. "I know you ain't going to treat me any better than you did before. I know your friends would give you too much trouble."

Victor was ashamed of himself. Whatever happened to the tribal ties, the sense of community? The only real thing he shared with anybody was a bottle and broken dreams. He owed Thomas something, anything.

"Listen," Victor said and handed Thomas the cardboard box which contained half of his father. "I want you to have this."

Thomas took the ashes and smiled, closed his eyes, and told this story: "I'm going to travel to Spokane Falls one last time and toss these ashes into the water. And your father will rise like a salmon, leap over the bridge, over me, and find his way home. It will be beautiful. His teeth will shine like silver, like a rainbow. He will **20** rise, Victor, he will rise."

Victor smiled.

MINI-LESSON: CRITICAL THINKING

Order of Events

Teach   The ability to order events in chronological order can be helpful in understanding a story's plot and characters. A writer might use a time line to keep the order of events clear in her/his mind even though the actual story may incorporate flashbacks.

Activity Idea   Have students create a time line or flowchart showing events in Victor's life from the time he was young. The chart might begin like this:

Thomas and Victor go to see fireworks.	Victor steps in wasp nest. Thomas saves Victor's life.	Victor gets drunk and beats up Thomas.	Thomas tells story about modern-day warriors.	The two go to the trailer.

Encourage students to discuss the promise Victor makes Thomas, and relate it to the story's overall meaning.

Questions

- What is the meaning of the promise that Victor makes? *(Possible responses: that he will listen to Thomas next time; that he will pay more attention to Thomas, that he will understand the importance of the stories.)*
- What might the story itself mean? *(Possible responses: that strange, crazy people may have something to teach us; that it is important to listen to other people's stories; that stories are part of what ties a community together; that dreams are important; that communities are important.)*

"I was planning on doing the same thing with my half," Victor said. "But I didn't imagine my father looking anything like a salmon. I thought it'd be like cleaning the attic or something. Like letting things go after they've stopped having any use."

"Nothing stops, cousin," Thomas said. "Nothing stops."

Thomas Builds-the-Fire got out of the pickup and walked up his driveway. Victor started the pickup and began the drive home.

"Wait," Thomas yelled suddenly from his porch. "I just got to ask one favor."

Victor stopped the pickup, leaned out the window, and shouted back. "What do you want?"

"Just one time when I'm telling a story

What is the mood of Laurie Brown's 1984 photo-series, *Journey Foretold, Launa Niguel, California?* Choose five adjectives that describe the work's mood, then tell whether the same five could apply to the story.

somewhere, why don't you stop and listen?" Thomas asked.

"Just once?"

"Just once."

Victor waved his arms to let Thomas know that the deal was good. It was a fair trade, and that was all Victor had ever wanted from his whole life. So Victor drove his father's pickup toward home while Thomas went into his house, closed the door behind him, and heard a new story come to him in the silence afterwards. **21**

This Is What It Means to Say Phoenix, Arizona **919**

Check Test

1. What is Victor's problem? *(His father is dead and he doesn't have enough money to travel to Phoenix to claim his father's ashes and his inheritance.)*

2. Who solves Victor's problem and how? *(Thomas offers to lend Victor the money, as long as he takes him to Phoenix with him.)*

3. Why aren't Victor and Thomas friends anymore? *(Thomas is kind of strange; he tells stories all the time. No one likes to listen to him.)*

4. Are Victor and Thomas friends by the end of the story? Why or why not? *(Answers will vary. Thomas is still very strange and Victor feels he can't really be friends with him, but they seem to have gained understanding of one another and perhaps friendship will come.)*

5. What does Victor promise to do for Thomas at the end of the story? *(He will stop and listen to one of Thomas's stories some day.)*

Unit 8 Resource Book
Alternate Check Test, p. 45

BUILDING ENGLISH PROFICIENCY

Making Cultural Connections

Encourage students to learn and think more about the role of storytelling and storytellers with these activities.

Activity Ideas

- Focus students' attention on Thomas's story about the importance of stories (page 917). Ask students to locate each story that Thomas relates. Invite them to decide to whom each story is important—person, family, culture group—and why.

- Suggest that students analyze stories told in their family to identify the reason each is told: to prove a point, to demonstrate an idea, or to give a sense of family and family history. Invite volunteers to share stories as well as reasons for the tellings.

- Encourage abler students to do basic encyclopedic research about storytelling in the Native American culture and in their own culture. Suggest that they share their findings in chart form.

After Reading

MAKING CONNECTIONS

1. Responses will vary based on how students respond to each character's traits.

2. Responses will vary. Students might choose one of the flashbacks or the end of the story.

3. Victor and Thomas travel to Phoenix and back; Victor's spiritual journey involves coming to a better understanding of Thomas and himself, through present events and past memories. Thomas's journey involves going deeper into what he already instinctively understands and helping another to understand it.

4. Possible response: They aren't interested in the old days any more, when a storyteller was important. They just think Thomas is crazy.

5. Possible responses: He loved Victor's father; he'd promised Victor's father to take care of Victor. He still thought of Victor as a friend.

6. Possible response: Most students will say that they aren't valid. Students may understand, however, the way in which pressure from friends can affect one's decisions. Thomas is still a "crazy storyteller" to Victor's friends.

7. Responses will vary. Students who believe his life will change may point to Victor's increased understanding of himself, his father, and Thomas. Students who believe his life won't change may point to the fact that Victor still hasn't changed enough to become friends with Thomas again.

After Reading

Making Connections

Shaping Your Response

1. Which of the two men would you prefer for a friend, Victor or Thomas? Why?

2. If you had to choose a section from this story for a dramatic reading, which section would you choose? Explain your choice.

Analyzing the Story

3. This story can be seen as being about two journeys, one real and one spiritual. Describe the journeys.

4. Why do you think people don't listen to Thomas Builds-the-Fire's stories anymore?

5. Why do you think Thomas Builds-the-Fire wanted to accompany Victor to Phoenix?

Extending the Ideas

6. Is Victor's reason for not being friends with Thomas valid in your opinion? Why or why not?

7. Do you think that Victor's life will change after his journey to claim the body of his father? Explain your answer.

Literary Focus: Flashback

Skim the story to find all of the flashbacks that Sherman Alexie uses to reveal the relationship of the two main characters. Make a map of the story showing the "detours" for the flashbacks. Your map might begin like this.

Plot:

> Victor's father dies. Victor tries to get to Phoenix.

Flashbacks:

> Young Thomas and Victor celebrate the Fourth of July.

920   UNIT EIGHT: AMERICAN VOICES TODAY

LITERARY FOCUS: FLASHBACK

After students have mapped the story, invite them to share what they learned from the flashbacks. They might note that the flashbacks cover the arc of Victor and Thomas's friendship from best buddies to Victor beating Thomas up. The flashbacks also explain why Thomas is strange and tell a little about Victor's father.

 *Unit 8 Resource Book*
Graphic Organizer, p. 41

Vocabulary Study

Use the vocabulary words in the list to complete the sentences below on a separate sheet of paper.

altitude
genetic
boycott
hover
cremate

1. The plane began to lose _____ as it approached Phoenix.
2. There were no _____ ties between Victor and Thomas.
3. Thomas planned to _____ around Victor's front door waiting to be asked to go along to Phoenix.
4. The authorities had to _____ the body of Victor's father.
5. The gymnast's chance for fame was ruined when the U.S. decided to _____ the 1980 Olympic Games.

Expressing Your Ideas _____

Writing Choices

Writer's Notebook Update Reread the writer's notebook entry about your childhood friend. Then think about your current friends. Consider what it is that makes a person a friend. Write an **explanatory paragraph** discussing the qualities that you value in a friendship.

In Loving Memory Write a **sermon** or **speech** that might be given at a memorial service for Victor's father by Thomas Builds-the-Fire.

Plateau Tribes Choose the Spokane Indians, the Coeur d'Alene Indians, or another Columbia River Plateau tribe and learn about the pre-reservation tribal history, customs, leaders, and economy. Write a **research report** describing the information you discover.

Other Options

Tell a Story Read another one of the stories about reservation life from Sherman Alexie's collection *The Lone Ranger and Tonto Fistfight in Heaven.* Prepare a **retelling** of the story to present to the class.

Scene 1, Take 1 Because of all of the flashbacks, this story would make a better movie than a play. If you were the screenwriter converting this story to a movie script, how many different sets would you have to describe for the director? Draw an **illustration** of one of the sets you would need for the production.

Heart to Heart Give Thomas Builds-the-Fire some advice. Should he continue telling stories or not? Why? Work with a friend and prepare a **conversation** that Victor might have with Thomas giving him helpful advice. Act out the dialogue for the class.

---

1. altitude
2. genetic
3. hover
4. cremate
5. boycott

More Practice   Students can define each vocabulary word orally.

Unit 8 Resource Book
Vocabulary, p. 43
Vocabulary Test, p. 46

WRITING CHOICES
Writer's Notebook Update

Students may value character traits such as a sense of humor, kindness, and empathy. They may also mention shared interests such as sports, music, art, or other leisure activities.

In Loving Memory

Thomas's memorial would probably build on the story that he tells Victor on page 916.

Plateau Tribes

Students might use either of these books in their research:

- *500 Nations, an Illustrated History of North American Indians* by Jack Leustig, et al. (Knopf, 1994)
- *The World of the American Indian* (National Geographic Society, 1989)

Selection Test

Unit 8 Resource Book
pp. 47–48

Transparency Collection
Fine Art Writing Prompt 14

OTHER OPTIONS
Tell a Story

If students can't locate this collection, they might consider reading a story by Louise Erdrich, another Native American who frequently writes about reservation life.

Scene 1, Take 1

Students might prepare a storyboard for each scene. The set illustrations could be sketches, or students might build scale models of the setting.

Heart to Heart

Review tips for writing natural-sounding dialogue with students. As appropriate, use:

- contractions
- sentence fragments or short sentences
- regional expressions and slang

Suggest that after the dialogue is written, pairs read the dialogue aloud to see if it sounds natural.

Before Reading

Building Background

A food chain is a series of organisms related by feeding habits, such as prey, predators, and animals that eat those predators.

Tropical forests cover 7% of the earth's surface, but they house between 50% and 80% of the planet's species. Forest destruction may be making an average of about 100 plant species extinct each day. The resulting ecological imbalance may prove disastrous.

Literary Focus

To illustrate **hyperbole** in satire, encourage students to bring editorial cartoon caricatures that exaggerate political figures' physical features or traits. Explain that literature can achieve similar humor, exaggerating the hypocrisy or faults of persons and institutions.

Writer's Notebook

Have students write a list of five things that they might do to address these concerns.

More About T. Coraghessan Boyle

Boyle's imaginative subjects have included a center for treating shopping disorders and the developers of breakfast foods. His fiction includes:

* *East Is East,* 1990
* *The Road to Wellville,* 1991

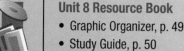

Before Reading

Top of the Food Chain

by T. Coraghessan Boyle

T. Coraghessan Boyle
born 1948

T. Coraghessan Boyle once said, "I would like to be a guy like [Kurt] Vonnegut for my generation, who could wake up people a little bit and show them that literature is fun and entertaining, and also serious at the same time." His writing career began in college at the State University of New York at Potsdam when he took an elective class in creative writing. He now teaches creative writing at the University of Southern California and writes both short stories and novels. One of his recent novels, *The Road to Wellville* (1993), was also made into a movie.

Building Background

Which Way to Borneo? Borneo is a large island southwest of the Philippines. Part or all of three different countries are included within the borders of the island. Brunei, the smallest of the three, is on the north coast of Borneo. It is an independent oil-rich sultanate, which means that the country is ruled by a sultan, an Islamic sovereign. Below Brunei are two states belonging to Malaysia, Sabah and Sarawak. South of these Malaysian states is Kalimantan, a region belonging to the Republic of Indonesia. This equatorial island, once colonized by the British, Portuguese, and Dutch, has a tropical climate and is covered with rugged mountains and large areas of rain forest. The rain forests of Borneo and other places in the world are important to the ecosystem of the planet. Locate Borneo on the map.

Literary Focus

Hyperbole "Top of the Food Chain" is a **satire,** and T. Coraghessan Boyle uses hyperbole, or obvious exaggeration, to create satiric humor. As you read the story, look for examples of hyperbole.

Writer's Notebook

Environmental Impact In your opinion, how well are human beings managing the resources of the natural environment? In your notebook, make a list of concerns that you have about the future of our environment.

SUPPORT MATERIALS OVERVIEW

Unit 8 Resource Book
* Graphic Organizer, p. 49
* Study Guide, p. 50
* Vocabulary, p. 51
* Grammar, p. 52
* Alternate Check Test, p. 53
* Vocabulary Test, p. 54
* Selection Test, pp. 55–56

Building English Proficiency
* Literature Summaries
* Activities, p. 239

Reading, Writing & Grammar Skillbook
* Vocabulary, pp. 7–8, 19–20
* Reading, pp. 104–106

Technology
* Audiotape
* Personal Journal Software
* Custom Literature Database
  Other satirical literature, such as "The Diary of Adam and Eve" by Mark Twain, can be found on the database.
* Test Generator Software

TOP
of the
FOOD CHAIN

T. Coraghessan Boyle

THE THING WAS, WE HAD A LITTLE PROBLEM WITH THE INSECT
vector[1] there, and believe me, your tamer stuff, your malathion and
pyrethrum[2] and the rest of the so-called environmentally safe products,
didn't begin to make a dent in it, not a dent, I mean it was utterly useless—we might as well have been spraying Chanel No. 5[3] for all the
good it did. And you've got to realize these people were literally covered with insects night and day—and the fact that they hardly wore
any clothes just compounded the problem. Picture if you can,
gentlemen, a naked two-year-old boy so black with flies and mosquitoes it looks like he's wearing long johns, or the young
mother so racked with the malarial shakes she can't even lift
a Diet Coke to her lips—it was pathetic, just pathetic, like
something out of the Dark Ages. . . . Well, anyway, the decision was made to go with DDT. In the short term. Just to
get the situation under control, you understand.

Yes, that's right, Senator, DDT: dichlorodiphenyl-   **1**
trichloro-ethane.

---

1. **vector** (vek′tər), *n.* organism that transmits disease
   germs, such as a mosquito or a tick.
2. **malathion and pyrethrum** (mal′ə thī′ on, pī rē′-
   thrəm), *n.* insecticides.
3. **Chanel No. 5** a brand of perfume.

Top of the Food Chain   **923**

During Reading

Selection Objectives

- To consider a serious theme conveyed comically
- To investigate the use of hyperbole
- To recognize jargon

Unit 8 Resource Book
Graphic Organizer, p. 49
Study Guide, p. 50

Theme Link

A government agent reacts to crises without considering the environment. Citizens
of tomorrow may face disaster if people
misuse nature.

Vocabulary Preview

vector, organism that transmits disease
germs, such as a mosquito or tick

domestically, having to do with one's
country; not foreign

contingent, a group that is part of another
group

eradication, complete destruction or
elimination

diatribe, a bitter, abusive criticism or
denunciation

exponentially, in a way that involves
unknown or variable quantities as
exponents; dramatically in number

efficacy, power to produce the effect
wanted; effectiveness

nemesis, an unbeatable rival

adverse, unfavorable; harmful

inadvertently, in an inattentive, careless,
or negligent way

SELECTION SUMMARY

Top of the Food Chain

The narrator, a United States government agent,
is defending his actions in Borneo before a
Senate committee. With a tone that is racially
condescending and remorseless, he describes
tragic and silly events that followed a decision to
spray the island with DDT, a toxic pesticide with
grave environmental effects. He defends his
actions as expedient solutions to an epidemic, the
nuisance of mosquitoes, and other woes. He also
chronicles the passage of the poison through various members of the food chain, casually noting its
catastrophic effects on the lives of the islanders.
As the narrative progresses, his solutions become
increasingly irrational, culminating with a parachute drop of stray cats imported from other
countries to control rats. The ecological chaos
and his flippant attitude, satirize the intervention
of world powers in the affairs of small nations.

 *For summaries in other languages, see
the **Building English Proficiency** book.*

1 Historical Note

DDT

DDT is a pesticide that kills insects by acting as a nerve poison. It has been proven
to cause cancer, and it causes severe environmental effects, such as the decrease of
bird populations. In 1972, the United States
banned the use and manufacture of DDT. It
remains in use around the world, however,
particularly as a means of malaria control.

2 Reading/Thinking Skills

Infer

Questions

- What question do you think was just posed to the narrator by a senator? *(Possible responses: Hasn't DDT been banned? Don't you realize that DDT is a toxic and illegal substance?)*

- Where might the narrator be speaking? *(Possible response: at a hearing in the U.S. Senate)*

3 Literary Element

Tone

Questions

- How would you describe the narrator's tone as he describes the indigenous people of Borneo? *(Possible responses: patronizing, bigoted, disgusted, intolerant)*

- An author's tone may be very different from the tone of a story character. How would you describe the author's tone? *(Possible response: mocking the narrator and people like him)*

4 Active Reading

Clarify

Response Borneo was plagued with insects, so he sprayed the area with DDT.

---

2 **YES, I'M AWARE OF THAT FACT,** sir. But just because *we* banned it domestically,[4] under pressure from the bird-watching contingent[5] and the hopheads down at the EPA, it doesn't necessarily follow that the rest of the world—especially the developing world—was about to jump on the bandwagon. And that's the key here, Senator, "developing." You've got to realize this is Borneo we're talking about here, not Port Townsend or Enumclaw. These people don't know from square one about sanitation, disease control, pest eradication[6]—or even personal hygiene, if you want to come right down to it. It rains 120 inches a year, minimum. They dig up **3** roots in the jungle. They've still got headhunters along the Rajang River, for God's sake.

And please don't forget they *asked* us to come in there, practically begged us—and not only the World Health Organization but the Sultan of Brunei and the government in Sarawak too. We did what we could to accommodate them and reach our objective in the shortest period of time and by the most direct and effective means. We went to the air. Obviously. And no one could have foreseen the consequences, no one, not even if we'd gone out and generated a hundred environmental impact statements—it was just one of those things, a freak occurrence, and there's no defense against that. Not that I know of, anyway . . .

CLARIFY: What is the problem that the speaker was asked to address, and what is the solution that he undertook?

CATERPILLARS? YES, SENATOR, that's correct. That was the first sign: caterpillars.

But let me backtrack a minute here. You see, out in the bush they have these roofs made of thatched palm leaves—you'll see them in the towns too, even in Bintulu or Brunei—and they're really pretty effective, you'd be surprised. A hundred and twenty inches of rain, they've got to

---

figure a way to keep it out of the hut, and for centuries, that was it. Palm leaves. Well, it was about a month after we sprayed for the final time and I'm sitting at my desk in the trailer thinking about the drainage project at Kuching, enjoying the fact that for the first time in maybe a year I'm not smearing mosquitoes all over the back of my neck, when there's a knock at the door. It's this elderly gentleman, tattooed from head to toe, dressed only in a pair of running shorts—they love those shorts, by the way, the shiny material and the tight machine-stitching, the whole country, men and women both, they can't get enough of them . . . Anyway, he's the headman of the local village and he's very excited, something about the roofs—*atap,* they call them. That's all he can say, *atap, atap,* over and over again.

It's raining of course. It's always raining. So I shrug into my rain slicker, start up the 4x4, and go have a look. Sure enough, all the *atap* roofs are collapsing, not only in his village but throughout the target area. The people are all huddled there in their running shorts, looking pretty miserable, and one after another roofs keep falling in, it's bewildering, and gradually I realize the headman's diatribe[7] has begun to feature a new term I was unfamiliar with at the time—the word for caterpillar, as it turns out, in the Iban dialect. But who was to make the connection between three passes with the crop duster and all these staved-in roofs?

Our people finally sorted it out a couple of weeks later. The chemical, which, by the way, cut down the number of mosquitoes exponentially,[8]

---

4. domestically (də mes′tik lē), *adv.* having to do with one's own country; not foreign.

5. contingent (kən tin′jənt), *n.* a group that is a part of another group.

6. eradication (i rad′ə kā′shən), *n.* complete destruction or elimination.

7. diatribe (dī′ə trīb), *n.* a bitter, abusive criticism or denunciation.

8. exponentially (ek′spō nen′shəl lē), *adv.* in a way that involves unknown or variable quantities as exponents. In everyday use, if objects decrease *exponentially,* they decrease dramatically in number.

MINI-LESSON: GRAMMAR

Recognizing and Avoiding Jargon

Teach Point out that the author creates satire through the use of jargon, or hard-to-understand language used among members of a group, such as people in a profession. For example, the speaker refers to "the insect vector" and to reducing the number of mosquitoes "exponentially." The person speaking seems to be hiding behind technical terms rather than using simple words.

Apply Although the use of jargon such as *cost overrun, efficacy,* and *the mosquito population* makes the narrator's report seem official, he seems to be using elevated rhetoric rather than admitting mistakes.

Question How might a person avoid jargon and express the ideas in the phrases *cost overrun* and *mosquito population* in simpler words? *(Possible responses: spending more than you planned, going over budget; the number of mosquitoes)*

Activity Idea Students can find other sentences in the story that contain jargon and rewrite them, using clearer language.

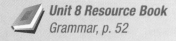

Unit 8 Resource Book
Grammar, p. 52

had the unfortunate side effect of killing off this little wasp—I've got the scientific name for it somewhere in my report here, if you're interested—that preyed on a type of caterpillar that in turn ate palm leaves. Well, with the wasps gone, the caterpillars hatched out with nothing to keep them in check and chewed the roofs to pieces, which was unfortunate, we admit it, and we had a real cost overrun on replacing those roofs with tin . . . but the people were happier, I think, in the long run, because, let's face it, no matter how tightly you weave those palm leaves, they're just not going to keep the water out like tin. Of course, nothing's perfect, and we had a lot of complaints about the rain drumming on the panels, people unable to sleep, and what have you . . .

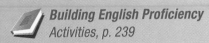 **YES SIR, THAT'S CORRECT—THE** flies were next.

Well, you've got to understand the magnitude of the fly problem in Borneo, there's nothing like it to compare it with, except maybe a garbage strike in New York. Every minute of every day you've got flies everywhere, up your nose, in your mouth, your ears, your eyes, flies in your rice, your Coke, your Singapore sling, and your gin rickey. It's enough to drive you to distraction, not to mention the diseases these things carry, from dysentery to typhoid to cholera and back round the loop again. And once the mosquito population was down, the flies seemed to breed up to fill in the gap—Borneo wouldn't be Borneo without some damned insect blackening the air.

Of course, this was before our people had tracked down the problem with caterpillars and the wasps and all of that, so we'd figured we'd had a big success with the mosquitoes, why not a series of ground sweeps, mount a fogger in the back of a Suzuki Brat, and sanitize the huts, not to mention the open sewers, which as you know are nothing but a breeding ground for flies, chiggers, and biting insects of every sort—at least it was an error of commission rather than omission. At least we were trying.

I watched the flies go down myself. One day they were so thick in the trailer I couldn't even *find* my paperwork, let alone attempt to get through it, and the next they were collecting on the windows, bumbling around like they were drunk. A day later they were gone. Just like that. From a million flies in the trailer to none . . .

Well, no one could have foreseen that, Senator.

The geckos ate the flies, yes. You're all familiar with geckos, I assume, gentlemen? These are the lizards you've seen during your trips to Hawaii, very colorful, patrolling the houses for roaches and flies, almost like pets, but of course they're wild animals, never lose sight of that, and just about as unsanitary as anything I can think of, except maybe the flies.

Yes, well don't forget, sir, we're viewing this with twenty-twenty hindsight, but at the time no one gave a thought to geckos or what they ate—they were just another fact of life in the tropics. Mosquitoes, lizards, scorpions, leeches—you name it, they've got it. When the flies began piling up on the windowsills like drift, naturally the geckos feasted on them, stuffing themselves till they looked like sausages crawling up the walls. Whereas before they moved so fast you could never be sure you'd seen them, now they waddled across the floor, laid around in the corners, clung to the air vents like magnets—and even then no one paid much attention to them till they started turning belly-up in the streets. Believe me, we confirmed a lot of things there about the buildup of these products as you move up the food chain and the efficacy[9]—or lack thereof—of certain methods, no doubt about that . . .

EVALUATE: How did the speaker compound the problems he created? **7**

---

9. **efficacy** (ef′ə kə sē) *n.* power to produce the effect wanted; effectiveness.

Top of the Food Chain **925**

---

5 Literary Element
Characterization

You might explain that *Singapore sling* and *gin rickey* are the names of alcoholic beverages.

Question What does the narrator's statement suggest about his work ethic? *(Possible response: that he was not too concerned with the crisis to indulge in leisurely drinking)*

6 Literary Focus
Hyperbole

Discuss the way people can use exaggeration figuratively, to make a point using images that are not literal.

Question What examples of hyperbole in this paragraph emphasize the quantity of flies? *(Possible responses: "I couldn't even* find *my paper work," "a million flies in the trailer")*

7 Active Reading
Evaluate

Response He ignored the environmental problems, used more DDT, and treated each problem as an isolated issue, instead of recognizing the connections between the consequences of his mistakes.

BUILDING ENGLISH PROFICIENCY

Understanding Story Sequence

Some students may find the story events difficult to follow, because they are interspersed with the speaker's opinions and the implied dialogue at the Senate hearing. Help students make a time line or sequential list of the events in Borneo. The example shown has been begun but not completed.

Building English Proficiency Activities, p. 239

ESL LEP ELD SAE LD

Events in Borneo
- The large insect population was causing problems.
- An American government agency was invited to help.
- They decided to spray DDT to kill mosquitoes.
- The DDT also killed wasps that preyed on caterpillars.
- The number of caterpillars then increased.
- The caterpillars ate the people's palm-leaf roofs.
- The roofs were destroyed and had to be replaced with tin roofs.

Art Study

Possible Responses to Caption Question Yes; the image of dropping cats by parachutes is silly, and the painting style matches it. The story has an underlying tragic humor that may not be very evident in the art.

When students first see the art, they will not know that the parachute drop is part of the action in the story.

This 1993 illustration of T. Coraghessan Boyle's story was done by Caty Bartholomew. Do you think the artist has done a good job matching the tone of "Top of the Food Chain"?

 THE CATS? THAT'S WHERE IT GOT sticky, really sticky. You see, nobody really lost sleep over a pile of dead lizards—though we did tests routinely and the tests confirmed what we'd expected, that is, the product had been concentrated in the geckos because of the number of contaminated flies they consumed. But lizards are one thing and cats are another. These people really have an affection for their cats—no house, no hut, no matter how primitive, is without at least a couple of them. Mangy-looking things, long-legged and scrawny, maybe, not at all the sort of animal you'd see here, but there it was: they

MINI-LESSON: VOCABULARY

Recognize Idioms

Teach Have students analyze the following idioms that appear in the story:

- "to make a dent in it"
- "to jump on the bandwagon"
- "had a field day"

Remind students that an idiom is an expression peculiar to a language. It has a meaning different from the literal meaning of the words.

Question What does each of the preceding idioms mean? *(Possible responses: to make progress; to have an impact on it; to follow a current trend; to join others; experienced great pleasure and activity)*

Activity Idea Students can write a new sentence using each of the above idioms. Students also can identify, define, and practice using other idioms from the selection.

loved their cats. Because the cats were functional, you understand—without them, the place would be swimming in rodents inside of a week.

You're right there, Senator, yes—that's exactly what happened.

You see, the cats had a field day with these feeble geckos—you can imagine, if any of you have ever owned a cat, the kind of joy these animals must have experienced to see their nemesis,[10] this ultra-quick lizard, and it's just barely creeping across the floor like a bug. Well, to make a long story short, the cats ate up every dead and dying gecko in the country, from snout to tail, and then the cats began to die . . . which to my mind would have been no great loss if it wasn't for the rats. Suddenly there were rats everywhere—you couldn't drive down the streets without running over half a dozen of them at a time. They fouled the grain supplies, fell in the wells and died, bit infants as they slept in their cradles. But that wasn't the worst, not by a long shot. No, things really went down the tube after that. Within the month we were getting scattered reports of bubonic plague,[11] and of course we tracked them all down and made sure the people got antibiotics, but still we lost a few and the rats kept coming . . .

It was my plan, yes. I was brainstorming one night, rats scuttling all over the trailer like something out of a cheap horror film, the villagers in a panic over the threat of the plague and the stream of nonstop hysterical reports from the interior—people were turning black, swelling up, and bursting, that sort of thing—well, as I say, I came up with a plan, a stopgap, not perfect, not cheap, but at this juncture, I'm sure you will agree, something had to be done.

9 PREDICT: What plan do you think the speaker has come up with? If you were in his place, what might you propose?

We wound up going as far as Australia for some of the cats, cleaning out the S.P.C.A.

facilities and what have you, though we rounded most of them up in Indonesia and Singapore—approximately 14,000 in all. And yes, it cost us—cost us up-front purchase money and aircraft fuel and pilots' overtime and all the rest of it—but we really felt there was no alternative. It was like all nature had turned against us. **10**

And yet, all things considered, we made a lot of friends for the U.S.A. the day we dropped the cats, and you should have seen them, gentlemen, the little parachutes and harnesses we'd tricked up, 14,000 of them, cats in every color of the rainbow, cats with one ear, no ears, half a tail, three-legged cats, cats that could have taken pride of show in Springfield, Massachusetts, and all of them twirling down out of the sky like great big oversized snowflakes . . .

IT WAS SOMETHING. IT was really something.

Of course, you've all seen the reports. There were other factors we hadn't counted on, adverse[12] conditions in the paddies and manioc fields—we don't to this day know what predatory species were inadvertently[13] killed off by the initial sprayings, it's just a mystery—but the weevils and whatnot took a pretty heavy toll on the crops that year, and by the time we dropped the cats, well—the people were pretty hungry, and I suppose it was inevitable that we lost a good proportion of them right then and there. But we've got a CARE program going there now and something hit the rat population—we still don't know what, a virus we think—and the geckos, they tell me, are making a comeback.

So what I'm saying is it could be worse, and to every cloud a silver lining, wouldn't you agree, gentlemen?

---

10. **nemesis** (nem′ə sis), *n.* an unbeatable rival.
11. **bubonic plague** (byü bon′ik plāg), *n.* a very serious contagious disease, usually carried to human beings by fleas from rats or squirrels.
12. **adverse** (ad vėrs′), *adj.* unfavorable; harmful.
13. **inadvertently** (in′əd vėrt′nt lē), *adv.* in an inattentive, careless, or negligent way.

Top of the Food Chain   **927**

8 Reading/Thinking Skills
Recognize Values

Question What negative aspect of the narrator's values or character is the author emphasizing? *(Possible response: He doesn't value animal or plant life; he doesn't even value the lives of people.)*

9 Active Reading
Predict

Response Students may predict some extreme and ecologically preposterous plan for killing rats, such as having an army shoot them or poison them. Students might propose that they set rat traps, concentrate on protecting people, or do nothing, to let nature get back into balance.

10 Reading/Thinking Skills
Make Judgments

Discuss the irony in the statement, "It seemed like all nature had turned against us."

Question Why is the narrator's claim absurd? *(Possible responses: because by carelessly contaminating nature he has turned nature against himself; because he is not the victim, since the people and animals are the ones suffering)*

Check Test

1. Why did the speaker's agency spray DDT on the area in question? *(to kill the many insects there)*

2. Why did the village roofs collapse? *(Caterpillars ate the palm leaves that comprised the roofs.)*

3. Why did the geckos die? *(They feasted on flies contaminated with DDT.)*

4. Why did the agency import cats from Indonesia and Singapore? *(to eat rats, because DDT had wiped out the cats)*

5. To whom is the narrator telling the story? *(a senator)*

 *Unit 8 Resource Book*
Alternate Check Test, p. 53

BUILDING ENGLISH PROFICIENCY

Analyzing Tone

Help students understand and appreciate the story's satiric tone.

- Remind students that tone is the writer's attitude toward the subject. In a story, tone is revealed by the characters' traits and actions and by descriptions of settings and events.

- Point out that an author's tone may be very different from a character's tone or attitude. The speaker in this story calls people who care about the environment

"the bird-watching contingent" and "hopheads," but the author uses these words to reveal what the speaker is like.

- Invite students to judge whether the writer presents the speaker as a "good guy" or a "bad guy" on the basis of the speaker's actions and statements. Ask students to support their judgment with details.

After Reading

MAKING CONNECTIONS

1. Responses may reflect disapproval of his dangerous incompetence and prejudiced attitudes.

2. People are at the top of the food chain. In the story, people poison insects, thus poisoning animals that eat those insects. Damage to these species affects humans.

3. Possible responses: He is arrogant, glib, prejudiced, short-sighted, criminally irresponsible, and lazy.

4. Possible response: The "developed" countries cause more harm than good when they apply their technology to environments they do not understand.

5. Students should be able to support their responses by quoting the text or giving historical examples.

VOCABULARY STUDY

A sample response is shown; crossword numbers will vary.

Across

1. The agency <u>inadvertently</u> killed wasps.

2. The insect <u>vector</u> was causing malaria.

3. The gecko had been the cat's <u>nemesis</u>.

4. The senator doubted the <u>efficacy</u> of the agent's actions.

5. The number of geckos dropped <u>exponentially</u>.

Down

1. The speaker may hear an angry <u>diatribe</u> from environmentalists.

2. His goal was the <u>eradication</u> of insects.

3. People in Borneo had to deal with <u>adverse</u> conditions.

4. DDT was banned <u>domestically</u> but not overseas.

5. The rat <u>contingent</u> grew without cats.

Unit 8 Resource Book
Vocabulary, p. 51
Vocabulary Test, p. 54

Selection Test

Unit 8 Resource Book
pp. 55–56

928

After Reading

Shaping Your Response

Analyzing the Story

Extending the Ideas

Making Connections

1. If you were the speaker's boss and had to write a job performance report on his work in Borneo, what would you say?

2. What is the significance of the title "Top of the Food Chain"?

3. How would you **characterize** the speaker of the story?

4. The purpose of **satire** is to instruct or inform. What do you think is the message of Boyle's satirical story "Top of the Food Chain"?

5. What role, if any, do you think the United States should play in the internal affairs of other nations?

Vocabulary Study

diatribe
vector
adverse
efficacy
inadvertently
eradication
domestically
contingent
nemesis
exponentially

Use the listed vocabulary words to make a "Top of the Food Chain" crossword puzzle. On a piece of graph paper, map out your puzzle with five words down and five across. Then, as clues, write sentences that relate to the story, leaving a blank in each where the vocabulary word fits in the sentence. Trade with a partner and see if you can solve each other's puzzles.

Expressing Your Ideas

Writing Choices

Writer's Notebook Update Choose one of the environmental concerns that you listed in your writer's notebook. Write what you know about the problem and explain the progress, if any, that is being made toward solving it.

Congressional Report You are one of the members of the congressional committee listening to the speaker's report on his activities in Borneo. Write a **report** summarizing the results of those activities and making recommendations for the future of the project in Borneo.

Another Option

What's for Dinner? The ecological balance in Borneo was upset when the speaker attempted to solve the insect problem there. Make an **illustrated diagram** of the food chains that he weakened in his misguided attempts to improve the living conditions on the island.

WRITING CHOICES
Writer's Notebook Update

You might suggest that students research the topics using library or media center—and online—resources. Periodicals include *Environment* (published by the Scientists' Institute for Public Information, Washington, DC) and *The Conservationist* (published by the New York State Department of Environmental Conservation, Albany, NY).

Congressional Report

Students might consult periodical references such as the United States *Congressional Quarterly* and *Congressional Digest* to research models for their report.

ANOTHER OPTION
What's for Dinner?

• Food chain one: palm leaves—caterpillars—wasps

• Food chain two: flies—geckos and rats—cats

Before Reading

A Blizzard Under Blue Sky

by Pam Houston

Pam Houston
born 1962

Born and raised in New Jersey, Pam Houston graduated with a B.A. from Denison University. After her graduation she took a cross-country bicycle trip with a friend and wound up in Colorado. There, in order to follow modern-day cowboys, she threw herself into mastering all kinds of outdoor activities. She has worked as a horse trainer, ski instructor, hunting guide, and rafting guide. In addition, she found time to complete her Ph.D. at the University of Utah. She currently writes during the winter and works as a river guide in the summer. She married a former safari guide from South Africa. The story you are about to read is taken from Houston's first book, *Cowboys Are My Weakness* (1992).

Building Background

More Than Just the Blues People often say that they are "depressed." More often than not, they are just suffering from a normal "down" mood. Usually these everyday "blues" evaporate by themselves. More severe depression may be caused by a chemical imbalance and usually requires medical attention. The depressed person may feel numb, may not want to get out of bed in the morning, may exhibit symptoms of physical illness, and may become irritable and unable to concentrate. People can overcome less severe depression by giving themselves special treats, by doing intense physical activity, by keeping busy with challenging tasks, or by getting outside of themselves by helping others. The main character of "A Blizzard Under Blue Sky" tries a new activity to help her overcome her depression.

Literary Focus

Setting Where and when a story takes place is its setting. Setting can help establish mood, reveal character, and affect the development of the plot. For example, "The Devil and Tom Walker" (page 240) takes place outside of Boston in a swamp in the year 1727. The dismal, dreary setting creates an ominous mood. The setting of "A Worn Path" (page 667), the rural countryside of Mississippi, reveals the character of Phoenix Jackson, the old woman who conquers the landscape to get medicine for her grandson. As you read "A Blizzard Under Blue Sky," note the details that describe the setting. Also, determine what effect, if any, the setting has on the mood, character development, and plot of the story.

Writer's Notebook

'Tis the Season Weather plays a big part in the story you are about to read. What is it like where you live during each of the four seasons? Are you mired in mud or socked in by heavy fog in spring? Are you parched by droughts or cooled by mountain breezes in the summer? In your notebook, write a list of descriptive phrases telling what your area of the country is like during your favorite season.

A Blizzard Under Blue Sky   **929**

Before Reading

Building Background

Although it helps to activate students' knowledge of many topics, the classroom is not a good milieu to share personal knowledge of depression. You might ask a counselor to speak briefly to the class, or consider another background topic such as students' knowledge of Utah, the story's setting.

Literary Focus

In "A Blizzard Under Blue Sky," the setting—the splendor and bitter cold in the mountains of Utah—is an integral part of the story. Suggest that, as students read the story, they note how the narrator changes through interaction with her surroundings.

Writer's Notebook

To help students compile phrases, suggest that they concentrate on one sense at a time. Students can imagine wet, damp, or dry air; dark, puffy, or low clouds; and the sounds of rain, birds, or wind through trees or other components of the environs.

More About Pam Houston

Houston's stories have been compared to Hemingway's by some critics. She portrays women in nontraditional roles. She also wrote *Women on Hunting: Essays, Fiction, and Poetry* (1994).

SUPPORT MATERIALS OVERVIEW

Unit 8 Resource Book
- Graphic Organizer, p. 57
- Study Guide, p. 58
- Vocabulary, p. 59
- Grammar, p. 60
- Alternate Check Test, p. 61
- Vocabulary Test, p. 62
- Selection Test, pp. 63–64

Building English Proficiency
- Literature Summaries
- Activities, p. 240

Reading, Writing & Grammar Skillbook
- Reading, pp. 52–53, 54–55
- Writing, pp. 119–120
- Grammar, Usage, and Mechanics, pp. 226–227

Technology
- Audiotape
- Personal Journal Software
- Custom Literature Database
  For another story set in extremely frigid weather, see "To Build a Fire" by Jack London on the database.
- Test Generator Software

Selection Objectives

- To consider themes of mental outlook, self-reliance, and survival in nature
- To recognize the effect of setting on mood, plot, and character development
- To recognize proper agreement between indefinite pronouns and verbs

Unit 8 Resource Book
Graphic Organizer, p. 57
Study Guide, p. 58

Theme Link

Young people, who are citizens of both today and tomorrow, face challenges and deal with issues of health and mental outlook. The protagonist of this story encounters depression and overcomes it during a daring overnight camping adventure.

Vocabulary Preview

rampant, unrestrained; unchecked

verge, the point at which something begins or happens; brink

primal, of early times; first; primeval

translucent, letting light through without being transparent

chastise, criticize severely; rebuke

Students can add the words and definitions to their Writer's Notebooks.

1 | Literary Focus

Setting

Students interested in the outdoors may enjoy finding the setting in Utah on maps. A detailed map may show places in the story such as Park City and Beaver Creek. The Alaska Clipper is a winter cold wind pattern that affects many northern and western states.

Question What details in the story establish the extreme cold that is an aspect of the setting? *(the thirty-two degrees below zero temperature, the Alaska Clipper, and later on the same page the images of cold sunshine and the hair in the narrator's nostrils freezing)*

A Blizzard
UNDER BLUE SKY

Pam Houston

The doctor said I was clinically depressed. It was February, the month in which depression runs rampant[1] in the inversion-cloaked Salt Lake Valley and the city dwellers escape to Park City, where the snow is fresh and the sun is shining and everybody is happy, except me. In truth, my life was on the verge[2] of more spectacular and satisfying discoveries than I had ever imagined, but of course I couldn't see that far ahead. What I saw was work that wasn't getting done, bills that weren't getting paid, and a man I'd given my heart to weekending in the desert with his ex.

The doctor said, "I can give you drugs."

I said, "No way."

She said, "The machine that drives you is broken. You need something to help you get it fixed."

I said, "Winter camping."

She said, "Whatever floats your boat."

One of the things I love the most about the natural world is the way it gives you what's good for you even if you don't know it at the time. I had never been winter camping before, at least not in the high country, and the weekend I chose to try and fix my machine was the same weekend the air mass they called the Alaska Clipper showed up. It was thirty-two degrees below zero in town on the night I spent in my snow cave. I don't know how cold it was out on Beaver Creek. I had listened to the weather

forecast, and to the advice of my housemate, Alex, who was an experienced winter camper.

"I don't know what you think you're going to prove by freezing to death," Alex said, "but if you've got to go, take my bivvy sack;[3] it's warmer than anything you have."

"Thanks," I said.

"If you mix Kool-Aid with your water it won't freeze up," he said, "and don't forget lighting paste for your stove."

"Okay," I said.

"I hope it turns out to be worth it," he said, "because you are going to freeze your butt."

When everything in your life is uncertain, there's nothing quite like the clarity and precision of fresh snow and blue sky. That was the first thought I had on Saturday morning as I stepped away from the warmth of my truck and let my skis slap the snow in front of me. There was no wind and no clouds that morning, just still air and cold sunshine. The hair in my nostrils froze almost immediately. When I took a deep breath, my lungs only filled up halfway.

I opened the tailgate to excited whines and whimpers. I never go skiing without Jackson and

---

1. **rampant** (ram′pənt), *adj.* unrestrained; unchecked.
2. **verge** (vėrj), *n.* the point at which something begins or happens; brink.
3. **bivvy sack** a bag designed to contain a sleeping bag and protect it from wind and water.

SELECTION SUMMARY

A Blizzard Under Blue Sky

After declining her doctor's offer of medication for depression, the narrator opts for winter camping to pick up her spirits. With her two dogs, on a bitterly cold Saturday, she drives to the mountains. During the day, as she skis over a trail through the wilderness, she finds herself in awe of the splendor of the natural world. Nevertheless, she still cannot forget her troubles. That night, while curled up in a handmade snow cave for fourteen hours, she chastises herself for risking her life and those of her dogs—and she battles the cold. On Sunday morning, while skiing back to the truck, she realizes that during the night she didn't think about her troubles. At daybreak she is happy to see a day beginning, for the first time in many months. This epiphany gives her hope that her depression will end.

 For summaries in other languages, see the Building English Proficiency book.

Describe your personal reaction to Paul Ladnier's *Grandy Snow Scene*. Does it make you want to step into the picture, or does it make you feel glad that you aren't there?

Art Study

Possible Responses to Caption The beauty of the winter scene makes me want to step in, put on cross-country skis, and explore. I'd step into the picture if it were possible to step back out; it looks great but might feel too cold.

Hailey; my two best friends, my yin and yang[4] of dogs. Some of you might know Jackson. He's the oversized sheepdog-and-something-else with the great big nose and the bark that will shatter glass. He gets out and about more than I do. People I've never seen before come by my house daily and call him by name. He's all grace, and he's tireless; he won't go skiing with me unless I let him lead. Hailey is not so graceful, and her body seems in constant indecision when she runs. When we ski she stays behind me, and on the downhills she tries to sneak rides on my skis.

The dogs ran circles in the chest-high snow while I inventoried my backpack one more time to make sure I had everything I needed. My sleeping bag, my Thermarest, my stove, Alex's bivvy sack, matches, lighting paste, flashlight, knife. I brought three pairs of long underwear—tops and bottoms—so I could change once before I went to bed, and once again in the morning, so I wouldn't get chilled by my own sweat. I brought paper and pen, and Kool-Aid to mix with my water. I brought Mountain House chicken stew and some freeze-dried green peas, some peanut butter and honey, lots of dried apricots, coffee and Carnation instant breakfast for morning.

Jackson stood very still while I adjusted his backpack. He carries the dog food and enough water for all of us. He takes himself very seriously when he's got his pack on. He won't step off the trail for any reason, not even to chase rabbits, and he gets nervous and angry if I do. That morning he was impatient with me. "Miles to go, Mom," he said over his shoulder. I

---

4. **yin and yang,** elements in Chinese philosophy representing opposing forces. The phrase is used to describe complementary opposites.

A Blizzard Under Blue Sky   **931**

Literary Element
Characterization

The description of the dogs develops them as characters, but it also characterizes the narrator more fully. She is the woman who cares about them, notices their traits, skis and camps with them, and responds to their needs.

Question How do you think Jackson says "Miles to go, Mom"? *(Possible responses: Jackson, a dog, probably uses a look back over his shoulder and a canine expression of impatience. The narrator is figuratively translating the dog's message as words.)*

The World of Work

For the experiences of another woman who has met challenges, as a **circus performer,** see the pages listed here.

The World of Work
pp. 27–28

BUILDING ENGLISH PROFICIENCY

ESL
LEP
ELD
SAE
LD

Understanding Key Terms

The main character uses terms from subjects such as psychology and camping to tell the story. Students who gain an understanding of such terms can appreciate the story more fully.

- "I was clinically depressed." While many people from time to time feel depressed, the expression *clinically depressed* suggests more than a personal impression. A doctor may diagnose depression in a person whose gloominess involves a physical condition. Psychologists believe that depression involves chemical activity in the brain and nervous system. Such depression often is diagnosed in a clinic.

- "... a man I'd given my heart to weekending in the desert with his

ex." To *weekend* is to spend a weekend. *Ex* is a slang term for a divorced person's ex-wife or ex-husband, a former mate.

- "... take my bivvy sack. ..." A *bivvy sack* can serve as a layer wrapped around a sleeping bag for camping in very cold or wet weather. Its name comes from the word *bivouac,* an encampment.

- Students can use context to figure out word meanings and can talk about expressions and various trade names in the story. Students familiar with camping may share information.

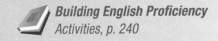

Building English Proficiency
Activities, p. 240

931

Making Personal Connections

The narrator says, "It was utterly quiet out there, and what minimal noise we made intruded on the morning like a brass band: the squeaking of my bindings, the slosh of the water in Jackson's pack, the whoosh of the nylon, the jangle of dog tags."

Question   Have you ever been in circumstances that drew your attention so intensely to sounds? If so, describe it. *(Possible responses: Some students may recount fearing an intruder in their homes. Others may recount trying to keep quiet while sneaking into a room. Still others may recount awakening on a camping trip or some other circumstance.)*

Imagery

Question   What image or images on page 932 strike you as most vivid? *(Possible responses: the landscape as a crystal palace; twigs and shadows seeming to leap out of the background; the squeaking, sloshing, whooshing, or jangling sounds; Jackson's tail thumping the snow; crystal-coated trees or diamond-studded sunshine; the translucent snow reflecting blues, purples, and grays)*

---

snapped my boots into my skis and we were off.

There are not too many good things you can say about temperatures that dip past twenty below zero, except this: They turn the landscape into a crystal palace and they turn your vision into Superman's. In the cold thin morning air the trees and mountains, even the twigs and shadows, seemed to leap out of the background like a 3-D movie, only it was better than 3-D because I could feel the sharpness of the air.

I have a friend in Moab who swears that Utah is the center of the fourth dimension, and although I know he has in mind something much different and more complicated than sub-zero weather, it was there, on that ice-edged morning, that I felt on the verge of seeing something more than depth perception in the brutal clarity of the morning sun.

As I kicked along the first couple of miles, I noticed the sun crawling higher in the sky and yet the day wasn't really warming, and I wondered if I should have brought another vest, another layer to put between me and the cold night ahead.

It was utterly quiet out there, and what minimal noise we made intruded on the morning like a brass band: the squeaking of my bindings, the slosh of the water in Jackson's pack, the whoosh of nylon, the jangle of dog tags. It was the brass line and percussion to some primal[5] song, and I kept wanting to sing to it, but I didn't know the words.

Jackson and I crested the top of a hill and stopped to wait for Hailey. The trail stretched out as far as we could see into the meadow below us and beyond, a double track and pole plants carving through softer trails of rabbit and deer.

"Nice place," I said to Jackson, and his tail thumped the snow underneath him without sound.

We stopped for lunch near something that looked like it could be a lake in its other life, or maybe just a womb-shaped meadow. I made peanut butter and honey sandwiches for all of us, and we opened the apricots.

"It's fabulous here," I told the dogs. "But so far it's not working."

There had never been anything wrong with my life that a few good days in the wilderness wouldn't cure, but there I sat in the middle of all those crystal-coated trees, all that diamond-studded sunshine, and I didn't feel any better. Apparently clinical depression was not like having a bad day, it wasn't even like having a lot of bad days, it was more like a house of mirrors, it was like being in a room full of one-way glass.

"Come on, Mom," Jackson said. "Ski harder, go faster, climb higher."

Hailey turned her belly to the sun and groaned.

"He's right," I told her. "It's all we can do."

After lunch the sun had moved behind our backs, throwing a whole different light on the path ahead of us. The snow we moved through stopped being simply white and became translucent,[6] hinting at other colors, reflections of blues and purples and grays. I thought of Moby Dick, you know, the whiteness of the whale, where white is really the absence of all color, and whiteness equals truth, and Ahab's search is finally futile, as he finds nothing but his own reflection.

"Put your mind where your skis are," Jackson said, and we made considerably better time after that.

The sun was getting quite low in the sky when I asked Jackson if he thought we should stop to build the snow cave, and he said he'd look for the next good bank. About one hundred yards down the trail we found it, a gentle slope with eastern exposure that didn't look like it would cave in under any circumstances. Jackson started to dig first.

Let me make one thing clear. I knew only slightly more about building snow caves than Jackson, having never built one, and all my knowledge coming from disaster tales of winter camping fatalities. I knew several things *not* to

---

5. primal (prī′məl), *adj.* of early times; first; primeval.
6. translucent (tran slü′snt), *adj.* letting light through without being transparent.

MINI-LESSON: GRAMMAR

Indefinite Pronoun-Verb Agreement

Teach   Indefinite pronouns such as *one, some, many,* and *most* can appear as sentence subjects. Singular and plural pronouns and their verbs should agree. Review the concept of present-tense verbs that work with singular or plural subjects.

Activity Ideas

- Have students write a sentence using each of the following singular pronouns as the subject: *each, every,* and *neither.* Have students write a sentence for each of the following plural indefinite pronouns: *both, few,* and *several.*
- Have students write a sentence for each of the following indefinite pronouns, which may be singular or plural: *all, most,* and *none.*

When a singular indefinite pronoun is used as a subject, a singular verb is required. *One of the unfortunate things about winter camping is that it has to happen when the da̲ are so short.*
When a plural indefinite pronoun is used as a subject, a plural verb is required. *Many of the toughest things about winter seem to occur when I go camping.*
Some indefinite pronouns may be singular or plural, depending on to whom or to what they refer: *all, none, any, some, more* and *most.*
• *Some of my food fits in this pouch.* (*Food* is a singular noun.)
• *Some of the items in my pack are heavy.* (*Items* is plural.)

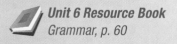

Unit 6 Resource Book
Grammar, p. 60

do when building a snow cave, but I was having a hard time knowing what exactly to do. But Jackson helped, and Hailey supervised, and before too long we had a little cave built, just big enough for three. We ate dinner quite pleased with our accomplishments and set the bivvy sack up inside the cave just as the sun slipped away and dusk came over Beaver Creek.

The temperature, which hadn't exactly soared during the day, dropped twenty degrees in as many minutes, and suddenly it didn't seem like such a great idea to change my long underwear. The original plan was to sleep with the dogs inside the bivvy sack but outside the sleeping bag, which was okay with Jackson the super-metabolizer, but not so with Hailey, the couch potato. She whined and wriggled and managed to stuff her entire fat body down inside my mummy bag, and Jackson stretched out full-length on top.

One of the unfortunate things about winter camping is that it has to happen when the days are so short. Fourteen hours is a long time to lie in a snow cave under the most perfect of circumstances. And when it's thirty-two below, or forty, fourteen hours seems like weeks.

I wish I could tell you I dropped right off to sleep. In truth, fear crept into my spine with the cold and I never closed my eyes. Cuddled there, amid my dogs and water bottles, I spent half of the night chastising[7] myself for thinking I was Wonder Woman,[8] not only risking my own life but the lives of my dogs, and the other half trying to keep the numbness in my feet from crawling up to my knees. When I did doze off, which was actually more like blacking out than dozing off, I'd come back to my senses wondering if I had frozen to death, but the alternating pain and numbness that started in my extremities and worked its way into my bones convinced me I must still be alive.

It was a clear night, and every now and again I would poke my head out of its nest of down and nylon to watch the progress of the moon across the sky. There is no doubt that it was the longest and most uncomfortable night of my life.

But then the sky began to get gray, and then it began to get pink, and before too long the sun was on my bivvy sack, not warm, exactly, but holding the promise of warmth later in the day. And I ate apricots and drank Kool-Aid-flavored coffee and celebrated the rebirth of my fingers and toes, and the survival of many more important parts of my body. I sang "Rocky Mountain High" and "If I Had a Hammer," and yodeled and whistled, and even danced the two-step with Jackson and let him lick my face. And when Hailey finally emerged from the sleeping bag a full hour after I did, we shared a peanut butter and honey sandwich and she said nothing ever tasted so good.

We broke camp and packed up and kicked in the snow cave with something resembling glee.

I was five miles down the trail before I realized what had happened. Not once in that fourteen-hour night did I think about deadlines, or bills, or the man in the desert. For the first time in many months I was happy to see a day beginning. The morning sunshine was like a present from the gods. What really happened, of course, is that I remembered about joy.

I know that one night out at thirty-two below doesn't sound like much to those of you who have climbed Everest or run the Iditarod[9] or kayaked to Antarctica, and I won't try to convince you that my life was like the movies where depression goes away in one weekend, and all of life's problems vanish with a moment's clear sight. The simple truth of the matter is this: On Sunday I had a glimpse outside of the house of mirrors, on Saturday I couldn't have seen my way out of a paper bag. And while I was skiing back toward the truck that morning, a wind came up behind us and swirled the snow around our bodies like a blizzard under blue sky. And I was struck by the simple perfection of the snowflakes, and startled by the hopefulness of sun on frozen trees.

---

7. **chastise** (cha stīz´), *v.* criticize severely; rebuke.
8. **Wonder Woman,** a comic book heroine.
9. **Iditarod,** a famous Alaskan dog-sled race.

A Blizzard Under Blue Sky   **933**

5 Reading/Thinking Skills
Recognizing Values

Question While curled up in the snow cave, the narrator chastises herself "for not only risking my own life but the lives of my dogs." What does this thought demonstrate about the character? *(Possible responses: She cares for others besides herself. She loves her pets.)*

6 Literary Focus
Setting

Question How has the bitter cold facilitated character development in this story? *(Possible response: Battling the cold takes the narrator's mind off her troubles, allowing her to feel joy or hope that she hasn't felt in months.)*

Check Test

1. What is the narrator's problem as the story begins? *(She is suffering from clinical depression.)*

2. How does she plan to try to solve the problem? *(by going winter camping)*

3. Who accompanies her on a trip? *(her dogs, Jackson and Hailey)*

4. Where does she stay at night? *(in a snow cave)*

5. What challenge does she face during the night? *(The temperature is well below zero, and she sleeps outside.)*

Unit 8 Resource Book
Alternate Check Test, p. 61

BUILDING ENGLISH PROFICIENCY

Exploring Key Concepts

Students can consider the problems the woman faces and how her healing process begins. They may want to write ideas in two columns on a notebook page. One column can contain the physical challenges posed by camping in the life-threatening weather, as well as the ways she protects herself. The other column can contain notes about her mental challenge, combating depression, as well as the ways she breaks free of the depression.

• Students should note the fact that she could have died in the cold and can determine how various actions prevented that.

• Students also can decide how much she was in control at any point in the story. They should understand that she took the initiative in trying to combat depression. She did accept help from her dogs and Alex, and information from the doctor, but she was the agent of change, turning down the medication, going camping, and surviving.

933

After Reading

MAKING CONNECTIONS

1. Possible responses: No; she's not an experienced winter camper in the high country, and it's incredibly cold. Yes; she's an experienced camper, and it will be an adventure.

2. Possible responses: She is depressed but adventurous. She seems self-reliant, athletic, and cool-headed. She's a woman with a strong sense of the natural world's wonders.

3. Possible response: This story is about the character's frame of mind during her adventure. A first-person narrative engages us with her thoughts and feelings.

4. Possible response: As she coped with natural elements, the narrator was able to stop dwelling on her problems.

5. Possible response: It is believed that depression is caused by a chemical imbalance in the brain, and certain medications can help restore a proper balance.

Vocabulary Study

1. b. tin foil

2. a. comment

3. c. ending

4. b. modern

5. a. diamonds

 Unit 8 Resource Book
Vocabulary, p. 59
Vocabulary Test, p. 62

Selection Test

 Unit 8 Resource Book
pp. 63–64

934

After Reading

Making Connections

Shaping Your Response

1. If the main character had asked you to accompany her on her camping trip, would you have gone? Why or why not?

Analyzing the Story

2. Describe the narrator, the main **character** in the story.

3. Why do you think Houston chose a **first-person narrator?**

4. What was it about the winter camping trip that proved to be therapeutic for the narrator?

Extending the Ideas

5. What do you know about the causes and remedies of depression from sources in the mass media?

Vocabulary Study

Which item in the group following each vocabulary word is *least* related to the numbered word?

translucent
chastise
verge
primal
rampant

1. *translucent*   **a.** sunglasses   **b.** tin foil   **c.** stained glass

2. *chastise*   **a.** comment   **b.** scold   **c.** rebuke

3. *verge*   **a.** beginning   **b.** brink   **c.** ending

4. *primal*   **a.** ancient   **b.** modern   **c.** original

5. *rampant*   **a.** diamonds   **b.** rumors   **c.** epidemic

Expressing Your Ideas

Writing Choices

Writer's Notebook Update Using the phrases you wrote in your writer's notebook about your favorite season, write a prose description of your part of the country during that season.

Wish You Were Here Write **postcard messages** that the narrator might have sent to her housemate, her therapist, and her ex-boyfriend.

Other Options

Sunny and Cold You are the meteorologist for a Salt Lake City television station. Prepare a **weather report** for the nightly news show predicting the weather for the day the narrator is to leave on her camping trip. Videotape your weather report and present it to the class.

Brrr! Research winter camping and present an **oral report** explaining any special supplies or clothing that winter campers need. Also, explain the dangers involved in winter camping.

WRITING CHOICES
Writer's Notebook Update

Suggest that students put the phrases into categories. Before writing, students can imagine strolling in the places that they will describe. Suggest that they prepare brief outlines for their sketches.

Wish You Were Here

In order to capture the tone of a post card—breezy, vivid and upbeat—have students contrast it with the tone of an answering-machine message or a formal letter.

OTHER OPTIONS
Sunny and Cold

Alternately, students can research and present a report on the GOES satellite launched into orbit in April 1994. How has this satellite advanced weather prediction?

Brrr!

Students might talk to knowledgable personnel in a store that sells camping supplies or they can compare the equipment of a winter camper from the 1950s to that of a winter camper today.

Before Reading

The Janitor

by August Wilson

August Wilson
born 1945

When August Wilson was sixteen he was accused of passing off his sister's schoolwork as his own. He left school and never returned. Wilson continued his education independently at the local library while holding various jobs to support himself. During this time he began writing poetry. In 1968 he founded the Black Horizons Theatre Company in St. Paul, Minnesota. He describes himself as "a cultural nationalist . . . trying to raise consciousness through theater." In 1982 Wilson wrote his first play, *Jitney,* and others followed, including *Ma Rainey's Black Bottom* (1985), *Fences* (1986), *Joe Turner's Come and Gone* (1988), *The Piano Lesson* (1990), and *Two Trains Running* (1992).

Building Background

Expert Advice If you were to attend a National Conference on Youth, which of these experts would you like to see on the program, and what topic would you like to hear each discuss? Copy a chart like the following into your writer's notebook and fill it in. In which three topics and experts are you and your classmates most interested?

Expert	Topic
teacher	
psychologist	
athletic coach	
doctor	
parent	
police officer	
other (specify)	

Literary Focus

Allusion A reference to a person, thing, event, or aspect of culture is called an allusion. Allusions may be drawn from art, myth, literature, history, religion, or any other aspect of culture. Can you explain the allusions in these sentences?

- Carl thought he was another Babe Ruth when he stepped up to the plate.
- My chemistry teacher has a Jekyll-Hyde personality.
- It's hotter than Hades in here!

Writer's Notebook

America's Youth If you could give a five-minute speech that would be heard by young people all across America, what would you say? Write your ideas in your notebook.

The Janitor **935**

Before Reading

Building Background

Professionals in different fields may see young people in different lights. Ask students how they think these people may view youth: a teacher, an athletic coach, a psychologist, a parent, and a police officer.

Literary Focus

Allusions in literary works usually refer to people or things that many readers (or theatergoers) will recognize.

Responses to Question

- Babe Ruth was a famous baseball hitter.
- Jekyll and Hyde are parts of a schizophrenic character in a novel by Robert Louis Stevenson.
- Hades is the hellish underworld in Greek mythology.

Writer's Notebook

Suggest that students decide what main idea or main points the speech would make.

More About August Wilson

Wilson has set various plays in different decades of the twentieth century. His plays have been acclaimed as a dramatic history of key parts of African American culture.

SUPPORT MATERIALS OVERVIEW

Unit 8 Resource Book
- Graphic Organizer, p. 65
- Study Guide, p. 66
- Vocabulary, p. 67
- Grammar, p. 68
- Alternate Check Test, p. 69
- Vocabulary Test, p. 70
- Selection Test, pp. 71–72

Building English Proficiency
- Literature Summaries
- Activities, p. 241

Reading, Writing & Grammar Skillbook
- Reading, pp. 100–103
- Grammar, Usage, and Mechanics, pp. 244–248

Technology
- Audiotape
- Personal Journal Software
- Custom Literature Database
  For a selection with thematic connections, see John F. Kennedy's Inaugural Address on the database.
- Test Generator Software

Selection Objectives

- To consider themes concerning youth and age
- To understand the meaning of allusions
- To recognize parallel construction

 Unit 8 Resource Book
Graphic Organizer, p. 65
Study Guide, p. 66

Theme Link

A janitor imagines himself giving a speech about youth and the future. He speaks of change and opportunities, poignantly exploring the theme.

Vocabulary Preview

lectern, a reading desk or stand, such as the kind used by speakers

literacy, ability to read and write

rife, full; abounding

resilience, power of springing back; elasticity

reap, to gather a crop

Students can add the words and definitions to their Writer's Notebooks.

1 Literary Focus

Allusion

The janitor's speech contains several allusions.

- The paraphrased line from Shakespeare may refer to Juliet's comment in *Romeo and Juliet,* Act III, Scene 2: "I am not I, if there be such an I." Other Shakespearean characters such as Hamlet also distinguish themselves from who they seem to be.

- Sam's remark about a river paraphrases a famous quotation from the Greek philosopher Heraclitus: "You cannot step twice into the same river, for other waters are ever flowing upon you."

- Jacob, in Genesis (in the Bible), dreamt that he wrestled an angel and was beaten, but bargained for a blessing to secure his future.

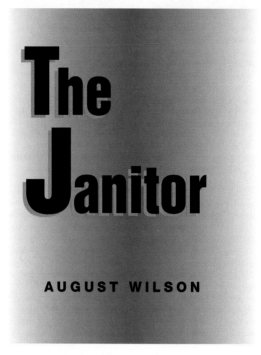

The Janitor

AUGUST WILSON

A hotel ballroom. Sam enters, pushing a broom near the lectern.[1] He stops and reads the sign hanging across the ballroom.

Sam. NATIONAL . . . CONFERENCE . . . ON . . . YOUTH. *(He nods his approval and continues sweeping. He gets an idea, stops, and approaches the lectern. He clears his throat and begins to speak. His speech is delivered with the literacy[2] of a janitor. He chooses his ideas carefully. He is a man who has approached life honestly, with both eyes open.)* I want to thank you all for inviting me here to speak about youth. See . . . I's fifty-six years old and I knows something about youth. The first thing I knows . . . is that youth is sweet before flight . . . its odor is rife[3] with speculation, and its resilience[4]—that means bounce back— is remarkable. But it's that sweetness that we victims of. All of us. Its sweetness . . . and its flight. One of them fellows in that

Shakespeare stuff said, "I'm not what I am." See. He wasn't like Popeye. This fellow had a different understanding. "I am not what I am." Well, neither are you. You are just what you have been . . . whatever you are now. But what you are now ain't what you gonna become . . . even though it is with you now . . . it's inside you now this instant. Time . . . see, this is how you get to this . . . Time ain't changed. It's just moved. Or maybe it ain't moved . . . maybe it just changed. It don't matter. We are all victims of the sweetness of youth and the time of its flight.

See . . . just like you I forgot who I am. I forgot what happened first. But I know the river I step into now . . . is not the same river I stepped into twenty years ago. See, I know that much. But I have forgotten the name of the river . . . I have forgotten the name of the gods . . . and like everybody else I have tried to fool them with my dancing . . . and guess at their faces. It's the same with everybody. We don't have to mention no names. Ain't nobody innocent. We are all victims of ourselves. We have all had our hand in the soup . . . and made the music play just so.

See now . . . this is what I call wrestling with Jacob's angel. You lay down at night and that angel come to wrestle with you. When you wrestling with that angel, you bargaining for your future. See. And what you need to bargain with is that sweetness of youth. So . . . to the youth of the United States I says . . . don't spend that sweetness too fast! 'Cause you gonna need it. See. I's fifty-six years old and I done found that out. But it's all the same. It all comes back on you . . . just like sowing

---

1. **lectern** (lek′tərn), *n.* a reading desk or stand.
2. **literacy** (lit′ər ə sē), *n.* ability to read and write.
3. **rife** (rīf), *adj.* full; abounding.
4. **resilience** (ri zil′ē əns), *n.* power of springing back; resilient quality or nature; elasticity.

MINI-LESSON: GRAMMAR

Parallel Construction

Teach Parallel ideas can be clearly expressed in parallel forms. Parallel structures in sentences or paragraphs include gerunds with other gerunds, as in the end of the janitor's comment: *It all comes back on you . . . just like sowing and reaping.*

Sam uses parallel structure when he says, ". . . the river I step into now . . . is not the same river I stepped into twenty years ago."

Activity Ideas

- Students can identify other examples of parallel phrasing in the play.

- Students can write sentences that are not parallel (such as: *The janitor has already started to mop the floor and clean the windows.*) Ask other students to rewrite the sentences using parallel structure.

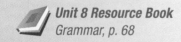 **Unit 8 Resource Book**
Grammar, p. 68

2 Literary Elements

Character and Allusion

This janitor must be well-read, judging from his allusions to traditional literature and lore.

Question How does Sam's speech, with allusions to scriptural figures such as the angel Gabriel and to other literature, contrast with many people's stereotypes about janitors? (*Possible answer: Most people don't consider janitors learned, but he thinks of ideas from classical works, religion, and philosophy.*)

Check Test

1. What event is about to take place in the ballroom? (*The National Conference On Youth*)

2. What does Sam stop to do instead of sweeping? (*give a speech about youth*)

3. What does Sam consider the primary characteristic of youth? (*its sweetness, which does not last a long time*)

4. Who does Sam feel is responsible if you find yourself "down and out"? (*yourself*)

5. What is the response to Sam's comments? (*His boss tells him to get back to work.*)

 Unit 8 Resource Book Alternate Check Test, p. 69

⌃ What personality traits would you say artist Hubert Shuptrine has captured in his 1976 painting, *Study of Williams?*

and reaping.[5] Down and out ain't nothing but being caught up in the balance of what you put down. If you down and out and things ain't going right for you . . . you can bet you done put down a payment on your troubles. Now you got to pay up on the balance. That's as true as I'm standing here. Sometimes you can't see it like that. The last note on Gabriel's horn always gets lost when you get to realizing you done heard the first. **2** So, it's just like—

Mr. Collins (*entering*). Come on, Sam . . . let's quit wasting time and get this floor swept. There's going to be a big important meeting here this afternoon.

Sam. Yessuh, Mr. Collins. Yessuh. (*He goes back to sweeping, as the lights go down to black.*)

---

5. **reap** (rēp), *v.* to gather a crop.

The Janitor **937**

BUILDING ENGLISH PROFICIENCY

Making Cultural Connections

Ask students to consider whether Sam's urge to share his ideas represents a universal desire to pass along one's knowledge of life.

- Ask students if adult relatives or other people have shared wisdom about life with them. Students can comment, either orally or in journals, about the knowledge shared and its usefulness.

- Invite students to consider how old they think a person must be to have enough

experience of life to pass it on to a younger generation.

- Ask students which famous (or not famous) people they would ask for advice about life.

Building English Proficiency Activities, p. 241

For summaries of the play in English and other languages, see the Building English Proficiency Book.

After Reading

MAKING CONNECTIONS

1. Sample responses: Do you have regrets about the path you've taken? If you could have any job, what would it be?

2. Possible responses: Sam is a survivor. He is wise, but he doesn't get many chances to share what he has learned.

3. Possible responses: The loneliness; the people who won't hear his ideas

4. Possible responses: Life is in constant change; nothing remains the same.

5. Possible responses: He might advise Salvador to hang in there while caring for his brothers, make some friends, and learn. He might advise Donny to return home and keep away from the troubles of adult life while he is young.

LITERARY FOCUS: ALLUSION

Students may these resources:

- Books such as *Who's Who in the Bible?*, edited by Peter Calvocoressi (Grossman, 1988) and *Familiar Quotations* by John Bartlett, Sixteenth Edition edited by Justin Kaplan (Little, Brown, 1992)
- Concordances to the Bible and to the plays of Shakespeare, available in print and multimedia formats
- Encyclopedia articles, including entries on Heraclitus

VOCABULARY STUDY

1. rife   **4.** resilience

2. literacy   **5.** reap

3. lectern

Unit 8 Resource Book
Vocabulary, p. 67
Vocabulary Test, p. 70

Selection Test

Unit 8 Resource Book
p. 71–72

Transparency Collection
Fine Art Writing Prompt 14

938

After Reading

Making Connections

Shaping Your Response

1. If you had heard Sam speak, what questions would you want to ask him?

Analyzing the Story

2. **Characterize** Sam, the main character in this play.

3. Sam speaks to an empty ballroom. What do you think the empty ballroom might **symbolize,** if anything?

4. What do you think Sam means when he says, " . . . the river I step into now is not the river I stepped into twenty years ago"?

Extending the Ideas

5. What advice do you think Sam might give to Salvador of "Salvador Late or Early" or Donny from "Teenage Wasteland"?

Literary Focus: Allusion

Sam's speech is rich with **allusions.** Working in groups, find the allusions that he uses and try to track down their sources.

Vocabulary Study

lectern
literacy
reap
resilience
rife

Complete the paragraph using the listed vocabulary words.

Sam, the janitor, is __(1)__ with ideas he would like to express to today's youth. Although his __(2)__ level is not as high as other experts on youth, when he approaches the __(3)__ and speaks to the empty auditorium, his wisdom begins to show. He emphasizes that the __(4)__ of youth does not last forever, and that what one sows in one's youth, one will __(5)__ in later life.

Expressing Your Ideas

Writing Choices

Writer's Notebook Update Reread your ideas for the speech to America's youth from your writer's notebook. Is there anything you would like to add or delete after reflecting on the topic? After organizing your thoughts, write a speech about youth to deliver to your class.

Stop and Reflect How do you feel about your youth? Is it as sweet as Sam says it is? Reflect on what you treasure about your youth and what aspects of youth you are anxious to leave behind. Write a **journal entry** reflecting your thoughts.

WRITING CHOICES
Writer's Notebook Update

Suggest to students that, when delivering a speech, many speakers use notes but do not read from a fully prepared text or memorize the speech. Students may want to videotape their speeches.

Stop and Reflect

Students also may want to interview family members and friends, asking them in what way they felt their youth is or was sweet. Some students may want to keep their journal entries private.

American Voices Today

A Glimpse Into the Future

Futurist Connection

As we begin a new millennium, America's eyes are turned toward the future. What will life be like as the twenty-first century progresses? The following pages explore possibilities for America's future, both serious and frivolous.

African Americans
Their ranks will almost double, from 32 million to 62 million.

Hispanics
Their numbers will more than triple, from 24 million to 81 million.

THE WAY WE WILL BE

By midcentury [the year 2050], seemingly small changes in birth, immigration, and mortality rates will have changed dramatically the way America looks. Here's a preview:

Age
The median age will climb from 33.4 years to 39.3, and senior citizens will make up almost 21 percent of the population, compared with just 13 percent today. Americans also will live longer than today's average of 75.8 years. A baby born in 2050 can expect to be around for 82.1 years.

Population
In the United States, it will have grown from 255 million to 383 million. World population will nearly double to 10 billion, from 5.6 billion today.

Whites
Their numbers will remain roughly the same, rising from 191 million now to 202 million in 2050, but they will drop from 75 percent of the population to just 53 percent.

Asians
The fastest-growing group by far, they will jump from 8.5 million to 41 million.

939

Interdisciplinary Study

Theme Link

By knowing our past, and understanding our present, perhaps we can predict what America will look like tomorrow.

Curricular Connection: Futurist

You can use the information in this interdisciplinary study to help students think seriously and frivolously about life in the future.

Terms to Know

biometric (bi⁄o met⁄rik) biological statistic or measurement

psychotherapeutic (si⁄ko ther⁄ə pyü⁄tik), of the treatment of mental or emotional disorders by psychological means

sanctuary (sang⁄chü er⁄e), a place of refuge or protection

annihilation (ə ni⁄ə la⁄shən), complete destruction

Unit 8 Resource Book
Interdisciplinary Study Guide, p. 73

BUILDING ENGLISH PROFICIENCY

Responding to Information

Encourage students to use their dialogue journals to respond to details that catch their attention. For example, in the left-hand column of a t-chart, they could summarize predictions or note details. In the right-hand column, they could comment or ask questions. Suggest to students that the comments and notes in their journals will help them participate in class discussion, respond to the article, and enhance their original writing.

Summaries/Details	My Response
By 2050, almost 21 percent of Americans will be senior citizens.	Hey! By then, I'll be a senior citizen!

ESL
LEP
ELD
SAE
LD

Art Study

In 1962 came *The Jetsons,* which placed George Jetson, his wife Jane, his teenage daughter Judy, and his son Elroy, with their dog Astro in an unidentified future time. A robot helps them with their housework, and all kinds of wonderful high-tech gadgets attempt, but often fail, to make their lives easier.

The Jetsons, a cartoon first aired in the early 1960s, is still popular today in reruns. It features a family living in the distant future, whose lives are surrounded by technological wonders. ➤

FUTURE TECHNOLOGY

DREAM OR NIGHTMARE?

One thing's nearly certain about the future: technology will advance by leaps and bounds. Will technology help us solve present problems, and make our lives easier and more comfortable? Or will it exacerbate our problems and add new ones we haven't yet imagined? The following articles discuss the advantages and drawbacks of life in a technological age.

Waking Up in 2025: A Scenario

It is November 28, 2025: You wake up at 7 A.M. and your biometric bed checks your vital signs. "The old blood pressure is a little high this morning, my friend," the bed warns in a soothing tone. You step into the shower, and the showerhead automatically adjusts from your father-in-law's 6-foot, 4-inch, 240-pound frame to your slimmer body; the spray is rousingly forceful. You listen attentively as the shower room's personal information system reports on the overnight stock activity from Tokyo. As the shower douses you with antibacterial suds, you ask the information system for a quick personality assessment from the psychotherapeutic expert system you installed. "Hey, relax! Try to image a sun-drenched beach," you're advised. "You'll be able to handle that marketing presentation much better."

You smile, thinking about the fun you had on your last vacation in Hawaii as the shower's heat jet blasts you dry. The robotic closet-valet brings out your color-coordinated, temperature-sensitive business suit, and you quickly dress. As you leave your bedroom, you sense the temperature going down behind you and the lights turning off automatically.

You peek into the kids' room to make sure they've transmitted their homework to school and have gotten dressed for their teleclass, which they "attend" for three hours in your home's media room during what used to be a long Thanksgiving holiday.

You are now ready to face an average workday in the twenty-first century.

MINI-LESSON: SPEAKING AND LISTENING

Reading Aloud for the Class

Teach Remind students that in a classroom setting, when reading aloud from a textbook, the reader needs to convey information to the entire class at once in a way that is clear, accurate, and true to the author's meaning. To prepare for reading aloud, the reader should

- search the text for difficult words
- check the author's tone
- understand the main idea of the paragraphs
- read in a moderately loud voice, enunciating clearly.

Activity Idea Ask volunteers to read aloud a portion of the text on pages 940–941. Allow students only a few moments for preparation. After they read, have them review the strategies they used, and discuss how they might revise their strategies for future application.

The Armored Cocoon

As the world grows more complicated, stressful, and dangerous, we are turning our homes into bunkers, cozy sanctuaries in which we can set up alarm systems, pull down the blinds, and imagine ourselves safe from the threats outside. A man's home was once his castle; today it has become an armored cocoon.

Technology has made this retreat from reality possible. A telephone call brings nearly all the essentials of life—from footwear to pizza—right to our doorstep. Computer games and home video supply entertainment on demand. Now a new technology, virtual reality, could send us ever deeper into our cocoons—or inspire us to emerge, like butterflies, and explore the world.

Virtual reality's power lies in its ability to simulate an alternative universe. The tiny monitors inside a virtual reality helmet depict three-dimensional computer graphics of a landscape that shifts as you turn your head. Sophisticated hand controls let you move about and manipulate objects in this artificial world. Virtual reality allows users to immerse themselves in environs they might never otherwise visit—or which exist only in the mind of a software designer. Armchair adventurers can explore the ocean bottom or visit an imaginary planet, and risk nothing more than eye strain.

The danger is that, as conditions outside our windows worsen, virtual reality may seem more appealing than reality itself. Why spend hundreds of dollars per family member to visit the Grand Canyon—fighting crowds of pushy tourists and spending the night in a grungy motel—when a computer will create a clean, quiet Virtual Canyon in the comfort of your humble abode? Especially when the computerized version lets you adjust the canyon's color scheme to suit your personal tastes? Virtual reality gives us another excuse to stay home, thereby depriving us of the social interactions that are so vital to our humanity.

Even if virtual reality doesn't supplant the physical world, it may well divert us from solving real world problems. Many of us have become addicted to video games; virtual reality's realism could make it the technological equivalent of a narcotic. We can't save the environment or fight crime if we're constantly donning a helmet and escaping to another universe.

Of course, any technological development has both positive and negative impacts. Nuclear weapons threaten us with unprecedented annihilation, but fear of their use has probably prevented several bloody conventional wars from occurring. Millions of us let our minds atrophy in front of the boob tube each night—but television also brings us valuable news shows and documentaries.

Perhaps instead of isolating us from the outside world, virtual reality will stimulate our imaginations. It is easy to think of intriguing educational applications for this technology. Instead of describing the French Revolution to school kids, we will be able to take them to 18th century Paris and let them experience it "firsthand." In college physics classes, a virtual Albert Einstein might teach relativity. Used as a mental launching pad, virtual reality might inspire us to climb off our couch and see the world—to break out of our armored cocoon.

At NASA Ames, scientist Rick Jacoby controls the movements of a virtual robot.

BUILDING ENGLISH PROFICIENCY

Checking Comprehension

As the article's main title suggests, virtual reality has advantages and disadvantages. Have groups of students evaluate their understanding by listing as many reasons as they can on either side of the argument.

- Have students organize the article's ideas into a two-column chart.
- Have students use the information in their charts to answer the question, "Do you think virtual reality is an 'armored cocoon'? Why or why not?"

Virtual Reality	
Advantages	**Disadvantages**
allows people to explore the world	people will prefer the virtual world to living in the real one
helps people be better informed	diverts us from trying to solve world problems

- Students working in small groups can review several current issues of high-tech magazines, such as *Wired*, to find out what the future looks like to the magazine editors.
- Students can use U.S. Bureau of the Census data to chart the statistics of ethnic group populations in the United States.
- Students can do an ethnographic study of their classmates. Suggest that they first devise a survey that elicits the information they want, such as ethnic group and ethnic group of parents and grandparents, number of years in the United States, other countries lived in, and so on. Students should then distribute their survey, and then collect, collate, and report their data.

Although Paris was the center of the fashion industry from the fourteenth century to the mid-twentieth century, since the 1960s, Britain, Italy, the United States, and Japan have made inroads into Paris's grip on the industry. Notable American designers include James Galanos, Rudi Gernreich, Halston, Adolfo, Perry Ellis, Calvin Klein, and Donna Karan.

Future Fashions

On the lighter side of the future, what will Americans be wearing by the middle of the 2000s? Film director Tim Burton and designer Donna Karan were asked to imagine what the fashion of the future might look like. The following are their visions of tomorrow's fashions.

Donna Karan believes that in the future clothing will merge with communications. "The future of fashion will focus on technology— in fabric and personal electronics," she says. Her basic "catsuit" clothing design, made of course from the latest temperature-sensitive fabrics, are enhanced by high-tech accessories, including an "info-wrist" that contains both a Filofax and a videophone.

SOLAR BAND

UNI

THERMAL CATSUIT

INFO--WRIST

MINI-LESSON: VISUAL LITERACY

Information through Illustration

Teach The illustrations on pages 942–943 provide information and convey the artist's vision of life in the future through the use of graphics, caption, and labels.

Activity Idea Have students create their own diagrams showing their ideas about how clothing will look in the future. Their approach may be serious or tongue-in-cheek. Encourage them to use captions, labels, arrows, and other methods to make their ideas clear to their readers.

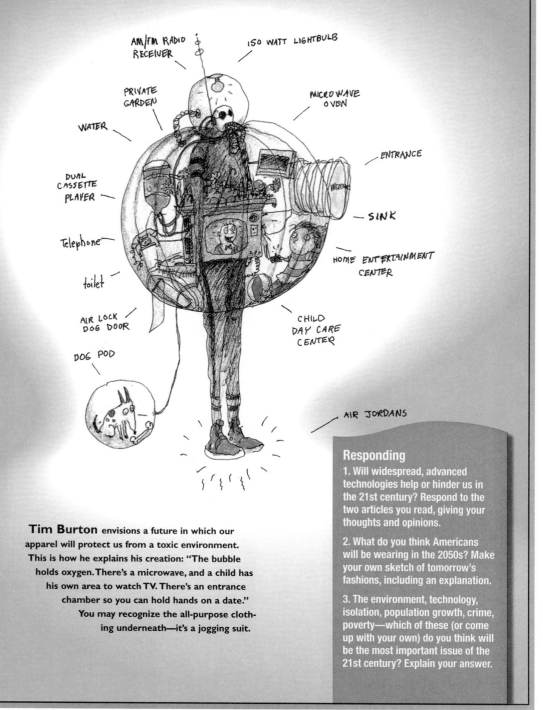

AM/FM RADIO RECEIVER

150 WATT LIGHTBULB

PRIVATE GARDEN

MICROWAVE OVEN

WATER

ENTRANCE

DUAL CASSETTE PLAYER

WELCOME

SINK

Telephone

HOME ENTERTAINMENT CENTER

toilet

AIR LOCK DOG DOOR

CHILD DAY CARE CENTER

DOG POD

AIR JORDANS

Tim Burton envisions a future in which our apparel will protect us from a toxic environment. This is how he explains his creation: "The bubble holds oxygen. There's a microwave, and a child has his own area to watch TV. There's an entrance chamber so you can hold hands on a date." You may recognize the all-purpose clothing underneath—it's a jogging suit.

Responding

1. Will widespread, advanced technologies help or hinder us in the 21st century? Respond to the two articles you read, giving your thoughts and opinions.

2. What do you think Americans will be wearing in the 2050s? Make your own sketch of tomorrow's fashions, including an explanation.

3. The environment, technology, isolation, population growth, crime, poverty—which of these (or come up with your own) do you think will be the most important issue of the 21st century? Explain your answer.

Additional Background

Tim Burton directed the movies *Beetlejuice* (1988), *Edward Scissorhands* (1990), *Batman* (1989), and *Batman Returns* (1992).

Responding

1. **Possible Response**   Technology will help or hinder us depending on how we use it. If we allow it to control us and take over our lives, it will hinder us. Not every new technology may be of equal service. We need to take the time to sort through what's available and decide what serves our needs and what wastes our time.

2. Responses will vary. Encourage creativity.

3. Responses will vary, but should include a clear and fact-supported opinion.

BUILDING ENGLISH PROFICIENCY

ESL
LEP
ELD
SAE
LD

Exploring a Theme

Both future fashions pictured on these pages combine a sense of style with convenience or practicality. Invite students to take a closer look at this combination.

• Have students write or dictate a head-to-toe description of one of the designs as if it were being presented in a fashion show. Suggest that their commentary include ways in which the fashion will make the wearer's life easier.

• Have students examine the details in Tim Burton's "bubble" design and then think about their own daily activities. Ask students to design a "bubble suit," to fit their lifestyles.

• Ask students to imagine that a futuristic movie will feature this clothing as costumes. Invite them to propose a title and plot outline for the film.

Interdisciplinary Study

Theme Link

Information today can help us predict and plan for a future that is based on realistic expectations.

Curricular Connection: Career

You can use the information in this interdisciplinary study to explore with students how statistical research can help us understand the changes we see today and plan for the future.

Responding

Possible Response   Students may discuss opportunities and experiences they have had as a direct result of cultural diversity. They may also discuss instances of prejudice and bias that have affected them.

Career Connection

How will increasing cultural diversity affect American society? Raul José Lopez has a unique perspective on this question. As Senior Vice President and Director of Syndicated Research at Strategy Research Corporation in Miami, Lopez has made it his career to keep tabs on the diverse Spanish-speaking peoples known as Hispanic Americans, who, combined, make up one of the fastest-growing groups in the United States.

Most immigrant groups in the past have been quickly absorbed into the 'melting pot' of America, but this phenomenon has not had the same influence on Hispanics. Many factors are responsible for this, including the proximity of the countries of origin, the increasing ease of communication and travel, the availability of media outlets (television, radio, magazines, and newspapers) in Spanish, and an increased focus on racial and ethnic pride in the United States in general.

The Changing Face of America

by Raul José Lopez

According to projections of the U.S. Bureau of the Census, Hispanic Americans will become the largest minority group in the United States, surpassing the Non-Hispanic Black population around the year 2006. By the year 2010 Hispanics will represent 13.5 percent of the total U.S. population, and by the year 2050, the total combined minorities of Hispanics, Non-Hispanic Blacks, and Asians will represent nearly half of the total population. Thus, by 2050 nearly one out of every two people in the United States will be a member of a minority group.

I have personally seen the changes here in Miami, a city with over 1.3 million Hispanics. When I went to high school, the ethnic mix in my school was roughly 35% Black, 35% Hispanic, and 30% White Non-Hispanic. That same high school today is 65% Hispanic, 25% Black, and 10% White Non-Hispanic.

The changes in the population have led to lifestyle changes for persons living in markets with large Hispanic populations. Bilingualism has become a virtual necessity rather than a simple advantage. The interaction of the cultures has seen both English and Spanish incorporate new words. Many Hispanic American children and teens in Miami speak a combination of both languages. Further, the mixing of the cultures has affected many lifestyle factors including the food people eat, the way people dress, and their forms of entertainment.

Responding

How has cultural diversity affected your life—in education, food, dress, entertainment, personal relationships, or other ways? List as many instances as you can in which America's cultural diversity has touched your life.

944

MINI-LESSON: STUDY SKILLS

Graphing Statistics

Teach   The statistical information in "The Changing Face of America" can also be presented in a table or a graph.

2050

total U.S. population   minority population

Activity Idea   Have students translate the ethnic statistics about Mr. Lopez's Miami high school into two tables or graphs.

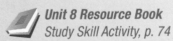

Unit 8 Resource Book
Study Skill Activity, p. 74

Language History

Computerese

 Although some grammarians undoubtedly abhor the use of the word *interface* as a verb, nowadays it's quite common to hear that people who don't get on well with each other don't interface as they should.

This observation, in a recent article by computer expert Edward Swart, suggests the extent to which our language has been affected by computers. The term *computerese* refers to the technical vocabulary and other jargon used by people who work with computers. This term dates from the latter half of the 1950s. In the last 50 years, this word and hundreds of others associated with computers have become part of American English.

One of the strengths of the English language is the ease with which it accommodates new words. In the 400 years since the first English speakers arrived in the Western Hemisphere American English has absorbed words from a great variety of sources: American Indian languages (see page 45), the foreign languages spoken by successive waves of immigrants (page 422), dialect and slang (page 624), government, the military (page 851), science and technology, fine art, and popular culture. One major recent source of new words for American English has been the computer.

Many of these words are used largely by people working with computers and are first employed generally in their technical senses. These words include such terms as *hypertext, cursor, database, download, hard drive, internet,* and *modem.* However, as computers assume an ever larger role in people's lives, the language associated with them comes into ever more general use in contexts that have nothing to do with computers, as Swart notes above.

Language History **945**

Language History

Teaching Objectives
- To recognize that the English language continues to develop and change
- To be aware of the adoption of computerese into our everyday language

Introduce

Ask students to name some expressions that are new to English in the past thirty years. You may wish to get them started with words such as *HIV, Internet, powerbook,* and *online.*

Point out that there are new terms in English that originate in computer technology. Then have students read the article.

Follow Up

Divide students into small groups, and challenge them to come up with more examples of computerese that have entered general English. Have groups compare and revise their lists.

CONTENT AREA READING

Keeping Up-to-Date

Encourage students to read and bring to class an article or a software or equipment review from a computer user's magazine such as *Macworld* or the technology section of a news magazine such as *Time Magazine.* Ask students to write a brief summary of the article and share the information with the class.

Writing Workshop

WRITER'S BLUEPRINT
Specs

The Specs in the Writer's Blueprint address these writing and thinking skills:

- analyzing character
- drawing conclusions
- making judgments
- using poetic format
- comparing and contrasting
- using figurative language for dramatic effect
- avoiding careless spelling errors

These Specs serve as your lesson objectives, and they form the basis for the **Assessment Criteria Specs** for a superior paper, which appear on the final TE page for this lesson. You might want to read through the Assessment Criteria Specs with students when you begin the lesson.

Linking Literature to Writing

Lead a discussion in which students talk about the characters in the literature in this part of the unit.

STEP 1 PREWRITING
Choose a character

For additional support, see the worksheet referenced below.

Unit 8 Resource Book
Prewriting Worksheet, p. 75

Citizens of Tomorrow

Narrative Writing

Writing Workshop

Poetic Insights

Assignment Among the characters in this part of the unit, which one stands out for you? Which one moves you most, interests you most? Answer these questions with a poem.

WRITER'S BLUEPRINT

Product   A poem
Purpose   To gain insight into a character
Audience   People who have read the literature
Specs   As the writer of a successful poem, you should:

❑ Choose a character from the literature you feel strongly about and write a poem about him or her.

❑ Imagine that this character could somehow read your finished poem. In it, try to give this character some real insight into his or her true self. You don't have to address the poem directly to the character ("You . . ."), but you might.

❑ Use either free verse or rhyme, whichever works best for you.

❑ Use imagery and figures of speech to dramatize your insights.

❑ Use punctuation suitable for the kind of poem you're writing. Make sure everything is spelled correctly.

OR . . .
Discuss these characters with a partner or small group. Listen to their choices and to their reactions to your choices. Use what you learn to help you choose the character you'll be focusing on.

STEP 1 PREWRITING

Choose a character. Review the literature in this part of the unit and choose three characters who stand out for you. Take a few minutes and jot down what it is about each character that makes him or her stand out. When you finish, look over your notes and choose the character who interests you most.

WRITING WORKSHOP OVERVIEW

Product
Narrative writing: A poem

Prewriting
Choose a character—Profile your character—Make comparisons—Try a quickwrite—Plan your poem
Unit 8 Resource Book
Prewriting Worksheets pp. 75–76

Drafting
Start writing
Transparency Collection
Student Models for Writing Workshop 27, 28

Revising
Exchange drafts—Strategy: Using Imagery and Figures of Speech
Unit 8 Resource Book
Revising Worksheet p. 77

Editing
Ask a partner—Strategy: Avoiding Careless Spelling Mistakes
Unit 8 Resource Book
Grammar Worksheet p. 78
Grammar Check Test p. 79

Presenting
Poetry Portrait
Cover Sheet

Looking Back
Self-evaluate—Reflect—For Your Working Portfolio
Unit 8 Resource Book
Assessment Worksheet p. 80
Transparency Collection
Fine Art Writing Prompt 14

Profile your character. Go back over the selection in which your character appears and take insightful notes on him or her. Use an outline like the one shown. For your character you may want to use a different set of categories. These categories will occur to you as you review the selection. Look for quotes from the selection to illustrate your insights.

Pam Houston from "A Blizzard Under Blue Sky"

- **Skills, Strengths**
  —sensitive, a sharp observer of life: Hailey's body "seems in constant indecision when she runs"
  —resourceful: knows little about snow caves but builds one herself
  and so on . . .

- **Problems, Weaknesses**
  —"When everything in your life is uncertain"
  —"The doctor said I was clinically depressed."
  and so on . . .

- **Likes**
  —"the natural world" because it "gives you what's good for you"
  —her two dogs, Jackson and Hailey
  and so on . . .

- **Dislikes**
  —the everyday, workaday world that deeply depresses her
  and so on . . .

Make comparisons to supply yourself with ideas for imagery and figures of speech you might use in your poem. Finish a sentence like this one for each of the boldfaced words and phrases, and for any other people, places, or things that might lead to vivid, lively comparisons:

If (my character) were a _____ (he, she) would be _____ because _____.

> **emotion, time of day, season, piece of furniture, jewel, plant, song, body of water, color, building**

For example: If Pam were an animal, she would be a butterfly because during her camping trip she emerges from her cocoon of depression.

Try a quickwrite. First, look over your comparisons and character profile and circle the ten words or phrases that stand out most. Then write for five minutes about your character, focusing on as many of your circled items as you have time for. Write quickly, getting your ideas down as fast as they come to you. On the next page is part of one student's quickwrite.

> **OR . . .**
> In addition to making comparisons, design a coat of arms with images and symbols (animals, flowers, colors, designs, etc.) that you feel reflect the essence of your character.

Profile your character

Suggest that students start by using the categories given. If a category doesn't apply to their character, have them add another category. They should develop four or five categories before they begin their poems. For additional support, see the worksheet referenced below.

Unit 8 Resource Book
Prewriting Worksheet, p. 76

Make comparisons

On the board, write one of the boldfaced words and the name of a character from the selections. Ask student volunteers to write five ideas for imagery and figures of speech on the board. Allow time for class discussion.

Try a quickwrite

Remind students that during a quickwrite, they should keep your pen moving—even if it is to write "I can't think of anything to say"—until a thought comes along. Have them write thoughts as they come without paying attention to organization.

BUILDING ENGLISH PROFICIENCY

Choosing Poetic Ideas

If students seem overwhelmed by the requirement to be poetic, offer them the option of creating a found poem.

1. Ask students to review and add to journal entries made about the chosen poem.

2. Have students tear a sheet of notebook paper into ten pieces. On each piece, have them write a phrase from their notes about the character.

3. After students experiment with and choose an order for their notes, ask them to copy the notes onto a single sheet of paper.

4. Have students share and comment upon the found poems.

Plan your poem

Have students plan whether they will use rhyme or free verse in their initial drafts. Assure them that their plans are flexible: it is in the writing itself that this particular decision begins to unfold.

Connections to Writer's Notebook

For selection-related prompts, refer to Writer's Notebook.

Connections to Writer's Resource

For additional writing prompts, refer to Writer's Resource.

STEP 2 DRAFTING
The Student Models

The **transparencies** referenced below are authentic student models. Review them with the students before they draft. These questions will help:

1. Evaluate model 27 on each point of the Writer's Blueprint, from 6 (superior) to 1 (inadequate).

2. The writer obviously made some mistakes in the third-from-last stanza in model 28. See if you can rewrite it so it makes sense.

3. Find examples of imagery and figures of speech in the two models that help give insights into the characters.

Transparency Collection
Student Models for Writing
Workshop 27, 28

STEP 3 REVISING
Exchange drafts (Peer assessment)

Suggest that partners meet after revising one another's drafts for a discussion. Allow them to help each other in any weak areas of their poems.

948

> Donny is a mess. He is a candle burning at both ends. On one end he feels burned. Hurt. On the other end, he burns others. Hurts them. And all the while he hurts himself. He keeps thinking that other people are somehow responsible for his problems. He can't seem to see that his biggest enemy is himself.

> STUDENT MODEL

Plan your poem. Look back at your prewriting materials and jot down answers to these questions:

✔ What are some important words and phrases I'll want to focus on?

✔ What are some images and figures of speech I might use?

✔ What shape will my poem take? Will I break it into stanzas?

✔ Will I use rhyme or free verse?

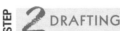

STEP **2** DRAFTING

Start writing. Concentrate on getting your ideas down on paper. Use your prewriting materials as guides. Here are some drafting tips.

- Don't forget that your primary objective is to give insight into your character's true self.

- Be vivid and specific. Use imagery and figures of speech to lift your writing from the ordinary and everyday to the extraordinary and poetic. See the Revising Strategy in Step 3 of this lesson.

- When you finish, look back at what you've written and give your poem an appropriate title.

STEP **3** REVISING

Exchange drafts with a partner before you revise. Mark the words, phrases, and figures of speech from your partner's poem that are most memorable to you. Then, beneath your partner's poem, complete this sentence:

The insights you provide into your character's personality are _____.

MINI-LESSON: WRITING STYLE
Using Imagery and Figures of Speech

Teach Work directly with the Editing Strategy feature on page 949. Go over it with students, including the edited model.

Activity Idea Return to the chart above the edited model and invite volunteers to add to it. First, add a number of entries for "Idea Stated Literally." Then have students respond in the "Idea Dramatized" column. These examples should help students apply this skill to their own drafts.

Apply Have students keep the extended chart in view when they revise their drafts in terms of strengthening their poems with imagery and figures and of speech, using it for inspiration.

Revising Strategy

Using Imagery and Figures of Speech

Don't just state your insights in a literal manner. Dramatize them with imagery and figures of speech. As you revise, look for places where an image or a figure of speech could bring an idea to life. For example:

Idea Stated Literally	Idea Dramatized
You have made things difficult for yourself	For the road you have chosen now Is nothing but bumps and ditches
He said your parents/had made life a game of survival for you	He said/you were an eagle/and you had wings/and your parents were the hunters

The image of a bumpy road brings the idea of *difficult* to life. The metaphor of an eagle being hunted brings the idea of *a game of survival* to life. Notice how the writer of the student model used imagery to bring ideas to life.

You live in a ~~place~~ *wasteland*

Of seemingly unending ~~misery~~ *emotional storms*

The ~~problems~~ *storm damage* can be ~~solved~~ *repaired*

Provided you ~~help~~ *do the cleanup.*

 STUDENT MODEL

STEP 4 EDITING

Ask a partner to review your revised draft before you edit. When you edit, look for errors in grammar, usage, spelling, and mechanics. Look over each line to make sure there are no careless spelling errors. See the Editing Strategy on the next page.

Writing Workshop   **949**

Revising Strategy: Using Imagery and Figures of Speech

Have students close their eyes and listen as you read the student model aloud both with and without the changes. Discuss how dramatizing the literal ideas gives them more life and interest.

For additional support, see the mini-lesson at the bottom of page 948 and the worksheet referenced below.

 Unit 8 Resource Book
Revising Worksheet, p. 77

 Connections to
Writer's Resource

Refer to the Grammar, Usage, and Mechanics Handbook on Writer's Resource.

STEP 4 EDITING

Ask a partner (Peer assessment)

Tell students that the same proofreading marks are used for editing poetry or prose. Have students try reading each line of their partner's poem backwards to look for careless spelling errors.

MINI-LESSON: GRAMMAR

Avoiding Careless Spelling Mistakes

Display this sentence: I no Mr. Smth from working at teh bank last summer.

Ask students to look for and suggest corrections for any misspelled words (no to know, Smth to Smith, teh to the). Then display the following sentences and have students make necessary corrections.

1. Their should be four guards at the front door. (Their to There)

2. We're going to get our new car on Teusday. (Teusday to Tuesday)

3. Wich bus should I take to get downtown? (wich to which)

4. I will be home at six an James should be here about eight. (an to and)

5. My freinds are out of town for the weekend. (freinds to friends)

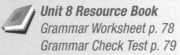 *Unit 8 Resource Book*
Grammar Worksheet p. 78
Grammar Check Test p. 79

Editing Strategy: Avoiding Careless Spelling Mistakes

For additional support, see the mini-lesson at the bottom of page 949 and the worksheets referenced below.

Unit 8 Resource Book
Grammar Worksheet, p. 78
Grammar Check Test, p. 79

Connections to
Writer's Resource

Refer to the Grammar, Usage, and Mechanics Handbook on Writer's Resource.

STEP 5 PRESENTING
Cover Sheet

The graphics on the cover sheet could include both colors and symbols. They would provide a visual introduction to the character described in the poem.

STEP 6 LOOKING BACK
Self-evaluate

The *Assessment Criteria Specs* at the bottom of this page are for a superior paper. You might want to post these in the classroom. Students can then evaluate themselves based on these criteria. For a complete scoring rubric, use the *Assessment Worksheet* referenced below.

Unit 8 Resource Book
Assessment Worksheet, p. 80

Reflect

After the students have answered the questions individually, you might encourage them to write a poem about themselves that would include some of the information from their answers.

To further explore the theme, use the Fine Art Transparency referenced below.

Transparency Collection
Fine Art Writing Prompt 14

950

Editing Strategy

Avoiding Careless Spelling Mistakes

We often misspell familiar words because we overlook them—words like these:

know	now	I'm	outside	where
our	which	their	Christmas	to
we're	don't	let's	friends	they

These mistakes make us look bad. If we could learn too notice these mistakes, we'd catch them. (Did you catch the misspelling in that last sentence?) Reading your work aloud and focusing on one line at a time are both good methods for proofreading for careless spelling mistakes. See the Computer Tip for more advice.

COMPUTER TIP
If your computer has a spell checker, use it—but don't rely on it to give you perfect spelling. A spell checker won't catch a mistake like substituting *too* for *to*. Proofread your writing carefully for spelling.

STEP 5 PRESENTING

- Create a poetry portrait by drawing a border around your poem as if you were making a picture frame for it. In this border, draw images and symbols from your poem.

- Make a cover sheet with graphics that reflect the essence of the character you describe in your poem.

STEP 6 LOOKING BACK

Self-evaluate. Look back at the Writer's Blueprint and evaluate your paper on each point, from 6 (superior) to 1 (inadequate).

Reflect. Think about what you've learned from writing this poem as you write responses to these items.

✔ In what ways is the character like you? different from you?

✔ Look back at the "Make comparisons" prewriting activity and write some comparison sentences about yourself.

For Your Working Portfolio Add your poem and reflection responses to your working portfolio.

ASSESSMENT CRITERIA SPECS

Here are the criteria for a superior paper. A full six-level rubric for this paper appears on the Assessment Worksheet referenced below.

6 Superior The writer of a 6 paper impressively meets these criteria:

- Captures the essence of a character from the literature and shows that the writer feels strongly about him or her.

- Reveals genuine insights into who this character really is: this character's true self.

- Dramatizes these insights through vivid figurative language and imagery.

- Uses a poetic format: either free verse or rhyme.

- Uses suitable punctuation and makes few, if any, spelling mistakes.

Unit 8 Resource Book
Assessment Worksheet, p. 80

Beyond Print

Analyzing Advertising

Wait! Before you read any further, take a look at the image below. Jot down the first fifteen words or phrases that come to mind as you look at it.

You can't explain funk.

Victoria Johnson

Your list of words may look something like: *freedom, graceful, funky, young, strong, independent, free-thinker, athletic, attitude,* and so on. Or it may not. But chances are you didn't include a lot of words and phrases like: *gym shoes, price, quality, materials, endurance, arch support,* and so on.

This advertisement is for athletic shoes, but that's not really what the ad is selling. Rather it's carefully constructed to sell a feeling, an attitude, a mind-set. The advertiser hopes that, unconsciously, the viewer will associate the product with the feeling so that, in a sense, buying the product is like buying the feeling.

A Closer Look

Now look at the ad again and analyze it. Start by thinking about the following concepts:

Symbolism Ads have only the split second you're looking at them to get their point across, so they often let symbols tell the story. Consider the ad on this page. What might a dancer symbolize? What message may be contained in her

Beyond Print **951**

Beyond Print

Teaching Objectives

- To increase awareness of advertisement messages
- To use criteria to evaluate advertisements

Curricular Connection: Critical Thinking

You can use the material in this article to give students practice viewing and thinking critically about the advertisements they see every day.

Introduce

To begin a discussion of advertisements, ask students to brainstorm elements that make up advertisements, such as music, words, pictures, and symbols. Ask students to describe or bring in their favorite advertisement and explain why they find it appealing. Then have students read the article and discuss the advertisements they described or presented in light of the information in the article.

BUILDING ENGLISH PROFICIENCY

Exploring Advertising Art

Preface this article by having students bring in a printed or videotaped ad that they think has a high visual impact. The ad may be in English or another language spoken by your students.

- Invite students to explain why they like the ad.

- Guide students in finding commonalities such as color, target audience, and medium, of the ad they brought in and the ad for the athletic shoes on page 951.

Activity 1 Have students present the advertisement they have chosen to a panel of people who might be representative of the ad's target audience. This is called a focus group. The purpose of the focus group is to gather information about the effectiveness of the advertisement. Students should prepare questions for the panel that are designed to gather information about each of the concepts discussed in this article.

Activity 2 Encourage students to begin their project by first choosing their target audience. This may help them choose their most effective advertising medium and write their message.

position—seemingly soaring through the air with arms flung out and arched above her? What might the colorful, wacky hat and sunglasses suggest? What is the advertiser trying to say through the contrast between the dancer's small, graceful, colorless body and the large, colorful, untied shoes?

Target Audience Advertisers carefully consider the age, income level, even gender and ethnic background of the people they think are most likely to buy the product. To what group do you think the ad on the previous page is targeted? Explain why you think so.

Medium Ads are everywhere—on television, radio, billboards, magazines, newspapers, trucks, even on the Internet. The medium an advertiser chooses depends on the advertiser's budget, as well as on the message and the target audience. For instance, if an advertiser wants to convince people to ride subways, a good place to advertise might be on billboards where those who are stuck in rush-hour traffic can read them.

Copy Words used in an ad are called *copy*. Often copy is kept to a minimum—perhaps even a slogan, if it's printed, or a jingle (song) if it's on radio or TV—so the audience can remember it easily. Why do you think the ad on the previous page uses the phrase, "You can't explain funk"? How do these words relate to the images, to the message or feel of the ad, and to the target audience?

Activity Options

A Critical View Choose an advertisement to analyze. What images does the ad include, and what might they symbolize? What overall feeling or message is the ad trying to convey? What is the medium, and why was it chosen? Who is the target audience? What copy is included, and why? Share your analysis with the class.

Shoe on the Other Foot Now you're the advertiser. You are selling a shoe. Decide whether it is a woman's or man's shoe, or both; an athletic, casual, or dress shoe; an expensive or economical shoe. Now plan an advertising campaign. Consider carefully your message, target audience, and medium. Create a TV commercial, magazine ad, radio jingle, or poster (billboard) for your product.

ANOTHER APPROACH

Without Visuals: Ads on the Radio

As an alternative, assign students an aurally-based activity instead of a visually-based activity. Invite students to read the article, and then discuss how the information, criteria, and questions could be adapted to analyze a radio advertisement.

Discuss the elements of speech that add nuance, innuendo, and other subtle or not so subtle suggestions to radio information. Ask students for ideas of how imagination can be exploited in radio ads, and how visual symbolism could be translated successfully into aural information.

Challenge students to choose a radio advertisement and analyze it, or to create a radio ad of their own.

Multicultural Connections

Change

Citizens of Tomorrow The Coble parents in "Teenage Wasteland" watch their son Donny change into someone they cannot understand or help. Gary Keillor's attitude changes when his mother stands up for their family, a "watershed moment" that seems to him to "open the door to show business." Generations of tradition were interrupted when "a sister . . . relinquished her name" in "Lost Sister." A winter camping expedition changes the narrator's outlook in "A Blizzard Under Blue Sky," and Sam in *The Janitor* reminds the youth of America that, "what you are now ain't what you gonna become." These are just some of the instances of change you have encountered in "Citizens of Tomorrow."

■ Based on the changes you've encountered in this unit, would you say that change is good, bad, or both? Explain, using examples from the literature.

Activities

Work in small groups on the following activities.

1. Do we change society or does society change us? Choose one of these views and make a list of reasons that led your group to its conclusion. Your reasons should include specific examples of individuals or events, past or present, that support your group's position. Compare your ideas with those of other groups.

2. Discuss changes that your group thinks need to occur at your school or in your community. Pick one that the group feels is the most important and brainstorm possible solutions for the problem. Write an editorial to a school or community newspaper that explains your proposed change, why you think it's necessary, and what you think will need to occur for the change to happen. Read your editorial to the class before sending it.

953

Unit Wrap-Up

MULTICULTURAL CONNECTION

Students are certainly familiar with the idea of change. It's probably the one constant in their lives. To facilitate the discussion of change as found in Unit 8, you can use the following ideas and questions.

Change

- Change can happen on a personal, community, generational, or societal level.
- Change can be good or bad.
- Sometimes we need strong foundations of the past to accept and understand the changes of the future.

Possible Response Encourage students to expand their answer by also drawing on their own experiences with change. Have them compare and contrast their experience of change with the issues of change in the literature.

Activities

Activity 1 Undecided or unresolved groups might begin with a list of specific examples for both sides of the issue and then choose the strongest and best supported side of the argument.

Activity 2 Students might want to present a well-thought-out plan beyond the editorial pages of the school newspaper. For example, in addition to an editorial they might

- talk to a school board member
- address the parent-teacher organization
- make a presentation to the student council.

Writing

Encourage students to visualize the future world twenty years from now and then place the characters into that world. Students might include characters'

- occupations
- environments
- friends
- relationships with the other characters from the story

Drama

Before students can write thoughtful dialogue consistent with the story characters, they may need to carefully analyze each character. A character web of each character's traits, hopes, dreams, and goals will be helpful.

Geography

Review with students the use of the map or atlas index and how to use a map grid for location. Students may find computer geography software helpful for this project.

Entertainment

Before students begin, have each group define "appropriate set," "a good show host," and "fabulous prizes." Encourage groups to come up with different approaches to the project.

Unit Test

Unit 8 Resource Book
New Selection, pp. 81–88
Test 1, pp. 89–90
Test 2, pp. 91–96

Independent and Group Projects

Writing

Looking Ahead Donny, Gary, Salvador, the boy in "Coca-Cola and Coco Frío," the woman in "Lost Sister," the character in "Top of the Food Chain," Victor, Thomas, the narrator in "A Blizzard Under Blue Sky": What will all of these characters be doing twenty years from now? What will the world they are living in then be like? Write a short paragraph for each of these characters, telling how their lives have progressed. Compare your future scenarios with those of other students.

Drama

Shared Wisdom Sam in *The Janitor* has a lot to say to the young people of today. Working with a partner, choose one of the other characters in this unit and pair him or her up with Sam. Create and present a conversation between Sam and the character in which the character confides in Sam some of his or her concerns and thoughts, and Sam shares the wisdom he has acquired through years of thoughtful living.

Geography

Where in the World is Borneo? Many of the selections in this unit mention a specific place. In a group, list all of the places mentioned in the works. Divide the places up among the group members. Locate the places on a map and do some research into each place's history, climate, and peoples. Present the information to the class in the form of a labeled world map, and take turns telling about the places.

Entertainment

Quiz Show In a group, create your own television quiz show by gathering bits and facts about the people and events from the Unit 8 literature. You will ask volunteer contestants from your classroom audience questions about the characters, events, settings, and so on, and assign points for each correct answer. Or, you may want to have students guess letters to fill in phrases from the literature, Wheel-of-Fortune style. Have fun with your quiz show: create an appropriate set, choose a good show host, and provide real or imaginary "fabulous prizes" as incentives for your contestants.

954

THE MEDIA

THEMES IN AMERICAN LITERATURE

THE MEDIA

PHOTOGRAPHERS LIKE THESE HAVE HOUNDED CELEBRITIES IN THE 20TH CENTURY AND HELPED CREATE THE FRENZIED ATMOSPHERE SURROUNDING "MEDIA EVENTS."

From the days of Benjamin Franklin's best-selling publication *Poor Richard's Almanac* in the mid-1700s to the Internet today, Americans have been enthusiastic users of an extraordinary variety of communication and entertainment media: books, newspapers, magazines, advertising, movies, radio, television, computers. The media have informed and misinformed, shaped and distorted, amused and annoyed Americans from the beginning.

Ballyhoo and Media Blitz

In the future,

everyone will be

world-famous for

fifteen minutes.

ANDY WARHOL (1968)

In Only Yesterday, *his social history of the 1920s, Frederick Lewis Allen describes the origins of what was known then as "ballyhoo" and might now be described as a "media blitz."*

It was the tragedy of Floyd Collins, perhaps, which gave the clearest indication up to that time of the unanimity with which the American people could be excited over a quite unimportant event if only it were dramatic enough.

Floyd Collins was an obscure young Kentuckian who had been exploring an underground passage five miles from Mammoth Cave. . . . Some 125 feet from daylight he was caught by a cave-in which pinned his foot under a huge rock. . . . Only a few people might have heard of Collins's predicament if W. B. Miller of

956

THEME LINK TO THE LITERATURE

Some other selections in the text that deal with the theme of the media are the following:

the *Louisville Courier-Journal* had not been slight of stature, daring, and an able reporter. Miller wormed his way down the slippery, tortuous passageway to interview Collins, became engrossed in the efforts to rescue the man, described them in vivid dispatches—and to his amazement found that the whole country was turning to watch the struggle. Collins's plight contained those elements of dramatic suspense and individual conflict with fate which make a great news story, and every city editor, day after day, planted it on page one. When Miller arrived at Sand Cave he had found only three men at the entrance. . . . A fortnight later there was a city of a hundred or more tents there and the milling crowds had to be restrained by barbed-wire barriers and State troops with drawn bayonets; and on February 17, 1925, even *The New York Times* gave a three-column page-one headline to the news of the dénouement:

Find Floyd Collins Dead in Cave Trap on 18th Day; Lifeless at Least 24 Hours; Foot Must Be Amputated to Get Body Out

Within a month, as Charles Merz later reminded readers of the *New Republic*, there was a cave-in in a North Carolina mine in which 71 men were caught and 53 actually lost. It attracted no great notice. It was "just a mine disaster." . . .

FREDERICK LEWIS ALLEN (1931)

A recent account of a media blitz surrounding a tragic event was reported in the following article from The New York Times *on television coverage of the earthquake that struck Los Angeles on January 14, 1994.*

There's always a positive media spin for tragedy. In Los Angeles, it is that a city racked by racial and class divisions has come together after the earthquake. On TV and in the papers we are told how African-Americans, Latinos, Asians, Middle Easterners, and Anglos have laid down their arms—literal and rhetorical—to pitch in and help their neighbors. But the truth is that even in disaster, the fault lines that divide L.A. are there for all to see.

Take the way the city's two largest ethnic groups have responded. The quake thrust Anglo suburbia into an unaccustomed dramatic role: when the shaking stopped, neighbors spilled into the streets, offering each other gallons of water, flashlights, words of reassurance. Normally, the brick walls between their homes are so high that neighbors rarely speak, much less borrow sugar. Now, with all those bricks in dusty piles on the sidewalks, people greet each other like long-lost relatives.

A world away in the Latino immigrant barrios, such solidarity is the survival mechanism of daily life. The firetrap apartment buildings have the thinnest of walls. Trained for disaster by war and poverty in their native countries, residents see tragedy as inevitable as a heart attack, a car accident or a stray bullet. After the quake, there was more resignation in the barrios than chaos or hysteria; once again tragedy had struck and once again it had to be overcome. . . .

On the morning of the quake, in the pancaked parking lot of the Northridge Fashion Mall, Salvador Peña, an immigrant from El Salvador, was trapped beneath tons of concrete. He was saved because the street sweeper he was driving around at 4:30 A.M. protected him from falling debris like a steel womb. Live on TV, firefighters worked for hours before freeing him. Throughout the ordeal, rescuers assured us, the man was in good spirits, although few could be sure what he was saying since only one spoke Spanish.

Yes, this rescue assured us, good will can guide us through tragedy. . . .

RUBÉN MARTÍNEZ (1994)

957

About Will Rogers

Rodeo performer, vaudeville and radio star, newspaper columnist, and movie actor, Will Rogers (1879–1935) endeared himself to audiences with a folksy amiability. Many Americans could quote his famous claim, "I never met a man I didn't like."

About Joseph Pulitzer

Born in Hungary, Joseph Pulitzer (1849–1911) bought the *New York World* in 1883. Within a year he had increased his newspaper's circulation from 15,000 to 100,000. Pulitzer later left money to the Columbia School of Journalism to fund the annual Pulitzer Prizes, awarded since 1917 in journalism, fiction, drama, biography, history, and (since 1921) poetry.

About William Randolph Hearst

Publisher William Randolph Hearst (1863–1951) played a leading role in causing the Spanish-American War. As tensions built between the United States and Spain, American writers and illustrators—including Frederic Remington—rushed to Cuba to be ready to cover the expected war. After weeks of inactivity, Remington wired Hearst that there would be no war. Hearst is said to have wired back, "You furnish the pictures and I'll furnish the war." The acclaimed movie *Citizen Kane* (1941) is modeled on Hearst's career.

"Yellow Journalism" and the Spanish-American War

> All I know is what I see in the papers.
>
> WILL ROGERS (1928)

In the late 1890s, two New York newspapers, Joseph Pulitzer's World *and William Randolph Hearst's* Journal, *were engaged in a circulation war. As part of their effort to attract readers, the two papers vied with each other in publishing lurid stories about Spanish atrocities in Cuba. This sensationalistic "yellow journalism" (from the name of a* World *comic strip, "The Yellow Kid") helped feed the war fever in the United States that led to the outbreak of the Spanish-American War in 1898. In the following passage, a correspondent who covered the war defends "yellow journalism."*

It has been said by those calm students of human events who were untroubled by the cries of oppressed Cuba, that the war between the United States and Spain was the work of "yellow newspapers"—that form of American journalistic energy which is not content merely to print a daily record of history, but seeks to take part in events as an active and sometimes decisive agent. . . . As one of the multitude who served in that crusade of "yellow journalism" . . . I can bear witness to the martyrdom of men who suffered all but death—and some, even death itself—in those days of darkness.

It may be that a desire to sell their newspapers influenced some of the "yellow editors," just as a desire to gain votes inspired some of the political orators. But that was not the chief motive; for if ever any human agency was thrilled by the consciousness of its moral responsibility, it was "yellow journalism" in the never-to-be-forgotten months before the outbreak of hostilities, when the masterful Spanish minister at Washington seemed to have the influence of every government in the world behind him in his effort to hide the truth and strangle the voice of humanity. . . .

If the war against Spain is justified in the eyes of history, then "yellow journalism" deserves its place among the most useful instrumentalities of civilization. It may be guilty of giving the world a lopsided view of a few things and ignoring others, it may offend the eye by typographical violence, it may sometimes proclaim its own deeds too loudly; but it has never deserted the cause of the poor and downtrodden; it has never taken bribes,—and that is more than can be said of its most conspicuous critics.

One of the accusations against "yellow journalism" is that it steps outside of the legitimate business of gathering news and commenting upon it—that it acts. It is argued that a newspaper which creates events and thus creates news, cannot, in human nature, be a fair witness.

There is a grain of truth in this criticism; but it must not be forgotten that the very nature of journalism enables it to act in the very heart of events at critical moments and with knowledge not possessed by the general public; that what is everybody's business and the business of nobody in particular, is the journalist's business.

JAMES CREELMAN (1901)

958

MINI-LESSON: READING/THINKING SKILLS

Identify Alternatives

Identifying alternatives is finding or proposing various ways to accomplish something, especially alternative solutions to problems.

Teach The critics of "yellow journalism" at the time of the Spanish-American War criticized the so-called yellow newspapers for manipulating events by their coverage of the news. Correspondent James Creelman defended this proactive journalism as being in a good cause. Discuss with students the alternative positions on the role of the media reflected in these two views.

Activity Idea Have students hold a panel discussion on the following question: Should the media ever go beyond gathering news and reporting it—for instance, to the point of staging news or pressuring the government—in the service of some "good cause"? *(Students' answers should explore the impact of different alternatives.)*

WILLIAM R. HEARST

THIS CARTOON SHOWS NEWSPAPER
PUBLISHER WILLIAM RANDOLPH
HEARST AS "THE YELLOW KID."

Congress shall make no law . . .
abridging the freedom of speech,
or of the press. . . .

1ST AMENDMENT (1791)

Nast Attacks Boss Tweed

In the years after the Civil War, Thomas Nast (1840–1902) became America's most influential political cartoonist. Nast's cartoons helped overthrow William Marcy "Boss" Tweed (1828–1878), leader of a group of corrupt politicians who controlled the government of New York City in the 1860s and early 1870s. Tweed himself admitted their effectiveness: "I don't care a straw for your newspaper articles. My constituents don't know how to read, but they can't help seeing them . . . pictures."

I will be as harsh as truth, and as uncompromising as justice—I am in earnest— I will not equivocate—I will not retreat a single inch— And I will be heard.

WILLIAM LLOYD GARRISON,
FIRST ISSUE OF HIS
ANTI-SLAVERY NEWSPAPER,
THE LIBERATOR (1831)

A GROUP OF VULTURES
WAITING FOR THE
STORM TO "BLOW
OVER"—"LET US PREY"

959

About the Yellow Kid

Generally identified as the first newspaper comic strip, Richard Outcault's *The Yellow Kid* began its run in the May 5, 1895 issue of the *New York World*.

About William Lloyd Garrison

One of the most determined abolitionists was William Lloyd Garrison (1805–1879). His antislavery agitation was so effective that the Georgia legislature offered a $5000 reward to anyone who would bring Garrison from Boston to Georgia to be put on trial.

About Thomas Nast

Thomas Nast created or popularized images including the elephant as the symbol of the Republican party, the donkey as the symbol of the Democratic party, and the familiar image of Santa Claus.

About the Tweed Ring

William Marcy Tweed and his cronies benefited from bribes and payoffs to the extent of perhaps $200 million. Most members of the Ring eluded punishment. Tweed finally went to jail, escaped, and was arrested in Spain after someone identified him with the aid of a Nast cartoon.

 *Art Study*

Visual Literacy A caricature is a drawing of a person in which one or more features are exaggerated. In this Nast cartoon, William Marcy Tweed is the vulture in the foreground with the diamond stickpin.

Question What features does Nast emphasize in his caricature of Tweed? *(Possible responses: deepset eyes, large nose, and obesity)*

ESL
LEP
ELD
SAE
LD

BUILDING ENGLISH PROFICIENCY

Debating the 1st Amendment

To help students grasp the importance of 1st Amendment guarantees of free speech and a free press, you might begin by quoting Chief Justice Oliver Wendell Holmes, Jr.'s famous opinion in the case of *Schenck* v. *U.S.*: "The most stringent protection of free speech would not protect a man in falsely shouting 'fire' in a theater and causing a panic." Then you might ask:

1. Are there any circumstances in which the government should be able to suspend 1st Amendment guarantees? *(Possible responses: wartime or national emergency; cases in which speech endangers others)*

2. Do you think an attempt to eradicate a social evil—such as child pornography— would justify defining or limiting 1st Amendment guarantees? *(Possible response: Freedom of speech can be limited to protect the rights of people affected by the speech or communication, such as victims of libel or children hurt by producers of pornography.)*

Art Study

Visual Literacy The bulk of the 11,000 magazines published today are trade magazines and academic journals. Of the rest, nearly 1,000 are called "consumer magazines"—women's and men's magazines, and magazines devoted to news, movies, hobbies, cars, sports, fiction, science, various cities, and so on.

Question Judging by John Vauhon's photograph, what were some of the popular interests of Americans in the late 1930s? *(Possible responses: movies, news, photography, cars, pulp fiction, sports)*

Origins of the Magazine in America

The first two American magazines, Andrew Bradford's *American Magazine* and Benjamin Franklin's *General Magazine*, premiered within a week of each other in 1741. Bradford's publication lasted three months; Franklin's survived for six. Writers in colonial America depended upon newspapers, magazines, and pamphlets to get their ideas to the public. Unlike newspapers circulated in a single city or colony, the magazines sought readers in all thirteen colonies. Usually selling for a shilling, the colonial magazines dealt with timely issues briefly and pointedly. Through such periodicals, the colonists acquired the magazine reading habit still characteristic of Americans.

THE NEWSSTAND

MINI-LESSON: READING/THINKING SKILLS

Synthesize

Synthesizing is combining information to form new, complex ideas.

Teach Point out to students that scholars who study ancient civilizations recover the artifacts created by the peoples of the past and use them to build up a picture of their culture.

Activity Idea Have students use the magazine covers from the photo of the 1938 newsstand and the contemporary supermarket tabloids as if they were archaeologists in the distant future attempting to synthesize a picture of "ancient" (that is, twentieth-century) America.

About Supermarket Tabloids

The first of today's crop of supermarket tabloids, *The National Enquirer,* established the now-familiar formula stories of alien landings and two-headed babies during the 1950s. Today's *Enquirer* is more restrained—largely as a result of a libel suit settled in 1981 for $800,000. Its competitors at the check-out line, however, continue the tradition of unabashed hokum, or nonsensical "news" stories filled with apparent scandal about celebrities, science fiction disguised as reportage, and trick photography.

A newsstand is a good introduction to the popular mythology of a culture. The one at left was photographed in 1938 by John Vauhon in Omaha, Nebraska. The supermarket tabloids above are contemporary.

Bigfoot Captured!

Elvis is Alive!

World War II Bomber Found on Moon!

63-year-old Mom Gives Birth to Alien Twins!

961

BUILDING ENGLISH PROFICIENCY

Considering Tabloid Headlines

Students can think critically and talk about the sample headlines from the kinds of tabloid newspapers sold in supermarket check-out lines.

- "Bigfoot" is the name used for a large, hairy creature believed by some people to live in the mountainous areas of western North America. Similar ape-like or human-like creatures have been rumored to live in Asia. There is no widely-accepted scientific proof of the existence of such creatures, much less the capture of one. Ask: Do you think most people who read reports such as the story of a captured bigfoot believe them?

- Elvis Presley, the extremely popular singer, died in 1977. Ask: Why might some people people claims that Presley is still alive?

- Ask: Do you think many people take seriously or believe a headline about an airplane of the 1940s found on the moon? Why might someone buy a newspaper with such a headline?

- Students may enjoy considering what other strange or silly headlines they think might fascinate readers or help sell tabloid newspapers.

ESL LEP ELD SAE LD

About Zines, or Fanzines

Although the medium, zines, is named after fan magazines, many are too topical or personal to reflect the interests of music or entertainment fans. Some zines do promote music groups, some resemble countercultural comic books, and many reflect whatever interests their creators choose.

There are zines that critics blast for pornography or poor quality, but others are innocent, quirky, or just irreverent. Most have print runs too small to interest commercial publishers.

Pagan Kennedy wrote *Zine: How I Spent Six Years of My Life in the Underground and Finally Found Myself, I Think* (St. Martin's Press, 1995).

 ## Art Study

Visual Literacy   The approach taken to cover design probably is the most significant design decision in creating a magazine. For mass-market magazines, the cover is a vital marketing tool. For publications with a very limited circulation such as fanzines, cover design can be more eccentric.

Question   Judging by the zine covers shown here, what impressions are these publications trying to convey? *(Possible responses: that their readers are young; that they are off-beat or funny)*

Fanzines

While much of the media has become more and more high-tech, one determinedly low-tech media phenomenon of recent years is the fanzine (short for "fan magazine" and abbreviated still further to zine or 'zine). Zines are generally addressed to small audiences of enthusiasts (typical print runs are usually fewer than 2,000 copies) and deal with a bewildering variety of subjects from the serious to the trivial. Diseased Pariah News, for example, gives a sardonically humorous view of living with AIDS; The I Hate Brenda Newsletter is devoted to attacking former Beverly Hills 90210 star Shannen Doherty. The basic point of zines is to give their creators a voice. A sampling of fanzines is shown below.

My zine is just about me. . . . about how I wanted to be a famous writer and about all the other stuff that occupied my narcissistic little mind. Hair trouble. My crush on Danny Bonaduce. My sinus problems.

PAGAN KENNEDY,
CREATOR OF *PAGAN'S HEAD*
(1995)

962

MINI-LESSON: READING/THINKING SKILLS

Synthesize

To synthesize ideas, readers recall information they have known, mentally revise and update it, and relate it to new ideas. This allows readers to recognize unfamiliar concepts and form complex thoughts.

Teach   Point out to students that the purpose of zines is to allow persons or small groups who publish the zines to express individualistic perspectives.

Activity Idea   Invite students to come up with ideas for their own zines. These can include titles, cover art, subjects for articles, and so on. Students with access to computers may want to publish trial issues.

TALK SHOWS

Talk shows are radio or television programs where the famous or just outrageous are allowed to spout their views on a chosen topic, the more controversial the better (for ratings if not for the moral tone of the proceedings). Among the most famous talk show hosts are radio's Rush Limbaugh and television's Oprah Winfrey.

[Talk shows] are on to something. The frayed edges should be cut off. These shows have great relevance to tens of millions, but sometimes the moral message is obscured by a burlesque theater.

GERALDO RIVERA (1995)

About Oprah Winfrey

Hugely popular with audiences for her spontaneity and sympathy toward her guests, Oprah Winfrey (born 1954) is the preeminent talk show host on television. She has worked in radio and TV news and acted in films. She also heads her own video production company. In 1985 she made her movie debut in Stephen Spielberg's film of Alice Walker's novel *The Color Purple.* Winfrey received an Academy Award nomination for her performance.

About Rush Limbaugh

Conservative and sarcastic, Rush Limbaugh (born 1951) hosts a popular talk show on radio. In 1992 he began appearing on television. He has written two best-selling books, *The Way Things Ought to Be* (1992) and *See, I Told You So* (1993). Limbaugh uses these media to bash persons and groups he opposes: liberals, feminists, environmentalists, advocates of minority groups, and others that he accuses of "anticapitalism, secular humanism, and socialism."

About Geraldo Rivera

Geraldo Rivera (born 1943) is a television talk-show host and has hosted other programs such as human-interest specials. He also worked as a TV journalist. Rivera has criticized some talk shows for questionable content, and likewise he has been criticized.

963

BUILDING ENGLISH PROFICIENCY

Recognizing Values

Recognizing values is identifying statements based on deeply held beliefs or philosophies. Students can do this as they read and as they hear statements in other media, such as television talk shows.

Teach Point out to students that a talk show is a forum for the expression of opinions and values—those of the host, the guests, and the studio audience (on TV), and callers (on radio and TV).

Activity Idea Students can examine various radio and TV talk shows, including those of Oprah Winfrey and Rush Limbaugh, and discuss what these programs reveal—individually and collectively—about American values or individuals' values at the present time. Students may want to report on or talk about the style of language on a program.

Literature and Computers, Video Games, and the Internet

Science fiction writers have cast computers in their works for generations. Many of their machines are large, humanity-controlling devices inspired by mainframe computers of the past. An example is Arthur C. Clarke's *2001: A Space Odyssey.*

Ray Bradbury explored virtual reality in his short story "The Veldt" (1951), and many authors have explored imagined societies in which real experiences have been replaced with computer-supported simulations. An example is the young-adult story "A Quiet One" by Anne McCaffrey, published in *2041,* edited by Jane Yolen (Delacorte, 1991). Students may be familiar with stories told in movies such as *War Games* (directed by John Badham, 1983), *Tron* (directed by Steven Lisberger, 1982), and more recent films such as *The Net* and *Sneakers.*

Many recent books and stories, by writers such as Michael Crichton and William Gibson, feature computers. You may want to preview works for suitability before recommending them to students.

Video Games

Among the most popular forms of interactive media are video games, played on television screens or video monitors hooked up to a microcomputer system. A sampling of video games is shown below.

964

The Internet

Perhaps the most dramatic event in recent media history has been the rapid development of the Internet, a worldwide network of linked computers that offer users access to a tremendous range of information and services. The home page for the Smithsonian Institution Internet site appears above.

RESPONDING

1. In your opinion, what are the most important characteristics of a "media event"?
2. What examples of "yellow journalism" (page 958) can you find in the media today?
3. What is your favorite headline from a supermarket tabloid?
4. In general, do you think radio and TV talk shows serve a useful purpose? Why or why not?
5. Should there be any attempt to control the content of material in video games or on the Internet? Why or why not?

Information About the Internet and Digital Communications

Two of the many books about computer communications and their impact on American society and culture:

- *The Road Ahead* by Bill Gates (Viking, 1995). An excerpt of this book by Gates, the chairman of the Microsoft software company, appeared in *Newsweek* (Nov. 27, 1995).
- *Being Digital* by Nicholas Negroponte (Knopf, 1995), the founding director of the Media Lab at Massachusetts Institute of Technology. This book is considered by critics informative and very readable but perhaps uncritical of some uses of digital networks. A compact disc edition is available.

About the World Wide Web

The World Wide Web is a system for computer users to find and present informational documents over the Internet. World Wide Web documents can include text, images, sound, animation, and "hypertext" links to other information. People and organizations use the World Wide Web, and many create Web sites, also called home pages, with Internet addresses. The address of ScottForesman educational publishers, for example, is: http://www.scottforesman.com

One kind of Web site is called a Webzine—a magazine on screen. A Webzine devoted to literary topics is *Salon* (http://www.salon1999.com). It publishes interviews with authors such as Amy Tan, as well as book information.

RESPONDING

1. Possible responses: Students might mention a dramatic "life-or-death" quality; the involvement of celebrities; or a scandalous or sexy angle.

2. Possible responses: Students may mention media coverage of political campaigns, "tabloid television" programs such as *Hard Copy,* or radio "shock jocks" such as Rush Limbaugh or Howard Stern.

3. Possible responses: Many students probably will need no prompting, but those who can't recall any headlines might be invited to invent some, based on the examples offered on page 961.

4. Possible responses: Students who think talk shows are useful may argue that they provide a forum for discussion of social issues that affect many people. Students who feel that these programs are not useful may argue that talk shows frequently sensationalize the subjects they address.

5. Possible responses: Students who agree may point to the violent content of many video games and some Internet material. Students who disagree may argue that First Amendment guarantees of free speech and a free press should include these forms of expression.

Glossaries, Handbooks, and Indexes

Glossary of Literary Terms

Words within entries in SMALL CAPITAL LETTERS refer to other entries in the Glossary of Literary Terms.

alliteration (ə lit′ə rā′shən), the REPETITION of consonant sounds at the beginnings of words or within words, particularly in accented syllables. It can be used to reinforce meaning, unify thought, or create a musical effect.

> *Sinuous southward and sinuous northward*
>   *the shimmering band*
> *Of the sand-beach fastens the fringe of*
>   *the marsh to the folds of the land.*
>   Lanier, from "The Marshes of Glynn"

allusion (ə lü′zhən), a brief reference to a person, event, place, real or fictitious, or to a work of art.

analogy (ə nal′ə jē), a comparison made between two basically different things. Frequently an unfamiliar object or idea will be explained through comparison to a familiar one.

anastrophe (ə nas′trə fē) See INVERSION.

antagonist (an tag′ə nist), a character in a story or play who opposes the chief character or PROTAGONIST. In Freeman's "The Revolt of 'Mother'" (page 468), "Father" is the antagonist.

aphorism See MAXIM.

apostrophe (ə pos′trə fē), a figure of speech in which an absent person, an abstract concept, or an inanimate object is directly addressed. Melville addresses an inamiate object, the Shenandoah Valley, in "The Portent" (page 308):

> *Hanging from the beam,*
>   *Slowly swaying (such the law),*
> *Gaunt the shadow on your green,*
>   *Shenandoah.*

assonance (as′n əns), the REPETITION of similar vowel sounds followed by different consonant sounds in stressed syllables or words. *Hate* and *great* are examples of rhyme; *hate* and *sail* are examples of assonance.

autobiography See BIOGRAPHY.

ballad, a NARRATIVE song or poem passed on in the oral tradition. It often makes use of REPETITION and DIALOGUE. "El Corrido de Gregorio Cortez" (page 398) is a ballad.

biography, an account of a person's life written by someone else. AUTOBIOGRAPHY is the story of a person's life written by the person who lived it.

blank verse, unrhymed IAMBIC PENTAMETER:
> *See the first four lines of "Birches" (page 639).*

cacophony (ka kof′ə nē), a succession of harsh, discordant sounds in either poetry or prose, used to achieve a specific effect. Note the harsh, somewhat explosive sounds in these lines:

> *Too much horrified to speak,*
> *They can only shriek, shriek,*
>   *Out of tune,*
> *In a clamorous appealing to the mercy of the fire,*
> *In a mad expostulation with the deaf and frantic fire. . . .*
>   Poe, from "The Bells"

characterization, the methods an author uses to develop a character. A character's physical traits and personality may be described, as in the first two paragraphs of "A Worn Path" (page 667); a character's speech and behavior may be presented, as in "The Life You Save May Be Your Own" (page 720); or the thoughts and feelings of a character may be shown, as in "The Jilting of Granny Weatherall" (page 611). Characters can be described as either round or flat. A round character is fully developed and exhibits a variety of human traits. A flat character displays few, if any, distinguishing features.

climax, the decisive point in a story or play when the problem must be resolved in one way or another. In "The Leader of the People" (page 676), the climax comes when Grandfather, after overhearing an angry Carl Tiflin, realizes that no one but Jody wants to hear his stories of westering anymore. Not every story or play has a dramatic climax. Sometimes a character may simply resolve a problem in his or her mind.
> *See also* PLOT.

comedy, a play written primarily to amuse the audience. Comic writing often appeals to the intellect, and the comic mode has often been used to "instruct" the audience about the follies of certain social conventions and human foibles.

concrete poetry, poetry in which the appearance of the poem on the page suggests the subject of the poem. "1(a" on page 577 is a concrete poem that sugests a falling leaf.

conflict, the struggle between two opposing forces. The four basic kinds of conflict are these: 1. a person against another person or ANTAGONIST, as in *Trifles* (page 455); 2. a person against nature, as in "Top of the Food Chain" (page 923); 3. a person against society, as in the excerpt from *Crusade for Justice* (page 483); and 4. two elements within a person struggling for mastery, as in Tim O'Brien's "On the Rainy River (page 812).

    See also PLOT.

connotation, the emotional associations surrounding a word, as opposed to the word's literal meaning or DENOTATION. Some connotations are fairly universal, others quite personal. The author of "Leaves" (page 774) explores the many personal connotations of grape leaves and pieces of paper with his father's writing on them.

consonance, the repetition of consonant sounds that are preceded by different vowel sounds.

    The autu*m*n-ti*me* has co*me*;
    On woods that drea*m* of bloo*m*. . . .
                Whittier, from "My Triumph"

Consonance is an effective device for linking sound, MOOD, and meaning. In the lines above, the *m* sounds contribute to a drowsy feeling.

couplet, a pair of rhyming lines with identical METER. See "The Spring and the Fall" (page 492).

denotation the strict, literal meaning of a word.

    See also CONNOTATION.

denouement (dä′nü mäN′), the RESOLUTION of the PLOT. The word is derived from a French word meaning "to untie."

dialect, a form of speech characteristic of a particular region or class, differing from the standard language in pronunciation, vocabulary, and grammatical form. "Ma Rainey" (page 528) is partly written in dialect.

dialogue, conversation between two or more people in a literary work. Dialogue can help develop CHARACTERIZATION of those speaking and those spoken about, create MOOD, advance PLOT, and develop THEME.

diary, a record of daily happenings written by a person for his or her own use. The diary makes up in immediacy and frankness what it lacks in artistic shape and coherence. Examples are the excerpts from *The Diary* of *Samuel Sewall* (page 56) and from Mary Chesnut's diary (page 302).

    See also JOURNAL *and* MEMOIR.

diction, the author's choice of words and phrases in a literary work. This choice involves both the CONNOTATION and DENOTATION of a word, as

well as levels of usage. In "The Devil and Tom Walker," (page 240) Irving refers to Mrs. Tom Walker as "a tall termagant," a choice of words that reveals something about Irving as well as about Walker's wife, whom another writer might have chosen to describe as a common scold.

drama, a literary work in verse or prose, written to be acted, that tells a story through the speech and actions of the characters.

dramatic convention, any of several devices that the audience accepts as reality in a dramatic work. For instance, the audience accepts that an interval between acts may represent hours, days, weeks, months, or years; or that a bare stage may be a meadow or an inner room.

dramatic irony See IRONY.

dramatic monologue (mon′l ôg), a LYRIC poem in which the speaker addresses someone whose replies are not recorded. Sometimes the one addressed seems to be present, sometimes not. "The Love Song of J. Alfred Prufrock" (page 568) is a dramatic monologue.

epigram, any short, witty VERSE or saying, often ending with a wry twist.

    Let us all be happy and live within our means,
    Even if we have to borrow the money to do it with.
                Artemus Ward

  Compare with MAXIM *and* PROVERB.

epigraph, a motto or quotation at the beginning of a book, poem, or chapter, often indicating the THEME. An example is found at the beginning of "The Love Song of J. Alfred Prufrock" (page 568).

epiphany (i pif′ə nē), a moment of enlightenment in which the underlying truth or the meaning of something is suddenly made clear. In O'Brien's "On the Rainy River"(page 812), that moment comes when he realizes that going to Canada to escape the draft is no longer a possibility for him.

essay, a composition that presents a personal viewpoint. An essay may present a viewpoint through formal analysis and argument, as in the excerpt from "Civil Disobedience" (page 231) or it may be more informal in style, as in "Harlem: The Culture Capital" (page 512).

exposition, the beginning of a work of fiction, particularly a play, in which the author sets the atmosphere and TONE, explains the SETTING, introduces the characters, and provides the reader with any other information needed in order to understand the PLOT. The exposition in Miller's *The Crucible* appears on pages 64-66.

extended metaphor, a comparison that is developed at great length, often through a whole work or a great part of it. "A Black Man Talks of Reaping" by Arna Bontemps (page 524) contains an extended metaphor, with *sowing* and *planting* representing the efforts of black people and *reaping* representing the meager rewards for black people, rewards that others mostly glean.

falling action, the RESOLUTION of a dramatic PLOT, which takes place after the CLIMAX.

fantasy, a work that takes place in an unreal world or concerns incredible characters or employs fictional scientific principles. Though it does not take place in an unreal world, Hawthorne's "Dr. Heidegger's Experiment" (page 276) has other elements of fantasy.

See also SCIENCE FICTION.

fiction, a type of literature that tells about imaginary people and happenings. NOVELS and SHORT STORIES are fiction.

figurative language, language used in a nonliteral way to express a suitable relationship between essentially unlike things in order to furnish new effects or fresh insights. When Twain writes that a frog whirled in the air "like a doughnut," he is using a figure of speech or figurative language. The more common figures of speech are APOSTROPHE, SIMILE, METAPHOR, PERSONIFICATION, HYPERBOLE, METONYMY, and SYNECDOCHE.

flashback, interruption of the narrative to show an episode that happened before that particular point in the story. Alexie's "This Is What It Means to Say Phoenix, Arizona" (page 911) contains several flashbacks.

foil, a character whose traits are the opposite of those of another character, and who thus points out the strengths or weaknesses of the other character. Dee and Maggie are foils in Walker's "Everyday Use" (page 644).

folk literature, a type of early literature that was passed orally from generation to generation, and only written down later. The authorship of folk literature is unknown. Folk literature includes MYTHS, FABLES, BALLADS, and LEGENDS. "How the World Was Made" (page 6) is folk literature.

folklore, the customs, proverbs, legends, superstitions, songs, and tales of a people or nation.

Literature often borrows elements from folklore. The old legend (common to the folklore of many countries) of someone who strikes a bargain with the devil is incorporated by Irving into "The Devil and Tom Walker" (page 240).

foot, a group of syllables in verse usually consisting of one accented syllable and one or more unaccented syllables. A foot may occasionally, for variety, have two accented syllables (a spondee) or two unaccented syllables. In the following lines the feet are separated by slanted lines.

At mid-/night, in/the month/of June.
I stand/beneath/the mys-/tic moon.

Poe, from "The Sleeper"

The most common line lengths are five feet (PENTAMETER), four feet (tetrameter), and three feet (trimeter). The lines above are iambic tetrameter.

See also RHYTHM.

foreshadowing, a hint given to the reader of what is to come. In "The Revolt of 'Mother'" (page 468), mother's revolt is foreshadowed from the moment her husband reveals that a new barn instead of a house is being built.

free verse, a type of poetry that differs from conventional verse forms in being "free" from a fixed pattern of METER and RHYME, but using RHYTHM and other poetic devices. Walt Whitman (page 360) was the first recognized poet to use free verse extensively.

genre (zhän′rə), a form or type of literary work. DRAMA, the NOVEL, the SHORT STORY, and the poem are all genres. Subheadings under these types are also called genres: the mystery, the myth, and fantasy, for example.

hero, the central character in a NOVEL, SHORT STORY, DRAMA, or other work of fiction. When the central character is a woman, she is sometimes called a *heroine.* The term *hero,* however, can be used to refer to both males and females.

historical narrative, a nonfiction prose account of real people, places, and events, such as Bradford's *Of Plymouth Plantation* (page 31).

hyperbole (hī pėr′bə lē), great exaggeration. The effect may be serious or comic. American folklore abounds with hyperbole, such as the story about the man who was so stingy that he stood on one foot at a time to avoid wearing out his shoes. There is hyperbole in "The Jumping Frog of Calaveras County" (page 390) by Mark Twain.

iamb (ī′amb), a two-syllable metrical FOOT consisting of an unaccented syllable followed by an accented syllable, as in the word *until.*

idiom, an expression whose meaning cannot be understood from the ordinary meanings of the words in it. To "smell a rat" indicates suspicion and to "get cold feet" describes an unwillingness to do something; both are idioms.

imagery, the sensory details that provide vividness in a literary work and tend to arouse emotions in a reader that abstract language does not. Houston's "A Blizzard Under Blue Sky" (page 930) contains many sensory details.

inference, a reasonable conclusion about the behavior of a character or the meaning of an event, drawn from the limited information presented by the author. After reading "In Another Country" by Hemingway (page 580), one might infer that this is a story about human isolation and that the physical wounds of the soldiers symbolize the emotional scars of alienation.

interior monologue, a technique used by writers to present the stream of consciousness of a fictional character, either directly by presenting what is passing through the character's mind or indirectly by the author's selection of and comments upon the character's thoughts. Olsen's "I Stand Here Ironing" (page 732) consists entirely of interior monologue.

inversion A reversal of the usual order of the parts of a sentence, primarily for emphasis or to achieve a certain RHYTHM or RHYME. In this example both lines contain inversion.

> In a branch of a willow hid
> Sings the evening Caty-did. . . .
>> Freneau, from "To a Caty-Did"

irony, the term used to describe a contrast between what appears to be and what really is. In *verbal irony,* the intended meaning of a statement or work is different from (often the opposite of) what the statement or work literally says. *Understatement,* in which an idea is expressed less emphatically than it might be, is a form of verbal irony often used for humorous or cutting effect. In "Gary Keillor" (page 876), Garrison Keillor uses understatement when he comments on two talent show acts by his fellow classmates: "I enjoyed watching these dogs, strictly from a professional point of view." *Irony of situation* refers to an occurrence that is contrary to what is expected or intended, as in "Richard Cory"

(page 576). *Dramatic irony* refers to a situation in which events or facts not known to a character on stage or in a fictional work are known to another character and the audience or reader.

legend, a story handed down from the past, often associated with some period in the history of a people. A legend differs from a MYTH in having some historical truth and often less of the supernatural. There are many legends about Pocohantas but relatively little is actually known about her.

local color, a type of regional writing that focuses on a particular locale and the peculiarities of speech, dress, custom, and landscape that make it distinctive. Willa Cather is a writer who explores the effects that setting has on character.

lyric, a poem, usually short, that expresses some basic emotion or state of mind. It usually creates a single impression and is highly personal. It may be rhymed or unrhymed. "One Art" (page 772) fulfills the qualifications of a lyric.

maxim, a brief saying embodying a moral, such as "Eat not to dullness: drink not to elevation" [Benjamin Franklin]. It is also called an aphorism.

memoir (mem′wär), a form of AUTOBIOGRAPHY that is more concerned with personalities, events, and actions of public importance than with the private life of the writer, for example the excerpt from Ulysses S. Grant's *Memoirs* (page 322).

metaphor, a figure of speech that makes a comparison, without *like* or *as,* between two basically unlike things. This comparison may be stated (She was a stone) or implied (Her stony silence filled the room).

(See also SIMILE and FIGURATIVE LANGUAGE.)

meter, the pattern of stressed and unstressed syllables in POETRY.

See also RHYTHM and FOOT.

metonymy (mə ton′ə mē), a figure of speech in which a specific word naming an object is substituted for another word with which it is closely associated, as when the term "city hall" is used to refer to a mayor, or "the bench" is used to refer to persons who sit as judges.

monologue, an extended speech given by one speaker. It differs from a SOLILOQUY, which is the extended speech of a character on stage who is in effect talking to himself or herself and expressing inner thoughts aloud.

Glossary of Literary Terms **971**

simile a figure of speech involving a direct comparison, using *like* or *as,* between two basically unlike things that have something in common.

soliloquy (sə lil′ə kwē), a DRAMATIC CONVENTION that allows a character alone on stage to speak his or her thoughts aloud. If someone else is on stage but cannot hear the character's words, the soliloquy becomes an *aside.*

Compare with DRAMATIC MONOLOGUE.

sonnet, a LYRIC poem with a traditional form of fourteen iambic PENTAMETER lines. Sonnets fall into two groups, according to their RHYME SCHEMES. "If We Must Die" (page 525) is an example of a Shakespearean sonnet. The rhyme scheme of a Shakespearean sonnet is *abab cdcd efef gg.* Another type of sonnet is called Italian or Petrarchan, after a fourteenth century Italian poet named Petrarch. Its rhyme scheme is usually *abbaabba cdecde.* Both types have fourteen lines.

sound devices, the choice and arrangement of words to please the ear and suit meaning. RHYME, RHYTHM, ASSONANCE, ONOMATOPOEIA, and ALLITERATION are examples of sound devices.

speaker, the person who is speaking in a poem, as in Eliot's "The Lovesong of J. Alfred Prufrock" (page 568).

stage directions, directions given by the author of a play to indicate the action, costumes, SETTING, arrangement of the stage, and so on. For examples of stage directions, see Miller's *The Crucible* (page 62), where they are in italic type.

stanza, a group of lines set off to form a division in a poem and sometimes linked with other stanzas by RHYME.

stereotype a conventional character, PLOT, or SETTING that possesses little or no individuality. Such situations, characters, or settings are usually predictable. Examples of literary stereotypes include the dead body in the library, the wandering lone hero, or aliens who terrorize a city.

stream of consciousness, the recording or re-creation of a character's flow of thought. Raw images, perceptions, and memories come and go in seemingly random fashion, much as they do in people's minds. Actually the author orders these images and perceptions, however, as in Porter's "The Jilting of Granny Weatherall" (page 611).

style, the distinctive handling of language by an author. It involves the specific choices made with regard to DICTION, syntax, FIGURATIVE LANGUAGE, and so on. For a comparison of two different styles, see Hemingway's "In Another Country" (page 580) and Tyler's "Teenage Wasteland" (page 866).

symbol, a concrete image used to designate an abstract quality or concept. A military medal may be a symbol of bravery, a dove a symbol of peace. Often the title of a work or a repeated image is a clue to symbolic meaning. See, for example, Ana Castillo's "Red Wagons" (page 898).

synecdoche (si nek′də kē), a figure of speech in which a part stands for the whole, as in "hired hands." *Hands* (the part) stands for the whole (those who do manual labor; those who work with their hands). The term also refers to a figurative expression in which the whole stands for a part, as in "call the law." *Law* (the whole) represents the police (a part of the whole system of law).

tale, a simple prose or verse NARRATIVE, either true or fictitious. Twain's "The Celebrated Jumping Frog of Calaveras County" (page 390) is a tale.

theme, the underlying meaning of a literary work. A theme may be directly stated but more often is implied. The topic of Hawthorne's "Dr. Heidegger's Experiment" (page 276) is the experiment involving a miraculous water, but the theme concerns vanity. Not every work has a theme.

tone, the author's attitude, either stated or implied, toward his or her subject matter and toward the audience. Cabeza de Vaca's tone (page 14) is sometimes matter-of-fact, sometimes wondering. Satanta's tone (page 403) is firm and forthright.

tragedy, dramatic or NARRATIVE writing in which the main character suffers disaster after a serious and significant struggle, but faces his or her downfall in such a way as to attain heroic stature.

verse, in its most general sense, a synonym for POETRY. Verse may also be used to refer to poetry carefully composed as to RHYTHM and RHYME SCHEME, but of inferior literary value.

Glossary of Vocabulary Words

a hat	ī ice	ü rule		
ā age	o hot	ch child		a in about
ä far	ō open	ng long		e in taken
â care	ô order, all	sh she	ə	i in pencil
e let	oi oil	th thin		o in lemon
ē equal	ou out	ŦH then		u in circus
ė term	u cup	zh measure		
i it	ù put			

abandonment (ə ban′dən mənt), *n.* freedom from restraint.

abashed (ə basht′), *adj.* embarrassed; ashamed.

abdicate (ab′də kāt), *v.* give up or relinquish formally.

abet (ə bet′), *v.* urge or assist in any way.

abolitionist (ab′ə lish′ə nist), *n.* person who advocates doing away with an institution or custom, such as slavery.

abruptly (ə brupt′lē), *adv.* unexpectedly.

accost (ə kost′), *v.* approach and speak to.

accursed (ə kėr′sid), *adj.* hateful.

acquiescence (ak′wē es′ns), *n.* consent given without objections; assent.

adrenaline (ə dren′l ən), *n.* hormone which speeds up the heartbeat and thereby increases bodily energy and resistance to fatigue.

adverse (ad vėrs′), *adj.* unfavorable; harmful.

affidavit (af′ə dā′vit), *n.* statement written down and sworn to be true, usually before an authorized official.

affiliation (ə fil′ē ā′shən) *n.* association or connection with a group or organization.

affirm (ə fėrm′), *v.* declare positively to be true.

afford (ə fôrd′), *v.* manage to give or spare.

aggregate (ag′rə git), *adj.* total.

agitated (aj′ə tāt əd), *adj.* disturbed; very upset.

alcove (al′kōv), *n.* a small room opening out of a larger room.

alien (ā′lyən), *adj.* strange; foreign.

alight (ə līt′), *v.* descend and lightly settle.

altitude (al′tə tüd), *n.* height above the earth's surface.

ambiguous (am big′yü əs), having several possible interpretations; lacking definiteness.

ameliorate (ə mē′lyə rāt), *v.* to make better or improve something.

amiably (ā′mē ə blē), *adv.* in a pleasant and agreeable way.

anguish (ang′gwish), *n.* great suffering.

anonymity (an′ə nim′ə tē), *n.* condition or quality of being unknown, nameless.

append (ə pend′), *v.* attach as a supplement.

aptly (apt′lē), *adv.* intelligently.

arbitrary (är′bə trer′ē), *adj.* based on one's own wishes, notions, or will.

arduous (är′jü əs), *adj.* hard to do.

articulate (är tik′yə lit), *adj.* able to put one's thoughts into words easily and clearly.

aspiration (as′pə rā′shən), *n.* a longing; ambition.

assiduously (ə sij′ü əs lē), *adv.* attentively; diligently.

assuredly (ə shùr′əd lē), *adv.* confidently, boldly.

atrociously (ə trō′shes lē), *adv.* shockingly badly.

audaciously (ô dā′shəs lē), *adv.* in a bold or impudent manner.

avarice (av′ər is), *n.* greed.

averted (ə vėrt′əd), *adj.* turned away or turned aside.

avid (av′id), *adj.* extremely eager.

azure (azh′ər), *adj.* the clear blue color of the unclouded sky.

barbarous (bär′bər əs), *adj.* not civilized; savage.

barren (bar′ən), *adj.* infertile or sterile; empty.

begrudge (bi gruj′), v. be reluctant to give or allow (something).

beguile (bi gīl′), v. entertain; amuse. Also deceive; delude.

belie (bi lī′), v. give a false idea of; misrepresent.

benevolent (bə nev′ə lənt), adj. kindly; charitable; wishing to promote the happiness of others.

bestow (bi stō′), v. give as a gift.

blatantly (blāt′nt lē), adv. obviously or flagrantly.

blithe (blīᵀH), adj. happy and cheerful; joyous.

bough (bou), n. one of the branches of a tree.

boycott (boi′kot), v. to abstain from using, buying, participating, or dealing with to express protest.

breaker (brā′kər), n. wave that breaks into foam on the shore, rocks, etc.

buxom (buk′səm), adj. attractively and healthily plump.

callow (kal′ō), adj. young and inexperienced.

capitulate (kə pich′ə lāt), v. surrender.

cardinal points (kärd′n əl points), n. pl. the four main points of a compass.

cavity (kav′ə tē), n. hollow place; hole.

cease (sēs), v. come to an end or stop.

censure (sen′shər), n. expression of disapproval; criticism.

cessation (se sā′shən), n. a ceasing, stopping.

chalice (chal′is), n. a cup-shaped blossom of a flower.

chaotic (kā ot′ik), adj. very confused; completely disordered.

charnel (chär′nl), adj. deathlike; ghastly.

chastise (cha stīz′), v. criticize severely; rebuke.

citation (sī tā′shən), n. honorable mention for bravery in war.

cite (sīt), v. summon officially to appear in court.

close (klōs), adj. private; reserved.

cognizance (kog′nə zəns), n. awareness.

commodious (kə mō′dē əs), adj. spacious; roomy.

compel (kəm pel′), v. drive or urge with force.

compensate (kom′pən sāt), v. make an equal return.

complacency (kəm plā′sn sē), n. a self-satisfaction; a sense of security.

comport (kəm pôrt′), v. conduct (oneself) in a certain manner; behave.

conclusive (kən klü′siv), adj. decisive; convincing.

condoning (kən dōn′ing), n. forgiving or overlooking.

conjecture (kən jek′chər), n. formation of opinion without sufficient evidence or proof.

conjurer (kon′jər ər), n. person who practices magic.

consanguinity (kon′sang gwin′ə tē), n. relationship by descent from the same parent or ancestor.

constrain (kən strān′), v. force; compel.

contempt (kən tempt′), n. open disrespect for the rules or decisions of a court of law.

contemptuous (kən temp′chü əs), adj. showing the feeling that a person, act, or thing is mean, low, or worthless.

contemptuously (kən temp′chü əs lē), adv. scornfully.

contention (kən ten′shən), n. struggle; competition.

contingent (kən tin′jənt), n. a group that is a part of another group.

convene (kən vēn′), v. meet for some purpose.

conviction (kən vik′shən), n. firmly-held belief, certainty.

coquetry (kō′kə trē), n. flirting.

cordial (kôr′jəl), adj. strengthening; stimulating; also warm and friendly in manner.

cornice (kôr′nis), n. an ornamental molding along the top of a wall, pillar, building, etc.

corroborate (kə rob′ə rāt′), v. confirm; support.

corroding (kə rōd′ing), adj. eating away gradually.

countenance (koun′tə nəns), n. expression of the face.

covenant (kuv′ə nənt), n. solemn agreement; compact.

craven (krā′vən), adj. cowardly.

cremate (krē′māt), v. to burn a dead body to ashes.

crimson (krim′zən), adj. a deep red.

crucial (krü′shəl), adj. very important; critical.

decisively (di sī′siv lē), adj. firmly, expressing no question or doubt.

deference (def′ər əns), n. respect.

deferential (def′ə ren′shəl), adj. showing respect for the judgment, opinion, wishes of another.

defilement (di fīl′mənt), n. an act of dishonoring.

defunct (di fungkt′), adj. no longer in use.

degenerating (di jen′ə rāt′ing), adj. worsening; showing a decline.

degraded (di grād′ed), adj. lower in rank, honor, quality.

demeanor (di mē′nər), n. way a person looks and acts, manner.

demented (di men′tid), adj. insane; crazy.

demur (di mėr′), v. show disapproval or dislike, take exception, object.

deposition (dep′ə zish′ən), n. testimony, especially a sworn statement in writing.

deprivation (dep′rə vā′shən), n. act of depriving; loss.

deride (di rīd′), v. scorn; ridicule.

desolate (des′ə lit), adj. deserted.

detached (di tacht′), adj. reserved, aloof.

diaphanous (dī af′ə nəs), adj. transparent.

diatribe (dī′ə trīb), n. a bitter, abusive criticism or denunciation.

digress (dī gres′), v. turn aside from the main subject; to ramble.

dilapidated (də lap′ə dā′tid), adj. fallen into ruin or disrepair.

diligent (dil′ə jənt), adj. hard-working; industrious.

discern (də zėrn′), v. perceive the difference between two or more things.

discerning (də zėrn′ing), adj. seeing clearly, perceiving the difference between two or more things.

disciplined (dis′ə plind), adj. well-trained.

discord (dis′kôrd), n. lack of harmony; contradiction.

disdain (dis dān′), n. a feeling of scorn.

disfigure (dis fig′yər), v. spoil the appearance of.

disposition (dis′pə zish′ən), n. one's habitual ways of acting toward others or of thinking about things; one's nature or attitude.

dispossess (dis′pə zes′), v. oust; deprive.

dispute (dis pyüt′), v. argue; disagree with.

dissemble (di sem′bəl), v. hide (one's real feelings, thoughts, plans, etc.); conceal one's motives.

dissipation (dis′ə pā′shən), n. a scattering in different directions.

diversified (də vėr′sə fīd), adj. varied.

doctrine (dok′trən), n. a principle taught by a church, nation, or group of persons; belief.

domestically (də mes′tik lē), adv. having to do with one's own country; not foreign.

dominion (də min′yən), n. power or right of governing.

dormant (dôr′mənt), adj. in a state of rest or inactivity.

dusky (dus′kē), adj. somewhat dark; dark-colored.

dwindle (dwin′dl), v. shrink; diminish.

eccentricity (ek′sen tris′ə tē), n. oddity; peculiarity.

ecstasy (ek′stə sē), *n.* condition of very great joy; overwhelming delight.

effaced (ə fāsd′), *adj.* rubbed out; blotted out; wiped out.

efficacy (ef′ə kə sē), *n.* power to produce the effect wanted; effectiveness.

elixir (i lik′sər), *n.* substance supposed to have the power of lengthening life indefinitely; cure-all.

emancipate (i man′sə pāt), *v.* release from slavery or restraint; set free.

emblem (em′bləm), *n.* object or symbol that represents an idea.

emerge (i mėrj′), *v.* come into view; come out.

eminent (em′ə nənt), *adj.* above most others; outstanding; distinguished.

enact (en akt′), *v.* pass (a bill), giving it validity as law.

enfranchisement (en fran′chīz mənt), *n.* the rights of citizenship, especially the right to vote.

enterprise (en′tər prīz), *n.* any undertaking, project, or venture.

enterprising (en′tər prī′zing), *adj.* showing initiative and readiness to undertake a project or venture.

entreaty (en trē′tē), *n.* an earnest request or appeal.

eradication (i rad′ə kā′shən), *n.* complete destruction or elimination.

erupt (i rupt′), *v.* burst forth.

escalation (es′kə lā′shən), *n.* act of being increasing or expanding something rapidly in stages.

etherised (ē′thə rīzd′), *adj.* unconscious from ether fumes.

evade (i vād′), *v.* avoid by cleverness; elude.

evasive (i vā′siv), *adj.* tending or trying to evade.

evident (ev′ə dənt), *adj.* easy to see or understand.

exalted (eg zôl′təd), *adj.* noble; elevated.

excommunication (ek′skə myü′nə kā′shən), *n.* a formal cutting off from membership in the church.

excruciatingly (ek skrü′shē ā′ting lē), *adv.* very painfully; torturously.

exile (eg′zīl), *v.* banish; force to leave one's country or home.

expedite (ek′spə dīt), *v.* do or perform quickly.

exponentially (ek′spō nen′shəl lē), *adv.* in a way that involves unknown or variable quantities as exponents. In everyday use, if objects decrease exponentially, they decrease dramatically in number.

extenuating (ek sten′yü ā′ting), *adj.* making the seriousness of a fault seem less; partially excusing.

exuberant (eg zü′bər ənt), *adj.* abounding in health and good spirits.

exultingly (eg zult′ing lē), *adv.* happily; joyfully.

fathom (faᴛʜ′əm), *n.* unit for measuring depth of water; a fathom is six feet.

fetch (fech), *v.* go to another place and bring back.

foeman (fō′mən), *n.* enemy in war; adversary.

fomenter (fō ment′ər), *n.* one who stirs up trouble or rebellion.

forbear (fôr bar′), *v.* hold back; keep from doing.

foreboding (fōr bō′ding), *n.* feeling that something bad is going to happen.

forlorn (fôr lôrn′), *adj.* wretched in feeling or looks; unhappy.

formidable (fôr′mə də bəl), *adj.* hard to overcome.

formulated (fôr′myə lāt əd), *adj.* reduced to a formula; expressed in a formula.

forsake (fôr sāk′), *v.* give up; abandon.

founder (foun′dər), *v.* fill with water and sink.

frankly (frangk′lē), *adv.* openly; expressing one's thoughts, opinions, and feelings freely.

frenum (frē′nəm), *n.* fold of membrane beneath the tongue.

furtive (fėr′tiv), *adj.* sly, stealthy.

furtively (fėr′tiv lē), *adv.* done quickly and stealthily to avoid being noticed; secretly.

futile (fyü′tl), *adj.* not successful, useless.

gainsay (gān′sā′), *v.* deny; contradict.

game (gām), *n.* wild animals, birds, or fish hunted or caught for sport or food.

gangling (gang′gling), *adj.* thin, tall, and awkward.

garret (gar′it), *n.* a space in a house just below a sloping roof.

garrulous (gar′ə ləs), *adj.* talkative.

gaunt (gônt), *adj.* very thin and bony.

genetic (jə net′ik), *adj.* having to do with origin and natural growth.

gentry (jen′trē), *n.* people belonging to the upper class of society.

gravity (grav′ə tē), *n.* serious or critical character; importance.

guile (gīl), *n.* crafty deceit, sly tricks, cunning.

gyration (jī rā′shən), *n.* a circular or spiral motion; whirling.

harass (har′əs, hə ras′), *v.* trouble by repeated attacks; harry.

hedge (hej), *v.* avoid giving a direct answer.

hegira (hej′ərə), *n.* departure; flight; journey.

helm (helm), *n.* the steering apparatus of a ship.

hinder (hin′dər), *v.* get in the way; make difficult.

hindrance (hin′drəns), *n.* person or thing that hinders; an obstacle.

homely (hōm′lē), *adj.* not good-looking; plain.

hone (hōn), *v.* to perfect or make more effective.

horizon (hə rī′zn), *n.* line where the earth and sky seem to meet.

hover (huv′ər), *v.* hang fluttering or suspended in air.

humiliate (hyü mil′ē āt), *v.* cause to feel ashamed.

humor (hyü′mər), *v.* give in to the whims of a person; indulge.

hurtle (hėr′tl), *v.* dash or drive violently.

hypocrite (hip′ə krit), *n.* person who is not sincere.

ideograph (id′ē ə graf), *n.* a graphic symbol that represents a thing or an idea directly, without representing the sounds of the word for the thing or idea.

imbibe (im bīb′), *v.* absorb; drink in.

immortality (im′ôr tal′ə tē), *n.* life without death, a living forever.

impassible (im pas′ə bəl), *adj.* not expressing feeling or emotion.

impatiently (im pā′shənt lē), *adv.* crossly; in a manner showing a lack of patience.

impeccable (im pek′ə bəl), *adj.* free from fault; irreproachable.

impedimenta (im ped′ə men′tə), *n.* pl. baggage, equipment, etc., which impedes movement or progress.

imperturbably (im′pər tėr′bə blē), *adv.* calmly.

impious (im pī′əs), *adj.* not showing reverence to God; wicked; profane.

implicate (im′plə kāt), *v.* show to have a part or be connected; involve.

implore (im plōr′), *v.* beg or pray earnestly for.

importune (im′pôr tün′), *v.* ask urgently or repeatedly.

imprecation (im′prə kā′shən), *n.* curse.

impregnable (im preg′nə bəl), *adj.* able to resist attack.

improvise (im′prə vīz), *v.* make up on the spur of the moment; perform without preparation.

impunity (im pyü′nə tē), *n.* freedom from punishment.

inadvertently (in′əd vėrt′nt lē), *adv.* in an inattentive, careless, or negligent way.

inconsistency (in′kən sis′tən sē), *n.* act that is lacking in agreement, harmony.

indecision (in′di sizh′ən), *n.* tendency to delay or hesitate.

indeterminate (in′di tėr′mə nit), *adj.* not definite or fixed.

indictment (in dīt′mənt), *n.* accusation.

indignant (in dig′nənt), *adj.* angry at something unworthy, unjust, unfair.

indiscernible (in′də zėr′nə bəl), *adj.* not distinguishable; imperceptible.

ineffable (in ef′ə bəl), *adj.* too great to be described in words.

ineptly (in ept′lē), *adv.* in an awkward or clumsy manner.

infamous (in′fə məs), *adj.* well-known, but with a very bad reputation.

infinitesimal (in′fi nə tes′ə məl), *adj.* so small as to be almost nothing.

infirmity (in fėr′mə tē), *n.* sickness, illness.

injunction (in jungk′shən), *n.* an authoritative or emphatic order; command.

insidious (in sid′ē əs), *adj.* wily; sly.

insular (in′sə lər), *adj.* standing alone like an island; isolated.

insuperable (in sü′pər ə bəl), *adj.* unable to overcome.

interminable (in tėr′mə nə bəl), *adj.* unceasing; endless.

interminableness (in tėr′mə nə bəl nes), *n.* endlessness.

interminably (in tėr′mə nə blē), *adv.* endlessly.

intricacy (in′trə kə sē), *n.* intricate nature or condition; complexity.

intricately (in′trə kit lē), *adv.* elaborately.

inundate (in′un dāt), *v.* overspread as if with a flood.

involuntarily (in vol′ən ter′ə lē), *adv.* in a manner that is not of one's own free will.

irked (ėrkd), *adj.* disgusted, annoyed.

jeopardize (jep′ər dīz), *v.* put in danger; risk.

jilt, *v.* cast off a lover or sweetheart after giving encouragement.

jocularity (jok′yə lar′ə tē), *n.* with a jocular (funny, joking) quality.

jubilant (jü′bə lənt), *adj.* joyful.

laudable (lo′də bəl), *adj.* worthy of praise.

lectern (lek′tərn), *n.* a reading desk or stand.

literacy (lit′ər ə sē), *n.* ability to read and write.

loathsomeness (lōŦH′səm nəs), *n.* cause of disgust.

maelstrom (māl′strəm), *n.* a turbulent whirlpool.

magnanimity (mag′nə nim′ə tē), *n.* nobility of soul or mind.

maize (māz), *n.* corn.

malign (mə līn′), *adj.* evil; injurious.

malinger (mə ling′gər), *v.* pretend to be sick in order to avoid work.

mandatory (man′də tôr′ē), *adv.* required by a command or order.

martinet (märt′n et′), *n.* a person who upholds and enforces very strict discipline.

marvel (mär′vel), *n.* something wonderful; an astonishing thing.

massive (mas′iv), *adj.* bulky and heavy; huge.

meager (mē′gər), *adj.* poor or scanty; sparse.

meanly (mēn′lē), *adv.* of a small-minded nature.

meditate (med′ə tāt), *v.* engage in deep and serious thought.

melancholy (mel′ən kol′ē), *adj.* sad; gloomy.

menacingly (men′is ing lē), *adv.* in a threatening manner.

mendicant (men′də kənt), *n.* beggar.

mentor (men′tər), *n.* a wise and trusted advisor.

meticulous (mə tik′yə ləs), *adj.* extremely careful about details.

mimic (mim′ik), *v.* make fun of by imitating.

morass (mə ras′), *n.* a difficult situation; puzzling mess.

morose (mə rōs′), *adj.* gloomy; sullen; ill-humored.

mute (myüt), *adj.* not making any sound; silent.

myriad (mir′ē əd), *n.* a very great number; countless; innumerable.

nadir (nā′dər), *n.* lowest point.

naive (nä ēv′), *adj.* not sophisticated.

nascent (nā′snt), *adj.* in the process of coming into existence; emerging.

nemesis (nem′ə sis), *n.* an unbeatable rival.

nominal (nom′ə nəl), *adj.* in name only.

nonexistent (non′ig zis′tənt), *adj.* having no being or existence.

notorious (nō tōr′ē əs), *adj.* well-known, especially for something bad.

obeisance (ō bē′sns), *n.* show of deference or respect.

oblivious (ə bliv′ē əs), *adj.* not mindful; unaware.

obscure (əb skyùr′), *adj.* not well known; attracting no notice.

obsequious (əb sē′kwē əs), *adj.* polite or obedient from hope of gain.

obstinate (ob′stə nit), *adj.* not giving in; stubborn.

obtuse (əb tüs′), *adj.* slow in understanding.

ominous (om′ə nəs), *adj.* unfavorable; threatening.

oppress (ə pres′), *v.* keep down unjustly or by cruelty.

opulence (op′yə ləns), *n.* wealth; riches.

organdy (ôr′gən dē′), *n.* a fine, thin, stiff, transparent material, used for dresses, curtains, etc.

ostentation (os′ten tā′shən), *n.* display intended to impress others.

pallor (pal′ər), *n.* lack of normal color from fear, illness, or death.

pandemonium (pan′də mō′nē əm), *n.* wild disorder or lawless confusion.

parched (pärcht), *adj.* hot and dry; thirsty.

parochial (pə rō′kē əl), *adj.* narrowly restricted.

parsimony (pär′sə mō′nē), *n.* extreme economy; stinginess.

pathos (pā′thos), *n.* quality that arouses a feeling of pity or sadness.

peer (pēr), *v.* look closely to see clearly.

perfidy (per′fə dē), *n.* being false to a trust; base treachery.

peril (per′əl), *n.* chance of harm or loss.

perjury (per′jər ē), *n.* crime of willfully giving false testimony or withholding evidence while under oath.

perplexed (pər pleksd′), *adj.* puzzled; bewildered.

persecuted (per′sə kyüt əd), *adj.* oppressed because of one's principles or beliefs.

persistently (pər sis′tənt lē), *adv.* continually.

pestilential (pes′tl en′shəl), *adj.* causing or likely to cause disease or death.

pettishness (pet′ish nəs), *n.* peevishness; crossness.

placid (plas′id), *adj.* pleasantly calm or peaceful.

plague (plāg), *v.* annoy or bother.

platitude (plat′ə tüd), *n.* dull or commonplace remark, especially one give out solemnly as if it were fresh and important.

plunder (plun′dər), *v.* rob.

poignant (poi′nyənt), *adj.* very distressing; deeply felt.

politic (pol′ə tik), *adj.* wise in looking out for one's own interests.

portfolio (pôrt fō′lē ō), *n.* holdings in the form of stocks, bonds, etc.

postponement (pōst pōn′mənt), *n.* delay.

precariously (pri kar′ē əs lē), *adv.* insecurely; uncertainly.

precipitate (pri sip′ə tāt), *v.* hasten the beginning of; bring about suddenly.

precipitation (pri sip′ə tā′shən), *n.* a hurrying.

preconception (prē′kən sep′shən), *n.* idea or opinion formed beforehand.

predilection (pred′ə lek′shən), *n.* a liking; preference.

premeditation (prē′med ə tā′shən), *n.* previous deliberation or planning.

preoccupied (prē ok′yə pīd), *adj.* absorbed; engrossed.

presage (pres′ij), *v.* give warning of.

presume (pri züm′), *v.* dare; take liberties.

prevail (pri vāl′), *v.* to be great in strength or influence; triumph.

prevalent (prev′ə lənt), *adj.* widespread; common.

primal (prī′məl), *adj.* of early times; first; primeval.

prismatic (priz mat′ik), *adj.* varied in color; brilliant.

profoundly (prə found′lē), *adv.* deeply felt; very greatly.

prominent (prom′ə nənt), *adj.* well-known or conspicuous.

propitious (prə pish′əs), *adj.* favorable.

proposition (prop′ə zish′ən), *n.* what is offered to be considered; proposal.

prosecutor (pros′ə kyü′tər), *n.* the lawyer in charge of the government's case against an accused person.

prostrate (pros′trāt), *v.* to bow down low in submission, worship, or respect.

prowess (prou′is), *n.* bravery; daring.

pulsate (pul′sāt), *v.* beat; throb.

pummel (pum′əl), *v.* strike or beat; beat with the fists.

pursue (pər sü′), *v.* follow to catch, chase.

pyre (pīr), *n.* large pile of burnable material.

quake (kwāk), *v.* shake or tremble.

quandary (kwon′drē), *n.* state of perplexity or uncertainty; dilemma.

radical (rad′ə kəl), *n.* person favoring extreme changes or reforms.

rambunctious (ram bungk′shəs), *adj.* wild and noisy.

rampant (ram′pənt), *adj.* unrestrained; unchecked.

rapt (rapt), *adj.* so busy thinking of or enjoying one thing that one does not know what else is happening.

raucous (rô′kəs), *adj.* hoarse; harsh sounding.

ravenous (rav′ə nəs), *adj.* very hungry; greedy.

reap (rēp), *v.* to gather a crop.

rebuke (ri byük′), *v.* express disapproval of.

recommence (rē kə mens′), begin again.

recusant (ri kyü′sənt), *n.* one who refuses to submit or comply.

redundant (ri dun′dənt), *adj.* needlessly repetitive.

reiterated (rē it′ə rāt′əd), *adj.* repeated.

relent (ri lent′), *v.* give in.

relinquish (ri ling′kwish), *v.* give up; let go.

remonstrate (ri mon′strāt), *v.* reason in protest.

removal (ri mü′vəl), *n.* a degree of distance; remoteness.

render (ren′dər), *v.* give in return; give; do.

rendition (ren dish′ən), *n.* a performance of a musical score or dramatic piece.

repentant (ri pen′tənt), *adj.* feeling regret; sorry for wrongdoing.

reprieve (ri prēv′), *n.* delay in carrying out a punishment, especially the death penalty.

repudiate (ri pyü′dē āt), *v.* refuse to accept; reject.

resign (ri zīn′), *v.* submit quietly; accept without complaint.

resilience (ri zil′ē əns), *n.* power of springing back; resilient quality or nature; elasticity.

resolute (rez′ə lüt), *adj.* determined; firm.

resolve (ri zolv′), *v.* break into parts or components.

restrictive (ri strik′tiv), *adj.* confining; limiting.

retaliation (ri tal′ē ā′shən), *n.* pay back for a wrong, injury, etc.

reticence (ret′ə səns), *n.* tendency to be silent or say little; reserved in speech.

reverential (rev′ə ren′shəl), *adj.* feeling deeply respectful, mixed with wonder.

rife (rīf), *adj.* full; abounding.

rivulet (riv′yə lit), *n.* a very small stream.

robust (rō bust′), *adj.* strong and healthy, sturdy.

rue (rü), *v.* to feel regret or remorse.

rummage (rum′ij), *v.* search thoroughly by moving things about.

scoff (skof), *v.* to show one does not believe something; mock.

scoffingly (skôf′ing lē), *adv.* mockingly; in a manner that makes fun to show one does not believe something.

scruple (skrü′pəl), *n.* a feeling of uneasiness that keeps a person from doing something.

sedulous (sej′ə ləs), *adj.* diligent; painstaking.

seethe (sēṯH), *v.* be excited; be disturbed.

semantic (sə man′tik), *adj.* having to do with the meaning of words.

serene (sə rēn′), *adj.* peaceful, calm.

sidle (sī′dl), *v.* move sideways.

skirmish (skėr′mish), *n.* minor conflict or contest.

smartly (smärt′lē), *adv.* in a lively, keen way.

smugness (smug′nes), *n.* overly pleased with one's own goodness, cleverness, respectability, etc.

solace (sol′is), *v.* to give comfort or relief.

solemn (sol′əm), *adj.* done with form and ceremony.

somber (som′bər), *adj.* melancholy; dismal.

spasmodically (spaz mod′ik lē), *adv.* in a manner characterized by sudden, involuntary contractions of a muscle or muscles.

speculative (spek′yə lā′tiv), *adj.* reflective.

stabilize (stā′bə līz), *v.* prevent changes in, hold steady.

stately (stāt′lē), *adj.* having dignity; imposing; majestic.

steadfast (sted′fast′), *adj.* loyal and unwavering.

stealthily (stelth′ə lē), *adv.* secretly; slyly.

stern (stėrn), *n.* rear part of a ship or boat.

stiffly (stif′lē), *adv.* not easy or natural in manner.

stigma (stig′mə), *n.* mark of disgrace.

stupor (stü′pər), *n.* a dazed condition.

subtle (sut′l), *adj.* so fine or delicate as to elude observation or analysis.

subtlety (sut′l tē), *n.* fine-drawn distinction, refinement of reasoning.

suffuse (sə fyüz′), *v.* overspread.

sullen (sul′ən), *adj.* showing resentment; somber.

sultry (sul′trē), *adj.* hot, close, and moist.

superfluous (sù pėr′flü əs), *adj.* more than is needed.

superlative (sə pėr′lə tiv), *adj.* of the highest kind; above all others; supreme.

surly (sėr′lē), *adj.* bad-tempered.

surmise (sər mīz′), *v.* infer or guess.

suspiciously (sə spish′əs lē), *adv.* in a mistrustful manner.

taboo (tə bü′), *adj.* prohibited; banned.

talisman (tal′is mən), *n.* anything that acts as a charm.

tamper (tam′pər), *v.* meddle improperly.

tauten (tôt′n), *v.* tighten.

teak (tēk), *n.* made of hard, durable, yellowish-brown wood from a large tree that grows in the East Indies.

tedious (tē′dē əs), *adj.* long and tiring, boring, wearisome.

thistle (this′əl), *n.* any of various composite plants with prickly stalks and leaves.

tranquil (trang′kwəl), *adj.* calm; peaceful.

transcribe (tran skrīb′), *v.* set down in writing.

transient (tran′shənt), *adj.* passing soon; fleeting.

translucent (tran slü′snt), *adj.* letting light through without being transparent.

transpire (tran spīr′), *v.* pass off or send off moisture in the form of vapor, through a membrane or surface, as from the human body or from leaves.

treacherous (trech′ər əs), *adj.* not reliable.

treasonous (trē′zn əs), *adj.* traitorous; involving betrayal of one's country.

trepidation (trep′ə dā′shən), *n.* nervous dread; fear.

tumult (tü′mult), *n.* emotional disturbance.

tumultuously (tü mul′chü əs lē), *adv.* violently.

turbulent (tėr′byə lənt), stormy; tempestuous.

unalienable (un ā′lyə nə bəl), *adj.* permanent; non-transferable.

unremitting (un′ri mit′ing), *adj.* never stopping; persistent.

unwittingly (un wit′ing lē), *adv.* not knowingly; unconsciously.

urgently (ėr′jənt lē), *adv.* in a manner demanding immediate attention.

usurpation (yü′zər pā′shən), *n.* the seizing and holding of the places or powers of another by force or without right.

vanity (van′ə tē), *n.* too much pride in one's looks, abilities, and so on.

vault (vôlt), *n.* something like an arched roof.

vector (vek′tər), *n.* organism that transmits disease germs, such as a mosquito or a tick.

vengeance (ven′jəns), *n.* revenge.

venturesome (ven′chər səm), *adj.* rash; daring.

veracious (və rā′shəs), *adj.* truthful.

verge (vėrj), *n.* the point at which something begins or happens; brink.

vile (vīl), *adj.* very bad; foul, disgusting, obnoxious.

vindicate (vin′də kāt), *v.* justify or support.

vindictive (vin dik′tiv), *adj.* feeling a strong tendency toward revenge.

visage (viz′ij), *n.* face, appearance or aspect.

wiry (wī′rē), *adj.* lean, strong, and tough.

wither (wiᴛʜ′ər), *v.* shrivel.

wrath (rath), *n.* very great anger; rage.

yearning (yėr′ning), *n.* strong desire; longing.

Language and Grammar Handbook

A

accept, except The similarity in sound causes these words to be confused. *Accept* means "to take or receive; consent to receive; say yes to." It is always a verb. *Except* is most commonly used as a preposition meaning "but."

◆ She did not hear the story as many women have heard the same, with a paralyzed ability to *accept* it.
   from "The Story of an Hour" by Kate Chopin

◆ She sat . . . quite motionless, *except* when a sob came up . . .
   from "The Story of an Hour" by Kate Chopin

active and passive voice A verb is said to be in the active voice when its subject is the doer of the action, and in the passive voice when its subject is the receiver of the action. A passive verb is a form of the verb *be* plus the past particple of the verb: *is written, had been written, will be written,* and so on.

ACTIVE: Jessica prepared dinner for the family.

PASSIVE: Dinner for the family was prepared by Jessica.

Active verbs are more natural, direct, and forceful than passive verbs. Passive verbs are useful and effective, however, when the doer of the action is unknown, unimportant, or obvious, or when special emphasis is wanted for the receiver of the action:

◆ Without elation, without an interval of moist glory, the cold was gone.
   from "Winter Dreams" by F. Scott Fitzgerald

◆ Evenings were spent mainly on the back porches. . . .
   from "To Be Young, Gifted and Black" by Lorraine Hansberry

p. 229
p. 236 **adjective** Adjectives are modifiers that describe nouns and pronouns and make their meaning more exact. Adjectives tell *what kind, which one,* or *how many.*

What kind:	*dusty* road	*red* bird	*brick* house
Which one:	*this* game	*that* person	*those* players
How many:	*five* weeks	*few* spectators	*many* ducks

See also **comparative forms of adjectives and adverbs.**

p. 253 **adverb** Adverbs modify verbs, adjectives, or other adverbs. They tell *how, when,* or *where* about verbs.

How:	quickly	courageously	slowly
When:	soon	now	tomorrow
Where:	here	there	near

See also **comparative forms of adjectives and adverbs.**

affect, effect *Affect* is a verb. It is most frequently used to mean "to influence." *Effect* is mainly used as a noun meaning "result" or "consequence."

◆ . . . seeing wise Seneca was so *affected* with sailing a few miles on the coast of his own Italy, as he affirmed, that he had rather remain. . . .
from *Of Plymouth Plantation* by William Bradford

◆ At home the *effects* were no less disturbing.
from *Black Boy* by Richard Wright

p. 228 **agreement**

1. subject-verb agreement

a. Most compound subjects joined by *and* or *both . . . and* are plural and are followed by plural verbs.

◆ The old woman and her daughter were sitting on their porch when Mr. Shiftlet came up their road for the first time.
from "The Life You Save May Be Your Own" by Flannery O'Connor

b. A compound subject joined by *or, either . . . or,* or *neither . . . nor* is followed by a verb that agrees in number with the closer subject.

Neither Josie nor the Riveras drive a van.

Neither the Riveras nor Josie drives a van.

Problems arise when it isn't obvious what the subject is. The following rules should help you with some of the most troublesome situations.

c. Phrases or clauses coming between the subject and the verb do not affect the subject-verb agreement.

◆ The helpless part of trying to do anything about it was that she did it all herself.
from "Winter Dreams" by F. Scott Fitzgerald

d. Singular verbs are used with singular indefinite pronouns—*each, every, either, neither, anyone, anybody, one, everyone, everybody, someone, somebody, nobody, no one.*

◆ Nobody seems to notice me.
from "Blue Winds Dancing" by Thomas S. Whitecloud

e. Plural indefinite pronouns take plural verbs. They are *both, few, many,* and *several.*

Many of the football players sleep on the way home.

p. 226 **f. The indefinite pronouns *all, any, most, none,* and *some* can be either singular or plural depending on their meaning in a sentence.**

<u>Singular</u>
All the neighborhood *was* dark.
Most of the night *was* calm.
None of the shopping *is* done.

<u>Plural</u>
All the streets *were* snowy.
Most of the cars *were* stuck.
None of the groceries *are* here.

g. The verb agrees with the subject regardless of the number of the predicate complement (after a form of a linking verb).

His one *dislike was* cats.
Cats were his one dislike.

h. Unusual word order does not affect agreement; the verb generally agrees with the subject, whether the subject follows or precedes it:

◆ In me was shaping a yearning for a kind of consciousness, a mode of being that the way of life about me had said could not be. . . .
from *Black Boy* by Richard Wright

In informal English, you may often hear sentences like "There's a sandwich and a cold drink for you on the counter." *There's* is a contraction for "There is." Technically, since the subject is a sandwich and a cold drink, the verb should be plural and the sentence should begin, "There are . . ." Since this may sound strange, you may want to revise the sentence to something like "A sandwich and a cold drink are on the counter." Be especially careful of sentences beginning with *There;* be sure the verb agrees with the subject.

◆ There were times when I thought I'd gone off the psychic edge.
from "On the Rainy River" by Tim O'Brien

◆ There is an incessant influx of novelty into the world, and yet we tolerate incredible dullness.
from *Walden* by Henry David Thoreau

2. Pronoun-antecedent agreement.

a. An antecedent is a word, clause, or phrase to which a pronoun refers. The pronoun agrees with its antecedent in person, number, and gender.

Alma will tell me if she can go.

The actors knew that the audience was filled with their relatives.

b. Singular pronouns are generally used to refer to the indefinite pronouns *one, anyone, each, either, neither, everybody, everyone, somebody, someone, nobody,* and *no one.*

antec.   pron.
Has somebody lost her jacket?

antec.   pron.
No one remembered his ticket.

The second sentence poses problems. It is clearly plural in meaning, and "everybody" may not refer to men only. To avoid the latter problem, you could write "No one remembered his or her ticket." This solution is clumsy and wordy, though. Sometimes it is best to revise:

No students remembered their tickets.

HINT: If you can use the word *ready* alone, without changing the meaning of the sentence, *all ready* is the one to use.

all ready, already *All ready* is an adjective phrase meaning "quite ready." *Already* is an adverb of time.

We are packed and *all ready* to go.

◆ . . . he lost consciousness and was as one *already* dead.
    from "An Occurrence at Owl Creek Bridge" by Ambrose Bierce

NOTE: The spelling *alright* is not accepted in either formal or informal writing.

all right *All right* is used both as an adjective and as an adverb.

◆ "I'm pretty hungry, *all right*," he said. "I'll tell you about that later."
    from "The Leader of the People" by John Steinbeck

ambiguity An ambiguous sentence is one that has two or more possible meanings. The most common causes of ambiguity are these:

1. misplaced modifiers Misplaced modifiers, because of their position in a sentence, do not clearly modify the word they are intended to modify. They are also often a source of humor that the writer does not intend.

Ambiguous: The tourists saw the tower on the bus.
Clear: The tourists on the bus saw the tower.
Clear: On the bus, the tourists saw the tower.

2. incomplete comparisons

Ambiguous: Seiko likes sushi as much as Eric.
Clear: Seiko likes sushi as much as Eric does.

amount, number *Amount* is used to refer to nouns which name things that can be measured or weighed; *number* is used in referring to nouns which name things that can be counted.

large amount of wood   large number of jewels
small amount of cloth   small number of books

NOTE: An apostrophe is not used in forming other plurals or in the possessive form of personal pronouns: "The tickets are theirs."

apostrophe (') An apostrophe is used in possessive words, both singular and plural, and in contractions. It is also used to form the plurals of letters and numbers.

men's league	Teresa's bracelet	can't
A's and *B*'s	6's and 7's	wasn't

Apostrophes may be used to indicate places in words in which the speaker does not pronounce certain sounds.

◆ "They're digging a cellar, I *s'pose,* if you've got to know."
from "The Revolt of 'Mother'" by Mary E. Wilkins Freeman

p. 176 **appositive** Apposition means, literally, a "putting beside." An appositive is a noun or phrase that follows a noun and identifies or explains it more fully. It is usually set off by commas or dashes.

◆ Mr Frank Davis, *the sheriff,* . . .
from *Crusade for Justice* by Ida B. Wells-Barnett

If, however, the appositive is used to specify a particular person or thing, it is not set off.

◆ . . . and burned the body of the poet *Shelley* who was drowned in a storm . . .
from *Lord Byron's Love Letter* by Tennessee Williams

as, like. *See* **like, as.**

awhile, a while *Awhile* (one word) is an adverb; use two words when *while* is a noun in a prepositional phrase.

◆ Stop and rest *awhile.*

◆ For a *while* I just drove, not aiming at anything. [*While* is object of the preposition *for.*]
from "On the Rainy River" by Tim O' Brien

B

bad, badly In formal English and in writing, *bad* (the adjective) is used to modify a noun or pronoun and is used after a linking verb. *Badly* (the adverb) modifies a verb.

◆ . . . though he knew it was *bad* for him, . . . [adjective used with linking verb *was*]
from "The First Seven Years" by Bernard Malamud

◆ She wanted to see John again and point to them and say, Well, I didn't do so *badly,* did I?
from "The Jilting of Granny Weatherall" by Katherine Anne Porter

HINT: To check yourself, mentally eliminate the first term. You would never say "between we," you would say "between *us*," us being the objective form of the pronoun *we*.

between you and me After prepositions such as *between,* use the objective form of the personal pronouns: between you and **me,** between you and **her,** between you and **him,** between you and **us,** between you and **them.**

The run-off will be between you and him.

◆ Those were the only times of peaceful companionship between her and Susan.

from "I Stand Here Ironing" by Tillie Olsen

capitalization

p. 258 **C**

1. Capitalize all proper nouns and adjectives.

Proper Nouns	Proper Adjectives
Canada	Canadian
China	Chinese
Victoria	Victorian

p. 260

2. Capitalize people's names and titles.

General Powell	Uncle Jack	Grandma
Justice Ginsburg	Bishop Clark	Senator Hanrahan
Ms. Sarah Stoner	Dr. Fernandez	

3. Capitalize the names of ethnic groups, languages, religions, revered persons, deities, religious bodies, buildings, and writings. Also capitalize any adjectives made from these names.

Indo-European	Buddha	Grace Lutheran Church
German	Catholicism	the Bible
Islam	Allah	

NOTE: Do not capitalize directions of the compass or adjectives that indicate direction: Front Street runs north and south. The weather map showed showers in the northwest.

4. Capitalize geographical names (except for articles and prepositions) and any adjectives made from these names.

Australia	Tampa Bay	the Red Arrow Highway
Gila River	Danish pastry	Zion National Park
Straits of Mackinac	Spanish rice	
the Rockies	Southern accent	
Arctic Circle	Gettysburg	

NOTE: Earth, sun, and moon are not capitalized unless used with the names of other planets: Is Venus closer to the Sun than Saturn? The earth revolves around the sun.

5. Capitalize the names of structures, organizations, and bodies in the universe.

the Capitol	the House of Representatives
Carnegie Hall	the United Way
the Eiffel Tower	Neptune
the Cubs	the Milky Way

6. Capitalize the names of historical events, times, and documents.

the Hundred Years' War	the Elizabethan Period
the Treaty of Versailles	the Emancipation Proclamation

NOTE: Do not capitalize the names of the seasons.

NOTE: Some modern poets do not begin each line with a capital letter.

NOTE: No c
when the cc
words are s

7. Capitalize the names of months, days, holidays, and time abbreviations.

February   Sunday

Thanksgiving   A.M. P.M.

8. Capitalize the first letters in sentences, lines of poetry, and direct quotations.

◆ Because I could not stop for Death—
  He kindly stopped for me
     by Emily Dickinson

◆ "If you see this boy," said the ballerina, "do not—I repeat, do not—try
  to reason with him."
     from "Harrison Bergeron" by Kurt Vonnegut, Jr.

9. Capitalize certain parts of letters and outlines.

Dear Mrs. Moore,   Sincerely yours,

I. Early types of automobiles
   A. Gasoline powered
      1. Haynes
      2. Ford
      3. Other makes
   B. Steam powered
   C. Electric cars

10. Capitalize the first, last, and all other important words in titles.

book	Dickens's *Great Expectations*
newspaper	story in the *Washington Post*
play and movie	starred in *Showboat*
television series	liked *Murphy Brown*
short story	read "The Monkey's Paw"
music (long)	saw *The Pirates of Penzance*
music (short)	sang "Swing Low, Sweet Chariot"
work of art	Winslow Homer's *Breezing Up*
magazine	*Seventeen* magazine

See also **Italics.**

p. 160
p. 162
p. 164
clause A clause is a group of words that has a subject and a verb. A clause is independent when it can stand alone and make sense. A dependent clause has a subject and a verb, but when it stands alone it is incomplete, and the reader is left wondering about the meaning.

<u>Independent Clause</u>

     s   v
Richard Wright wrote *Black Boy.*

<u>Dependent Clause</u>

              s   v
Because Richard Wright wrote *Black Boy.*

Superlative: That documentary was the most interesting one I've ever seen.

See also **modifiers.**

p. 255 **conjunction** A conjunction is a word that links one part of a sentence to another. It can join words, phrases, or entire sentences. Coordinating conjunctions *(and, but, for, yet, or, nor, so)* connect words, phrases, and clauses of equal value. Subordinating conjunctions *(after, because, so that, unless, while, and so on)* connect dependent, or subordinate, clauses with main clauses.

Coordinating
rose *and* fell
She came yesterday, *but* left today.

Subordinating
Sara worked quickly *until* the dishes were done.

 dangling modifiers A modifier that has no word in a sentence which it can modify is said to be dangling. The italicized words in the first sentence seem, illogically, to modify *concert.*

Dangling: *Seated in the balcony,* the concert sounded magnificent.

Revised: The concert sounded magnificent to the audience seated in the balcony.

dash (—) A dash is used to indicate a sudden break or change of thought in a sentence:

◆ And yet she had loved him—sometimes.
from "The Story of an Hour" by Kate Chopin

dialogue Dialogue is often used to enliven many types of writing. Notice the punctuation, capitalization, and paragraphing of the following passage.

◆ "What is that? he asked.
"A story," I said.
"A news story?"
"No, fiction."
"All right, I'll read it," he said.
He pushed my composition book back on his desk and looked at me curiously, sucking at his pipe.
"But I want you to read it *now,*" I said.
from *Black Boy* by Richard Wright

See also **quotation marks.**

direct address *See* **Comma Rule 3**

ellipsis (. . .) An ellipsis is used to indicate that words (or sentences or paragraphs) have been omitted. An ellipsis consists of three dots, but if the omitted portion would have completed the sentence, a fourth dot is added for the period.

◆ "Well, what can we expect" "Yes, eighty years old. . . .
from "The Jilting of Granny Weatherall" by Katherine Anne Porter

◆ She was too vulnerable for that terrible world of youthful competition, of preening and parading, of constant measuring of yourself against every other, of envy, "If I had that copper hair," "If I had that skin. . . ."
from "I Stand Here Ironing" by Tillie Olsen

exclamation point (!) An exclamation mark is used at the end of an exclamatory sentence—one that shows excitement or strong emotion. Exclamation points can also be used with strong interjections.

◆ "Free! Body and soul free!" she kept whispering.
from "The Story of an Hour" by Kate Chopin

See also **quotation marks.**

fewer, less *See* **less, fewer**

fragment *See* **sentence fragment.**

friendly letter form A typical form for a friendly letter contains five parts: the heading, which provides the writer's address and the date, the greeting, the body of the letter, the closing, and the signature. Note the sample below.

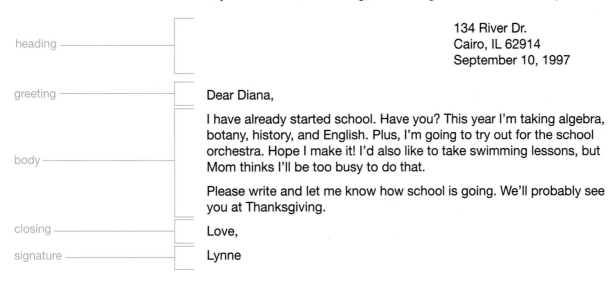

heading

134 River Dr.
Cairo, IL 62914
September 10, 1997

greeting

Dear Diana,

body

I have already started school. Have you? This year I'm taking algebra, botany, history, and English. Plus, I'm going to try out for the school orchestra. Hope I make it! I'd also like to take swimming lessons, but Mom thinks I'll be too busy to do that.

Please write and let me know how school is going. We'll probably see you at Thanksgiving.

closing

Love,

signature

Lynne

p. 244 **G**

gerund A verb form ending in *-ing* that is used as a noun.

◆ It means *dancing* to the strings of custom and tradition; it means *living* in houses and never knowing or caring who is next door.
from "Blue Winds Dancing" by Thomas S. Whitecloud

HINT: When you are referring to health, use *well* if the meaning is "not ill." "I am quite well, thank you." If the meaning is "pleasant" or "in good spirits," use *good.* "I feel good today."

good, well *Good* is used as an adjective to modify a noun or pronoun. Do not use it to modify a verb. *Well* is usually used as an adverb to modify a verb.

◆ But I stayed *good* friends with the boy who had been wounded. . . .
from "In Another Country" by Ernest Hemingway

◆ And as for the decks and upper works, they would caulk them as *well* as they could . . .
from *Of Plymouth Plantation* by William Bradford

H

hopefully This is often used to mean "it is hoped" or "I hope," as in the following sentence, "*Hopefully,* I can relieve at least some of the pressure." However in formal writing, avoid this usage.

◆ I'm hoping to relieve at least some of the pressure on my dreams.
from "On the Rainy River" by Tim O'Brien

however Words like *however, moreover, nevertheless, therefore, consequently,* etc. (known as conjunctive adverbs) require special punctuation. If the word comes within a clause, it is generally set off by commas:

◆ Tom Walker, however, was not a man to be troubled. . . .
from "The Devil and Tom Walker" by Washington Irving

If the conjunctive adverb separates two independent clauses, a semicolon is used preceding the word. If it begins a sentence, a comma is used after it:

◆ He did not argue; however, as the days went by . . .
from "The First Seven Years" by Bernard Malamud

p. 247 **I**

infinitive The infinitive is the simple form of the verb, usually preceded by *to.* Infinitives are used as nouns, adjectives, or adverbs. In the following sentence, each infinitive acts as a noun:

◆ *To play* is *to win* something.
from "To Be Young, Gifted and Black" by Lorraine Hansberry

p. 257 **interjection** An interjection is a word or phrase used to express strong emotion.

◆ Never lost a ball! Willing! Intelligent! Quiet! Honest! Grateful!
from "Winter Dreams" by F. Scott Fitzgerald

italics Italic type is used to indicate titles of whole works such as books, magazines, newspapers, plays, films, and so on. It is also used to indicate foreign words and phrases, or to emphasize a word.

◆ . . . perished usually at the *autos-da-fé,* and one of those had been held. . . .

from "The Pit and the Pendulum" by Edgar Allan Poe

See also **Capitalization Rule 10** for titles that are italicized.

NOTE: In formal English the correct way to respond to a question such as, "Who's there?" is "It is I." This sounds too formal in some situations, however. While it is not correct to say, "It's them," "It's him," "It's us," or "It's her," "It's me" is generally accepted as standard usage.

its, it's *Its* is the possessive form of the personal pronoun *it; it's* is the contraction meaning "it is."

lay, lie This verb pair presents problems because, in addition to the similarity between the words, the past tense of *lie* is *lay.* The verb *to lay,* means "to put or place something somewhere." The verb *to lie* means "to rest" or "to be at rest."

Present	Past	Past Participle	Present Participle
lay	laid	(has) laid	(is) laying
lie	lay	(has) lain	(is) lying

Notice how the verbs are used in the following sentences:

◆ Special emphasis was laid upon them. [Stress was placed on them.]
from *Crusade for Justice* by Ida B. Wells

NOTE: *Lied* refers only to not telling the truth: "The jury was convinced that the defendent lied."

◆ . . . he lay perfectly quiet and listened. [He rested quietly.]
from "Winter Dreams" by F. Scott Fitzgerald

less, fewer Use less to refer to amount or quantity (things that are measured). Use fewer to refer to number (to things that are counted).

less heat	fewer houses
less work	fewer jobs
less poverty	fewer scholarships

M

media *Media* is the plural of *medium.* Many people use a singular verb when referring to the mass media. In formal writing it is best to use a plural verb.

All the media *are* focused on the trial.

misplaced modifier *See* **ambiguity.**

p. 238
p. 249
modifier A modifier is a word or group of words that restrict, limit, or make more exact the meaning of other words. The modifiers of nouns and pronouns are usually adjectives, participles, adjective phrases, and adjective clauses. The modifiers of verbs, adjectives, and adverbs are adverbs, adverb phrases, and adverb clauses. In the following example, the italicized words modify the words in bold-face type.

◆ **Moving** *slowly* and from *side to side,* she went into the *big* **building,** and into a tower of steps where she **walked** *up* and *around* . . .
from "A Worn Path" by Eudora Welty

See also **comparative forms of adjectives and adverbs; dangling modifiers.**

myself (and **himself, herself,** and **so on**) Be careful not to use *myself* and the other reflexive and intensive pronouns when you simply need to use the personal pronoun *I* or its objective form *me.*

> Incorrect: Robert called Evan and myself into the office.

> Correct: Robert called Evan and me into the office.

HINT: When trying to decide which pronoun to use, remember that you would not say, "Myself is going to the game" You would use *I*. Use *I* with a compound subject, too.

Reflexive pronouns reflect the action of the verb back to the subject. An intensive pronoun adds emphasis to the noun or pronoun just named.

◆ ". . . with which I amuse myself here in my study."
   from "Dr. Heidegger's Experiment" by Nathaniel Hawthorne

◆ Even I didn't have, myself, the slightest inkling . . .
   from *The Autobiography of Malcolm X* by Malcolm X and Alex Haley

p. 178
p. 180
p. 182

noun A noun is a word that names a person, place, thing, or idea. Most nouns are made plural by adding *-s* or *-es* to the singular. When you are unsure about a plural form, check a dictionary.

parallel construction Items in a sentence that are of equal importance should be expressed in parallel (or similar) forms. These can take the form of noun phrases, verb phrases, infinitive phrases, and prepositional phrases:

◆ I've got my own mind an' my own feet, an' I'm goin' to think my own thoughts an' go my own ways, an' nobody but the Lord is goin' to dictate to me unless I've a mind to have him.
   from "The Revolt of 'Mother'" by Mary E. Wilkins Freeman

◆ She had treated him with interest, with encouragement, with malice, with indifference, with contempt.
   from "Winter Dreams" by F. Scott Fitzgerald

◆ Nobody was smarter than anybody else. Nobody was better looking than anybody else. Nobody was stronger or quicker than anybody else.
   from "Harrison Bergeron" by Kurt Vonnegut, Jr.

parentheses ( ) Parentheses are used to enclose words that interrupt or add explanation to a sentence. They are also used to enclose references to page numbers, chapters, or dates. Punctuation marks that belong to the sentence come after the parentheses, not before.

◆ Now, when it is too late (as if she would let me hold and comfort her like I do the others), I get up and go to her at once at her moan or restless stirring.
   from "I Stand Here Ironing" by Tillie Olsen

p. 242 **participle** A participle is a verb form used in forming various tenses of verbs. The present participle ends in *-ing: growing.* The past participle usually ends in *-ed, -t, -d, -en,* or *-n: scared, wept, said, risen, grown.* Participles are also used as adjectives, modifying nouns and pronouns.

◆ White *waving* ribbons that seem to pulsate with the rhythm of the drums.
from "Blue Winds Dancing" by Thomas S. Whitecloud

plagiarism Using the words, ideas, or expressions of others as if they were your own is called plagiarism. Plagiarism problems usually grow from the following circumstances: l. copying a passage from a source without giving credit; 2. paraphrasing a source so closely that only a few words or phrases are changed; 3. using someone else's ideas without giving credit. In a short paper credit is usually given directly in the text. In a longer piece of writing, you will need to footnote your sources.

possessive case The possessive case is formed in various ways. For singular nouns and indefinite pronouns, add an apostrophe and -s:

my *brother's* car   *no one's* notebook   *everybody's* children

For plural nouns ending in an -s, add only an apostrophe:

the *doctors'* offices   the *babies'* shoes   the *teachers'* rooms

If the plural is irregular and does not end in -s, add an apostrophe and then an -s: women's clothing.

p. 251
p. 253
prepositions Prepositions are words such as *about, between, during, from, in, of, over, under, until,* and *with* that show the relationship between a noun or pronoun and some other word in a sentence.

p. 251
prepositional phrase Prepositional phrases are groups of words that begin with a preposition and end with a noun or pronoun (the object of the preposition). These phrases act as modifiers and create vivid pictures for the reader. Notice the prepositional phrases in the following sentence:

◆ The investigator followed, *through a stout paintless gate in a picket fence, past a broad brick walk between two rows of shabby cedars, toward the rambling and likewise paintless sprawl of the two-story house in the open hall* of which the soft lamplight glowed and the lower story of which, as the investigator now perceived, was of logs.
from "The Tall Men" by William Faulkner

pronoun A pronoun is a word used instead of a noun to designate a person or object. Subject pronouns are used as subjects of sentences. Object pronouns can be used as direct objects, indirect objects, or objects of prepositions.

HINT: When you are uncertain about whether to use a subject pronoun or an object pronoun, take out the first pronoun to test the sentence. (You wouldn't say "Me played yesterday" or "Tom asked I to stay.")

p. 186,188,192
p. 192,194,198
p. 200

When a pronoun is used as the subject, it is in the nominative case. When a pronoun is used as an object, it is in the objective case.

Subject Pronouns			Object Pronouns		
Singular:	I	you	he, she, it	me	you	him, her, it
Plural:	we	you	they	us	you	them

He and I played yesterday	Tom asked her and me to stay.

p. 96
p. 268

quotation marks (" ") Quotation marks enclose a speaker's words. They are also used to enclose some titles. When you use someone's words in your writing, use the following rules:

1. Enclose all quoted words within quotation marks.

> Thomas Jefferson wrote, "All men are created equal."

2. Introductory and explanatory expressions *(he said, I replied)* **are set off by a comma, or if they interrupt a sentence, by two commas.**

3. Periods and commas are always put inside quotation marks. Semicolons are put outside quotation marks.

> "I've read several of his poems," he said, "and liked them."

4. A question mark or exclamation point is put inside the quotation mark if it applies only to the quoted matter, outside if it applies to the complete sentence that contains the quotation.

> Didn't Thomas Jefferson write "The Declaration of Independence"?

5. When both the sentence and the quotation ending the sentence are questions or exclamations, only one mark is used—inside the quotation marks.

> Who wrote "What Was It?"

6. A long quoted passage is often presented without quotation marks and indented instead, sometimes in smaller type.

See also **dialogue.**

real, really *Real* is used as an adjective, and *really* is used as an adverb.

> We couldn't tell the *real* diamond from the fake one.

> Our vacation was *really* great. [not "real great"]

p. 152 **run-on sentence** A run-on sentence occurs when there is only a comma (known as a comma splice) or no punctuation between two independent clauses. Separate the clauses into two complete sentences, join them with a semicolon, or use a comma and a coordinating conjunction

> Run-On: Anita saw the play, then she wrote a review.
> Correct: Anita saw the play. Then she wrote a review.
> Correct: Anita saw the play; then she wrote a review.
> Correct: Anita saw the play, and then she wrote a review.

Often, in narrative writing, authors purposely choose to use run-ons for effect, as in the following passage:

◆ Although, as we walked to the Cova through the tough part of town, walking in the dark, with light and singing coming out of the wineshops, and sometimes having to walk into the street when the men and women would crowd together on the sidewalk so that we would have had to jostle them to get by, we felt held together by there being something that had happened that they, the people who disliked us, did not understand.

from "In Another Country" by Ernest Hemingway

See also **stringy sentences.**

p. 266 **S** **semicolon (;)** Use this punctuation mark to separate the two parts of a compound sentence when they are not joined by a comma and a conjunction.

◆ Adoniram did not reply; he shut his mouth tight.
from "The Revolt of 'Mother'" by Mary E. Wilkins Freeman

p. 150 **sentence fragment** A fragment often occurs when one sentence is finished, but another thought occurs to the writer and that thought is written and punctuated as a complete sentence. Experienced writers often use fragments for effect as in the following passage.

◆ Northward again. Minnesota, and great white fields of snow; frozen lakes, and dawn running in dusk without noon. Long forests wearing white. Bitter cold, and one night the northern lights.
from "Blue Winds Dancing" by Thomas S. Whitecloud

stringy sentences A stringy sentence is one in which several independent clauses are strung together with *and.* Since all the ideas seem to be treated equally, a reader may have difficulty seeing how they are related. Correct a stringy sentence by breaking it into individual sentences or changing some of the independent clauses into subordinate clauses or phrases.

Stringy sentence: Saturday morning I have to take my brother to his music lesson and pick up some dry cleaning and then I'm supposed to let Mom have the car so she can shop and I guess I'll have to walk or hitch a ride to football practice.

Corrected: Saturday morning I have to take my brother to his music lesson and pick up some dry cleaning. Since I'm supposed to let Mom have the car so she can shop, I guess I'll have to walk or hitch a ride to football practice.

p. 202
p. 204
p. 208 **T** **titles** *See* **Capitalization Rules 2** *and* **10.**

p. 210
p. 212
p. 216 **V** **verb** A verb is a word that tells about an action or a state of being. The form or tense of the verb tells whether the action occurred in the past, the present, or the future.

p. 206 **verb shifts in tense** Use the same tense to show two or more actions that occur at the same time.

> Incorrect: She *went* [past] to the mall with friends and she *buys* [present] a sweater and earrings.

> Correct: She *went* [past] to the mall with friends and she *bought* [present] a sweater and earrings.

When the verb in the main clause is in the present tense, the verb in the subordinate clause is in whatever tense expresses the meaning intended.

Mr. Washington *thinks* that the dinner *was* a success.

voice *See* **active and passive voice.**

 p. 196 **who, whom** Use *who* as the subject of a sentence or clause. *Whom* is used as a direct object or the object of a preposition.

> ◆ The doctor told me that the major's wife, *who* was very young and *whom* he had not married until he was definitely invalided out of the war, had died of pnuemonia.
> from "In Another Country" by Ernest Hemingway

who's, whose *Who's* is a contraction meaning "who is"; *whose* is a possessive.

> ◆ "Howdy, Rafe," the marshal said. "*Who's* sick?"
> from "The Tall Men" by William Faulkner

> ◆ . . . in her eyes, *whose* gaze was fixed . . .
> from "The Story of an Hour" by Kate Chopin

 your, you're *Your* is the possessive form of the personal pronoun *you; you're* is a contraction meaning "you are."

> ◆ "Is she *your* baby girl?" he asked.
> from "The Life You Save May Be Your Own" by Flannery O' Connor

> ◆ "Tom, *you're* come for," . . .
> from "The Devil and Tom Walker" by Washington Irving

Index of Skills and Strategies

■

Writing Forms, Modes, and Processes

Reading/Thinking Strategies

Active reading model, xxvi–xxxv

■

Speaking, Listening, and Viewing

Interdisciplinary Connections

Multicultural Awareness and Appreciation

Index of Fine Arts & Artists

Index of Authors and Titles

Acknowledgments

continued from page iv

■

335 From *"Co. Aytch": A Side Show of the Big Show* by Sam R. Watkins, with a new Introduction by Roy P. Basler, pages 109–11. Copyright © 1962 by Macmillan Publishing Company. Reprinted by permission of Simon & Schuster Inc. **354–357** "Much Madness is divinest Sense," "The Soul selects her own Society," "This is my letter to the World," "A Bird came down the Walk" and "Because I could not stop for Death" by Emily Dickinson. Reprinted by permission of the publishers and the Trustees of Amherst College from *The Poems of Emily Dickinson,* Thomas H. Johnson, ed., Cambridge, Mass.: The Belknap Press of Harvard University Press, Copyright 1951, 1955, 1979, 1983 by the President and Fellows of Harvard College. **398** From *With His Pistol in His Hand: A Border Ballad and its Hero* by Américo Paredes, Copyright 1958, renewed 1986. By permission of the author and the University of Texas Press. **400** "Gold Mountain Poems" from *Songs of Gold Mountain: Cantonese Rhymes from San Francisco Chinatown* by Marlon K. Hom. Reprinted by permission of the University of California Press and the author. **420** From "Eleven" from *Thousand Pieces of Gold* by Ruthanne Lum McCunn, pages 105–108 and 109–110. Copyright © 1981 by Ruthanne Lum McCunn. Reprinted by permission of Beacon Press. **421** From *Down the Santa Fe Trail and into Mexico: The Diary of Susan Shelby Magoffin 1846–1857,* edited by Stella M Drumm, pages 37–39. Copyright 1926 by Yale University Press. Reprinted by permission of Yale University Press. **432** "The Setting Out" by N. Scott Momaday. Reprinted by permission. **432** "Night Journey" by Theodore Roethke from *The collected Poems of Theodore Roethke.* Copyright 1940 by Theodore Roethke. Reprinted by permission of Doubleday, a division of Bantam Doubleday Dell Publishing Group, Inc. **433** From *Blue Highways* by William Least Heat Moon. Copyright © 1982 by William Least Heat Moon. First appeared in *The Atlantic Monthly.* By permission of Little, Brown and Company in association with the Atlantic Monthly Press. **433** From Chapter 1 from *Mississippi Solo: A River Quest* by Eddy L. Harris, pages 1–2. Copyright © 1988 by Eddy L. Harris. Reprinted by permission of Lyons & Buford Publishers. **435** Excerpt from *The Grapes of Wrath* by John Steinbeck. Used by permission of Viking Penguin, a division of Penguin Books USA, Inc. **435** "Peregrinacion, Penitencia, Revolucion" by Cesar E. Chavez. Reprinted by permission of the Cesar E. Chavez Foundation. For additional information about Cesar E. Chavez and the UFW, please contact the Cesar E. Chavez Foundation, P.O. Box 62, Keene, CA 93531, (815) 882-5571, ext. 256. **436** Excerpt from *Diary of an Overland Journey* by Lydia Rudd. This item is reproduced by permission of The Huntington Library, San Marino, California. **440** "Speed" by May Swenson (Originally published in *The New Yorker*) from *Nature:*

Poems of Old and New. Copyright © 1994 by The Literary Estate of May Swenson. Reprinted by permission of Houghton Mifflin Company. All rights reserved. **440** "The Moth and the Star" by James Thurber from *Fables for Our Time* (HarperCollins). Copyright © 1940 by James Thurber. Copyright © 1968 by Rosemary A. Thurber. Reprinted by permission of Rosemary A. Thurber. **442** "Homesick Blues" from *The Dream Keeper and Other Poems* by Langston Hughes. Reprinted by permission of the publisher. **442** "Indian Boarding School: The Runaways" from *Jacklight* by Louise Erdrich. Copyright © 1984 by Louise Erdrich. Reprinted by permission of Henry Holt and Company, Inc. **483** From *Crusade for Justice: The Autobiography of Ida B. Wells,* edited by Alfreda M. Duster. Copyright 1970 by the University of Chicago. Reprinted by permission. **492–493** "The Spring and the Fall" and "On Thought in Harness" by Edna St. Vincent Millay from *Collected Poems* (HarperCollins). Copyright 1923, 1934, 1951, © 1962 by Edna St. Vincent Millay and Norma Millay Ellis. Reprinted by permission of Elizabeth Barnett, Literary Executor. **498** From *Complaints and Disorders: The Sexual Politics of Sickness* by Barbara Ehrenreich and Deirdre English. Reprinted by permission. **512** "Harlem: The Culture Capital" by James Weldon Johnson from *The New Negro,* edited by Alain Locke. With introduction by Arnold Rampersad, pages 301–311. **526** "Harlem Wine" by Countee Cullen. Reprinted by permission. **527** "Youth" from *The Dream Keeper and Other Poems* by Langston Hughes. Copyright 1932 by Alfred A. Knopf, Inc. and renewed © 1960 by Langston Hughes. Reprinted by permission of the publisher. **528** "Ma Rainey" by Sterling A. Brown from *The Collected Poems of Sterling A. Brown,* edited by Michael S. Harper. Copyright 1932 by Harcourt Brace & Company. Copyright renewed © 1960 by Sterling A. Brown. Reprinted by permission of HarperCollins Publishers, Inc. **533** "How It Feels to Be Colored Me" by Zora Neale Hurston. Reprinted by permission of Lucy Ann Hurston. **558** From "Which Side Are You On?," words by Florence Reece. Copyright 1946 by Stormking Music Inc. Reprinted by permission of Stormking Music Inc. All rights reserved. **559** Studs Turkel, *Working.* New York, N.Y.: Random House, Inc. **560** Mary Crow Dog, *Lakota Woman.* Grove Weidenfeld, 1990. **568** "The Love Song of J. Alfred Prufrock: from *Collected Poems 1909–1962* by T.S. Eliot. Reprinted by permission of Faber & Faber Ltd. **577** "1(a" by E.E. Cummings from *Complete Poems: 1904–1962,* edited by George J. Firmage. Copyright © 1958, 1986, 1991 by the Trustees for the E.E. Cummings Trust. Reprinted by permission of Liveright Publishing Corporation. **580** "In Another Country" by Ernest Hemingway, from *Men Without Women.* Copyright 1927 Charles Scribner's Sons; copyright renewed 1955 Ernest Hemingway. Reprinted with the permission of Charles Scribner's Sons and Jonathan Cape Ltd. **586** "Winter Dreams" reprinted (with slight deletions) with permission of Scribner, and imprint of Simon & Schuster, Inc., from *All the Sad Young Men* by F. Scott Fitzgerald. Copyright 1922 by Metropolitan Publications, Inc. Copyright renewed 1950 by Frances Scott Fitzgerald Lanahan. **605** From *Black Boy* by Richard Wright. Copyright 1937, 1942, 1944, 1945 by Richard Wright. Copyright renewed © 1973 by Ellen Wright. Reprinted by permission of HarperCollins Publishers, Inc. **611** "The Jilting of Granny Weatherall" in *Flowering Judas and Other Stories,* copyright 1930 and renewed 1958 by Katherine Anne Porter, reprinted by permission of Harcourt Brace & Company. **620** From Chapter Five, "The Revolution In Manners and Morals" from *Only Yesterday: An Informal History of the Nineteen-Twenties* by Frederick Lewis Allen, pages 89–92. Copyright 1931 by Frederick Lewis Allen. Copyright renewed © 1959 by Agnes Rogers Allen. Reprinted by permission of HarperCollins Publishers, Inc. **636, 637, 639** "Stopping By Woods On A Snowy Evening," "Mending Wall," and "Birches" from *the Poetry of Robert Frost* edited by Edward Connery Lathem. Copyright © 1962 by Holt, Rinehart, and Winston, Inc. Reprinted by permission of Henry Holt and Company, Inc., the Estate of Robert Frost, and Jonathan Cape, Ltd. **644** "The Tall Men" from *Collected Stories of William Faulkner* by William Faulkner. Copyright 1941 and renewed © 1969 by Estelle Faulkner and Jill Faulkner Summers. Reprinted by permission of Random House, Inc. **658** "Blue Winds Dancing" by Thomas S. Whitecloud in *Scribner's Magazine,* Vol. CIII. Copyright 1938 Charles Scribner's Sons; copyright renewed. Reprinted by permission of Charles Scribner's Sons, and imprint of Macmillan Publishing Company. **667** "A Worn Path" from *A Curtain of Green and Other Stories,* copyright 1941 and renewed 1969 by Eudora Welty, reprinted by permission of Harcourt Brace & Company. **676** "The Leader of the People" from *The Red Pony* by John Steinbeck. Copyright 1933, 1937, 1938, renewed © 1961, 1965, 1966 by John Steinbeck. Reprinted by permission of Viking Penguin, a division of Penguin Books USA Inc. **690** *Lord Byron's Love Letter* by Tennessee Williams. Reprinted by permission. **699, 700, 702** From *The Homefront: America During World War II* by Mark Jonathan Harris, Franklin D. Mitchell, and Steven J. Schechter, pages 69–70, 109–111, 251–252. Copyright © 1984 by Mark Jonathan Harris, Franklin D. Mitchell, and Steven J. Schechter. Reprinted by permission of The Putnam Publishing Group. **720** "The Life You Save May Be Your Own" from *A Good Man is Hard to Find and Other Stories* by Flannery O'Connor. Copyright 1953 by Flannery O'Connor and renewed © 1981 by Regina O'Connor. Reprinted by permission of Harcourt Brace & Company. **732** "I Stand Here Ironing" from *Tell Me a Riddle* by Tillie Olsen, introduction by John Leonard. Copyright © 1956, 1957, 1960, 1961 by Tillie Olsen. Reprinted by permission of Delacorte Press/Seymour Lawrence, a division of Bantam Doubleday Dell Publishing Group, Inc. **742** "Separating" from *Problems and Other Stories* by John Updike. Copyright © 1979 by John Updike. Reprinted by permission of Alfred A.

Knopf, Inc. **754** From *The Woman Warrior: Memoirs of a Girlhood Among Ghosts* by Maxine Hong Kingston. Copyright © 1975, 1976 by Maxine Hong Kingston. Reprinted by permission of the author. **760** "Everyday Use" from *In Love & Trouble: Stories of Black Women* by Alice Walker. Copyright © 1973 by Alice Walker. Reprinted by permission of Harcourt Brace & Company. **771** "Mirror" from *Crossing the Water* by Sylvia Plath. Reprinted by permission of HarperCollins Publishers, Inc. and Faber & Faber Ltd. **772** "One Art" by Elizabeth Bishop from *The Complete Poems 1927–1979.* Copyright © 1979, 1983 by Alice Helen Methfessel. Reprinted by permission of Farrar, Straus & Giroux, Inc. **773** "Legacies" from *My House* by Nikki Giovanni. Copyright © by Nikki Giovanni. Reprinted by permission of William Morrow and Company, Inc. **774** "Leaves" by Hamod from *Dying With the Wrong Name: New and Selected Poems* 1958–1979 (Smyrna-Anthe Press, New York, N.Y.). Copyright © 1980 by Hamod. Reprinted by permission of the author. **775** From *Blood Root* by Alma Villanueva (Place of Herons Press). Copyright © 1977 by Alma Luz Villanueva. By permission of the author. **779** Abridged from *The Great Leap: The Past Twenty-Five Years in America* by John Brooks. Copyright © 1966 by John Brooks. Reprinted by permission of Harper & Row, Publishers, Inc. and Harold Ober Associates Inc. **794** "Chicago: Southside Summers" from *To Be Young, Gifted and Black: Lorainne Hansberry in Her Own Words* (A Prentice-Hall Publication), adapted by Robert Nemiroff, pages 17–21. Copyright © 1969 by Robert Nemiroff & Robert Nemiroff as Executor of the Estate of Lorraine Hansberry. Reprinted by permission of Simon & Schuster Inc. **797** "Dream Deferred" from *The Panther and the Lash* by Langston Hughes. Copyright 1951 by Langston Hughes. Reprinted by permission of Alfred A. Knopf, Inc. **800** From "Letter from a Birmingham Jail" by Dr. Martin Luther King, Jr. Reprinted by permission. **806** From Chapter Nineteen 1965 from *The Autobiography of Malcolm X* by Malcolm X, with the assistance of Alex Haley, introduction by M.S. Handler, Epilogue by Alex Haley, pages 364–367 and 377–378. Copyright © 1964 by Alex Haley and Malcolm X. Copyright © 1965 by Alex Haley and Betty Shabazz. Reprinted by permission of Random House, Inc. **812** Adapted from "On the Rainy River" from *The Things They Carried* by Tim O'Brien. Copyright © 1990 by Tim O'Brien. Reprinted by permission of Houghton Mifflin Company/Seymour Lawrence. All rights reserved. **828** From "The Year of the Monkey" from *Where the Ashes Are: The Odyssey of a Vietnamese Family* by Nguyên Qúi Dú'c. Reprinted by permission of Addison-Wesley Publishing Company, Inc. **838** "The Village" by Estela Portillo. Copyright © 1989 by Estela Portillo. Reprinted by permission of the author. **866** "Teenage Wasteland" by Anne Tyler from *Seventeen Magazine,* November 1983, pages 145 and 167–169. Copyright © 1983 by Martín Espada. Reprinted by permission of W. W. Norton & Company, Inc. **876** "Gary Keillor" from *The Book of Guys* by Garriosn Keillor, pages 175–192. Reprinted by permission. **888** "Salvador Late or Early" from *Woman Hollering Creek: and Other Stories* by Sandra Cisneros. Published by Vintage Books, a division of Random House, Inc., New York and originally in hardcover by Random House, Inc. Copyright © 1991 by Sandra Cisneros. Reprinted by permission of Susan Bergholz Literary Services, New York. **893** "Coca-Cola and Coco Frío" from *City of Coughing and Dead Radiators* by Martín Espada, pages 26–27. Copyright © 1993 by Martín Espada. Reprinted by permission of W. W. Norton & Company, Inc. **894** "Lost Sister" from *Picture Bride* by Cathy Song. Reprinted by permission. **896** "Naming Myself" ("Poniendome Un Nombre") from *Another America (Otra América)* by Barbara Kingsolver, with Spanish Translations by Rebeca Cates, pages 56–57. Copyright © 1992 by Barbara Kingsolver. Reprinted with permission of Seal Press. **898** "Red Wagons" from *My Father Was a Toltec: And Selected Poems* by Ana Castillo, page 5. Reprinted by permission. **902** "Mother Tongue" by Amy Tan, first published in *The Threepenny Review.* Reprinted by permission. **911** Adaptation of "This Is What It Means to Say Phoenix, Arizona" from *The Lone Ranger and Tonto Fistfight in Heaven* by Sherman Alexie. Reprinted by permission. **923** "Top of the Food Chain," Copyright © 1993 by T. Coraghessan Boyle, from *Without a Hero* by T. Coraghessan Boyle. Used by permission of Viking Penguin, a division of Penguin Books USA Inc. **930** "A Blizzard Under Blue Sky: from *Cowboys Are My Weakness* by Pam Houston, pages 133–139. Copyright © 1992 by Pam Houston. Reprinted by permission of W. W. Norton & Company, Inc. **936** *The Janitor* by August Wilson. Copyright © 1985 by August Wilson. Reprinted by permission of the author. **939** "The Way We Will Be" from *U.S. News & World Report,* Oct. 25, 1993, vol. 115, No. 16, page 71. Copyright © 1993 by U.S. News & World Report. Reprinted by permission of U.S. News & World Report. **941** "Waking Up in 2025: A Scenario" from *The Futurist,* November–December 1994, page 38. Copyright G 1994 by World Future Society. Reprinted by permission of World Future Society, 7910 Woodmont Avenue, Suite 450, Bethesda, MD 20814. **942** "The Armored Cacoon" by Faith Popcorn from *Psychology Today,* Jan./Feb. 1995. Reprinted by permission. **956** From *Only Yesterday: An Informal History of the Nineteen-Twenties,* page 193–195. Reprinted by permission. **957** "1 Quake, 2 Worlds" by Rubén Martínez from *The New York Times,* January 20, 1994. Reprinted by permission.

■

Illustrations

Unless otherwise acknowledged, all photographs are the property of Scott, Foresman and Company. Page abbreviations are as follows: (t)top, (c)center, (b)bottom, (l)left, (r)right.

cover & frontispiece The Greenwich Workshop, Inc. Courtesy of The Greenwich Workshop, Inc., Shelton, CT (detail) on cover only **ii** The Greenwich Workshop, Inc. Courtesy of The Greenwich Workshop, Inc., Shelton, CT **viii** Charles Bird King, "Young Omahaw, War Eagle, Little Missouri and Pawnees"/National Museum of American Art, Washington, D. C./Art Resource **x** William Walcutt, "Pulling Down the Statue of George III," Private Collection **xii** National Museum of American Art, Washington, D. C./Art Resource **xix** Ralph Goings/O. K. Harris Gallery **xvii** Edward Hopper, "Nighthawks," Art Institute of Chicago/Superstock, Inc. **xvii** Robert Marcus Collection **0–1** Charles Bird King, "Young Omahaw, War Eagle, Little Missouri and Pawnees"/National Museum of American Art, Washington, D. C./Art Resource **1, 52, 54, 136, 142, 148** (icon) Delaware Art Museum **1, 2, 4, 41, 46, 51** (icon) Ohio Historical Society **3** Stock Montage, Inc. **7–8(c)** Philbrook Museum of Art, Tulsa, Oklahoma **9** Willard Clay **10** Jerry Jacka **12(br & tc)** Courtesy, Virginia Historical Society, Richmond **12(bcr& 13b)** Los Angeles County Museum of Art **12(bcl & 13t)** Historical Society of Pennsylvania **12(bl&cr)** National Archives of Canada, Ottawa **13** Granger Collection, New York **18** San Antonio Museum Association **21** Granger Collection, New York **24–25** Life Picture Service/Time-Warner Inc. **29** American Antiquarian Society **31** Pilgrim Society, Plymouth, Massachusetts **35** Jolene Rickard, "Two Canoes," 1987, color photograph collage, 28 x 17 inches, The M. & T. Bank Collection at the Burchfield Penney Art Center, Buffalo State College, Buffalo, New York **41(tobacco)** Arents Collection/New York Public Library, Astor, Lenox and Tilden Foundations, (pig) Library of Congress **42** Mireille Votter/Woodfin Camp & Associates **43** Bancroft Library, University of California, Berkeley **52–53** David Hiser/Photographers/Aspen, Inc. **52–53** Cynthia Clampitt **55(t)** Corbis-Bettmann Archive **55(b)** Granger Collection, New York **57** Peabody and Essex Museum **58** Massachusetts Historical Society **61** UPI/Corbis-Bettmann **68–132** Joan Marcus **137** U. S. Army photo **138(tr&br)** Archive Photos **138(bl)** Granger Collection **138(tl), 139(tl)** UPI/Corbis-Bettmann **139(tr)** Archive Photos **140** AP/Wide World **141** Metropolitan Museum of Art, New York, George A. Hearn Fund, 1956 **150** Charles Bird King, "Young Omahaw, War Eagle, Little Missouri and Pawnees"/National Museum of American Art, Washington, D. C./Art Resource **151(b)** Jerry Jacka **151(t)** Joan Marcus **152–153** William Walcutt, "Pulling Down the Statue of George III," Private Collection **153, 154, 156, 188, 193, 199(icon)** Tsing-Fang Chen, "Independence and Freedom," (detail)/Lucia Gallery, New York City/Superstock, Inc. **154(b)** The Fine Arts Museums of San Francisco, Gift of Mrs. Eleanor Martin **154(t)** Montana Historical Society **154–155** map, Diana Cole **154–155** title, Janice Clark **155(b)** Granger Collection **155(c)** New York Public Library, Astor, Lenox and Tilden Foundations **155(t)** Albany Institute of History & Art, New York **159** National Archives of Canada, Ottawa **161** Philadelphia Museum of Art, The Mr. and Mrs. Wharton Sinkler Collection **165** State Historical Society of Wisconsin, Museum Collection **169(b)** Corbis-Bettmann Archive **169(t)** National Portrait Gallery,

London **173** Collection of the Brandywine River Museum, Purchased through a grant from the Mabel Pew Myrin Trust **177** Independence National Parks & Monument Association/Eastern National Parks & Monuments Association **178–179** Library of Congress **184** Massachusetts Historical Society **188(r)** Library of Congress **188(c)** Robert Frerck/Odyssey Productions **188(l)** Schomburg Center for Research in Black Culture, New York Public Library **189(b)** S. Ferry/ Gamma-Liaison **189(tr)** Charlie Cole/Sipa Press **189(tl)** UPI/Bettmann **190** Smithsonian Institution **191** Courtesy of Petty Officer Maureen Sims **199(b)** Yale University Art Gallery **200(b)** Courtesy, The Henry Francis du Pont Winterthur Museum **200(t)** National Gallery of Art, Washington, D. C., Andrew Mellon Collection **201** William Walcutt, "Pulling Down the Statue of George III," Private Collection **202(b)** State Historical Society of Wisconsin, Museum Collection **202(t)** Library of Congress **205** National Museum of American Art, Smithsonian Institution, Gift of Mrs. Joseph Harrison, Jr./Art Resource **206** Private Collection, Photograph Courtesy of Kennedy Galleries Inc., New York **209** Gilcrease Institute of American History & Art, Tulsa **210** The Hudson Bay Co. **212** Courtesy Carol Hoy **213** National Park Service History Collection, Harper's Ferry Center, Harper's Ferry, West Virginia **216–217** National Museum of American Art, Washington, D. C./Art Resource **217, 298, 300, 332, 338, 344(icon)** Library of Congress **218(r)** Metropolitan Museum of Art, Gift of the Sculptor, 1906 (07.101) **218(l)** New York Public Library, Astor, Lenox and Tilden Foundations **218–219** title, Marilyn Reaves (for Eliza Schultz Lettering Design) **219(b)** Smithsonian Institution **219(cr)** Library of Congress **219(cl)** New Hampshire Historical Society **219(t)** White House Collection/Superstock, Inc. **221** George Eastman House **222** Private Collection **225** Concord Free Public Library **227** Elliot Porter **233** *Trodden Weed* by Andrew Wyeth, Tempera on panel, 1951. Collection of Mr. and Mrs. Andrew Wyeth, copyright 1995 by Andrew Wyeth **236** Sophia Smith Collection, Smith College **237** San Francisco Museum of Modern Art, Gift of Mrs. E. D. Lederman **239** Sleepy Hollow Restorations **240–241** Illinois State Museum **244** Indianapolis Museum of Art, Gift of Mrs. Morris Clark **247** Culver Pictures Inc. **252** Manuscripts Dept/Lilly Library, Indiana University, Bloomington, IN **266** National Gallery, Oslo, Norway/Superstock, Inc. **268** Courtesy of Tony Angell **275** Essex Institute, Salem, MA **277** Detroit Institute of Arts, Gift of Dexter M. Ferry, Jr. **279** Bequest of John T. Bowen, in memory of Eliza M. Bowen, Courtesy, Museum of Fine Arts, Boston **286(bl&br)** Kobal Collection **286(t)** Photofest **286–289** sky background, Sarah Marciniak **286–287** title, Janice Clark **287(br)** From the Collection of the Memory Shop **287(t&bl)** Kobal Collection **289** Courtesy of the Art Institute of Chicago **290** Universal Pictures **297** Photofest **298(b)** National Portrait Gallery/Transfer from the National Gallery of Art, Washington, D. C./Gift of Andrew W. Mellon **298–299(b)** St. Louis Museum of Art **298–299** Library of Congress **298(t)** The Metropolitan Museum of Art, Gift of I. N. Phelps Stokes, Edward S. Hawes, Alice Mary Hawes, Marian Augusta Hawes, 1937. (37.14.2) **299(t)** Stowe Day Foundation **301(b)** Library of Congress **301(t)** Granger Collection, New York **303** *Harpers Weekly*, May, 1861 **304–305(b)** Library of Congress **304–305(t)** National Archives **307** Corbis-Bettmann Archive **309** Metropolitan Museum of Art, Gift of Mr. and Mrs. Carl Stoecker, 1897 **311** Corbis-Bettmann Archive **312(inset)** British Film Institute **312** Yukimasa Hirota/Photonica **317(inset)** Lester Glassner Collection **317** Yukimasa Hirota/ Photonica **320** Dali, Salvador, THE PERSISTENCE OF MEMORY. 1931. Oil on canvas, 9–1/2 x 13". Collection, The Museum of Modern Art, New York. Given anonymously. Photograph © The Museum of Modern Art, New York. **321(all)** Library of Congress **323** West Point Museum, United States Military Academy **325(r)** Chris Nelson **325(l)** Fort Ward Museum, City of Alexandria, VA **328** Library of Congress **332** Museum of the Confederacy, Richmond, Virginia, photograph by Katherine Wetzel Museum of the Confederacy **333** National Archives **334** Courtesy of the Louise May Alcott Memorial Association **335** Collection of Mr. & Mrs. Franklin Fulton **337** Courtesy of Dennis Kelly **348–349** Walter, Ufer, "Where the Desert Meets the Mountain," The Anschutz Collection **349, 386, 388, 416, 423, 427(icon)** Library of Congress **349, 350, 352, 377, 381, 385(icon)** Culver Collections/Superstock, Inc. **350(tl)** Berry-Hill Galleries, New York **350(bl), 351(bl)** Library of Congress **350(br)** Edison Historic Site, National Park Service **350(t)** Museum of the City of New York **351(br)** Chicago Historical Society **351(c)** International Ladies Garment Workers Union Labor Management Documentation Center, Cornell University **351(t)** Brown Brothers **353** Trustees of Amherst College **355** National Gallery, Berlin/Superstock, Inc. **356** James Wyeth **360** Pennsylvania Academy of Fine Arts **361** Terra Museum of American Art **363** John Hancock Financial Services **364** Superstock, Inc. **369** Corbis-Bettmann Archive **370** "Photo Icon" by Gilles Larrain **373** Newark Public Library photo **374–375** Private Collection **377–380** background art, Cybele Grandjean **377** Terra Museum of American Art, Daniel J. Terra Collection, 1992.27 **378(b)** Museum of Fine Arts, Boston, Bequest of Miss Edith Nichols **378(t)** Cleveland Museum of Art, Purchase from the J. H. Wade Fund **379(b)** Museum of Fine Arts, Springfield, MA, The Morgan Wesson Memorial Collection **379(t)** Museum of Fine Arts, Boston, Bequest of Thomas G. Appleton **380** National Museum of American Art, Washington, D. C./Art Resource **386** map, Diane Cole **386(b)** Photograph courtesy History Division, Los Angeles County Museum of Natural History **386(c)** Union Pacific Museum Collection **386(t)** National Archives/Photo: Jonathan Wallen **387(b)** From *A Pictographic History of the Oglala Sioux*, The University of Nebraska Press **387(c)** Clara McDonald Williamson, "The Old Chisholm Trail," The Roland P. Murdock Collection, Wichita Art Museum, Wichita, Kansas **387(tr)** Union Pacific Museum Collection **387(tl)** Private Collection **388** Library of Congress **389(t)** North Wind Picture Archives

391 Laura Phillips/Bernstein & Andriulli **398** Gilcrease Museum of American Art, Tulsa, OK **400** Library of Congress **403** Smithsonian Institution **405** Museum of Western Art, Denver **406** Willa Cather Pioneer Memorial Collection/Nebraska State Historical Society **408–409** South Dakota Memorial Art Center Collection, Brookings **411** Museum of Fine Arts, Boston **416(b)** William Franklin McMahon **416(t)** Historical Pictures Service/Stock Montage, Inc. **417(br)** Western History Department/Denver Public Library **417(bl)** Western History Collections, University of Oklahoma Library **417(tr)** Library of Congress **417(tl)** California State Archives **419** The Thomas Gilcrease Institute of American History and Art, Tulsa, Oklahoma **419** Superstock, Inc. **420** Idaho State Historical Society **428** Everett Collection, Inc. **429** John Hancock Financial Services **430(b)** South Dakota Memorial Art Center Collection, Brookings **430(t)** Gilcrease Museum of American Art, Tulsa, OK **433** Jack and Pearl Resnick Collection **437** The Greenwich Workshop, Inc., Trumbull, CT **438** Philadelphia Museum of Art: Given by Carl Zigrosser **439(all)** Akita Collection **440–441** Courtesy David Hockney **442** Phillips Collection, Washington, D. C. **444–445** Charles Alston, "Walking," Sydney Smith Gordon Collection **445, 508, 510, 538, 543, 548(icon)** Aaron Douglas, "Rise, Shine for Thy Light Has Come," 1932/The Gallery of Art, Howard University, Washington, D. C. **445, 446, 448, 495, 501, 506(icon)** Claude Monet, "Woman With a Parasol," (detail), Musee D'Orsay, Paris/A. K. G., Berlin/Superstock, Inc. **446–447** Library of Congress **446(br)** Museum of the City of New York **446(t)** Old Life **446(bl)** Underwood/Corbis-Bettmann **447(b)** Library of Congress **447(t)** J. C. Allen & Sons **449** Missouri Historical Society **451** National Gallery of Art, Washington, D.C., Gift of Curt H. Reisinger **454** AP/Wide World **457** © Bob Timberlake **458** National Museum of American Art, Washington/Art Resource **461** The Phillips Collection, Washington, D. C. **466** Edgar William & Bernice Chrysler Garbisch Collection/National Gallery of Art, Washington, D. C. **467** Granger Collection, New York **469** Shelden Swope Art Museum, Terre Haute **474** Eric Sloan **479** Metropolitan Museum of Art, George A. Hearn Fund, 1942 **482** University of Chicago Library **486** U. S. Postal Service **491** Courtesy of Vassar College **492–493** Thyssen-Bornemisza Museum, Madrid/Art Resource **495(icon)** Musee D'Orsay, Paris/A. K. G., Berlin/Superstock, Inc. **496** Museum of the City of New York, Harry T. Peters Collection **498** Culver Pictures Inc. **499** Colorado Springs Fine Arts Center **502–503** Edward Hopper, "Nighthawks," Art Institute of Chicago/Superstock, Inc. **508(b)** AP/Wide World **508(t)** Dr. E. David Cronin, University of Wisconsin **509(tl)** Beinecke Rare Book and Manuscript Library, Yale University **509(br)** Globe Photos, Inc. **509(bl)** The estate of Carl Van Vechten, Joseph Solomon, executor **509(tr)** Schomburg Center for Research in Black Culture, New York Public Library, Astor, Lenox and Tilden Foundations **511** National Portrait Gallery, Smithsonian Institution/Art Resource **512, 514** Photograph by James Van Der Zee, Courtesy of Donna Van Der Zee **517, 523(c)** Corbis-Bettmann **523(b)** New York Times **523(tc)** Schomburg Center for Research in Black Culture, New York Public Library **523(t)** AP/Wide World **525** Phillips Collection, Washington, D. C. **527** The Gallery of Art, Howard University, Washington, D. C. **528** Courtesy Estate of Romare Howard Bearden **532** Courtesy The Estate of Carl Van Vechten **535** Norton Gallery of Art, West Palm Beach, Florida 1932/The Gallery of Art, Howard University, Washington, D. C. **538–539** Museum of Afro American Art, Boston **538(l)** Hampton University Museum, Hampton, VA **540(r)** Museum of African American Art **540(l)** National Museum of American Art, Smithsonian Institution, Gift of Benjamin and Olya Margolin/Art Resource **540–541** Schomburg Center for Research in Black Culture, New York Public Library **541** Whitney Museum of American Art, New York **553** Boatmen's National Bank of St. Louis **554–555** Courtesy Kansas State House **558** New York State Historical Association, Cooperstown **559** Paul Davis **560** National Geographic Society **563, 564, 566, 620(icon)** Grant Wood, "American Gothic," (detail), © 1996 Grant Wood/VAGA/Superstock, Inc. **563, 564, 566, 620, 625, 631(icon)** Edvard Munch, "The Scream," (detail), National Gallery, Oslo, Norway/A. K. G., Berlin/Superstock, Inc. **564–565** diorama, Diane Cole **564–565(background)** Holland McCombs **564(br)** Holland McCombs **564(t)** Brown Brothers **564(bl)** Library of Congress **565(r)** Detroit News **565(cr)** Culver Pictures Inc. **565(cl)** Culver Pictures Inc. **565(l)** Library of Congress **567** AP/Wide World **569** Private Collection **575(b)** Corbis-Bettmann Archive **575(t)** Corbis-Bettmann Archive **576** Private Collection **577** Private Collection **579** UPI/Corbis-Bettmann **580** Heerers Museum, Vienna **584** National Gallery of Art, Washington, D. C./Superstock, Inc. **585** Ivan Massar/Black Star **586, 593, 599, 600** Courtesy, Cluett, Peabody & Co., Inc. **604** AP/Wide World **607** Vaga, New York, NY **610** Jill Krementz **613** Carnegie-Stout Public Library **614** Minneapolis Institute of Arts **620** Culver Pictures Inc. **623(b)** AP/Wide World **623(t)** Old Life **632(b)** Metropolitan Museum of Art, New York, Alfred Stieglitz Collection, 1952 (52.203) **632(t)** Library of Congress **633(br)** Country Music Foundation Library and Media Center, Nashville **633(tl)** Detroit Institute of Arts, Gift of the Edsel B. Ford Fund **635** Dartmouth College **637** Eric Sloane **639** Metropolitan Museum of Art, Gift of Dr. and Mrs. Robert E. Carroll, 1979. (1979.138.2) **643** Bern Keating/Black Star **644, 647** The Oakland Museum of California, The City of Oakland, Gift of Paul B. Taylor **659** © Richard Red Owl **666** Jill Krementz **668** Eudora Welty Collection, Mississippi Department of Archives and History **676–677** Courtesy David DeMatteo **680** Library of Congress **683** Superstock, Inc. **688** Private Collection **689** NPA **691** Courtesy of Audrey Flack **695** Courtesy of Sandra Burshell **699(b)** Schomburg Center for Research in Black Culture, New York Public Library **699(t)** National Archives **701** AP/Wide World **714–715** Ralph Goings/O. K. Harris Gallery **715, 790, 792, 846, 852, 857(icon)** UPI/Corbis-Bettmann **715, 716, 718, 779, 784,**

789(icon) Superstock, Inc. **716(b)** Fred DeWitt/Time-Warner Inc. **716(c)** Brown Brothers **716(t)** Sovfoto **717(tr&b)** & Superstock, Inc. **717(tl)** CBS **719** AP/Wide World **720–721** Courtesy Billy Morrow Jackson **725** Collection of the Whitney Museum of American Art, Purchase **731** AP/Wide World **733** Walker City Art Gallery, Liverpool/Superstock, Inc. **736** Collection of Whitney Museum of American Art, Purchase, and gift of Gertrude Vanderbilt Whitney, by exchange **741** Michael Chikiris **743** Parrish Art Museum, Southampton, NY **747** The Pennsylvania Academy of the Fine Arts, Gift of Mrs. Fairfield Porter **753** © Franco Salmoiraghi **755** Courtesy Tomie Arai **759** AP/Wide World Photos **761** Copyright © 1985 by S. Hill Corporation. All rights reserved. Used with permission. **765** The Bob Timberlake Gallery, Lexington, North Carolina **770(tc)** Courtesy HarperCollins Publishers **770(t)** Courtesy Farrar, Straus and Giroux, Photo: Thomas Victor **770(bc)** Courtesy Nikki Giovanni **771** Photo by Wilfredo Q. Castano **771** Addison Gallery of American Art, Phillips Academy, Andover, Massachusetts, Gift of R. H. Donnelley Erdman (PA.1956) **773** The Howard University Gallery of Art, Washington, D. C. **775** Courtesy Fatima Del Real **779** Brown Brothers **781(l&r)** Everett Collection, Inc. **782(t&b)** Photofest **783** CBS News **790–791** Bernie Boston/*Washington Evening Star* **793** Nat Fein/New York Herald Tribune **794** Art and Artifacts Division, Schomburg Center for Research in Black Culture, New York Public Library **801** Courtesy Martin Luther King Memorial Library, Washington, D. C. **806** UPI/Corbis-Bettmann **811** AP/Wide World **813** Gerold-Wunderlich Gallery, New York **819** Courtesy of the artist **823** Thomas Barry Fine Arts, Minneapolis **828–829** William Albert Allard/ © National Geographic Society Image Collection **837** Courtesy Achilles Studio **839** Courtesy Rachael Romero **845** Susan Meiselas/ Magnum Photos **846** UPI/Corbis-Bettmann **847(t)** AP/Wide World **848(br)** Owen Franken/Stock Boston **848(bl)** James Pickerell/Black Star **848(tr)** Peter Amft **848(tl)** Bob Fitch/Black Star **849(b)** John P. Filo **849(c)** UPI/Corbis-Bettmann **849(t)** Elliott Landy/Magnum Photos **850(tl)** Michael Abramson/Black Star **850(b)** Alex Webb/Magnum Photos **850(tr)** UPI/Thai Khad Chuon/Corbis-Bettmann **858** Ralph Goings/O. K. Harris Gallery **859(b)** Gerold-Wunderlich Gallery, New York **859(t)** Art and Artifacts Division, Schomburg Center for Research in Black Culture, New York Public Library **860–861** Robert Marcus Collection **861, 862, 864, 939, 946, 951(icon)** Diana Ong, "Family Unit," (detail)/Superstock, Inc. **862–863(b)** Jack Parsons **862(bl)** Ernst A. John **863(br)** Lawrence Migdale **863(tr)** David R. Frazier **865** Jerry Bauer **867** Hirshhorn Museum and Sculpture Garden, Smithsonian Institution, The Joseph H. Hirshhorn Bequest, 1981, photograph by Lee Stalsworth **871** Marlborough Fine Art Ltd. **875** AP/Wide World **877** © Curt Teich Postcard Archives, Lake County (IL) Museum **882** Bob Verlin/Monkmeyer Press Photo Service, Inc. **887** Rubin Guzman **889** Private Collection, Courtesy of Ruth Benzacar Galeria de Arte, Buenos Aires **892(bc)** Courtesy HarperCollins Publishers, Photo: Steven L. Hopp **892(b)** Courtesy W. W. Norton, Photo: Barbara Seyda **892(tc)** L. Tom **893** Metropolitan Museum of Art, Purchase, Anonymous Gift, 1984 (1984.2) **895** Collection of Dr. Connie Christine Wheeler, Photography by Oren Slor **896–897** Steinbaum Krauss Gallery **898** Mary MacDonald **903** Courtesy Pacita Abad **910** Courtesy HarperPerennial, Photo: Rex Rystedt **913** The Greenwich Workshop, Inc., Trumbull, CT **914–915** Collection of the Oakland Museum of California, Burden Fund **922** Courtesy Viking Press, Photo: Pablo Campos **923–927** animals, Ralph Creaseman **926** Courtesy Caty Bartholomew **929** Courtesy W. W. Norton **931** Gallery Contemporanea, Jacksonville, FL/Superstock, Inc. **935** AP/Wide World **937** Copyright © 1976 by Hubert Shuptrine. All rights reserved. Used with permission **939** Superstock, Inc. **940–941(background)** Superstock, Inc. **940** Everett Collection, Inc. **941** Roger Ressmeyer © 1995 Corbis **942** Donna Karan **943** Tim Burton **944** Courtesy Raul Jose Lopez **953** Robert Marcus Collection **954(b)** Collection of Dr. Connie Christine Wheeler, Photography by Oren Slor **954(t)** Copyright © 1976 by Hubert Shuptrine. All rights reserved. Used with permission **956** Photoworld/FPG International Corp. **959(t)** Culver Pictures Inc. **960–961** Library of Congress **963(t&b)** Kevin Horan.

Handlettering by Eliza Schulte.

Electronic Illustrations by Bruce Burdick, Lena Checroun, Scott J. Jordan, Steven Kiecker, and Gwen Plogman.

Custom Literature Database

The *ScottForesman Custom Literature Database* is a collection of over 1400 literary selections. Over 200 titles in the database have lessons to support students as they read. Eight indices—Title, Author, Genre, Subject, Nationality, Literary Themes, Anthology Correlations, and Lessons for Selected Titles—help you navigate through the database, allowing you to search for, view, and print the exact selection you want. The Anthology Correlations index lets you identify titles in the database correlated to *ScottForesman Literature and Integrated Studies*.

Address to the Apostles from Bible, Matthew, 10:5–42*

African Proverbs

"Aladdin, or The Wonderful Lamp" from *A Thousand and One Nights*

"Ali Baba and the Forty Thieves" from *A Thousand and One Nights*

Anglo-Saxon Riddles

Apocalyptic Utterances from Bible, Matthew 24:4–25:46

Articles of Confederation

Babylonian Law from *The Hammurabi Code*

Battle of Brunanburh, The

"Battle of Otterbourne, The"

Bhagavad Gita

Bible, Acts of the Apostles

Bible, Corinthians 1:13

Bible, Genesis 1–3

Bible, John

Bible, Luke 10:25–37*

Bible, Mark

Bible, Psalm 1

Bible, Psalm 8

Bible, Psalm 23 in Six Translations

Bible, Psalm 24

Bible, Psalm 91

Bible, Psalm 100*

Bible, Psalm 137

Bible, Ruth*

"Birth of Hatshepsut, The"

Birth of Jesus, The from Bible, Matthew 1:18–4:17

"Bonnie George Campbell"

"Bonny Barbara Allan"

Book of Jonah, The from The Hebrew Bible

"Brahman, the Tiger and the Six Judges, The"*

Brown v. *Board of Education of Topeka**

"Caedmon's Hymn"

Chinese Exclusion Act*

Civil Rights Act of 1964*

"Clementine"

Code of Manu, The

Constitution of the Confederate States of America, The

Constitution of the United States

Death of Jesus, The from Bible, Matthew 26:14–28:20

"Deep River"

"Demon Lover, The"

"Descent of Ishtar into the Underworld, The"

Dred Scott v. *Sandford*

"Egyptian Love Song"

"Emergence Song"

"Enchanted Horse, The" from *A Thousand and One Nights*

Everyman

"Experiences of a Chinese Immigrant" from *The Independent**

"Follow the Drinking Gourd"*

"Get Up and Bar the Door"

Gibbons v. *Ogden*

"Go Down, Moses"*

Hammurabi Code, The

"How Thoutii Took the Town of Joppa"

"Joshua Fit de Battle ob Jericho"

Kingdom of Heaven Parables from Bible, Matthew 13:1–52

Laws, The from Bible, Exodus 19:1–23:33

"Little Old Sod Shanty on the Claim, The"

"Lord Randal"

Magna Carta

Marbury v. *Madison*

"May Colvin"*

Mayflower Compact, The

NAACP v. *Alabama*

"Old Chisholm Trail, The"

On Humility and Forgiveness from Bible, Matthew 18:1–35

Parables from Bible, Luke*

"Pat Works on the Railway"

"Peasant and the Workman, The"

Plessy v. *Ferguson*

Preamble to the Constitution of the Knights of Labor

Prince Shotuku's Constitution

Resolution of the Stamp Act Congress

"Scheherazade" from *A Thousand and One Nights*

"Seafarer, The"

Second Shepherd's Play, The

Seneca Falls Declaration of Sentiments and Resolutions, The

Sermon on the Mount from Bible, Matthew 5:1–7:27

"Seven Voyages of Sindbad the Sailor, The" from *A Thousand and One Nights**

"Shenandoah"

"Shipwrecked Sailor, The"

*Sir Gawain and the Green Knight**

"Sir Patrick Spens"*

Song of Creation

"Story of Rhampsinites, The"

"Story of the Fisherman, The" from *A Thousand and One Nights*

"Sumer is icumen in"

Sura LXXV—The Resurrection from *The Koran*

Sura LXXVI—Man from *The Koran*

"Swing Low, Sweet Chariot"

"Three Ravens, The"

Treaty of Peace with Great Britain

Trustees of Dartmouth College v. *Woodward*

"Twa Corbies, The"

Virginia Bill of Rights

Vishnu Purana

Volstead Act, The

"Wanderer, The"

"Western Wind"

"Wife of Usher's Well, The"

Adams, Henry
Education of Henry Adams, The, Chapter XXV, "The Dynamo and the Virgin"

"Prayer to the Virgin of Chartres"

Addison, Joseph
"Artifices in Tragedy" from *The Spectator*

"Party Patches" from *The Spectator*

"Sir Roger at Church" from *The Spectator*

"Westminster Abbey" from *The Spectator*

"Will Wimble" from *The Spectator**

"Wit: True, False, and Mixed"

Aelfric, Abbot
"Colloquy on the Occupations, A"

Aesop
"Crow and the Pitcher, The"

"Fox and the Crow, The"

"Fox and the Grapes, The"

---

*This selection includes background information, a study guide, and comprehension and critical thinking questions in a lesson on the disc.

Custom Literature Database

"Hound and the Hare, The"

"Mice and the Weasels, The"

"North Wind and the Sun, The"

Alcaeus

"Drinking Song"

"Summer"

"Winter"

Alcott, Louisa May

"Amy's Valley of Humiliation" from *Little Women**

Hospital Sketches

"Old-Fashioned Thanksgiving, An"*

"Onawandah, Fourth Spinning Wheel Story"

Alighieri, Dante

Divine Comedy, The, " The Inferno," Canto I

Divine Comedy, The, "The Inferno," Canto III

Divine Comedy, The, "The Inferno," Canto XXXIV

Alline, Henry

"The Conduct of Most Sailors"

Anacreon

"Beauty"

"Combat, The"

"Cup, The"

"Love"

Andersen, Hans Christian

"Emperor's New Clothes, The"*

"Little Mermaid, The"

"Red Shoes, The"

"Snow Queen, The"

"Steadfast Tin Soldier, The"

"Swineherd, The"

"Thumbelina"

"Tinder-Box, The"

"Ugly Duckling, The"*

Anderson, Sherwood

"Discovery of a Father"*

"Stolen Day"

Anonymous

Independent, The

"My mind to me a kingdom is"

"There is a Lady Sweet and Kind"

Anthony, Susan B.

On Woman's Right to Suffrage*

"Political Economy of Women"

Antin, Mary

"Immigrant Goes to School, An" from *The Promised Land**

Aristotle

Poetics, The

Arnold, Matthew

"Isolation, To Marguerite"

"Last Word, The"

"Requiescat"

"Scholar-Gipsy, The"

"Self-Dependence"

"Thyrsis"

Aspinwall, Alicia

"Upsidedownians, The"

Aulnoy, Comtesse d'

"White Cat, The"

"Yellow Dwarf, The"

Aupaumut, Hendrick

A Short Narration of My Last Journey to the Western Contry

Babur

Babur-nama*

Bacon, Francis

"Of Studies"

"Of Truth"

Bambara, Toni Cade

"Blues Ain't No Mockin Bird"*

"Happy Birthday"*

Barbour, Ralph Henry

"Brewster's Debut"

Beach, Lewis

Clod, The*

Bede

Ecclesiastical History of the English People, The, Book II, Chapters 9–13*

Ecclesiastical History of the English People, The, Book IV, Chapter 24

Behn, Aphra

"Lady's Looking Glass, The"

"Love in Fantastic Triumph Sat from Abdelazar"

Oroonoko

Bellamy, Edward

Looking Back*

Belloc, Hilaire

"Lion, The"

"Yak, The"

Benét, Stephen Vincent

"By the Waters of Babylon"

Benet, WIlliam Rose

"Skater of Ghost Lake, The"

Bennet, John

"Fritz the Master Fiddler"

Bierce, Ambrose

"Occurrence at Owl Creek Bridge, An"

Blackwell, Alice Stone

Indifference of Women, The*

Blake, William

"And did those feet" from *Milton*

"Chimney Sweeper, The" from *Songs of Experience*

"Chimney Sweeper, The," from *Songs of Innocence*

"Divine Image, The" from *Songs of Innocence*

"Holy Thursday" from *Songs of Experience*

"Holy Thursday" from *Songs of Innocence*

"Human Abstract, The" from *Songs of Experience*

"Infant Joy"

"Infant Sorrow"

Introduction ("Hear the voice of the Bard") from *Songs of Experience*

Introduction ("Piping down the valleys") from *Songs of Innocence*

"Lamb, The" from *Songs of Innocence*

"Nurse's Song" from *Songs of Experience*

"Poison Tree, A"

"Proverbs of Hell" from *The Marriage of Heaven and Hell*

"Sick Rose, The"

Song ("How sweet I roamed")

"Tyger, The" from *Songs of Experience*

Bleecker, Ann Eliza

"On the Immensity of Creation"

Boas, Franz

"Raven's Adventures"

"Sedna, Mistress of the Underworld"

Boswell, James

Life of Samuel Johnson, LL.D, The

London Journal, 1762–1763

Bradstreet, Anne

"Contemplations"

"Prologue, The"

"To My Dear and Loving Husband"

"Upon the Burning of Our House, July 10th, 1666"

Brontë, Emily

"No coward soul is mine"

"Remembrance"

Song ("The linnet in the rocky dells")

Brooke, Rupert

"Peace"*

Brooks, Gwendolyn

"Pete at the Zoo"

Brothers Grimm

"Bremen Town Musicians, The"*

"Elves and the Shoemaker, The"

"Fisherman and His Wife, The"

"Frog Prince, The"

"Gallant Tailor, The"

"Hansel and Grethel"

"Juniper Tree, The"

"Rapunzel"

"Rumpelstiltskin"*

"Sleeping Beauty, The"

"Snow-white"

"Twelve Dancing Princesses, The"

Brown, Dee

"Katlian and the Iron People"*

Brown, John

Last Speech

Browning, Elizabeth Barrett

Sonnet 1 ("I thought once how Theocritus had sung") from *Sonnets from the Portuguese*

Sonnet 14 ("If thou must love me, let it be for naught") from *Sonnets from the Portuguese*

Sonnet 26 ("I lived with visions for my company") from *Sonnets from the Portuguese*

Sonnet 28 ("My letters! all dead paper, mute and white!") from *Sonnets from the Portuguese*

Sonnet 43 ("How do I love thee?") from *Sonnets from the Portuguese*

Browning, Robert
"Andrea del Sarto"*
"Caliban Upon Setebos"
"Childe Roland to the Dark Tower Came"
"Fra Lippo Lippi"
"Home Thoughts, From Abroad"
"How They Brought the Good News from Ghent to Aix"*
"Love Among the Ruins"
"Meeting at Night"*
"Parting at Morning"
"Pied Piper of Hamelin, The"
"Porphyria's Lover"
"Prospice"
"Rabbi Ben Ezra"
"Soliloquy of the Spanish Cloister"
"Summum Bonum"
"Year's at the spring, The"

Bryan, William Jennings
Cross of Gold, The

Bryant, William Cullen
"Thanatopsis"
"To a Waterfowl"
"To the Fringed Gentian"
"Waiting by the Gate"

Bulfinch, Thomas
"Adventures of Aeneas, The"
"Adventures of Ulysses"
"Apollo and Daphne"
"Apollo and Hyacinthus"
"Atalanta"
"Bacchus and Ariadne"
"Bellerophon, Pegasus, and the Chimaera"
"Cadmus"
"Castor and Pollux"
"Centaurs, The"
"Cupid and Psyche"*
"Daedalus"*
"Death of Baldur, The"
"Diana and Actæon"
"Echo and Narcissus"

"Golden Fleece, The"*
"Hercules"
"Hero and Leander"
"Medea and Jason"
"Meleager"
"Midas"
"Minerva"
"Myrmidons, The"
"Niobe"
"Of the Joys of Valhalla"
"Orpheus and Eurydice"
"Perseus and Medusa"
"Phaeton"*
"Prometheus and Pandora"*
"Proserpine"
"Pygmalion"
"Pyramus and Thisbe"
"Sphinx, The"
"Theseus"
"Trojan War, The"
"Venus and Adonis"

Bunyan, John
Pilgrim's Progress, The

Burnett, Frances Hodgson
"Editha's Burglar"

Burney, Fanny
Diary, The

Burns, Robert
"Ae Fond Kiss"
"Auld Lang Syne"
"Cotter's Saturday Night, The"
"Highland Mary"
"John Anderson My Jo"
"Man's a Man for A' That, A"
"My Heart's in the Highlands"*
"My Jean"
"O, wert thou in the cauld blast"
"Red, Red Rose, A"
"Sweet Afton"
"Tam o' Shanter"
"To a Louse"*

Byron, Lord (George Gordon)
Childe Harold's Pilgrimage, Canto IV, Stanzas CLXXVIII–CLXXXIV

Don Juan, Canto I, Stanzas 1, 6–10, 13, 15, 17–20, 23–27, 32, 33, 37–41, 44, 45, 47–50, 54, 55, 60–62, 69–72, 75–79, 86, 87, 90–92

Don Juan, Canto III, Stanzas 1–16
"On This Day I Complete My Thirty-Sixth Year"*
"She walks in beauty"
"So we'll go no more a-roving"
"Sonnet on Chillon"
"Stanzas for Music"
"When We Two Parted"
"Written After Swimming from Sestos to Abydos"

Cabeza de Vaca, Alavar Nunez
Relation of Alvar Nunuez Cabeza de Vaca, Chapter VII

Cain, Reverend Richard H.
Address of the State Convention to the White Inhabitants of South Carolina

Calhoun, John Caldwell
Slavery

Campion, Thomas
"Cherry-Ripe"
"Man of Life Upright, The"
"My Sweetest Lesbia"
"Now Winter Nights Enlarge"
"Rose-cheeked Laura"
"When to her lute Corinna sings"

Carlyle, Thomas
French Revolution, The*
"Midas" from *Past and Present*

Carroll, Lewis (Charles Lutwidge Dodgson)
Alice's Adventures in Wonderland
"Crocodile, The" from *Alice's Adventures in Wonderland*
"Father William" from *Alice's Adventures in Wonderland*
"Jabberwocky" from *Through the Looking Glass*
"Mad Carpenter's Song, The"*
"Mock Turtle Song, The" from *Alice's Adventures in Wonderland*
"Walrus and the Carpenter, The" from *Alice's Adventures in Wonderland*

Cather, Willa
"Sculptor's Funeral, The"*
"Sentimentality of William Tavener, The"*

Cervantes, Miguel de
Don Quixote*

Chaucer, Geoffrey
"Clerk's Prologue, The" from *The Canterbury Tales*
"Clerk's Tale, The" from *The Canterbury Tales*
"General Prologue, The" from *The Canterbury Tales*
"Nun's Priest's Tale, The" from *The Canterbury Tales*
"Pardoner's Tale, The" from *The Canterbury Tales*
"Prologue to the Nun's Priest's Tale, The," from *The Canterbury Tales*
"Wife of Bath's Prologue, The" from *The Canterbury Tales*
"Wife of Bath's Tale, The" from *The Canterbury Tales**

Chekhov, Anton
"Bet, The"
"Bishop, The"
Boor, The*
Cherry Orchard, The, Act One
Cherry Orchard, The, Act Two
Cherry Orchard, The, Act Three
Cherry Orchard, The, Act Four
"Darling, The"
"Day in the Country, A"
"Kiss, The"
"Lady with the Dog, The"
"Misery"
"Upheaval, An"*

Chesterfield, Lord (Philip Stanhope)
Letters to his Son

Chesterton, G. K.
"Two Taverns, The"

Chief Joseph
I Will Fight No More Forever

Child, Lydia Maria
Letter to Colonel P. H. Anderson

---

*This selection includes background information, a study guide, and comprehension and critical thinking questions in a lesson on the disc.

T51

Custom Literature Database

Chopin, Kate
"Pair of Silk Stockings, A"*

Christie, Agatha
"Third-Floor Flat, The"*

Churchill, Winston
Blood, Sweat, and Tears
Dunkirk
Iron Curtain Has Descended, An*
Their Finest Hour

Clay, Henry
On the Compromise of 1850

Clough, Arthur Hugh
"Epi-Strauss-um"
"Latest Decalogue, The"
"Say not the struggle nought availeth"

Cobb, Frank I. and Walter Lippmann
Interpretation of President Wilson's Fourteen Points

Coleridge, Samuel Taylor
Biographia Literaria
"Christabel"
"Eolian Harp, The"
"Frost at Midnight"
"Kubla Khan"
"Rime of the Ancient Mariner, The"
"This Lime-Tree Bower My Prison"

Colum, Padraic
"Aegir's Feast: How Thor Triumphed"
"Baldur's Doom"
"Building of the Wall, The"
"Children of Loki, The"
"Dwarf's Hoard, and the Curse That It Brought"
"How Brock Brought Judgement on Loki"
"How Freya Gained Her Necklace and How Her Loved One Was Lost to Her"
"How Thor and Loki Be-Fooled Thrym the Giant"
"Iduna and Her Apples: How Loki Put the Gods in Danger"

"Odin Goes to Mimir's Well; His Sacrifice for Wisdom"
"Sif's Golden Hair: How Loki Wrought Mischief in Asgard"
"Sigurd's Youth" from *The Children of Odin*
"Thor and Loki in the Giants' City"
"Twilight of the Gods, The"
"Valkyrie, The"

Conrad, Joseph
Secret Sharer, The
Youth*

Crane, Stephen
"Bride Comes to Yellow Sky, The"
"Do not weep, maiden, for war is kind"
"Episode of War, An"
"I met a seer"
"Man saw a ball of gold in the sky, A"
"Mystery of Heroism, A"
"Open Boat, The"*
Red Badge of Courage, The
"Think as I Think"

Crevecoeur, Michel-Guillaume Jean de
Letters from an American Farmer

Curtin, Jeremiah, and Hewitt, J. N. B.
"Woman Who Fell from the Sky, The"

Curtis, Natalie
"Creation"
"Deathless One and the Wind, The"
"Morning Star and the Evening Star, The"
"Origin of Corn and Pemmican, The"
"Stories of Wak-Chung-Kaka, the Foolish One"
"Story of Gomoidema Pokoma-Kiaka, The"
"Story of the First Mother, The"
"Story of Wakiash and the First Totem-Pole, The"*
"Vision of the Earth-Maker, A"*

Davis, Jefferson
Inaugural Address of Jefferson Davis
Last Message to the People of the Confederacy
Message to Congress

Davis, Richard H.
"Midsummer Pirates"

de la Mare, Walter
"All But Blind"
"All That's Past"
"Cake and Sack"
"Dwelling Place, The"
"Flight, The"
"Listeners, The"*
"Nobody Knows"
"Silver"
"Song of the Mad Prince, The"
"Tartary"
"Up and Down"

De Quincey, Thomas
"On the Knocking at the Gate in *Macbeth*"
"Poetry of Pope, The"

Defoe, Daniel
Essay Upon Projects, An
Journal of the Plague Year, A

Dekker, Thomas
"Lullaby"

Delgado, Reverend Father Fray Carlos
Report Made By Reverend Father Fray Carlos Delgado

Dickens, Charles
David Copperfield
"Signalman, The"*

Dickinson, Emily
"Alter! When the Hills do"
"Apparently with no surprise"
"Because I could not stop for death"
"Bustle in a House, The"
"'Faith' Is a fine invention"
"'Hope' is the thing with feathers"
"I felt a Funeral, in my Brain"
"I heard a Fly buzz – when I died"
"I like to see it lap the Miles"
"I taste a liquor never brewed"
"I Years had been from Home"
"I'll tell you how the Sun rose"
"If you were coming in the Fall"
"Morns are meeker than they were, The"
"Much Madness is divinest Sense"
"Narrow Fellow in the grass, A"*

"Of all the Souls that stand create"
"Some keep the Sabbath going to Church"
"Success is counted sweetest"*
"Surgeons must be very careful"
"There's a certain Slant of light"
"This is my letter to the World"
"To make a prairie it takes a clover"
"Triumph – may be of several kinds"*

Dixon, Roland B.
"Creation, The"
"Theft of Fire, The"

Donne, John
"Bait, The"
"Ecstacy, The"
"Flea, The"
"Indifferent, The"
Meditation 17 from *Devotions*
"On His Mistress"
Song ("Go and catch a falling star")
Sonnet 4 ("At the round earth's imagined corners, blow") from *Holy Sonnets**
Sonnet 6 ("This is my play's last scene; here heavens appoint") from *Holy Sonnets*
Sonnet 10 ("Death, be not proud, though some have called thee") from *Holy Sonnets**
Sonnet 14 ("Batter my heart, three-personed God; for You") from *Holy Sonnets*
"Sun Rising, The"
"Valediction: Forbidding Mourning, A"
"Woman's Constancy"

Dorsey, George and Kroeber, Alfred L.
"Star Husband, The"

Douglass, Frederick
Life and Times of Frederick Douglass, The*
Meaning of July Fourth for the Negro, The*
Narrative of the Life of Frederick Douglass, The
Oration in Memory of Abraham Lincoln

*This selection includes background
information, a study guide, and
comprehension and critical thinking
questions in a lesson on the disc.

Custom Literature Database

Harte, Bret
"Baby Sylvester"
"Brown of Calaveras"
"Iliad of Sandy Bar, The"
"Luck of Roaring Camp, The"
"Miggles"
"Outcasts of Poker Flat, The"*
"Plain Language from Truthful James"
"Tennessee's Partner"

Hawthorne, Nathaniel
"Birthmark, The"
"Dr. Heidegger's Experiment"
"Drowne's Wooden Image"
"Golden Touch, The"*
"Maypole of Merry Mount, The"
"Minister's Black Veil, The"*
"My Kinsman, Major Molineaux"
Notebooks, The
"Rappacinni's Daughter"
"Young Goodman Brown"*

Hayford, J. E. Casely
"As in a Glass Darkly" from *Ethiopia Unbound*
"Black Man's Burden, The" from *Ethiopia Unbound*
"Gold Coast Native Institutions"
"Saving the Wind" from *Ethiopia Unbound*

Hayne, Paul Hamilton
"Aspects of the Pines"

Hazlitt, William
"Macbeth"
My First Acquaintance with Poets
"On Going a Journey"

Heine, Heinrich
"Loreley, The"*

Henley, William Ernest
"Invictus"

Henry, Patrick
Speech in the Virginia Convention, March 23, 1775

Herbert, George
"Altar, The"
"Avarice"
"Bitter-Sweet"
"Collar, The"
"Easter Wings"*

"Love (III)"
"Man"
"Pulley, The"
"Redemption"
"Virtue"*

Heredia y Heredia, Jose Maria
"Ode to Niagara"

Herrick, Robert
"Argument of His Book, The" from *Hesperides*
"Corinna's Going A-Maying"
"Ode for Ben Jonson, An"
"To the Virgins, to Make Much of Time"
"Upon Julia's Clothes"

Hobbes, Thomas
Leviathan, Part I, Chapters 13–15

Holmes, Oliver Wendell
"Ballad of the Oysterman, The"
"Chambered Nautilus, The"
"Last Leaf, The"
"My Last Walk with the Schoolmistress"
"Old Ironsides"

Hoover, Herbert
Philosophy of Rugged Individualism, The

Hopkins, Gerard Manley
"Carrion Comfort"*
"Felix Randal"
"God's Grandeur"
"Habit of Perfection, The"
"No worst, there is none"*
"Pied Beauty"
"Spring and Fall"
"Thou Art Indeed Just, Lord"
"Windhover, The"

Horace
"Ad Leuconeon"
"Death of Cleopatra, The"
"Golden Mean, The"
"Ship of State, The"

Housman, A. E.
"Loveliest of trees, the cherry now"
"Night is freezing fast, The"
"Oh, when I was in love with you"

"On moonlit heath and lonesome bark"
"To an Athlete Dying Young"
"White in the moon the long road lies"

Howard, Henry, Earl of Surrey
"Alas, So All Things Now Do Hold Their Peace"
"Love, that doth reign and live within in my thought"
"Lover's Vow, A"

Howe, Julia Ward
"Battle Hymn of the Republic, The"*

Howells, William Dean
"Christmas Every Day"*
"Editha"

Hudson, W. H.
Idle Days in Patagonia, The, Chapter XII*

Hughes, Rupert
"Latest News About the Three Wishes, The"

Hunt, James Henry Leigh
"Abou Ben Adhem and the Angel"

Huxley, Thomas Henry
"Method of Scientific Investigation, The"

Irving, Washington
"Early Life in Manhattan" from *A History of New York*
"Legend of Sleepy Hollow, The"*
"Rip Van Winkle"
Tour on the Prairies, A

Jackson, Andrew
Second Inaugural Address

Jacobs, Harriet Ann
Incidents in the Life of a Slave Girl, Chapter I*

Jacobs, Joseph
"Dick Whittington and His Cat"*
"Jack and the Beanstalk"
"Jack the Giant-Killer"

Jacobs, W. W.
Monkey's Paw, The

James, Henry
"Four Meetings"
"Middle Years, The"
"Real Thing, The"

James, William
"On a Certain Blindness in Human Beings"

Jefferson, Thomas
Declaration of Independence, The
Jefferson's First Inaugural Address
Virginia Statute of Religious Liberty

Jewett, Sarah Orne
"Courting of Sister Wisby, The"
"Hiltons' Holiday, The"
"Miss Tempy's Watchers"
"Native of Winby, A"*
"White Heron, A"

Johnson, Andrew
Johnson's Proclamation of Amnesty

Johnson, James Weldon
Autobiography of an Ex-Colored Man, The, Chapters 1–2*
Autobiography of an Ex-Colored Man, The, Chapters 3–4*

Johnson, Lyndon
Speech at Johns Hopkins University

Johnson, Pauline
"Corn Husker, The"
"Silhouette"

Johnson, Samuel
Dictionary of the English Language
Life of Milton, The
London
"On Choosing Friends" from *the Rambler* No. 160
"On Fiction" from *the Rambler* No. 4
"On Forgiveness" from *the Rambler* No. 185
"On Self-Indulgence" from *the Rambler* No. 155
"On Spring" from *the Rambler* No. 5
"On the Death of Dr. Robert Levet"
"On the Tyranny of Parents" from *the Rambler* No. 148
Preface to Shakespeare, The

Jonson, Ben
"Elegy, An"
"Ode to Himself, An"
"On My First Daughter"
"On My First Son"
"Song: To Celia"
"Still to Be Neat"

---

*This selection includes background information, a study guide, and comprehension and critical thinking questions in a lesson on the disc.

Custom Literature Database

Major, Charles
"Big Bear, The"

Malory, Sir Thomas
"Arthur Marries Gwynevere"
Morte d'Arthur, Le, Book 21, Chapters 5–7

Marlowe, Christopher
"Passionate Shepherd to His Love, The"*
Tragical History of Doctor Faustus, The, Act One
Tragical History of Doctor Faustus, The, Act Two
Tragical History of Doctor Faustus, The, Act Three
Tragical History of Doctor Faustus, The, Act Four
Tragical History of Doctor Faustus, The, Act Five

Marshall, George C.
Marshal Plan, The

Marvell, Andrew
"Bermudas"
"Dialogue Between the Soul and Body, A"
"Garden, The"
"Picture of Little T. C. in a Prospect of Flowers, The"

Masefield, John
"Cargoes"*
"Sea-Fever"*

Masters, Edgar Lee
"Cooney Potter"
"Dow Kritt"
"Hortense Robbins"
"Mrs. Kessler"
"Samuel Gardner"

Mather, Cotton
Wonders of the Invisible World, The*

Maupassant, Guy de
"Boule de Suif" (Ball of Fat)
"Devil, The"
"Diamond Necklace, The"
"Horla, The"
"Piece of String, The"*
"Two Friends"*

McCrae, John
"In Flanders Fields"*

McNeil, Everett
"King of the Golden Woods, The"

Melville, Herman
"Art"
"Bartleby the Scrivener"
"Maldive Shark, The"
"Portent, The"
"Shiloh"

Meredith, George
"Lucifer in Starlight"

Mill, John Stuart
Autobiography of John Stuart Mill, The
On Liberty
"Black Hero of the Ranges, The"*

Milton, John
"Il Penseroso"
"L'Allegro"
"Lycidas"
"On Shakespeare"
"On the Late Massacre in Piedmont"
Paradise Lost, Book VI
Paradise Lost, Book IX*
Paradise Lost, Book XII
"When I consider how my light is spent"

Monroe, James
Monroe Doctrine, The

Montagu, Lady Mary Wortley
"Answer to a Love-Letter in Verse, An"
"Lady's Resolve, The"
"On The Death of Mrs. Bowes"

Moore, Milcah Martha
"Female Patriots, The"

Moore, Thomas
"Harp that once through Tara's halls, The"
"Minstrel Boy, The"

More, Hannah
"Slavery, a Poem"

Morris, William
"Apology, An" from *The Earthly Paradise*
"Defence of Guenevere, The"*
"Haystack in the Floods, The"
"Love Is Enough"

Morton, Sarah Wentworth
"African Chief, The"

Nashe, Thomas
"Autumn"
"Litany in Time of Plague, A"

Nesbit, E.
"Beautiful As the Day"
"Jungle, The"
"Plush Usurper, The"*
"Pride of Perks, The" from *The Railway Children**

Newman, John Henry Cardinal
"Lead, Kindly Light"

Nightingale, Florence
Cassandra

Northup, Solomon
"Christmas on the Plantation" from *Twelve Years a Slave*
"Picking Cotton" from *Twelve Years a Slave*

O. Henry (William Sidney Porter)
"After Twenty Years"
"Cop and the Anthem, The"*
"Furnished Room, The"
"Hearts and Hands"*
"Man Higher Up, The"*
"Ransom of Red Chief, The"*
"Retrieved Reformation, A"*
"Unfinished Story, An"

Owen, Wilfred
"Anthem for Doomed Youth"*
"Strange Meeting"

Ozaki, Yei Theodora
"Momotaro, or the Story of the Son of a Peach"
"Story of Urashima Taro, the Fisher Lad, The"*
"Tongue-Cut Sparrow, The"

Paine, Thomas
American Crisis, The
Common Sense

Palou, Francisco
Life of Junípero Serra

Parris, Robert
"Refusal to Pay Taxes, A" from *The Liberator*

Peacock, Thomas Love
"War Song of Dinas Vawr, The"

Pepys, Samuel
Diary, The

Perrault, Charles
"Bluebeard"
"Cinderella"
"Little Red Ridinghood"
"Puss in Boots"

Plato
Apology
Crito
Phaedo

Po Chu-i
"After Passing the Examination"
"Chu Ch'en Village"*
"Escorting Candidates to the Examination Hall"
"Golden Bells"*
"In Early Summer Lodging in a Temple to Enjoy the Moonlight"
"Old Man with the Broken Arm, The"
"On Board Ship: Reading Yu Chen's Poems"
"Prisoner, The"
"Remembering Golden Bells"*
"Watching the Reapers"

Poe, Edgar Allan
"Annabel Lee"
"Bells, The"
"Cask of Amontillado, The"
"Eldorado"
"Fall of the House of Usher, The"*
"Hop-Frog"
"Israfel"
"Ligeia"
"Masque of the Red Death, The"
"Oval Portrait, The"
"Philosophy of Composition, The"
Poetic Principle, The
"Purloined Letter, The"*
"Tell-Tale Heart, The"
"To Helen"*
"Ulalume"
"William Wilson"

*This selection includes background information, a study guide, and comprehension and critical thinking questions in a lesson on the disc.

Custom Literature Database

Steele, Sir Richard
"Alexander Selkirk"
"Country Manners" from *The Spectator*
"Spectator Club, The" from *The Spectator*

Stevens, Wallace
"Anecdote of the Jar"*

Stevenson, Robert Louis
"El Dorado"
"Lantern-Bearers, The"*
"Lodging for the Night, A"
"Requiem"
"Sire de Maletroit's Door, The"
"Thrawn Janet"

Stockton, Annis Boudinot
"Exemptore Ode in a Sleepless Night by a Lady Attending on Her Husband in a Long and Painful Illness, An"

Stockton, Frank
"Castle of Bim, The"*
"Floating Prince, The"
"How the Aristocrats Sailed Away"
"Lady, or the Tiger?, The"*

Stowe, Harriet Beecher
"Ghost in the Mill, The"*
"Slave Warehouse, The" from *Uncle Tom's Cabin*

Suckling, Sir John
"Constant Lover, The"
"Out Upon It!"
Song ("Why so pale and wan, fond lover?")

Swift, Jonathan
"Description of a City Shower, A"*
"Satirical Elegy on the Death of a Late Famous General, A"
"Voyage to Brobdingnag, A" of *Gulliver's Travels*
"Voyage to Lilliput, A" from Chapter 1 of *Gulliver's Travels*
"Voyage to Lilliput, A" from Chapter 3 of *Gulliver's Travels*

Swinburne, Algernon Charles
"Garden of Proserpine, The"
"When the Hounds of Spring Are on Winter's Traces" from *Choruses from Atalanta in Calydon*

T'ao Ch'ien
"In the Quiet of the Morning"
"Peach-Blossom Fountain, The"
"Reading the Book of Hills and Seas"
"Returning to the Fields"
"Substance, Shadow, and Spirit"

Taylor, Edward
"Huswifery"
"Upon a Spider Catching a Fly"
"Upon What Base?"

Tecumseh
Sell a Country! Why Not Sell the Air?*

Tennyson, Alfred Lord
"Break, Break, Break"
"Charge of the Light Brigade, The"*
"Eagle, The"
"Flower in the crannied wall"
"In Memoriam" 1, 2, 7, 11, 27, 28, 34, 50, 54, 55, 56, 67, 88, 95, 106,115, 119, 121, 130*
"Kraken, The"
"Lady Clare"*
"Locksley Hall"
"Lotos-Eaters, The"
"Merlin and the Gleam"*
"Morte D'Arthur"
"Now Sleeps the Crimson Petal"
"Song of the Brook, The"
"Splendor Falls, The"
"Tears, Idle Tears"
"Tithonus"

Thayer, Ernest L.
"Casey at the Bat"*

Thomas, Edward
"Adlestrop"
"Cat May Look at a King, A"*
"Cherry Trees, The"
"Look Before You Leap"
"Never Look a Gift Horse in the Mouth"
"Owl, The"
"Rain"
"Tears"

Thompson, Francis
"Hound of Heaven, The"

Thomson, James
"Rule, Britannia!"

Thoreau, Henry David
Civil Disobedience
Walden

Thucydides
Funeral Speech of Pericles
Melian Dialogue, The

Timrod, Henry
"Charleston"
"Ethnogenesis"

Truman, Harry S.
Truman Doctrine, The*

Truth, Sojourner
Ain't I a Woman?

Tu Fu
"Farewell of an Old Man"
"Meandering River, Two Poems"
"Night Thoughts Aboard a Boat"
"Random Pleasures: Nine Quatrains"
"Recruiting Officer of Shih-hao"

Turell, Jane Colman
"Lines On Childbirth"

Twain, Mark
Adventures of Huckleberry Finn, The
"Baker's Bluejay Yarn"
"Californian's Tale, The"
"Cat and the Pain Killer, The" from *The Adventures of Tom Sawyer*
"Cecil Rhodes and the Shark"
"Celebrated Jumping Frog of Calaveras County, The"
"'Cub' Pilot's Experience, A" from *Life on the Mississippi*
"'Cub' Wants to be a Pilot" from *Life on the Mississippi*
"Diary of Adam and Eve, The"
"Dog's Tale, A"
"Great French Duel, The"
"Invalid's Story, The"
"Legend of the Capitoline Venus"
"Man That Corrupted Hadleyburg, The"
"Punch, Brothers, Punch"*
"Story of the Bad Little Boy, The"
"Story of the Good Little Boy, The"
"Story Without an End, A"
"Tom and the Loose Tooth" from *The Adventures of Tom Sawyer*

Tzu, Lao
Tao Te Ching

Vallejo, Mariano Guadalupe
Recuerdos historicos y personales

Vargas, Don Diego de
Letter on the Reconquest of New Mexico

Vaughan, Henry
"Retreat, The"

Vega, Luis Lazo de
History of the Miraculous Apparition of the Virgin of Guadalupe in 1531

Villeneuve, Madame de
"Beauty and the Beast"*

Virgil
Aeneid, The, from Book Two*

Walker, David
"Walker's Appeal"

Walters, Joseph J.
"Guanya Pau, A Story of an African Princess"

Wang Wei
"Enjoying Coolness"
"Red Peonies"
"Seeing Someone Off"
"Suffering from the Heat"
"To Subprefect Chang"

Washington, Booker T.
American Standard, The*
Atlanta Exposition Address
"My Struggle for an Education" from *Up from Salvery*
Up from Slavery

Washington, George
Farewell Address to the People of the United States*
Washington's First Inaugural Address

Wharton, Edith
"Afterward"*
"Angel at the Grave"
"Other Two, The"

---

*This selection includes background information, a study guide, and comprehension and critical thinking questions in a lesson on the disc.

Custom Literature Database

Wheatley, Phillis

Letter to Rev. Occum

"To His Excellency General Washington"

"To S. M., A Young African Painter on Seeing His Works"

"To the Right Honourable William, Earl of Dartmouth"

Whitman, Walt

"A Child's Amaze"

"As Toilsome I Wander'd Virginia's Woods"

"Beat! Beat! Drums!"*

"Beautiful Women"

"Bivouac on a Mountain Side"

"Cavalry Crossing a Ford"

"Crossing Brooklyn Ferry"*

"For You O Democracy"*

"I saw in Louisiana a live-oak growing"

"Joy, Shipmate, Joy!"

"Noiseless patient spider, A"

"On the Beach at Night"

"On the Beach at Night Alone"

"Passage to India"

"Sight in Camp in the Daybreak Gray and Dim, A"

"Song of Myself," 1,16,17,24

"Song of Myself," 3

"Sparkles from the Wheel"

"We Two Boys Together Clinging"

"When I heard the learn'd astronomer"

"When Lilacs Last in the Dooryard Bloomed"*

Whittier, John Greenleaf

"Barbara Frietchie"*

"Hampton Beach"

"Ichabod"

"Kansas Emigrants, The"

"Telling the Bees"

Wiesel, Elie

Acceptance Speech for the Nobel Peace Prize

Wilde, Oscar

"Ballad of Reading Gaol, The"*

"Birthday of the Infanta, The"

"Canterville Ghost, The"

"De Profundis"

"Few Maxims for the Instruction of the Over-Educated, A"

"Grave of Shelley, The"

"Happy Prince, The"

Importance of Being Earnest, The, Act One*

Importance of Being Earnest, The, Act Two

Importance of Being Earnest, The, Act Three

"Phrases and Philosophies for the Use of the Young"

"Prison Reform" from the *Daily Chronicle*

"Symphony in Yellow"

Wilson, Woodrow

First Inaugural Address

Peace Without Victory

Wordsworth, William

"Composed upon Westminster Bridge"*

"Elegiac Stanzas"

"Expostualtion and Reply"

"I travelled among unknown men"

"I Wandered Lonely as a Cloud"

"It is a beauteous evening, calm and free"*

"Lines Written in Early Spring"

"London, 1802"

"Lucy Gray"

"Michael"

"Nuns fret not at their convent's narrow room"

"Ode: Intimations of Immortality from Recollections of Early Childhood"*

Preface to *Lyrical Ballads*

Prelude, The, Book 1

"Resolution and Independence"

"She Dwelt Among the Untrodden Ways"

"slumber did my spirit seal, A"

"Solitary Reaper, The"

"Strange fits of passion have I known"

"Three Years She Grew"

"To a Skylark"

Wyatt, Sir Thomas

"Divers Doth Use"

"He is not dead that sometime hath a fall"

"My lute awake!"

"They Flee from Me"

"Varium et Mutabile"

"Whoso List to Hunt"

Zimmermann, Arthur

Zimmerman Note, The

---

*This selection includes background information, a study guide, and comprehension and critical thinking questions in a lesson on the disc.

GREYSCALE

BIN TRAVELER FORM

Cut By _Michael A Huerta_ Qty _11_ Date _8-2_

Scanned By _Jakeyra Hearn_ Qty _11_ Date _8-3-2024_

Scanned Batch IDs

_23740 237289192_ _____ _____

Notes /Exception

_____

_____

_____

_____

_____